INFORMATION

INFORMATION
A HISTORICAL COMPANION

Edited by Ann Blair, Paul Duguid,
Anja-Silvia Goeing, and Anthony Grafton

PRINCETON UNIVERSITY PRESS
PRINCETON AND OXFORD

Published by Princeton University Press
41 William Street, Princeton, New Jersey 08540
6 Oxford Street, Woodstock, Oxfordshire OX20 1TR

press.princeton.edu

Library of Congress Cataloging-in-Publication Data

Names: Blair, Ann, 1961– editor. | Duguid, Paul, 1954– editor. |
    Goeing, Anja-Silvia, editor. | Grafton, Anthony, editor.
Title: Information : a historical companion / edited by Ann Blair,
    Paul Duguid, Anja-Silvia Goeing, and Anthony Grafton.
Other titles: Information (Blair, Duguid, Goeing, Grafton)
Description: Princeton : Princeton University Press, [2021] | Includes
    bibliographical references and index.
Identifiers: LCCN 2020025889 (print) | LCCN 2020025890 (ebook) |
    ISBN 9780691179544 (hardback) | ISBN 9780691209746 (ebook)
Subjects: LCSH: Information science—History. | Information resources—History |
    Information science—Encyclopedias.
Classification: LCC Z665 .I57815 2021 (print) | LCC Z665 (ebook) |
    DDC 020.9—dc23
LC record available at https://lccn.loc.gov/2020025889
LC ebook record available at https://lccn.loc.gov/2020025890

British Library Cataloging-in-Publication Data is available

Editorial: Anne Savarese and Jenny Tan
Production Editorial: Natalie Baan and Karen L. Carter
Text Design: Carmina Alvarez
Jacket Design: Layla Mac Rory
Production: Erin Suydam
Publicity: Kate Hensley, Jodi Price, and Amy Stewart
Copyeditor: Kathleen Kageff

This book has been composed in Charis

Printed on acid-free paper. ∞

Printed in the United States of America

10 9 8 7 6 5 4 3 2 1

CONTENTS

INTRODUCTION

Information: A Historical Companion explores how information has shaped and been shaped by human society across ages past and present. It offers readers views of history through the lens of information and views of information through the lens of history.

Such a project might seem paradoxical. In 1964, the media scholar Marshall McLuhan declared his the "age of information." The idea was widely taken up, so that in the following decade an IBM advertisement could announce, "Information: there's growing agreement that it's the name of the age we live in." Both announcements thrust information to the fore but in the process suggested that it and related information technologies of the sort IBM made had created a fundamental break from the past. History, by these and similar accounts, can seem retrograde, irrelevant to forward-looking information. This book is built on the belief that, contrary to IBM's assertion, "growing agreement" might reasonably be claimed to point another way. Since the 1970s, books, conferences, and university courses have shown increasing interest in information in prior ages. In the process, a growing body of information-focused research has thrown new light on both the past and the present, drawing the two together rather than separating them. Indeed, as this book goes to press, two other significant collections, *Information Keywords* and *Literary Information in China: A History*, are also coming into print. Together those volumes and this one reveal the remarkable range of approaches to and topics in information history that are raising interest and enthusiasm within academia and beyond.

For its part, this book assembles researchers who have engaged directly with information in historical context to illustrate for scholars and general readers alike the breadth and the depth of these developing perspectives. The contributors look at the emergence across history of new information practices, technologies, and institutions as these developed to address informational challenges of their day. In particular, they look at moments of confrontation and transition—beginning, for example, with Columbus's legendary encounter with Caribbean societies in 1492—to reveal how approaching these as part of a history of information provides fresh insight into how they unfolded at the time and how they might be better understood today. From this starting point, the thirteen long articles in part 1 of the book present a cumulative narrative bringing this exploration of information in history to the present. The 101 short entries in part 2 examine in depth particular topics that are critical to such an exploration. Together, contributors to *Information: A Historical Companion* show how information and information technology were crucial to earlier ages, as they are to our age today.

Information, of course, is an expansive term. Consequently, any starting point for an investigation can seem arbitrary, and convincing arguments can always be made for starting elsewhere. But given inevitable constraints of space and time in a publishing venture such as this, the editors have chosen to focus principally on the *early modern and modern periods, from circa 1450 to the present. Nonetheless the early articles and many of the entries look back well before this to allow the overall collection to develop a continuous, information-focused narrative across many historical contexts down to the present in the scope of a single volume and with sufficient depth to reveal emergent and enduring themes. Within this constraint of continuity, the editors sought entries that engaged diverse issues and places and took distinct approaches to the topic of information. The attempt to achieve both continuity and diversity makes no claim to comprehensiveness. While it is hoped that this selection will appear judicious, all contributors, as well as the editors, are aware of inevitable gaps. They hope that the collection as a whole can indicate how topics omitted might nonetheless be illuminated by the overall information perspectives of the collection. Together, the articles reveal recurring responses to social change, thereby making evident over time and across cultures the resilience of attitudes familiar today, such as information optimism and information anxiety or faith in information "solutions" and surprise at their unintended consequences.

The opening account of Columbus and the Silk Road introduces globalization as one of the volume's major themes, represented by emerging networks of travel and communication across Asia, the Islamic world, and Europe. Informational connections inevitably shaped this "road" as not only silk and spices but also word of supply and demand and technologies such as paper and forms of writing and mathematics passed back and forth, opening new worlds, both literally and metaphorically, to recipients. These exchanges also fostered spiritual and scientific engagements, as intrepid Buddhists, Muslims, and Christians traveled in opposite directions along these interconnecting pathways, appearing in new environments and before new audiences, then sending back reports of such encounters. Supporting this circulation, the Silk Road and similar communication channels emerge as complex sets of social, institutional, and geographical networks, continuously circumscribed by short- and long-distance demands of and for information. In response to these demands, practices from printing to record keeping developed to formalize and reify information in different ways, and new communication channels able to carry such reifications arose, including crucially important forms of postal networks.

These developing interconnections played a significant role in shaping what we now think of as information technologies. Printing, which appeared first in the Sinosphere and centuries later in Europe, was crucially transformed and transforming in interactions with state, market, and culture. Analyses of these different settings and the information practices they favored add complexity to the simple determinism that accounts of information technology otherwise often assume. New information techniques also accompanied the formation of commercial relations, including the emergence of accounting devices for making and recording market exchanges, such as the financial "ledger" (a historical, transnational technology whose enduring contribution is evident today in the ledgers of Bitcoin and other digital currencies). On the one hand the articles track an increasing use of information to control and stabilize markets, as well as attempts by markets to control information in order to commodify and commercialize it. On the other hand the articles also explore the drive to resist control by removing restrictions and liberating the circulation of information. This resistance to control is particularly noticeable in the accounts of scientific groups and educational institutions that sought autonomy for members and also for their information so both could circulate across national, political, and religious boundaries. In particular the development and spread of new forms of scholarly information included natural histories, encyclopedias, and other kinds of reference works (all in different ways, of course, forerunners of this book).

One of the most influential developments explored across this volume is the rise of the "information state" and its informational apparatus—chanceries, secretaries, surveillance, archives, and the like—designed to help assert political control over populations. Among the most pervasive state-driven contributions revealed in these accounts are the standardization of information, through such things as forms and questionnaires, and the quantification such standardization allowed as populations were counted in different ways for different reasons. The passport, as one article shows, offers an unexpected and insightful view of the state's attempts to standardize both information and population and of their normative impact. Conversely, as the state sought to control people through information, others sought to use information to help control the state, and inevitably states pushed back. Thus articles in part 1 move from the rise of "public information" in Japan to the periodical and the press in the West and the emergence of the information media of the "public sphere" along with state initiatives to control the press and public opinion directly or indirectly.

The cluster of articles focused on the nineteenth century and early twentieth century track the development of electromagnetic and then electric technologies, including the telegraph, telephone, phonograph, radio, and television, showing how these technologies transformed prior assumptions about the relation between information, nation-states, and the public. Nonetheless, despite these apparently transformative technologies, themes of unequal distribution, problematic standardization, commodification, normativity, and state control return, along with new bouts of anxiety about increasing quantities of information and contrasting optimism about its potential to create efficient and effective markets and democracies. The final articles in part 1 take the collection from telephone and telegraph into IBM's "information age" with discussions of new communication and search technologies, exploring ways in which, despite claims of "revolution," recent developments and enthusiasms often parallel those discussed in earlier chapters. Throughout, these discussions repeatedly raise important questions of information politics and ethics that run from Magellan's (and Columbus's) willingness to lie to their crews to the development of propaganda to support state interests and the appropriation of personal information to improve search and surveillance technologies.

While part 1 builds a chronological narrative from the early modern period to the present, each of the entries in part 2 focuses on a particular topic critical to understanding information in history, from accounting, algorithms, and archivists to secretaries, social media, surveilling, and much more. The 101 short entries, which appear alphabetically, are also grouped together under a series of thematic categories (the category "objects," for instance, includes essays on coins, government documents, and inscriptions) and are linked to one another by cross-references. The book also contains a glossary, collecting and elaborating terms that may be unfamiliar to readers or that are used in distinctive ways in this volume. The cross-references and the glossary seek to support both the autonomy and the focus of particular pieces as well as the cumulative interdependence of the collection as a whole.

Information's complex character presents challenges to anyone trying to undertake this sort of historical enquiry. As noted, influenced by arguments like those of McLuhan and IBM about the "information age," many assume that information is a critical feature for the present age alone. Conversely, other scholars have followed the linguist and computer scientist Anthony Oettinger, who in 1980 argued that "every society is an information society." *Information: A Historical Companion*, while recognizing changes over time, clearly takes the latter view. But in so doing, it faces questions about whose notion of information is at stake. Is it the historian's notion or that of the subjects of historical study? The latter perspective is exemplified in the words of the historian Peter Burke, whose *Social History of Knowledge* (2000–2012) seeks to trace "what early modern people—rather than the present author or his readers—considered to be knowledge." This is an important distinction; hence this book highlights people becoming aware of information as a critical aspect of their lives. But the alternative view, allowing examination of historical actors who did not have the term or the concept but whose behavior can nonetheless be illuminated with insight from current perspectives of information, is equally important here. Contributors have taken what they have seen as the appropriate approach for each topic.

Using the term *information* itself presents further challenges. Not only does the word favor particular (i.e., Latinate) languages, but even within those languages, *information* has been used in quite different ways in different times and contexts. Given these complexities, it might seem plausible to define *information* as a technical term to be shared among this book's contributors, thus putting to one side both historical and contemporary variations. Unfortunately, such definitions are as likely to generate as to resolve difficulties. For instance, it seems unexceptional to take "information" as a carrier of meaningful ideas between people. Such views, however, must confront the pioneering information theorist Claude Shannon, whose work, discussed in several of the pieces that follow, probably did more than any other to promote ideas of an "information age." Shannon's theory held meaning as irrelevant to information. Many also assume that information is an objective entity. Yet Geoffrey Bateson's famous definition of information as "a difference that makes a difference" (which is, deservedly, one of the most cited definitions in this book) portrays information as personally subjective: the ability to make a difference depends not only on the communication, but also on what the recipient knew before. Similarly, some take information as an autonomous entity that can be removed from one context and unproblematically presented in another. McLuhan, however, famously argued that in the age of information "the medium is the message," suggesting that context is inescapable.

Overall, the problems of definition are perhaps best exposed in a study in 2007 by the information scientist Chaim Zins that compiled definitions of *information* (and *data* and *knowledge*) offered by forty-five information scholars from sixteen countries. The compilation revealed 130 distinct notions, with different degrees of compatibility with one another, but no one capable of encompassing all the different variations. Contributors to this collection proceeded using their own understandings rather than subordinating themselves to a single definition. Their contributions reveal both common and distinctive threads across the volume's different historical and thematic explorations. Nonetheless, one aim of the book is, where possible, to encourage contributors and readers to weave these threads together.

While following the development of current scholarship, another goal of this book is to engage readers outside the academy. Consequently, the book eschews scholarly footnotes and long bibliographies, offering instead short "further reading" lists. (For those seeking more depth, the editors are maintaining a fuller bibliography of works explicitly and implicitly invoked in articles. This can be reached through the Princeton University Press website for this book at https://press.princeton.edu/books/hardcover/9780691179544/information.) Overall, both long and short pieces work individually and together to illustrate key facets of information's *longue durée* and wide reach from multiple perspectives. Again, this collection makes no claim to be comprehensive but rather aspires to be illustrative. Its editors hope that it will provide a range of audiences with useful and reliable insights, but also that it will prompt readers in the developing field of information history to pursue new questions and fill gaps made evident by this attempt.

Paul Duguid

ACKNOWLEDGMENTS

The editors would like to extend deepest thanks to the contributors to *Information: A Historical Companion*. Their enthusiasm in the process of putting the volume together, their responsiveness to comments, the help that they lent to one another, and the quality of their final submissions all lie quite beyond initial expectations and will be, we are confident, appreciated as much by the readers as by the editors. In particular, we would like to acknowledge the work of the authors of the articles in part 1 for both their remarkable contributions and their significant collaborations with the editors and with one another. The editors extend similar thanks for their oversight to the project's advisory board, Jean Bauer, Arndt Brendecke, Peter Burke, Michael Cook, Richard Drayton, Markus Friedrich, Randolph Head, Matthew Kirschenbaum, Carla Nappi, Daniel Rosenberg, and Jacob Soll, several of whom also contributed to the book. The editors are also deeply grateful to Princeton University Press and Anne Savarese and her staff, in particular Thalia Leaf, Jenny Tan, and Natalie Baan, for the extraordinary support and responsiveness provided throughout the process of assembling the book, and also to Kathleen Kageff for scrupulous copyediting and Tobiah Waldron for indexing the volume. Warm thanks also go to Jeremy Norman for the support of his History of Information website (HistoryofInformation.com) and to Theodore Delwiche for his work on the preparation of the glossary and related materials. All these people helped make a long process much easier for the editors, resulting in what, it is hoped, will be for all an informative and rewarding endeavor.

HOW TO USE THIS BOOK

Part 1 contains thirteen long articles that together provide a chronological narrative of the history of information from the early modern period to the present. Part 2 contains 101 short entries, focused on particular issues central to that history.

The short entries are arranged alphabetically. Each concludes with cross-references (labelled "see also") pointing to other entries in the volume that explore related topics.

For readers interested in further research, each entry concludes with a "further reading" list of books and articles important to the topic under discussion. In a few cases, such as quotations drawn from secondary sources, brief parenthetical references within the entry point to their source.

Words marked with an asterisk (*) on first mention within an entry can be found in the glossary, which defines terms used in specific ways within this book. Foreign words appear in italics on their first mention within each entry. Foreign terms and titles of books, newspapers, and the like have generally been translated if they are not explained. Translations often appear in parentheses after the original name—for example, *Tiangong Kaiwu* (The exploitation of the works of nature) or *Frankfurter Postzeitung* (Frankfurt postal newspaper).

A general index aids navigation across the multiple topics and issues that make up the volume as a whole.

Finally, an expanded bibliography offered by our contributors on their several topics can be found through the book's website, which will be linked from the Princeton University Press website and updated periodically.

Ann Blair, Paul Duguid, Anja-Silvia Goeing, and Anthony Grafton

ALPHABETICAL LIST OF ENTRIES

THEMATIC LIST OF ENTRIES

CONTRIBUTORS

Jeremy Adelman, *Princeton University*
10. NETWORKING: INFORMATION CIRCLES
THE MODERN WORLD

Monica Azzolini, *University of Bologna*
HOROSCOPES

Melinda Baldwin, *University of Maryland*
JOURNALS

Lionel Bently, *University of Cambridge*
INTELLECTUAL PROPERTY

Susanna Berger, *University of Southern California*
PRINTED VISUALS

Ann Blair, *Harvard University*
4. INFORMATION IN EARLY MODERN
EUROPE; SCRIBES; SECRETARIES;
SERMONS

Lina Bolzoni, *Scuola Normale Superiore, Pisa*
ART OF MEMORY

Paul Botley, *The University of Warwick*
LETTERS

Dan Bouk, *Colgate University*
QUANTIFICATION

Arndt Brendecke, *Ludwig-Maximilians-Universität, Munich*
GOVERNANCE (COAUTHOR)

John Brewer, *California Institute of Technology*
NETWORKS

Michael K. Buckland, *University of California, Berkeley*
PHOTOCOPIERS; STORAGE AND SEARCH

Peter Burke, *University of Cambridge*
KNOWLEDGE

John Carson, *University of Michigan*
INTELLIGENCE TESTING

Hwisang Cho, *Emory University*
LAYOUT AND SCRIPT IN LETTERS

Frederic Clark, *University of Southern California*
READERS

Brian Cowan, *McGill University*
PUBLIC SPHERE

Peter Crooks, *Trinity College Dublin*
BUREAUCRACY

Lorraine Daston, *Max Planck Institute for the History of Science, Berlin*
OBSERVING

Surekha Davies, *Utrecht University*
MAPS

Paul M. Dover, *Kennesaw State University*
DIPLOMATS/SPIES

Johanna Drucker, *University of California, Los Angeles*
BIBLIOGRAPHY

Paul Duguid, *University of California, Berkeley*
INTRODUCTION; 12. COMMUNICATION,
COMPUTATION, AND INFORMATION

Dennis Duncan, *University College London*
INDEXING

Matthew Daniel Eddy, *Durham University*
DIAGRAMS

Alexander J. Fisher, *University of British Columbia*
BELLS

Devin Fitzgerald, *University of California, Los Angeles*
3. INFORMATION IN EARLY MODERN EAST
ASIA (COAUTHOR)

Christian Flow, *University of Southern California*
PROFESSORS

Markus Friedrich, *Universität Hamburg*
ARCHIVISTS

John Frow, *The University of Sydney*
COMMODIFICATION

John-Paul A. Ghobrial, *University of Oxford*
5. NETWORKS AND THE MAKING OF A CONNECTED WORLD IN THE SIXTEENTH CENTURY

Tarleton Gillespie, *Microsoft Research and Cornell University*
PLATFORMS

Lisa Gitelman, *New York University*
9. NINETEENTH-CENTURY MEDIA TECHNOLOGIES (COAUTHOR)

Anja-Silvia Goeing, *Harvard University/ University of Zurich*
APPRAISING; LEARNING; TEACHING

Anthony Grafton, *Princeton University*
1. PREMODERN REGIMES AND PRACTICES; SCROLLS AND ROLLS

Sean Gurd, *University of Missouri, Columbia*
PUBLICITY/PUBLICATION

Earle Havens, *Johns Hopkins University*
FORGERY; PLAGIARIZING

Kenneth Haynes, *Brown University*
ERROR

Randolph C. Head, *University of California, Riverside*
6. RECORDS, SECRETARIES, AND THE EUROPEAN INFORMATION STATE, CIRCA 1400–1700; REGISTERS

Daniel R. Headrick, *Roosevelt University*
TELECOMMUNICATIONS

David M. Henkin, *University of California, Berkeley*
POSTAL CUSTOMERS

Niv Horesh, *Western Sydney University*
MONEY

Hansun Hsiung, *Durham University*
LITHOGRAPHY (COAUTHOR)

Sabine Hyland, *University of St Andrews*
KHIPUS

Sarah E. Igo, *Vanderbilt University*
SURVEYS AND CENSUSES

Richard R. John, *Columbia University*
11. PUBLICITY, PROPAGANDA, AND PUBLIC OPINION: FROM THE *TITANIC* DISASTER TO THE HUNGARIAN UPRISING (COAUTHOR)

Adrian Johns, *University of Chicago*
PRIVACY

Matthew L. Jones, *Columbia University*
PROGRAMMING

Lauren Kassell, *University of Cambridge*
CASES

Vera Keller, *University of Oregon*
LISTS

Eric Ketelaar, *University of Amsterdam*
GOVERNMENT DOCUMENTS

Matthew Kirschenbaum, *University of Maryland*
COMPUTERS

Valerie Kivelson, *University of Michigan*
PETITIONS

Markus Krajewski, *Universität Basel*
CARDS

Josh Lauer, *University of New Hampshire*
SURVEILLING

Diana Lemberg, *Lingnan University*
INFORMATION POLICY

Rebecca Lemov, *Harvard University*
CYBERNETICS/FEEDBACK

Erik Linstrum, *University of Virginia*
POLITICAL REPORTING

Pamela O. Long, *Independent scholar*
MANUALS

Jack Lynch, *Rutgers University*
REFERENCE BOOKS

Ian Maclean, *Universities of Oxford and St Andrews*
BOOK SALES CATALOGS

Hannah Marcus, *Harvard University*
CENSORSHIP

Erin McGuirl, *The Bibliographical Society of America*
OFFICE PRACTICES; SALES CATALOGS

David McKitterick, *University of Cambridge*
LETTERPRESS

Emily Mokros, *University of Kentucky*
DOCUMENTARY AUTHORITY

Elias Muhanna, *Brown University*
2. INFORMATION IN THE MEDIEVAL
ISLAMIC WORLD

Thomas S. Mullaney, *Stanford
University*
9. NINETEENTH-CENTURY MEDIA
TECHNOLOGIES (COAUTHOR)

Leos Müller, *Stockholm University*
MERCHANTS

Carla Nappi, *University of Pittsburgh*
3. INFORMATION IN EARLY MODERN EAST
ASIA (COAUTHOR)

Paul Nelles, *Carleton University*
LIBRARIES AND CATALOGS

Geoffrey Nunberg (1945–2020),
University of California, Berkeley
INFORMATION, DISINFORMATION,
MISINFORMATION

Elisa Oreglia, *King's College London*
GLOBALIZATION

Andrew Pettegree, *University of
St. Andrews*
NEWSPAPERS

Jamie L. Pietruska, *Rutgers
University*
FORECASTING

Andrew Piper, *McGill University*
DIGITIZATION

Richard K. Popp, *University of
Wisconsin–Milwaukee*
MEDIA

James Raven, *University of Essex*
BOOKS

Joad Raymond, *Queen Mary University
of London*
NEWSLETTERS

Craig Robertson, *Northeastern
University*
8. DOCUMENTS, EMPIRE, AND CAPITALISM
IN THE NINETEENTH CENTURY; FILES

Daniel Rosenberg, *University of
Oregon*
13. SEARCH; DATA

Joan-Pau Rubiés, *ICREA and Universitat
Pompeu Fabra, Barcelona*
ETHNOGRAPHY

Annie Rudd, *University of Calgary*
CAMERAS

Bruce Rusk, *The University of British
Columbia*
XYLOGRAPHY

Paolo Sachet, *Université de Genève*
PROOFREADERS

Neil Safier, *Brown University*
TRANSLATING

Haun Saussy, *University of Chicago*
ARCHAEOLOGICAL DECIPHERMENT

Kathryn A. Schwartz, *University of
Massachusetts Amherst*
LITHOGRAPHY (COAUTHOR)

David Sepkoski, *University of Illinois,
Urbana-Champaign*
DATABASES

Zur Shalev, *University of Haifa*
TRAVEL

William H. Sherman, *The Warburg
Institute, London*
ENCRYPTING/DECRYPTING

Will Slauter, *Sorbonne Université*
7. PERIODICALS AND THE
COMMERCIALIZATION OF INFORMATION IN
THE EARLY MODERN ERA

Daniel Lord Smail, *Harvard University*
INVENTORIES

Jacob Soll, *University of Southern
California*
ACCOUNTING

Alan M. Stahl, *Princeton University*
COINS

Benjamin Steiner, *Ludwig-Maximilians-
Universität, Munich*
GOVERNANCE (COAUTHOR)

William Stenhouse, *Yeshiva
University*
INSCRIPTIONS

Ted Striphas, *University of Colorado
Boulder*
ALGORITHMS

Emily Thompson, *Princeton University*
RECORDING

Heidi J. S. Tworek, *The University of British Columbia*
11. PUBLICITY, PROPAGANDA, AND PUBLIC OPINION: FROM THE *TITANIC* DISASTER TO THE HUNGARIAN UPRISING (COAUTHOR)

Siva Vaidhyanathan, *University of Virginia*
SOCIAL MEDIA

Alexandra Walsham, *University of Cambridge*
LANDSCAPES AND CITIES

Alexis Weedon, *University of Bedfordshire*
STEREOTYPE PRINTING

Kirsten Weld, *Harvard University*
READING AGAINST THE GRAIN

Elizabeth Yale, *The University of Iowa*
ALBUMS

JoAnne Yates, *Massachusetts Institute of Technology*
MEMOS

Richard Yeo, *Griffith University*
NOTEBOOKS

Helmut Zedelmaier, *Ludwig-Maximilians-Universität, Munich*
EXCERPTING/COMMONPLACING

PART ONE

PART ONE

1

PREMODERN REGIMES
AND PRACTICES

On the sixth of November 1492, Christopher Columbus was exploring Cuba. In his journal, he recorded what the native inhabitants told him: information that filled him with excitement. They "said, by signs," that he could find plenty of cinnamon and pepper—samples of which he had brought and showed them—nearby. A couple of days before, old men had reported that locals wore gold "on their necks, ears, arms, and legs, as well as pearls." True, he also learned that "far away, there were men with one eye, and others with dogs' noses who were cannibals, and that when they captured an enemy, they beheaded him and drank his blood, and cut off his private parts." Even this unpromising report did not dismay Columbus. On the contrary, it confirmed what he had believed and hoped since he reached land in October: that he had arrived, by traveling west across the Atlantic, at the Indies, near China, "the land of the great Cham."

Columbus knew where he was: at or near the eastern sources of the two great sets of trade routes that brought luxuries from the East to Latin Christendom and trade goods and money from Latin Christendom to the East: the Silk Road and the Spice Route. Both had functioned, more or less regularly, since the early centuries of the Common Era. Both had generated wealth for those who created silk and harvested spices to sell and for the numerous intermediaries who brought them to market. And both had been the sources of information of many kinds, about everything from distant lands to the properties of foods and spices. But both routes had been disrupted, in the thirteenth century and after, by the rise of Mongol power in the steppes of central Asia. In Columbus's day, both were dominated by Muslim merchants and powers, whom most Christians regarded as enemies—but from whom they bought, indirectly or directly, glossy consumer goods. When he heard tales of gold, pearls, and monsters in his vicinity, he knew he had arrived at the source of luxuries of many kinds. Immediately he inferred that he could enrich his masters, the Catholic Kings, both by eliminating middlemen and by domesticating the natives and putting them to productive work.

Columbus was wrong, of course, about the geographical facts. He was in the Caribbean, not the Pacific, the very existence of which was unknown to him and all other Europeans. And the local knowledge that he gleaned from the Cubans proved inaccurate as well. Accounts of gold, pearls, and spices in Cuba turned out to be greatly exaggerated. Investigation—as Columbus later informed the Catholic Kings—turned up no men of monstrous form. This comes as no great surprise, since Columbus seems to have extracted these reports from the signs made by Cubans with whom he shared no language. Yet he had some reason to think as he did. An imaginary map of the world and its resources had formed over the centuries, as sailors and travelers told, and later wrote, tales. Monsters appeared on it, at the far end—from a European perspective—of the world, next to the lands from which silks and pepper were imported to Europe. These ancient images hung before Columbus's eyes and shaped and colored what he saw.

After Columbus, travel—and the collection of information about the world— underwent a transformation. The Catholic Kings established permanent colonies and trade networks. They sponsored continuing, systematic collection of information, re- corded and transmitted by pilots with formal training and credentials and military com- manders with royal commissions. They and their rivals worked with sailors, merchants, and soldiers to begin the process that historians refer to as globalization: the uniting of the globe by institutions, sometimes paper thin but still constructed for the long term (Ghobrial, chap. 5).

Information travels: it moves, often unpredictably, with the people or the mediums that carry it. Information matters: states need reliable ways to collect, store, and access information and to provide it to their subjects, and merchants and bankers need it to serve their customers and outwit their rivals. Information abides: so long as its owners also possess a medium that can store it. This chapter sketches three histories of infor- mation. It follows the trading routes that brought luxuries from China and India across the world. It re-creates the information regimes that were created to govern the Roman Empire. And it examines the history of paper, a single medium for writing that had a powerful impact. The result will not be a survey but a sketch map of some of the ways in which information was collected and stored, transmitted and accessed, before the full process of globalization began.

SILK ROAD AND SPICE ROUTE

Exchange of goods and ideas is as old as human settlement. By 3000 BCE, caravans connected cities and markets across the Fertile Crescent and beyond. But the forms of trade that took shape early in the Common Era—and that eventually connected two great but distant empires, China and Rome—differed in scale, as well as distance covered, from anything that had preceded them. In the third century BCE, the Qin dynasty, based in the wealthy state of the same name, conquered the other six Warring States and cre- ated a unified government with a powerful military and civil service. It and its succes- sor, the Han dynasty, ruled from 221 BCE to 220 CE. Always confronted by the neces- sity of feeding their large population, China's rulers had to encourage agriculture. To do so it was necessary to protect their farmers from the Xiongnu, horse-riding nomad archers who lived on the steppes to their north and defeated them in 200 CE. Early military expeditions were unsuccessful. Gradually, it became clear that the silk that the Chinese had learned to produce, in the Yangtze valley and elsewhere, was unique and desirable. The heavier and more complex brocades, produced by specialists for the im- perial court, were reserved for the Chinese elite. But farming families also cultivated mulberry trees, grew silkworms, and produced thin, simple silks, with which they paid their taxes to the state. These silks, the Chinese found, could be traded to the nomads of the steppes in return for horses, which they needed for agriculture. The Han extended the walls that protected China from the nomads. But they also pierced them with gates, which in turn became the centers of trading stations. From these sprang the immense trade network conventionally called the Silk Road.

Across Eurasia, meanwhile, Rome developed great military power, which enabled it to defeat the trading power Carthage in the third and second centuries BCE. In the next century, Rome conquered Gaul and Britain, establishing farms and founding new cities, and took Egypt, which had been ruled since the time of Alexander by a Greek-speaking dynasty, the Ptolemies. Roman rule stretched from North Africa to Gaul and from Syria to Britain. New cities were founded, and older Greek cities prospered under imperial authority. As the elite of aristocrats and entrepreneurs who dominated Rome under the emperors became wealthier and wealthier, new luxuries, arriving from China and elsewhere in the East, found an eager market. Silk shocked Roman traditionalists, who complained that dresses made from it were immodest. But it became fashionable nonetheless. Roman merchants began to look for larger supplies. Fleets sailed from Alexandria to the eastern Mediterranean. Others traveled down the Nile and across land to the Red Sea coast, from where they could sail to India in search of silk and other goods.

Contacts between Rome and China were not direct. Intermediaries ruled the thousands of miles of territory between them. Alexander the Great's expedition from Persia across Afghanistan and the Hindu Kush in the fourth century BCE did not extend his empire to the ends of the earth, as he may have hoped it would. But it transformed much of the world nonetheless. Alexander's conquest of Persia and looting of the immense royal treasury spread precious materials through the known world, making possible the creation of more coined money than had ever existed before. His hard-fought journey to India and back proved in the most dramatic possible way that large numbers of people and animals could move from the Mediterranean to Asia. The Greek-speaking cities that he founded across central Asia and the spread of the Greek language and Greek styles in art and religion, finally, brought lands and peoples that had previously existed in separation into contact with one another—contact that became more intense and regular as his successors invested in massive port facilities that supported trade.

Other intermediaries, equally vital, worked on a more local level. In the first century BCE the Yuezhi, another nation of steppe-dwelling nomads, founded the Kushan Empire in Bactria and India. They created cities modeled, in their layout and architecture, on those of the Greek world. Trade generated new forms of settlement, and these, in turn, perpetuated the trade. Caravan routes developed, which came to dominate central Asian trade. They also sponsored the growth of what became a new brand of Buddhist religion: one centered on monasteries, gifts to which were strongly encouraged, and which soon collected massive endowments. Further west, the Nabateans—an Arab people who lived in northern Arabia and the Levant—engineered water systems that enabled them to settle in the desert. They built caravan cities, whose traders moved silk into Parthian and Roman territory, and ports. Though the Nabateans were conquered by the Romans, the wealth that trade generated for them enabled the creation of Petra, a city cut from the rocks of a gorge in Jordan. Sculpted façades deftly combined Greek and Roman architectural forms with local ones. By the third century the Sogdians—an Iranian people whose lands were centered on Samarkand, in modern Uzbekistan—were also actively trading along the Silk Route. They set up trading zones everywhere from the Byzantine Empire to China itself, where they settled in large numbers. These and other nations created the aggregate of trading routes that made up the Silk Road.

Meanwhile a second set of trade routes grew up—one that intersected with the first but involved maritime as well as overland trade. For centuries, the inhabitants of southern Arabia—Arabia Felix—had tapped trees that flourished in their desert habitat for aromatic resins like frankincense and myrrh—the gifts that the Magi, wise men from the East, bring to the baby Jesus in the Gospel of Matthew. Employed in incense, perfumes, and medicaments, the oil from these resins came to be valued from China to Greece. Traders who used camels as their beasts of burden (since they could cross the desert on their thickly padded feet and required far less water than horses) formed caravans to carry them to Parthia and Rome. The Nabateans and other intermediaries offered vital help and shelter. As Roman sailors based in Egypt mastered the prevailing winds of the Indian Ocean, they moved back and forth between East Africa and western India, where they could exchange these precious resins and other products for the even more precious spices made in India and beyond: pepper above all.

The silk and spice trades linked China, Rome, and many lands between in a complicated but effective system of exchanges, one that brought gold and silver, slaves, and other products from the lands to the west and exchanged them for pepper and incense as well as fine silks. These systems were supported more by self-interest and curiosity than government policy, more by traders cooperating than by formal institutions. Yet they proved flexible and resilient. As the western Roman Empire weakened after the fourth century, the new city founded by Constantine at the meeting point of Asia and Europe, New Rome (later Constantinople), turned into one of the great entrepôts for trade in luxury goods between the edges of the world. Even the Mongol invasions of the thirteenth century and after did not cut these trade routes, though they changed them in important ways. While the techniques used by traders and the sailors who transported their goods changed over time, these long-distance trade routes proved strikingly durable.

Information and its transmission were woven into these trade routes from the start. The Han emperor Wudi (147–87 BCE) called for an official to undertake an embassy to the Yuezhi, in the hope of allying with them against the Xiongnu. Only Zhang Qian, a minor official, proved willing. His embassy turned into an epic. It lasted for thirteen years, most of which he spent in captivity. He failed to make the treaty Wudi had sought. But he succeeded in something of much greater import in the long run. His reports, preserved in later Chinese histories, show that he was a sharp observer with an eye and ear for detail, who used his time in outside lands to learn an immense amount. He drew up crisp ethnographies, informative about resources, crops, and potential trading conditions.

> An-si [Parthia] may be several thousand li west of the Ta-yue-chi. The people live in fixed abodes and are given to agriculture; their fields yield rice and wheat; and they make wine of grapes. Their cities and towns are like those of Ta-yuan. Several hundred small and large cities belong to it. The territory is several thousand li square; it is a very large country and is close to the K'ui-shui [Oxus]. Their market folk and merchants travel in carts and boats to the neighboring countries, perhaps several thousand li distant. They make coins of silver; the coins resemble their king's face. Upon the death of a king the coins are changed for others on which the new king's face is represented. They paint [rows of characters] running sideways on [stiff] leather, to serve as records. West of this country is T'iau-chï; north is An-ts'ai.

One observation in particular reveals the quality of attention that Zhang Qian brought to watching everyday life: "When I was in Ta-hia [Bactria]," he told the king, "I saw there a stick of bamboo of Kiung [Kiung-chóu in Ssï-ch'uan] and some cloth of Shu [Ssï-ch'uan]. When I asked the inhabitants of Ta-hia how they had obtained possession of these, they replied: 'The inhabitants of our country buy them in Shon-tu [India].'" Wudi, impressed by the active trading systems and range of goods that Zhang Qian's report described, tried to follow his recommendation and forge routes to India and Bactria that did not pass through the lands controlled by the steppe nomads. This enterprise failed, but Wudi extended the northern wall far to the west and founded garrisons and trading posts. As trade expanded, the Chinese obtained Indian spices and cloth, Roman glass, and other exotic trade goods—as well as further knowledge about the kingdoms that produced them. Information made the Silk Road.

It also traveled. Languages and knowledge of languages expanded. Chinese, for example, rapidly became a language of world trade. Trading centers became zones where several languages might be in use. Palmyra, for example, was a caravan oasis northeast of Damascus. Once Petra was conquered by Rome, Palmyra became a dominant node in the caravan routes that brought goods to and from the Persian Gulf. The city established garrisons and trading sites in other cities. Many Palmyrenes spoke Aramaic, the lingua franca of the eastern Mediterranean, and wrote it in a distinctive alphabet. Others used Arabic, and still others were conversant in Greek and the Iranian language of the Parthians. In Dunhuang, a city of some thirty thousand inhabitants near the border with Tibet, forty thousand surviving scrolls reveal that the languages used there included Tibetan, Sanskrit, Chinese, Sogdian—and, as attested by one scroll, Hebrew. In this small but cosmopolitan community, as Jacob Mikanowski has written, "Buddhists rubbed shoulders with Manicheans, Christians, Zoroastrians, and Jews, and Chinese scribes copied Tibetan prayers that had been translated from Sanskrit by Indian monks working for Turkish khans."

Cultural practices and styles moved as far—and as erratically—as words, transmitted by the artisans who made them, by the products that embodied them, and, above all, by missionaries and other migrants. Palmyra was constructed as a magnificent Greek city. Its main trading street ran between immense colonnades built in three stages, more than a kilometer long, supported by several hundred Corinthian columns. At its core were an agora, a theater, and a senate house. The reliefs on the sarcophagi of its wealthy inhabitants showed them reclining, like Greeks, on couches and drinking from goblets. They were following the practices of the Greek symposium, a fundamental part of social life. Yet they dedicated their main temple to Bel, a Semitic god, and—unlike the cities of Hellenistic and Roman Egypt and Syria—never developed a local culture based on the Greek language; nor did they build the gymnasium that was as central to Greek cities as the agora was. Christianity was carried all the way to China by followers of Nestorius, a fifth-century theologian; fleeing condemnation by the church council of Ephesus in 431, they established a separate church in Persia. In 781, Nestorians described the history of their church in China in a long inscription on a stele in the inland city of Xi'an, which was both the terminus of the silk route and the capital of the ruling Tang dynasty. They told their story in Chinese and placed special emphasis on both the imperial favor that had allowed them to proselytize and the pursuit of perfection and purity, which they treated as the core of Christianity. Yet even they were no more skillful in portraying themselves in the languages of distinct cultures than the Sogdian officials in sixth-century Xi'an, whose families commemorated them with monuments in both Sogdian and Chinese, which emphasized completely different traits and accomplishments. It is often hard to know what a particular style of building or sculpture, hair or clothing, or a particular turn of phrase in a second or third language, meant to those who enthusiastically adopted them.

Technical information—especially about the goods traded on the silk and spice routes—traveled these roads as well. Surviving letters written by Sogdian traders in the fourth century offer little information about markets beyond brief lists of goods on sale in a particular locality. It seems that trade on the Asian silk routes was often relatively modest in scale, carried on by peddlers. But monks also traveled these routes, as we have seen, bringing elaborate scriptures and complex doctrines with them. Sometimes their packs may have included much more. In the middle of the sixth century, according to the Byzantine historian Procopius, "there came from India certain monks; and when they had satisfied Justinian Augustus that the Romans no longer should buy silk from the Persians, they promised the emperor in an interview that they would provide the materials for making silk so that never should the Romans seek business of this kind from their enemy the Persians, or from any other people whatsoever" (*History of the Wars* VIII.xvii.1–2). Justinian had long planned to cultivate silk, and archaeological evidence suggests that sericulture, like the fashion for silk garments, had spread from China over the centuries. Once the monks—or someone else—provided the silkworm eggs, the emperors made Byzantium a western center of silk manufacture, which remained an imperial monopoly. Brilliantly colored silks, stitched with gold designs, served for centuries to come as material for court garments and as gifts to foreign powers. Like the transfer of religions, the transfer of technologies was often encouraged by royal authority.

The trade routes that carried spices—and, eventually, silks—across the Indian Ocean and up the Red Sea were also polyglot and cosmopolitan. They carried the spices that gave food in Rome and medieval and *early modern Europe its sharp, varied flavors. At first, spices came without much cultural framework. The Roman natural historian Pliny, writing in the first century CE, complained that "pepper has nothing in it that can plead as a recommendation to either fruit or berry, its only desirable quality being a certain pungency; and yet it is for this that we import it all the way from India" (*Natural History* XII.xiv.29)—though even Pliny recommended it for many medicinal uses. Over time, spices developed multiple preferred functions, as Greek and Arabic medical writers observed their effects and analyzed their working. By the eleventh century, Constantine the African—a Muslim physician from Tunisia, steeped in the traditions of Arabic medicine, who ended his life as a Benedictine monk at Monte Cassino in Italy—revealed to readers in the Latin world that cloves, ginger, cinnamon, anise, and several other spices could remedy sexual impotence.

Those who traveled the long distances of the spice trade collected technical information, to an extent not documented for their counterparts in central Asian caravans. In the middle of the first century CE, a Greek-speaking merchant captain based in Egypt took the time to write down, in spoken rather than literary Greek, a record of the useful knowledge he had accumulated in his time as a trader. The *Periplus [Coasting Voyage] of the Erythraean Sea* is, first and foremost, a practical guide to navigation and trade.

It moves from the Egyptian ports where the author was based south along the Red Sea. The author describes natural features, ports, and markets on the Horn and southeast coast of Africa, in Arabia, and in the Indian subcontinent. He also makes clear how dangerous expeditions across the oceans that separated them could be. A captain had to be in command not only of the prevailing winds, which carried ships across the Indian Ocean in both directions, but also of the challenging geography of many coasts: "To set a course along the coast of Arabia is altogether risky, since the region with its lack of harbors offers poor anchorage, is foul with rocky stretches, cannot be approached because of cliffs, and is fearsome in every respect." Even major ports could be dangerous. At Barygaza, a major entrepôt on the west coast of India, the tides "are much more extreme . . . than elsewhere." The flood tide, which was so powerful that it made the sea floor visible, overturned small ships and grounded larger ones on the shoals.

But the *Periplus* spends much more time on the opportunities for trade available in the "designated harbors"—the cities where established trade routes met and permanent markets flourished. To reach Barygaza from Egypt, one had to set sail in July. There one could sell wine from Italy, Laodicea, and Arabia; copper, tin, and lead; coral; and textiles and clothing; as well as silverware, unguent, and female slaves for the ruler. Exports included ivory, onyx, Chinese silk and silk yarn, and pepper, but "Roman money, gold and silver, which commands an exchange at some profit against the local currency," could also be traded. Passages like these make clear how rich and varied the major markets were: Barygaza served both the silk and the spice trades and many others. Such passages also reveal the striking range of knowledge needed by a trader: mastery of exchange rates and knowledge of both valuable exports and desirable imports in multiple different trading zones.

Above all, the trader had to be able to make expert judgments of a vast range of goods. In the course of the *Periplus*, the author evaluates the quality of cloth, garments, nard, incense, tortoise shell, and slaves available in different markets. Evidently, he and his colleagues had to cultivate skilled eyes and hands in order to learn the preferred colors, weights, and textures of many forms of goods and to subject the goods offered them for sale to expert scrutiny. When Columbus interrogated the inhabitants of Cuba and scrutinized their ornaments and the plants they brought him, he was practicing skills and depending on knowledge developed long before in the silk and spice trades.

Traders were curious. In the course of their voyages, they learned something of the methods used to create the products they bought and sold. The *Periplus*, which devotes close attention to the "frankincense-breeding land" of Yemen and the resins produced there, describes their production in grim, unsparing detail: "The frankincense-bearing trees are neither very large nor tall: they give off frankincense in congealed form on the bark, just as some of the trees we have in Egypt exude gum. The frankincense is handled by royal slaves and convicts. For the districts are terribly unhealthy, harmful to those sailing by and absolutely fatal to those working there—who, moreover, die off easily because of the lack of nourishment." This is probably accurate. Even now the desert highlands where frankincense is harvested are forbidding, and those engaged in the harvesting are said to live ascetic lives while at work. Pearl diving in India, the *Periplus* notes, was also "carried out by convicts."

Occasionally, the text provides information that is not strictly practical. For example, it describes an Indian shrine: "men who wish to lead a holy life for the rest of their days remain there celibate; they come there and they perform ablutions. Women, too, do the same. For it is said that at one time the goddess remained here and performed ablutions." More often, the author reports information about inland markets and the trades performed there, which could derive from conversations in the port city markets he frequented rather than direct experience. For example, he describes the yearly fair held at the border between northeastern India and Tibet, attended by people whom he calls Sêsatai, who "come with their wives and children bearing great packs resembling mats of green leaves and then remain at some spot on the border between them and those on the Thina side, and they hold a festival for several days" and provide the locals with the materials for making malabathrum, balls of dried leaves from cinnamon-like plants, in three distinct grades. Officials and merchants from other societies had eyes as sharp as those of the author of the *Periplus*. In southern India, in the years when he was plying the Indian Ocean, a literary work recorded the striking presence at Arikamedu, near modern Pondicherry, of "abodes of [Romans], whose prosperity was never on the wane. On the harbor were to be seen sailors come from distant lands, but for all appearance they lived as one community."

Much remained unknown. The author of the *Periplus* broke off his account after describing the Tibetan fairs: "What lies beyond this area, because of extremes of storm, bitter cold, and difficult terrain, and also because of some divine power of the gods, has not been explored." He thought of China as a land to the north of India and mistakenly believed that the Greek kingdom of Bactria still existed in his time. Misinformation derived from tradition as well as from misunderstood experience. Ancient myths survived into modern collections of information. The monsters that Columbus expected to find in the Indies had first been described not by traders or soldiers but by Greek writers, Ctesias and Megasthenes, from whom a Roman authority on natural history and ethnography, the elder Pliny (d. 79 CE), took them over into his own compendium, the *Natural History*. Yet as Columbus's interest in them suggests, traders and sailors undoubtedly included such creatures, as well as information about winds and coasts, currencies and goods for sale, when they told tales and advised the young. To put to use the information that moved down these networks always required a critical mind and a quick wit.

EMPIRE AND INFORMATION: THE CASE OF ROME

The description of the kingdom of Da Qin—possibly Rome—in the Chinese dynastic histories includes some striking details. Da Qin has four hundred walled towns and many dependent kingdoms. The walls are made of stone. More impressive still, "at regular intervals, it has built postal relay stations, which are all plastered and whitewashed." The king moves every day from one of his five palaces to another, giving justice, and "each palace has a staffed archive." In these passages at least, the kingdom in question sounds like Rome. It is a massive empire, a mosaic of towns and nations under the rule of a single monarch. And it makes provision—extensive provision—for receiving inquiries and pleas from the citizens of those lands and communicating its decisions to them. A postal service and a system of archives are both in place, to conserve and move the documents on which this kingdom seems to run. The Chinese—who built their own formidable road system and bureaucracy, which managed immense amounts of information—were naturally sensitive to these features of Roman life. But they were not the only observers to note the sheer mass of record keeping that Roman government required. A Jewish scholar who lived in the Babylonian town of Sura, under Roman rule, is reported to have made the same observation: "Rav said: Even if all the seas were ink, and the reeds were quills, and the heavens were parchment, and all the people were scribes; all these are insufficient to write the intricacies of governmental authority" (*Babylonian Talmud Shabbat* 11a). Chinese and Jewish observers were both right. Rome functioned as much by its systems of records and communication as by its armies and navies.

The Roman Empire—which grew, first through Italy and then, in the last century BCE and the first century CE, into Gaul, Egypt, England, and beyond—covered a staggeringly large and varied territory. At its height, according to the Stanford ORBIS project, which has created "a geospatial network model of the Roman world," it "ruled a quarter of humanity through complex networks of political power, military domination and economic exchange" that covered one ninth of the world's surface. These vast land holdings were wrapped around an enormous inland sea. As Fernand Braudel, a pioneering historian of the Mediterranean, argued long ago, distance was the enemy: it constantly hindered the exertion of political power and military force in predictable time spans.

Rome's leaders fought distance from the start of the city's rise to power. They constructed a system of roads that eventually extended from the city of Rome east to Constantinople and then to Trebizond; to the west across Gaul to London and then to northern Britain, and across Iberia to Gades, at the entrance to the Mediterranean. Across from Gades, another road system began in Banasa, in what is now Morocco. This ran eastward, along the southern shore of the Mediterranean, to the Levant, and joined the northern system of roads in Syria. Republican magistrates had begun constructing the Italian part of the system, not only building roads but also lining them with milestones to mark distances. But the emperors built the great roads that connected the parts of the empire. The system consisted, at its peak, of 372 roads, more than four hundred thousand kilometers in total length. (By way of comparison, the American Interstate Highway System is 77,556 kilometers long.)

Though forms of paving varied, some eighty thousand kilometers were paved with cut blocks of stone or lava resting on layers of earth and rubble. Roads were cambered—made convex—so that water would run off into the drainage ditches that flanked them. Rows of curbstones held the layers of pavement in place. Oak pilings made it possible to build roads across marshy land. Stone bridges supported by piers carried roadways directly across rivers and valleys. The longest of these runs 2,437 meters. The section of it that spans the bed of the Danube is 1,137 meters long. Roads were built, largely, by the Roman armies, using the same engineering skills seen in their camps, pontoon bridges, and siege weapons, but slaves and prisoners of war were also conscripted to work on them. Once these vast projects had been completed, local magistrates were responsible for maintaining them from their own funds or by raising taxes. This system functioned well for centuries. Many of the roads survive to this day.

Roman roads were open to all: to the Roman military and officials, but also to merchants and ordinary citizens. From the start, though, they existed to carry information, as well as to project military power and support trade and travel. Suetonius, the biographer of the early Roman emperors, records that the first of them, Augustus, systematically reorganized the *cursus publicus*, or postal service: "First he set young men at reasonable intervals on the military roads, then he placed vehicles there, so that what was happening in each province could be known as swiftly as possible." He added the vehicles in order to receive and analyze important news as soon as possible: "This seemed the most convenient way, so that those who brought a letter from a given place could be questioned about it, if necessary" (*Life of Augustus* 49.3). When the system was complete, couriers (*tabellarii*) riding horses or post carts carried the news, changing horses at designated changing places (*mutationes*), ten to twenty kilometers apart. Full rest stops (*mansiones*), set a day's journey from one another, offered lodging, artisans, veterinary surgeons, and police, to support the couriers.

Imperial power also depended on travel by water. The empire included navigable rivers and canals that stretched some twenty-eight thousand kilometers, and its oceangoing ships followed hundreds of routes in the summer sailing season. Roman ships could carry substantial cargoes—up to three thousand amphoras, or 150 metric tons. Thanks to Rome's hold on the Mediterranean littoral and to its vast naval power, travel by ship was safe and, by historical standards, inexpensive. Emperors, accordingly, often chose to send crucial dispatches and instructions by ship. Fleets carried hundreds of thousands of tons of Egyptian grain to Pozzuoli in Campania: the philosopher Seneca describes the eager crowds, greeting the mailboats that arrived first and announced the coming of the larger fleet.

Imperial authority rested on this immense communications network. Political changes and military developments in, around, and outside the Roman world had to be observed. Decrees, legislation, and verdicts that affected the empire's immense and scattered body of citizens and subjects had to be circulated. From the time of Julius Caesar, scribes prepared and posted the *Acta diurna*: an official record of important events. This began as a record of deliberations in the Senate and the assemblies of the people but expanded to include news of major bequests, prodigies of nature, and victories of gladiators. When Cicero was away from Rome, he followed events in the *Acta*, complaining that they contained too much trivial matter. He was not wrong. The emperor Caligula not only gave good and bad marks to the married women with whom he had sex but in some cases made out bills of divorce in their husbands' names and "ordered that they be inserted into the *Acta*" (Suetonius, *Life of Caligula* 36.2). Still, the *Acta* did much to make the operations of government visible, if not transparent.

Roman emperors did not provide, or promise to provide, much of what even an austere modern government might offer: public education for all, health care, security in old age. But they did need to maintain armed forces around the empire: soldiers had to be equipped and paid. Citizens of Rome, moreover, were entitled to "bread and circuses"—a ration of wheat and free entertainment. Citizens and subjects across the immense empire had to be taxed to cover this vast expense. Surviving documents from Egypt show that local officials kept careful registers of land ownership, which noted the legal status and state of cultivation of each plot. *Coded marginal annotations—a single letter or a pen stroke—indicate that these records were consulted and used, though their exact meaning is unclear. When an official suspected that a given landowner was not paying a proper share, he could check the tax return in question against census records. The same officials also recorded troop movements and accommodations and ordered shipments of the materials they needed.

At a higher level, the imperial government in Rome regularly promulgated edicts, issued other official documents, and provided verdicts on legal cases appealed to the highest authority. Archives in Rome and in the provinces stored these documents. Requests for new copies regularly reached Rome and shed light on the procedures used to produce and validate them. In 39 BCE the city of Aphrodisias in Anatolia sent an ambassador to Rome, partly in order to obtain copies of four distinct documents. Octavian—not yet Augustus—replied, sending a letter to which the copies were attached. When the city government received the emperor's communication, it gave orders that both Octavian's reply and a senatorial decree should be recorded in public inscriptions. The whole system required the employment of many scribes, as well as skilled artisans who could inscribe texts on stone or bronze tablets.

Given the distances between cities—and between the provinces and Rome—such documents had to bear clear signs of their authenticity. References to archival practices were common. Octavian, writing to Aphrodisias, noted that the copies he forwarded came "from the public records," and he expressed his "wish" that the citizens of Aphrodisias would "register them among your public records." Many surviving documents contain declarations that they were "copied and approved," or statements that "I have signed it. I have approved it"—presumably to be attributed, as Clifford Ando has shown, not to the emperors who appear as the authors of the decrees in question but to the scribes who copied them. Roman magistrates also took responsibility for making new legislation known to the empire's subjects. Gradually, uniform procedures developed. Even in the Republican period, the governors of the vast Roman provinces sent copies of decrees or instructions to all major cities, with instructions that they be inscribed on stone pilasters "in the most conspicuous place, so that justice might be established for all time uniformly for all the province." Under the principate and empire, these became the norms for imperial decrees as well. Even matters not important enough to be preserved on stone had to be formally announced. A standard principle held that no one could be held accountable to obey a new ordinance until it had been posted—normally in the form of a text on *papyrus or wood—for at least thirty days.

The empire, in short, built a sophisticated system for producing and distributing official documents—one whose vast Roman core was mirrored by local archives and workshops. Yet it would be wrong to imagine that this system embraced all the tasks of government. Around 110 CE, the emperor Trajan appointed the younger Pliny, the nephew of the natural historian, as governor of Bithynia in Asia Minor. Pliny repeatedly passed the buck, forwarding requests from the citizens of his province to the emperor: "It is my custom, Sire," he remarked, his tail wagging as he dictated his letter, "to refer to you in all cases where I am in doubt, for who can better clear up difficulties and inform me?" (*Letters* X.xcvi.1) Pliny would not give permission for Prusa to build a new bath or Nicomedia to create a fire department until he had asked Trajan's assent (which was forthcoming for the former, not for the latter). When he encountered followers of a new superstition, some of them denounced by informers, he reported in detail to the emperor. Pliny composed what remains the earliest description of a

Christian service, which he confirmed by torturing two deaconesses: "they declared their guilt or error was simply this—on a fixed day they used to meet before dawn and recite a hymn among themselves to Christ, as though he were a god. So far from binding themselves by oath to commit any crime, they swore to keep from theft, robbery, adultery, breach of faith, and not to deny any trust money deposited with them when called upon to deliver it. This ceremony over, they used to depart and meet again to take food—but it was of no special character, and entirely harmless" (X.xcvi.7). What matters most about these letters, for our purposes, is the manner of their survival. The road system made it possible for the governor and the emperor to discuss official business, at the slow pace that distance required but still in detail, reflecting the granular, prosaic nature of everyday administrative work. These texts are cast in an economical, formulaic language, which enabled Pliny to report *facts, express his uncertainty about how to deal with difficult cases, and ask for advice. The emperor's replies include friendly if patronizing personal letters to his trusted governor and official rulings. "The correspondence between Pliny and Trajan," comments Kathleen M. Coleman, "lets us overhear two bureaucrats running the empire at an absolutely nuts-and-bolts level." But their surviving correspondence was not simply preserved—so far as we know—in an official archive. Pliny himself included it as the tenth book of his letters, which he may have collected and redacted from his own records, inserting the emperor's replies in the proper places, omitting many attachments mentioned in the texts, and deleting what he saw as superfluous or potentially awkward details. Some scholars have argued that Pliny assembled this collection, with Trajan's permission, to serve as a portrait of the empire in action. In this case—and in dozens of others—important documents were created and preserved in ways that suggest that important Romans saw them as their private property.

Information gathering in the empire as a whole, moreover, depended on multiple systems. The elder Pliny served the emperor Vespasian in multiple capacities. He died doing his job as prefect of the fleet, trying to rescue friends from the eruption of Mount Vesuvius—and to study it close up—in August 79 CE. He believed in seeing for himself. But in compiling his enormous *Natural History*, an *encyclopedic survey of the wonders of nature and art—especially those of the Roman Empire—he drew his information chiefly from written sources, which he listed. He probably worked from the immense notebooks full of excerpts that, the younger Pliny tells us, he compiled, using the help of slaves. Despite his official position, Pliny often compiled facts and traditions passed down in ordinary texts: for example, the descriptions of the monstrous races to be found in India. From Augustus on, Romans liked to suggest that they had conquered, and knew, the whole world. Yet Claudius Ptolemy, who folded thousands of place names and vast amounts of other information into the maps and text of his atlas, the *Geography*, in the second century CE, depended on written sources and his own conjectures for his knowledge of the Indian Ocean and seems to have had no access to military maps and itineraries, which would often have allowed him to correct his own work.

The efficiency and comprehensiveness of the Roman information state, in short, were anything but absolute. The entire corps of Roman officials numbered no more than thirty thousand to thirty-five thousand—just over a quarter as many as are employed by the American Department of Justice. Even the most important documents were not systematically classified and preserved. The first full collection of imperial edicts, the Theodosian Code, was not commissioned until 429 CE: it was promulgated nine years later. The Senate saw to it that carefully made official copies were dispatched to multiple archives. So far as its sources were concerned, though, it was a patchwork. The committee that composed it had to scour local as well as central archives, family papers, law school libraries, and other collections to find the texts of the emperors' proclaimed new laws. Transport of documents—though rapid by ancient standards—was often too slow and too unpredictable to have the desired effect. The last letter that the emperor Caligula sent to Publius Petronius, the governor of Syria, who had disobeyed what he thought an unreasonable command, threatened him with execution. Fortunately for Publius, the Jewish historian Josephus explained, "It happened that the carriers of Caius [Caligula]'s letter were caught in a storm for three months on the ocean, while the others that brought the news of Caius's death had a good voyage. Accordingly, Petronius received the letter concerning Caius twenty-seven days before he received the one against himself" (*Jewish War* II.203).

Yet the system functioned for centuries. Early in the fourth century, Eusebius of Caesarea, a Christian bishop who had avoided martyrdom during the Great Persecution, wrote a triumphant history of the Christian Church. Later he would write the life of the emperor Constantine, who had adopted the Christian God and religion. Both texts were unusual, because Eusebius filled them with documents quoted word for word—a violation of the normal conventions of narrative history in Greece and Rome. He drew them from both the archives of the more established Christian churches—especially that at Jerusalem, not far from him—and the official archives of the Roman Empire. The documents in his life of Constantine have been accused by more than one historian of being forgeries. Yet one of them has now turned up in an independent copy on papyrus, and current opinion is that they are genuine. In one case, Eusebius even stated that he was citing his text "from an authenticated copy of the imperial edict preserved in my possession, on which the personal subscription, by Constantine's right hand, signifies its testimony to the trustworthiness of my speech" (Eusebius, *Life of Constantine* II.23). Clifford Ando maintains that Eusebius saw himself as following Roman practice when he emphasized that his histories rested on authentic documents. And it is certain that he knew and used the imperial information system. When the emperor asked Eusebius to have his *scriptorium produce fifty large Bibles for the new churches of Constantinople, he sent the necessary *parchment—too much for even a rich bishop to provide—by the post carts of the *cursus publicus*. And when Eusebius himself compiled his work on the topography of Palestine, he drew on military records for the positions of towns and the directions of roads. No wonder that Chinese and Jewish observers, like Eusebius, found much to admire in Rome's imperial information culture.

In one respect, though, Eusebius's admiration was qualified. When he quoted his official copy of Constantine's letter, he explained that "I think it well to insert [it] here as connected with my present subject, in order . . . that a copy of this document may be recorded as matter of history, and thus preserved to posterity." The implicit point of this remark is clearly true. The archives that held the emperor's letters have disappeared, taking the vast majority of their contents with them. Yet Eusebius's literary work remains, attesting to the power of writing and the materials on which it is inscribed to preserve what governmental power could not.

FRAGILE INFRASTRUCTURE: PAPER

Writing materials, like trade, are ancient and varied. More than two thousand years ago, the Chinese were the first to realize that plant fibers, now known as cellulose, could be beaten, mixed with water, and then left on a screen to drain until a sheet of paper remained. This practical discovery changed the world. Millennia before anyone knew what cellulose was, papermakers separated it strand by strand from wood and silk, cotton and seaweed, and devised a writing material that is still cheaper and more adaptable than any other. The Chinese themselves had long since developed elaborate systems for incising their characters on bones and tortoiseshell, and for writing them with ink on strips of bamboo, as well as for inscribing them on bronze bells and cauldrons and boulders. But paper rapidly showed its advantages. It could be created from different raw materials, from various plants to waste rags, and in many different forms and qualities. Brilliant white paper made from the bark of paper mulberry was used for the largest scrolls; bright green paper, perhaps from mulberry bark, for writing; white rattan paper for the Inner Chamber edicts of the Tang government. Paper could also be used for many purposes, from wiping the nose to doing the same for the rear—a use attested by the sixth century (for its later diffusion see Fitzgerald and Nappi, chap. 3).

Made from inexpensive materials, paper could be produced in sufficient quantities to be used for printing. For millennia the Chinese had used seals to make impressions of reverse images with ink. They also found paper useful for taking rubbings, copies of reliefs and inscriptions. By the beginning of the seventh century, carved woodblocks were in use to print images and characters on paper. During the Tang (618–906) and Song (960–1279) dynasties, woodblock printing spread. At first it was used chiefly for practical works, such as medical texts and almanacs. By 868, a Chinese translation of the Diamond Sutra, a Buddhist text on the pursuit of perfection, had been printed. The only known copy of it, now in London, was found, appropriately, at Dunhuang. Over the centuries to come, woodblock printing would become the standard method for reproducing Chinese texts of every kind, from the classics and the commentaries on them to novels. At first, the government dominated production, but in the course of the Song dynasty, commercial printers also appeared, competing to dominate the market with what they and their editors described as critical editions, produced by comparing many versions of the classic texts, preserved in academy libraries. Though printing with movable metal type was also invented in China, in the eleventh century, woodblock printing, which was cheaper when used for large editions, remained the standard method. Printing moved from China to Korea and then to Japan. There too it sparked innovation. By the fourteenth century, Korean books were being printed with movable metal type.

"The Silk Road," as Lothar Müller observed, "was also a paper road." In the eighth and ninth centuries, Chinese paper texts bearing everything from inventories to short Buddhist scriptures traveled as far as the Caucasus Mountains, near the Black Sea. More important, the methods of papermaking also traveled. By the time the storeroom at Dunhuang was closed off, it contained thousands of documents, from astrological charts to scriptures: hundreds of them are written on paper. The new religion of Islam took shape—and its followers captured vast territories, from central Asia to

Spain and Africa—in the seventh and eighth centuries. At first, Muslims used the writing materials that had been most common in the ancient Mediterranean. Scribes normally used parchment, the writing material made from the skins of sheep and calves, for the Quran. Egypt was the home of papyrus—the paper, made from reeds that grew in the Nile, that had been the standard writing material for ancient Greece as well as Egypt. It found use in bureaucratic documents, as the new government grew.

But paper had much to offer the followers of Islam. The Chinese had already found that rags, as well as bark, could be turned into paper. In central Asia and beyond, mulberry bark was not available. But used clothing and cordage were. As great new cities took shape at Baghdad, Damascus, and elsewhere, paper mills were created. They took advantage of a ready-made wealth of raw material. Cheaper than parchment, which depended on the availability of livestock and required intensive preparation, more flexible and durable than papyrus, paper could be used for many purposes. The fifteenth-century historian Ibn Khaldūn explained that a vizier who had served the caliph Hārūn al-Rashīd, eight hundred years before, sponsored the manufacture of paper in Baghdad because parchment was in short supply. His decision, Ibn Khaldūn held, had transformed politics and culture: "paper was used for government documents and diplomas. Afterwards, people used paper in sheets for government and scholarly writings, and the manufacture [of paper] reached a considerable degree of excellence."

Gradually paper did become the writing material of choice, for the Quran and other texts as well as for government registers and inventories. Paper mills spread across the Islamic world, all the way to Iberia. New techniques were developed. Rags had to be beaten before they could be spread across the racks to form paper. The mills of Samarkand, in modern Uzbekistan, used water to power mechanical hammers, known in the West as stampers, to carry out this part of the process.

The ready availability of paper, as Jonathan Bloom has shown, transformed possibilities in many fields. Though the Quran always remained as much an oral as a written text, meant for recitation, a world of commentaries and further traditions grew up alongside it, recorded—like the Quran itself—on paper. Another vast world of philosophy and *philology, based on translations from Greek into Syriac and from Syriac into Arabic, grew up in fields from medicine to metaphysics. Imaginative writers began to rework stories and fables into works on a grander and more elaborate scale—like the *Thousand and One Nights*, the title of which appears on one of the earliest Arabic documents to survive, a ninth-century fragment preserved in Chicago.

Muslims learned to compute, using Arabic numerals, with pen and ink on paper rather than an abacus or dust board. Cartographers who revived and expanded the techniques inherited from the Greek and Roman world made their maps on paper. Architects used paper to draw up formal plans for buildings. Paper, the nomadic medium, provided essential aid to societies that were remaking themselves in the pursuit of many forms of knowledge. It made possible the founding of libraries from Damascus to the Abbasid *"House of Wisdom" in Baghdad and the tenth-century library of Caliph al-Hakam II al-Mustansir in Cordoba, and the flourishing of book markets like the one that Ibn Baṭṭūṭa found in fourteenth-century Damascus, near the great Umayyad Mosque, and the one in Istanbul, still the largest in the Mediterranean world in the seventeenth century (see Muhanna, chap. 2). On a more humdrum level, it provided vital infrastructure for the growth of the trade networks documented by the thousands of letters and contracts, court documents, and pilgrim records, fragments of which were stored in the Cairo Genizah, the storeroom of the Ben Ezra Synagogue in Old Cairo—networks that stretched from Morocco to India.

Paper mills were not altogether good neighbors. They were noisy; they processed vast piles of dirty rags, collected by male and female ragpickers; and they stank of ammonia, often derived from human urine, which was used to break down the rags' fibers. Neighbors hated them. Yet their workers developed extraordinary skills, working "so quickly and with such agility that you can scarcely see their hands." More important, they produced something mysteriously strong and beautiful. As an observer wrote on visiting a paper mill in seventeenth-century Genoa: "the way paper is made is a marvelous thing, because, as we have said, the materials from which it is made are merely rags and water, which have no viscous or resistant qualities, and yet the sheets of paper made from them have such consistency that they are better than cloth."

Some early reactions to paper in Christian Europe were negative. Peter the Venerable complained around 1144 that Jews wrote on a material made not, as it should be, from animal skins, but from "scraps of old rags or even viler stuff." A century later Emperor Frederick II forbade its use in official records. Others, however, adopted it eagerly. Once King Jaume the Conqueror had fought his way to mastery of the Iberian coastal realm that he called the kingdom of Valencia, his government produced thousands of documents. More than ten thousand of them, written between 1257 and 1276, are now preserved in twenty-nine immense volumes. From the start he issued charters in paper as well as parchment, to Christians as well as Muslims, using the products of the Muslim paper mill at Játiva and then establishing his own mill. Soon paper mills opened in southern France and in Fabriano in the Italian Marches, where wire molds produced paper with handsome surface patterns and distinctive watermarks.

Innovation never stopped. European technology for making scissors improved in the fourteenth century, making it possible to cut the rags that went into paper more evenly. So did methods for wire drawing, which enabled papermakers to make finer sieves than ever before, with which they could produce an absolutely smooth form of paper. European papermakers devised a way to size paper with gelatin, giving it a smooth surface that was impervious to ink and resisted abrasion and soiling. Many grades of paper were available. When the Nuremberg printer Johannes Petreius was trying to convince Erasmus Reinhold to publish with him, he promised that his work would appear on "fine crown paper." Early printers used parchment for deluxe copies of particular books. But Vincenzo Conti, who owned the press at Cremona, did not need to have animals skinned when he brought out the first three-volume edition of the *Zohar*, the core text of the kabbalah from 1558 to 1560. Instead he followed a precedent set by Daniel Bomberg and used a rich blue paper for some copies.

By the fourteenth century, paper played a substantial role in book production in the Latin West. Most authors still preferred parchment, especially for the fine presentation copies of their works destined for patrons. Some thirty extant documents contain Petrarch's handwriting. Only two are on paper. A generation later, Christine de Pizan still preferred parchment for the splendid *illuminated copies of her French writings. In them she herself appeared, wielding the penknife with which she would have both sharpened her quill and scraped away slips of the pen. But secular scribal work was expanding, in city governments and state bureaucracies. *Vernacular literature of all kinds was being written and copied. The Latin literature of the humanists was also finding a larger market. Several of the translations and treatises of the most popular fifteenth-century humanist, Leonardo Bruni, are preserved in two or three hundred manuscript copies each, all, or all but a handful, written on paper. Paper production grew to meet the need, and more—so much so that it began to dominate the Muslim as well as the Christian market. In 1409 a worried client asked the Maghrebi jurist Ibn Marzûq for a formal opinion on whether a devout Muslim could use Christian paper—particularly Christian paper with a watermark that might include Christian symbols—for the Quran and other texts. In an elaborate fatwa, Ibn Marzûq argued that one could. The holy text, after all, transformed the mere medium that held it.

Paper made possible the rise of movable-type printing in Europe in the fifteenth century, which is treated in detail below (Blair, chap. 4). But it made other developments possible as well. A vast expansion of writing took place at the same time as printing, which became the dominant form of publication. Even as printers filled the world with books, governments invested in vast new paper management systems, diplomats filed endless reports in cipher, impresarios produced handwritten newsletters for select clients, and scholars devoted their lives to filling notebooks with excerpts taken from the vast production of the presses and systematically classified. The age of Gutenberg was also the age of the "paper king," Philip II of Spain, who took to signing documents with a stamp and waved them around at meetings like a *Renaissance Joseph McCarthy (Head, chap. 6).

It seems completely appropriate that Columbus, trying to understand what he was seeing in the Indies, used pen and paper as his tools. In this as in other ways, he was the heir of generations of travelers and traders, missionaries and skippers. Some of their ways would soon be transformed beyond recognition. Others continued to rest on foundations laid long before and far away.

Anthony Grafton

See also bureaucracy; commodification; diplomats/spies; documentary authority; ethnography; globalization; governance; knowledge; letters; maps; merchants; networks; notebooks; observing; travel; xylography

FURTHER READING

Clifford Ando, *Imperial Ideology and Provincial Loyalty in the Roman Empire*, 2000; Timothy Barrett, "Early European Papers/Contemporary Conservation Papers," *Paper Conservator* 13 (1989): 1–108; Jonathan Bloom, *Paper before Print: The History and Impact of Paper in the Islamic World*, 2001; Fernand Braudel, *The Mediterranean and the Mediterranean World in the Age of Philip II*, 1949, translated by Siân Reynolds, 1973; Socha Carey, *Pliny's Catalogue of Culture: Art and Empire in the "Natural History,"* 2003; Kathleen M. Coleman, "Bureaucratic Language in the Correspondence between Pliny and Trajan," *Transactions of the American Philological Association* 142, no. 2 (2012): 189–238; Paul Freedman, *Out of the East: Spices and the Medieval Imagination*, 2008; Anthony Grafton and Megan Williams, *Christianity and the Transformation of the Book: Origen, Eusebius and the Library of Caesarea*, 2006; Valerie Hansen, *The Silk Road: A New History with Documents,*

2017; Friedrich Hirth, "The Story of Chang K'ien, China's Pioneer in Western Asia," *Journal of the American Oriental Society* 37 (1919): 89–152; Christopher Kelly, *Ruling the Later Roman Empire*, 2004; Xinrue Liu, *The Silk Road in World History*, 2010; John Matthews, *Laying Down the Law: A Study of the Theodosian Code*, 2000; Jacob Mikanowski, "A Secret Library, Digitally Excavated," *New Yorker*, October 9, 2013; Lothar Müller, *White Magic: The Age of Paper*, 2012, translated by Jessica Spengler, 2014; Walter Scheidel, "ORBIS; The Stanford Geospatial Network Model of the Roman World" (online); Romolo Augusto Staccioli, *The Roads of the Romans*, 2003; Frances Wood, *The Silk Road: Two Thousand Years in the Heart of Asia*, 2002.

2

REALMS OF INFORMATION IN THE MEDIEVAL ISLAMIC WORLD

This chapter considers the history of information in the medieval Islamic world. Before setting off, a few remarks about the words *information* and *Islamic* are necessary. The diverse readings of the concept of information found in this volume testify to the difficulty of saying what it is, particularly outside the context of the information age. Scholars of historical civilizations are accustomed to thinking about the development of intellectual disciplines, scribal traditions, educational institutions, and other subjects related to the history of knowledge. But what about information? Are knowledge and information the same thing? Some have drawn on a familiar metaphor from structuralist anthropology to distinguish between the two concepts, suggesting that information is "raw" while knowledge is "cooked." Others describe information as free-floating and value neutral, and knowledge as holistic and rooted within a particular epistemological regime. Information is often said to be "harvested" or "gathered" while knowledge is "produced." Are these meaningful distinctions, or has knowledge been information all along?

In Classical Arabic and Persian, the literary languages of the contexts I will be exploring, a distinction is detectable between terms associated with knowledge (Arabic: *ʿilm, maʿrifa, ḥikma*; Persian: *dānist, dānish, maʿrifat*), and a rich stock of words denoting a class of entities that, while related to knowledge, aren't quite the same thing. An important term in this regard is *khabar* (pl. *akhbār*), which Lane's *Arabic-English Lexicon* defines as "*a piece of information; a notification; intelligence; an announcement; news; tidings . . . what is related from another or others*: to which authors on the Arabic language add, that it may be *true* or *false*." *Akhbār* is the stock-in-trade of historians; many chronicles have the word in their titles. Like information, a *khabar* may be disseminated, investigated, circulated, published, and suppressed. It can be scrutinized, falsified, deemed unreliable, taken out of context, or colored by bias, and it is sought out through reading and research (*muṭālaʿa*) or interrogation (*istifsār*). Information of this kind is often granular, described as a small particle, portion, or trace (*luṭkha, nubdha, athar*), and may take different shapes: a narrative (*riwāya*), an announcement (*nabaʾ*), or a strange report (*ṭurfa*).

Many of these Arabic terms are also found in Persian, where the word *khabar* is connected with a wide array of professions, from scholars to explorers, investigators, spies, historians, informers, and scouts. The methods of acquiring information are strongly associated with the five senses, reflected in the Persian word for "ear" (*gosh*), which may refer figuratively to a spy, sentinel (*goshchī*), rumor (*gosh-zad*); and "tongue" (*zabān*), which is connected with the act of taking a prisoner to gain information (*zabān giriftan*) about an enemy. Perhaps the most common word for spy in Arabic, Persian, and Turkish—*jāsūs*—derives from the Arabic verb *jassa* (to touch, feel, take the pulse of). All this is to say that while *information* is a term that has certainly been reshaped by developments in digital technology since the middle of the twentieth century, there is no shortage of concepts from medieval Islamicate languages pointing to a category that looks quite a bit like "information," in the looser sense of "reports supposed to be truthful or useful that could be spread in various media," as Ann Blair has written. This is the sense I will be using in this chapter.

So much for information—what about *Islamic*? A history of information in the medieval Islamic world is difficult to imagine in light of the great diversity of peoples, cultures, and languages encompassed by that term. It would include over a millennium's worth of attitudes, artifacts, and practices across a large part of the Earth, from Indian tax records and Syrian cookbooks to the teaching circles of medieval Fes and the libraries of Mamluk Cairo. In other words, too much information. How to go about synthesizing it into knowledge? And why would such an exercise be useful? I propose to address these questions by introducing some of the most important tokens of the creation, circulation, transmission, authentication, and interpretation of information in three historical contexts: ninth- and tenth-century Iraq, the heart of the Abbasid Empire; fourteenth-century Egypt and Syria, which were ruled by the Mamluk sultanate; and Timurid Iran and Khorasan in the fifteenth century. A history of information in just one of these contexts would fill an entire book. This discussion is, therefore, necessarily macroscopic and intended as a survey as well as an attempt to rethink the history of knowledge through the lens of information.

IRAQ, NINTH AND TENTH CENTURIES

In the late ninth century the city of Baghdad was a hundred years old, the capital of an empire that stretched from North Africa to Transoxania. Never again would a single Islamic polity exert its dominion—however tenuously in some territories—across such a wide span of the globe. When people today speak of the golden age of Islamic civilization, many have Abbasid Baghdad in mind, a glorious city inhabited by scientists, translators, poets, musicians, and philosophers. The stories of its rulers and their courts, their soirees filled with learned and witty conversation, would be told in the literature and lore of the Islamic world for centuries.

According to some early accounts of the city's founding, the specific time and place chosen for Baghdad's erection were decided by information. An ancient prophecy foretelling that the caliph al-Manṣūr would erect a great city on the banks of the Tigris was found in a Christian text. A Persian astrologer in al-Manṣūr's court cast a horoscope establishing that July 30, 762, was an opportune moment to commence work on the foundation. Alongside astrological information and prophecies, geopolitical concerns played a deciding role. The new city sat on a fertile plain where the Tigris and Euphrates Rivers were only thirty kilometers apart. Baghdad was positioned more centrally than the old Umayyad capital at Damascus with respect to the empire's expansion into Iran and central Asia. It sat along the road to Khorasan, serving as a waystation for caravans from the East traveling to the Levant and Egypt, and for pilgrims making their way to Mecca for the annual hajj pilgrimage. In this respect, Baghdad was a place to and from which many things flowed: people, commodities, and information. The book markets of the city, like its palaces and gardens, would become proverbial in Islamic history. Before visiting them, it is worth considering the backdrop of Baghdad's bookish culture. Both before and after the arrival of paper in the eighth century, the world of information was profoundly shaped by knowledge practices rooted in orality.

Orality and Information

The origins of all the major disciplines of Islamic thought are connected to orality in some way, none so firmly as the area of prophetic tradition (hadith). In the years after the death of the Prophet Muḥammad in 632 CE, there emerged a large body of tradition about his biography. This took many shapes: narratives about his political career following the revelation of the Quran, details of his ethical views, anecdotes about his dealings with different groups of people, and general data about his life. Insofar as the Quran did not provide answers to every practical, legal, or theological question that medieval Muslims would meditate on in the centuries after the revelation, the traditions about Muḥammad's life and customs, as well as those of his closest companions, acquired tremendous significance.

At first, these traditions, like the Quranic revelations, circulated almost exclusively in oral form. Muḥammad's companions were the keepers of this data, but as they relayed it on to their own disciples and followers in the growing Muslim community, the population of transmitters grew larger, as did the number of utterances and actions attributed to Muḥammad. By the ninth century, a *canon of authoritative selections was beginning to emerge in the form of respected compendia compiled by traditionists. Relying on a sophisticated methodology of authentication through the use of the *isnād*— or chain of transmitters—compilers like Muḥammad ibn Ismāʿīl al-Bukhārī pulled together the hadiths that merited special status on the basis of the trustworthiness of their transmitters. This mode of authenticating information was initially associated with the hadith literature, but it would have an important impact on other forms of knowledge transmission throughout the Islamic world.

Even as the methodology for certifying the trustworthiness of information about the Prophet became more robust, the traditions that were deemed suspect (or even confirmed as forgeries) were not universally discarded. Many continued to be recorded and transmitted. Some scholars became specialists in compiling hadiths known to be problematic or abrogated by other, more reliable reports, as well as hadiths that were authenticated by only a single chain of transmission. This practice of preserving information even while recording its abrogation had parallels in the study of the Quran. The concept of abrogation (*naskh*) is one of the most important principles in Quranic *exegesis and Islamic legal theory. It offered to the exegete a way to harmonize and explain contradictions, inconsistencies, and ambiguities that emerged from the study of the Quran and the hadith canon, particularly when such problematic elements bore on legal issues.

In its most common form, the ruling expressed in one Quranic verse could be overruled or superseded by the ruling in a different verse. Such an approach to the Quran renders it a kind of divine palimpsest, overwriting itself while continuing to preserve the abrogated verses. Sanction for a theory of abrogation comes from the Quran itself (Q 2:106, "And for whatever verse We abrogate [*nansakh*] or cast into oblivion, We bring a better or the like of it"). The verb *nasakha* has several meanings, among them: to obliterate, abandon, replace, nullify, erase, copy, transfer, and others. In interpreting Q2:106, the medieval exegetes explained the word *nansakh* in terms of either suppression or supersession. For the first meaning, scholars referred to Q13:39 ("God blots out and establishes what He pleases, and with Him is the Mother of the Book"), which suggests that God can (and does) erase or suppress parts of the Quran for unknown reasons. For the second meaning, the relevant verse adduced was Q16:101 ("When We replace one verse with another"), which suggests a process of divine "editing" or supersession within the revelation history of the Quran. These two processes are central to the history of Quran's reception in the medieval Islamic world and reveal how self-consciously preoccupied with issues of authentication, contradiction, and supersession Muslim learned cultures have been throughout history.

What were some of the other emerging disciplines influenced by the oral lifeworld of ninth-century Iraq? Even as the empire was becoming more ethnically and linguistically heterogeneous, there remained tremendous cachet associated with the Arabic language and the poetry of the pre-Islamic Bedouin tribes, who were thought to speak the purest and most eloquent form of the language. Beginning in the eighth century, *philologists from the emerging grammatical schools of Kufa and Basra began to systematize Classical Arabic. The medieval sources report that individuals like Sībawayh, a scholar of Persian extraction and the author of the first grammar of Arabic, *al-Kitāb* (The book), would go out into the desert and spend time with the Bedouins, observing their speech patterns and asking them questions about unusual expressions and rare words. The results of these exploratory missions found their way into grammars, word lists, dictionaries, and other philological texts. The earliest scholars of poetry built their corpora in similar ways, collecting their data—individual verses, fragments, and entire poems—from the mouths of tribal poets. The Arabic word for poetic criticism (*naqd*) derives from the idea of assaying currency to determine its authenticity. This is to say that the act of criticism was, from the start, concerned with determining the authenticity of poetic information.

The codification of Classical Arabic on the basis of what we might call today a form of ethnolinguistic dialectology would serve an infrastructural purpose for the apparatus of learned culture in the Islamic world for over a thousand years. Besides standardizing what would become one of the world's great cosmopolitan languages, the work of philology played an elemental role in a major cultural project: the exegesis of the Quran. The urban environments of Baghdad, Kufa, Basra, and Mosul were far removed from the Meccan setting in which the Quran had been revealed two centuries earlier, and the context for making sense of many of the Quran's references and its allusively evocative language was increasingly remote. As such, the ninth century witnessed the composition of some of the most influential works of exegesis (*tafsīr*) in Islamic history, none more important than Muḥammad ibn Jarīr al-Ṭabarī's thirty-volume work. The scholarship of al-Ṭabarī, a Persian *polymath who also authored the ninth century's most significant chronicle, the forty-volume *History of the Prophets and Kings* (*Tarīkh al-rusul wa-l-mulūk*), is an example of how different streams of information flowed together in the work of interpreting the Quran. Al-Ṭabarī's commentary brought together narratives of tribal exploits, linguistic analysis, accounts of prophetic history, and traditions about Muḥammad's life, all by way of stitching together the backdrop for the revelatory material.

A Well-Rounded Education

Al-Ṭabarī was in a class of his own in terms of the significance of his monumental works of history and exegesis, but ninth-century Baghdad was full of polymaths. The Abbasid Empire's secretarial class abounded in individuals well versed in a variety of disciplines, a quality seen as necessary for the duties of a scribal bureaucrat. A famous description of this many-sided competence is found in a manual on secretaryship by Ibn Qutayba, another ninth-century polymath:

> The Persians always used to say, "He who is not knowledgeable about diverting water into channels, digging out courses for irrigation streams and blocking up disused well-shafts; about the changes in the length of the days as they increase and decrease, the revolution of the sun, the rising-places of the stars and the state of the new moon as it begins to wax, and its subsequent phases; about the various weights in use; about the measurement of triangles, four-sided figures and polygons; about the construction of bridges and aqueducts, irrigation machines and water wheels; and about the materials used by various artisans, and the fine points of financial accounting—such a person must be considered only partly-qualified as a secretary." (Bosworth, "Pioneer")

Descriptions like this are plentiful in the historical sources, and while they smack of hyperbole and self-aggrandizement—after all, many of the authors of such descriptions were scribes themselves—there are a few important things to note in the description. One is the Persian connection: the secretarial tradition of the new Islamic empire was strongly shaped by the bureaucratic cultures of earlier polities. Under the Umayyads, who ruled from Damascus, many of the scribal families had come from the Byzantine Empire and brought with them a knowledge of Greek, Aramaic, and other languages of the Levant. In Iraq, most of the scribal elite had Persian ancestry, descending from families who had served the Sasanian Empire. This intermixing of cultures had an effect on the texts that circulated in the growing cities of Iraq. The ideal of encyclopedic education represented in Ibn Qutayba's description would, over time, come to apply to the materials of that education rather than just the ideal itself. The notion of *adab*—a term that means "good breeding," "good manners," a well-rounded education—emerged during this time as the name of a bibliographic *genre: an umbrella category that included poetry, belletristic prose narratives and reports about important historical figures, quotations from scripture and the hadith literature, proverbs, rare words and other lexicographical oddities, and materia medica (i.e., ingredients of medical recipes). One of the most important works in this genre, *Choice Reports* (*ʿUyūn al-akhbār*) was written by Ibn Qutayba himself and launched a tradition of adab *encyclopedias that aimed to provide an overview of the topics that any aspirant to a certain status of cultural literacy would be expected to know. *Choice Reports* contained ten chapters on the topics of sovereignty, war, governance, traits and morals, knowledge, piety, friends, achieving one's ends, food, and women. A few decades later, *The Unique Necklace* (*al-ʿIqd al-farīd*) of the Andalusian courtier and poet Ibn ʿAbd Rabbih (d. 328/940) had swelled to nearly twice as long as *Choice Reports*. Following in the footsteps of these two foundational texts, adab encyclopedias proliferated throughout the Islamic world.

Classifying the Sciences

The explosion of books in the ninth century created a familiar problem: How to organize all this information? One solution took the shape of yet another bibliographical category, books on the classification of the sciences. Less voluminous than the adab encyclopedias, these texts included curricula of the disciplines like al-Fārābī's *Enumeration of the Sciences* (*Iḥṣāʾ al-ʿulūm*), dictionaries of technical terms such as al-Khwārizmī's *Keys of the Sciences* (*Mafātīḥ al-ʿulūm*), and programs for the integration of the rational and religious sciences, such as Abū ʿAlī Miskawayh's *The Classification of the Sciences and the Classification of Happiness* (*Tartīb al-ʿulūm wa-tartīb al-saʿādāt*). These works were the outcome of a larger process of consolidation that many disciplines would undergo, reflected in the growing conventionality of book arrangements, page layouts, tables of contents, and titles, and of generic categories. By this time, a canon was beginning to emerge in different disciplines, with respected oral authorities being replaced by textual sources. The textualization of information meant, among other things, that it could travel to places it hadn't before. Scholars with the means to devote all their time to study and teaching often moved from one city to another with their books. In their new homes, surrounded by new students, these books would serve as the progenitors of new textual seedlings, as the students copied texts from exemplar manuscripts. The oral tradition, however, never died away. Even in this new textualized form, remnants of the memory-based transmission of information persisted in the mechanisms by which information was passed along. Students earned the right to copy a text by reading it aloud to their master to ensure that there were no flaws in the process of copying. Once a perfect copy had been made, the student would receive a certificate (*ijāza*) to make additional copies of the text. This process of certification represented an essential mechanism for authenticating textualized information in the premodern Islamic world. It would last for centuries and was used in the madrasas of Pakistan and the Sufi lodges of Marrakesh.

One of the most important encyclopedic works produced in tenth-century Iraq was *The Epistles of the Sincere Brethren* (*Rasāʾil Ikhwān al-Ṣafāʾ*), a collection of letters on various philosophical themes including the "mathematical sciences," the "corporeal and natural sciences," the "sciences of the soul and of the intellect," and the "nomic, divine, and legal sciences." Who were the Sincere Brethren? The identity of this collective remains relatively obscure, but scholars believe that they were a group of Ismāʿīlī Shīʿī figures interested in Neoplatonic and Neopythagorean thought, with influences from other traditions such as Gnosticism and Hermeticism. Although the *Epistles* circulated widely, they did not exert much influence on the future of the philosophical encyclopedic tradition, which was dominated by Ibn Sīnā (d. 449/1037, also known as Avicenna) and his commentators. However, as we will see later in this chapter, the career of the Sincere Brethren would inspire other clandestine intellectual networks in the Turko-Persianate world.

Besides codicological means of consolidating knowledge, this era witnessed another important phenomenon: the emergence of knowledge practices concerned with the theoretical underpinnings of other disciplines. Characterized by the term *principles* or *origins* (*uṣūl*) in their titles, these fields sought to uncover the elemental assumptions and logical processes that lay at the basis of disciplines like grammar (*naḥw*), jurisprudence (*fiqh*), and lexicography (*lugha*). Today, we refer to information about information by the term *metadata*; by this token, one might call these knowledge practices *metadisciplines*. They sought to make sense of how disciplines operated and how they thought about their constitutive data.

The Paper Revolution

The transition from a culture in which information was transmitted orally to a written ecosystem was aided by the appearance of a revolutionary technology in the Islamic lands. Paper first arrived in Iraq in the eighth century, having been unknown in the lands governed by the Sasanian and Byzantine Empires before the rise of Islam. Prior to that, other materials had been used for record keeping. The Arabic word for account book, *daftar*, is derived from the Greek word *diphthera*, meaning "skin, hide," pointing to the practice of using prepared animal skins (parchment) as well as *papyrus for bureaucratic accounting. A paper mill was built in Baghdad in 794–95 CE, during the reign of the caliph Hārūn al-Rashīd, and paper began to replace more costly writing surfaces. Some reports suggest that the use of paper in al-Rashīd's administration was both a matter of cost savings and a safeguard against forgery, as writing on paper was more difficult to erase or scratch out than texts on parchment. From Iraq, paper would travel swiftly across the Islamic empire, reaching Spain within two hundred years of its discovery in central Asia.

The market for books in Baghdad meant that there was always a demand for the trade of the copyist (*warrāq*), who made copies of manuscripts that were in demand and sold them. The most famous bookseller in Islamic history was one such copyist: Abu l-Faraj Muḥammad ibn Isḥāq, known as al-Nadīm. Born in the first half of the tenth century in Baghdad, al-Nadīm was introduced to the trade at a young age. He traveled across Iraq, studying with notable teachers and frequenting the court circle of one of the grandees of the Abbasid Empire. His travels brought him to libraries and book markets, exposing him to the contours of the growing ocean of books. By way of mapping this ocean, al-Nadīm composed a work entitled *The Index* (*al-Fihrist*), a bibliographic compendium divided into ten chapters, cataloging all the Arabic books that he had come across during his travels. The chapters were organized thematically. The first six addressed subjects related to what were already, by then, considered to be the "traditional" subjects of the Arabic-speaking world (holy scriptures, grammar, historical works, genealogy, and belletristic prose, poetry, theology, and law). The last four chapters took up books translated from the "foreign" (mainly Greek) sciences, on subjects like philosophy, magic, fables, storytelling, syncretistic religions, and alchemy.

Al-Nadīm's *Index* provides an invaluable window into the culture of bookmaking in the tenth century, and also a sense of its bibliographic categories. He includes information about the length of books and their authors, and reports about well-known libraries and patrons of letters. The *Index* also provides rare insight into one of the most famous libraries in history, the *House of Wisdom (Bayt al-Ḥikma), an institution connected with the early Abbasid caliphs al-Rashīd and al-Maʾmūn. The House of Wisdom was a palace library staffed mainly by officials of Iranian descent, responsible for collecting books about Persian heritage and ancient Arabian lore. Among its holdings, al-Nadīm records, were old manuscripts written in different scripts and a book believed to be in the hand of Muḥammad's grandfather ʿAbd al-Muṭṭalib ibn Hāshim. Al-Nadīm also mentions that some of the employees of the House of Wisdom were engaged in translating Persian books into Arabic. This report, along with another that connects the library's director, Salm, with a translation of Ptolemy's *Almagest*, fed the supposition among many scholars during the twentieth century that the House of Wisdom was a kind of research academy, the hub of a caliphate-sponsored project to translate Greek scientific and philosophical texts into Arabic. Recent scholarship has corrected that view; the name of the library was likely a translation of the Middle Persian term used for the palace libraries of the Sasanian empire of Iran, reflecting the influence of the bureaucratic traditions of Iran on the new Islamic empire.

The Abbasid translation movement was a watershed in the history of information. As Dimitri Gutas has written, "One can justly claim that the study of post-classical Greek secular writings can hardly proceed without the evidence in Arabic, which in this context becomes the second classical language, even before Latin." Beginning in the mid-eighth century, during the reign of al-Manṣūr, the builder of Baghdad, and reaching its apogee in the ninth century, the campaign to translate works of philosophy, medicine, mathematics, geometry, and other disciplines from Greek, Syriac, and Pahlavi would have a great impact on the transmission of these sciences throughout the Islamic world and into medieval Europe. The question of why translation was an imperial policy of the Abbasids is one that would require too much space to explore here, but, as we have already seen in the excerpt from Ibn Qutayba's manual on secretaryship, the benefits of astrology, geometry, arithmetic, and other sciences to the practice of statecraft are readily apparent. It is important to stress that this movement, which lasted over two centuries, was supported not just by the political elite of Abbasid society but also by its scholars, bureaucrats, and merchants. It was a widespread cultural project that cut across different confessional, ethnic, and class lines.

During the ninth century, the most famous figure associated with the translation movement was Ḥunayn ibn Isḥāq, a Christian Arab from southern Iraq. Ḥunayn studied medicine in Baghdad at a young age and then traveled to the Byzantine lands— probably Constantinople—where he continued his studies and attained a mastery of Greek. His translations of the works of Galen from the Greek into Syriac and Arabic were commissioned by members of the Abbasid court and other wealthy patrons. Working with his son and nephew, he translated much of the Galenic corpus, along with works by Dioscorides, Artemidorus, and Aristotle, as well as the Old Testament. As a translator, Ḥunayn was a singular talent, but as a multilingual individual he was emblematic of the linguistic pluralism of Abbasid Iraq. The literate community of Iraq was familiar with Persian, Greek, and Syriac and almost certainly spoke a very different variety of Arabic than it wrote. The language of writing was what we today call Classical Arabic (*al-ʿarabiyya*, or *al-ʿarabiyya al-fuṣḥā*) while the languages of everyday speech—the dialects of Baghdad, Mosul, Basra, and Kufa, and all the subdialects within those *vernaculars—were grouped under the broad category of the demotic (*lughat al-ām*). Why should this matter to the history of information? Simply, because such a history is more than a catalog of official records and learned culture; information takes many forms. The existence of a prestige dialect in the Islamic lands served as a gatekeeper to the fields of privileged information. Like Latin in medieval and *Renaissance Europe, Classical Arabic predominated as the language of high culture, thus regulating the production of certain genres of information and delimiting the boundaries of the channels through which it flowed. In later centuries, evidence of information circulating in other registers of Arabic attests to the widening of those channels.

EGYPT AND SYRIA, FOURTEENTH CENTURY

In 1258, the armies of the Mongol Ilkhanids led by Hülegü, a grandson of Genghis Khan, sacked the Abbasid capital at Baghdad and brought an end to a dynasty that had reigned for half a millennium. The Mongol conquests created great upheaval in the Near East, laying waste to cities and causing the deaths of millions through war, disease, and deprivation. The campaigns in the Russian steppe during the 1220s and 1230s transformed the slave trade and facilitated the rise of a regiment of slave-soldiers (*mamlūks*) who would overthrow their masters and rise to power, ruling over Egypt, Syria, and parts of northwest Arabia until 1517. Over the course of the fourteenth and fifteenth centuries, the territories of the Mamluk sultanate emerged as the intellectual and cultural hubs of the Arabo-Islamic world. Learned individuals emigrated from lands where bureaucratic and scholarly institutions had been thrown into upheaval by the invasions, and many of them found new homes in Cairo and Damascus, the flourishing school cities of the Mamluk realms.

Many of these immigrants were professional scholars, a vocation made possible by the rise of a relatively new institution: the madrasa. Formally a college of jurisprudence, madrasas also offered instruction in the Quranic sciences, Prophetic traditions, Arabic grammar, rhetoric, theology, logic, mathematics, and other subjects. Students came from around the Islamic world to benefit from the hundreds of madrasas that had been established in Cairo and Damascus, endowed by wealthy members of the political and civilian elite. Many students sought careers as jurists, hoping to find employment as bureaucrats or judges in the imperial administration. Others intended to become madrasa professors themselves. Many made a living in the book trade, copying sought-after manuscripts and selling them to other scholars, interested laypeople, and the many libraries attached to the colleges. In these school cities, there was a large market for texts of a pedagogical character—commentaries, supercommentaries (i.e., commentaries on commentaries), glosses, digests, epitomes, abridgments—which offered guidance to the staples of a madrasa curriculum. A well-known work on the classification of the sciences by a fourteenth-century physician, Ibn al-Akfānī, entitled *Guiding the Seeker to the Most Splendid Destinations* (*Irshād al-qāṣid ilā asnā l-maqāṣid*), included descriptions of sixty disciplines and six hundred books associated with them. The fifteenth-century historian al-Sakhāwī prepared a list of texts mastered by graduates licensed to teach in madrasas, and it included more than a thousand works. In comparison with other premodern societies, these numbers are striking. It is not uncommon to find accounts of libraries attached to Mamluk madrasas containing thousands of books. In a study of one such institution, the Ashrafiyya (an "average" Syrian library founded in the thirteenth century), Konrad Hirschler has suggested that its holdings were comparable in size to those of all the libraries of Cambridge University combined, two centuries later.

An Age of Compendia

This bookish environment not only facilitated the work of a compiler but also, in certain ways, engendered it. Insofar as the growing numbers of books and learned people circulating within the network of scholarly institutions created a sense of the expanding boundaries of knowledge, they also made it possible to envision a solution to the problem of too much information. This partly took the form of the capacious compilatory texts that began to appear in such profusion during this period. Anthologies, manuals, encyclopedias, dictionaries, commentaries, and chronicles all depended on the act of sorting and arranging existing information into new forms. The historical sources make apparent the fact that being a learned individual in this period meant devoting a great deal of time—perhaps a majority of one's working life—to copying, editing, abridging, commenting on, excerpting, anthologizing, and reorganizing information. Even texts that declared their own originality depended heavily on the work of earlier authors. As has been observed in other contexts, the importance of information-management techniques for gathering and sorting the textual materials that found their way into finished works was paramount. The historian and polymath al-Maqrīzī completed his many books by gathering his sources together, excerpting them, summarizing them, and then composing them into rough drafts and then finished drafts. Some scholars kept a *commonplace book or aide-memoire (tadhkira) in which they made copies and excerpts of works they found to be useful in the course of their reading. The Tadhkira of Khalīl ibn Aybak al-Ṣafadī, a prolific author and bureaucrat of the fourteenth century, contained thirty volumes.

Among the many types of books that organized information in encyclopedic dimensions was the biographical dictionary. Compendia of famous individuals had been written in the Islamic world prior to this period, but the Mamluk realms saw an efflorescence and diversification of this genre. In its outlines, a biographical dictionary is a collection of biographies of famous individuals (mostly men, but famous women make appearances as well), grouped according to a theme. There are biographical dictionaries devoted to the members of a certain occupation (such as lawyers within a particular legal rite, musicians, hadith transmitters, Quran reciters, grammarians, etc.); people from a particular city; people born during a given century; and universal dictionaries that summed up all these other categories. It has been supposed that biographical dictionaries functioned as a kind of historiographical record, an alternative to the annalistic chronicle that served as a history of states.

Other types of compendia included enormous *lexicons, commentaries on the Quran and hadith, geographical works, cosmographical works, and universal histories. Similarly comprehensive in outlook, books on the classification of the sciences outlined a curriculum of study for the novice. Three of the most famous encyclopedias of the fourteenth and fifteenth centuries were composed by bureaucrats in the Mamluk administration. Shihāb al-Dīn al-Nuwayrī's thirty-one-volume work The Ultimate Ambition in the Arts of Erudition was a compendium of universal knowledge arranged into five divisions: (i) the cosmos, comprising the earth, heavens, stars, planets, and meteorological phenomena; (ii) the human being, containing material on physiology, genealogy, literature, music, proverbs, political rule, and chancery affairs; (iii) the animal world; (iv) the plant world; and (v) a universal history, beginning with Adam and Eve, and continuing all the way through the events of al-Nuwayrī's life. To flip through

The Ultimate Ambition's pages is to encounter a dizzying array of subjects: poetry about the sleepiness of cheetahs; recipes for the production of aphrodisiacs; boilerplate legal language for marriage contracts; a biography of Muḥammad and the history of the Islamic world; anatomical and literary descriptions of electric eels, turtles, falcons, and cats; administrative minutiae concerning promissory notes, joint partnerships, commercial enterprises, loans, gifts, donations, charity, transfers of property; and much more.

Another fourteenth-century encyclopedia, Ibn Faḍl Allāh al-ʿUmarī's *Routes of Insight into the Civilized Realms*, was a geographical-historical compendium consisting principally of biographies of famous personages arranged by professional categories and organized to demonstrate the supremacy of the Islamic East vis-à-vis the Maghrib. Aḥmad ibn ʿAlī al-Qalqashandī, another Mamluk bureaucrat, composed a fourteen-volume scribal encyclopedia entitled *Dawn for the Night-Blind: On the Craft of Chancery Writing*. Although the main portion of his book was devoted to furnishing the aspiring clerk with sample letters and *protocols of official address, it also covered such diverse topics as meteorological phenomena, foreign relations, the operation of water clocks, the geography of the Mamluk Empire and neighboring realms, and many other subjects.

It is in these encyclopedic texts that one best appreciates the wealth of information that circulated within the Mamluk cities. Some encyclopedists saw themselves primarily as compilers; others as synthesizers. Al-Nuwayrī and Ibn Faḍl Allāh are instructive examples in this regard. The former exhibits a mostly deferential attitude toward the information that he brings together. He makes a distinction, echoed in other sources, between different kinds of sciences, the traditional (*al-ʿulūm al-naqliyya*) and the rational (*al-ʿulūm al-ʿaqliyya*). His preference was for the former, favoring the authenticating transmission of traditional knowledge over the fickle, precarious operations of a single mind. Ibn Faḍl Allāh, by contrast, was more skeptical about time-honored knowledge. He writes in his preface that the books on geography are full of outdated information, and that he saw his role as an arbiter of fact: "Having consulted all of the books written about the states and contents of the terrestrial climes, I did not find any that scrutinized their conditions or depicted them accurately, for most of these books only contain old reports about the conditions of long-gone kings, extinct civilizations, and customs that have vanished along with their peoples. There is not much point in simply recounting them. The best statement is the truest one, and people resemble their own times more than they resemble their own ancestors" (Muhanna, *World*).

Information and Bureaucracy

It is no accident that many authors of encyclopedic texts and other compilations were employed in the Mamluk sultanate's administration. The bureaucracy, like the madrasas, cultivated a foundation in a range of disciplines and imparted many of the practical skills that proved essential to large-scale compilers, such as bookmaking, record keeping, and other forms of archival practice. The bureaucracy comprised an expansive network of learned individuals with diverse intellectual interests. Many of them spent time in the madrasas, studying jurisprudence and mastering the canons of traditional scholarship. But there are differences between the scholarly and bureaucratic realms that are worth paying attention to, not least because they help make vivid the distinction between "knowledge" and "information" at this time.

To put it simply, the information procured in the service of governance was of a different character than the knowledge imparted in a madrasa education. Gathered, recorded, and instrumentalized by the political administration, this bureaucratic information was almost exclusively contemporary in its outlook. Scribes collected information from visiting envoys about the conditions of other kingdoms. They toured the agricultural hinterlands outside the school cities and took notes on crop yields so as to make adjustments to their tax levies. They recorded the hiring and firing of provincial governors and other bureaucrats. While the path to scholarly excellence in the madrasa world involved, in its essence, the mastery of a curriculum of canonical texts, success in the bureaucratic sphere required an ability to negotiate the social, communal, and economic networks that constituted the contemporary sultanate. Al-Nuwayrī and Ibn Faḍl Allāh's encyclopedias contain massive amounts of such data on the daily events of the Mamluk sultanate and the lives of its notable subjects. They detail the troop movements of the army as it went out to put down rebellions; financial information that emerged from cadastral surveys; and data about the flooding of the Nile, earthquakes, and other environmental phenomena.

These practices of record keeping were immensely important, and the historical sources testify to their sophistication and complexity. The administrative encyclopedias shed light on the structure of the administration and its various offices, which scholars have used to learn about how this society produced, disseminated, and preserved documents. While relatively few repositories have been found, there is ample evidence of an elaborate system used to keep track of the circulation of documents around a decentralized imperial administration, what Konrad Hirschler has called a "meta-layer" of indexes, lists, and registers that facilitated the retrieval of individual documents. Because such documents were not universally stored in a single state archive but rather in other locations such as regional bureaus and in the private papers of military officers, tax farmers, and provincial governors, this metalayer provided a way to keep tabs on the circulation of information throughout the various branches of the bureaucracy.

Army secretaries, for example, were responsible for maintaining lists of all the soldiers and their commanding officers, the auxiliary troops from among the Turkoman and Bedouin tribesman along with the number of horses and camels they contributed to the royal stables, and the details of their compensation through land grants, currency, or fungible commodities. Al-Nuwayrī tells us that the administrator in charge of the sultan's larder required accounting each day for all the "meats, seasonings, vegetables, spices, sweets, and nuts, as well as perfume, incense, fire logs, and other things" consumed by the royal kitchens, which received a continuous stream of shipments from around Egypt and Syria. In the sultan's buttery, the responsible official oversaw the preparation and stocking of "sugar drinks, theriacs, medicinal powders, pastes, pastilles, raisin drinks, near beer, dates, herbs, sweets, electuaries" and various other types of refreshments and restoratives. The treasury may have been the hardest office to keep track of, as al-Nuwayrī's description attests:

> Integrity and trustworthiness are the mainstays of this position, for the treasuries of kings in our age cannot be fully inventoried due to their size, abundant contents, and the immensity of their treasures. Were a scribe commissioned to prepare an account of the financial revenues of the sultan's treasury for a single year,

he would have to be appointed solely to this task for an entire year without work-ing on anything else. By the time the account was complete [at the end of the sec-ond year] and corrected by the secretary of the treasury [during the third year], its anticipated benefit would have long passed. Furthermore, the secretary of the treasury would have neglected the receipts of the third year, having been occu-pied with the first year's bookkeeping.

Procuring contemporary, reliable information in the service of the state was the com-mon thread uniting the many professions that composed the administration—from fi-nancial comptroller to *notary to army secretary. There were similarities between the duties of the Mamluk bureaucrat and those of the scholarly compiler, which helps ex-plain why so many learned individuals were active in both domains. Gathering large quantities of information from a wide range of sources, collating them and ensuring their authenticity, and distilling them into new forms represented the core activities of both professions. What set them apart, however, was the essential difference between what we have been calling information and knowledge.

Finally, it is worth noting that Mamluk Egypt and Syria, like Abbasid Iraq, were places of linguistic multiplicity. Even though Classical Arabic remained the preeminent lan-guage of literature, scholarship, and administration, other languages had begun to en-croach on its domain. In the late thirteenth century, the North African judge Ibn Manẓūr composed a twenty-volume work entitled *The Arab Tongue* (*Lisān al-ʿArab*), the largest Arabic dictionary written to date. Ibn Manẓūr was a tireless compiler; one of his biog-raphers noted that his abridgments amounted to five hundred volumes. He had con-densed Ibn ʿAsākir's encyclopedic *History of Damascus* to a quarter of its size, and rear-ranged Abū Faraj al-Iṣfahānī's celebrated *Book of Songs* according to alphabetical order. In other words, Ibn Manẓūr had an immense stock of raw material with which to com-pose *The Arab Tongue*, in which individual entries spanned many pages, assaying the nuances of Arabic roots and their many shades of meaning. There is some irony in the fact that Ibn Manẓūr's desire to produce this book stemmed partly from a deep anxiety about Arabic's future, a belief that its position as the civilized world's language of so-cial prestige, literary eloquence, and religious knowledge was under threat. Even within the Arab lands, Ibn Manẓūr saw signs of a looming threat. "In our time, speaking Ara-bic is regarded as a vice," he wrote in the dictionary's preface. "I have composed the present work in an age when men take pride in using languages other than Arabic, and I have built it like Noah built the Ark, enduring the sarcasm of his own people."

Which languages did Ibn Manẓūr have in mind? Persian and Turkish were becoming increasingly prestigious languages and would have been heard widely in the Mamluk territories, for reasons that will become clearer later in this chapter. But it's likely that Ibn Manẓūr was also thinking of the proliferation of literary production in Arabic ver-naculars, an area that scholars have only lately begun to explore. Traditionally dismissed as the uncouth writings of semiliterate authors, this vernacular literature has begun to receive greater attention. It encoded spheres of contemporary information and subjec-tive experience that were not often expressed in the high language, by individuals whose stories have been left out of traditional historiography. Given that Classical Arabic, as discussed earlier, has played a gatekeeping role in Islamic intellectual his-tory, the inclusion of texts composed in nonstandard Arabic holds out the possibility of teaching us more about how information, and not just knowledge, circulated in the Islamic world.

IRAN AND KHORASAN, FIFTEENTH CENTURY

At the start of the fifteenth century, much of central Asia was ruled by Tīmūr Lang, the Turko-Mongol conqueror known to Europe as Tamerlane. Thirty-five years of military campaigning had knit together a vast patchwork of territories. Tīmūr's armies had reached as far west as Anatolia and as far east as northern India, and at the time of his death in 1405 CE Tīmūr was marching at the head of an army intent on invading China. The Timurid dynasty would rule over this domain—including most of modern-day Iran, Afghanistan, Iraq, Azerbaijan, Georgia, Turkmenistan, Uzbekistan, Kyrgyzstan, and Pakistan—until the end of the fifteenth century. Cities like Bukhara, Isfahan, Merv, Shiraz, Tabriz, Nishapur, and Balkh had produced some of the greatest thinkers of the Islamic world in earlier centuries, but the Mongol conquests of the 1200s coupled with Tīmūr's devastating campaigns in the 1300s had ravaged many of these historic centers of learning. During the fifteenth century, a period of relative stability, some of them would recover and flourish.

One of the distinctive features of intellectual and cultural production under the Timurids was its courtly context. As we have seen, patronage played an important role in the world of knowledge under the Abbasids. The translation movement was supported by the caliphs and their courts, who cultivated entourages of literati, scientists, philosophers, and musicians. In the Mamluk period, however, the sultan's court was eclipsed by the madrasa and the chancery as the preeminent spaces of intellectual exchange. These spaces were still, in most cases, financially supported by the political elite, but they were managed by networks of scholars and bureaucrats whose works were increasingly divorced from a strict relationship of patronage, and oriented toward other members of the network.

The Timurid period exhibits features of both these earlier contexts. Its princely courts were the sites of a cultural efflorescence often referred to as the Timurid Renaissance. The cities of Samarqand and Herat, in particular, witnessed an outpouring of royal patronage in the areas of astronomy, architecture, calligraphy, the occult sciences, miniature painting, and literature. They attracted some of the luminaries of the Persian world: Jāmī, the great Persian poet and Sufi scholar; Mīr ʿAlī Shīr Navāʾī, the father of Chagatay literature; Sharaf al-Dīn Yazdī, the historian and biographer of Tīmūr; Vāʿiẓ Kāshifī, the prominent preacher and occultist; and Bihzād, the most famous of Persian miniature painters. Some of the Timurid princes were themselves practitioners of the arts they patronized, such as Bāysunghur (d. 1433 CE), who oversaw the Herat *scriptorium (kitābkhāna) and was a talented calligrapher. The political economy of the Timurid dynasty, with its decentralized tax base, facilitated the independence of its different branches, allowing the courts to compete with each other in their patronage projects.

A second social feature of Timurid intellectual life was the importance of scholarly networks. As in the Mamluk sphere, these included formal networks of students who had studied with well-known teachers or who belonged to particular legal rites. The prominence of Sufi networks in both contexts has been noted by scholars, along with the extensive cultural contacts between the Timurid and Mamluk realms. There were also informal networks of individuals committed to, as Evrim Binbaş has written, "a specific political, ideological, and aesthetic view," and were often engaged in Neopythagorean philosophy and the occult sciences. The case of Sharaf al-Dīn Yazdī, the historian, provides an instructive example. He and his teacher, Ṣāʾin al-Dīn Turka, both traveled to Cairo at the end of the fourteenth century to study with Sayyid Ḥusayn Akhlāṭī, a well-known occultist. Akhlāṭī was a member of a clandestine network that called itself the Brethren of Purity (Ikhvān al-ṣafā, a nod to the famous tenth-century Ismāʿīlī collective that authored the encyclopedic *Epistles*), which extended across Egypt, Ottoman Anatolia, and the Balkans. Such interregional associations were important channels for the flow of information, which traveled through written correspondence (*munshāʾāt*)—a network that has been described as a fifteenth-century Islamicate *Republic of Letters.

Information and the Occult

The occult sciences were a chief interest of many scholars of this era. They included various forms of divination—for example, on the basis of dreams (oneiromancy), celestial phenomena (astrology), or sand (geomancy)—each with its own procedures and subsumed within a broader Neoplatonic and Neopythagorean philosophical framework. At the foundation of these divinatory methods was the science of letters or lettrism (*ʿilm-i ḥurūf*), a program for uncovering the secrets of the unified cosmos by studying the mystical properties of the Arabic alphabet. Similar in ways to kabbalistic traditions in Judaism, lettrism in fifteenth-century central Asia was used as a hermeneutic to interpret both the texts of sacred scripture as well as the hidden or interior nature of reality. Divinatory practices had existed for millennia, but the fifteenth-century Persianate world marked a golden age for this activity, attracting some of the period's foremost thinkers to its ranks. Astrologists, geomancers, and dream interpreters held high-ranking positions in Timurid courts. Some scholars eschewed these methods as heretical, but few discounted them as charlatanry. Ibn Khaldūn, the great fourteenth-century historian, famously denounced astrology and alchemy in his *al-Muqqadimah* (The Prolegomenon) (earning praise from nineteenth- and twentieth-century historians who cast him as a skeptical empiricist), but he was the exception that proved the rule. Furthermore, even Ibn Khaldūn did not doubt the reality and efficacy of magic and divination but rather categorized them as forms of illicit sorcery.

Why did the occult sciences attract so much interest? From our perspective, practices like alchemy, astrology, and geomancy (a form of "terrestrial astrology" similar to the *I Ching*) may not count as sciences at all, but it is necessary to recognize that these methods were enmeshed in a philosophical program that sought to explain the natural world by studying a code immanent in the universe. Lettrist thought intersected with messianic, apocalyptic, and mystical thought, holding out the promise of prophetic intuition for those who mastered its secrets. While historians have traditionally regarded such practices as belonging to a prescientific age, scholars such as Matthew Melvin-Koushki have increasingly recognized the place of magic and esoteric practices in the thought of many Renaissance and Enlightenment figures "from Pico to Bruno and Kepler to Newton, [who have] been shown to be profoundly occultist in orientation and methodology—and profoundly dependent on Arabic sources in the same vein."

Astronomy and Mathematics

Alongside the copious writings devoted to astrology, the Timurid era witnessed advances in the field of astronomical observation and measurement. One of Tīmūr's grandsons, Ulugh Beg (d. 1449 CE), built a great observatory in Samarqand, the Timurid capital. At forty-eight meters wide, it contained an internal graduated trench that formed part of a massive sextant, which, because of its size, could measure the angles between planets and stars with an unprecedented degree of accuracy. Ulugh Beg was a mathematician and astronomer himself, and he brought together a large staff of scientists who taught at the observatory and worked on devising new instruments and solving theoretical astronomical problems. Around 1441, a set of star tables—the *Zīj al-Ṣulṭāna'ī*—was completed and disseminated throughout the Islamic world, eventually also translated into Latin. Such works, of which Ulugh Beg's was the last great example in the Ptolemaic tradition, were used to calculate the positions of the planets, the sun, and the moon, as well as the time of the sunrise and sunset.

One of the significant theoretical advances made by astronomers at the Samarqand observatory concerned the relationship of their discipline to Aristotelian physics and metaphysics. Islamic astronomy had long been grouped with the mathematical disciplines following Ibn Sīnā, but some concepts from Aristotelian natural philosophy remained essential. The doctrine of the earth's stasis, for example, was held by Naṣīr al-Dīn al-Ṭūsī, the thirteenth-century savant, to be unprovable solely on the basis of mathematical reasoning. Arguing against this long-standing view, one of the astronomers at the Samarqand observatory, ʿAlī Qūshjī (d. 1474 CE), would propose that astronomy had no need of Aristotelian metaphysics and could rest entirely on a mathematical foundation. As many of the Samarqand astronomers and mathematicians were themselves committed occultists, some have speculated that this "mathematicization of astronomy" was itself strongly influenced by the occultist renaissance of the fifteenth century, which was rooted in Neoplatonic and Neopythagorean philosophy.

The Timurid Renaissance ended as the dynasty itself was brought down in the early sixteenth century. Many of the intellectuals and artists patronized by the Timurids left the glorious courts at Herat and Samarqand in search of new employers. Bābur, a fifth-generation descendant of Tīmūr (and of Genghis Khan, on his mother's side), would establish the Mughal sultanate in India, where the miniature painting traditions developed by Timurid artists would continue. The philosophical and scientific activities of the fifteenth century carried over into the Safavid and Ottoman Empires.

CONCLUSION

Nearly all the practices of disseminating, authenticating, and contesting information discussed here continued well up to the late nineteenth century. Under the Ottoman Empire, familiar institutions like the madrasa proliferated, along with public libraries, courts, and bureaucratic archives. Scholars continued to compose encyclopedic works and compilations of different kinds, relying on similar modes of textual reproduction. However, the early modern period brought with it new technologies of information management and publication. The arrival of print in the Ottoman lands in the late eighteenth century had a transformative effect, as might be expected, leading to the rise of newspapers and publishing houses, even if manuscript traditions did not disappear.

What has been left out of this survey of the history of information in the medieval Islamic world? I have not addressed the subject of hospitals as realms of medical information, or judicial courts as zones of legal information. What about markets, barracks, prisons, and private households? There has been no mention of postal systems, maps, diagrams, magic squares, or censuses. Some of the giants of Islamic thought—al-Ghazālī, Ibn Rushd, Fakhr al-Dīn al-Rāzī, and others—have not even made an appearance. This has to do with the contexts I have chosen to examine, but also my focus on information rather than knowledge. As should be apparent, the line between these two categories is difficult to draw. The purview of occult science was certainly considered by its practitioners to be *knowledge*, no less firmly rooted than any of the other disciplines I've addressed. Hadith collections, encyclopedic adab works, and astronomical tables were all seen as containing knowledge alongside information. Keeping both categories in mind as we study Islamic history attunes us to the processes by which knowledge and information were mutually constitutive and ever changing.

Elias Muhanna

See also accounting; bibliography; bureaucracy; diplomats/spies; documentary authority; excerpting/commonplacing; governance; horoscopes; indexing; inventories; knowledge; learning; libraries and catalogs; merchants; reference books; scribes; secretaries; teaching; travel

FURTHER READING

Jonathan P. Berkey, *The Transmission of Knowledge in Medieval Cairo: A Social History of Islamic Education*, 1992; İlker Evrim Binbaş, *Intellectual Networks in Timurid Iran: Sharaf al-Dīn ʿAlī Yazdī and the Islamicate Republic of Letters*, 2016; Ann Blair, "Managing Information," in *Oxford Illustrated History of the Book*, edited by James Raven, 2020; Jonathan Bloom, *Paper before Print: The History and Impact of Paper in the Islamic World*, 2001; C. E. Bosworth, "A Pioneer Arabic Encyclopedia of the Sciences: Al-Khwārizmī's Keys of the Sciences," *Isis* 54, no. 1 (1963): 97–111; Sonja Brentjes, "Teaching the Mathematical Sciences in Islamic Societies: Eighth–Seventeenth Centuries," in *Handbook on the History of Mathematics Education*, edited by A. Karp and G. Schubring, 2014, 85–108; Adam Gacek, "Tazwīr," in *Encyclopaedia of Islam*, 2nd ed., edited by P. Bearman, Th. Bianquis, C. E. Bosworth, E. van Donzel, and W. P. Heinrichs, 1960–2007; Dimitri Gutas, *Greek Thought, Arabic Culture: The Graeco-Arabic Translation Movement in Baghdad and Early ʿAbbāsid Society (2nd–4th/8th–10th Centuries)*, 1998; Konrad Hirschler, "From Archive to Archival Practices: Rethinking the Preservation of Mamluk Administrative Documents," *Journal of the American Oriental Society* 136, no. 1 (2016): 1–28; idem, *Medieval Damascus: Plurality and Diversity in an Arabic Library: The Ashrafiya Library Catalogue*, 2016; Ibn Qutayba, *Adab al-kātib*, edited by Max Günert, 1900; E. W. Lane, *Arabic-English Lexicon*, 1984; Matthew Melvin-Koushki, "Introduction: De-orienting the Study of Islamicate Occultism," *Arabica* 64, nos. 3–4 (September 13, 2017): 287–95; idem, "Powers of One: The Mathematicalization of the Occult Sciences in the High Persianate Tradition," *Intellectual History of the Islamicate World* 5 (2017): 127–39; Elias Muhanna, "Encyclopaedias, Arabic," *Encyclopaedia of Islam Three*, 2007–; idem, *The World in a Book: Al-Nuwayrī and the Islamic Encyclopedic Tradition*, 2018; Muhsin Jāsim Mūsawī, *The Medieval Islamic Republic of Letters: Arabic Knowledge Construction*, 2015; Aḥmad ibn ʿAbd al-Wahhāb al-Nuwayrī, *The Ultimate Ambition in the Arts of Erudition: A Compendium of Knowledge from the Classical Islamic World*, translated by Elias Muhanna, 2016; Carl F. Petry, "Scholarly Stasis in Medieval Islam Reconsidered: Mamluk Patronage in Cairo," *Poetics Today* 14, no. 2 (Summer 1993): 323–48; F. Jamil Ragep, "Freeing Astronomy from Philosophy: An Aspect of Islamic Influence on Science," *Osiris* 16 (2001): 49–71.

3

INFORMATION IN EARLY MODERN EAST ASIA

Recent histories of information describing premodern East Asia have little to say about "revolutions" in information. The impact of the early invention of paper and printing has mostly been obscured, and while *"early modernity" has been a topic of great debate, there is little consensus about when or if the concept fits East Asia as a whole. That said, scholars of East Asia, particularly of Japan and China, have long focused their attention on histories of information circulation in the region during the "late imperial" period (roughly 1000–1840 CE). Structural shifts in China dating to the Song dynasty (960–1279), such as the popularization of printing, widespread proto-industrialization, the abolition of a landed aristocracy in favor of a bureaucratic elite, and the rise of autocratic governance, changed political and intellectual cultures across the region. The cosmopolitan Sinographic culture first developed in China during antiquity also extended throughout East Asia. However, in the fourteenth century after the collapse of the Mongol Empire the reconstitution of self-conscious, increasingly "ethnicized" culture undermined the universalist claims of the Sinitic tradition, as actors throughout the region began to clearly articulate what it meant to pass beyond the borders of one place into another cultural region. This survey of information in early modern East Asia aims to combine attention to transnational trends with attention to the impact of the Sinitic cultural model on local and regional scales.

From this perspective it is possible to argue that from roughly 1000 CE until the arrival of modern industrial technologies, a series of information revolutions continually remade East Asia, and these revolutions contributed to the rise of new concerns about the role information played in everyday life. In this essay we will proceed through five sections to consider how methods of disseminating, then storing, sorting, and controlling information interacted with the material and linguistic realities of the region.

DISSEMINATING INFORMATION

China has a long history of written culture, dating back to the origins of writing in the early Shang dynasty circa 1700 BCE. Despite disruptions during periods of political instability and war, its linguistic and ideographic tradition has been continuously transmitted down to the present and widely dispersed geographically to neighboring areas. A few written artifacts (e.g., bamboo strips and scrolls) from ancient China survive thanks to modern archeological discoveries in caves at Dunhuang or tombs in Yinqueshan, but the bulk of the texts we have from ancient and medieval China survive only in later printed versions, produced during or after the great expansion of printing in the sixteenth century.

On Paper and Books

Unlike in the West, most premodern East Asian papers were made entirely from raw plant materials. East Asian paper production was therefore agrarian. Farmer-papermakers made paper to supplement household income during periods of agricultural quiet, although some regions produced year-round. In terms of material composition, it is almost impossible to speak of a "typical" paper. Chinese papers were highly local products, relying on plants endemic to the region of production. According to the *Tiangong Kaiwu* (The exploitation of the works of nature), a late Ming technological manual, to make paper from bamboo, young bamboo was harvested, cut into small sections, and soaked for several months in either a pool or running water. After soaking for roughly three months, the bamboo was ready to be processed by "killing its green." The phrase means that the husks of the plant were removed, and the fibers left over were then combined with lime and either left to soak for up to a month or boiled for seven to eight days. Both methods weakened the long fibers so that they could be processed more efficiently.

Once the first boiling or monthlong soaking was done, the strands of bamboo were washed in clean water. The fibers were then recombined with ash, boiled, and strained in an almost-continual cycle for ten days. In some places, such as Jiangxi province, they were also left to bleach in the sun, sometimes for months. When the fibers had "ripened," they were drained and pulped by wooden beaters until they had a clay-like consistency. The pulped paper would then have some form of sizing added to optimize its absorptive qualities (every region had its own preference), and only then was the mess transferred to a vat. A vat man would then use a bamboo screen to pull individual sheets of paper from the slurry in the vat. As in Europe, the paper sheets would be couched in piles and pressed to remove moisture. In the final stage of drying, the paper would be brushed onto a wall for drying. A team of four, working the screens, couching, and drying, could produce over sixty pounds of paper in a day—which probably amounted to more than two thousand sheets. After the paper was dried, it would be assembled into bundles for transport to the market. It was at this time that the Chinese version of a "watermark" would be added, with an inked stamp noting the manufacturer's name.

The description of production above stems from the Ming dynasty (1368–1644), when Chinese papers were already common and inexpensive. In the earlier Song period (960–1279) paper was still scarce enough as to be frequently recycled, and few printed books from this period survive as a result. But in the fifteenth and sixteenth centuries paper became much cheaper and more widely available. Cheap paper meant that books, in both manuscript and print (by woodblock), were inexpensive in East Asia from a relatively early period.

After the medieval period, the most frequently encountered premodern East Asian books were codices, rather than scrolls (although scrolls never vanished). The *codex form emerged in the Tang dynasty (618–907), likely owing to the influence of palm-leaf (*pothi*) books entering China from Inner Asia. Pages, literally "leaves" (*yezi*), were new to the Chinese world, and they provided scholars with the unprecedented ability to randomly access bodies of texts. Codices became dominant almost simultaneously with the invention of printing by woodblock (or xylography). Scholars disagree over when to date the first use of woodblock printing in China, though it seems to have happened sometime between the seventh and eighth centuries. A copy of the Diamond Sutra, published in 868 and found in a cave in the Buddhist monastic complex in Dunhuang in northwest China, is widely regarded as the world's oldest extant printed book. Unlike paper, however, printing was not widely adapted or sustained in regions outside China. Despite an initial burst of energy (we see printing in eighth-century Japan), the technology failed to win early popular support in Korea and Japan.

In China, population growth, commercialization, and urbanization that had begun in the late Tang dynasty continued through the Song dynasty, providing essential conditions for an early print revolution. The expansion of the elite class beyond hereditary nobility, along with the establishment of a standard curriculum for the imperial examinations, created a market eager to consume print. Scholars were not necessarily happy with the rise of printing. The eleventh-century thinker Cheng Ju (1078–1144) described the dangers of print to textual transmission, noting that

> earlier dynasties transmitted the Classics and Histories by transcribing them on paper and silk. Even though errors were made, still, the versions could be compared and collated. Then in the Five Dynasties, officials began to use inked-[wood] blocks to print the Six Classics. . . . With this, the manuscript versions of the Histories and Six Classics that had been transmitted down to that time were no longer used. Yet the inked-blocks were riddled with errors. They were never correct. . . . Later scholars will not be able to turn to other versions to discover and rectify the mistakes in them. (Cherniack, 34)

While print was not the actual cause of the loss of textual authority in the classics (similar concerns were present before the invention of printing), "inked-blocks" removed the agency of individual scholars, because their manuscripts could be corrupted by the processes of carving, printing, and circulating them.

The printed matter created to satisfy the Song market included works belonging to almost every *genre. Buddhist texts with elegant illustrations for lay devotees circulated next to cheap imprints from Jianyang Fujian, an early center of commercial publication. Song dynasty trends continued through the Mongol conquest in the thirteenth century and the early Ming (1368–1644). Government printing and commercial printing met most needs, but the volume of production seems to have remained relatively low until a second print revolution in the sixteenth century. The sixteenth-century Ming commercial boom—spurred in part by silver from the New World—heated the Chinese economy to the melting point. Costs for book production fell with the expansion of an available labor pool of people who could more cheaply transcribe and carve the script of a text into woodblocks. Several economic historians have recently shown that the cost of woodblock printing, while initially higher than the cost of printing with letterpress, was actually far lower than that of letterpress printing after print runs passed approximately fifteen hundred copies. Given that blocks could be used for hundreds of years if they were properly maintained, the economic benefits of East Asian printing made them a wise investment in several different regions around the empire. Ming and Qing printers grew into *publishers with transnational reach. By the middle of the seventeenth century, Chinese imprints could be found in Korea, Japan, Vietnam, and even Europe.

While print flourished early in China, it took a different trajectory in Korea, Japan, and Vietnam. After its early introduction to Korea and Japan, printing remained confined mostly to monasteries. Since the reproduction of Buddhist texts brought religious merit, print technology allowed for industrial-scale merit production. Alongside its Buddhist uses, printing emerged as the preferred mode of textual distribution only in conjunction with major shifts in the political cultures of each region.

In Korea, the long-lived Chosŏn dynasty (1392–1897) consolidated state ideologies around a Confucian *canon of classical texts and histories. While Buddhist printing continued in monasteries, the Chosŏn court became the primary producer of official calendars, texts required for education in the classics, and works promoting morality. The centralization of printing at the court had a notable influence on early Chosŏn print technology. While movable type had been invented in the twelfth century in East Asia, the level of resources required to print a wide range of texts in classical Chinese in movable type prevented its widespread adoption. When the Korean court asserted almost exclusive rights to print and distribute important texts, movable type became its preferred mode of textual production. In 1444, experiments with movable type for Chinese ideograms resulted in the emergence of one of the finest fonts ever created, the *kabin* type, which borrowed heavily from Song and Yuan aesthetics. The type was recast seven times over the course of the Chosŏn period. While the court promoted and used movable types given the predilection prevailing for an expensive luxury product, woodblock (or xylographic) printing remained the predominant form of printing in Korea. Popular texts—or texts that needed to be printed in especially high numbers— were usually printed via woodblocks. Moreover, the commercialization of print in the eighteenth and nineteenth centuries, when we see evidence of a popular market in Korea, was primarily a xylographic phenomenon.

As in China and Korea, in Japan the earliest printed matter consisted of Buddhist texts produced in temples. In the twelfth and thirteenth centuries the use of print in Buddhist institutions increased along with the geographical spread and range of those temples; at the same time the printing of secular works, such as the *Analects of Confucius*, began. But here too the success of printing depended on cultural factors in addition to technical know-how. The Tokugawa unification of the islands in the seventeenth century laid the foundation for a spectacular expansion of printing. Publication centers in Osaka, Kyoto, and Tokyo emerged to dominate a newly integrated state-scale market. Like late Ming China, where commercial print expanded rapidly, Tokugawa Japan also experienced a significant expansion in commercially published texts. As a result, a wide range of texts became newly available to urban readers. These included books, which were often beautifully illustrated, and news broadsides. The printed books ranged from classic Japanese texts to newer works like maps, travel guides, how-to manuals, picture books, and the ukiyo-e prints of the "floating world" that often depicted the entertainment and pleasure quarters and, with the advent of multicolor woodblock printing in the middle of the eighteenth century, could be cheaply mass-produced in vibrant colors (see figure 1). Printed books of non-Japanese authorship also circulated. By the

Figure 1. *Ehon azuma asobi*, 1802. A multicolor woodblock print of a shop selling ukiyo-e, illustrated by Hokusa. UCLA East Asian Library.

end of the eighteenth century, these included imported and reprinted Chinese books, Dutch books and Dutch translations of books from other European languages, and Korean books.

Printing seems to have arrived in Vietnam sometime after the Song dynasty. As in other parts of East Asia, temples assumed a leading role in the publication of texts. However, the early history of printing is murky. The biography of Tín Học (d. 1190) noted that his family had been "carving blocks" for printing Buddhist scriptures for many generations. Despite this early reference, the high cost of printing and the tropical climate of Vietnam have left us with only a small amount of material dating to before the nineteenth century, with the earliest surviving printed text dating to 1665. While this early archive is fragmentary, a great deal of material testifying to potential productivity remains. Tens of thousands of blocks, as well as a large number of unstudied books, still survive from the Nguyen dynasty (1802–1945).

The rise of printing in East Asia never eclipsed manuscript production and transmission. As scholars have recently emphasized for early modern Europe, printing and manuscript production existed as mutually complementary modes of managing and circulating texts. In Japan, manuscripts allowed authors to carefully control the circulation of their works. Many of the works central to the Japanese literary canon, such as the *Tale of Genji*, were produced and transmitted via manuscript even after printed editions became common. Just as print never displaced manuscript in Europe, East Asian cultures continued to value manuscripts for a number of complicated reasons.

The relationship between print and manuscript technology in China was regionally specific. (Indeed, throughout the history of books, print, and information, it is important to be wary of generalizations about large units like states, as there was a great deal of regional variation in the price, availability, medium, and distribution of books.) While the Song government sponsored massive printing initiatives in medicine, the classics, and official and government forms of all sorts, and in some areas of China, such as the economically prosperous regions around Hangzhou, print overtook manuscript as the form in which people read and collected books, elsewhere in the empire imprints began definitively to outnumber and replace manuscripts in popularity only in the sixteenth century. Regardless of locality, even at its height the popularity of print did not eclipse the production and use of manuscripts.

Commercialization and Vernacularization

As in other regions of the premodern world, the relationship between *vernaculars and written languages was complex in East Asia. One of the major changes that occurred in East Asia during the early modern period was the widespread emergence of written and printed vernacular languages. Literary Sinitic (sometimes referred to as Classical Chinese, or simply Chinese) was the language of the educated elite throughout premodern East Asia. Although the language changed over time, when compared to the challenges posed by the paleographic and linguistic shifts in other parts of the world, Sinitic was remarkably stable, but like Latin in the West, its stability was imposed by the veneration of certain styles and grammars. This stability also applied to its grammatical difficulty, especially when studied by linguistic groups outside of the Sino-Tibetan family. Challenges to its hegemony began to emerge during the Song dynasty, when Inner Asian kingdoms such as the Khitan Liao (916–1125) and Tangut Xixia (1038–1227) invented their own scripts. At the same time, Japanese Kana (a phonetic syllabary derived from Sinitic) began to become more popular, partly because of the rise of late medieval literary culture. The rise of the Mongol Empire, with its policy of "divide and rule," continued to undermine claims of Sinitic centrality, as is demonstrated dramatically by the 1345 sexaglot inscriptions (Chinese, Tibetan, Mongolian, Uyghur, Sanskrit, and Tangut) of the Cloud Platform, near the Great Wall outside modern Beijing. Each of the inscriptions records a Buddhist text, and the platform is seen as an example of Mongol commitment to Buddhist rulership.

With the dissolution of Mongol imperial rule, East Asian multilingualism entered a new phase. While some scripts, such as semiphonetic Jurchen and character-based Tangut, faded, new scripts, such as the Korean alphabet, were invented (some of these languages belonged to the Sino-Tibetan family; others were Tungusic). When King Sejong (r. 1418–50) proposed promulgating the Korean alphabet for writing vernacular Korean, Choe Malli condemned the writing system because of the association of phonetic alphabets with "barbarians." He wrote: "Although winds and soils vary from region to region, there has been no separate writing system for local dialects. Only such peoples as the Mongolians, Tanguts, Jürchens, Japanese, and Tibetans have their own writings. But this is a matter that involves the barbarians and is unworthy of our concern. It has been said that the barbarians are transformed only by means of adopting Sinitic ways; we have never heard of Sinitic ways being transformed by the barbarians" (adapted from Lee, 519). For Choe, the problem at the root of the new script was that it promised to alter the nature of the relatively young Chosŏn state. While it may not seem so on first appearance, Choe's argument was fundamentally historical. Adopting "barbarian" ways, in this case a phonetic script, explicitly harkened to the Yuan (Mongols), the Jurchen Jin, and the Tangut Xixia. Korea was different from these places *precisely* because it had never stepped away from Sinitic practices by adopting a "barbarian" script. Despite Choe's concerns, the Korean alphabet would eventually become an important script in Chosŏn Korea, particularly in later periods when *literacy expanded to include greater numbers of women and non-elite men (see figure 2). Sinitic remained the working language of state and scholarship until the modern period, but it coexisted alongside other forms of literacies.

Across the sea, Sinitic became less important to many readers in Japan after the Heian period (794–1185). Although the printing of Buddhist texts and some Confucian classics (as well as occasional monastic missions to China) kept Sinitic language alive, most Japanese literature, such as the *Tale of Genji*, was written in the vernacular. After the rise of the Tokugawa shogunate in the early seventeenth century, the fortunes of Sinitic improved, but it never displaced the dominance of texts written in colloquial Japanese— which included translations from Sinitic and semivernacular Chinese. In early modern Japan, the expansion of available texts that came with a burgeoning print market helped generate an increasingly accessible body of public information. According to Mary Elizabeth Berry's *Japan in Print*, this market helped to create a "library of public information," which manifested as something like an available pool of common knowledge and a collective memory. This "library" included *encyclopedic lists of flora and fauna, cookbooks, calendars, guides to etiquette, guidebooks for travel to various cities and localities, useful vocabularies for various circumstances and professions, and books on poetry composition, gardening, healing, the arts of the bedchamber, ritual and social customs of all sorts, and many other topics.

China, too, underwent a great vernacularization during the late Ming. During the sixteenth century commercial printers attracted new readers by issuing a wide variety of books for entertainment. Medieval stories were translated into *baihua*, semivernacular Chinese, which was more accessible to less educated readers. Under Manchu rule during the Qing dynasty (1644–1911), the print market expanded to include materials in non-Han languages. From the middle of the seventeenth century the Manchu language grew into a key language of empire, political instrument, and medium of translation and communication across eastern Eurasia. Manchu-language translations of Chinese poetry, fiction, history, and classic texts were printed alongside a growing library of original manuscript materials in a wide range of genres, both for the court and for a Manchu-reading public. Because not all Qing subjects had access to a Manchu-language

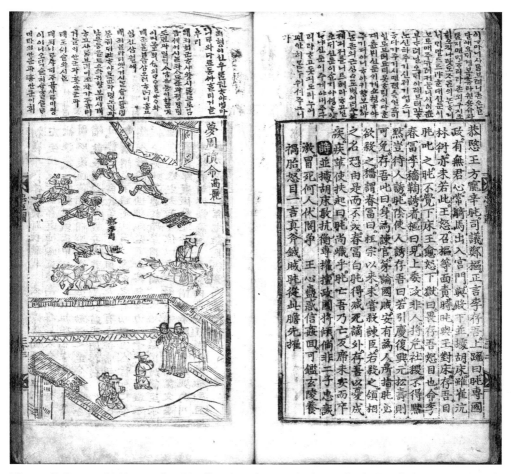

Figure 2. *Samgang Haengsilto* (An illustrated record of moral relationships), seventeenth century. A Korean morality primer in which the Chinese was printed with movable type, while the Korean alphabet was printed by xylography. UCLA Library Special Collections.

education, composing a text in Manchu and refusing to translate it into Chinese was also a way to limit it to Manchu readers, like the Kangxi (r. 1661–1722) era *Dergici toktobuha ge ti ciowan lu bithe* (Complete record of the body, imperially commissioned, more commonly known as *The Manchu Anatomy*). This medical text mixed East Asian and Western medical traditions into a hybrid style, allowing the Qing court to position itself as a center of cosmopolitan "imperial" science that existed only in Manchu. Tibetan monasteries were key sites of printing, storing, and making available works on religious, literary, medical, historical, and other topics, and the seventeenth and eighteenth centuries saw major shifts in Tibetan and Mongolian print cultures.

Similarly in Vietnam a distinctive script was developed for writing in the vernacular. Chữ Nôm script appeared sometime in the twelfth century, as a local adaptation of Chinese to represent Vietnamese pronunciation. The script gained in popularity during the Ming invasion of Vietnam in the early fifteenth century, eventually becoming the preferred language for literary composition. While Sinitic remained important in various Vietnamese courts, the elite composed and circulated (in manuscript and print) works in the vernacular.

STORING INFORMATION

Like any information culture, East Asian societies prioritized storing materials for later retrieval. For the most part, it is difficult to find firm distinctions between libraries and archives. Instead, repositories of books and manuscripts existed in a continuum. While archives (for which there was no single Sinograph, although many were "storehouses," e.g., Chinese *ku* / Japanese *ku* / Korean *ko* / Vietnamese *khổ*) might be devoted exclusively to manuscript materials, they often held print as well. Nonetheless, in the following subsections we treat each separately.

Storing: Libraries

Libraries, by which we mean book collections that were accessible beyond the scale of a single individual or controlling family, became increasingly common in East Asia through the late imperial period. As book production increased, so did the number of libraries. Initially, most libraries were associated with institutions such as academies, government offices, or monasteries. But over time, libraries belonging to families that were accessible through personal introduction became important to scholarly communities.

Academies spread throughout East Asia (beginning in the 1200s in China, the 1400s in Korea, and after 1600 in Japan) as the principal institutions of higher education, each of which had its own books available for student perusal. Most academies owned standard works such as the Confucian classics and important historical chronicles but also displayed a great deal of regional variety. Since academies could often be traced to important intellectuals or specific lineages, they owned unique texts in manuscript or ones that had been produced in limited print runs (in some cases published by the academy) that differentiated their holdings from collections elsewhere. This meant that while scholars could use academy libraries to lay a common foundation, their more intensive research in a given library was often inflected by a particular intellectual tradition.

The academies of Chosŏn Korea are some of the best surviving institutions for understanding the nature of academy libraries. In the sixteenth and seventeenth centuries, Korean academies emerged as significant centers for both education and consolidation of their intellectual factions. Affiliation with a particular academy's educational lineage involved affiliation with a particular political faction. This was reflected not only in national politics, which began to divide around famous lineages and their teachings, but also in library collections. In a survey of thirty-three surviving collections, most of which were built in the eighteenth century, Yi Chun'hŭi has recently discovered that academies from the Namin faction held none of the collected works of the major thinkers from rival factions.

Like academies, monasteries also held significant collections of books. Veneration of the Buddhist canon played a major role in East Asian Buddhist piety. During both the Ming and the Qing dynasties, imperially printed editions of the Buddhist canon, in Mongolian, Tibetan, and Chinese, were disseminated to select monastic institutions to demonstrate imperial commitment to the faith. The presence of the canon attracted both scholars and lay devotees to monasteries and even contributed to the creation of a unique architectural feature: the rotating library case. Because "turning the wheel" of Buddhist doctrine was the metaphor for disseminating Buddhist teachings, it was seen as a devotional act to be able to literally rotate portions of the canon. Sometime in the late Tang dynasty, large rotating shelves containing the canon became popular features of some monasteries, and they became particularly popular in Japan during the Tokugawa period (and there are over 110 rotating libraries in Japan today).

Private libraries also played a major role in the circulation of knowledge through the sharing of their holdings. The late Ming dynasty saw the emergence of several important private libraries in south China. The most famous library, the Tianyi ge library in Ningbo, was founded in 1561 by the bibliophile official Fan Qin. The library set new standards for book preservation and storage, becoming the model for other libraries, and it is still in use today with many of its original features. While not "public," the Fans permitted scholars with connections to the family (either directly or through social introduction) to access the seventy thousand or so books in the collection.

Government offices also maintained book collections. The collections developed by the Ming and Qing courts were especially large. Books printed in China were also central to government libraries in Korea and Japan. A memorial to the throne (a formal suggestion to the ruler) by the Korean official Kim Kŭnsa (d. 1539) on the importance of book collecting captured the role of books in government collections. He explained in his memorial to King Chungjong (r. 1506–44): "The collection of books dates to antiquity. . . . All governance, disorder, as well as the rise and fall of different historical periods are in them." Kim complained that collecting was unfortunately no longer a major priority: "That we have neglected books in this way, is it not heart breaking?" At the end of his memorial, he asked Chungjong not only to seek out old texts from among his subjects, but also to request books from the Ming.

A month after Kim's memorial, Chungjong released an official edict on the importance of books to the Korean throne. He reiterated Korea's commitment to books in a memorial to the Board of Rites:

> Books are the abode of the way of governance. . . . Since the time of the ancestors of our dynasty, we have elevated the art of classicism, the sagely scriptures and traditions of the worthies, as well as all of the collections of the historical masters. We have done this so that we could gather all lost or neglected texts. We not only preserve them in secret government collections, but we also distribute them. . . . Today, we order our emissaries who go to the central court [of China] to seek books without limits . . . [and for those within Korea] to submit books, for which I will richly reward them.

This edict, which was circulated "domestically and abroad" made Chungjong's commitment to learning a matter of public record.

By 1600 the shogun of Japan, Tokugawa Ieyasu, had formed important collections of books produced abroad, often by relying on books looted from Korea, comprising both Chinese and Korean editions. Tokugawa Ieyasu collected books not only to bolster his legitimacy, but also to draw on the knowledge they contained as he patronized the new "Confucians" of Japan, the most famous of whom was Hayashi Razan (1583–1657). Razan looked at the Tokugawa collection in Sunpu with some ambivalence. He viewed himself as something of a hostage to the books in the shogunal collection for which he was responsible. The books, not the shogun, kept him loyal: "I myself feel as if I am [more and more] going in for fame and profit. . . . It is shameful. It is terrible. However, I hold the keys of the library in Sunpu. I try one of the buildings, and the boxes are filled [with books]. I leave it to my hand [which one] to pick. The happiness of reading a book I have not yet read. . . . My only pleasures are books. . . . This is a favour from my lord, and one thing that I have gained. Is it not also [a reason] to be glad?" (Boot, 236). As Razan's anxiety shows, collections of books were powerful enticements. Razan and his lineage founded one of the most impressive libraries in Tokugawa Japan. While printing enabled many scholars to amass impressive collections of their own, they could not hope to compete with the collecting agenda of the state. Royal collections, like those associated with the shogun Yoshimune (r. 1716–45), became centers for the creation of knowledge.

Over the course of the seventeenth century, the commercial production of books increased in Japan, fueling expanded individual collections but also new forms of access to books. By the end of the century, commercial lending libraries were open to readers who paid a subscription fee. By the end of the Tokugawa period in the nineteenth century, commercial libraries were common throughout Japan, and some domains could even boast entirely free "public" libraries housed in shrines. In Qing China there were commercial lending libraries, but the existence of "public" libraries is debated. Lending libraries for popular literature also became popular in nineteenth-century Korea.

Storing: Archives

Although premodern intellectuals in East Asia were keen collectors of information from all sources, when compared to libraries, archives were relatively uncelebrated. Materials worth saving became parts of books, and it was presumed that ephemeral papers would vanish over time. Moreover, the presence of overwhelming amounts of paper made archives a focus of official anxiety. By the late sixteenth century, paperwork overload worried the Ming official Lu Kun. He blamed documentary disorder for the decline of the state: "Methods of governance are in decline because of the flood of written text; the disaster has come from the overabundance of registers. . . . In their thousands, they pile up on hundreds of shelves, eaten by insects and rats, and inside they all contradict one another!" Lu Kun's concerns would have resonated at the time with readers in Europe struggling under similar archival burdens.

In Japan, archival practices and systems took a multitude of forms. Each domain and each office had its own particular modes of handling paperwork. The Nagasaki magistrates (bugyō), charged by the shogun with the management of the city and its extensive international trade, owned their own archival records. When they left office, they took their personal papers with them. Although archives moved with officials, continuity in practices was maintained because Japanese governance relied on networks of archives. Official translators in Nagasaki, for example, maintained their own archives, as did local neighborhood organizations. While there was disruption in the continuity of governance when officeholders left with their papers, vested subordinates could domesticate new officials to local practices and standards.

While the records of specific posts were often tied to the collections of the individuals who held them, various domains (which were controlled by lineage) maintained detailed archival records. The Tsushima domain, ruled by the Sō family (r. twelfth century–1871), managed trade between Chosŏn Korea and Tokugawa Japan. Its retainers kept records of both domain affairs and international relations in the family compounds on the island of Tsushima and in its estate in Edo. These chronologically organized registers were subdivided by topic, which could lead readers to full versions of documents. These records have been exploited by historians to great results.

Governance by archive was also a characteristic of the Chosŏn and the Ming and Qing courts. In Ming and Qing China archival collections were essential tools for tracking government accountability, and registers linked readers in different offices with originals presumed to be in an archival collection. Unfortunately, our knowledge of the actual organization of archives of Chinese offices is anecdotal, since most were destroyed or reorganized in the twentieth century. One Ming compilation, a 1540s official manual for the Rear Lake Archive, where census records were stored, provides a sense of some of the changes in archival practices. For example, the manual explains a basic change in the material composition of registers. Early in the Ming, registers were bound in paper wraps, which were stuck to the spine of the text using wheat paste. But the wheat paste attracted rodents and insects, and archival managers discovered extensive damage in the collection in the 1470s. This led to a debate about format—and a shift to the use of registers bound with paper twists and threads.

While preservation was clearly important in East Asian archives, destruction was also normal. In Chosŏn Korea, local-level government archives were routinely destroyed after they had been processed into summary registers. Only a small proportion of central-level archival documents survive from the Chosŏn period. But this was by design. Throughout East Asia, almost every member of society understood the power of political archives, and both states and their subjects knew better than to leave documents in archives "undomesticated" by historical narratives. History bureaus were formed by most courts to bring records into order. In Chosŏn Korea, historians were also officially prohibited from holding any other government positions, to ensure impartiality in processing records.

Officials were not the only collectors of papers. Family archives became increasingly important throughout the region as the state became increasingly capable of making its presence felt. Lineages in south China managed their archival materials with exceptional acuity in their efforts to manage their interactions with the state. In Huizhou, a commercially prosperous center of south China, many families held the Ming tax receipts into the twentieth century—even when the tax registers held by the state had long since been lost. In Korea and Japan family collections are some of our best-preserved collections for understanding and interpreting the premodern period. Although little has been written on these collections in English, East Asian scholars have long been aware of the importance of family archives for premodern history.

In addition to family collections, almost every corporate body in premodern East Asia maintained records of its activities. Large firms, such as those operating in the city of Chongqing during the Qing dynasty, kept their own records and also made sure to get important contracts on file in the county archives. Temples throughout East Asia kept collections of deeds and, in Tokugawa Japan, even assisted that state by holding records that were used to certify that no subject secretly harbored Christian beliefs.

SORTING INFORMATION

Since all premodern East Asian societies could boast sizable collections of texts, different methods for sorting and classifying information were created to manage materials. From a macro perspective, the tools available for managing information were similar on both ends of Eurasia. Library catalogs in codex form linked book locations to shelf numbers; paper files were organized according to paper registers; and filing systems used complicated taxonomies. Despite similarities in their technologies for information organization, the ways in which states and individuals interacted with materials created striking differences between premodern Asia and the West.

One easy example to consider is bibliographic classification. Most East Asian societies shared bibliographic categories that emerged during the medieval period of Chinese history, particularly as they were outlined in the "bibliography" section in the *History of the Sui* (compiled in the 620s). Libraries and catalogs in many parts of East Asia followed the order of categories outlined in the *History*—with the "classics, histories, masters, and compilations" as supercategories under which many subcategories were organized. However, the subcategories under each section were subject to regular change and debate. Books moved from "standard history" to "unofficial history" at the whims of bibliographers influenced by political changes. This could have social consequences beyond the library, as it led to the censorship of texts, and in some exceptional circumstances, the posthumous punishment of the earthly remains of their authors. In East Asia, as in other parts of the world, how things were sorted was political, and sorting was a major focus of intellectual activity.

Sorting Spaces

Sorting information was guided by any number of different priorities. One topic of great interest to East Asian intellectuals was sorting by place. In the Chinese context, this was exemplified in the transformation of a genre known as a *gazetteer (difang zhi)*, a textual compilation of information about the geography, peoples, history, and other features of a particular locality, culled from any combination of texts, in situ observations, and conversations. From their popularization in the Song period, there was a long-term rise in the production of local gazetteers, with periods of increased compilation during the founding and consolidation of dynasties and in the context of some imperial projects, and periods of decline during times of war.

Local gazetteers were crucial to the information history of China because they gathered local information in the material form in which it circulated to local and nonlocal readers. Gazetteers helped local elites connect to and influence central government officials and policy, and they helped a centralizing imperial state incorporate peripheral areas into the empire. Although they were intended primarily for an audience of officials and literati, the actual readership varied.

No two gazetteers are identical, but the genre is unified by similar topical arrangements. They often began with a series of maps, then related the administrative history of the area, and predictably drilled down with further details about a locale. Gazetteers sorted the empire by contributing to court debates about how to classify regions according to their governability. Their functionality meant that in the borderland peripheries of the empire, gazetteers were seen by Chinese officials as tools for assimilating native peoples into Chinese culture and political order. They were often the first Chinese-language literary projects in these places, and they helped facilitate the circulation and translation of information between Chinese and non-Chinese societies.

The influence of gazetteers extended far beyond China. The shogun Yoshimune viewed gazetteers as important tools to understand the politics of his Qing neighbor. This reading of Chinese gazetteers occurred alongside the continual production of gazetteers (*Fudoki* and other genres) in Japan, which had begun in the 700s. Tokugawa authors, like their Ming and Qing neighbors, also displayed an interest in classifying and sorting spaces on a local and global scale. In both East Asian contexts, attending to locality was bound up with attention to frontiers and boundaries, and much information was contained in gazetteers' discussions of border affairs, relations and networks across borders, and the characteristics that separated entities at various scales from one another.

Gazetteers were also a popular genre in Vietnam. The earliest surviving gazetteer was compiled in 1425. The Nguyen dynasty (1802–1945) sponsored a large number of gazetteer projects as it asserted rule over a united northern and southern Vietnam. Court enthusiasm for classifying the realm spurred individual scholar-officials, like Phạm Thận Duật (1825–85), to draw on their experience in border regions, as well as on their extensive reading in Chinese and Vietnamese sources, to compose their own local histories. Korea also inherited the gazetteer tradition. The Chosŏn court oversaw the production of gazetteers about important government offices. The *Gazetteer of the Translation Bureau* (T'ongmun'gwan chi), compiled in 1708, was a record intended to outline the duties and responsibilities of government translators. This kind of office gazetteer, which drew on earlier precedents, illustrates how officials could use textual genres to sort out bureaucratic responsibilities.

Stepping back from the issues associated with individual gazetteers, it is evident that the genre was essential for the transformation of space into specifically governed place. During the Qing dynasty, different counties throughout the empire were given "importance ratings" based on their governability. Although gazetteers were not directly mentioned in these ratings, the process that sorted the empire occurred at the gubernatorial level. The 1782 governor of Shandong county noted, for example: "Among the 110 districts, departments and garrisons [in Shandong], there are many where local conditions in the past and local conditions today are not the same. The importance ratings of such positions should be adjusted. One should go with the times and make changes. [It would be] for the sake of good government. . . . If we swap importance ratings [in the way outlined above], each place would end up with an appropriate label, human resources would be allocated according to local conditions and it would be to the benefit of local administration" (Koss, 166). Labeling counties with reference to archival and gazetteer-based reports sorted the empire in two ways. First, it made the state's difficulties legible by linking counties to particular problems of governance. Second, it allowed for the sorting of the people responsible for government. Counties ranked as "difficult" received more attention from more experienced magistrates than counties with few problems.

Sorting Sciences

The sorting of spaces went hand and glove with the sorting of human bodies and nature. Chinese natural historians in the late Ming period developed new methods for evaluating the many kinds of evidence available in the libraries, compendia, and collectanea of an expanded information economy. In addition to textual sources, scholars ascribed new evidentiary value to first-person witnessing of natural phenomena. Li Shizhen's *Bencao gangmu* (Systematic materia medica), first printed in 1596, exemplified this approach by drawing on poetry, dictionaries, histories, medical texts, first-person interviews, and self-experimentation to explain and organize the natural world.

This work became one of the most influential works on natural history across East Asia. In the seventeenth and eighteenth centuries, natural history encyclopedias in China and Japan continued to combine lexicographical research and personal observation in descriptions of plants, animals, and other natural objects. The booming commercial market for these works in both places helped foster a concern for accuracy as a virtue, and at the same time anxieties about identifying and assessing accuracy.

Like Li Shizhen, Hŏ Chun, a Chosŏn court physician active after the Japanese invasions of Korea (1592–98), compiled an encyclopedic collection of medical information that was both cosmopolitan and specific. It was cosmopolitan in its agreement with the basic practices of the Sinitic medical tradition, especially those in the *Bencao gangmu*. But like some before him, he also believed that a distinctly Korean body had emerged, along with distinctly Korean materia medica, which demanded special treatment and localized knowledge. The publication of his medical compendium in 1614 led to the work's eventual reprinting, in several editions, in both Qing China and Tokugawa Japan. His lessons about the specificity of the Korean body and Korean herbs placed the importance of locality at the center of increasingly transnational medical practices.

Throughout East Asia, the expanding print economy fostered methods of measuring, describing, and valuing natural objects that allowed for the further circulation of this information. Plants and animals became physical and intellectual commodities, and accounts of them strove for accuracy and precision. (Scholars and officials also learned to strategically deploy misinformation in order to further their political or social goals.) The commercialization also favored illustrations. A pictorial archive emerged as a result of the commodification of plants and animals, and with it connoisseurship practices around objects and images.

Images and accuracy not only were important in medical works but also played an important role in evidentiary scholarship. Like medical doctors, antiquarians valued the ability of print to reflect and circulate discoveries. One particularly stunning example of the speed with which such news traveled was the discovery of a Chinese Christian stele. In 1625, Chinese laborers excavated a nine-foot-tall, three-foot-wide limestone stele on the outskirts of Xi'an. The stone, dating to the late eighth century, was entitled *Jingjiao liuxing zhongguo bei* (A stele on the spread of Nestorianism in the Central Kingdom). It celebrated the progress of the Nestorian Church in China between 635 and 791. A rubbing of the stele was sent to Li Zhizao, who shared it with his *Jesuit colleagues. Li produced a xylographic edition and commentary of the text, while the Jesuits sent the inscription back to Europe with a translation. The inscription was eventually used as a basis for a copper-plate engraving of the monument when Athanasius Kircher published his *China monumentis qua sacris qua profanis nec non variis naturae et artis spectaculis aliarumque rerum memorabilium argumentis illustrata* (China illuminated by sacred and profane monuments, as well as varied spectacles of nature and art and tales of other remarkable matters) in 1667.

In the case of the Nestorian stele, the Jesuits were interlocutors in translating a Chinese archeological discovery for European readers, but in the case of calendrical sciences, they played a major role in transmitting Copernicanism and more accurate astronomy to East Asia. During the seventeenth and eighteenth centuries, Jesuit contributions to astronomical observation and recording, timekeeping, and mapmaking generated maps, charts, diagrams, and illustrations by woodblock printing for East Asian scholars. Their introduction of perspective to paintings also served informational purposes, notably when such paintings were designed to represent political reforms at the court or were exchanged in private communications as a form of social currency. One unintended consequence of the growing emphasis on observation, measurement, and identification was the emergence of anxieties about precision and accuracy in the production and circulation of such information across space and time.

CONTROLLING INFORMATION

Sorting information inevitably involved selection and control. Compilers, librarians, and archivists were constantly making choices about what to keep and what to remove, and these choices were driven by political concerns. Even the grandest encyclopedia in world history, the imperially commissioned 1405 *Yongle Encyclopedia* (which, at the size of 370 million characters, was surpassed only by Wikipedia in 2007), was selective about which information to include. The act of selecting contributed directly to the standardization of information. In China and Korea, the predominance of court projects and the bureaucratic system of recruitment of officials ensured a relatively high level of central control of information cultures. Standardization and censorship were often closely related in the bureaucracies of East Asia. In China, the state's leadership in scholarly projects contributed to the creation of literary canons and allowed officials to check work for potential offenses to the throne.

Examinations and Standardizing Education

The civil service examination system stands out as one of the most remarkable features of premodern East Asian governments. While the examination system began in the Tang dynasty, it emerged as central to bureaucratic recruitment during the Song and Chosŏn dynasties in China and Korea, respectively. The premise of the system was simple enough: in order to earn appointment as a state official, scholars needed to pass a series of tiered examinations that would qualify them for office. This idea spawned massive investments by states and by aspiring officials. In China, by the thirteenth century there were already tens of thousands of scholars competing in the triennial examination.

The examinations brought about different types of standardization. First, they integrated the interests of state and society. Broad social networks were necessary for a candidate to pass the exams and gain office (and this was increasingly the case already during the transition from the Tang to the Song dynasty), and conversely exam credentials garnered social prestige and lucrative official appointments for successful candidates. An expansion of the exam system in the late tenth century helped undermine long-standing social hierarchies for a time, but by the Ming period the exams were producing long-lasting new literati groups. Competition for the civil exams created a status group of degree holders who shared a common classical language that served as a kind of lingua franca of classically educated men, a shared canon based on Song "Confucian learning" that they memorized, and a shared literary writing style (the eight-legged essay) (see figure 3).

Second, examinations contributed to the standardization of education. One need look no further than the book market to see the impact of the examination system on reading

Figure 3. Palace Examination paper of Xiong Wentao, 1889. An example of a Qing period examination paper. From the Han Yu-shan Collection, UCLA Library Special Collections.

and learning habits. Publishers around the empire all sold their own editions of the core texts of the examination, the Confucian four books and the Chinese classics. No scholar has attempted to estimate the total number of distinct editions of these texts (attempting to count them would be as bibliographically difficult as enumerating the number of Bible editions for early modern Europe), and the commentarial tradition that developed to make them accessible beggars comprehensive description. Already in the southern Song, sample examination essays and discussions of examination curriculum formed an important part of the print market. By the Ming and Qing, winning examination essays were frequently printed to serve as models for the reading public. With the fall of the Ming and the rise of the Qing state, examinations were adapted to further integrate the conquering Manchu and Mongolian soldiers. The state established special dynastic schools for the eight military banners, a school for the imperial Manchu family, and examinations in Manchu and Mongolian. Examinations for the banner men emphasized martial and translation skills, considered essential for those who would extend Qing rule over Inner Asia. The book market responded by making relevant textbooks available.

Examinations played an important part in Chosŏn Korea as well. The Chosŏn court limited participation in the civil service examinations to members of elite lineages (*yangban*). Scholar-bureaucrats, however, were unprepared for many of the more technical problems facing the state. Tackling those was the purview of *chungin* ("middle-people"), the technically trained classes of the Chosŏn government, including translators, scribes, doctors, and geomancy specialists. Like other members of the bureaucracy, they were recruited through examinations and trained for these in specialist schools that developed "practical" skills.

Vietnamese regimes were also early adopters of the examination system. By the 1230s, the Trần made examinations a regular part of bureaucratic recruitment. The first examinations recruited only small classes of bureaucrats, but by the middle of the sixteenth century, the examinations were routinely drawing thousands of candidates in the economic centers of the region. While later examinations would never prove as popular as they were during the sixteenth century, a strong test-taking culture ensured that a standard set of classics and texts unified "Confucian scholars" in China, Vietnam, and Korea.

In Japan the state was not powerful enough to impose such a system. Early Tokugawa Confucians admired the system, but the hereditary elite of various domains could never be abolished through shogunal fiat. Still, experiments with examinations were irresistible to the shogun's scholars. In 1792 the shogun began experimenting with educational reforms that culminated in a standardized examination. These experiments were inspired in part by fears of decline. The scholar Koga Seiri (1750–1817) noted these problems in the Saga domain: "As our country is under a regime of generals, the path of selection/election is closed. Particularly in domains [controlled by Daimyo] such as ours [Saga], the damage of the hereditary system is not to be avoided. Those with hereditary status are negligent, and those without it do not serve. This is why the spirit of the gentleman/samurai cannot be enacted and why custom can so degenerate" (Paramore, 88). The 1792 establishment of shogunal examinations based at the Shōheizaka Academy in Edo was one attempt to provide a new model for training scholars in the sorts of virtues necessary to prevent state decline. As with everywhere else in East Asia, Confucian books were at the center of the curriculum.

Throughout the region, the examination system contributed to the making and remaking of a Confucian canon tailored to the interests and needs of the government and its ruling bureaucrats. Certain texts were universally perceived as important, but debates about *which* commentary to adapt, and a philological approach to analyzing the classics and their compilation, created contention over a common canon.

Censorship

The existence of curricula worthy of universal study throughout East Asia coexisted with the other extreme of standardization: the formation of lists of banned and heterodox works. Hints of lèse-majesté or the violation of taboos led to books being banned and burned. Despite occasional censorship campaigns, attempts to ban books also met with considerable resistance. This resistance was perhaps facilitated by technology. Woodblocks, after all, were highly mobile, so printers could forestall their confiscation. But it is also likely due to the "chilling" effect of bans and the practice of self-censorship by authors and printers that we have relatively few cases of book burning.

Despite the reputation it has today as a period of strict censorship, the Qing dynasty was not always harsh. In the famous case of Zeng Jing (1679–1735), a moderate Yongzheng emperor pardoned Zeng for attempting to incite an anti-Manchu rebellion among the Han Chinese. In a long tract arguing for cosmopolitanism, the emperor condemned Zeng's writings, noting that place of origin had nothing to do with one's suitability to rule. He castigated Zeng for being someone who "wrongly conjured the selfish idea of 'this border' and 'that line' . . . [and for] not knowing that this dynasty being Manchurian is the same as the Chinese having native places. After all, [the sage king] Shun was a person from the Eastern tribes and [the sage king] Wen was a person from the Western tribes. Was this any detriment to their sagely virtue?" Zeng's works were banned, but he was released from prison after his imperial reeducation.

Zeng's pardon in his lifetime proved only temporary. The following ruler, the Qianlong emperor (r. 1735–96), declared Zeng's crimes against the Manchu throne unpardonable. Zeng's body was exhumed and beaten in public, a spectacle befitting the ruler who began one of the longest censorship campaigns in Chinese history. There are many reasons why the Qianlong emperor pushed for censorship. Some scholars have argued that he feared Manchu assimilation and interethnic tension. Others have seen his drive to censor as part of the court's attempt to shape intellectual culture through the empire. Regardless of its causes, the compilation of the *Complete Library of the Four Treasuries* (*Siku Quanshu*) and the resulting censorship campaign have become emblematic of Qing despotism.

In brief, the *Four Treasuries* was an encyclopedic project initiated by the Qianlong emperor in the early 1770s. The purpose of the project was to scour the empire in order to collect and reproduce books of literary and philosophical merit. Approximately eleven thousand titles were collected and submitted to court inspectors. Thirty-five hundred of these titles were printed in seven copies each (in movable type!) and stored in official libraries for scholarly use around the empire. The book collection campaign served the purpose of rendering the textual landscape of the empire legible to the court. In the process of collecting books to reprint, others were found unacceptable and confiscated. Approximately three thousand titles were burned, and in many more, taboo words, such as "barbarian," which the emperor deemed offensive to the Manchu elite, were expunged.

Despite the censorship accompanying the *Four Treasuries*, many censored works survived. But the influence of the campaign was felt far beyond China. Regular visitors from Chosŏn Korea learned about Qing censorship, and their reports likely inspired more censorship at the Chosŏn court. Despite this moment of shared censorship, censorship was not new to Korea. During the Ming dynasty Chosŏn sensitivity over perceived insults to the Chosŏn founder led the court to petition the Jiajing emperor to revise the chapter of *The Collected Institutions of the Ming* (*Daming huidian*) describing Korea. Factional politics also played a role in determining what was censored. In 1709, the chief councillor of state Ch'oe Sŏkchŏng (1646–1725) became the target of impeachment in a lengthy memorial. Yi Kwanmyŏng accused Ch'oe of attempting to outshine the classical commentaries of the Song thinker Zhu Xi (1130–1200), who had written the orthodox commentaries on the classics. Ch'oe's commentary on the *Book of Rites* was condemned for subtly changing Zhu Xi's perspective on the classics, and all copies of the text were burned.

Sensitivity toward dynastic founders also inspired selective forgetting in Nguyen Vietnam. The state banned histories from the Le period (1428–1788) that cast doubt on the legitimacy of its origins. But such measures seem to have been exceptional rather than ordinary in Vietnam before the nineteenth century. Phillipe Binh, a Vietnamese priest who spent much of his life in Lisbon, praised the Portuguese ability to censor printed works before publication. His description of the process illustrates that while he considered it desirable for the state to have a hand in selecting which texts should be printed, this perspective was exceptional for someone from the southern part of Vietnam.

Tokugawa Japan censored works it found potentially damaging to state interests. Beginning in the 1630s, Christian works were almost universally prohibited because of their perceived dangers to the state. The ban remained in effect for most of the Tokugawa period, but there was a loosening in the 1720s after Yoshimune began to promote the study of Western sciences. Other forms of censorship in the Tokugawa period are harder to trace. A large number of ad hoc edicts occasionally banned the circulation of certain works, and authors were occasionally imprisoned. One way around taboos seems to have been through the circulation of manuscripts. A large number of manuscript accounts of foreign places *leaked from government offices into wider circulation. These texts contained sensitive information and, while not explicitly banned, were accessible only to trusted members of a scholarly network.

In sum, banning books was a common tactic of rulers throughout East Asia, although it rarely was entirely successful. Instead, as in much of the world, taboos and government restrictions created a chilling effect. Scholars understood the sorts of books they were supposed to publish, and they kept anything potentially controversial in manuscript to circulate among limited groups of readers.

Archival Compilations

The control of information was typically entwined with summarizing or condensing. When texts were too long, or when space was limited, the ability to condense information efficiently and accurately was critical. Summarizing became important in encyclopedias—many of which were astonishingly long. In fact, the length of some books, even affordable household encyclopedias, could be something of a joke. A 1797 Japanese text complained that "the eighty-two chapters" of the *Japanese Illustrated Universe* (*Sancai tuhui*) were too much for a child. The author decided to summarize the entire text in fifteen pages so that even a three-year-old (*sanzai*, a homophone for "universe" in Japanese) could manage to learn its key points. The humorous illustrations throughout the work's fifteen pages poked fun at the conceit of encyclopedism, while also providing useful points for a pleasant education.

Summarizing was important not just for popular readers; it was also at the core of government labor. Every Qing office functioned on a much larger scale than any European bureaucracy from the same period. Groups of officials and clerks coordinated and merged vast textual burdens of print, manuscript, and correspondence into succinct summaries for imperial perusal. They developed standard forms for submitting information to the throne that facilitated summarizing a legal document of several hundred pages in a handful of sentences. Information processing was the work of hundreds of officials working in concert and without individual recognition; for an individual to emerge as a moderating node (as Jean-Baptiste Colbert did under Louis XIV in seventeenth-century France) would have been perceived as a fundamental flaw and failure.

One place to begin considering the strengths of the summarizing system of premodern Asia is with the state and its archival burden. Vertically integrated bureaucracies like those in China, Korea, and Japan governed through a series of registers. Registers made important parts of local government visible to the central government and allowed for the formation of appropriate policy. One challenge with trying to centrally legislate empire, however, was the need to keep everything up-to-date and synchronized.

In the early Ming, Zhu Yuanzhang (r. 1368–98), the founder of the dynasty, attempted to keep government offices working by commissioning the compilation and publication of a text containing the regulations of central government offices, entitled *Duties of All Government Offices* (*Zhusi zhizhang*). The compilation guided Ming governance until the 1470s, when officials began complaining that the nearly one-hundred-year-old compilation was out of date.

In the 1490s, the court ordered officials to begin searching through their archives for updated regulations. These updates were submitted to the court and compiled into a new work entitled the *Collected Institutions of the Great Ming* (*Daming huidian*). Completed in 1509, the preface by the Zhengde emperor (r. 1505–21) highlighted the importance of the text as a compilation that brought order to the chaos of contemporary administrative practice. He summarized the need for the *Collected Institutions* as follows:

> [Zhu Yuanzhang ordered] the writing of *Duties of All Government Offices* which recorded the guiding principles. . . . Truly it may be called a [collection] of laws of unprecedented greatness. But if we examine it as a text, then we see that it was made in the middle of the Hongwu reign [of Zhu Yuanzhang]. Matters which were fixed later in the reign, even if the offices were named in the text, had been altered. The late sagely rulers followed time, and circumstances made changes that both increased and decreased [regulations]. Since every age differs, they did not fall short of the intentions of the sagely ancestor [Taizu]. . . . So it is that over the years there has been much accumulated. Registers and texts have piled up. Some of the separate boards and respective offices are unable to completely know what is within them.

The book that the government printed was a snapshot of the fragments of the archive. The hundred or so pages of *paratext before the work explained its compilation and created trust in the hundreds of chapters of archive-derived rules that followed.

While government offices rarely preserved drafts of books created from the archive, surviving compilations provide useful insight into scholarly working methods. The scholar-official Qi Biaojia (1602–45) was keenly interested in compiling a record of the Wanli reign (1563–1620). He began his work by cutting important entries from his father's manuscript notes on the court gazette, a manuscript newspaper circulated to officials throughout the Ming empire to report on court news. He supplemented these notes by making and cutting out his own notes on the Wanli reign. With his cutting done, he arranged all these materials, whatever their origins, in chronological order and pasted them into a series of blank notebooks. The cover of each notebook listed its main concerns and topics, a form of indexing that made the twenty-volume manuscript navigable.

Qi Biaojia's methods of managing information were likely shared by scholars across East Asia. The archives of the preconquest Manchu (which started its central archives around the year 1616) exist in a variety of different states, preserving a rare example of government work. Notes in a local register recording runaway enslaved peoples show that government scribes carefully selected what information to transfer into hierarchically superior registers of state precedent. Those registers, known as the "original Manchu archives" (*Manwen yuandang*), were subsequently edited into an even more condensed record—*The Manchu Veritable Records* (*Manzhou Shilu*)—after being carefully examined by officials in the National History Office.

The selection and use of archival and printed materials for practical matters was common throughout East Asia. In foreign relations, China's neighbors often had to do research into precedent as a matter of course. In 1462, when Zuikei Shūhō was charged with composing letters to the Ming court, he wrote a history of Japanese foreign relations. In 1470, he completed his *Precious Record of Benevolent Neighbor States* (*Zenrin kokuhōki*). The text is a tour de force of Chinese and Japanese sources. Shūhō used Ming texts, such as the *History of the Yuan,* and several different Japanese sources to reproduce the documentary exchanges between Japan and China, and Japan and Korea, from 600 to 1400. This work seems a clear antecedent to the anti-Manchu *The Barbarization of Civilization* (*Ka'i Hentai*), compiled by Hayashi Gahō (1618–88). This work gathered and presented documents relating to the Manchu invasion of China and circulated in manuscript for much of the Tokugawa period. The sources of the documents were (1) letters and requests written from Ming officials to the shogun, (2) translated summaries of news from China based on interviews with Chinese merchants in Nagasaki, and (3) documents such as edicts and letters that were circulating within China and were brought to Japan. Like Zuikei and Qi Biaojia, Hayashi Gahō seamlessly blended the archival and the printed to create a narrative of recent history.

CONCLUSION: INFORMATION ALTERS TIME AND SPACE

Whether we call them early modern or late imperial, the fifteenth to nineteenth centuries in East Asia saw major structural shifts in information practices. Printing grew from its early invention and limited use to play a major role in societies throughout the region. The period witnessed the emergence of many different types of popular compilations. Encyclopedic compilations spread knowledge about states and their place in the world. A concept of the nation was built through print publications that circulated different kinds of information beyond the classical canon and government-sponsored projects. Formerly closed forms of knowledge became common knowledge, as commercial publishers poached and recycled information from one another and from the collections they could access.

Across East Asia, an increased volume and variety of texts accompanied significant increases in urbanization, literacy, and travel. This early modern textual archive helped to shape how time and space were conceived and performed, at scales that ranged from the household to the state and the empire and helped to generate new approaches to history and cartography. These texts reflected a new emphasis on completeness and holistic coverage and associated anxieties about any potential lack thereof. A holistic vision of the polity characterized cadastral and cartographic surveys of the land such as those seen in gazetteers, whose form and style tended to convey a sense of the unity of that which was being mapped. This knowledge became part of a shared stock of information and cultural memory; it taught users how to read the state and the empire, and to think of themselves as part of both entities.

Information practices and the early modern transformations they wrought were deeply shaped by the transnational circulation of information. As this essay has illustrated, the region of East Asia shared information practices, starting with a learned language, script, and textual canon, and including the high value placed on scholarship, the collection of books and records, and performance on examinations. Local information cultures within this large geographic area (including China itself) emerged from a negotiation between the local and more distant cultural centers made possible by the circulation of people, manuscripts, and printed books. For every inhabitant in the region, persistent engagement with the foreign and novel, as well as growing confidence in their own places in the world, contributed to the reshaping of identities that both created and unbound ideas of the nation.

But this outline is still limited. Our focus on the coherence of an "East Asian Mediterranean" has excluded interactions within a still larger geographic framework of Inner Asia, such as the Persian-reading astronomers of the Yuan court, the Arabic- and

Persian-literate Confucian Muslim scholars of the Qing, and the hybrid Tibetan Mongolian Buddhist scholars of Inner Asia. An Inner Asia–oriented history of East Asia would illustrate how China went from peripheral in the Ming to central in the Qing, as the Qing court became a center for polyglot practices. It would also illustrate how scholars in Japan and Korea grappled with the "barbarization" of Chinese civilization as Manchu rulers transformed Sinitic traditions for their own end. The history given above coexists with the Inner Asian history of early modern East Asia, and scholars are only now beginning to bring these stories together.

Devin Fitzgerald and Carla Nappi

See also archivists; bibliography; books; bureaucracy; censorship; learning; letters; libraries and catalogs; manuals; public sphere; reference books; registers; scrolls and rolls; surveys and censuses; travel; xylography

FURTHER READING

Mary Elizabeth Berry, *Japan in Print: Information and Nation in the Early Modern Period*, 2006; Willem Jan Boot, "The Adoption and Adaptation of Neo-Confucianism in Japan: The Role of Fujiwara Seika and Hayashi Razan," PhD dissertation, Leiden University, 1983; Cynthia J. Brokaw and Kai-Wing Chow, eds., *Printing and Book Culture in Late Imperial China*, 2005; Susan Cherniack, "Book Culture and Textual Transmission in Sung China," *Harvard Journal of Asiatic Studies* 54, no. 1 (1994): 5–125; Kai-wing Chow, *Publishing, Culture, and Power in Early Modern China*, 2004; Joseph R. Dennis, *Writing, Publishing, and Reading Local Gazetteers in Imperial China, 1100–1700*, 2015; Hilde De Weerdt, *Information, Territory, and Networks: The Crisis and Maintenance of Empire in Song China*, 2015; George Edson Dutton, *A Vietnamese Moses: Philiphê Bỉnh and the Geographies of Early Modern Catholicism*, 2017; Benjamin A. Elman, *Civil Examinations and Meritocracy in Late Imperial China*, 2013; Jahyun Kim Haboush and Martina Deuchler, eds., *Culture and the State in Late Chosŏn Korea*, 2002; Matthias Hayek and Annick Horiyuchi, *Listen, Copy, Read: Popular Learning in Early Modern Japan*, 2014; Catherine Jami, *The Emperor's New Mathematics: Western Learning and Imperial Authority during the Kangxi Reign (1662–1722)*, 2012; Daniel Koss, "Political Geography of Empire: Chinese Varieties of Local Government," *Journal of Asian Studies* 76, no. 1 (2017): 159–84; Peter H. Lee, *Sourcebook of Korean Civilization*, vol. 1, *From Early Times to the 16th Century*, 2010; Federico Marcon, *The Knowledge of Nature and the Nature of Knowledge in Early Modern Japan*, 2015; Osamu Oba and Joshua A. Fogel, *Books and Boats: Sino-Japanese Relations and Cultural Transmission in the Eighteenth and Nineteenth Centuries*, 2012; Kiri Paramore, *Japanese Confucianism*, 2016; Kurtis R. Schaeffer, *The Culture of the Book in Tibet*, 2014.

4

INFORMATION IN EARLY MODERN EUROPE

The period of European history from roughly 1450 to 1789 is now commonly called "early modern" on the notion that various features of "modernity" originated then. An earlier label for the period of "*Renaissance and *Reformation" emphasized the contents and impacts of those movements, whereas the preference for "early modern" that has spread since the 1980s invites attention to a broader array of developments and their interactions. In devoting multiple chapters to the fifteenth to eighteenth centuries in Europe and elsewhere, this volume seeks to highlight the presence and significance of information practices before the term and concept were in use in their current acceptations. In using the term *modern* we reject abstract definitions of modernity (e.g., as advanced by modernization theory in the 1950s and 1960s); instead we use the term pragmatically to describe developments that endured into the later period called "modern" by convention and convenience. These early modern chapters focus on expanded travel and trade linking long-separate parts of the globe (Ghobrial, chap. 5); the consolidation of political power through bureaucratic and archival practices in city-states, nation-states, and colonial empires (Head, chap. 6); the circulation and impact of news (Slauter, chap. 7); and the parallel and distinct cultures of information in the Islamicate world (Muhanna, chap. 2) and East Asia (Fitzgerald and Nappi, chap. 3). These topics were selected from among many other possible areas of study especially because of the depth of existing scholarship on them.

This chapter, focusing on the chronologically earlier part of the early modern period, roughly 1400–1650, will set the stage for subsequent chapters on European information culture by examining the situation circa 1400 and the invention (around 1450) and rapid spread of printing by metal movable type (or typography). It will consider the transformation of medieval information practices and the rise of new ones in the wake of printing and the information explosion that it fueled and will close by emphasizing a second major contemporaneous development—the improvement of the postal system in western Europe. The confluence of these developments with others that were quite independent of them generated a remarkable spate of changes for which the period is famous: not only Renaissance and reformations, the consolidation of nations and empires, and the globalization of commerce, but also (with consequences for all those processes) new ways of producing, managing, and disseminating information.

THE CONTEXT OF THE EARLY FIFTEENTH CENTURY

A number of the features of the information landscape that we associate with the early modern and modern periods were already well established in medieval Europe, so that the history of information involves long continuities as well as sudden innovations. A new technology like printing is best understood as the product of its historical context and its impacts as resulting from a whole range of factors, some of them technical, many of them social and cultural. Europe in 1400 featured the technical prerequisites for the invention of printing as well as the conditions for a rapid commercialization of this method of mechanically reproducing texts.

The manuscript culture of late medieval Europe was grounded in centuries of continuous growth, including the Carolingian Renaissance (around 800 CE), noted for the foundation of new schools offering instruction in Latin, and the "twelfth-century Renaissance," which featured the transmission of Aristotelian philosophical works to the Latin West from the Arabic translations circulating in Spain (see Muhanna, chap. 2), the foundation of universities where those and other texts were studied, and the spread of the manufacturing of paper first in Italy and Spain and later north of the Alps (see Grafton, chap. 1). Strong demographic and commercial growth between 1000 and 1300 had made possible the rise of cities as centers of government, commerce, and culture, and of trade routes between them sustained by roads, rivers, and regular fairs. The medieval church was a widely distributed institution featuring multiple branches—secular (priests), regular (following rules in monastic house), and mendicant (the Dominican and Franciscan orders founded in the thirteenth century). After the Christianization of Scandinavia in the twelfth century and of Lithuania in 1387, it spanned all of western Europe.

Experiences of information in the Middle Ages varied widely by place and social standing. The spoken word (in sermons or proclamations or other texts read aloud) and sounds (like bells and tocsins) were typically accessible to all the inhabitants of villages and towns. Writing was encountered in legal and administrative contexts, in complex mercantile operations, and among the clergy and the educated. Historians have moved away from the blunt categories of literate and illiterate to identify kinds of *literacy. "Pragmatic literacy" (as coined by Michael Clanchy) enabled people even of lower social orders to manage basic legal and business affairs that increasingly involved written documents. Those who lacked the requisite skills depended on intermediaries, friends, family members, or experts who could be hired. Mercantile literacy included reckoning and reading followed by writing in the vernacular. A career in any branch of the clergy (including all forms of higher education) theoretically involved literacy in Latin, a sacred language that was also a living language common to the learned across Western Christendom. Critics of the church at the time claimed that many clerics were not properly literate and celebrated the Latin Mass by rote; churchgoers too likely acquired a partial literacy in the components of the Mass through force of habit even without being able to read. By the late Middle Ages there was also a growing audience for and production of vernacular manuscripts in a wide range of *genres, from the literary (including Dante and Boccaccio in Italian and Chaucer in English) to practical books like almanacs and how-to manuals that could convey information by pictorial as well as textual elements. New scripts designed for speed and efficiency as well as the increasing availability and use of paper lowered the production costs of manuscripts and facilitated access to them, in response to and further fueling an increase in readership.

It is fiendishly hard to estimate how many manuscripts were produced or in circulation at the time, given the losses suffered as they were reduced to tatters by use or recycled for the material they were written on (since both *parchment and paper were serviceable in other contexts) and given the paucity and unreliability of records of book ownership. Our principal evidence rests in the details about production, circulation, and use contained in the manuscripts themselves that survive. Arguments from surviving manuscripts are of course complicated by the many factors affecting their survival (including a general correlation of greater rates of loss with the greater passage of time). Nevertheless, the explosion in the number of surviving manuscripts produced in the early fifteenth century leaves no doubt about a surging demand for texts across a variety of genres especially in the Italian and German contexts. In each of these areas the number of surviving manuscripts produced each year rose from about five thousand in 1400 to twenty thousand in 1460. In considering examples of two different motives for publication in this period, I will emphasize how late medieval manuscript culture met demands for both the rapid circulation of short texts and the durable preservation of longer ones. In this context the merits of printing in accomplishing both of these goals were readily apparent; in other words, the new technology was developed in a place and a time where it was put into use right away.

Daniel Hobbins has recently given us insight into the life and writings of Jean Gerson (1363–1429), a major French cleric (chancellor of the University of Paris, bishop then archbishop and cardinal) and a prolific author. Gerson wrote sermons delivered orally then circulated in writing, devotional works, learned treatises, poetry, and, most distinctively, *tractatuli* or short tracts written rapidly and widely disseminated, which offered clearly labeled interventions in current events, such as the Council of Constance (1414–18, which ended the papal schism and declared the Czech church reformer Jan Hus a heretic) and the final phases of the Hundred Years' War (including the rise of Joan of Arc). Gerson wrote in Latin as was the norm for clerics, but also in French in order to reach a wider audience. He often composed in his own hand although few of his autographs survive, and he added features to guide and attract his readers such as a *colophon, unusually placed at the beginning of the text, announcing title and author, and "rubrics" and "little rubrics" indicating the divisions and subdivisions throughout the text to facilitate browsing. In doing so Gerson drew on practices of manuscript organization or *ordinatio* that were first developed in scholastic contexts in the thirteenth century alongside alphabetical finding devices like the first biblical *concordances (ca. 1247), alphabetically ordered dictionaries (like the *Catholicon* of 1286), and indexes of contemporary works (like the *encyclopedic *Speculum maius* of Vincent of Beauvais, composed 1240–60, and its index composed separately by Jean de Hautfumey in 1320–23). In major centers like Paris, scribes also prepared manuscripts for sale without a prior commission, confident of the demand for their products, although Gerson's writings did not fit into the best-selling categories on which they focused (Bibles, chronicles, moral treatises, and romances, many of the latter in the vernacular).

To disseminate his works Gerson took advantage of church gatherings, from regional synods to the massive Council of Constance that attracted as many as eighteen thousand clerics from all over Western Christendom. A great deal of copying happened during the council, resulting for example in some eighty surviving copies of Gerson's tract *On Ecclesiastical Power* made there, which were often transported back to their owners' hometowns. Outside these special events Gerson's works were also disseminated through the networks of the Carthusian and Celestine orders to which Gerson had strong ties, but principally north of the Alps rather than in Italy. The late medieval culture of oral debates and sermons and extensive manuscript copying, combined with the clerical infrastructure of large gatherings and interconnected religious houses, made it possible for someone like Jean Gerson to achieve an immediate impact in current events through wide and rapid diffusion of his short tracts. Gerson did not live to see Gutenberg's invention, but he modeled attitudes and behaviors of authorship that later clerics ambitious to have an immediate impact in the world could follow even more effectively thanks to printing.

Gerson's methods of publicity owed a great deal to the scribal culture of Italian city-states in which the humanist movement had started to develop already in the fourteenth century, inspired most famously by his own favorite modern author, Francesco Petrarca (Petrarch, 1304–74). Italian contexts also experienced a surge of manuscript production in the fifteenth century, with distinctive humanist emphases. The humanist project involved cultivating classical Latin (as opposed to the scholastic forms of Latin common in clerical and university contexts) and when possible learning Greek in order to appreciate the ancient texts in their original languages. With the patronage of wealthy backers like the Medici who covered the significant expenses involved, humanists searched for manuscripts of ancient texts that had been neglected or forgotten in order to copy them and collect them in libraries. They sent agents to purchase Greek manuscripts before and after the fall of Byzantium in 1453, and they scoured monastic libraries in Europe looking for hidden treasures that had been copied onto parchment centuries earlier. The Council of Constance proved a fruitful base of operations, for example for Poggio Bracciolini (1380–1459), a Tuscan whose skill in humanist Latin landed him employment as papal secretary for some fifty years. In 1416–17, while the council wrestled with appointing a new pope, Poggio was on hiatus and used the time to visit monastic libraries in Switzerland and Germany. There he recovered manuscripts of hitherto lost works by Cicero, Quintilian, Statius, and most spectacularly Lucretius, whose "De rerum natura" was fascinating for its expansive vocabulary and skillful poetry rather than for its shocking Epicurean ideas about the universe, which only a few—such as Niccolò Machiavelli—pursued in detail. Although the copy that Poggio made of Lucretius does not survive, it served as the basis for subsequent manuscript copies. The flurry of copies that resulted marked the first time Lucretius's text had been read since the ninth century, when the manuscript Poggio found had been made.

Humanist manuscripts commissioned by noble patrons were often lavish productions, sometimes made on parchment even though paper was available, typically bearing colorful floral decorations and the patron's coat of arms. They were copied in new scripts that the humanists had devised first by imitating older manuscripts (such as Carolingian minuscule, resulting in our "roman" fonts), then by adding a *cursive slant (which inspired italic fonts) for greater speed. The major collectors of this period amassed significant libraries comprising hundreds of manuscripts. The Florentine collector Niccolò Niccoli (1364–1437), for example, gathered one of the largest collections of his time, with eight hundred manuscripts. After his death these books formed a crucial core of the new library of San Marco founded in 1444 by Cosimo de Medici as the first public library of Florence. Although that institution did not endure past the early modern period, its manuscripts did, while the ideal of forming a vast secular library for the "use of all men of letters of our own age and of subsequent time" was realized in the Vatican Library, founded in 1451 by Pope Nicholas V. Nicholas's plan was to gather the best manuscripts of ancient texts in order to serve as a reference library. His successors invested further in manuscripts and then printed books, in addition to bigger quarters beautifully outfitted. With the exception of a few restrictive decades during the Counter-Reformation in the later sixteenth and early seventeenth centuries, the Vatican Library has served as a major resource for scholars down to the present.

Keenly aware of the masses of ancient texts that they would never manage to recover, humanists aimed to preserve for all time all the classical texts that they could find, to spare posterity the trauma of further losses. As a result they soon appreciated how printing could contribute to preservation and transmission of painstakingly recovered texts. To be sure, some were hostile to the new technology. One scribe of luxury humanist manuscripts, Vespasiano da Bisticci (1421–98), complained about the cheap production values of a book printed in black and white on paper that could never be as valuable nor as durable as parchment manuscripts. Nevertheless his favorite customer, Federigo da Montefeltre, Duke of Urbino, also owned many printed books even while he too affected to despise them. Poggio's great find was one of many classical texts printed soon after Gutenberg's invention. The *editio princeps* (or first printed edition) of Lucretius appeared in 1473, at a price that made it accessible to many who could not have afforded a manuscript copy; although only four copies from this first edition survive today, other editions followed, and printing played a powerful role in the survival of vast numbers of texts (recovered from antiquity but also composed at the time) that would otherwise have been lost.

Printing originated in a cultural context in which many were eager to put to use a new technology that could achieve at lower cost and more quickly what manuscript copying was already producing—a wide spectrum of texts both learned and vernacular, designed for rapid impact or for long-term transmission or both.

THE DEVELOPMENT AND FEATURES OF TYPOGRAPHY

Printing could reproduce a short text fast (to satisfy a Gerson) and ensure the preservation of scholarly texts far into the future (to satisfy a Poggio). Indeed, Gutenberg himself likely printed texts in both of these modes: his famous 42-line Bible took an estimated two years to produce and was surely not the first thing he printed. He no doubt ran his first successful experiment on a short text, such as a twenty-eight-page grammar book by Donatus, or an *indulgence, printed on just one side (in a broadsheet that would be cut into multiple indulgences). Both types of texts could be sold rapidly in large numbers—respectively to students and to the church, which took charge of retail sale of indulgences to penitents. Both were the kind of practical imprint that survives very poorly (at a rate of about 0.003 percent in the case of indulgences). By contrast, when Gutenberg printed a Bible, presumably in order to showcase his new technology and gain respect for it, it survived at an unusually high rate of almost 33 percent; in addition many fragments of lost copies also survive, as Eric White has shown. This book was large in size and sacred in content, its early owners were mostly religious institutions, and its later ones were book collectors—all factors that contributed to its high survival rate.

Given that our evidence for early printing largely rests on what has survived, we can be sure that vast numbers of ephemeral imprints have been completely lost. These likely included printed forms to be filled out by hand (such as contracts, receipts, and bills in addition to indulgences that called for the name of the penitent to be written in) and leaflets of many kinds (such as government notices, news, songs, and religious prayers and messages, with or without accompanying images). Ephemera were the cheapest imprints, accessible to the greatest number of buyers, who in due course reused the paper on which they were printed for many purposes from starting fires to wrapping or wiping things. That reuse has occasionally led them to be found, notably as the endpapers inserted into the binding of later books. Despite its poor survival, cheap print was especially powerful in reaching a wide audience rapidly and at low cost. Government proclamations, reports of recent events from far and near (whether reliable or not), and religious exhortations and prophecies were among the major genres of ephemera that kept printers financially afloat and readers in the sway of political and religious trends. In earlier periods similar information was diffused orally (through sermons and town criers, formal meetings and informal gossip) and by manuscript copying. Oral and manuscript media remained essential (and indeed still are), but printing lent a new level of impact to whatever was selected for publication, whether by the official authorities of church and state, or by the private calculus of printers hoping to make a profit. That profit motive and the fear of punishment generally discouraged printers from challenging the authorities under which they operated. But the fragmentation of competing European polities and the trade in printed matter among them also made it possible for ephemera to circulate content that one church or state considered undesirable while others did not (such as Protestant broadsheets).

Gutenberg was still experimenting when he printed his first Bible: he drew on his skills as a goldsmith to create multiple separate sorts for each letter. This method resulted in multiple versions of each letter, which differed slightly and were recycled through the book, as scholars have tracked with the aid of digital imaging. Over time Gutenberg streamlined the production of letter sorts, by forming one perfect punch for each letter, which could be used to shape the matrix in which to cast (using molten lead) as many identical copies of the same letter as needed. Gutenberg must also have experimented with inks that would stick to the metal but transfer cleanly onto the paper, and with sizing for the paper, treating it with alum to prevent the ink from seeping too deeply into the paper and becoming illegible. Oil-based paints devised a few decades earlier and most famously adopted by the Flemish panel painter Jan van Eyck may have inspired Gutenberg's use of oil-based ink. The screw press that was characteristic of the handpress era, down to 1800, was familiar from wine and oil presses. The idea of imprinting a pattern by woodblock was also familiar from the long history of creating patterned cloths. But the latest assessment is that block books formed by woodblocks containing a mix of image and text did not predate Gutenberg's invention, but rather coincided with the first decades of typography.

Another crucial ingredient was paper, but for commercial not technical reasons since one could print on parchment. Indeed, Gutenberg printed some of his Bibles on *vellum, presumably on commission for wealthy buyers. Imprints on vellum were exceptional, reserved for copies to be presented to special patrons. Paper was expensive enough to account (given the vast quantities necessary) for about half the expense of a print run; using parchment for a whole print run would have been punitively expensive. Finally, printing required more workers and more division of labor than scribing: a compositor to set the type (upside down and backward) and lay it in the bed of the press; another to prepare and apply the ink to the type; a pressman to pull the bar, pressing the blank sheet onto the inked text so that it was transferred onto the page. Large printing houses would run multiple presses at once and would hire specialists to proofread, draw up an index, or make woodblocks for illustrations. Binding was the purview of another expert whom printers or buyers hired to assemble the book from the printed sheets; whether they used a costly material like stamped leather or the less expensive vellum, a bound book was easier to store and more likely to be saved and transmitted than one left unbound in lightly stitched folded sheets.

It is impossible to measure the odds of someone else inventing printing if Gutenberg had not, but I suggest that they were high. Claims of a simultaneous invention by Laurens Janszoon Coster seem grounded only in a sixteenth-century attempt at burnishing the reputation of Coster's hometown of Haarlem, in the Netherlands. But all the elements were readily available, as well as existing demand for what printing could offer, so the idea could plausibly have occurred to someone else around the same time. We now appreciate that printing by both woodblock (xylography) and (more rarely) movable characters (made of wood or porcelain but also metal) was in use centuries earlier in multiple East Asian contexts. Nevertheless, there is no good evidence of a westward transmission of printing from Asia to Europe, although gunpowder and papermaking clearly were transmitted in that way. Xylography and typography involve distinct affordances that become erased in our use of the single term *printing* to denote both of them. The distinctive features of typography include the inflexible nature of the initial decision of how many copies to print. Once each sheet was printed in a given number of copies, the metal sorts used to print it were distributed back into the case from which they would be used to compose the next sheet. To print more copies of a sheet that had already been printed and dismantled would require investing the labor of setting type all over again (although the labor of planning the layout could be reused). On the contrary, a woodblock could be saved once it was carved and reused a long or a short time later to reprint a great number of extra copies. Woodblocks used in European imprints for illustrations and decorative elements were similarly stored, traded, and reused; but the text printed alongside these blocks by metal movable type could not be. By the early eighteenth century a few innovative printers had experimented with the casting of full pages of type that could be stored and extensively reused; stereotype printing was deployed in this early phase in the printing of inexpensive Bibles, before its heyday in the nineteenth century.

While East Asian xylography offered the advantages of print on demand (provided the blocks were stored in good condition, which might entail significant expense), European typography was always a more speculative and risky undertaking, involving high expenditures up front and no way to profit from strong sales beyond the copies that had already been planned without incurring most of the production costs again. For example, Gutenberg raised the number of 42-line Bibles he produced partway through that first edition, evidently for fear of missing out on the opportunities for profits that those extra copies could offer. It meant resetting the pages that had already been printed at the point when he decided to raise the size of the print run; the small differences between the two settings of type on these pages provide the evidence for this decision. The second distinctive feature about the development of typography in Europe is its immediately commercial nature. In East Asia books were for the first five hundred years mainly printed by Buddhist temples, central or local governments, or families—these were commissioned and private printings rather than commercial ones.

On the contrary, in Europe printing was a commercial and capitalist venture from the start. Printers who lacked the necessary funds partnered with publishers who provided the capital. For example, Gutenberg could not repay the loan taken out to cover his initial expenses and lost his business to his creditor Johann Fust. Variations of that pattern would be repeated many times over, in the initial explosion of interest in the new business and even once the industry had matured. In Italy printers set up in eighty different towns and cities in the fifteenth century; the resulting overproduction led the vast majority of them to fail. By 1500 Italian printing was consolidated in eleven locales, with four cities accounting for 80 percent of the total output for the peninsula. The same was true on the scale of Europe, where a few major centers dominated the business. Venice, Frankfurt and Cologne, Paris and Lyon, Basel, and Antwerp each had the crucial advantage of being located on a major river and at the intersection of existing trade routes. Since any local market would soon be saturated, access to more distant ones was crucial. Partnerships were a common method of sharing in the risk of producing a book and seeking broader markets. Printers would band together to publish a book, with each member of the partnership receiving a share of the printed copies proportional to their investment. Some partnerships were formed among colleagues in one city (like the three Johanns of early sixteenth-century Basel: Amerbach, Petri, and Froben). Other partnerships spanned multiple cities, whether based on family ties or international contracts. The Giunti family, which started printing in Venice in 1489 and Florence in 1497, involved some thirty family members down to the 1620s in producing, warehousing, and selling books in dozens of cities in at least six countries. In addition, learned books especially, being expensive and written in the international language of Latin, were the object of partnerships where the reciprocity of commercial interests rather than family ties kept multiple parties faithful to their agreements, even across national and confessional differences. Finally, book professionals throughout Europe used the major fairs (Frankfurt being the largest among them, overtaken by Leipzig after 1632) to trade stock and information with colleagues and competitors every fall and spring. Despite all these methods of distributing risk, many printers died with lots of debt and unsold stock.

The risks inherent in the business could be offset by job printing—the production of small items that would sell quickly (e.g., pamphlets with exciting claims or news) or that were paid for in advance by church or government. Some genres were steady sellers and reliable sources of revenue, thanks to strong buyer demand—notably devotional, liturgical, and pedagogical books. More generally, whenever the same printer published a second edition of a work we can presume the first one had sold well. A wise printer would plan a mix of projects, so that risky ones could be covered by safer ones. A study of the practice at the university press in seventeenth-century Cambridge revealed a complex choreography of presses being assigned to short-run pamphlets in the midst of printing much larger works. For works produced on speculation, profit depended on the correct choice of print run: print too few and miss out on profit, print too many and incur uncompensated expenses that could prove ruinous. A rare case of a book colophon mentioning a print run of three hundred copies gives us one data point for the period of incunabula (i.e., books printed before 1500). In the sixteenth century print runs usually ranged up to 1,000–1,250 copies, since this was the number of copies of one sheet that could typically be printed in one day (as we know from the exceptional set of archives that survive from the Plantin Moretus shop in Antwerp starting in 1564), but higher print runs were also possible.

A crucial feature of a printed item is that it was never produced alone: from one surviving copy we can deduce that hundreds more were produced at the same time, even if they do not survive. Imprints that were never bound, especially printed forms and short practical works and pamphlets, have often been completely lost; but new finds continue to be made—as lost books are identified from fragments found in the bindings of other books, or appear during house renovations centuries after they were hidden to avoid religious persecution. Overall printing generated quantities of texts on an unprecedented scale: at least twenty-seven thousand editions of incunabula were printed by 1500, followed by more than 320,000 editions in the sixteenth century. The number of printed books that resulted (likely more than three hundred million, excluding the many ephemera that have been completely lost) dwarfed not only the estimated number of European manuscripts surviving from the sixth to the sixteenth century (1.3 million) but also the number of manuscripts estimated to have been available in 1500 (six to seven million).

Printing was a business but a special one given the intellectual content of the product. Books circulated ideas and connoted the power of the written word. In setting up printing presses in various colonies, Europeans valued them as tools to achieve their various goals of converting Indigenous populations, creating cohesion among the colonists, or representing imperial power, even though they were not very successful commercially. In Mexico the Seville printer Juan Cromberger produced his first books in 1540, with the support of the bishop there, but probably profited more from his monopoly on importing books than from the one on printing them, both granted to him by Spanish royal decree. Printing started in Goa on the west coast of India in 1556 thanks to a press transported from Portugal by the Jesuits. The first press in the British colonies in America was brought over in 1639 to aid the population of one thousand colonists in Boston and the college they had just founded three years before. The production from these presses was not very great but was symbolically important. Conversely printing was forbidden in places where the authorities feared it would foster further resistance, for instance, in the Latin-occupied Greek Levant (such as Crete) where the Roman Church hoped to spread its control in the wake of the fall of Byzantium and banned printing lest it be used to shore up Orthodox Christianity instead. Cracow and Prague were the largest printing centers in eastern Europe, producing books in a range of languages and scripts. The first incunabula and Bible printed in Cyrillic type were published there in 1490–91 and 1517, respectively, as well as many Hebrew imprints for the Jewish communities of Ashkenaz.

More generally European printers needed to cultivate favorable relations with the government under which they operated. Unlike East Asian xylography, which could be practiced almost anywhere without leaving a trace, typography required considerable capital and could not easily be carried out in secret—the press and metal type were so heavy that some printshop floors collapsed under their weight. Portable presses were devised and used clandestinely in special circumstances, as in the production of the

Marprelate pamphlets in England in 1588–89, but in most cases the new industry operated in full view of its urban environment and subject to regulations of two kinds: commercial and ideological. Printers themselves set up commercial regulations to protect
their ability to recover the great expense of publishing a book by preventing others from
printing the same work. On the continent printers would seek a privilege that granted
them a monopoly on printing a work for a certain number of years, free from competition within the jurisdiction of the grantor. Privileges issued by monarchs or the pope or
the emperor were never automatic—they required the favor of the grantor (which could
prove difficult to obtain) and the payment of a fee. In England the Stationers' Company,
founded in 1557, operated like a guild and issued licenses to print specific works or kinds
of works to members who bid for them. The trade relations that printers and publishers
maintained across jurisdictional boundaries also served to regulate behavior; although
piracy (which undercut a printer's market) was a real threat, the fact that printers could
retaliate against one another and controlled a powerful medium in which to voice their
complaints worked against rampant piracy.

The second form of regulation came from outside the industry, as churches and states
sought to control the content that was printed. Censorship did not originate with printing. Producers of texts both oral and written (including preachers, teachers, authors, and
scribes) had long since been held responsible for content deemed heretical or seditious.
The medieval church issued general condemnations of certain positions and persecuted
individuals who seemed to espouse them, especially once heresy became a major concern in the thirteenth century. Self-censorship of speech and writing was a natural by-
product of the efforts to enforce religious, political, and social norms that were widespread across most medieval and early modern contexts. Printing introduced new players
in the production of written texts, and printers were soon required to include their name
on all their imprints, so they too could be held responsible; one evasive maneuver was to
list a false printer's name and address. Prepublication censorship was common in both
Catholic and Protestant contexts, whereby printers had texts approved by the authorities
before investing in publishing them, in order to spare themselves the risks of their stock
being destroyed or their persons punished. The Catholic Church was unique in forming
(in 1559, as part of the Counter-Reformation) a bureaucratic wing of the papacy devoted
to postpublication censorship. The Index of Prohibited Books published lists of banned
authors and texts, and of specific passages in otherwise allowable texts that Catholics
should refrain from reading as dangerous to their faith. Of course a large area of Europe
had become Protestant by this point and produced these "bad" books in abundance, beyond the sway of Rome. Depending on their location Catholics could access more or less
easily such books through the market, and some—especially experts, such as medical
men seeking to keep up with the latest publications—even did so with permission, which
the church granted to trusted individuals. Protestant contexts also exercised postpublication censorship. In Tudor and Stuart England, for example, royal authorities removed
from circulation books they judged offensive and sometimes staged public burnings of
them, occasionally accompanied by the corporal punishment of their authors or distributors (as in the cases of John Stubbs and William Page in 1579, and William Prynne in
1634 and 1637). Public book burnings, complete with many symbolic elements, were
designed to display the power of the state or the condemnation of rebels against authority (as in the case of the schismatic Jan Hus or the burning of antiroyalist books at the

restoration of Charles II in 1660), but that power did not extend to the contemporary reaction, which could include voices of sympathy for those condemned.

Publishing new ideas could be risky but also supremely successful. The German reformer Martin Luther was especially adept at marshaling the power of the press. His printers at Wittenberg and elsewhere ended up benefiting handsomely from the brisk sales of his works starting with the ninety-five theses of 1517; the books helped to bring about a religious schism that protected their makers from Catholic repression. In other cases, when new ideas did not catch on, printers could pay a heavy price for advancing a cause in which they believed or on which they had wagered; the Lyon printer Etienne Dolet, for example, was executed for heresy in 1546. Authors could hope to keep their identity secret, and some succeeded in doing so; thanks to elaborate ruses, Jonathan Swift avoided being identified as the author of texts that would have been grounds for conviction of *libel. But printers had more limited options—a false imprint was the most common evasive maneuver and not always successful as the authorities could identify printers by the characteristics of their work much as bibliographers do today. As a result, manuscript remained the medium of choice for the distribution of texts that risked legal proceedings against their makers as intolerable on religious, political, or moral grounds. Identifying the culprits was more difficult, and the authorities generally cared less about what circulated in manuscript once printed books were available to cause greater damage.

IMPACTS OF PRINTING

Contemporaries were struck by the power of printing: the ability to produce in one day what would have taken many men more than a year to write, as multiple contemporaries noted as early as 1470, and the remarkable drop in price that resulted for a text that was printed rather than manuscript (which one contemporary estimated at 80 percent). Printing was the optimal way to produce very many copies of a text, and, given the commercial incentive to produce enough copies to ensure a profit if they sold, the technology favored abundant output. One modern bibliographer, Hugh Amory, astutely observed that as a result most printed books (i.e., individual copies of books) have never been read. A good number were never even purchased but lingered unsold, reused to make new works (as I discuss below), or recycled for the paper. Printing became a new option for publication but was not the medium of choice for making a small number of copies for narrow circulation. In other words, printing never replaced manuscript copying, although the production of manuscripts declined steeply in the fifty years following its height around 1470.

The need for professional scribes dropped significantly, but their activities did not disappear entirely. Most important was probably their continued primacy in producing official documents—charters, treaties, and the like. They also provided models for type design and took on new kinds of work in the printing business; others retooled themselves as teachers of handwriting and authored printed books to showcase their skills and attract students. A few carried on producing manuscripts commercially, in various specific genres such as chamber music parts, which were expensive to print and were needed only in small numbers, and newsletters produced for subscribers that would be customized to meet their interests and could contain news considered unfit to print.

Printing also likely encouraged the use of handwriting, since it was no longer associated with the mere copying best delegated to scribes. The Benedictine abbot Johannes Trithemius (1462–1516), drawing on medieval sources, depicted the work of monastic scribes as literally holy, in a way that the mechanical work of compositors and pressmen was not. Nevertheless humanist pedagogues introduced new grounds for handwriting: they advocated taking reading or classroom notes in one's own hand in order to retain them better in memory (indeed this advice has been reiterated recently in response to digital note taking). The great humanist Desiderius Erasmus (1466–1536) also portrayed autography as an important skill for a gentleman because "a man's handwriting, like his voice, has a special, individual quality." Correspondents were increasingly expected to write letters to family and associates in their own hand, though using a secretary was considered appropriate for writing to social superiors or inferiors and for keeping copies of outgoing correspondence.

The earliest printed books were designed to look like manuscripts, but by 1530 the printed book had acquired many crucial features that we expect in a book today. In order to replicate the role of color in manuscripts to guide the reader's eye to key points in the text, incunabula were printed with blank spaces for initial letters and headings to be filled in by a scribe using red (or sometimes blue) ink. Two-tone printing was possible and used in some cases throughout the handpress era, but since it involved running the sheet through the press twice, to apply the black and red inks separately, it was time-consuming and expensive. Over time printers devised other methods to distinguish the different sections of a text, including the use of blank space and lines (e.g., paragraphing), varying sizes and types of fonts, and the little symbols known as dingbats. Most of the abbreviations common in medieval scripts were gradually dropped (but the suspension of nasals persisted for another century or more, and the ampersand has remained in use until now). Books in romance languages were usually printed in roman or italic font, whereas Germanic languages used versions of Gothic script. If a text shifted between Latin and English or German the font shifted according to this convention; in England blackletter signaled popular (since it was the font of the hornbook from which children first learned to read) or old-fashioned by around 1600, but it continued to be used in some genres like royal proclamations into the eighteenth century. In German Fraktur remained common until the mid-twentieth century.

Printing increased access to the written word for those reading and those writing alike. The earliest imprints were existing texts that circulated in manuscript—liturgical and pedagogical texts in particular. Humanists soon sought to print their recent finds of ancient texts, hoping to gain reputation for themselves and for the recovered ancient author through a learned edition, including translation into Latin as needed for texts in Greek, and often some commentary. But a growing percentage of books were new compositions by authors from many walks of life. In addition to learned authors (e.g., in the clergy, law, medicine, or education) who dominated textual production in the Middle Ages, artisans and merchants had greater access to books as they became cheaper. Although there were medieval autodidacts (e.g., the prolific Islamic medical author Ibn Sīnā, known in Europe as Avicenna, d. 1037), the phenomenon of teaching oneself from books became more feasible; similarly, publishing a book was within reach of a broader range of writers. Craftsmen and artists shared their practical expertise in how-to books or collections of "secrets," which proved a long-lived genre in Latin and the vernaculars. Many factors were involved in these developments, including the rising status of an elite of artisans who received princely patronage, and efforts to improve schools that originated in both the Reformation and the Counter-Reformation.

Literacy is hard to define (see the different types of literacy mentioned above) and even harder to measure, but the mandate of parish record keeping common among Catholics and Protestants starting in the sixteenth century has been used to track rising rates in the ability to sign documents (rather than leaving simpler marks such as crosses). Literacy rates varied widely by place (with urban rates higher than rural ones), by gender (with male literacy rates usually double those for women), and owing to specific circumstances. For example, unusually high rates of literacy resulted in Sweden by 1700 from its being mandated by the church there as a precondition to marriage; English Quakers and the men of New England reached near universal literacy in the eighteenth century, while these rates were reached more broadly in Europe only around 1900. Overall literacy rates rose in western Europe from the fifteenth to the eighteenth century, from estimated averages of 5–15 percent in 1500 to 50–75 percent in 1750, and the greater availability and lower price of books was both a cause and an effect of that rise.

With more and new readers to address, printing prompted the development of new ways of guiding the reader: title page, errata lists, and pagination. The title page was rarely present in medieval manuscripts; instead bibliographers identify manuscripts by their incipit or first words of the text. The title page played a key role in attracting buyers who in a shop or fair faced many options of books to purchase. The title page included identifiers (author, title, printer, place, and date of publication) and made alluring claims about the topic of the book or its special features, like "a most abundant index" or a "most correct and enlarged" text. Since the purpose of the title page was above all to prompt a sale, exaggerations and inaccuracies were common. The errata list was another feature new to printed books. Scribes committed errors too, but whereas their errors were unique to each manuscript, typographical errors affected every copy of the print run. Sometimes errors were corrected partway through a print run in a "stop-press correction." This practice resulted in variations among the extant copies within one edition, because printers were typically reluctant to dispose of the sheets containing the error and, as a result, some copies of the book for sale would contain the error while in others it had been corrected (the two different versions that resulted are called "issues" within an edition). Occasionally errors were also corrected in the printshop with a manuscript annotation or by pasting a correction slip over the error. But the easier remedy was to include (typically at the back of the book) a list of errors and their corrections. This list of errata was designed to forestall complaints of readers by enjoining them to make the corrections in their copies by hand and to guide those producing future editions of the text. Errata lists occasionally also featured short blurbs in which the author or the printer could take or assign blame for the faults; these shed light on the multiple people involved in book production and the potential for tensions among them.

Errata lists referred to specific passages by page or folio numbers, which were also innovations linked to printing. Uniform numbering of pages was rare in manuscripts. Early printed books, formed by folding each printed sheet into a cluster of pages called a quire, featured signature numbers in the lower right of the first pages in each quire; these were meant to guide the compositor and the binder to ensure the proper assembly of the quires. For the use of readers, incunabula introduced foliation (which appeared on the recto, or front, of every page); then pagination (on both recto and verso, or back of the page) became the norm by 1530. Paratexts (i.e., front matter or back matter) that referred to the text (such as errata lists but also tables of contents and indexes) did so by page or folio numbers, whereas medieval indexes used layout-independent forms of reference such as book and chapter number that could apply to any manuscript. An index tied to a specific edition represented some loss of information since it was not easily transferable to another edition (or to a manuscript copy), but by making the index specific to each edition printers may have hoped to lure buyers for an edition with a "new and improved" index even if they already owned an earlier edition of the text. Indexes were clearly an attraction for readers. Some were drawn up in haste as a short list of the marginal summaries printed in the text; but large informational books typically featured detailed indexes and often multiple ones—for different languages, thematic headings, proper names, "memorable things and words," or for "things of note not contained in the earlier indexes." The first page of the enormous *Nuremberg Chronicle*, a world history published in 1493, advertises the index ("Registrum") of the book, rather than the text itself, in large Gothic type. Early indexes often featured with short explanations of how to use them, that is, by searching alphabetically and following the references provided—a clear sign that this practice was not widely known even among the educated. But by the end of the sixteenth century these explanations were uncommon. Thanks to printing, many more readers had become familiar with the use of indexes than the small numbers of scholars who had access to them in the Middle Ages. Few paratextual elements were truly unique to printed books, but, more consistently than medieval manuscripts, printed books featured more different kinds of paratexts, and longer ones. Table of contents, dedication (occasionally more than one, with each attached to a different part of the book), preface by author or printer or both, commendatory odes, alphabetical indexes, and errata lists were the most common types. These were variously designed by authors and printers to help a book sell by vaunting its merits and the support of respected contemporaries and by offering aids to encourage its reading and use.

More generally printing facilitated the production of longer works. Just as the *codex had proved more efficient in storing text than the papyrus roll, so too the printed page could pack in more words per page than a manuscript. The two-column layout developed in medieval manuscripts remained in continuous use through the early modern period and indeed well beyond, down to the present, for longer texts including the Bible and reference works. But denser typesetting and smaller fonts made possible pages with many more words—a page in Gutenberg's Bible held about 480 words whereas a page of the *Magnum Theatrum Humanae Vitae*, a massive reference work of 1631, held fifteen hundred words, and the whole work spanned more than ten million words in seven volumes. Of course some very large works were composed in the Middle Ages: the encyclopedic *Speculum maius* (Greater mirror) of Vincent of Beauvais topped six million words in the thirteenth century. But long works rarely circulated entire in the manuscript era: instead users commissioned copies of only the parts that they wanted. Of the *Speculum* we have only two complete manuscript copies and three hundred partial copies, most of which are of the *Speculum historiale* (the most popular of its four parts) and often only subsets of that part. Every manuscript could be tailored to the interests that motivated that particular copy. By contrast a printed book had to be produced in the same form in a large number of copies, so each copy had to include all the parts that would appeal to every subset of its target audience. In the incunabular period the four parts of Vincent's *Speculum* were published singly multiple times, then the whole work was published together in four volumes in 1591 and again in 1624. Printing a long work was of course more expensive than printing a shorter one, but printing greatly reduced the production costs in any case, and the profit margins on expensive books were typically higher because their buyers were wealthier. Since a printed book did well if it appealed to as many readers as possible, genres based on compilation, like collections of recipes or sayings or reference books more generally, typically became larger in each successive edition. The additions or enhancements offered in a new edition would also help it compete against earlier ones, which would remain available as used books even if the print run had sold out initially.

Given its ability to produce more books, larger books, and massively more copies than manuscript copying (and which proved equally durable except insofar as they were less expensive), and given cultural dynamics that produced plenty of supply and demand for texts to print—medieval, ancient, and recently written—printing rapidly generated an unprecedented accumulation of books. Complaints about too many books predate printing, including the biblical lament "of making many books there is no end" (Ecclesiastes 12:12) or the thirteenth-century prologue in which Vincent of Beauvais complained of "the multitude of books, the shortness of time, and the slipperiness of memory" that motivated him to write a compendium of all knowledge. While only a narrow elite of scholars had experienced it in earlier periods, after the first century of printing a broad cross section of the educated articulated a concern about what we would call *"information overload"—the sense that there were too many books for an individual to read and to master. Complaints about an overabundance of books became a well-worn refrain throughout early modern Europe and were used to justify any number of postures: railing about the base commercial motives of printers who produced whatever sold without a care for quality or intellectual merit, mocking the vanity of bookish learning, worrying about the end of civilization from too many people writing (bad) books and no one reading good ones anymore, or on the contrary worrying that authors with new ideas would be discouraged from writing by the mass of what already existed.

These complaints about the consequences of printing were of course made in printed books, which added to the abundance of which they complained while offering various remedies to the overload: advice on how to read well, for example by taking good notes; judgments and reviews of books to aid in selecting them (a prime content of learned periodicals starting in the late seventeenth century); bibliographies to identify existing books (and possibly to deter the unnecessary composition of new ones); and reference works designed to collect the best parts of the best books to spare readers the trouble and expense of making these selections themselves. Printing prompted a new awareness of the need to manage information in and about books and also facilitated the development of new methods for doing so, among them printed questionnaires and lists, images and tables, cutting and pasting from printed books, or using the backs of printed playing cards.

MANAGING AN INFORMATION EXPLOSION IN EARLY MODERN EUROPE

The complaints about overabundance that strike a familiar chord today should not obscure an equally widespread attitude in early modern Europe that played a crucial role in causing the explosion of printed books: enthusiasm for the accumulation of information of all kinds. The development and rapid growth of printing coincided with and was fueled by a number of independent cultural movements focused on info-lust or a desire to accumulate information in many forms—texts but also things natural and artificial, including natural specimens or images of them, paintings and sculptures, medals and coins. Renaissance humanists with their focus on classical antiquity recovered and studied not only texts but also methods of architecture (e.g., the dome) and art (sculptures large and small), coins and inscriptions, and other cultural remains. At the same time exploratory travel, most famously to the Americas, but also to Asia far and near, to Africa, and all over Europe, generated a new fascination for collecting plant and animal specimens and the artifacts of cultures distant in space and time. The two movements were linked in that ancient works of history and natural history recently recovered or brought to renewed attention—like those of the Roman encyclopedist and natural historian Pliny the Elder (23–79 CE), the Greek botanist Dioscorides (40–90 CE), and Aristotle on the parts of animals—provided models for the observation and description of fauna, flora, peoples, and places both familiar and newly encountered.

The travelers (merchants and diplomats, missionaries and scholars, soldiers and adventurers) brought back reports of their interactions but also objects that by gift or purchase ended up in collections formed by the wealthy and the great throughout Europe. The trade in collectibles enabled members of local elites to form collections in emulation of the large and famous ones. Some collections were focused on particular kinds of objects. Botanical gardens became de rigueur for the best medical faculties in the late sixteenth century; zoos, being much more expensive, became symbols of power that only the greatest monarchs could maintain. Collections of coins and other remains appealed to antiquarians, who studied them for clues about the past. Sixteenth-century antiquarians surveyed ruins in various Italian cities, in Istanbul and Anatolia (Pierre Gilles and Ogier Ghiselin de Busbecq), the Holy Roman Empire (Conard Celtis and Conrad Peutinger), England (John Leland and William Camden), and elsewhere; their studies ranged from Egyptian obelisks to Nordic runes and medieval remains, like the Merovingian tomb of Childeric discovered in 1653 during the digging of the foundation of a hospital in Tournai (in today's Belgium). By contrast those with less specialized interests formed *cabinets of curiosities that reveled in a miscellaneous mix of items, natural or human in origin, local or exotic; highlights might include a crocodile or a horn of a unicorn (in fact from a narwhal), a Native American artifact, or a decorative piece beautifully wrought around a gem or a shell. We have a glimpse of these remarkable collections, despite their dispersal in the interim, through the catalogs drawn up at the time, which applied to new objects the methods of recording sacred relics in the later Middle Ages.

Some of these collections resulted in the foundation of museums that still exist today, such as the Uffizi in Florence founded by the Medici family or the Ashmolean in Oxford founded by the wealthy antiquarian Elias Ashmole in 1677. Whereas in the Middle Ages royal and ecclesiastical treasuries were kept out of public view, the owners of cabinets of curiosities typically welcomed visitors (at least with a letter of introduction), as we know from some guest books that have survived. A few images of early collections (printed in books about them) show a room full of items of many kinds in close proximity and little apparent order. Surviving inventories and catalogs (usually manuscript but occasionally printed) show a concern to organize the collections, at least on paper but also in specially labeled drawers or cabinets. In the eighteenth century Hans Sloane (whose massive collection became the seed of the British Museum) and his amanuenses (or secretaries) recorded provenance and date of acquisition and location codes that corresponded to labels on the objects that were attached or sometimes written directly on them. At the Francke Foundation in Halle, Germany, one can visit today the eighteenth-century collection formed for the education of the pupils (many of them orphans) in this pietist Lutheran school. It featured one section of *naturalia* or natural specimens and another of *artificialia*, including not only exotic artifacts (with an unusual emphasis on written media from around the world) but also miniature models of many trades from the time. Teaching from objects was a pedagogical technique advocated already by Jan Amos Comenius (1592–1670), who as a member of the Moravian Brethren and religious refugee had difficulty creating durable institutions. But Comenius's innovative textbook for children with illustrations, *Orbis sensualium pictus* (World of the senses in pictures, 1658), was the object of many translations and reeditions and surely helped to inspire the pedagogically oriented Wunderkammer in Halle. At the other end of the European world, eighteenth-century Harvard created a Philosophy Chamber for its students, including specimens and scientific instruments. There is much to be learned still about the way objects (including everyday items such as clothes, tools, and cooking utensils) were vehicles of information in early modern Europe and can be for historians today, as recent work has begun to explore.

Methods of managing texts have been better studied, thanks to a variety of sources including advice books about reading and writing books, manuscript notes and drafts, and many examples of large printed compilations of information. These kinds of books, which are rarely extant from the Middle Ages, became more common in many early modern fields thanks to the increasing amounts of information available and the opportunities that printing offered for financial and reputational gains from publishing them. Although they were often large and thus expensive books, reference genres included some steady sellers like dictionaries and *florilegia (collections of quotations by classical or religious authorities sorted under thematic headings) in addition to works that appeared only once but then inspired imitations. The large books I offer as examples bring into sharper relief practices that applied to informational genres in smaller sizes and across many areas of compilation, from ancient inscriptions to medical recipes to political treaties. Some of the practices of information management—like alphabetization, chronological order, the use of topical headings, and the morselization of information into discrete units—were already known in the Middle Ages and became more widespread through printing. Other techniques, including making images from life, weighing conflicting sources, and the use of mobile slips to store and sort information either temporarily or for the long term were new or newly emphasized in the early modern period.

Images were of course not new as vehicles of information, but printing and a new emphasis on close observation among natural historians gave them a new prominence. In medieval manuscripts, diagrams and illuminations were copied along with the text by the scribe or a specialist. We know less about the presence of illustrations in ancient papyrus rolls, but it is plausible to imagine that drawings of plants and animals were copied along with accompanying text from ancient originals onto the parchment of medieval manuscripts. Judging from these manuscripts, even near-contemporaries in antiquity varied in their attitude toward images: many surviving manuscripts of Pliny's *Natural History* have none, while those of Dioscorides typically include an image for each plant described. Just like texts, images were subject to modification in transmission; but unlike with texts, changes introduced in images could not be identified and corrected as easily as textual variants, which could seem suspect on philological grounds. In the Renaissance, natural historians devoted much energy to studying the ancient sources in combination with natural specimens they could observe directly. A new attention to observation and an expansion of travels not only to the New World, but also within the known "old" worlds of Europe and the Near East especially, generated an explosion of new flora and fauna to describe. Whereas in 1550 the most complete enumeration of known plants was a humanist edition of Dioscorides with some five hundred specimens, by 1623 Caspar Bauhin published a massive tome describing six thousand of them. The major authors of Renaissance natural history were keen to integrate direct experience with textual descriptions and commentaries and strove to offer images of plants and animals made "from life." This meant drawing plants and animals where they could be seen live in botanical gardens or displays of exotic animals, or when climbing up mountains or traveling to distant locations; but in some cases images "from life" in fact involved drawing from the more or less reliable reports of others who had traveled. Image making also required decisions about whether to depict features specific to the particular specimen on view (like a wilted leaf or a damaged stem) or to aim for a more abstract representation of the species; those decisions were especially difficult when only one specimen of an otherwise unknown species was available to view.

Printing an image from life was costly, since it involved hiring a draftsman before the usual stages of transferring the image to woodblock and carving the block (each of which was performed by a specialist). Color (essential in many cases, e.g., for identifying plants, birds, or fish) could be described verbally but was not part of a printed image. Printed images could be colored by hand according to directives provided by the makers of the book (available at the printer's in one colored copy to serve as a model) or without such guidance on a simply decorative basis. In either case the addition of color was a considerable extra expense for the buyer, but one that conveyed valuable information if carried out well; of course that work could also be completed in haste and inaccurately, as the Swiss naturalist Conrad Gessner (1516–65) complained of the colored copies of his natural histories that his printer commissioned. The expense of making the original image motivated as much reuse of it as possible. Since the original editions for which the images were made were generally large-format and expensive Latin works, they might not warrant a reedition. Instead the publishers could reuse the images in vernacular translations, or in an abridged "picture book" version focused mainly on the images, or in smaller format editions that would reach a broader market; the latter would require carving new woodblocks to fit the smaller size of book but could rely on the same original drawings. This tactic of selling the most expensive edition first to tap the wealthiest buyers, followed by less expensive editions that would have broader appeal was favored for illustrated books and other expensive genres.

The value of natural historical works lay in the trustworthiness of their information and in their ability to persuade readers of it. The German botanist Leonhard Fuchs (1501–66) accompanied his massive *History of Plants* (*De historia stirpium*, 1542) with unusual images not only of himself but also of the three men responsible for the abundant images; by showing and naming them he presumably meant to offer evidence to support his claim of images made "from life." The near contemporary Gessner prefaced each of his four volumes of natural history on quadrupeds (1551), reptiles (1554), birds (1555), and fish (1558) with other displays of the trustworthiness of his work. Many Renaissance books (including some of Gessner's earlier works) opened with a list of authorities cited as a bare list of names of authors alphabetically ordered, including even ancient authors whose works did not survive and who were known only secondhand through the citations of others—suggesting that the list was more a show of erudition than a list of sources actually used. By contrast, in each of the volumes of his natural history Gessner included a detailed bibliography of books published, from ancient and medieval times down to the recent books of contemporaries. He concluded with a list of experts whom he had consulted in person or by correspondence. Gessner named them ostensibly in order to thank them, but in so doing he also highlighted how well connected he was to many expert scholars, doctors, and apothecaries, who gave him information and thus lent further credibility to his work.

After naming these sources in the paratext Gessner did not try to cite them at every relevant point within the text. There he occasionally mentioned books and correspondents as sources, but also things he saw himself or learned from personal contact with "an old woman" or anonymous fishermen. Gessner and other early modern naturalists embraced sources of all kinds—including *canonical ancient works but also practical knowledge that they or their correspondents gleaned from experience and from talking to contemporaries even of low social standing. While they were aware of the merits of identifying their sources, their practice of citation was principally designed to make unusual information more convincing or to provide the evidence available in cases where conflicting information from different sources needed to be weighed (leaving the final judgment to the reader). A more systematic culture of citation developed piecemeal starting in the later seventeenth century, and the footnote originated around then too, though it served other purposes than citation alone, as the famously mocking and critical footnotes in Gibbon's *Decline and Fall of the Roman Empire* (1776–89) make clear.

Most early modern compilations were driven by the supply of information from their sources rather than systematic inquiry. Nevertheless Gessner made a concerted effort to treat for every quadruped a series of eight topical sections labelled by a letter of the alphabet: (a) on the names of the species in different languages; (b) on the places where it lives; (c) on its bodily habits (nutrition, reproduction, and death); (d) on its moral habits; (e, f, and g) on the uses of the animal for humans (e.g., for labor, food, or medical remedies); and (h) on philology, focused on the appearance of the species in proverbs, poetry, metaphors, or other literary settings (and this section was further subdivided into eight types also labelled a–h). Gessner's history of quadrupeds spanned 1,096 pages, followed by eight pages of supplements (*paralipomena*) devoted to images of animals for which he could not offer a systematic treatment, and a further nine pages of corrections and additional information (to be inserted according to page and line number). Gessner clearly labored hard to make this work as complete, systematic, and correct as possible, although he also apologized for being too prolix in the philological sections. Interestingly, in the later volumes in the series Gessner abandoned the scheme of answering the same questionnaire for each species and proceeded as other contemporaries did, by generally following a similar outline, but without calling attention to it and thus to places where he lacked answers to all the questions. (On other questionnaires, see Ghobrial, chap. 5.)

Fuchs and Gessner and others like them were attentive to the problems of ordering their vast material. Many Renaissance compilers hoped to find a systematic order that would match the order "of the things themselves." Of course there were conflicting views on what such a perfect order should be; one scholar has counted over two dozen kinds of systematic order in Renaissance encyclopedic works, including the order of Creation, of the Decalogue, of the biblical narrative or the catechism; various chronological and geographical orders; and hierarchical orders of the disciplines or of the chain of being. In addition, some authors, like the great humanist Desiderius Erasmus (1466–1536) in his *Adages* (a vast collection of ancient sayings explained), embraced a miscellaneous order as particularly pleasant owing to the unpredictable variety of the reading experience. The ancient precedent of the "haphazard order" (*ordo fortuitus*) of Aulus Gellius's *Attic Nights*, rediscovered by the humanists, lent miscellaneity a new respectability; this method also avoided the logistical difficulty of physically reordering the material according to a change of plan. By contrast the encyclopedist Theodor Zwinger (1533–88) devised and revised an elaborate hierarchical system for his *Theater of Human Life* (*Theatrum humanae vitae*, in three editions of 1565, 1571, 1586, each of which was enlarged and rearranged), which he touted as teaching ethics by example rather than precept. Despite the complex branching diagrams that extended over multiple pages to lay out the logical structure of his system, it was no better than a random order in the judgment of one contemporary who recommended using the alphabetical indexes instead to access the text.

Whatever the order chosen for the text of a large informational book, one or more alphabetical indexes provided the most predictable kind of access. Erasmus drew up himself, with the help of one or more amanuenses, not only an index of adages by opening words, but also an index according to 257 topics or "loci" that listed relevant adages for each. While the first kind of indexing can be considered fairly mechanical, the second kind involved both expert and personal judgment. But he and others were aware of a basic problem with topical indexing: that the same concept could occur under different keywords or headings. Indexes in the sixteenth century opened with explanatory blurbs for readers who might not be familiar with how to use them. In one of these Zwinger recommended explicitly: "If things do not occur under one heading, look for them under a synonym." Zwinger introduced occasional cross-references in his text, but never systematically, and almost none were offered in his indexes. As Erasmus noted in one of his "index blurbs": "Remember that what pertains to generosity is at the same time considered as pertaining to avarice under the heading 'avarice' and thus in different instances of the same kind." As a result, using indexes in the sixteenth century was "often unpleasant" as Gessner observed and required intelligent reflection and diligent labor in consulting multiple entries and across multiple indexes. In the seventeenth century some encyclopedic works (like Alsted's *Encyclopaedia* of 1630 or the sequel to Zwinger's *Theatrum*) palliated this problem by consolidating separate indexes into a single one and introducing more cross-references.

The problem of heading choice was a concern not only for great compilers like Erasmus, Zwinger, and Gessner in indexing but also for ordinary readers who had been enjoined by their teachers to take notes by excerpting memorable passages from the books they read and store them for later consultation and retrieval in notebooks. These were called commonplace books because they were organized according to the common "places" (*loci* or *topoi*) of argumentation. Humanist pedagogues offered advice on the selection of headings for these notebooks, and the number of headings considered optimal ranged widely. Erasmus used 257 in his index by places; others recommended only thirty headings. By contrast, Vincent Placcius in 1689 touted a piece of furniture, first described by Thomas Harrison in the 1640s—a "literary closet" that could accommodate up to three thousand separate headings, each with a hook on which to stick relevant note slips; but such a closet was costly, and we know of only two exemplars that were actually built, neither of which survives. There was no attempt to create an equivalent to the controlled vocabulary for subject indexing or book cataloging until the nineteenth century. In these earlier periods, teachers and some printed books no doubt prompted some to imitate their categories in their notes; in particular, the vices and virtues had been traditional topics since the florilegia of the Middle Ages. Overall, though, choice of headings and methods of taking notes more generally were left up to each individual; even Renaissance pedagogues who articulated the "best practices" of the day acknowledged that individuals should modify the general pattern of note taking to suit their purposes. The grip of humanist pedagogues further loosened over time, and eighteenth-century methods of note taking were especially varied.

The mobile paper slip became a key tool for the organizing and reorganizing of material according to keywords or alphabetical order. The slip, cut up from a sheet of paper before or after it had been written on, was a new tool of information management in the early modern period. Although some have argued that alphabetization in antiquity and the Middle Ages must have been performed with movable slips, there is no firm evidence to support these rational reconstructions. The earliest surviving slips glued into notebooks date (to my knowledge) from the fifteenth century. The cheapness of paper facilitated the practice since to make slips one could write on only one side of a sheet and would waste the verso in order to glue the slips in place. The first explicit advice about the use of slips likely dates to Gessner's 1548 description of his method of indexing. A few years before his works of natural history Gessner had published a universal bibliography of books in learned languages, extant and not, manuscript and printed, totaling about twenty-five thousand items by five thousand authors. He accompanied this *Bibliotheca universalis* (Universal library, 1545) with a topical index to the contents of as many of those books as he could access, the *Pandectae* (1548—the title, by alluding to the Pandects of Roman law, connoting a summary treatment of a large subject). For each topic within the major fields of study Gessner listed all the relevant books in over six hundred pages of such lists. Clearly Gessner spent a lot of time ordering a vast set of textual information and had optimized his working method in the process. Following the section of the *Pandectae* on dictionaries Gessner explained how to make abundant and accurate indexes: cut the material into loose slips that can be stored in bundles or envelopes and rearranged as needed until the proper order is reached, at which point glue the slips into place. This method allowed for fully alphabetized indexes by contrast with medieval and early printed indexes, which were typically sorted only by first or first two letters. Partial alphabetization of that kind resulted from listing the items to index on to separate sheets for each first (or first two) letter(s) in the order in which the items occurred in the text. By contrast the use of slips became the norm for alphabetization (or ordering of other kinds) in the early modern period. We have many examples of surviving manuscripts prepared for print, collections of notes, library catalogs, and manuscript indexes that take the form of slips glued into place, most often in alphabetical order. Placcius's note closet remained unique in recommending keeping the slips fully mobile, so they could be moved around indefinitely, and sorted in different ways, or shared with others without jeopardizing the whole collection. In most cases scholars stored their slips in bundles or containers of some kind (pigeonholes, envelopes, or pouches).

Gessner's advice on indexing was not limited to the use of mobile slips, which may well have predated his published mention of them and certainly became standard practice. More unusually Gessner also recommended, as in 1548, cutting and pasting from printed books in order to save the labor of creating slips by copying out the passages to index. Indeed, some of Gessner's surviving notebooks feature short excerpts cut from books printed in Latin or German and glued in place. The excess copies that were inevitably generated by printing presumably played a role in suggesting this practice. Copies of books with no or low commercial value (either because they had been marked up for making a new edition or because they were damaged or left unsold, like our remaindered books) could be cut up for note taking or indexing purposes, or reused as material in a new publication. Zwinger's *Theatrum* served in this way as the basis for a much expanded *Magnum theatrum vitae humanae* (Great theater of human life, 1631), as described in the preface of that work. Cutting and pasting likely remained within the narrower purview of those engaged in bulk compiling rather than a widespread practice. It attests nonetheless to the relative cheapness of printed material that could be used to aid in information management. Similarly, in the eighteenth century a new form of slip came into use for note taking and (accidentally at first) for cataloging the holdings in a library: printed playing cards featuring blank backs and in some cases space to write on the front as well.

Every society is an information society, as Robert Darnton and others have pointed out, but early modern Europeans became uniquely aware of their information technologies in comparison with earlier periods. Printing was perceived as a major innovation, famously cited by Jean Bodin and Francis Bacon alongside gunpowder and the compass as crucial inventions unknown to the ancients. Printing prompted both admiration and complaints, but also new practices and explicit discussions of them—from censorship to methods of compiling. Renaissance compilers took medieval practices of excerpting and ordering to new levels by handling much greater quantities of materials—objects, images, and texts—and experimenting with many ordering principles including miscellaneous order, which was considered especially pleasant. Alphabetical indexes of many kinds served as the main points of access for collections of written information, and their use became so widespread that indexes no longer featured explanatory blurbs after the sixteenth century. Mobile slips, cut from sheets of paper, first recommended for indexing, proved versatile, for example, for note taking, sorting of many kinds, and cataloging books; for the latter task stiffer playing cards used in the eighteenth century prompted the development of standardized index cards in the nineteenth.

COMMUNICATION

The impact of information is constrained by the means of its circulation. Essential to the success of printing in the mid-fifteenth century was the mercantile network that made possible the distribution of books far and wide throughout Europe. At just around the same time Europe developed a postal system that could convey letters and messengers at speeds similar to the ancient Roman *cursus publicus* or the medieval Islamic *Barīd*. The crucial element was a network of relay stations with fresh mounts. In the centuries since the decline of the Roman system, merchants' posts had been the most reliable form of mail. Major rulers also kept a staff of messengers to deliver diplomatic messages. But since there was no provision for a change of horses, deliveries on foot were the norm, yielding a maximum speed of sixty to seventy kilometers per day. In the fifteenth century innkeepers started to retain their own couriers, each covering their own portion of well-defined routes. When these inns served as a source of fresh horses and riders more ground could be covered (up to 170 kilometers per day). The Habsburgs' engagement of the Taxis family to provide a standing post service of that kind from Milan to Innsbruck (notably after Maximilian's marriage in 1494 with Bianca Sforza from Milan) set up the backbone of a network that was soon extended throughout the Habsburg territories to include Spain and Flanders and neighboring areas, and onto which the English and French monarchies each grafted their own system of relay riding. Wolfgang Behringer has called the resulting speeds a "communications revolution" within western Europe. In 1505 the Taxis system guaranteed delivery times that in some cases rival those of today's regular mail—for example, from Brussels to Paris in less than two days, to Lyon in four, and to Innsbruck in five and a half, although it took twelve days to Toledo and fifteen to Granada. (These were summer delivery times; winter deliveries took longer.) The mail system allowed for transportation of letters and small packets, not heavy goods, so that Europe was integrated intellectually far more successfully than agriculturally during this period when it continued to suffer from localized famines even when crops were abundant elsewhere.

Letters circulated in truly vast numbers throughout the early modern period. A small fraction of them were printed by senders or recipients, during their lifetimes or after their death. One scholar has estimated that by 1627 forty thousand letters had been printed in Italy alone. Far, far more had been written and sent. Untold numbers of letters have of course been lost, yet large collections also survive. Among the earliest are the letters of the Paston family from the English gentry (1,088 letters between 1422 and 1509); large surviving collections include four thousand letters to and from Erasmus, ten thousand for the French polymath Nicolas-Claude Fabri de Peiresc (1580–1637), and nineteen thousand for Voltaire (1694–1778) in the French Enlightenment. The *Republic of Letters (respublica litterarum)* described a pan-European community united by "letters" ("litterae") in the sense of learning, but the second meaning (at least in English and French) of letters as epistolary can serve as a reminder of the crucial role of the medium in stoking the friendships and rivalries that existed within this complex community. The terms and ideals of the Republic of Letters and its practices of communicating by letter and printed matter remained remarkably stable throughout the early modern period despite a major shift in its emphasis, between Erasmus and Voltaire, from a humanist focus on classical learning to a focus on the arts and sciences of the "moderns" carried out in the vernacular, especially in French, which had replaced Latin as the dominant language of international communication by around 1700.

The mail enabled the exchange of information over larger distances than correspondents could actually travel. Some of these letters preceded or followed personal travel, but many were also exchanged between people who never met in person, for example, after learning of one another through other people or through printed matter. Conrad Gessner maintained correspondence directly and indirectly with hundreds of contacts; though he rarely traveled far from his native Zurich, Gessner gathered information about natural historical species and books and manuscripts from all over Europe with which he filled his major publications. Gessner also applied his habit of cutting up useful information in the letters he received, parts of which can be found pasted into notebooks (with care taken that both the front and the back of the letter can still be read). Conversely Gessner sought to elicit new correspondents through the distribution of his printed books to unknown and distant readers. In his *Historia animalium* on birds (1555), Gessner ended the list of those he thanked for sending him information with a general plea to other readers to join the effort, especially those from "remote regions" like Spain or Scandinavia where he had few contacts. Gessner explained to his readers how to send him something via a local merchant who frequented the major fairs and could there pass on to a merchant from Zurich material to reach Gessner. Gessner promised to answer by the same route in reverse with a countergift if desired; and he had already shown that he used print to publicly thank helpful contacts so a new correspondent could hope for recognition in one of Gessner's future publications as well.

Gessner's advice is a reminder that the Taxis postal system did not eliminate the more informal networks of communication through merchants. Services were never perfect, and anxious correspondents sent duplicate letters through different routes to maximize the chances of success. All these communication channels played a crucial role in circulating information in print and manuscript at speeds, distances, and quantities that had not been experienced before in Europe. The confluence of technical and cultural innovations, from postal service and printing to the discoveries, recoveries, and schisms for which the period is famous, made possible and motivated a desire to collect and consume information across many fields on unprecedented scales and also to discuss the best ways of doing so.

Ann Blair

See also books; book sales catalogs; cards; censorship; error; indexing; letterpress; letters; libraries and catalogs; notebooks; printed visuals; reference books; scribes; secretaries; stereotype printing

FURTHER READING

Wolfgang Behringer, "Communications Revolutions: A Historiographical Concept," translated by Richard Deveson, *German History* 24, no. 3 (2006), 333–74; Ann Blair, "Printing and Humanism in the Work of Conrad Gessner," *Renaissance Quarterly*, 70, no. 1 (2017): 1–43; Blair, *Too Much to*

Know: Managing Scholarly Information before the Modern Age, 2010; *British Library Treasures in Full: Gutenberg Bible* (online); Eltjo Buringh, *Medieval Manuscript Production in the Latin West*, 2011; James Delbourgo, *Collecting the World: Hans Sloane and the Origins of the British Museum*, 2017; Paula Findlen, ed., *Early Modern Things: Objects and Their Histories, 1500–1800*, 2012; Findlen, *Possessing Nature: Museums, Collecting, and Scientific Culture in Early Modern Italy*, 1994; Jonathan Green, Frank McIntyre, and Paul Needham, "The Shape of Incunable Survival and Statistical Estimation of Lost Editions," *Papers of the Bibliographical Society of America* 105, no. 2 (June 2011): 141–75; Daniel Hobbins, *Authorship and Publicity before Print: Jean Gerson and the Transformation of Late Medieval Learning*, 2009; Markus Krajewski, *Paper Machines: About Cards and Catalogs, 1548–1929*, 2002, translated by Peter Krapp, 2011; Sachiko Kusukawa, *Picturing the Book of Nature: Image, Text, and Argument in Sixteenth-Century Human Anatomy and Medical Botany*, 2011; Hannah Marcus, *Forbidden Knowledge: Medicine, Science, and Censorship in Early Modern Italy*, 2020; Joseph P. McDermott and Peter Burke, eds., *The Book Worlds of East Asia and Europe 1450–1850: Connections and Comparisons*, 2015; David McKitterick, *Print, Manuscript, and the Search for Order 1450–1830*, 2003; Paul Needham, *The Printer and the Pardoner: An Unrecorded Indulgence Printed by William Caxton*, 1986; Andrew Pettegree, *The Book in the Renaissance*, 2010; Aysha Pollnitz, *Princely Education in Early Modern Britain*, 2015; Christoph Reske, "Hat Johannes Gutenberg das Gießeninstrument erfunden? Mikroskopischer Typenvergleich an frühen Drucken," *Gutenberg Jahrbuch*, 2015; Mary Rouse and Richard Rouse, *Authentic Witnesses: Approaches to Medieval Texts and Manuscripts*, 1991; Rouse and Rouse, *Manuscripts and Their Makers: Commercial Book Producers in Medieval Paris, 1200–1500*, 2000; Nikolaus Schobesberger et al., "European Postal Networks," in *News Networks in Early Modern Europe*, edited by Joad Raymond and Noah Moxham, 2016, 19–63; Angus Vine, *Miscellaneous Order: Manuscript Culture and the Early Modern Organization of Knowledge*, 2019; Eric White, *Editio Princeps: A History of the Gutenberg Bible*, 2017.

5

NETWORKS AND THE MAKING OF A CONNECTED WORLD IN THE SIXTEENTH CENTURY

One should fear more the nib of a Jesuit's pen than the point of an Arab's sword.

—Niccolò Manucci, a Venetian merchant in the Mughal
   Empire (1638–1717)

Long before modern prophets foretold the rise of a "network society" in the twentieth century, information underpinned what historians have often referred to as a "connected world" in the *early modern period. On the heels of the discovery of the Americas, scholars, statesmen, and clerics alike reimagined their world through the sometimes unpredictable circulation of letters, handwritten news, and printed documents, which connected the newly discovered worlds of the Atlantic to the "old worlds" of the Mediterranean, Africa, and Asia. Although building on old practices, these novel forms of circulation connected unfamiliar societies to each other in surprising and powerful ways.

Consider, for example, two books published in the space of twenty years of one another in the last decades of the sixteenth century. The first was an Ottoman Turkish work called the *Tarih-i Hind-i garbi*, or *A History of the India of the West*, the earliest manuscripts of which date to 1580. The work is the first ever account of the discovery of the New World written for an Ottoman audience in Istanbul. Although we know almost nothing about the person who wrote it, clues in the text suggest that the Anonymous Chronicler drew primarily on classic Spanish accounts of the New World that had been published in the sixteenth century, alongside several passages lifted directly from Spanish, Italian, and Portuguese news accounts. To access this world of printed information in Istanbul, the Anonymous Chronicler almost certainly relied on the help of a local European merchant or renegade in Istanbul, someone, at least, with a good working knowledge of European and Ottoman languages. Out of this act of collaborative translation, the *Tarih-i Hind-i garbi* presented the exotic wonders of "New India," or the West Indies, to an Ottoman audience. Readers in Istanbul could read firsthand the tales of the Spanish conquest of Mexico, descriptions of the Inka Empire of Peru, and fantastical observations of the great mining center of Potosí, in the Andes, from where American silver was transported into the Ottoman world and further east. In some surviving copies, intricate Ottoman miniatures have been added in an attempt to capture the wild variety of flora and fauna in the Americas, for example, manatees, tapirs, turkeys, bison, jaguars, avocados, and papayas—all wondrous discoveries to an audience in Istanbul.

More than ten thousand kilometers away, around the same time, a book was published in Mexico City called the *Repertorio de los tiempos*, or *Repertory of the Times*, which set out to satisfy the curiosity of readers in New Spain with two chapters focused on the Ottoman Empire. Both chapters reflected on distinctly presentist matters: the first explored "the way in which one deduces from predictions, prognoses, conjectures and natural reasons the fall and the destruction of the monarchy and the empire of the Turks," while the second chapter sought to explain "the origins of the Turkish Empire, and the way in which it grew and in which it achieved the power it wields today." Unlike in the case of the *Tarih-i Hind-i garbi*, we know much more about the man behind the book: one Heinrich Martin, a German migrant from Hamburg whose family settled in Spain during Martin's youth in order to take up work at the center of the thriving print trade. At some point, Martin traveled to the New World and set up a print shop in Mexico City in 1599, where the *Repertory* was published in 1606. Like the *Tarih-i Hind-i garbi*, the *Repertory* was assembled from information, individuals, and texts in motion in the sixteenth century. While Martin was unlikely to have had any Ottoman informants to guide his work, he was able from Mexico City to access some of the most authoritative accounts of life in the Ottoman Empire in his time, many of them written by individuals who had observed the Ottoman Empire directly for themselves.

Mexicans imagining life in Istanbul, Ottomans reflecting on the wonders of Mexico City: taken together, these two works reveal the extent to which, already in the sixteenth century, the circulation of information connected societies separated not only by huge distances but also by profound differences in language, culture, and religion. Information contributed to a certain lived experience of global simultaneity, that is, a consciousness shared by separate societies that they inhabited the same world even if the actual movement of information continued to require weeks or even months to travel around the earth. And yet both works were also intensely "local" in their genealogies: both emerged in very specific contexts—colonial Mexico and the literary milieu of the Ottoman capital—through the somewhat haphazard intersection of a handful of texts and individuals able to read them. The presence of Ottoman histories in Mexico City and Spanish conquest narratives in Istanbul was itself a reflection of recent political, religious, and financial transformations unleashed by the discovery of the New World and the proliferation of empires in this period. In this way, early modern global historians have argued compellingly for the importance of information in the "world making" of the sixteenth century: a first phase of global integration through the circulation of information that predated by four centuries the phenomena usually conjured up by the term "globalization" for the twentieth century.

This chapter explores the role information played in the making of connectedness on a global scale. After briefly describing the historical transformations in trade, politics, and religion that defined this period, the chapter focuses on two types of human networks—merchants and missionaries—that contributed in important ways to the flow of information before the advent of modern technologies of communication. These groups drew on the prevalent media of the day—especially handwritten letters and questionnaires—as ways of circulating information to communities far beyond their own networks. In the last half of the chapter, we concentrate on a case study—European knowledge of Islam—as a way of understanding the many intellectual, political, and religious consequences of information flow in the age of early modern globalization.

COMING INTO FOCUS: EARLY MODERN GLOBALIZATION

Worldwide integration in the early modern period set the stage for the emergence of the first global networks of information. It is impossible to understand the way in which information became global in this period without reference to how political, economic, and religious transformations of this period all contributed to the circulation of information. Four central changes deserve mention. First, this was a period during which genuinely global commercial exchange networks emerged for the first time. Of course, long-distance trade had always been an important feature of the ancient and medieval worlds, but it was only in the early modern period that the regular and predictable movement of peoples, commodities, and capital would connect the distant reaches of East and West, the Americas and Asia. Information moved hand in hand with this trade, and indeed the mechanics of long-distance trade networks relied on a wide array of practices that influenced the spread of information, for example, information gathering about local markets, the dissemination of information to business partners through correspondence, and the standardization of new *bookkeeping and accounting practices.

Second, and arising in part from the establishment of global trade flows, this was a period of large-scale migrations of people and, with them, increased contact between different languages, cultures, and societies. In such a context, information brokers thrived, especially those who commanded multiple languages or specific chancery skills of use to political powers.

Third, the discovery of new worlds set into motion a period of worldwide biological exchanges. The movement of New World seeds, plants, and foodstuffs, for example, introduced both new challenges and new opportunities into European societies. At the most basic level, questions arose about the identification of biological species that had never been seen before, but there were also more complicated questions that demanded collaboration and information gathering: Which plants could be cultivated in different climates, which plants could be eaten, which could be smoked or made into drinks, which had medicinal properties, and which were, put simply, dangerous?

Finally, this was a period of great religious upheaval as much for Christianity as for Islam. The Protestant and Catholic *Reformations of Europe unleashed a particular interest in the spread of Christianity to the new worlds now firmly planted in the European imagination. Similarly, the emergence of Muslim powers like the Ottoman, the Safavid, and the Mughal empires witnessed the spread of Islam to new geographies far from the core caliphates of the medieval Middle East. Missionary strategies required close engagement with native and local societies, the collection of information about religious practices and beliefs, and the careful comparison and handling of all this information in a meaningful and organized way.

Trade, migration, biological exchanges, and the spread of religion were all central to the emergence of new global networks of information in the early modern period and underpinned by long-term demographic trends in which the world's population doubled between 1500 and 1800. To be sure, there was much that was old in these new networks. One marker of continuity with the past was the perseverance of the letter as a most important medium of communication that carried on from the medieval period into the early modern. One need only consider S. D. Goitein's classic study of medieval Jewish trading networks to know that letters had always been an important instrument of communication: the Cairo Genizah alone holds some three hundred thousand fragments of letters, written in Hebrew, Arabic, and Aramaic, a testament to a world of trade that stretched across Egypt, Palestine, Lebanon, Syria, Tunisia, Sicily, and as far as India. Similar stories could be told about trade around the Mediterranean, the South China Sea, and the Indian Ocean, each area animated by its own distinct networks of communication in the medieval period. In contrast, early modern networks transcended familiar regional configurations, creating new and sometimes surprising geographies that reflected the preoccupations of political and mercantile actors in this period. Indeed, if early modern global networks were distinct from their medieval predecessors, it was not only in the truly global reach of their networks but more importantly in the extent to which information networks were embedded in the distinct political and financial institutions of this period. The consolidation of power by maritime empires, the profit motives of trading companies, and the expansion of global missionary orders: all depended in critical ways on the scale and reach of information flows.

Of course, there were also imbalances and asymmetries in these information networks. Europeans, for example, played a disproportionate role in the movement of goods, information, and cultures connecting port cities across Asia, the Atlantic, and the Mediterranean world. Once overseas empires were established by the Spanish, the Portuguese, the Dutch, the English, the French, and even the Scandinavian empires, much of the work of global information networks would cater specifically to their needs. Alongside these imperial networks, regional information networks continued to thrive, but it was often Europeans who played the critical role as agents who connected American, Asian, and Middle Eastern information networks not only with Europe but also with each other. This is an important reminder that networks never existed in the ether, simply to be uncovered or connected into, but rather they were fashioned, constructed, subverted, managed, and organized according to the interests and needs of specific actors. In what follows, attention is given therefore to two main sets of actors—merchants and missionaries—and the effects they had on the circulation of information in the early modern period.

THE POWER OF MERCHANTS: TRADING COMPANIES AND TRADING DIASPORAS

Information was the dark matter that connected the early modern world. Much of this circulation was organized around the preoccupations and interests of merchants whose global careers straddled both the old worlds of the East and the new worlds of the West. In Europe, with the support of patrons normally in positions of authority in the state, several trading companies emerged and competed with one another to establish themselves in markets scattered across the Middle East, Asia, Africa, and the Americas. Although local, regional patterns of trade had always existed in such places as the Indian Ocean, European merchants created new hubs of communication as trading companies sought to consolidate their supply chains in sites far from their home countries. The Dutch East India Company is a case in point. Established in 1602 with its innovative structure of a joint-stock corporation, the company was given a twenty-one-year monopoly on the Dutch spice trade. Key to its success was the development of a vast administrative machinery, which effectively meant the creation of a second headquarters of operations in Batavia, present-day Jakarta. Because much of the company's success in the Indian Ocean relied on its access to intra-Asian trade, the company employed a host of translators, go-betweens, and intermediaries whose main job was to make communication possible between Dutch merchants and their local, Asian counterparts. In port cities like Makassar in eastern Indonesia, entire family dynasties arose to command these roles as translators and interpreters for much of the eighteenth and nineteenth centuries, a reminder of the extent to which information was also a business in the early modern world.

Some scholars have seen in such ventures as the Dutch East India Company the emergence of a "modern business infrastructure," where information networks paved the way for the rise of the stock exchange and institutions like the Royal Exchange in London. That may be the case, but more important in its time was the series of transformations in the handling of information occasioned by the rise of trading companies. Apart from the basic task of gathering information about markets, commodities, and the foreign societies in which they operated, trading companies dealt with a series of challenges related to the management of information. On the micro level of everyday practicalities, they developed systems for dealing with the sheer mass of accumulated information, including filing systems, the organization of documents, and techniques for retrieving information efficiently when needed. How busy merchants were with information management is clear from the archives of the Dutch East India Company, which alone amount to some twenty-five million pages of paperwork scattered today in repositories in Jakarta, Colombo, Chennai, Cape Town, and The Hague.

Alongside official trading companies whose work necessarily carried information across great distances, it was trade diasporas (that is, communities of merchants settled in foreign lands) that were responsible for the intricate ways in which information crossed languages in this period—the Armenian merchants of New Julfa, for example, or the Sephardic merchant networks based around Livorno. Like trading companies, trade diasporas had a similar structure that combined a central hub with the operation of multiple nodes separated by immense distances, all of which functioned to help circulate merchants, credit, goods, and especially information around the globe. In the case of the Armenian networks studied to such great effect by Sebouh Aslanian, the central hub could be found in New Julfa, a suburb of Isfahan in present-day Iran. But beyond New Julfa, the activities of Armenian merchants were spread across several other nodes in such a range of places as Amsterdam, Venice, Izmir, Madras, Canton, Manila, and even St. Petersburg and Jakarta. These sites were connected by the circulation of personal and business correspondence through a well-developed courier system. The vagaries of weather, warfare, and piracy could all cause significant delays, yet even so the Armenians remained connected through a regular, stable, and remarkably efficient communication network.

Trade diasporas played key roles in the circulation of information thanks to the specific structures and institutions of trade in the early modern world. In the case of both Armenian and Sephardic merchants, the *commenda* system of trade provided the organizing framework for most legal contracts. In this system, a junior partner would begin working in New Julfa with a senior partner, often connected by local family and kin networks, and this collaboration offered the junior partner an opportunity to learn the trade under the supervision of a skilled merchant. Once he had achieved a certain level of expertise, the junior partner could sign a commenda contract, wherein he would undertake to leave New Julfa in order to carry out trade using the capital and investment of the senior partner. At the same time, the senior partner undertook to look after the agent's family while he was away, which acted as an important mechanism to securing trust between the two agents. Importantly, commenda contracts included explicit clauses directing the junior agent to keep his partner informed through regular, detailed, and frequent correspondence. A strict set of expectations governed this sort of business correspondence, and merchants abroad would fall foul of their partners if they did not adhere to such conventions. In one case in 1711, for example, a merchant was reprimanded by his senior partner because his "letter was without flavor or salt because it contained no news about purchases and expenditures," the salt being the crucial ingredient of news about purchases and expenditures. A similar case could be made for the array of documents and instruments of trade used in this period: printed bills of exchange, letters of recommendation, broadsides with price descriptions, and advertisements all contributed crucially to early modern trade by circulating information in oral, written, and printed media.

In the case of trade diasporas, these networks played a central role in connecting European trading companies to the Mughal, Ottoman, and Safavid empires of the East. When a French merchant ship leased to Armenian merchants was taken captive off the coast of India in April 1748, the British privateers who inventoried the ship found that it contained more than seventeen hundred letters intended for Armenian merchants around the world. If we consider that this was only a single ship of the hundreds in motion around the world, we can capture a glimpse of the scale of information networks constructed around trading diasporas. And yet, we should also view such evidence with some caution: merchants typically sent several copies of a single letter by various routes as a way of managing the routine uncertainties of postal communication in this period.

Information was important to merchants, therefore, but it also played a crucial role in the forms that empire took in this period. In part, this is because so much of early modern colonialism was based on the informal partnership of merchants and state authorities. The relationship between information, capitalism, and empire crystallized in important ways in this period. The English East India Company, and its role in establishing British empire in India, provides a good example. Different modes of communication functioned as sinews of power in the expanding world of empires. Merchants carried royal letters that were deployed to forge new commercial relationships in the East Indies. Forms of accounting and bookkeeping were developed in coastal trading posts to help the company organize and most efficiently use this information of trade. Even pamphleteers and propagandists used communication and information to protect the monopoly rights of the companies, while the development of new forms of stock keeping and price watching contributed to the idea of a self-regulating and quasi-independent market system. Information was wielded in manuscript and in print, in the work of surveillance, imperial administration, and information gathering by a growing imperial bureaucracy. In this way, entire empires were forged from the work of communication, writing, information inscription, record keeping and correspondence. The British Empire was built on communication—of handwritten letters and printed forms—as much as on trade, governance, and sheer military power.

JESUIT INFORMATION NETWORKS, LOCAL AND GLOBAL

Even more important than merchants in bringing different cultures into contact with one another were the extended networks of missionaries, both Christian and Muslim, that spread into new geographies in this period. In the case of Christianity, this phenomenon was driven mainly by the development of Catholic missionary organizations who aspired to revitalize Catholicism in the wake of the challenges posed by the Protestant Reformation. In this context early modern Catholicism developed an acute sense of the importance of its global mission to the world beyond Europe. The Counter-Reformation Church dispatched Catholic missionaries to the Middle East, Africa, Asia, and the Americas and established sophisticated communication networks to manage the movement of people, funding, relics, sacred objects, and of course information. The main hub of this emerging Catholic network was located at the Vatican in Rome, but new hubs of Catholicism crystallized in other centers, for example, across Germany, in the New World centers of Mexico City and Lima, and as far away as China. Between these centers of gravity, new and unexpected geographies were created through the spread of information between Mexico, Europe, and China.

In his excellent study of the global *Jesuit network, Luke Clossey offers perhaps the best case study for understanding the role of missionary networks in the circulation of information. From the moment of the establishment of the Jesuits' mission to the world, information was seen as a vital element in the mission. The first General Congregation of the Jesuits included clear orders about the importance of establishing a system of epistolary exchanges such that "in every place . . . [the superiors] should know about the things that are being done in other places" (Clossey, 194). This insistence on the acts of writing, reading, and circulating information explains how someone like Niccolò Manucci, a Venetian merchant living in Goa in the late seventeenth century, could warn his readers that the "nib of a Jesuit's pen" was mightier than the "point of an Arab's sword." The tens of thousands of letters that circulated across this global geography are a telling reminder that the work of the missionaries went far beyond the goal of conversion and proselytization to include important consequences for the spread of information.

The Jesuits were a truly global network, whose members were scattered across the world and also moved efficiently from one node to another. Clossey's meticulous research offers an intriguing snapshot of detailed aspects of communication in the Jesuit information network. Of the sample of Jesuits under study, Clossey identified some fifty-three Jesuits who were known to have been active in at least two of three missionary theaters in this period, including in Germany, Mexico, and China. The output of these fifty-three individuals alone comes to some twelve hundred surviving texts, mostly letters. Almost half are written in Latin, and another quarter in Spanish. A fifth survive as copies or summaries, mostly in German. The rest are written in Chinese, Dutch, French, German, Italian, and Portuguese. The physical circulation of these documents is evident from the fact that only a few are preserved today in the Roman archives of the Jesuit order; most of them in fact are scattered about in manuscript collections in Europe and the Americas. Of course, these fifty-three Jesuits were only a small part of a network that numbered around over fifteen thousand Jesuits scattered across the early modern world over the course of two centuries of the order's existence. And they wrote as many letters to other Jesuits as they did to private correspondents, such as relatives and friends. In one three-year period, for example, a missionary based in China by the name of Adam Gerstl wrote some twenty-six letters to his father in Germany.

Surprisingly perhaps, the information that circulated in this vast network was not mainly, or even primarily, about conversion practices. Rather, the letters included a wide array of information, mostly covering current news, but also science, climate, theology, travel, and what we might term today cultural ethnography or anthropology. In addition to this diversity of subjects, the actual practices of letter writing by Jesuits magnified the impact of their individual letters. First, they often sent letters in multiple copies to different correspondents in Europe, encouraging them to forward the letters on to others. In the short term, the writers hoped that their letters would be copied and read aloud to larger audiences, but in the long term the order aimed to print them. Although the earliest books of Jesuit letters were published in Rome in 1552 in Italian, publication also took place in several Catholic centers across Europe—in Germany as well as across Italy, Portugal, Spain, Bohemia, and France. At multiple sites, therefore, popular Jesuit works were being printed in standard print runs of a thousand copies. This geographically wide publication history, combined with the preference for publishing the letters in inexpensive editions, meant that letters rooted in specific, distinct, local networks abroad managed to find a wide reading audience at home in Europe.

The information circulated in these ways was durable. The vagaries of communication meant that letters could have long, and often surprising, afterlives in the Jesuit communication network. A copy of the first letter written by Frances Xavier from Goa in the mid-sixteenth century arrived in 1664 in Vilnius, Lithuania, more than a century after Xavier himself had composed it. In another case, a "Chinese narrative from the letter of Father Joannis de Haynin," written in 1669, was still circulating in the Upper German province of Regensburg as late as 1726. In this context, modern conceptions of communication are ill suited to understanding the attitudes of individuals to the speed and route of communication in the early modern world. There was, for example, a regular and dynamic exchange of letters that connected Jesuits in China to their counterparts in Mexico. Although news over the Pacific could face severe delays, the Jesuits involved in this particular exchange only began to complain when they didn't hear from their counterparts after a period of three years.

Similarly, information traveled in surprising ways that defied any straightforward descriptions of standardized "routes" of communication. News from China was normally sent first to Jesuits in Mexico before being forwarded on to correspondents in Europe. Even so, there were instances where Mexican Jesuits would write to Europe with requests for news about China, when they seemed unable to receive it directly. Contemporaries had expectations about the spread and speed of information travel, which were vastly different from our own assumptions of near instantaneous communication in the age of *digital technologies. Put simply, the speed and efficiency of information might have been less important in the sixteenth century than the dependability of its arrival and the completeness of its account.

In Clossey's sample, the lion's share of letters focused not on the exchange of "best practices" of conversion but rather on local news and current events from the various outposts in which the Jesuits were scattered. In many ways, this made Jesuit correspondence somewhat distinct from merchants' letters, where current events were reported only inasmuch as they appeared to have an impact on business, trade, and commodities. Within the global geography of Jesuit networks, certain centers came to function as unique clearinghouses for the circulation of news from one region or another. The Jesuits in Mexico, for example, received news directly from Asia, and they would come to play a natural role in the gathering, editing, rewriting, and publishing of information about China for audiences in America as well as Europe. In this way, someone like Juan González de Mendoza (1545–1618), a missionary who never set foot in China, could become a major authority on the Chinese Empire. In 1586, he published his *History of the Most Notable Things, Rites and Customs of the Great Kingdom of China*, which became one of the earliest and standard introductions to the history of China for European audiences. Information flows could turn writers who never traveled into sources of authority distributed across the world.

Beyond current events and news, Jesuit networks also played a central role in the collection, circulation, and dissemination of scientific information. Scattered as they were across the world, they were ideally and uniquely suited to gathering comprehensive information on such things as comets, astronomical data, weather, longitude and latitude, and other aspects of the study of the natural world. For good reason the emergent scientific societies of this period sought to cultivate their connections with the Jesuits. Clossey's study describes how in 1667, Henry Oldenburg, the first secretary of the Royal Society of London, wrote to Robert Hooke of his hope "to procure for the Royal Society a correspondency all over the world by means of missionaries." The Jesuit network was also the target of the interests of the architects of royal power, for example, Jean-Baptiste Colbert, who envisioned that the first expedition of French Jesuits to China should have as its primary goal the collection of astronomical data. Through such processes, Jesuit networks provided the foundation for several types of knowledge formation in this period. Athanasius Kircher, who has been called the "last man who knew everything," proposed making a *Consilium Geographicum*, or Geographical Council, tasked with gathering measurements collected in Jesuit colleges around the world. Even Gottfried Wilhelm Leibniz, who was renowned in his time for his interest in Chinese philosophy and politics, could joke with a friend in 1697 that he relied so much on news obtained from the Jesuits that he had considered putting a sign over his door saying "post office for China" (as reported by Clossey).

Centuries before multinational corporations would dream up taglines like the "world's local bank," the Jesuit information network managed to operate effectively both on a local scale, in specific regions across the world, and on a global one by circulating the information it produced throughout its worldwide network. This global reach was even a recurring theme in the titles of its publications, such as *On the Society of Jesus Fighting in All Parts of the World* (1675), *Catholic Christendom Spread through the Whole World* (1678), and *The Society of Jesus have moistened the whole World with their Sweat* (1701). Titles like these underscored the global frontiers of Jesuit information but also contributed to the feeling of simultaneity and global consciousness that connected people separated otherwise by space, religion, and language.

LETTERS AND QUESTIONNAIRES: TWO MODES OF COMMUNICATION

The physical letter—ink inscribed on a sheet of paper—appears to be under threat of extinction today. But in the early modern period, letters continued to be one of the most critical instruments of communication; it is difficult to exaggerate their ubiquity. If we focus on what might be called with some imprecision "learned letters," something like twenty thousand collections of learned correspondence might have been printed between 1500 and 1800. Even more survive in manuscript. The Oxford-based Cultures of Knowledge project—which has pioneered an ambitious attempt to catalog and document all this correspondence in a single database—has estimated that a million letters survive from this period, perhaps even twice that many. Other anecdotal measures of the scale of letter writing are available in the attitudes toward letter writing expressed in early modern literary culture. The anonymously published *Letters of a Portuguese Nun* in 1669 or Aphra Behn's *Love-Letters between a Nobleman and His Sister* (1684–87), among other examples, speak to the rise of the epistolary novel in the late seventeenth century, itself a reflection of the growing importance of the *genre of letters to early modern Europeans.

The importance of letter writing was obviously not just restricted to Europe, but rather it reflected a practice that connected individuals across Europe, the Middle East, and Asia. Across the globe there were men and women who spent their time scribbling, copying, crossing out, reorganizing, and dispatching letters, while waiting for new ones to arrive to fill their time. As Gagan Sood has shown for eighteenth-century India, European merchants and missionaries existed in a shared world of epistolary exchange, in which similar conventions, practices, and processes united European merchants and missionaries to their Indian counterparts. Evidence for this can be gleaned from the distinct terminology used in multiple languages to signify the set of agents who were central to everyday communication: scribes and clerks—who might be referred to alternatively as kātibs, nivisandahs, écrivains, escrivãos, writers—and translators, that is, interprètes, linguas, tarjumāns, dubashis, and gumashtahs. Beyond this terminology, epistolary cultures across Islamic Eurasia had much in common, from the general structure of letters to the specific forms of address and opening and closing formulas, and in the array of topics normally discussed in letters. They also shared similar strategies aimed at restricting the flow of information to all but the intended recipient: techniques of seeking privacy, for example folding, sealing, and in some cases the use of ciphers.

In a global context, one of the challenges facing the spread of information was how to transcend linguistic diversity across different locales. To this end, lingua francas existed in specific regions—a form of Italian in the Ottoman Empire, Portuguese in India—and they helped individuals overcome language barriers. Nonetheless the circulation of information owed much to collaborative translation carried out by several individuals working together. Gagan Sood has described, for example, the revealing case of Bernard Picot de la Motte, a French merchant based in Mahe in Malabar in the latter half of the eighteenth century. A native speaker of French, La Motte likely dictated the first draft of his letters in French, then wrote them (or had them translated) into Portuguese for the Indigenous Malabar clerks who were more likely to know Portuguese than French. The clerks then sought out someone who was able to translate the Portuguese into Arabic, the language spoken by La Motte's trading partners in India. In his own records, La Motte preserved all three versions of his letter: the original French draft, the neat copy in the Portuguese lingua franca, and the final Arabic version intended for his recipient. This was the distinct process through which information could transcend language barriers in multilingual contexts, which required the collaboration of several people working together.

Apart from multilingualism, there were other more mundane challenges to the spread of such information. No matter where they originated across the globe, letters in this period shared a common set of complaints and refrains. The lack of letters was a constant source of worry, even unhappiness; recipients were not writing often enough or in enough detail; handwriting was hasty and difficult to read; important subjects had gone neglected; reminders were made, in vain, that more letters should be sent; and genuine pleasure was expressed at the perfect letter, swift in its arrival and comprehensive in its reporting. It is difficult to know how to read these complaints: a reflection of anxieties about information before the twentieth century or, more likely, a reminder that for most people in this period, information was precious and highly valued especially when it traveled across great distances.

How far these global networks of information relied on personal contacts is clear from the short, general phrases used to address letters to their recipients. A European merchant in India could tell his associates in Lisbon to write to him simply by name "at the Portuguese factory in Surat," and it was assumed the letter would get to him. Likewise, a correspondent in London could tell his Oxford correspondent: "Sir, send me two lines in reply to [my] letter without fail, and when you send them address them to the printing shop. For when a letter is addressed to that house it will reach me, because everyone there knows me." The global world of information was so personal that even the most basic information—a name and a city—could carry a letter across the world to its intended recipient.

Alongside letters, other instruments of communication played an important role in the making of information networks. Unlike the long traditional genre of the letter, questionnaires appeared as a novel feature of the media landscape of the sixteenth century, as a means of collecting mass information long before the advent of modern research methods. In 1671, for example, while preparing for his travels to the Islamic world, the diamond merchant Jean Chardin received a questionnaire from a savant in Paris called Cabart de Villermont. Known by his friends as a "curieux," or someone with a voracious appetite for information, Villermont had spent his career collecting as much information as he could on the customs, practices, and realities of the East. When he learned of Chardin's intention to travel to Persia, he sent him a questionnaire complete with 107 questions about the East. The subjects of interest ranged wildly across a vast array of topics: mostly about the Dutch and French trade in spices, drugs, and tea, but also about Eastern customs and manners, the state of ports in the Middle East, and the quality of manufactured goods produced there. Through this questionnaire, Villermont hoped to gain certainty on some of the topics he had been discussing with friends in Paris. It would be several years before Chardin finally replied to Villermont's questions, but the questionnaire grew in importance, particularly for those individuals who could not manage to carry out the global travels of merchants and missionaries in this period.

Questionnaires were important not only to individuals like Villermont but also for the aspirations of political and religious elites. In 1580, royal officials in Spain distributed around New Castile a set of printed questionnaires called the *Relaciones Topográficas* (Topographical Accounts), which contained several questions aimed at collecting information about the economic resources of the country. Interestingly, the *Relaciones* included questions on local religious practices, offering invaluable insight into religion in sixteenth-century Spain. Questionnaires had already been deployed in the New World as a form of administration, an innovation that inspired new procedures and practices back in Europe. Questionnaires showed how information could be standardized around the interests of those doing the collecting. In this way, local information could also become the basis for larger, state-led initiatives dealing, for example, with conversion and conquest. Yet for all the effort carried out in the circulation of these questionnaires, in most cases religious officials never actually did anything with the information contained in them.

Nonetheless questionnaires acted as bottom-up modes of communication that played a role in forging new regional identities on the basis of local information gathering. This was the case in the seventeenth and eighteenth centuries when scholars and antiquarians based in *learned societies around Britain began to disseminate questionnaires to various shires, communities, and urban centers in Wales, Scotland, and Ireland. Such ventures had an earlier history, for example, in the "enquiries" that had been circulated from time to time in local parishes during the fifteenth century. But it was only in the sixteenth and seventeenth centuries that these occasional, ad hoc efforts began to be systematized in the form of printed questionnaires. Francis Bacon formulated "heads" or "articles of inquiry" aimed at identifying questions for future study and to structure empirical research in natural history. By the end of the seventeenth century, the printed questionnaire had become a natural method for learned societies in search of antiquities, as in the 1677 publication of *That the Northern Counties which abound in Antiquities and Ancient Gentry, may no longer be bury'd in Silence Information is desired concerning the following Queries as they lye in order.* Questionnaires of this kind contributed to the rediscovery and the development of histories and identities that transcended any single parish or locality in England, Ireland, Scotland, or Wales.

As with the Spanish questionnaires, the circulation of these questionnaires did not always result in direct answers, or any at all. Of four thousand questionnaires sent out by the Dublin Society in the late eighteenth century, for example, responses to just forty are preserved (as studied by Fox). As today, all sorts of factors dissuaded individuals from replying: some people simply ignored circulars, perhaps out of indifference or apathy; others lacked the ability, or sufficient time, to respond to the sorts of detailed questions being asked of them; still others simply found the questionnaires to be "bothersome" and "intrusive" meddling from strangers. Whatever the case, it is striking that questionnaires of this sort continued to be produced well into the nineteenth century and, indeed, would become a familiar tool in the arsenal of modern social science researchers presaging such things as the founding of Mass Observation in Britain in the 1930s. That individuals remained so optimistic about the promise of these questionnaires is evidence of the faith placed in such modes of communication, even if their ambitions were not always realized.

THE CASE OF EUROPEAN KNOWLEDGE OF ISLAM

Not only were the information networks of this period important for the discovery of new, unknown worlds, but they also contributed to profound changes in the understanding of societies about which much was already known. This final section examines how European knowledge of the Islamic world was transformed in the early modern period. Before the sixteenth century, knowledge of Islam in western Europe stemmed mainly from a handful of texts that circulated primarily among European theologians and scholars working in Latin. These works were mostly of a polemical and ideological nature: even works that appeared to be straightforward—for example, European translations of the Quran or accounts written by medieval travelers who had witnessed Islamic societies firsthand—were intended to serve an anti-Islamic purpose. In such a world, Shakespeare could write in *Henry VI, Part I*: "Was Mahomet inspired with a dove? / Thou with an eagle art inspired then," a reference to a medieval trope according to which the Prophet placed corn in his ear to attract a dove, as a sign of revelation from the Holy Spirit. By the end of this period, such a polemic may have persisted in its appeal to some people, but it competed with a range of new evidence about the Islamic world that was circulating in Europe.

This new information drew, in the first instance, from the emergent networks of diplomacy and trade that connected Europe to the Ottoman Empire. Starting in the 1530s, European powers agreed to a set of treaties, or capitulations, with the Ottoman sultan, which paved the way for the establishment of permanent European embassies and consuls in the Ottoman Empire. First the French in 1535, then the English in 1579 and the Dutch in 1612: one by one, new communities of Europeans were established in Istanbul, Smyrna, Aleppo, Cairo, and further afield in Basra and Isfahan. By the end of the eighteenth century, Istanbul had become one of the few places in the world where all the major European powers—both Catholic and Protestant—encountered one another, a virtual clearinghouse of information exchanged between the representatives of Austria, Russia, Sweden, Sardinia, Denmark, Prussia, Spain, and, by 1830, even the United States. European embassies and consulates in the Ottoman Empire became critical hubs of information where the daily business of trade and diplomacy brought together individuals from a wide range of social and cultural backgrounds. In 1687, the English embassy alone counted among its staff several Turkish scribes, Italian doctors, local Eastern Christian translators, English merchants, the family and household of the English ambassador, the English secretaries of the Levant Company (one of whom was married to the daughter of a local Greek notable), and Turkish janissaries guarding the doors, not to mention the countless travelers, scholars, and missionaries who stopped at the embassy during their travels to and from the East. In this way, European embassies became dynamic hubs of information, rumor, and gossip that circulated orally, in the first instance, but with important consequences for handwritten and printed news in the wider world. Indeed the business of diplomacy in the Ottoman Empire required European ambassadors to spend much of their time writing and reporting local matters to their correspondents and superiors at home.

Information first obtained from the official and private correspondence of European diplomats in turn fueled the news diet of European readers with reports about the contemporary Islamic world. News of the deposition of the Ottoman sultan Mehmed IV in

1687 is a case in point. A contemporary of Louis XIV, Mehmed IV was the longest reigning sultan in Ottoman history until November 1687, when he was deposed in a series of events that were covered in some detail in both English and French printed news. Both the *London Gazette* and the *Mercure Galant,* for example, recounted how Mehmed's obsession with hunting had created so many costs for the Ottoman court—and during a period of extended warfare with Europe—that the janissaries would no longer accept his presence as ruler. An earlier generation of scholarship might have seen in such stories a symptom of European orientalism—that is, exotic and fanciful imaginations about the Orient—but in this particular case, many of the printed news reports had a genealogy that stretched back to actual letters first written in Istanbul as the events of the deposition were unfolding. In the case of the *London Gazette,* most of the reports that ended up in print in London repurposed a set of intelligence dispatches that had first been compiled by a secretary working in the English embassy named Thomas Coke. His letters, in turn, drew on oral rumors and reports that he had gathered personally from Ottoman and Greek informants working in the Ottoman palace. In this way, oral information that circulated originally in Turkish was reported by Coke in English in letters and became front-page news in the printed gazettes of England and France. In this way, networks of information exchange operated on a small-scale level across many localities in the Ottoman Empire and even in the "border zones" along the Ottoman-Habsburg frontiers, thereby carrying political intelligence and diplomatic news directly and effectively to the Ottoman imperial capital.

Political news represented only a small part of the information that Europeans sought about the Islamic world in this period. Even landlocked scholars who never set foot in the Ottoman Empire might turn to trading and diplomatic networks for information about a wide range of things. Nicolas-Claude Fabri de Peiresc (1580–1637) offers an excellent example. Peiresc was a man of insatiable curiosity, a *polymath, philologist, and cat lover ("I really like that kind of animal") whose interests stretched across a remarkable variety of objects—manuscripts, printed books, coins, fossils, gems, pottery, mummies—and subjects ranging from the rhythms of the tides to the movements of Jupiter to the contemporary practices of Samaritans, Copts, and Muslims, to name just a few. His wonder about the world around him, particularly about the East, is reflected today in the more than seventy thousand pages of correspondence by which someone in the South of France became so well informed on the Islamic world. His particular asset was his connections to Mediterranean merchants: the familiar factors of Marseille but also those faceless agents further afield whom Peiresc could identify only by their handwriting. Moreover, individuals like Peiresc acted as important sources of information to the work of orientalists, university scholars with interests in Arabic, Persian, Turkish, and Syriac. Oriental studies was one field of study that developed in dramatic ways on the back of new information networks. Consider, for example, the career of Edward Pococke, who spent six years as a chaplain at the Levant Company factory in Aleppo. He devoted this period of his life to studying Arabic, learning about the Islamic tradition, and working with local Arab scholars. When he returned to England, Pococke kept up a regular correspondence with one Darwish Ahmed, a scholar based in Aleppo, who kept Pococke supplied with the latest works to excite the interests of Muslim scholars in Aleppo. Some of Pococke's seminal publications are indebted to the networks of trade and diplomacy that supplied him with manuscripts and information from the Ottoman Empire.

Trade, diplomacy, scholarship—sometimes these impulses intersected in a single person with important effects on the circulation of information. The appointment of Charles Marie François Olier, the marquis de Nointel, as French ambassador to the Ottoman Empire in 1669 was one such case. While his official work in Istanbul focused on the everyday business of diplomacy and trade, he had also been approached by the Jansenist scholars of Port-Royal in hopes that he could collect information of use to them in their ongoing debates with Protestants. The specific matter concerned the doctrine of transubstantiation, and Nointel was asked to learn as much as he could about the practices of the Eastern churches in this regard. From September 1673, therefore, Nointel made a tour of the Ottoman Empire that lasted over seventeen months. During this period, he met with priests, bishops, and patriarchs of the various Eastern Christian communities living in Chios, the Cyclades, Palestine, and Egypt. In these encounters, he directed a series of questions at his interlocutors about their beliefs and practices, requesting detailed written answers. The confessions of faith produced out of these encounters functioned much like the questionnaires discussed above, and these texts were duly sent back to France, where they eventually became part of great polemical projects like Antoine Arnauld's *Perpetuité de la foi* (The perpetuity of the faith, 1669–79). In this way, not only did diplomatic information networks provide material to Europe in the form of dispatches and letters, but Europeans like Nointel participated in the creation of specific documents and forms of record keeping about the Ottoman world. It is not an exaggeration to say that the frontiers of knowledge about the Christian and Muslim East developed in ways that were a direct representation of European preoccupations.

In a very practical sense, information moved in the form of the manuscripts, antiquities, coins, and objects that Europeans carried with them from the Ottoman Empire back to Europe. Acquisitions were made during trade missions by the Dutch, English, and French trading companies, but specific missions were also sponsored by powerful political figures like Louis XIV's minister Jean-Baptiste Colbert, who funded several missions to collect manuscripts in the East. In England, Archbishop Laud insisted that every Levant Company ship returning from the Middle East should carry with it at least one Arabic or Persian manuscript. The movements of all these materials created new problems of their own, and they should not be taken as a sign that Europeans always understood the information they obtained. One anecdote tells of the discovery by the archbishop of Paris during an Easter procession in 1709 that the luxurious fabric that had been used to wrap the bier carried in the procession was not simply an expensive cloth obtained from the East but rather a flag bearing the Islamic credo "There is no God but God." With abundant information came new opportunities for misunderstanding.

Information obtained through personal relationships had a transformative impact on literary cultures in Europe. The case of the discovery of the *One Thousand and One Nights* is revealing in this regard. The French orientalist and scholar Antoine Galland had traveled to the Ottoman Empire in the 1670s as one of a small number of people tasked with the collection of manuscripts, antiquities, and coins. During this journey, Galland developed an interest in the popular tales that he found circulating in the mouths of storytellers but also in Arabic manuscripts. Years later the personal relationships he had forged in the Ottoman Empire contributed to one of the greatest literary events of the eighteenth century. In 1709, a young Syrian merchant named Hanna Diyāb through a set of peculiar circumstances found himself in Paris and face-to-face with Galland, who, at the time, was working furiously to complete a French translation of the fantastic tales of *One Thousand and One Nights*. Galland was convinced that there were in fact 1,001 stories corresponding to each of the nights, but despite his best efforts, he could come up with only a few hundred based on the manuscripts he had obtained thus far. When he heard of Hanna's presence in Paris, therefore, Galland sought him out and asked him whether he knew of any tales that he could add to his collection. The two men, Hanna and Galland, met together at Galland's home for several weeks, during which time Hanna recounted stories to him while Galland scribbled them down hastily. (Hanna told the stories in Arabic, and Galland wrote them out in French.) Today, *Nights* specialists refer to the stories that Hanna told Galland as the "orphan tales," a reference to the fact that, curiously, there is no known manuscript tradition in Arabic that corresponds to any of the stories that Hanna told to Galland. In other words, oral improvisation and information lay at the roots of the first Western telling of the *One Thousand and One Nights*. It is especially striking that some of the most popular stories from the book—such as "Aladdin and the Lamp" and "Alibaba and the Forty Thieves"—can be traced back only to the stories that Hanna shared with Galland in Paris.

Yet Europeans' exposure to more information about Islam did not always mean that contemporaries knew how to read, understand, and interpret that information. One should not overestimate the relationship between the mobility of information in this period and the extent to which it was intelligible to contemporaries. The growing array of information, manuscripts, and texts in foreign languages created its own set of problems for Europeans tasked with having to understand and make sense of them. For example, the growing presence of Arabic, Persian, and Turkish manuscripts in manuscript libraries in Europe necessitated the assistance of Middle Eastern Christian and Muslim translators who took up posts in these libraries to make this information intelligible to European orientalists. Purposeful use of the new information circulating about Islam in this period required a particular form of expertise, not simply in the strict sense of record keeping but also in all the related practices of copying, translating, cataloging, and, perhaps most importantly, determining the authenticity of information. As in other areas of *information overload in this period, the possession of information about Islam opened a host of new problems: Who would read and translate these works? How might they be copied, organized, and managed? Who could authenticate and date these documents? Above all, who could identify the salient information in them while discarding what was ephemeral, unlikely, and not useful?

Beyond these circles of scholars, merchants, and missionaries, information about the Islamic world was also accessible to a wider and more diverse segment of European society. Among a broader public, perceptions of Islam more often involved an encounter with stories and information rather than direct contact with Ottoman subjects. "Stories of the East" circulated in a wide range of oral, scribal, and printed media, from songs about the Turks sung in taverns to cheap print sold by itinerant chapmen. This information came in all shapes and sizes to suit the diverse interests of readers. Most readers in Europe learned about Islam in the pages of newsletters, broadsides, cheap print, and novels; these sources give us a firsthand glimpse of how Europeans knew what they knew about the Ottoman world. Consider, for example, a story that circulated in Paris: the curious tale of a man called Padre Ottomano, as revealed in a book published in 1665 by a Maltese knight who claimed to have knowledge of the "true history" of the

"Reverend Father Dominique Ottoman." As the knight told the story, Dominique Ottoman was an Ottoman prince who had been captured by corsairs and imprisoned in
Malta, where he converted to Christianity and ultimately became a Dominican friar
(hence the "Padre"). This man now traveled from one European court to another on a
mission to raise money so that he might lead a crusade against the Ottomans and,
thereby, restore himself as a new Christian sultan of the Ottoman Empire. Looking at
such stories today, we might immediately dismiss them as little more than the imaginative musings of Grub Street hacks. But for seventeenth-century readers who were inun-
dated with fanciful tales, the boundaries between fact and fiction were rarely so clear.
As for Padre Ottomano, there was indeed a man living in seventeenth-century Italy who
called himself Dominique Ottoman and claimed to be the son of the Ottoman sultan.
His identity was a subject of great debate that kept European writers arguing well into
the eighteenth century.

The abundance of information, therefore, did not always lead in a teleological way to
increased certainties of knowledge about the Islamic world. If scholarly orientalists were
able to challenge old misrepresentations of Islam, they did so mainly because they had
access to more, and more diverse, information about the Islamic world. But this is not
to say that such information produced more tolerant, ecumenical people: Ludovico Mar-
racci, who drew extensively on new sources to write his Latin translation of the Quran,
did so with the clear goal of better refuting the Quran. The establishment of a regular
presence of diplomats, merchants, and travelers to the Islamic world meant that entirely new, and neglected, realms of information became available to Europeans for the
first time. Their knowledge of Muslims was no longer limited to core texts but drew on
direct experience of their politics, but also of their families, social practices, and dining
habits, which formed the basis for real ethnographic study. As Alexander Bevilacqua
has shown, the consequence was that European scholars of the seventeenth and eighteenth centuries made remarkable efforts to understand Islam on its own terms, un-
clouded by the polemical biases of their time. As Barthelemy d'Herbelot wrote in the
introduction to his *Bibliothèque Orientale* (Oriental library), "The reader shall judge
whether the Orientals are as barbarous and as ignorant as public opinion would suggest." It was the connected world of this period that made it even imaginable for
d'Herbelot to offer this possibility to his readers.

CONCLUSION

Information was crucially important to the "world-making" of the early modern period.
This was a period when the coalescence of religious, political, and financial networks
brought people into contact with one another across huge expanses of space. Animated
by such modes of communication as correspondence and questionnaires, information
could move efficiently across both space and language barriers. We are right to see in
these interactions the first stirrings of a global network of information. But two caveats
require mention. First, while these networks were global, they also remained intensely
local, personal, and rooted in close interactions between a circumscribed set of individuals. At the heart of early modern global flows of information, therefore, we find
not strangers reaching out to one another but systems of communication developed out
of familiar relationships.

Second, in these cross-cultural and cross-confessional networks that spanned the whole globe, information took circuitous and unpredictable routes. Even if there were obvious nodes—Rome, New Julfa, Batavia, London, Istanbul—there was also an emergent multipolarity in this world where several nodes further afield also projected themselves onto the world stage. In this polycentric world of information, those who commanded unique linguistic skills—multiple languages, writing abilities, forms of oral and written communication—would thrive most. If vagaries and uncertainties existed in these information networks, they represented nonetheless a first phase in the globalization of information that would, by the twentieth century, become truly global in its aspirations and its mechanics.

John-Paul A. Ghobrial

See also accounting; bureaucracy; diplomats/spies; documentary authority; ethnography; globalization; letters; merchants; networks; scribes

FURTHER READING

Sebouh David Aslanian, *From the Indian Ocean to the Mediterranean: The Global Trade Networks of Armenian Merchants from New Julfa*, 2011; idem, "'The Salt in a Merchant's Letter': The Culture of Julfan Correspondence in the Indian Ocean and the Mediterranean," *Journal of World History* 19, no. 2 (2008): 127–88; Francisco Bethencourt and Florike Egmond, eds., *Correspondence and Cultural Exchange in Europe, 1400–1700*, 2007; Alexander Bevilacqua, *The Republic of Arabic Letters: Islam and the European Enlightenment*, 2018; Michael Carhart: *Leibniz Discovers Asia: Social Networking in the Republic of Letters*, 2019; Luke Clossey, *Salvation and Globalization in the Early Jesuit Missions*, 2008; Filippo de Vivo, "Microhistories of Long-Distance Information: Space, Movement and Agency in the Early Modern News," in John-Paul A. Ghobrial, ed., "Global History and Microhistory," *Past and Present* supplement 14 (2019): 179–214; Paula Findlen, ed., *Athanasius Kircher, the Last Man Who Knew Everything*, 2004; Adam Fox, "Printed Questionnaires, Research Networks, and the Discovery of the British Isles, 1650–1800," *Historical Journal* 53, no. 3 (2010): 593–621; John-Paul A. Ghobrial, *The Whispers of Cities: Information Flows in Istanbul, London and Paris in the Age of William Trumbull*, 2013; Serge Gruzinski, *What Time Is It There? America and Islam at the Dawn of Modern Times*, 2008, translated by Jean Birrell, 2010; Peter N. Miller, *Peiresc's Mediterranean World*, 2015; Miles Ogborn, *Indian Ink: Script and Print in the Making of the English East India Company*, 2007; Robyn Radway, "Vernacular Diplomacy: The Culture of Sixteenth-Century Peace Keeping Strategies in the Ottoman-Habsburg Borderlands," *Archivum Ottomanicum* 34 (2017): 193–204; Gagan Sood, "'Correspondence Is Equal to Half a Meeting': The Composition and Comprehension of Letters in Eighteenth-Century Islamic Eurasia," *Journal of the Economic and Social History of the Orient* 50, nos. 2–3 (2007): 172–214.

RECORDS, SECRETARIES, AND THE EUROPEAN INFORMATION STATE, CIRCA 1400–1700

Informatio enim incipit a sensu. At universum negotium desinit in Opera; atque quemadmodum illud principium, ita hoc finis rei est.

For information commences with the senses. But the whole business terminates in works, and as the former is the beginning, so the latter is the end of the matter.

—Francis Bacon, *Novum Organum* 2:XLIV

Information occurs ubiquitously in human societies whenever human senses perceive phenomena and treat them as data; perceived data, in turn, informs the creation of knowledge by individuals and shapes how they respond to their world. Information is thus at one level an ephemeral process transacted in a moment: when a worshipper hears the bell announcing services, when a storyteller's listeners absorb elements that shape their consciousness, and in innumerable other ways. As human interactions and the political systems that frame them intensify, more and more informational moments also result in durably recorded traces, or records, which can be saved and conveyed through time. In consequence, the term *information* generally comprises both the (potential) *content* of such traces and also the underlying *processes* by which people became informed. Whereas information theory since Claude Shannon's pathbreaking work concentrates primarily on processes of communicating information and their reliability, semantic information as discussed by historians emphasizes the content that is transmitted. Notably, recorded information plays a disproportionate role in all historical thinking. Only records enable us to reconstruct any sense of how the world informed human minds at specific times and places. Written records play a core role in such reconstruction, although information could always also take place through images, by performances (possibly based on recorded scripts), and in various other ways. A focus on written records, in turn, privileges literate societies—such as late medieval and *early modern Europe— and literate individuals within them, while also drawing our attention to the institutions that enabled the creation and preservation of written records.

Western Europe experienced major developments in its management of recorded information from the fifteenth to early eighteenth centuries. Shifting cultural contexts and new media technologies not only changed the scope of information but also changed the relationship between the world, institutions, and records in consequential ways. This chapter probes society-wide transformations by focusing on one exemplary site where information practices intensified after 1400: the writing offices and archives of political domains. Such offices, not coincidentally, were also a focal point for the expansion of European states' knowledge about their own territories and subjects and about the complex world beyond Europe. Growing state knowledge paralleled expanded erudition in the *Republic of Letters and burgeoning scientific knowledge about the heavens and nature that emerged over the same period. Indeed, learned knowledge management techniques, first from the Scholastic learning of medieval universities, then from humanist pedagogy and from scientific analysis, provided vital resources for the growth of the information states analyzed below. Such information states operated through and become visible in their accumulated records, in part; indeed, new ways of organizing such records helped give intelligible form to the abstract concept of a state. After delving into how European states transformed their information systems between the 1400s and the 1700s, this chapter also briefly considers noninscribed information such as ceremony and architecture, reflects on the limits on early modern state information, and concludes by asking how changes in the media, organization, and cultural contexts of information may have been connected with changes in cognition and reasoning.

FRAMEWORKS FOR FORMAL INFORMATION IN EUROPE AFTER CIRCA 1400

Information's role in transmitting knowledge always depends on larger frameworks of meaning, which help make information intelligible or simply recognizable as informative in the first place. Information becomes trustworthy and knowledge develops in coherent ways when the actors involved share languages and effective channels for communication. Equally, failed or distorted communication can lead to misinformation or disinformation or can block information processes altogether. Understanding the expansion and intensification of written information systems that characterized early modern European states therefore begins by considering the larger communicative environment and the assumptions that educated Europeans brought to it.

In premodern Europe, well-developed cultural ideas lay behind the way various actors understood information and its value. In particular, theology and law provided ways to assess the value and reliability of political information from various sources. Most broadly, Europeans understood a single Creator as the ultimate guarantor of meaning, and they valued sources of information in part by their association with a divine order. In the words of Baldassare Bonifacio in his *De Archivis* of 1632, "Through order, [God] gave form to formless things. Deservedly, order is called the soul of the world." Roman law and its reinvention in high medieval Europe (ca. 1000–1300 CE) provided a second powerful way to assess information. Indeed, the language of neo-Roman law suffuses both early modern and modern knowledge terminology: information itself, along with *fact, evidence, testimony, and data, were all originally legal terms, honed by the endless work of courts seeking to weigh the reliability of conflicting human statements. Legal practices, notably those developed by the Roman Church's inquisitions, provided powerful tools for gathering and deploying information. Additionally, God's demand for justice required rulers to be "fully informed" before adjudicating disputes, which encouraged their systematic collection, use, and preservation of evidence. Theological and legal discourses profoundly shaped the information orders developing in European political chancelleries.

Medieval ways of framing information, always contested and fluid, began to change systematically after about 1400. Both new social contexts and improved media tools enabled new approaches. Paper and then printing greatly reduced the cost of reproducing texts and images, enabling more people to access more recorded information in more ways (Blair, chap. 4). Intensifying commerce across the Mediterranean and around the globe stimulated communication and reporting, while also providing the resources that allowed officials, scholars, and merchants to produce and preserve records (Ghobrial, chap. 5). As record keeping expanded, the sites where records were gathered, preserved, and organized took on new importance. After 1400, we see rulers across Europe shifting their record keeping from strongboxes full of charters to writing offices that managed archives filled with letters, reports, and deliberations. These archives became an important new site for producing information of value to rulers.

INFORMATION MEDIA AND TOOLS: CONTINUITIES AND SITES OF CHANGE

Edward Higgs defines "information states" as polities that rely on the "generalized and *structured collection of information . . . the creation of routine administrative records, and of databases, paper and electronic." In such states, accumulated written records played a growing role in the circulation of information. The analysis of their growth in early modern Europe here will follow two paths. The first looks at the media used for recording and regenerating information—whose basic forms remained remarkably stable from the fifteenth to eighteenth centuries, but whose deployment became both more intensive and more extensive. The second considers the architecture of state information systems, which evolved in ways that connected the world beyond chancellery offices to the operations of a new imagined actor, the European bureaucratic state. Both rely on a second important theoretical concept, namely the "information order." Understanding the connections between the "state's intelligence and social communication," as Christopher Bayly notes, requires us to look at "the generators of knowledge, the institutions of information collection and diffusion and the discourses to which they give rise." Equally, analyzing the evolving architecture of state information systems helps us further explore both the potential and the limitations of what James C. Scott characterized as "seeing like a state," that is, relying on the information gathered in reports, offices, and archives, especially after the sixteenth century.

Becoming informed through the use of records inherently means responding to signs and symbols that convey meaning; such signs, in turn, depend on durable physical media that allow them to be transmissible between persons and between eras. The basic medial equipment that European rulers used to build bureaucratic states changed only slowly from the late Middle Ages to the eighteenth century. Letters from the Roman alphabet and Roman or Arabic numerals were inscribed in Latin or a *vernacular language onto either parchment or paper surfaces. Images and maps, while rare, conformed to contemporary *canons of visual representation. Nontextual objects of various kinds played a decreasing role in political record keeping as the period went on, despite their continuing importance in ceremonial and performative contexts.

At the next level of organization, too, media technologies changed relatively slowly from 1400 to 1700. Inscribed leaves either could circulate independently—as letters, charters, reports, and so on—or could be gathered into folded quires and books, or into bundles wrapped or strung together or placed in a box or sack. Many domains built chests and armoires to house larger accumulations of paper and parchment, leading to various schemes to organize the resulting spaces. For use in chancelleries' daily routine, the book reigned supreme throughout this period. Books offered a powerful suite of organizational technologies that had emerged from Europe's universities in the twelfth century. As they created *concordances, *Summae*, and other tools of learning, Scholastic intellectuals learned how to use pagination, page layout (*mise-en-page*), indexing, alphabetization, and similar tools to make vast amounts of data accessible. Like their colleagues in the thirteenth-century Inquisition, who collected thousands of testimonies in books tracking suspected heretics in southern France and elsewhere, chancellery secretaries working for Europe's princes and cities found these Scholastic tools effective and economical as they sought to gain control of their informational treasures.

The same suite of tools supported the erudite humanism that emerged outside European universities after 1350, and humanist scholarship developed further innovations in reference and organization as chancelleries grew. Since early modern administrative secretaries typically had some university education, the flow of techniques between scholarship and secretaryship is not surprising. Just as humanists routinized and disseminated methods for excerpting key texts as *commonplaces, urban and princely secretaries refined their ability to capture key points in *protocols and finding aids: both practices contributed to the parcelization of data that underlay later developments in both erudition and bureaucracy. European scholars also pioneered schemes to use glued slips, cards, book wheels, or tricky cabinets to disaggregate and organize many separate texts. Chancelleries were slower to turn to card files and long relied on book-form registers connected to masses of loose records in either chronological or topical order. Still, the shared experience of too much to know, and the shared challenge of finding the right information among thousands of paper leaves, connected scholars and secretaries.

INFORMATION ARCHITECTURE IN POLITICAL CHANCELLERIES, 1400-1700

The records accumulated by political authorities serve to illustrate how records from the past became information for the future during this era. To be sure, most political life both before and after the transformations discussed here took place beyond the sphere of written records. Still, the scope of written records grew explosively after 1400 (depending on region), which changed how records informed rulers in the course of governance. The case studies below trace three distinct modes of using written records. First, documents could serve as performative objects bearing signs with emotional and social meaning. Charters and other documents could be displayed in court ceremonies, promenaded in processions, and take center stage when urban citizens swore loyalty to their communes. Second, documents could preserve information about either occasional or systematic inquiry and action on the part of political authorities: from the charters recording specific deeds to Inquisition registers recording testimonies to the vast information-collecting efforts that the Spanish crown undertook in the sixteenth century, chancelleries preserved records about specific circumstances that could be accessed in the future. Finally, records became tools of administration, oriented to the needs and actions of the state. Such use of records, while taking account of particulars, also transformed political life by framing resources or burdens as parts of a systemic whole, as in tax rolls, military census records, or land cadasters; or by framing the flow of information as part of state processes, as in the document registries discussed below. Importantly, the aggregation of information that took place in early statistics prioritized knowledge gained by combining records, rather than by what was found in any one record. All these approaches already existed in Europe before 1400 (or in any polity with institutionalized administration), but the balance among them shifted, ultimately justifying our description of some European polities as information states by the later 1600s.

The Medieval Background

The societies that emerged after the collapse of the Western Roman Empire remained literate throughout the following period. Christianity's reliance on canonical texts ensured clerical *literacy, and political life also produced formal records for certain occasions, though far less often than under the Roman bureaucracy. Written documents' roles expanded again during the High and later Middle Ages, ranging from memorials of specific grants or transactions (such as charters and *notary records) to treaties, settlements, and verdicts, to statutes and ceremonial records. Both those claiming political authority and those subject to it made and kept records with increasing frequency after 1000 CE, which they deployed in multiple ways. The later developments discussed here rested on this rich and complex foundation.

A large proportion of surviving political records from before 1400 purported to transmit authentic memories of an authoritative *action*: the general term for such documents is *charter* or *instrument*. In form and words, charters served as evidence of an act or deed—in itself performative and oral—that they preserved "for perpetual memory." Charters were treated as material objects of value and rested in rulers' treasuries among money, jewels, and other evidential objects such as swords, flags, or even clods of earth. At the same time, a charter's evidence could be reproduced in other documents; indeed, the text of many a medieval charter survives today only as an entry in a register or a cartulary. Charters typically demonstrated their authenticity through tangible signs such as signatures, witness lists, seals, or notary signets (although many of the earliest European charters are in fact inauthentic). The status of a document's possessor could also lend a document credence, especially after Roman-law rules of evidence were reintroduced after the eleventh century.

This view of records—as traces proving past actions—was the focal point for earlier research but has recently been supplemented by studies of documents' use in multiple communicative contexts, both at the time of their creation and later. As Geoffrey Koziol shows, in the mid-ninth century, a document's material and textual features reveal only part of what was significant during the political act of its creation. In one case Koziol analyzes, the most important feature was which persons did *not* appear among the parties named in the document's text, since such absence communicated a powerful statement about ruptured alliances. Peter Brun's study of the charters that Emperor Sigismund issued after 1415 to his regional allies in Switzerland shows that Sigismund gave his urban supporters charters that had no content at all: they simply confirmed, without details, whatever privileges each town might already possess. The point of such charters was not to inform anyone about past actions, Brun concludes, but rather to demonstrate that Sigismund was empowered to grant imperial privileges. Notably, when he appealed to local aristocrats, Sigismund relied on ceremonial feasts instead of charters, since these nobles made little use of written evidence.

Close study of how documents could be deployed after their production shows similar results: the performative context of displaying a document was separate from, and often just as important as, the words it contained. Ron Makleff, for example, traces how documents belonging to Liège and several other cities defeated during a rebellion in 1408 were handed over to the victorious bishop. The bishop's agents cataloged the trove and destroyed some records, while returning others with physical marks of cancellation, all as part of a theater of authority. For Lucerne, Jeanette Rauschert has reconstructed how city fathers repeatedly changed the text of their *Geschworener Brief*, the allegedly ancient contract that bound the citizens and validated their law. Careful research can sometimes retrieve the information communicated during such documentary performances, but much is lost, even though performative contexts were vital to establishing documents' meaning at the time.

Multiple factors led to an explosion in political record making and record keeping across Europe in the fourteenth and fifteenth centuries. Increasing formalism in the law, the growing influence of administrative specialists, and the expansion of mercantile record keeping all contributed to the habit of making written records, accelerated by the appearance of paper as a durable and inexpensive medium. Political functionaries responded to the resulting masses of documents with new ways of authenticating and preserving them. The resulting accumulations of original documents, copies, registers, summaries, finding tools, and more became a source of anxiety for those responsible for managing it all. Secretaries wrote about "swimming in a world of paper" with "many lovely parchment charters trodden under foot and crumpled up," evoking tropes of being overwhelmed that emerged across multiple intellectual spheres in this period.

While the sheer volume of records produced after 1400 was impressive, extensive record production also transformed the relationships between human communities and their records, as suggested by Simon Teuscher. Making or using a record remained a political act, always conditioned by the immediate context's contention. In the fifteenth century, however, these contexts shifted in ways that increased the salience of other documents and their texts at the expense of performances and communities. Teuscher illustrates this change on a local scale in an early sixteenth-century dispute between a Swiss village, Dürnten, and its bailiff from the city of Zurich. During a boundary dispute, the bailiff, Jürg Berger, sought a copy of the bylaws (*Weistum*) that the Dürnten villagers had accumulated in a book. The villagers, however, refused his request to use the Weistum unless a delegation of villagers could accompany their statutes: in their view, only the community's presence ensured proper reading of the bylaws' words. In the end, Berger did get his copy, which he placed on a shelf next to copies of other villages' bylaws in a compact corpus of documents. In place of a community, texts came to rest among other texts, right down to the present.

This development paralleled contemporary changes in legal process, as adjudication by expert judges relying on written evidence displaced face-to-face confrontations before a community. Texts surged in importance relative to performances, which allowed documents to be viewed as sources of information by themselves apart from their original interpretive community. This shift only accelerated as energetic scribes produced whole new *genres of documents on paper, which increasingly piled up in offices, storerooms, and attics. By the late fourteenth century, we see systematic efforts across Europe to organize such materials. As Gerard de Montaigu put it in the first systematic inventory to the French royal treasury of documents, created in the 1370s, he organized the repository "so that it would be possible to find at once and promptly whatever letter was sought by a particular person." Management of political and legal information increased in intensity and sophistication during the late Middle Ages and continued to evolve after 1500, although it remained focused on recovering evidence about particular persons and properties. More and more political actors—rulers, councils, and bureaucrats—expected to become informed by consulting documents that were provided by their archives, which thus became vital parts of Europe's evolving political information order.

The Architecture of Political Record Keeping after 1400

We take it for granted that formal governance today takes place through offices that rely on written records (or *digital resources), which may ultimately be conserved in a public archive. In contrast, a large part of early modern governance, especially in smaller political units, took place through face-to-face interactions and performative events that did not necessarily find their way into council protocols or charters. Even in Europe's great courts, interactions between kings and their most important subjects remained personal, neither relying on nor producing many documents. High medieval royal families and towns did have documentary treasures, often kept with other treasures such as money and gems. Sometimes these traveled along with itinerant kings, at risk of capture as happened when King Philip II of France lost most of his records to the English at the 1194 Battle of Fréteval. Generally, though, nobles and towns preserved their most precious charters in safe places such as the sacristy of a cathedral or in a family monastery. Ecclesiastical institutions, which combined Christian respect for the power of words with reliance on gifts from the powerful for their survival, also preserved ancient document collections. Few clear distinctions existed among various sites for accumulated records, which largely lacked dedicated keepers.

Efforts to organize records after 1400 generally proceeded through a series of differentiations, as originally small and unordered bodies of documents (such as chests and sacks) grew and split into increasingly large and systematically organized bodies, gathered in bundles or boxes or copied into books. As the distinctions between different kinds of records became more stable, new principles for arranging and describing them also developed, eventually producing sophisticated registries that could track the documentary trail of important matters over years and decades. According to Robert-Henri Bautier's influential periodization, many state-like actors from about 1400 to 1800 sought to create documentary *arsenals* that they could use to maintain control over their subjects and to fend off threats from other domains. As German archivist Georg Aebbtlin put it in 1669, a properly ordered archive allowed "documents to be drawn just like weapons, so that the interests of a lordship can be battled for, defended, stiffened, preserved and maintained." In consequence, the ability to respond to specific conflicts about particular lands or rights remained at the forefront of *archival thinking well into the eighteenth century. Only slowly did officials across Europe begin to use accumulated records to understand their states as a whole, introducing new practices of collection and analysis that are generally associated with the beginning of statistics (that is, the science of the state).

The short studies that follow illustrate how early modern European rulers and their bureaucrats understood accumulated records, which helps us see how they thought these could inform their decisions and actions. Our cases include systematic efforts to manage information by means of books in Portugal and in Austria, and to organize archival spaces in France and Switzerland. Later examples will include the comprehensive information gathering undertaken in late sixteenth-century Spain, followed by the development of state information management tools such as censuses, land cadasters, and administrative registries across Europe.

Organization and Access: Case Studies and Contrasts

As written communication burgeoned across the fifteenth and sixteenth centuries, so did the benefits of organizing the growing masses of material that writing produced: strong positive feedback loops drove the rapid proliferation not only of writing itself, but also of the registering, indexing, and sorting that followed. Two exemplary projects to compile information in books just after 1500, from different parts of Europe, show how willing Europe's most successful rulers were to invest in their record-keeping priorities. In Lisbon, the thriving Portuguese state began creating carefully organized and materially splendid register books after 1460 that reproduced in accessible form a large number of older privileges that the Crown had given out. In Innsbruck, an administrative and financial center for the Austrian Habsburgs, the elevation of a new ruler in 1523 spurred the creation of paper copybooks to systematically record correspondence between the ruler, the regional administration, and the territories it supervised. Both projects drew directly on well-established media technologies in book form, including layout, pagination, and indexing with page references to help searchers quickly find what they sought.

Like most European crowns, the kings of Portugal issued charters to individuals, towns, and noble families as part of their exercise of power. By the mid-fifteenth century, the royal chancellery had accumulated voluminous records about such issuances, mostly on parchment quires that provided a date and a summary for each issued privilege. The passage of time rendered these primitive registers increasingly hard to read, however. In 1460, responding to complaints from the kingdom's estates, the royal chancellery launched an ambitious program to select grants of privilege "suitable for perpetual memory" for copying into new, high-quality parchment books. A generation later, with the accession of Manuel I, who could draw on revenue from Portugal's growing overseas empire, this initiative grew into a carefully articulated series of copybooks known as the *Leitura Nova*, the "new reading." Using fine parchment and calligraphy, and embellishing the volumes with illuminated frontispieces that celebrated royal power, the royal chancellery between 1505 and the 1550s compiled over sixty volumes of privileges organized by region, type, or category of recipient. These splendid volumes helped the Crown manage its relations with Portugal's powerful patrimonial nobility and towns while displaying the king's wealth and knowledge in material form. Yet these refined chancellery products were backward looking as information tools. They preserved traces of royal acts with meticulous notarial authentication, but the project's design did not include alphabetical indexes, and its sketchy entries gave only scant details about long-past actions. In short, the project's focus on materially reproducing authentic acts limited its value as a source of broader information.

In Innsbruck, Habsburg administrators faced rather different challenges. As rulers over a composite monarchy that stretched from Spain to the Netherlands to Hungary, the Habsburgs relied on regional administrators to manage conflicts and revenue flows, while family members (including Emperor Charles V, his brother Ferdinand, and royal mothers, sisters, and wives) traveled to the places that most needed their attention. Rather than jockeying with a tightly knit aristocracy, the Habsburgs needed to stay informed about developments in territories with divergent needs. A series of volumes produced in Innsbruck after 1523 reflected these circumstances in the way it captured the correspondence among king, administrators, and subjects in book form. At the system's heart lay two chronologically organized series of copybooks whose names reveal their purpose: one, filling a volume every year or so, was entitled "To the princely Highness," the other "From the princely Highness"; additional series recorded the princely chancellery's correspondence with regional agents and the courts. In the first series, every letter from the Innsbruck chancellery to its itinerant prince was copied before sending; in the second, every incoming letter from the prince was copied before going to the relevant officers. The books used mise-en-page tools such as marginal keywords and highlighting to enable searching, while alphabetical indexing made key terms in each copied letter accessible. In contrast to the Portuguese *Leitura Nova*, therefore, which continued to privilege acts, the Innsbruck copybooks privileged communications about particulars: names, actions, events, and conflicts made accessible for an audience of future administrators.

The similarities and differences between these two projects to organize records are instructive. In the first place, both projects selected and copied records into books, in the process silencing material and performative aspects of the originals. Both projects also changed records' contexts by locating copies or abstracts side by side with copies of other documents that had not originally been placed there. This increased the salience of intertextual relations among records by assimilating them within a shared environment. Both, finally, drew extensively on the technologies of the book that scholars had perfected in the Middle Ages to manage large amounts of textual data.

Their two projects' differences are equally telling. The *Leitura Nova* and its fifteenth-century predecessor kept a sharp focus on acts by Portugal's kings and invested heavily in capturing such acts in honorable and authenticated form. The volumes' audience consisted of the Crown and aristocracy, mediated by the notaries in the royal chancellery. In Innsbruck, royal commands and administrative responses were also central but were represented as an ongoing conversation, copied into alphabetically indexed registers that covered all sorts of matters. Its audience consisted of Habsburg regional agents who sought to be informed about the domains they were charged to oversee and about the wishes of their prince. Rather than acts, the Innsbruck copybooks therefore focused on commands and reports, while incorporating far more systematic browsing tools and indexing than the *Leitura Nova*—all in paper copybooks that were relentlessly utilitarian in appearance. Ultimately, both projects, which absorbed substantial labor over many decades, illustrate just how important access to records was becoming for European rulers.

Selecting and copying records into books created powerful reference tools for those who could afford to create and sustain them. The explosive increase in stored documents, however, led many chancelleries after about 1450 to begin organizing the actual records within their storage spaces instead, thus avoiding the labor of recopying them. In place of the haphazard chests and sacks of medieval collections, chancellery staff dreamed about defining a place for every document that would make it easy to find. Organizers' ideas about how records could inform future users shaped their organizational schemes, which thus provide evidence about the information order at the time. Notably, almost all early modern archival plans concentrated on content, or pertinence, as a key locational principle: secretaries wanted to group documents according to what they were *about*, in contrast to the modern archival principle of provenance, which organizes records based on their role in the creator's operations. By focusing on content, early modern archiving derived order from the world outside the chancellery, rather than from the institution itself.

Two cases illustrate the ways premodern chancelleries organized separate documents. Further investigation would reveal a wide variety of intermediate and intersecting approaches, however, emphasizing how variable and creative the organizing work of early modern chancellery staff could be. The first case, from Paris in the 1360s, shows that many tools for organizing archival spaces were already available at that time. When Gérard de Montaigu became warden of the French royal charters, the *Trésor des Chartes*, in 1370, he found in the storeroom of the Sainte Chapelle "an ocean of letters and registers confused as by a storm." As he worked on the collection over the next eighteen months, ease of finding was a central concern. Older organizing schemes already shaped the *Trésor*—in this case, a system of boxes dedicated to specific regions such as Delphinatus, Flandria, Navarre and labeled with two letters, which apparently confused users. Montaigu preserved the topical boxes but chose to number them, because of the "infallible continuity of numbers." He also created an inventory, consisting of an alphabetized register that included various subtopics. As he observed, "there is no name of a prince nor sobriquet for a country or city that does not begin with some letter of the alphabet, and it is thus impossible to fail to find the one you want whenever you look." Topically focused boxes linked to an alphabetical inventory created an effective way to move from a particular name or place to a specific document, and variations on this approach can be found all across Europe.

Many early modern archivists chose a different path, however, and created systematic architectures of storage spaces that reflected their understanding of the world. This approach, defined by Peter Rück as ideal-topographical organization, started with topically defined units of accumulation (usually boxes or bundles) but added a systematic dimension by arranging the resulting masses according to a coherent worldview. An illuminating example comes from mid-seventeenth-century Zurich, where city secretary Johann Heinrich Waser undertook a complete reorganization of the city's repositories and finding tools in 1646. As in Montaigu's *Trésor*, subject-oriented boxes remained the basic organizational unit in Zurich. In his oversight of the city's information resources, the *Index archivorum generalis* (Comprehensive Index of the Archives), Waser sketched the major divisions among the city's documents, from the courts to the finance office, before turning to 475 core boxes of material under his direct authority. Action was urgent, since Waser, like his predecessor Montaigu, had found rooms and boxes with "everything overfilled."

When Waser was done, his boxes were arranged in careful order, with boxes arranged in storage and mapped onto the pages of the *Index archivorum generalis* according to an identical sequence. The first two boxes contained documents pertaining to the Holy Roman emperor and corresponded to the first two pages of the inventory, the third (surprisingly!) to the "Turkish" emperors in Constantinople. European monarchs from France and England to Poland found their places in boxes and pages 5 through 17, while lesser principalities and towns occupied the following boxes and pages through 45. A new series started with the papacy and cardinals (box 46) and continued with bishops, abbots and abbesses, and so forth. Waser's boxes and inventory thus tracked first the worldly and then the spiritual hierarchy of western Europe from top to bottom. To find material about a particular actor, a user did not rely on alphabetization, but only on the actor's rank in the hierarchies mapped onto the pages of Waser's *Index*. Eventually, to enable searching by specific names or places, Waser also laid out an alphabetical *Index specialis*, which allowed "matters that are connected [to] come together even if they are located in different boxes."

Critical similarities as well as important differences connect Montaigu's 1370 inventory and Waser's 1646 *Index generalis*. Each was a sophisticated finding tool created during the physical reorganization of an archive. Each archive relied on boxes as a key organizational unit, with each box or group dedicated to a single topic, often a domain or office. As a direct consequence, other features of documents—their material form, the context of their creation, and their genre—were subordinated in the finding system. A charter issued by the pope and a dossier about relations with the pope both belonged in Waser's box 1, for example. The logic by which these boxes were placed in their archives' space was very different, however. Montaigu placed his numbered boxes so that they would fill his armoires efficiently, although he sought to keep related material in the same general section. To allow users to find the right box, he depended on alphabetical indexes to topics more specific than the box titles. Waser started by organizing the boxes themselves into a systematic architecture, following the strategy that Rück identified as "mirroring relationships between the archival and the state organism" so that "the mental and material orders should match." This allowed Waser to defer the laborious work of indexing in favor of a summary index that was sufficient for most searches (although users' interest in particulars ultimately made an alphabetical register necessary, too). Alphabetical indexing and mapping according to the order of the world each solved the problem of too much material to recopy, but in very different ways. Still, each approach prioritized the content, not the administrative function or provenance, of the documents involved.

Fully Informed: Grand Schemes and Limited Practices in Sixteenth-Century Spain

Although traces of authentic actions remained a core concern for most involved, early modern chancelleries also sought to collect and control ever more information about multiple topics. The growing primacy of informing rulers becomes particularly visible in several projects launched by King Philip II of Spain during his long reign from 1556 to 1598. The earliest evidence of Philip's approach appears in a memorial that his humanist adviser Juan Páez de Castro submitted to the then crown prince in 1555. Páez proposed that Philip establish a new knowledge center with three major chambers: the first would contain a library of books, the second would collect maps and scientific instruments useful in geography and seafaring, and the third would include crucial charters from the pope or pertaining to the royal family, but also reports from agents in the Indies and across Europe. After ascending the throne, Philip created several institutions that embodied this plan, including the royal archive in Simancas outside Valladolid and the royal library at his monastery-palace at El Escorial. At these and additional sites, the founding documents called for the creation of guides in book form that would help in finding information. At each site, as well, a "libro de hystoria" was ordained, whose purpose was to provide narrative highlights from the assembled materials.

In parallel with these collecting institutions, Philip and his agents also ordered enormous data-gathering projects across his realms in Iberia and around the world. A key figure, along with Páez de Castro, was Juan de Ovando, who first inspected, then led the Council of the Indies after 1567. During his inspection, many complaints arose about the council's ignorance, its susceptibility to corruption, and the spiritual harm to the Crown that abuse of the Indigenous peoples was causing. A powerful faction inspired by Bartolomé de las Casas complained that little was known about the Americas, and such information as did arrive was distorted by the self-interest of those who sent it. Ovando proposed that henceforth the council should follow a scheme much like Castro's, including a new codification of the laws, a new cosmographer-chronicler to collect information, and the creation of a new book of descriptions, constantly updated, to guide the council in its decision making. Whereas in the past, the council "had not had, and could not have information (*noticia*) about the Indies' affairs and those of each province, upon which governance can and must rest," henceforth "it is necessary that they have full information (*entera noticia*) of such affairs."

In response to Ovando's urging, the Spanish state turned to a familiar information tool, namely interrogatory questionnaires. Standardized questions already played an important role in Inquisition procedures, and Ovando had served as an Inquisitor before presiding over the Council of the Indies. The council's interrogatories ultimately reached many parts of the Spanish government in the Americas in printed form in 1577 and 1584; over two hundred responses trickled back to Spain, which are known as the *Relaciones Geográficas* (Geographical Accounts) A similar approach to gathering reports from parishes across Spain produced the parallel *Relaciones Topográficas* (Topographical Accounts) after 1574. Drawing on the humanist discipline of chorography (geographical description), the lists of questions asked for information about physical features, animals and plants, recent history, religious life, and Indigenous languages.

These initiatives in Spain display three important features: a desire to be comprehensively informed, the systematic establishment and organization of repositories, and broad questioning of royal agents to gain knowledge about local circumstances around the empire. The entire initiative, notably, served a king who notoriously so disliked face-to-face interaction and ceremonial events, preferring to manage affairs on paper, that he gained the epithet *rey papelero*, the paper king. Philip's initiatives produced results: the archive at Simancas and library at El Escorial were built and quickly filled, among other things with the reports arriving in response to royal interrogatories. Surprisingly, however, these enterprises had little impact on what the Spanish crown knew in the succeeding decades, or on how it made decisions. By the 1620s, when inspected by a royal commission, the archive in Simancas had become moribund, with much material disordered or lost. The *Relaciones Geográficas* and *Relaciones Topográficas*, meanwhile, were packed up and rarely accessed. Particularly surprising from a modern perspective is the absence of compilation of the data that came in. For example, the council asked local authorities to estimate the number of Hispanic and Indigenous people in each district—which local administrators loudly complained they had no means to do—but there is no evidence that the results were compiled to create statistics about the overall population. Indeed, the absence of statistical handling is typical for this period, as will be discussed below. Gathering information and creating sites to preserve it, though necessary for the operation of an information state, were not sufficient to bring it into being.

While the technical challenges involved in registering, copying, or indexing the rivers of paper flowing into Philip's chancelleries contributed to the meager results of his initiatives, early modern archival practice was also simply not oriented toward producing statistics (in the sense of calculated conclusions about the state as a whole). Behind even the most sophisticated early modern organization and indexing lay the assumption that archivists were there to reveal particulars about the world on demand—"to find at once and promptly whatever letter was sought by a particular person," as Montaigu had put it in the 1370s. Similar assumptions shaped approaches to organizing records, which continued to rely on pertinence—that is, records' connection to the outside world—as the natural approach to large accumulations of documents. Only when the administrative state itself became the primary frame of reference did it become urgent to categorize and use stored records primarily in relation to that state and its operations.

From Collection to Knowledge: The Riddle of the Emerging Bureaucratic Information State

An enormous amount of research shows that bureaucratic states with effective information management capabilities did evolve from the fifteenth to the eighteenth centuries, however unevenly, but the causes for this development remain controversial. Phenomena ranging from the rise of the bourgeoisie to intergenerational dynamics among elites have been proposed as the key driver, as have mechanical printing, colonial expansion, and climate change. Rather than adding to possible causes, the following section will focus on shifts in the relationships among political actors, stored records, and processes of information, with particular attention to the mundane techniques of gathering, organizing, and using written records that were employed to inform rulers and their agents. As the history of the largely fruitless Spanish *Relaciones* of the late sixteenth century shows, the mere gathering of reports was not enough. Despite commands from the highest level that every administrative officer should respond to a detailed list of specific questions, the Spanish *Relaciones* never became information in operative terms because the people with access to them did not frame them as comprehensive data about an imaginary but increasingly salient actor, the state.

Large-scale efforts to gather data were nothing new in the sixteenth century: we need only point to the English Domesday Book, completed in 1086, which described land tenancies in some thirteen thousand places. Enumerations of population became common in Italian cities by the late fourteenth century, and amazingly detailed tax rolls survive from towns as modest as Zurich (1467) and as prosperous as Florence (1427). The key point in defining information states is therefore not simply the accumulation of large amounts of recorded information, but rather how such records were understood and how they could be used. The discussion here will begin with two illustrative examples before reviewing more systematic approaches to collected data, such as the creation of censuses and cadastral maps. The final section on archival registry will argue that changes in archival practice reveal an intensification of information use and the consequent emergence of information states after 1600.

A first illustration of the challenges that early modern rulers faced in synthesizing information from a broad range of records comes from the France of Louis XIV. Fiscal oversight is one logical place to look for such synthesis: not only did the quantum nature of money make it easy to consolidate multiple records into sums or debits, but the maturation of double-entry *bookkeeping after 1500 also provided a clear method for transforming fiscal transactions into actionable information. Yet as Jacob Soll demonstrates for France, applying accounting tools to the monarchy's finances became possible only in the later seventeenth century. Despite many earlier demands for better accounting, Jean-Baptiste Colbert was the first to provide his king, Louis XIV, with compact budget documents for each year. These pocket ledgers (abrégés) started in 1669 and showed Louis the state's receipts and expenditures in major categories with year-to-year comparisons. The books were richly illuminated and compact enough that Louis could carry them in his sleeve for ready reference. In these short volumes, the finances of France as an ongoing fiscal-military enterprise became visible as a whole: the books thus represented France as single actor, the state—embodied, famously, in its king— that received income and incurred expenses.

In another corner of Europe a few years later, the Swiss city of Lucerne in 1698 illustrates another key shift in perspectives. In Lucerne, decades of poor order among the city's records (which covered the city, its rural territory, and its partners in the Swiss Confederation) finally provoked the construction of a dedicated repository in 1698, along with a reorganization of the documents by the city's chancellor, Johann Karl Balthasar. Balthasar found the records haphazardly arranged in a typical content-oriented system. He responded with two radical changes. The first was to separate out many older records that were rarely used, thus creating a true archive in the sense of papers withdrawn from routine use. The second was to completely reorganize how documents were ordered within the archival space. Instead of mirroring people and places in the external world, Balthasar's new organization rested on categories of state action, such as legal disputes, commerce, or cloisters. This switch—from nouns to verbs, so to speak—aligned the material with the evolving needs of Lucerne's rulers, who increasingly saw themselves as presiding over a state. Balthasar's reorganization project is revealing in another way. The new system revolved around a detailed index to the entire body of material, but this index was never completed, since local crises apparently drew the chancellor away from the project even before his death in 1703. A report commissioned a generation later showed that the entire archive was nearly unusable without an index. The sheer drudgery of information management in tediously copied parchment and paper books should never be ignored, and it lies behind many archival failures in the early modern period.

Information State Practices before the Nineteenth Century: Census, Cadaster, Registry

Studies of how comprehensive record collection projects like the Spanish *Relaciones* were *used* are still rare. Some research discusses censuses and cadastral maps, which became transformative genres of informational record in the eighteenth century. Comparing the evolution of census taking and cadaster making is useful because the first also invited quantification, and thus shared features with fiscal bookkeeping, whereas cadastral mapping, while equally valuable to the state, produced largely relational and visual rather than quantified knowledge. Other studies consider the appearance of educational tracks for state service, for example in the *Kameralwissenschaft* (Science of state service) that appeared at German universities after 1727, or the establishment of a chair in diplomatics whose graduates had a monopoly on validating archival records in Coimbra, Portugal, late in the eighteenth century. Such education was critical for fiscal management, which encouraged numeracy and quantification among the men who were trained in this way, but also required familiarity in reading and interpreting older records. Even less attention has been paid to the registry systems for tracking administrative processes that developed after 1500 in intimate connection with developing state machinery. Further research from the perspective of the history of information is still needed to understand the deep shifts in knowledge, practice, and culture that accompanied the emergence of both modern states and modern informational consciousness in Europe.

Counting the inhabitants of a territory or social group is an old and widely distributed practice around the globe, as the Roman etymology of the word census suggests. Control over citizens and knowing who owed revenue or military service were typical reasons to enumerate individuals both in Mediterranean antiquity and in European societies as they emerged in later periods. Most premodern enumerations did not include everyone, but only those households owing taxes or service, omitting the indigent and exempt. In Europe after the *Reformation, both the Catholic and the Protestant authorities began ordering local clerics to register births, marriages, and deaths, which transferred earlier concerns about controlling citizenship into the spiritual sphere. European authorities were willing to invest in extensive data collection for such ends, but little evidence suggests that early modern authorities used the resulting material to synthesize new information about the population as a whole. Inquisitors might use parish registers to help track down dissidents, and tax rolls could be used to distribute taxes within a community (often long after the data was obsolete), but even the simple totaling of population from such sources was rarely undertaken until the eighteenth century. Indeed, quantification itself has a history that begins surprisingly late in Europe; as Daniel Headrick notes, only in the *Enlightenment did Europeans come to the conclusion that "numbers could be used to analyze something other than money, such as population, health and illness, nature, or even divine Providence."

Some of the earliest efforts to use the data that states and other public actors were collecting took place in England, where private authors such as John Graunt (1620–74) and William Petty (1623–87) began compiling information about deaths published by London's parish clerks to understand the city's population. Petty coined the phrase "political arithmetic" to describe such calculations, which he attempted to apply to land values, manufacturing, navigation, agriculture, and other areas of public life as well.

By the late seventeenth century, the powerful incentives driving England's (and Europe's) fiscal-military states made state officials ever more interested in participating in such arithmetic and the synthesized information it could provide. Although this interest appeared under different names in each major kingdom—political arithmetic, political economy, Kameralwissenschaft—the forces driving it and the resources available for understanding populations and their characteristics were similar. The transition from record keeping that gathered information about individuals or families to censuses that sought to comprehend entire populations was complete only after 1800.

Another area in which statistical approaches emerged was the creation of cadasters, that is, systematic land maps showing the possessor of each parcel, forest, meadow, and so forth. In contrast to conventional topographic maps, which visually represent a terrain and its human geography, cadasters visually represent ownership as meticulously as possible, with topographical features playing a secondary role. Cadasters, not surprisingly, are closely linked to both tax collection and judicial disputes over land ownership, including the great disentangling of communal and individual rights over land that took place across Europe in the eighteenth and nineteenth centuries. Some land maps (usually not to scale and not comprehensive) had been created by landholders from Italy to the Netherlands in the late fifteenth and sixteenth centuries for their own use in tax collection. Other early efforts to visually represent landholding came from areas with strong communal traditions, such as the polder authorities, who maintained the dikes in the Netherlands. Only in the seventeenth century, however, did public authorities begin making comprehensive cadastral maps; as Roger Kain and Elizabeth Baigent conclude, these quickly became "a highly contentious instrument for the extension and consolidation of power, not just of the propertied individual, but of the nation-state and the capitalist system that underlies it."

The long-term enterprise to create systematic cadasters in the German principality of Hesse is described by Karin Gottschalk. Tax collection was a primary driver of the Hesse project. When traditional revenues failed to cover costs during the Thirty Years' War, a direct tax on real property, the *Kontribution*, had been introduced, which was made permanent after the war. The tax was levied on the basis of long-past statements of wealth, however, which led to a widespread perception of unfairness. After several failed starts, Hessian officials began creating a comprehensive cadaster in 1736, which was completed only in 1791—demonstrating just how many obstacles such projects faced. Tensions between central agents and local officials interested in preserving the status quo slowed progress, as did evolving survey technology and differing goals that divided the stakeholders in the process; as Gottschalk notes, "questions about which data [*Informationen*] should be collected and processed by which agents and at what accuracy kept being raised anew and answered differently."

The government's initial questionnaires for gathering data proved to be so unreliable that by 1750, the program ground to a halt after central commissions agreed with local complaints about the inconsistency of assessments. Meanwhile, the central authorities kept raising their expectations for the uniformity of results, causing repeated cycles of remapping and reregistration. When local maps and property lists were finalized, another problem immediately arose: with three copies—one held locally, one in the district's center, and one at the landgrave's court—keeping versions synchronized as properties changed hands proved to be impossible. Land gained new owners, or boundary stones were (often illegally) moved, but the registers were not updated. Even if the local version was up-to-date, moreover, reproducing the changes in the district and central copies was entirely beyond the capacity of this early modern administration. Nevertheless, central officers pursued ever-expanding expectations about the accuracy and amount of detail the newly created maps and land registers should include.

As the problem of synchronization shows, creating large bodies of data created considerable challenges for record keeping. Gathering systematic reports was relatively easy by the sixteenth century, though the responses to the *Relaciones* and the struggles over measurement in Hesse show that even collecting faced resistance. Rendering the collected data useful, and learning to see in them not just individual places and people, but also features of a new actor, the state, required greater effort, both technical and conceptual. This transformation clearly affected every part of European political culture, from intellectuals' debates over sovereignty to local communities' efforts to find a modus vivendi with increasingly obtrusive rulers and their book-toting bureaucrats.

In addition to supervising large data-gathering projects like censuses and cadasters, seventeenth- and eighteenth-century chancelleries also increased their ability to manage documents consistently, and thus to track matters of interest out in the world. A general term for this development is registry (from the German term *Registratur*), with three key features: (1) new administrative structures dedicated to managing documents and the information in them, with the documents (2) organized in ways that privileged the internal processes of the state involved and (3) intentionally held accessible to support decision making by rulers and their agents. Registry focused record keepers' attention on making and executing decisions within a political apparatus, rather than on circumstances beyond. In a registry, the outside world became raw material for state action, rather than providing the framework that shaped the internal architecture of the archives.

An early form of registry appeared in the book-form protocols that European cities began creating in the High Middle Ages. Items in such protocols were entered chronologically, which tended to dissociate people and conflicts from their circumstances and reduce them to one item on a list. Registers and protocol books in various political units grew in volume and became more specialized in their content over the sixteenth century, adding more and more *metadata that oriented individual records to contexts defined by offices, councils, or other state institutions. Such registers reveal that their creators were beginning to understand the state—an abstract entity, in principle—as the actor whose existence linked records over time. Registry further expanded this perspective by organizing records, in the first instance, by their relation to state processes rather than in relation to the world. The most intensive form of registry emerged in the north German and Netherlandish transaction-file registry (*Sachaktenregistratur*) after 1700, but related practices can be found in every city, lordship, and monarchy in western Europe.

Such systems have received relatively little scholarly attention, and the way that the sophisticated transaction-file registries of nineteenth-century Prussia and its neighbors developed still needs considerably study. Comparing the starting point and the end point of this process is nevertheless useful for tracking a fundamental shift in what political information meant. To simplify, for many early modern secretaries and archivists (and, by extension, scholars, merchants, and princes), information involved a process of communication from world to political actors, which took place when traces of a past action or situation (increasingly in writing) informed a political actor in the present. Records, when viewed from this perspective, consisted primarily of signs about the world. Logically enough, secretaries and archivists therefore preserved and organized records according to the action or circumstance they pertained to (pertinence, in archival science). They also developed sophisticated ways to articulate archival space and used the powerful technologies of the book to enable later users to find records according to the persons or places involved. This approach did not go away in the eighteenth century, to be sure, and persists in commonsense notions of archiving today. However, this orientation was supplemented and eventually superseded in state repositories by a different conception of information that derived from, and also shaped, new ways of organizing and accessing records. A symptomatic example of this new view appeared in the Lucerne reorganization of 1698: here, not the world, but the actions of a state provided the primary framework for accessing records.

As collected records across Europe expanded in volume and became differentiated into more categories, specialized agents emerged who could mediate between the user and the records. A key step in some German states, notably Brandenburg-Prussia, took place late in the seventeenth century, when a dedicated office, the Registratur, began supervising this mediation. When fully developed in the nineteenth century, this office stood between the world and the state apparatus, but also between the chancellery that gathered information and guided the deliberation of the ruler and his councils, on the one hand, and the archive (now meaning the corpus of closed cases) on the other. Incoming correspondence was all directed to the Registratur, where each item triggered the creation of a transaction file that was placed into a preexisting system of categories. Whether a petition from a subject, a query from a lower court about how to handle a case, or a bill for river dredging, each incoming message went into the same system. The Registratur added relevant past documents to the file and routed it to the appropriate officers and councils for deliberation. The authority's decision and the final communication of the outcome entered the same transaction file in the registry, all documented according to a complex tracking system.

In such a system, the term "information" gained a second, novel meaning: rather than being the process by which the world informed rulers, information became the raw material that entered the registry. Divided into categories and circulated in *coded documents, information in a registry became a thing, a substance to be processed by the state. The work of the state, from this perspective, consisted of identifying the right information and the right office to analyze it, leading to a decision (another piece of information) that could then be sent out into the world. The subject's petition was denied, the court was instructed how to sentence the defendant, and the dredger's bill was either paid or returned for further proof of work completed. Events and actions in the world were still vital to an administration that operated in this mode: "the whole business terminates in works," as Francis Bacon (himself an administrator) proclaimed. But for the offices involved—and specifically for their management of records—the world was approached through bundles of information that could be stored, moved, divided, categorized, and otherwise processed to reach a decision. At every step, the organization of records revolved around their place in an administrative process, carried out not by a fully informed lord but by the state itself. As the most famous eighteenth-century Prussian king, Frederick II, put it, he was simply the first servant of the state.

The archival principle that (slowly) captured this new orientation—in which documents are organized by and for the institutional actor that produces or collects them—is provenance or *respect des fonds*. Provenance rests on the following argument: because state records are meaningful primarily in the context of the actions of a state and its agents, only preservation in the order created by the state's offices can preserve their intelligibility. If removed from their transactional context, their meaning will be corrupted or lost. Therefore, the shift from pertinence to provenance in archival theory is one marker of shift from public records as evidence about the world itself to records as evidence about administrative processes by which a state deals with the world.

BEYOND TEXTS IN POLITICAL INFORMATION PROCESSES

While writing played a central role in the transmission of political information in Europe from at least the thirteenth century, other ways to communicate information remained important. Research has begun exploring many of these ways, such as ritual forms that recapitulated important informational moments and architectural and other monumental self-representations erected by rulers and communities. Moreover, we must not imagine that the sphere of dusty records tediously scrutinized by withered clerks was separate from alternate spheres of public performance or celebration. Political information flowed through various channels by means of different media in ways that ensured no sharp boundaries existed between written, oral, and sensory information. In addition, European political actors were perfectly capable of self-conscious reflection about how they became informed, and to combine or distinguish different informational channels when it suited them. The world of political paperwork provides only one perspective on a more complex world.

Francis Bacon's epigram cited above offers one way to approach the wider universe of nontextual informational processes. Information commences with the senses, he claimed, and ends with works, that is with human action. Recent historical research on the senses—hearing, smell, even touch—makes it clear that each could provide a channel, given appropriate media, for signs to move from the world into human minds. A first challenge in considering such forms of information lies in the ephemerality of much sensory experience: smells and sounds are difficult to record directly and largely lack a shared language for preserving traces of them. Sight—the sense most at work in reading written records—can be evanescent, too, but the marks that provoke it are not, since writing preserves traces of language in a durable visual medium, making them seemingly easy to recover or reperform. It is this ease enabled by writing, as much as the durability of paper and parchment per se, that lies behind the way that written material predominates in most historical research and analysis. However, visual images can be analyzed according to the grammar of iconology and iconography, and ceremonies too have their own structures and rhetorical dimensions. Discussions of visual and ceremonial communication and how they can create recorded traces therefore offer rich potential for information history.

INFORMATION AND TRUTH IN EARLY MODERN EUROPE

So far, this essay has not addressed questions of truth in political information—that is, whether the insights that early modern European rulers and their growing staffs of officers derived from the information available to them corresponded to conditions in the larger world. This is because actors became informed through reading official records whether or not the records were authentic, accurate, or manipulated. In reality, however, chancellors, secretaries, and princes were acutely aware of how unreliable records could be: erroneous, incomplete, or actively forged to misrepresent the truth. To assess the reliability of records, these agents first turned to their religious and legal frameworks to assess whether what they read was trustworthy, and to sharpen their ability to discern misinformation. The oaths that accompanied much record making threatened eternal sanction for false statements, while a large body of legal literature reaching well back into the Middle Ages addressed problematic evidence by establishing criteria for trusting some records and dismissing others.

In addition to assessing records' truth, any work with durable informational traces has to confront the many possibilities that existed for loss and silencing. Loss was possible in multiple ways, even within the paradigm that described charters as authentic traces of authorized actions, and only grew in importance as the scope of recorded information expanded. In the first place, recording anything in textual form necessarily left out much about the record it claimed to describe. Such omission was inevitable, and indeed necessary: records concentrated on what seemed important to the actors involved while parsing out everything from the weather on the day a charter was issued to what the king had for breakfast. Omissions could also be entirely intentional, like the missing witnesses that were so important in the charters analyzed by Koziol (discussed above). In a context where the absence of certain words or people could convey meaning just as much as their presence, omission was both effective and largely invisible to later readers. Such processes of omission and silencing, inherent in the recording of information, also enabled the exercise of power in part by blotting out knowledge about much of life—notably, the life of those excluded from power by their race, gender, religious difference, or other forms of subalternity, as trenchantly analyzed by Michel-Rolph Trouillot.

Loss could take place later as well. Beyond the traditional archival terrors of fire, flood, and hungry vermin, documents could fade or be stolen, altered, or simply misplaced. Another cycle of loss began at the moment of rereading, especially when this took place long after the material had been written down. Changes in language or legal expectations could make what had been clear at one time cryptic or incomprehensible later. The Swiss villagers' assumption that someone from the village had to be present to understand their statutes shows considerable hermeneutic sophistication on their part: they recognized that without their contribution, an outsider might simply fail to comprehend the intention of a village bylaw or a description of its boundaries.

Beyond issues of truth and silencing, the commodification of information implicit in the early modern developments raised further challenges to the reliability and accessibility of records and the information processes they enabled. Most obvious are the various forms of concealment or censorship of documents and their texts that early modern states were happy to undertake. Denying particular parties access to the archives was routine (whether they requested a specific document known to exist or sought to search for records about some issue). At least formally, archives and chancellery papers were closed to anyone not authorized by the ruler, and secretaries' oaths of service contained detailed stipulations about not reading, copying, or otherwise circulating anything without explicit orders from above. A notorious example appears in the Venetian archives' policy of appointing only illiterates as service personnel in the Archivio Segreto—though as Filippo de Vivo shows, such prohibitions had become little more than a formalized pretense by the seventeenth century. In Spain, access to material in Simancas required an authorization signed personally by the king, while litigants seeking information about events in the Indies were generally turned away, and some documents were kept in chests to which even the archivists lacked a key. Like political information in other media, the history of misinformation and disinformation is an open topic waiting for more research. From spies and codes to the material fate of records during wars, floods, and fires, political information was never a passive and fixed quantity.

As information became increasingly packaged and commodified, financial incentives to hide or reveal it grew, leading to veritable information markets. In Venice, the detailed reports filed by the city's ambassadors across Europe and in the Ottoman sphere became desirable commodities owing to the trust that readers developed in the legates' perspicuity. As de Vivo shows, transcripts of these *Relazioni* were available for sale in the city and beyond, despite repeated prohibitions, giving rise to an entire economy of political knowledge emanating from the Venetian chancellery. Print provided another avenue for both welcome and unwelcome divulgence of political records from Europe's chancelleries. By the early seventeenth century, much political literature—especially the more polemical sort—included an appendix of "genuine" documents to support the author's points. Erudite scholars (who often worked in the chancelleries and administrations) jumped on board, so that by midcentury thousands of pages of documents could be consulted by learned readers. Even petty oligarchs in political backwaters joined the game: in 1622, amid invasions, political murders, and the plague, one local faction in the Swiss Grisons added twenty-nine documents from between 1289 and 1570 (translated into contemporary German) to a print manifesto protesting an Austrian military occupation. Naturally, the ability of various parties to publish documents favoring their arguments encouraged authorities with opposing views to censor such books, which in turn encouraged curious buyers to seek them out and savvy printers to churn out new editions. A complex overlap developed in the print world between political and commercial interests, and between affairs of state and public rhetoric, which supplemented the older world of face-to-face and manuscript circulation of information.

Ultimately, it follows from the fraught nature of human communication that political information in early modern Europe—and in any society—remained dynamic and unstable in both process and content. The manifest significance of changing information practices for any society has been highlighted by recent research in media and memory studies and finds considerable resonance in recent investigations into early modern humanist practices such as making *commonplace notebooks. At the intersection of these trends, a few scholars have suggested that the changing ways that European intellectuals and secretaries coped with the flood of "too much to know" had consequences not only for politics and erudition, but also for the cognitive structures of

European readers. Following in the footsteps of Marshall McLuhan, Alberto Cevolini and Markus Krajewski each analyze the evolution of card-filing systems, as found first in bibliographical and encyclopedic projects and eventually in libraries and archives. Cevolini claims that card files brought about a "radical transformation to the relationship between memory and time" by parcelizing knowledge in ways that fundamentally changed how intellectuals found, managed, and circulated texts. Ann Blair has also explored how the development of reference books since the Middle Ages drove the trend toward packaging information in discrete parcels—whether as index entries, index cards, or *encyclopedia entries—while at the same time creating networks of linkages among them. So far, the consideration of how such techniques found entry into secretarial and political contexts has scarcely begun; we need to investigate what was taking place in chancelleries as well as in scholars' studies much better before we can understand the implications of new excerpting and organizing practices for thought and society.

CONCLUSION

Close examination of official record keeping in post-medieval Europe suggests that unraveling the shifting cultural foundations from the practical architecture of information orders as they existed in different contexts can reveal new perspectives on multiple developments. Behind European cultures of record keeping lay the contentious ways Europeans understood the human political order with its spiritual and legal foundations, as well as the channels of communication at different scales that crisscrossed European societies. Correspondingly, behind European information architectures lay the media technologies by which political communication was transacted and embodied and the durable traces of such communication that accumulated in the hands of various political actors in rapidly increasing volumes after the fourteenth century.

Turning first to the symbiosis between political communication and the evolving political order in western Europe after 1400, the evidence presented above offers fresh perspectives on a very old question, namely the transformation of Europe from a patchwork of domains into a system of increasingly national states. Comparing the way various polities organized their records helps us understand not only what kings and chancellors could know, but also how they understood the political landscape on which they operated. Two broad organizational principles predominated through most of the early modern period. The first was that a repository's organization should privilege key actors outside the repository in the political world, such as emperors, kings, popes, and so on. The second was that the most important purpose of accumulated records was to memorialize the authentic actions of particular actors in the form of proofs that could be "drawn like weapons" in later contention. Even as archivists differentiated more genres of documents and accumulated more informational records, these priorities—in concord with medieval understandings of political order—continued to predominate in archives large and small. Meanwhile, the book technologies developed by medieval Scholasticism provided powerful tools for implementing rulers' and their officers' understanding of how records could and should be used.

By the sixteenth century, motivated in part by critical perspectives from humanism but also by the capacities of Scholastic media tools and by Europeans' confrontation with Asia and the Americas, chancelleries across Europe began collecting information in larger amounts than they ever had before. Agents at every level received commandments to send more reports to central offices: parish priests had to record baptisms, marriages, and deaths; citizens had to declare their wealth for taxation; and in Spain, the Crown circulated extensive questionnaires throughout its new empire in search of information. Meanwhile, the growing effectiveness of archival tools created new possibilities for information tracking and management. Although the media that were used (paper, writing, boxes, strings) and the available media technologies (alphabetization, registers, topographic and chronological articulation of storage spaces) changed very slowly if at all, the simple fact of accumulation in ordered spaces by increasingly professional staff created new opportunities for use and action.

Most importantly, as seen in initiatives for systematic censuses and cadasters, and even more through the development of registry techniques that categorized and managed documents in relation to their place in a state's decision-making processes, the growing mounds of paperwork accumulating across Europe made a new actor legible and intelligible, namely the abstract state itself. Combining old conceptions of office with a proliferation of specialized officers (often to the anger of traditional noble elites), this state became visible through its paperwork practices in resonance with emerging theoretical discussions of sovereignty (Bodin), unitary state power (Hobbes), and state service (German Kameralwissenschaft). Like these theories, the practices emerging in chancelleries and the capabilities for deploying information offered by registries did not at first directly challenge older regimes of kinship-based princely dominion and documents viewed as proofs of privilege. What they did do was to add a new layer of reified information, whose practical successes and ideological implications eventually transformed Europe's political information orders.

Randolph C. Head

See also archivists; bureaucracy; cards; governance; indexing; information, disinformation, misinformation; information policy; letters; merchants; secretaries

FURTHER READING

C. A. Bayly, *Empire and Information: Intelligence Gathering and Social Communication in India, 1780–1870*, 1996; Ann Blair, *Too Much to Know: Managing Scholarly Information before the Modern Age*, 2010; Arndt Brendecke, *The Empirical Empire: Spanish Colonial Rule and the Politics of Knowledge*, 2009, translation by Jeremiah Riemer, 2016; Peter Brun, *Schrift und politisches Handeln: Eine "zugeschriebene" Geschichte des Aargaus 1415–1425*, 2006; Alberto Cevolini, *Forgetting Machines: Knowledge Management Evolution in Early Modern Europe*, 2016; M. H.-François Delaborde, "Les Inventaires du Trésor des Chartes Dressés par Gérard de Montaigu," in *Notices et Extraits des Manuscrits de la Bibliothèque Nationale et autres Bibliothèques*, vol. 36, pt. 2, 1900; Filippo de Vivo, *Information and Communication in Venice: Rethinking Early Modern Politics*, 2007; Markus Friedrich, *The Birth of the Archive: A History of Knowledge*, 2013, translated by John-Noël Dillon, 2018; Karin Gottschalk, "Wissen über Land und Leute: Administrative Praktiken und Staatsbildungsprozesse im 18. Jahrhundert," in *Das Wissen des Staates: Geschichte, Theorie und Praxis*, edited by Peter Collin and Thomas Horstmanneds, 2004; Randolph Head, *Making Archives in Early Modern Europe: Proof, Information, and Political Record-Keeping, 1400–1700*, 2019; Edward Higgs, *The Information State in England: The Central Collection of Information on Citizens since 1500*, 2004; Roger Kain and Elizabeth Baigent, *The Cadastral Map in the Service of the State: A History of Property Mapping,*

1984; Geoffrey Koziol, *The Politics of Memory and Identity in Carolingian Royal Diplomas: The West Frankish Kingdom (840–987)*, 2012; Markus Krajewski, *Paper Machines: About Cards and Catalogs, 1548–1929*, 2002, translated by Peter Krapp, 2011; Ron Makleff, "Sovereignty and Silence: The Creation of a Myth of Archival Destruction, Liège, 1408," *Archival Journal* (2017); Marshall McLuhan, *The Gutenberg Galaxy: The Making of Typographic Man*, 1962; Jose Luis Rodríguez de Diego, *Memoria Escrita de la Monarquia Hispanica: Felipe II y Simancas*, 2018; Peter Rück, "Die Ordnung der herzoglich savoyischen Archive unter Amadeus VIII (1398–1451)," *Archivalische Zeitschrift* 67 (1971): 11–101; Andrea Rusnock, *Vital Accounts: Quantifying Health and Population in Eighteenth-Century England and France*, 2002; James C. Scott, *Seeing Like a State: How Certain Schemes to Improve the Human Condition Have Failed*, 1998; Jacob Soll, *The Information Master: Jean-Baptiste Colbert's Secret State Intelligence System*, 2009; Simon Teuscher, *Lords' Rights and Peasant Stories: Writing and the Formation of Tradition in the Later Middle Ages*, 2007, translated by Philip Grace, 2012; Michel-Rolph Trouillot, *Silencing the Past: Power and the Production of History*, 1995; Cornelia Vismann, *Files: Law and Media Technology*, 2000, translated by Geoffrey Winthrop-Young, 2008; Geoffrey Yeo, *Records, Information and Data: Exploring the Role of Record-Keeping in an Information Culture*, 2018; Cornel Zwierlein, ed., *The Dark Side of Knowledge: Histories of Ignorance, 1400 to 1800*, 2016.

7

PERIODICALS AND THE COMMERCIALIZATION OF INFORMATION IN THE EARLY MODERN ERA

This chapter emphasizes two long-term changes: the commercialization of timely information and the proliferation of periodical publications. The two phenomena were linked, and together they had profound effects on the information cultures that developed in many parts of the world in the seventeenth and eighteenth centuries. There are earlier examples of treating information as a commercial product and of publishing at somewhat regular intervals; calendars and almanacs, for example, had long been produced annually. But beginning in the seventeenth century, commercialization and periodicity combined to create new forms of publication that were to have remarkable futures. These included newspapers, magazines, and learned journals as well as specialized periodicals covering commerce, urban health, and criminal justice. The story was not the same in Spain or Russia as it was in the British Isles or North America, not to mention South Asia, the Middle East, or the islands of the Caribbean. But the overall pattern is unmistakable: by around 1800, a growing number of periodicals containing reports of recent developments—in politics, commerce, science, literature, and other areas of inquiry—were transforming the information landscape.

Periodicals are open-ended publications (with no end date announced) issued at regular intervals (daily, weekly, monthly, and so on) and with a stable title or other recognizable features, such as a consistent format or numbering. There is nothing natural about publishing information on a regular schedule, and to the extent that we can speak of the rise of periodicals it was a process that involved experimentation, adaptation to local circumstances, a fair amount of risk, and quite a bit of failure. But over time periodicals became the medium of choice for the rapid exchange and discussion of information in many domains. The success of periodicals did not result from the inherent advantages or affordances of periodicity so much as from the strategies and conventions developed over time by writers, printers, government officials, advertisers, and readers. Individuals and groups developed formats and modes of distribution that they exploited to achieve various goals.

By commercialization I mean simply the process of turning something into a product that can be sold. Of course, information of various sorts was exchanged among individuals without any expectation of a monetary transaction, and the business of selling information should not be conflated with the broader cultural experiences of information in any given time and place. But there is little doubt that contemporaries in the seventeenth and eighteenth centuries perceived a process that can be referred to as the commercialization of timely information. By the 1620s, when the Thirty Years' War (1618–48) increased demand for foreign news and the ongoing expansion of postal networks facilitated the more regular delivery of this news across Europe, the English playwright Ben Jonson could mock the greed of printers and the gullibility of readers caught up in the incipient news cycles of his day. The title of one of Jonson's plays—*The Staple of News* (first performed in 1625)—evoked the sense that news had become a commodity that flowed into and out of the merchant's emporium or staple. Some contemporaries indeed used the term *commodity* to describe the way reports of recent events were being sold for a profit. Samuel Butler, another English writer of the seventeenth century, defined a newsmonger as "a retailer of rumor" who "deals in a perishable commodity, that will not keep. . . . True or false is all one to him; for novelty being the grace of both, a truth goes stale as soon as a lie." It was the timeliness of news that made it a viable commercial product, which in turn raised questions of authenticity and trustworthiness.

News and other sorts of information were sold in various forms, including books, pamphlets, and broadsides, but it was the open-ended nature of periodicals that troubled critics most. Periodicals created an appetite among readers, a forum for ongoing discussion, and an obligation to fill the available space even in the absence of verifiable reports. While critics worried about the financial and political interests that shaped accounts, authorities weighed the benefits and risks of setting up official periodicals or tolerating unofficial ones. It was periodicity combined with commercialization that created the first news cycles, for better and for worse.

And yet periodicity did not just affect the world of political and military news; it also structured information about commerce, literature, and scientific endeavor. In the late seventeenth century, the editors of the first scientific and literary journals highlighted the advantages of publishing timely reports at regular intervals. During the eighteenth century, writers in many places celebrated the role of journals in spreading *enlightenment and facilitating discussion of economic, social, and philosophical questions. By the end of the century, faith in the newspaper as a democratic medium was expressed by leaders on both sides of the Atlantic. Individuals highlighted the capacity of newspapers to foster an informed citizenry by relaying information cheaply and quickly over vast distances. These ideals were not always realized, but their expression became commonplace. Information in the form of reference books, maps, and single-sheet broadsides remained important, but regular and timely access to newspapers and other periodicals was increasingly seen as vital to understanding the world and effecting change within it.

Even in areas where printing presses did not exist, the proliferation of periodicals could still be felt. Periodicals traveled alongside letters in the post, reaching readers in far-flung places. And periodicals did not have to be printed. Manuscript newsletters were also periodicals that made timely information available in exchange for money. The audience for newsletters was more restricted, but they were a semipublic form of correspondence that continued to matter long after the creation of the first printed newspapers. For example, by the late eighteenth century, a number of printed gazettes and journals circulated in the Italian peninsula and in France, but the manuscript accounts known as *avvisi* and *nouvelles à la main* continued to attract subscribers because they provided information that could not be printed for reasons of censorship. Even in Britain, where prepublication censorship effectively ended in 1695, handwritten newsletters remained crucial for certain kinds of information—such as parliamentary proceedings—well into the eighteenth century. Newsletters also thrived in places without a printed newspaper, such as Iceland before the 1790s and many areas of Latin America during the wars of independence in the early nineteenth century. In India, there were no printed newspapers until the 1780s, and none in Indigenous languages until the 1820s. But the English-language and *vernacular Indian press built on a rich information ecosystem that included newsletters known as *akhbarats*, which were produced by professional news writers on behalf of rulers who paid for regular updates from other regions. These were the Indian counterparts to the newsletters in multiple languages that circulated through the expanding postal networks of Europe.

Without a functioning postal system, the collection and distribution of timely information in periodical form would have been next to impossible. Printed periodicals, like manuscript newsletters, were embedded in correspondence networks because their editors relied on information that arrived in the mail to fill their columns. The *publishers then used the post to distribute their final product to subscribers. Postal schedules enabled weekly publication in many places and semiweekly or triweekly publication in some places. Daily publication was reserved to a few cities where the concentration of customers and sufficient local sources of information made it viable. Working in tandem and traveling together in the mail, letters and periodicals connected people and facilitated the circulation of information of all sorts. The way periodicals and correspondence reinforced each other enabled information to travel faster and farther than before and encouraged the development of what Brendan Dooley has called "contemporaneity"—the sense among individuals in different places that they were living through a shared present, paying attention to the same events.

In reality, communication over vast distances was unpredictable and often frustrating. But the fact that people were expecting more regular updates was an important development. The quantity and variety of information that was publicly available was not everywhere the same, and within a given society access to information depended on one's location, social status, gender, race, professional affiliations, degree of *literacy, and other factors. But by 1800 individuals in many places sought out timely information and looked for ways to manage that information to advance their goals in the present. These were not information societies in the sense that the production of information was the primary economic activity—far from it. But these were societies in which information was increasingly seen as an important factor in political, economic, intellectual, and social life.

Recent scholarship has emphasized the benefits of studying the interaction of oral, written, and printed media as well as the need to avoid the reification of "print culture" and teleological narratives of the rise of the newspaper. The chronology of printing and the types of periodicals produced varied by place. Moreover, the fact that a newspaper or journal existed somewhere does not tell us how people at the time used it in relation to other sources of information at their disposal. In many places and fields of inquiry, printed periodicals could not compete for freshness or level of detail with what individuals could learn through conversation and private letters. Information came in many forms, and the emphasis here on periodicals does not mean that other modes of communication were not important to people at the time.

But if we take a long view of the history of information—rather than trying to understand all the ways information mattered in a given context—then one fruitful way to think about the *early modern period is to highlight the growth in the number and variety of publications that were delivered at regular intervals and devoted to information about recent occurrences. This process began with the creation of the business press in the sixteenth century and entered a new phase with the development of printed newspapers and scientific journals during the seventeenth century. This chapter covers these early developments before turning to the eighteenth century, which witnessed major changes in the scale, density, and perceived significance of periodicals as media of enlightenment and revolution.

THE PUBLICITY OF COMMERCE AND URBAN HEALTH

It is nearly impossible to sell information independently of its representation in words, figures, or illustrations. Information can be shared without any financial transaction, but it cannot be sold unless it is embedded in some material object—such as a handwritten newsletter or a printed pamphlet—or part of some service—such as a subscription reading room where the information is displayed. Information is nonrivalrous (one person's enjoyment does not diminish the quantity available for others) and only partly excludable (publishers can charge for access, but information permeates most borders). In the case of a printed ballad or a newspaper, for example, some people purchased copies while others learned the information by listening to the ballad sung on the street or by perusing the newspaper in a *coffeehouse. Still, the availability of this information to the public generally depended on its appearance in publications that were produced in order to be sold.

Specialists of the history of news, including C. John Sommerville, Joad Raymond, and Andrew Pettegree, have pointed out that periodicals were not the most obvious or efficient way of commercializing news. When an event occurred that seemed likely to interest paying customers, it often made more sense to issue a broadside or pamphlet, both of which could be produced quickly, cheaply, and anonymously. Periodicals required a production schedule in a fixed location—which made them easier for the authorities to monitor—and a continuous supply of copy. Events of public concern do not normally occur on a predictable schedule, though news publishers have long been attracted to events that are announced in advance, such as ceremonies, trials, and public executions. Ongoing events such as wars and treaty negotiations also lent themselves to publishing in installments, and some periodicals engaged in speculative commentary while awaiting confirmation of what actually happened. But many writers and publishers censored their comments in order to avoid trouble with the local authorities. Independent of the question of censorship, periodical publication required that there was something to print and that it arrived in time to go to press. In the case of reporting foreign news, this problem was overcome gradually as a result of the creation of more regular and reliable mail services after 1600. The fact that the first weekly newspapers developed only in the early seventeenth century, about 150 years after the invention of printing, is due in large part to the expansion of private and public postal networks.

A specialized business press developed even earlier. Indeed, the first printed periodicals devoted to timely information focused on commerce rather than politics or diplomacy. Merchants and brokers needed reliable sources of information about market conditions, such as the prices of goods and the movement of ships. Such information had long been exchanged in private letters, and much of it had been closely guarded since knowledge of market conditions could be a serious advantage in trade. But beginning in the mid-sixteenth century, as John McCusker has shown, merchants in important trading centers in the Italian peninsula and northern Europe adopted a new approach. They recognized that publicizing certain kinds of information on a regular basis was mutually beneficial. The result was the creation of commodity price currents, which were single-sheet publications listing the prices at which goods were trading, and exchange rate currents, which itemized the rates at which foreign bills were being exchanged locally. Though specialized, these business papers were to provide a model for subsequent newspapers and journals.

The earliest surviving printed price currents are from the 1580s in Frankfurt, Amsterdam, and Venice, but there is evidence that they existed in Antwerp as early as 1540 and probably even earlier in Italy. Exchange rate currents soon followed. Florence had one by 1598, though it seems likely that the French city of Lyon, whose international trading fair also served as a major money market, had one as early as the 1550s. By the early seventeenth century, many trading centers had either commodity price currents or exchange rate currents or both. Amsterdam had a price current by 1585, Hamburg probably by 1592, and London from at least 1600. Eventually they existed in ports on the Mediterranean and the Atlantic, such as Lisbon, Bordeaux, and Cádiz. This chronology makes sense. The Italian cities were the center of trade in the fourteenth and fifteenth centuries. In the mid- to late sixteenth century, Antwerp was the most important hub of commercial news, but by the early seventeenth century Amsterdam had taken over. In 1617, the English diplomat James Howell was able to refer to Amsterdam as the "Great Staple of News," using the same term that Jonson would for his satire of news culture a few years later. The Amsterdam price currents were available not only in Dutch but also in English, French, and Italian, making them useful to merchants across Europe. During the Dutch golden age, the prices at Amsterdam served as a benchmark; though a broker might have fresher information or find a way to buy lower or sell higher, the published weekly prices remained an important international reference.

The sale of commercial information at regular intervals represented a conscious effort to use publicity to promote certain interests. In Amsterdam, for example, members of the *guild that ran the *beurs* or exchange envisioned the publication of an officially sanctioned price current as a means of attracting more buyers and sellers to Amsterdam. The municipal authorities also recognized that carefully managing the flow of information could help boost the local economy. Individual merchants and brokers also benefited from access to a trusted source that other traders were also using. The adoption of such benchmarks lowered the cost of gathering information and reduced risk. Finally, these business newspapers were profitable ventures in themselves—profitable enough, in fact, to lead members of the exchange to outbid each other to have the privilege of being the official *courantier*. Such privileges constituted an official monopoly on a whole category of information for which merchants were willing to pay. The brokers' guild that ran the exchange had an interest in making sure the information was accurate and reserved the right to cancel the privilege and assign it to a more trustworthy courantier.

Over time, London overtook Amsterdam as the single most important hub of commercial information, and its business press took off. In seventeenth-century England, as in the Low Countries, business periodicals were treated as official monopolies governed by privileges. In addition to price currents, there were bills of entry, which provided a digest of the goods entered in the custom house books, and marine lists, which detailed arriving and departing ships. These were all published as periodicals protected by letters patent. In the 1690s, the creation of the Bank of England and the growth in joint-stock companies spawned a new kind of business paper: the stock-exchange current. This was not protected by patent, and there was competition in this field at times—such as in the years leading up to the South Sea Bubble of 1720—but in most decades merchants and brokers gravitated toward a single source, John Castaing's *Course of the Exchange* (see figure 1).

Price currents offer a good example of how publishing a periodical by subscription helped overcome a paradox identified by the economist Kenneth Arrow. Most people want to know what they are buying before they commit to paying. But Arrow pointed out that when it comes to information, if customers are allowed to see the product—or enough of it to ascertain its value to them—then their incentive to purchase that information is reduced. Periodicals sold by subscription provided a solution for cases in which individuals wanted timely access to information of a certain kind. Merchants and brokers wanted the latest prices, whatever they might be, and they were willing to pay an annual fee to receive them from a trusted source. They might not use the price current every week, but it was better to have access just in case. Meanwhile, for the publisher, selling by subscription meant having dedicated customers in known locations; that made it easier to know how many copies to produce and where to deliver them. These factors provided an incentive for the ongoing collection and distribution of certain kinds of information.

Another area where regular updates of numerical data underpinned a long-standing periodical was what we would now call vital statistics. The rather exceptional example here is the London bills of mortality, which provided weekly updates on the number of christenings and burials (especially plague burials) in each parish of London, Westminster, and nearby districts. The collection of this information was of interest to the English monarchy and the City of London, but details leaked out in manuscript copies from the late sixteenth century, and starting in 1603 (a plague year) printed copies were sold to the public through annual subscription and one-off street sales. By the following decade, the Worshipful Company of Parish Clerks had a royal charter recognizing its duty to deliver weekly reports to the authorities and the exclusive right to sell bills of mortality to the public. The clerk of each parish tallied the christenings and burials in his district and relied on individuals known as searchers, usually elderly women supported by the parish, to determine the cause of death of each victim. These weekly tallies

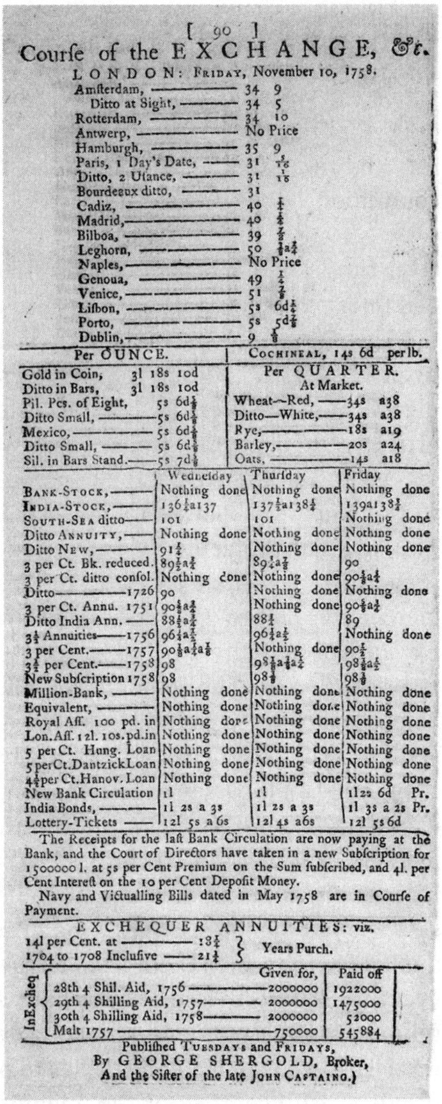

[90]

Course of the EXCHANGE, &c.

LONDON: Friday, November 10, 1758.

Amsterdam,	34 9
Ditto at Sight,	34 5
Rotterdam,	34 10
Antwerp,	No Price
Hamburgh,	35 9
Paris, 1 Day's Date,	31 5/16
Ditto, 2 Usance,	31 1/16
Bourdeaux ditto,	31
Cadiz,	40 1/2
Madrid,	40 1/4
Bilboa,	39 7/8
Leghorn,	50 1/8 a 1/4
Naples,	No Price
Genoua,	49 1/4
Venice,	51 7/8
Lisbon,	5s 6d 1/4
Porto,	5s 5d 7/8
Dublin,	9 1/8

Per OUNCE.		Cochineal, 14s 6d per lb.	
Gold in Coin,	3l 18s 10d	Per QUARTER. At Market.	
Ditto in Bars,	3l 18s 10d		
Pil. Pcs. of Eight,	5s 6d 5/8	Wheat—Red,	34s a38
Ditto Small,	5s 6d 5/8	Ditto—White,	34s a38
Mexico,	5s 6d 5/8	Rye,	18s a19
Ditto Small,	5s 6d 5/8	Barley,	20s a24
Sil. in Bars Stand.	5s 7d 1/8	Oats,	14s a18

	Wednesday	Thursday	Friday
Bank-Stock,	Nothing done	Nothing done	Nothing done
India-Stock,	136 1/4 a137	137 1/2 a138 1/4	139a138 3/4
South-Sea ditto	101	101	Nothing done
Ditto Annuity,	Nothing done	Nothing done	Nothing done
Ditto New,	91 1/4	Nothing done	Nothing done
3 per Ct. Bk. reduced.	89 1/2 a 3/4	89 1/4 a 7/8	90
3 per Ct. ditto consol.	Nothing done	Nothing done	90 1/8 a 1/4
Ditto 1726	90	Nothing done	Nothing done
3 per Ct. Annu. 1751	90 5/8 a 3/4	Nothing done	90 5/8 a 3/4
Ditto India Ann.	88 1/2 a 3/4	88 1/4	89
3 1/2 Annuities 1756	96 1/4 a 1/2	96 1/4 a 1/2	Nothing done
3 per Cent. 1757	90 1/8 a 1/4 a 1/8	Nothing done	90 1/2
3 1/2 per Cent. 1758	98	98 1/8 a 3/8 a 1/4	98 3/8 a 1/2
New Subscription 1758	98	98 3/8	98 3/8
Million-Bank,	Nothing done	Nothing done	Nothing done
Equivalent,	Nothing done	Nothing done	Nothing done
Royal Aff. 100 pd. in	Nothing done	Nothing done	Nothing done
Lon. Aff. 12l. 10s. pd. in	Nothing done	Nothing done	Nothing done
5 per Ct. Hung. Loan	Nothing done	Nothing done	Nothing done
5 per Ct. Dantzick Loan	Nothing done	Nothing done	Nothing done
4 1/2 per Ct. Hanov. Loan	Nothing done	Nothing done	Nothing done
New Bank Circulation	1l	1l	1l 2s 6d Pr.
India Bonds,	1l 2s a 3s	1l 2s a 3s	1l 3s a 2s Pr.
Lottery-Tickets	12l 5s a 6s	12l 4s a6s	12l 5s 6d

The Receipts for the last Bank Circulation are now paying at the Bank, and the Court of Directors have taken in a new Subscription for 1500000 l. at 5s per Cent Premium on the Sum subscribed, and 4l. per Cent Interest on the 10 per Cent Deposit Money.

Navy and Victualling Bills dated in May 1758 are in Course of Payment.

EXCHEQUER ANNUITIES: viz.

14l per Cent. at — 18 1/4 } Years Purch.
1704 to 1708 Inclusive — 21 1/4 }

In Excheq	Given for,	Paid off
28th 4 Shil. Aid, 1756	2000000	1922000
29th 4 Shilling Aid, 1757	2000000	1475000
30th 4 Shilling Aid, 1758	2000000	52000
Malt 1757	750000	545884

Published Tuesdays and Fridays,
By GEORGE SHERGOLD, Broker,
And the Sister of the late John Castaing.)

Figure 1. A copy of the twice-weekly London *Course of the Exchange* from 1758. Lewis Walpole Library, Yale University.

were given to a central clerk who aggregated the data and prepared the bills for the printer (see figure 2).

It may be surprising that the bills of mortality were sold to the public instead of being reserved for government use, but in fact the timely collection of the information depended on the decentralized and commercial nature of the operation. Beyond their sense of duty, the parish clerks had a financial incentive: in exchange for making timely reports to government they had the exclusive right to sell the printed bills in their respective parishes. The City of London and the king also saw the advantages of publishing an official record rather than letting rumors and misinformation take over, especially during epidemics. Those who read the bills or heard their contents being discussed were able to track the progress of the epidemic; the listing of individual parishes made it possible to see at a glance which areas were affected. Contemporary letters and diaries reveal that people paid most attention to the increase or decrease in

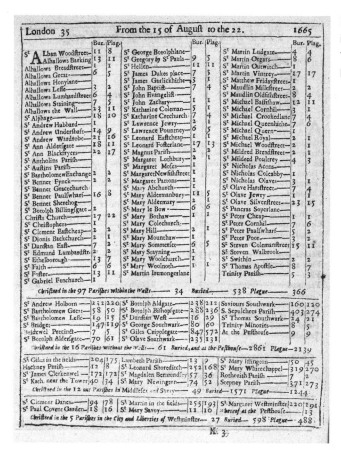

Figure 2. London bill of mortality for the week of August 15–22, 1665. The Wellcome Collection (CC BY).

burials from one week to the next, a telling example of how periodicity could structure the way people made sense of events. As with price currents, knowing the latest figures—whatever they were—was valuable to people and it influenced their decisions. Wealthy individuals who had the luxury of being able to leave London during the plague used the bills to know when to depart and when it was safe to return. London was unusual in having this weekly publication available in print from the early seventeenth century, but variants later existed in other places, including the French city of Rouen, where merchants and municipal leaders had an interest in managing information about epidemics, thereby counteracting rumors affecting trade with their city.

NEWS THROUGH THE POST

The first periodicals reporting political and military news were handwritten newsletters that began to circulate in the sixteenth century. In Italian the newsletters were called *avvisi*, and the individuals who produced them were known as *reportistas* or *novellistas*; in French, the *nouvelles à la main* were put out by *nouvellistes*; in English the compilers of newsletters were known as "intelligencers," a name that was subsequently adopted in the titles of printed newspapers such as the *Publick Intelligencer* (1655–60). Similarly, in German the term *Zeitung* was used for both printed relations and handwritten newsletters. The most well-known of the latter are the *Fuggerzeitungen* (Fugger newsletters) associated with the Fugger banking family and preserved by the Austrian National Library. Over the course of several decades beginning in the 1560s, the brothers Octavian Secundus Fugger and Philipp Eduard Fugger received and collected thousands of letters compiled by professional news writers and other individuals based in cities across Europe. The collection, which has recently been digitized and indexed, offers an exceptional window into how information circulated in sixteenth- and seventeenth-century Europe.

In general, the compilers of newsletters worked for clients who paid them to receive regular updates of news from other places (local news spread orally). Some had numerous subscribers and hired clerks to make copies. Others worked alone in fly-by-night operations. But by around 1620 they could be found in many cities and courts of Europe. The newsletters were largely tolerated because they met the information needs of well-connected people. Indeed, the sources of information included reports leaked by diplomats and spies as well as rumors gathered locally and newsletters from other cities. In that sense, we can speak of networks of newsletters, rather than just one-to-one relationships between intelligencers and their customers. The newsletters fed into each other and later became crucial sources for printed newspapers.

In the early seventeenth century, individuals began to reproduce newsletters in print for sale to a larger clientele. The first may have been Johann Carolus of Strasbourg, a city that was at the crossroads of European trading and postal networks. In 1605, Carolus began to produce a printed version of his existing manuscript newsletter. Thanks to a privilege from the municipal council, he was the only person in Strasbourg who had the right to put out such a publication. Printers elsewhere, including Basel, Frankfurt, Berlin, and Hamburg, soon followed Carolus's lead. But they faced competition from officials of the imperial post, who were uniquely positioned to collect intelligence and exploit their free use of the mails to distribute their periodicals to customers. The weekly publications that they produced were known as *Postzeitungen*, the first of many titles to announce the essential link between news and postal transmission. The *Frankfurter Postzeitung* (Frankfurt postal newspaper), for example, was founded in 1615 by the local imperial postmaster. In other places *Zeitungen* were the initiatives of printers or merchants, such as Johann Meyer in Hamburg, who used his connections in business to create a manuscript news service and then switched to print with the *Wöchentliche Zeitung* (Weekly newspaper). This paper had a rather exceptional circulation of about fifteen hundred copies owing to Hamburg's importance as a trading center. Most of the early news periodicals had print runs in the low to mid hundreds, but this could still be enough to turn a profit.

Meyer's experience also shows how periodical publishing involved struggles for control of a given territory. Pettegree has explained how the Hamburg city council sought to appease local booksellers, who also wanted to profit from demand for news. The city council decided that Meyer could sell his paper directly to customers for the first three days of the week, after which point local booksellers would have their turn. But in the 1630s a new imperial postmaster declared that he had a monopoly on news in Hamburg and tried to drive Meyer and his widow, Ilsabe, out of business. Ultimately the city council gave the postmaster exclusive use of the title *Postzeitung* but denied that he had a monopoly on printed news in Hamburg, allowing Ilsabe Meyer to compete directly with him.

Like Carolus and Meyer, the publishers of news often sought privileges in order to protect their investments against competition. A privilege could be a valuable monopoly for the publisher as well as an instrument of control for the authorities, but enforcement depended on a number of factors. In the Dutch Republic, for example, the close proximity of cities, each with its own privileges, meant that an individual who was excluded from issuing a newspaper in one place might succeed in obtaining a privilege in another. Moreover, the privilege to print news in one city did not automatically come with the right to stop the importation of publications from other cities. Postal policy was a separate lever that authorities could use to manage the flow of information, as the example of France discussed later reveals.

By 1618 or so, Amsterdam had a regular newspaper or *courante*. This term and related ones in several languages, including *coranto* and *currant*, evoked the idea of messengers (couriers) and the mail they carried, not to mention the idea of being up-to-date or *au courant*. By the 1640s, Amsterdam had nine different corantos, though according to an agreement between city officials and the publishers they had to appear on designated days of the week so as to avoid ruinous competition. Because of its importance as a trading center and the relative openness of its government—it is no coincidence that merchants were at the center of municipal politics—Amsterdam had a thriving information culture that included the production of quality maps, polemical pamphlets, and the business press already mentioned. But in order for regular news periodicals to succeed, there had to be an ongoing story to capture the attention of readers and make them willing to subscribe. Apart from the Thirty Years' War, which boosted demand for news across Europe, the story that caught the attention of Amsterdamers, as Michiel van Groesen has shown, was the fledgling colony of Dutch Brazil. The struggle between the Dutch and Portuguese for control of Brazil was framed as part of a broader conflict between Protestants and Catholics, but it also had major financial stakes for the Dutch West India Company and individual merchants. It was the perfect recipe for a thriving news culture that supported the sale of corantos as well as news maps—a popular visual medium—and polemical pamphlets. The Dutch West India Company and city leaders were initially able to manage the flow of news from Brazil, but over time this became more difficult, especially after soldiers and colonists returned to Amsterdam and shared their firsthand observations of life in Brazil.

As news periodicals cropped up in various places, from the Dutch Republic and the Habsburg Netherlands to the German lands and the Italian peninsula, it was common for the local authorities to govern these publications through privileges. The princes or city councils that granted such privileges sometimes gave explicit instructions about what topics should be avoided and what tone should be taken. Some of them required each issue to be submitted to a censor. From the standpoint of political or religious authorities, ongoing periodicals were easier to monitor than one-off publications like broadsides and pamphlets, many of which were anonymous and sold on the street. Periodicity also encouraged self-censorship. In exchange for a monopoly in their geographic territories, most publishers could be counted on to avoid certain subjects; it was generally understood that domestic politics was off limits and that reports should be presented in a neutral tone without editorial commentary. The need to attract subscribers and advertisers similarly led publishers to avoid topics that might alienate them. Periodicals made the sale of timely information viable, but they also required catering to political patrons and customers.

In more centralized states, such as France and Spain, monarchies established official gazettes. The French *Gazette* dates to 1631 and the Madrid *Gaceta* to 1661. In England the idea of an official newspaper was proposed as early as 1620, when two "intelligencers" with experience producing handwritten newsletters petitioned the king for a privilege. They argued that the creation of an official printed periodical would enable the monarchy to counteract rumors and better control the flow of news. But King James I (r. 1603–25) was not ready for this idea. Instead, he appointed a censor to authorize news publications by a few members of the London Stationers' Company, which had a monopoly on printing and bookselling in England. The stationers knew that they were on a tight leash with respect to political news. During the English Civil War (1642–51), publishers enjoyed greater freedom, though Parliament still monitored the press and called writers and printers to account for the occasional article. During the 1640s the publication of news became truly regular, with several competing periodicals appearing each week. The idea of an official newspaper became more of a reality in England during the 1650s under the Protectorate of Oliver Cromwell, when only two news periodicals (one covering Parliament and the other foreign news) were authorized. But a true state-run newspaper did not exist in England until 1665, when the *London Gazette* was created.

The example of the *London Gazette* illustrates how secret and public intelligence were intertwined during this period. The secretaries of state, who oversaw diplomacy and espionage, were also given responsibility for the gazette. The post office was central to all three. Postal officials were expected to monitor correspondence and report back details that might be of interest to government. In exchange they received copies of the *London Gazette* to sell to local customers, thereby facilitating the spread of the official version of events. The undersecretaries of state who supervised the *London Gazette* also ran subscription newsletter services for a more restricted clientele. By sharing fresh news with these elites, they received other information in return, plus the profit from the sale of the newsletters.

This connection between secret and public intelligence existed elsewhere in Europe, including France, Spain, the Habsburg lands, and later Russia. The official gazettes tended to include edited selections from the diplomatic correspondence of the realm. They provided a means of counteracting rumors and promoting a particular image of the monarchy. It was also hoped that they would provide readers with enough information to reduce demand for unofficial publications. In France, for example, the monarchy adjusted its policies over time in an effort to limit the creation of rival sources of information. After printers in the provinces began to pirate the official *Gazette* in the early eighteenth century, the monarchy responded by setting up official franchises. Printers in various towns were licensed to issue local reprints of the *Gazette*, thereby giving the printers a source of profit while encouraging the wider dissemination of the official news.

The need for some kind of information policy had long been evident to rulers, as early privileges for printing and postal monopolies make clear. Princes and city councils often worried about how to manage the production and circulation of information. By the late eighteenth century, the question of what kinds of information should be made available to the public was the subject of debate among writers and government officials in several countries. Periodicals received special attention because they offered a regular channel of communication with subjects but also the danger of encouraging ongoing criticism of institutions or policies.

BEYOND NEWSPAPERS: SCIENTIFIC AND LITERARY JOURNALS

In the German lands, a complex patchwork of political jurisdictions combined with high literacy led to a vibrant periodical press. As Jeremy Popkin has explained, by the end of the seventeenth century, newspapers had become common enough to be the subject of the first book-length celebration of the medium, Kaspar von Stieler's *The Pleasure and Utility of Newspapers* (1695). Stieler had worked as a court secretary, where his responsibilities included reading gazettes and diplomatic dispatches. He championed newspaper reading not only for statesmen and merchants, but also for landowners, clergy, teachers, soldiers, artisans, and literate women. Stieler thought all people had a natural curiosity to follow events. He remarked on the way individuals hurried to the printing shop or post office, impatient to learn the latest developments. But unlike most writers before him, Stieler saw periodical news as a positive development for people of various walks of life. To understand the world, he claimed, it wasn't enough to read history. One also needed newspapers to be well informed about the present.

The sense that periodicals enabled people to be up to date was not limited to the realm of politics and trade. The late seventeenth century saw the first scientific and literary journals, and their creators also highlighted the advantages of timely reports of new books and recent discoveries. The French *Journal des Savants* (Journal of the learned), created in 1665, announced that it would appear once a week "because things would become too dated if we waited a month or a year to talk about them." Some of the journal's prospective subscribers had also made it known that they would prefer short weekly installments to a copious annual volume that would lack "la grâce de la nouveauté" (the charm of novelty). Receiving each week's issue would be a pleasant diversion and would enable people to tune in to the latest conversations among the *curieux* of Europe. Still, like many subsequent journals, the *Journal des Savants* had continuous pagination so the weekly numbers could be bound into annual volumes with indexes to help readers locate information. Periodicals were a flexible *genre: they promoted the exchange of what was new while enabling readers to take stock of the accumulation of knowledge that each year was sure to bring. The destiny of many information-rich periodicals was thus to serve as a kind of reference book. For the same reason, political gazettes often had continuous pagination as well. Surviving collections of periodicals reveal that some readers indeed gathered individual numbers into bound volumes, made annotations in the margins, and even created their own indexes to facilitate subsequent consultation, sometimes quite self-consciously turning newspapers and journals into material for the writing of history.

Interest in what was novel and timely and the desire to foster more regular communication of knowledge encouraged the creation of learned journals. By the time Pierre Bayle began to edit the *Nouvelles de la République des Lettres* (News of the Republic of Letters) in 1684, he anticipated the objection that there were already too many journals. Why start another? In response, Bayle insisted that journals could complement each other by covering different subjects and even by providing different reviews of the same book. Over the next century, learned journals were set up in many places, often in connection with academies or *learned societies, from London and Paris to Copenhagen and Stockholm, Berlin, Saint Petersburg, and Philadelphia.

Learned journals emphasized the benefits of timeliness and periodicity, and like other periodicals they were embedded in correspondence networks. Journals were often consciously envisioned as a public form of correspondence that enabled collaboration and debate among geographically dispersed individuals. Beginning with the *Philosophical Transactions of the Royal Society* in 1665, learned societies used their journals not just to communicate their proceedings, but also to create a forum for further observations and criticism of published reports. General-interest magazines and journals, which developed in parallel to learned journals, also encouraged reader submissions. The *Mercure Galant* (Courtly mercury), which began publication in 1672 and became the *Mercure de France* (French mercury) in 1724, contained literary and cultural news, court gossip, discussion of etiquette and fashion, obituaries, and other material. As an early example of a society journal, it was to inspire many European magazines during the eighteenth century. The *Gentleman's Magazine*, established in London in 1731, was the first monthly miscellany to use the word *magazine* in its title. Its many imitators in Britain and abroad published a mix of essays, poetry, book reviews, and information of various kinds, from mortality figures and observations on the weather to reports of inventions and short digests of political news.

We should not assume a sharp distinction between the kinds of information of interest to members of the *Republic of Letters and those of interest to the mercantile and political elite. These worlds overlapped. In England, many of the virtuosi who orbited around the Royal Society owned stocks in overseas trading companies. They frequented the same coffeehouses as merchants; they read price currents as well as foreign gazettes and learned journals. The development of political arithmetic—the systematic study of economic and demographic data—depended on the networks of the Royal Society and its counterparts in other countries. But it is hard to imagine early scholars of population change such as John Graunt and William Petty being able to treat numbers of births and deaths as data *series* if these numbers hadn't first been collected and published in a weekly *serial*, namely the bills of mortality. A fellow of the Royal Society named John Houghton was also an apothecary and dealer of colonial imports such as tea, coffee, and chocolate; his shop was very close to the Royal Exchange. Much like the Royal Society itself, Houghton used print to disseminate useful information. The title of his weekly periodical, *A Collection for the Improvement of Husbandry and Trade* (1692–1703), indicated that his goal was to provide readers with information that was useful to them (such as explaining how the Bank of England worked) while actively promoting agricultural improvements and the growth of trade.

A clever use of correspondence to facilitate the exchange of information was developed by John Dunton and his associates on the *Athenian Mercury*, which appeared twice a week in London from 1690 to 1697. Dunton's journal was nominally produced by the Athenian Society, which consisted of Dunton and a few friends in a coffeehouse answering letters from readers. Women and men alike were encouraged to ask the Athenian Society questions on a range of subjects, from religion and family life to history, economics, and science. In 1693, Dunton also launched the first journal explicitly aimed at women, the *Ladies' Mercury*, but it only lasted four weeks. Yet the success of the *Athenian Mercury* confirmed readers' curiosity about everyday phenomena and their desire to interact through the medium of a periodical.

Although most subsequent journals did not imitate the question-and-answer format developed by the *Athenian Mercury*, reader submissions remained central. The *Spectator* (1711–12), produced in London by Joseph Addison and Richard Steele, encouraged readers to send in queries and observations. Addison and Steele printed some of these and used others as the basis for their own essays on social, economic, and cultural topics. The *Spectator* spawned numerous reprintings in bound volumes and imitations in French, German, Dutch, Swedish, Russian, and other languages. Such essay-based periodicals could be seen as privileging comment and informed opinion rather than information per se, but it should be remembered that readers turned to them not only for essays, poems, and book reviews, but also for numerical information such as the prices of goods, estimates of state budgets, the relative size of European armies and navies, and casualty figures in a century of almost incessant warfare.

A good example of the connections between correspondence networks, periodical publishing, and information exchange can be seen in a newspaper genre that flourished in France in the second half of the eighteenth century known as the *affiches*. (They are called *affiches* because they usually appeared with some variation of the title *annonces, affiches, et avis*, but they should not be confused with posters, which are also called *affiches* in French.) Because the official *Gazette de France* had a monopoly on political news, the affiches largely eschewed politics. But as Elizabeth Andrews Bond has shown, these periodicals were crucial vectors for the exchange of practical information and should be seen as counterparts to loftier enlightenment projects such as Diderot and D'Alembert's *Encyclopédie* (Encyclopedia) (1751–72). In addition to official notices, advertisements, and market news, the affiches gave significant space to correspondence. Readers were encouraged to make queries or contribute observations on practical issues of health, nutrition, agriculture, manufacturing, architecture, astronomy, and botany, among other subjects. Most of the contributors were anonymous, and they represented a range of backgrounds, though scientists and doctors wrote more than clergymen, lawyers, or artists (see figure 3).

The affiches appeared in many provincial towns, and it is not surprising that one was also set up in the increasingly prosperous sugar colony of Saint Domingue in the 1760s. The affiches catered mainly to local subscribers and advertisers, but they were embedded in wider correspondence networks, and the way publications in different regions reprinted each other's articles allowed the information provided by readers to circulate. The affiches therefore had something in common with other vectors of enlightenment, such as provincial academies, learned journals, and *encyclopedias: they embodied the ideal that knowledge could be known and that its circulation was beneficial to society. The affiches are also a good example of how correspondence and printed periodicals reinforced each other, enabling individuals to share information and discuss its reliability and significance. Readers of the affiches debated the efficacy of various medical remedies, agricultural techniques, and methods for repairing things.

The affiches were different from question-and-answer journals such as the *Athenian Mercury* or essay-based journals like the *Spectator*, but all three types of periodical catered to the intellectual curiosity of readers and created new habits of information

Figure 3. A page from the weekly *Affiches* published in Toulouse with notices advertising property, books, and a young clergyman seeking employment as a tutor. Bibliothèque municipale de Toulouse.

exchange. Editors and readers exploited key features of periodicals—their regular interval of publication and their dependence on the post—to engage in an ongoing quest for beneficial and reliable information. The role of periodicals in the spread of enlightenment can be traced back to the first scientific journals of the seventeenth century through to the essay contests that appeared in the journals of learned academies and general-interest monthlies such as the *Berlinische Monatsschrift* (Berlin monthly), which published Immanuel Kant's essay "What Is Enlightenment?" in 1784. As Kant admitted in a letter to Johann Gottlieb Fichte in 1797, "My choice of the journal *Berliner Blätter* (Berlin pages) [which succeeded the *Monatsschrift*] for my recent essays will make sense to you and to my other philosophizing friends . . . for in that paper I can get my work published and evaluated most quickly, since, like a political newspaper, it comes out almost as promptly as the mail allows" (Maliks, 4). The affiches were more focused on commerce than the periodicals Kant contributed to, but their editors believed that economic progress depended on the timely circulation of information of all sorts, not just the prices of goods and the arrival of ships.

THE RISE OF ADVERTISING

Advertising was crucial to the survival of many kinds of periodicals, not just trade-oriented ones like the affiches. By the end of the eighteenth century, advertising was viewed by publishers as essential to the profitability of most newspapers and quite a few journals. The process began in the Dutch Republic, where the weekly corantos of the 1620s already contained advertisements. Most of the early advertisements were for books sold by local printers and booksellers, but by the 1650s they included notices for goods and services paid for by private individuals and public money (such as notices for wanted criminals or information about market days). In France, Théophraste Renaudot, whose Paris-based *Gazette* had a monopoly on political news starting in the 1630s, also had an advertising business protected by privilege, the *bureau d'adresse*, which facilitated communication between employers and job seekers and between buyers and sellers of goods. Notices were posted at the office and printed in a periodical that was separate from the *Gazette*. The *Gazette* itself rarely included advertisements, but unofficial gazettes and journals, which were tolerated beginning in the late eighteenth century (more on this later), sometimes contained ads for luxury products, property, and employment.

The rise of advertising was particularly noticeable in Britain and its American colonies. In the 1650s, some English news periodicals contained ads, but the real growth came after 1695, when parliamentary legislation governing the printing trades was allowed to lapse, putting an end to prepublication censorship and the monopoly of the Stationers' Company. The extent to which 1695 marked a turning point in book publishing remains a matter of debate (big London booksellers continued to dominate), but it was clearly a boon for the periodical press. As newspapers and journals proliferated after 1695, publishers turned to advertising as an important source of revenue in addition to subscriptions. Even for essay-based journals like the *Spectator*, paid notices were a crucial source of profits. Although the *Spectator* had a print run of about three thousand copies a day, Joseph Addison suggested that the readership was twenty times that number, since copies were consulted in coffeehouses and shared among friends. As Pettegree has suggested, the multiplier of twenty readers per copy also represented a bit of salesmanship on the part of Addison, who no doubt had advertisers in mind when he boasted about the *Spectator*'s reach. The *City Mercury*, a paper that contained only advertisements, gave a similar figure of twenty readers per copy back in the 1690s, and the goal was clearly to attract further paid notices.

The printer of the *New York Gazette* in 1769 referred to advertisements as "the Life of a Paper," a claim that would have been confirmed by his counterparts on both sides of the Atlantic. By the mid-eighteenth century, the daily and triweekly London newspapers devoted between one-third and three-quarters of their space to ads. Newspapers in English towns outside London were published weekly, but they were similarly reliant on advertisements as the main source of profits. By the 1760s, a type of newspaper that for lack of a better term might be called the "commercial advertiser" dominated English-language journalism on both sides of the Atlantic. Its mix of news paragraphs, essays, letters to the printer, accounts of trials, excerpts from books and pamphlets, and shipping news made it harder for separate essay-based journals to survive after midcentury. The daily, triweekly, and weekly commercial advertisers became the primary means of selling timely information and an important venue for political debate.

Many English-language papers had the word *advertiser* in their title, though it should be remembered that advertisement, news, and information were related terms at the time. In Samuel Johnson's English *Dictionary* (1755), the verb *to advertise* was defined as "to inform another; to give intelligence." *Advertiser*, meanwhile, referred both to "he that gives intelligence or information" and to "the paper in which advertisements are published." Paid advertisements became crucial to most English-language newspapers, which were not protected by privileges (as many gazettes on the continent still were during the eighteenth century) and which catered largely to the mercantile and political elite. Even the European gazettes, however, tended to contain at least a few ads— often for luxury goods and property—and in the Netherlands and Germany, advertising was very present in the newspapers of the period. The German *Intelligenzblätter* (intelligencers), which existed in roughly two hundred cities by the end of the eighteenth century, were advertising-based newspapers.

AN EXPANDING NETWORK

The eighteenth century witnessed tremendous growth in the periodical press, but there were important differences by country and region. In England, the lapse of press licensing in 1695 was the result of disagreements among members of Parliament about how best to regulate the press. At the time it was assumed that some sort of legislation was forthcoming, and many bills were proposed over the next fifteen years. But developments in state finance such as the creation of the Bank of England and the national debt, coupled with an increasingly interventionist foreign policy under William III (r. 1689–1702) and his successors, created a situation in which the circulation of timely information about trade, finance, and diplomacy became crucial. In hindsight it is clear that the lapse of licensing in 1695 enabled the growth of the newspaper press, but it also affected literary and scientific periodicals. It was now possible for private commercial ventures to compete with officially sanctioned publications such as the *London Gazette* and the *Philosophical Transactions of the Royal Society*.

In addition to ending prepublication censorship, the lapse of licensing in 1695 cancelled the Stationers' Company's monopoly and the restriction that presses had to be located in London. Soon printers began to set up in provincial towns, and most of them started a newspaper. By 1750 there were over forty provincial newspapers, and by 1800 there were over seventy. In addition to reports collected locally and reader submissions, the provincial papers reproduced material from London periodicals, and, over time, their counterparts in other towns. Copying enabled news and commentary to spread. Although Britain enacted its first *copyright statute in 1710, the law did not explicitly protect writings in newspapers and periodicals. Moreover, the business and culture of news publishing that developed in Britain and its American colonies worked against the very idea of literary property for time-sensitive information and commentary on recent events. Newspapers actively relied on each other, and news collection was a casual affair. Most newspapers did not have paid reporters. In addition to material produced by the printer or editor, they relied on reader submissions, the occasional letter from a correspondent in another city or country, and articles copied from other publications. The main expenses were paper, printing labor, and government taxation in the form of stamp and advertising duties; together these dwarfed the occasional amounts spent paying a writer or collector of news. Copying was common, and it was generally viewed in positive terms as a means of spreading information and facilitating commentary.

Britain, like the Netherlands, enjoyed a relatively open information culture. Reports of political decisions, fiscal policy, and the progress of wars were laid before the reading public and vigorously debated in clubs and coffeehouses. Such an information culture reflected the interconnected nature of business and government. In the Netherlands, merchants and trading companies had long enjoyed influence in politics. In Britain, the parliamentary system and the mechanisms of state finance that developed in the late seventeenth and early eighteenth centuries made the regular circulation of information increasingly important. Reports of trade and finance were not just of interest to merchants and brokers; they were essential to the political fortunes of the state in an age of imperial rivalry and warfare on an entirely new scale. Investment in the national debt by individuals and the large trading companies meant that financial news was inherently political and political news had financial stakes. It seems inconceivable that the British monarchy could have borrowed the money it needed to finance the increasingly costly wars of the eighteenth century without allowing its activities to be publicized and scrutinized by those who were loaning money to the state.

And yet certain activities remained closed to public scrutiny longer than others. By the 1720s, British writers were developing arguments about the role of newspapers in monitoring the actions of politicians and sounding the alarm against corruption and abuse of power. But coverage of Parliament was for many decades restricted to manuscript accounts and veiled and somewhat speculative reports, such as Samuel Johnson's imaginative accounts of proceedings "in the Senate of Lilliput," which appeared in the *Gentleman's Magazine* in the early 1740s. In the early 1770s, actions by John Wilkes and several printers finally led both Houses of Parliament to accept regular newspaper coverage of proceedings. By this time some members of Parliament argued that the public had a right to be informed of proceedings, but others complained that printed accounts distorted their words, a problem exacerbated by the way newspapers spun accounts to serve political ends. Still, open coverage of Parliament in the 1770s was a turning point as important as the end of press licensing in 1695. The statements of government ministers and members of Parliament were henceforth reported, scrutinized, and criticized in the press. Gazettes and journals in other cities and countries copied and translated from London newspapers, allowing debates in Westminster to reverberate throughout Europe and North America, sometimes with effects that the speakers could never have imagined.

The Seven Years' War (1756–63) was a watershed for the periodical press across Europe and the Atlantic World. In France, the government adopted a new policy in the late 1750s whereby gazettes and journals printed outside France were admitted into the French royal post on favorable terms. The monarchy realized that a two-tiered information system, with an official channel represented by the *Gazette de France* and an unofficial one represented by the foreign gazettes, provided a means of monitoring criticism while allowing elites to have access to information they wanted. Rather than relying on prepublication censorship, the monarchy kept these foreign gazettes within bounds by threatening to deny them access to the French post, which would have cut them off from most of their subscribers. The result of this policy was a much richer variety of information coming into France from Amsterdam, Leiden, The Hague, the free cities of Hamburg and Altona, the Prussian enclave of Cleves, the Duchy of Zweibrücken, and other communication hubs. The international French-language gazettes had a reputation for providing reliable information. Between 1760 and 1789 about sixty of them were produced outside of France aimed primarily at a French audience. In addition, a number of European cities saw the creation of French-language gazettes and scientific and literary journals for the local population. These include Berlin, Cologne, Vienna, Warsaw, Copenhagen, Stockholm, and St. Petersburg, not to mention the French colonies of Saint Domingue (which had a newspaper from 1764), Martinique (1766), Grenada (1779), Guadeloupe (1785) and Francophone areas in British Canada (Quebec City had a bilingual gazette from 1764).

The growth was even more spectacular in the German lands. By the end of the eighteenth century, there were perhaps two hundred newspapers in Germany, most of them serving an average of between five hundred and one thousand subscribers, although some had much higher figures. The best-selling newspaper in the world around 1800 was the *Hamburgische Unpartheyische Correspondent* (Hamburg impartial correspondent), which printed an estimated thirty-six thousand copies per issue. But there was much more to the German periodical press than newspapers. Scholars estimate that as many as three thousand new journals were created in the second half of the eighteenth century. Many of them were short-lived, and print runs varied from a few hundred copies to a couple thousand. There were journals covering literature, theater, economics, and various branches of science, but the most common were general-interest periodicals containing a mix of practical information, news of scientific discoveries, historical essays, medical advice, and literary pieces. These journals were like miniature encyclopedias delivered in regular installments. Rolf Engelsing has referred to a "reading revolution" in eighteenth-century Germany, a term that he used to describe a general shift from "intensive reading" of a small number of books to "extensive reading" of a wide range of printed sources. Though the thesis is debatable—many readers read both extensively and intensively—it is clear that many contemporaries discussed what they perceived to be an "addiction" or "mania" for reading; they worried about how new reading habits affected individuals and society as a whole.

In the Italian peninsula, Milan and Florence joined Venice as the most important information centers. The Florence-based *Notizie del Mondo* (News of the world) achieved the relatively high circulation of seventeen hundred at a time when most Italian papers were selling only a few hundred copies. By translating reports from English, French, and German sources, gazettes and journals in the Italian peninsula kept elites fairly well informed despite the existence of censorship in many regions. As in the German lands, political fragmentation meant that press policies varied. In Lombardy and Tuscany, the struggle between the ruling Habsburg family and the church for control of culture led to a freer atmosphere than in Rome, where the *Diario ordinario di Roma* (Journal of Rome) was the official voice of the papal government. In some places, such as Naples, governments saw periodicals as a means of building consensus rather than a force of opposition that needed to be suppressed.

This point holds for other areas of Europe as well. Many periodicals were linked to government initiatives. The development of the press and the cultivation of public opinion was often promoted by authorities, rather than always developing in opposition to the state. In many places, the printing trades were not as tightly controlled as the official decrees might make us think. Frederick the Great of Prussia (r. 1740–86) approved more than forty decrees regulating the press during his forty-six-year reign, but enforcement was uneven, and many authors were affiliated with the regime in some way, making it hard to distinguish between official and unofficial publications. In Russia, the Muscovite rulers repeatedly modified their policies with respect to newspapers in an effort to maximize the benefits for local and imperial administration. Under Catherine the Great (r. 1762–96), there was an expansion of the periodical press that included essay journals on the model of the *Spectator* as well the creation of official newspapers in Moscow, St. Petersburg, and the provincial capitals.

According to some writers at the time, the circulation of periodicals helped to foster a cosmopolitan public. In 1764, Cesare Beccaria published an essay on the role of periodicals in the Italian journal *Il Caffè* (The coffeehouse). He claimed that gazettes and journals "make us citizens of Europe; they produce a continuous commerce among the different nations and destroy that diffidence and contempt with which isolated nations look on foreign ones. Everything in Europe tends to become closer and more similar, and there is a stronger tendency towards equality than in the past" (Barker and Burrows, 209). Beccaria saw periodicals as promoting social and political harmony, but many of his contemporaries expressed a more pessimistic view. The words *journaliste* and *gazzettiere* often had negative connotations, and the diaries and letters of the period contain plenty of remarks about the unreliable and suspect nature of reports circulating in the periodical press. But such remarks constitute further evidence of engagement with timely information and the mutually reinforcing nature of periodicals and correspondence.

During the American Revolutionary War, the London press became the primary source of information for newspapers and journals across Europe. The American politician John Adams, who spent several years on diplomatic mission in Paris, described the London press as "an engine, by which everything is scattered all over the world" (September 8, 1783). He noted that an article inserted in a London newspaper was bound to be reprinted in other countries. As Adams observed, the key to understanding how information could be manipulated was the way newspapers and gazettes copied and translated from each other, enabling false and exaggerated reports to spread. "Stock jobbers are not the only people, who employ a set of scribblers to invent and publish falsehoods for their peculiar purposes," Adams wrote. "British and French, as well as other politicians, entertain these fabricators of paragraphs, who are stationed about in the various cities of Europe, and take up each other's productions in such a manner, that no sooner does a paragraph appear in a French, Dutch or English paper, but it is immediately seized on, and reprinted in all the others" (June 24, 1783). Adams lamented that some of these dubious paragraphs were being reprinted in American newspapers. Periodicals were interdependent, and they were open to anonymous submissions, for better and for worse.

INFORMING REVOLUTION

The French Revolution was another major turning point for the periodical press, leading to an explosion of newspapers in Paris and the French provinces and a corresponding decline of the international French-language gazettes. Between the storming of the Bastille in 1789 and Napoleon's coup d'état in 1799, more than two thousand different newspapers appeared in France. The French Revolutionary and Napoleonic Wars also led to the tightening of press controls in countries across Europe and the Atlantic World; these reactions revealed the extent to which newspapers and periodicals were seen as channels for the spread of revolutionary ideas. In 1793, as he tracked the news from his home city of Montreal, a young writer named Henri-Antoine Mézière explained, "The French Revolution has electrified the Canadians and enlightened them more about their natural rights in a year than a century of reading would have been able to do. . . . Every day, they assemble in the towns in small groups, tell each other about the latest news received, rejoice with each other when the news is favorable to the French and grieve (but not desperately) when it is unfavorable" (quoted in Taylor). But for Mézière, newspapers and correspondence were not only a means of learning about distant events. They enabled the spread of revolutionary consciousness. An anonymous piece in the *Montreal Gazette* that Jordan E. Taylor plausibly attributes to Mézière dismissed the importance of writings by Locke and Voltaire and stressed how international commerce led to "reciprocal communications" through the press that enabled the "genius of information" to awaken people to the fundamental "rights of man."

Mézière was not alone in highlighting the connection between information circulation and democratic revolution. Thomas Jefferson famously declared in 1787 that if given the choice between government without newspapers and newspapers without government he would choose the latter. But the quote should not be taken out of context. Jefferson was describing the potential of newspapers to create an informed citizenry essential to a functioning democracy. For him, this could work only if everyone had access to newspapers and was able to read them. In 1792, the US Congress put its full support behind this idea by creating a new postal system that encouraged the circulation of newspapers (which were charged a very low postage rate) and subsidized the process of news gathering itself (printers were allowed to exchange their newspapers free through the mail, thereby treating news as a shared resource). By 1800, there were over 230 newspapers in the United States, including more than twenty dailies, compared to a total of approximately thirty-five newspapers in 1783.

On the other side of the Atlantic, amid debates over press regulations in revolutionary France, the deputy J.P.F. Duplantin made explicit why periodicals were the democratic medium par excellence: they enabled ideas to spread quickly among a large and dispersed population. According to Duplantin, "separate writings" such as books were slower to produce and less affordable. Citizens needed the "rapid and secure communication that only periodicals can offer, to circulate opinion and enlightenment from the center to the periphery and to bring them constantly together from each point to the opposing extremes, just as in the biological world the fluids necessary for life carry the essentials of survival to all parts of the human and vegetable body" (Barker and Burrows, 189). Then as now, circulation was the most common metaphor for the movement of information, and it was the fact that periodicals were faster to produce and cheaper than books that made them seem like the ideal medium. Periodicity also encouraged ongoing discussion. The openness to reader contributions was not inherent to periodical publishing, but its development makes perfect sense given the strong links between postal correspondence and periodicals.

The remarks by writers and political leaders quoted above represent idealized views of newspapers and their role in democratic societies. But it is important not to assume too sharp a distinction between political news and other kinds of information that appeared in periodicals and circulated through the post. Philosophical debates took place in journals; newspapers and magazines contained summaries and excerpts from books. News, science, literature, and practical information mingled in the pages of periodicals. The Dutch patriot movement, constitutional changes in Poland, Thomas Paine's *Common Sense*, the American Declaration of Independence, the debates in the French National Assembly and the colonial assemblies of Saint Domingue and Martinique—all this and more was printed in local periodicals, which traveled outward to be copied and translated into other periodicals, acquiring new meanings for readers in new contexts.

A recent forum in the online journal *Age of Revolutions* entitled "(In)forming Revolution" provides a sample of how specialists of the late eighteenth and early nineteenth centuries have recently been studying the role of information in varied and sophisticated ways. Examining not only Europe and North America but also the Caribbean, South America, Eastern Europe, Japan, and China, scholars are illuminating the agents and media of information as well as the different ways individuals collected, exchanged, manipulated, and recorded information. Contributors note the role played by newspapers and other periodicals, but they also stress the importance of oral and written communication, not only for places where printing was nonexistent but also in cases where the speed of events made other modes of communication paramount.

Many places in the Americas and the Caribbean lacked locally printed periodicals, but publications sent by mail were available to those who could afford the postage and subscriptions. In colonial Venezuela, as Cristina Soriano has shown, between 1770 and 1810 roughly one in five postmortem inventories of private libraries included newspapers and other periodicals, with some elites owning lengthy runs of periodicals in Spanish, French, and English that had been printed on one side or the other of the Atlantic. Official gazettes appeared in colonial Mexico (1722), Peru (1743), and Guatemala (1729–31, revived 1794). At the end of the eighteenth century, journals such as the Lima-based *Mercurio peruano* (Peruvian mercury) (1791–94) offered a forum for discussion of economics, politics, and science.

But in most places the freshest information spread orally or through manuscript newsletters. Several of the islands in the French Antilles had presses with officially sanctioned newspapers, but reports of the French and Haitian revolutions mostly spread by word of mouth. The momentous nature of events combined with delays in receiving verified reports allowed speculation and rumor to thrive. Cuba had an official newspaper in Havana starting in 1790, and the authorities tried to stop the spread of reports about slave insurrections on neighboring islands, but the news still arrived via sailors and French refugees from Saint Domingue. In India, the English-language and vernacular Indian press built on what C. A. Bayly referred to as the "information order" of the Mughal Empire, which included manuscript newsletters, running spies, and newsmongers in the bazaars who provided grist for the rumor mill. These modes of communication provided a base on which the vernacular Indian press would build in the mid- to late nineteenth century.

CONCLUSION

This chapter has highlighted the commercialization of timely information in periodical form as an important development of the early modern period. Clearly, any history of the age of enlightenment and revolutions would be incomplete without also considering information that was not perceived as time sensitive—from dictionaries and encyclopedias to recipe books and instruction manuals, not to mention government surveys and scholarly investigations. Much information was never published, either because it was held secret or because it was more effectively transmitted orally. In addition, timeliness is a relative concept. Information about medical remedies or the latest farming techniques had a sense of urgency for people suffering from illness or in need of a good harvest; such information may have been entirely new to them even if it was not to others. Periodicals contained a lot of practical information of these sorts, and some encyclopedias were published as serials, with subscribers receiving installments that they could later bind into volumes. Many journals had continuous pagination so that each new issue—fresh in itself—could be preserved and consulted for years to come. The editors of magazines and reviews often described their compilations as materials for future historians.

So not all information published in periodicals was time sensitive, and periodicals were not the only source of information. Print did not reduce the importance of writing or conversation. Periodicals did not eliminate the value of other kinds of informational works—maps, charts, and reference books are obvious counterexamples to any such claim. Even in places where printed newspapers gained prominence at a relatively early date, such as the Low Countries, the German lands, and England, they did not reduce the importance of receiving information through private letters. Indeed, correspondence was the lifeblood of the periodical press. Without it, most newspapers and journals could never have existed. They simply would not have had a reliable means of obtaining information to include in their periodicals. Political newspapers, scientific journals, literary reviews, and price currents—all depended on what came in the mail. Many periodicals invited readers to submit queries or information; they relied extensively on such unpaid submissions. In some places, printers doubled as postmasters; in others, postal officials acted as wholesaling agents for periodicals. Printed publications traveled through the post alongside letters, and many people enclosed them in their correspondence, sometimes commenting on the authenticity or significance of the information they contained. The proliferation of periodicals and the commercialization of timely information went hand in glove, and together they were central to the information cultures that developed in many places during this period. The process was neither inevitable nor linear, but it transformed the way people shared, analyzed, and commented on information about the world around them.

Will Slauter

See also censorship; intellectual property; journals; letters; newsletters; newspapers; public sphere

FURTHER READING

Adams Papers Digital Edition; Kenneth J. Arrow, *The Rate and Direction of Inventive Activity*, 1962; Bryan Banks, ed., "(In)forming Revolution: Information Networks in the Age of Revolutions," *Age of Revolutions* (online journal), 2017; Hannah Barker and Simon Burrows, eds., *Press, Politics and the Public Sphere in Europe and North America*, 2002; Christopher A. Bayly, *Empire and Information*, 1996; Elizabeth Andrews Bond, "Circuits of Practical Knowledge: The Network of Letters to the Editor in the French Provincial Press, 1770–1788," *French Historical Studies* 39, no. 3 (2016): 535–65; Samuel Butler, *Characters and Passages from Notebooks*, edited by A. R. Waller, 1908; Robert Darnton and Daniel Roche, eds., *Revolution in Print*, 1989; Brendan Dooley, ed., *The Dissemination of News and the Emergence of Contemporaneity in Early Modern Europe*, 2010; Brendan Dooley and Sabrina A. Baron, eds., *The Politics of Information in Early Modern Europe*, 2001; Richard R. John and Jonathan Silberstein-Loeb, eds., *Making News*, 2015; Reidar Maliks, *Kant's Politics in Context*, 2014; John McCusker, "The Demise of Distance: The Business Press and the Origins of the Information Revolution in the Early Modern Atlantic World," *American Historical Review* 110, no. 2 (2005): 295–321; Miles Ogborn, *Indian Ink*, 2007; Andrew Pettegree, *The Invention of News*, 2014; Jeremy Popkin, "New Perspectives on the Early Modern European Press," in *News and Politics in Early Modern Europe*, edited by Joop W. Koopmans, 2005; Joad Raymond and Noah Moxham, eds., *News Networks in Early Modern Europe*, 2016; Will Slauter, "The Paragraph as Information Technology: How News Traveled in the Eighteenth-Century Atlantic World," *Annales HSS* [English edition] 67, no. 2 (2012): 253–78; idem, *Who Owns the News?*, 2019; C. John Sommerville, *The News Revolution in England*, 1996; Cristina Soriano, *Tides of Revolution*, 2018; Jordan E. Taylor, "Information and Ideology in Henri-Antoine Mézière's Canadian Age of Revolutions," *Age of Revolutions*, September 18, 2017, https://ageofrevolutions.com/2017/09/18/; Michiel van Groesen, *Amsterdam's Atlantic*, 2016.

DOCUMENTS, EMPIRE, AND CAPITALISM IN THE NINETEENTH CENTURY

In 1859, Sarah Remond, a thirty-five-year-old "freed person of color," arrived in London with a US passport. In the two years she spent in London Remond delivered more than forty-five antislavery lectures as she studied for a degree at Bedford College for Ladies. Neither of these activities attracted the attention of newspapers in the United States. The press paid attention to Remond only once a US official in London refused to recognize her passport.

The controversy around the issuance and rejection of Remond's passport that I outline below brings to the foreground important aspects of the debate generated by the belief that governments and organizations needed to collect a large range of information that could be easily circulated, at times on a global scale. Concerns included the reliability of information, the conditions necessary for the production of accurate information, who controlled the production of information, and whom information was used to control. The struggle to use, and make sense of, documents amid these issues and in response to significant changes in scale provides the contours of the history of information addressed in this chapter.

To start with a controversy over a passport is a deliberate decision intended to emphasize that many of the anxieties that states and organizations had about information in this period came from the belief that it was necessary to know more about individuals combined with a heightened concern about the effectiveness of the documents used to circulate information. In this context the function of passports was beginning to change. Reflecting a dominant existing perception of a passport as a letter of introduction, the *New York Times* approvingly reprinted Remond's letter of complaint and endorsed her right to have a passport before commenting that the official "seems to have been instructed to take his cue from the face of the bearer rather than from that of the document." Someone's face and appearance (and documents) could be seen, and represented as information, in very different ways. The notary public in the United States who prepared Remond's passport application described her hair, complexion, and face as "dark"; in contrast the official in London described her as "dark mullato with wooly hair and negro features." Seeing her as "Black" identified Remond as someone who prior to the Fourteenth Amendment could not be a US citizen and therefore was not entitled to a passport.

So how did Remond come to have a US passport? In a world of few documents and limited administrative reach, the State Department still had to trust the honesty of local officials and applicants to provide the information required to issue a passport. Department memos noted an expectation that a person applying for a passport would state if they were a "person of color." Remond's passport application did not mention her race but it identified her as a citizen of Salem, Massachusetts, where she lived. Her application took the form of a handwritten affidavit, not the recently introduced preprinted application form; it would be several more decades before the State Department started returning applications that did not use the form. When it arrived in Washington, DC, one of the twenty-eight officials and clerks who made up the State Department would have read it; some of those clerks and officials had "passports" listed as one of their designated responsibilities. These duties likely included signing a passport in the name of the secretary of state. This practice became a necessity in the 1850s when the department issued forty thousand passports, which totaled twice the number issued in the previous five decades.

In an era when passports were not required, but with passport numbers increasing and the definition of citizenship becoming even more contested, the State Department, along with its officials abroad, sought to establish the passport as a certificate of citizenship. This was a work in progress in 1859. In arguing that Remond should be able to carry a passport, the *New York Times* saw no necessary connection between the document and citizenship. Because it did not see a passport as an identification document, it presented a passport in its traditional role as a letter requesting protection and, therefore, something a woman traveling alone definitely needed. The *New York Times*'s stance could also be a case of playing dumb in support of abolitionism.

In the middle of the nineteenth century, while uncommon, it was definitely not unusual for a Black person to apply for and receive a passport. Beginning in the 1830s, the abolitionist movement had strategically used US passport applications to further its cause. These applications attempted to exploit not only a lax federal administrative structure, but also loose passport laws and differences between federal and state citizenship laws. Remond (coming from a family steeped in abolitionism) deliberately sought to manipulate the still-developing relationship between information and documents, particularly the understanding of documents as "objective" evidence of *"facts" such as citizenship. This faith in official documentation was particularly prone to manipulation with documents used to constitute an ever-expanding administrative space.

The controversy around Remond's passport highlights a still-developing relationship between information and documents, between authority and evidence, which is the focus of this chapter. The nineteenth century saw the aspirations to collect information according to an increasingly pervasive faith in centralized standards and practices paired with a lack of administrative reach. This lack manifested itself in the need to rely on information generated by the work of people who often had at best an ambiguous relationship to a centralized authority, be it a government or a large business concern. As the Remond incident illustrates, this could easily mean that an individual's opinion or action could subvert or trump the authority of a document as a record or evidence. This could be done intentionally or through a failure to understand the logic of the procedures used to produce official documents.

In response to problems of scale, people acting in the name of institutions created documents to collect, collate, and circulate information. These documents needed to be easily stored and retrieved, but more importantly they had to be able to move information across territories and into different social and cultural contexts. The intention was that the circulation of documents would contribute to the work of governing or "managing" (the profession of management emerged out of larger US business enterprises at the end of the nineteenth century). However, this goal involved a struggle over the status of documented information that illustrated not only an attempt to establish a new set of relationships between information and people, but also a historically specific understanding of information as instrumental. In this period, neither the form of information presented in documents nor the authority of documents was a given. A focus on the details of forms, structures, and systems that mediated people's interactions with information makes this apparent. Or put another way, this chapter explores a period when the people that institutions empowered to organize the production and circulation of information acted with little or no knowledge of the previous attempts to articulate paper and information in the name of control discussed in previous chapters. Therefore, in some cases, they reinvented the proverbial wheel in the form of previously used classification techniques and filing systems, while in other cases they invented new technologies and systems to record and store documented information.

This discussion begins with an examination of documents that governments introduced to manage and control the movement of people. Then the broader structures introduced to support these documents are analyzed by widening the focus to consider the articulation of an ideal relationship between documents and information in the extension and maintenance of empires and an examination of how that relationship played out in practice. The final section of the chapter moves away from empire and government as a site of organization to a more localized effort to produce and organize relatively large amounts of information: the nineteenth-century reorganization of capitalism on a corporate scale.

GLOBAL MOBILITY

The example of Sarah Remond illustrates the informality of state practices when it came to collecting and presenting the information used to identify individuals in the middle of the nineteenth century. This would change as the long century wound its way to an end in 1914. The outbreak of World War I is often presented as the end of an era of freedom of movement in the Western world, signaled in part by the emergence of a global passport regime. However, the impetus and groundwork for the standardization of official identification practices emerged in a nineteenth-century world increasingly on the move.

An expanding industrial economy (within a developing international state system) provided the context for the movement of people. Readily available ideas to make sense of this changing world included the rights of individuals, national identity, and the free movement of goods, money, and people. Racism often mediated the contradictions between these liberal ideas and governing practices; this was definitely the case when it came to the establishment of a global system of migrant identification between the 1880s and 1910s.

In the decades after Remond's encounter in London, migration around the world increased dramatically. In the middle of the nineteenth century the annual number of migrants totaled fewer than half a million people. By the late 1890s, this had increased to 1.5 million people, and in the first decade of the twentieth century it doubled to more than three million migrants a year (as the arguments in this chapter about record keeping make clear, such numbers should be taken as a rough approximation). Much of this migration involved a transatlantic journey; however, a considerable number of migrants came from East Asia and South Asia (and there were large circulations of people within those regions). Racism directed at Chinese and Indian migrants produced many of the principles and techniques central to the development of modern border control, particularly the use of documents to create stable *individual* identities increasingly articulated to *nation*-states. Managing mobility and difference was central to the work of empires, which functioned both as political orders grounded in difference and as systems that depended on mobility, whether of slaves, indentured or free workers, soldiers and police, or administrators.

The attempt to manage the movement of particular people centered on documents that used standardized categories to present the information governments believed necessary to identify a person. However, officials at borders greeted the introduction of such documents with indifference at best. To function as identity documents to police migration the papers presented to officials had to be recognizable as official and authentic, and be accurately and easily linked to the bearer. Officials assigned to ports of entry did not trust the papers to do any of these things. Instead they continued to believe that as they were the people on the spot, their own face-to-face judgment was all that was necessary to verify identity.

Identifying Chinese and Indian Migrants

In 1882, the federal government halted the migration of Chinese laborers to the United States. Documents were issued to Chinese exempt from exclusion. These included merchants and their families, college students, travelers, and laborers already resident in the United States; women could enter only if married to a man in one of the exempt categories. The complicated set of documents used to manage the exemptions from the act was the first of its kind at US borders. However, officials trusted neither the "Chinamen" who presented the documents, nor the absent official they did not know whose signature authorized the document. Therefore, customs officers charged with enforcing the act tended to prioritize evidence from what was present: the body and appearance of the person who presented the document. The bodies of Chinese who claimed to be merchants were read to provide evidence of labor: calluses, sunburnt legs or arms, the size and shape of fingers, clothing, and demeanor were all accepted as proof that the applicant was a laborer pretending to be a merchant. The legal system was less certain about the use of this evidence. Chinese denied entry did enjoy some success in using courts to overturn decisions. However, most reversals occurred because of the presentation of other proof; judges upheld personal appearance as an acceptable criterion equal in value to documents.

Similar identification practices were followed at seaports in the South African colonies. In the early twentieth century the estimated forty thousand Indians in the southwest Indian Ocean area were quickly perceived as a threat to local trade and culture and became subject to immigration bans and restrictions. In the Cape Colony, Indian boys under eighteen years old whose fathers already lived in the Cape constituted an exempt category from such bans. As the historian Uma Dhupelia-Mesthrie shows, officials favored visual evidence centered on the applicant's body to verify a claim under this exemption. There were efforts to make this reading of bodies produce more "objective" evidence that the applicant was less than eighteen years old and related to the person who presented himself as his father; officials introduced formal medical exams centered on teeth, genitals, and body hair, along with x-rays (similar techniques and technologies were used at other borders around the world). When papers were used to assess the identity of a boy they tended to be statements that officials had taken from interviews with resident Indians who claimed to be related to the applicant. Although Cape officials introduced a requirement for documents issued by Indian authorities, they tended to ignore the document when an Indian boy presented it upon arrival in Cape Town.

Significant changes to the US enforcement of Chinese exclusion changed the role of documents in border control. As the historian Adam McKeown argues, this first attempt to systematically manage a range of identities through documents produced a template that would be used to manage the movement of Chinese migrants (and other targeted populations) around the world. The shift away from personal appearance toward a faith in documents occurred partly in response to the number of Chinese who claimed exemption through familial relationships. This increased faith in documents occurred during a period in which the US government began to adopt increasingly more rigorous administrative structures and methods.

In the 1890s, the arrival of a Chinese person generated a handful of pages that as a "file" offered little if any assessment of the evidence used to approve or deny entry. Officials did not use standardized forms or a standardized set of questions. However, by the end of the 1920s, the arrival of a Chinese person generated a case file that usually contained a single-spaced typed manuscript of around thirty pages and a multipage explanation of the decision to admit or exclude an individual. Standardized forms and an improved indexing system indicate that officials created files in anticipation of future use. These files were prepared on the assumption that someone with no previous knowledge of a case could read it and understand it. Cross-referencing and the production of monthly reports in triplicate illustrated a new understanding of accountability and predictability intended to prevent individual discretion from affecting cases.

Equally significant were attempts to better control the work of US officials who issued documents in China. This involved the standardization of methods of investigation and the introduction of comprehensive filing systems to improve communication among officials. The former was relatively successful; the latter proved harder to maintain. In both cases the increased use of documents sought to relocate US officials and Chinese into a centralized administrative network where procedures would produce reliable identification. The local knowledge previously used to verify identities was now considered unreliable. In this scenario, local Chinese were considered "interested parties," in contrast to the administratively neutral US government officials whose endeavors to enforce the act apparently did not come with any "interest."

Therefore, in practice the identity of "merchant" originated in the criteria outlined in Chinese exclusion law and policy, not the social networks within which Chinese lived. Policy directed officials not to use evidence and witnesses provided by Chinese. The application centered on an interview. In recording his impressions on a standardized form, the US official determined the applicant's fate. These impressions became "objective" owing to the belief that the categories in standardized forms would discipline officials to ignore other information outside the document, especially personal bias. This paper-based procedure was intended to produce a fixed identity constituted by information comprehensible to multiple officials and institutions, regardless of their location. The claim to objectivity through procedure masked the political and racist worldview that created Chinese exclusion.

The increased use of documents did not decrease the problems associated with policing migration. Problems arose from both the failure and the success of documentary systems. In the newly created Union of South Africa, corruption scandals in 1915 revealed officials who worked with Indian agents to exploit the system (or lack of system) for profit. These officials removed or destroyed existing documents and provided Indian immigration brokers with blank forms to create false identities. If thumbprints were required, some officials ensured they were deliberately smudged to make them ineffective or had them added to fraudulent documents after arrival. The subsequent reforms in record keeping, salaries, and fingerprint detection, along with the standardizing of rules across departments, did result in more efficient identification of migrants at seaports. However, as the historian Andrew MacDonald shows, an unintended consequence of the success of the reforms was to shift the site of illegal entry to land borders. A market in fake identity permits developed along South Africa's eastern frontier with Mozambique and Swaziland. Networks of local officials on either side of the border colluded with Indian merchant houses of the coastal West, syndicates from Madeira, and "tropical" African migrants to move permits, people, and money across the region.

While corruption occurred among US officials, the main impediment to enforcing Chinese exclusion came from the successful attempt to limit the information used to verify identity to categories outlined in law and policy. The reality that the documentary system produced the identity used to manage the movement of Chinese resulted in the creation of "paper families." These "families" came into existence when on his return to China a man exempt from exclusion through US citizenship sold his status as a "father" to men who could then enter the United States as the child of a citizen. Frequently the "children" received coaching to prepare them for their arrival in the United States, in addition to fraudulent papers.

In response, officials doubled down on their reliance on documents. They closely read documents to find inconsistencies between statements and comments from a "son" with those already recorded in the files of other "family" members. A system developed in which inspectors were usually able to cross-check an applicant's answers with those provided in previous interviews with people identified as family members, even if those interviews had taken place several years earlier and at another immigration office. In a typical case, twelve additional files would be pulled for comparison. However, despite these attempts at verification, in 1950 it was estimated that nearly one-quarter of Chinese in the United States had illegally entered as "paper children."

Travelers and Passports

At the same time governments sought to use documents to better police the movement of migrants, passport laws were removed or simply lay dormant in most European states; South American countries introduced constitutions that granted citizens and foreigners a right to travel without passports. This changed with the outbreak of World War I, when emergency wartime passport laws were introduced to secure borders. In the 1920s, under the guidance of the League of Nations, these temporary passport laws became a permanent system used to manage the movement of individuals through a system of nation-states.

In a society that had frequently relied on local reputation to identify someone, the idea that a government could replace respectability with an impersonal document seemed preposterous. Therefore, some people viewed a required passport not as a privilege, but as a symbol of eroding trust between citizens and their government. The request for supporting documents in an application over and above someone's statement underscored this. To demand information in the form of official documents instead of accepting a person's word was understood not as evidence of identity but as evidence a government did not trust you, that government officials considered you dishonest and untrustworthy.

This criticism of passports came from a particular part of the population, those who could afford to travel for leisure. This was a group whose class and race meant in most cases they had not been placed in a position where documents had been required to prove their identity. Although the origin of the passport as a required document to systematically manage people's mobility is attributed to regulations introduced during the French Revolution, most people who traveled through Europe for leisure did not encounter a demand for passports. In the nineteenth century, the European states that followed the French model used passports (along with permits and registration systems) to control mobility, criminality, and military desertion. This practice arose particularly as paupers and vagabonds became the target of regulations introduced in response to the perceived danger of unemployment and the fear of revolution in the 1830s and 1840s. However, by the middle of the century, passports largely ceased to play a role in the policing of mobility.

Therefore, required passports introduced a wider population to the world of identification documents. The anxiety and concerns this created is captured in the reaction to the use of photographs on passports, which was part of the so-called passport nuisance. From an official point of view, a photograph promised to erase bias from the identification process. Prior to photographs most passports contained a written physical description usually in the form of a list that people added single-word descriptions to, for example, Face: Oval; Nose: Roman. Officials came to see this as too subjective. Some applicants immediately considered this representation of identity to be unnecessary and inappropriate. The belief that a physical description presented an affront to a person spoke to the lingering idea of the passport as a letter. This association conveyed a very different understanding of identity and a person's relationship to information. From this point of view identity was not a thing to be reduced to a handful of categories generated by administrative procedure. Rejecting such an approach, an English novelist ignored the list of descriptors and completed his passport application describing himself as "of melancholic appearance."

However, when photographs supplemented a written description on a passport a photographer had to follow a set of guidelines to produce an image that officials considered objective evidence. These included photographing the subject in natural light looking straight at the camera in front of a light background. This photographic style, borrowed from criminal identification, sought to eliminate context to bring to the foreground information that could be seen as neutral or objective. This version of photographic accuracy clashed with the understanding of photographic truth shared by most applicants. Borrowed from portrait painting, this "truth" depended on a dark background with a three-quarter pose often including the whole body, not just the face. The clashing of these two different styles resulted in claims that a passport photograph in its similarity to a rogues' gallery image misrepresented a person as a criminal.

The idea that someone did not look like their passport photograph captured the anxiety at the core of the resistance to passports that emerged in small pockets in the early twentieth century. For critics of the passport a fundamental misidentification existed at the very core of this purported identity document. It appeared the government had created an identity separate from a person's sense of self; an honest trustworthy person had become an object of inquiry.

Concerned citizens considered the government was telling people who they were. In fact this was precisely what was happening. Well-to-do-travelers were encountering the consequences of faith in the purportedly objective information that officials used to identify migrants. Instead of using information from existing social networks, states chose to use administrative procedures to reduce personal identity to the minimum information necessary to know and recognize an individual for the purposes of governing. Therefore, accuracy and reliability created an identity that individuals had to measure up to when they presented a passport.

GOVERNING EMPIRES

The difficulties officials encountered using documents to manage the movement of migrants is one example of the problems associated with using paperwork to govern over distance. With its investment in extending markets, developing forms of government, and promoting specific ideas of progress and civilization, empire involved an intensification of the problems that distance created for rule within states. In addition, empire in the nineteenth century experienced both continuity and change. The century saw the fragmentation of the Ottoman and Chinese empires and the decline in imperial power of Spain, Portugal, and the Netherlands along with the rise of Japan and the United States. Britain, France, Germany (after unification in 1871), and Italy became the major European imperial powers. The end of the nineteenth century also saw the beginnings of a marked increase in struggle against empire that would intensify throughout the twentieth century. At the same time, the exploitative economic possibilities that drove empire increased as the use of the steamship and steam locomotive made it easier to move goods over long distances (aided by the opening of the Suez Canal). Along with the telegraph these technological developments also increased the speed at which information could travel.

In this context, despite the problems it generated, the systematic collection of documentary information became a key part of how governments responded to the ambitions and uncertainties that nineteenth-century empire raised. As we have seen in the attempts to identify migrants, the introduction of documents did not guarantee control. However, this did not lessen the desire to ground government in the use of documents to name, constitute, and know people and things. This mode of governing produced information that was "local" in the sense it was about specific people and places and "local" in the sense that it was collected and classified in a specific place by specific people. However, if it was to be used to make sense of events and to determine actions, local information had to be mediated through the worldview of the officials located in an empire's administrative center.

Attempts to establish the reliable participation of officials from the imperial power or local community became a critical part of administrative practices. The role of local information and colonial intermediaries emphasizes that the colony and the "metropole" need to be considered together, not isolated as two discrete entities. Increasingly historians have come to view empires as structures always in process, not static units. From this perspective, whether subordinate agents actually ran the show, or whether the pervasiveness of "investigative modalities" limited the role of local workers, is a subject of debate among historians. Aspects of that debate are evident in the following discussion. However, the focus remains on the changing role and status of information in the administration of empires (and reflecting the historiographical bias toward the dominant empire of the period, it centers on the British Empire). To look at imperial documents from this point of view is to recognize their role in a system of control, not simply as a means to transmit information; it emphasizes the centrality of information to the maintenance of imperial rule in colonies. However, while it is important to recognize that empire was conceived through a desire for order, this aspiration did not result in total control; failure and improvisation marked the administration of empire.

Changing Local Information Practices

Imperial governing involved claims to authority that depended on articulating localities and local knowledge to the centralized authority of the empire. In the late 1840s, the Dutch government introduced a policy to manage schooling in the Dutch Indies (present-day Indonesia) that made clear the status of the local in the production and circulation of knowledge. The policy sought to have Dutch parents send their sons to be educated in the Netherlands. Dutch Indies schools that were run on European principles could educate Dutch children, but colonial officials believed a child's education would be more successful if it took place in the Netherlands, where students would receive an authentic Dutch education. In addition, officials expressed confidence that anything the children learned about the Dutch Indies would be presented within a framework that recognized the superiority of European-based knowledge. The policy resulted in a series of protests from the Dutch population who had decided to stay in the colony. They viewed it as a challenge to their status as full Dutch citizens and a bid to intervene in their familial relationships.

The use of paperwork and specific documents provided a more common mechanism to relocate local information production and transmission within the dominant ideas of imperial powers. However, in contrast to the Dutch policy, this attempt to articulate local knowledge occurred in a documentary network that connected colonial territories and imperial centers. Procedure and documents were assumed to provide a structure to bring "native" ways of knowing fully into the imperial project. The use of paper involved challenges to existing knowledge practices such as storage and memory. This resulted in an instrumental mode of information that became critical to governing an empire. Officials privileged information produced through procedures instead of knowledge based in the expertise and experience of a "knower."

Nineteenth-century encounters with local cultures that did not use paper make explicit the importance of the materiality of paper to changes in administrative authority.

Paper enabled the movement of information across space rather than the transmission of knowledge over time; it was less dependent on the presence and singular expertise of authoritative figures. This becomes apparent in the colonization of New Zealand in the nineteenth century.

Maori cultural authority depended on embodied knowledge embedded within rituals. Knowledge was stored in a range of objects. Made by skilled experts from wood, bone, or *pounamu* (jade), these objects while durable were relatively scarce. Because the knowledge contained in the objects required expertise and rank to be accessed, this system ensured the reproduction of traditional authority and protected *tapu* knowledge.

The paper that the British used to facilitate communication in New Zealand and within the empire offered a new mode of storing information to Maori communities. In the far south of New Zealand, Kāi Tahu Whānui (the primary Indigenous community in the region) used whatever paper became available to create new archives of information. Unlike in British society, the look of paper did not affect its authority and status in Maori culture. Instead, Kāi Tahu were attracted by paper as a new disembodied and, therefore, more portable way to store knowledge.

As the historian Tony Ballantyne argues, the experiences of Kāi Tahu suggest the arrival of paper in New Zealand transformed Maori cultural practices and political traditions. Print undeniably diluted traditional power, but it did ensure that elements of old knowledge would survive the violence and ruptures of colonialism. Kāi Tahu did not abandon traditional cultural frameworks such as *whakapapa* (genealogy). Letter writing, diaries, minutes from meetings, and whakapapa books gave these frameworks a new archival form. Paper also facilitated engagement with European colonizers. Literate Maori attempted to navigate the paper world that supported the colonial order, and they used paper as a key medium to fight against the inequities of colonial rule.

Another example from the British Empire illustrates how intentional attempts to train people to work with information within the developing paper world of empire challenged existing conceptions of memory and knowledge. As the historian Bhavani Raman shows, from the mid-eighteenth century the presence of missionary schools offered an alternative role for memory in education that initiated a new function for written language in colonial India.

In southern India, existing Tamil *tinnai* (verandah) schools used texts to cultivate memory as a mode of learning. Memorization was taught as a skill to discipline the mind and senses. Regarded in this way, memory training assisted in the development of students' capacity to understand and comprehend their social world. In contrast, schools run by missionaries came to emphasize memorization as a way to teach the more practical skills of writing and reading. Brought back to England, a version of this technique known as the "monitorial system" became popular as an effective way to teach reading and writing to poor children in the first half of the nineteenth century; Quaker networks spread it to North America.

In the Tamil region this technique helped reorient schools toward lessons that would give their upper-caste students the skills required to work in the offices of mission stations and the East India Company. This alternative school model introduced an Anglo *vernacular that prized and restricted English to upper classes. Transcription and dictation became common as schools became places to learn to read and write rather than sites to hone intellectual prowess. The source of lessons became prose, not poetry, as the focus of education turned to mastering the written language, not the spoken language. In textbooks and lessons the teaching of grammar was frequently subsumed under lessons that treated reading and writing as clerical skills.

Establishing the Authority of Documents

Missionary education fits in a wider structure that became the source of a legitimation crisis for British rule in India. Beginning in 1600, the East India Company had governed India through a royal charter that gave it a monopoly over British trade with India in return for customs revenue. At the turn of the nineteenth century, the East India Company introduced administrative reforms intended to make its records transparent and uniform. These changes were a product of parliamentary pressure following scandals and allegations of nepotism triggered by articles of impeachment against Warren Hastings, the first governor-general of Bengal. Hastings was acquitted, but in a trial that lasted seven years, the role of the East India Company in an expanding British Empire became a focus of public debates and political intervention.

The faith that written procedures would provide the transparency and uniformity needed to check abuses of power changed the administrative model the company used in India. This structure continued to depend on local offices overseen by a British collector. However, the documents produced in these offices now had to satisfy the evidentiary requirements of British courts whether they were intended for the British Parliament, company directors, shareholders in London, or colonial subjects. The assumption was that if these standards were followed any interested party would easily understand the information in the documents. Specific forms of attestation became critical to a document's status as transparent and self-evident and, therefore, not subject to local bias. This emphasis on procedures to verify company documents in India gave new status to acts of signing, stamping, and registering, in contrast to traditional practices that depended on the collective validation of people the community identified as respectable.

As in other instances, the attempt to create authority through new verification practices provided the means to challenge or manipulate that authority. The East India Company reforms instituted an administrative structure in which a British collector and judges supervised caste notables, village accountants, native revenue officers, and judicial men. The documents created to record transactions at this local level became subject to fraud based in the signatures and stamps used to verify documents. This fraud contributed to a system that proved to be wasteful and costly. However, instead of changing the conditions in which documents were produced, the official solution reduced documentary requirements for local workers. Company supervision continued, but minor local officials no longer had to maintain detailed records. This decreased the potential for fraud, but it also made supervision more difficult, with the result that abuses of power continued. Raman argues that although these changes did little to prevent abuse of power they did enhance the authority of documents. Put simply, fraud and corruption were no longer a problem of paperwork. Instead, they were attributed to "native duplicity." The response to this was to bring paperwork in as the solution rather than categorize it as the problem: complaints generated written documents and petitions.

Presenting Information

The early nineteenth-century debates over corruption in India also revealed the British Colonial Office lacked basic information, such as a list of the civil and military officials who held appointments throughout the empire. Although the Colonial Office was relatively small in size, a lack of staff to compile such lists was not the cause of its absence; the information necessary to make these lists did not exist in London. The knowledge that did arrive in London from its colonies usually took the form of correspondence. The lack of uniform content across these letters hindered any endeavor to control or envision the empire as a whole, or to make individual colonies legible as discrete entities. The historian Zoe Laidlaw argues that in the first half of the nineteenth century the desire to know the empire and colonies in this way saw the beginnings of a transition away from correspondence to more uniform and numerical-based reports.

An attempt to standardize annual reports from colonial officials produced documents that became known as "Blue Books." Separated from correspondence these annual returns came to provide numerical information on revenue and expenditure, population, exports, and details of explorations. However, once in London, Blue Books were not used in any comprehensive way. The Colonial Office did not produce a digest of contents or publish information from the reports, nor did it circulate information from the Blue Books to other government bodies; it still lacked the administrative capacity and desire to use the reports for comparative analysis. While Blue Books remained largely unread, officials in London did read the descriptive report that a governor had to compile. Governors were reminded that they had to write these reports, not delegate them to junior officials, as was expected to be the case with the Blue Book.

The importance given to a descriptive report and the status of its author underscored the type of information the Colonial Office continued to value. This information took the form of the written words of people in positions of authority. The Colonial Office remained more comfortable dealing with correspondence from networks established via personal connections between senior London-based officials and administrators and other Englishmen known to the office.

The reliance on personal-based information ended in the late 1830s when an abrupt change in Colonial Office leadership resulted in a renewed effort to create a collection of information less dependent on specific individuals. A desire for transparent information that could be more easily examined reoriented the Colonial Office to the type of information found in Blue Books rather than in the reports that accompanied them. The new leadership sought greater centralization and control of information from the colonies with the belief that it would enable collation and comparison.

The use of numerical information to understand colonies and the empire existed alongside the recognition that this information was frequently inaccurate. Notably, officials circulated Robert Montgomery Martin's *Statistics of the Colonies of the British Empire* even though they knew it contained errors. The origin of the errors seemed to be evenly shared between Martin's transcriptions and the Blue Books he based his volume on. However, Martin's novel use of classifying, recording, and mapping made the book an attractive resource. For example, he included a tabular index and a statistical chart with a foldout sheet that used thirty categories to describe every British colony.

The use of numbers to describe the empire and the uniform presentation that statistical charts and tables offered were part of a shift away from a personal mode of information based in narrative and description. More and more the latter was viewed as a form of information that did not travel well. It was also information that did not enable comparison at a time when governing on a large scale was increasingly seen to require comparative thinking. This was the beginning of a mode of colonial governance and policy implementation that depended on structures of collection and categories of analysis based on an understanding that information should be transparent and therefore easily understood outside of the context in which it was produced.

Compiling Local Information: *Gazetteer and Census

In India, the change to prioritize numerical information picked up momentum in the second half of the nineteenth century when the British government took over colonial rule of India from the East India Company. This was a period during which concerns about security and the loyalty of the population began to replace revenue collection as the driving force behind the gathering of information. The Great Rebellion of 1857 was the catalyst for this. The focus on loyalty brought with it an investment in understanding people and culture to help explain the behavior of specific groups. As the historian Nicholas Dirks contends, British authorities increasingly believed that if they improved their knowledge of the social organization of India it would be easier to maintain social order; numbers could be analyzed and compared to suggest reasons for unrest. Specifically, this information could be directed toward military recruitment, policing, land settlement, and legal policy.

Reflecting the rise of comparative thinking in government, officials believed that if they could take local information and make comparisons across common categories "India" would reveal itself and become an object that could be governed more effectively. Various compendiums, notably manuals and gazetteers, became more important than collections of local information and texts. The key was a format that lent itself to consultation, not reading. Narrative descriptions and explanations were reduced in favor of numerical tables in the belief they allowed information to be more easily digested and compared. However, at the local level, reports and manuals still tended to mix discursive accounts with statistics.

In 1869, W. W. Hunter was appointed director-general of statistics to the government of India; eight years later he became director-general of gazetteers. The existence of these positions represented an attempt to centralize and systematize the collection of information. The goal was to create a single statistical account at the provincial level and then consolidate these provincial gazetteers into a single volume. Hunter was not tasked with collecting information but with coordinating information. His appointment as director-general of gazetteers occurred after he had produced the twenty-volume *Statistical Account of Bengal*. Other provincial gazetteer projects began to be published after 1881.

Hunter's early forays into statistical volumes drew heavily from an all-India census, which took place in 1871 and 1872 (the 1857 rebellion derailed an earlier census). This census built on methods used in previous tabulations. However, earlier efforts to enumerate people in specific territories had been part of the East India Company's goal to enhance revenue collection. The innovation in the early 1870s census came in the attempt to generate uniform procedures, standards, and categories for enumeration within the logic of a census.

Although the subsequent census in 1881 is viewed as much more successful, in both instances problems of definition and categorization thwarted the effort to compare and contrast information collected across India. Difficulties began with the choice of caste as the main organizational category. While this made sense within the orientalist ideas of hierarchy and race shared by British colonizers, it proved impossible to implement with any consensus in a census (as well as in gazetteers). Problems included the definition of specific castes and the consistent spelling of caste names. How to rank castes proved to be particularly fraught especially when officials chose to use the varna principle to determine ranks. Between 1871 and 1881 the number of castes identified in the census increased from 3,208 to 19,044, even though officials had decided to include only castes with more than one hundred thousand people. In 1891, occupation replaced caste as the main organizing category. However, with similar definitional issues and an intensification of ethnological interest in India, caste returned in 1901. Prior to the 1911 census, caste associations formed to petition to have their caste recognized and to contest their position in the official hierarchy; these petitions weighed in at 120 pounds. With the 1911 census it was decided to collect caste information but not classify castes by status.

In Egypt the nineteenth-century development of a census and the collection of vital statistics came directly from a military-based response to security needs and the need to maintain power. Although part of the Ottoman Empire, Egypt's somewhat independent governor, Mehmed Ali, sought to create a modern army to give him more power in his relationship with Istanbul. While he was not from a leading Istanbul household, Egyptian pressure had led to Ali (an Albanian military leader) being appointed in 1805 to restore Ottoman authority after Napoleon's unsuccessful occupation of Egypt. Ali's efforts to create an army of loyal Egyptian soldiers relied on the introduction of a medical and public health administration that provided the foundation for a system to update figures for the numbers of births and deaths and, in 1848, a national census.

The precensus attempts to monitor and police the population in the interests of conscription had centered on the bodies of potential soldiers. Officials rounded up peasants with ropes around their necks or tattooed peasants to make it easier to identify deserters. A registration system was introduced as another attempt to manage the local population. The registers recorded a person's name, physical description, village, and province. It was supplemented with a "passport" issued to people who moved from their home village.

Official concern about the health of soldiers accompanied these fears about desertion. The effort to limit the effect of disease similarly boosted the authority of experts, documents, and record keeping. A new medical school, founded in the late 1820s, trained doctors for the army. Graduating doctors also became involved in public hygiene programs that depended on the systematic collection of information. They worked on smallpox vaccination, enforced quarantine regulations, and established systems to help the police in murder cases. Trained midwives became instrumental in these programs and in the creation and implementation of a system to record births.

According to the historian Khaled Fahmy, the change to systematic record keeping had legal consequences unique within the Ottoman Empire. A legal system centered on public law was created separate from sharia courts and a focus on private law. This began as a system to target elite households. Drawing from the techniques applied to the military and public health it introduced a documentary system to identify individuals that was distinct from the traditional system that relied on witnesses embedded in social networks. The public law system used to identify people outside of specific social relations introduced a category previously unknown in Egypt's legal system: the individual as an autonomous, isolated person.

Ali's actions in Egypt and the Ottoman Empire in the 1830s (including taking over the Sudan and Syria and his threatening gestures to Istanbul) caused the sultan to grant his family hereditary right to govern Egypt. The fraught relationship with Egypt and increasing economic subordination to European powers contributed to the belief in Istanbul that, as the Ottoman Empire fragmented and decreased in power, its stabilization required the centralization of power and the downplaying, or ignoring, of intermediaries. The resulting changes occurred as part of the Tanzimat ("Reorganization," 1839–71). This included a transformation of the sultan's scribal corps into something closer to a civil service or bureaucracy. A restructured Ministry of Foreign Affairs embraced specialization with a range of offices including the Translation Office, Foreign Correspondence Office, Free Military Press Office, and the Bureau of Nationality. Although consular and diplomatic services were also reorganized, the creation of empire-wide infrastructure often proved too challenging.

"Ethnographic" Information

The movement to numerical and statistical information evident in the census in India and Egypt did not signal the abandonment of the collection of more descriptive information. The ethnographical interest that saw caste maintain its organizational status in the Indian census produced a large body of written literature. For its advocates such literature was essential to interpreting the numbers presented in the census and gazetteers. This investment in what was becoming known as "anthropology" became important to the governing of a number of empires in the last quarter of the nineteenth century. French rule of Algeria provides one example.

From the 1880s, a series of administrative changes increased political ties between the colony of Algeria and France. Algeria had never been regarded as a colony for French settlement. It had been claimed from Ottoman North Africa in the 1830s in the context of domestic politics and power struggles with European states, not from any direct imperial drive. Following the fall of the Second Empire in 1870, French rule of Algeria became linked to the redefinition of empire within a republic not a monarchy. At the same time that the secular Third Republic increasingly viewed Algerian Islam as a threat, the settler population (including not only French citizens, but also Italian, Maltese, Spanish, and Jewish settler groups) sought to claim Algeria as its own. In this context French officials sought information about Muslim groups with the goal of controlling them. The information took the form of systematically organized narratives. These publications provided the framework the French used to understand Algeria.

The published reports and books comprised narratives, analyses, and descriptions drawn from personal interactions. The historian George Trumbull argues that these interactions were interpreted as typical, that informants became archetypes, and that the authenticity of firsthand observation created "facts" that gave these descriptions the force of truth. Administrators with local language ability became critical to documenting events and social groups. Travelers and scholars also contributed to this literature. However, through logistical aid, its influence on publishing, and the work of colonial societies, the colonial state exerted a critical role in these nonstate publications.

Administrators persisted in writing books and reports as a sideline to their official work into the early twentieth century. They continued to base their expertise in participant observation and a belief in the authority of long-term studies' ability to synthesize and analyze information to make it useful for government. The systematic narrative writing about culture these efforts produced fits into the category of "ethnography." It was an implicit rejection of what administrators viewed as the superficial and limited expertise that questionnaires relied on and that the French authorities had begun to use in the mid-1890s. Surveys were introduced to complement field reports from administrators. Authorities sought statistical information, general descriptions, and photographs of each Sufi order. Questionnaires were produced to guide the collection of information, often completed by officials who lacked the networks of Indigenous informants and language skills of administrators. However, despite the concerns this raised for the colonial administrators steeped in claims to "participant observation," the survey provided the substance of an 1897 report the governor-general commissioned.

CAPITALISM AND INFORMATION

The development of modern industrial enterprises provides another site from which to consider the specific relationship between paper, information, and decision-making processes that emerged in the nineteenth century. As with empire and government these new conditions tended to encourage more impersonal modes of information. However, this should not be read as a before-and-after narrative in which preindustrial financial dealings were solely personal, in contrast to the impersonal information industrial economics used to focus on productive investment and that determined credit decisions. Elements of the personal and impersonal existed in both periods.

Credit Networks

To loan money a lender has to decide if a borrower can be trusted. This depends on information. If the borrower is not part of a network of personal ties another source of information is required, which introduces an impersonal element into the transaction. The relatively limited territory in which most financial dealings took place prior to the nineteenth century has fostered the belief that only personal knowledge underwrote the lending of money. However, from the middle of the eighteenth century, Parisian notaries were the main players in the city's long-term credit market. They functioned as intermediaries who mobilized capital. As the economic historians Philip Hoffman, Gilles Postel-Vinay, and Jean-Laurent Rosenthal argue, *notaries were at the center of a mode of borrowing that mixed the personal and impersonal. While the loans depended on a notary's personal knowledge of borrowers and lenders, the lack of a preexisting relationship between the borrower and lender lent the transaction an impersonal element.

In Paris notaries had begun as legal experts who could draw up papers covering a range of transactions involving property and other assets. However, because the law required them to keep copies of the documents they created, notaries maintained a detailed collection of information about their clients' wealth. It was this information that allowed them to arrange loans between their clients. Notaries could offer information that was more precise than public opinion. Lenders wanted the service of notaries on the assumption that they had evidence of the legitimacy of collateral being offered, for example knowing that the property being put up was not already mortgaged to other creditors.

At the turn of the nineteenth century, Parisian notaries annually brokered new loans for private borrowers and new debt for the state equivalent to the annual earnings of 750,000 day laborers. However, legal and administrative reforms soon made relevant information easier for lenders to access. A system that required real estate transactions and liens to be registered made public the information that used to be the preserve of notaries, which contributed to the rise of other intermediaries like banks. In the early 1840s, new legislation restricted the role of notaries in credit markets.

Credit Reporting

In the United States a challenge to the question of who to trust as a buyer or seller of goods occurred as nationally organized circuits of exchange and finance emerged in the first half of the nineteenth century. Strangers had always been part of local business interactions, but a more nationally focused market increased the potential opportunities to transact with strangers, which exposed the drawbacks of an understanding of trust limited to locally generated reputations. As the media historian Josh Lauer shows, the response to trading in a national market was an attempt to systematically collect local knowledge so it could be nationally circulated as information about an organization or individual's creditworthiness. By the 1920s, this provided the basis for a viable market in information bought and sold within business and financial communities.

In 1841, the businessman Lewis Tappen started a centralized subscription-based service to report on the creditworthiness of firms. In an era without financial statements and annual reports Tappen relied on local correspondents (usually unpaid lawyers) to supply information. In reporting on this new phenomenon, newspapers labeled credit reporters "spies" or "private detectives." Articles played up the acquisition of local knowledge as the collection of gossip from a businessman's family, friends, and domestic staff. As one early critic put it, for all intents and purposes credit reporting was "an organized system of espionage." The extent to which it was either systematic or espionage is debatable, but what is not up for debate is the fact that in the United States the history of documentary surveillance begins in the private sector not in the actions of the federal government.

In the 1860s, the main commercial credit-reporting companies began to make significant changes in a bid to make their product more useful and appealing to existing and potential customers. Full-time credit reporters were hired to replace local correspondents, and a ratings system replaced descriptive entries. For credit companies a more abstract conception of creditworthiness not only solved the problem of understanding narrative reports, but also made it easier to present large amounts of information. A coded reference book published in 1868 contained information on 350,000 firms; an 1886 edition listed one million firms.

At the same time, organizations emerged to collect information on consumers. They also used alphanumeric *codes to signify relative creditworthiness. This information centered on establishing a person's character rather than listing income and property. Lauer argues that the creation of consumer credit reporting introduced the idea of a "financial identity," an impersonal, disembodied identity that could affect a person's social interactions.

The ongoing struggle to get information from merchants, the time and labor needed to produce reports, and an inability to stop subscribers sharing information with non-subscribers combined to make consumer credit reporting a difficult way to make money. In an attempt to become a viable industry, consumer credit agencies sought to "modernize" their operations. In line with turn-of-the-century paperwork initiatives this meant standardization of application forms and record-keeping practices, as well as elaborate systems to code, update, and communicate information. Index cards became critical to organizing and storing the information used to identify creditworthiness. These new technologies and techniques in commercial paperwork had emerged to manage the increased volume of information generated when capitalism entered its corporate phase.

Corporate Management and Office Work

Modern industrial enterprises signaled a new alternative to businesses personally run by owners. This occurred when the scale of individual businesses increased. As part of the reaction to this change in scale a new set of organizational structures and techniques (at least new to business) became increasingly pervasive in the second half of the nineteenth century as "managers" arrived to oversee large-scale enterprises, eventually bringing with them the profession of "management." The United States became a global reference point for these developments; in 1913 the United States accounted for 36 percent of the world's industrial output, followed by Germany (16 percent) and Great Britain (14 percent).

The new business enterprises tended to take on a corporate form as production facilities were organized in response to technological changes and as manufacturing enterprises moved into purchasing and distribution through mergers and (what would now be called) vertical integration. The organizational structure had two main characteristics: distinct operating units and a hierarchy of full-time salaried executives to manage the units.

This structure was quickly presented as necessary to exploit the economies of scale and scope enabled by the deployment of changes in production, distribution, transportation, and communication. These changes increased the volume of economic activities to a point where the "visible hand" (of management) replaced the "invisible hand" (of the market); administrative coordination became more efficient and profitable than market coordination. This resulted in a demand for information on a scale not previously encountered in manufacturing and finance.

The new administrative structure placed operating decisions in the hands of managers; hence some historians have taken to call these changes "managerial capitalism" instead of corporate capitalism or industrial capitalism. In the United States, management as a profession developed from the 1880s as engineers began to occupy many of the new management positions. The new profession advocated the gathering, handling, analyzing, and circulating of information as a way to better control production. The "machine" with its ideas of harmony and order became central to the idea of business as a managerial problem. This explicitly carried the assumption that all problems had technical solutions. The technocratic approach of early management provided the context for mechanical engineer Frederick Taylor's writings on factory management and equipment standardization, as well as his decision to emphasize the rationalization of labor when he promoted his program of scientific management.

However, while the techniques that belonged to management, especially Taylor's form of scientific management, are usually associated with the corporation and the factory, they did not need modern forms of capitalism to develop. The historian Caitlin Rosenthal shows that techniques akin to scientific management existed among American and West Indian slaveholders. On plantations there were hierarchies similar to the multidivisional form of the corporation, a standardization of accounts enabled a form of separation of ownership and management, and, most significantly, there was a commitment to the productivity analysis attributed to scientific management. In the case of the latter the regularity of picking records shows that regimented procedures for measurement of work existed on plantations and that this information when collected was recorded systematically. Plantation owners and scientific management proponents shared a mechanistic view of human labor underwritten by the belief that careful observation would reveal laws that could be used to extract the maximum amount of labor from workers; the information on the picking ability of individual slaves was put to work to determine how to improve the productivity of slaves and therefore the plantation.

In the last quarter of the nineteenth century the new discourse of "efficiency" became central to the articulation of these techniques and to ideas of productivity within industrial capitalism. While establishing maximum capacity and productivity for specific tasks and then using that as a baseline to assess individual workers remained the key, these ideas were articulated as part of a wider set of temporal anxieties. "Saving time" would become one of the major concerns of twentieth-century society as efficiency emerged as the goal not only of modern business but also of the economy and society in general.

However, efficiency was not only about reducing the time it took to complete a task. Efficiency in business also involved knowing what needed to be produced and when. As the business historian JoAnne Yates argues in *Control through Communication*, individual memory was replaced with "organizational memory." This went beyond monetary transactions and correspondence with distant places to facilitate the emergence of written internal communication. Planning became critical as day-to-day business increasingly viewed predicting the future as the path to profit. Information related to production, sales, finance, and accounting had to be coordinated to ensure that corporate capitalism fulfilled its promise to increase production and profit. Managers believed that information would provide the certainty that modern business required.

The quest for predictability transformed record keeping into an analytic exercise, not a descriptive one; this was part of a broader social turn to prediction as a path to certainty (or better managing uncertainty) that included crop estimates and weather forecasting. Cost accounting provides an important example of the rethinking of information and planning within finance. This new technique allowed management to compare and evaluate internal operations. By recording and classifying the costs associated with each aspect of production, cost accounting presented specific information intended to give management the ability to control and modify the production process.

While information became critical to realizing efficiency, the logics of efficiency also structured the production of information and, therefore, changed the way people encountered information. Similar in approach to managing labor, the aim was to break information apart into the smallest functional detail. The key was to do this in such a way that information could still be coordinated, that managers would not lose sight of the big picture.

As Yates shows, the application of principles of standardization to the production and circulation of information led to the increased use of standardized forms and the emergence of the memo. These documents arrived with the promise that impersonality would foster efficiency and enable control of large organizations. The memo eliminated wordy formalities associated with writing conventions to create an impersonal mode of writing centered on information as an easily identifiable unit.

The index card was another important information technology in this period. Tabulated information increasingly appeared on index cards that were stored in drawers and cabinets invented for library catalog cards. Cards were celebrated as part of a broader fetishizing of speed and a more specific desire for easy access to information. They became the home for information on sales, production statistics, and central accounts. The tables on cards became more complex as different techniques and technologies were used to make it easier to see specific information: notches, different colored metal tabs, and punched holes. The index card became the symbol of system. In the first decade of the twentieth century, *System: The Magazine of Business* began publishing in the United States. Almost every other page of the early volumes of *System* carried an illustration of an index card ruled to create a table to store information; on the rare occasion it was not a card it was a drawing of a ledger page. To apply "system" to shipping or insurance businesses, police records, a dentist's office, or a real estate office was to use specifically formatted cards. In the early decades of the twentieth century, as the volume of information increased in finance and insurance, another card would become increasingly important—the punch card, credited to Herman Hollerith, and celebrated for its use in processing the information collected in the 1890 US census.

The information work associated with these new technologies and techniques brought women into the office as clerical workers. In the United States in 1880 about 5 percent of clerical workers were women; in 1930, almost half of clerical workers were women. In the same period the number of employed adults who worked in offices increased from one in forty to one in twelve. A similar pattern occurred in offices throughout the Western world.

An articulation of cultural, social, and economic beliefs contributed to employers' conviction that women provided a competent and affordable supply of labor for new forms of office work. A belief in an innate feminine dexterity, exhibited in knitting and piano playing, aligned with the new technology and new specialization of work. This belief naturalized as feminine the tasks associated with paper and new office machines. When equipment like the typewriter, billing machines, and filing cabinets was exported from the United States, it arrived in countries gendered as something women should operate.

A woman was paid less than a man based on the assumption she was not a household's primary income earner. The belief that work constituted a temporary phase in a woman's life between school and marriage resulted in women leaving or being fired upon marriage: a practice known as the "marriage bar." The extent to which employers actively used the marriage bar is unclear, but enforced or not, it successfully underwrote the association of women with jobs that required limited training and skill and little opportunity for advancement. Nonetheless, women wanted to be clerical workers. Newspapers and popular culture represented clerical work as one of the best employment options for women regardless of class: better working conditions than in a factory, the potential for better pay than teaching, and a job that allowed a woman to use her education.

Therefore, gender was critical to legitimating and naturalizing the introduction of a particular form of work in the office. In the modern office, men held positions that involved responsibility while women did routine work to assist men. This assistance took the form of working with information. This information and work fitted in the reorganization of capitalism instituted in response to increased production. Through a new mode of manual labor women recorded, produced, and circulated information. This created a more functional relationship to information in which feminine clerical work did not involve skills associated with knowledge of the business.

CONCLUSION

Throughout the nineteenth century the creation of order became one of the primary roles of information. The employment of women as clerical workers and the emergence of management as a profession occurred as part of the dramatic increase in the speed and volume of production known as the Industrial Revolution. This response constituted an attempt to create order by controlling production at this new scale. Through the influence of a group of men trained as engineers this became an effort to manage a distinct form of capitalism more efficiently. In the development, expansion, and contraction of empires, information also became critical to dreams of total order. Priority was given to information that could be used to know populations and individuals. It was assumed such information would make government more effective. This was information that would make populations and territories "legible." Colonial rulers became increasingly aware of the need for the information they collected to accurately represent "reality" and to be understood as such far from the colonial territory.

These aspirations to order were not benign. Government and business brought specific worldviews to their understandings of how to order the world. Corporations, care of engineers and efficiency, understood order through a set of technocratic ideas. In practice these ideas sought to generate a specific form of control and power through making labor and information visible. Governments, in the creation and maintenance of empires, colonies, and national borders, used information to legitimate hierarchies based on race, religion, class, gender, and sexuality.

A specific conception of information served these aspirations to order. Framed by the scale of empire and corporations this was information that when compiled would stand in for the memory of individuals. This understanding of information suggests what would in the twentieth century be labeled a bureaucratic mode of information and organization, that is, a perception of information that enabled organizations to work beyond the capacities of individuals. Acknowledging the limitations of personal memory in the context of the scalar dynamics of the nineteenth century, the information governments and businesses sought became something that could be comprehended by anyone who read it. Information became distinct from knowledge through this claim to perspectival neutrality. This was not simply a turn to quantitative information, to statistics. It is better understood as information with an instrumental bias. Conceptualized in this way, information became something that could be processed, possessed, and exchanged. To be circulated information had to be less dependent on context. In the nineteenth century, this created an increased sensitivity to the role of documents as the sole source of context and therefore authority. Whether it took the form of an index card, a passport, or gazetteer page, paper was intended to support information so it could be read as self-evident. Paper as an object facilitated an understanding of information as a thing that existed separately from the person who created it. If paper was to fulfill this function the collection and production of information had to be centralized and made as uniform as possible. The goal was a manner of information production that privileged procedure over people. To that end, policies, technologies, and techniques were introduced to limit the discretion of the people who produced documents and those who read them. An important aspect of the nineteenth-century history of information was the attempt to forge a relationship between documents and information so that documents had the authority to make a person known to the state or represent his or her character to businesses, to allow for comparative thinking, and ultimately to make information understandable so it could be used for planning.

Craig Robertson

See also bureaucracy; cards; documentary authority; files; governance; information policy; memos; quantification; secretaries; surveilling; surveys and censuses

FURTHER READING

Tony Ballantyne, *Webs of Empire*, 2013; Christopher Bayly, *Empire and Information*, 1996; Antoinette Burton and Tony Ballantyne, *Empires and the Reach of the Global 1870–1945*, 2012; Bernard Cohn, *Colonialism and Its Forms of Knowledge*, 1996; Uma Dhupelia-Mesthrie, "False Fathers and False Sons: Immigration Officials in Cape Town, Documents and Verifying Minor Sons from India in the First Half of the Twentieth Century," *Kronos* 40, no. 1 (2014): 99–132; Nicholas Dirks, *Castes of Mind*, 2001; Khaled Fahmy, "Birth of the 'Secular' Individual: Medical and Legal Methods of Identification in Nineteenth-Century Egypt," in *Registration and Recognition: Documenting the Person in World History*, edited by Keith Breckenridge and Simon Szreter, 2012; Delphine Gardey, "Culture of Gender, Culture of Technology: The Gendering of Things in France's Office Spaces between 1890 and 1930," in *Cultures of Technology*, edited by Novotny Helga, 2006; Philip Hoffman, Gilles Postel-Vinay, and Jean-Laurent Rosenthal, "Information and Economic History: How the Credit Market in Old Regime Paris Forces Us to Rethink the Transition to Capitalism," *American Historical Review* 104, no. 1 (1999): 69–94; Zoe Laidlaw, *Colonial Connections 1815–45*, 2002; Estelle Lau, *Paper Families*, 2007; Josh Lauer, *Creditworthy*, 2017; Andrew MacDonald, "Forging the Frontiers: Travellers and Documents on the South Africa–Mozambique Border, 1890s–1940s," *Kronos* 40, no. 4 (2014): 154–77; Adam McKeown, *Melancholy Order*, 2011; Bhavani Raman, *Document Raj*, 2012; Craig Robertson, *The Passport in America*, 2010; Caitlin Rosenthal, *Accounting for Slavery*, 2018; Radhika Singh, "Passport, Ticket, and India-Rubber Stamp: The Problem of the Pauper Pilgrim in Colonial India c. 1882–1925," in *The Limits of British Colonial Control in South Asia: Spaces of Disorder in the Indian Ocean*, edited by Ashwini Tambe and Harald Fischer-Tine, 2008; George R. Trumbull IV, *An Empire of Facts*, 2009; Joanne Yates, *Control through Communication*, 1989.

9

NINETEENTH-CENTURY MEDIA TECHNOLOGIES

Two concepts emerged in the nineteenth century that were to prove essential to our present-day understanding of information. These were the concepts "media" and "technology." While it is commonplace today to apply the terms *media* (or *medium*) and *technology* anachronistically to earlier developments—such as in reference to Gutenberg's printing press—neither concept was available in its present configuration until the late nineteenth century, and putting the two together as we have in our chapter title would have been unimaginable until quite recently. Only after media technologies emerged explicitly as such would information take on its present characteristics as the relatively abstract entity it is, the alienable "content" that can move across contexts and that comes in discrete chunks like *bits or packets. In what follows we will offer a highly selective history of nineteenth-century media and the ways that communication technologies like telegraphy and photography helped to underwrite information as a matter of interest and concern to historical actors around the globe. As they joined existing and evolving methods of communication, telegraphy, photography, and other innovations helped broadly to imply that -*graphy* (from the Greek *graphos* for writing) was relevant to information. Since the concept of information itself would remain emergent, however (as explored in subsequent chapters of this volume), we begin with a brief acknowledgment of the abstract terrain on which the concepts of media and technology would come to achieve their relevant force.

According to the literary scholar John Guillory, the concept of media that emerged in the nineteenth century had been wanted for some time, existing as a kind of gap in the Anglophone intellectual tradition as thinkers grappled with the characteristics of human communication as such. Whereas *media* and *medium* had long referred to intervening or intermediary entities—such as "filtering media" used to clarify solutions, or the "medium of gears" used to transmit motion within mechanical devices—the terms eventually came to refer to technical forms of communication: telegraphs, telephones, phonographs, and so on. Likewise, according to the historian Leo Marx, "technology" in its current sense arrived belatedly. Once used to designate a kind of knowledge—the useful or mechanic arts—the term eventually came to denote the cumulative accomplishment of that knowledge, redolent with assumptions about progress and the historical efficacy of innovation and industrial development. "Technology" thus became a dangerously sloppy concept in Marx's telling, the term too easily reified, its referent granted a seeming autonomy that would belie the complexity of actual objects and processes of modernization. The coincident latency of both concepts—their oddly belated necessity—ended as the keywords *media* and *technology* were adapted in relation to the social and cultural formations that they would come to designate. Crucial in the first instance was the proliferation of new technologies of communication, and crucial in the second were whole sociotechnical systems—like railroads—unprecedented in scale and complexity.

While telegraphs and other technical means of communication proved essential for the emergence of the media concept, the ground had already been softened by the philosophical tradition that Guillory explores. Thinkers within this tradition had variously come to appreciate writing as (what would eventually be called) a medium. Celebrations of letterpress printing by Francis Bacon and others, for instance, acknowledged print as a medium for writing. The growing familiarity of printed texts made nonprinted writing newly recognizable as manuscript. At the same time, Bacon and his contemporaries reckoned with the world's diverse writing systems in ways that helped to affirm writing as (what would eventually be called) a medium for thought. The so-called real character of Chinese was instructive in this regard. Chinese characters were "real" to European observers because they were thought to refer directly to ideas and entities themselves rather than referring first to the sounds of speech. It was a gross mischaracterization of Chinese if also an inspiration for John Wilkins's *cryptographic *Essay toward a Real Character and a Philosophical Language* (1668). In short, writing came to beg the concept of media, on the one hand as a sort of back-formation in light of printing, and on the other hand in speculative inquiries addressed to diverse writing systems. Thus it should come as no surprise that writing—broadly in the form of -*graphy*—would play a starring role in the conception of the media technologies that became essential to the developing notion of information in and after the nineteenth century. These media technologies were apprehended within and against structures and practices that they helped partly to reconstruct as and in terms of writing.

The first two -graphies warranting our attention in this context are telegraphy and photography. Etymologically these imply distance writing (tele-) and light writing (photo-). If both were somehow (like) writing, the former emphasizes a transmission function (writing *at a* distance), while the latter by contrast emphasizes a storage function (writing *with* light), telegraphs writing across space (like writing a letter and mailing it away) and photographs writing across time (like taking some notes to consult in the future). Both telegraphy and photography emerged in the late 1830s to become subjects of intense interest, celebrated in the decades that followed while also absorbing the attentions of inventors and entrepreneurs. Too easily reified then as now—telegraphy consolidated singularly as "the telegraph," for instance—neither ever existed in a stable form, as a single technical device or process. Each was instead an area of specialized inquiry and the site of ongoing aspiration and development, productive of variation at almost every turn—technical improvements, specialized applications, and new political economies—amid changing sociocultural landscapes around the world. Our account cannot encompass all this variation. Instead and in the interests of pursuing media technologies as groundwork for the emergent information concept, we focus first on telegraphy and photography as open questions of use. What functions were telegraphy and photography intended and then embraced to fulfill and in what contexts? How did the situations in which they were developed and deployed help to indicate the ways their functions were reimagined? Later we broach similar questions about additional media technologies that arrived on the scene beginning in the 1870s.

TELEGRAPHY

Electronic communication was the subject of intense inquiry and experimentation starting in the 1830s. The electromagnetic telegraphs developed in Europe and the United States were understood to be improvements on earlier optical systems like the French *télégraphe* of Claude Chappe, which relied on visible signals passed laboriously along a line-of-sight chain of towers constructed for that purpose. Electromagnetic telegraphs by contrast promised communication over greater distances at unprecedented speeds, using that most modern if still mysterious power, electricity. British inventors William Cooke and Charles Wheatstone had railroad safety in mind when they patented their telegraph as an "Improvement in Giving Signals and Sounding Alarms in Distant Places" (1837), while an American inventor, Samuel Morse, was known for asserting that his telegraph would revolutionize the relay of "intelligence," a contemporary word for news used in a way that presaged "information." The devices and systems developed by these and other experimenters in the mid-nineteenth century all involved coded communication, so while the distance writing of telegraphy offered a novel encounter with transmission—instantaneously across wires—it also required a self-conscious encounter with *semiotics, as the *binary off/on of an electrical circuit was variously enrolled to produce a sequence of symbols within an invented system of signs that referred to linguistic equivalents. The improved *Morse code that was eventually adopted as an international standard in 1865 used sequences of dots and dashes to represent alphabetic characters and numerals 0 to 9.

As distance writing, electromagnetic telegraphy made a virtue of inscription. To that end, many telegraph-receiving devices produced printouts—the most desirable of these printing messages decoded into alphabetic characters—and specialized telegraphs were eventually adapted to print market information out on ticker tape. But by 1860 sending and receiving by sound had become a common telegraphic practice wherein skilled telegraph operators tapped out messages to each other and listened for the sequence and rhythm of clicks made by the receiving device. A message written out on paper by a customer was encoded on the fly, transmitted across the line, and decoded by an operator at the other end who had internalized the code sufficiently to translate dots and dashes also on the fly, writing out the corresponding words for delivery by messenger to the telegram's addressee. Thus the virtue of inscription morphed to imply the virtues of skilled labor across an extensive network infrastructure, and soon additional virtues of automaticity and efficiency took hold as institutions like the British Post Office and the monopolistic Western Union corporation helped to inspire innovations in multiplex telegraphy—sending more than one message at a time across a single wire—and other improvements. Though the word *information* was still seldom used in telegraphic practice, electromagnetic telegraphy represented a decisive, even a revolutionary step in the ongoing reconceptualization of communication. As the media theorist James Carey explains, the age-old identity of communication and transportation was at an end, since messages—effectively dematerialized as electronic signals—could finally be sent without being physically carried.

Telegraphy had many applications and effects. In the United States, where the first working telegraph line was completed in 1844, uptake by competitive private interests was swift and diverse. Two early ventures are especially suggestive in light of the future for information that lay ahead: the Associated Press, a wire service for New York news-papers, was founded in 1846, and the Chicago Board of Trade, an exchange for com-modity futures, was founded in 1848. News agencies like the Associated Press would provide telegraphic reports to subscribing newspapers, helping to quicken the pace of the news cycle while intervening in the already intricate geographies of newsprint. Like the contemporary practice of reprinting snippets from other publications, printing tele-graphic reports in metropolitan dailies helped to affirm the status of news as alienable content and abstract commodity, what the linguist Geoffrey Nunberg called the "mor-selized substance" of an informative press. Meanwhile financial exchanges like the Chi-cago Board of Trade would provide subscribing members with simultaneous access to telegraphic market data, helping to create a single market out of previously disconnected locales. As Carey elaborates, one result would be the displacement of speculation into the temporal dimension. Speculation had forever been a question of geography—guessing which local market would garner a better price, for instance—but now new financial markets arose in which the buying and selling of commodities like wheat was abstracted into the buying and selling of derivatives. These were financial instruments like wheat futures, which represented agreements to buy or sell a certain amount of wheat of a certain quality at a certain date in the future for a certain price. Investors effectively bet on prices across time, trading in futures rather than in bushels of wheat. Telegraphic market data was thus a new and abstract commodity that enabled further abstractions of the kind that enable finance capitalism.

The new technology fostered its own forms of anxiety as well. The shock of near-instantaneous communication—the very feature of telegraphy that proved its greatest asset to speculators, among others—was also, for some, the greatest cause for concern that the telegraph raised. In an era when mechanization and advanced industrializa-tion were simultaneously objects of awe and terror, late nineteenth- and early twentieth-century society increasingly drew analogies between telegraphy and the human ner-vous system, imagining the world as an organism in which signals were transmitted at tremendous speeds from the "brain" (understood, in the West, as Western metropoles such as London and New York) to the "organs" and "limbs" (extra-urban outposts and non-Western peripheries). As an organism, it was thought, this increasingly global sys-tem might be susceptible to the same kinds of human ailments as those that featured increasingly in discussions of the industrial era: of "panic" and "hysteria." For those who took part directly in the new technology, for example, new medical conditions were coined—such as "telegrapher's palsy" (involving the cramping of the hand as part of a nervous condition), a pathology of the industrial age that took its place in medical trea-tises alongside other neologisms such as "railway spine" and "traumatic neurasthenia."

Quickly adopted by railroads, newsmen, and brokers, telegraphy became essential for armies and empires. The 1860s in particular witnessed the accelerated expansion of modern colonialism and with it a rapid development of the global telegraphic net-work. In 1864, cables were laid in the Persian Gulf that, when connected to the existing landline system, put India into direct telegraphic connection with Europe. In 1870, a further rapid expansion saw cables laid from Suez to Aden and Bombay, and from Ma-dras to Penang, Singapore, and Batavia. During this period, indeed, the expansion and maintenance of Western empire came to depend on telegraphy, just as the spread and governance of telegraphy relied on Western empire. From the Indian Mutinies of 1857–58, through the Anglo-Egyptian War of 1882, into the period of the Boer War (1899–1902), and beyond, the British Empire in particular increasingly depended on the communicative speed afforded by the new and growing network. What is more, the great cartographic enterprises of British and European empire—so pivotal to the modern imperial project—relied increasingly on techniques of trigonometric surveying that themselves relied on telegraphy (among other emergent and preexisting technologies) to carry out. Arguably no part of the British imperial map was of greater importance than India, where a full three-quarters of all British imperial subjects lived. It also served as a vital transmission node in the overland telegraphic link between Britain and the Far East. One gets a sense of the importance of this area by the speed with which telegraph cable was laid down. In February 1855, the "Electric Telegraph Department in India" opened; two short years later, India was home to just over forty-five hundred miles of telegraphic cable. Throughout the early history of this new communication technology, electric telegraphy and modern colonialism depended on one another in a tight-knit symbiotic relationship.

Telegraphy's primary function, however, remained business. By 1865 telegraphy was a globalizing force, subject of the world's first multilateral organization—the International Telegraph Union—and of feverish investment and construction. Initial attempts at a transatlantic cable had failed, but by 1866 there were two in operation, and cables had crossed the Mediterranean, the Persian Gulf, and the Red Sea to connect Europe with Ottoman Turkey, Persia (Iran), and India. This was just a beginning. In the decades that followed a web of terrestrial and undersea cables established a global infrastructure for communication. Governments played a role—especially by granting concessions to cable companies—but the prime movers behind the construction and exploitation of this architecture were international cartels. Corporations capitalized largely in the West competed together to carve up global connectivity as effectively as the European imperial powers were carving up African territory into colonies. News agencies—the Associated Press, Reuters, Havas—internationalized, and multinational enterprise enjoyed an expanding marketplace. A similar global architecture and a similar global liberalism persist today, as fiber-optic cables for *internet transmissions follow many of the same routes as the original telegraph lines and are largely the purview of multinational corporations that operate in the contexts of multilateral associations for the adjudication of international standards.

While often viewed through the lens of its material infrastructure—submarine cables, gutta percha, transmission poles, and so forth—telegraphy was in equal measure a linguistic and semiotic infrastructure as well. At telegraphy's inception, the entrepreneurial Samuel Morse referred to the new invention as "the American telegraph" and, even more intimately, "my telegraph." Even as Morse eagerly promoted the technology in Russia, western and southern Europe, the Ottoman Empire, Japan, Egypt, and parts of the African continent, the telegraph code on which it was based remained fundamentally connected to the Latin alphabet and the English language—that is, to the fabric of Morse's linguistic world. With the short "dot," the long "dash," and code sequences ranging primarily from one to four units in length, the code was originally designed to accommodate thirty discrete units: just sufficient to encompass the twenty-six English letters, with four code spaces remaining. Essential symbols—such as Arabic numerals and a select few punctuation marks—could then be relegated to the less efficient realm of five-unit code sequences (later expanded to the even less efficient six-unit sequences in "Continental Morse").

While the code was ideally suited to handle English, the same could not be said for other languages—even alphabetic ones. With its thirty letters, German bumped up against the limits of the code's capacity, while French and its multiplicity of accented letters spilled out beyond it. Nevertheless, such Anglocentrism was further reinforced by the International Telegraphic Union in its original list of signifiers permitted for telegraphic transmission. At the ITU conference in Vienna in 1868, the collection of acceptable symbols was confined to the twenty-six unaccented letters of the English language, the ten Arabic numerals, and a small group of sixteen symbols (being the period, comma, semicolon, colon, question mark, exclamation point, apostrophe, cross, hyphen, e-acute [é], fraction bar, equal sign, left parenthesis, right parenthesis, ampersand, and guillemet or quotation mark). The expansion of telegraphy's authorized list of transmittable symbols was an extremely conservative and slow affair, moreover. It was not until 1875, for example, that the St. Petersburg conference of the ITU finally expanded the original list of twenty-six letters to include a twenty-seventh: the accented "e" (é), now no longer sequestered to the specialized list of "signes de ponctuation et autres" (punctuation marks and other signs). The conference further stipulated that, for those using Morse code, it would now be possible to transmit six other special, accented symbols: Ä, Á, Å, Ñ, Ö, and Ü. It was not until the London conference of 1903, almost two decades later, that this supplemental list of accented letters was granted admission into the "standard" semiotic repertoire.

The history of Chinese telegraphy is particularly illustrative of the limits of Morse, and the challenges faced when extending this code to writing systems that it was not originally designed to handle. In 1871, the growing network of telegraphic communication reached the shores of the Qing Empire, with a single line opened between Shanghai and Hong Kong in April of that year. Carried out by two foreign companies—the Great Northern Telegraph Company of Denmark and the Eastern Extension A&C Telegraph Company of the United Kingdom—the installation of this line marked the initial step in the construction of an empire- and then nationwide communications web, woven one filament at a time. A line was installed between Saigon and Hong Kong in June 1871, another between Shanghai and Nagasaki in August, and a third between Nagasaki and Vladivostok in November. In the ensuing years, this network expanded to encompass Xiamen (Amoy), Tianjin, Fuzhou, and other cities throughout the empire. Chinese authorities and companies would steadily gain ownership of this web and expand it to a total length of approximately sixty-two thousand miles by the middle of the Republican period (1911–49).

With the entrance of China and the Chinese language into international telegraphy, a vexing question emerged: as the globalization of telegraphy brought Morse code into contact with scripts it had not been originally designed to handle, would the inclusion of new languages, scripts, alphabets, and syllabaries prompt a radical reimagination of telegraphy itself, or would they be absorbed and subordinated to the logic and syntax of existing approaches? How could Morse code, dependent as it was on alphabets for its functioning, possibly be able to handle Chinese script, which is entirely nonalphabetic? What is Morse code *without letters*?

What ensued was not a reimagination of the modes or syntax of telegraphic transmission. Instead, the Chinese telegraph code of 1871—invented by two foreigners—left the global information infrastructure of Morse code unaltered, while placing Chinese script in a position of structurally embedded inequality. Developed by a Danish professor of astronomy named H.C.F.C. Schjellerup and formalized by a French harbormaster in Shanghai, Septime Auguste Viguier, the *code of 1871 encompassed a group of approximately sixty-eight hundred common-usage Chinese characters. These characters were organized according to the leading Chinese dictionary of the age, the *Kangxi Dictionary*, and then assigned a series of distinct, four-digit numerical codes running from 0001 to 9999. Approximately three thousand blank spaces were left at the end of the code book, and a few blank spaces left within each radical class, so that individual operators could include otherwise infrequently used characters essential for their work. To transmit a Chinese telegram using this system, the telegrapher began by looking up a character in the code book, finding its four-digit cipher, and then transmitting this cipher using standard Morse signals.

The code designed by Schjellerup and Viguier thus placed Chinese script within a fundamentally different relationship with telegraphic transmission *protocols than alphabetic and syllabic scripts. The 1871 code was premised on an additional or double mediation of Chinese: a first layer mediating between Chinese characters and Arabic numerals, and a second layer mediating between Arabic numerals and the long and short pulses of telegraphic transmission. By contrast, the transmission of English, French, German, Russian, and other languages involved only one layer of mediation—from letters or syllables directly to the machine code of dots and dashes. In order for Chinese to enter the machine code of telegraphy, then, Chinese script would first need to pass through an additional (foreign) semiotic layer—in this case, that of Arabic numerals, but also conceivably the letters of the Latin alphabet.

Because of its reliance on numerical transmission, this telegraph code had immense implications for China's starting position within the global telegraphic infrastructure, due to the history of the international telegraphic community prior to 1871. From an early moment within the history of telegraphy, a pressing issue facing cable companies and governments was the rapid spread of *coded languages and ciphers. These systems of encryption were geared toward protecting the content of the message and toward reducing the cost of transmission by creating short codes and ciphers that stood in for longer sequences and even entire sentences. While a boon for individuals and companies, these codes and ciphers threatened to erode the profits of telegraph companies and were quickly subjected to higher tariffs and certain limitations on usage (for example, it was stipulated that telegram addresses had to be transmitted "in the clear" and not in code).

The moment that the Chinese language entered into the international telegraph system, then, it immediately fell under the rubric of a "numbered language" and was subject to the entire body of laws that had been developed to confront encryption. From 1871 onward, that is, there was de facto no such thing as a "plain language" in the case of Chinese transmission. Telegraph companies with vested financial interests in the Qing—particularly the Danish company Great Northern and the British company Eastern Extension Australia and China Telegraph Company—focused on compensating for the disadvantaged position of Chinese script by establishing preferential transmission rates.

They also advocated special status for the Chinese number code, securing agreements as early as 1893 such that the price of Chinese transmissions would be assessed differently than conventional "numbered language" transmissions. Domestically, various Chinese regimes also promulgated preferential pricing systems. Circa 1933, for example, a regulation was passed that exempted customers from paying the cost of encipherment and decipherment, deferring it instead to the telegraph offices themselves. Even with such makeshift exemptions, however, the Chinese telegraph code was not on equal footing with codes for other languages.

PHOTOGRAPHY

Whether because it is less explicitly semiotic or because it is less inherently transmissive, the medium of photography may seem at a greater remove from the history of information than telegraphy. Yet from its initial public acclaim in 1839, photography emerged entangled with reigning notions of the real, becoming instrumental within changeable regimes of truth and habits of sociality in ways that would provide key contexts for the recognition of information as such and that remain profoundly relevant today. The earliest observers of daguerreotypes (named after Louis Daguerre in France) were staggered by their precision, the way they reproduced the minutest particulars of a scene. And like observers of the first calotypes (from the Greek for beautiful impression) or Talbotypes (named by William Henry Fox Talbot in Britain), they were amazed at the nonhuman agency involved, as sunlight itself seemed to be the artist responsible for these images. "Heliography" was one early term for photography, as experimenters developed multiple techniques and processes, and as the new medium became widely enjoyed. The precision and automaticity, or light-activated quality, of photographic images helped to lend them a seeming objectivity as representations of the real. Photographs were assumed to capture the world as it really was. Some early processes (daguerreotypes, ambrotypes, tintypes, for example) resulted in one-of-a-kind images, the seeming usurpation of one-of-a-kind paintings or drawings. Later techniques involved developing negatives that could then be used to produce as many identical images as desired, a seeming usurpation of xylography (woodblock printing) and engravings that would help to suture the presumptive objectivity of the photographic image to the effects of its infinite reproducibility.

Unlike telegraphy, photography would become fully domesticated, part of the way that everyday people could see and be seen in new ways. As photographic images turned into consumer goods, landscape "views" and portraits quickly became dominant photographic *genres, tangible, discrete, and finite slices of time to be saved and shared. Home or amateur photography—photographs that consumers could take themselves and have developed—would arrive only in the late 1880s and thanks to Eastman Kodak, which advertised, "You push the button, we do the rest." Also in the late 1880s, halftone technology enabled the incorporation of photographic images into printed materials, aiding in the proliferation of illustrated newspapers and magazines, a stimulus to both an explosive growth of advertising and the nascent practices of photojournalism.

Although early processes were cumbersome, involving dangerous chemicals and intricate manipulations, photography spread quickly around the world, taken up in an ever-widening field of practice. Metropolitan "galleries" and itinerant portraitists traded in showing people to themselves, newly fixed by the camera. Showing people their "others" also clearly had appeal. The acquisitive logic of "taking" pictures seems to have jibed immediately with the logics of imperial conquest and administration, as photography became a new means of knowing colonial sites and subjects. Taken in 1839, a photograph of Muḥammad ʿAlī's palace at Raʾs al Tin in Alexandria is believed to be the first photograph taken in the Middle East. Five years later the Frenchman Jules Richard brought photography with him when he traveled to Persia, where he taught French and English, and ultimately converted to Islam. Other practitioners of photography in Persia included those from Austria and Italy, such as Luigi Montabone, and the Neapolitan colonel Luigi Pesce, first dispatched to the region as commander in chief of the Persian infantry. By the end of 1848, the first calotype business in Calcutta was open, helping to popularize the method across India. In short order, increasing numbers of British and European photographers turned their lenses on India, and other regions of the world were no less well attended. Americans took photography with them to the Mexican-American War (1846–48), for instance, and soon there were photographic images of the conflict in the Crimea (1853–56).

Colonial subjects would eventually take up cameras themselves. In Persia, for example, Naṣr al-Dīn Shāh became well known for his photography and helped lay the groundwork for the introduction of photography into the curriculum of Dar al-Funun College circa 1860. By the 1890s, professional Chinese-run photography studios could be found in China. Meanwhile in Burma, photography studios such as F. Beato Ltd. and Johannes & Co. Mandalay began to employ Burmese staff members, such as Maung Pot Chit and Maung Win. The increasing number of native-born practitioners raised the possibility of decolonizing photography in Asia, Africa, the Middle East, and elsewhere. Students who excelled at Dar al-Funun were sometimes afforded the opportunity to study abroad, where they deepened their aesthetic and technical understandings of the new medium. Photographic societies eventually opened in Bengal, Madras, Calcutta, and elsewhere, their membership and leadership populated by many local Indian photographers. Photography also began to be celebrated at the highest rungs of the state. In Persia, cameras were given as gifts to the shah's cherished courtiers, and, with newly designed cameras, court photographers sometimes accompanied the shah on travels. In China, rulers eventually began to incorporate photography into their repertoire of official gifts, as a means both of generating publicity abroad and of cementing personal ties with the heads of foreign states and delegations.

At the same time, non-Western photography retained its close relationship with its colonial origins. Cameras continued to be produced abroad, serviced by European and American companies. Photographic societies were in many cases dominated by foreigners, and Europeans and Americans in many ways matched the output of local journals and manuals with their own treatises on photography, such as George Erwin's *Handbook of Photography for Amateurs in India*, published in 1895. The customers for photography also remained, in large part, Europeans and Americans. This had a profound and enduring influence on the choice of photographic subject matter. Orientalist themes persisted, with one paradoxical result that the realism of photography—its claims to objectively reproduce the real—became marked in association with the exotic. Nowhere was this more true, perhaps, than in pornography, which became a lucrative if typically clandestine form of photography, promising to reveal the harem and other titillating secrets to the male gaze.

Less clandestine links between photography and exotic subjects were legion, endemic for instance within the Western vogue for stereoscopes and the accompanying stereograph views, which offered a means of vicarious travel. Stereoscope photography involved the production of two images, one for each eye, which when viewed appropriately created a three-dimensional effect. Throughout the second half of the nineteenth century and well into the twentieth, European and American companies competed to supply their well-to-do consumers with sets of stereographs and the stereoscopes with which to view them. A parlor diversion, the consumption of these mass-produced diptychs purported to show the world beyond the parlor as it really was. The alien and exotic were domesticated—tourist sites, modern marvels, distant climes—and realism enhanced as much by the gimmick of the 3-D effect as by assumptions about the objectivity of the photographic image over and against other forms of imagery.

In general the photographic view was a popular genre that helped to inscribe the natural and human-made wonders of the world as such, creating a visual iconography for collective recognition. Obviously, the spatial terrain of one's individual or collective life was not photographed evenly or with consistent intensity. Certain sites of life became nonplaces: quotidian, forbidden, or in-between zones that, for a variety of reasons, were rarely if ever incorporated into photographic documentation. Meanwhile, other sites of life came to be photographed incessantly, creating an ever-thickening *palimpsest of commemoration and remembrance, so much so that the visual representation of places might seem to eclipse the very places themselves. Certain sites and landmarks were visually consumed as never before. The Holy Land and Niagara Falls, for instance, began to lose their identity as preexisting sites that were then captured in photographic form. Rather, it was the incessant act of capturing sites like these photographically that began to create or reshape them as known and knowable sights. Photography helped to prepare travelers (actual or armchair) with visual cues, expectations, and itineraries that they might re-create in their lived experience. This was not completely without precedent, of course, since images of other kinds had circulated in similar ways. Prior to the advent of photography Chinese travelers had long employed famous works of poetry and landscape painting to prefigure particular parts of the empire, such that when they themselves arrived, they were in many ways sojourning inside a poem or painting, as much as in geographic space itself.

Just as the genre of the view helped create visual iconography for collective recognition, so the genre of the portrait eventually came to structure or crystalize certain elements of lived experience and to affirm the self as a specifically photographic subject. The "events" of a person's life might increasingly be defined as those moments worthy of, or particularly amenable to, being captured in photographic form. By the same token, photography equally helped to shape the formation of "nonevents": those moments that, for any number of reasons, tend not to be photographed. Photography helped quietly to transform and to forge a new aesthetic grammar through which to signpost a lifetime and to knit kinship, becoming a vital technique of commemoration and remembrance. Events and nonevents varied from place to place, of course, shaped by longer-standing cultural norms that predated or that arose in conjunction with the adoption of photography. In turn-of-the-century Burma, for instance, cameras were used to record not only wedding ceremonies—the kind of life event that would be photographed across many cultures—but also a person's acquisition of particularly fine new clothing or dress. Dour, unsmiling portraits were the cultural norm in America during the nineteenth century, taken frequently against painted backgrounds. Children were held still for the camera, tightly clasped on laps or from behind curtains, but many were also photographed dead and laid out in their coffins.

The self as a photographic subject was produced both by the cultural conventions of photographic representation—by poses and occasions, for instance—and by conventions related to the collection and circulation of photographs as objects. Albums were adapted to preserve photographs as keepsakes, and photographic portraits became important mementos to be shared and given to loved ones. Increasingly mobile populations required a growing traffic in photographs, as dislocations associated with migration, immigration, or military service, for instance, induced individuals to send or exchange pictures of themselves. Portrait photography became in this sense a social medium for the circulation of self-presentations—today we'd say "profiles"—in the production and maintenance of associations among friends and family members as well as aspirational associations among strangers. A token of remembrance, the photographic portrait was thus also a unit of transaction productive of social relations and social capital, a fact made manifest by the enormous numbers of photographs sent through the mails as well as by the eventual emergence of celebrity photographs, which were sold in the tens of thousands as souvenirs by theatrical stars, platform lecturers, and other notables. A midcentury vogue for the so-called *carte de visite* affirmed the photograph as a transactional form. The carte de visite was a portrait printed on a small card and intended, like visiting cards, to be given to and exchanged with others. Immensely popular in America and Europe for a decade or so, the carte de visite became a collectible, a way of making and maintaining social connections.

The ostensible objectivity of photography—the medium's reality effect—was thus an intricate and ongoing project that depended on the emergence of conventional subjects for photographic images as well as conventional practices for producing and then proliferating and using photographic prints. More than simply a visual medium, photography was a collection of materials, processes, norms, and associations. The "truth" of photography was and remains complex, as cameras were used to frame and select certain things and not others, and as images were developed—and potentially cropped, edited, tinted, or otherwise manipulated—often for specific ends. The doctoring of photographic plates and negatives was one of the most important and historically widespread modes of intervening in the space between exposure and final image. Through careful, well-timed alterations of standard development and printing sequences, it became possible for the photographer to transmute his or her work in sometimes subtle, sometimes vibrant, ways. Photographic prints in the Palace Museum collection in Beijing, for instance, are known to have been retouched so as to present a wrinkle-free Empress Dowager. In portraits of Yu Xunling, a Qing dynasty bannerman, meanwhile, the young man's face was carefully hand painted, and elsewhere techniques of retouching employed brushstrokes, tonalities, and shading designed intentionally to mimic those of traditional Chinese brush painting. Nor were darkroom manipulations always an act of homage or the benign mystifications of power. Hoaxers like the American William H.

Mumler perpetrated fraud, embarking on a practice known as "spirit photography," in which double exposures and other tricks were used photographically to suggest the presence of ghosts, fodder for spiritualists and a means of fooling and fleecing the recently bereaved.

For all of this, photography achieved and retained its authority as a means of representing the real. It stabilized into a taken-for-granted element within a whole repertoire of techniques and practices for visual representation and became enrolled within a widening web of truth regimes, both bureaucratic and scientific (and pseudoscientific). "Rogues' galleries" and later mug shots helped to tie photography to policing and made photographs an early form of biometric registration, a means of collecting data about people for the purposes of categorizing them. In Britain the eugenicist Francis Galton employed a technique of composite photography, superimposing images of multiple subjects, in an attempt to identify types. In France Alphonse Bertillon concocted a whole system for analyzing criminality in which mugshots were supplemented by anthropometric measurements, while Cesare Lombroso did something similar in Italy. Both Etienne-Jules Marey and Eadweard Muybridge adapted serial photography to study animal locomotion. Anthropologists, art and architectural historians, epigraphers, naturalists, astronomers: for these and for many others photography became a form of evidence, a way to document and thus to compare and distinguish, to argue and persuade.

TELEPHONY AND RECORDED SOUND

The dissemination of telegraphy and photography that occurred with such power and rapidity in the nineteenth century was of course but one element amid a confluence of changes that can be broadly if weakly described as modernization. However uneven and chaotic experiences of this process must have been, it became (and remains) commonplace to understand modernity in relation to technological progress. Where telegraphs and photographic technologies were concerned, progress clearly entailed an encounter or reencounter with reigning assumptions about communication, the very substance of communication—be it linguistic or visual, instantaneous or not, inscribed and by whatever means—as well as its functions and effects. These encounters or reencounters, we have been suggesting, formed some of the groundwork on which the concept of information would achieve its ultimate and enduring force. Myriad other developments—in business methods and journalism, for instance—have a bearing, but we will conclude this chapter selectively in reference to two new media technologies of the late 1870s, telephony and recorded sound.

Developed as a form of "acoustic telegraphy," telephony was an offshoot of the earlier electromagnetic communication, losing its -*graphy* as direct voice transmission across wires was hailed as a breakthrough. Alexander Graham Bell captured public attention when he demonstrated a telephone at the US Centennial Exposition in 1876, but telephone devices and telephonic transmission were the subjects of such intense experimentation in Europe and the United States that numerous experimenters might legitimately be given credit for "the telephone," and many played a role in making it practical. Nor did this technology ever fully stabilize; active research and development would continue throughout the next century. (It should be noted that Claude Shannon's 1948 mathematical conception of communication—the basis of contemporary information theory—was an outgrowth of signal-processing research conducted at Bell Labs.) With the telegraph companies as their model, capitalization by Bell Telephone Company and others was swift, and telephone networking became an arena for monopolistic or oligopolistic exertions as well as regulatory schemes. In keeping with its telegraphic origins, telephony was conceived first as a business technology and only later succeeded more broadly as a form of networked sociality. The new telephone infrastructure articulated localities, connecting private businesses and homes to the outside world, and then interurban and rural-to-urban lines integrated localities with one another.

The American inventor Thomas Edison was experimenting with telephony in order to invent around Bell's patents when he stumbled across sound recording. (Scientists had successfully inscribed sound waves before, but now inscription would be the prelude to auditory reproduction of the sounds inscribed.) The crude recording device Edison made and named "the phonograph" was soon given public demonstrations and hailed around the world. It was a proof-of-concept moment and with Bell's 1876 prototype seemed indeed the presentation of modern wonders. Only after a decade or more would the makers of phonographs, related "graphophones," and gramophones identify and exploit markets for the technology. Like telephony, sound recording felt primarily like a business technology at first, a way of taking dictation without a stenographer or a pencil. (*Phonograph* was an adaptation from *phonography*, a form of *shorthand reporting.) Besides the recording and reproduction of business letters, Edison imagined a world of talking clocks and talking dolls as well as the preservation of dying words, important speeches, and famous voices. Only later would prerecorded sounds be exploited as a new commodity form: canned performances of music or recitation for the enjoyment of listeners equipped with a machine for playback. By the late 1890s and into the new century, phonograph and gramophone records had become the content objects of a new global culture industry, akin to and contemporary with other developing culture industries, like movies, an outgrowth of Auguste and Louis Lumière's *cinematograph* and related innovations.

The uptake of telephony in the non-Western world commenced in the late 1870s and early 1880s. As in Meiji Japan, which imported its first telephone in 1877, there was little choice for non-Western modernizing elites but to build new telephone communications infrastructures with foreign-bought or financed components, such as Western Electric switchboard equipment in Japan in 1889. In part reflective of dominant approaches to telephone infrastructure, but also of Japan's experience as the target of fierce western European colonial intrusion (in the form of Commodore Perry's infamous Black Ships), Japanese officials viewed telecommunications as a matter of vital national security. This view resulted in the state's subsidization of the industry, and eventually, the formation of a state monopoly over telecommunications. Over time, moreover, the Meiji state undertook an aggressive domestication policy, with the goal of producing as much of its telecommunications infrastructure as possible through homegrown means. One major outgrowth of this policy was the formation of Nippon Telegraph and Telephone Company, as well as a network of smaller, support-level firms that acted as the beneficiaries of NTT's sizable R&D budget.

As in other parts of the world, the construction of telephone infrastructures in non-Western locales often mapped onto preexisting cartographic and transportation frameworks. In the case of India, for example, where British colonial officials installed the first telephone in 1881, telephone lines were laid down along established routes of information—notably those already stretching from Bengal northward toward Peshawar, via Lucknow and Delhi—which had been in existence during the Mughal Empire (1526–1857).

The history and experience of telephony in the non-Western world was shaped by other preexisting technosocial, geopolitical, and sociocultural frameworks as well. First, the case has been made that India's comparatively slow uptake of telephony was in no small part attributable to the way in which telephony was conceptualized by British imperialists at home in the UK. Viewing the telephone as a device well suited for intra-house communication, but perhaps for little else, the British Post Office announced as late as 1879 that it had no plans in place for the installation of telephone communications as part of its broader, long-distance telegraph branch. Such attitudes were reflected in the sluggish uptake of the technology in the UK, where the number of telephones rose from just 45,000 circa 1890 to only 818,000 by 1915. By comparison, the number of telephones in the United States is estimated to have risen from around three thousand in 1876, to approximately twenty million by the end of the 1920s. Circa 1910, moreover, the United States is estimated to account for a full 67 percent of all telephones in use globally at that time. British telephone use paled by comparison.

Long-standing ideas about the telephone in Great Britain had repercussions for the levels of growth (or, more accurately, the lack of growth) of telephone infrastructure in British India. From the time of its introduction to British India in 1881, telephony grew at a similarly slow rate: from an estimated fifty-six state-owned telephones in 1882, to just around twelve thousand in 1924, just over forty years later. Also telling is the fact that automatic switching systems, in use as early as 1892 in the United States in some places, 1901 in Canada, and 1908 in Germany, were not introduced to Bombay—one of India's most important metropoles—until 1923. As late as 1923, moreover, there were no public call facilities in the whole of India (rising to only seven by 1932).

For those telephone lines that the British did build, these in turn were shaped by still other geopolitical frameworks. In particular, investment in telephone infrastructure in British India was skewed dramatically toward northern India, propelled by threats of Russian incursion during the so-called Great Game. For those telephone lines that were installed, then, construction efforts were concentrated in cities and military cantonments in north India and the North West Frontier Province (NWFP). Incidentally, the choice of where British Indian officials decided to build, and not to build, telephone infrastructure laid the groundwork, some have argued, for a long-standing *"digital divide" in India today, with north India enjoying a far more advanced information infrastructure than the south.

Sociocultural frameworks also shaped the uptake and transformation of telephony in the non-Western world, as illustrated in the case of Japanese switchboard operation. Specifically, the categorization of telephone switchboard operation as a form of "women's work," as it came to be viewed early on in the United States and elsewhere in the West, was not an association that came naturally in Japan. To the contrary, many in Japan regarded it as inappropriate that young women, often from middle-class families, should work not only outside of the home, but also in a profession that placed them in regular contact with strangers of both sexes, sometimes even at night. What is more, the physical location of one of the main switchboard exchanges circa 1890, in Tatsunokuchi, was itself considered a place of ill-repute frequented by gamblers and thieves. Over time, however, gendered conceptualization of switchboard work in Japan began to sync with more common global tropes, with young women—who were cheaper to employ— steadily being presented as better suited to the work than young men thanks to their "inherent" gentleness, patience, and politeness. By the year 1905, male telephone operators effectively ceased to exist, with men taking on supervisory positions only.

The same kinds of sociocultural frameworks were significant for the development of recorded sound as a popular medium. Women's voices proved challenging to record well and so became a standard against which the fidelity of recordings might be judged. At the same time, as home phonographs and gramophones started to become popular amusement devices in the mid-1890s, prerecorded music intervened in social norms that separated public and domestic life. Like the contemporary player pianos that "read" music off a perforated paper roll, commercial phonograph and gramophone records upset long-standing associations between the middle-class home and amateur music making as a sacralized and sacralizing womanly accomplishment that was productive of domesticity and helped to distinguish it from public life. Records and piano rolls brought professionally produced music home, where previously public sounds—suggestive of the music hall, bandstand, opera, or vaudeville house—might now be enjoyed in private. Phonograph and gramophone companies plugged opera at home as a kind of touchstone, although more lowbrow fare clearly predominated. The after-dinner sing-along was doomed, observers warned, and sheet music *publishers saw their revenues plunge.

Commercial recording was a global endeavor from the outset, as American and European record companies sent representatives around the world to obtain recordings and as they developed outlets abroad. The British Gramophone Company recorded widely and established subsidiaries in India in 1901, Russia in 1902, and Persia in 1906. A few years later there were record labels established in Lebanon, Argentina, and elsewhere, while record-pressing plants were operating in China and Japan. Operations remained transnational at multiple levels. The Lebanese Baidaphone label, for instance, had its records manufactured in Berlin from masters produced in Beirut. The Argentine Discos Nacional label pressed its own records to supply domestic markets, but it arranged to issue its tango recordings in Europe under European labels as well. Meanwhile so-called foreign records were profitable within the United States, as companies like Columbia supplied immigrant audiences and niche markets. In short, the success of sound recording as a popular medium meant the circulation and consumption of culture and cultural differences in the form of mass-produced musical recordings. Records remained brief—most were only about two minutes long—so this wasn't the capture and dissemination of preexisting musical forms as much as it was the creation of new popular musics, plural, selectively representative, and transformative of existing performance traditions.

Largely forgotten amid the success of recorded music as an industrial commodity form were the initial shocks of the late 1870s, when the -graphy of phonographs had amazed listeners worldwide with the possibility—as yet imperfectly realized—of capturing sounds for later reproduction. If seventeenth-century European savants had the "realness" of Chinese script (supposing a direct—that is, nonphonetic—reference to ideas and things), here finally was reality of a different sort. Sound waves delicately inscribed onto a recording surface could be reproduced at will. It was as if some new, futuristic form of written quotation could suddenly speak itself, or as if a new form of musical notation could be made automatically to play itself aloud. Novelty wore off quickly. Sound recording became a familiar idea, and then phonographs and gramophones became commonplace. Only lawyers and judges and policy makers would continue to puzzle the -graphy of sound recording, as musical *copyright remained an open question into the twentieth century and as the publishers of sheet music argued that the new delicately inscribed recordings (and perforated piano rolls) were infringements of their printed scores.

Some nineteenth-century encounters with the -graphy of media technologies prompted explicit questions about writing and written communication: among those who wrestled to adapt telegraphic signals to different writing systems, for instance, or those puzzled by the nonauthored character of phonographically recorded speech. Other encounters prompted implicit adjustments to assumptions about human communication, its character and extent. More than any one technology or one medium, however, it was the proliferation of so many new processes and then habits of communication that would prove particularly salient to the history of information. As the multiplicity of forms came to be understood in common—as media technologies—the very obvious differences among them helped to encourage an abstracted sense of the communicative functions they seemed to share. In light of so many and such diverse options for messaging, so many new ways of meaning and knowing, content itself appeared alienable, the abstract substance available to be communicated: information.

Lisa Gitelman and Thomas S. Mullaney

See also art of memory; bureaucracy; cameras; forgery; globalization; journals; knowledge; letterpress; networks; newspapers; printed visuals; recording; travel

FURTHER READING

Erik Baark, *Lightning Wires: The Telegraph and China's Technological Modernization, 1860–1890*, 1997; James Carey, *Communication as Culture: Essays on Media and Society*, 1989; Deep Kanta Lahiri Choudhury, "Of Codes and Coda: Meaning in Telegraph Messages, circa 1850–1920," *Historical Social Research/Historische Sozialforschung* 35, no. 1 (2010): 127–39; idem, "Sinews of Panic and the Nerves of Empire: The Imagined State's Entanglement with Information Panic, India c. 1880–1912," *Modern Asian Studies* 38, no. 4 (2004): 965–1002; John Guillory, "Genesis of the Media Concept," *Critical Inquiry* 36, no. 2 (Winter 2010): 321–63; Leo Marx, "Technology: The Emergence of a Hazardous Concept," *Social Research* 64 (Fall 1997): 965–88; Thomas Mullaney, *The Chinese Typewriter: A History*, 2017; idem, "Semiotic Sovereignty: The 1871 Chinese Telegraph Code in Global Historical Perspective," in *Science and Technology in Modern China, 1880s–1940s*, edited by Jing Tsu and Benjamin Elman, 2014; Geoffrey Nunberg, "Farewell to the Information Age," in *The Future of the Book*, edited by Geoffrey Nunberg, 1996; Dwayne R. Winseck and Robert M. Pike, *Communication and Empire: Media, Markets, and Globalization, 1860–1930*, 2007; Kerim Yasar, *Electrified Voices: How the Telephone, Phonograph, and Radio Shaped Modern Japan, 1868–1945*, 2018.

10

NETWORKING

Information Circles the Modern World

In the early 1890s, American newspapers went into a frenzy with reports about Spanish atrocities in Cuba. In selling the news they cleared the ground for America's first overseas war, which itself became a great story business. William Randolph Hearst was locked in combat with his former mentor, Joseph Pulitzer; they dueled to out-sensationalize each other with appalling stories of distant wrongdoings. Until then, Hearst's pride and joy, the *New York Journal*, had been a struggling money pit. On December 12, 1895, he broke new ground with a headline: "SPANIARDS INHUMAN CRUELTY." Based on eyewitness reports, the article described how Spanish troops were mowing down innocent civilians, including children. Hearst even sponsored a rescue operation of the damsel in distress Evangelina Cisneros, locked in a Cuban jail, as a story to plaster on the front pages. He sent his fellow Ivy Leaguer and illustrator Frederic Remington to get some images of humanitarian desperation. Remington, a racist boor, used to dip his Yale football jersey in slaughterhouse blood before a big game. Now, he was in Havana's Hotel Inglaterra, a beehive of reporters hustling for an angle. But Remington got bored hanging around the lobby and cabled his boss, "there is no trouble here." Months later, the boiler room of the USS *Maine* blew up, and the chest beaters finally got their pretext. (Hearst, though, was livid because Pulitzer's *New York World* got the scoop first; not to be outdone, Hearst's headline the next day blared: "THE WHOLE COUNTRY THRILLS WITH WAR FEVER.") During the Spanish-American War, sales of Pulitzer's *World* and Hearst's *Journal* soared to one million each.

Fast forward to the 1960s, when journalists and illustrators again teamed up over atrocity news. This time, the tables had turned. During the Vietnam War, Saigon hotels also had their sweaty lobbies. But by then the media business had become professionalized; the self-defined fourth estate was emerging as autonomous from official truth peddlers and thus able to hold the latter accountable. The Associated Press had a hyperactive bureau in Saigon committed to reporting the truth about a war that defied Yankee heroism. The German photographer Horst Faas turned it into a new-style media hub. He'd figured out how to send photographs instantly by wire to editorial offices in North America and Europe using cylindrical wire photo drums. On February 1, 1968, the seasoned photojournalist Eddie Adams came in, deposited a roll of thirty-five-millimeter film taken on the streets of Saigon, turned around, and went back out. Faas took the roll and retreated to the darkroom. He picked out a few samples from the contact sheets, including the image in figure 1, the execution of a Viet Cong assassin, Nguyên Vā Lém, and cabled it to New York. By then, news consumers were becoming accustomed to horror filling the pages of their newspapers and magazines. This image was more: it was

Figure 1. *Saigon Execution* by Eddie Adams, 1968. AP Photos/Eddie Adams.

evidence of how reporters were truth tellers, pulling back the veil of official claims about soldierly sacrifice and distant do-gooding.

For the century in which print media created and then dominated how strangers learned about faraway places, information became news, a business, then a very good business, a staple of conversation in dining rooms and dentists' lounges, and a matter of boardroom and government fretting. Distant events got packaged for sale; by circulating information and making it a commodity, the news business played a vital role in collapsing expanses between the world's parts, turning readers into remote yet instant spectators long before our globalization.

This essay is about two entangled stories: how news became *the* news and in so doing became a big business, and how mass circulating information went global. It starts with the laying of telegraphic cables and the making of the first kind of cable news. It ends when television—what Marshall McLuhan would famously call "hot" media—challenged dailies and weekly news magazines as the main sources of global news information and representation. It stresses three factors: first, technological shifts, second, business structures that managed and controlled supply chains through hierarchies and networks, and third, the practices of reportage and information gathering as investigative reporters and self-described "photojournalists" managed news. The essay ends with the break of the 1960s. For along with the rise of McLuhan's hot, screen-based media and the blurring of news and entertainment, another line got crossed. Up until the late 1960s, journalists as information brokers largely self-identified as reporters of objective truths. By 1970, a split was opening between a professionalization of the fourth estate, symbolized above all by the reporting on the Vietnam War, and the emergence of activist reportage, which argued that journalists were not just information brokers but ethically and politically committed to social change and justice. One might argue that our contemporary truth wars in the media can be traced back to this split. A new age was upon us in the business of packaging global information as news.

MAKING NEWS GLOBAL

Before 1800, most of the printed news business concerned itself with the information of commercial value. Print costs were relatively high, transportation was slow and expensive, and readership circles were small. The demand for news focused on information about markets near and far, from the price of cotton in New York to insurance rates for shipping to Canton, mainly for merchant classes who sought out more information to assess risks and opportunities of their bills of exchange and, after the Napoleonic Wars, investments in public bonds. Articles read more like opinion pieces and long-form essays than like reportage. Still, the commercial press was important for the functioning of capital and commodity markets—and for starting the process of making information about distant parts into circulating news.

In the 1820s, it could take over four months for the news from London to reach India and then New South Wales, two to three months to reach Buenos Aires or Cape Town. Even before the advent of the telegraph and cabling, transmission times of information were declining thanks to organizational changes in information business. Indeed, news, especially commercial and coveted financial news, became a business, so that the maritime journal *Lloyd's List* went from being published twice a week to six days a week in 1837, and new economic newspapers and magazines began to flourish, stoking demand for relevant news. The British Admiralty took over the running of ocean mail packets. American packet boats muscled into the Royal Mail business, cutting round trips between New York and Liverpool to five weeks. This was called "steamship news" for a reason.

It was in the middle of the nineteenth century that the marketplace for information about the world surged. Some of this had to do with expanding supply, linked to technological shifts. Some of it was tied to demand, especially as investors with access to pools of money in European capital markets wanted to know more about distant ventures in River Plate mining or Indian railways. But in both supply and demand for news, national government policy played a crucial role in creating markets for global information. Most important was the rise of the idea of "press freedom"—to join the other freedoms in trade and labor. *Libel laws underwent profound changes, which immunized writers and reporters from prosecution by the powerful. Information flows were also considered private goods, even if in some cases governments owned or controlled some of the land cables. The British government advocated "free trade in cables" in part to protect the British advantage as the first movers in the news business; it charged that no one could lay cables and discriminate against other national (read: British) competitors.

Government policies were also crucial in technical diffusion. Long-distance and underwater cables expanded the reach and rapidity of information gathering. Poles went up to raise the lines above ground; new coating techniques employing colonial Malaysian latex and Bengali hemp allowed cables to be laid underwater. A cable linking Dover to Calais got laid in 1851; after that, lines got stretched all over the planet to link commercial and political entrepôts. The number of days it took between dispatch and receipt of news from London went from one month to two days to New York, from 145 days to three to Bombay, from ninety-seven days to three to Buenos Aires. From 1865 to 1903, the global reach of cables went from 4,400 kilometers to 406,000 kilometers. Wartime spending and subsidies for strategic capacities spurred the placement of even more cables where private investors steered clear of laying down infrastructure.

Along with a revolution in transportation and communication, there was also a change in printing technologies. Here there was not one big disruptive breakthrough, but a cluster of innovations. Woodblocks gave way to casting metal type. By the late 1860s (as a response to the cotton shortage of the US Civil War), newspapers were adapting wood pulp as a source of paper. The effect, eventually, was to reduce dramatically the cost of paper, creating the prospects for large rolls of printable sheets and thus unimaginable economies of scale for *publishers who sought to render information about the day or week's events into immediately legible "news." Approximately four thousand copies could be produced, without interruption, by printing on rolls of paper up to 3.5 miles in length. By 1860, printing on rolls had become a standard practice. Many of the first daily outlets self-identified as *news*papers. The *Daily Telegraph* (named to capture the edge of the new technology) launched in 1855; within three years it could boast unprecedented print runs of three hundred thousand. Prices dropped sharply, down to one penny (or sou or cent) per issue (with the halfpenny paper, like the *Mercury Leader* and the *Daily Mail*, to follow in the 1890s).

Once stamped sheets gave way to rolls, tinkerers tackled typesetting. This lagged a bit, until by 1890, printers had devised a system known as linotype, which eventually became an industry standard, though there remained many newspapers that hung on to their own techniques—which gave printers and typesetters important control over production and made them often into vanguards of the modern labor movement. Still, there was no denying the effect of mechanical casts. By 1900, the Wicks Rotary Typecaster could lay sixty thousand characters an hour.

There was also booming demand for information made into news. Thanks to the spread of basic public education, from the United States to Japan, *literacy rose, and with it the spread of mass readership and a middle-class cult of being seen to be a reader. Investors wanted to know about what was happening to their stocks in western Canadian railways or Peruvian guano. There were also geostrategic forces at work. The outbreak of the Mexican-American War in 1846 created a surge in demand for news from the front. Tensions between Britain and Russia over the Dardanelles in 1851 produced a news frenzy. Getting information was crucial to drumming up public support and for winning wars. Then, when underwater cables got laid to Sebastopol, good reporting became invaluable intelligence. Russian commanders grumbled during the Crimean War that they learned more about the movements of their troops from the *Times* than from their own horse-powered information chains. (Little did they know that British and French commanders were also poring over the news to figure out what was going on.) Crimea was the first war fought with little or no censorship and a burgeoning press— which eventually brought the first photographs of war's lethal results back home. The 1854 *Times*—even the very name of the paper denoted the immediacy of the reporting— became the most influential newspaper in the world thanks in part to its wartime reportage, though it was the *Daily Telegraph* that pioneered sensational headlines, stop-the-press columns, and the all-important filler stories. The result: buoyed by the rising rates of literacy and by the declining costs of print production, news became a global commodity to join the flow of rubber, wheat, and tea. News became not just the way in which information got packaged and distant events got represented; news made information an industrial product. It was not a coincidence that the new journalism was tied so intimately to the new imperialism.

MAKING GLOBAL NEWS

By the century's end, any self-respecting city was wired in and boasted any number of telegraph offices. Many of them were manned by a new actor on the stage: the telegraph company, and out of their network sprang information brokers and "agencies." Among the enterprises that grew in the wake of the cables was the news business—which went global as it went mass. Managing information as news brought us some industrial-age organizations—and indeed a new business model for managing global flows of information, cartels of national monopolies. It started in Paris, with Charles Havas's agency (later Agence France-Presse or AFP). On the heels of the Dover-Calais cable, Julius de Reuter created his news agency in London (Reuter's Telegram Company, later Reuters). Bernhard Wolff carried the model to Germany. Reuters became among the first truly multinational corporations with agents and "bureaus" scattered all over the planet. The Americans' Associated Press or the AP joined the club a bit later. It was not mere coincidence that these networked firms reflected the imperial molds from which they had sprung. They partitioned the planet like their ruling classes. Reuters made a grab for Asia. AP, in the shadow of the Monroe Doctrine, wanted the Western Hemisphere. Havas mopped up the Middle East. Wielding such market power, the cartel struck pricing deals with equally concentrated telegraph companies; lower, exclusive cable rates helped lock down their edge over other sources of global news, though Australians, Canadians, Japanese, and Russians responded with agencies of their own to rival the informal empires of the cartel. The Japanese Foreign Ministry opened bureaus in Shanghai and New York; later, the Kokusai and Tōhō News Agencies were prewar ventures to feed reports to China to frame East Asian "news" in a common esprit against non-"Orientals." It didn't work. After the Russo-Japanese War, Japanese, Russian, Chinese, and British reporters were crawling all over Manchuria digging up stories of imperial entanglements and encounters. As with so many other facets of the world economy at this stage, the business side of news circulation was a picture of oligopoly and upstart competition.

National news agencies generally operated below the middle-sized agencies. Their activity was strictly domestic. Before 1860, only five news agencies existed: the "Big Three" (Reuters, Havas, and Wolff), the New York Associated Press (the AP's forerunner), and the Torino-based Agenzia Telegrafica Stefani. Between 1860 and 1870, a dozen more were established, and between 1870 and 1900 that number doubled again. Below the national organizations were smaller, regional ones. In the United States, for example, the Western Associated Press and the Southern Associated Press relied on the New York Associated Press for reports.

The result was less a frenzy of competition than an elaborate hierarchy. The Big Three supplied national agencies with world news in return for a subscription fee and national news; those agencies in turn bundled the news for regional agencies and local outlets. This interdependence suited both the national press and global agencies that exercised a monopoly on world news, leaving them free to secure fees from cable companies and to commission news from a network of low-cost reporters.

Here is an example of the multilayered system. The French agency, Havas, took the Latin regions of Europe, including Spain and Italy. With the laying of the South Atlantic cable in 1874 from Carcavelos, Portugal, to Pernambuco, Brazil, Havas also took

South America and its existing regional webwork of cables and information production. It opened nine offices around South America and enlisted local subscribers for its global news service, which published daily telegrams about news in Eurasia. It was expensive for outlets to pay the monopoly agency and cable company rates. With the advent of the expanded "duplex" system and later the 1894 "fat cables," which allowed some competition, clients got a bit of a reprieve. Still, they were fed hundreds of words a day from Havas in part because the agency commanded a wider network of information gatherers and was able to negotiate cut-rate transmission contracts to keep its edge over any competition. Buenos Aires's *La Nación* (The nation) boasted a special section of Havas's selection of world news called "Telegrams, Telegraphs, or Telegraphic Bulletin" to connect Argentine readers to the wider world. The daily also sprinkled cable news throughout the rest of the paper to fill in the empty sections, creating something of a random collage of world and South American happenings. From a reader's perspective, it felt as if *La Nación* was the source; behind the datelines, however, was an elaborate supply chain managed by a single firm and its network.

The result was a thickening web of contracts and cables that linked sources to readers through daily newspapers and the first glossy magazines. In spite of the sprawl, there was in fact a high degree of uniformity of sources on which outlets drew, especially when it came to news beyond local sources. So, while social, technological, and legal revolutions gave more people more access to higher-quality, instant, and differentiated information, these changes encouraged the rise of a global media cartel.

PICTURING THE WORLD

The last piece of the puzzle in making information news was the advent of another industrial by-product: photography. Mixing light and chemicals to create images of the world that could be transported and reprinted at no extra cost required several separate steps. Photojournalism, traditionally dated to the 1842 launch of the *Illustrated London News*, did not imply direct reproduction of photographs. Before 1870, photographs appeared in mass-circulation periodicals translated into wood engravings and line drawings. Most photographs were made in studios, or if shot in the field, required elaborate setups for long exposures and for plates to dry. Reproduction on cheap sheets of paper was impossible. But George Eastman's 1888 "Kodak" was a simple handheld box capable of taking multiple exposures on paper negatives. Kodak made capturing the everyday life of strangers and strange lands possible—and the goal. It became a global booster of its own. The firm sponsored Hiram Bingham's Yale Peruvian Expedition, equipping it with the tools to showcase its marvels. In return, Bingham was quick to advertise the camera in his visual exposés of Machu Picchu and other finds in *Harper's Weekly* and *National Geographic*—which put on a full spread of over two hundred images in 1913. Kodak returned the favor with Peruvian panoramas in its promotional sales.

Journalists, like the Danish American Jacob Riis, immediately saw the potential. He tinkered with flashes to shoot nocturnal portraits of New York's squalor. In 1889, *Scribner's Magazine* published a montage called "How the Other Half Lives"—which shocked the city's bourgeois readers. It also became a model publication of the Gilded Age; soon, many booming metropolises had their own Jacob Riis to add photographic news to the print narrative. Black-and-whites got easier to print in 1897, when it became possible to reproduce photographs on the cheaper paper of newspapers; the photo was no longer exclusive to higher-quality paper magazines—just in time for the spasm of war in South Africa, the Philippines, Cuba, and China. The 1898 war brought the power of photography to the newsrooms of New York's cut-throat newspaper rivals. When the war began, it became the first war in which photographers would use their new mobile devices to capture living images of the conflict for readers back home. Jimmy Hare, the Brooklyn-based photographer, was dispatched by *Collier's* to shoot the new war after the sinking of the USS *Maine*. Within days, he was in Havana and would establish a reputation for his willingness to expose himself to gunfire to get the right shot. When one American soldier told him that he wouldn't tempt shooters if he didn't have to, Hare replied, "neither would I, but you can't get real pictures unless you take some risk!" And there was a page in *Collier's Weekly*, April 2, 1898 (figure 2), a collage of Hare's photos of "liberated" Matanzas, which linked the work of American liberators to the rescue of colonial peoples from the "concentration camps" created by the Spanish military.

The 1898 war anticipated how photography got used to document expansion and catastrophe during the Boer War (1899–1902) and the Russo-Japanese War (1904–5), so images would become instruments in the contest over public opinion in war and moral entanglement with strangers.

Between 1850 and 1900 the news industry changed dramatically. It made news valuable; increasingly, packaged information provided a platform to get the attention of readers—something that advertisers coveted. "Agents" sprung up to place ads in papers and magazines, which yielded publishers' revenue streams and padded profit margins. This in turn added to a frenzy to control local market shares, less to monopolize news than to grab and to monopolize readers' attention to parcel and sell to advertisers and specialized agencies. If in 1800, merchant presses were mainly weekly affairs dominated by dense columns of prices and text-heavy essays or letters, by 1900, the modern newspaper and literary and increasingly glossy magazine dominated the market.

By 1900, news making was also a profession. It created the modern journalist and the idea of the itinerant reporter working a beat—like policemen—to get the story. The drive to report "the truth" meant going to the scene. Stringers, often attached to the news agencies and their web of offices, were information gatherers on the spot. Major metropolitan newspapers dipped into their books to dispatch foreign correspondents to hot spots. The *Toronto Star*, for instance, hired a former ambulance driver with writerly ambitions to report back on how the peace was being settled in Europe after 1918. His name was Ernest Hemingway; his reporting for the *Star* influenced his gritty prose. By 1900, photographers were leaping onto trams and ships when they heard rumors or got cables about happenings, rushing to be the men on the spot to get the shot.

Newspapers and magazines were, in effect, bricolages of local social news with wider political reporting. The layout and eventually the creation of special sections for wives and children—and even dedicated "Sunday Editions" for working families without the means to afford the dailies but who aspired to belong to the reading class—yielded to an increasingly familiar structure. They were public scrapbooks made up of editorials and letters, clippings and wire service notices. At the high-end papers with their own writers and photographers, editors had more control over content and stories, though for budget reasons they deployed in-house staff more for local news; beyond, they relied on the wire services. For publishers on meager budgets, editing mainly comprised

Figure 2. Jimmy Hare's photos of Matanzas, Cuba. *Collier's Weekly*, April 2, 1898.

selecting pieces and letters, and framing the bylines. Beyond the local variations and social news, newspapers and magazines bore a certain resemblance to one another. And they all ran ads.

This did not make them identical. Though they depended on the informal empires of the wire services for the stories from distant places, the bricolages could be assembled with similar content put to diverse local purposes. For instance, before becoming a nonviolent activist, Mahatma Gandhi cut his teeth as an editor in South Africa. His newspaper, *Indian Opinion*, started in Durban in 1898. Aiming to provide an alternative outlet to the white supremacy of empire and appealing to readers of the raj's diaspora, *Indian Opinion* provided a pastiche of world news from the wire services, patches from Ruskin, Tolstoy, and Thoreau, and long editorial ruminations on the idea of India seen from afar. Indeed, the drafts of Gandhi's famous pamphlet *Hind Swaraj* (Indian home rule) (1909) first appeared as editorials in *Indian Opinion*, albeit surrounded by columns about upheavals of the Boxer Rebellion in China and meltdowns on Wall Street. When Gandhi finally returned to India in 1914, he regarded the printing press and the newspaper as indispensable arsenals in his nonviolent campaigns to give his readers a sense of location in a wider, new world.

The result was a global reporting regime that looked something like an hourglass. It was squat and decentralized at two ends: reporters and readers were scattered and particularized. Connecting them was a narrow, concentrated neck where government regulators, private cartels, and advertisers managed the flow of news information from sources to consumers. Private enterprise, which owned about 90 percent of the world's telegraph lines, dominated the capital-intensive nature of cables; naturally, they concentrated on routes that generated high traffic and returns on investment. Where there was competition between lines, managers rushed to consolidate. For instance, the Eastern Extension Telegraph Company absorbed several smaller entities in 1872–73. For the rest of the century, this firm alone handled around one-half the world's cable traffic. In the middle of this bottleneck, connecting the wash of newspapers, advertisers, and readers, were the news agency intermediaries. The agencies bargained and bundled their way to control over the circulation of global news. With such control over circulation, they bargained with cable operators to lower charges in a way that individual newspapers could not and then charged news outlets for "subscriptions" to their information services. In the biggest of all news markets in 1900 (the United States alone sold half of the world's newspapers), the Associated Press was sending fifty thousand words per day to twenty-three hundred newspapers around the country. It was in this fashion that the Big Three cartel (AFP, Reuters, and the AP) became the world's principal supplier of news, even as the number of publications dependent on it proliferated. The effect was to standardize the information they procured and packaged between distant corners of the world.

Eventually, even the outlet side of the news market succumbed to concentration along with the rest of the industrial sector. One method was syndication, mergers of local papers into chains. Another was sprawling behemoths opening up competitor papers and using bargain deals with news agencies to drive down the cost of newspapers—and to drive incumbents out of business. In England in 1910, for example, three "newspaper barons" (Lord Northcliffe, George Cadbury, and C. A. Pearson) published papers that accounted for one-third of all morning circulation and four-fifths of all evening circulation. In Germany, by contrast, a large market was extremely segmented and scattered, perhaps reflecting the deeply regional commitments of readers; most papers were one-man or one-family shows with short print runs of one thousand. Late to the industrial revolution and to urbanization that fueled the newspaper business, Japan's market was very small, and its 250 papers in 1910 looked more like the German model on a smaller scale.

In effect, by the outbreak of the Great War, the market for news exploded worldwide. With it came standardized content and consolidated ownership. This trend, despite the folklore of American competition, was more acute in the United States than in Europe. Britain's degree of standardization and consolidation stood in the middle.

BRAVE NEW WORLD

After 1910, the basic elements of the production and circulation of print news were set and spread. Every city on the planet had its daily, often many dailies. Newsstands and delivery services were hallmarks of urban life everywhere. One of the challenges for the next five decades was spreading print news into the countryside, where markets were more dispersed, literacy rates much lower, and the consumer base poorer. But even villages soon had print news outlets, even if they did not exactly mimic big-city papers. In Shaanxi Province in north China (where Mao Tse-tung would finally end the Long March in October 1935), rural papers and newsletters did not mirror the vibrant Shanghai press, which looked a lot more like London's. More often, provincial papers were organs to recite official proclamations and documents. The provincial governments set up newspaper reading rooms in towns and villages to ensure that their version of the news got around. But there were limits to the circulation of news via print. In some ways, big cities like Shanghai and Beijing were more connected to Paris than to outposts in the Ordos Desert. In early May 1919, when students at the University of Peking got the news of humiliating terms conceded by the peace negotiators in Paris—news they got from the wire services connecting Europe and Asia—they rose up against what they saw as a supine government and foreign delegations in the capital. People in Shaanxi learned of the uprising only once students straggled home from Beijing to study for their exams. Word of mouth conveyed the news across the provincial hinterlands. Despite the power of the press, isolation was still a watchword in much of the world; rumor and oral forms of communication remained a resilient form of diffusion. To the extent that newspapers reached into hinterlands, they looked less and less like the "Western" press, while *Shenbao* in Shanghai and *Dagongbao* in Tianjin resembled their cousins in San Francisco or Lima. In more impenetrable markets, radio would soon become a competitor, especially with the arrival of the portable transistor radio in the 1950s.

The basic technologies from 1900 lasted for over a half century. It would not be until the 1960s that new devices disrupted mechanical typesetting. Since 1890, words and lines had been arranged by keyboard to assemble the "hot metal" casts that stamped pages and sheets. Though the days of the old artisanal composer were over, skilled machine operators could control the pace of production. Their days became numbered with the advent of "cold type" systems, or phototypesetting, in the 1960s—by which time the newspaper business was feeling the pressures from other media, especially the television. We will get to that story shortly.

Continuity in basic production, telegraphic diffusion, and retail advertising also meant basic continuity in the business structure. The Big Three remained the paramount purveyors of global news, with secondary regional and national agencies functioning for subglobal news markets. The hourglass remained more or less intact. If it faced major threats it was from states that wanted to control the news business, to harness public opinion making to rulers' ambitions.

One of the perils of the hourglass structure of the news business was its vulnerability to pressures by governments, especially autocrats. In some authoritarian regimes, like the Soviet Union, and later China, "official" news agencies came into being. They seized private firms and turned them into government monopolies over the flow of news. Occasionally, they inherited an official agency but put the clamps down on any autonomy. During the Cold War, TASS (Russian News Agency) controlled the networks of information flowing into the Soviet Union and its satellite states. Created in 1902 by the Ministry of Finance as a telegraph agency, TASS was Russia's answer to the Big Three. When the Bolshevik Revolution broke out, the leadership immediately saw the importance of information control, seized the agency, and turned it into the mouthpiece of the Communist Party. Thereafter, TASS controlled information flowing in and out of the country, with a lock on the nearly four thousand newspapers across the USSR and in command of a vast network of bureaus around the world—which, not surprisingly, often doubled as intelligence agencies for the Soviet state. Alexander Ivanonich Alexeyev, a seasoned diplomat and intelligence officer, was sent to Cuba in early 1959; he could get a visa only as a TASS reporter—and it was under that aegis that he negotiated the alliance between Moscow and Havana, leading to the broken ties with Washington. It was more challenging for TASS to control the flow beyond the Soviet borders, as newspapers like *Le Monde* (The world) and the *New York Times* or highbrow magazines like *Der Spiegel* (The mirror) and the *Economist* had permanent stringers dispatching stories. These writers had to be cautious about their reporting, lest they face deportation.

Monopolizing the news business and putting it into the state was one strategy; ruling by fear and controlling vital inputs, like paper supply and advertising revenue, provided more indirect tools for control. The Nazis in Germany, Franco in Spain, and the Fascists in Italy put the screws on private news purveyors to report proregime news through direct censorship. In 1933–34, the Nazis merged Wolff and the Telegraphic Union to create the Deutsches Nachrichtenbüro (DNB) to be a concentrated news distributor and collector of information for the regime. The private press, in effect, subsidized official intelligence through subscriptions to DNB services. Sometimes, the control could take a more indirect form: when Juan Domingo Perón came to power, he managed Argentine paper supplies and prices, favoring papers that lavished praise on him, and taking away advertising and cheap paper sources from those that did not.

The relationship between the press and the state could also take cozier forms; some would say mutually opportunistic. Perhaps the most notorious was the comfortable relationship—"tribal friendship" in the words of Joe Alsop, the ubiquitous columnist for the *Saturday Evening Post* and later *New York Herald Tribune*—between influential editors of the *Washington Post* and the politicos of the American capital. Over dry martinis, Cold War elites of the government and fourth estate reenacted ancien régime salons and catered to each other's news-making needs; insider reporters would get their scoops while politicians and policy makers could manage the message behind the scenes. What was known as "the Georgetown Set" had similar counterparts in Ottawa, Delhi, London, and elsewhere—albeit without the breezy confidence born of American hegemony. Whether controlled or cozy, the relationship between news makers and global elites would start to fracture in the 1960s and break wide open in the 1970s.

In the meantime, changes occurred more in the practices of news making rather than in the business organization or technology that these involved. One was the turn to increasing professionalization of journalists and editors who shared a common drive to be information purveyors first and opinion makers second. While newspapers like Gandhi's or the National Association for the Advancement of Colored People's *Crisis* (est. 1910) had more explicit ideological purposes, the large, mass-circulation papers imagined themselves as news outlets, even if their selection of what to report and how to frame the news could tilt to extremes. Mass circulation meant that, increasingly, writers could make a living as reporters. Reporters, accordingly, became public figures. They also designed regimes of professional certification and gatekeeping. Not unlike experts concerned with universal weights and measures, sanitation, meteorology, money, and law, journalists formed their own nineteenth-century International Press Congress (IPC), which called on editors and reporters from around the world to convene and adhere to common standards of ethics and freedoms.

As was so often the case, professionalization got tracked through higher education. In 1899, the fifth IPC in Lisbon called for the creation of schools of journalism. The University of Missouri and the École Supérieure de Journalisme lay claim to being the first. University degrees in journalism, by the 1950s, were becoming a prized certificate to get jobs in top-echelon papers in the United States. It was none other than Joseph Pulitzer, who dreamed of journalistic training—despite his own lack of it, and his affection for sensationalism—that got the ball rolling with a gift to Columbia University to create a graduate school of journalism. It opened in 1912. London University opened its small journalism school in 1919, though for the most part, British reporters learned on the job. France saw the École Supérieure de Journalisme de Lille open in 1924. The model took longer to catch on in Europe and Latin America. For the most part, training relied on older, artisanal models and personalized networks of recruitment, socialization, and promotion. But even here, higher education was a training ground—if there was no formal journalism school, the proliferating papers and magazines of student life incubated graduating reporters. Then came news guilds (unions for journalists) and reporter associations to monitor ethical behavior and to safeguard professional integrity. By 1950, under Cold War pressures and as the strife over decolonization worsened, journalists founded the International Press Institute to defend principles of freedom for reporters, effectively replacing the old nineteenth-century congress as journalists became more than just witnesses; they were becoming targets. The degree of professionalism should not, however, be pressed too far. Journalism and the news business—bereft of technical expertise and dependent on basic savvy and narrative skills—never went as far as lawyers' or accountants' guilds in governing credentials and professional access. The barriers to exit and entry for aspiring news makers were simply too low. In the end, associations could not bare much tooth in the realpolitik of reporting.

If there was a major disruption, it came less from the men and women with pens than those who wielded cameras. News of the world increasingly took illustrated form as the camera turned the consumption of news into a "being there" moment. News consumers were invited to be spectators. Action photography had to wait for two decisive innovations. The first was getting beyond the constraints of plates and paper to photos that could be made and reproduced more easily. In 1889, George Rochester and Thomas Edison invented a thin, portable, sensitized film made from cellulose acetate that could be used in still or motion picture photography. It was not until 1925 that German engineers developed the portable Leica, a camera capable of swapping out canisters of rolled film. A person behind the lens could cock and repeat up to thirty-six shots a roll before having to switch films.

It is hard to exaggerate the Leica effect. The photographer, now a subspecies of reporter, was spared the "reload" problem; she or he could replace canisters in seconds, stash the exposed film in a bag or pocket, continue shooting, and save the "developing" for later. In turn, the chassis got lighter and more discrete and became a better instrument for "shooting" the action. Thus began a journalistic scramble to exotic parts and distant wars in search of late-breaking stories and exotic landscapes. No one took this path to greater heights than the Hungarian-born Robert Capa, the celebrity photojournalist and iconic war photographer who followed the frontiers of global conflict. Unlike those who shot previous war photography, which was too slow and cumbersome to enable them to be part of the action, Capa could get close, perilously close. When he jumped off the landing vessel at Normandy in 1944 to shoot the first moments of D-Day, he sent his rolls immediately back to London for developing so he could follow the action for *Life* magazine. He didn't have to worry about the darkroom, or about setting up his gear. He shot like the GIs around him, to record how "the next mortar shell fell between the barbed wire and the sea, and every piece of shrapnel found a man's body. The Irish priest and the Jewish doctor were the first to stand on the 'Easy Red' beach. I shot the picture. The next shell fell even closer. I didn't dare take my eyes off the finder of my Contax and frantically shot frame after frame. Half a minute later, my camera jammed—my roll was finished. I reached in my bag for a new roll, and my wet, shaking hands ruined the roll before I could insert it in my camera" (*Slightly Out of Focus*, 1947). Pictures blurred and out of focus, Capa could shoot alongside the soldiers, oftentimes not bothering with the viewfinder. Like the shooters around him, Capa was shooting the air.

The emergence of action photography coincided with, and provided fodder for, a new *genre of magazine. The German *Berliner Illustrierte Zeitung* (Berlin illustrated newspaper) was the only German magazine that ever approached American-scale circulation. With almost two million in circulation on the eve of the Nazi takeover in 1933, *BIZ* had experimented with the use of feature photographs since the 1890s and pioneered the photo-essay to convey the news. Indeed, the photo became the news: glamour shots, aerials, stop-action sports, behind-the-scenes images—the camera gave reader-viewer-consumers the full range of perspectives, from intimate insider to outsider in the skies. In 1931, Willi Ruge rolled out *I Photograph Myself during a Parachute Jump*, turning the photographer from the spectator to the subject. *BIZ* was so influential that Joseph Goebbels seized it and made it part of his Propaganda Ministry. During the war, one of its most celebrated photographers, Eric Borchert, was embedded in General Erwin Rommel's North Africa campaign. The French *Vu* pushed the genre even further with innovative layouts and double-page spreads. An American magazine entrepreneur, Henry Luce, watched European innovators closely. The founder of *Fortune* and later *House and Home* and *Sports Illustrated*, he bought a struggling weekly called *Life* with the idea of making it the first outlet especially dedicated to print photojournalism. It would be in *Life* that Capa, and many more to follow, would exhibit their portraits of history. Luce also hired the talented Margaret Bourke-White, who'd been among the first western photographers to shoot photos of Soviet industry in 1930. *Life*'s first issue was full of her dramatic wide-angle shots of the Fort Peck Dam. The February 15, 1937, issue of the magazine carried her portraits of despairing Black flood victims standing forlorn below a placard reading "World's Highest Standard of Living." A decade later, she and the French photographer Henri Cartier-Bresson would use their cameras to chronicle the epic of Indian independence and the human toll of the refugee crisis that followed its wake, all in *Life*.

By the 1950s, the age of print news, a mixture of text and graphic reportage from around the world, was at its zenith. Henry Luce's *Time* magazine, with separate editions niched for different markets, was tailor made for the age of the organization man. Its slogan, "Take Time—It's Brief," aimed at the busy executive who wanted to get the world's news compressed into an hour's read, oftentimes digesting the news by flipping through the graphics and reading the captions. In some cases, the textual narratives were being compressed into standardized three-line diminutive text under the graphic spread. Its "People of the Year" marketed celebrity as news. It became the world's largest circulating world news magazine. At its peak, it had tens of millions of weekly readers; it sat on newsstands in Spanish and brought world news to Asia through the Hong Kong–based *Time Asia*. A reader-viewer of *Time*, *Life*, or *Paris Match* could be excused for confusing the graphic ads with graphic news—and often enough the photographers who took both came from the same studios.

There was a conceit to the glory days of news making: it was that reporters, photographers, editors, and publicists could have it all. They could make news and make money at the same time. And not just at the same time: news making made money, and money could help turn distant, costly information into news. It relied on a virtual monopoly over the means to circulate information about distant happenings.

But that monopoly was also vulnerable to manipulation and control. Thus, it fell to the fourth estate to burnish its commitment to objective reportage in order to sustain the impression that the news business could have it all ways. Despite the surface breeze with which news appeared to circulate, there was enormous pressure on the points at which state control and journalistic autonomy found themselves at odds.

Consider two ways in which readers and audiences learned about the horrific potential of nuclear weapons. By definition, the making of the atomic bomb was a secret. Dropping it, and later testing it, was a shock—a shock that had to be managed. Dropping the bomb on Hiroshima on August 6, 1945, was thus also a news bomb. Around two hundred thousand died in one detonation. The US military sought to keep a grip on the message. The first reportage was bland and lifeless. The photographs issued to editors consisted of air force aerial shots—which conveyed the impression that the first victim was the cloud cover pierced by the massive mushroom that erupted into the skies over the unseen (and invisible) city below. Thereafter, the image of the mushroom cloud would become a dominant impression of the new weapon's lethal potential. Getting the human story from the ground was a challenge for the fourth estate, not least because once Japan did surrender, the occupying allied forces under the US military kept their grip over who and what got published. This did not stop intrepid efforts. In May 1946, the editors of the *New Yorker* magazine dispatched John Hersey to the scene of the first atomic blast. He and his editors were seasoned enough to know that timing was of the essence; Hersey slipped into Hiroshima and spent three weeks in the wreckage interviewing helpers and survivors. The result was an issue of the magazine devoted to a single story, simply called "Hiroshima." When it hit the stands on August 31, a year after the blast, it was a sensation. In 1949, it was released in translation in Japan. "Hiroshima" conveyed to readers what it was like to be bombed in a new way. The key was giving to the survivors, the *hibakusha*, voice and chronicling those first days in which humans collapsed in puddles of their own vomit, blood, and excrement from diarrhea, nausea, and fevers. Hersey's was not the only account. How others got their information stories out also tells us about message management. On August 9, at the military base at Hakata, one Japanese propagandist photographer, Yosuke Yamahata, was ordered to the scene of another bombing, this time in Nagasaki, to shoot images for the military. Driving through the night, he had to wait till dawn for there to be enough light to start shooting. As the sun rose, the scale of the ruin appeared. Stepping through the smoldering fires—he would later recall the macabre horror as "a strangely beautiful scene"—Yamahata spent the next twelve hours shooting the day-after wreckage. His was the most comprehensive visual record of the aftermath of the bomb. Within two weeks, his images appeared in the Japanese newspaper *Mainichi Shimbun* (Daily news). To staunch the controversy, the occupying American military shut it down. With the end of US occupation, censors finally lifted restrictions in 1952. In September of that year, *Life* started to print Yamahata's work. Bordered by Pepsodent and Westinghouse ads, the lunar black-and-whites and freeze-framed images of the aftermath hit the stands of middle America. On the twentieth anniversary of the Hiroshima bombing in 1965, Yamahata started to vomit and turned violently ill. He died a year later from cancer caused by the radiation he picked up while shooting the wreckage of Nagasaki.

Controlling how the Japanese learned about how Americans bombed and burned them continued to be a matter of contention and diplomatic conflict. Indeed, getting information and news about civilian and military uses of nuclear capabilities of states anywhere would remain a point of standoff between officials and investigative reporters.

THE BROKEN HOURGLASS

The hourglass regime depended on how print technology, telegraphy, and oligopolies mediated millions of consumers and their sources. It was layered over with the idea that reporters were committed to objective reporting, which would make the news worthy. It was sustained by a delicate balance of mass advertising and ambivalent government regulation, at once adhering to principles of press freedom while trying to control the message. Both sides of the regime, the technological foundation and reportorial distance, took a hit in the 1960s and occasioned a full-blown crisis of the fourth estate in the 1970s. Television drained away advertisers. A new generation of journalists and photographers cast aside their professional identities as neutral witnesses to become advocates for the voiceless and the powerless in an adversarial world.

The first hit to tele*graphy* came from the advent of tele*vision*. The radio was not a blow to the print news business, though in areas where papers were expansive and literacy rates lower, the radio did take a bite out of potential demand for print news. Unlike radio, television was much more concentrated than the print industry. It also developed a more global programming reach. Early broadcasting systems relied on partnerships across borders and the import of entertainment product—*I Love Lucy* for Asian markets, Argentine soap operas for the vast Spanish-speaking markets—in a scramble for viewers and advertisers. In the mid-1950s, America's NBC and CBS took in well over half the profits of the entire television industry. The BBC had a grip on Britain. They called themselves "networks"—a bland term for oligopoly. In most of Europe, governments simply added television broadcasting to existing state communications monopolies, keeping the new medium under government authority. Beyond Europe, countries bereft of nascent television industries in the 1950s offered a new commercial frontier as far as American television interests were concerned. During the 1950s, Latin America, noncommunist East Asia, and Turkey established US-style private broadcast systems and abided by US broadcasting standards to facilitate imported products. In some cases, American interests worked with foreign governments and invested in local media conglomerates (as in Brazil, Mexico, and the Philippines). Elsewhere in the world, television industries conformed to colonial legacies. Francophone and Anglophone Africa, for example, inherited the centralized state broadcasting bureaucracies of their former colonizers.

TV changed the production and circulation of news. The daily television newscast became morning and evening rituals. By 1960, network news was broadcast daily from 7 to 9 a.m. and early on Sunday evenings, with half-hour "specials" common in the wake of major news events. In Britain, the BBC's *Tonight* news program drew an average of seven million evening viewers, blending "hard" news with "human interest" stories to attract viewers. The turning point of the crisis was, one might say, 1960. In that year, Americans bought more news emitted from television sets than from the printed page. A national poll in 1959 showed that 57 percent of respondents got their news from papers; by 1963, a majority had turned to television. The TV shock was almost instantaneous. New York City's four evening newspapers in 1950 had been halved by 1960 and halved again—to one—in 1970. Hallmark magazines also got whiplashed. Between 1969 and 1972, three of the most widely read newsmagazines in America (the *Saturday Evening Post, Life,* and *Look*) closed down. The neck of the hourglass got tighter. Advertisers slipped away and poured their resources into the more livid potential of television.

The crisis was more than economic and technological. The concept of objectivity that had nurtured journalistic professionalization and global reportage, bolstered by the notion of the camera as the "eye of history" (as the American Civil War photographer Matthew Brady put it), came under assault. I won't go into detail on this except to note that the 1960s brought a new generation of reporters to the fore. They relied on the old networks and still dispensed their reporting into the same old (increasingly beleaguered) outlets. But the stories and montages were taking a decisive turn, making reporters into advocates of justice or defenders of the weak. The most famous was of course the way in which reporting on the Vietnam War unfolded to make it less and less an episode of Yankee heroism and more and more a tale of hubris, peasant killing, and jungle burning. Eddie Adams's shot *Saigon Execution* mentioned at the start of this chapter was one lurid episode—though, to be true to Adams, he was unhappy with the way his picture got, as it were, framed as an indictment of the South Vietnamese puppet state. But there was the reporting on the clamor for *free speech in Czechoslovakia, the photos of Gilles Caron of the stately rue Saint Jacques in Paris, torn up by student demonstrations and littered with charred vehicles, and the efforts of the Mexican government to suppress the massacre of students gathered in the center of the capital to demonstrate against the one-party state's lavishing resources on the Olympic Village. Indeed, 1968, the year of these uprisings, was something of a symbolic turning point. Don McCullin was already making himself famous as the photographer of Cold War Berlin, London gangs, and Vietnamese bloodletting. The year 1968 had him shooting the Beatles during their *White Album* recording and flying off to Nigeria to shoot the savagery of the Biafran civil war in unflinching black and white, as if to draw the observer's eye to the distortions of the famished human body and to the flies preying on sores and eyes. McCullin, heir to Capa's gritty realism, threw aside Capa's avowed noninvolvement. For McCullin, chronicling the suffering of the poor was political, and he meant to play a political role. He, and his Nikon F, became celebrities in a new style of committed reporting. His imagery of Vietnam invited news consumers to wonder whether the GI was not just another victim of warmongers in Washington.

By the end of the 1960s, a paradox loomed over the global news business. Torn from the threat of television competition, it was also the stage for a new idyll of heroic reporting. It was no coincidence that the notion of embedding went by the wayside—and that reporters were increasingly shot in the crossfire or going down in helicopter crashes—as Gilles Caron, a close friend of McCullin's, did in 1970 on Route 1 between Cambodia and Vietnam in territory controlled by the Khmer Rouge. The lens of McCullin's own Nikon deflected a bullet that was meant to take him out. There was a problem with this new style of advocacy reporting, though it took some time to pan out. Less committed even to the illusion of objectivity, the news threatened to become a matter of interpretation, a battle over the narrative, and from there, the *facts themselves. Anyone with an active memory of how fascists or TASS throttled the news business to produce stories to suit their agenda could warn progressive activists that this was a dangerous game; those who did get the message were in turn reminded that it was always in the interests of business to depoliticize the message. Between competition and heroism, print media was under assault and under fire.

Advocacy journalism was one response to the dissolving postwar consensus. Another form of adversarial stance taking by the print media was fueled by the spectacle of state violence—and reporters' commitment to informing publics about hidden truths about repression. This form disavowed partisan loyalties. Instead, truth tellers claimed to be objective and found themselves in conflicts with authorities. In France, exposés of torture and civilian casualties during the Algerian War embarrassed the government. There was already a furious debate over whether the *presse de la trahison* (traitorous press) had betrayed the nation in Indochina. But Algeria was worse: closer and more intractable, the state clamped down on television and radio, over which it still had direct regulatory powers—but it had less power over print media, which (like the leftwing *Libération*) documented repressive counterinsurgency and (like *Algérie française*) reported bombings by Algerian militants in a bitter feud over national loyalties. The Charles de Gaulle administration looked ever weaker and more ham fisted in its efforts to control the reporting by seizing newspapers and magazines or threatening legal actions on trumped-up charges about, in the case of the highbrow *Le Monde*, its finances. The effect was to embolden even more hostility between the press and the Fifth Republic.

If the war in Indochina let loose French truth seeking in the 1950s, it also unleashed a contest over information in the United States a decade later. As the Vietnam War worsened, members of the government of Lyndon B. Johnson began to despair. The secretary of defense, Robert S. McNamara, in June 1967 secretly commissioned a lengthy report on how the country had gotten into the quagmire. But instead of disclosing what was learned, the government kept a lid on it—until 1971, when an insider named Daniel Ellsberg released the three-thousand-page top-secret narrative on the US role in Indochina (and another four thousand pages of appendixes). The *Washington Post* and the *New York Times* proceeded to publish what would be called the Pentagon Papers to an already frustrated and polarized public.

Ellsberg represented a new type in the history of information. The *leaker had always been around. For as long as media existed, politicians and the powerful had used such figures surreptitiously to convey news that served their interests; leaking was an effective way to manage the circulation of news. It was also, by definition, a métier reserved for the insider. Very occasionally, there would be a sensational announcement. But so long as the press had a cozy relationship with power, it more often colluded and covered up. The wars of the 1960s changed the balance. Insiders fed secret information to outsiders, using the press as the medium, setting in motion a long process that culminated in entire organizations—exemplified above all by WikiLeaks formed in 2006—devoted to disclosing secret information by using insiders and leaky vessels of state. A military analyst in the Defense Department and later RAND Corporation, Ellsberg had what was called "privileged access" to information. Like others in the intelligence community, he had become disillusioned with the war and especially what he considered the systematic misinformation and lying by the government and the high command. He approached the *Times* reporter Neil Sheehan, who took the scoop to his editors. The aspect of the Pentagon Papers that caused the most uproar and street protests was the degree to which the public and Congress were kept in the dark about key decisions that led to escalation and disaster. It was hard to pinpoint any single incident in what was an astonishing catalog of deliberate dis- and misinformation. But the cover-up of clandestine provocations against North Vietnam that led two patrol boats to attack a US vessel (the USS *Maddox*) in the Gulf of Tonkin in August 1964, and which was used as a pretext for a congressional resolution to authorize the president to take any actions "necessary" to defend the US against attacks, was pivotal. It was this resolution that triggered formal involvement. The White House used it as a legal means to escalate the war. Within twelve hours, bombers were en route to shower the North with their payloads. Eight years later, the newspapers were revealing to the public that the whole Tonkin "incident" had been manufactured.

Distrustful of the press and wanting to control the narrative about the war, the government of Richard M. Nixon in 1972 sought to clamp down on the publication of the Pentagon Papers by issuing restraining orders. In the end, the US Supreme Court freed the papers to continue printing the documents—arguing that the First Amendment freedom of speech and press trumped the arguments about national defense.

Meanwhile, Ellsberg surrendered to authorities in Boston. "I felt that as an American citizen, as a responsible citizen, I could no longer cooperate in concealing this information from the American public. I did this clearly at my own jeopardy and I am prepared to answer to all the consequences of this decision," he declared. A Los Angeles grand jury indicted him on charges of stealing and holding classified documents. But in a case that would only intensify the hostility between the press and authorities—and would illustrate the paranoid style of the Nixon White House—the judge announced a mistrial. It turned out that the White House had sent agents, illegally, to break into the office of Ellsberg's psychiatrist to steal files and thus "leak" information that would stain his reputation. The slippery slope continued. Members of Nixon's administration approached the trial judge with a job offer: directorship of the FBI. The government's lawyers were then caught with illegal wiretaps on Ellsberg—which they claimed to have lost. It was a fiasco. And it was all public information. So it was that the cycle of leaking, breaking, *hacking, smearing, and more effort to leak and indict seeped into journalistic practice.

Indeed, while the Pentagon Papers rocked world opinion about the US conduct of the war in Vietnam and the bizarre trial against the leaker unfolded, the Nixon circle would not be daunted from relying on secret dirty tricks. On June 17, 1972, White House "plumbers" were sent to break into the Watergate Hotel in Washington to get confidential information on the Democratic presidential campaign. They got caught. The White House scrambled to cover up the story in an increasingly ornate pile of lies. A few journalists, most notably Bob Woodward and Carl Bernstein of the *Washington Post*, with congressional staffers and ultimately some key leakers on the inside, brought the saga to light—which eventually helped lead to the president's resignation. Watergate became a metonym for official skullduggery and journalistic exposé.

Torn between advocacy and objectivity, and faced with the mounting competition of television in particular, the fourth estate was in a furious debate—and gathering anxiety. It took decades, but the pressure had compound effects on the business. Closing print sources and shrinking newspaper budgets meant less work for staff photographers. Working on tight margins, editors turned ever more to wire services for distant images. Nowadays, five image providers dominate the picture industry: Getty Images, Corbis (Microsoft), AP, AFP, and Reuters. With the advent of *digital images and the billowing volume, editors review thousands of photographs a day (as opposed to a few dozen per day in the predigital photography age), hunting for the most riveting, if not always the most complex or subtle, shot. The effect is a tilt toward simple, tightly focused compositions over wider contextual frames. Speed and affective shock value are prized over complexity and accuracy. Framing and photoshopping have only accentuated this trend. Some photographers have lashed out against the quest for the "too-perfect picture" and advocate a return to film to spend more time on composition, perspective, and exposure— slowing things down to be more creative with the shots than spending time on a laptop and relying on Adobe software.

The same fate befell the writer. Belt-tightening editors cast off their stringers. Newspapers had to rely ever more on wire services. In recent decades, the notion of a "week's" digest in an age of acceleration was becoming an anachronism. One of the remaining popular mass-circulation news (as opposed to entertainment) weeklies, *Time*, has threatened to go belly up more than once. With readers wanting around-the-clock reportage— or more, instant notification with a headline "feed" or a digital "gram" of news—the magazine's circulation has plunged to two million. The British writer Nick Davies levied a devastating blast against his industry, charging modern journalism with repackaging unverified, secondhand material gleaned too often from dubious, unchecked sources, to line the profit margins of the commercial interests who produce and circulate what passes as "news." The new regime is no longer an hourglass. It is, in his words, "Flat Earth News"; gone is the art of double-checking, of editing; churnalism masquerades as journalism. This is, no doubt, an overdrawn and excessively pessimistic bottom line. But the current malaise in our day about truth and news has been gathering for decades.

It is worth noting, however, that despite the appearance of rising and falling hegemony of print media and telegraphic circulation, there has been an undercurrent of continuity. Even considering the transformation with digital media, a few names remain uncannily familiar. Some are family names with cunning staying power: Murdoch, Getty, McClatchy, or Hearst. Others are household institutions: the BBC, the Associated Press, Reuters, or NBC, all of which predate the first Wall Street crash of 1929.

In 1962, two scholars published pathbreaking books about the media, especially print media, and the modern condition. The German philosopher Jürgen Habermas wrote a book about what he called the *bürgerliche Öffentlichkeit*, the bourgeois public sphere. The English translation had to wait until another fateful year, 1989. Habermas made the case for the rise and fall of an autonomous domain of journalism, reading *salons, and *coffeehouses, where the literate and "polite" classes would gather and debate information from and about the world in spaces reserved apart from the marketplace and the polity. Print culture played a vital role in informing and influencing with information and learned opinion. He lamented the way in which mass print media became a new technology for managing consensus and promoting sales. This pessimistic narrative was at odds with the other pathbreaking book of 1962, by the Canadian Marshall McLuhan. *The Gutenberg Galaxy: The Making of Typographical Man* became a cult classic. It announced the arrival of what he called "the Global Village," laced together by wires—hence "Typographic Man"—and electronic interdependence. In this account, print media and news circulation had cleared the stage for a higher order of intervisibility; instead of depending on two-dimensional, static print, consumer-villagers could tune into their television sets. This hot media mobilized more senses to intensify the awareness of what was going on elsewhere. Hence the making of a global village.

Habermas and McLuhan stood at either end of the spectrum of debate about the media. But they shared a sense of passing. Part technological, part economic, part in the practices of production and consumption of information about distant happenings, the media was the stage and the source of *epistemological mayhem that would gather force in the 1960s—and one might say has ripened in our day. McLuhan and Habermas could look back on a century in which it appeared to be the other way around. The printed word and image claimed to speak as self-evident truths. Yes, some accused photographers of staging shots. Yes, others charged writers of putting words into the mouths of subjects. But on the whole, the long century of print was one in which the hourglass created the medium for managing the flow of information from sources to consumers worldwide.

Jeremy Adelman

See also cameras; censorship; diplomats/spies; globalization; information, disinformation, misinformation; merchants; networks; newspapers; printed visuals; readers

FURTHER READING

Gerald J. Baldasty, *The Commercialization of News in the Nineteenth Century*, 1992; Jeremy Black, *The Power of Knowledge: How Information and Technology Made the Modern World*, 2014; Oliver Boyd-Barrett, "'Global' News Agencies," in *The Globalization of News*, edited by Oliver Boyd-Barrett and Terhi Rantanen, 1998, 19–34; idem, *The International News Agencies*, 1980; Oliver Boyd-Barrett and Terhi Rantanen, eds., *The Globalization of News*, 1998; Robert W. Desmond, *The Information Process: World News Reporting to the Twentieth Century*, 1978; Juan Gonzalez and Joseph Torres, *News for All the People: The Epic Story of Race and the American Media*, 2011; Daniel R. Headrick, *The Invisible Weapon: Telecommunications and International Politics, 1851–1945*, 1991; Carol Sue Humphrey, "Coming of Age: The Growth of the American Media in the Nineteenth Century," in *The Rise of Western Journalism, 1815–1914: Essays on the Press in Australia, Canada, France, Germany, Great Britain and the United States*, edited by Ross F. Collins and E. M. Palmegiano, 2007, 173–201; Richard R. John and Jonathan Silberstein-Loeb, eds., *Making News: The Political Economy of Journalism in Britain and America from the Glorious Revolution to the Internet*, 2015; Simon J. Potter, *News and the British World: The Emergence of an Imperial Press System, 1876–1922*, 2003; idem, "Webs, Networks, and Systems: Globalization and the Mass Media in the Nineteenth- and Twentieth-Century British Empire," *Journal of British Studies* 46, no. 3 (2007): 621–46; Matthew Pressman, *On Press: The Liberal Values That Shaped the News*, 2018; Tehri Rantanen, "The Globalization of Electronic News in the Nineteenth Century," *Media Culture Society* 19, no. 4 (1997): 605–20; idem, "The Struggle for Control of Domestic News Markets (1)," in *The Globalization of News*, edited by Oliver Boyd-Barrett and Tehri Rantanen, 1998, 35–48; Donald Read, *The Power of News: The History of Reuters*, 2nd ed., 1999; Dana Schwartz, "Objective Representation: Photographs as Facts," in *Picturing the Past: Media, History, and Photography*, edited by Bonnie Brennen and Hanno Hardt, 1999, 158–81; Jonathan Silberstein-Loeb, *The International Distribution of News: The Associated Press, Press Associations and Reuters, 1848–1947*, 2014; Anthony Smith, *The Newspaper: An International History*, 1979; John Steel and Marcel Broersma, "Redefining Journalism during the Period of the Mass Press 1880–1920: An Introduction," *Media History* 21, no. 3 (2015): 235–37; Heidi Tworek, "The Creation of European News: News Agency Cooperation in Interwar Europe," *Journalism Studies* 14, no. 5 (2013): 730–42; Dwayne R. Winseck and Robert M. Pike, *Communications and Empire: Media, Markets, and Globalization, 1860–1930*, 2007; Timothy Wu, *The Attention Merchants: The Epic Struggle to Get Inside Our Heads*, 2016.

11

PUBLICITY, PROPAGANDA, AND PUBLIC OPINION

From the *Titanic* Disaster to the Hungarian Uprising

The *Titanic* disaster is an unlikely landmark in the history of information. Yet a landmark it was. The world's largest and most opulent oceangoing vessel, the *Titanic* unexpectedly collided with an iceberg and plunged into the frigid North Atlantic in 1912, drowning over fifteen hundred passengers and crew. No one seriously believed the *Titanic* could sink. But it did. Some interpreted the disaster as a Greek tragedy, a Dickensian social commentary, or a love story. For others, it became a parable about the power of information: a portentous warning about the terrible things that could happen when a message failed to reach its intended destination, or, even more ominously, when access to information was denied.

The presumption that something as ephemeral as information could be invested with world-historical significance is a modern invention. For much of human history, contemporaries rarely regarded information as an agent of change. This was largely because so much of what we today would define as information remained tightly controlled. Priests, political leaders, merchants, and government officials enjoyed privileged access to time-specific updates on religion, politics, commerce, and public life. Each would have regarded the idea of broad access to information as strange, if not downright dangerous. Not until the eighteenth-century *Enlightenment would it become commonplace, at least in Europe and North America, for moral philosophers, social theorists, and statesmen (an apt turn of phrase, since political leaders were almost all men) to embrace the daring presumption that improvements in popular access to information would promote the public good. In some circles, it would even become fashionable to credit technical advances in what we would today call information technology with hastening moral progress, an assertion familiar to today's digital utopians, social media enthusiasts, and smart phone advertisers. Ours is not the first age when visionaries proclaimed that "information wants to be free."

For the US sociologist Charles H. Cooley (1864–1929), the influence of technical advance on moral progress was an article of faith. Innovations in information technology, such as the mail, telegraph, or telephone, Cooley confidently predicted in his landmark 1909 exploration of "social organization," would inexorably usher in a new era of "moral progress" (his phase) in which "the public consciousness" would expand outward from the locality to the nation and beyond, until eventually the "world itself" would be included in "one lively mental whole."

Cooley's identification of technical advance with moral progress shaped the popular understanding of the *Titanic* disaster. Not until 1900, a mere dozen years before the

Titanic sank, would it become possible to send or receive messages through the air. This technical advance was known as wireless telegraphy to distinguish it from wire-based telegraphy, an innovation first popularized in the mid-nineteenth century. Wireless telegraphy in 1912 remained a one-to-one narrowcast medium whose proper operation demanded a high level of technical expertise. Only after the First World War would it become the one-to-many broadcast medium for speech and music that is today known as radio.

The movie director James Cameron did not cast the *Titanic*'s wireless operator as his hero, let alone make a blockbuster film about him (almost all wireless operators were male). Yet he might have. For the *Titanic* wireless operator's frantic calls for help hastened the arrival of a nearby ship that rescued almost half of the ship's passengers. Had circumstances been different, even more could have been saved. For on the night of the disaster, the ships best positioned to rescue passengers stranded in lifeboats had all turned off their wireless receivers. To make matters worse, the Marconi Company (then the leading supplier of wireless equipment) limited access to its network. Had information flowed more freely, or so many contemporaries quite plausibly believed, fewer passengers might have drowned.

This essay traces the shifting understanding of the Enlightenment truism that improving popular access to information is a public good. It spans the "age of radio"—an epoch that can be said to have begun in 1912, the year of the *Titanic* disaster, and to have ended in 1956, the year in which US-backed radio broadcasts failed to catalyze a political revolution in communist Hungary. Technical advances in information technology, of course, continued after 1956; they included, in particular, the widespread commercialization of the digital computer, the technical advance most central to today's information age. In some quarters, the Enlightenment faith in the emancipatory promise of information never died.

Yet the age of radio remains a watershed in the history of information. For it challenged, without entirely undermining, the Enlightenment faith that technical advance in information technology could bring moral progress. This challenge can be traced by examining the evolution of three media *genres—publicity, propaganda, and public opinion—and three media organizations—the metropolitan newspaper, the government messaging agency, and the radio broadcasting station. In particular, we examine how media insiders—political leaders, government officials, business elites, journalists, and social scientists—understood the relationship between publicity, propaganda, and public opinion.

This understanding changed over time. Early on, many if not most media insiders presumed that public opinion was shaped by, and often identical with, the information published in the press. Beginning in the 1910s, a small but influential group of social scientists challenged this premise. The audience for news, they demonstrated, was often unpersuaded by the information they read in the newspaper or heard on the radio. Building on this insight, they transformed an amorphous phenomenon that was familiar to the Enlightenment political theorists and that was known variously as the "public," "public opinion," or "public sentiment" into a theoretical construct that could be precisely measured using quantitative techniques. In so doing, they invented the modern concept of public opinion.

In the age of radio, the production and distribution of international news, as well as its systematic analysis by social scientists, was the work of a tiny elite. Almost entirely excluded from this process was the vast majority of the world's peoples—women, the illiterate, the colonized, the nonwhite. Sadly, but perhaps not surprisingly, journalists only rarely depicted these groups with sympathy or insight. This elitist bias did not go unremarked. The Indian anticolonial activist Mahatma Gandhi challenged prevailing assumptions about news management, as did government officials in Japan and the Soviet Union. These critiques notwithstanding, international news remained dominated by a relatively small number of Western organizations that enjoyed close ties to political leaders, government officials, business elites, and journalists. In the United States, the United Kingdom, and Germany, their ranks included a constellation of social scientists who set the terms for a mid-twentieth-century debate about the relationship between publicity, propaganda, and public opinion that remains influential today. The information-related organizations, individuals, and ideas that shaped this debate are the main focus of this essay.

The United Kingdom, the United States, and Germany each had distinctive national histories, institutional arrangements, and intellectual traditions. Yet in all three countries, media insiders shared a surprisingly similar understanding of the relationship between information, power, and social change. Intellectual developments in one country often crossed national borders, and in some instances, academics physically relocated from one country to another. Of these intellectual migrations the most consequential was the exodus of social scientists from Germany to the United States in the 1930s following the Nazis' rise to power.

THE INFORMATION INFRASTRUCTURE

The metropolitan newspaper and the government messaging agency each took advantage of technical advances that predated their emergence. Among the most important was the vast network of undersea (or "submarine") telegraph cables that by 1914 encircled the globe. The best-known and most intensively utilized cable network spanned the North Atlantic, beginning with the first successful Atlantic cable in 1866. Contemporaries hailed this network for annihilating time and space, fostering sociability, and promoting world peace. While historians sometimes assume that this language was unique to electrical communications, identical claims had been previously advanced to characterize the steamship, the railroad, and the mail.

The novelty of the cable network is easily exaggerated. The North Atlantic cables followed the same route, and served the same market, as the Cunard steamships that the British post office had relied on since 1840 to carry the mail. Though the Atlantic cable was faster, it was really more of an incremental change than a fundamental rupture. Cable rates were extremely high, discouraging the transmission of long messages. The vast majority of merchants active in the Atlantic trade in the early 1900s continued to rely on the mail—just as they had before 1866.

Cables were big business. The most important cable lines were owned and operated not by governments, but by a relatively small number of companies that ranked among the world's largest and most powerful multinational corporations. Cable company managers assumed that they would earn more by keeping prices high and volume low. As a consequence, cables were used primarily by government officials, journalists, and the global commercial elite—the Victorian equivalent of today's 1 percent. Prior to the post-1970 restructuring of global telecommunications, it was extremely rare for ordinary people to send a telegram overseas. If you wished to stay in touch with a distant friend or a family member, you posted a letter. The "Victorian *internet" was not the telegraph, but the mail.

The landline telegraph network, in contrast, was often government owned and government operated. This made landlines even more nation centric than submarine cables. In many countries, landlines were administered by the same government agency that coordinated the mail, in an arrangement that was popularly known as a PTT. This was true not only in the United Kingdom and Germany but also in France, Switzerland, and Japan. These institutional arrangements profoundly influenced the rate structure for long-distance intranational communications. This was because, in these countries, it was almost always cheaper to send a telegram a long distance inside the country's borders than to send it even a short distance to a neighboring country. In some countries—spurred by nationalization of the landline telegraph network and the emergence of a robust transnational reform movement known as "postal telegraphy"—it became almost as cheap in the late nineteenth century to send a telegram as a letter. Despite this reform, for most people the posted letter, whether handwritten or typed, retained—as a telegram did not—a palpable reminder of the sender's presence, making it a superior medium for the conveyance of personal information.

In the United States, in contrast, the postal telegraph movement failed, and the telegraph would not be configured as a popular medium for in-country messages until 1910, several decades after the postal telegraph movement had lowered in-country telegraph rates in the United Kingdom and Germany. The telephone, in contrast, had by 1910 already been configured for a decade as a low-cost way to circulate information over short distances. The popularization of the telegraph and telephone was coordinated not by the government but, rather, by a nexus of corporations that was dominated by a vast combine popularly known as Bell. Bell leaders touted this combined low-cost long-distance-telegraph-short-distance-telephone service as "universal service," an arrangement that they were forced to abandon in 1913 after the Justice Department instituted a lawsuit on behalf of a rival network provider. The popularization of the telephone in the United States was much remarked on by British visitors; it set the United States apart from the United Kingdom and France, though not from Germany and Sweden.

Cables had politics. By far the largest and most extensive cable network operated out of the United Kingdom, a fact well understood by British imperial officials, who used their dominant position in the information infrastructure to project imperial power overseas. Other countries with a sizable cable network included the United States, whose government subsidized cable-laying projects in Latin America to try to bolster US political influence and promote overseas trade. The German government also looked to information technology to bolster its international standing. Intent on challenging the British, the French, and the Americans, it invested heavily in wireless telegraphy, then the newest *new media of its day.

The close relationship between cable corporations and national governments dated back to the 1890s. Prior to this period, though nominally British, the world's largest

cable corporation—the Eastern and Associated Company, which linked the United Kingdom with its colonies in India and East Asia—operated largely independently of political control. The one vital exception concerned landing rights. Every cable corporation
needed government permission to land its cables on the shoreline of another country, a
seemingly minor issue that became increasingly salient as governments tightened their
control over the transnational flow of information.

In the 1890s, everything changed. It was in this decade, but not before, that the Great
Powers came to regard the cable network as a strategic asset in international relations,
military planning, economic policy, and geopolitical prestige. In recognition of this fact,
the British, German, and US governments each began to invest heavily in laying new
cables. The British government, for example, subsidized a cable connection between Van-
couver, Canada; Australia; and New Zealand that opened in 1902. The Vancouver-
Australia cable completed the final link in an imperial "All-Red Route"—a global network of cables that landed only on British or imperial soil. British government officials
no longer needed to fear that a rival power could tap their cable lines and intercept
messages cabled between London and their imperial possessions. Henceforth, the cable
network became a tool of empire, and not an open market, a distinction that would
loom large in the interwar debate over the emerging information order. To put it differently, the British government was committed to improving the information infrastructure within the British Empire, rather than around the globe. (British postal policy in
this period had a parallel goal: when imperial postal officials championed "universal"
penny postage, they had in mind cheap postage within the British Empire, and not cheap
postage anywhere in the world.)

The All-Red Route deeply troubled German government officials, who feared that the
British government could mobilize it in wartime to control the informational environment. The widespread conviction that the British government had censored cables between South Africa and Europe during the Second Boer War (1899–1902) lent credibility to this concern. Further confirmation came in 1903, when the British government
denied a German cable promoter the right to land a transatlantic cable in Great Britain.

Any lingering questions about the political significance of the cable network were
decisively answered when the First World War began in August 1914. Within days, the
British government had cut every important cable linking Germany to the United States.
For the duration of the war, the cable network became an "invisible weapon," a key
military resource in what one historian has aptly dubbed the "information warfare that
pitted Germany against the United Kingdom and its allies," which after April 1917 included the United States.

British control over the cable network led directly to one of the greatest publicity
coups of the period. To counteract the negative effect of the potential entry of the United
States into the war as an ally of the United Kingdom and France, German secretary of
state Arthur Zimmerman sent a top-secret telegram in January 1917 to a high-ranking
Mexican government official over hostile telegraph lines (the German lines having
already been cut). In this telegram, Zimmerman offered Germany's support for returning territory to Mexico that the country had lost to the United States in the Mexican-
American War (1846–48), should Mexico declare war on the United States in response
to the anticipated US declaration of war on Germany. The British government intercepted Zimmerman's message and decoded it, a major triumph for British intelligence.

When the decoded message became public, it outraged many Americans, a sentiment that intensified when, a few months later, Zimmerman acknowledged its authenticity. In combination with Germany's resumption of unrestricted submarine warfare, the Zimmerman telegram contributed to President Woodrow Wilson's decision, in April 1917, to seek and obtain congressional support to declare war against Germany.

Here is one example, of many, when information technology brought war, not peace. US president James Buchanan had hopefully predicted in 1858 that a transatlantic cable would insure "perpetual peace" between the United Kingdom and the United States. Buchanan could not have been more mistaken. Had an Atlantic cable linked the United Kingdom and the United States in 1861, or so contended the British minister to the United States shortly thereafter, near-instantaneous communication would have heightened the mounting diplomatic tensions between the two countries and almost certainly led to war.

The consequences of the cable network extended far beyond its role in diplomacy, espionage, and surveillance. It also fostered a new kind of news broker: the international news agency. The first international news agencies were founded in the mid-nineteenth century to gather news from around the world and to supply it directly to newspapers. The vast majority of newspapers could not afford correspondents in their nation's capital, let alone foreign correspondents. International news agencies solved this problem by saving newspapers the cost of foreign correspondents and of transmitting news by cable to the press.

Just as the cable network was a tool of empire, so too were the most important international news agencies. For in addition to greatly increasing the volume of information on world affairs, they promoted the interests of the nations with which they were linked. Each had close ties with one of the world's major powers: Reuters with the United Kingdom; Agence Havas with France; Wolff's Telegraphisches Bureau with Prussia and, later, Germany. The dominant US international news agency was the Associated Press, the successor to a Chicago-based news agency that dated back to the Civil War. Each of these news agencies cooperated with the others in a cartel that lasted from the mid-nineteenth century until the outbreak of the Second World War. (The principal exception was the Associated Press, which pulled out of this arrangement in 1934.)

THE METROPOLITAN NEWSPAPER AND ITS CRITICS

The rise of international news agencies owed much to the concurrent rise of metropolitan newspapers, a new medium that emerged more or less simultaneously in the late nineteenth century in the United Kingdom, Germany, and the United States. The metropolitan newspaper, with its growing readership for international news and large and growing advertising base, would provide the international news agencies with a large and steady revenue stream, while elevating publicity to an unprecedented prominence in public life.

The ubiquity of the metropolitan newspaper was one of the wonders of the age. Though its predecessors dated back to the seventeenth century, they contained relatively little content and rarely reached more than a few thousand copies. Almost no single issue exceeded four pages (one sheet of paper folded once). In the late nineteenth century, everything changed. Printed in an attractive format, sometimes with multicolor supplements, individual issues ran to eight, sixteen, or even more pages filled with original content written by a permanent staff of full-time reporters. All were dailies, with hefty Sunday editions; the most successful published as many as six editions at least five days a week. Some stories originated with beat reporters or out-of-town correspondents. Others reached the newsroom by wire. If an unusually important news story broke, *publishers interrupted their regular press run to print a one-page extra, sometimes within ten minutes of receiving the information.

This new medium was, by definition, urban. Small towns, villages, and rural districts had to make do with less. Here daily newspapers remained unusual, with local coverage spottier, and original news stories fewer and less varied.

The most successful metropolitan newspapers reaped large profits from advertisements, subscriptions, and street sales. Rapid urbanization had increased the size of their readership, making them an attractive advertising medium for the many new businesses that had begun in the late nineteenth century to churn out a multitude of branded, packaged products. Flush with revenue, editors invested in high-speed machinery that could print thousands of copies in minutes on cheap paper made from wood pulp rather than rags.

The novelty of metropolitan newspapers was obvious to contemporaries. In the United Kingdom, they were called the "new" journalism, a phrase coined in 1887 by cultural critic Matthew Arnold. In Germany they became known as "boulevard papers." In the United States, they were the "yellow press," a phrase that derived not from the supposedly lurid content of their articles, but from the popularity of a cartoon character known as the "yellow kid."

Journalists dubbed the publishers of the most successful British and American metropolitan newspapers "barons." The feudal barons of medieval Europe commanded the labor of a legion of retainers; fin de siècle publishers presided over media fiefdoms in which they had become a new aristocracy. Perhaps the most celebrated British newspaper baron was Alfred Harmsworth, the first Viscount Northcliffe (1865–1922). Among Harmsworth's US-based counterparts were William Randolph Hearst (1863–1951) of the *New York Journal*, Joseph Pulitzer (1847–1911) of the *St. Louis Post-Dispatch* and *New York World*, Adolph S. Ochs (1858–1935) of the *New York Times*, and Robert R. McCormick (1880–1955) of the *Chicago Tribune*.

Northcliffe rose from a humble background to found a media empire that targeted newspapers at new kinds of readers. The *Daily Mail*, which he founded in 1896, catered to a lower-middle-class audience. Priced at half the cost of its London rivals, it swiftly became the largest-selling newspaper in the world—a million copies daily by 1902. The following year, Northcliffe created the *Daily Mirror* to reach female readers. After a rocky start, Northcliffe changed its format to incorporate more visual material, including photographs. Six years later, Northcliffe bought and revived the prestigious London *Times*, a testament to his emergence as one of the most influential press barons of the age.

Less ambitious than Northcliffe, yet no less influential, was W. T. Stead (1849–1912). As editor of the *Pall Mall Gazette*, Stead pioneered the exposé, a demanding literary form that combined ethnographic detail, florid language, and religious fervor. Buoyed by an unshakeable faith in the redeeming power of publicity, Stead piled up *fact upon fact in emotionally riveting, morally charged, and often lurid prose that chronicled urban evils ranging from prostitution and police corruption to unsanitary housing.

Stead was fascinated by the United States and crossed the Atlantic frequently to re-port on its industrial expansion and urban squalor. Among the most celebrated of his exposés was *If Christ Came to Chicago* (1894), a perceptive and deeply reported investi-gation of everyday life in a metropolis that many contemporaries, including Stead, re-garded as the most revealing "shock city" of the modern world. Though Stead would not have considered himself a sociologist, his block-by-block diagrams of Chicago's slum neighborhoods bore a family resemblance to the information-packed monograph, *Hull-House Maps and Papers*, that Jane Addams compiled the following year on her Chicago neighborhood or that W.E.B. Du Bois published in *The Philadelphia Negro* (1899). Like the municipal socialist Delos Wilcox, each regarded publicity as a key to social reform.

Stead's zest for original reporting proved his undoing. Intent on expanding his cov-erage of the United States, he booked a ticket on the *Titanic*—and perished in the mid-Atlantic. Yet his pioneering form of information-intensive reporting would be emulated by the rising generation of investigative journalists, popularly known as "muckrakers," that included, in the United States, Ida B. Wells, Lincoln Steffens, Ida Tarbell, and Upton Sinclair. These journalists combined in-depth reporting with compelling story lines to reach large audiences. Like President Theodore Roosevelt, who gave the muckrakers their name in a 1906 speech in which he criticized their excesses, they believed in the power of publicity as an agent of reform. Each marshaled reams of information to in-spire people to action.

"Facts, facts piled up to the point of dry certitude, was what the American people then needed and wanted," declared the journalist Ray Stannard Baker in 1945 in as-sessing the early twentieth-century popular fascination with information-packed prose. Publicity, or so contemporaries assumed, was the handmaid of reform. "'Let there be light!'" proclaimed President Woodrow Wilson in his political testament—"The New Freedom"— in 1913: "Publicity is one of the purifying elements of politics. The best thing you can do with anything that is crooked is to lift it up where people can see that it is crooked, and then it will either straighten itself out or disappear. . . . There is no air so wholesome as the air of utter publicity." For progressives of all stripes, information and reform seemed inextricably linked.

Wilson's words serve as reminder that, in the period before the First World War, pub-licity had a broader, and more positive, meaning than it would after 1918. Today pub-licity often refers to the subjective presentation of information to cast a favorable light on a person, organization, or cause. Should a corporation find itself confronted with negative news coverage, it might mount a publicity campaign. Prior to the First World War, in contrast, publicity retained its close association with the core Anglo-American journalistic value of transparency. In a 1901 message to Congress in which he called for the investigation of big business, President Theodore Roosevelt made this identifi-cation of publicity and objective information explicit: "The first essential in determin-ing how to deal with the great industrial combinations is knowledge of the facts— publicity." Though Roosevelt admired facts, he recognized that they had a limited ability to shape public opinion. To reach the public, Roosevelt sardonically observed, the most relevant art form was not the finely wrought "etching" but the flamboyant "circus poster." Over time, the boundary between publicity and transparency blurred, and publicity became identified with the overtly promotional appeals later known as "public relations." Among the pioneers in this field were two journalists: George Mi-chaelis, who in 1900 founded the Publicity Bureau in Boston to burnish the image of railroads, public utilities, and universities, and James E. Ellsworth, who in 1907 be-came a publicity agent for Bell, which was well on its way to becoming one of the larg-est corporations in the world.

The late nineteenth-century press baron was a familiar figure in Germany too. The most famous German press barons were Leopold Ullstein (1826–99) and Rudolf Mosse (1843–1920). Ullstein purchased his first newspaper in the late 1870s. In the early 1900s he founded the first German tabloid, *B.Z. am Mittag* (B[erlin] n[ewspaper] at noon); shortly thereafter, he purchased the prestigious *Vossische Zeitung* ([C. F.] Voss's newspaper), a decision reminiscent of Lord Northcliffe's purchase of the London *Times* in 1908. Mosse founded a number of successful German newspapers, including the long-lived *Berliner Morgen-Zeitung* (Berlin morning newspaper), which he operated in con-junction with a highly successful advertising business that he used to increase the page counts of his publications.

Ullstein and Mosse were liberal and Jewish. During the First World War, they were joined by Alfred Hugenberg, an industrialist who created a publishing empire that fea-tured more conservative content. During the Weimar Republic (1919–33), their ranks included the communist Willi Münzenberg, who briefly became the second-largest pub-lisher in the country, before being driven out of business by the Nazis.

While metropolitan newspapers in the three countries had much in common, national variations remained. Per capita newspaper readership was much higher in the United States and Germany than in the United Kingdom. London was the metropolitan news-paper hub in the United Kingdom, while metropolitan newspapers originated in many cities in the United States and Germany. The United Kingdom did boast a flourishing provincial press whose ranks included the *Manchester Guardian*, the *Liverpool Echo*, and the *Birmingham Post*. Yet this press remained, as its name implies, provincial compared to London. In the United States, metropolitan newspapers flourished not only in New York City but also in Chicago, St. Louis, and San Francisco. In Germany, similarly, metropolitan newspapers thrived not only in Berlin but also in Frankfurt, Munich, and Cologne.

The training of journalists also differed from country to country. In the United States, Joseph Pulitzer championed the founding of specialized journalism schools to train new reporters; British publishers, in contrast, remained committed to hiring journalists who learned their trade on the job. In Germany, a third journalistic tradition emerged. In the United Kingdom and the United States, journalists regarded the reporting of infor-mation to be their primary task. In Germany, journalists subordinated reporting to in-terpretation. Many newspapers had political or religious affiliations, and journalists were expected to hew to the party line. One example was *Germania*, a Berlin-based newspaper founded in 1871 to support the Catholic Center Party. *Germania* played a critical role in mobilizing German Catholics during the Kulturkampf, the anti-Catholic campaign that Chancellor Otto von Bismarck would launch in the following year. Ex-ceptions existed. Following the abolition of newspaper taxes in the 1870s, a new kind of newspaper—the *Generalanzeiger* or general advertiser—emerged in many cities. In-tended to appeal across the political spectrum to a rapidly growing urban audience, these newspapers relied heavily on advertisements.

The metropolitan newspaper prompted an outpouring of commentary, positive and negative. Much focused on the sheer volume of information. Each morning, remarked the British journalist Ford Madox Ford in 1911, the newspaper reading public was "overwhelmed" with a "white spray of facts" that were "more or less new, more or less important, more or less veracious."

Newspaper reading did not necessarily render the public well informed. "The [prewar] inhabitant of London," the British economist John Maynard Keynes nostalgically observed in 1919, "could order by telephone, sipping his morning tea in bed, the various products of the whole earth, in such quantity as he might see fit, and reasonably expect their early delivery upon his doorstep." For this inhabitant, Keynes elaborated, the "projects and politics of militarism and imperialism" and the "racial and cultural rivalries" that divided the world were "little more than the amusements of his daily newspaper, and appeared to exercise almost no influence at all on the ordinary course of social and economic life," a remark that revealed the inhabitant's—and Keynes's—obliviousness not only to the precariousness of the international order, but also to the violence wrought by British imperialism on its colonial subjects.

German press critics fixed their sights on the influence of commercial considerations on newspaper coverage. Too many publishers ran their newspapers like a schnapps distillery in order to intoxicate their audience by blunting awareness of pressing social issues, complained the German media scholar Robert Brunhuber in 1907. German newspapers had an obligation, contended a prominent journalist eight years later, to reject their alliance with a profit-seeking news agency that was linked to the government. As an alternative, they sought out a news broker modeled on the Associated Press, an organization owned by newspapers and operated on their behalf. Economic autonomy, or so the journalist elaborated, would free the metropolitan newspaper from government intervention in news supply. Though the news broker model was much discussed, it would not come to fruition until 1949, with the founding in West Germany of the Deutsche Presse-Agentur (dpa).

The relative importance in German journalism of interpretation, as distinct from reporting, set it apart from journalism in the United Kingdom and the United States. In looking back on his years as a journalist in the Weimar Republic, the Hungarian British journalist Arthur Koestler reflected on this distinction. Anglo-American journalists, Koestler reminisced, believed in "impersonal and objective reporting of facts." German journalists, in contrast, had a "tendency towards subjectivity." One German editor, Koestler scathingly recalled, had proclaimed facts not to be "fit for the reader when served raw." Instead, "they had to be cooked, chewed and presented in the correspondent's saliva." Such an outlook, Koestler believed, predisposed German readers to reject fact-based journalism in favor of the Nazis' deliberately slanted propaganda.

Whether or not voter behavior correlated so directly with newspaper reporting was a question that a later generation of social scientists put high on its research agenda. Yet the relationship that Koestler identified was real. Journalists *had* undermined Weimar democracy by scandal mongering and indicting the "system" as corrupt. In so doing, they unintentionally helped to bolster nationalists who insisted that only a strong leader could save Germany from economic ruin.

US journalists echoed the British and German critique of the metropolitan press. The subservience of journalists to advertisers was deplorable, contended the editor and publisher Hamilton Holt in 1910. As an alternative Holt called for a foundation-based "independent" press. Upton Sinclair's *The Brass Check* (1919) was a blistering exposé of journalists' willingness to publish false and misleading information to protect vested interests while undermining the public good. Like Brunhuber, Sinclair accused journalists of bowing to the profit motive in their coverage of the news.

While journalists penned the most acerbic press criticism in this period, they were hardly alone. Academics quickly followed, spurred by the simultaneous rise of the metropolitan newspaper as a popular medium and sociology as an academic discipline. Germany in the late nineteenth century had emerged as a world leader in the social sciences; it was hardly surprising that German scholars led the world in this field too. Though Max Weber is best known as a sociologist of religion, science, and politics, he was also fascinated by journalism and urged his colleagues to analyze its character and significance. Following Weber's lead, social scientists founded the Institute for Newspaper Science in Leipzig in 1916, a mere eight years after the University of Missouri established the first professional school of journalism in the United States.

German scholarship on the press proliferated in the interwar period with dozens of books and doctoral dissertations. While politicians continued to regard the citizenry as gullible and easily manipulated, academics knew better. In this debate, the critique of mass culture popularized by sociologists like Ferdinand Tönnies (1855–1936) anticipated later arguments about communications and public life advanced by the Austrian émigré Paul Lazarsfeld.

German scholarship on the press found a receptive audience in the American academy. Social scientists should investigate the "natural history of the newspaper," declared the University of Chicago sociologist Robert Park in 1923. Park's interest dated back to the prewar period, when he had toiled away as a graduate student in Germany. The influence on the American academy of this German tradition would soon be eclipsed by a second German tradition—known as the Frankfurt school—that would be pioneered by a talented generation of German-speaking refugee scholars who had fled Germany for the United States in the 1930s. Park focused on the relationship of journalism and democracy. Members of the Frankfurt school, in contrast, had witnessed the collapse of democratic institutions in Germany and Austria; not surprisingly, they found it more compelling to analyze the press as a tool of mass persuasion and to devise novel techniques to measure its effects.

GOVERNMENT PROPAGANDA AND THE LEGACY OF THE GREAT WAR

The First World War marked a watershed in the history of information. The catalyst was not technological: radio broadcasting had yet to emerge, and wireless remained important primarily for military communications. Rather, governments on both sides of the war mobilized the press to get their message across. These messaging campaigns generated an enormous volume of information, often labeled propaganda, that in the postwar period would be widely criticized for hastening the rise of fascism.

Propaganda was hardly new. To defend itself against the heresy of Protestantism, the Catholic Church in the early seventeenth century established an organization that it officially called the Sacra Congregatio de Propaganda Fide, which became in English the Congregation for the Propagation of the Faith, or, simply, "the Propaganda." The effectiveness of this clerical organization impressed government leaders, who borrowed freely from its methods in times of crisis to buttress their authority. The British government led the way, using its control of the cable network to spread (and suppress) atrocity stories during the Boer War (1899–1902).

Government messaging campaigns reached unprecedented heights of sophistication during the First World War, when all the major belligerents established agencies designed specifically to rally the troops and stiffen civilian morale. It is sometimes assumed that journalists in the Anglo-American world operated independently of the state. In fact, they worked covertly or overtly with the governments in their respective countries. To keep the public informed, government agencies relied on two very different techniques: censorship and messaging. Sometimes governments suppressed information about the war; sometimes they shaped coverage. In the United States, government messaging was coordinated by the aptly named Committee on Public Information (CPI), a bit of nomenclature that reflected the intimate linkage (honed in the prewar period by the metropolitan press) between information and publicity. The CPI was led by a pair of crusading journalists: George Creel (1876–1953), who oversaw domestic messaging, and Walter S. Rogers (1878–1965), who coordinated the circulation of US-based press coverage outside of the country.

Creel won the admiration of President Woodrow Wilson for his earnest disparagement of publicity bureaus, which Creel regarded as morally suspect. Like the muckrakers, with whom Creel can be profitably compared, Creel told stories to move minds. CPI-generated messaging, Creel insisted, was not propaganda, but advertising: the marshalling of facts to shape public opinion.

The CPI prepared newspaper copy, designed posters, and commissioned movies and public talks. Rogers's mandate was to expand US based messaging overseas, with a focus on positive news stories that he hoped would crowd out the often-unflattering coverage in the foreign press of race riots, lynchings, and sensational crimes. The US government, in Creel's view, did not circulate propaganda, a word he deplored. Rather, it trafficked in truth. Not everyone agreed, a conflict that would prove highly contentious following the war.

In the United Kingdom, the relationship between the metropolitan press and wartime government messaging was equally tight. Eager to run British government messaging, the press baron Lord Northcliffe turned down Prime Minister David Lloyd George's offer to run the air ministry. Following brief stints on a succession of government advisory committees, Northcliffe got his wish and served during the final months of the war as the director of government messaging for enemy countries. A second press baron, the British Canadian publisher Max Aitken (1879–1964)—better known as First Baron Beaverbrook because of the knighthood that he received just before the war—was tapped in March 1918 to head the British government's new Ministry of Information.

Only belatedly would the Germans follow suit. Although the German high command understood the importance of propaganda to counter enemy messaging and bolster civilian morale, its initial foray into government messaging was bureaucratically disorganized. Not until 1917 would it establish a centralized government press bureau.

The different approaches that the three belligerents adopted to government messaging were reflected in the nomenclature they adopted. The British and American messaging agencies included the word "information" in their official name. The German ones did not. The agency responsible for much of the German government's messaging, including its surveillance of enemy propaganda, was the emergent German Secret Service, the Nachrichtendienst (intelligence service). The word *Nachrichten* refers not only to "news," in the sense of messaging, but also to "intelligence," in the sense of espionage. The Germans used both tools in the Middle East, where they tried to undermine British imperial rule by fomenting anticolonial sentiment. For the Germans, messages could be not only broadcast, but also censored, and even surveilled.

This conflation of news and espionage was by no means unique to Germany. Though the British and American wartime messaging agencies were purportedly in the information business, like their German counterpart, they combined broadcasting, censorship, and surveillance. This conflation of news and espionage continued long after 1918. The Office of War Information established by the US government in 1942 to coordinate US domestic and international messaging during the Second World War would be dissolved and folded into the Central Intelligence Agency (CIA) in 1947.

The German defeat in 1918 led to much soul searching about the ineffectiveness of the German government's wartime media policy. Right-wing critics of the postwar Weimar regime bitterly complained that the war had been lost not on the battlefield but in the press, pointing their fingers incorrectly at journalists and publishers, of whom several were Jewish. Military leaders also found much to deplore. Colonel Walter Nicolai, chief of the German Secret Service between 1913 and 1919, contended that the German government could not communicate effectively with its population because of the widespread popular confusion between the Nachrichtendienst (intelligence service) and the Pressedienst (press service). Germany's poor wartime messaging, contended the German journalist Edgar Stern-Rubarth in 1921, had been a "political instrument" critical to Germany's defeat. Stern-Rubarth even blamed Anglo-American messaging for demoralizing Germany's Austrian ally in 1918 so effectively that Austria's troops summarily surrendered. The widespread conviction that Anglo-American propaganda had won the day was reinforced by the translation into German of a number of English-language books such as Sir Stuart Campbell's *Secrets of Crewe House* (1922) that detailed the allies' wartime media policy.

Germany was not the only country to entertain sober second thoughts about the relationship between its government's messaging and the war. In both the United Kingdom and the United States, contemporaries derided their government's messaging campaigns as "propaganda," a term that in the prewar period had a largely neutral, or even affirmative, connotation. The policy implications of this rapidly shifting intellectual terrain troubled the US political scientist Harold Lasswell (1902–78). Propaganda, Lasswell sardonically observed in the introduction to *Propaganda Technique in the World War* (1927), had come to acquire an "ominous clang." In response, Lasswell countered that every government had an obligation to channel in a positive direction the "mighty rushing wind of public sentiment." Propaganda, Lasswell elaborated, deliberately using the now-suspect word with pride, was an indispensable—and ethically unobjectionable—political resource: "Propaganda as a mere tool is no more moral or immoral than a pump handle. . . . The only effective weapon against propaganda on behalf of one policy seems to be propaganda on behalf of an alternative." Building on the work of the German Edgar Stern-Rubarth and the Briton Sir Stuart Campbell, Lasswell elaborated that the purpose of propaganda was to convince the public that its military opponents were "incorrigi-ble, wicked, and perverse" and that by "a circularity of psychological reaction the guilty is the satanic and the satanic is the guilty." Defeated countries like Germany, Lasswell perceptively added, were "predisposed" to attach "very great importance" to foreign propaganda in explaining their defeat.

Lasswell was right. Postwar German governments *had* invested heavily in new media to try to influence populations abroad. British and US insiders also learned lessons from the war. Buoyed by the apparent success of their government's media policy, each de-rided propaganda as a dirty word, and, misleadingly, as a failed media policy that nei-ther government had pursued. The governments of the United Kingdom and the United States had purportedly circulated not propaganda, but information. This distinction was not entirely spurious: the German government *had* intentionally spread falsehoods dur-ing the war more than the British or the Americans. Yet no government had a mono-poly on truth. A few like Lasswell strenuously resisted this seemingly incontrovertible proposition. *Only* the enemy had deliberately set out to mislead, Lasswell contended, a failed messaging policy that demoralized its audience by persuading it that news was inherently false and unreliable.

The discrediting of wartime messaging proved so successful that, in the 1920s, few public figures other than Lasswell proved willing to defend propaganda explicitly. Among the outliers was the American public relations and marketing pioneer Edward Bernays (1891–1955). Bernays, like Lasswell, recognized the utility of propaganda as a tool for mobilizing public support in domestic politics. In *Crystallizing Public Opinion* (1923) and *Propaganda* (1928), Bernays did his best to salvage the concept of propaganda as an ana-lytical tool. Echoing Lasswell's premise that propaganda was not necessarily malign, Bernays defined it in *Propaganda* as nothing more than "the establishing of reciprocal understanding between an individual and a group." Bernays justified his defense of the concept by appealing to psychology, which was perhaps not surprising, since he was a double nephew of the psychologist Sigmund Freud. In so doing, Bernays evaded the larger ethical issues that government propaganda raised for liberal champions of demo-cratic institutions such as the philosopher John Dewey and the journalist Walter Lipp-mann. Only when, to his horror, Bernays discovered that Hitler's propaganda minister Joseph Goebbels owned a copy of *Crystallizing Public Opinion* would he reluctantly "speak up for democracy"—publishing a book of this title in 1940.

Dewey and Lippmann differed in occupation, temperament, and perspective. Dewey never lost his faith that journalists could elevate the tone of public debate by cultivat-ing in the public an aptitude for the free and full discussion of the leading issues of the day. Lippmann, in contrast, in two important books—*Public Opinion* (1922) and *Phan-tom Public* (1925)—came to believe that the fundamental task of journalism was not to engage the many, but to provide accurate information for the few. "There seems to be no way of evading the conclusion," Lippmann wrote just after the war, "that liberty is not so much permission as it is the construction of a system of information increasingly independent of opinion. . . . The administration of public information toward greater accuracy and more successful analysis is the highway of liberty."

Dewey found much to admire in Lippmann's critique. Lippmann's indictment of demo-cratic theory, Dewey memorably declared in a famous book review of *Public Opinion*, was "perhaps the most effective indictment of democracy as currently conceived ever penned." Yet Dewey faulted Lippmann for presuming that, in a democracy, the purification of information at its source could substitute for the ongoing nurturing of civic engagement. For Dewey, information became consequential only when it engaged the entire citizenry in forums that reached far beyond the corridors of power. The solution was to revive bottom-up civic engagement, informed by the best scientific knowledge. For Dewey, journalists were high-profile players in an ongoing contest to interest the public in the public interest. For Lippmann, in contrast, journalists should remain discreetly on the sidelines and patiently counsel elites.

While Dewey and Lippmann differed in their prescriptions concerning the role of information in public life, it would be a mistake to contend—as have, unfortunately, many social theorists, media scholars, and historians—that they were antagonists in an epochal public debate over the possibilities and limitations of democratic institutions. No such debate occurred. Both Dewey and Lippmann championed liberalism, democracy, and pluralism—value commitments that distinguished them not only from the pro-Nazi German political theorist Carl Schmitt, but also from the avowedly Nietzschean Baltimore newspaper columnist H. L. Mencken, an unabashed pro-German monarchist who built an enormous popular following with his searing take-downs of American political ideals. Both were skeptical of the pre–First World War assumption that if the citizenry were sufficiently well informed, it could make wise decisions about public affairs. And both were relentless in their condemnation of information that had been intended to deceive, a common definition of propaganda. Nothing angered Lippmann more than the deliberate misreporting in the 1910s of the Russian Revolution by the *New York Times,* the subject of his pioneering indictment in 1920 of what might today be called "fake news." Dewey, for his part, enthusiastically defended the scientific method, a process that, almost by definition, valorized the judgment of a meritocratic elite. For both, it was, in the end, a relatively straightforward task to distinguish between public opinion, which they approved of, and propaganda, which they did not.

While Dewey and Lippmann remained wary of what Lasswell and Bernays persisted in calling propaganda, German, French, and Soviet policy analysts championed aggressive government messaging as an effective tool for promoting a positive national image abroad, an initiative that they rebranded as "cultural diplomacy." French interwar diplomats launched cultural initiatives to boost the country's public image, such as establishing educational institutes in Poland and other newly created eastern European nation-states. Not to be outdone, Soviet diplomats invited travelers from the West to tour Soviet factories and power plants. Following one such Soviet-sponsored tour, the American journalist Lincoln Steffens famously remarked that he had seen the future and that it worked.

The interwar debate over propaganda shaped the messaging agencies of the belligerents in the Second World War. The Nazis embraced the term *propaganda* and created a Ministry of Public Enlightenment and Propaganda. Convinced that Germany had lost the last information war, the Nazi propaganda minister Joseph Goebbels unleashed a torrent of information to embolden its population and demoralize its foes. While Weimar scholars such as Ferdinand Tönnies had tried to refine the concept of "public opinion" as an analytical tool, the Nazis rejected the concept outright as a "rallying cry of liberalism." To explain how people understood the world, Goebbels posited that their mental outlook could be divided into two categories: *Stimmung* (mood) and *Haltung* (attitude). Stimmung was fleeting and idiosyncratic and could be influenced by daily fillips of information. Haltung, in contrast, was rooted in a person's deeply rooted habits and could be changed only slowly over an extended period of time. Nazi propaganda relied on this distinction to cultivate and sustain a pro-Nazi frame of mind. Among the Nazis' most effective policies was their systematic denigration of all non-Nazi information outlets as false and all non-Nazi information providers—including journalists, public figures, and even celebrities—as liars.

To spread their message, the Nazis relied on newspapers, films, posters, speeches, and radio, a rapidly evolving new media in the 1930s whose potential had yet to be tapped. For radio listeners at home and abroad, Nazi-approved broadcasts supplied an alluring mix of news and entertainment. German radio was so effective that, in 1938, the American radio executive Cesar Saerchinger published an essay in *Foreign Affairs* entitled "Radio as a Political Instrument" in which he characterized the German shortwave radio station at Zeesen as the "most terrific agency for the spread of political doctrine that the world has ever seen." When Germany negotiated the surrender of France in the summer of 1940, Nazi radio broadcasts in thirty-one different languages could be heard in Europe, Asia, Africa, and the Americas: German radio, alongside the German army, seemed poised to conquer the world.

The British government stepped up its messaging as well. To maintain British imperial cohesion while preempting the colonization of its radio audience by rival Italian and German broadcasters, the BBC established a shortwave radio network in 1932. Originally called the Empire Service, this network is known as the BBC World Service today. To shape public opinion in the United States and cultivate support for Britain should it find itself once again at war, British officials built a sophisticated radio broadcasting office in the Rockefeller Center in New York City. In addition to overseeing the BBC's North American Service, this office secretly planted stories in the US press to outrage public opinion against Germany. Before long, both the Rockefeller Center office and the North American Service would be folded into the British Information Service, a prototype for the US government's own overseas broadcaster, the Voice of America (VOA).

Mindful of American hostility toward propaganda, British government officials took care to conceal their penetration of the US media market. The effectiveness of British propaganda during the First World War was by this time well known through books such as James Duane Squires's authoritative *British Propaganda at Home and in the United States, from 1914 to 1917* (1935). Many Americans were highly skeptical of British intentions, convinced, not entirely implausibly, that Britain had duped the United States into declaring war on Germany in 1917. British officials shared the American fascination with the lessons of the First World War. To understand Germany's burgeoning information empire, for example, British government officials in the 1930s resurrected their own assessments of German news agencies from the First World War.

The US government was no less determined than the Germans or the British to avoid the mistakes of the past. Troubled by the capacious mandate of Creel's Committee on Public Information, President Franklin Delano Roosevelt deliberately parceled out authority over government messaging to a panoply of government agencies. Of these agencies, perhaps the one closest in spirit to Roosevelt's own ideas about government messaging was the Office of Fact and Figures. Under the leadership of Archibald MacLeish (1892–1982), the librarian of Congress, this government agency helped generate information relevant to the war effort following the Japanese attack on Pearl Harbor. Mac-Leish pursued a "strategy of truth." "A democratic government," MacLeish explained in a 1942 public radio debate with Lasswell, is "more concerned with the provision of information to the people than it is with the communication of dreams and aspirations. . . . The duty of government is to provide a basis for judgment [on the part of its citizens]; and when it goes beyond that, it goes beyond the prime scope of its duty."

Critics charged that Roosevelt needed an American Goebbels to maintain civilian morale and countermand Nazi propaganda. "If democracy is to endure," Lasswell wrote in 1941, "democracy must make propaganda in favor of itself and against propaganda hostile to itself. This is the propaganda aspect of civic education." In 1942, MacLeish set up a study group, the Committee on War Information, to devise a way forward. In Lasswell's view, MacLeish's "strategy of truth" had proved to be woefully inadequate as a policy goal. To be effective, Lasswell believed, government messaging had to have a "large element of fake in it."

Roosevelt had committed the United States to countering German propaganda even before Pearl Harbor pushed the country into the war. To push back against Nazi radio broadcasts in South America, US lawmakers in 1940 established the Office of the Coordinator of Inter-American Affairs (CIAA). In the following year, CIAA would broadcast the US government's first international direct radio programming. Voice of America (VOA) followed shortly thereafter. Intended to counter German propaganda and supplement the BBC, VOA had been established with a mandate that was unusually expansive. By 1945, it was broadcasting around the world in forty languages, a remarkable achievement for an organization with such a short history.

The most important US wartime messaging agency was the Office of War Information (OWI). Established by Roosevelt in June 1942 under the direction of the popular radio broadcaster Elmer Davis, the OWI boasted a talented staff that included Milton Eisenhower, the brother of the general. In Eisenhower's view, the OWI should not set policy, as many believed the CPI had in the First World War. On the contrary, Eisenhower contended, it should "continue to be thought of primarily as an *information* agency." MacLeish left the OWI the following year. "I hated information work," he later reminisced, having found it virtually impossible to walk the fine line between publicity and propaganda: "I suppose in times of peace . . . you could probably devote yourself to information, trying to help a self-governing people to govern themselves. By seeing that they got the information they had to have. But in war you were always on the verge of propaganda."

The Office of War Information outlasted the war and, in 1953, was rechristened the United States Information Agency (USIA). The primary mission of the USIA was to combat propaganda originating in the Soviet Union, which had emerged as the country's principal postwar ideological rival. To counter the Soviet threat, the USIA relied on a battery of social-scientific techniques known as "psychological warfare." To streamline its operations, it absorbed the Voice of America and collaborated with the Central Intelligence Agency, which covertly funded a number of information-related organizations that included Radio Free Europe and the Congress for Cultural Freedom.

Not everyone approved. Psychological warfare, warned Walter Lippmann, compromised journalistic integrity and undermined democratic values: diplomats, and not radio broadcasters, should communicate the government's message overseas. The pollster

George Gallup disagreed. The Soviet threat had become so dangerous, Gallup warned in 1952, that lawmakers had no choice but to establish a "Department of Ideological Warfare." Though Gallup never got his agency, the postwar contest between the United States and the Soviet Union that Lippmann had foreseen, and that he would label the "Cold War" in 1947, severely restricted journalists' ability to obtain freely the information they had customarily used to report on public affairs. This problem would become so serious that, in 1954, the *New York Times* columnist James Reston, a consummate Washington journalistic insider, complained to Congress about the executive branch's "news management" of the press.

WIRELESS, RADIO BROADCASTING, AND THE FREE FLOW OF INFORMATION

The new Cold War rivalry was not the only impediment to Reston's idealized free flow of information. Another was the ability of radio broadcasting to transcend the traditional geographical constraints that had limited the circulation of print. Newspapers could be impounded at national borders. While radio broadcasts could be jammed, they crossed borders invisibly and without permission, making information warfare far harder to contain.

The emergence of radio in the 1920s as a broadcast medium was an event that no one could have predicted. The Italian Irish wireless promoter Guglielmo Marconi had originally intended to build a business around real-time point-to-point communication, for which a ready market existed, rather than one-to-many broadcasting, a medium with uncertain commercial prospects. Marconi was an Edwardian Steve Jobs, an image-conscious promoter who crafted a public image of himself as a lone-wolf genius inventor. Yet he was no fool. Though the share price of his business fluctuated wildly in response to rumors floated in the press, Marconi had by 1914 found a niche in the lucrative business of maritime logistics—a service of self-evident utility to merchants, shippers, and naval officers. In many countries, navies had invested heavily in the new medium to coordinate from afar the movement of their ships at sea.

Under different circumstances, radio might have remained point-to-point. Instead, it emerged in the 1920s as a broadcast medium, an innovation with far-ranging implications for the history of information, journalism, and public policy. In the United Kingdom and Germany, lawmakers devised regulatory safeguards to limit commercialization. In the United States, in contrast, regulatory safeguards gave way to wide-open commercialization, an outcome backed not only by radio promoters and Bell, which hoped to profit from its ownership of the nation's most sophisticated long-distance wire network, but also by advertisers and the many amateur radio buffs who did not want to be shut out of the spectrum. Just as many lawmakers remained wary of a government-operated radio network, so, too, promoters and radio buffs looked to the nation's long commitment to antimonopoly to guarantee their continued access to the radio spectrum.

It is a historical truism that old media does not expire following the advent of new media in an irreversible death spiral. For the technological determinist, it might seem foreordained that radio broadcasting would swiftly supersede the metropolitan newspaper. Yet this did not happen. In most countries, the metropolitan newspaper remained the primary outlet for breaking news until the Second World War, when it would be supplemented, though rarely rendered obsolete, by radio.

Radio proved useful to journalists long before Germany invaded Poland in 1939. For the most part, however, the medium was deployed in this period less to broadcast information from radio stations to their audience than to circulate information from reporter to publisher. Even here, radio's role was limited. Of the news items that found their way into European newspapers in 1934, fully 70 percent had arrived by mail—with the rest arriving via cable, radio, or telephone.

The regulatory framework for radio broadcasting that emerged in the 1920s built on precedents for regulating not only wireless but also municipal public utilities such as gasworks and electric power plants. Though the US government had in the 1900s sent delegates to the world's first two international radio conferences, the new medium was regulated primarily by the courts. Following the *Titanic* disaster in 1912, this all changed. Lawmakers and journalists deplored Marconi's refusal to interconnect with his rivals and found it outrageous that amateur radio operators had flooded the airwaves with misleading and possibly fraudulent information about the doomed ocean liner's final hours. The *New York Times*, for example, had published a false news story, based on a wireless report, that the *Titanic* had survived its collision with the iceberg, and was being safely towed to Halifax with all its passengers aboard.

To bring order to the electromagnetic spectrum, Congress required every wireless operator to obtain a license. Following US entry in the First World War, the navy purchased Marconi's US assets, including its manufacturing facilities and patent rights, so that it could build out a government-owned and government-operated wireless network to facilitate wartime naval communications. Commercial radio broadcasting emerged only in 1919, following the navy's transfer of control over its radio assets to the Radio Corporation of America, a commercial venture founded to manufacture radio equipment. Henceforth radio broadcasting in the United States would be not only US owned and US operated, but also regulated in accordance with a principled antimonopolism that rested in municipal utility law.

The influence of municipal public utility law on radio regulation is often overlooked. In the 1920s, and for many decades thereafter, almost all the most powerful and influential commercial radio broadcasters in the United States were based in New York City, Chicago, and other leading metropolitan centers. US radio policy was *not* shaped by a lack of regulation, as is often assumed. In fact, it was molded by an antimonopoly regulatory tradition, rooted in municipal utility law, that privileged civic ideals over private profit. Antimonopoly did not necessarily lead to the atomization of big business. On the contrary, in radio broadcasting, as well as in telecommunications, and, eventually, television broadcasting and even digital platforms, it helped to enshrine the bedrock presumption that corporate management and not government administration was not the exception but the rule.

The negative example of the United States decisively shaped British radio regulation. The most important British broadcaster in the 1920s was the British Broadcasting Corporation (BBC), a government-owned and government-operated content provider funded by user fees. The British government had chartered the BBC not only to forestall the nightmare scenario that the British radio spectrum might come to resemble the commercially driven, advertising-drenched chaos that had prevailed in the United States, but also to slow the importation of cheap German-made radio receivers.

Radio regulation in Germany took a somewhat different path. Just as US wireless promoters derided Marconi as an obstacle to progress, so did German government officials. From their perspective, Marconi's primary threat was not to naval communications, but to foreign policy. Troubled by the dominant position of the United Kingdom in the global cable network, they hoped to build a global wireless network that could circumvent the All-Red Line. Spurred in part by the fascination of Germany's Kaiser Wilhelm II with new media, government officials pushed two private companies in 1903 to launch a joint subsidiary named Telefunken, a high-tech start-up devoted to cutting-edge innovations in wireless equipment. Telefunken quickly become a major rival to Marconi. For a decade, however, its commercial expansion was frustrated by Marconi's refusal to interconnect. To solve this problem, the Telefunken executive Hans Bredow lobbied at a 1912 London wireless conference to draft *protocols obligating rival wireless networks to interconnect. With the *Titanic* disaster grabbing headlines, Bredow prevailed, and, before long, Telefunken and Marconi entered into various patent-sharing agreements, a business strategy that hastened the integration of the global wireless network.

For the German government, a German-based global wireless network had the potential to liberate it from the British-dominated All-Red Route of globe-encircling cables. Finished in early 1914, the German "All-Wireless Route" linked Germany to its far-flung colonies in Africa and the Pacific. Both Germany's emerging wireless network and its rudimentary cable network proved highly vulnerable to attack. Within days of the first gunfire on the western front, the British cut the most important German overseas cables, while Australia made it a military priority to capture the Pacific islands housing German wireless towers. In response, the German government teamed up with Telefunken to build an alternative world wireless network, a venture that never quite got off the ground.

Wireless energized the decades-old vision of liberal postal reformers that information might one day flow freely and unimpeded around the world. Though Marconi was based in the United Kingdom, this vision had less appeal there than in Germany and the United States. The reason was simple. The United Kingdom already enjoyed a dominant position in the global cable network, reducing the lure of a rival network. In Germany and the United States, in contrast, wireless became a tool with which to bypass the British.

In Germany, this vision was embraced after the First World War by Bredow, who had by this time left Telefunken for a series of high-level positions in radio broadcasting and government radio regulation. Bredow's positions enabled him to shape the future of German radio. Skeptical of amateurs, Bredow lobbied for government control not only of wireless receivers but also of wireless information. Should wireless information remain privately held, he warned, speculators might trade on inside information regarding the fluctuation in exchange rates and security valuations to defraud the public. Bredow clamped down on private use of wireless, but that did not stop Germany's slide into hyperinflation in 1922–23.

The US journalist-turned-government-official Walter S. Rogers championed a sweeping vision of an information-abundant future in a rhetorically effusive, multipage memorandum that he prepared at the request of US president Woodrow Wilson in February 1919, four months after the cessation of hostilities, and twenty-one months before the first regularly scheduled US-based radio broadcast. Rogers was based at this time in Paris, where he was coordinating news coverage of the US delegation to the Paris Peace Conference, a logical follow-up to the work he had performed in New York City for the CPI during the war. "Barriers to the flow of news from nation to nation," Rogers declared in his preamble, should be "removed in the general public interest": "The ideal is a world-wide freedom for news, with important news going everywhere."

Under existing conditions, Rogers elaborated, the unimpeded global flow of information had become an indispensable prerequisite for world peace: "The steady extension of democratic forms of government and the increasing closeness of contact between all parts of the world point to the conclusion, that the ultimate basis of world peace is common knowledge and understanding between the masses of the world. Hence the distribution of intelligence in the form of news becomes of the utmost importance." To hasten the free flow of information across national borders, Rogers looked to the League of Nations, which, he hoped, would become a center for the exchange of technical information on wireless and radio, and the promulgation of the international protocols necessary to transform global news into a single integrated market.

RADIO BROADCASTING AND THE CRISIS OF DEMOCRACY

Radio broadcasting evolved differently in the United Kingdom, Germany, and the United States. It was, thus, perhaps surprising that, in the 1920s, commentators in all three countries hailed radio as a savior of the nation. By creating an imagined community of listeners, or so they assumed, the new medium could combat parochialism, foster common understanding, and encourage a laudable spirit of civic engagement. This project would only gradually come to be associated with the broadcasting of news.

The rise of radio news popularized a new way of gaining access to time-specific information about the outside world. For the first time, it became possible to learn about current events by listening to them as they unfolded—or "broke," a bit of nomenclature that radio broadcasting helped to popularize in the 1920s—rather than merely by reading press reports. Radio bulletins announcing breaking news predated the emergence in the late 1930s of regular radio news broadcasts. Not everyone approved. In the view of Sir John Reith, the first director of the BBC, the new medium was best suited to the broadcast of classical music and similar kinds of high-toned entertainment and popular lectures aimed at uplifting the masses. News broadcasts did not fit comfortably into either category. At least in the 1920s, relatively little news found its way onto the BBC. When news did find its way onto the air, it was almost always morally salubrious, or, as the phrase went, "worthy." Newspaper accounts of fires, deaths, and motorcar accidents were deemed insufficiently weighty. On Good Friday in 1930, for example, a BBC announcer reported, regretfully—though, conceivably, not without a touch of sacrilegious irony—that there was simply no news to report that night. Beginning in the 1930s, a combination of circumstances prompted the BBC to begin to gather and broadcast its own news inside the United Kingdom, throughout its empire, and, increasingly, to radio listeners around the world, including those in the United States, Asia, and Latin America who might have been otherwise tempted by broadcasts from fascist countries.

Radio news proved, if anything, even more controversial in Germany. In the 1920s, German radio expert Hans Bredow had warned that radio news broadcasts might stoke panic among German listeners, given the divisiveness of the political landscape in the Weimar Republic. To limit political instability, Bredow lobbied successfully in the late 1920s and early 1930s for government supervision of radio broadcasting, including radio news. Bredow was a principled critic of the Nazis and resigned his government post when Hitler came to power in January 1933. Ironically, however, the radio regulations that Bredow had backed to limit political controversy during the Weimar era proved to be a huge boon for the Nazis, since they made it relatively easy for Nazi publicists to silence their critics, once their party had gained control of the state.

Nazi publicists made full use of radio to get their message across. Hitler's speeches were routinely broadcast on the air, as was pro-Nazi news. In addition, they enlisted the British fascist William Joyce to broadcast German propaganda to a British audience. Lord Haw-Haw, as Joyce would be derisively nicknamed by the British press, reached a large audience in the United Kingdom.

Before long, however, radio listeners who were not true believers found the Nazis' radio fare monotonous and unreliable. During the Second World War, Nazi officials waged an information war to block foreign new reports from reaching German listeners—primarily by jamming their signals—and to do everything they could to ensure that domestic and foreign news reports that originated in Germany or German-occupied lands toed the party line. German radio listeners quickly caught on to the deception. In fact, during the Second World War millions of ordinary Germans increasingly tuned in to radio stations that originated in enemy countries—particularly the BBC—to hear more reliable information about the war.

The challenge of radio news extended beyond issues of form and content. An even more basic question confronted regulators, station managers, and listeners: Who was the audience? The publishers of metropolitan newspapers had begun in the late nineteenth century to answer this question by providing data on the size and demographic makeup of the publication's readership to the advertising agencies that purchased newspaper space for their clients. The resulting information, which would become widely accepted as a proxy for consumer preferences, helped to rationalize the newspaper advertising market, stabilizing a critical revenue stream for the publishers and, not incidentally, the job security of the journalists who reported the news.

Radio was different. Though station managers did their best to persuade advertisers that their audience was large, well-to-do, and consumption minded, it was notoriously difficult to determine just who was listening in. This conundrum was particularly vexing in the United States, where advertising was the primary revenue stream. In the absence of audience data, it was hard to calculate advertising rates. Newspaper publishers, working in conjunction with advertising agencies, had devised a workaround. Radio stations had not. To help solve this problem, a new industry—public opinion polling—emerged.

Public opinion pollsters built on and helped to promote a new way of thinking about human nature. In the United States, the new thinking was popularized by advertisers who questioned the presumption that consumers based their purchasing decisions on rational criteria. Consumer decisions, in their view, were often influenced by emotional appeals that tapped into irrational and, in some instances, unconscious fears and desires. The "product" of advertising, declared one US advertising man shortly after the war, was "public opinion." In Germany, similar assumptions, drawn in part from academic research on group behavior, informed specialists in the emerging field of *Werbepsychologie* (advertising psychology).

In the United States and Germany, advertisers built on the disparaging analysis of crowd behavior that had been popularized in the late nineteenth century by the French social theorist Gustave Le Bon (1841–1931). Le Bon's critique met with a responsive audience in the United Kingdom, where elites had warned for decades that metropolitan newspapers might inspire "irrational" crowd behavior. In 1920s Germany, this critique became a staple of the anti-Semitic journalism of the right-wing newspaper magnate Alfred Hugenberg, who castigated Jewish publishers as a pack of manipulative Pied Pipers guilty of "deluding" a gullible German public into rejecting conventional assumptions about politics and culture.

Public opinion, like propaganda, has a venerable history. The origins of the concept went back to ancien régime France, where political economists invoked it to monitor shifting attitudes toward public finance. Originally, the concept referred to the attitudes not of the many, but of the few—and, above all, to well-informed bourgeois men. In their quest to understand what a later generation would call mass society, the concept would be swiftly embraced by political theorists ranging from David Hume and James Madison to Alexis de Tocqueville and John Stuart Mill.

Interestingly, none of these political theorists devoted more than passing attention to the technically demanding, and conceptually fraught, question of how public opinion might be measured. When contemporaries considered the issue, they were mostly content to sample newspaper articles. In the United States, for example, the Baltimore journalist Hezekiah Niles clipped articles from hundreds of publications in compiling *Niles's Weekly Register*, the most influential news digest of the early republic, while in the 1880s the editors of *Public Opinion*—a magazine that, as its title implied, tried to gauge the popular mood—reprinted editorials from publications espousing different points of view. In Germany, similarly, journalists routinely conflated public opinion with the pronouncements of contemporaries that they had gleaned from the press— pronouncements that they would then reprint or summarize in their own columns. To streamline the process, newspaper clipping services sprang up to provide their clientele with articles on particular topics of interest.

In the interwar period—hastened by the rise of radio—public opinion would cease to refer to the considered judgments of a discerning, and presumably well-informed, elite. Instead, it would be reconceptualized as the cultural beliefs of the many. Two modes of cultural analysis proved to be particularly influential. The first traced public opinion to material conditions that rested ultimately in economic power; the second to the subjective preferences of the audience itself. Both were pioneered by a small but influential group of German émigré scholars who fled Nazi Germany for the United States.

The materialist mode of cultural analysis originated at the Institute for Social Research in Frankfurt, Germany. Founded in the interwar period, the Frankfurt school— as this movement became known—critiqued institutional arrangements and cultural norms from a neo-Marxist perspective. The Frankfurt school produced a body of scholarship on new media that remains influential today. Siegfried Kracauer explored why working-class German shop girls flocked to the cinema. Walter Benjamin analyzed how the "mechanical reproduction" of famous works of art—for example, through photography—destroyed their ineffable aura of authenticity.

While modern technical contrivances devalued certain modes of cultural expression, they amplified others. The desacralization of art, Benjamin argued, would enable propagandists to aestheticize politics—rendering the masses vulnerable to fascist appeals. Information, Benjamin contended in an essay on Russian storyteller Nikolai Leskov, was a new literary genre, created by the metropolitan newspaper for the middle class to consume. Spawned by the "fully developed capitalism" of modernity, it challenged such venerable storytelling forms as the epic in a "more menacing way" than had other older literary forms, such as the novel: "This new form of communication is information."

Benjamin's work intertwined with certain ideas of Theodor Adorno and Max Horkheimer. Like Benjamin, Adorno and Horkheimer were Jewish, which obliged them to flee Germany for the United States after the Nazis came to power. Horkheimer had been the head of the Institute for Social Research in Frankfurt. When the Nazis came to power in 1933, he moved the Institute first to Geneva, and then New York City, where it found a home at Columbia University.

Adorno's first project following his arrival in the United States was a Rockefeller Foundation–funded study of the relationship between radio broadcasting and Hitler's rise to power. Like the first generation of public opinion pollsters, Adorno drew on social psychology to probe the relationship between form and content. Radio broadcasts, Adorno provocatively concluded, predisposed certain listeners to become fascists, including, in particular, those individuals who harbored what he would famously label an "authoritarian personality." While Adorno would later be faulted for psychological reductionism, his analysis of the authoritarian personality generated an innovative tradition of scholarship on the relationship of culture and politics.

The most influential of Adorno's publications on the relationship of media and society was the *Dialectic of Enlightenment* (1944), which he coauthored with Horkheimer. *Dialectic* traced the origins of present-day "culture industries"—a capacious conceptual category that included radio broadcasting, movies, and popular music—to the Enlightenment belief in reason, a faith that they presumed, somewhat paradoxically, would inexorably undermine the promise of rational thought.

Neither Adorno nor Horkheimer had much confidence in the objective measurement of subjective preferences. This task would fall to their sometime colleague Paul Lazarsfeld, an Austrian Jew who helped to found the new field of communications research. Shortly after his arrival in the United States, Lazarsfeld obtained funding from the Rockefeller Foundation to investigate radio listening habits—the same project on which Adorno had briefly worked. Lazarsfeld originally based his research center at Princeton, before moving it to Columbia University, where it would become the Bureau for Social Research, a center that still exists today.

The most influential contribution of central European émigrés to US communications research was methodological. Though Lazarsfeld was not the first to rely on focus groups and longitudinal panel surveys to measure public opinion, he would become their most devoted champion. Similar techniques would soon take root in the United Kingdom. The longitudinal panel survey, for example, would be used extensively by the Mass Observation project, a British social research organization, founded in 1937, that was best known for its three-decade-long investigation of the living conditions of the British working class.

No comparable methodological innovations in communications research would originate in Germany until after the Second World War. A key figure in German postwar media scholarship was Elisabeth Noelle-Neumann, who is best known for *The Spiral of Silence: Public Opinion—Our Social Skin* (1980; English translation 1984). Noelle-Neumann completed a PhD dissertation at the University of Missouri in 1940 on US public opinion research. Following her return to Germany, she wrote widely for Nazi publications. In a newspaper article entitled "Who Informs America?," for example, she blamed Jewish publishers for monopolizing the American press. Following the Nazis' defeat, Noelle-Neumann built on her American training in public opinion research to establish in 1948 the Allensbach Institute, the first center for quantitative communications research in West Germany.

The Frankfurt school would remain an influential center for communications research following the Second World War, especially following its return to Germany in 1953. A key figure in the postwar generation was the philosopher Jürgen Habermas. In his *Structural Transformation of the Public Sphere* (1962; English translation 1989), Habermas built on his predecessors' long-standing interest in the influence of communications media on public life to trace the rise and fall of the "bourgeois public sphere," a social form, he contended, that originated in the *coffeehouses and cafés of early eighteenth-century England in which men could rationally exchange information on public affairs.

Habermas's characterization of this novel social space as "bourgeois" paid homage to the Frankfurt school's materialist mode of cultural analysis. So too did his mordant, and at times despairing, assessment of the political consequences of modern media. Like Adorno, Habermas criticized the "cultural industries" of the nineteenth and twentieth centuries for debasing public life by commercializing domains that had formerly fostered the rational exchange of information.

The translation of Habermas's *Structural Transformation* into English in 1989 helped to popularize the concept of the "public sphere" in the English-speaking world. For the next two decades, this concept helped set the agenda for communications research in both the English-speaking and the German-speaking worlds. The resulting information exchange was a two-way street. Only after *Structural Transformation* had been translated into English would historians, philosophers, sociologists, and media scholars join together to publish a critical reassessment—*Habermas and the Public Sphere* (1992)—that faulted Habermas for idealizing a communicative realm that marginalized women, nonwhites, and the poor. Habermas himself would join this transnational information exchange, contributing an essay to this volume in which he acknowledged his critics.

CONCLUSION

The history of information in the first half of the twentieth century was profoundly shaped by three media organizations: the metropolitan newspaper, the government messaging agency, and the radio broadcasting station. The popular fascination with the sinking of the *Titanic* in 1912 fit neatly into an oddly optimistic, resolutely progressive morality play as old as the Enlightenment. Had the distress signals broadcast by the *Titanic*'s wireless operator been more widely circulated, the disaster could have been averted. Limited information imperiled; abundant information saved. An analogous logic shaped the popular understanding of the metropolitan newspaper: publicity was good; more publicity was better.

Following the First World War, when the British, German, and American governments fought an information war alongside the war on the ground, thoughtful observers in all three countries came to regard this prewar faith in publicity as misguided and naive. No one could possibly possess the intellectual bandwidth—or so Walter Lippmann observed in *Public Opinion*, pointedly including himself—to process intelligently the information that would be necessary to pronounce competently on all the issues of the day. By deliberately manipulating the public through propaganda, messaging agencies only made a bad situation worse. No longer was the citizenry omnicompetent; no longer could information save. No longer did public opinion bear any relationship to the carefully calibrated judgment of the few. Henceforth, it would become increasingly conflated with the often-inchoate preferences of the many.

The prewar faith in the free flow of information persisted, especially in the United States. Yet with the rise of radio broadcasting, it became obvious to media insiders in the United Kingdom, Germany, and the United States that the new medium challenged basic assumptions about the relationship between information, freedom, and power. No longer could the beneficence of information be taken for granted.

The Hungarian uprising of 1956 furnished a fitting epilogue to the often-extravagant expectations that accompanied the long-standing US commitment to the free flow of information. Though the leaders of the Hungarian resistance were driven primarily by internal considerations, CIA-backed Radio Free Europe broadcasts emboldened protesters to overplay their hand by demonizing the Soviet-backed regime and raising the possibility of outside military support. Few events better symbolized how the Enlightenment dream in the salvific power of information could become a nightmare. For the Hungarian rebels, information was not freedom and the CIA's news management a death sentence for an audience primed to listen in.

Though US-backed radio broadcasts had not instigated the uprising, and figured little in internal Soviet decision making, they helped to fan the flames of a failed insurgency that left as many as twenty thousand dead. The reputation of Radio Free Europe never entirely recovered. Even sympathetic observers termed its conduct in the uprising a "debacle." It was not the ethereal airwaves, but the tangible presence of Soviet tanks, that won the day, at least for the time. What had changed since 1912? Not only the absence of information, but also its abundance, could be a harbinger of disaster. Nothing was as simple as it seemed.

Richard R. John and Heidi J. S. Tworek

See also bureaucracy; censorship; data; diplomats/spies; documentary authority; globalization; information, disinformation, misinformation; information policy; merchants; networks; political reporting; public sphere; publicity/publication; surveilling

FURTHER READING

Theodor W. Adorno, *The Culture Industry: Selected Essays on Mass Culture*, 1991; Jonathan Auerbach and Russ Castronovo, eds., *The Oxford Handbook of Propaganda Studies*, 2013; Colin B. Burke, *America's Information Wars: The Untold Story of Information Systems in America's Conflicts and Politics from World War II to the Internet Age*, 2018; John Dewey, *The Public and Its Problems*, 1927; David Greenberg, *Republic of Spin: An Inside History of the American Presidency*, 2016; Julia Guarneri, *Newsprint Metropolis: City Papers and the Making of Modern Americans*, 2017; Jürgen Habermas, *The Structural Transformation of the Public Sphere: An Inquiry into a Category of Bourgeois Society*, 1962, translated by Thomas Burger with the assistance of Frederick Lawrence, 1989; Daniel R. Headrick, *The Invisible Weapon: Telecommunications and International Politics, 1851–1945*, 1991; Andrew Hobbs, *A Fleet Street in Every Town: The Provincial Press in England, 1855–1900*, 2018; Max Horkheimer and Theodor W. Adorno, *Dialectic of Enlightenment*, 1944; Richard R. John, *Network Nation: Inventing American Telecommunications*, 2010; Richard R. John and Jonathan Silberstein-Loeb, eds., *Making News: The Political Economy of Journalism from the Glorious Revolution to the Internet*, 2015; Walter Lippmann, *Liberty and the News*, 1920; idem, *The Phantom Public*, 1925; idem, *Public Opinion*, 1922; Simone M. Müller, *Wiring the World: The Social and Cultural Creation of Global Telegraph Networks*, 2016; John Nerone, *The Media and Public Life: A History*, 2016; Elisabeth Noelle-Neumann, *The Spiral of Silence: Public Opinion—Our Social Skin*, 1980, English translation 1984; Marc Raboy, *Marconi: The Man Who Networked the World*, 2016; Paul Starr, *The Creation of the Media: Political Origins of Modern Communications*, 2005; Heidi J. S. Tworek, *News from Germany: The Competition to Control World Communications, 1900–1945*, 2019; idem, "The Savior of the Nation? Regulating Radio in the Interwar Period," *Journal of Policy History* 27, no. 3 (2015): 465–91.

COMMUNICATION, COMPUTATION, AND INFORMATION

Surrounded as we are by informational devices such as smart phones, watches, and speakers, along with computers, tablets, and similar *digital devices, all interlinked through *internet connections, it is generally uncontentious to assert that we live in the "information age." Such an assumption distinguishes this chapter, bringing this book up to the present, from its predecessors. They principally use modern notions of information to explore the past. From such a perspective, as the historian Robert Darnton notes, "every age was an age of information." But this chapter concerns an age whose inhabitants regularly invoke "information" to distinguish their age from every other, often citing information technologies of the sort mentioned above as the cause of the age's distinctiveness. Indeed, some see these as making our age so distinct that history is irrelevant. Anthony Levandowski, a prominent Silicon Valley engineer, told a *New Yorker* journalist in 2018, "The only thing that matters is the future. . . . I don't even know why we study history. . . . In technology, all that matters is tomorrow." Yet such claims, paradoxically, must assume some knowledge of the past in order to be able to dismiss it, for in asserting that the current age is so distinct they presume some idea of what the past was like, how we got here from there, and when that transition occurred. As Steve Jobs, a better-known Silicon Valley guru, put it, "You can't connect the dots looking forward, you can only connect them looking backwards." The same could even be said for disconnecting the dots, as Levandowski and information age champions try to do, for that too needs an understanding of the past. Connecting the dots, as this chapter (and, indeed, this book) seeks to do, helps reveal the extent to which our age is (or is not) distinct. The chapter investigates, in particular, the way in which over time the realms of computation and communication were combined to form the "information technology" that is assumed to have shaped the new age.

CHANGE AND CONTINUITY

Breaking history into ages has a long history itself. In the eighteenth century, the economist Adam Smith identified his own society as having reached the "state or age" of commerce, distinguishing this from prior ages of hunters, shepherds, and agriculture, while, infused with similar ideas of progress, his contemporary George Washington distinguished their era from a prior "gloomy Age of ignorance." Of course, Smith's age of commerce and Washington's "Auspicious period" certainly relied on what we might now classify as "information technologies," such as printing, *bookkeeping, timekeeping, and the postal service that carried Washington's "circular." But it is our age that conceptually connected such a diverse array into a unitary category of devices that are together seen as creating an entirely new era by, on the one hand, underwriting new kinds of labor, production, distribution, and consumption, as well as particular kinds of goods or commodities; and, on the other hand, instigating new kinds of connectivity and sociality to support communication in the "public sphere" and develop unprecedented forms of "social network."

To investigate the attendant claims about the new age, we need first to explore when it is seen as beginning, and by extension when its distinctive technology is seen to emerge. For the first, we might explore when the occupants themselves began to claim "information" as a marker of their own age.

In July 1977, IBM ran an advertisement in *Fortune* magazine asserting "Information: there is growing agreement that it is the name of the age we live in." IBM supported its claim by noting "changes in our perception of information itself" driven by an "explosion" in the "volume of information" before consoling readers with the promise that there "exists today remarkable technological capacity for dealing with it," capable of turning information from a threat into "an inexhaustible resource." IBM then highlighted its own contribution to such technological capacity, invoking its machines from "computers to copiers" and including a "vast array of electronic techniques."

As IBM's own history can, as we shall see, be traced back into the nineteenth century, its advertisement, while recognizing a certain level of self-awareness, fails to mark a cutoff. For instance, its invocation of distinctive technology pushes us back two decades to an article in *Harvard Business Review* in 1958 that noted that the "new technology" that had "begun to take hold in American business" largely after World War II "does not have a single established name." The article decided to call it "information technology." (A little later, IBM called its contribution to the 1964 World's Fair the "Information Engine.") This definition pushes us back in turn yet another decade to 1949, when *Scientific American* claimed a revolution was taking place, "based on the transformation and transmission of information" and enabling "information processing," driven by "mathematical machines." In giving primacy to such accounts from the world of business and science, we should not overlook the claim of the literary critic Marshall McLuhan, who announced the "age of information" a decade before IBM's advertisement, but similarly claimed this age was driven by electrical machines through which "commodities themselves assume . . . [the] character of information."

Such observations reflect a coming together in the postwar years, and no doubt in part as a result of wartime innovation, of ideas about computation and communication, resulting in IBM's "growing agreement." But IBM's long history in making "machines," *Harvard Business Review*'s imprecise "largely after World War II," *Scientific American*'s claim that its revolution succeeded a prior one in the nineteenth century, and McLuhan's vagueness about "electrical" machines all make it tricky to know when to look for the origin of the transformation they all want to mark. Indeed, their own decade-by-decade regression illustrates how claims to historical antecedents can prod us back indefinitely, so that, investigating "information technology," we slide irresistibly toward such devices as the ancient Greek Antikythera device or the Chinese abacus. To limit such a slide, we might invoke those smart devices, portable computers, and the internet that, as I suggested above, are regularly offered as unproblematic indicators of our distinctive age, and explore their roots and commonalities. These exemplars embrace communication and computation in ways many would agree transformed access to and use of information. Thus homing in on generally accepted antecedents of such tools, particularly those explicitly cited by developers in that postwar period that *Harvard Business Review* portrayed as critical, might plausibly allow us to stop an indefinite if not infinite regression.

In tracing such a path, however, we should not assume that those three notions—communication, computation, and information—were always as readily associated as they are today. For example, if we were to say "calculation" rather than "computation," the connection would be far less clear, yet the ancestors of modern computers were, as we shall see, primarily calculating devices. Consequently, until quite recently, communications and computation were for many fundamentally distinct. McLuhan's work, for example, focuses almost wholly on the former while IBM's advertisement involves primarily the latter, yet each assumes that it embraces the devices that produced the "information age." Similarly, in the early 1980s, the software pioneer Joe Weizenbaum disputed an account of the rise of the "information society" offered by the sociologist Daniel Bell. Bell, in Weizenbaum's words, saw the "information society" as the "child of the marriage between modern communication and computer technologies." Weizenbaum, by contrast, like many before (and after), argued that these two were fundamentally distinct species.

Nonetheless, today it can be hard to see the two as anything other than interrelated. And one critical notion making such confidence possible may be their shared identity as "information" devices. Thus, connecting some of the dots that brought communication and computation together, as I attempt in what follows, will I hope tell us something about our claims to a distinctive "age" marked by information.

COMPUTING ENGINES

From the 1949 *Scientific American* article to the issue of *Time* magazine that nominated the computer as the "machine of the year" in 1983 to contemporary TED talks, Charles Babbage (1791–1871) is widely portrayed, in *Time*'s terms, "as the first man to conceptualize a true computer." As so often with technology heroes (e.g., Gutenberg, Morse, Jobs), Babbage is perhaps not quite as original as conventionally portrayed. Nonetheless, he conceptualized two distinct types of machine, the "Difference Engine" and the "Analytical Engine," in which later computer pioneers saw the roots of their own work. (Accounts of Babbage are limited to "conceptualization" because, continuously enticed by new possibilities, he failed to complete a version of either.)

With the Difference Engine, Babbage sought to automate the production of reliable mathematical tables. Such tables of figures could turn complex mathematical calculations into more simple and so manageable ones. Logarithms, for example, transformed baffling multiplication and division into straightforward addition and subtraction. Unfortunately, the work of calculating and printing such tables required challenging mathematics and tedious typesetting, both of which contributed to published tables being notoriously error strewn. Babbage sought to produce more reliable figures, driven by the hope "that all these tables . . . might be calculated by machinery," which, with automated printing, would overcome human frailties. Surveying earlier table-making attempts, he found that one of the best, devised by Gaspar de Prony (1755–1839) for the

French government, was quite machine-like. Drawing on Adam Smith's famous "division of labor," Prony had broken down the calculating task into columns of people working together, the more proficient disassembling difficult calculations into manageable subtasks that they passed to their less proficient colleagues. Developing Prony's insight, Babbage sought to build a "mechanism for assisting the human mind in executing the operations of arithmetic" with columns of calculating cogs replacing the columns of calculating people and taking up the disassembled tasks and passing partial results to neighboring columns for completion.

The British government funded Babbage's work, but when Babbage lost interest, the government withdrew support, and the project dwindled. A major distraction for Babbage was that engine's more sophisticated sibling, the Analytical Engine, with which he hoped to bypass many of the assisting human minds required for the earlier engine by "teaching the engine to see and then act [with] foresight." This theoretically self-controlling machine relied on "operations," driven by a "mill," whose results could be put in a "store" until needed. Babbage appropriated these terms from the industrial production of grain, but with them he envisaged the programming, central processing, and memory of modern computers. Moreover, as Prony's division of labor had inspired Babbage to divide computational tasks, so another Frenchman, Joseph Marie Jacquard (1752–1834), who had developed punched cards to control elaborate silk-weaving machines, inspired Babbage's card-fed input system. In essence, by reworking insights and tools of the industrial era, Babbage foreshadowed its end, which his intellectual heirs would help to instantiate.

Babbage's work cultivated the attention of eager enthusiasts who were more capable than he of addressing a broader audience. These included the Italian mathematician (and later prime minister) Luigi Menabrea (1809–96) and the English mathematician Ada Lovelace (1815–52). Menabrea wrote an enthusiastic account of the potential of both engines in French, which Lovelace then translated into English and annotated with insightful notes twice the length of the original. These commentaries revealed, perhaps even to Babbage, unanticipated possibilities for his engines.

Machines that presage the future tend to provoke thoughts of "technological determinism," suggesting that once envisaged, such machines irresistibly push forward and transform society in the process. Yet, despite the support of his enthusiasts and the accolades of our contemporaries, rather than pushing forward, Babbage and his work sank into oblivion. Intermittently, engineers stumbled upon the work and attempted to complete one or the other of his engines. During Babbage's lifetime, a Swedish father and son, Georg and Edvard Scheutz, supported by the Swedish government, built a version of the long-abandoned Difference Engine, receiving a gold medal (and Babbage's approval) at the Great Exhibition in Paris in 1855. Nevertheless, in 1871, *Scientific American* allotted Babbage a cursory one-paragraph obituary, dismissing the "calculating machine" as "valueless for general use."

Despite this limited contemporary appreciation, more recent historians and computer scientists have seen essential precursors of the modern computer in Babbage's devices. They have, however, revealed no similar anticipation of the communication aspects of modern technologies, despite Babbage's living in the era of transformational communication systems, such as trains, steamships, telegraphs, and telephones. Babbage was well aware of these. Indeed, he blamed "railway mania" for making it hard to find engineers for his engines, while the ability of the telegraph to convey "information over extensive lines with great rapidity" impressed him greatly. But though Babbage saw communication devices dealing with "information," that concept had, for him, no bearing on his engines or on his idea of computation. If we see the computer as critical to an "information revolution," Babbage and his supporters almost certainly did not. Billed as "father" of the computer, he evidently was not aware of what Daniel Bell and others saw as the inevitable suitor for his child.

As Babbage and his machines sank, another central figure in histories of computation, Herman Hollerith (1860–1929), rose to prominence in the United States. Not only did advances in engineering make building his machines easier, but Hollerith, unlike Babbage, found customers for them, first in the government, then in corporations, both of which, as populations, workforces, and industrial production grew, found keeping track of their charges more challenging and looked to machinery for help.

Hollerith began with the government. After leaving university, he had gone to work on the 1880 US decennial census. Though mandated by the country's constitution, US census work was disorganized. (That other countries were better organized probably made them less interested in developing innovative machines.) Faced with a growing population, tabulation of the 1880 census was slower, more demanding, and more expensive than ever before, and the task barely finished when work on the 1890 census began. The difficulty of extracting accurate statistics inspired a colleague of Hollerith's to insist, with a vision reminiscent of Babbage's, that "there ought to be a machine for doing the purely mechanical work of tabulating population and similar statistics." Hollerith designed such a machine and won a government competition to automate the 1890 census. Though the population had grown by some 25 percent and the census asked twice as many questions as in 1880, Hollerith's calculator made the 1890 tabulation both faster and cheaper, saving two years in time and $5 million in costs.

Previous attempts at automation in the Census Office had used a machine fed by a paper strip that was indefinitely long and consequently made access to particular points cumbersome. Hollerith's major insight was to feed in data with discrete cards. Where Babbage took inspiration for his cards from the silk industry, Hollerith took his from the railways, where tickets were issued as cards printed with a selection of identifying features that an inspector's punch would perforate to create a "punch photograph" of individual travelers ("light hair, dark eyes, large nose"). Hollerith adapted the idea, using more census-like characteristics (sex, age, birthplace, conjugal status, occupation) for a census "photograph." The machines made electrical connection through the punched holes, allowing indicated data to be selected, sorted, accumulated, and enumerated.

Though Hollerith's preeminent biographer refers to him as a "forgotten" giant, his recognition was more immediate than Babbage's. Census offices in Europe and Russia and manufacturing, railway, insurance, and finance corporations on both sides of the Atlantic sought his machines. To meet demand, Hollerith formed the Tabulating Machine Company, which, in the early twentieth century, transformed itself, via the Computing-Tabulating-Recording Company, into International Business Machines, or IBM. This transformation can make the transition from the nineteenth century to IBM's advertisement about the "information" age seem inescapable. Yet, while Hollerith's company explicitly invoked "computing," notions of "information" and "communication" played little role in his work, nor, for a long time in IBM's. By the time of its 1977 advertisement, IBM was eager to embrace "information," as that had by then come to be seen as a facet of computing, but the company still did not associate its machines with communication.

Moving from Babbage to Hollerith and from there to IBM, the story inescapably seems another of Anglo-Saxon men advancing technology. The "second industrial revolution," which, as James Beniger's influential *Control Revolution* argues, spurred the development of modern computers, took place primarily in Britain and the United States in an era of white male dominance, so it is not surprising that a tale connecting the conventional dots should reflect these privileged features. But this preponderance should not allow us to underestimate contributions from Ada Lovelace as a critical interpreter of Babbage's work to the anonymous female "computers" who ran Hollerith's machines, each processing up to ten thousand cards per day and overcoming the inevitable challenges and failings of emerging technologies that early workers have to surmount but retrospect tends to hide. Nor should the Anglo-Saxon focus allow us to ignore Hollerith's German heritage, the critical contributions from France of Jacquard and Prony, nor the Italian Menabrea and the Swedish Scheutzes. Further, conventional championing of market entrepreneurialism in the information age should not obscure the critical role of government in this history, funding Babbage and then Hollerith, building infrastructure, and overseeing standards. And while the story also resembles whiggish accounts of irresistible, emancipatory forward progress, applauded by Beniger, as society found ways to gain control over information, we should note ominous foreshadowing of the technology's converse control over people: Babbage's work anticipated Frederick Winslow Taylor's (1856–1915) "Scientific Management," which from the nineteenth-century factory to Amazon warehouses has treated people themselves as cogs in machines, while Hollerith's "punched photographs" point to later forms of surveillance, from IBM's role in helping the Nazis monitor their population and impose race law to India's use of biometrics to avoid railway ticket scalpings.

COMMUNICATIONS AND INFORMATION

The nineteenth century primarily saw "information" as an aspect not of machine calculation, but of human communication, in particular of writing, books, and libraries. Hence to see the trajectory of information and communication we need to look at this alternative context. Moreover, there is an intriguing link between the two. The colleague of Hollerith's at the Census Office who raised the Babbage-like idea of a tabulating machine fed with cards was John Billings (1838–1913), a doctor working on census "vital statistics." Previously, Billings had conducted research at the US surgeon general's office and, overwhelmed by its resources, attempted to reorganize its library. Such challenges were common at the time. Scientific endeavor increasingly suffocated under its growing output, with new articles, reports, commentaries, and books accumulating at unprecedented rates. Scientists and librarians desperately sought ways to make this output accessible. Billings played both roles, and in the surgeon general's library he pioneered a card catalog for books and articles while also developing the scholarly *Index Medicus* in 1879, a still-published, innovative monthly index of new medical research. Both projects relied on library cards, no doubt inspiring Billings's suggestion to Hollerith. (In 1896, Billings became the first librarian of the consolidated New York Public Library.)

The explosion of research in the late nineteenth century prompted numerous such attempts to make scholarly output accessible. One of the most adventurous, again organized around cards, was undertaken by the Belgian scholar Paul Otlet (1868–1944), who pioneered the field of "documentalism." While history recognizes Babbage for foreshadowing the computer, applause is often as loud for Otlet presaging the *World Wide Web. Like Billings, whose work he knew, Otlet sought to track the content of publications. But rather than merely pointing to the source, as Billings's cards did, Otlet attempted to liberate the *facts, ideas, and information, as he variously referred to these (in French, *faits, idées, information*), from books and the like, which, to Otlet, an enthusiast of telegraph, telephone, radio, television, and cinema, appeared as outdated physical constraints on the communication of information. Otlet envisaged the product of such liberation as "informations sans préoccupation d'ordre" ("[pieces of] information without any concern for order") and began to accumulate the key facts of human knowledge extracted from books and inscribed on cards so that they could be easily reordered. Extracted facts were indexed for author and source by another set of cards, creating "informations documentées" ("documented [pieces of] information"). All these cards (later, microfiches) were organized in files that were in turn collected in a library-like center, the Mundaneum, to be replicated in, connected to, and distributed from similar venues throughout the world. For the Mundaneum, Otlet planned a multimedia, desk-like device, the *mondothèque*, to give users means to access this atomized information and reassemble it into new structures of knowledge. Information and communication were, in this view, inseparable aspects of human knowledge, and Otlet's grand notion of "documentalism" envisioned technology (some admiringly modelled on Hollerith machines) to further all three across the world. In the process, Otlet idealistically hoped to liberate not only information but humanity.

Otlet's vision embraced extant notions of information and communication and in the process revealed many assumptions that would become critical as these two embraced computation. People had come to see information as a fundamental, countable, and transferrable unit of human knowledge accumulated in books—since the eighteenth-century *publishers' advertisements had regularly boasted that there was "more" information in their books than in their rivals'—and Otlet by extension sought the independence and subsequent reassembly of such units in new forms connected by networks of links into what he envisaged as a "mechanical brain." While his dream of a worldwide network was never fulfilled, he built nodes of this vision in Belgium, stocking them with hundreds of thousands of indexed and conceptually interconnected cards.

Over time, librarians took up such views of "information" from Billings, Otlet, and also the influential library scholar Melvil Dewey (1851–1931), the proponent of decimal classification for library books. Subsequently, the worlds of documentalism and librarianship would claim the identity of "information science," a trajectory that can be traced in the successive names of one journal from *Journal of Documentary Reproduction* (1938), to *American Documentation* (1950), to *Journal of the Association of Information Science* (1968), to *Journal of the Association of Information Science and Technology* (2001). Yet librarians' work had little direct influence on computer science, which reached its views of "information" and "communication" from other directions. The resilient distance between these two worlds is indicated in an article from the early 1970s in the *Journal of Librarianship* that, echoing Weizenbaum's insistent separation noted earlier, inveighed against the "erroneous notion that computers were able to handle or even to produce information (when all they can ever do is manipulate data)."

INFORMATION DEFINED

In many ways a visionary, Otlet imagined the world of information networked through the Mundaneum as leading to world peace. As if in response, the two world wars of the twentieth century helped to sideline his work. Turning attention back to calculating machines, the wars played a central role in advancing computing, where development was once more driven by government investment and national interests, as we shall see. But the evolution of modern technology and the concept of "information" nonetheless took a significant nonmilitary turn between the wars, guided by corporate research with little direct interest in either library science or computation, in particular in the work of a major communications company, AT&T, seeking to address challenges of the wired network whose potential, as we have seen, Babbage admired.

In the 1920s at Bell Laboratories, AT&T's research center, the engineer Ralph Hartley (1880–1970), exploring the "manufacture of telephone apparatus" and "long distance telephone lines," sought to measure "the capacity of the physical system to transmit information." Hartley saw information as the common underpinning of telegraphy, telephony, and television, which forward-looking eyes could see converging on telephone lines. That idea of "information" may seem unproblematic today, but Hartley was cautious about it, noting that "information is a very elastic term," that elasticity making objective measurement difficult. Consequently he decided to "eliminate the psychological factors" and "establish a measure of information in terms of purely physical quantities." Thus his research was deliberately and profoundly separated from discussions of information and knowledge at play in, for instance, documentalism and libraries.

In his search for an objective measure, Hartley echoes the French engineer Émile Baudot (1845–1903), who in the 1870s recognized that in using "long" and "short" pulses (as well as a "medium" gap to mark the separation of letters and a "long" gap for the separation of words) to compose messages, Morse had introduced subjectivity into telegraphy (one person's long might be another's short) and thus the system often required that the recipients of a signal guess at the meaning of the message under transmission in order to interpret the *code. Baudot replaced *Morse code with Baudot code, a mathematical cipher that antedated modern *binary codes (for which Baudot is still recognized in the use of *baud* as the unit of measurement for the speed of a signal along a channel). Baudot signals were particularly significant for international telegraphy. First, they could be transmitted accurately to recipients who did not understand the message. And second, they could handle nonalphabetic writing more easily than Morse code. Baudot's work resembled experimentation with numerical codes, which were being developed in China to suit its nonalphabetic script at the same time (see Gitelman and Mullaney, chap. 9).

Hartley's more celebrated AT&T colleague Claude Shannon (1916–2001) developed Hartley's insights, leading to Shannon's enormously influential "mathematical theory of communication" (often erroneously referred to as the "mathematical theory of information"). Shannon defined communication as "reproducing at one point . . . a message selected at another," and to measure the accuracy of that reproduction without reinvoking the psychological factors that troubled Hartley, Shannon dismissed "meaning" as irrelevant to the task, further distancing semantic understandings of communication. (As his colleague Warren Weaver noted, the mathematical theory was indifferent to whether the signal indicated "the text of the King James Version of the Bible" or the word "Yes.") With such assumptions, Shannon was able to calculate the most efficient way to send "information" over a line. Where Hartley's model had also had to ignore "noise" or interference on the line, Shannon was able to incorporate that and deduce optimal ways of dealing with it. More significantly, Shannon's meaning-neutral account of information was also able to address the computer: "This case has application not only in communication theory, but also in the theory of computing machines," he noted at one point. Shannon mentioned this only in passing and clearly felt that the connection was not obvious; nonetheless, influenced by Shannon's work, the notion of "information" as autonomous signal started to connect dots between "computation" and "communication." With psychology, meaning, and semantics omitted, however, the notion of information in play is self-evidently a restricted one. Nevertheless, Shannon's theory spread from the telephone to any domain willing to claim "information" as part of its provenance, particularly those looking for mathematical validation. This wide embrace (implicitly assuming that more information was more informative) troubled Shannon, who remained ever conscious of the restrictions of his definition and feared that in many appropriations of his work these were being ignored.

The adoption of Shannon's work for "computing machines" became central to the growth of those machines following military-supported research of World War II, in which Shannon himself took part. Indeed, Shannon's theory in part developed from his attempts to design impenetrable encryption. Among other things, wartime research helped rediscover Babbage: Alan Turing (1912–54), who worked on the innovative Colossus computer at Bletchley Park to crack the German Enigma encryption machine, reported that Babbage was regularly discussed there. Turing himself went on to instantiate ideas behind Babbage's Analytical Engine in the development of stored-program digital computers, naming his machine the "Automatic Computing Engine" in tribute to the "engines" Babbage and Lovelace had described. (Turing's US contemporary John von Neumann [1903–57] also drew on Babbage for what he called his "Electronic Computing Instrument.") These engines or instruments were number crunchers, having little to do with conventional interhuman communication. Fittingly, Bletchley interoffice communication relied on paper messages pulled on wires along underground tunnels rather than the advanced computation machines being built above ground.

ANIMAL AND MACHINE

As wartime insights developed in the postwar years, however, the new "computers" fostered increasing elision between descriptions of people and of machines. Following wartime work on the "feedback" needed to track moving targets, Norbert Wiener (1894–1964) developed the concept of "cybernetics," which saw information feedback as common to "communication in the animal and the machine." Turing took computation in a similar direction with his attribution to machines of information-related concepts for-merly reserved for animals, such as "memory," "stimulus," and "search." Attributions of this sort, leading to concepts like *"artificial intelligence" and "thinking machines," raised questions about when such usage was primarily metaphorical, indicating simi-larities between two worlds, and when, rather, it assumed a single, homogeneous world in which the same concepts could be applied unproblematically to both man and ma-chine. Information's elasticity, which Hartley and Shannon sought to limit, helped fos-ter this elision.

The influential computer scientist Vannevar Bush (1890–1974) made similar assump-tions. Before the war, working to make power lines more efficient (much as Hartley and Shannon had worked with telephone lines), Bush, though unaware of Babbage, built a Babbage-like machine. During the war he supervised scientific research for the mili-tary and after helped to found the US National Science Foundation (NSF) to propagate that research in the peacetime world. Apparently unaware of Otlet, too, Bush's cele-brated postwar essay "As We May Think" raises similar issues. Like Billings, Bush dis-played a heightened sense of scholarly anxiety, noting that wartime military funding had produced a surge in scientific discovery that, without better means of storage and access, would probably be lost. Bush proposed that a "record" be made of such find-ings. "To be useful to science," he argued, this record must be "continuously extended" and "stored." In response, he conceptualized a small camera (a little like Google's infa-mous "Glass") to be worn on the forehead for scientists to record whatever they encoun-tered and the *"memex," rather like Otlet's mondothèque, a machine to store and sort such records, giving people "access to and command over the inherited knowledge of the ages" and allowing them to build links between previously unconnected ideas to produce new insights or "creative thought." The memex, Bush argued, would relieve the intellectual burdens of humanity because "whenever thought for a time runs along an accepted groove—there is an opportunity for the machine."

Again, I should pause to acknowledge that the conventional story continues to re-volve around white males in the Anglo-American world—though figures from Baudot to Otlet, Wiener, and von Neumann challenge those geographical boundaries. Equally, the invisible but essential women that ran Turing's machines, and the "girls" that Bush can barely bring himself to acknowledge running his, faced and survived demanding work to make these machines viable. Indeed, despite their significant contribution, the highly productive work of wartime women "computers" was suppressed in postwar years as they were pushed to one side to give precedence to returning male soldiers. Hence, as recent scholarship such as Marie Hicks's *Programmed Inequality* (2017) has shown, even those who did pioneering work with early computers, programming the pathbreak-ing ENIAC and UNIVAC machines, writing the COBOL language, or developing Small-talk, among them Marlyn Meltzer, Betty Holberton, Jean Bartik, Grace Hopper, Adele Goldberg, and many others, remained almost invisible.

SWITCHING

Both inside the military and out, the machines and the organizations that used them tended to instantiate centralized, hierarchical structures. Over time, however, chang-ing designs of computers challenged these structures, and with them dominant concepts of communication and information. The first digital machines, huge assemblies of interdependent vacuum tubes, were inherently centralizing. Organizations that adopted them allocated "computer rooms" to hold the machines and the people that ran them. Those requiring their services went to the machine, into which, for the most part, their calculating needs were fed on punched cards. One of the first corporate machines, LEO, developed in the early 1950s by J. Lyons and Co. in England, was used to centralize the firm's control over a supply chain that stretched from tea fields in India to teahouses in London.

Limitations of such centralization provoked the idea of time-sharing, enabling several people to use the same machine simultaneously, a far more efficient use of expensive machine time (and, usually, of people's time too). Time-sharing took advantage of the Babbagean process of breaking down tasks into subunits. These ran independently, amid the work of other users, to be reintegrated and reassembled when the subtasks were completed. This alternative approach also prompted a shift from cards to keyboards for the input, which allowed access points to be distributed more widely. In turn, distributed access raised the possibility of long-distance use, allowing people without local machines to seek access to and run programs on computers far away. As Hartley and Shannon had shown, the lines both had studied could support reliable access from remote terminals, further decentralizing computer use and introducing "communication" as a term for interaction with a computer.

Designers sought the most efficient way to arrange this. The answer turned out to be "packet-switching": once again, breaking down messages into elemental units (or "packets") to be sent independently across communication lines. This idea emerged at two separate venues, and their different paths to a similar conclusion reveal yet more about the changing relationship of computers and communication.

One version developed in the early 1960s at the Research and Development or RAND Corporation in California, under the eye of the electrical engineer Paul Baran (1926–2011) and funded by the US government at the height of the Cold War. Researchers addressed the problem of "survivable communications": how branches of the military might communicate in response to attack if their lines of communication, still of the sort that Hartley had studied, were vulnerable. Baran and colleagues proposed "distributed communications," building networks of multiple lines between any sender and receiver, thus providing multiple paths for a message to take. The message would be broken down into numerous subunits, each able to travel by different routes to the destination, where they would be reassembled. Which route each part would take could be decided at interconnected "store and forward" nodes along the way, depending on the state of the network at the time. The system could thus route around trouble: if one path was impassable at some point, packets could be sent along another. Only if the entire network was destroyed would communication collapse. "Survivability," Baran proposed, "is a function of switching flexibility." Both military and nonmilitary communication systems took on the structure Baran had envisaged, less to avoid bombing than, as with time-sharing, for the efficiency and flexibility it promised for the system as a whole.

Simultaneously, another "communication" project was getting underway at the National Physical Laboratory (NPL), a British standards institute. Donald Davies (1924–2000), who had worked with Turing, oversaw the project. Where RAND was investigating interhuman communication networks, the NPL was responding to the spread of computers and the challenge of "real-time communication" among them. The strategy was to replicate aspects of time-sharing and batch-processing or "methods used in multi-access computers" in order to allow what Davies called "a conversation between the user and the computer." Where Baran sought to avoid destruction, Davies sought to avoid congestion, but both came to a similar conclusion, now known under the name given to the NPL work, "packet-switching."

Both Baran and Davies made predictions for what Baran called the "wired city" that such networks would enable. The differences between these predictions reflect some of the differences between their initial assumptions. Along with "computer-aided school instruction," Baran foresaw users managing "bus, train, and air scheduling" and "person-to-person" communication, whereas Davies envisaged, among other things, "editing and typesetting of text," "booking of transport," "banking," "remote access to national records," and, reflecting British proclivities, "betting." Overall, where Baran was building networks that allowed interpersonal communication, Davies focused more on "computer to computer conversations" and the "communication needs" of "remote on-line data processing." These differences reflect ways in which information as an aspect of interpersonal communication was still in the early 1960s seen as distinct from "information-processing" computation.

"The Computer as a Communication Device," a 1968 essay by Joseph Licklider (1915–90) and Robert Taylor (1932–2017), each of whom played seminal roles in developing the internet, recognizes these distinctions while envisioning their pending merger. The authors saw themselves engaged in a struggle to portray the computer not "as a mathematical device, but as a communication device," as Taylor later put it in an interview. This portrayal was a challenge because, as the two wrote, a "communications engineer thinks of information from one point to another in codes and signals," which is very much in the spirit of Hartley, Shannon, and Davies. But, Licklider and Taylor insisted, "to communicate is more than to send and receive." In the process of pulling ideas of communication, computation, and information together, while building on send-and-receive models, they implicitly started to add back issues of psychology and meaning, which Hartley and Shannon had explicitly extracted to make their theories work. Licklider and Taylor, however, saw the separation as primarily historical and institutional: "Information transmission and information processing have always been carried out separately and have become separately institutionalized." Their new vision predicted the beginning of the end of such separation and projected the idea of new social communities emerging "face to face through a computer" from this united but enlarged notion of "information."

Licklider and Taylor exemplified their vision by describing an online meeting they had taken part in organized by Doug Engelbart (1925–2013) of Stanford Research Institute. In 1968, Engelbart caused a sensation with what became known as the "Mother of All Demos," in which he demonstrated real-time communication with remote colleagues through a computer and for which one of the key devices was the computer "mouse," on public display for the first time. The amalgamation of notions of "information," supported by the combined insights of Baran, Davies, Licklider, Roberts, and Engelbart, was leading toward what would be called the "internet," a packet-switching network using computers and related devices to transmit and process "information" not only among machines but among communities of people. Distinct ideas developed by Babbage, Hollerith, Otlet, Hartley, Shannon, and Bush began to coalesce in modern "information technology," but the commonalities, taken for granted now, were not, as this history suggests, self-evident then. Bernard Strassberg of the US Federal Communications Commission acknowledged twenty years later that "the first awareness that we had of the fact that computers and data processing had something in common with communications started in early '65." In all, Licklider and Taylor's title, "The Computer as a Communication Device," was designed to envision the future provocatively rather than describe the present complacently.

LAYERING

The internet as we know it today is the outcome of these multiple attempts to interconnect different types of device. (The word *internet* indicates that the initial goal was to *inter*connect multiple, different *net*works with one another, though the term today tends to invoke an all-embracing, single network.) Interconnections require common standards: a telegraph message written in Morse code but sent on a network built to expect Baudot codes, for example, would fail. Telecommunications companies, computer companies, governments, and militaries all had interests in what sort of networking should evolve, but each had different priorities.

Consequently, it proved difficult to find acceptable common standards. After complex and contentious battles, most parties eventually converged around a pair of standards or *"protocols" known as "Transmission Control Protocol" and "Internet Protocol" or TCP/IP, features of almost every connected device today.

The TCP and IP standards developed under the aegis of the Advanced Research Projects Administration (ARPA), a branch of the US military. Through the 1970s, ARPA had sought to interconnect a set of computing research centers it had established at different sites (mostly universities), primarily to allow Davies-like time-sharing among them. The central challenge was to enable Davies's "data communications" not only among different sites but also between computers built on different principles. For this, protocols standardized the means of "translation" from different "layers" of different machines and across different networks so that each contributor, rather than needing to understand the diverse workings of the whole network, only had to know how to use the "application layer" of the local device and how to transfer files produced there up to the shared "transport layer" (TCP) and "network layer" (IP), which could remain indifferent to all that happens locally below in much the same way that the post office does not have to understand what goes into producing a particular letter, but only how to take that to the address on the envelope, on the condition that the address conforms to protocol. Many different sets of protocols were suggested, some claiming to be superior to ARPA's. ARPA had the advantage, however, that the military could command all who wanted access to its network to use its protocols. It delivered such a command, demanding all those already on or aspiring to join its network to accommodate TCP/IP by January 1, 1983. Conformity was not quite so instantaneous, but ARPA protocols became the de facto international standards.

ARPA's focus remained machine-to-machine communication and its users primarily researchers. Lawrence Roberts, one of the early proponents of email, noted that personal communication was "not an important motivation for a network of scientific comput-ers." From the early 1970s, however, users designed various systems to make interhu-man communication easier. The engineer Ray Tomlinson transformed a time-sharing messaging protocol into a forerunner of email in 1971, in essence combining Baran's network vision with Davies's (and in the process introducing the now-familiar "@" for addresses). But he told his colleagues to keep his innovation secret as it was not what he was meant to be working on. Similar improvisation led to the development in 1981 of SMTP, a widely accepted, IP-compatible mail transfer protocol. In the eyes of Janet Abbate, the preeminent historian of the internet, email was the "smashing success" that reinvigorated languishing networks and encouraged private corporations to set up and interconnect subnetworks, leading ultimately, in the mid-1990s, to the internet being privatized as a communications network, supporting person-to-person, machine-to-machine, and person-to-machine exchanges all embracing the term "information." Privatization reflected the increasing participation of commercial companies in the networks, whose rise to dominance is signaled by the prevalence of ".com" addresses. The first of these was acquired in March 1985, just before the NSF created its own net-work, NSFNET, an initial step away from the military control of ARPA and toward the privatization of the internet in the 1990s, during which time the number of connected computers grew from about two thousand to two million. Initial purchasers of the ".com" addresses were computer companies. A decade later they were companies offer-ing public access, usually via subscription, to the range of services Baran and Davies had envisaged.

The initial failure of network designers to see the potential for both types of com-munication seems plausibly to rest on the two distinct "institutions" of "communica-tion" and "information" that Licklider and Taylor described. Actual users, like Tomlin-son, by contrast, pragmatically ignored this separation, adapting networks for both intermachine and interpersonal connection.

A similar story of user interests and adaptations transformed another packet-switching network, Transpac in France. In 1976, fearful of falling behind the United States in computer development, the French government commissioned a report to outline a competitive strategy. (The NPL packet-switching work in the UK was driven by similar concerns.) The report, *L'Informatisation de la Société*, introduced the term *télématique* (telematics) to recognize the "mariage entre les ordinateurs et les réseaux de transmis-sion" or that, as Daniel Bell, who as we have seen would go on to claim such a "mar-riage" as critical to the birth of the information society, put it in his introduction to the US edition, "the computer is not only a computational machine, but a communication device." (The US edition was entitled *The Computerization of Society*, which suggests that some US scholars still did not recognize the "mariage.") In pursuit of broader "infor-matization" and well ahead of the United States, the government-owned French tele-phone service developed a packet-switching network to connect consumers rather than, as with ARPANET and NSFNET, to connect researchers and deprecate communication. The service provided free MINITEL (Médium Interactif par Numérisation d'Information Téléphonique) terminals to households throughout France. These keyboard-driven terminals supported *videotext*, bridging typewriter, telephone, and television, which Hartley had sought to combine. The initial service offered a relatively unexciting digi-tal telephone book. But private corporations were encouraged to offer other services over the network and soon gave users the opportunity to engage in many of the activities that Baran and Davies foresaw—telebanking, online bookings, grocery shopping, and newspaper reading. Consequently, through the 1980s, France was probably the best exemplar of Baran's "wired world." The most popular MINITEL service were its *messageries*. These, precursors of internet "chat rooms" that later reached similar levels of popularity elsewhere in the world, were built initially by users who, rather like the early email protagonists, *"hacked" the system to enable users to interact with one another rather than just with banks or betting shops.

For all its success, MINITEL was a closed network controlled from above. Elsewhere, as network protocols spread, different public and private networks were interconnecting. One of particular importance developed across the border from France at a nuclear research center, CERN (Conseil Européen pour la Recherche Nucléaiare) in Switzerland. An international collaboration, CERN confronted many of the problems faced by NPL and ARPA, because, despite shared goals, researchers were often isolated from colleagues who worked on different, incompatible machines. To address this problem, CERN created its own internal network in the 1970s. It changed to TCP/IP in the mid-1980s, becoming by 1990 the largest European internet site. Despite this push toward interconnection, an English engineer at CERN, Tim Berners-Lee (b. 1955), remained frustrated with the difficulty of finding out what his colleagues were up to. He believed that "once someone somewhere made available a document, database, graphic, sound, video . . . it should be accessible (subject to authorization . . .) to anyone . . . [with] a link." Equally, he saw value in allowing people to build new associations between documents and the like, something, he noted, "that the brain can do easily." Pursuing such thoughts he became aware of earlier ideas from Bush and Engelbart and the computer maverick Ted Nelson, who had introduced the notion of *"hypertext" as a way to link digital objects without having to go through a centralized machine or institution.

With an international group of CERN colleagues, Berners-Lee developed a system that fulfilled many of the goals espoused by these early proponents of linked systems. He initially thought of his as something like a phone book, providing addresses of fellow researchers and their documents, which makes his path a little like MINITEL's. And as with MINITEL, the ultimate system developed far beyond this idea, producing the World Wide Web, whose protocols standardized document formats and provided unique addresses for each document with the links to reach them from any computer on the network. The outcome was in many ways a digital instantiation of Otlet's worldwide vision from some ninety years before of decentralized connectivity. Stanford University's Linear Accelerator Center (SLAC) established the first US web server in 1991. One champion there was the laboratory's librarian, Louise Addis, who saw the potential for opening access to SLAC's online documents. Her contribution implicitly recognized a convergence of the semantic sort of bibliographic information of Otlet's vision with the signal-based sort of Shannon's.

GOING WORLD WIDE

While the development and spread of the internet can occasionally appear as an irresistible, technologically driven force emerging primarily from Silicon Valley entrepreneurs, the contributions of ARPA, MINITEL, and CERN indicate that the forces at play were more complex and more diverse. Among these three pioneers alone, we see the power of the military in ARPA, of state telecommunications systems in MINITEL, and of international scientific research in CERN. Equally, not only did MINITEL develop in France, but the web, while developed in Switzerland, was a truly international effort: the first paper its developers published had Belgian, Danish, English, Finnish, and French coauthors. And it was in this work that the interhuman communications potential of these networks was more directly explored. Moreover, while ARPA and the web drew on government funding to address a specialized audience, MINITEL, while launched with state funding, was designed to draw on French corporations and consumers for funds. The different ways of developing software have been opposed as the "cathedral" versus the "bazaar," to suggest hierarchical versus market forces as alternative structures. For the spread of the internet, we have to consider these two not simply in opposition, but in complex combinations of "top-down" and "bottom-up" forces, as governments sought to retain political stability while keeping pace with developments elsewhere, and to encourage markets and enjoin or resist "natural monopolies" in telecommunications, while being pushed to respond to the demands of an inventive and adaptive public. This transition is perhaps best exemplified in the standards of the internet, which as we have seen were first issued from on high, by ARPA, taking advantage of what the historian Andrew Russell calls the "advantages of autocratic design," but increasingly were "opened" to democratic decision making within standards organizations, of which the NPL was a precursor.

Similarly contending forces were evident as the networks spread worldwide. Japan, where in the 1970s perhaps the earliest discussions anywhere of an "information society" (*joho shakai*) appear, also adopted ideas of "informatization" (*johaka*), a notion that became popular throughout Asia, with the establishment of its Center for the Informatization of Industry in 1985. Japan's telecommunications monopoly, however, made illegal the sorts of improvisation that, as we have seen, pushed popular development elsewhere. Consequently, insular, proprietary, unconnected subscription networks developed first. It took time (and the disbanding of the monopoly) to produce an open, interconnected network. In China, the state controlled developments, but, seeking like others to keep up with the West, it introduced a program of popular "informatization" at the beginning of the twenty-first century. Elsewhere, developing countries explored the idea that information and informatization could produce economic development, for which, it was assumed, what the French had called *télématique mariage* was necessary and thus increasingly adopted, though control from above, which drove many such developments, often had to contend with desired autonomy from below (manifest in such things as the development of internet cafés). Political structures played a curious role in these developments. As Benjamin Peters argues in *How Not to Network a Nation*, a Soviet internet project failed because, where "the capitalists behaved like socialists . . . the socialists behaved like capitalists." In these different contexts, the elasticity of terms like *information* and *informatization* helped different sociopolitical circumstances accommodate local desires to join the networks that were visible elsewhere. In India, for instance, scientific research initiated packet-switching developments, but state monopolies restricted broader access. Enthusiasts returning from other countries and determined to replicate their more open networked systems, however, gradually forced state and corporate accommodation.

STRETCHING INFORMATION

In the international adoption of "informatization," we literally see the idea of "information" being stretched, despite both Hartley's and Shannon's resistance. It can be useful to think of this elasticity being achieved less by stretching than by layering, deploying the structure on which the internet and the web were built, and which has roots reaching back through much of the work discussed above.

Berners-Lee called layers "simple rules for global systems." More elaborately, Abbate describes the internet as a "layered system . . . organized as a set of discrete functions that interact according to specified rules . . . arranged in a conceptual hierarchy . . . from the most concrete . . . (such as handling electrical signals) to the most abstract functions (e.g., interpreting human language commands from users)." Overall, this structure represents for Abbate a "division of labor." That phrase takes us from the World Wide Web back to Babbage and his insights from Prony and Smith that the way to build a calculating machine was to divide it into layers, with each layer able to execute its own task and pass the result down to the next, which could in turn perform its tasks while remaining usefully ignorant of what went on above. Such a structure, from Babbage to Berners-Lee, provided efficient coordination among both devices and people. Similar assumptions can be seen in the economics of Shannon's time. The economist Friedrich Hayek, a Nobel laureate, had argued in the 1930s that markets work efficiently by providing consumers with prices for goods, "information" that allows consumers to make rational decisions without needing to understand the complex forces that produce the goods or bring these to the market. The "information" encoded in price is a product of but also efficiently excludes the information carried by people active in the market.

In such arguments, "information" is used at different levels, but the notion of information differs with the layer. We can see such layering in Hartley's and Shannon's work, as each isolated signals for machine communication by excluding human dimensions of psychology and semantics. Shannon portrayed this process in his famous "Schematic diagram of a general communication system" (figure 1).

In Shannon's account the "*information source* . . . produces a message." Then a "*transmitter* . . . operates on the message . . . to produce a signal suitable for transmission." The "*channel* is merely the medium used to transmit the signal." The "*receiver* . . . performs the inverse operation of that done by the transmitter," and the *destination* is the person (or thing) for whom the message is intended" (italics in original). It would not be unreasonable to use *information* at each layer: as the input, as the stripped-down message, as the signal transmitted, and as the outcome at the destination. But it would not be the same notion at each layer.

At its heart, with psychology and meaning stripped out, all that counts for successful communication in Shannon's terms is for the destination to end up with the signal sent. Reception is the mirror image of transmission. Transmission is predictable, and anything unpredicted a malfunction. Licklider and Taylor classified this as the "engineer's" view of communication. "But to communicate," they argued, "is more than to send and to receive." So saying, they take information to another level. At this level we do not always condemn the unpredictable as malfunction or failure (what Babbage was trying to overcome in human "computers") but sometimes see that as understandable, and sometimes even laudable "interpretation" (this was often required, for instance, of Morse's telegraph operators), something we might even classify as insight or innova-

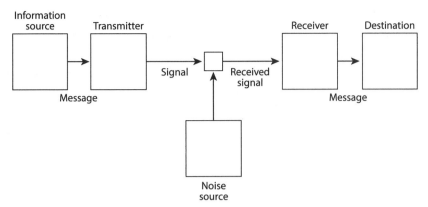

Figure 1. Schematic diagram of a general communication system. Figure 1 in Claude Shannon's "Mathematical Theory of Communication," *Bell Systems Technical Journal* 27, no. 3 (1948): 379–432. Reused with permission of Nokia and AT&T Archives.

tion. From this we get the originality that prompts Otlet, Bush, and Berners-Lee to extoll connections made through links that have never been made before. Yet, as Licklider and Taylor themselves show, we tend to use this same term *information*, across the different levels, sometimes using it to denote something objective, independent, autonomous, and countable, while sometimes using it for something context bound and consequently subjective and interpretable.

Moreover, while layers may help to separate people from machines, they can also contribute to ideas of people as themselves layered systems. At times "information" is the stuff of thought, ratiocination, and conscious decision making. At other times, it is the stuff of signals, something that lies beyond our consciousness and reflection. Vannevar Bush, for example, used *information* the latter way, arguing that "when the eye sees, all the consequent information is transmitted to the brain by means of electrical vibrations in the channel of the optic nerve." (Bush even suggested these signals could fruitfully be intercepted and understood by machines.) For the products of ratiocination, by contrast, he reserved words like *knowledge* and *record*. Where Hartley removed psychology and Shannon meaning, Bush thus extracted awareness, self-consciousness, and reflection from human information, which is reduced to signals along channels, sounding very like electric impulses along power lines, the focus of his early work. And as with those lines, he assumed that the impulses in the nervous system are unproblematically and unreflectively received. From these perspectives, "communication in the animal and the machine," as Wiener had put it, start to look the same, with "information" helping to unite the two. If "information" allows us to pull together computation and communication, by extension it can also allow us to pull together people and machines. Thus von Neumann started to account for both as kinds of "automata."

STRETCHED TO THE LIMIT?

Our "age of information" has inherited these elastic accounts. In his book on advertising, *The Attention Merchants* (2016), for instance, the lawyer Timothy Wu notes at one point that "information cannot be acted upon without attention" while, at another point, noting that "every second, our senses transmit an estimated 11 million bits of information." It is hard to see us giving attention to 11 million *bits a second. Yet the assimilation of computation and communication, with information as the common factor, is generally unproblematic.

"Information processing" is often taken as common to both and seen as a mechanical process. With "information" as the key ingredient of exact and correct calculation, the abundance of information has offered an optimism that arose with the age and is evident in the areas of economics and the public sphere mentioned earlier as critical venues for appraising the age's distinctive use of information. Economics, which helped propel ideas of an "information economy" and "information work" to vindicate claims for an "information age," embraced notions of "complete" or "perfect" information, the former in particular suggesting that with more information people's decision making will improve and as a result markets will become more efficient, coordinating the needs of all involved through welfare "optimization." Similarly, the economic idea of "asymmetric information" as the reason for market failure has implicitly assumed that "symmetrical information" will lead to success, implying that if everyone has the same information their behavior will synchronize into Shannonian mirror images, leaving aside concerns about whether people who have the same information might interpret it differently. Context, history, personal reflection disappear in these visions just as they did in Shannon's, though he was more explicit about the move in his models.

Similarly, modern notions of "information" underwriting the democratic public sphere have led to assumptions that increases in availability of information will lead to increased democracy. From here arise enthusiasms for social media as means to overcome undemocratic control, and claims that they will lead irresistibly to freedom follow. These views build on ideas of Licklider and Engelbart that technology would set us free, which in turn echo earlier views of Otlet's. Moreover, Otlet's notion (echoed later by Bush) that information was sufficiently autonomous that it could be isolated from its source and recombined with other pieces of information reflects ideas, emphasized by the historian of the public sphere Jürgen Habermas, that democracy feeds on information independent of its source. Ideally, we don't enter the Habermasian public sphere, but rather our information goes in alone and is judged on its merits, not its source or context. Here we can see similarities once again to Hartley's and Shannon's attempt to atomize and isolate units of information. Related assumptions can be found in the libertarian, anti-institutional streak that runs through many modern champions of the information age, who unquestioningly link computation and communication. The cyberlibertarian John Perry Barlow, for instance, declared the "independence" of cyberspace," renouncing the old world for a new world in which computation strips information from institutional control (much as Otlet sought to strip it from books), and so doing underwrites the autonomy of both information and individuals. Similar anti-institutionalism can be read in prophecies that the "quantified self" will allow people to manage their own health and so bypass the institutions of medicine, that "blockchain" will do away with central banks, or that MOOCs (massive open online courses) will eviscerate schools and universities.

Through all such accounts runs a pervasive "techno-optimism" that has heralded control over information as giving us control over the world in which we live. Thus we see a lot of "info-solutions" in which information is offered as a solution to our problems based on the assumption that those problems can be coherently and comprehensively diagnosed in terms of information. If education is the delivery of information, for example, schools can be replaced with computers. Not only do such solutions play the informational equivalent of the "man with a hammer," but they also tend to overlook, while nonetheless depending on, the elasticity of the use of the notion of *information* used in such diagnoses, an elasticity that has allowed us to weave very different ideas of information, communication, and computation into an apparently harmonious whole.

The optimism that runs through these claims has to confront contrary feelings that rather than more information being a good thing, it can be highly problematic; and that while control over information may be beneficial, we are often in danger of being controlled by information and the algorithms it feeds. Both the optimistic and the pessimistic views have a curiously long history. Though we may claim information as a distinctive feature of the twenty-first century, the phrase "age of information" first appeared in the eighteenth, at the height of the *Enlightenment, just as Smith was declaring the age of commerce and Washington denouncing the age of ignorance. And then, too, it supported a unifying and optimistic view of that period's social, political, and economic transformation. Declaring his to be an "age of information," the essayist Vicesimus Knox assumed, like some today, that the book, as the fount of communicable information, would probably kill the university and claimed that if people were given the right information, they would do the right thing. Hence, at the end of that century as at the beginning of this one, people enthusiastically embraced information as both uniting and transformative, weaving society into an egalitarian network of autonomous individuals. Critics, however, then as now, cautioned that different ideas of information were in play, some of which espoused information as the necessary ingredient for open deliberation and debate and the convergence of different people into a harmonious society; and others of which took information as an autonomous force to which people were irresistibly subject. Perhaps, after all, the dots of our "information age" are more closely connected to the past than those who deem history irrelevant realize.

Paul Duguid

See also algorithms; commodification; computers; cybernetics/feedback; databases; digitization; encrypting/decrypting; error; files; media; networks; platforms; public sphere; social media; storage and search; telecommunications

FURTHER READING

Janet Abbate, *Inventing the Internet*, 1999; Kenneth J. Arrow, "Information and Economic Behavior," in *Collected Papers*, edited by K. Arrow, 1984, 136–52; Geoffrey D. Austrian, *Herman Hollerith: Forgotten Giant of Information Processing*, 1982; James R. Beniger, *The Control Revolution: Technological and Economic Origins of the Information Society*, 1986; Tim Berners-Lee and Marl Fischetti, *Weaving the Web: The Original Design and Ultimate Destiny of the World Wide Web by Its Inventor*, 1999; M. K. Buckland and Z. Liu, "History of Information Science," *Annual Review of Information Science and Technology*, no. 30 (1995): 385–416; Vannevar Bush, "As We May Think," *Atlantic Monthly* 176, no. 1 (1945): 101–8; Martin Campbell-Kelly and William Aspray, *The Computer: A History of the Information Machine*, 1996; Robert Darnton, "An Early Information Society: News and Media in Eighteenth-Century Paris," *American Historical Review* 105 no. 1 (2000): 1–35; Paul Duguid, "The Ageing of Information: From Particular to Particulate," *Journal of the History of Ideas* 76, no. 3 (2015): 347–68; Gerard Goggin and Mark McLelland, *The Routledge Companion to Global Internet Histories*, 2017; Marie Hicks, *Programmed Inequality: How Britain*

Discarded Women Technologists and Lost Its Edge in Computing, 2017; Richard John, "Rendezvous with Information? Computers and Communications Networks in the United States," *Business History Review*, no. 75 (Spring 2001): 1–13; J.C.R. Licklider and Robert W. Taylor, "The Computer as a Communication Device," *Science and Technology* 76 April (1968): 21–41; Julien Mailland and Kevin Driscoll, eds., *MINITEL: Welcome to the Internet*, 2017; Armand Mattelart, *The Information Society: An Introduction*, 2001; Marianna Mazzucato, *The Entrepreneurial State: Debunking Public vs. Private Sector Myths*, 2014; Benjamin Peters, *How Not to Network a Nation: The Uneasy History of the Soviet Internet*, 2016; Andrew L. Russell, *Open Standards and the Internet Age: History, Ideology, and Networks*, 2014; Claude Shannon and Warren Weaver, *The Mathematical Theory of Communication*, 1964 [1948]; Joe Weizenbaum, "Once More, the Computer Revolution," in *The Microelectronics Revolution: The Complete Guide to New Technology and Its Impact*, edited by Tom Forrester, 1981; Hans Wellisch, "From Information Science to Informatics: A Terminological Investigation," *Journal of Librarianship* 4, no. 3 (1972): 157–87; Norbert Wiener, *Cybernetics: Or Control and Communication in the Animal and the Machine*, 1948; Shoshana Zuboff, *In the Age of the Smart Machine: The Future of Work and Power*, 1988.

13

SEARCH

At a conference in Australia in April 1998, two Stanford University graduate students described the challenge of searching for information on the *World Wide Web and a new tool called "Google" that they had designed to address it. The challenge of search in this evolving domain, as Sergey Brin and Larry Page explained it, reflected at once the size, dynamism, and character of the web. Though not even ten years old, the web was already big, and its growth was rapidly accelerating. One could foresee a time in the near future when it would dwarf even the largest electronic database then extant. This was the problem to which Brin and Page nodded when they named their search engine Google, evoking the mathematical term "googol," meaning ten to the one hundredth power. Google was designed to process what would later come to be called *big data. It was built specifically to scale with the web. It was also built to mirror the web's dynamism. In contrast to the *structured data found in traditional databases, information on the web was heterogeneous, conforming to no predetermined subject categories. Older techniques of information retrieval designed for searching databases foundered in this new environment. In 1998, Brin and Page wrote, only one of the top four commercial web search engines could find even itself.

In hindsight, it is bracing to reread Brin and Page's paper, "The Anatomy of a Large-Scale Hypertextual Search Engine." It offers a remarkable snapshot of the world just before the emergence of Google and the web as we know it, that last fleeting crepuscule of the twentieth century before search became ubiquitous in everyday life. Their paper is full of details that now feel either charmingly quaint, terribly ominous, and sometimes both. When Brin and Page unleashed their first crawler onto the web to collect and index everything it could find, many system administrators had no idea what to make of the hits it was giving them. "It turns out," Brin and Page write, "that running a crawler which connects to more than half a million servers, and generates tens of millions of log entries generates a fair amount of email and phone calls. . . . Almost daily, we receive an email something like, 'Wow, you looked at a lot of pages from my web site. How did you like it?'"

And it is not just those perplexed administrators whose voices echo from a former world: Brin and Page, too, sound like time travelers. Unlike commercial search engines of the day such as Lycos and Altavista, which kept their algorithms and data closely guarded as proprietary secrets, Google was to be open and noncommercial. "We believe," Brin and Page write, "the issue of advertising causes enough mixed incentives that it is crucial to have a competitive search engine that is transparent and in the academic realm." That was April 1998. Google incorporated in September of the same year. It went public in August 2004. By 2018, its parent corporation, Alphabet, was valued at over one trillion dollars. The algorithms that Google uses today are as closely guarded as any corporate secret.

What is search? What role does it play in our information culture? Where did it come from? Consider what made Google's first algorithm distinctive. As Brin and Page observe in their paper, in 1998 existing approaches to web search worked, if just barely. At that time, the various strategies of information retrieval used by the major search engines were all showing strains in handling the unstructured data of the web. Because the information content of the web was not organized by categories, representing it as such was both difficult and limiting. Yet, in one way or another, this was what the state-of-the-art search engines were doing. At the time, one of the most popular search portals, Yahoo!, still employed human indexers to make categorized lists of websites. These were often useful, but, in addition to imposing categories that might differ from those of both creators and consumers of information on the web, it was hard to see how this approach could scale with the web as it grew. The word-indexing techniques favored by other search engines were automated, but at scale even vector space models and similarly sophisticated statistical approaches overlooked important references and produced a lot of irrelevant hits. These "tended to prefer results that were textually similar to query terms, regardless of their thematic relevance," so, for example, a search on the phrase "Bill Clinton" using a popular search portal produced as its top result the "Bill Clinton Joke of the Day" page. Another engine gave a top ranking to a page that said only, "Bill Clinton sucks," while entirely missing the website www.whitehouse.gov. To use terms from the field of information retrieval itself: when applied to the web, the Yahoo! approach offered precision at the expense of recall, while the word-indexing approach offered recall at the expense of precision. Neither reflected the inherent logic of the web itself.

According to Brin and Page, the difference between web search and database search came down to two main factors: scale and heterogeneity. Whatever advantages there were in existing approaches to web search, most operated on taxonomic principles that had characterized the field of electronic data processing since its emergence a century earlier with the punch cards and machine tabulators applied to the US Census of 1890 by Herman Hollerith. Such systems could process large volumes of data efficiently, so long as that data fell into rigidly delineated categories. Indeed, historically, it was the control of categories itself that transformed otherwise heterogeneous information into data in the first place, going back all the way to mortality rolls, censuses, and other ambitious enumerative enterprises dating to the *early modern and medieval periods. In contrast to this structured universe of data, write Brin and Page, "the web is a vast collection of completely uncontrolled heterogeneous documents." Yet, as they well knew, the problem of uncontrolled heterogenous documents endemic to the web was in no way original to it. To the contrary, it was a problem that scholars and other searchers had been dealing with continuously since the beginning of documentation itself in fields quite different from those in which the database had grown up. The approach to web search proposed by Brin and Page was derived not from an earlier development in electronic data processing but from the history of scholarly notation techniques.

The specific formula for web search that Brin and Page first proposed—an algorithm they called "PageRank"—drew from a tradition that extended as far as that of the data roll, running parallel to it, sometimes interacting, but remaining through it all distinct.

To determine relationships among pages on the web and to determine the value of particular pages as responses to a given query, Brin and Page made an analogy between the *hyperlinks that connected web pages and the notes and bibliographies that connected traditional scholarly texts to one another. In traditional print scholarship, Brin and Page observed in their 1998 paper, writers use footnotes to point to the prior research and argumentation on which their own work relies. In doing this, they also ratify the value of these sources. A footnote, they said, is a kind of vote for the relevance of a specific source to the matter at hand. Compare the notes in a few related books, and you begin to get a picture of who the authorities are in that field. And it is not just general importance to which these references attest; they also indicate the specific relevance of a source to a given subject, which is, of course, the precise aim of a web search. The geneticist may never have considered the possibility of DNA computing, but repeated citation of earlier genetics research in articles on DNA computing by biochemists and computer scientists confirms the relevance of the earlier work to the subject.

To achieve a view of this network of references, Google used its crawler to follow links all over the web and to map them. Borrowing an idea from academic citation analysis, its PageRank algorithm characterized a web page according to its so-called back links—not the list of links found on that page but rather the list of links to that page from others—and the link graph accounting for the network of such connections across the web. Of course, assembling a comprehensive list of back links for the web, to say nothing of mapping them, was no trivial task, but as it emerged at Google, the assembled graph offered a metric for establishing the importance of web pages as well as characterizing their subject matter. Using this approach, Google would need no predetermined categories. Those would write themselves.

From a conceptual point of view, Google's break with received approaches in information retrieval was decisive. And yet, what Brin and Page were proposing drew directly on long-standing tradition. The most immediate precedent was Eugene Garfield's bibliometrics, from which also derives the so-called *impact factor often employed today as a quantitative measure of the influence of academic publications. Through this, their approach drew on very old traditions of commentary and interreference. In effect, they treated the web as a kind of literature, but this should not be surprising: the notion that the structure of the web might look something like the referential structure of a literature was baked into the enterprise from the start.

This was axiomatic for the gadfly computer theorist Theodor Holm (Ted) Nelson, who, already in the early 1960s, envisioned an electronic network of documents that encompassed much of what would eventually be realized in the World Wide Web and more. In his 1974 samizdat manifesto *Computer Lib/Dream Machines* and his 1980 *Literary Machines*, Nelson argued that a web of documents such as he imagined would create new possibilities for writing, while also bringing into view and activating nonlinear structures implicit in *analog text. *Hypertext*, Nelson's term for the cross-linking, associative, nonlinear, and nonhierarchical aspects of texts and collections, was thus a new name for a basic and pervasive textual structure. In Nelson's words: "Many people consider [hypertext] to be new and drastic and threatening. However, I would like to take the position that hypertext is fundamentally traditional and in the mainstream of literature. Customary writing chooses one expository sequence from among the possible myriad; hypertext allows many, all available to the reader. In fact, however, we constantly depart from sequence, citing things ahead and behind in the text. Phrases like 'as we have already said' and 'as we will see' are really implicit pointers to contents elsewhere in the sequence." And elsewhere, "Hypertext can include sequential text, and is thus the most general form of writing. (In one direction of generalization, it is also the most general form of language.)" To Nelson, literature was not a collection of independent works, but a docuverse, "an ongoing system of interconnecting documents." In his own proposal for an electronic document network, these interconnections were paramount. Quotations would offer dynamic windows into source texts, intellectual property would be traceable, and content creators could take advantage of a decentralized micropayment mechanism incorporated into the underlying exchange *protocol.

Both backward- and forward-looking, Nelson's would have been a very different web from the one that was implemented by the World Wide Web Consortium in the 1990s. For historians, the backward-looking aspects of Nelson's vision have particular resonance: over the course of many centuries, Nelson argued, textual scholars had worked out systems for connecting heterogeneous fields of inquiry into a great web of knowledge, in which factors such as importance and interrelationship were constantly represented and evaluated, and through which practiced readers could move fluidly and with intelligence. While the old paper universe had limitations that electronic media might mitigate, the basic principles at work should be considered all that much more robust for that very fact. The old media could not do everything that electronic media would be able to, but over centuries the scholarly traditions of manuscript and print worked. This was something that had not yet been shown for the electronic word. Nelson insisted on attention to precedent. Why? "Literature is debugged," he said.

All this is notable for several reasons. First, it helps to clarify what was new about Google when it was introduced: as Brin and Page explain it, the basic insight behind PageRank was the realization that in its link structure, the web provided its own *metadata; that is, in its network of links, the web expressed its native relational structure. As a consequence, PageRank was able to do autonomously what Yahoo!, for example, was using human readers to accomplish. Second, it illuminates a fundamental tension in the application of Brin and Page's technique to the accumulated wealth of information accessible on the web. While Google took its inspiration from time-tested traditions of bibliographic interreference, at the same time, it systematically disregarded the metadata that this tradition had generated and preserved over a long period of time. Third, it shows how centrally the project of the web reiterates old and persistent problems of information seeking. Brute-force solutions common in the digital era were mostly impractical if not out-and-out impossible in analog media. Predigital systems of interreference were, by force of necessity, models of elegance.

There are exceptions. In the early 1940s, for example, before he had regular access to a computer, the digital humanities pioneer Roberto Busa composed a dissertation on the use of the Latin preposition "in" found in the works of St. Thomas Aquinas, itemizing by hand on notecards each instance of "in" among the roughly thirteen million words that Aquinas wrote. For his next feat, the fifty-six-volume *Index Thomisticus* (Index to Thomas), Busa used an IBM computer to apply a similar method to every word in Aquinas's works. The example of Busa—and that of other early adopters including Paul Tasman (working on the Dead Sea Scrolls) and David W. Packard (working on Livy)— makes clear how directly certain kinds of analog research models could be adapted to the context of the computer and what becomes possible once a computer is unleashed on repetitive tasks of this sort.

We should note that in many cases, and this was certainly true in the 1940s when Busa began his *Index Thomisticus,* the image of the computer working autonomously is misleading. Much computer processing takes place without human intervention, but even in today's world of data processing, a great deal of repetitive data labor, ranging from the sorts of tasks done by gold farmers in online gaming to the piecework one finds through Amazon's Mechanical Turk, is still performed by people. Some of this labor, such as the image recognition processing we perform each time we decode a captcha or the unannounced A/B testing constantly implemented by web services, we barely notice, if at all. Busa himself employed a large staff of women to key in Aquinas's texts. He explained that he employed women in these tasks because they were more reliable and accurate than men. (And surely they could be paid less too.) On these lines, it is worth noting that even in the 1940s, the term *computer* was still mostly used to name a human worker whose job was to perform mathematical calculations, and that this particular job was frequently done by women. The persistence and intensification of this kind of work in the age of the web, as well as its outsourcing to various locations in the developing world, has led to an emergent critique of the digital sweatshop.

PageRank is only one expression of a common pattern in the history of information of implementing and transforming old techniques using new technologies. Other statistical search strategies have similar genealogies. The practice of alphabetical indexing fundamental to electronic search, for example, is quite old. It significantly predates the printed book, though in the West its efflorescence came in the first decades of movable type print in the fifteenth century. In printed books, mechanical reproduction brought with it standardized pagination. This, in turn, allowed for standardized page indexes. As Ann Blair has noted, such indexes were often selling points for new books. And, of course, new editions required new pagination, and new indexes, and potentially new purchases.

Even in the era before print, very important books—in Europe, this meant especially the Bible—were already indexed with microscopic precision. As early as the thirteenth century, the French Dominican friar Hugh of St-Cher produced a *concordance index containing nearly every word in the Bible. In 1445, the Jewish scholar Isaac Nathan completed a concordance to the Hebrew scripture, printed first in Venice in 1523, along similar lines. Nathan's work listed not only the words that it indexed but also those that it excluded by rule. In the 1950s, IBM engineer Hans Peter Luhn would recommend the same practice, the application of what he called a stop list, in automated concordance indexing systems. Created in two different languages five hundred years apart, Nathan's and Luhn's lists, both of which contained mostly so-called function words such as articles, prepositions, conjunctions, closely resemble one another.

Early on, Google explicitly signaled which words its searches were stopping. Users had to take an extra step if they wished to search certain very common words including those on Luhn's and Isaac's lists. At the start of 2007, a Google search on a phrase that included common function words such as "the Fourth of July" or "A Room with a View" would elicit a set of results along with a message that the search had been conducted only on the words "Fourth July" or "Room View." Google wagered that in most cases the result of searching the shorter phrase would be close to that of searching the longer one and that the savings thereby achieved in processing power and time favored searching the stopped phrase rather than the complete one. This was precisely the reasoning that Luhn had employed when he composed his first sixteen-word stop list for his electronic Keyword-in-Context (KWIC) indexing system and that Nathan had used in composing his concordance to the Hebrew scripture. In Luhn's case, the economy could be measured in boxes of paper punch cards and machine time, just as, in the case of Nathan, it could be measured in paper and scribal labor.

Because the Bible and the Bible concordance are both books, it is easy to overlook just how substantial a technical intervention the latter represents. In the concordance format pioneered by Hugh of St-Cher, the words of the source text are disassembled and then reassembled as an alphabetical word list. Hugh's concordance contains the full text of the Bible and nothing but that text. And yet, his concordance is not the Bible. In it, the text of scripture appears in an entirely different order from the source text. As the early concordance format developed in the thirteenth century, it came to include the presentation of contextual passages—what we would today call snippets—so that users could see immediately how words were being used and could evaluate whether those instances were relevant to their search. A passage that contained two or more words deemed significant might appear in the concordance more than once, resulting in a work that, though it contains only words from the Bible, would be longer than the Bible. It also, very importantly, resulted in a text that could be read on its own.

Over time, Bible concordances proved enduringly popular. After nearly three centuries, Alexander Cruden's 1737 *Complete Concordance to the Holy Scriptures*, for example, has still never been out of print. Concordances have also remained a terrain of scholarly innovation, offering a notable variety of formats and schemes of linguistic stemming. And after Cruden, the concordance approach was applied increasingly to texts other than the Bible. In 1741, Cruden himself published a "verbal index" to John Milton's *Paradise Lost*. In time, other writers including Dante and Shakespeare got their own concordances, in itself an indicator of their cultural significance. Among the most notable modern concordance systems is the one published in 1890 by the American Methodist scholar James Strong, providing an alphabetical index to every word in the King James Bible along with a numerical reference system—"Strong's Numbers"—assigning to each English word in the King James Version a corresponding Hebrew or Greek word.

Of course, readers understood concordances as reference tools. No medieval reader would have imagined that Hugh's concordance meant something independent of the Bible. Its purpose was to aid in reading scripture, but the very fact that medieval Christian scholars knew the text of the Bible so well facilitated the relative independence of the concordance in use. Leaving aside the theological question, from the point of view of the history of information, the practice of reading a concordance, or, to generalize, the practice of reading an index, is distinctive, just as is the practice of scanning the snippets presented as the result of a Google search. These come from the web pages that Google indexes, but they are not those pages, and reading Google results is not equivalent to reading web pages, a fact that is reinforced with some intensity each time it turns out that a Google result links to content hidden behind a pay wall. Reading a Google results page is an information practice of a different sort, a kind of scanning or mapping operation similar to what Hugh hoped his concordance would allow biblical scholars to perform. In our culture, however, the place of this kind of index reading is transformed. What in the Middle Ages was a rarified scholarly practice serves us increasingly, in our age of search, as the very model of reading itself.

The practice of information seeking is as old as any historical record we have. It is a fundamental concern for any library, archive, or repository. Among the most famous losses in that most famous information catastrophe, the destruction of the Library of Alexandria, was that of the *pinakes* or tables of categories composed by the scholar-poet Callimachus in the third century BCE. This, as much as the texts in the library, contained precious information, metadata, as we would say today. Self-evidently, the larger a given collection, the more complex a problem search becomes; hence the composition of the pinakes for what was said to be the world's largest library; hence too, Brin and Page's shorthand, ten to the one hundredth power, in their name for Google. So, we should not make the mistake of thinking that the amount of information to be searched nor the rapidity of its growth is a new concern in our period.

The contemporary docuverse is indeed large and rapidly growing. But the problem of scale is endemic to the world of documents, and both the worry about it and the fantasy of mastering it have reappeared with regularity throughout the long history of information, inspiring new cataloging systems and devices in each era, including a kaleidoscope of what Markus Krajewski has called "paper machines," ranging from the "literary closets" of Thomas Harrison and Vincent Placcius in the seventeenth century (Blair, chap. 4) to the "Mundaneum," the card-based "Universal Bibliographical System" of the Belgian documentalist Paul Otlet at the start of the twentieth (Duguid, chap. 12). If there is a point somewhere back in history before which scholars fretted about it, it must have been very long ago indeed. Socrates famously worried about the corrosive effects of writing: in his age memorization was understood to be a crucial technical and intellectual skill. Having information memorized allowed a thinker not only to access but to spontaneously interrelate different ideas. For him, the prospect of a society in which important knowledge was committed to writing but not to memory presented a serious danger. Of course, his admonition did nothing to slow down the offloading of memory onto external media such as manuscript scrolls, even by his own acolytes including Plato and Xenophon. Had it, we likely would know little if anything about Socrates today. (In fact Socrates also acknowledged the value of writing in preserving what had been lost to memory, notably when he praised in the *Timaeus* the Egyptians' written records of events that the Greeks, dependent on memory, had forgotten.)

Nor, for that matter, was the idea of a mechanical search engine itself novel in the twentieth century. The great visionary of search Vannevar Bush, who headed the US Office of Scientific Research and Development (OSRD) during World War II, the same agency that oversaw the Manhattan Project, described his work as extending a tradition of information machines going back to those proposed by the German philosopher Gottfried Wilhelm Leibniz late in the seventeenth century and the English mechanical engineer Charles Babbage early in the nineteenth century. Each envisioned a kind of computer. Babbage actually designed two, one called the "Difference Engine" and another, the "Analytical Engine," for which the mathematician Ada Lovelace wrote programs. But in the cases of both Leibniz and Babbage, writes Bush, "the economics of the situation" were against bringing the designed machines into existence. Before the age of mass production, the labor necessary to build and run such machines exceeded what they could save the user. Even in July 1945, when Bush published his classic essay

"As We May Think," describing a hypothetical search machine called the *"memex," the mechanical computer was still a relative novelty. Hollerith's tabulating machines were only a half a century old. The ENIAC computer at the University of Pennsylvania, which used punch cards for input and output, would not debut publicly until early the following year.

Bush's moment was one of enormous technical innovation in the area of electronic computing. For this, ENIAC is emblematic. And yet, the important insights in Bush's great article on search did not rely fundamentally on that technology. Tellingly, his own system would have mostly employed analog photographic technology such as microfilm rather than the electronic technology such as was found in ENIAC, to compress libraries into a desk-sized device. Tellingly, too, some of the key features of Bush's proposal, including a ubiquitous, forehead-mounted wearable visual recording device, remain embryonic seventy-five years later despite efforts in multimedia life logging by experimenters such as Gordon Bell and Stephen Wolfram, and innovations in wearable devices such as Google Glass.

The idea of applying technology to problems of information search was fundamental to Bush's project, but the specific technologies of his day were less so. More important to his thinking was a problem, sometimes referred to as *information overload, for which there are abundant precedents in the history of information. For Bush himself, the pressing problem, as well as the unique opportunity, emerged directly from the technical research that flourished during the Second World War. In the article in which he described the memex machine, Bush argued that with the war now done, scientists could and should turn their attention to the "mountain" of knowledge that society had amassed but not mastered. "The summation of human experience," he wrote, "is being expanded at a prodigious rate, and the means we use for threading through the consequent maze to the momentarily important item is the same as was used in the days of square-rigged ships." To address the problem Bush proposed a kind of Manhattan Project of the mind.

Elevated as were the goals that he articulated, the instigating problem for the director of OSRD was military and industrial. Indeed, at war's end, in addition to taking account of its own burgeoning literature in science and technology, the United States was faced with the felicitous problem of absorbing parallel literatures captured from its defeated adversaries. In the following decades, Cold War competition too would figure centrally in the imperatives of information retrieval. As scientific journals multiplied and industrial reports piled up, information pioneers such as Douglas Engelbart, whose Augmentation Research Center at the Stanford Research Institute (SRI) was responsible for crucial early work on both the computer mouse and the graphical user interface, framed their work in this light. In a 1958 article on the "information problem," Engelbart and his collaborator Charles Bourne articulated the need: "Recent world events have catapulted the problem of the presently unmanageable mass of technical information from one that should be solved to one that must be solved." The Soviet approach, they continued, was to throw bodies at the problem, including twenty-three hundred dedicated translators and abstractors "who publish over 400,000 abstracts of technical articles from more than 10,000 journals originating in about 80 countries." The American response, they said, ought to both match and advance on what the Soviets were doing. On the one hand, it was incumbent on the United States to establish its own National Technical Information Service parallel to the Soviet All Union Institute of Scientific and Technical Information. On the other, it would be essential to deploy within it a "highly mechanized" system of information search. As Engelbart and Bourne wrote, "Technology, so adept in solving problems of man and his environment, must be directed to solving a gargantuan problem of its own creation. A mass of technical information has been accumulated and that has far outstripped means for making it available to those working in science and engineering."

Many of the influential technical information systems developed in this period imposed controlled vocabularies and prefabricated systems of classification on their subjects. That is to say, they applied precisely the kinds of approach that Brin and Page considered typical of the field of information retrieval prior to Google. These systems enhanced the slip and card systems of earlier innovators such as Placcius and Otlet, allowing more search factors to be coordinated, but as Brin and Page argue, in the end, they could be only as good as the categories around which they were constructed. And even in their time, they were put in question by more flexible indexing approaches such as those proposed by Bush and Luhn.

The urgency of Engelbart and Bourne's language reflects the real demands of the moment—not least among these, that of garnering funding from US government defense agencies—yet, in the longer history of information, the postwar context of Engelbart and Bush appears epiphenomenal, as does the specific technological character of both the challenge and the proposed solution that each articulates. Consider another statement of the "information problem" from two centuries earlier when the broadside and the newspaper represented the bleeding edge of new media, when an explosion of published books worried researchers as much as did the explosion of technical literature that concerned Bush, Luhn, and Engelbart.

That world, at the midpoint of the eighteenth century, argued the French philosopher Denis Diderot, was poised at the edge of a fundamental and irreversible transformation of knowledge and media. In his words, "As long as the centuries continue to unfold, the number of books will grow continually, and one can predict that a time will come when it will be almost as difficult to learn anything from books as from the direct study of the whole universe." Perhaps for Diderot, that time had not yet quite arrived, but the forces at work appeared both intensifying and inexorable. Diderot's proposed solution to the problem was technical. With his collaborator, the mathematician Jean le Rond d'Alembert, he would create a new kind of *encyclopedia that would make it practical to navigate this flood of books.

Diderot and d'Alembert were not alone in their concerns: to illustrate the problem, their contemporary the French journalist and critic Louis-Sébastien Mercier invented a new literary form, the novel of the future. Mercier's 1769 book, *The Year 2440: A Dream If Ever There Was One*, described politics, society, and knowledge in a speculative world located seven centuries in the future. In one of the most famous scenes in that book, the narrator, a time traveler from the eighteenth century, makes his way to the building that in his day housed the Royal Library of France. The traveler finds the building still there, looking much as it did in his own time. But when he enters, he gets a shock: the great halls that had once been filled with printed books are now empty, or nearly so. All that remain are a few volumes.

The time traveler, knowing the stories of the great Library of Alexandria, approaches a librarian and ventures to ask if some "fatal conflagration" had not devoured the king's collection. To this, the librarian replies, "Yes, it was a conflagration; but we lit it with our own hands." Faced with a crushing, ever-growing accumulation of books, "what remained for us to do, but to rebuild the structure of human knowledge?" From shelves and shelves of books, the good information was sorted out from the bad and, in the end, not much was left. This was condensed into clear language and assembled.

Book burning aside, Mercier's plan echoes that of Diderot and d'Alembert. They gathered the best writers they knew and made an encyclopedia that contained key knowledge from a wide range of technical and humanistic fields that could serve as a kind of index to all. The resulting work, one of the great monuments in the history of information, also contained eleven volumes of illustrations that set a standard for contemporary information graphics. The organization of the work was novel, and, for its creators, as much as for Bush, Engelbart, or Brin and Page, it was this technical dimension that distinguished it. Diderot and d'Alembert believed that in their explosive information environment, above all, knowledge had to be searchable so that it could be found and accessed quickly and then reassembled creatively according to the changing needs of the user and the demands of the moment.

To achieve these search capabilities, the *Encyclopédie* of Diderot and d'Alembert combined several older technical strategies. The typical encyclopedia of the time, according to Diderot and d'Alembert, was organized thematically and in a general sense hierarchically. They called this kind of organization *encyclopedic order. In a work organized this way, discoveries in natural history and in the study of language, for example, would occupy entirely different sections of the work. Moreover, within each thematic section, information was often deeply buried. A researcher interested in one specific aspect of natural history, perhaps bird calls, might need to read everything about birds to learn anything useful on the subject, and a researcher interested in somehow connecting information about bird calls to information about human language was in a still greater bind. This was, of course, part of the problem that Socrates had envisioned resulting from the abandonment of the ancient arts of memory, but for Diderot and d'Alembert, three centuries into the age of print, the solution had to emerge from print itself.

As with many such innovations, the full implications of Diderot and d'Alembert's adaptation of the encyclopedia format were not all immediately apparent. Indeed, the publisher's 1745 prospectus for the *Encyclopédie* promised readers little more than a translation of the English *Cyclopaedia* published by Ephraim Chambers in 1728. By 1751, when the first volume of the work appeared, the project had changed fundamentally. Chambers's book remained an inspiration, and some of its features were emulated in the new work including its alphabetical organization and its cross-references; his text, by contrast, was abandoned. By 1755, when the fifth volume of Diderot and d'Alembert's work appeared, including the self-reflexive entry ENCYCLOPÉDIE, the encyclopedia embodied a fully conceptualized *epistemological program.

Diderot and d'Alembert's work turned out to be an encyclopedia of a new kind. Unlike a thematic encyclopedia, theirs was divided into discrete chunks—articles—each placed under a headword—what today we would call a keyword. The information in these articles was sourced from a crowd of writers selected for their knowledge and special perspective, a *société de gens de lettres*, as Diderot and d'Alembert put it, though the gendered English translation, *society of men of letters*, was in fact more accurate. In their argument and presentation, these different contributions were not to be integrated.

Instead, they would be interlinked through a web of embedded cross-references operating according to several different logics. The idea that knowledge could be usefully grouped into hierarchical categories, a branching tree of the sort suggested by Francis Bacon's classification of knowledge, was not abandoned. To the contrary, in his preliminary discourse, d'Alembert sketched his own version of Bacon's tree. But instead of organizing the text around this tree, Diderot and d'Alembert embedded its logic in the network of cross-references woven throughout.

In an important way, this move strengthened the tree of knowledge, because it unburdened it: now that it could be understood to represent only one possible projection of complex and overlapping fields of knowledge, problems of hierarchization disappeared. Trees of different kinds could be imagined, as could linking structures that were horizontal rather than hierarchical. Diderot, ever the wit, even described a satirical style of cross-reference familiar in today's world of hashtags, in which the reference itself *serves as a form of commentary*. He counseled his readers to look out for these signals, "carefully weighing" the significance each cross-reference. For example, says Diderot, at the end of one article in the *Encyclopédie* (on Grey Friars), the attentive reader will notice an incongruous cross-reference to MONK'S COWL. The reader who follows that cross-reference will be amused to discover an account of a pointless sartorial debate that once (for a century) raged among the Franciscans. Put the two entries together, and the reader will understand that what looked like praise of argument in the first article "was meant ironically." References of this sort, Diderot suggests, allow the *Encyclopedia*'s authors to criticize "ridiculous customs," afford "a delicate and amusing way to pay back an insult," and offer "an excellent means of snatching off the masks from the faces of certain grave personnages."

The way into Diderot and d'Alembert's *Encyclopédie* was distinctive, too. Here again, the French editors borrowed from the Englishman Chambers, who, two decades before, had eschewed encyclopedic order in favor of a more humble dictionary order. Like him, Diderot and d'Alembert organized their encyclopedia alphabetically. In the perspective of electronic information technology, this hardly seems much of an innovation, but the implications were substantial and the significance enduring. What Diderot and d'Alembert noticed in their reading of Chambers was that individual words shorn of syntactic context were excellent tools for search.

In retrospect, the *Encyclopédie* appears a visionary document. But we should not be taken in by what looks like foresight in Diderot any more so than by the science fiction future of Mercier's *2440*. Rather, we should understand both the *Encyclopédie* and *2440* as telling documents of their time. The *Encyclopédie* of Diderot and d'Alembert *feels* modern because the imperatives and conditions—the feeling of overload, the sense of acceleration—that drove it resemble the imperatives that drive our own information society. Neither Diderot nor Mercier saw the future. What they saw, powdered wigs or no, was a media present that we are still living out. And, as they understood it, the core problem of modern information society was the problem of search.

This is also the deeper message behind Mercier's vision of burning books. Presented as it was, his account of the destruction of the books in the Royal Library was neither utopian nor dystopian. Mercier was a prolific writer who certainly did not want *his* books burned, but he really did believe, as did Diderot and d'Alembert, that a great encyclopedia could do more good in the world than a vault filled with mediocre, redundant, or unfindable books. His efforts were aimed at changing the perspective of the reader on the problem of knowledge in general. For all these *Enlightenment writers, more information ceased to be a useful objective. The goal was better and more accessible information, information that could be used and recombined in previously unimagined ways.

This brings us to what is the most striking observation made by Vannevar Bush in his famous article on the memex, one influential in both the design and the ultimate coming into being of the web itself. Bush's vision revolved around two key desiderata. First was a mechanical system providing access to an enormous amount of information from diverse sources through a single interface. Second was a way of traversing this information in crisscrossing associative trails. To achieve the first, Bush proposed microfilm. This turned out not to be the best technology for the application, although it took some time for this to become obvious: late in the twentieth century, vast archiving projects still employed microfilm. To achieve the second, Bush proposed something so simple that it harked back to early modern *commonplace books and the rearrangeable note slips and index cards of scholars such as Desiderius Erasmus, Conrad Gessner, and Vincent Placcius. As individual readers worked their way through the subject matter on the memex, they would create trails that would allow them to retrace their own paths through the forest of information and to share them with others. The tool for doing this would be a new, technical feature of the memex machine. But the underlying idea was as traditional as scholarship itself.

The notion of automating the process of association was more novel. Here, Luhn was an exemplary contributor. At IBM in the early 1950s, Luhn began work on what he called a "business intelligence system." His goal was to design a computer program to examine new technical literature, summarize it, and direct it to appropriate engineers at IBM. Like Diderot's *Encyclopédie* and Bush's memex, Luhn's system was meant to break out of the rigid categories of field specialization that would, for example, send articles on chemistry exclusively to chemists. Appropriately, Luhn's work in this area was eagerly followed not only by computer scientists but by a wider community of documentalists drawn from diverse institutions ranging from libraries to scientific societies to national security agencies for which the management and processing of information were central. This grouping of fields was represented, among other places, in the American Documentation Institute, later the Association for Information Science and Technology, or ASIS&T, where Luhn would for a time serve as president. In itself, this grouping was important, and the combination of approaches that it fostered is strongly echoed in the genealogy of PageRank.

Luhn's procedure was simple in concept. The computer first had to determine which words used in a text were most important. This was to be achieved statistically first through an analysis of word frequency: words that appeared often in an article were considered significant so long as they were not so frequent that they represented nothing more than the regularities of the language or of the present field of research. Thus, for example, the computer would be instructed to ignore function words such as the articles *the* and *a* as well as more content-laden terms such as *doctor* or *illness* when preparing an abstract from a medical journal. Words that were determined to be significant were ranked by the algorithm. High-ranking terms were then assessed to be the keywords of the source article and were used to characterize and to classify it.

Luhn proposed further that, following this approach, key sentences might also be identified, extracted, and arranged in order. What resulted would serve as an "automatic abstract" of the source article. Users of Luhn's "business intelligence system" would characterize themselves by selecting a set of keywords of interest to them. The system could then match abstracts to readers. On the basis of feedback gleaned as users accepted and rejected abstracts suggested by the system, keyword profiles for both users and articles could be refined. Notably, in Luhn's system, the reader and the text were *both* characterized by profiles made up of keywords: from the point of view of the system, the searcher and the searched were interchangeable.

Luhn worked for IBM, which had an immediate business interest in information retrieval both for its internal operations and as a commercial product that it could market to others. And much of early web search too was driven by commercial concerns. Yet some search projects emerged from academia as well. The most successful of these was Google itself, which began as a graduate student research project. Indeed, at the start of 1998, Google was still an academic project, and though that would soon change, it remained then a characteristic that its creators considered important. "Up until now," they write, "most search engine development has gone on at companies with little publication of technical details. This causes search engine technology to remain largely a black art and to be advertising oriented." By contrast, they continue, "With Google, we have a strong goal to push more development and understanding into the academic realm." In their paper, they envision Google as a "Spacelab-like environment" where "other researchers can come in quickly" and "process large parts of the Web." At the time, this was just a premise, but so, for that matter, was the entire project of making Google a tool for the everyday web user, which Brin and Page convey in what must be some kind of record-setting understatement: "we believe our solutions are scalable to commercial volumes with a bit more effort." Time would show that Google scaled very well to commercial volumes; at scale, it would come to dominate the field of web search, despite concerted, well-funded competition by Microsoft and other corporate rivals, and state-protected companies such as Baidu in China and Yandex in Russia. To say that the web grew exponentially in the following two decades barely hints at the pace of change. In 1998, Brin and Page's first crawler was able to collect and index a total of one hundred forty-seven gigabytes of data. A recent estimate put the size of Google's index at approximately one hundred million gigabytes, a growth of six orders of magnitude.

Of course, once reconfigured as a commercial project, Google would become expert in the same "black art" that Brin and Page had criticized. While the implications were enormous, the reasons were banal. Some were proprietary: once it was in the market, a search engine was competing with others, and not only other search engines, also other interested parties such as site administrators who would attempt to *game* search engine results in order to obtain high rankings for their sites. Entire businesses emerged specializing in this kind of search engine optimization, and varieties of web spamming including link farming, redirection spamming, and visual cloaking became common. Search engines had a stake in preventing their results from being manipulated by outsiders, whether because they wanted to be able to offer better results, or because they wanted to be able to pick winners themselves. Other issues were technical: search algorithms were becoming more complex, and with the application of *machine learning to their optimization, the connection between specific intentionality on the part of engineers and the operation of the search mechanism became more distant and harder to fully comprehend, even for the engineers themselves.

Part of what allowed web search to become so ubiquitous to begin with is that, to the individual user of a search engine, search appeared to be a free service. From a certain perspective, it was: neither Google nor its main competitors charged individual customers for web search, and search is a powerful tool. Certainly, consumers of search experienced real costs, including charges by ISPs (*internet service providers) and by consumer electronics companies that make and sell the devices used to conduct searches. This is to say nothing of the many economic and environmental externalities of the communications infrastructure underlying the internet. But, remarkably, search itself, in the form provided by Google, Microsoft, and other commercial services in the early twenty-first century, generally incurred no direct charge.

For these companies, the incentive structure worked the other way around: when users searched, search companies made money, and the more people searched, the more money the search companies made. The same incentive structure led these companies to offer a variety of other products—including social media, document and spreadsheet software, web browsers, mobile phone operating systems, low-cost computer equipment, *cloud storage, and internet connectivity—that lowered barriers to participation and helped keep users within a given data ecosystem. In the case of Google, this included also massive absorption and service of web content, including from 2004, the Google Books text digitization project, and from 2006, the video streaming service YouTube, which quickly became the second most visited site on the web, surpassing Facebook, Amazon, and other web heavyweights, and ranking behind only its mother corporation, Google.

From the point of view of the history of the web, both YouTube and Google Books were enormously important. From the point of view of the history of reading and scholarship, Google Books was transformative. With it, Google leapfrogged the many digitization projects already being conducted by libraries and other information providers. In one fell swoop, it created the largest repository of books on the web and integrated it into a search environment shared by everything else that Google indexed. As Google presented it, Google Books was a realization of the age-old dream of the universal library. In its own words, Google's aim was to make "the full text of all the world's books searchable by everyone." That idea was reinforced early on by the agreement of several major research libraries including the New York Public Library and the libraries of the University of Michigan, University of Oxford, Stanford University, and Harvard University to participate in the project. Google would scan their holdings, process them using OCR (*optical character recognition), and make them searchable. The libraries too would get copies of the resulting electronic documents, which they would then pool through the academic consortium Hathi Trust. Libraries and foundations, of course, continued their own digitization work and constructed valuable interfaces such as those as for the manuscript collection in the Vatican Library's online DigiVatLib and the early books collection at the Bayerische Staatsbibliothek's Münchener DigitalisierungsZentrum. For most users, however, it seemed likely that the principal gateway to "the world of information contained in books" would be Google itself.

Google Books was a big idea and a big project, and its ambitions were amplified by enthusiasts such as technology theorist and *Wired* magazine founder Kevin Kelly. In Google, Kelly wrote, the world's books become "one very, very, very large single text: the world's only book," "a single liquid fabric of interconnected words and ideas." For him, "turning inked letters into electronic dots that can be read on a screen is simply the first essential step in creating this new library. The real magic will come in the second act, as each word in each book is cross-linked, clustered, cited, extracted, indexed, analyzed, annotated, remixed, reassembled and woven deeper into the culture than ever before. In the new world of books, every bit informs another; every page reads all the other pages."

In some respects, Kelly was undoubtedly right. In Google Books, and everywhere else on the web, too, the experience of reading was changing. Boundaries between texts were becoming more malleable, and the difference between reading and searching was increasingly blurred. At the same time, in the version of the web that emerged at the end of the twentieth century, and in the version of Google Books developed for it, none of these utopian longings was fulfilled. This was less a failure in innovation than in imagination, argued Theodor Nelson. The basic protocols on which the web was running—including HTTP (hypertext transfer protocol) and HTML (Hypertext Markup Language), proposed in 1989 by Tim Berners-Lee—limited the relationships among documents that could be implemented.

Not all visions of the universal library have been utopian. For Denis Diderot, as for many of his contemporaries, the idea of the universal library was as much cautionary as it was visionary. During the Enlightenment, as we have seen, the story of the destruction of the Library of Alexandria resonated strongly. When Enlightenment thinkers thought about the Alexandrian Library, they mostly thought about the fragility of knowledge and of media, a subject of renewed importance in our own age of digital ephemerality. For them, the Library of Alexandria represented an Icarian dream: the greatest library in the history of the world, and it went up in flames. In the charter for his encyclopedia project, Diderot alluded to that catastrophe, promoting his *Encyclopédie*, of which there would be many copies, as a kind of starter kit for a new world of knowledge after the next, ineluctable information holocaust: "The most glorious moment for a work such as this would be that which might come immediately in the wake of some revolution so great as to suspend the progress of science, to interrupt the labors of craftsmen, and to plunge a portion of our hemisphere into darkness once again. What gratitude would not be lavished by the generation that came after this time of troubles upon those men who had discerned its approach from afar, and who had taken measures to ward off its worst ravages by collecting in a safe place the knowledge of all past ages!" As Tung-Hui Hu has argued, a related kind of apocalyptic, or necropolitical, thinking underlay Paul Baran's original design for a distributed and thus un-nuke-able ARPANET in the 1960s as well as the *data bunkers* that today inhabit the husks of old fallout shelters deep below ground.

However comprehensive the Library of Alexandria in fact was, and however precisely it came to its end, it must have been a remarkable resource. No physical library ever again made the same claim to universality. This has something to do with the fact that over time, as Diderot pointed out, the world of books kept expanding. It also has much to do with the history of empires. In the West, after Alexandria and before Google, no political or commercial entity had the wherewithal to engage in a comparable project. The Library of Alexandria was impracticable apart from Egypt's military and infrastructural dominance. When ships docked at Alexandria, they were meant to send any book on board to be copied at the library. An ancient account describes books acquired this way piled up in warehouses. The extent to which this actually happened is a mystery, but the principle is illuminating. While Egypt's wealth and passion for Greek culture gave it the power to make such a demand, it was its domination of infrastructure that allowed it to channel information into its repository.

The Google Books project began in 2004 when Google proposed two book initiatives, one aimed at contemporary *publishers and one aimed at libraries. Google Print, announced at the Frankfurt Book Fair in October 2004, was to allow digital search and access to current books through agreement with publishers. The Google Books Library Project, announced in December 2004, was to do much the same with material obtained from libraries. In 2010, a Google Book Search engineer estimated that since the beginning of print in the West, approximately 130 million unique titles had been published—actually, the number he gave was 129,864,880. Eventually Google intended to obtain and digitize the vast majority of these. By October 2015, it had made a respectable start by scanning twenty-five million books from its research library partners. By that time, Google Print and the Google Library Project had been subsumed under the common rubric of Google Books.

From the start, Google Books provoked controversy. Problems of *fair use and *copyright had to be settled. A major legal issue was whether Google would be allowed to operate its book projects on an opt-in or an opt-out principle, in other words, whether Google would have to ask authors and publishers for permission before or after digitizing their works. Google's preference and its initial approach were decidedly for opt-out: Google tried to hoover up everything it could first and to deal with the niceties later. And while publishers and writers initially sued regarding this approach to copyrighted materials, Google's partnership with research libraries allowed it to plunge into scanning headlong. Authors and publishers argued that Google's approach "shifts the responsibility for preventing infringement to the copyright owner rather than the user, turning every principle of copyright law on its ear."

Some governments, too, including those of France and Germany, argued that Google's approach placed "unchecked, concentrated power" over the shared fund of human knowledge, as well as the unique cultural heritage of nations around the world, in the hands of an unaccountable US commercial entity. The research libraries partnered with Google tried to find a middle ground. Harvard's librarian, the eminent book historian Robert Darnton, for example, made a case for using Google's scanning to build up digital materials for a network of noncommercial digital libraries, the DPLA or Digital Public Library of America, which would guarantee that access to out-of-copyright books would remain in public hands. Darnton found models for such networks of collective agreement in library initiatives developed in Europe and especially in Europeana, a pan-European network of networks. Others argued for even more ambitious, public efforts such as the Human Knowledge Project proposed by historian and media scholar Siva Vaidhyanathan.

For its part, Google defended the notion of amassing "the world's knowledge stored in books" in its own repository, arguing that digitizing books and then making them searchable through a single, unified interface transformed them fundamentally, using the legal term of art. In its legal arguments, Google focused on the claims of authors and publishers to works still in copyright. These, it argued, could be addressed by assuring that copyrighted items stored by Google would not be viewable except as permitted by copyright holders. It argued that its search product would provide specific benefits to authors and publishers by making their properties discoverable and by driving traffic to them, whether on the web, in a physical library or bookstore, through on-demand printing, or in some other way. It argued further that the public good that it would create relied on the comprehensiveness of its underlying data. That, in turn, demanded the opt-out approach. Though complex, a settlement agreement reached in 2008 affirmed Google's basic strategy. It also permitted Google to monetize its collection of digitized books through a variety of mechanisms. And it affirmed the premise that the "world's knowledge stored in books" would be rendered searchable through Google's proprietary interface under terms mostly set by Google itself.

Many worried that the Google Books project would crowd out others. The scope and cost of its book digitization were enormous, and, despite dedicated efforts by a number of public and nonprofit entities, once Google had advanced to a certain point, these critics argued, it was hard to imagine another institution doing the same heavy lifting. Indeed, evidence to support these concerns was abundant: many likely competitors to Google Books, including the nonprofit Internet Archive and the library partners in the Google Books project themselves, had already opted to rely on Google to provide digitized texts for their own collections. This was, for the libraries, a principal incentive to participate in Google's project in the first place. Thus, whatever Google did in its digitization project was likely to endure and to propagate through many channels. Consequently, as readers relied increasingly on digital means to access books, their experience of books would be increasingly shaped by Google, by its selections, its scanning procedures, its treatment of bibliographic metadata, and so forth. The looming dystopian possibility was not a Google that dominated the treasury of world literature. Rather, it was a Google that for one reason or another never fully took the problem of books seriously, that abandoned the task only partway done, or both. And a decade or so in, many of these fears seemed more than justified. After a largely successful legal struggle to defend its approach to digitization, Google Books appeared to evolve rather little, and Google stopped saying much about it.

Early studies quickly demonstrated a wide range of problems and peculiarities in Google's approach. For example, the algorithms applied by Google Books frequently attributed to books the wrong publication dates. In a review in the *Chronicle of Higher Education*, Geoff Nunberg pointed out that according to Google Books, Raymond Chandler's *Killer in the Rain* was published in 1899, the same year as "*The Portable Dorothy Parker*, André Malraux's *La Condition Humaine*, Stephen King's *Christine*, *The Complete Shorter Fiction of Virginia Woolf*, Raymond Williams's *Culture and Society 1780–1950*, and Robert Shelton's biography of *Bob Dylan*." Classification was similarly problematic. "H. L. Mencken's *The American Language* is classified as Family & Relationships. . . . An edition of *Moby Dick* is labeled Computers; *The Cat Lover's Book of Fascinating Facts* falls under Technology & Engineering. And a catalog of copyright entries from the Library of Congress is listed under Drama (for a moment I wondered if maybe that one was just Google's little joke)."

As Paul Duguid showed, Google Books had similar problems interpreting what was inside of books. It failed to read drop capitals, the large initial letters common at the beginning of book chapters; it mistook book illustrations for scanning errors; it read book plates as title pages; its optical character recognition functioned poorly on older books, particularly those published before 1800. Various features such as hyperlinked tables of contents worked inconsistently, and, depending on the quality of the initial digital scan, Google often failed to recognize entire sections of works. All this created serious problems for text search within the corpus and even greater problems using the corpus for quantitative analysis—including the briefly ballyhooed culturomics, or quantitative analysis of culture, emblematized by the Google Books Ngram Viewer—or anything else. Of course, Google had every intention to provide the best digitization possible at scale, and it had some very good reasons to want to do this. As Nunberg pointed out, the fact that in 2009 Google was still displaying ads for gardening supplies to readers of Walt Whitman's *Leaves of Grass* could not have particularly pleased ad buyers at Home Depot. Regardless, this was the situation.

In all this, most worrisome perhaps was Google's programmatic lack of interest in bibliographic metadata, the very stuff that makes a library a library rather than just a storehouse of books. This was an ironic development, since the catalog was in principle the aspect of the traditional library *best* adapted to the digital framework, as well its most comprehensive tool for information search. Indeed, historically, the library card catalog was the very paradigm of the humanistic database, and massive digitization— retroactive *conversion, as it is called—of library catalogs had begun long before the advent of Google Books. Nicholson Baker's famous essay "Discards," a *cri de coeur* for the library card catalog and against the "national paroxysm of shortsightedness and anti-intellectualism" that had led to its devaluation and destruction, was published in the *New Yorker* in 1994, four years before the founding of Google and a full decade before the announcement of the Google Books Library Project. And Baker's essay was already belated: New York Public Library, for example, had microfilmed and disposed of its card catalog in the late 1970s.

Others followed. As Baker recounts in his essay, even Harvard University, with a massive catalog containing more than five million cards, was doing a retrocon, sending off boxes of cards, a week at a time, to OCLC, the Online Computer Library Center in Dublin, Ohio, which then rendered them in "machine-readable form," specifically the so-called MARC or Machine Readable Cataloging format developed in the early 1960s with the Library of Congress. In fact, the standardization of library catalogs had begun earlier still. At the very start of the twentieth century, the Library of Congress in the United States began selling printed copies of its own catalog cards. To create or augment their card catalogs, libraries in the United States and elsewhere could order cards from Washington. A 1969 study of the Rice University Library, for example, found that fully two-thirds of the library's catalog cards had been purchased from the Library of Congress. This system had many advantages: catalogers at the Library of Congress were skilled professionals, and their system was detailed, standardized, and represented the bibliographic state of the art. From the late 1960s, OCLC offered a similar service, printing cards for libraries on demand. But OCLC also offered another feature, exploiting the possibilities offered by MARC. The OCLC not only could send copies of individual cards to libraries, but it could sort those according to MARC fields providing drawers for author, title, and subject, for example, or for more rarefied categories such as shelf list or catalog number when requested.

The OCLC approach was both bibliocentric and economically clever. A preprinted OCLC card cost more than a similar Library of Congress card, but in addition to the advantages offered by the automatic sorting that it could perform, OCLC offered libraries a way of offsetting their costs. While a library would pay to purchase a card that was already in the OCLC database, when it discovered an item for which OCLC had no record, it could earn credit by creating a new master record for OCLC through a dedicated computer terminal obtained through the OCLC consortium. As Baker writes, "there was plenty of incentive for all libraries, engaged in the creation of a kind of virtual community long before there were such things as Usenet and listservs, to pump up the burgeoning database. What began mainly as a handy, unilateral way of delivering the Library of Congress MARC files to member libraries turned into a highly democratic, omnidirectional collaboration among hundreds of thousands of once isolated documentalists." When libraries began shifting from card catalogs to OPACs (Online Public Access Catalogs) from the late 1970s, the existing OCLC database provided the foundation.

For many libraries, then, the shift to online catalogs was both welcome and intuitive. While a library employing duplicate OCLC cards might hold card sets representing *several* MARC fields, a library employing a computerized catalog could sort records according to *any* MARC field down to the most obscure. Even so, there were difficulties. Some problems endemic to the OCLC approach even before OPAC were intensified by it. In the OCLC system, for example, the master record that governed what was on a given OCLC card was determined the *first* time that data was entered. If the first record contained an error, omission, or idiosyncrasy, it would be perpetuated in every catalog that employed that record. Additionally, OCLC lacked a good system of authority control, a major issue for any database. If one catalog used the name Mark Twain and another Samuel Clemens, an OPAC might end up with conflicting records or overlooking a work entirely. In general, OCLC was resistant to variation. If a Harvard card contained information that was either more detailed than what was in the OCLC record or particular to the Harvard Library, this information was at serious risk of being lost in translation. Even if OCLC's error rates were low, irreplaceable information was always at risk, and along with it, aspects of the unique scholarly history embodied in every library.

By the time that Google Books started up, many of these concerns seemed comparatively minor. After all, the digital retroconversion of card catalogs was meant to preserve and enhance their traditional functionalities, and the path from MARC to OCLC to OPAC was conducted within the institutional framework of libraries. Something very different was happening in Google Books. From the beginning, as Brin and Page stated, their system was meant to work in a way distinct from catalog-type search. Google Books would itself have no catalog. Not even an accession list. So there was no simple way to even determine what books Google Books contained. And when Google absorbed the textual content of libraries, it did not do the same for their indexing systems. Rather, it expected readers entering its corpus to rely on the same kind of search tools that it applied to the web more generally.

Consistent with the big data ethos that governed its search strategies, in Google's digitization projects, quality mattered, but quantity mattered more. Thus, the difficulties Baker pointed to in the digital retroconversion of library catalogs in the 1980s and 1990s were amplified in the digitization of the books enumerated therein. A digitized book, whatever its virtues, simply was not the same variety of object as a printed book or manuscript; having multiple copies of one digital scan was not the same as having multiple books; and the convenience offered by remote access was often paid for by an inferior product.

The result of all this—though it became more difficult to perceive as libraries themselves increasingly relied on electronic tools—was a search experience unlike what libraries had until then provided. Without question, Google's search was powerful and the advantages many, particularly when, to use Nunberg's words, one's purpose was only to "find a chunk of a book that answers our needs." In such cases, a Google-type search offered a means to enter books "sideways." But this was very often at the expense of knowing exactly what it was that one was entering, why one ended up there, or where that there was. Was a searcher looking at a first edition, a revised edition, an extract, a compilation, a plagiarism, a parody? These sorts of questions were of particular importance for scholars, but, in fact, they were issues for every reader, and, in an age of widespread digitally generated *disinformation*, all the more so. In traditional libraries, the curation provided by librarians and the metadata provided by catalogs served these ends, even if most readers never noticed. In the framework of Google Books, these services were absent.

At all events, by the second decade of the twenty-first century, as readers relied increasingly on the web as principal source of information, algorithmic search displaced structured approaches to search to a great extent. Unlike the pinakes of Callimachus, versions of the old library catalogs—or at least their digital shadows—remained available through libraries, but the seamlessness of the delivery of textual content in Google, the great extent of its reach, and its integration into the ubiquitous environment of search increasingly made the web a likely first stop, and for the same reason, often also a last stop in information search in the world of books.

What Wendy Hui Kyong Chun called the "conflation of memory and storage" also presented new problems for the history of information. As digital media increasingly supplanted analog media, and as the web increasingly connected to everything around it, old archival mechanisms faced new threats. Digital media became obsolescent quickly, and the graveyard of *dead media grew crowded as paper punch cards were replaced by magnetic tapes and tapes by magnetic disks and these by optical disks and these by solid state memory and this by cloud storage and so on. Archives in the digital era began requiring that donors provide, along with digitally stored materials, the computer equipment necessary to read them; and this was often not enough, as old computer systems themselves often failed when they could not be virtualized or emulated on a newer system. Ironically, many archives began asking for paper versions of anything delivered digitally. Only decades into the digital era, foundational works of interactive digital art were already disappearing into the ether. In the condition that Chun referred to as "the enduring ephemeral," curators debated how to preserve an experience of (now old) new media art without altering it substantially.

Even bigger problems of preservation were presented by the link graph of the web and by the interactive structures of web search. Organizations such as the Internet Archive and rhizome.org made efforts to address the first of these challenges. Recognizing that the web had no self-archiving function, the Internet Archive set out to take snapshots of it every day and to make these available through what it called the Wayback Machine, allowing users not only to view individual stored pages but also to *surf* a stored version of the web on a given date in the past. Rhizome.org, focusing on the problem of viewing art rather than information, provided a tool for viewing the web through vir- tualized historical *web browsers* going all the way back to Marc Andreesen's *NCSA Mosaic*, first issued in 1993. The second problem, that of archiving search itself, proved less tractable. While the Internet Archive could make available the websites that Google or AskJeeves or another search engine might in the past have recommended as well as the links among them, it could not emulate the generation of search results as such. For the early decades of the web, these results, crucial information artifacts in and of them- selves, proved as ephemeral as any expression of traditional oral culture had ever been.

This situation was of immense concern to activists such as the creators of the Long Now Foundation including the writer Stewart Brand and the computer engineer Danny Hillis. Brand writes,

> "Back when information was hard to copy," said Hillis, "people valued the copies and took care of them. Now, copies are so common as to be considered worthless, and very little attention is given to preserving them over the long term." He noted that thousands of years ago we recorded important matters on clay and stone that lasted thousands of years. Hundreds of years ago we used parchment that lasted hundreds of years. As a result, Hillis suggests, we are now in a period that may be a maddening blank to future historians—a Dark Age—because nearly all of our art, science, news, and other records are being created and stored on media that we know can't outlast even our own lifetimes.

To achieve their goal of encouraging long-term, "generational" thinking, the Long Now Foundation produced a number of compelling artifacts including Hillis's Ten-Thousand- Year Clock, "the world's slowest supercomputer," and the Rosetta Disk, a durable three- inch nickel plate micro-etched with over one hundred thousand pages of culturally important texts readable under a microscope. In 2004, one Rosetta Disk was launched into space. Others have been readied to survive an information apocalypse here on Earth.

As Brin and Page noted in their 1998 paper, in the first years of the web, the princi- pal financial basis of search was advertising. A user searching the web with a major search engine would get results relevant to query terms along with advertisements the system determined to be relevant and that sponsors paid for through programs such as the AdWords auction that Google launched in 2000. As we have seen, this model had the great virtue of making search nominally free, but as Brin and Page argued at the time, it also produced incentives for "search engine bias" and "poor quality search re- sults." In part, Brin and Page suggested, the market would take care of these. Obvious examples of bias, such as "selling companies the right to be listed at the top of the search results for particular queries" were likely to cause "an uproar." However, products of "less blatant bias are likely to be tolerated by the market. For example, a search engine could add a small factor to search results from 'friendly' companies and subtract a factor from results from competitors. This type of bias is very difficult to detect but could still have a significant effect on the market." And studies of search, particularly in the e- commerce sector, bear out this hunch.

At the same time, as Brin and Page predicted, the market did a reasonably good job of clearing out search engines that provided obviously distorted results or that failed to adequately defend against spammers. Actually, the market did a reasonably good job of clearing out *everyone* except Google. Surviving search engines including Google promoted their results as objective and unbiased by human judgment. In fact, they found the principle of algorithmic neutrality so valuable that they were willing to defend it even in the face of strenuous public protest, as in 2004 when Google was criticized for allowing an anti-Semitic website to achieve a top ranking in response to the search query "Jew." But, as Tarleton Gillespie has argued, the implications of algorithmic neutrality are equivocal, and the fact that an algorithm is unsupervised does not mean that it is value-free. Some algorithmic values are explicit. As we have already seen, Google's algorithms are designed to promote search results of high quality and relevance and filter out or demote fraud and spam. In SafeSearch mode, Google's algorithm filters pornographic material. And there are large parts of the web including the so-called dark web that Google does not search at all. As Siva Vaidhyanathan has argued, Google has an important stake in making the web that its users experience as safe as possible. Users who trust Google and the web use both more. But "safe" and "trustworthy" are not the same as "complete," "enlightening," or "urgent."

The principle here is a general one: algorithms pick and choose by rule not by whim, but that does not mean that their selections lack character. When the algorithm is black boxed, that character becomes hard to determine and hard to critique. From time to time, one gets a view of just how particular a search engine's interpretations can be. In 2013, UN Women published a series of public service ads entitled "The Autocomplete Truth," to demonstrate how pervasive sexism remained in the world and in the world of information. Each ad from the United Nations group featured a photograph of a woman's face. Over her mouth was superimposed the image of a Google search box (along with the note "Actual Google search 9/3/13") and a partial query phrase including "Women shouldn't . . ."; "Women cannot . . ."; "Women should . . ."; and "Women need to . . ." Below each query was the list of suggestions made by Google's autocomplete feature. After "Women need to . . . ," for example, the list read, "be put in their place"; "know their place"; "be controlled"; "be disciplined." None of these suggestions represented the editorial views of the corporation, just as the anti-Semitic link that Google suggested in 2004 for the query "Jew" did not represent anti-Semitism on Google's part. At the same time, together they show that, depending on how it is tuned, a search engine may reflect and even amplify common prejudices and presuppositions.

On some points, Brin and Page's 1998 critique of the "mixed incentive" structure produced by the advertising revenue model proved durable, but after they wrote their paper, that model substantially gave way to a new approach centered on harvesting and analyzing data on user habits and preferences. This newer model in turn reinforced the incentive for search companies to offer still more products. Google's Gmail and Google Maps services, for example, collected data on individuals at a level of detail rivaling or exceeding that of social media services such as Facebook whose entire premise was user profiling. In the first decades of the twenty-first century, profiling of this kind enabled web search companies to offer increasingly personalized results. For consumers, this was convenient, and many welcomed it, authorizing web services to read and store great volumes of personal data such as location histories, calendars, and contact lists, in order to get better results. But as data on individuals became available from more and more sources, explicit permission to access any particular data stream diminished in importance. Predictive analytics became both more powerful and more intrusive as users increasingly engaged entities such as Google through portable and wearable technologies, AI assistants, and ubiquitous sensor technologies communicating through the internet of things.

In the era of personalization, search became increasingly bidirectional. As users searched the web, they accumulated data profiles that were themselves cross-referenced and searched. By 2018, the Google personalization algorithm, for example, considered more than two hundred factors or signals. And Google's approach in this regard was less extraordinary than exemplary. Still in 2018, how such data was assembled and shared remained mostly obscure and unregulated, despite some important legislative efforts, especially the robust General Data Protection Regulation of the European Union, which became enforceable that same year.

As these changes took place, public awareness came along only in fits and starts. Not long before, in 2011, German Green Party politician Malte Spitz could still make headlines in the German weekly newspaper *Die Zeit* (The time) by revealing that his cellular telephone provider, Deutsche Telekom, was automatically creating and storing records of his geolocation history. Within a short span of time, it became clear that Spitz's discovery only scratched the surface of what data was being captured, stored, and shared on a routine basis by commercial and government entities. In 2013, former US National Security Agency contractor Edward Snowden *leaked documents detailing the NSA's enormous arsenal of data collection instruments, as well as its powerful internal tools for searching that data.

And the revelations kept on coming. In 2018, a whistle-blower revealed how the political data mining firm Cambridge Analytica acquired the data it used to target individuals for messaging during the 2016 US presidential election campaign. The data came from a third party who had offered a seemingly innocuous quiz app on Facebook. More than 250,000 users signed up for the app and, in ticking off its EULA or end-user license agreement, intentionally or unintentionally provided the app permission to access much of their Facebook data, as well as that of more than eighty-seven million of their Facebook friends, even those who had not themselves signed up for the app.

Each of these cases provoked public outcry, and each highlighted just how much was still left to do to regulate the use of *personal data*. In most, no laws were broken. Lawsuits, such as the one filed by Spitz against Deutsche Telekom, and leaks such as Snowden's mostly served to shed light on the voracious appetite for data among large commercial and state actors. All this, as Matthew Jones has argued, reflected quickly changing attitudes toward data itself. As recently as 1996, the US National Security Agency identified the exploding volume of data that it had to handle as one of the top three problems it faced. About the same time, Microsoft research engineer Usama Fayyad framed the issue this way:

If I were to draw on a historical analogy of where we stand today with regards to digital information manipulation, navigation, and exploitation, I find myself thinking of Ancient Egypt. We can build large impressive structures. We have demonstrated abilities at the grandest of scales in being able to capture data and construct huge data warehouses. However, our ability to navigate the digital stores and truly make use of their contents, or to understand how they can be exploited effectively is still fairly primitive. A large data store today, in practice, is not very far from being a grand, write-only, data tomb.

Under the old information retrieval regime, too much data, and particularly too much miscellaneous data, only made the system more unwieldy. But, as Jones explains, in the regime of big data, the problem was reversed: in 2006, a top-secret memo circulated within the NSA opened with the words, "Volume is Our Friend."

Of course, none of this was entirely without precedent. In the twenty-first century, government surveillance was not new. In fact, the word *statistics* itself was coined originally to name the science of data analysis developed by the eighteenth-century bureaucratic state. And businesses, too, had long taken an interest in customer behavior and preferences. Beyond the scale of the data collection, what made these newer projects so striking was that now individuals were donating their data directly to the institutions that were surveilling them, and they were doing it incessantly. Indeed, in some cases, as for example, in genetic genealogy services such as 23andme.com and ancestry.com, individuals were paying to have their most immutable, personally identifiable data decoded and made searchable with few guarantees about its eventual use.

Beyond the question of privacy, personalization changed the way search itself functioned. It influenced the ranking of standard search results so that users in different locations and with different search histories saw different results for the same query. Different ads fired. News feeds featured different stories. Again, the convenience was real. A regular *New York Times* reader was more likely to be served a story from the *Times* than from the *Daily News*. A basketball fan was more likely to be served basketball stories than stories about hockey. But this development was widely criticized. The activist and critic Eli Pariser, for example, argued influentially that personalization tended to build walls between people, what he called filter bubbles, reinforcing prior experiences, preferences, and beliefs at the expense of surprise and learning on the one hand and of common culture on the other.

In some respects, search was always personal. The "literary closets" of Thomas Harrison and Vincent Placcius allowed scholars to assemble, preserve, and share textual finds. Bush's memex machine was meant to standardize and to automate the process. But the black-boxed personalization employed by the major web services operated differently, simultaneously centralizing the service of information and fragmenting—narrowcasting—its presentation in unprecedented ways. What one user saw as the result of search was different from what was seen by their neighbor. And as the Cambridge Analytica affair made clear, the accumulated effect of serving targeted information to targeted audiences could be substantial, not least in reinforcing, by providing common information to subgroups, the groupings that resulted in the differential service of information in the first place.

In the environment of big data, the importance of words, which had been the lifeblood of search technology, changed too. On the front end, users increasingly gained the ability to search using nonlinguistic representations including maps, images, and music, for example. Meanwhile, on the back end, search services such as Google acquired the ability to combine many different kinds of data with user queries. For entities such as Google, words were precious, yet they had always been proxies for something else, such as desires, behaviors, or identities. In this new environment, proxies were everywhere.

Search in the early twenty-first century differed importantly from search in preceding epochs. Pixels replaced paper. Data became big. Searchers themselves became the subject of search. Search was everywhere integrated into everything. Yet, somehow, the big transition from "looking something up" to "googling it" seemed to happen quite naturally. A long history of search helps us understand how a technology so world changing as Google could be so quickly and thoroughly assimilated into information culture and practice: in fact, Google was something that users had at least a millennium to prepare for. At the same time, this history helps clarify how great was the cultural change the modern search engine effected. While a search engine such as Google employed a format strongly reminiscent of the indexes that preceded it, implemented as it was, it enabled a style of reading so extensive and aleatory—so deeply rooted in the experience of the *index*—that even peak print did not foreshadow it. Ironically, in some ways, it produced an experience more similar to that of a medieval textualist such as Hugh of St-Cher than to that of a typical reader of the late twentieth century.

The history of information was always also the history of information search. This was no less true at the advent of the *codex book or of movable-type print than at that of the web. Like those earlier changes in the mediascape, the emergence of the web produced tensions between tradition and innovation. Old practices did not go away. Instead, web search contributed new tools to an existing repertoire including indexes, concordances, file systems, encyclopedias, and others, many of which were enhanced and extended through their implementation on the web. Nor was the era of Google the first in which designers of search systems sought alternatives to older hierarchical taxonomies. Hugh of St-Cher and Denis Diderot both aimed to flatten information hierarchies. Vincent Placcius and Vannevar Bush innovated techniques of navigating through text corpora by creative association rather than by categorical rule.

Yet, by the second decade of the twenty-first century, web search had become more than one kind of search among others; it had become the paradigm of search in general, even as search had integrated itself into nearly every aspect of daily life. The benefits were enormous. When you could hold up your smart phone, camera on, and layer a contextual search over the world before you, *reality*, the boosters said, was *augmented*. But the trade-offs were substantial too. Many of these were already suggested in Brin and Page's original charter for Google. There, they had argued for a transparent, accountable, not-for-profit search engine. There, they had argued for the application of principles deeply embedded in the traditions of humanistic scholarship. There, they had warned about the incentives that the market imposes on a search company driven by profit. Two decades into the twenty-first century, Brin and Page's 1998 paper had become both a telling artifact in the history of search and a promising launch point for future critique.

Daniel Rosenberg

See also algorithms; art of memory; books; cameras; cards; commodification; cybernetics/feedback; data; databases; digitization; documentary authority; excerpting/commonplacing; files; globalization; indexing; information, disinformation, misinformation; information policy; knowledge; libraries and catalogs; lists; media; networks; quantification; reference books; storage and search; surveilling

FURTHER READING

Ann Blair, *Too Much to Know: Managing Scholarly Information before the Modern Age*, 2010; Sergey Brin and Lawrence Page, "The Anatomy of a Large-Scale Hypertextual Web Search Engine," in *Computer Networks and ISDN Systems* 30, nos. 1–7 (April 1, 1998): 107–17; Vannevar Bush, "As We May Think," *Atlantic Monthly* 176, no. 1 (July 1945): 101–8; Wendy Hui Kyong Chun, *Updating to Remain the Same: Habitual New Media*, 2016; Robert Darnton, *The Case for Books: Past, Present, and Future*, 2009; Tarleton Gillespie, "The Relevance of Algorithms," in *Media Technologies: Essays on Communication, Materiality, and Society*, edited by Tarleton Gillespie, Pablo J. Boczkowski, and Kirsten A. Foot, 2014; Anthony Grafton, *The Footnote: A Curious History*, 1999; Tung-Hui Hu, *A Prehistory of the Cloud*, 2015; Matthew Jones, "Querying the Archive: Data Mining from Apriori to PageRank," in *Science in the Archives: Pasts, Presents, Futures*, edited by Lorraine Daston, 2017: 311–28; Hans Peter Luhn, *H. P. Luhn, Pioneer of Information Science: Selected Writings*, edited by Claire K. Schulz, 1968; Theodor Holm Nelson, *Computer Lib / Dream Machines*, 1974; Eli Pariser, *The Filter Bubble: How the New Personalized Internet Is Changing What We Read and How We Think*, 2011; Frank Pasquale, *The Black Box Society*, 2015; Daniel Rosenberg, "An Archive of Words," in *Science in the Archives: Pasts, Presents, Futures*, edited by Lorraine Daston, 2017, 271–310; idem, "An Eighteenth-Century Time Machine: The Encyclopedia of Denis Diderot," in *Postmodernism and the Enlightenment*, edited by Daniel Gordon, 2001, 45–66; Trebor Scholz, *Uberworked and Underpaid: How Workers Are Disrupting the Digital Economy*, 2017; Nanna Bonde Thylstrup, *The Politics of Mass Digitization*, 2019; Siva Vaidhyanathan, *The Googlization of Everything (and Why We Should Worry)*, 2012.

PART TWO

ACCOUNTING

All major civilizations have had versions of some form of storehouse and, consequently, single-entry accounting that measured asset holdings or cash income and expenditures. Mesopotamian accounts provide the earliest form of writing to measure bread storehouse inventory. However, the advent of double-entry *bookkeeping, a method that endures to this day, in medieval Tuscany transformed accounting into the central tool for managing financial information.

The double-entry system balances the recording of transactions of debits and of credits and the calculation of their sum, equaling profit or loss. Debits are kept in the left-hand column and credits in the right. Since a debit in one account offsets a credit in another, the sum of all debits must equal the sum of all credits, following the underlying precept that Liabilities + Equity = Assets. That is: accounts showing a net credit (positive) are classified in the asset section of the balance sheet, while accounts that total a net debit (negative) are shown in the liability section.

Double-entry accounting has, remarkably, remained stable since its inception, though concepts such as pure business profit and depreciation became standard only in the eighteenth and nineteenth centuries. The methods involved in double-entry accounting evolved from a business practice into a method for the large-scale management and archiving of financial data for government administration, or public finance. Indeed, double-entry accounting would become a vital foundation to both modern science and modern industry. At the same time, effective accounting was predicated on a certain level of transparency and flourished where cultures of auditing were more prevalent.

In *The Machiavellian Moment: Florentine Political Thought and the Atlantic Republic Tradition* (1975), J.G.A. Pocock proposed that a tradition of republican government spanned from *Renaissance Florence to the early United States. Pocock argued that Machiavelli's idea that one must run government with the idea of maintaining civil peace and constitutional stability and continuity (*vivere civile*) was the basis of a long tradition of relatively free commercial societies. They enjoyed a rule of law that, in turn, allowed the maintenance of commercial credit through stability and trust from Florence and Venice to Holland, Great Britain, and the United States.

While this political paradigm has been disputed, it provides a remarkable road map for understanding the history of double-entry accounting. As a historically minded, systematic mode of financial management, it was born in the traditions of Florentine and Venetian Renaissance republicanism and flourished only where public checks and balances existed both in government and in business. Legal constitutions provided a mechanism for citizens to hold governments accountable and relied on the right to call for audits of financial records of states and companies, which is where the very term and concept of "accountability" derives. They also relied on the "artifice" of commercial finance.

Though historians cannot pinpoint who, exactly, invented double-entry accounting, it first emerged in Tuscany, where it was used by medieval bankers and leading international merchants who had access to Roman numerals, which allowed the calculation of condensed large sums with fractions. Advanced commercial cultures with multipartner, long-distance trading firms were key in creating the need for a mathematical measure for profit and equity in real time. As goods left the storehouse, double-entry accounting could measure that as a loss, while awaiting confirmation of income from sale. Only the balancing of debits and credits could guarantee that the action of both sending goods out and receiving income from them could be tallied.

The first systematic double-entry ledgers come from the Rinieri Fini brothers' firm (1296), which traded in fairs across Europe, and the Farolfi merchant house (1299–1300), which traded between Florence and Provence. Rather than a simple ledger, the Farolfi archive exposes something extraordinarily modern: a system of books designed to compute business transactions and holdings in real time. Cross-referencing of debits and credits shows that they were indeed offsetting each other. Moreover, the Farolfi ledger records prepaid rent as a deferred expense, thus conceptualizing it in the manner of double-entry accounting.

Even Italian city-states, such as Genoa, employed double-entry accounting for public finance. The famed 1340 Genoese state pepper account gives a sense of how important complex accounting and balance sheets were to city management: the book is filled with rules, such as double signatures to close each account, and material guarantees of authenticity (such as special paper and strings) so that the republic's public financial records and their bilateral matching totals could be audited, verified, and trusted. The *res publica* was represented by the verifiable and relatively public accounts books of its finances. If the balance and profit of an account book showed business and managerial acumen, it was also a moral reckoning. By the sixteenth century, *Jesuits would develop formalized "spiritual account books" to balance sins and good acts.

As double-entry accounting became central to the republican systems in medieval and Renaissance Italy, it also became prone to fraud. The Medici bank's collapse in 1479 was due in part to Lorenzo the Magnificent's poor accounting and public financial management. Practical, financial mathematics had its detractors. In particular, nobles did not always respect the mercantile ethos of accounting. The Neoplatonist Pico della Mirandola's *Oration on the Dignity of Man* (1486) was a great manifesto of high Renaissance, princely values of knowledge. For Pico, numbers had to remain pure, beyond the earthly interests of business. One should not confuse "divine arithmetic," he warned, "with the arithmetic of merchants."

This problem plagued the Dominican friar and mathematician Luca Pacioli (1445–1517). Often depicted as the inventor of double-entry accounting, Pacioli actually innovated by describing in print techniques previously transmitted in manuscripts by abacus masters. His manual of the relevant techniques formed part of his *Summa de Arithmetica, Geometria, Proportioni, et Proportionalita* (Treatise on arithmetic, geometry, proportion, and proportionality), which appeared in 1494, the same year the invasions of Italy began, which disrupted regimes and brought French and Spanish monarchical power to the peninsula. Double-entry accounting had existed for around two hundred years. And yet only at that point, as the rule of the Renaissance Italian merchants waned, were its rules printed.

Pacioli's book had no great success, and his chapter on accounting, "De computis," was not very original and still equated household and business expenses in one account. Still, it would become the basis for a tradition of works on accounting. Its message echoed the values of Italian mercantile republicanism and mirrored the common manuscript accounting manuals. Merchants who mastered the techniques of bookkeeping could count, calculate, and manage "abundance" and "war," "famine" and "pestilence," which appeared as headings in the books. Republics, Pacioli stated, needed well-educated, disciplined, and moral merchants, who could manage financial information and manage private and public finance. He insisted that a good merchant kept clear books that could be easily audited by city officials. The identity of all handwriting used in them, for example, must be verified by notes or personal presentation to officials. However, he also explained how to approach accounting when dealing with tax or excise officials. The good order of financial books was the very essence of the wealth and stability of republics. While recognizing that accounting could pose certain problems—it was always possible to keep two sets of books—Pacioli hoped that early training, based on strict religious ideas, would produce a form of accounting that was both ordered and moral.

Pacioli's printed guide offered the merchant the basic and essential tool of capitalism: the capacity to calculate and record his assets and liabilities at all times. Indeed, Pacioli's manual was a lesson not only in accounting, but also in data management and archiving. The first step in good accounting was to make an inventory. This was the capital holding from which debits and credits were made. Books had to be regularly updated, measuring spending, income, and other liabilities as related to capital holding.

To make the system work, four books were necessary: the inventory of assets; the memorandum (*Memoriale*); the journal (*Giornale*); and the ledger (*Quaderno*). The memorandum was the first step in good accounting, a notebook in which a merchant wrote down or pasted receipts from the day's transactions, "hour by hour," detailing "everything he sells or buys." Its pages had to be numbered and marked for clarity and to avoid any suspicion of falsification. The memorandum was necessary not just for real-time recording of information, but also for recording all the different monetary transactions that could take place in a number of different currencies. They would have to be converted into a single currency value. At the end of each day, the notes in the memorandum had to be systematically transferred into the journal as debits and credits.

The journal is a chronological record that gives all pertinent information for each transaction, noting the dates, agents, merchandise, and currency. All would be noted under *per* (for) to be debited, or *avere* (to have) to be credited. These chronological debits and credits would then be transferred to the ledger. Each time a transaction was transferred to the ledger, a letter (A, B, or C) was written to mark where the transaction could be found in the corresponding book. Then a red line was drawn through the transaction to show that credit had been transferred, and a second red line when it was balanced with a corresponding debit. Ledgers were to be systematically organized under headings such as "Ginger," or specific business ventures.

Pacioli's *Summa* went through only two editions, one of which he probably paid for. The spread of double-entry accounting followed a mercantile and then a republican trajectory as Dutch accounting masters translated Pacioli and other manuscript and printed Italian works on accounting. The Flemish merchant Yan Ympyn de Christoffels (1485–1540) first partially translated Pacioli in the *Niewe Instructie ende beweijs der looffelijcker consten des Rekenboeks* (New manual and proof for the valuable arts of accounting) (Antwerp, 1543). It and other Dutch manuals became the primary conduit of the double-entry method into Dutch, German, French, and English.

Flemish and Dutch municipal accounting schools proliferated, often alongside the prestigious and more formal universities, though erudite scholars and educators like Isaac Beeckman, principal of the influential Dordrecht Latin School, also had detailed knowledge of accounting practices. Influential mathematicians like Valantijn Mennher (1521–71), Claes Pietersz (Nicolaus Petri), and Simon Stevin maintained the republican tradition of combining the teaching of formal mathematics with merchant bookkeeping, which was seen to be the "finishing touch" on a good education and an essential management practice for commerce, politics, and everyday life.

Trust developed from civic financial *literacy, and precise management was one reason the Dutch were able to create the first publicly traded company, the Dutch East India Company (Vereenigde Oostindische Compagnie or VOC), and the Amsterdam stock exchange, both in 1602. Dutch investors were comfortable asking for a "reeckening," or "shauw," literally to see the books, and could read them when they did. Thus political and even corporate accountability was part of a material process of accounting. Flemish and Dutch painters from Quentin Matsys (1466–1530) to Marinus van Reymerswaele (1490–1546) produced major paintings depicting the practice of double-entry accounting, with all the relevant books and papers. In some cases, such as van Reymerswaele's *Two Tax Gatherers* (1540), Dutch painters both celebrated double-entry accounting's complex paperwork and warned against abusing it with financial hubris. Such technically fine paintings reveal a striking level of cultural expertise and care. As Pieter de la Court (1618–85) would rightly note, the Dutch Republic excelled in private and public financial accounting, while absolute monarchies in Spain and France failed again and again not only to implement ambitious accounting within their states—in spite of the massive efforts of Louis XIV's accountant-turned-minister Jean-Baptiste Colbert—but also to make it a widespread public practice. Still, though they surpassed other entities of their time, in practice both the VOC and the Dutch Republic would, nonetheless, struggle with maintaining accurate double-entry accounting.

Louis XIV's famous minister Jean-Baptiste Colbert (in office 1661–83) used the systems and forms of accounting archives to create the massive French archival and library complexes. However, it was impossible to maintain high accounting standards and practices for public financial management in an absolute monarchy that had no concept of public audits or transparency. In spite of Colbert's efforts to apply and circulate accounting literacy, the French government and many leading commercial entities struggled, as did such entities under other absolute monarchies. At the same time, Colbert used accounting methods of archiving and documentary organization for his famous library projects, injecting a mercantile, *encyclopedic ethos into the organization and categorization of books.

Following the Pocockian trajectory of political and commercial artifice, it was via the British commercial emulation of Dutch accounting that the method continued flourishing. Indeed, the powerful movement of Baconian science and practical mercantile methods helped propagate accounting in British merchant and governmental culture. Skilled in double-entry accounting, Francis Bacon pioneered the idea that looking into nature and its management via science and commerce was part of the Godly act of researching God's presence through observation. Keeping balanced accounts was part of this process. Thomas Hobbes, who served as Bacon's amanuensis and worked in his youth collecting receipt books, saw the keeping of account books as a tool not just for management, but also for thinking about politics. In his *Leviathan* (1651), Hobbes used the metaphor of accounting not only in questions of self-control, but also in his very definition of reason. He ascribed the birth of logical reasoning to accounting and its processes of formal reasoning. He wrote in *Leviathan*, "REASON in this sense, is nothing but Reckoning (that is Adding and Subtracting) of the Consequences of Generall names agreed upon, for the *marking* and *signifying* of our thoughts" (5, 18, 31). The connection of accounting culture and politics started in earnest in England with the old Commissions of Accounts from 1644 and the 1660s led by William Prynne. There followed a significant demand for good accounting and transparent accountability within the English state. While ethical management was a challenge, governments from Walpole to Pitt used high-quality double-entry techniques for government administration, and on a limited scale, balance sheets came to represent political management. English political life was full of accounts both within the government, in parliamentary debate, and within the nascent financial press, which comprised, in great part, the publication of accounts.

The British world was permeated with accounting literacy and consciousness. British Puritans and Dissenters saw the writing of diaries and autobiographies as a way first to measure good works and sin, and ultimately, to record and celebrate economic success. The Presbyterian Daniel Defoe included descriptions of bookkeeping in *Robinson Crusoe* (1719), a fictional autobiography in which Defoe—who had written expert accounting manuals and was a prolific financial critic—had Crusoe account for himself, as the Jesuits had, "like Debtor and Creditor," trying to balance the positive and negative moral prospects of his life once stranded on a deserted island. The impact of accounting was palpable throughout most European polities and in the administration of their colonies. Slave traders and plantation managers also relied on advanced bookkeeping.

In 1740, eleven accounting academies were active in Britain. By the end of the eighteenth century, there were more than two hundred. John Rule's Islington Academy claimed to form the "gentleman, scholar, and the man of business." Some heads of academies were self-made men, while at least nine were well-known scientists or members of the Royal Society. A backbone of the Industrial Revolution, these academies mixed scientific, experimental training with practical merchant arts.

The development of complex cost accounting in the mid-eighteenth century in Britain led to the idea of breaking economic or industrial processes into measurable units and pricing them. Although rudimentary forms of cost accounting had existed since the Middle Ages, the inventor of its modern, labor-oriented form was the pottery industrialist Josiah Wedgwood. He scoured every element of economic data in his accounts in order to create efficiency in industrial production. By evaluating time, space, materials, and labor, cost accounting changed Western society. Workers would not simply follow Benjamin Franklin's adage that time is money; they would carry clocks and hurry. Indeed Adam Smith, professor and accountant of the University of Glasgow, used cost accounting to develop his theory of the division of labor in his 1776 *Wealth of Nations*.

Following Defoe, in 1781 the utilitarian philosopher Jeremy Bentham tried to account for the "greatest happiness principle" with a "hedonic, felicific calculus," which was a double-entry method of valuing pleasure. Bentham called for an "account" of pleasure and pain. Thus the science of bookkeeping became a way of thinking about happiness and individual worth, and not simply sinful and virtuous acts. Even more, balanced books began to symbolize not only personal virtue but also political virtue. Accounting data played a major role in the apotheosis of commercial culture as balanced accounts and proven surpluses became the signs of modern good government. The Protestant director of finances in France, Jacques Necker, in his *Compte rendu* of 1781, held up a physical balance sheet of accounting data to represent his political "virtue." The early American republic would follow suit with a primitive balance sheet that year, and the Grand Duchy of Tuscany published perhaps the finest public balance sheet of the *early modern era, the *Rendiconto* of 1790.

Thomas Malthus used the analogy of a numerical balance in his *Essay on the Principle of Population* (1798). In a pessimistic parallel to Bentham, Malthus also believed in two sides balancing each other out. In a biological reckoning, human subsistence requirements and the fatalities of vice would oppose human population in a natural system of checks and balances by which "the superior power of population is repressed, and the actual population kept equal to the means of subsistence, by misery and vice." Malthus was not alone in seeing the very essence of life and death through the analogy of balanced books. In 1859, Charles Darwin—a reader of Malthus—wrote *On the Origin of Species*. The word *species* was also a medieval term for money. For Darwin, there was a link between the world of accounting and his categories and lists of species that showed the course of evolution and nature's fine but violent system. Darwin, it should be noted, was Josiah Wedgwood's grandson. When in 1873 Darwin was asked about his "Special Talents" Darwin answered, "None, except for business as evinced by keeping accounts, replying to correspondence, and investing money very well. Very methodical in my habits." But as novelists from Dickens to Joseph Conrad showed, the coldness of accounting data could lead to inhumanity, atrocity, and slavery. Financial order, as Taylorism illustrates, did not always equate with human felicity. Then as now, accounting was a powerful tool that, when mishandled, could cause catastrophe.

Yet what is most remarkable about the double-entry method is that it remains the finest measure and organization for financial analysis. Today, it has been replaced with a more complex modern system of financial accounting, but one that still rests on the same principle that revenue minus expenses equals net income, and that assets minus liabilities equal profit or net worth. What has changed over the past decades is that, as in so many spheres, the material books of accounting have mostly disappeared, replaced by *digital data. Today computer programs and forms permeate the process by which people collect, manipulate, and use financial information, perpetuating with new tools the search for balanced books that, on paper, changed the way Europe and great swathes of the world perceived themselves in the early modern period.

Jacob Soll

See also books; bureaucracy; governance; indexing; inventories; libraries and catalogs; lists; memos; notebooks; quantification; registers; scribes

FURTHER READING

Raymond De Roover, "The Development of Accounting Prior to Luca Pacioli According to the Account-Books of Medieval Merchants," in *Studies in the History of Accounting*, edited by A. C. Littleton and B. S. Yamey, 1956; Florence Edler de Roover, "Francesco Sassetti and the Downfall of the Medici Banking House," *Bulletin of the Business Historical Society* 17, no. 4 (October 1943): 65–80; Geoffrey A. Lee, "The Coming of Age of Double Entry: The Giovanni Farolfi Ledger of 1299–1300," *Accounting Historians Journal* 4, no. 2 (1977): 79–95; A. C. Littleton, *Accounting Evolution to 1900*, 1933; Neil McKendrick, "Josiah Wedgwood and Cost Accounting in the Industrial Revolution," *Economic History Review* 23, no. 1 (1970): 45–67; Edward Peragallo, *Origin and Evolution of Double Entry Bookkeeping: A Study of Italian Practice from the Fourteenth Century*, 1938; Gary John Previts and Barbara Dubis Merino, *A History of Accountancy in the United States*, 1998; Jacob Soll, *The Reckoning: Financial Accountability and the Rise and Fall of Nations*, 2014.

ALBUMS

Begin with an object: a book, kept by Althea Beatrice Moore, an African American student at the University of Iowa, from 1924 to 1928. The item's archival catalog entry describes it with various terms: scrapbook, address book, and autograph album. It bears the university's seal on its cover: an eagle grasping a laurel and a bow in its talons, an arrow in its beak; around the eagle, the university's name and founding date.

Page by page, this album presents a curated record of Moore's college experience. On preprinted forms friends signed their names, each with their address and a "toast." Moore listed athletic contests, "theatres and entertainments," and "social functions" on similar forms, which gave her space to record where and when the entertainment was, with whom she went, and a few notes about her experience. A concert put on by the Midnight Ramblers Jazz Orchestra was "wonderful. All the players really knew music and gave it to us. Men were sharp." Moore filled blue and black pages with photographs, programs, invitations, greeting cards, and newspaper clippings. One page is taken up by a collage: Madison Avenue phrases cut from magazine pages ("You can't beat it"; "For all needs"; "Delightful and so inexpensive"; and "The results will convince you") surround a magazine photo of an African American couple, clinched in a kiss.

In her album, Moore expresses and records herself. She mediates herself through paper forms, through the set expectations they communicate that college is a whirl of athletic games, social events, and friends. She grounds her identity in a formal institutional affiliation and in the social connections that blossomed in that context. One page in particular suggests how the album mediates the personal, the institutional, and the social: on the first of a series of photograph pages, Moore has constructed the figure of an "I" from six small portraits of herself and her friends. In Moore's "I," she and her friends are the building blocks of the "I" of her institution, the University of Iowa. *I have a place here. I am Iowa.*

As a material text, Althea Beatrice Moore's album expresses the tensions and creative possibilities that have defined the album as a *genre from the *Renaissance to the present in the West. Albums have long been used to communicate and reinforce social order, rank, and cultural expectations for what it means to be a literate, educated person. They have also been venues for the expression of individual and corporate identity. As a result, albums are prime sites for exploring how individual experience and self-fashioning happen with and against cultural norms and expectations.

In ancient Rome, an "album" was a white-painted wooden board (*albus* meaning white in Latin), posted outside official locations, such as the Roman Senate, to publish the official lists of senators. Edicts were officially published on alba. Here the official aspect of the album predominated: it was a tool for ordering and ranking society and communicating the dictates of power.

In sixteenth-century Europe, German-speaking students, among others, revived the album as the *album amicorum*, or album of friends. It took *codex form, with written, drawn, printed, and collaged elements. These books—in which individuals (usually men) collected signatures, drawings, scraps of verse, printed woodcuts cut out and personalized with coats of arms and other marks of personal identity—were popular with students, travelers, scholars, and physicians. Alba amicorum began as makeshift affairs, but soon press professionals got in on the game. Binders neatly interleaved emblem books with blank pages for album entries, and *publishers, such as the Frankfurt bookseller Sigmund Feyerabend (1528–91), printed books with purpose-made woodcuts and forms for including all the requisite marks of personal esteem and association. Artists produced drawings and watercolor paintings for bespoke albums. The "album verse" became a byword for canned couplets.

Like Moore's album, the album amicorum displayed the self—a person's journey through life, collecting associates and experiences. It was a semipublic record, in that album keepers expected associates to peruse the book and note the company they would enter in signing. It reflected and reinforced the distribution of power in society, as individuals signed the book in an order that reflected social status (kings in the front, artisans at the back) and signers perused each other's books for clues to their relative places in the world. It was a memory device, to be returned to in later life to muse over past friendships and travels.

In the eighteenth and nineteenth centuries, the album gathered women as keepers and contributors. Articles in nineteenth-century general-interest and women's magazines recommend the keeping, care, and decoration of friendship albums, and, by the end of the century, photograph albums. In the 1820s, the *Saturday Evening Post* printed album verses, with themes of death, friendship, the contrast between one's outer gaiety and inner sadness, and the swift passage of youth. (A sample from 1825: "But ah! Just as its rich array / The opening bud display'd / Some rude hand snatch'd the flower away, / And left the Rose-bush, no more gay, / To droop its withering head.") Album keeping trended in and out of fashion: *Harper's Bazaar,* in 1883, lamented that the kids these days had abandoned it. The magazine urged readers to keep original, clever albums, rather than fall prey to the temptation to water the *Saturday Evening Post*'s rose bushes.

In the nineteenth century, albums were a natural site for preserving photographs, given the ways in which they had long captured memory and identity. Women tended their photograph albums as domestic furniture, encasing them in velvet slipcovers embroidered with their monogram. Albums available for purchase might be bound in fine, gilded leather, decorated with curlicues and clasps, with pages precut for round and square portraits. Both exterior and interior of the album displayed the keeper's place within an extended world of family, friends, and acquaintances. Such albums might, as Moore's does, incorporate text as memories, quotes, and lists of friends, as well as labels for the photographs. The boundary between "scrapbook" and "album" is fuzzy (witness the multiple archival tags applied to Moore's book), but add social life's paper ephemera—dance and concert programs, menus, visiting cards, and magazine pages—and you have an album that could also be called a scrapbook, the making of which still tends to be the province of women. Through handwork and careful consumption of ready-made goods, wives, mothers, sisters, and daughters have long kept their families' memories and conserved and promoted their families' places in the world.

The word *album* continued to spread as a label for various media genres, often, but not always, retaining its list-like character, its sense of miscellany, and its connections with sentimental domesticity. Late nineteenth-century sheet music publishers sold collections of short, sweet musical vignettes, appropriate for gifting, such as the *Little Folks' Album of Music* (1882). In the early twentieth century, with the commercialization of recorded sound, record companies broke longer pieces of music (such as the movements of a symphony) across multiple records (each three to five minutes per side) and packaged them as a boxed collection, to be displayed on the shelf like a photograph album. Perhaps because these first music albums were coherent, longer works, the record album evolved as a less miscellaneous, more story-like genre in the mid-twentieth century, with some artists insisting that each album trace a narrative.

For many, memory keeping, and the performance of social identity that it entails, began shifting to the online realm in the 1990s, first through photo-sharing sites and then through social media platforms like Facebook, Instagram, and Twitter. These services unite the functions of the album amicorum and the photograph album: Facebook, famously, emerged from a university milieu, like Moore's album and the *early modern German album amicorum. The social network photograph album is a collaborative performance distributed across space and years, as relatives and friends see, share, and remember photographs of significant events in their lives: births, weddings, trips, deaths. The experience is organized and reorganized by the creators themselves and by the hosting company's programmers as they tweak how their algorithms display information.

As ever, albums oscillate between official, printed, or preprogrammed forms and an individuality achieved through personalization of those forms. In the digital era, tensions between originality and individuality and the prepackaged formulas of social expression (emojis, "like" buttons) are as deeply felt as they were in the early modern period. As albums have moved online, they have been shaped by tensions between privacy and publicity; permanence and evanescence; and corporate versus personal control of information. In the online realm, the relative publicity or privacy of one's comments, memories, and photos depends on decisions made by companies and governments to use, sell, and regulate personal data. Albums are seemingly everywhere, visual and textual records to be searched and recalled, many years hence. Yet albums are also nowhere, scrolling by, fragmenting, and disappearing, as successive technological waves barrel on, as governments and companies delete content, as users abandon outdated social networks.

Return for one last look at Althea Beatrice Moore's collegiate album. Though her photographic *I* opens the pages of snapshots, it is not the first page of the album. The printed frontispiece depicts vignettes from college life: a white man carries a briefcase, contemplates a letter, and plays football. A white woman casts her gaze down toward a shelf of textbooks. Moore did not tear this page out; she could have. But she did counterbalance this image with her own. Moore's album powerfully reminds us of the creativity and play in human identity making, and the ways in which the forms of social life channel, constrain, and distort that creativity.

Elizabeth Yale

See also art of memory; cameras; digitization; letters; platforms; public sphere; social media

FURTHER READING

Marisa Bass, *Insect Artifice*, 2019; Phyllis Culham, "Archives and Alternatives in Republican Rome," *Classical Philology* 84, no. 2 (1989): 100–115; Donell Holloway and Lelia Green, "Mediated Memory Making: The Virtual Family Photograph Album," *Communications* 42, no. 3 (2017): 351–68; Vera Keller, "Forms of Internationality: The Album Amicorum and the Popularity of John Owen (1564–1622)," in *Forms of Association: Making Publics in Early Modern Europe*, edited by Paul Yachnin and Marlene Eberhart (Amherst: University of Massachusetts Press, 2015), 220–34; Ilse O'Dell, "Jost Amman and the 'Album Amicorum' Drawings after Prints in Autograph Albums," *Print Quarterly* 9, no. 1 (1992): 31–36; June Schlueter, "Michael van Meer's *Album Amicorum*, with Illustrations of London, 1614–15," *Huntington Library Quarterly* 69, no. 2 (2006): 301–14; Althea Beatrice Moore Smith, Scrapbook, 1924–28, African-American Historical Museum and Cultural Center of Iowa and Iowa Digital Library (online).

ALGORITHMS

When was the last time you went a day without crossing paths with an algorithm? Run a search on Google or Baidu, or query Siri or Alexa, and you trigger algorithms that determine which information to feature, and in what order of priority. Visit Amazon, Alibaba, or eBay, and you're greeted with an algorithmically generated list of products you may be interested in buying. Popular news apps behave similarly, either surfacing or burying stories based on what algorithms have deemed relevant to you. Interested in watching a movie or television show? Hop on over to Netflix, where the company's algorithms have produced a list of content "recommended for you." Need a ride? Request an Uber, and in milliseconds an algorithm will process location, productivity, and ratings data to determine which driver to dispatch. Looking for love? The algorithms working behind the scenes at Tinder, Match, Grindr, and elsewhere have you covered. Tired of seeing Facebook posts from that errant cousin of yours? Algorithms have much to do with the frustration (and pleasure) you feel on social media.

In less than three decades, algorithms have become a ubiquitous part of daily life, affecting all manner of human affairs in ways that may be helpful, irritating, surprising, and, sometimes, even a little creepy. This is especially true of societies that have invested heavily in digital tools and accompanying infrastructure. Algorithms seem to be everywhere these days, helped along by the explosive growth of mobile devices, apps, and wearable technologies, all of which provide remote access to powerful, back-end computational systems.

Algorithms have become widespread in popular culture, too. Since the late 1990s, algorithms have become a favorite MacGuffin for scriptwriters, which is to say, a seemingly incidental plot device that nonetheless propels the narrative forward. On television, there are episodes and even whole series in which algorithms figure as such: *Numb3rs* (2005–10); *The Big Bang Theory* (2007–19); *The Good Wife* (2009–16); *Person of Interest* (2011–16); *Black Mirror* (2011–); *Halt and Catch Fire* (2014–17); *Blindspot* (2015–); *Mr. Robot* (2015–); *Billions* (2016–); *Silicon Valley* (2016–); and surely more. The same is true of popular film, in movies including *Office Space* (1999), *The Social Network* (2010), *Transformers: Age of Extinction* (2014), and *The Circle* (2017, based on the book published in 2013), among other notable examples. You know algorithms have gone mainstream when a family-friendly feature film like Disney's *Ralph Breaks the Internet* (2018) includes in its cast an algorithm named "Yesss," voiced by Academy Award nominee Taraji P. Henson.

If algorithms are everywhere now, then so too is what you might call an "algorithmic imagination." Ed Finn (2017) uses the phrase to describe how computational systems such as Google engage in a type of abstract thinking in predicting what you want to search for. Thus, he argues, the category "imagination" is no longer the exclusive provenance of human beings. Maybe so, but this usage misses a critical dimension of the phenomenon it sets out to identify: namely, instances in which ordinary people become aware of, and possibly self-reflexive about, their relationships to formalized, computationally based decision systems. Yesss, arbiter of trends on the fictitious website BuzzTube, is a prime example of this phenomenon, insofar as the character embodies a host of popular assumptions about how algorithms help to curate material online, and how, in doing so, they can affect one's reputation.

It may be tempting to describe this historical time period as "the age of algorithms," much as previous generations coined "the machine age," "the computer age," "the information age," and similar catchphrases to mark earlier technological and cultural turning points. Yet, to do so would be to overlook one critical fact: *algorithms are nothing new*. Physicians have been talking about and utilizing "diagnostic algorithms" since at least 1960, or almost forty years before Google was founded. The expression refers to formalized processes by means of which (human) doctors either confirm or rule out the presence of illness—processes that are in some sense programmed to ensure rigor, consistency, and efficiency. Some of these processes have even begun to be automated. Such is the case in the screening for cervical cancer in which, routinely, computer algorithms now determine the initial test results. Mammography may be soon to follow.

Similarly, one could make a case for how the algorithmic feats of Amazon, Facebook, Tinder, and company duplicate, in significant respects, those of human "cultural intermediaries." The term, coined by sociologists, refers to classes of knowledge workers whose job is to match cultural goods, broadly defined, to the tastes, needs, and desires of their clients. Examples include librarians; critics, both professional (e.g., literature scholars and film reviewers) and lay (e.g., booksellers and [erstwhile] video store clerks); matchmakers; news editors; retail buyers; museum curators; and more. At the risk of overgeneralizing, cultural intermediaries determine which goods to recommend and which to exclude by weighing a calculus of values against an awareness of their clients' interests. Their work may not be as systematic as that of their silicon counterparts; they also tend to address a smaller-scale clientele. Even so, doesn't Spotify essentially do what a perceptive DJ or record store clerk used to do, formally speaking?

Algorithms may be nothing qualitatively new, but, until recently, *algorithm* was a term belonging almost exclusively to mathematicians, engineers, and computer scientists. Today, ordinary people are trading in it too—so much so that it seems reasonable to suggest it is entering conventional usage. A search for the term in the Google Books database shows a substantial increase in the word since 1950. Not only are algorithms everywhere in digital culture; so, it seems, is the signifier *algorithm*.

A word's leap from one semantic context to another is rarely an innocent occurrence. When a term suddenly changes definition or assumes new meanings, or when it experiences a rapid expansion of its user base, it is often behaving along the lines of what the cultural studies scholar Raymond Williams in 1983 called a keyword. Typically, *keyword* denotes an important term that performs a representative function. The keywords of an academic article are supposed to stand in for, or point to, its major themes. While this definition is somewhat consistent with Williams's thinking, it is not exhaustive of it. Instead, keywords are terms whose semantic twists and turns betoken shifts in material and social reality and, thus, in our capacity to be and act in the world. An exemplary instance is the word *culture*, which, until about 1800, referred almost exclusively to the raising of plants and animals in agrarian settings.

Could it be that the word *algorithm* is undergoing a comparable shift today, or even perhaps that it is helping to usher in different modes of thinking about, conducting, and expressing ourselves?

If *algorithm* is on our collective minds and in our vocabulary to a newfound degree, and if indeed it is engaging in some deep existential work, then perhaps it makes sense to figure out what it means, more or less definitively. According to computer scientist John MacCormick (2012), an *algorithm* is "a precise recipe that specifies the exact sequence of steps required to solve a problem." Procedure figures prominently in this definition as do, implicitly, the values, objectives, and pathways that must be painstakingly prescribed—programmed, if you will—for an algorithm to work not only effectively, but efficiently. Little wonder that in addition to *recipe*, the metaphorics of *algorithm* often include words like *plans, instructions, flow charts, blueprints, tricks*, and *templates*. Collectively they emphasize form, and thus the extent to which apparently idiosyncratic choices and behaviors may in fact follow predictable patterns. They also provide insight into why algorithms have a tendency to serve up the same types of products, services, and ideas again and again, and to classify groups of people on the basis of racist, sexist, homophobic, classist, ageist, ableist, and other deplorable stereotypes.

The preceding definition of *algorithm* may provide some context for current dreams and anxieties about algorithms. But, like the word *culture*, *algorithm* did not always mean what it means today. It is better to approach prevailing understandings not as definitions but as temporary settlements, or articulations: that is, as semantic resting places carved out at this unique moment in history. This of course begs the question, where else has *algorithm* come to rest? And what, if any, older senses and meanings endure today as "traces without an inventory," as Antonio Gramsci (1971) stated in *The Prison Notebooks*? The question is not "what does the word *algorithm* mean?" but instead: "in what semantic and social history do you participate whenever you cross paths with an algorithm?"

Apropos, algorithm refers to a person: Abu Jafar Muḥammad ibn Mūsā al-Khwārizmī. He was a mathematician and astronomer of the ninth century CE who lived and worked for most of his professional life in Baghdad, then the capital of the Persian Empire. There he was a member of the *House of Wisdom, a think tank (to impose an anachronism) established by al-Mamun, caliph of Baghdad, to promote knowledge and learning and to assert the intellectual superiority of the Persian Empire. Algorithm is a name, moreover. I mean this not only in the simple, nominative sense but also in the sense of a "principle of authority" as captured in the ancient Greek root, *onoma*. It is to this sense of the word *name* that one appeals when one utters phrases such as, "stop in the name of the law." The authoritative sense of *algorithm* comes chiefly from an unattributed eleventh-century Latin translation of al-Khwārizmī's manuscript on arithmetic, which repeats the phrase "*dixit algorizmi*"—"algorithm said"—throughout. Significantly, this manuscript was the principal source through which both the word *algorithm* and its alternative spelling, *algorism*, wound their way into the English language. In other words, al-Khwārizmī was at intellectual ground zero of the "golden age of Islam" and, indeed, a critical player there. More to the point, algorithms may be established authorities both in and beyond the West today, yet they are not strictly of the West, historically speaking.

Thus, they bear witness to the complex and often troubling movement of people, goods, and ideas across the surfaces of this planet, and also then to the territorialization of the planet into distinct, albeit imagined and unequal, cities, empires, regions, and more. *Algorithm* isn't just a person, therefore, but also a place, in addition to a language associated with that place. To wit: though al-Khwārizmī worked in Baghdad, his family hailed from Khwarizm, now the modern-day city of Khiva, located on the border of present-day Uzbekistan and Turkmenistan, an area known for exquisite textiles. Although al-Khwārizmī wrote in Arabic, he or his ancestors were likely to have spoken Khwarizmian, a linguistic distant relative of modern Persian. The language would have indicated their belonging to an ethnic minority that was conquered by the Persian Empire in sometimes brutal acts of political and cultural repression. Algorithms, therefore, have long been implicated in the machinations of culture, power, and politics; that is their long-standing predicament. Observers of digital culture have only now rediscovered it.

Culture, yes, but also computation: *algorithm* additionally refers to a system of numeration. The aforementioned manuscript by al-Khwārizmī not only introduced the word *algorithm* into European *lexicons; it also was instrumental in popularizing the use of Indo-Arabic numerals. They were called, even into the early twentieth century, the "numbers of algorism." And here it is important to stress that although numerals may seem more or less given (2 is two, after all, right . . . ?), they are nonetheless specific tools for representing quantity. And, like any tool, they have their own affordances. Have you ever tried performing long division with Roman numerals? This is tantamount to saying that algorithms may be helpful in performing certain types of tasks, yet they also encourage path dependencies that make it difficult to imagine alternative ways of performing those tasks, or alternative outcomes.

Similarly, *algorithm* refers to technology, particularly to commercial technology. The first recorded instance of the word in the English language occurs in Chaucer's *Canterbury Tales* (1387–1400), specifically "The Miller's Tale," where the author refers, in Middle English, to "augrim [algorithm] stones." The reference is to a calculating device resembling an abacus or, more precisely, to one whose stones had been modified by etching Indo-Arabic numerals—the numbers of algorism—onto them. The resulting object embodied both dominant (manipulable) and emergent (symbolic) systems for calculating quantity, generally in commercial settings. In other words, Google, Netflix, and company were hardly the first to monetize algorithms. Chaucer, the great humanist author, happened upon the political economy of algorithms six centuries ago.

Despite their centuries-long public presence, algorithms—or rather, their inner workings—have tended to be shrouded in mystery. Protected as they often are today by intellectual property laws, users rarely know what "ingredients" make up the proverbial "secret sauce." One also hears from engineers and computer scientists about how the very algorithms they have created function in ways they do not fully comprehend. The mysteriousness has everything to do with the fact that *algorithm* also refers to a *code. Until the twentieth century the number zero was regularly referred to as "cypher in algorism," and it was al-Khwārizmī's manuscript on arithmetic that helped to introduce zero into Western systems of numeration. Previously, the idea of a numeral "signifying nothing" was apt to seem antithetical to the very concept of number, which denoted only positive quantity. Significant, too, is the manuscript's introduction of the concept of place value (1s, 10s, 100s, etc.) and the use of zero as a stand-in, or place-holder, in the event of a nonvaluation. This may be the basis for what Gillespie in 2016 identified as the "synecdochical" function of *algorithm*, in which algorithms become convenient proxies for an otherwise opaque network of actors and actions.

Lastly, *algorithm* refers to the giving of order. Another manuscript for which al-Khwārizmī is known helped to popularize the principles of *al-jabr*, or algebra, also translated as the "art of reckoning," or of "restoration and balancing." The book set out to proceduralize mathematics, laying out a series of rules by means of which to discover the value of unknowns—placeholders, like algebra's ever-present *x*—in all manner of problems. As the word *algebra* diffused into Moorish Spain, it coalesced into the word *algebrista*, now an archaic form of the word for orthopedist, or bonesetter. The metaphor is an apt one, for the purpose of al-Khwārizmī's algebra was to cull all the pieces of a disjointed system and set them aright according to predefined rules. This proceduralism, however, is also why some observers considered algebra to be a lesser form of mathematics. The philosopher Edmund Husserl dismissed it as "a mere art of achieving results according to technical rules," a view that carries over into critical accounts of contemporary algorithmic culture and its tendency to encourage filter bubbles.

What to take away from all these latent and manifest meanings of *algorithm*? First, an algorithm is a *topos* or enunciative ground from which to produce authoritative statements about the world. Paradoxically, an algorithm is both a principle of authority and that which grounds the principle itself. Similarly, algorithms are both placeholders for some unknown aspect of reality and the procedures by means of which to fabricate the missing aspect. All this circularity may get at why Gillespie in 2016 referred to algorithms as "talismans"—objects of the human world that appear to be endowed with magical capacities, as if beyond our control. But lest we conclude that we live in a world in which algorithms now perform their work autonomously: the figure of al-Khwārizmī is a startling reminder of the raced, classed, gendered, colonized, and sexualized human bodies that subsist, persist, and insist in every algorithm and in every query. Much the same might be said of the etchings on Chaucer's augrim stones, which epitomize humanity's imprint on algorithmic tools—and, indeed, the imprint they have left on us, in the form of an algorithmic imagination.

If *algorithm* is a keyword, its status as such hinges on the latter insight—namely, on a popular awareness of the degree to which code and computational decision making now orient human affairs. Its status also hinges on our bearing witness to the ways in which long-standing human repertoires are, today, overlaid with and mediated by technical infrastructure. The larger point is to appreciate both the functional and the semantic proximity human beings have shared with algorithms for more than a millennium; it is also to accept that we are hardly the first generation to inhabit an "algorithmic culture." Algorithms may be programs for solving problems, but they are better imagined, in the abstract, as sociotechnical assemblages—temporally and culturally unique entanglements of people and technology that are nonetheless historically freighted.

Ted Striphas

See also bureaucracy; computers; data; databases; encrypting/decrypting; information, disinformation, misinformation; programming; quantification; social media; surveilling

FURTHER READING

Corona Brezina, *Al-Khwarizmi*, 2005; John Cheney-Lippold, *We Are Data*, 2017; Ed Finn, *What Algorithms Want*, 2017; Tarleton Gillespie, "Algorithm," in *Digital Keywords*, edited by Benjamin Peters, 2016; John MacCormick, *Nine Algorithms That Changed the Future*, 2012; Safiya Umoja Noble, *Algorithms of Oppression*, 2018; Cathy O'Neil, *Weapons of Math Destruction*, 2016; Frank Pasquale, *The Black Box Society*, 2015.

APPRAISING

Browsing the *internet, we are collectors of search results. We appraise and discard our findings on a rolling basis; we download and store only very few of them. We let search machines do much of the categorizing and arranging for us. Through the internet, we have access to information concerning all kinds of general knowledge. In the past by contrast, *encyclopedias, libraries, scientific collections, and museums had a role in shaping how people—scholars and citizens, children and adults—accessed general knowledge. These collections presented their own forms of categorization and organization, and they put forward modes of comparison and appraisal that helped establish in that context what was valuable, beautiful, right, and morally acceptable, and what was not. When the English traveler and collector of curiosities John Evelyn (1620–1706) visited the Venetian island of Murano in Italy in 1645, he wrote in his diary that it was "famous for the best glasses in the world, where having viewed their furnaces, and seen their work, I made a collection of divers curiosities and glasses, which I sent for England by long sea. It is the white flints they have from Pavia, which they pound and sift exceedingly small, and mix with ashes made of a seaweed brought out of Syria, and a white sand, that causes this manufacture to excel." Evelyn valued the use of rare and very specified materials together with the makers' craftsmanship, an assessment that brought him not only to marvel at the artisans' work, but also to buy a number of samples for his own collection. Collectors such as Evelyn followed their own version of the categories and rules of appraisal when they purchased texts and rearranged, erased, or put into storage what was not desired at that moment.

Throughout history, humans have appraised and discarded not only objects, but also information, including knowledge that affects the appraisal of objects. Terms, technologies, and conditions for the activity of appraising have changed. Starting with terms: *appraise* was what official valuers or appraisers did, a meaning captured by the *Oxford English Dictionary* as early as 1424, the act of assigning a price for a good. In this capacity, appraisers are roaming the world still today. For example, Alison Gay at the US company EquiAppraisal is described by her client G.S. as "a must for anyone in need of a certified equine appraiser." While Gay would set the monetary value of a horse according to market research and analysis, based on the median price of transactions at the horse's location, other appraisers would value a horse long before the market value kicks in. The horse breeding associations put forward a catalog of criteria to set the standards of a breed, making it possible to estimate whether a foal will prove to be a good jumper or dressage athlete. The association of Hanoverian horses in Germany revises its goals for breeding Hanoverian horses every year, but it always centers them on exterior appearances—specific to a breed owing to its evolution—and performance. It and other breeding associations use statistical methods to determine the genetic influence of animals on their offspring. Several times a year, the Hanoverian breeding association organizes important auctions of Hanoverian horses in the German town of

Verden near Hannover, where the best of Hanoverian breeds (according to those criteria) are auctioned off. The auction prices that are realized then contribute to setting the market value of the horses. A goal of appraisals is to set standards within a community of buyers and sellers.

Technologies and methods for professional appraising have changed over time. What today is a projecting science based on statistics did not use scientific methods in earlier times. A study of 335 probate inventories written for the small town of Thame in Oxfordshire in the seventeenth century invites comparisons. The inventories, made after the death of the proprietor, recorded the possessions of the deceased and their values. They represented an official record but were not written by officials or *notaries, as elsewhere in Europe. Amateurs, such as family, friends, and neighbors, prepared these inventories and organized them differently from one another. An account of the estate appraiser Andrew Parslow in the second half of the seventeenth century shows that he developed and popularized a new method to deal with ever increasing numbers of household goods. Instead of recording items individually, and room by room, as had been the custom, he summarized items by type and assigned them a common value. Other appraisers in Thame followed this use at the end of the seventeenth and beginning of the eighteenth century. The new format left individual values of single objects more obscure than before, while emphasizing the overall material wealth of the family; it also speeded up the process of reaching the desired estimate. But the evaluation did not document how the value of objects was calculated.

Taken in its general form as judging or estimating value, other methods of appraisal were practiced during the *early modern and modern period that were imprecise and not formulaic, such as the development of categorizations or topical lists in natural philosophy (see the entry "lists" in this volume) or acts of religious self-appraisal. Various religious denominations called on their constituents to use accounting and diaries to estimate and attest to their own moral weight in front of God and in preparation for the last judgment, or, as the Quakers did, to progressively dissolve the self and reveal the presence of God in daily events. The journal of George Fox (1626–91), the founder and religious leader of the Society of Friends, as the Quakers call themselves, is typical of many early Quakers' narratives of journeys and sufferings as it displays "a sense of a divine plan emerging from apparently arbitrary events" that transcends the account of many all-to-human occurrences.

Cultural change had an impact on the dynamics of appraisals and led to reappraisals. Following the reception of object *taxonomies over a number of generations illustrates how cultures have changed their value systems. In a case study about the significance of the category "monsters" for late medieval and early modern European beliefs, Lorraine Daston and Katharine Park focus on three types of appraisal that changed in relevance over the years: monsters were objects of horror, as they represented divine portents of future doom; monsters were entertaining, as they were objects of spectacle and an artful manifestation of the playfulness of nature; and monsters were repugnant, as they infringed the standards of order and decency set by society and the university disciplines. All three interpretations developed in parallel to each other, but their emphases shifted. A stress in the sixteenth century on religious horror shifted in the eighteenth century toward one on the violation of cultural standards. This emotional turn from wonder to repugnance occurred in anatomical and natural philosophical accounts of monsters, in late seventeenth-century aesthetics, where monsters chiefly violated taste, and found its way into encyclopedias for the wider public.

Individual appraisals are informed by cultural patterns of choice and preference. In the 1960s and 1970s, the sociologist Pierre Bourdieu researched modern aesthetic judgment (interlaced with morals and beliefs), what we call in short "taste." In his book *Distinction: A Social Critique of the Judgement of Taste"* (1979, English translation 1986), he maps out the results of two large surveys conducted in 1963 and 1967–68 in France on a sample of 1,217 people. He examined the preferences of his contemporaries, organized by professional groups. His questionnaire included twenty-five questions on tastes in interior decoration, clothing, singers, cooking, reading, cinema, painting, music, photography, radio, pastimes, and more. Question 10 about choices in food asked: "When you have guests for a meal, what kind of meals do you prefer to serve: simple but well presented; delicate and exquisite; plentiful and good; pot-luck; appetizing and economical; original and exotic; traditional French cuisine; other (specify)." Bourdieu claimed to be able to match certain cultural preferences to individual professional groups, and to their home background and formal education. In his category of food, items such as charcuterie, pork, pot-au-feu, and bread would represent food materials that manual workers would prepare and eat, with the value grid salty-fatty-heavy-strong-simmered and cheap-nourishing, while the dominant middle class would rather settle on beef, fish, and fruit as delicate, lean, refined, and light nourishment that didn't take long to prepare. He concludes that "to the socially recognized hierarchy of the arts, and within each of them, of genres, schools or periods, corresponds a social hierarchy of the consumers." Bourdieu's theory that taste is firmly linked to class, education, and upbringing encourages us to view appraisals historically, as constructions that change through time and across cultures, though this was not Bourdieu's primary purpose.

Scrutinizing the Scottish delicacy "offal" and its ingredients over a period of time and through cookbooks for different social groups, Jeremy Strong has criticized Bourdieu's approach, suggesting how his theory could be reformulated as an explicit historical analysis of cultural taste. Offal is an ingredient that forms part of the Scottish heritage dish haggis and refers collectively to the edible parts that are cut off in preparing the carcass of an animal for food, mainly internal organs and entrails. Clearly, Bourdieu would have located this ingredient on the "manual workers'" side of his roster, among the "salty-fatty-heavy-strong-simmered and cheap-nourishing" meals. However, around the year 2000, offal had a revival among British and American diners who made up a subgroup of increasingly discriminating consumers belonging to the wealthy middle class. This subgroup was interested in knowing and preparing the food they ate. Strong interpreted this relocation in the register of Bourdieu's social distinction "as a consequence of . . . [the offal's] appropriation and re-presentation by influential tastemakers." Bourdieu had not anticipated a fluidity of his terms of difference.

The place of information in past and present cultures and societies is shaped by practices such as appraising. To give value to an object or belief is an elementary form of appraising as a cultural practice. Every person individually who expresses taste builds and rebuilds implicit taxonomies of preferences and dependencies. The individual agent not only codefines interdependent cultures of society; he or she also uses this roster as an important directive for the order and interpretation information to receive and transmit. Appraising methods and practices interact with and filter the information we get and give.

Anja-Silvia Goeing

See also book sales catalogs; censorship; encrypting/decrypting; indexing; inventories; knowledge; learning; lists; media

FURTHER READING

Pierre Bourdieu, *Distinction: A Social Critique of the Judgement of Taste*, 1979, translated by Richard Nice, 1986; Lorraine Daston and Katharine Park, "Monsters, a Case Study," in *Wonders and the Order of Nature, 1150–1750*, 2001, 173–214; John Evelyn, *The Diary of John Evelyn*, edited by William Bray, vol. 1, 1901; German Hanoverian Association, Auctions, https://en.hannoveraner.com/verden-auction/collection-of-the-135th-elite-auction/; Hilary Hinds, *George Fox and Early Quaker Culture*, 2012, 82–99; G. Riello, "'Things Seen and Unseen': The Material Culture of Early Modern Inventories and Their Representation of Domestic Interiors," in *Early Modern Things: Objects and Their Histories, 1500–1800*, edited by P. Findlen, 2013, 125–50; Donald Spaeth, "'Orderly Made': Re-appraising Household Inventories in Seventeenth-Century England," *Social History* 41, no. 4 (2016): 417–35; Jeremy Strong, "The Modern Offal Eaters," *Gastronomica* 6, no. 2 (2006): 30–39.

ARCHAEOLOGICAL DECIPHERMENT

To think about archaeological decipherment is to leave behind many of the assumptions now current in the *humanities, such as: context determines meaning; form is an aesthetic category detached from reality; all interpretation is subjective; the text means whatever readers through history want it to mean; interpretation is a free play with no consequences. A document in an unknown script cannot be read for content or context: these may be guessed at (and in practice often are, repeatedly) but not assumed. The reading of an unidentified script can proceed in only one way: a formal methodology that captures statistical properties of recurrent elements of the corpus, leading to attempted correlations with the properties of known languages. Imagination, under these conditions, is usually a hindrance. The other side of this restricted mode of reading, confined to material features, is that interpretations can and must be tested against one another: there are better and worse answers to the question, *what does this text say?*, and in the end, perhaps, one and only one satisfactory answer. In decipherment it is not enough to say that the meaning of the text is what you make of it. The prospect of recovering lost archives and adding a new cultural province to the world's stock of memories sets a goal for the activity.

Because a decipherment, unlike an opinion, can be deeply and demonstrably wrong, the annals are populated by cautionary examples. Consider Athanasius Kircher, *Jesuit, professor at the Collegio Romano and one of the seventeenth century's most famous *polymaths. Primed by a *philosophia perennis* that treated earthly things as emblems and ciphers of celestial mysteries, Kircher saw in the hieroglyphic inscriptions covering the obelisks of Rome elaborate sermons in an allegorical mode: "Supramundane Osiris . . . flows down into the Osiris of the elemental world, Apis, beneficent Agathodemon, who distributes the power imparted by Osiris to all the members of the lower world," translated Kircher from an inscription that present-day Egyptologists read as saying "Horus, strong bull, beloved of Maat . . . king of Upper and Lower Egypt," and so forth. For Kircher, a hieroglyph was an image, and thereby a portent, an omen, a password, an initiation. Deciphering Egyptian writing required, first of all, putting oneself in the right frame of mind, and then calling up to memory the many esoteric Hellenistic texts that, for example, bestowed on the hippopotamus a moral character (bad) and saw promises of immortality in the outlines of the sun and moon. Knowledge of Coptic might smooth some edges. So inspired, one could ascend from the sensory images to a Platonic anamnesis of archetypes that brought the saving doctrines of Osiris once more to view.

A hundred and seventy years after Kircher's *Oedipus Aegyptiacus* (Egyptian Oedipus) the efforts of Thomas Young and Jean-François Champollion had opened the way to reading the hieroglyphics effectively. They had the advantage of a key—the *Rosetta Stone, discovered in 1792, which bore one and the same inscription in hieroglyphic, demotic, and Greek—and of a method that treated meaning not as the precondition for interpretation but as its delayed reward. Rather than starting from analogies and assumed commonalities (the picture of the sun depicting the source of light, therefore standing for the origin of all beings, therefore denoting Osiris, the pharaoh's celestial equivalent, and so forth), Young and Champollion sought to determine what value and function the graphs had in the different sentences where they occurred, allowing for the possibility that the writing system might use the same graph in several different capacities (as sign of an idea, as sound, as substitute for another sound, as silent classifier). Instead of beginning with the most exalted concepts of the Egyptian language (Osiris, the sun), they began with the transliteration of foreign names—a nearly nonconceptual use of the Egyptian characters. In the landscape of a language's semantics, proper names are already at the very edges of meaning; foreign names even more so; foreign names transcribed are practically nonsense. But it was the non-Egyptian names "Ptolemaios" and "Kleopatra," enclosed in cartouches to mark their pharaonic status, that opened the way to identifying the hieroglyphic signs that had been borrowed to write the sounds P, T, O, L, M, I, S, L, and A. From there it was only a short step to recognizing other names, including some of Egyptian origin: "Ramesis," "Thutmosis." From these beginnings, gradually the whole congeries of expedients that makes up the system of Egyptian writing came into view, with the range of "mimic," "tropic," and "phonetic" values that might variably be assigned to a character.

Admittedly, Egyptian hieroglyphic is a particularly complex writing system, which had a long history and a user base of professional scribes with no motive to reform it in the direction of simplicity. No one can say how long it would have taken to decode it without the Rosetta Stone's parallel inscriptions in two forms of the unknown language and one in a known language, Greek. But the means of Champollion's discovery are those common to all decipherments of unknown scripts. The underlying language, the principles of its writing system, the uniformity of the textual corpus—none of this could be assumed. Young and Champollion had to frame hypotheses and test them, discarding those that yielded nonsense (while allowing for the possibility that the standard for nonsense differs from one culture to another) and retaining those that made it possible to gain one more letter, one more name.

The methods are the same, that is, as those of cryptanalysts, with the circumstantial difference that the ancient scribes had no intention of disguising their meaning. Indeed many archaeological decipherers gained expertise in wartime cipher offices. Intentional *cryptography aims at leaving behind no trace of the regularities of the original language (the redundant formulas, the standard percentage of e's or k's, vestiges of syntax or accidence). The would-be *code breaker, in the words of a spy in the service of Louis XIV, "has no idea whether a certain sign stands for A or B or C or some other letter of the alphabet, whether it is a syllable or a word or perhaps a null sign; he hesitates everywhere, he doubts everything, and has nothing sure on which to fix his attention." The very purpose of code clerks in foreign ministries, spy agencies, and armed forces is to ensure that their writings will be unreadable to the unauthorized—a series of genuinely arbitrary signs. But writing at any length with no meaning or pattern at all seems to be beyond human capabilities.

Since Champollion, translation from so-called dead languages has claimed a series of successes: Babylonian, through names and royal titles preserved in the otherwise unrelated language of modern Persian; Akkadian, working through Old Persian and relying on the verbal tics of self-important monarchs; Hittite, using Akkadian letter equivalents and a grammar recovered through Indo-European analogs; Brahmī and Tokharian through bilingual inscriptions and analogies with known scripts. After holding out for centuries, Mayan glyphs were finally decoded, proceeding through the usual first steps: numbers, dates, regnal names, and astronomical data.

What David Kahn calls "the most elegant, the most coolly rational, the most satisfying, and withal the most surprising" of archaeological decipherments, that of Linear B script, took place in the years 1945–52 after many false starts. The first tablets containing Linear B inscriptions were brought to light by Arthur Evans in 1900. Evans's apparent reluctance to publish and two world wars delayed the appearance of significant numbers of Linear B texts from Knossos and Pylos until the early 1950s. No one could identify the language of the inscriptions, much less the structure of the writing. With little to go on, archaeologists experimented with solutions that involved analogies to Cypriot, Etruscan, even Basque. In 1952, building on work by Alice Kober, Michael Ventris published his solution, which has been received as definitive. Kober had recognized in the unknown graphs certain regularities that recalled the shape of words having a constant stem and varying case endings—a common word structure in Indo-European languages like Greek and Latin. Ventris, an architect, seems to have had the orderly mind and tolerance for detail required to document the behavior of each of eighty-seven signs, tabulating their co-occurrences and mutual exclusions. Phonetic equivalences were not yet in play; up until the publication of his solution Ventris had been skeptical of the suggestion by Kober and others that Linear B represented an earlier form of Greek. In discerning the organizing principles of the writing system, comparisons were useful, but only indirectly so. The large number of signs suggested a syllabary rather than an alphabet. Some pictograms and numerals had already been distinguished by E. L. Bennett. In addition to the sequences that stood in relation to one another recalling those of the inflected forms of a noun, there were apparent classifiers, marks that seemed most likely to preface a noun with a category such as "boy," "girl," "grain." But the classifiers appeared also in the middle of words, as one would not expect from mere labels. Reasoning from the apparent catalog style of the tablets (a *genre well represented in the Bronze Age eastern Mediterranean), Ventris took the hypothetical step of supposing that some of the inflected modifiers that headed lists of commodities might be place names, and he experimented with inserting a few nearby Greek localities. *A-mi-ni-so*, representing later Greek Amnisos, *Ko-no-so* for Knossos, and *Tu-li-so* for Tulissos were at least plausible readings for those sequences and suggested substituting equivalent sounds wherever the same graphs occurred in the corpus. Ventris soon produced six or eight recognizable Greek words from the marks on the clay, and that was the turning of the corner. Phonetic equivalents for nearly all the remaining graphs followed, and by June 1952 it could be declared that Linear B was Greek and legible.

The elegance of Ventris's solution is partly a product of its unusual history. Until the very end Ventris was not persuaded that the language of Linear B was Greek, and so his initial hypotheses were not jiggered to favor Greek (consciously or subconsciously). Analogies with other scripts were called in only rarely and with reservations. Ventris circulated his working notes among the ten or twenty researchers who had attempted to crack Linear B, whose assumptions varied greatly. Well before attempting to read words, regularities of a minimally semantic kind (numbers, evidence of inflection, categories appearing from layout) were amassed, until finally it was possible to begin ascending the "chimney" (as rock climbers might call it) of the place names and thence to attempt reconstructing nouns and verbs.

A bit of linguistics jargon has found its way into anthropology—the difference between "etic" and "emic" description. An "etic" description of behavior, say the organization of an annual temple feast in Taiwan, supplies an account of what goes on from the perspective of an outsider, perhaps a Dutch missionary with an inherited set of definitions (what is a ritual, what is devotion, what are favors, why do people attend festivals, and so on). An "emic" description, by contrast, attempts to clarify and explain what is going on in the terms available to the participants. (The linguistic analogy is to the difference between phonetics, which situates the sounds of a language on a putatively universal grid like the International Phonetic Alphabet, and phonemics, where every sound is charted in its relations of analogy and opposition to other sounds within the same language.) The project of decipherers like Ventris can be said to be quite literally "emic": one must draw up the inventory of units first and then catalog their combinations and other ways of behaving. Supposing no language had been found that corresponded to Linear B, and thus no sound or meaning equivalents been assigned to its "words," a complete description of the distribution of the signs in the spirit of Zellig Harris would nonetheless have been possible; and with some scripts it may be that that is as far as knowledge can go. The leap from forms to meanings may always be desired—in most eyes it is the definition of successful decipherment—but it is not always to be had.

Upon decipherment, mute signs begin to speak. We can overhear ancient scribes committing to writing the matters that they or their rulers thought were important: lists of commodities, tax rolls, tribute, kingly titles, and eventually dates, proclamations, laws, and treaties. The general message is, as Shelley put it while the Egyptian writings were still unreadable: "My name is Ozymandias, King of Kings! / Look on my works, ye Mighty, and despair!" Not every civilization writes down its myths, poems, epics, tales, fables, philosophies, and jokes. The great majority of recovered ancient writings consists of receipts, inventories, law contracts, and business letters; the *Epic of Gilgamesh* is the rare exception, preserved by a school curriculum that maintained it in the *canon of three successive languages. For recovering the daily life of ancient societies these dry records nonetheless have their poetry.

Haun Saussy

See also accounting; archivists; art of memory; bureaucracy; diplomats/spies; encrypting/decrypting; inscriptions; landscapes and cities; translating

FURTHER READING

John Chadwick, *The Decipherment of Linear B*, 1963; Jean-François Champollion, *Grammaire égyptienne* [Egyptian grammar], 1836–41; idem, *Lettre à Monsieur Dacier* [Letter to Monsieur Dacier], 1822; Michael D. Coe and Mark L. Van Stone, *Reading the Maya Glyphs*, 2005; J. P. Devos and H. Seligman, eds., *L'Art de deschiffrer* [The art of deciphering], 1967; Zellig S. Harris, "Distributional Structure," *Word* 10, nos. 2–3 (1954): 146–62; David Kahn, *The Codebreakers: The Story of Secret Writing*, 1967; Daniel Stolzenberg, *Egyptian Oedipus*, 2013.

ARCHIVISTS

Among the key developments that shaped the history of information in premodern Europe was the growing presence and visibility of an ever-widening group of self-designated information specialists claiming to have exceptional skills and expertise concerning the production, management, and processing of information. By developing a growing body of mental habits, social practices, and working skills; and by reflecting on these practices, by making them explicit, and by promoting them actively, often in a competitive and conflict-ridden way, these partisan information specialists structured and drove the impact of information on European history. In a way, information specialists were enthusiastic prophets of a self-fulfilling prophecy: they advocated what they were doing best, that is, caring for and working with information.

Information specialists came and come in many stripes and colors, some claiming to be specialists in information "in itself" (e.g., information scientists), others more narrowly focused on particular media forms that are assumed to carry information. Of particular importance among the latter are the many professionals dealing with written information: a particularly prominent subgroup are those carrying out specialized work in the archives, often simply subsumed under the label *archivist*. For conceptual clarity, it is helpful to distinguish between "archival workers" (i.e., people doing archival work) and "designated 'archivists.'" In premodern Europe, the two were by no means coextensive, and even in the twenty-first century by no means all archival work is done by officially designated archivists. Thus, the term *archivist* as used in the following paragraphs is generally understood loosely, including, but by no means limited to, officially designated "archivists."

Often, the role of archivists has been described in a paradoxical way: On the one hand, their presence is considered of utmost importance. Without adequate personnel, so the well-rehearsed trope goes, no archive can ever function properly. On the other hand, the archivist's presence in the archive should be almost invisible. "Personal judgment" should be totally avoided, according to Hilary Jenkinson, the most important Anglophone archival theorist in the early twentieth century (as quoted by Elizabeth Shephard). It is only more recently and in the wake of important theoretical work by Michel Foucault and Jacques Derrida that this idea has been fundamentally challenged, not least by scholars working in a postcolonial framework. Contrary to Jenkinson's notion, most scholars would now insist that the archive actually was a prime arena for different actors to enact their "personal judgments" or social agendas. Approaching the history of archives and record keeping via a closer look at archivists will thus highlight the close connection that archives had to surrounding social, political, and cultural developments.

While archival practices have been part of human history for many millennia, specialized archivists make an appearance in European sources only relatively late in that long history. Initially, certain individuals probably simply acquired increasing familiarity with governmental repositories in connection with other administrative duties. Among various secretaries or counselors, for instance, one person may eventually have assumed the role of de facto archival expert because he had developed a habit of working in and caring for certain documents. This, it seems, was initially the case with Thierry Gherbode in Flanders (ca. 1350–1421) before he became formally employed as archivist in 1399. Only gradually did such activities become more formalized, but from the fourteenth and fifteenth centuries onward, the sources do mention with growing frequency that certain men were employed by princes and other owners of documents as "guardians of records" (*garde des chartes*) (e.g., Flanders, 1399) or "archivist" (*archivarius*) (e.g., Sicily, 1401). The emergence of such language is important, since it shows that the management of written documentation came to be seen as a set of specialized tasks. At least ideally, caring for records became an office in its own right, separated and potentially independent from other governmental functions.

But we should not overestimate such early archivists' professionalism. It is important to look beyond the words and study the actual practices of archival work. "Archivist" had become an official title, but by no means did that mean that de facto archival work was carried out only by these officeholders. Quite to the contrary, many so-called archivists worked in the archive only part-time, and a wide variety of other jobs could be combined with the functions of an archivist. Some, such as Adrian vander Ee (d. 1464) in Flanders, combined active (and, in his case, effective) archival work with diplomatic service. Others worked primarily as counselors or secretaries. In such arrangements, the archival duties were not always of primary importance, and the title of archivist was often nothing but a lucrative sinecure. In Switzerland well into the nineteenth century, most state archivists worked in the archives only part-time, often combining their record-keeping duties with other governmental charges. We could characterize this development by saying that in these (more and more frequent) cases political work acquired an (albeit often only modest) archival dimension.

On the other hand, much archival work was (and still is) often taken over by people who were not called archivists. Scribes, secretaries, and other men working in princely and urban chancelleries carried out much archival work. Many smaller and medium-sized archives had, for most of their history, no dedicated personnel caring for them. Consider the parish archives, increasingly organized after the Council of Trent (1545–63): these important caches of documents generally remained under the care of parish priests with little or no previous expertise in record keeping. Entire areas of record keeping became professionalized only in the very recent past. Throughout economic history, for instance, private businesses—even if they held enormous amounts of records, as did the Datini, Fugger, or Welser firms—rarely employed dedicated specialists that could be meaningfully called archivists, yet their papers were often well cared for by people also charged with other tasks. In the private sphere of the family, women sometimes acted as archivists. Recent research has highlighted the role of wives and mothers in family accounting and account keeping as well as in the preservation, management, and transmission of the household papers. Well-known is the case of Lady Anne Clifford in Stuart England, who in her diaries displays significant interest in and mastery of her family's papers. Similarly, in the case of scholarly families, often the widows took care of the papers of their late husbands.

It would thus be wrong to link the rise of archival practices in Europe exclusively to the emergence of a distinctive social class of dedicated specialists. And yet, there can be no doubt that the keeping and managing of records increasingly became a specialized task and eventually a proper profession. Several early and effective archivists are now well known to scholars, including Gérard de Montaigu in Paris (d. 1391), Diego Ayala in Spain (1512?–94), and Carlo Cartari in Rome (1614–97). Certainly their number was growing, their professionalism deepening, and their impact on the wider archival culture increasing. As more and more men were hired as archivists, their employment documents and instructions started to show a coherent, if idealized picture of the perfect archivist. The growing body of theoretical works on archives since the sixteenth century, which usually included at least a few paragraphs on archival personnel, helped to establish this image. By the end of the sixteenth century, the profession of archivist (together with its twin, the librarian) was well on its way to acquiring a distinctive profile. The ideal archivist was a man of honorable birth, dedicated and steadfast, trustworthy, and morally upright. Loyalty to his employer was his most important quality, and most official instructions contained stern admonitions not to divulge any governmental or dynastic secrets that the archivist might have learned while working in the archive. All instructions typically insist that this obligation to keep the arcana secret held for life ("bis in die Gruben," into the grave, as the formula usually went), even in the case that the archivist should change employment.

These depictions of an ideal archivist were primarily moral in nature or focused on character traits but had little or nothing to say about technical capabilities, except for the very basic and mostly tacit assumption that every archivist should be able to read and write. That the Dukes of Württemberg in 1550 explicitly asked for knowledge of two languages (Latin and French) in addition to German was already an unusually specific request. Even the particularly elaborate description of the ideal archivist that Jakob von Ramingen gave in 1571 in the first (printed) monograph on archives contains almost nothing on technical expertise—his most specific point was simply that the archivist should "know about the law and politics." With no clearly defined skill set for archivists conceptualized, no professional education for archivists could be institutionalized. Proper training institutions with academic standards of teaching emerged only in the nineteenth century in Paris, Vienna, Munich, and Marburg. France is an interesting example here. In 1821, King Louis XVIII founded the École Nationale des Chartes, today the major training center for archivists and librarians in France. Almost immediately the idea came up that the graduates of the École could (and should) staff the regional archives (*archives départementales*) created during the French Revolution. Yet it took until 1850 for that idea to become law (decree of February 4), and it took still further decades for the well-trained *chartistes* to actually take over regional and local archives. The establishment of these new cadres often went hand in hand with significant conflicts between exponents of older traditions of archival work and the newer, more academic and "scientific" archivists. Local pride, local customs, and local power arrangements could be significant barriers against the imposition of a coordinated archival workforce by the central government.

While explicit standards of education may have been lacking before the second half of the nineteenth century, many archival specialists prior to that time were nevertheless knowledgeable and experienced. Significant bodies of experiential knowledge accumulated and circulated among those working in archives. Families played an important part in the transmission of archival expertise. Fathers and uncles bequeathed their knowledge to sons or nephews. It is best to understand premodern archival training as a sort of apprenticeship: prospective archivists acquired familiarity with record keeping by observing experienced specialists, either while working in closely related administrative offices like chancelleries or by becoming adjuncts to senior archivists. Even today, while academic archival training is the high road to becoming an archivist, many countries still offer additional, more practice-oriented types of archival education, for instance through formal apprenticeships or internships.

Archivists were confronted with two major types of tasks. The archivist's first responsibility was "to keep and conserve writings" (*onus detinendi et conservandi scripturas*) (Sicily, 1436). Archivists also had to create and maintain order in the archive. This meant, first and foremost, ordering the records in some meaningful way and creating reliable finding aids. In many employment contracts, the cataloging of documents and the creation of inventories were named as primary tasks. The ordering of knowledge implied significant *epistemic decisions: According to what structure should archivists sort the records? How should they (re)arrange them—in alphabetical order, in geographical, or in topical order? What categories should they use to divide the mass of documents into more manageable portions? How were they to create meaningful shelf marks?

In addition, ordering the archive implied a wide range of bodily labors. Archivists had to clean the rooms where the records were kept, control the physical arrangements of the storage facilities, and check on the material condition of the records themselves. Archivists carried piles of papers and *parchments, climbed ladders, chased rodents, and fought against the elements, sometimes quite literally, for instance when saving the precious materials from fire, water, or wind. To achieve their goals, archivists also had to work manually with individual documents. They had to glue and pierce documents, and they sewed them together, hung them on strings, or carefully placed them in boxes, envelopes, or folders. To do this, archivists relied on many utensils; today, they may rely on punchers, staplers, and, of course, computers for their work. Not least, the archivists of today use shredders, for they are responsible for deciding what documents are to be destroyed (in quantitative terms, more than 95 percent of all records produced today will never enter an archive). Organizing archives also meant looking beyond one's own repository to understand its place in the bureaucratic structure. Archivists were key actors in governmental attempts to consolidate and centralize documentation. Traditionally, ministers or secretaries had kept in their private possession most of the papers they had worked with. During the *early modern period, this habit was increasingly seen as problematic, and archivists were more often charged with bringing such dispersed materials under government control. Inversely, archivists had to keep track of all documents checked out of the archive. Usually, they would keep specialized notebooks or registers for that purpose.

For most of European archival history, there were few instructions on what such an archival organization should look like. Employers in most cases often simply trusted the expert experience of their new employee. All that was specified was the hope that thanks to the good work of the archivists, the records could be better and more efficiently used in the future. This was an idea that became more and more important. With bureaucratic forms of government on the rise and with the administrative function of archives accordingly ever more explicitly expressed, the responsibility to feed records into decision-making processes became a second dimension of the archivists' job description. They would search for and transport to councillors the relevant documents needed for decision making. In some cases, archivists actually sat in on the deliberations, allowing them to be dispatched to the archives more easily. Occasionally, this went beyond simply providing decision makers with requested documentation. Archivists could be called on to produce position papers summarizing what could be learned from archived documentation about specific areas of policy. We could characterize this development by saying that not infrequently archival work acquired a political and administrative dimension.

Also, archival work increasingly acquired a scholarly dimension. *Renaissance archivists such as Augustin Kölner in Munich (ca. 1470–1548) were regularly members of humanist circles. Like librarians (though perhaps to a lesser extent), archivists became, in the words of the historian Mario Rosa, "mediators in the *Republic of Letters." They provided scholars with documents and, in more than one case, combined their work in the archive with scholarly investigations of their own, often leading to prominent publications. In the nineteenth century, the "historian-archivist" became dominant. The two professions of historian and archivist were both rapidly professionalizing and intimately connected. Individuals moved easily back and forth between the two careers. Friedrich Meinecke (1862–1954), for instance, who became one of the most influential German historians of the first half of the twentieth century, had initially trained as an archivist. One wonders if and how this amalgamation of archival and historical thinking shaped subsequent developments of historiography. The ideal of the scholarly archivist, while never universally shared, remained prominent and widespread until well after World War II. In later decades, however, an alternative and much more restricted vision emerged under the label of "records management," of a more technical and managerial approach to archival work. In most Western countries, this led to sharp debates about job ideals (in German: *Berufsbilddebatte*) among archivists and, along similar lines, also among librarians.

Who were the archivists, and where did they come from in social terms? By and large, it seems, the social recruitment of archivists follows the broader patterns of other *literacy-dependent professions. Initially, clerics played a significant role, and even today, the major part of the Catholic Church's archives are headed, at least nominally, by clerics. Well into the nineteenth century, priests such as Andreas Baumgartner (Chur) or Leonard Ennen (Cologne) could also occasionally be found leading important secular repositories. By and large, however, clerical influence quickly waned, beginning in the fifteenth century. Archivists came to be seen as important cogs in the machinery of bureaucracy, making administrative experience and familiarity with the law important criteria for recruitment. This meant that a growing percentage of archivists was university trained. According to Ottnad, in sixteenth-century Württemberg, for instance, of fourteen archivists, eleven had attended university, of whom six had studied the law, a percentage that only increased over the next centuries (in the eighteenth century, seventeen out of nineteen had studied law). Two other characteristics changed in Württemberg over these two centuries: the age of entry declined significantly (from age 39 to 29.5), and the length of stay in the archive increased. Toward 1800, about 90 percent of the men stayed in the archive throughout their professional lives. By 1800, many examples to the contrary notwithstanding, being an archivist was thus on its way to becoming a proper profession that was chosen comparatively early in life and pursued for long periods. While many people working in European archives did come from lower strata of society, and while a few members of the (minor) nobility found pleasure in the archive, archival work attracted mostly members of the middle classes. Sons of pastors, doctors, and teachers, and especially sons of state employees abounded. And it was, most of the time, exclusively sons, since women entered into professional archival contexts only very late in this history. It is only around 1900, for instance, that a first wave of female archival experts became clearly visible in England. Only from the 1930s onward did women archivists such as Joan Wake or Ethel Stokes figure prominently in the British Records Association. In 1951, Ernst Posner spoke of a "large and increasing number of women members" of the Society of American Archivists. Five years later, one-third of its members were female. While setbacks and continuing gender imbalance should not be overlooked, it seems obvious that in the early twenty-first century the profession has significantly opened up toward women in the profession.

Markus Friedrich

See also bibliography; computers; documentary authority; information policy; learning; libraries and catalogs; scribes; secretaries; teaching

FURTHER READING

H. Bots and F. Waquet, eds., *Commercium litterarium, 1600–1750. Forms of Communication in the Republic of Letters*, 1994, 81–99; F. de Coussemaker, "Thierry Gherbode, premier garde des chartes de Flandre et secrétaire de ducs de Bourgogne Philippe le Hardi et Jean sans Peur, étude biographique," *Annales du Comité flamand de France* 26 (1901–02): 175–385; Filippo de Vivo, Andrea Guidi, and Alessandro Silvestri, eds., *Archivi e archivisti in Italia tra Medioevo ed età moderna*, 2015; Markus Friedrich, "Being an Archivist in Enlightened France: The Case of Pierre-Camille Le Moine (1723–1800)," *European History Quarterly* 46 (2016): 568–89; Olivier Guyotjeannin, "Un archiviste du XIVe siècle entre érudition et service du Prince: Les 'Notabilia' de Gérard de Montaigu," in *Histoires d'Archives: Recueil d'articles offert à Lucie Favier par ses collègues et amis*, 1997, 299–316; Wolfgang Leesch, *Die deutschen Archivare 1500–1945*, 2 vols., 1985–92; Bernd Ottnad, "Das Berufsbild des Archivars vom 16. Jahrhundert bis zur Gegenwart," in *Aus der Arbeit des Archivars: Festschrift für Eberhard Gönner*, edited by Gregor Richter, 1986, 1–22; Elizabeth Shepherd, "Pioneering Women Archivists in England: Ethel Stokes (1870–1944), Record Agent," *Archival Science* 17 (2017): 175–94.

ART OF MEMORY

In 1968, Alexander Lurija, a Russian neuropsychologist, published *The Mind of a Mnemonist: A Little Book about a Vast Memory*, which recounted—with scientific rigor and considerable narrative skill—a clinical case that he had studied. He discussed a man, Šereševskij, who from childhood was burdened by an excessive memory that prevented him from forgetting anything. When, in the 1930s, Šereševskij performed as a mnemonist, he put in place a series of techniques to discipline his memory. These techniques—associations, images giving visual form to words, the construction of a spatial route, that is, a succession of places in which images were gathered—are identical to those practiced by an age-old tradition that neither Lurija nor Šereševskij knew: the art of memory, also known as artificial or spatial memory. From ancient Greece until the *Renaissance, this tradition played an important role in European culture, transforming itself gradually through contact with diverse philosophical and scientific cultures, changes in the modes of communication, and the different needs to which it responded. At the same time—as Lurija's case shows us—the principles on which it rested seem to have some basis in how the brain works. After all, more recently anthropologists have shown that these techniques also exist in non-European cultures, although they manifest differently.

In this entry I trace not so much the different theories of memory and the treatises that taught how to develop it, but rather how mnemonics were used between the Middle Ages and the end of the sixteenth century as a means to make information that might otherwise be forgotten memorable. We must begin with the classical texts that were the foundations of the tradition. These were rhetorical texts, since the orator had to rely on a well-trained memory both in the phase of *inventio*—the creation of the discourse—and in that of *actio*—the recitation in public. Cicero's *De oratore* (On the orator) (II.86–88), the pseudo-Ciceronian *Rhetorica ad Herennium* (Rhetoric to Herennius) (III.16–24), and Quintilian's *De institutione oratoria* (On the training of the orator) (XI.2) (which also expresses doubts and reservations about traditional mnemonic practices) transmit the basic components of a technique that was developed in Greece and has its roots deep in oral society. The Aristotelian texts are also essential, especially *De anima* (On the soul) (III.3.427b–432a) and *De memoria et reminiscentia* (On memory and recollection) (451b–452a), which highlight the link between memory and imagination and describe the procedures underlying the associations that facilitate recollection: similarity, opposition, and contiguity. From the classical world onward, then, the art of memory taught not how to record memories, but how to transform them. Memory's riches thus became an extensive treasury for discovering more: from which to create new words, concepts, and images.

In addition to the rhetorical texts, we find medical ones. Avicenna in particular harmonized diverse traditions regarding the location of the soul's functions. In general, the function of memory was located in the lower part of the brain. These texts gave instructions about diet and therapies that could improve the physical conditions that sustain memory.

In the Christian world, the classical tradition was revived and transformed. The great Dominican writers Albertus Magnus and Thomas Aquinas commented on Aristotelian psychology and on the precepts of Cicero and of the *Rhetorica ad Herennium*. But the meaning of mnemonic techniques changed. They assumed a strong religious connotation: remembering the passion of Christ, one's own sins, the pains and joys of the afterlife, the articles of faith, and the most important prayers became an essential task that concerned the salvation or damnation of the soul. At the same time, the ancient techniques were combined with the practices of monastic meditation, which taught how to construct in the mind an ordered path that gradually produces an interior transformation and lifts one up to God. An extraordinary example of this is the *Divina Commedia* (*Divine Comedy*). Dante the pilgrim crosses Hell, Purgatory, and Paradise, meeting historical characters that are also *exempla* of all the sins and all the virtues. As he progresses, he purifies himself morally and grows in his knowledge of the order that governs the world. When he reaches the end of his journey through Paradise, he experiences the vision of the mystery of the Trinity, and at this point "memory yields to such excess" (*cede la memoria a tanto oltraggio*) (*Paradiso*, XXXIII, 57).

Before and after Dante, Dominican and Franciscan preachers used mnemonic techniques both to construct and recall their sermons, and to imprint them in the memory of a largely illiterate public. To this end, they employed the logical and rhetorical divisions of the subject in question, but also images from civic iconography. For example, St. Bernardino of Siena (1380–1444), a Franciscan preacher who enjoyed enormous success thanks also to his unconventional theatrical performances, connected the contents of his sermons in Siena to famous local images like the Annunciation by Simone Martini in the Duomo, or the frescos of Good and Bad Government by Ambrogio Lorenzetti in the Palazzo Pubblico. He gradually directed the gaze of his listeners and gave instructions for the use of images, in the sense that painters' images should be transformed into *imagines agentes* (acting images), images capable of recalling the moral teachings that the preacher associated with them (in the case of the Annunciation, how women should behave, in the case of Lorenzetti's frescos, how governors should secure peace). In this way, every time a member of the public saw these images, she or he would recall the teachings of St. Bernardino.

Many categories of people in addition to preachers practiced the art of memory in the fifteenth century: men of letters, doctors, ambassadors, students and professors engaged in university disputations, and, above all, jurists. There were also other reasons to employ the techniques of memory: contemporary treatises taught how to remember the cards already played in a card game, credits, debts, dates, and the names of creditors and debtors, and also how to remember the merchandise loaded on ships. Moreover, we also find these techniques in didactic practices, especially at the intersection between pedagogy and play that was so prominent in European culture between the fifteenth and seventeenth centuries. For example, in 1507, Thomas Murner, a Franciscan from Strasbourg, published the *Chartiludium logice seu logica poetica vel memorativa* (Logical card game or poetic and mnemonic logic) in which a game of cards teaches students to recall the *Summulae logicales* (Brief summaries of logic) of Peter of Spain, a thirteenth-century text still present in university curricula despite its outdated contents and its difficult and barbarous Latin. In 1518, Murner's *Chartiludium institute summarie* (Card game in brief) proposed the same method, though with different images, to facilitate the memorization of complex case law. This mnemonic use of playing cards was very durable: at the end of the seventeenth century, a great scholar, Francesco Bianchini, constructed illustrated books and playing cards in parallel to outline, condense, and make memorable universal history.

In the fifteenth and sixteenth centuries, mnemonic techniques were the object of criticism and satire on the part of men of letters and philosophers like Erasmus, Melanchthon, Agrippa, and Rabelais. The masters of memory were criticized for the useless tasks they inflicted on their pupils, for the purely passive and repetitive nature of their practices, and for their pretensions to transmit with great speed a knowledge that was based on words instead of matter. The diffusion of printing, moreover, helped to create a situation in which the art of memory seemed to lose its importance: the book, the dictionary, and the catalog provided modern readers with the basic tools to cultivate their own learning and to write new works. And yet, even in this moment of crisis and polemic, the art of memory found new life and enjoyed great prominence in European universities, courts, and printing presses.

Various components led to this apparently paradoxical state of affairs. On the one hand, printing was very well suited to interact with those currents of thought—as in the case of Petrus Ramus (1515–72)—that made memory a part of logic, linking memory to the problem of the method to be followed in research and in the transmission of knowledge. It became typical of Ramism to use diagrams and large tree structures in which the logical path taken could be visualized and its memorization and presentation were both made easier. The page of the printed book offered an ordered and reproducible space in which diagrams and large synoptic tables based on taxonomic division could be inserted. In this way, it was possible to render "knowledge visible," as the editorial project of the Accademia Veneziana della Fama (1558–61) proposed—a project entrusted to Paulus Manutius, heir and descendant of the famous printer Aldus Manutius.

There were also other important elements of the new sixteenth-century culture that worked well with the art of memory. The rebirth of arts and letters was often connected to the imitation of the ancients, in an effort to revive in new forms a world that was perceived to be the guardian of the secrets of beauty. In this context, imitating classical models became crucial. To imitate them (and to emulate and surpass them, perhaps) it was necessary to have them present in one's memory. Here the techniques of memory integrated traditional modes of reading and of memorizing texts and interacted with the new tools offered by the printed book, such as rhyming dictionaries, lists of sources, *commonplaces, and illustrations that translated the text into a gallery of images.

The art of memory also drew new strength from different philosophical and religious currents—such as Neoplatonism, hermeticism, and kabbalah—that exalted the powers of imagination and of the human mind. The techniques of memory were not only an aid to make up for the weaknesses of man, but a symbol of his almost divine potential. The memory theater of Giulio Camillo (ca. 1480–1544) is exemplary in this sense; it presents itself both as a kind of machine for literary memory, in that it offers the tools to remember and imitate model texts, and as a guide to attain the highest powers and knowledge of which the mind was capable. Camillo's theater in fact aims to reproduce the divine order that expresses itself on the different levels of reality. Camillo believed that the order uncovered was not arbitrary, but one that reproduced and made visible the very order of the cosmos. The structure is a type of grid, based on seven. At the base there are seven columns that represent the seven planets and the divinities that Greek mythology associated with them, the days of the creation, and also the *sefirot*, the divine attributes in Hebrew mystical tradition, as well as the first principles of Pythagorean and hermetic philosophy. The seven columns of the theater thus became the images of memory in a syncretistic attempt that had its celebrated model in the approach of Pico della Mirandola. The theater is presented as the synthesis of the truths that form part of various philosophical and religious traditions.

The columns constitute the vertical order of the theater; seven steps mark its horizontal order. One begins from divine ideas, first principles, to ascend through man and nature to the arts and sciences. The model is the classical theater, but the structure is reversed: at the center, on the stage, stands the spectator, who sees around him, in the places and images of the theater, all reality as his mind perceives it. We know that Camillo had a wooden model of his theater constructed and that he had the images painted by great artists, like his friend Titian. This project embodied in itself the myths of the Renaissance. The theater must of course provide the tools to master rapidly the secrets that made ancient texts so beautiful. It must at the same time guarantee access to the *encyclopedia—but not only that. For anyone who knew how to attain the wisdom kept hidden in the theater, it opened the paths to the fulfillment of the alchemical opus and to deification. Indeed, in its creator's intentions, the theater gave men divine powers, because it offered them the keys to the three arts of transformation: eloquence (the metamorphosis of words), alchemy (the metamorphosis of things), and deification (the metamorphosis of the soul).

Precisely these characteristics of Camillo's theater help us understand the fascination that the art of memory exercised in the sixteenth century, and the reasons behind its crisis. Both its allure and its crisis were related to the encyclopedic character that the art assumed, and to its magical and esoteric components. The expectations that the art created could be dangerous, as one famous case demonstrates. Giordano Bruno (1548–1600), philosopher and great master of the art of memory, was in exile in various European countries because he was considered a dangerous heretic. He returned to Italy in 1591 because the Venetian patrician Giovanni Mocenigo wanted him to teach him the secrets of the art, and he died burnt at the stake in the Campo de' Fiori in Rome on February 17, 1600.

Between the sixteenth and seventeenth centuries the production of texts about the art of memory continued, but the preconditions for a crisis materialized. The mistrust toward occultism, the rejection of magic, the growth and specialization of knowledge, the decline of a unitary conception of the world and of knowledge, all contributed to a radical crisis in the tradition of the art of memory.

At the same time, however, in the last decades of the sixteenth century, its techniques were used by missionaries as valuable tools to make distant, different worlds communicate with each other. In 1579, the Franciscan Diego Valadés published in Perugia his *Rhetorica christiana* (Christian rhetoric) in which the use of the art of memory builds a bridge between the world of conquistadors and that of Indigenous peoples. Against those who denied local populations human dignity, reducing them to the state of beasts,

Valadés pointed out that even if they do not use alphabetical writing, they nevertheless use images to communicate and to remember, exactly as the ancient Egyptians once did and Europeans do still. To defend Indigenous populations, Valadés carried out a reverse cultural translation. The mysterious and unsettling images of pre-Columbian civilization are framed in a way that renders them accessible to the Western eye, in that it reveals their resemblance either to a remote antiquity that the West views with reverent awe (the hieroglyphs of ancient Egypt) or to a practice diffused throughout Western culture, namely that of the art of memory. This maneuver was similar in some ways to that which the Jesuit Matteo Ricci attempted in China in the last decades of the sixteenth century, when he committed the fundamental truths of Christianity to a *"memory palace" and created a parallel between Chinese ideograms and European mnemonic images.

The capacity of images to communicate beyond linguistic differences meant that in the sixteenth and seventeenth centuries, the art of memory, with its *imagines agentes* (acting images), was intertwined with utopia. For example, in the *City of the Sun* by Tommaso Campanella (1568–1639), all the sciences and arts were depicted in images painted on seven walls that encircle the city, reproducing the cosmic order. The children of the city of the sun could thus learn the encyclopedia of knowledge just by looking at the painted images while they played. The *Orbis sensualium pictus* (World of the senses in pictures, 1658) of Jan Amos Komensky (or Comenius) was a great success, with its promise to communicate knowledge in an efficient and pleasing manner, using all the traditional resources of mnemonics, especially images. For Comenius, as for Campanella, the renewal of knowledge had a strong utopian charge: in his view, pansophism, or universal knowledge, would bring peace. The images make possible the rediscovery of a common ground beyond divisions and, at the same time, the ascent from the *orbis sensualis* (sensual world) to the *orbis intellectualis* (intellectual world)—to a united and peaceful vision of reality.

Lina Bolzoni
Translated by Madeline McMahon

See also diagrams; excerpting/commonplacing; knowledge; learning; professors; sermons; teaching

FURTHER READING

Aleida Assmann, *Cultural Memory and Western Civilization: Functions, Media, Archives*, 2011; Lina Bolzoni, *The Gallery of Memory: Literary and Iconographic Models in the Age of the Printing Press*, 1995, translated by Jeremy Parzen, 2001; idem, *The Web of Images: Vernacular Preaching from Its Origins to St. Bernardino da Siena*, 2004; Mary Carruthers, *The Book of Memory: A Study of Memory in Medieval Culture*, 1990; idem, *The Craft of Thought: Meditation, Rhetoric, and the Making of Images*, 1998; Paolo Rossi, *Logic and the Art of Memory: The Quest for a Universal Language*, 1960, 2nd ed., 1983, translated by Stephen Clucas, 2000; Frances A. Yates, *The Art of Memory*, 1966.

BELLS

This article reviews the history of bells as information sources, with particular emphasis on their use in the premodern West. Until the advent of modern acoustic technology, bells—defined here as open, cup-shaped vessels as opposed to *crotals* (hollow spheres)—were one of the most widespread and effective means of communication over distance. Usually made of metal, bells are idiophones that vibrate over most of their surface when struck and may be oscillated or remain in a fixed position (as is typical in the Western and Eastern traditions, respectively). Bells are thought to have developed in southeast Asia before 3000 BCE, spreading subsequently to India, China, the Near East, and eventually the Mediterranean basin; ancient examples are also known in Africa and in the pre-Columbian Americas. Bells have been cast in a wide variety of sizes, ranging from under a centimeter to the 6.6 meter diameter of the "Tsar Kolokol III" bell at the Kremlin in Moscow (1735), weighing some two hundred thousand kilograms. The sound of a bell consists of a complex series of sounding partials: the characteristic pitch or "nominal" of the bell is only one of a series of partials (component vibrations) both below and above, which may or may not be in a harmonious relationship. Western bells in particular were tuned from the Middle Ages onward to produce more concordant relationships between these partials, supporting more purely musical traditions such as change ringing in England and carillons in the Low Countries.

From an early stage bells fulfilled both spiritual and practical functions. Smaller bells were commonly attached to animals as a means of locating herds and frightening predators, and they were attached to vestments to signal the approach of important persons or to emphasize bodily movement and gesture. Spread by Celtic missionaries between the fifth and ninth centuries, the earliest known bells in medieval Europe signaled the times of monastic canonical prayer. By the twelfth century church towers, originally built as defense structures, were being equipped with bells, their numbers and size gradually increasing in subsequent centuries. Bells thus became a sonic marker of ecclesiastical authority and complemented the symbolic position of the church tower as the visual center of the community. Bells were traditionally accorded spiritual essences as well: their sound moved both gods and men; they attracted beneficent spirits and drove away evil spirits and influences. Bells were sounded within the church, especially to mark the moment of Eucharistic transubstantiation or the beginning of the sermon.

Bells were typically rung for sacramental rites of passage: baptism (especially for highly placed persons), marriage; and for priests bearing the Eucharist to the sick. Most significant was the ringing of bells to mark death or its approach. Differences in the duration or intensity of ringing conveyed information to a community on the class, gender, or age of the deceased and compelled collective prayers for the sake of the soul. However, this informative function was balanced by an apotropaic function, in that the sounds of consecrated or blessed bells were thought to keep at bay the evil spirits who might disturb the soul's passage. Thus the "passing bell" commonly was heard at the moment of death, and other bells would accompany the body to the church and to the place of burial. Bells proved to be especially useful as a signal to compel collective prayer, for the living and the departed. The so-called Angelus bell, at whose sound devotees were to pray the "Ave Maria" (Hail Mary), was especially fostered through papal pronouncements and *indulgences. By the fourteenth century more or less distinctive prayer bells were rung at morning and evening, and in 1456 Pope Calixtus III made a midday prayer bell mandatory as well, increasingly associated with prayers against the Turkish military threat ("Turk bell"). By the sixteenth century a threefold cycle of the Angelus at sunrise, noon, and sunset was commonly heard in European towns and was joined by additional signals on Thursdays and Fridays to commemorate Christ's agony and Passion. By popular demand the ringing of the Angelus was sometimes maintained in the Protestant *Reformation, but its theological significance changed: the midday Angelus, for example, was shorn of its Marian associations and reinterpreted as a call for peace (*pro pace*).

The cultic importance of bells in the traditional church followed from a ritual of consecration that resembled that of baptism. Known as early as the eighth century and later ratified by the Roman Church, the rite required the priest to wash the bell with salt and oil, chant psalms and prayers of consecration, and anoint the bell with chrism. This ritual, together with the common identification of bells by proper names and the addition of inscriptions in the first person ("I call the living, I lament the dead, I shatter the lightning") only deepened the sense of the bell as invested with spiritual power, its sound able to disperse threatening storms and the demons and witches that stirred them up. In a broader sense bells were thought to project the voice of the Lord and the mysteries of the Gospel: the consecrated bell became not only a source of apotropaic power, but a vessel of proclamation as well. The arrival of the Protestant Reformation brought significant changes to the traditional uses of church bells, as the former density of liturgical ringing was variously reoriented and theologically reinterpreted. Martin Luther attacked bell consecrations as an idolatrous ritual, and many theologians reinterpreted bell sounds as compelling the prayers that were the only sure way of staying God's wrath. If Lutheran officials uniformly rejected bell consecrations and apotropaic notions, this did not lead to any widespread silencing of bell sounds, which continued to invite the faithful to services, call for collective prayer in the face of calamities and threats, observe the passing of persons both prominent and ordinary, and serve for timekeeping and for civic safety. Despite the admonitions of the theologians, many Christians on both sides of the confessional divide continued to invest bell sounds with apotropaic power well into the eighteenth century and even beyond.

For many centuries there was not necessarily a clear distinction between cultic, ritual, and "secular" uses of bell signals. Given the political dominance of the medieval church, its bells could readily serve as civic signals and as symbols of communal identity. As communes increasingly asserted themselves against ecclesiastical and territorial lords, complex patterns of ownership emerged in that certain bells in church towers were designated for civic purposes, such as striking the hours or warning in case of fire or other disturbances. A timbral distinction between religious and profane signals could be achieved, for example, by tolling the bell instead of setting it in oscillation; or by striking the bell with a hammer or other device. Between the twelfth and fourteenth centuries cities began to erect municipal buildings and towers in which bells emerged as a sonic focus of civic authority: fine examples may be found in the grand palazzi of Florence (1322) and Siena (1348). Civic bells were rung to convene popular assemblies, to announce judicial proceedings and the collection of taxes, and to mark the execution of malefactors; town criers, moreover, carried smaller bells to disseminate important and officially sanctioned news. More generally bells emerged in the Middle Ages as instruments for the regulation of trade, commerce, and internal civic order. Bells were rung for the opening and closing of gates at morning and evening, and for marking the period of sanctioned commerce. Countering the potential dangers and disturbances of the premodern night would make bells necessary for the closing of taverns and the imposition of curfew. During the night hours watchmen in towers would periodically strike bells to reassure the populace of their wakefulness, and roving watchmen would also sometimes carry handbells to signal their presence: bell signals, then, were an aural symbol of safety and vigilance.

A range of bells—including tower bells in elevated locations as well as smaller bells hung in towers, gates, and guard houses—warned the populace in case of fire or the approach of enemies. An alarm bell (tocsin) was often distinguished by rapid striking with a hammer or by an inherently discordant sound. Some bells were associated directly with a military function: Florence's "La Martinella," for instance, rang to assemble troops and alert the citizenry in the face of external threats and was carried into battle as a physical and aural symbol of the commune. Military victories and other celebratory occasions compelled cities to ring all bells together, creating a stereophonic sound that could be augmented by gunfire or fireworks.

Collective ringing of this nature, though aurally impressive, was rare. The soundscape of premodern towns and cities was characterized by a complex interlocking of liturgical and secular cycles of ringing that structured routine experiences of space and time, augmented by distinctive signals that conveyed information of a more urgent nature. It is likely, moreover, that premodern populations readily distinguished subtleties of rhythm and timbre that have been largely effaced in the modern age. Industrialization and the destructive effects of modern warfare have fundamentally changed the communicative function of bells, whose sound, for many, now incites nostalgia for a lost age.

Alexander J. Fisher

See also governance; sermons

FURTHER READING

Niall Atkinson, *The Noisy Renaissance: Sound, Architecture, and Florentine Urban Life*, 2016; Jean-Daniel Blavignac, *La Cloche, études sur son histoire et sur ses rapports avec la société aux différents âges*, 1877; Alain Corbin, *Village Bells: Sound and Meaning in the Nineteenth-Century French Countryside*, translated by Martin Thom, 1998; Ansgar Hense, *Glockenläuten und Uhrenschlag: Der Gebrauch von Kirchenglocken in der kirchlichen und staatlichen Rechtsordnung*, 1998; Heinrich Otte, *Glockenkunde*, 1884; Percival Price, *Bells and Man*, 1983; Wendell Westcott, *Bells and Their Music*, 1970.

BIBLIOGRAPHY

Bibliography is fundamental to a historical understanding of the ordering of information and has impacts across multiple scholarly and professional disciplines. The term *bibliography* chiefly refers to practices for listing, describing, and organizing books. For manuscripts and archival material, the term *cataloging* is used to refer to similar practices. Bibliography can be extended to include description and classification applied to organization, search, access, and retrieval within higher-level knowledge management systems. Bibliography has close connections to diplomatics, document studies, and critical editing, where its descriptive and analytic tools are an aid to authentication, collation, comparison, forgery detection, and the study of texts. Bibliographical records structure information through standards and professional practices that are themselves objects of study.

Bibliography and textual editing have long histories in the West and are closely linked to the transmission of biblical and classical corpora. Book and manuscript cataloging also play a role in the inventory and transfer of personal and institutional collections, as well as their access through surrogates (descriptive records) and spatial arrangement (shelving). Newer approaches to bibliography have challenged its Western bias in choice of objects—particularly its emphasis on printed books, and methods—with their positivist underpinnings. Understanding what is at stake in those challenges requires an introduction to the outline of the field.

In the common historicizing narrative, the earliest bibliographical system is considered to be Callimachus's *Pinakes* (*Tables of Those Who Have Distinguished Themselves in Every Form of Culture and What They Wrote*), created in the third century BCE for the Library of Alexandria. From the handful of remaining fragments, Callimachus's work appears to have been a detailed descriptive reference, containing biographical material on authors as well as commentary on their works. The *Pinakes* was reputed to run to 120 scrolls while the library may have contained as many as five hundred thousand scrolls. Callimachus divided texts by field and *genre into rhetoric, law, history, medicine, mathematics, natural sciences, then epic, tragedy, comedy, lyric poetry, and miscellanies, with all materials organized alphabetically within these sections.

Using the *Pinakes* as a point of origin shows how quickly lines blur between description and classification. Even the simplest act of assigning an author name, title, or date embodies assumptions, while assigning a genre or theme to a work implies a larger system of organization. These systems carry powerful hegemonic and intellectual weight but are often invisible except in the material instantiation of shelf organization and physical display—an aspect of information management that is changing rapidly in *digital systems. Early acquisition records frequently added items sequentially and relied on shelf "marks" or numbers to link items to their storage location. Much bibliographical work is intimately bound to knowledge classification schemes (for instance, *Library of Congress subject headings or *Universal Decimal Classification). The invention of card catalogs, with their flexible cross-referencing system, did not occur until the late eighteenth century, when they appeared as part of cultural patterns of social management in Revolutionary France. As Patrick Wilson argued in his much-cited text *Two Kinds of Power* (1968), bibliography asserts controls over knowledge through descriptive as well as purpose-driven systems.

Modern rules for cataloging rely on bibliographical concepts. These may be quite elaborate when used for rare materials but are often streamlined and simplified for efficiency. The practice of copy cataloging, for instance, greatly reduces overhead on creating records for library systems, since it uses the information in authoritative resources (like the Online Catalog of the Library of Congress). However, this technique often ignores the features of individual books (signatures, provenance markings, annotations, or other elements of an individual copy).

Bibliography is usually divided into enumerative, descriptive, and analytic methods. Enumerative bibliography basically lists items in a collection. Early library lists, estate inventories, and sales catalogs are examples of enumerative bibliography. These lists do not have to contain any cross-referencing or indexing, and the use of the alphabet as an organizing principle (by author, title, or subject) is so common it goes unremarked. Alphabetical order is a legacy of Western historical transmission and cultural exchange, just as bibliographical standards are grounded in the study of manuscript scroll and *codex book. In cultures that use character-based writing, glyphic systems, monumental inscriptions, or ephemeral traces, the imposition of alphabetical schemes (including transcriptions and surrogates) is associated with colonial practices and abuses.

Enumerative bibliography has a long history. Ashurbanipal's library at Nineveh had a catalog in the seventh century BCE, and medieval monastic libraries kept records of their holdings. Johannes Trithemius, remembered for his 1492 essay *In Praise of Scribes* (questioning the advantages of print), produced various catalogs of German scriptoria in the decades following the spread of printing in Europe. In 1545, the classical scholar and polymath Conrad Gessner published his *Bibliotheca universalis* (Universal library) an attempt at an exhaustive catalog of all then-known texts in Greek, Latin, and Hebrew. The intellectual influence of this work is marked by the repetition of its title phrase in similar reference works for several centuries. In the seventeenth century, Sir Thomas Bodley, founder of Oxford's Bodleian Library, argued for the necessity of cross-referencing author names and subjects to index collections. Printed lists of famous collections were thus produced well before the seventeenth and eighteenth centuries, when scholars, like the renowned bibliographer and philologist Bishop White Kennett, encouraged these techniques.

The information that appears in the handwritten pages and printed inventories of older libraries is often richly descriptive, if idiosyncratic. Cataloging protocols carrying fuller descriptions of the size, binding, number of pages, illustrations, and other features were only formally proposed by the head of the British Library Anthony Panizzi in his "Ninety-One Cataloging Rules" in 1841. The French bibliophile and bookseller Charles Brunet created an organizing scheme, *Table Méthodique* (A method in tabular form), in the 1860s in the final, sixth, volume of a reference work meant to provide a standard for professional librarians. Melvil Dewey's decimal system, which also became the basis of the European Universal Decimal Classification, was developed beginning in the 1870s, with its major rival, the Library of Congress system, developed through efforts of the librarian Herbert Putnam (aided by Charles Cutter) beginning in the 1890s. Both systems were used to organize shelving arrangements as well as create catalog listings by subject. Library organization prior to this had often been by author or general subject areas like medicine, law, theology, rhetoric, which becomes unwieldy for large collections.

The publication of library catalogs, such as Charles Coffin Jewett's 1856 *Index to the Catalogue of a Portion of the Public Library of the City of Boston* and Charles Ammi Cutter's 1876 *Rules for a Dictionary Catalogue* (a catalog with dictionary-like features, not an inventory of dictionaries), set precedents for principles still used into the present. As part of broader trends in the rise of professionalization, the American Library Association was founded in 1876, and the Bibliographical Society in the United Kingdom was established in 1892. The first library schools were established in the 1880s, replacing apprenticeship systems with courses of study designed to professionalize practices of classification and organization in public libraries, and in business institutions and cultural repositories. The Columbia School of Library Economy offered its first classes in 1887, under the stewardship of Dewey, who promoted his system of organization with the idea that cataloging and bibliography, the basis of search and access, were the cornerstones of the library profession.

As collections grew, questions of spatial organization and arrangement became pressing. It was clear that organizing books by size took much less space than ordering them by subject. John William Wallace, addressing the Congress of Librarians in Philadelphia in 1876, asked whether collections "are to be disposed by subjects, by size, by alphabetic arrangement, by order of publication to the world" and so on. His list of possibilities gives an indication of the practices in play. Wallace saw the librarian's role not simply in terms of creating an order to things, but rather, as someone standing "between the world of authors and the world of readers." This interface role bore responsibility that intensified as technological changes and the increased scale of knowledge management led to developments in the twentieth century. Alongside these were utopian dreams of total access and instant retrieval, like H. G. Wells's *World Brain* in the 1930s, and Vannevar Bush's midcentury vision of *memex, sometimes seen as precursors to the *World Wide Web.

For centuries, the practice of organizing volumes by language and size also prevailed. The Romans divided their libraries, associated with temple complexes, into two chambers, one for Greek and one for Latin texts. Theology, classics, and literature of the modern world (e.g., Milton and Shakespeare) were relegated to their own neighborhoods on shelves. When the first printed catalog of the Harvard Library was produced in the early 1720s, it listed around three thousand titles, the vast majority of which were theological texts in Latin. Older libraries, like the Bodleian and Vatican, had collections whose scope far exceeded any manageable scale of inventory. Repositories were unruly and disorganized or contained pockets of materials with liabilities attached. The Vatican Library, for instance, had a collection of adulterous letters from Henry VIII to Anne Boleyn to which access was severely restricted. Locked cabinets for salacious or erotic materials still exist. The political dimensions of cataloging and access practices became apparent with Sanford Berman's landmark 1971 publication *Prejudices and Antipathies: A Tract on the LC Subject Heads Concerning People*. For instance, Berman pointed out that texts on homosexuality had been long classified under pathologies and perversions. Debates about the ethics of cataloging have increased, opening topics for consideration that reflect changing values in the culture and profession that challenge long-held beliefs.

Library alcoves were often inscribed with names of renowned figures or contained sculptures of them and could be referenced by these figures. The library built by Eumenes the Second at Pergamon, for instance, was organized by the portrait busts of Herodotus, Homer, Alcaeus, and Timotheus of Miletus. But the pressures brought by acquisitions and the problems of continued need for reshelving and reorganization were noted from the earliest times. Mark Antony's gift of over two hundred thousand scrolls to Cleopatra carried significant administrative overhead. Medieval monastic libraries in the West were often modest in scale, and books were stored in cabinets with shelf marks. Work by Albert Derolez on the subject of medieval book lists provides a major reference source for library organization in this period. The habit of using busts of classical figures as an organizing principle continued, as in the Cotton Library in Ashburnham House, which provided a significant contribution to the fledgling British Museum.

While enumerative bibliography blurs into cataloging, descriptive bibliography is closely aligned with critical editing practices. Descriptive bibliography is based on exhaustive observation of the physical features of a work, including collation formulas used to guide the folding of signatures (gatherings of pages) in preparation for binding. Such description can be used to compare individual copies, to check for changes and variations, and for standardization of the text.

Analytic bibliography analyzes the production history of a physical object and opens the way to studying the history of printing, publishing, the business and marketing of books, editions, binding, and other aspects of the book trade. Where descriptive bibliography remains focused on the object, and restricts its field of inquiry to the material features of the book, analytic bibliography connects these elements to cultural conditions of production, reading the social history of print from the material evidence in books. Similar descriptive practices occur in diplomatics and the traditions relevant to handling government and institutional records. The French Benedictine monk Jean Mabillon's *De Re Diplomatica* (On the study of documents) (1681), one of the first significant contributions to that field and still a major reference, consisted of detailed facsimiles of features like handwriting, scripts, forms, seals, and visual elements of documents that could be used to detect attempted falsification.

These methods of bibliographical description are fundamentally forensic, grounded in empirical approaches and assumptions. They use physical or material evidence to identify features that distinguish one object from another. Attention to paper, watermarks, the number of words to a line or characters to a font, changes made on press partway through a print run, specific details of bookplates, binding, provenance, or other aspects of experience that leave a physical trace are all central to bibliographical practice. Even in the twenty-first century, bibliography does not call forensic evidence into question and has largely remained resistant to critical challenges that question the positivist assumptions underpinning its methods.

In 1986, Donald F. McKenzie published a collection of essays, *Bibliography and the Sociology of Texts*, that offered a radically different reading of material evidence. The collection argued vividly for the extent to which the meaning of evidence was a matter of cultural perception. McKenzie argued that a major political document, known in New

Zealand as *The Treaty of Waitangi*, could be understood only through the parallax of differing cultural viewpoints—Indigenous peoples and chiefs, settlers, colonial government officers, a printer, a translator, and other participants. McKenzie's work challenged the notion that evidence was simply self-evident. The social implications of forensic evidence take on varied meanings when linked to social and ideological concerns. But for the most part, traditional bibliography has not reflected on its own hegemonic biases or cultural assumptions. The codex book, a product of the early Christian era in the West and long ignored in other cultures, remains its central object, unproblematically situated within the discourses of analysis and description. By contrast, in the latter half of the twentieth century, critical hermeneutic approaches in French critical theory, particularly the work of Jacques Derrida and Paul de Man, questioned the autonomy and identity of the text. The shift toward constitutive acts of reading, rather than positivist modes of describing, is a tenet of this critical practice but has not been integrated into standard bibliographical methods.

The connection between bibliography and textual editing links the descriptive and interpretative traditions. The quest to establish authoritative textual records for classical, biblical, and *canonical works drove critical editing practices at least as early as the first centuries of the Common Era. The work of textual scholars from the third century, Origen and Eusebius, depended on assessing the authority of multiple witnesses (manuscripts) on which to establish biblical passages. The comparative and collational work involved was partially aided by the invention of a technique of tracking variations. Known as the "hexapla," this was a tabular structure used by Origen to compile his version of the Old Testament in the first half of the third century. Scribal traditions of copying and editing increased the bibliographical inventory, proliferating errors in the process. Textual editing of biblical and classical works formed a crucial part of Western *Renaissance publishing as these manuscripts were migrated into print.

In the eighteenth century, the prominent bibliographer Joseph Ames produced an account of printing in England in his *Typographical Antiquities* (1749). One of his emenders and followers, Thomas Frognall Dibdin, was among the early codifiers of bibliographical practice. In 1802, Dibdin published his *Introduction to Knowledge of the Rare and Valuable Editions of the Greek and Latin classics; including the Scriptores de re rustica, Greek romances, and lexicons and grammars: to which is added a complete index analyticus: the whole proceeded by an account of polyglot Bibles, and the best editions of the Greek Septuagint and Testament.* Within the many phrases of the title, the bibliographical focus for which Dibdin became well known is evident. Dibdin's mania for books was reflected in two other renowned texts, *Bibliomania* (1809) and *Bibliophobia* (1832), both of which contain much idiosyncratic thought and wit. Such bibliographical eccentricity was ridiculed in Alexander Pope's early eighteenth-century poem *The Dunciad*, where he mocked the classical philologist and pedant Richard Bentley in his elaborate notes.

Bibliography cannot, however, be simply associated with quaint or obsolete antiquarianism. The German tradition of genealogical classification of manuscripts was established by the philologist Karl Lachmann in the early to mid-nineteenth century. His "family tree" approach organized textual variants by degrees of similarity. Committed to metaphors of natural science, the approach gained authority through its associations with scientific methods. In another approach, the highly influential twentieth-century bibliographer Roger McKerrow articulated a concept of the *"copy text" as the version of a work closest to the author's (presumed) intentions. Recovering this state of the text became a goal for many textual editors following his lead. In 1950s, the Shakespeare scholar W. W. Greg pushed editing practices toward an ideal text that was a composite work drawn from all the "best" versions of a particular work. Greg's studies focused on canonical literary figures—Shakespeare, Marlowe, Jonson—and addressed problems of editorial judgment, errors, and transmission. This tradition was taken up in modified form in the work of later bibliographers, among them Fredson Bowers. The titles of two of Bowers's major works show the connections between bibliography and editing: *Principles of Bibliographical Description* (1949) and *Some Principles for Scholarly Editions* (1964). This work was continued by Philip Gaskell in *A New Introduction to Bibliography* (1972), by Thomas Tanselle, and in professional societies for textual editing and scholarship. The academic Jerome McGann's fundamental challenge, *A Critique of Modern Textual Criticism* (1983), argued for the social production of texts by suggesting that literary works, in particular, were the result of many participants—authors, editors, confidants, printers, and so on.

A very different challenge to the traditions of bibliography came from Hugh Amory. Extending the work of McKenzie, Amory argued in "The Trout and the Milk" (1997) that evidence was not self-evident. The presence of a page of a Bible, found as part of a medicine bundle in the colonial-period grave of a Native American girl, could not simply be read is if it were a symbol of Christian faith. Amory coined the term *ethnobibliography* to address the complexities of situating physical evidence in cultural conditions. With other ethnographically inclined scholars of the written record, notably Walter Mignolo, Amory pushed for decolonization of the methods, not merely the objects, of bibliographical inquiry. Much remains to be done in reworking fundamental principles and addressing biases built into bibliographical approaches. Recent work on Lachmann, for instance, by Yii-Jan Lin, explores the alignment between a critical language of purity and corruption in textual transmission and its similarity to racial biases in nineteenth-century practices.

An alternative bibliographical approach would need to begin differently. By taking the broad field of inscriptional practices as a starting point, rather than the scroll or codex, it might establish practices for studying the codification, transmission, and mediation of meaning-producing objects along with the study of intangible knowledge production. Borrowing forensic, collational, comparative techniques from traditional bibliography, along with ethnographic approaches and critical interpretative methods, such an approach might be constituted *from* its objects of study, rather than being imposed *on* them.

As twenty-first-century knowledge management progresses, other considerations relevant to the historical traditions of bibliography also come to the fore. The use of cataloging systems for spatial organization of shelving is at risk of disappearing. Electronic records management, remote storage, and robotic retrieval blind the user to the once evident system of knowledge organization that was structured into library spaces. The organization of libraries into zones and neighborhoods, identified by subject or theme, established its own priorities and biases, as well as sometimes peculiar groupings embodying local systems. But such space was legible to the user who cared to read the physical organization. Though cataloging standards are changing under challenges to their legacy biases, the costs for implementation and restructuring are impediments.

The idea of a plurality of ontologies, of the multiverse of voices and viewpoints for organization, description, and access that could be supported in networked environments, has not yet come to pass. The trend toward using online catalogs as the only access point to collections complicates this matter. Rather than creating a better way to expose the organizational structure and intellectual and cultural values, it obscures these and emphasizes a consumer-satisfaction model, rather than one that embodies historical and intellectual awareness.

Johanna Drucker

See also books; cards; diplomats/spies; forgery; indexing; inventories; libraries and catalogs; lists; scrolls and rolls; storage and search

FURTHER READING

Craig S. Abbot and William Proctor Williams, *An Introduction to Bibliographical and Textual Studies*, 2009; Hugh Amory, *Bibliography and the Book Trades*, 2005; Sanford Berman, *Prejudices and Antipathies*, 1971; Femi Cadmus, "Things in Common: Challenges of the 19th and 21st Century Libraries," *Green Bag* 14, no. 2 (2011): 193–99; Yii-Jan Lin, "Chapter 3: Lachmann and the Genealogy and Corruption of Texts," in *The Erotic Life of Manuscripts*, 2016; Jerome McGann, *A Critique of Modern Textual Criticism*, 1983; Donald F. McKenzie, *Bibliography and the Sociology of Texts*, 1986; Patrick Wilson, *Two Kinds of Power*, 1968.

BOOKS

Read, reread, or even unopened, books make up familiar, comforting, and reproving provisions in our lives. The reading of certain books, at certain times and in certain circumstances, can be life changing, enlightening, terrifying, and consoling. And when we ask what a book is, a strong material image comes to mind. Books, the vessels of information, knowledge, instruction, and entertainment, carry their contents in recognizable and culturally specific physical forms.

Many of us, if asked whether books or weapons have changed most in human history, would probably opt for weapons. We might trace a succession of armaments from spears and bows and arrows to cannons and guns to chemical and nuclear bombs. By contrast, we probably think that what we know as a book has been relatively unchanging. A book has words, a cover, and a spine. It might carry pictures. If a work of reference, it will probably include a contents list and an index. We instinctively think that it will be printed. But after further reflection, the apparent stability of books unravels.

If you are reading these words in paper and bound form, then you are implicated in the idea of the book as *codex. Taken from the Latin *caudex* for "trunk of a tree" or "block of wood," the codex is usually defined as a book constructed of a number of sheets of paper, *parchment, *papyrus, or similar material bound together. In ancient Rome the codex form likely developed from the practice of binding together the boards of waxed tablets that were used for temporary writing in antiquity, when the medium for long-term storage was the papyrus roll. The codex spread in the second to fourth centuries CE as the form of choice for Christians; some scholars argue that it appealed to Christians engaged in itinerant proselytizing because it could encompass more writing in a smaller-sized object, which was thus easier to carry. In some cases papyrus rolls were cut up to be bound in a codex, but for a variety of reasons (including the fact that papyrus sheets fray at the edges) parchment became the writing surface of choice for the codex. Except for the use of scrolls in specific *genres like genealogies or grand documents, manuscripts in medieval Europe set the patterns of the Western codex, which continued unchanged in printed books down to our own time. Although the codex is often associated with handwritten books, it has also become universally coupled with printed books from the Western world.

From the ancient period we have also inherited the notion of a book as a unit of text, typically limited to the amount of text in a papyrus roll. Thus the Hebrew and Christian Bibles are divided into dozens of books (which vary in number by religious denomination); and ancient works of all types were often transmitted with divisions into books, such as the eight books of Aristotle's *Physics*, the thirty-seven books of Pliny's *Natural History* (plus one book for the table of contents), or the twelve books of Virgil's *Aeneid*.

In all parts of the globe, however, and in societies past and present, books have existed in many other manifestations. The fullest history of books therefore describes how different peoples in different parts of the world, in different ways, for different reasons, and with very different consequences have striven to store, circulate, and retrieve knowledge and information. In such a history, print—word and image—is far from the only means of graphic communication used to convey messages in books. Texts might be impressed, imprinted, inscribed, written, drawn, stenciled, block or letterpress printed, engraved, stereotyped, lithographed, or photographically or digitally reproduced. The comparative challenge is remarkable: from cuneiform tablets to digital tablets, of a succession and a simultaneity of forms, of scrolls and codices, of Inka *khipus*, Chinese and East Asian bamboo books and woodblock printing and xylography, Buddhist *thanka* scrolls, Singhalese leaf books, and Dakota buffalo hides. In East Asia, the term *shuji* (書籍 in traditional Chinese and Korean) commonly translates as "book" and can describe unbound papers bearing written or printed characters or a mixture of both. More specifically, since about 1000 CE, the word *banben* 版本 has distinguished different, but usually printed, editions of an essentially unchanged text.

As a gathering of written words, books have existed for at least five thousand years. The thirty-third century BCE is claimed by some scholars as the date of the earliest surviving object to fulfill the definition of a book as a durable, portable, replicable, and legible transmitter of texts. Thousands of clay tablets attributed to circa 3200 BCE have been found impressed with cuneiform in southern Mesopotamian cities such as Uruk and Babylon. From roughly the same centuries, Egyptian grave goods bear the earliest hieroglyphic inscriptions. The earliest surviving blank papyrus rolls in Egypt date from circa 3000 BCE, while the earliest known inscribed papyrus scrolls and wooden writing boards, also from Egypt, are dated to 2600 BCE. This is roughly contemporaneous with the most ancient examples of Chinese writing, as found on pottery and bronze containers. Three hundred years later, scribes in Mesopotamia used waxed wooden writing boards, and a few centuries later still, in circa 1800 BCE, alphabets intended to simplify hieroglyphs were incised on rocks in quarries in the Sinai Desert.

Writing in what we call Linear B began on clay tablets in Crete in about 1400 BCE, only a hundred or so years before Indian scribes composed the books of the Vedas, Hinduism's most sacred texts. Surviving from about a century later, and inscribed on tortoiseshell, are the earliest Chinese divination books. Their texts also offer evidence for lost bamboo-strip books of the same period. The earliest surviving bamboo books date from circa 450 BCE, but older are other book survivals, such as Old Hebrew collected letters and legal documents on leather and papyrus of about 670 BCE; the library established by Ashurbanipal in Nineveh, Assyria, in 650 BCE; and, from China itself, the first known writing on silk (also ca. 650 BCE). The Sanskrit *Ramayana* epic was created about 500 BCE, and copies of the Sanskrit *Mahabharata*, the world's longest epic poem, date from as early as 400 BCE, from the same century as the earliest surviving Indian and Sinhalese potsherds bearing Brahmi inscriptions. The earliest surviving papyrus roll from Greece has been dated as circa 340 BCE, about forty years before the creation of the first of the Hebrew and Aramaic Dead Sea Scrolls. Birch-bark and palm-leaf books were first used in south Asia in about 200 BCE, at a time when silk began to replace bamboo as a writing material in China. The earliest known surviving fragments of Chinese paper (from the Han capital Chang'an or Xi'an) are dated to between 140 and 87 BCE, with the traditional date of 105 CE given to the supposed invention of modern paper by Cai Lun, a senior official of the Han dynasty.

It is also in the second century CE that codices originate in the form that we most often associate with books. From about 150 CE codex production began to replace that of scrolls in the Middle East and Mediterranean. The earliest fragment of a Latin codex yet found is a small part of a historical work known as *De Bellis Macedonicis* (On the Macedonian Wars). In a quite different part of the world, the earliest known paper book, a copy of the Buddhist *Piyujing Sutra*, dates from 256 CE. The Codex Sinaiticus, one of the earliest and most complete Greek Bibles, was created in about 350. From the early eighth century survive a number of important codices including the Codex Amiatinus, the earliest extant complete manuscript of the Latin Vulgate Bible, and the illuminated Lindisfarne Gospels created in the monastery at Lindisfarne, off the coast of Northumbria. The Book of Kells, an illuminated manuscript of the four Gospels in Latin, and one of the most celebrated early medieval manuscripts in Europe, was created in a Columbian monastery in Ireland or Britain in about 800. In China during these centuries, book production similarly increased. In the Later Tang dynasty, a woodblock publication of a complete set of the Confucian Classics was completed in 130 volumes in 954. The earliest known book printed by movable earthenware type in China dates from between 1041 and 1048. Collections of books in both East and West also became more numerous, and with the establishment of a chained library at the Sorbonne between 1289 and 1292, we have one of the earliest medieval examples of a room in which books were not only stored but also consulted in situ.

Across so many textual traditions transmission has depended on not only physical but also cultural factors. Maya petroglyphs survive but without the transmission of the cultural knowledge for us to decipher them. On the other hand, the ancient texts of many cultures have come down to us despite the fragility of their original media and thanks instead to their status as *canonical texts that were regularly memorized and copied. But physical factors have also played a crucial role. Some quite durable media made it possible to recover texts after up to a millennium of benign neglect, as in the case of early medieval codices on parchment rediscovered in excellent condition during the European *Renaissance. And in exceptional circumstances even fragile media have transmitted texts after very long periods of neglect, as in the Dead Sea Scrolls, Dunhuang Caves, or the Cairo Genizah. As we transition to electronic media we face many unknowns about the physical durability of the formats in which we transmit texts. How well would these texts survive a period of oblivion, without continued cultural "maintenance" including upgrades to new software and hardware?

The definition of a book most obviously relates to the manner in which thought and information are materially produced and consumed, and how this, in turn, depends on ideographic, pictographic, alphabetic, and other writing systems recording verbal sounds, and graphic signs, script, print, and other technologies conveying them. The book has been successively remodeled and reformed over time and in different parts of the world. The unexpected parallels and contrasts between book making and reading continue to challenge comparatively localized ideas of writing and publication practices. Nonetheless, the global history of the book is also one of constants and residual forms, of key moments of transition, and of the coexistence of contrasting functions and materials over long periods.

Such temporal and geographical diversity of books astonishes. Whether made of terracotta, a skin, or a natural fiber, or enabled by a *digital screen, central processing unit, random access memory, or a graphics card, books constitute a durable, portable or mobile, replicable, and legible (that is, readable and communicable) means of recording and disseminating information and knowledge. If we think radically, we might even ask whether a person could be a book. Storytellers, teachers, and preachers, ancient or modern, memorize their tales or knowledge and speak or sing to order. Such persons are mobile and in a sense portable; they are relatively durable, they communicate, and (if not exactly replicable) they can be copied by others. Most of us, however, would discount the concept of a person-book because we believe that a book has to be a vehicle for encoded signs that are visually read. But in thinking through the question we are forced to hone our definitions and begin to realize that many of our concepts are culturally and temporally conditioned. Take, as another example, the book as digital download or an online text read on screen. The text is clearly mobile in that the reader scrolls through it or otherwise accesses it, and some screens—on smart phones or tablets or laptops—are clearly portable. But what of the fixed-site computer in a library or even on a desk at home? The "portability" of the material form within which the text is read (however that reading is done) is more like that of a chained book in a medieval library. The mobility of the digital text, moreover, is now more than manual, moving and changing by automated means if desired—and capable of apparently limitless replication. "Online" books can be read only when their readers are connected to the *internet. With links to other sites, *hypertext books are also liberated from certain conventional modes of textual appearance and reading.

Even within the general domain of the codex, map books, music books, scrapbooks, flip-out books, and comic books (such as Japanese manga) suggest the diversity of genre and form. Telephone books and Filofaxes suggest how quickly new and innovative forms of book can become outdated and unfamiliar within a couple of generations. Above all, we live today with a diversity of digital book forms capable of very different textual composition, handling, encounter, and reading experiences. All this unsettles our definitions of a book's "text" and its relationship to its material form and conveyance. The changing valorizations of our own time offer insights into how the relationship between book form and the signs conveyed by and within it has changed and is described differently in different ages. Popular reference to a "text," for example, is currently given new meaning by the sending of a "text" message, just as worldwide word processing and text messaging have brought about the rejuvenation but also the reconfiguration of the word "font." Font (or "fount") is a word that only thirty years ago needed explanation to those introduced to typography—but now, exactly because of its casual usage, it requires even more careful explanation by students of books.

The residual influences of earlier forms also distinguish the design of even "born-digital" books. This *"skeuomorphism" appears, for example, in the way that the majority of online books and e-resources resemble the page-based and *paratextual forms of codices, with traditional formatting parameters. Electronic pages are normally available to read sequentially and are skippable by "flipping" in a reading mode familiar to all uses of codices (and in which search engines still offer sequential results). Many electronic journals retain volume and issue structures with contents lists, even when they publish on a continuous basis, and, as with e-books, indexes are replaced by word searching, at once more particular but also less capable of generic and guided assistance. The remediating of books and of print in the digital age questions anew what knowledge is, how it is created and transmitted, and what it looks like.

Changes to modes of reading are equally transformational. Digital books offer revisions and tests to our consideration of sign and character design and recognition, of the composition and comprehension of the page, of what a "page" is and where it ends, of the complexity of "paratexts," and of the variety of our reading practices and motivations. How might we now measure the overwhelming quantity and ephemerality of reading and reader response evidence such as Goodreads, digital reading group records, Amazon order histories, and easily accessible and monitorable school and university reading lists? The history of reading, however problematic, often provides the most, and sometimes only, significant historical claim in the analysis of the influence of a text. The very act of reading eschews recording—few readers write down what they do in reading—and yet the understanding of reading and literacies involves consideration of motivations, experiences, skills, and aptitudes and is fundamental to most of the cultural transactions epitomized by the history of books.

The history of reading can also diverge from the history of books, where the material object might have been collected, displayed, or otherwise used for symbolic, speculative, aesthetic, spiritual, emotional, sexual, pathological, or other reasons. Many books were and are, of course, never read at all, and the majority of the copies of certain misconceived editions are pulped, but what is now the digital equivalent of the unread and the destroyed? Loss, deletion, and redundancy take on different and challenging meanings.

What then, is the future of the book in the age of makerspaces, *hackerspaces, and a "shared knowledge economy"? In the world of digitized texts and of Google Books we are challenged by questions not only of the archiving and retrieval of knowledge and information through "books," but also of what *copyright is and of the implications of *open access, licensing agreements, and inequitable information supply. Authors, *publishers, and readers confront new forms of global pirating, of how censorship operates, and of how new technologies change and are changed by commercial, political, religious, and national interests. Publishers are digitizing backlists and keeping books "in print" to an unprecedented extent. The digital revolutionizes the commercial structure and business models of modern book publishing and international conglomerates.

Changes to physical means of communication have therefore clearly affected our sense of "the book." The appearance of portable computers, smart phones, and scrollable texts challenges assumptions about the makeup, effect, and purpose of books. We text (moving that word from noun to verb), we use and customize e-books, and we create and ostensibly control our own publications. Popular and academic critics explore contrasts between *analog and digital media, between paper and pixels. Electronic books generate new reading and knowledge experiences—and ones that question not only our understanding of material forms but the definition, design, and networking of information and knowledge. Many commentators associate contemporary "books" less with their material *form* than with their *function* as a means of communicating information. The revival and adaptation of such words and concepts as *icon, font, table, scrolling*, and *the virtual* are cyphers for a reconceptualization of what a book is. Hyperlinked texts, digital editions and the e-book, screen adaptations, audiobooks, and podcasts change the ways in which texts are acquired, transmitted, circulated, read, interrogated, searched, and stored. Authorship identities and rights are made more complex, and automated cross-lingual translation accentuates issues of untranslatability. And in such transformative times, more books are published than ever before whether through conventional means, by print-on-demand, or on the World Wide Web, Twitter, and other social media; and more formalized modes of book self-publishing open to everyone the possibility of publication, extensive dissemination, and unknown readerships.

James Raven

See also knowledge; layout and script in letters; letterpress; libraries and catalogs; notebooks; printed visuals; publicity/publication; readers; reference books; storage and search

FURTHER READING

Cynthia Brokaw and Kai-wing Chow, eds., *Printing and Book Culture in Late Imperial China*, 2005; Robert Darnton, "What Is the History of Books?," *Daedalus* 111 (Summer 1982): 65–83; Caroline Davis and David Johnson, eds., *The Book in Africa: Critical Debates*, 2015; Lucien Febvre and Henri-Jean Martin, *The Coming of the Book: The Impact of Printing 1450–1800*, 1958, translated by D. Gerard, 1976; Joseph P. McDermott, *A Social History of the Chinese Book: Books and Literati Culture in Late Imperial China*, 2006; David McKitterick, *Print, Manuscript, and the Search for Order 1450–1830*, 2003; James Raven, *What Is the History of the Book?*, 2018; Henry Woudhuysen and Michael Suarez, eds., *Oxford Companion to the History of the Book*, 2 vols., 2010.

BOOK SALES CATALOGS

From the very beginnings of printing, printers and *publishers needed to advertise books, both to individual purchasers and to other members of the burgeoning book trade. Itinerant and sedentary booksellers also needed to provide information about their holdings for their potential clients. This need is still felt, but it is now much easier to engage in publicity and to provide much more information about the merchandise than was the case in the past. Potential purchasers can now expect to be told about authors (and their other works, where relevant), the title of their work, where and when it was (or is to be) produced, whether it is illustrated or not, how long it is, its size, and its price. Shoppers can also expect to find a summary of its contents and may even be given some short reviews by experts in the field rehearsing its strengths. Electronic forms of advertisement can even provide long excerpts as a further incentive. Until recently, purchasers would have expected to acquire a book in some form of binding, but now it is possible to possess a given work only in an electronic form.

These elements of bookselling were not all present from the beginning. In the second half of the fifteenth century, book advertisements by printer-publishers either were broadsides or formed part of one of their publications, whose title page, by the 1480s, had come also to act as an advertisement for the contents of a book, and possibly also an indication of the sort(s) of purchasers for whom the book was intended. The great Venetian printer Aldus Manutius's (1449/52–1515) separate printed broadside of 1498 listing his Greek books with their prices in five subject classes ("in grammatica," "in poetica," "in logica," "in philosophia," "in Scriptura sacra") is often seen as the first book sales catalog proper. The earliest catalogs were addressed to retail customers; thereafter book advertisement came to address itself to the wholesale trade too. It adapted itself to the commercial and legal context and the structure of the book trade, in which printers, publishers, and various kinds of booksellers all engaged. Their roles could overlap, and in some cases be united in one person: any of them might decide to issue a catalog of their stock, or of new books, or of books about to appear.

At this time, books did not have a fixed price. They were sold inclusive or exclusive of transport costs, and at variable discounts to the trade and to retail customers; prices were mainly not printed in catalogs, although they might be added in handwriting for a specific client. This happened in Aldus's second catalog of 1503, which covered his Latin books and small formats as well as the Greek. The date of a given entry in the catalog was also more often omitted than included: this was done to allow book merchants to produce simultaneously an edition with title pages bearing sequential dates, to give the impression that they were selling books "hot off the press."

By the middle of the sixteenth century, a clear distinction emerged between "mart catalogs" (produced for a specific occasion of sale) and "stock catalogs" (which might list the production of a given printshop, or a bookshop, or a mixture of the two). In the 1540s, sales catalogs in Paris were printed for the first time in the form of small booklets rather than broadsides or appendixes; that of Chrétien Wechel (1495–1554) provided the sparse information that became a widely accepted model: author, short title, place of publication or sale, printer or publisher, and format. Wechel's contemporary Robert Estienne (1503–59), on the other hand, gave more information about each of his publications. The use by international booksellers of book fairs, notably that of Frankfurt, led to the emergence of printed fair catalogs, of which the earliest known is that of the Augsburg book merchant George Willer in 1564. These catalogs, which were quite expensive, did not state prices, as they were issued for both retail customers and the trade; but they all specified format. The date of the edition was also implied by the requirement that the entry was a "new, improved or enlarged edition," but the practice referred to above of producing simultaneously sequential editions helped merchants to circumvent this, and make repeated declarations of their wares. Declarations were usually in the tersest form, but publishers of important works (such as Galileo's *Sidereus nuncius* [Starry messenger] of 1610) were allowed to extend their entries to highlight their importance.

Fair catalogs were organized by language (Latin before German) and subject (the university higher disciplines of theology, law, medicine, followed by history, arts, poetry, and music). A very small entry of *vernacular books in languages other than German followed. In most fair catalogs, the books were listed in the order that notice of them was received by the fair authorities, who took over the administration of the fair catalogs in 1597. Redacted versions of the Frankfurt fair catalog appeared in Italy and England; these were designed for use by both book collectors and merchants.

The attendees at the fairs also affixed "nomenclaturae" or broadside printed lists of most of or all the products of their presses to their stalls. These were usually organized so as to highlight the specialties of the publisher in question. By the end of the sixteenth century, booksellers too began to produce printed lists of their holdings, sometimes indicating that these extended well beyond the titles included in their catalogs. One striking example is Cornelis Claesz's Amsterdam bookshop catalog of 1604, whose title page announced the availability on request of "a huge multitude of bound books in every faculty." While much of this material was printed, there were still manuscript catalogs sent in letters by booksellers to their clients: Duke August of Braunschweig-Lüneburg's library at Wolfenbüttel is testament to his remarkable assiduity in collecting books of all sorts and contains many of these that were sent to him by his agents throughout Europe in the first half of the seventeenth century. Many of those sent by Lyonnais book merchants such as the Huguetans to the Italian book agent and librarian Antonio Magliabechi in the second half of the century survive. Publishers of books had from the beginning seen the benefit of adding to the last gathering of their productions short catalogs of other books available from their presses, often with prices fixed at the retail rate: the very successful group of Genevan publishers led by Jean Antoine Chouët and Samuel de Tournes did this regularly from the final years of the seventeenth century onward.

Meanwhile, the market for secondhand books grew in importance. First, a generation of European itinerant book merchants purchased these from a variety of places and then offered them for sale, whether bound or unbound, in printed catalogs. From the end of the sixteenth century, sales catalogs were issued when libraries were auctioned. One of the earliest (if not the earliest) of these was Jeremias Martius's *Catalogus bibliothecae,* which appeared in Augsburg in 1572. Auction and secondhand book catalogs contained mostly bound books and were mainly organized in the sequence of fair subjects, and within each rubric, by size, with folios preceding the smaller formats. These sorts of catalog were a very notable feature of the Dutch market, in which inventories of the possessions of a deceased person were a legal requirement; they also appeared in Spain, though rarely in printed form, from a similar date. There are some French and a very few Italian examples, for in those countries there was no legal requirement to publish such inventories. In several European contexts, censored books could be excluded from catalogs, but not in the United Provinces with its laxer relationship to regulations; in some catalogs there was even a rubric "*libri prohibiti.*"

Bibliophilia—the taste for books considered rare because of their content or their provenance—formed a subsection of the trade in secondhand books. Books from the library of a famous scholar, for example, had been sought after from the very beginnings of printing. The collecting of books for their other features (specialized subjects, illustrations, bindings) came a little later. In the early nineteenth century, other desirable features were listed by Thomas Dibdin (an early commentator on bibliophilia) as "first editions, true editions, blackletter-printed books, large paper copies; uncut books with edges that are not sheared by binder's tools; illustrated copies; unique copies with morocco binding or silk lining; and copies printed on *vellum." Octavo editions of the Aldine classics (books produced by Aldus Manutius in the fifteenth and early sixteenth centuries) constitute an early example of collecting not motivated by the consumption of the content: these were avidly snapped up by purchasers in the 1510s. Rare and beautiful bindings became an object of collection by the second half of the sixteenth century; patriotic collections of vernacular literature, such as that by the duc de la Vallière in the latter half of the eighteenth century, began somewhat later.

After the French Revolution, the release on to the market of very large numbers of aristocratic and monastic libraries boosted the trade in incunabula and other rare books. These were first sold by agents; later, specialist booksellers and auctioneers developed the *subgenre of the antiquarian book catalog of rare material in England (Maggs, Quaritch, Sotheby's), France (Morgand), Switzerland (Gilhofer und Ranschburg), Germany (Rosenthal), and Italy (Olschki). The most recent examples of these are lavishly produced, often with copious illustration, and provide scholarly information about editions, their provenance, and any points of rarity, which can help justify the eye-watering prices ascribed to the items. In the late nineteenth and twentieth centuries, publishers' catalogs also became more lavish: long descriptions, blurbs from authorities, and pictures were used to sell new as well as old books.

A final development of sales catalogs worth noting is their transformation into bibliographical reference tools. Already in the sixteenth century Conrad Gessner (1516–65) had noted the utility of lists of books available for a sale from a given printer, many of which he reproduced in the dedications to his *Pandectarum sive partitionum universalium libri XXI* (Twenty-one books of pandects or general categories) of 1548–49. Later bibliographical authors followed suit, including Antonio Possevino (1533/4–1611) in compiling his *Bibliotheca selecta* (Select bibliography) (1593) for Catholic use, and Gabriel Naudé's in authoring his advice on library building: *Advis pour dresser une bibliothèque* (Instructions concerning erecting of a library) (1627). Daniel Elzevier's compendious bookshop catalog of 1674 appeared in Amsterdam, then a city on the way to becoming "the bookshop of the world." It was almost immediately acquired as a bibliographical reference guide to the disciplines and subjects that it contained. Its purchasers no doubt settled down to peruse it studiously and fruitfully as an object in its own right, much in the spirit of Anatole France's fictional scholar Silvestre Bonnard, for whom there was "no easier, more attractive and sweeter reading than a catalog." Since the 1990s, this kind of entertainment has been provided by Amazon as well as many secondhand booksellers and has been available in vast quantities to anyone with a computer.

Ian Maclean

See also bibliography; books; censorship; commodification; digitization; inventories; libraries and catalogs; merchants; publicity/publication; readers; sales catalogs

FURTHER READING

Frédéric Barbier, Thierry Dubois, Yann Sordet, and Verona, Bortolazzi, eds., *De l'argile au nuage: Une archéologie des catalogues (IIe millénaire av. J.-C.—XXIe siècle)*, 2015; Christian Coppens and Angela Nuovo, "Printed Catalogues of Booksellers as a Source for the History of the Book Trade," *JILS.it* 9 (2018): 166–78; Giovanna Granata and Angela Nuovo, eds., *Selling and Collecting: Printed Book Sale Catalogues and Private Libraries in Early Modern Europe*, 2018; Kristian Jensen, *Revolution and the Antiquarian Book: Reshaping the Past, 1780–1815*, 2011; Graham Pollard and Albert Ehrman, *The Distribution of Books by Catalogue from the Invention of Printing to A.D. 1800, Based on Material in the Broxbourne Library*, 1965; Günter Richter, *Verlegerplakate des XVI. und XVII. Jahrhunderts bis zum Beginn des Dreissigjährigen Krieges*, 1965; Archer Taylor, *Book Catalogues: Their Varieties and Uses*, revised by W. P. Barlow, 1987; Reinhart Wittmann, ed., *Bücherkataloge als buchgeschichtliche Quellen in der frühen Neuzeit*, 1984.

BUREAUCRACY

As is the case with information, bureaucracy as a phenomenon is considerably older than *bureaucracy* the word. An *Enlightenment physiocrat, decrying excessive regulation of trade, invented it to deride a new form of government. French radicals, struggling to achieve the promise of the revolution, lambasted it as an impediment to social reform. English political theorists, observing complacently the centralization of continental European monarchies, congratulated themselves on avoiding it. Theorists of social organization, seeking the harbingers of modernity, praised and feared it as a technology of machine-like efficiency for controlling the flow of vast quantities of information. Cynics, appalled by its clandestine procedures and extravagant inefficiency in clawing information to the center, satirized it witheringly. Public officials, promoting their administrative efficacy and espousing an ethos of service, deny that they might embody it. Populist leaders, stoking fears that it thwarts the will of the people, threaten emptily to destroy it.

Ever since "it" was first named in the mid-eighteenth century, bureaucracy has carried unambiguously pejorative connotations. So it remains in our collective consciousness, even as the phenomenon of bureaucracy has come to saturate our every action and interaction. As the anthropologist David Graeber notes, in the literary sphere of "sword and sorcery" fantasy fiction, when good and evil are invariably locked in combat, only the evil people are depicted as bolstering their rule with bureaucracies.

What, then, is "it"? We may profitably begin by distinguishing between the word, the wide range of connotations it has provoked, and the phenomena it has been taken to denote. For the sake of clarity, the following characteristics may be offered as a working definition of bureaucracy as a category of analysis: *bureaucracy describes a system of administration in which routine administrative activity is delegated to officeholders (who are often, but not always, professional career administrators), conducted on the basis of information (typically in the form of written records), with some differentiation and specialization of offices that are organized hierarchically and are reliant on systems of communications.* By this definition, bureaucracy existed as a system of administration long before it entered our vocabulary. Already in the fifteenth century, the sheer drudgery of routine administration was recorded in the verse of the English poet and clerk Thomas Hoccleve (d. 1426), who labored by day in the hierarchy of the Privy Seal Office, where he stared in silence "upon the sheep's skin" (membranes of *parchment) keeping his songs and words within. A history of bureaucracies will not, then, be commensurate with, nor englobed within, the conceptual history of the word. On the other hand, scholarly efforts to comprehend bureaucracy sociologically or to investigate specific instantiations of bureaucratic administration historically cannot ignore the cultural freighting of the term and the contested nature of the concept.

In 1745, the French economist Jacques-Claude Marie Vincent, Marquis de Gournay, is said to have quipped: "We have an illness in France that appears likely to ravage us;

this illness is called bureaumania"—*bureaumanie*. De Gournay saw this malady as the outcome of a new form of government—rule by officials—which he dubbed, *bureaucratie*. This conjoining of the French *bureau* with the Greek κράτος (*kratos*, "governing power")—by analogy with the classical Greek forms of government such as aristocracy and democracy—marks the arrival of *bureaucracy* into our common *lexicon.

From French, *bureaucracy* passed into German (1799), English (1818), Italian (1828), and Russian (mid-nineteenth century), without shedding its pejorative connotations. Uniformly hostile, the polemicists varied subtly in the targets of their hostility. Some followed de Gournay in using *bureaucracy* to refer to illegitimate rule by overweening officialdom. It is in this sense that the French term made its debut in English prose when in 1818 Lady Morgan described British rule over Ireland as "the *bureaucratie* or office tyranny by which Ireland had been so long governed." For others, it was the officials specifically, not the system at large, who were suspect. To describe this ruling caste, the French Revolution created another neologism—"the bureaucrat" (first documented in 1791). Soon a whole social class—the bureaucrats—found itself satirized in pictorial and literary form. The lithographs of Henri Monnier, published under the title "Scenes from bureaucratic life," depict low-level functionaries idling the day away in reading daily newspapers and sharpening their quills (figure 1). Honoré de Balzac in *Les Employés* (1836) refers to the birth of bureaucracy after the French Revolution, describing it as a "gigantic power set in motion by dwarves" (*La bureaucratie, pouvoir gigantesque mis en movement par des nains, est née ainsi*).

Many authors depicted bureaucracy as a societal malignancy. A Prussian pamphlet published in 1844 describes bureaucracy—in the sense of ranks of salaried officials ever increasing in numbers—as a "powerful cancer [that] feasts voraciously, insatiably, and lives on the marrow and blood of the people." The paradox of bureaucracy was its indispensability, and ineluctable growth, in the face of this distaste. Friedrich von Schulte (1880) wrote of the "tumor of bureaucracy" but noted the irony that: "Everybody blames the Bureaucracy and asks from it everything he needs."

It was primarily through the sociology of Max Weber (1864–1920) that bureaucracy was rescued from polemic and redeployed, analytically, as a sociological concept to refer to a particular form of rational administration. The pithiest formulation of Weber's conception is found in his political writings. "Parliament and Government in Germany under a New Political Order" (1918) was a controversial essay first published in serial form in the *Frankfurter Zeitung* (1917). Here Weber links the modernization of the state with the rise of "bureaucratic officialdom," whose characteristics he lists as being "based on recruitment, salary, pension, promotion, professional training, firmly established areas of responsibility, the keeping of files, hierarchical structures of superiority and subordination." Notably, *bureaucracy* refers to a system of administration, not the new form of government invented by de Gournay; for the latter, Weber employed the word *Beamtenherrschaft*—"domination" or rule by officialdom.

Weber's most elaborate account of bureaucracy was composed earlier, about 1912, and published posthumously in his unfinished opus magnum: *Wirtschaft und Gesellschaft* (Economy and society). This account is often summarized as a checklist of ten constituent elements. In fact, Weber provides a fully worked out "ideal type" with reflections on historical precursors and preconditions. The opening section describes the features of "bureaucratic authority" and then moves to the role of the official within that struc-

Figure 1. *Dix Heures: Lecture des journaux, Déjeuners, Taille des Plumes* (Ten o'clock, reading the papers, lunch, sharpening of the quills). Engraving from *Moeurs administratives* (1828) by Henry Monnier (1799–1877). Courtesy of Gallica and the Bibliothèque nationale de France.

ture of rulership. The chief elements of bureaucratic authority are its delimited jurisdictional competence ordered by fixed administrative rules and regulations. This permanent, public "bureaucratic authority" is, in Weber's view, historically exceptional, typical only of modern officialdom. The second characteristic concerns structure, specifically the hierarchical office with graded levels of authority. Weber sees the development of hierarchy and specialization as typical of all bureaucratic structures, whether public (the state), ecclesiastical, political (the political party), or private (enterprise and industry). The third characteristic concerns control of information. Here "the files" assume a vital role in the management of the modern office: written records are the means by which information is systematized and channeled, and their maintenance requires a vast staff of clerks and scribes.

From this outline of the structure of bureaucratic authority, Weber advances a description of the ideal-typical official who holds office as a vocation. Office is not a personal or family possession that can be inherited, nor is it a mechanism for personal enrichment; rather, it is a duty. The pure type of bureaucratic official serves not out of personal loyalty to the ruler nor by election from below but rather achieves office through impersonal qualifications, training, and expertise, with office work constituting the primary activity of working life. The bureaucrat enjoys a career within the hierarchical structure of the bureaucracy and is salaried, moving progressively from lower- to higher-paid positions.

Weber's contribution is widely acknowledged as seminal. It has also been widely misunderstood. Critics object that real historical examples never precisely fit the profile of the ideal type. This is to miss the methodological point. Weber deliberately intensified the elements of the ideal type to throw into relief the salient features of real historical examples, which never occur in a pure form. Actual historical bureaucracies are likely, to lesser or greater extents, to reflect wider societal norms and attitudes concerning such matters as patronage and personal probity. By way of illustration, George Washington famously established a bureaucratic ethos in which the only bars to attaining office were "family relationship, indolence and drink," whereas in Britain at the same time, as Samuel Finer observed, "the last two criteria were no barrier to office, and the first was a positive recommendation" (Mann, 458).

Where one can quite justifiably query Weber is in his value judgment about the technical superiority of bureaucratic organization. Bureaucracy is a precision instrument for achieving goals, the pinnacle of formal or "means-end" rationality (*Zweckrationalität*): "The fully developed bureaucratic apparatus compares with other organizations exactly as does the machine with non-mechanical modes of production. Precision, speed, knowledge of the files, continuity, discretion, unity, strict subordination, reduction of friction and of material and personal costs—these are raised to the optimum point in the strictly bureaucratic administration."

Contemporaries disagreed. The Russian *Encyclopaedic Dictionary* of 1891 includes the comment that "bureaucracy observes form for the sake of itself and sacrifices the essence of the matter to it." The idea of essence and meaning being sacrificed to serve futile and relentless office formulas suffuses the work of Weber's contemporary the Czech author Franz Kafka (1883–1924). It is likely that Kafka met Alfred Weber (1868–1958), younger brother of Max Weber, who taught at Charles University Prague during Kafka's time there as a student, graduating in 1907. Certainly, Kafka encountered an essay by the younger Weber published in 1910 under the title "Der Beamte" (The official), which describes the alienation of administrative life and the dangers of a coming "age of bureaucracy." The influence is felt directly in Kafka's short story "In the Penal Colony," and the theme of impenetrable bureaucracy is prominent in Kafka's prose more generally. In his final, and incomplete, dystopian novel, *The Castle*, Kafka emphasizes the symbolic power of documents and power of (mis)information. The life of the protagonist, K., is thrown into confusion by the misplacement of a file appointing him as surveyor of the local village. Seeking to have the error rectified, K. learns of an official in the Castle named Sordini, whose office is stacked with paperwork. Officials rush to and fro, piling up further bundles and removing others, so that the files are always collapsing, and "the constant sound of one pile after another crashing to the floor has become associated with Sordini's office." The crashing files are not, however, taken as a sign of inefficiency; rather, they betoken Sordini's conscientious effort to control the flow of information and prevent error within a complex administrative organization. As the head of the village explains to K.: "Is there a bureau of control? There are only bureaux of control (*Kontrollbehörden*). Of course, they are not meant to detect errors in the crude sense of the word, for errors are not made, and even if one is made, as in your case for instance, who can say for certain that it is an error?" Kafka does not use the German word for *bureaucracy* here, but he creates an indelible image of "it" as a rules-based system of menacing absurdity and farcical bureaucratic infallibility.

Sociologists in the generations after Weber argued that informality was a necessary characteristic of efficient administration, and excessive adherence to formal rules rendered bureaucracy ineffective. But ineffective need not mean powerless. This takes us to the unintended consequences of how bureaucracies think. It is not simply that the effectiveness of bureaucracy falters when it fails to comprehend the real social complexity it was created to administer. It is rather that bureaucracy reshapes society in the effort to render it comprehensible or "legible." Bureaucratic institutions simplify radically, imposing external categories and insisting on uniformity and standardization in the effort to count populations, control the environment, and extract wealth. As James C. Scott describes: "The necessarily simple abstractions of large bureaucratic institutions . . . can never adequately represent the actual complexity of natural or social processes. The categories that they employ are too coarse, too static, and too stylized to do justice to the world that they purport to describe." The outcome of such abstract and schematized institutional thinking, when imposed on the scale of mass social engineering, has often been tragic in its impact on environments and populations.

One point on which the interpretation advanced by Scott sits in agreement with Weber is in depicting bureaucracy of this kind as a project of high modernism of the twentieth century. For Weber, bureaucracy in its pure ideal-typical form was a "structure of domination" characteristic of legal-rational forms of authority, closely associated with "modernity," and distinct from patrimonial administration, which Weber depicted as personal, traditional, and normally premodern. This is a view that remains influential, notably in the work of neo-Weberian social theorists such as Michael Mann, who places the most intensive phase of bureaucratization in the last quarter of the nineteenth century (well over a century after the arrival of "it" as a word) and describes bureaucracy as a project encouraged by ideologists pursuing rational administration to augment the power of the nation-state.

A different angle of critique complicates the chronology and the assumed causal connection between bureaucracy, "modernity," and the state. In long-range historical perspective, the "state" as a territorially bounded and (more or less) uniformly ruled political formation is very much the exception. Much more typical was extensive rule over various peoples or ethnicities—the rule of "empires." While empires developed formal institutions of administration, few (if any) had the manpower or economic resources to communicate with their subjects directly. Power was necessarily delegated to or mediated through local power brokers, whether natives or settlers or bureaucrats on the ground—the "kings of the bush," as they were termed in French colonial Africa. For bureaucracy to be operable in situations of this kind, it required flexibility. Efforts to expand imperial bureaucracies, to exercise direct rule, or to override local power structures often proved destabilizing. The *early modern Spanish monarchy provides an example of a colonial bureaucracy that possessed much greater administrative latitude than its formalized hierarchy might at first suggest. This flexibility is summed up by the famous formula "I obey, but do not execute." The formula provided colonial bureaucrats located thousands of miles away from Spain with a necessary degree of autonomy and discretion in choosing to implement the central directives of the monarchy, without altogether denying the overarching authority of the monarch.

There is, then, a twofold risk: first, of foreshortening the history of bureaucracies as a form of administration by examining their operations solely in the context of the formation of modern states; second, of exaggerating the capacity of bureaucracy to exercise power extensively, especially in imperial contexts. Our empirical evidence for studying historical bureaucracies was, more often than not, produced by the bureaucrats themselves, whether in the form of the "files," the procedures they prescribed, or the moralizing claims they made for their own legitimacy and indispensability. All this evidence is potentially self-aggrandizing and needs to be unpicked. Tolstoy captures the reality neatly in his parable of the ruler-administrator—the bureaucrat—on the sea of history in *War and Peace*:

> In quiet and untroubled times it seems to every administrator that it is only by his efforts that the whole population under his rule is kept going, and in this consciousness of being indispensable every administrator finds the chief reward of his labour and efforts. While the sea of history remains calm the ruler-administrator in his frail bark, holding on with a boathook to the ship of the people . . . naturally imagines that his efforts move the ship he is holding on to. But as soon as a storm arises and the sea begins to heave and the ship to move, such a delusion is no longer possible. The ship moves independently with its own enormous motion, the boat-hook no longer reaches the moving vessel, and suddenly the administrator, instead of appearing a ruler and a source of power, becomes an insignificant, useless, feeble man.

For historians, whose interpretations are shaped by the information that is preserved when bureaucratic files become historical archives, the chief danger lies in writing history from the viewpoint of the bureaucrat adrift in his bark, holding on to a boat-hook.

Peter Crooks

See also accounting; archivists; cases; databases; diplomats/spies; documentary authority; files; governance; information, disinformation, misinformation; information policy; lists; political reporting; recording; registers; secretaries; surveilling

FURTHER READING

Martin Albrow, *Bureaucracy*, 1970; Peter Crooks and Timothy H. Parsons, eds., *Empires and Bureaucracy in World History: From Late Antiquity to the Twentieth Century*, 2016; H. H. Gerth and C. Wright Mills, eds. and trans., *From Max Weber: Essays in Sociology*, new ed., 1991; Eugene Kamenka and Martin Krygier, *Bureaucracy: The Career of a Concept*, 1979; Michael Mann, *The Sources of Social Power*, vol. 2, 2012; James C. Scott, *Seeing Like a State: How Certain Schemes to Improve the Human Condition Have Failed*, 1998.

CAMERAS

Since the early nineteenth century, the term *camera* has been used to describe a tool that, while highly variable in its physical composition and its functioning, has generated a consistent result: a photographic image. If one interprets *camera* in this colloquial, modern sense, the camera's importance for the history of information has been predicated on the functions of storage and transmission: it has depended on the camera's ability to generate photographs that are permanent rather than transient, and on cameras' connections with communications networks that have enabled photographic images to circulate widely and to be consumed across a range of contexts.

Cameras have a history that extends beyond photography, encompassing not only ancient and *early modern iterations of the camera obscura—a dark chamber or box with a small lens that admits light, creating an inverted image of the visual material outside the chamber—but also cameras used to make motion pictures. However, the present essay concentrates on cameras used to make photographs.

Photographs, whose name, deriving from the Greek, denotes a process of drawing with light, are recorded through the camera's lens and displayed on metal plates, paper, or, beginning in the late twentieth century, digital screens. Identifying a single origin point for the photographic camera is bound to fail, because "photography" denotes a heterogeneous array of inventions, but the diverse experiments toward photography that occurred in early nineteenth-century continental Europe and Britain were united by an interest in discovering a system of chemical formulas and material supports that would enable the permanent mechanical recording of the fleeting images that appeared in the camera obscura. Ultimately, these experiments resulted in two distinct approaches to registering and fixing images generated by light, which were both made public in the late 1830s: in France, the daguerreotype, introduced by Louis Daguerre but owing a substantial debt to his predecessor and collaborator Nicéphore Niépce's heliograph, and in England, the calotype, invented by Henry Fox Talbot.

Of these two processes, daguerreotypes prevailed, becoming the first widely practiced form of photography. Daguerreotypes, images on polished metal plates that were sharp and intricately detailed, combined positive and negative images in one and therefore were unique rather than *reproducible images. A decisive factor in daguerreotypes' success was the way that instructions on their production were allowed to circulate: in 1839, the French government purchased the rights to the process and offered it as a gift free to the world, though Daguerre obtained a patent for the process in England. Daguerre's instructions were published in a manual that quickly appeared in many editions and translations, enabling the process to spread widely, and the first commercially produced cameras, licensed by Daguerre and manufactured by Alphonse Giroux, went on the market immediately.

The exactitude and precision of the daguerreotype drew enthusiastic responses, but the camera had something of a divided identity: contemporaries discussed—and in some cases balked at—the camera's use as an artistic tool, but they also avidly discussed its potential importance in many fields of scientific inquiry. Early uses of photography reflected these plural priorities: cameras were swiftly applied to portraiture, but they were also used to make images of objects of scientific interest ranging from botanical specimens to astronomical phenomena.

In scientific as well as artistic discourses, the camera was often described as a tool that would allow for the direct and unmediated capture of reality. Influential early accounts of the medium downplayed the importance of human labor in the production of the photographic image, instead ascribing agency to natural or technological forces. Early descriptions of photography by Daguerre and Talbot framed it as a process by which nature reproduced itself. Other readings emphasized the mechanical qualities of photography, suggesting that photographs were the products of neutral technological processes rather than the creations of human photographers. These discourses, which elided the role of human actors and human work in the production of photographs, had a lasting impact, supporting a positivist image of photographic objectivity that helped to legitimize the use of photographs as visual evidence across many fields, including some that used photography's purported evidentiary power to repressive ends, like criminology and physiognomy.

Starting in the 1850s, paper photographs made using collodion processes began to replace daguerreotypes. Collodion processes, which used glass negatives, generated reproducible photographs, and this signaled an important shift in the camera's cultural role, aligning it with the production of inexpensive, standardized images rather than unique ones. Sliding-back cameras that accommodated multiple plates without the need to reload between each exposure helped support an understanding of photographs as multiple and sequential rather than singular and static. As large volumes of portrait photographs were sold in small, paper-based formats as *cartes de visite* and cabinet cards, photography came to be understood as an industrially produced commodity and, arguably, a mass medium.

With photographs circulating in unprecedented quantities, some contemporaries began to speak of photographic representation superseding embodied experience. Stereographs, double photographs or photomechanical prints that, when viewed through an optical device called a stereoscope, simulated three-dimensional vision, presented spectators with seemingly lifelike views that afforded vicarious visual access to places, events, and people that they might not be able to see by other means. Oliver Wendell Holmes Sr. wrote that with this technology, cheap and transmissible "form"—the photographic image—was decisively divorced from "matter," the physical referent of the photograph. "Give us a few negatives of a thing worth seeing . . . and that is all we want of it. Pull it down or burn it up, if you please," he wrote. According to Holmes, the capacity to generate lifelike, reproducible, and transmissible photographs of the world meant that the physical substance of the world's places and people became less important than their availability as visual representations—an observation that prefigured twentieth-century discussions of spectacle culture and pseudoevents.

Beginning in the late nineteenth century, the camera itself became a consumer product targeted to a mass market of buyers. While cameras had been commercially available since photography's earliest years, their technical complexity and expense prevented most people from using them. In the 1880s, however, camera manufacturers began to market compact and affordable box cameras for general use, including the Kodak cameras sold by the Eastman Company from 1888 onward with the slogan "You press the button, we do the rest." Kodaks were black boxes both literally and figuratively: they appeared preloaded with rolls of film, a new invention, and were mailed back to Eastman headquarters for processing, printing, and reloading. This system foregrounded the camera's role in the photographic process: cameras were framed as picture-taking machines while virtually all the technical labor that produced photographs was rendered invisible to consumers. Advertisements and manuals encouraged new legions of photographers to use their cameras as a kind of visual diary, chronicling everyday experiences and stepping out into the public realm to take pictures.

It took longer for professional photographers to adopt compact, mobile cameras. Starting in the 1920s, news photographers, accustomed to using larger-format cameras that necessitated glass plates and tripods, gradually began to adopt 35 mm film cameras like the Leica. The use of compact film cameras opened up the possibility of capturing events as they unfolded and made it possible for photographers to move about freely while photographing. They also enabled photographers to work discreetly, and some photographers used this capability to photograph public figures without their consent. Popular discourses surrounding these "candid camera" photographs cast them as possessing special *epistemic value because they divested their subjects of the ability to pose. In a culture glutted with cameras in public space, the discernibly posed photograph began to appear, to professionals and amateurs alike, less truthful than the candid image.

Photographs had been appearing in the press since the halftone process came into use in the late nineteenth century; this image reproduction technique allowed newspapers and magazines to publish photographs alongside text. However, in the 1920s and 1930s, photographs became far more central to print journalism. The interwar period saw the flourishing of photographically illustrated magazines that featured photo-essays, in which multiple photographs and brief captions were placed in dialogue to create a story. The introduction of services for the instantaneous wire transmission of photographs, like the Associated Press's Wirephoto service, launched in 1935, allowed periodicals to incorporate photographs that were timely, matching the temporal structures of textual news. Another important shift in photography's relation to time occurred with the introduction of instant cameras. Beginning with the first Polaroid cameras in 1948, the processes of exposure and development were integrated fully into the camera, allowing images to be viewed immediately.

The introduction of digital cameras beginning in the late twentieth century elicited lively popular discussion about the altered epistemic value of the photograph in a digital age. Some cultural critics contended that digitization signaled the "death" of photography, nullifying the camera's status as an information source; these critiques often focused on the widespread availability of tools for digital manipulation. However, the numerous connections between cameras' *analog and digital functions suggest that these death reports were premature, and that narratives that have presented the relationship between past and present photography in terms of radical rupture may have elided some important affinities. In an age of networked, camera-equipped smart phones, certain features present in predigital modes of photography—such as cameras' integration with communications networks enabling rapid image transfer, and cameras' capacity to generate instantly viewable images—have become more central than ever to photography rather than going into abeyance.

Moreover, the manipulability of the photograph in an age of digitization should be seen as an acceleration of existing capacities rather than an existential shift: photographic manipulation is virtually as old as photography itself, though the tools required to manipulate photographs convincingly have now become more widely accessible. And in spite of the cliché, in the twenty-first century, that the camera can "lie," the continued institutional uses of photographic images as visual evidence in many realms—from closed-circuit television to face-recognition technologies—suggest that even if individuals may distrust the camera's veracity, its practical epistemic power remains significant in an era of digital imaging.

Annie Rudd

See also digitization; manuals; media; networks; newspapers; observing; printed visuals; surveilling

FURTHER READING

Oliver Wendell Holmes, *Soundings from the Atlantic*, 1864; Reese Jenkins, *Images and Enterprise: Technology and the American Photographic Industry, 1839–1925*, 1975; Mary Warner Marien, *Photography and Its Critics: A Cultural History, 1839–1900*, 1997; Allan Sekula, "The Body and the Archive," *October* 39 (Winter 1986): 3–64.

CARDS

Visiting cards, playing cards, business cards, notecards, index cards (even trade cards) all possessed a crucial role in predigital information processing. They were only partially replaced at the start of the twenty-first century by the email signature and other small personalized media—except for the visiting card, which had its heyday from the *Renaissance to the Belle Époque, while the trade card enriched modern marketing campaigns in the second part of the nineteenth century. They both belong to the category of *dead media, however, since invitations to visits or appointments are now initiated by *digital text messages, and advertisements for brands and products have been circulated differently long since. Among others, cards functioned as handheld representatives and manageable paper-based proxies. The early use of notecards and card index boxes, especially, illustrates the card's importance as an inconspicuous, though indispensable, medium of information processing and knowledge transfer. For centuries, cards were made from paper, which afforded the allegedly modern features of mobility, portability, flexibility, modularity, representativity, transitivity, manageability, updateability, legibility, combinability, and, last but not least, the organization of information in terms of *big data, long lists, and vast amounts of accumulated knowledge. (For a closer examination of those ten properties, see Krajewski, "Cards," in the further reading section.)

Ever since the Swiss doctor, *polymath, and mountaineer Conrad Gessner (1516–65) recommended the index card as an aid for scholarly and textual production in his *Pandectae* of 1548, this medium has been set on a unique, albeit often secluded career. The main advantage of discrete cards consists in their mobility, which enables the words and text modules stored on them to be combined and reordered. Although others might have used the technique of cutting up pieces of information on paper so as to (re)arrange them more readily, Gessner's explicit description and reflection of this process may constitute the earliest account of conveniently generating extensive lists in alphabetical and systematic order. In this sense, Gessner is the inventor of index cards for scholarly purposes, and he marks the beginning of both the history of the card catalog and the thinking with index cards.

Next to mobility, the simple portability of a stack of cards is what makes working with the individual elements incomparably easier, especially in comparison to the difficulty of working with a catalog in book form. As a consequence of portability, a book no longer needs to be present on the shelf—a circumstance that deeply altered the scholarly community's modus operandi to date. In 1790 Albrecht Kayser, librarian to the German prince of Thurn and Taxis, explained, "For librarians, the second advantage of writing down the titles of all the works on hand in a library on individual slips of paper and then laying these out in alphabetic order is that they can now produce a general-purpose alphabetic catalog whenever and wherever they want. They no longer need to pick up a book itself, and whenever they do need one, they can specify its location at a distant site from their own homes." In other words, the slip of paper, or notecard, becomes a proxy of the actual text, a procedure that would prove to be extraordinarily practical for information processing and knowledge production. Notecards consequently represent an entire personalized system of symbols consisting of flexible vehicles for signs whose combinatorics serve to produce surprising constellations and to create completely new connections between the cards themselves by pointing to other parts of the card collection. It resembles a deeply interwoven *hyperlink system on a paper basis.

Card catalogs serve mainly two purposes. On the one hand they were installed and curated in libraries since the end of the eighteenth century, where they gathered the book collection in both alphabetical and systematic order. On the other hand, a card catalog is operated by an individual scholar who compiles excerpts, ideas, references to books, data about persons, and notes of any kind. No doubt the task of a library catalog consists in referring to *all* addresses of available books in as complete and logically consistent an order as is feasible at any given time. Questions to the catalog—whether asked by the mediating librarian or later by readers themselves—customarily comply with this general schematized form: whether and where a text is to be found (author catalog), or which text can be found in the stacks (subject catalog). Thus, the catalog may be expected to be able to answer if the pattern is followed, regardless of how peculiar a query might be. In other words, the library catalog, built on cards, serves as a dynamic, collective search engine. Its data input comes from numerous sources, but it always works in accordance with strictly regulated instructions, so that it can be queried by anyone. Owing to its flexible order it may be always up-to-date. The difference between the collective search engine and the learned box of paper slips lies in the latter's contingency, and the resulting possibility that queries in one's own terms can be posed to the arrangement. While a search engine is designed to register everything randomly, the scholar's machine makes the determination whether or not to record a piece of information, and whether or not to draw a connection from a new entry to an old one. With the aid of these connections, the user succeeds in tracking down new connections following the reference structure of entries, uncovering unintended readings.

On the basis of keywords and short forms, every point of the index card box can refer precisely to another. In contrast to a book with its fixed connections and unchangeable format defaults, every slip of paper represents a finite, extendable information unit, an expandable, elementary piece of information that can easily be cited—for every index card carries an unequivocal address thanks to its position in the set order or in the form of a call number others can refer to. A card always remains a pure reference and a relation to something else: it refers to something beyond itself. This logic also seems to apply in the case of knowledge proxies such as the library: a card catalog simultaneously makes one curious and provides information, occasionally to the extent that consulting the source documented on an index card may seem superfluous. References always refer to something else, be it a keyword on an index card, a catalog entry, books in a library, names on other notecards, absent interlocutors, or overarching structures, all of which get gathered together in bundles of notes. The principle of transitivity or relationality always prevails. Consequently, surprises pop up, thanks to an unexpected reference to aspects not previously considered. Thus, the advantage of the index card box consists not only in its ability to deliver precise answers to specific inquiries, but above all in its infallible ability to remember associations, to say nothing of the value added that is offered by (semi)automatic associative linking. Every input is preserved and retrievable, either as an isolated piece of information or as a building block for a larger line of argument. Equipped with sufficient (material) flexibility, the notecard as a single information carrier can enter into circulation; mixed forms can now be created out of the heterogeneous material recorded on them; and new orders can emerge out of cards that had not previously been located next to each other. Getting involved in constant communication with such a *secondary memory means trusting not only in the fact that the apparatus faithfully returns the stored information—there is also the reliable fact that information successively fed in over time will generate future knowledge.

In the apparatus's connectivity of preformed elements, it achieves a configuration of potential states of knowledge that are merely actualized by the user at a given time in certain combinations—when they are called up. "The text knows more than its author," as one of the basic assumptions of *philology has it. One could transfer this statement easily to the relation between constellations of index cards and their users. Text fragments held at the ready by the apparatus in their potential connectivity offer incomparably more connection points than the user is aware of at any given moment. Thus, the interface offers a range of possible connections, and along with them it delivers potentially new lines of argumentation. Storing states of knowledge and (via their contacts with the interface) helping to catalyze future thoughts, index cards know more than their author. One might say that the communication between database and user is purely theoretical, in the etymological sense of the word *theoria*, "view." For the arrangements of paper slips allow their user an instant view, an overview of possible constellations or different arguments. The variety of the slips of paper opens a perspective onto different possible considerations at the same time, allowing one to see various mental constellations in their contingency. Theory is nothing else, at least in etymological terms. It is up to the users to commit themselves to a view, to select certain lines of arguments or readings according to scientific practice as the basis of their own textual production.

If modularity depends on the statistical completeness of information, each card must constitute a distinct, self-contained data container with limited storage space. A card is a fundamental unit of meaning. Conrad Gessner made a similar observation in his stipulation that each discrete thought be recorded on a new line, which should then be put on its own slip of paper. This is how information grows—through the accumulation of scattered thoughts and the formation of discrete modules. One of the most well-known examples of this approach can be found in Niklas Luhmann's theory and in his own note-taking system. Niklas Luhmann (1927–98) was a German sociologist who developed Talcott Parsons's system theory into a very subtle and all-encompassing theory of society. Less known, though no less efficient, was Johann Jacob Moser, an eighteenth-century figure who, like Luhmann, had been trained as a legal scholar. In both cases, the patchwork system of juridical knowledge seems to favor a card-based organization scheme. What Moser and Luhmann had in common was not only their immense productivity but also their emphasis on the reusability of their note-taking systems. While there has recently been much scholarship on Luhmann's note-taking system, Moser's practices remain underappreciated in spite of detailed information about the secret of his productivity. The advantage of a modular notecard, in comparison to an entire note-book consisting of collectanea, is that it can "be used right away, as it is; whereas if collected passages are entered into books, they need to be written down again." For this reason, modular loose leaves make drafting a new text easier than working with books. Moser's process is also more conducive to selecting specific information or even concealing it: "If I wish to communicate only one of my collected passages to other people, or to have someone transcribe something without seeing the rest of the material, then I need only take out the sheets I wish to retain. If, on the other hand, the collected passages have been entered into books, then I have to provide the entire volume, or multiple volumes, in which things might be located that I would not want to be made known to just anybody."

A module is something self-contained, self-enclosed, which can be understood as a unit. Moser also describes, again in detail, his practice of rereading his excerpts, and effortlessly generating a new text out of them. Out of all his notes, Moser would first select only those slips of paper that seemed most auspicious for his present argument and then arrange them according to some specific classification scheme. Next, he would refine the order of the slips of paper for each subpoint and subsequently furnish them with additional marginal notes. With the aid of this outline, Moser would then search through his library for further quotations, references, and new ideas, noting these down on their own slips of paper, which he would combine with the previously selected slips of papers into a new order. After further review, additions, and a round of self-editing, he would finally add a table of contents to this entire bundle, consisting only of little slips of paper, and hand the whole thing over to a printer's shop, or the censorship board, without expending any further effort on the material. Two things would come back in return—a new book, which would get put back on his bookshelf, and the box containing the old slips of paper, which would get refiled into his note-taking system, allowing the loop to repeat. Thus, Moser's data stream alternates between two different media: An excerpt from a book turns into a card, which represents a book, which will be turned back into more cards, which will, in turn, become new books.

Ultimately, the historical analysis of index cards and card catalogs is able to bridge the gap between premodern principles of knowledge production and modern modes of data distribution as they (at least partly) fulfill common functions: Both, paper cards and electronic data in specific formats, are unified in their performance as standardized knowledge carriers. Though their specific formats differ—information requires formats—their status as proxies resembles each other as does their ability to accomplish organizational tasks, and finally their main function as placeholders—or rather representatives—that have the potential to create ever new connections—even out of the smallest pieces of information.

Markus Krajewski

See also accounting; bibliography; books; book sales catalogs; databases; documentary authority; excerpting/commonplacing; indexing; inventories; knowledge; notebooks

FURTHER READING

Alberto Cevolini, "Where Does Niklas Luhmann's Card Index Come From?" *Erudition and the Republic of Letters* 3, no. 4 (2018): 390–420; Albrecht Christoph Kayser, *Ueber die Manipulation bey der Einrichtung einer Bibliothek und der Verfertigung der Bücherverzeichnisse nebst einem alphabetischen Kataloge aller von Johann Jakob Moser einzeln herausgekommener Werke—mit Ausschluß seiner theologischen, und einem Register*, 1790; Markus Krajewski, "Cards," in *The Oxford Handbook of Media, Technology, and Organization Studies*, edited by Timon Beyes, Robin Holt, and Claus Pias, 2020; idem, *Paper Machines: About Cards and Catalogs 1548–1929*, 2002, translated by Peter Krapp, 2011; Pamela Walker Laird, *Advertising Progress: American Business and the Rise of Consumer Marketing*, 1998; Niklas Luhmann, *Die Gesellschaft der Gesellschaft*, 1998; Johann Jacob Moser, *Einige Vortheile vor Canzleyverwandte und Gelehrte in Absicht auf Akten-Verzeichnisse, Auszüge und Register, desgleichen auf Sammlungen zu künfftigen Schrifften und würckliche Ausarbeitung derer Schrifften*, 1773.

CASES

Cases are good to think with. This entry is about their status as carriers of information. For much of the twentieth century, they were considered a literary form, typically used by lawyers and doctors. Modern scientists, in contrast, used evidence in the form of data and rules: *facts, not examples and narratives. Then, philosophers of science and sociologists of knowledge, spurred by the challenges of *artificial intelligence (AI) and rise of bioethics, with its focus on the case as the unit of study, began to question the dominance of evidence-based knowledge and to consider cases as a style of reasoning. We now have histories of cases running from ancient Mesopotamia to the present day, with especially rich bodies of work on the emergence of collections of medical cases in *early modern Europe and China.

We can think with cases, but they are also objects. In this sense a "case" usually means a container or frame and often extends to its contents, such as a case of wine, a suitcase. In most European languages, the term derives from the Latin *capsa*, a cylindrical container for books, relics, or money. Its obsolete meanings extended to clothing, pelts, and bodies, suggesting a limiting of the term around 1700, as these colloquial usages fell away and legal and medical professions began to use the term more formally. In China, *an* (案) designated a footed tray or vessel, and later a judgment in the form of a document (in contrast to *shi* [事], meaning event, often used when narrating history), either paired with *gong* (公), to mean legal cases, or, in a sixteenth-century innovation, *yi* (醫), to mean medical cases. Like bureaus and tables, cases conflate the act of producing the record and the record itself.

Cases are a central part of how we understand the histories of scholarship, bureaucracy, and information. As an object of study, they allow us to slip between a focus on the conventions of collecting multiple cases and of documenting particular cases, whether in the moment, like account books, or after the fact, as case histories and observations. These are different, though related practices. In fact, as we will see, the relationship between recording a series or collection of cases and describing a single anomaly or exemplar is a central feature of their history. It could even be considered the pivot at which the material record, the document, meets the episteme. Accordingly, before describing the history of cases, we need to consider cases as a style of reasoning.

THINKING IN CASES

John Forrester's 1996 article "If P, Then What? Thinking in Cases" has informed much of the scholarship on cases over the past two decades. Following Ian Hacking and others, Forrester proposed that "thinking in cases" is a "style of reasoning." He set out three tangled threads: the psychoanalytic case history, the historical sociology of the sciences, and the individual in the human sciences. In disentangling these, he traversed the whole history and philosophy of Western science, beginning with Aristotle, who teaches us that there is no science of the individual at the same time as laying down the gauntlet for a future science of the individual. Individuals and populations, particulars and generalizations, examples or experiments and rules or laws, the personal and the scientific, inductive and deductive logic are all thrown into relief when considering the history of the case. The genealogy of the psychoanalytic case history, Forrester's ultimate concern, leads him to test Michel Foucault's account of "the examination" in *Discipline and Punish* (1975). Toward the end of the eighteenth century, Foucault posits, the emergent clinical sciences admitted the individual into scientific discourse, through objective examinations and their associated procedures of writing and registration, and thus created cases, making individuals both objects of knowledge and subjects of power. Cases, previously the purview of priests and lawyers, became instruments of medicine and the state. Forrester challenged Foucault's story of a shift from theological and legal cases to clinical ones with a discussion of medical ethics and the analogical arguments, and the forms they take, of modern casuistry. Ultimately he concluded with a question that can be parsed: what work do cases do in the disciplines and practices that we recognize as the domain of the professional expert?

This survey follows up on Forrester's work. It traces the history of cases, paying particular attention to practices of recording, retaining, and using them.

Chinese Cases

China, with its awesome imperial bureaucracy and even longer tradition of written practices, has much to teach us about cases. The first comprehensive *code of imperial law was established in the Tang dynasty (618–907). Under the Song dynasty (960–1279), with the expansion of the legal apparatus, massive numbers of legal case records accumulated in local and central government archives. As magistrates engaged with this body of cases and navigated elaborate legal code, they produced more cases. Add in imperial memos, edicts and commentaries, and supplementary legal rulings, and the result was a volume of summary compilations too unwieldy for working jurists to use.

With the advent of print in the tenth century, the earliest surviving collections of printed legal cases began to be produced. These drew on cases from dynastic histories that illustrated the actions and achievements of important officials. Forms of written and printed cases (*an*) proliferated in the Ming (1368–1644) and Qing (1644–1912) dynasties. These included various sorts of legal handbooks, anthologies, and memoirs. As part of the economic growth, urbanization, increase in social mobility, and decline of the state that makes the late Ming period distinctive, the school system expanded, and printed books circulated more widely as recognized sources of authority and expertise. Bureaucratic positions became more competitive, and printed examination primers, including collections of legal and medical cases, were targeted at aspiring civil servants. The model of the judge, and the act of judgment, was adopted by other late imperial experts, especially doctors, as they began to produce case collections of their own.

Cases are foundational to the modern practices often called Traditional Chinese Medicine, and they feature in a legitimating history that begins with Shang oracle bones in the second millennia BCE and arrives at a fully developed form in the sixteenth century that persists to the present day. Individual medical cases do date from antiquity, and the form underwent marked changes in the sixteenth century, but this is more a story of socially embedded changes than of disciplinary continuities.

Chinese physicians may have recorded details of their consultations from around the third century BCE. As part of an idealized account of government structures, *Zhouli* (Rites of the Zhou) includes a medical master who provides annual reckonings of successful cures. A thousand years later, Song dynasty regulations for medical students similarly prescribed annual submissions of case records.

Evidence of actual practices of recording cases seems to have been common from at least the Han dynasty (206 BCE–220 CE). The *Shiji* (Records of the grand scribe), a universal history completed around 90 BCE by Sima Qian, records the troubles of the physician Chunyu Yi. When questioned about his expertise, Chunyu Yi allegedly produced twenty-five case histories and declared, "In every case where your vassal has conducted a medical consultation, he has always made a consultation record" (chapter 105, 2813, Cullen, 305). Chunyu Yi used the term *zhenji* (診籍), meaning consultation record, not *yi'an*, a later designation meaning case history or case statement. By the third century CE, detailed accounts of seventeen cases of the physician Hua Tuo (ca. 141–208) began to circulate in histories. Various texts dating from the seventh century onward included medical cases to illustrate successful prescriptions or provide instances amid theoretical discussions of diseases. This trend was amplified with the growth of a scholarly apparatus of government under the Song dynasty, as thirteenth- and fourteenth-century physicians included cases in their writings. Thus, individual medical cases were recorded in private practice or, like legal cases, within bureaucratic contexts before the Ming dynasty. Then things changed.

The collection of medical cases (*yi'an*) was a Ming innovation; the phrase seems not to have been used before the sixteenth century. This innovation was part of an increase in *publishing more generally. In the case of medicine, it marked a shift in authority from hereditary physicians whose reputation rested on lineage to scholarly physicians who demonstrated their expertise in writing. Collections of cases, focused on particulars, joined *canonical works, in which particular cases illustrated general rules. The *genre was self-consciously new, intended, as authors reflected, on establishing a standard process for conducting consultations and recording cases. For instance, in a treatise published in 1522 the physician Han Mao listed the six stages of a consultation and specified, "Whenever you treat any disease, make a case statement on a piece of paper in this format" (Cullen, 313). Medical cases, like legal cases, were to take a prescribed format. Formats became forms: a senior Ming bureaucrat, in guidance for good governance, recommended providing qualified physicians with a blank volume of yi'an to be completed by the physician and patient then, as we saw hundreds of years before, subjected to annual reckonings. Whether or not provincial governors actually reviewed yi'an annually, physicians considered recording cases good practice. Individual cases could be shared with patients and their families to enable them to choose between the recommendations of different physicians, and later printed, either by physicians or by their families and followers, in didactic collections. Whatever the audience, cases were intended to demonstrate a physician's expertise.

The practice of writing cases for a patient and her or his family, complete with prescription, rationale, and the physician's name, continued through the twentieth century. Such cases were central to Chinese medical encounters, though we should be cautious about generalizing from elite, literate families to less privileged spheres. During the Republican period (1912–49), some physicians took efforts to revise the format of cases in line with biomedical categories, an appropriation of, rather than a capitulation to, Western medicine aimed at unifying and bolstering Chinese medicine and ensuring the support of a government with inclinations to scientism. Han Mao had specified that a case should set out what a physician knew from conventional diagnostic methods: looking, listening, smelling, and questioning the patient, feeling the pulse, reasoning through this information, and providing a treatment. In contrast, He Lianchen (1861–1929), one of the leading modernizers of Chinese medicine, specified that a case should follow Western standards: the patient, the disease name, the disease cause, the symptoms, a diagnosis, treatment method, prescriptions, and results. He Lianchen rewrote case records by esteemed physicians from across the centuries into this new format. Most notably, old cases were organized by symptoms, new ones by diseases. This was a new medicine in the name of the old.

Collections published by physicians and their families and associates present a clear, self-conscious lineage from the cases of Wang Ji (1463–1539) gathered by his disciplines in 1531 and those of eminent physicians assembled by Jiang Guan and his son Jiang Yingsu in 1591 to the present. Joined by a further thirty-one works of the yi'an genre in the seventeenth century, and forty-six more in the eighteenth century, they went through many editions in subsequent centuries. In the Republican period, manuscript cases by renowned physicians of previous ages were printed too. These collections advertised physicians' expertise and provided instruction in their methods. Despite gestures toward standardization, late Ming and Qing cases (manuscript and printed) continued to range in length, detail, and emphasis, reflecting a physician's individual style and the intellectual lineage with which he aligned himself. By the twentieth century, as we have seen, Republican physicians favored more rigorously standardized, less discursive cases, focused on explaining the theories that informed therapeutic choices. Collections of printed medical cases were brought into line with the government ideals of a standardized, systematic, and internally consistent science.

Cases in European Traditions

The history of European cases typically begins in Greece, around 400 BCE, with Hippocrates, the father of medicine. In fact, Mesopotamian cuneiform tablets, some from as early as the fourth millennia BCE, detailed particular legal, medical, and divinatory cases. But these traditions were known only indirectly until relatively recent times, when archaeologists recovered them. Hippocrates, a legendary figure even in his own time, found followers who assembled a heterogeneous body of writings, known as the Hippocratic *Corpus*. This included the *Epidemics*, a work that contains more than three hundred cases, some focused on symptoms, others on therapeutics, together with weather observations and general medical rules. The cases date from circa 410 to 350 BCE, take place in various locales, and were probably written by three or more different physicians whose names are not recorded. *Epidemics* circulated in manuscripts through the Middle Ages in Greek, Arabic, and Latin and was included in a Latin edition of the *Corpus* printed in Rome in 1525, with a Greek edition the following year in Venice. Sixteenth- and seventeenth-century physicians modeled themselves on Hippocrates, writing cases on paper just as he had written them on wax tablets, or rolls made of papyrus or animal skins. Good doctors wrote cases.

So did good priests. Fourteen hundred lead tablets found at the oracular sanctuary of Dodona, dating from the sixth to the second centuries BCE, set out specific questions for the gods. The public inscriptions at the shrine of Asclepius at Epidaurus (ca. 400 BCE), where patients slept in a dormitory and received advice in their dreams, recorded individual cases, mounted as expressions of thanks to the gods for successful cures. Despite the absence of a theoretical literature, these are instances of thinking in cases.

We do not know whether the doctors who assembled the cases in the Hippocratic *Epidemics* were motivated by didactic interests, philosophical debates, or other purposes. Given that 60 percent end in a patient's death, they seem not to be showcasing expertise. The cases recorded at the shrine of Asclepius claim a much higher rate of success. When Galen, the immensely influential second-century Greek physician who worked in Rome, systematized the Hippocratic teachings, he did not collect cases. Rather, he used them selectively, as examples. This suggests that he recorded some cases, perhaps assisted by his slaves, if even just the most exemplary, didactic, cautionary, or self-promoting ones. The Greek Empiricists, defenders of Hippocratic medicine against the Rationalists, seem to have recorded cases in their now-lost works. Twenty-one cases attributed to the first-century Greek physician Rufus of Ephesus survive in an Arabic translation. The famous Arab physician al-Rāzī (854–925) recorded his own cases, modeled on Hippocratic writings and informed by Galen's teachings. He used them as examples in his treatises and, less formally, for instructing his students, who collected and circulated more than nine hundred of them after his death. Al-Rāzī also collected the cases of other physicians, from works or collections now lost.

Cases, medical and otherwise, featured throughout medieval Arabic literary works. Professional court physicians typically included cases to illustrate how their methods triumphed over another's. But cases do not feature as examples or anecdotes in Ibn Sina's (Avicenna) monumental *Canon of Medicine*, the *encyclopedic synthesis of medical knowledge that was foundational to medical teaching from its composition in eleventh-century Persia through European universities in the 1700s. Cases of a sort do feature in Ibn Sina's autobiography, completed posthumously by his student al-Juzjani. Within Arabic medical writings more generally, authors recorded *muyarrabat*, particular remedies or techniques, often with details of the case in which it was tried and proven.

Through the Middle Ages on both sides of the Mediterranean, as Galen's brand of rational medicine dominated learned teachings, individual cases featured as examples in theoretical works. While experience was valorized in some medieval Latin scholarship—mysticism, alchemy, parts of medicine, and increasingly astronomy (which encompassed astrology and astrometeorology)—in most copies of ancient texts, observed evidence from the natural world, often constituting a case, was noted, if at all, in the margins. *Experimenta*, like muyarrabat, might include details of a case, and case narratives (*narrationes, exempla*) typically were written in the margins of medical and religious works. From the early thirteenth century, theologians conducted theoretical debates about the increasing use of this sort of homiletic story in scholarly texts and everyday sermons by the mendicant orders. Surgical textbooks, as pioneered by Rolando Cappellutti in the mid-thirteenth century, used *narratio* that borrowed tropes from miracle stories to introduce new techniques and demonstrate the surgeon's skill. Physicians included narrationes and exempla in their *practicae*, inserting stories into manuals of regimen that reminded the reader of the experiential basis of book learning. By the fourteenth century, medical narrationes appeared independent of surgical textbooks or medical practicae, as the collections by the famous Montpellier physician Arnau of Villanova and the English surgeon John of Arderne demonstrate. In the fifteenth century, Michele Savonarola, physician at the court of Ferrara, used individual cases in his medical and historical writings. Thousands of European manuscripts survive, initially in Latin then in the *vernacular, from the twelfth through seventeenth centuries that include experimenta singly or gathered into collections as the observed and experienced knowledge—the case—moved from the margins to the center of the text.

We need to pause over *consilia*. A *consilium* was a consultation, often framed as a response to a question, theological, legal, or medical. In Republican Rome, distinguished jurists delivered consilia on issues that carried the force of judicial opinion. The practice continued into the classical period of Roman law, where consilia were held to have the approval of the emperor, then seems to have lapsed from the third century before emerging again in northern Italy around 1200. Where local judges could not settle a case, an esteemed jurist was consulted. When a person of note fell ill, the case might be put to a learned physician. These cases later became the building blocks of elaborate regimen, treatises on disease, or didactic collections. Whether legal or medical, a consilium typically began with a statement of the case, naming the litigants or patient and narrating the history of the matter to date, including opinions on it by other authorities. In legal cases, the contentious arguments were then set out. In medical cases, the second part was a regimen to prevent illness or restore health and a treatment, often listing numerous remedies, sometimes borrowing the argumentative style of legal cases. In both forms, consilia concluded with a summary describing the outcome. By the end of the fourteenth century, collections of legal and medical consilia were commonplace in Bologna. They soon spread to neighboring universities. Physicians ordered their collections, following other genres of practical medicine, by disease from head to toe; Bartolomeo Montagnana's is the best-known medieval example (1476). By the fifteenth century, astrologers—many of whom were medical men—were following this example to make collections of horoscopes, again combining details with prescriptions to improve health, avoid danger, and obtain riches.

None of these developments would have been possible without a shift in the balance between memory and written records beginning in the eleventh century. Fragmentary evidence of links between medieval scholarly practices and bureaucratic innovations survive in memoranda of medical and astrological cases from the decades around 1400. A century later, novel habits of account keeping and interests in testimonials and natural particulars converged at bedsides, consulting rooms, and doctors' desks, framed as an imperative to improve medicine. Some doctors' records focused on treatments and payments, others on narratives of diseases and cures, often written from rough notes or memory at the end of the day. Practices were local. Professors at Ferrara and Padua in the 1540s encouraged their students to record case histories. Toward the end of the century, Gemma Frisius, the Dutch physician and mathematician, reputedly kept a pair of notebooks, one of observations about the stars and weather, the other for medicine. His compatriot Pieter van Foreest noted that he began recording medical cases when he turned his attention from heavenly observations to microcosmical (earthly) ones. The resulting manuscripts seldom survive: several hundred, ranging from fragments of a few cases to many thousands, have been located, variously labeled diaries, journals, registers, observations, and casebooks.

At the same time, within scholarly publications, as Gianna Pomata has argued, *observationes* developed as a distinct "epistemic genre." Instead of dropping examples into theoretical works, humanist physicians collected what they termed *curationes* or *observationes medicinales* (medical treatments or observations respectively). *Philological works similarly assembled notes on discrete, disputed parts or words of an ancient text, producing observationes with a whiff of ritualized observances. While earlier legal consilia were collections of a single jurist, *observationes legales* or *forenses* were collections of cases decided by a court of law, connected to the development of case law and the publication of reports of tribunal rulings, all of which grew through the seventeenth and eighteenth centuries. In England, where common law originated and from whence it spread to her colonies, these were standardized as the *Law Reports* from 1865.

From the sixteenth century, medical professors harnessed print to extend their case-based methods of teaching from face-to-face meetings with their pupils to the nascent *Republic of Letters. Amatus Lusitanus, a Jewish physician living in Italy, published seven hundred cases, a hundred at a time between 1551 and 1566. His *Centuriae curationum* (Hundreds of treatments) established a new genre. Other collections, like al-Rhasis's, were eclectic by design: Johan Schenck von Grefenberg's *Observationes medicae, rarae, novae, admirabiles et monstrosae* (Rare, new, admirable and monstrous medical observations, 1585–97), the most significant late sixteenth-century collection, combined observationes from ancient and medieval texts, his network of correspondents, and his own practice. Producing observationes was an epistolary and bibliographical exercise, an instance of the drive to collect that shaped sixteenth- and seventeenth-century inquiry. By 1700, around a hundred authors had published collections of cases. Individual cases became staples of the new periodicals published by Europe's *learned societies. Collections of cases continued to be produced through the eighteenth century, some following old head-to-toe orders, others ordered by diseases. Thus, despite innovative technologies—physical examinations, quantitative testing, postmortem investigations—doctors relied on a vast medical library, reaching back through the centuries, to classify diseases. Medical knowledge, as Volker Hess and Andrew Mendelsohn have argued, was produced through the study of published cases, old and new.

We have arrived at the point where we began. Cases were an integral part of authoritative legal, medical, and theological traditions in eighteenth-century Europe and its empires. Collective investigations, predicated on standardized cases, were fundamental to the rise of scientific medicine and clinical sciences. This is when the examination, as Foucault argues, conducted in institutions like schools, prisons, legal courts, and hospitals, came to regulate social norms. An individual became a case to be described, judged, measured, and corrected according to norms and classifications. From the middle of the nineteenth century, practices of recording and collecting cases exploded. We now know much more about the histories of particular aspects of cases. To the formalizing of case histories in the Paris hospitals from admission to autopsy, we can add, for instance: the ways that male practitioners and their female patients negotiated authority and experience through manuscript casebooks and printed observations; increasingly rigorous hospital documentation through the 1800s, including standardized recording of pulse and temperature at regular intervals; competing models of case writing in nascent disciplines from sociology to neurology; the introduction of the case method of teaching at Harvard Law School in the 1870s and to medical education several decades later; subtle, extended psychoanalytic and postpsychoanalytic case narratives, and readings of them; the genesis of the unitary patient record—when patients became file numbers—in the early twentieth century; the aesthetics of fictional representations, written and pictorial; and the importance of case-based studies in biology, medicine, sociology, and business and case-based logic in AI. Debates are ongoing about whether computer-assisted case records will allow doctors to return to an idealized medical encounter before writing tools ostensibly diverted the medical gaze, or whether *digital tools are simply part of a continuous tradition, with advantages and shortcomings, of other information technologies. This sketch of the history of cases, East and West, has also been an account of how techniques to produce, share, and archive knowledge relate to notions of an individual as a constructed entity. Cases matter most when rules and those who maintain them are being challenged. If we are living in an era when the notion of the individual is legally, medically, and morally in crisis—think about, for instance, health inequalities, immigration, data protection, and reproductive rights—what constitutes a case matters more than ever.

Lauren Kassell

See also bureaucracy; documentary authority; governance; knowledge; learning; memos; notebooks; professors; teaching

FURTHER READING

Cristina Álvarez Millán, "The Case History in Medieval Islamic Medical Literature: *Tajarib* and *Muyarrabat* as Source," *Medical History* 52 (2010): 195–214; Christopher Cullen, "*Yi'an* (Case Statements): The Origins of a Genre of Chinese Medical Literature," in *Innovation in Chinese Medicine*, edited by Elisabeth Hsu, 2001, 297–323; John Forrester, "If P, Then What? Thinking in Cases," *History of the Human Sciences* 9 (1996): 1–25; Charlotte Furth, Judith Zeitlin, and Hsiung Pingchen, eds., *Thinking with Cases: Specialist Knowledge in Chinese Cultural History*, 2007; Volker Hess, "A Paper Machine of Clinical Research in the Early Twentieth Century," *Isis* 109 (2018): 473–93; Brian Hurwitz, "Narrative Constructs in Modern Clinical Case Reporting," *Studies in History and Philosophy of Science* 62 (2017), 65–73; Lauren Kassell, "Casebooks in Early Modern England: Astrology, Medicine and Written Records," *Bulletin of the History of Medicine* 88 (2014): 595–625; J. Andrew Mendelsohn, "Empiricism in the Library: Medicine's Case Histories," in *Science in the Archives: Pasts, Presents, Futures*, edited by Lorraine Daston, 2017, 85–109; Gianna Pomata, "Observation Rising: Birth of an Epistemic Genre, 1500–1650," in *Histories of Scientific Observation*, edited by Lorraine Daston and Elizabeth Lunbeck, 2011, 45–81.

CENSORSHIP

The saying "information wants to be free" has become a cliché in contemporary society, but in the *early modern world the unimpeded circulation of information was never a reality. Published texts were subject to censorship by political and religious authorities, and self-censorship by authors and *publishers was pervasive, though often difficult to document. Censorship—regulations on how and to whom information circulated—was a ubiquitous part of early modern information systems. Censorship in the early modern world is resonant with, and materially different from, censorship in our present. One major difference between early modern and contemporary censorship lies in its degree of secrecy: while early modern censorship was explicitly recognized and publicly enacted, governments today censor with a greater degree of secrecy. Indeed, the extent of the "classified universe" is now so vast that it impedes our ability to precisely track what information is censored and what is free.

Information in the early modern world was published, or rather made public, in manuscript, in print, and orally. The public circulation of information exposed it to scrutiny, especially from governments and religious institutions. Some of these systems required that governments or religious officials review and grant permission for a text to circulate prior to publication. These prepublication licensing systems were widespread in Europe. In early modern England, for example, state censors would confirm before printing that texts were free of treasonous ideas that were harmful to the Crown. Prepublication censorship of print in Catholic states took the form of an *imprimatur* (or formal permission to print, from the Latin for "let it be printed"), which was then printed in the opening pages of a book to show that ecclesiastical censors had approved the text. In addition to stifling the spread of certain kinds of ideas, prepublication censorship went hand in hand with patents (or "privileges") and registers that served as forms of intellectual property protection against piracy.

While states and religious authorities implemented prepublication controls, authors and printers devised several ways to bypass these systems. Manuscript production was harder to police than printing houses, so some authors chose to circulate information that would not pass the censors in manuscript instead of print. Other materials, like erotic texts and images, heterodox religious ideas, and political sentiments that undermined standing governments, circulated illicitly. In some cases, printers skipped the prepublication controls and disguised texts with false imprimaturs that made them appear legal when they had never actually been approved. Since prepublication controls were implemented by state and religious authorities within cities, printers occasionally disguised illicit material by adding a false location of printing, inventing a false printer, or even neglecting to include any of this information within the printed text, relying on anonymity to protect authors and printers alike. Neapolitan imprints were famously suspicious, and most early modern censorship laws explicitly forbade anonymous texts for this very reason. These underground networks and black-market strategies were the proxies and VPNs of early modernity, circumnavigating censorship using alternative text technologies.

Public book burnings have been some of the most visible spectacles of censorship systems. In a Christian context, book burnings followed the precedent laid out in the Bible in Acts 19:19: "And many of them who had followed curious arts, brought together their books, and burnt them before all." Book burnings were intended as instructive public demonstrations in addition to a means of destroying texts. The Catholic Church oversaw many mass burnings of the Jewish Talmud; the most infamous of these episodes took place in Paris in 1242 and in Rome in 1553. The *Reformation and resulting confessional fracture in Western Christianity was propelled by the wide circulation of printed texts and images and also ushered in a new era of book burning in Europe. In 1520, Martin Luther symbolically set ablaze Catholic theological texts with which he disagreed and also burned the papal bull announcing his excommunication. Throughout the Counter-Reformation, Catholics burned Protestant religious texts and books written by heretical authors in piazzas and squares across Italy. In Jean Calvin's Geneva in 1553, the city council publicly burned Michael Servetus on a pyre with his own writings. The human as well as cultural toll of censorship could be profound, and we must not overlook that efforts to control information have often led to violence.

Not all censorship sought to destroy texts in their entirety. Expurgation is a method of censorship that involves removing particular words or passages or altering the meaning of a text so that it could then comply with authorities' religious, political, and moral sensibilities. Prepublication censorship was a form of expurgation, but texts were also expurgated after publication. Some editions of the Catholic *Index of Prohibited Books* provided for certain books to be banned until they were expurgated (*donec expurgentur*, or *donec corrigantur*). Catholic authorities struggled to produce lists of official sets of expurgations that could then guide readers as they emended their books with pen and ink, knives, wax, glue, and scraps of paper. Catholic censors also took up their pens to expurgate material from Hebrew books, leaving traces on the opening or closing pages with their signatures and dates. There were many material solutions to censorship other than book burning. Expurgation became a widely used compromise in Catholic Europe at the end of the sixteenth and beginning of the seventeenth centuries, one that preserved expensive books and their often useful content while manually removing the errors they contained.

Censorship systems had widespread effects, but it is important to remember that censorship affected readers in different ways. Catholic prohibitions against and burnings of *vernacular translations of the Bible contrast with Protestant approaches to Bible readership and lay piety. However, learned and pious readers (especially men) in Italy could apply to obtain reading licenses that would allow them to read some prohibited texts. We might helpfully consider that early modern censorship was about controlling not only how information was spread, but also how it was consumed. Different classes of readers were permitted access to more information than others deemed less trustworthy. This observation remains true in the *longue durée* since censorship systems rely on censors who are granted access to information with the goal of suppressing it. News sources recently estimated that China's Great Firewall employs over two million people to censor the *internet. Censorship changes and controls how information circulates to particular audiences, rather than destroying that information in its entirety.

Self-censorship is the most insidious, widespread, and difficult to track effect of censorship regimes. Leaving few traces, self-censorship led authors and readers alike to dissimulate about the intent of their texts and the possible interpretations their reading suggested. When Galileo testified to the Roman Inquisition in 1633 about the accusation that he endorsed Copernicanism in his *Dialogue concerning the Two Chief World Systems*, his initial defensive strategy was to reread his book to determine whether "through my oversight, there might have fallen from my pen not only something enabling readers or superiors to infer a defect of disobedience . . . [but even something that would lead them to] think of me as a transgressor of the orders of Holy Church." Authors encoded multiplicities of meanings within texts and embraced dissimulation in response to censorship laws.

The greatest difference between early modern and contemporary censorship is its degree of secrecy. In early modern Europe, the extent of censorship, the identities of censors, and precise details about what information could not circulate were all common knowledge. In the sixteenth century in response to the Protestant Reformation, the Catholic Church printed and published versions of an *Index of Prohibited Books* in Spain, Portugal, France, and many Italian states. These laws were implemented in Catholic communities across the globe until 1966. The *Index of Prohibited Books* made public what knowledge was disallowed and often had the effect of ensuring an audience for prohibited texts by publicizing their existence. By contrast, China's Great Firewall is a vast and flexible system of censorship that constantly and secretly adapts its prohibitions to respond to current events. In the United States, which protects *free speech under the First Amendment to the Constitution, there are still extensive realms of classified information that are formally excluded from Freedom of Information Act requests. Secrecy about information control is characteristic of contemporary censorship systems and makes them distinct from those of past eras.

Censorship is fundamentally a material and interpretive process. As authors and publishers carefully composed texts to avoid triggering censors' responses and censors pored over manuscripts and printed books looking for indications of treason, heterodoxy, and depravity, both faced the problem of the slippery nature of interpretation. While there may have been many possible interpretations of a given text, censorship ultimately gave state and religious systems power over inscribing particular meanings to texts. The material censorship of texts through processes like expurgation sought to further restrict interpretation by removing prohibited text and physically altering books to warn future readers of the potential dangers inside. While information may not want to be free, it has inspired many authors, publishers, printers, and readers to resist controls placed on both interpretation and form. The thin lines of ink of an expurgator with dubious intentions might have the effect of calling attention to problematic material, rather than hiding it, and dissimulated language could hold different meanings for different audiences. These interpretive and material processes have changed between the distant past and the present, but the paradoxes they present about information and its circulation remain relevant.

Hannah Marcus

See also books; excerpting/commonplacing; governance; intellectual property; lists; media; networks; publicity/publication; readers; reading against the grain; registers; surveilling

FURTHER READING

Cyndia Susan Clegg, *Press Censorship in Elizabethan England*, 1997; Robert Darnton, *Censors at Work: How States Shaped Literature*, 2014; Maurice A. Finocchiaro, ed., *The Galileo Affair: A Documentary History*, 1989; Peter Galison, "Removing Knowledge: The Logic of Modern Censorship," in *Agnotology: The Making and Unmaking of Ignorance*, edited by Robert Proctor and Londa Schiebinger, 2008, 37–54; Adrian Johns, *Piracy: The Intellectual Property Wars from Gutenberg to Gates*, 2009; Peter F. Kornicki, *The Book in Japan: A Cultural History from the Beginnings to the Nineteenth Century*, 2007; Hannah Marcus, *Forbidden Knowledge: Medicine, Science, and Censorship in Early Modern Italy*, forthcoming 2020; Margaret E. Roberts, *Censored: Distraction and Diversion Inside China's Great Firewall*, 2018.

COINS

Coins and medals are similar in format and content but are distinguished in that coins (as well as banknotes and tokens) bear indications of the role that they play within the monetary economy, while medals exist only for the information they convey about the people, places, and events they depict or those who display them.

It is a commonplace of classical and medieval numismatics that coinage was the emanation of political authority most frequently encountered by the populace as a whole, and hence constitutes direct evidence for the information that the issuer wished to be disseminated to the users. Even in the modern era, coins are ubiquitous in the hands and pockets of most of the world's population and represent a message that is aimed at the public, but it is difficult to estimate the degree of reception of the information contained on them. Though endless discussion, plans, and drafts went into the series of circulating quarters issued from 1999 to 2008 by the United States with reverses commemorating the individual states, it is difficult to imagine that many of the users made more than a glancing perusal of them—to say nothing of deriving significant information about the various states from their representation on the coins.

The information carried by coins is conveyed by three elements—physical aspects of them as objects, plus the images and inscriptions stamped onto their two surfaces. It is actually the physical aspects of color, size, and edge treatment that constitute the most common information used by consumers to classify frequently encountered coins—observations that, taken together, form an almost subliminal identity of the piece in question. Only with unfamiliar coins would the average user examine the images or inscriptions to identify and hence evaluate a coin. Color serves the function of distinguishing gold-, silver-, and copper-based coins, which generally fall in that order in terms of relative valuation. Size is mainly a matter of diameter, but the combination of diameter and thickness (plus the relative density of the metal) determines the weight, which is only rarely used today in identifying coins but played a regular role in the medieval and *early modern marketplace. Edge treatment usually refers to the placing of ridges on the edges of coins (milling), which sometimes distinguishes denominations (as in the difference between the US nickel and quarter). Even in contemporary coinages in which all denominations are made of the same cupro-nickel alloy, traditional distinctions of color, size, and edge treatment are maintained to aid in the recognition of denominations.

The images (types) placed on a coin are usually identifiers of the issuing authority. Since the fifteenth century, most monarchical polities of Europe and the Americas have placed a portrait bust of the current ruler on the obverse of the coin. Since classical antiquity, it has been the practice of nonmonarchical states to avoid portraits and to use as the obverse type a representation meant to identify and symbolize the state as a whole, such as an animal, an allegorical figure, a building, or a cityscape. In the course of the twentieth century, many nonmonarchical states adopted the practice of using a portrait of a deceased individual of national significance as the obverse type of their coins.

The most common reverse image has been a heraldic device representing the issuing authority as a whole or the family of the ruler; in many cases these are extremely detailed in their quarterings, mottos, helms, crests, and supporters, probably more for the sake of impressing the viewer with the prestige of the tradition than with offering useful and readable information. The same range of symbols that appear on the obverse of nonmonarchical issues also may appear on the reverses of their coins.

The inscriptions on coins (legends) are secondary to the images on coins of the European tradition but dominate the surfaces of both sides of the coin on most pre-twentieth-century Asian issues. These commonly bear information on the authority, place, and date of issue, as well as religious expressions, and can be arrayed across the whole surface of each face or in various configurations. Legends on European coins generally go clockwise around the central type and were in Latin in an ancient epigraphic style with all uppercase letters on coins of early modern Europe, but in the course of the nineteenth century most issuers changed to *vernacular language (with the exception of Great Britain), and often to a more readily legible lettering font. The obverse legends usually identify the individual represented, often with long and abbreviated lists of titles, or the name of the issuing nonmonarchical authority.

Coin reverses often have technical information in their legends, including the denomination, the year of minting, the mint, and even the mint master's initials, sometimes arrayed horizontally beneath and separated from the reverse type by a line (exergue). Especially on low-value coins, the identifications of the denomination may take up all or most of the reverse, in either words, numbers, or symbols. In general, it can be supposed that the only aspect of the written information on either face of a coin relevant to most users would be the denomination.

As paper money is manufactured from a nonvaluable basic material, the information provided by size and color is seldom relevant to users. Most of what goes onto paper money in terms of types and legends has a primary purpose of discouraging counterfeiting, not only by such obvious exhortations as "To counterfeit is death," but through elaborate scrollwork, mismatched type fonts, intentionally misspelled words, and hand-inked signatures and serial numbers. The one crucial piece of information put on a banknote is its denomination, usually both in numerals and spelled out; in the case of the earliest paper money of China in the fourteenth century the denomination is illustrated with an image of the string of coins for which the note could be redeemed. The larger surface of the banknote allows much more complicated depictions than that of the coin, frequently including vignettes related to the industry and the architecture of the issuing state or regional entity.

The manufacture of low-denomination copper-based coinage by a state is often done at a financial loss to the issuer, so in many times and places there has been no officially minted small change. This gap has sometimes been filled by privately issued tokens, most notably in England in the seventeenth and eighteenth centuries and in the United States in the nineteenth; these are generally the size of the coin they're meant to replace. The issue of tokens was often sponsored by local businesses, especially store owners, and they usually bear the name of the issuing place and establishment; as such they constitute an early and widespread form of private advertising. *Jetons* resemble tokens in general appearance but usually have a nonmonetary function, such as use on counting boards, in gaming, or as calling cards of individuals.

Medals are totally nonmonetary objects but are close to coins in their appearance and manufacture; they have no function other than to be collected and displayed. The medium took its inspiration in the fifteenth century from large, high-relief ancient Roman bronze coins called *sestertii*, which were thought by many scholars in the *Renaissance and through the eighteenth century to have been commemorative rather than monetary in nature. The earliest medals were produced on behalf of Renaissance princes as personal gifts to friends or followers; because of technical limitations on the ability to strike coins of high relief, especially in bronze, they were cast in only a few examples and survive mainly as aftercasts (that is, made later from a mold formed from the original casting). The obverse generally bears the portrait of an individual while the reverse bears a heraldic device or, more commonly, a scene considered emblematic of the spiritual nature of the individual whose physical aspect is presented on the obverse.

In the course of the sixteenth century, as minting technology evolved, medals were struck rather than cast and took on the proportions and general appearance of Roman sestertii. Rulers began to issue series of medals with scenes of their achievements represented on the reverses, often imitating ancient precedents; Medici princes and Habsburg emperors figure importantly in these developments. Individuals began to collect medals in order to have sets of three-dimensional representations of contemporary and historical figures, and artists produced pieces specifically to sell to such collectors, often depicting ancient or even mythological individuals for whom no genuine coins had been produced.

As in many aspects of the culture of the early modern age, the disparate developments of the medal came together in the court of Louis XIV, who created the Académie des Inscriptions to invent the allegorical scenes and Latin legends for the reverses of his series of medals and gave sets of this Historia Augusta in various metals to visitors as a portable invocation of the glories of Versailles. In succeeding centuries, the governmental issue of medals was joined by their issue by cities and organizations and by entrepreneurs producing series for the benefit of collectors; as these medals had no official or monetary value, the information they carried was their prime raison d'être. The nineteenth-century invention of die-engraving machinery brought the work of sculptors rather than engravers to the medium, with a growing emphasis on the artistic aspects of pieces over the information they conveyed. In the twentieth century, medals sometimes bore political and patriotic themes, often mirroring the graphic arts of the period. In recent decades, there has been a growing interest among artists and collectors in the medal as small sculpture, often bearing little or no information.

Decorations constitute a source of information on an individual, for instance, his or her membership in a group or receipt of an award, destined to be physically worn on the person, and hence constitute a conspicuous form of identity information in social life. Particularly prestigious, and still widely used, are the decorations known as orders. These began as the insignia of the military monastic communities of the Middle Ages and in the early modern period were extended to societies of members of royal families and individuals of high status recognized by a sovereign. Napoleon created the Légion d'honneur as recognition for both military and civil service; though it has all the grades of membership and sashes, crosses, and stars of other orders when worn on formal attire, it is the small rosette of the order worn in the button hole of daily clothing that most commonly identifies its wearer as one of the elite of French society. Military award insignia (usually called medals) constitute another wearable sign of achievement that came into widespread use in Napoleonic Europe and spread throughout the world; as in the case of orders, they are commonly issued in a series of sizes and formats to reflect the status of the recipient. Medals for war service sometimes have the names of the various battles in which the individual participated on bars attached to the ribbon from which the medal itself is suspended.

Alan M. Stahl

See also commodification; forgery; inscriptions; money

FURTHER READING

Walter Cupperi, "Coins and Medals," in *The Classical Tradition,* edited by Anthony Grafton, Glenn Most, and Salvatore Settis, 2010, 207–8; Richard G. Doty, *The Macmillan Encyclopedic Dictionary of Numismatics,* 1982; *Standard Catalogue of World Coins,* various editors and editions, separate volumes for 1601–1700; 1701–1800; 1801–1900; 1901–2000.

COMMODIFICATION

Commodities have existed since well before the advent of capitalist production. In the ancient world there were markets for the sale of surplus agricultural product, of pottery or cloth or dyes, of slaves and cattle, or of the bodies of women and boys. In the Christian Middle Ages there were markets in *indulgences and holy relics and church offices, as well as in grain or textiles or tools. What is distinctive about capitalism is that the commodity form comes to be the dominant way in which goods are exchanged, and it is progressively extended to everything on which it can gain purchase; in recent years this has increasingly included information. Capitalism seeks to endow all goods with exchange value (to put a price on everything), and to create new needs that can then be satisfied by new goods. There are markets in money that establish its price, and there are markets in speculation on the future price of money or of any other good. Organized sports have gone, over about the last fifty years, from an amateur pastime to an industry in which salaried players are traded for large amounts of money, and the spectacle of the game is sold for large amounts of money to television broadcasters. The care of our bodies is catered to by cosmetics companies and gyms and personal trainers and weight-loss programs, and the care of our souls, for a price, by licensed or unlicensed professionals. Friendship and the liking of our friends' opinions are the tokens that allow social media companies to sell us to advertisers, and the appearance of friendship is sold to us in the service economy that requires a waiter to smile or a barista to chat with us. Rebellion and revolution are now the currency of the fashion and popular music industries. This is, of course, not to say that everything can now be bought and sold: it is to say that this is the tendency of the system in which we live.

The dominance of the commodity form does three things. First, it channels capital into an area of production in order to expand it to its fullest capacity, at the same time destroying all existing activities in that area that are not themselves commodified. Industrial-scale tourism, for example, transforms landscapes and traditional patterns of habitation, as well as traditional forms of unremunerated hospitality. Second, it makes the world more abstract: commodity production is interested not in the particular qualities of the thing or service produced but solely in the profit it can generate; its qualities are purely a means to this end. Third, it privatizes common resources (common grazing land, for example, or folk music and fairy tales, or publicly owned utilities); those resources are then allocated according to economic criteria (ability to pay rather than moral or civic entitlement), and the effects of these resources' commodification may be either restrictive or expansive. In the case of most cultural production—for example, of books, perhaps the oldest of all commodities, or of movies, which would not have come into being without extensive capital investment—the effects of commodification have been massively expansive.

The current phase of capitalist development is characterized by the fact that information has become a major productive resource. This has been evident since at least the *early modern period (Will Slauter's chapter 7 in this volume, "Periodicals and the Commercialization of Information in the Early Modern Era," examines the commodification of "timely information" by the periodical press in the seventeenth and eighteenth centuries), but the process was intensified in the course of the Industrial Revolution, when the knowledge embedded in technologies became the key to a radically increased industrial productivity, beyond the capacity of the bodies (of horses or human beings) that had previously powered machinery. This technological revolution transformed knowledge of the natural world into the basis of its systematic and concerted exploitation. More recently, however, information has become a means of production in its own right: a means of production, that is, of further information for which there is a demand and which is therefore economically valuable. Knowledge systems—elaborate systems of organization and management of information—have underpinned the development of finance capital in its many-layered complexity; of automated or semiautomated production lines; of biotechnology; of the entertainment industry in its digitally disseminated form; of social media; of the analysis of terrestrial resources; of the insurance industry, which controls risk in its every dimension; of *digital warfare (including the digital dimensions of conventional weaponry) and digital espionage; of aerospace and automotive technologies; and of a range of mediated human services to which value is attached. And the digital revolution has had the effect of turning the information previously embedded in material phenomena into pure, disembodied data controlled by new forms of property right: rather than being deposited primarily in an interlocking ensemble of open, "library" systems with minimal entry requirements, it is increasingly managed within a system of private intellectual property where access is regulated by the payment of rent.

Information is, in its "wild" state, a public good: "nonexcludable" and "nonrivalrous," as an economist would put it. In a letter of August 13, 1813, Thomas Jefferson said it a little more eloquently: it is difficult to make an idea someone's exclusive property because "its peculiar character . . . is that no one possesses the less, because every other possesses the whole of it. He who receives an idea from me, receives instruction himself without lessening mine; as he who lights his taper at mine, receives light without darkening me." Unlike material goods, then, information is not consumed by use and is not diminished (indeed, it may be enhanced) by being shared. It is structured as an open system without scarcity.

Two obstacles to commodification develop immediately from the public-good nature of information. The first is the problem of defining and enforcing exclusive property rights in something both intangible and diffuse. The simple solution to this problem is to treat information as a secret. The flow of information is restricted in this way in most precapitalist societies, and it continues to be an important weapon of statecraft and of industry. But Western legal systems have elaborated a more complex solution over the last three centuries: restricting access to and use of information, without necessarily restricting possession of it (that is, without enforcing exclusive property rights). Thus *copyright law allows me to own a book or a movie and restricts only the making of unauthorized copies; patent law makes an idea or a system freely available but restricts commercial exploitation; and so on.

This is also part of the solution to the second obstacle to commodification, the problem of attaching exchange value to an entity that has an almost limitless use value:

that is, of making an abundant good scarce. Using information as a way to make money is inherently risky: sophisticated information products tend to have relatively high costs of initial production and relatively low costs of subsequent copying; a software program or a new drug might take years to develop but will be highly profitable if it is accepted by the market, *and* if the ability of others to copy it cheaply is controlled.

Risk can be minimized by flooding the market with similar products (movies and pop songs are perhaps the paradigm cases) only some of which will be successful, but whose success will subsidize the losses made on the failures; and more broadly by a combination of control of access and regulation of demand. Nicholas Garnham has detailed five strategies elaborated by the culture and information industries to this end. They are (1) the production of scarcity by controlling the right to copy; (2) the control of distribution channels (for example, by vertical integration of film production and distribution); (3) the building in of obsolescence through the manipulation of time (for example, by the creation of rapidly decaying information in technology or fashion or journalism); (4) the sale of audiences or users (of Google or Facebook, for example) to advertisers rather than, directly, of cultural and informational goods to consumers; (5) the socialization of production costs by means of state patronage and subsidy. To these we could add the role of branding and authorship (the names of movie or sports stars, for example) in classifying and certifying information goods.

The commodification of information, as of any other domain, doesn't happen in a single stroke. Rather, it takes place on a number of different semiotic levels corresponding to a roughly sequential historical development. In the case of written texts we could distinguish between an initial commodification of the *material object* ("the book"), which happens more or less at the same time as the invention of the printing press; a second stage of commodification of the *form of expression* of information contained within the material object (and conceptualized in legal doctrine as "the work"), of which the major historical manifestation is the development in the eighteenth century of copyright law and the modern system of authorship; and a third, contemporary moment, developed in relation to electronically stored information, which, in addition to the copyrighted expression of information itself, commodifies *access* to that information (for example, by subscription to a streaming or market information service). These developments are sequential in the sense that this sequence is normally linear (although it may be condensed, its different moments may overlap, and it is by no means uniform in its effects), and it corresponds both to an application of property rights to increasingly immaterial entities and to the development of markets that are increasingly fine-grained in their scope. Each of these moments is, paradoxically, at once a way of restricting control of the commodity and of making it available to as broad an audience as possible.

Every model of the control and dissemination of information supposes and is underpinned by a specific set of social and economic relations. Making information fully available to anyone who wants to use it is a form of gift giving; keeping it secret corresponds to authoritarian social relations based on exclusive possession; copyright and patent law are grounded in nonexclusive private property rights; the model of sale of access to subscribers corresponds roughly to the relation between a franchisor and a franchisee. Finally, the metaphor that I used before of the "library" model of access to information is based on a hybrid set of social relations.

A library is a collection of informational materials, traditionally but not necessarily printed matter, which have typically been bought in the market but which, in most public library systems, do not circulate as commodities. But neither do these materials circulate as gifts; they are, rather—to pick up a term used by Marcel Mauss—prestations, "gifts" that are exchanged without conferring any rights of ownership or permanent use. At the same time, loaned library materials create no personal ties of obligation and lack the coerciveness of the forms of prestation that Mauss describes in his essay on the gift. In this sense, they partake of the impersonality and the abstractness of the commodity form. Unlike commodities, however, they have also been largely free of the constraints on access and use that tend to flow from the price mechanism. While the library model thus tends to collapse rather than to dichotomize the categories of gift and commodity, it does nevertheless represent a genuine alternative to the privatization of the commons in information.

Public libraries as we know them came into being as part of that massive expansion of state institutions in mid-nineteenth-century Europe and North America that also produced the public schooling system, post offices, railways, public museums, and public hospitals, and which set an ethos of public service against the monopolistic tendencies of the uncontrolled market. Their present existence is framed by a tension between that expanded model of the state and its role in the provision of free (that is, subsidized) public services, and a more restrictive view of the state that seeks to open the provision of information to market forces. To put it crudely, a model centered on the informing of citizens has been replaced, at least in part, by a model of choices made by consumers. The causes of this shift are many and complex, but a major one in the case of the public library system has been a change in the status of information itself, from being economically more or less valueless to being a primary source of value. Google's plan with its Google Books project—now in at least temporary abeyance—to digitize all existing print literature and to make it available on commercial terms is one model of this shift.

The tension between free public provision and the pressures to treat information as a commodity with a price is an aspect of the aporia that organizes the capitalist market. In order to work efficiently and fairly, any market relies on perfect information (information that is free and immediately and universally available); at the same time, however, information is more and more a commodity, deliberately kept scarce and costly and therefore in practice *never* freely available. The profit structure of markets directly undermines the basis of the market system itself. To the extent that structural breakdown is avoided, it is because this tension can be displaced into an endlessly deferred promise of the overcoming of information scarcity: on the one hand in the ongoing production of new information, and, on the other, in an increasing mining of the commons in information through the ongoing privatization of the public domain.

The concept of the *public domain has a precise application in modern legal systems, where it forms the cornerstone of copyright law and indeed of intellectual property doctrine generally. Yet the concept is a purely residual one: rather than being itself a set of specific rights, the public domain is that space, that possibility of access, that is left over after all other rights have been defined and distributed. It has had a shadowy legal presence through common-law principles such as *fair use, through administrative measures such as freedom-of-information regulations, or through statutory protection of *free speech, but its lack of positive content leaves it vulnerable to erosion. It is a concept that is in many ways in crisis.

Yet some such concept of public rights in the commons in information—a commons of which everyday talk would be one model, and scientific knowledge another—is crucial if we are to resist the pressures toward private and highly controlled ownership of information resources. This is not necessarily because of some attachment to communal existence or a blanket refusal of market relations, but rather because of the structural peculiarity of information itself: that the more it is shared the more it tends to increase in value, and the more value it is likely to add, both economically and in the realm of social and personal relations. Some restrictions on access to it, through the mechanisms of the secret or of commodification, may be necessary and even productive under some circumstances; as long as pharmaceutical research is conducted by for-profit corporations, new drugs will be developed only if they are protected for a term by patent law. In the long run, however, scientific knowledge will advance only if it can feed on itself; information not only wants but needs to be free.

John Frow

See also digitization; information, disinformation, misinformation; intellectual property; knowledge; libraries and catalogs; money; public sphere; publicity/publication; travel

FURTHER READING

James Boyle, *The Public Domain: Enclosing the Commons of the Mind,* 2008; Peter Drahos and John Braithwaite, *Information Feudalism,* 2002; John Frow, *Time and Commodity Culture,* 1997; Nicholas Garnham, *Capitalism and Communication: Global Culture and the Economics of Information,* 1990; J. K. Gibson-Graham, *A Postcapitalist Politics,* 2006; Marcel Mauss, *The Gift: Forms and Functions of Exchange in Archaic Societies,* 1923–24, translated by Ian Cunnison, 1954, repr. 1966; Margaret Radin, *Contested Commodities,* 1996; Katherine Verdery and Caroline Humphrey, eds., *Property in Question: Value Transformation in the Global Economy,* 2004.

COMPUTERS

"Computer" was a vocation before it was a thing. From the seventeenth century onward, a computer was an individual tasked with carrying out mathematical computations. In the first half of the twentieth century, most computers were women who worked in science or industry. Computers in the more familiar sense of inanimate information technologies are associated with two qualities above all others: they are understood to be mechanical or automated; and they are understood to perform operations with numbers. Yet this cold, mechanistic idea of what computers are fails to capture the intimacy they have come to claim in our daily lives, where a computer may nestle in our pocket or balance on our lap. Computers as we now know them—sleek, lightweight, and stylish products that afford us access to software, entertainment, and social networks—seem to have little to do with numbers as such. They are platforms for delivering media for personal consumption; instruments enabling us to communicate over great distances; and tools for enhancing productivity and creativity through the discovery, management, and sharing of information. Only in certain cases are computers still used for crunching numbers, as in the kind of work an accountant or a research scientist might enlist one to perform.

Even the word itself can sound distant and out of place in everyday speech: nowadays it is just as common to say *phone* or *laptop* or even *machine* as to say *computer*. But the term *computer* retains an aloofness that can serve to remind us of why they have come to be so pervasive, the one device that has replaced so many others. Paul Ceruzzi defines the essential characteristics of computers through three basic functions: calculation, as we have seen; automated control via sequences of instructions (what we more commonly think of as software, or a program); and the representation of stored data that are encoded in ways tractable to manipulation by calculation and control by automation. Note that all these functions are abstracted from any particular material implementation. Computers have been designed, and in some cases built, out of gears and rods, switches and relays, Tinkertoys, water and plumbing, paper, and, of course, electrical circuitry miniaturized and mounted on silicon wafers or "microchips." Also absent from this imagining are the iconic array of peripherals we tend to associate with computers, like display screens, keyboards, and the mouse, or storage formats like magnetic disks or tape. Ceruzzi's computer, by contrast, is a computer simply because it is a machine capable of following instructions (including forks and branches in those instructions) in order to manipulate stored data through arithmetical operations, whether or not the data themselves finally take the form of numbers.

From these characteristics—calculation, autonomous control, and encoded data—come all the functions of computers as we know them, from doing actual math to sharing a picture of a cat. Whereas once calculation was its own end, it is now a means to an end, a method for manipulating symbolic values so that they can form the basis for other types of representations (like a sound or an image). Because sequences of programmed instructions can also branch and repeat themselves, computers are efficient not just at addition and multiplication but also at iteration—the ability to repeat the same set of instructions, with or without variance, over and over again. In practice, computation is performed through iteration, and it is through vast quantities of iterations—we expect them to be lightning fast—that computers gain the awesome power to emulate and extend the world around us. Alan Turing presented the mathematical foundation of these principles in his paper "On Computable Numbers" in 1936. John von Neumann expressed them in what has come to be their most influential formulation in his *Draft Report on the EDVAC* in 1945, which contributed the idea of storing data and instructions for operating on those data in the same substrate as part of the computer. Charles Babbage and Ada Lovelace clearly understood the essence of the computer's principles a century earlier.

So much for what computers are, in theory. As actual artifacts—working things—computers have a long and messy history. Indeed, like many exemplars in the history of information, simplicity in concept is realized only through extreme ingenuity in implementation. Whereas once computers filled entire rooms, now they fit in our pocket (or indeed, in our bloodstream). Computers are often assumed to be interchangeable with *digital systems or technologies, but this is a matter of convenience in the engineering; likewise, we associate computation with the binary numeric system of 0 and 1, but this too is just a matter of convention for the more elemental condition of presence or absence (on or off) that is the most efficient schema we have yet devised to encode information and allow for its manipulation. Because digital systems operate with discreet symbolic or numeric tokens, error checking can be formalized and the inevitable imprecisions of the analog world can be modulated through discreet values with high tolerances for ambiguity. As W. Daniel Hillis puts it, "computers must produce perfect outputs from imperfect inputs, nipping small errors in the bud." Digital systems serve to mediate between the mundane stuff out of which computers are made and the formal requirements of mathematical computation, effectively ensuring that a given value is always unambiguous and that the result "checks out."

Computers thus support an illusion, or call it a working model, of an immaterial or "virtual" environment: copies are indistinguishable from originals, keystrokes can be backspaced and corrected without a trace, email flashes around the globe in the blink of an eye. In reality, however, these effects are carefully designed efficiencies. To achieve them, computers must have energy sources, such as comes from fossil fuels. They generate heat, which must be cooled with fans and air-conditioning. Computing's infrastructure has changed the landscape (including the ocean floor and low earth orbit), and, with much else, it is contributing to changing the climate. The raw materials out of which computers are made (gold, silver, copper, coltan, silicon, and palladium) must come from somewhere and are often extracted and manufactured under unjust labor conditions. For all the precision and perfection we expect from computers, they are a *part of* the world not apart from the world.

Computers have often been associated with predictive functions, whether related to the natural world, theoretical physics, economics, society, or warfare. In 1952 American television audiences were treated to the spectacle of a computer correctly predicting Eisenhower's victory over Adlai Stevenson in the presidential election. Displays like that undoubtedly contributed to the mythology around computers as autonomous or artificial intelligences, with interests potentially inimical to our own—a theme mined by science fiction ever since. (The first popular book about computers, published in 1949, was entitled *Giant Brains, or Machines That Think*.) In recent years such anxieties have increased again with new public awareness and concern over *"big data," privacy, surveillance, and algorithmic decision making.

But a computer, on its own, can do little besides compute. Its inputs and outputs are always embedded in a human context. Initially those contexts were determined by the government entities that possessed the resources to design, build, and operate computers: the military and scientific establishment. Computers became commercialized in the second half of the twentieth century, contributing to automation in a wide range of industries and professions; in the early 1980s, computers became affordable to an upper-middle-class segment of the population in the global North, and a consumer marketplace quickly took hold. Computers thus became associated with office work, household tasks, and recreation (games). At about the same time, computers started to become integrated into national and international telecommunications networks. The combination of telecommunications, individual ownership, and increasingly sophisticated audio and graphical capabilities ensured that by the twenty-first century computers would become the foundational technology for media production, distribution, and consumption. For many of us, our computer is also our telephone, typewriter, calculator, daybook, bookshelf, atlas, almanac, *encyclopedia, newspaper, television, cinema, stereo, family photo album, game room, mailbox, and soapbox. Computers as we know them are thus a realization of Turing's principles for what he termed a "universal" machine. As such, computers as we now know them are the instruments of politics, culture, and commerce as much as they are science and engineering.

As computers approach physical limits in both their size and their speed, the technical frontier has shifted to so-called quantum computers, which, if achievable, would allow for exponential increases in processing power. Nonetheless, even quantum computers would still be machines that iterate through discretely encoded units of information along programmable and controllable paths. In 1803 the poet and painter William Blake expressed a desire to "see a World in a Grain of Sand." Blake, of course, was not writing about computers. But the line serves to capture the contrast between today's computers built on microscopic silicon chips and their enormous capabilities and consequences for nearly every segment of human society. By virtue of innumerable individual operations repeated in immense quantities with exquisite accuracy in a mere instant, computers—and the ways we have all chosen to use them—have changed how we see the world.

Matthew Kirschenbaum

See also accounting; data; digitization; encrypting/decrypting; error; files; media; networks; programming; quantification; social media; storage and search; telecommunications

FURTHER READING

Janet Abbate, *Recoding Gender*, 2012; Edmund Berkeley, *Giant Brains, or Machines That Think*, 1949; Chris Bernhardt, *Turing's Vision*, 2016; Martin Campbell-Kelley et al., *Computer*, 2014; Paul Ceruzzi, *Computing*, 2012; idem, *A History of Modern Computing*, 1998; Thomas Haigh et al., *ENIAC in Action*, 2016; Marie Hicks, *Programmed Inequality*, 2017; W. Daniel Hillis, *The Pattern on the Stone*, 1998; Noam Nisan and Shimon Schocken, *The Elements of Computing Systems*, 2005.

CYBERNETICS/FEEDBACK

Cybernetics is a term that does not ring bells anymore for most people. It refers to a formerly in-vogue science that the MIT engineer and mathematician Norbert Wiener originated and about which he wrote a surprising best seller in 1948. According to recent sources, cybernetics is notable for marking a "moment" that slipped by and subsequently gave way to the "information age" as a way of defining the present. Still, when examined as a science that unified natural and social methods of study at mid-twentieth century—one that put feedback at the center of its understanding of reality—cybernetics was a paradox, a field that died unmourned but lives again around the globe, arguably, in almost everyone's increasingly feedback-driven twenty-first-century lives. In insisting on the centrality of feedback, cybernetics made critical contributions to the modern concepts of information and of an information society.

Although Wiener did not coin the term *cybernetics* until after World War II, its origins lie two decades earlier. In the late 1920s, a Cambridge anthropology graduate student with outstanding biology credentials—he was the second son of a famous British naturalist—sailed to a fieldwork site along the Sepik River in Papua New Guinea to work with the Iatmul people. The student was named Gregory Bateson, and he was on his way to a legendary career that would play out at the intersection of anthropology, biology, and psychiatry. When he reached Iatmul territory, however, Bateson knew neither the word *cybernetics* (for of course it did not exist) nor *feedback*. Still, he was struck by a dynamic that seemed both familiar and strange. The Iatmul were absorbed in their own thoughts and responsive actions, which he called "logical tangles." Their actions intensified in reaction to others' actions, and the result was a kind of recursively intensifying loop of responses, as he described in his book *Naven*. While Iatmul men, as the result of these loops, became ever more aggressive, Iatmul women became ever milder and more retiring. Iatmul society emerged out of this intersecting behavior as a kind of arms race. Bateson called this toxic dynamic "schismogenesis" ("complementary schismogenesis" referred to male-female oppositional dynamics whereas in-gender competition was called "symmetrical schismogenesis"). Ratcheting between male and female factions, in Bateson's view, would lead to unending, extremely disruptive polarization in the village.

Yet there was an escape hatch: each year, in a ceremony called "Naven," men and women reversed their roles for a short period, the women leaping to become aggressive by dressing and acting like men, the men melting into subordination and even submitting to ritualized rape and humorous humiliation. This transformed Iatmul schismogenesis into a self-regulating system, and Naven's effect, like a thermostat being adjusted, was to bring down the temperature in the Iatmul world. Note that the concepts of negative feedback and positive feedback existed already, having been used by the engineer James Clerk Maxwell in a publication in the 1860s to describe steam engines and how "steady states" could be achieved by regulation through a "governor" valve that would let off steam when necessary; further, in technologies dating to ancient Greece, China, and Korea—such as water clocks—closed-circuit and open-circuit control mechanisms could be found. And although in the 1920s Bateson was not familiar with "feedback" concepts, he would apply them, soon, to areas beyond steam engines—to human society itself. The insights provided from this fieldwork experience would grow in other sites. Bateson continued to work in New Guinea with his new wife, the anthropologist Margaret Mead, and later, also with Mead, in Bali.

The term *schismogenesis* took off—although not particularly in anthropological studies, nor in understandings of Melanesian society. Rather, Bateson during World War II became one of the founders of cybernetics. By the time he and Mead amicably divorced, the two were leaders of the new cybernetics movement. Its moment had arrived.

Following Bateson in Papua New Guinea has served to sketch the origins of cybernetics. One reason for this is that cybernetics' official beginnings are somewhat murky. In certain accounts it is said to lack a single, clear moment of genesis: "It is difficult to say precisely where and how cybernetics began," argues Geoffrey Bowker. Others, however, stress the high-demand settings of World War II and the collaborations the war fostered across disciplines, when experts in different fields pursued common practical aims such as learning how to chart the behavior of an aircraft pilot confronted in mid-air with enemy planes—how could evasions of enemy gunfire be graphed and anticipated? How could airmen's fatigue be predicted and avoided? Engineers, mathematicians, sociologists, and psychologists collaborated to solve problems. Success in such endeavors led to scholars wanting to enter into more collaborations. Most historians agree cybernetics emerged out of the environment of new technological possibilities occasioned by the war, and a new sense of possibility for academics to engage in practical problem solving. Cybernetics did not depend on a definition of information as essentially *digital (contra Claude Shannon's view); rather, Wiener envisioned a grand interdisciplinary science encompassing human and nonhuman elements in a penetrating communication network.

Cybernetics from the outset was characterized by its tendency to combine many fields. In fact, cybernetics has been described as a sort of long and multisited conversation that took place over many years and involved people talking to each other who almost never talked to each other. It never became centralized; it never got its own laboratories in one spot; it never got its own institutions but relied on threads of ongoing discussion and networks of research relations. Yet despite its lack of centralization and institutional solidity, cybernetics can be considered a significant contributor to the birth of the modern information age.

The legendary Macy Conferences, held from 1946 to 1953, were key arenas for the emergence of cybernetics, but in fact there was an important precursor to these "official" meetings that brought cybernetics more clearly into being, in effect: a kind of pre-Macy Macy meeting took place in 1942, in New York. The topic was one on the surface unlikely to lead to a grand synthesis of human social and biological systems: cerebral inhibition and the workings of hypnosis. An interdisciplinary group gathered, including the Mexican-born, Harvard-trained physiologist Arturo Rosenblueth, the neurologist and poet Warren McCulloch, the philanthropic foundation officer Frank Fremont-Smith, and the intellectual entrepreneur Lawrence K. Frank, as well as the husband-wife team of Mead and Bateson. At the New York meeting, Rosenblueth came forward to present a preview of the basic ideas for a paper he was to publish the next year, 1943, along with the mathematician Norbert Wiener and the computer engineer Julian Bigelow. Its seemingly unremarkable title, "Behavior, Purpose and Teleology," belied its boldness: in fact, it was a bridge spanning existing behaviorist research and the new unnamed idiom that would soon be called (by Wiener himself) *cybernetics*. The published paper by the three begins, in fact, by redefining "behavior" in terms of input and output rather than stimulus and response. Quite radically, Rosenblueth and his collaborators were rescuing *teleology and purpose*, concepts "rather discredited at present," and showing them "to be important." In this, the three felt they had sketched the lines of a new approach to the engineering of living beings in concert with machines: they argued that a uniform behavioristic analysis would apply to any machine or living organism, no matter its degree of complexity. The paper was really a manifesto arguing that one could now talk about teleological behavior (that is, behavior that led to an ultimate purpose) in any system while also remaining true to the demands of adequate explanation. This little presentation was in fact the "seed" of all future cybernetics meetings.

On exposure to this paper heralding—in essence—the possibility of a dynamic "control system" applied to human societies, several attendees of the 1942 conference felt something momentous had occurred. Margaret Mead, for one, was so excited (she reported later) that she broke her tooth and didn't notice until after the meeting was over. Bateson, too, saw immense possibilities. What came across was this message: Owing to negative feedback, also known as teleological mechanisms or servomechanisms (essentially, akin to the "Naven" ceremony Bateson had described twenty years earlier), one didn't have to throw out the baby (of adequate scientific models) or the bathwater (of the formerly metaphysical realm of teleology and purpose). Machines and mice were no longer *models* for human function, as they had been in earlier behaviorist experiments; they were animated by the same mechanism.

In the view of the Yale philosopher F.S.C. Northrop, commenting on the paper by Rosenblueth and his colleagues, it had shown that negative feedback (inverse feedback) mechanisms can be built to carry out social-engineering purposes. This mechanism could work for humans or robots, or some combination of the two. Cybernetics would mean the possibility of revolutionizing all "traditional theories" of human activity and upending philosophy itself. Some saw this as the dawn of an age of *ideological engineering* by means of these mechanisms. Citing the work of several early cybernetics researchers (including neural networks research by Walter Pitts and Warren McCulloch), Northrop declared that, now, social theories could be programmed into humans via the "firing of motor neurons." Social and institutional *facts would be determined—as Northrop put it—"literally." Needless to say, such an ability to engineer *programmed beliefs* within human nervous systems (in effect) bore implications for the fight in the war on communism—for if normative belief itself and the strength of ideas in guiding behavior were capable of being engineered, this was big news in the age of the Manichaean struggle between Soviet and Western worldviews.

The 1942 event inspired the creation of a series of later meetings under the rubric and title of "Circular and Causal Feedback Mechanisms in Biological and Social Systems"—later changed, but not until 1947, to the single term *cybernetics*. (These are now referred to as the Macy Conferences.) It was because of Bateson's formative presence and his anthropological concerns, in particular, that the conference planners added a fateful "and Social" to the title. Soon there were enthusiastically collaborative meetings under the banner of "Teleological Mechanisms"—including a conference in 1946 expressly for social scientists titled "Teleological Mechanisms in Society" and another in 1948 hosted by Lawrence K. Frank of the Caroline Zachary Institute of Human Development. To these events flocked many of the most creative social scientists of the day (including Mead and Bateson, Clyde Kluckhohn and Talcott Parsons, and, from Columbia, Paul Lazarsfeld and Robert K. Merton), as well as some of the most powerful mathematical theorists (Norbert Wiener, Warren McCulloch, Claude Shannon, and John von Neuman; the British mathematicians Alan Turing, Grey Walter, and W. Ross Ashby were also closely involved).

In 1948, the cybernetics movement achieved its most audible public voice with a popular book by Wiener. Announcing the invented word *cybernetics*, or "the art of the helmsman," Wiener argued in *The Human Use of Human Beings* that in the face of an onslaught of chaotic forces—the implacable second law of thermodynamics, dictating that, in essence, things fall apart and entropy rules—men and machines shared the capacity to fight back, to create local zones of order against entropy by "contribut[ing] to a local and temporary building up of information." As a result of this call to arms, many social science and behavioral science endeavors arose in the United States to attempt to build such shored-up information zones, which took the form of new social- and political-planning projects. Three US-based examples: the Nobel Prize–winning organizational expert Herbert Simon applied feedback principles to create an "ultrastable" homeostatic model for management systems; physiologist Hans Selye reenvisioned the dynamics of stress as a continual adaptation to the expectations of others; and the Harvard sociologist Robert Freed Bales designed a "special room" for research in which human-to-human interactions could be tracked and adjusted through feedback mechanisms. Essentially each human entity was the sum of their information exchanges within a system. In a variety of fields, what was called the "human factor" arose as a potential object of engineering.

In the two decades after World War II, cybernetics spread around the globe and grew its own independent "cultures," notably among left-leaning and communist regimes (whereas it had tended toward conservatism or middle-of-the-road liberalism in the US contexts). Soviet cybernetics, decrying the "bourgeois" cybernetics of the West, thrived from the 1950s through the 1970s; French cybernetics influenced the development of computer-education programs for children; and Chilean cybernetics embraced the task of developing a central-command-style cockpit—called Project Cybersyn under Salvador Allende—that would aggregate all existing information and feed it back into local programs. Most "applied" cybernetic programs eventually fell out of fashion because they were ineffective, despite ambitious aims to revolutionize human society. Second-wave cybernetics arose to add a partially Buddhist-inspired twist to cybernetics, characterizing "self-organizing systems" as forms of interdependently co-arising phenomena (in contrast to the command-and-control approach of the 1950s).

In recent years, a *New York Times* review firmly dismissed cybernetics as an obscure dead end—a "science [that] simply failed in the court of ideas." Most people know cybernetics, if at all, through the notion of *cyberspace*, a term the writer William Gibson thought up in 1982; Gibson recalls finding the *cyber* prefix "weird"—yet "I thought it sounded like it meant something while still being essentially hollow." His neologism now widely stands for the digital world as a whole. Another thread connects early cybernetics with Silicon Valley pioneers, as when, in 1976, *Whole Earth Catalog* founder Stewart Brand conducted a wide-ranging conversation with Gregory Bateson and Margaret Mead about the roots of cybernetic research. Bateson recalled gradually realizing, through the Macy meetings, that "the whole of logic would have to be reconstructed for recursiveness."

A more direct link with cybernetics today can be made by looking more closely at the ubiquitous role of feedback in technological transactions, especially those facilitated by social media encounters. Every aspect of communications, it is probably fair to say, is being remade by recursive feedback to an extent that might not have surprised Bateson. "Pernicious feedback loops" appear in the growing use of predictive-policing algorithms—those addressing vagrancy, "broken windows" crimes, sentencing, and "heat lists" generated to identify juveniles likely to become criminals. Where certain neighborhoods are targeted, more crime is found, more data is generated, and the result can be more proof of justified targeting, which results in more targeting, a kind of schismogenesis. Political strategists use feedback data from online interactions to choreograph twenty-five thousand (or many more) iterations of a candidate's ad message, each shaped by feedback. As *"big data" becomes increasingly entwined in real-time pervasive data gathering on ever-more-intimate areas of human experience, the use of feedback to amplify the power of machine learning and AI systems grows. The effects of this neocybernetic practice, however, are as yet unknown.

Rebecca Lemov

See also computers; data; databases; digitization; files; networks; platforms

FURTHER READING

Gregory Bateson, *Naven: A Survey of the Problems Suggested by a Composite Picture of the Culture of a New Guinea Tribe Drawn from Three Points of View*, 1958; Geoffrey Bowker, "How to Be Universal: Some Cybernetic Strategies, 1943–1970," in *Social Studies of Science* 23, no. 1 (1993): 107–27; F.S.C. Northrop, "The Neurological and Behavioristic Psychological Basis of the Ordering of Society by Means of Ideas," *Science* 107 (1948): 411–17; Arturo Rosenblueth, Julian Bigelow, and Norbert Wiener, "Behavior, Purpose and Teleology," *Philosophy of Science* 10 (1943): 18–24; Norbert Wiener, *The Human Use of Human Beings: Cybernetics and Society*, 1954 (1948).

DATA

Data is everywhere today, not only in the domains of science and technology, but in business, politics, sports, and the arts. And while claims about the ubiquity of data in our environment may be more or less accurate, even as claims, they represent something powerful: the idea of data has become central to contemporary culture, to our understanding of our world, our times, and ourselves.

Of course, neither the idea of data nor the technical practices that support it are entirely new. In one way or another, we have inhabited data cultures since the first tax rolls were inscribed and populations counted. Yet the need to call data "data," to distinguish it from other sister concepts such as records, *facts, information, or evidence is much newer. If we use the invention of the modern term "data" as an indicator, we may consider the seventeenth century as the beginning of our era.

There are a number of reasons why thinking "data" in the perspective of four centuries is useful today. In the first place, it gives a larger view than that offered in discussions of data limited to the electronic age. The seventeenth and eighteenth centuries belong to what historians call *"early modernity." This is our world, the world of globalization, technology, and capital at its first coalescence, when many of the institutions and ideas we now take for granted were still new and often shocking. While we may say that computer technology drove data to the center of culture, we may equally say that a preexisting early modern culture of data generated the demand for computer technology in the first place. The seventeenth-century world was steeped in many kinds of data immediately recognizable as such today, ranging from John Graunt's mortality tables to the gold-clasped accounts book that Louis XIV kept in his pocket to the "weather clock" designed by the great architect Christopher Wren to automatically record measurements of temperature and barometric pressure.

Yet in the seventeenth century, the word "data"—our own favored term for this kind of information—was still emergent and in usages unfamiliar today. Indeed, a glance at the most accessible historical data on "data" for this period, the Google Books ngram for the word, reinforces this hunch. By counting and plotting how many times a word appears in its data set in a given year relative to the total words occurring in that year, the Google Ngram Viewer gives us a clue about when terms have been more or less important in languages.

The results of the Google ngram for "data" are both striking and intuitive (figure 1). In the years before 1800, the curve hugs zero. Around 1800, we see a very gradual rise until the twentieth century, when the curve is flat, and then at midcentury and late in the century it approaches vertical. It is easy to look at the graph and infer a relationship with the modern history of computing technology, with inflection points roughly aligned with, say, the paper punch card, the electronic computer, and the *internet.

Interestingly, however, the term "data" turns out to be a good case for how difficult it can be to interpret results from a data tool such as the Google Books Ngram Viewer.

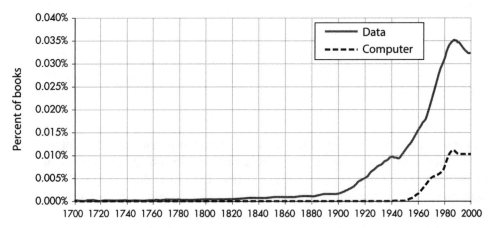

Figure 1. Results of the Google ngram for "data."

Here, the tip-off—and irony abounds—comes not from comparative quantitative data but from an older kind of qualitative data, an entry in the *Oxford English Dictionary* (*OED*). It is worth saying that the methods of the *OED* are not as dusty as one might assume. A monument of pen-and-paper scholarship, the *OED* was actually crowd-sourced using the networking methods of its day, press and post. Quotations were contributed by ordinary readers, which were mailed to the *OED*, sorted, and then filed in a purpose-built data collection center known as the *scriptorium.

From the *OED*, we learn that the term "data" emerged in English usage not in the 1940s but in the 1640s. We learn too that the usage of the term changed and flourished during the century and a half that followed. We also learn that these early usages both resembled and differed from what we expect "data" to mean in telling ways. The very first use cited by the *OED*, from the Anglican controversialist Henry Hammond, turns out not to refer to quantitative information, but rather, to theological precepts. What are we to make of this? And how are we to fit it into our modern cultural and linguistic picture?

There are a number of reasons for Google's relative blindness to the early history of the word "data." In general, Google Books presents challenges for researchers, not least because when it has digitized library books, it has not also digitized bibliographic *metadata from donor libraries. Many errors, including errors in assigning publication dates, have resulted. Often, books that Google claims were published in the eighteenth century and before turn out to be twentieth-century books that Google's *machine learning algorithm has coded incorrectly. Typeface in old books often boggles Google's *optical character recognition. And, for quantitative research, both problems are exacerbated by the relatively small sample that Google Books works with. Prior to the nineteenth century, the panacea of so-called *big data is absent. There are other reasons, too, more specific to the history of the term "data." One of the most notable things about the four-character string "d-a-t-a" is that it is very common in Latin, the language from which the modern term "data" is derived. Yet the uses of "data" in Latin are different from and more various than those in modern languages. Today's buggy optical character recognition technologies still have serious trouble distinguishing "data" from "date" and other visually similar character strings in pre-nineteenth-century typefaces. Moreover, the early modern usage history of the term "data" in European *vernaculars throws a screwball at any simple counting operation: at the beginning of the period in which we are interested, there was a lot of Latin being published, even in books that were otherwise written in modern languages.

In the general culture of the seventeenth and eighteenth centuries, "data" still evoked specialized kinds of argumentation and the special situation of argument. As the etymology of the word indicates—"data" is the neuter past participle of the Latin verb *dare* (to give)—"data" in the early modern period were "givens." What "data" meant depended on what kind of argument one was making, what kind of facts, principles, or values, might be "given" in a particular argument. In that first *OED* citation, "data" were theological propositions, and this was no anomaly. "Data" during the seventeenth century was frequently used to mean something like the opposite of recorded facts. This was to change around 1750, when something resembling our current expectations emerged. The story of how this shift took place is at once the story of modern *epistemology and the prehistory of our information culture.

If Henry Hammond's usage in 1641 strikes us as odd, the same is not true for the usage we find in an October 1775 letter from Benjamin Franklin to the English scientist and theologian Joseph Priestley, which employs the term "data," with some irony, to describe a kind of political calculus not at all foreign today. There, Franklin suggests that Britain reconsider its opposition to American independence. He writes, "Britain, at the expence of three millions, has killed 150 Yankies this campaign, which is 20,000£ a head; and at Bunker's Hill she gained a mile of ground, half of which she lost again by our taking post on Ploughed Hill. During the same time 60,000 children have been born in America. From these data his mathematical head will easily calculate the time and expense necessary to kill us all, and conquer our whole territory."

In Franklin's writing, "data" refers to quantitative facts gathered through observation and collection and subject to mathematical analysis. That Franklin might use the term "data" so casually strongly suggests that he took his usage to be transparent, if perhaps still neologistic. In the mid- and late eighteenth century, Hammond's usage was waning, and the sense employed by Franklin was catching on.

The term "data" appears in a wide variety of contexts in eighteenth-century English writing. But what were these early usages? What was their importance in the language and culture of the eighteenth century? And what was their connection to the usages familiar today? It is a bit surprising that we don't know more of the answers to these questions already. During the past decade, we have seen excellent books published on related terms including "fact," "evidence," and "truth." Lorraine Daston has referred to this kind of scholarship as *historical epistemology*, the study of the conditions of knowledge in different periods.

In this field, "data" has a complex and dynamic role to play. A "datum" in English is something given in an argument. This is in contrast to a "fact," which derives from the Latin verb meaning "to make" or "to do," so that a "fact" is that which was done, occurred, or exists. The etymology of "data" also contrasts with that of "evidence," from the Latin verb "to see." There are important distinctions here: facts are ontological, evidence is epistemological, data—something given in argument—is rhetorical.

This distinction was essential to the early modern usage, and it remains so today. For early modern theologians, statements given in scripture were "data" in the most fundamental sense. Because they were known to be true, they were not to be put into question. In early modern usage the term "data" was also widely used to refer to values given in mathematical problems. These data were to be taken for granted because they were given arbitrarily; from them, there was no underlying truth to discover. "Data" in these two realms was given in the *same sense* but for precisely the *opposite reason*. In both cases, the label "data" served to distinguish the propositions or values in question from facts that could be profitably interrogated.

In early modern usage, a datum could also be a fact, just as a fact could be evidence. But, from its first formulation, the term "data" was useful—and distinct from these other terms—because it set to the side the question of referential truth. In this respect, the contrast with "facts" is particularly revealing. For facts to be facts, they must be true. Data, on the other hand, may be—and very often is—erroneous or confected. None of this affects its status as data. Facts proven false cease to be facts. Data proven false is false data.

From the beginning, then, "data" had this peculiar and powerful character. Its ontology was forward looking. Yes, "data" of the sort that Franklin discusses could be more or less accurate. Yes, "data" that claims to represent things in the world can and should be interrogated in these terms. Yet what makes "data" data is that one may operate on it without posing that question. As we have seen in Hammond, in early modernity, "data" and "facts" were as often as not conceptualized as contraries. In the age of Cambridge Analytica, this fact feels arrestingly relevant.

In the mid-eighteenth century, the terminological water became muddier. Over the following two centuries, "data" mattered more and more, but mostly in fairly restrictive scientific and bureaucratic settings. During this period, "data" and "facts" seemed less opposed to one another, and finally, in many situations, they could be substituted for one another freely.

To a great extent, this situation endured all the way until the mid-twentieth century. Here the Google ngram is right on the money. Throughout the nineteenth century and into the twentieth, the term "data" was used more frequently in more contexts. Its history in this period roughly parallels that of "facts" and for good reason: in contrast to the seventeenth- and early eighteenth-century usage, from the *Enlightenment forward, scientific givens were increasingly expected to be factual.

And then something changed again. With the emergence of information theory and electronic computing, a more general terminological need arose. Just as in the seventeenth century, in the second half of the twentieth, through to the age of derivatives, it became important to distinguish between facts and givens. This second time around, the need arose because some term had to describe the values on which computation is effectuated independent of any question of representational truth.

Here, then, is something that is hard to perceive from the quantitative data on language that one may extract from a resource such as the Google Books Ngram Viewer, which seems to make "data" a twentieth-century development. One part of the story the Google data tells quite well: as an idea in our general culture, "data" matters more in the nineteenth century than in the eighteenth, more in the twentieth than the nineteenth, and, at the end of the twentieth century, more than ever before. Another part of the story, the Google data misses entirely: as a cultural tool and an intellectual razor, "data" matters now in a way that more resembles its importance in the seventeenth century than at any time since. From this perspective, this is a story of profound epistemological circularity.

Surprisingly, then, in the case of the history of "data," the *OED* is right, and Google is wrong. Or at least, Google on its own is not very helpful on the question. There are definitive trends in both the currency and the usage of the term "data" prior to the late modern period. But Google, with its massive resources, does almost nothing to make them visible.

For the moment, it is a win for nineteenth-century scholarly practices, but it is not a victory that is likely to stand for long. Even the venerable *OED* is moving to embrace a data-driven approach, which must be as good a signal as any that we should be ready to engage with quantitative approaches in the *humanities in a strong, critical fashion.

In the end, what does the history of the term "data" have to tell us about data today? There are a number of possible answers to this question, but one is worth particular attention: from the beginning, "data" was a rhetorical concept. "Data" means—and has meant since the beginning—that which is given. As a consequence, "data" serves as a kind of historical and epistemological mirror, showing us what, in any period, we take for granted. Without changing meaning, over the course of time, "data" has repeatedly changed referent. It went from being reflexively associated with things outside of any possible process of discovery to the very paradigm of what one seeks through experiment and observation.

Because data matters so much in our world, it is tempting to want to discover its essence, to define exactly what kind of fact it is. But this misses the most important reason why the word is useful. The data concept was innovated as a way of setting aside the question of facts. It reemerged at the center of our general culture as it came more and more to produce facts of its own.

Daniel Rosenberg

See also computers; cybernetics/feedback; databases; digitization; quantification; storage and search

FURTHER READING

Elena Aronova, Christine von Oertzen, and David Sepkoski, eds., "Data Histories," special issue of *Osiris* 32, no. 1 (2017); Soraya de Chadaravian and Theodore M. Porter, eds., "Histories of Data and the Database," special issue of *Historical Studies in the Natural Sciences* 48, no. 5 (2018); James K. Chandler, Arnold Ira Davidson, and Harry D. Harootunian, eds., *Questions of Evidence: Proof, Practice, and Persuasion across the Disciplines,* 1994; Lorraine Daston, ed., *Science in the Archives: Pasts, Presents, Futures,* 2017; Lorraine Daston and Peter Galison, *Objectivity,* 2010; Lisa Gitelman, ed., *"Raw Data" Is an Oxymoron,* 2013; Mary Poovey, *A History of the Modern Fact: Problems of Knowledge in the Sciences of Wealth and Society,* 1998; Daniel Rosenberg, "Data as Word," *Historical Studies in the Natural Sciences* 48, no. 5 (2018), 557–67; Steven Shapin, *A Social History of Truth: Civility and Science in Seventeenth-Century England,* 1994.

DATABASES

A database is a structured collection of aggregated, commensurable data capable of being sorted and accessed for some purpose of knowledge production, normally through the application of algorithms. A common feature of all databases—and perhaps the central one—is that they permit the *recontextualization* of information derived from multiple, often heterogeneous sources. It is common in the digital age to define databases as only those collections of data stored on electronic computers (and accessed via computerized algorithms), but this overly narrow and restrictive definition ignores the history, usage, and even etymology of the term. In the first instance, many of the key structural features of today's electronic databases (and the algorithms used to operate with them) were present in data collections dating back hundreds of years and encompassing a variety of (nonelectronic) media. Second, while the term *database* can be used as a noun, it also invokes a variety of practices of information management and analysis that again long predate electronic computers: databases are defined as much by *how they are used* as by what format they take. Some scholars have even suggested that the term can be employed as a verb: "to database." There is no question, however, that in the modern computer era databases have emerged as perhaps the preeminent technology both for managing increasing economies of scale of information and for structuring and managing our social, political, and economic lives. Nonetheless, attention to the broader historical trajectory of the database is vital to understanding how this particular form of information management has acquired such enormous importance in the current *"big data" ecology.

It is generally accepted that the first published use of the term in the specific context of computing occurred in a 1962 technical memorandum produced by System Development Corporation (a spin-off of the RAND Corporation devoted to developing command and control systems for the US military), which stated that a "'data base' is a collection of entries containing item information that can vary in its storage media and in the characteristics of its entries and items." While this reference is an important point of departure in the genealogy of today's modern electronic databases, the term was in fact adopted from a wider contemporary usage not strictly limited to computer applications. Since at least the early 1950s, the term *data base* was often used to refer to large collections of economic or social data in any form that served as the basis for analysis. For example, in what may be the earliest example of the term, a 1953 article in the journal *Sociometry* on the measurement of interpersonal communications described large collections of survey reports and interviews as "a data base" for conducting sociological analysis. Indeed, during the period between the early 1950s and the mid-1960s (by which point it acquired its more narrow, specific association with electronic computers), the term *data base* appeared in more than a dozen publications across a variety of social science disciplines without reference to computers. Thus, while the *Oxford English Dictionary* reflects common current usage by defining a database as "a structured set of data held in computer storage and typically accessed or manipulated by means of specialized software," it appears that the term was adapted from a wider convention in which it referred simply to any large, structured collection of information.

Why is this significant? Beyond simply making an etymological point, the broader application of database (or "data base") supports the legitimacy of applying the term to practices and technologies that predate electronic computers, perhaps by a century or more. While technically anachronistic, referring to earlier data collections as databases helps recover important continuities in information management across material cultures, and it highlights developments in the social and political functions of data collections that directly influenced the culture of data we live in today. Databases are not just tools for storing and processing large volumes of data: they are also systems of rational organization that create categories of people and phenomena, define relationships, and impose structure on our perceptions of reality. The technical and social functions of today's massive electronic databases are the product of a genealogy that began long before computers, and which encompasses a variety of forms and practices that are not specific to any particular technology.

In suggesting the value of this deliberate anachronism, it should be noted that there are probably limits to its usefulness. In the broadest possible sense, it could be argued that a great many collections of data, perhaps dating back centuries or millennia, could be considered "databases," including astronomical observations, accountings of economic goods and taxes, botanical and zoological taxonomies, medical records and reports, and a wide variety of other kinds of compendia of information recorded on paper, *parchment, *papyrus, and even clay tablets. While it is true that many of these collections are antecedents and analogs to modern databases, they do not always share some of the most vital characteristics of modern databases. One such characteristic relates to the structure of databases: they are organized in such a fashion that accommodates the dis- and reaggregation of information—in other words, they are amenable to some degree of recombination, sorting, and random access. If this is technically possible (though laborious) with a static list or catalog recorded on paper or other media (particularly if one is willing to recompose it to accommodate new information or order), it is far more practical if some type of movable medium is employed—whether paper slips, index cards, or another transposable system.

Techniques involving the collection of information on slips of papyrus or parchment may have been used in Roman antiquity, although few of the large reference works that were composed then have survived, and some have argued that such practices were employed in the composition of indexes to scriptural and philosophical works during the European Middle Ages. By the sixteenth century, these methods were evidently common, and reference works like Conrad Gessner's *Bibliotheca universalis* (Universal library, 1545–48) were no doubt composed, in keeping with Gessner's own advice, by collecting and organizing slips of paper containing bibliographical entries that could be rearranged in preparation for the production of the printed text. In the eighteenth century, Carl Linnaeus composed his massive *Systema naturae* (System of nature, 1750) and other taxonomic works thanks, in part, to an elaborate system of slips and cards, and there is evidence that he used this technique not just to lay out and rearrange the text for publication, but as a private data repository (he even had a cabinet constructed for the purpose) to which he could continually add and refer.

Practices like Linnaeus's card index appear to have been inspired by new systems for the organization of libraries developed during the second half of the eighteenth century, particularly in France, Germany, and Austria. The use of standardized cards (at first these were playing cards) for the storage of information was becoming widespread by the end of the century, and the first example of a general card catalog—at the court library in Vienna—was assembled during the 1780s. Indeed, libraries (and bibliographic practices more generally) have always been on the forefront of data management, from the catalogs (or *pinakes*) of the famed Library of Alexandria to the first publicly accessible electronic catalog systems (Online Public Access Catalogs, or OPACs) of the 1970s. In addition to introducing techniques of movability and random access to data, library catalogs also contributed to another key feature of databases: the organization of data by tagging or encoding them with *metadata (or "data about data"). Metadata—like references to the shelf on which a book is located or additional works by an author— allow data to be recombined and recontextualized in new ways and provide a means for random access. Above all, they help structure the data in a collection in terms of their *relationships* to one another, a crucially important feature of today's massive electronic databases that was, nonetheless, available in more limited forms in card and paper collections as well.

While schemes for the mechanical sorting of collections had been proposed in the eighteenth century (by G. W. Leibniz and others), the first truly effective technology for automated sorting was developed by Herman Hollerith, who invented an electromechanical punched-card sorting machine that was used to compile the 1890 US census (and which was immediately adopted by census takers in Europe and elsewhere). The Hollerith machine is rightly considered an immediate precursor to the first electronic computers—indeed, Hollerith's company became part of a conglomerate later renamed International Business Machines, or IBM—and the card collections processed by mechanical tabulating machines certainly qualify as databases in the modern, more narrow sense. But a variety of other practices emerged in the nineteenth century that were equally important in the development of the broader technical and cultural characteristics of modern databases.

One especially important feature of late eighteenth- and nineteenth-century data collections is their role in creating and defining new phenomena and categories of natural and social relationships. Linnaeus's data collection, for example, helped to produce the view that the organic world is structured as a nested hierarchy of taxonomic categories (families, genera, species, etc.) that to some degree have a real, if abstract, existence. Data collected about the fossil record and organized in massive compendia during the first half of the nineteenth century revealed genealogical relationships between organisms that led to theories of evolution, which helped scientists identify processes like diversification and extinction that contributed to the understanding of the natural world as having a directional history. In a more sobering case, analysis of organized collections of data on human physical and cultural characteristics—such as Samuel Morton's famous collection of human skulls—contributed to the belief in a hierarchy of human races and underwrote social and economic practices of division and discrimination. Such "databases," then, helped construct and reify categories that were implicit in other kinds of data collections, such as census tabulations (which to this day use "race" as a category for sorting data) and early life and medical insurance databases (which often informed restriction or denial of coverage to people who fell into undesirable racial categories).

Databases are not just collections of information, but, as tools for the accounting of resources and people, they are sources of power. As statistical practices became widespread during the second half of the nineteenth century that allowed for new kinds of analysis and prediction to be applied to large data sets, databases became a central tool for governments to regulate the lives of citizens, and for private interests (insurance companies, banks, etc.) to extend or deny opportunities to individuals. A central feature of the emergence of databases in this era is that the logic of aggregation—that is, the belief that patterns identified in large numbers can serve to make meaningful generalizations that cannot be observed from individual cases—became entrenched in modern statistical rationality. Databases themselves did not produce this rationality on their own, but as the main tools for decision making in a wide variety of social spheres, they came to be encoded with it. This feature was inherited during the transition to the era of computers and is not specific to any particular form of technology.

The first computerized electronic databases were developed during the early 1950s and 1960s, as engineers developed data-processing applications for military and administrative uses. Strictly speaking, what are commonly referred to as "databases" are in fact an interaction between "database management systems" (DBMS), which is the software that allows access and control of data, and the data tables stored on punch cards or magnetic media. The first electronic databases were hierarchical, meaning that data were stored in nested categories that could be accessed only by following a specific path, and the only way the database could be re-sorted was to essentially re-create the order in which the data were arranged, an often complicated and laborious process. A major innovation was the introduction of "relational" databases in the 1970s, in which data are organized in a matrix of multiple tables organized according to particular "keys," allowing access to individual data without needing to proceed linearly through the entire database. Most complex databases today are variations on "object-oriented" or "object-relational" databases, in which data and associated metadata are treated as independent "objects" rather than being keyed to predetermined fields. This allows for much greater flexibility and speed for querying enormous sets of data, and object- or document-oriented DBMS software are the primary applications for everything from simple address books on personal computers or smart phones to massive distributed databases used in big data computing.

Despite the increasing complexity and sophistication of DBMS software over the last several decades, however, there remains a fairly direct and tangible genealogy connecting paper and electronic databases. Though a distinction is sometimes made between *"analog" and "digital" collections of data, in point of fact nearly all databases, regardless of medium, are "digital," in the sense that they are composed of discrete symbols or numbers. A collection of numerical (or even textual) data stored on paper can be transferred to electronic storage media to be accessed by DBMS, and indeed many of the earliest electronic databases in a variety of fields were simply transcriptions of paper databases to electronic format. When census bureaus began using electronic data, records held on mechanical punched card storage were often directly transferred to magnetic tape. A number of important early scientific databases, including the records of the US National Weather Records Center, the National Library of Medicine bibliographic index, the Atlas of Protein Sequences and Structures, the fossil record, and other collections, began their lives in paper format or other transportable media (e.g., microfilm), and users of these data collections still often refer to pre- and postelectronic versions as "databases." Indeed, no crucial distinction need be drawn between the media on which data are stored; rather, the advent of computers is notable for the software applications that allow access to data, reporting, and analysis, most of which is now performed by complex automated software algorithms. The database is a dominant feature of modern life in countless, inescapable ways, but its emergence as a "central cultural form" is part of a much longer history of collecting, storing, analyzing, and valuing data stretching back centuries.

David Sepkoski

See also algorithms; bibliography; cards; computers; data; excerpting/commonplacing; indexing; observing; quantification; storage and search; surveilling; surveys and censuses

FURTHER READING

Ann Blair, *Too Much to Know*, 2010; Geoffrey Bowker, *Memory Practices in the Sciences*, 2008; Lisa Gitelman, ed., *"Raw Data" Is an Oxymoron*, 2013; Thomas Haigh, "'A Veritable Bucket of Facts': Origins of the Data Base Management System," *SIGMOD Record* 35 (2006): 33–49; Albert H. Rubenstein, "Problems in the Measurement of Interpersonal Communication in an Ongoing Situation," *Sociometry* 16 (1953): 78–100; David Sepkoski, "The Database before the Computer?," *Osiris* 32 (2017): 175–201; Bruno J. Strasser and Paul Edwards, "Big Data Is the Answer . . . but What Is the Question?," *Osiris* 32 (2017): 328–45; System Development Corp., "Technical Memo," TM-WD-16/007/00, 1962; Paul Wright, *Cataloging the World*, 2013.

DIAGRAMS

Diagrams are schematic figures or patterns comprising lines, symbols, or words to which meanings are attached. Throughout human history they have been used to represent concepts, objects, processes, or systems as linear forms of information. Early examples include prehistoric engravings such as the crisscross patterns incised on ochre rocks in the Blombos Cave in South Africa around 70,000 BCE (figure 1). Diagrams exist within most systems of communication. As noted by anyone who has attempted to follow IKEA assembly instructions, the longevity of a diagram is closely linked to its utility and to the presence of other competing forms of representation.

Diagrams are often not self-explanatory. Those made during the past three millennia featured labels, or they required descriptions that were memorized, inscribed, or printed. The Babylonian "Pythagorean theorem" tablet of 1900 BCE, for instance, consisted of a transected square that was labeled with cuneiform numeric headings. Even though modern scholars have been able to translate the headings, there is still debate as to how to interpret the diagram, thereby illustrating the fact that the meanings of diagrams, both ancient and modern, are often influenced by the context in which they were made and used.

Some of history's most iconic diagrams were remarkably simple and based on efficient combinations of long-standing visual elements such as circles, squares, chiasms, crosses, squiggles, arrows, and branches. The oldest known diagram from the geometry of Euclid (active around 300 BCE), found at Oxyrhynchus, Egypt, consisted of only a square and a rectangle. The sixteenth-century astronomer Nicholas Copernicus used concentric circles to represent the orbs of planets in his new heliocentric system. Charles Darwin visualized the process of speciation with a branching tree. The physicist Richard Feynman used H-shaped and Y-shaped arrows and squiggles to represent quantum relationships. All these diagrams blended simplicity and familiarity. The lineages depicted in Darwin's diagram, for instance, were presented as an evenly spaced array of branching lines. This kind of tree diagram was a form of representation that had been used for centuries to depict family genealogies.

The accessibility of a given diagram throughout history was often influenced by how it functioned in relation to other diagrams. As evinced in the first printed edition of Euclid's *Elements*, published by Erhard Ratdolt in 1482, different combinations of squares, circles, and rays could operate collectively as a group, a visual system, of Euclidean geometry presented in one place. Some of Ratdolt's quattrocento contemporaries, notably Leonardo da Vinci, argued that diagrams could provide information more clearly and more usefully than prose. This notion would continue to grow within the new knowledge economies that emerged as the printing press spread across the globe during the sixteenth and seventeenth centuries.

By the time of the *Enlightenment, reference works regularly displayed hundreds of thematically related diagrams. Those presented in the French *Encyclopedia*, one of the

Figure 1. Ochre stone etched with a geometric pattern, Blombos Cave in South Africa around 70,000 BCE.

era's most recognizable publications, ranged from a key to all human knowledge to schematic depictions of farming ploughs. Though diverse, the *Encyclopédie's* diagrams were used together in a way that allowed readers to make links between different kinds of useful knowledge. For instance, D'Alembert's chart of the disciplines in the front matter of the work, presented branching dichotomies grouped according to three categories: memory, reason, and imagination. Within the tree of reason, "raison," included agriculture, among many other fields, a categorization that helped explain why the plough diagram was conceptually relevant to the publication.

The diagrams of the *Encyclopédie* and Euclidean primers worked best as visual systems when they were used in real time, when viewers flipped the pages and compared them with each other. In recent centuries the real time aspect of diagrams has come to play an increasingly important role in the ways that they are used to represent data, blurring the line between what counts as a diagram and what counts as a graph. In many respects this interface was a reoccurring feature of diagrams from the *Renaissance forward. Though Copernicus's circles were neatly presented as singular shapes, other kinds of diagrams, especially those based on copious data, were not presented as freestanding forms, nor were they constrained by the binding of a book. Perhaps most notable among these were the rectangular, gridded, unfoldable charts used by chronologers to represent data as timelines.

Concurrent with the rise of quadriform diagrams, early modern diagrammers increasingly turned to circular, graticuled, and rotatable volvelles to represent everything from planetary motion to months of the year: these printed circles were cut out and mounted on the page around a string in order to demonstrate the effects of circular motion. Using charts and volvelles diagrammatically required bodily movement. Charts often needed to be scrolled out of a book across a desk. They were often large and required users to either move them around with their hands, or move around them as they sat on a table. Volvelles needed to be rotated so that new connections between different kinds of information could be made. Though they became popular in the *early modern period, charts and volvelles continue to be used as real-time diagrams today.

Diagrams were of course not confined to technoscientific settings. Geometric, geographic, and metric diagrams played an important role in the everyday life of learning in schools and literate households. Johannes Amos Comenius's *Orbis sensualium pictus* (World of the senses in pictures, 1658), arguably the most influential Latin primer across

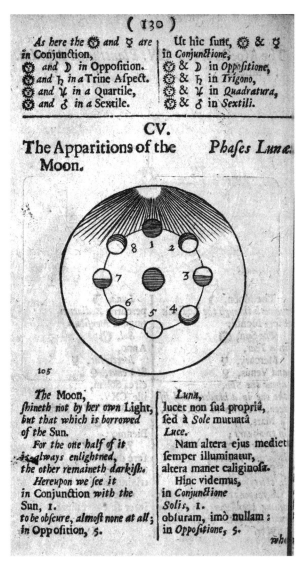

Figure 2. Johannes Amos Comenius, *Orbis sensualium pictus: Hoc est, Omnium principalium in mundo rerum, & in vita actionum, pictura & nomenclatura*, translated by Charles Hoole (1705), 130. Image courtesy of the Boston Public Library.

early modern Europe and its colonies, featured diagrams of numbered objects that students could match to vocabulary words presented in sentences above or below the image (figure 2). Frontispieces of popular Enlightenment primers and manuals such as George Fisher's *The Instructor* featured students in classrooms with diagrams hung on the walls around them.

Outside schools, domestic and commercial diagrams from the sixteenth century onward visualized everything from sewing patterns to the place settings of dining-room tables. By the nineteenth century, books like Eliza Acton's *Modern Cookery* (1860) featured diagrams of utensils, kettles, pots, saucepans, ovens, "smoke jacks," "weighing machines," ingredients, and various dishes. Advertisements in Victorian magazines such as the *World of Fashion* invited readers to buy diagrammatic sewing patterns, a trend that continued well into the twentieth century. Like those used in scientific settings, domestic diagrams were interpreted and used communally, oftentimes in shared spaces like parlors, kitchens, and gardens.

The components of diagrams evolved over time in relation to the knowledge possessed by their designers and users. Lines and labels were removed and added. Meanings were attached and detached. Most diagrams operated within communities, and their designers often took this factor into account. Here educational or training practices played a key role in influencing how diagrammers came to understand how to make and use diagrams as key elements of coherent visual systems. It would have been difficult for Newtonian calculus, for instance, to take hold in Britain were it not for the diagrams developed by several elite tutors based at Cambridge University. Likewise, Newton's younger contemporary Joseph Black would have struggled to communicate his discovery of carbon dioxide to his University of Edinburgh students were it not for a collection of simple diagrams that he used to explain chemical affinity.

Until recent times diagrams were made by hand, which means that designing or replicating one through copying was an adaptable and kinesthetic mode of knowledge acquisition, formation, and circulation. In this sense diagrams were similar to written notes in that they were thinking tools that allowed diagrammers to manipulate information on paper in real time. The Victorian astronomer John Herschel recognized this function in the meticulous diagrams of nebulae that he observed and then drew. He called them "working skeletons," a term that gestured to the long-standing interactive and schematic facets of handmade diagrams. His sketches built on diagramming traditions present in his own family, which also doubled as a scientific community. Caroline Herschel, his aunt who helped raise and educate him, had been making diagrammatic star charts since the 1780s to plot the movement of comets. Whether they were drawn in a notebook or read in a book, diagrams played an increasingly prominent role as thinking tools after the invention of the steam press. The proliferation was often countered or mediated through iteration. Marie Curie, for instance, employed diagrams to remember the specialized apparatus that she used for her radiation experiments. Indeed, the diagrams she drew in her circa 1900 laboratory notebook are still radioactive. The direct interface between diagramming and drawing remains with us to this day. The ribbon diagrams used by scientists and the public alike to illustrate the structures and functions of protein molecules, for example, were first hand drawn by the molecular biologist Jane S. Richardson and then photographed so that they could be printed in articles (figure 3). Like Herschel, Richardson used diagramming as a mode of thinking. In her words, "making a drawing can change one's scientific understanding of a protein."

Richardson's view on the relationship between thinking and diagramming resonates with the ways in which diagrams have been employed ever since humans began using visual forms of representation. The twentieth-century philosopher Ludwig Wittgenstein acknowledged this point when thinking about the relationship between logic and language. He was especially fascinated with arrows, perhaps one of the most popular forms of representation used in modern diagrams. In his words, "The arrow points only in the application that a living being makes of it." In many respects, this view accurately pinpoints the essence of diagrams and the role that they play as dynamic entities that are usually designed or iterated for a specific purpose. Whether carved with a stone tool in a rock or crafted on a screen with a mouse, they work best when they are adapted to

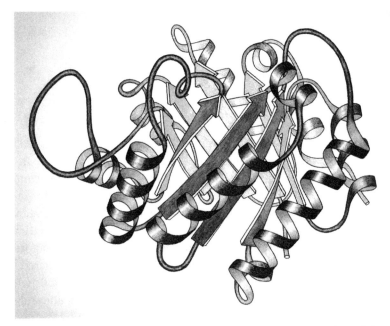

Figure 3. Jane Richardson, ribbon schematic (hand drawn and colored, in 1981) of the three-dimensional structure of the protein triosephosphate isomerase. The barrel of eight beta-strands is shown by green arrows and the eight alpha-helixes as brown spirals.

the needs of their makers and users. As such, they are multistable artifacts that will remain indispensable informatic tools for years to come.

Matthew Daniel Eddy

See also books; knowledge; learning; maps; observing; quantification; teaching

FURTHER READING

Michael Baxandall, *Painting and Experience in Renaissance Italy*, 1988; John Bender and Michael Marrinan, *The Culture of Diagram*, 2010; Lee E. Brasseur, *Visualising Technical Information: A Cultural Critique*, 2003; Matthew Daniel Eddy, "How to See a Diagram: A Visual Anthropology of Chemical Affinity," *Osiris* 26 (2014): 178–96; Reviel Netz, *The Shaping of Deduction in Greek Mathematics: A Study in Cognitive History*, 2003; Theodore W. Pietsch, *Trees of Life: A Visual History of Evolution*, 2013; Daniel Rosenberg and Anthony Grafton, *Cartographies of Time: A History of the Timeline*, 2012.

DIGITIZATION

In 1951, David H. Shephard invented what the newspapers called a "robot reader-writer." He spent $4,000 of his own money and worked in his attic for over a year. Two years later he took out a patent for what would eventually be known as the Scandex, one of the earliest *optical character recognition machines. He initially called it the "Gismo."

Shephard's invention was part of a growing postwar connection between the world of business and that of machines. Automated reading, or what we might think of more primitively as the processing of information from one written format to another, emerged as a core business concern with the rise of consumer-centered businesses. One of Shephard's first clients was *Reader's Digest*, who by the mid-1950s was shipping fifteen to twenty million books per year. Digitizing customer orders allowed companies to achieve an unprecedented scale and speed of service.

Alongside the booming postwar culture of business machines (think IBM), Shephard's work was also participating in a much longer tradition of thinking about the *conversion of information more generally. The Scandex, or the process of "scanning" that lent it its name, was based on the principle of turning written letters into electric current through the reflection of light. As light reflected off of a surface onto photoconductive cells, a current of varying strength was produced by the absence or presence of letters (dark or light shapes). This current could then be translated from its *analog voltage into a digital or *binary representation.

The principle of conversion behind Shephard's invention was intimately related with other conversional forms of transmission that would emerge most notably over the course of the nineteenth century, from telegraphy (the conversion of letters into electromagnetic signals) to telephony (the conversion of spoken words). "Seeing by electricity," as the editors of *Scientific American* called it in 1880, was first demonstrated as a functioning device by George Carey in the late 1870s. According to the editors, "The art of transmitting images by means of electric currents is now in about the same state of advancement that the art of transmitting speech by telephone had attained in 1876, and it remains to be seen whether it will develop as rapidly and successfully as the art of telephony." It did not. Nevertheless, Carey's device underlies all subsequent attempts at developing machines that can reproduce text or images through the use of photoelectric cells, from Shephard's Gismo to the printer/scanner in your office today.

If the history of digitization owes a deep debt to such nineteenth-century forebears, the fascination with signal conversion that underlay it was part of an even longer humanistic tradition of thinking about converting information from one form to another, whether from image to letter (or vice versa), from manuscript to print (or vice versa), or from one language to another. In its earliest form, dating back to the late fourteenth century, "to scan" meant to analyze a line of verse for its metrical qualities (now falling under the heading of prosody). It signaled an attempt to quantify speech, to transform letters into their appropriate numbers. When we think about digitization as a form of binarization, it is important to remember the scholastic origins of the quantification of information. By the nineteenth century, scanning could also mean "to look searchingly," as in scanning the heavens or someone's facial features. There was a synthetic quality to this aspect of scanning, the attempt to take the parts of an observed world and condense them into a single judgment. Scanning was about not just taking things apart, but also putting them back together into a more unified whole. By the middle of the twentieth century, to scan had assumed its modern meaning of distilling information—it combined the swift synthetic qualities of its nineteenth-century visual heritage with the discretizing and quantifying aspects of its bibliographic and scholastic origins.

Much of the historiography on media and information has been guided by a notion of *reproducibility. Each subsequent technological revolution brings with it a more intense level of reproductive potential, whether of text, image, or sound. As copies abound, space is shrunk. This is how the editors of Scientific American, for example, couched the novelty of Carey's device. "By this means any object so projected and so transmitted will be reproduced in a manner similar to that by which the letter, A [the initial projection], was reproduced." In focusing on the notion of reproducibility, historians have tended to think more about questions of proliferation and access—"more" as both a problem and a solution. But in doing so we lose a sense of the differences produced between techniques of inscription, the transformations that occur as we move from one form or format to another. Reproducibility, like its theoretical offshoot remediation, presupposes that information doesn't change as it travels. There is a fundamental notion of presence that resides within a theory of reproducible or remediable information.

One of the ideas that digitization introduces into the history of information, I would argue, is a new way of thinking about organizing the history of information around the notion of *conversion* rather than that of reproducibility. Conversion is the means of moving between *semiotic and material systems, of representing something in a new way rather than simply reproducing it in the same way. Conversion has been integral to how we have thought about and handled the idea of information. Similar to the practice of translation, conversion allows us to experience the knowledge of holding two incommensurable things together, to feel what it is like to be in between different worlds of signs. But it is also a powerful engine of discovery, much like its theological origins of implying a profound personal transformation. In translating information from one form to another we enter into a space of novelty, of something unknown.

While we often think about digital culture in terms of increasing resolution or fidelity ("high definition" [HD], "dots-per-inch" [dpi], or the next "generation"), at its base, digitization involves a process of sampling and discretization. It brings with it notions of error and uncertainty, but also redundancy, into the definition of cultural objects, whether as images, sounds, or texts. Digitization consists of a two-step process wherein an analog signal is sampled at discrete time intervals (discretization) and then those values are rounded or standardized (quantization) to produce a binary representation. As with any translational process, information is lost in making information accessible in new ways. Conversion, the act of turning around, also involves the act of leaving behind. It highlights all the losses that occur and uncertainties that are introduced through the practice of transformation.

The problem of information loss would become central to Claude Shannon's *Mathematical Theory of Communication*, one of the most influential works in the history of information theory. "The fundamental problem of communication," writes Shannon, "is that of reproducing at one point either exactly or approximately a message selected at another point." Understanding the reliability of communication channels—whether a message could be exactly or approximately reproduced—depended for Shannon on understanding the underlying redundancy *encoded in the initial message. For Shannon, knowledge of this redundancy allowed for more efficient engineering of communication channels. His work would engender an entire industry devoted to the problem of *compression, the practice of encoding information using fewer *"bits" than the original representation (which could be either "lossless" or "lossy" depending on one's goals or the nature of the underlying information). This is one more way that the principle of conversion, and the ideas of loss and uncertainty, stand behind the practices of digitization. For a subsequent generation of linguists and cultural theorists, Shannon's insights would drive a growing consensus about the probabilistic nature of communication more generally—the way an information-theoretic model underlies human communication and cognition. According to this thinking, meaning isn't a function of what stands out as radically novel or unique but emerges in the space between deviation from norms and the array of repetitions that shape cultural practices and human behavior.

Error is fundamental to any understanding of digital culture. We can measure the degree of error of OCR (optical character recognition), that is, the amount of mistranscription when machines read documents. But accounting for error is also essential in all *machine-learning-based approaches to understanding culture at large scale. If we want to write the history of scientific notation using a collection of over thirty million pages, for example, we can never be entirely certain as to the *overall* presence of the graphical practices, the tables, footnotes, diagrams, and figures, that underpin modern truth claims. We can only ever estimate and then account for the degree of our uncertainty. If you have not already heard of terms like *precision* and *recall*, which measure different kinds of error, they will become increasingly central to *humanities research. They allow us to quantify and thus communicate the degree of one kind of uncertainty about the past (there are of course multiple kinds of historical uncertainty).

In order to combat this aspect of uncertainty, conversion also typically involves the practice of standardization. Standards are essential to control the losses of conversion. In a literary context, we talk about the definitive translation or the authorized or critical edition. Over the course of the nineteenth century, scholars like Friedrich von der Hagen or François-Juste-Marie Raynouard devised a variety of techniques to transform the various manuscript sources of national cultural heritage into definitive print editions. As von der Hagen scoured the royal library in Copenhagen for handwritten versions of the medieval Icelandic *Edda* to produce a new print edition, he was in the process establishing the rules through which one could translate information from one format to another. Today, textual scholars like Ryan Cordell are drawing attention to the ways in which digitization produces even more variability and error in the archival record. Far from universalizing the inherited print record, the vagaries of optical character recognition mean that we end up with a polyphony of potentially heretical versions of texts. Von der Hagen reemerges in a digital world, this time as an algorithm to collate digital variants.

In the field of music, the development of digital standards follows a similar logic. The sampling frequency that was developed for CDs of 44.1 kilohertz was based on compatibility with video formats that were used for audio storage in the 1970s. As the sound historian Jonathan Sterne has written, standards are often translational tools to move between and make commensurable different material formats. The history of optical character recognition provides another case in point. Faced with the realization of the multiplicity of written characters across historical time and different world cultures, pioneers in document scanning advocated for the creation of a single standard font, the Esperanto of typeface. A committee was formed in 1966 as part of the American National Standards Institute (ominously called Committee X3A), whereupon it produced a template for the most efficient machine-readable typeface. If you look at the numbers on your credit card you will see it in action. At roughly the same historical juncture that produced large amounts of social unrest in Europe and North America in the late 1960s, engineers were busily working on reducing the unruliness of written documents. Along with what is now informally called OCR-A or officially ISO 1073–1:1976, there also emerged, not unsurprisingly, a second (European) version that was created at roughly the same time (OCR-B or ISO 1073–2:1976). The human efficiency of standardization always runs into the problem of cultural difference. Babel continues to lurk in our machines.

But such problems also run through our bodies. The story of digitization is not simply one of miraculous machines. It is also the set of practices through which knowledge of the human sensorium is encoded into material form (known as "perceptual encoding"). The .mpeg, .jpeg, and other formats of compression are designed to remove information based on the limits of how we think we see and hear. Standards of digitization encode a theory of human embodiment.

If uncertainty, standardization, and embodiment are key terms by which to think about digitization as conversion, a final one would be the idea of the model. The digitized representations circulating in the world today are models, of either some things out in the world or, like compressed files, other digitized representations. And like a compressed file, they are meant to make life more manageable by being smaller or more manipulable (the latter-day version of "hand"-books). In this sense, digital files are technologies of scale. And like any good model (*early modern globes or nineteenth-century ships in bottles), they can oscillate between being tools and being toys, useful techniques for understanding a highly complex world or giant wastes of time.

With the growing digitization of so many facets of contemporary life, computational modeling has entered into a vast array of academic fields, including the humanities. We might think of modeling as a second wave of digitization, where the first wave involved the act of scanning, converting, and reproducing historical records (a very lossy process). Computational models allow humanists to simulate not only different versions of the past, but different explanatory mechanisms. They explicitly place a degree of fictionality within the historical method, what Hans Vaihinger called the philosophy of the "as if," which he saw as the foundation of all knowledge. Just as the modeling of possible worlds has become essential to understanding the future, whether it is predicting the path of a storm or the end of the Anthropocene, so too do digitized historical documents allow for a more hypothetical relationship to the past. Computational modeling emphasizes the idea of "possible histories," once again foregrounding the prominence of uncertainty to the process of digitization. Possible history not only emphasizes the sense of constructedness about the past (by no means a novel idea); it also emphasizes the importance of testability (far more novel). It shifts the accountability of verification from one based exclusively on personal authority to one distributed between a person and a model (a person-model to use language inspired by the philosopher-anthropologist Bruno Latour). Models acknowledge their contingency but also open themselves up to verification by others. As forms of conversion, models interweave humans.

When it comes to the history of digitization, the media of sound, text, and image have their own genealogies. They are far from fully fleshed out. And yet one of the effects of digitization is to put pressure on these disciplinary boundaries that have historically been so mediacentric. Bits ("binary digits," the fundamental unit of digital forms) are emerging as an analytical lingua franca. The field of optical character recognition, for example, has expanded to include the larger heading of "document image analysis," where the *page image* replaces the letter or character as the ultimate referent of a text. It incorporates the multisensorial ways we engage with documents beyond a notion of immersive reading. In the field of musicology, researchers are using vector-space models pioneered by linguists in the field of information retrieval to think about the large-scale relationships of musical forms. And acoustic measures are now being applied to the study of texts through digitized collections of poetry readings. While each of these domains requires subspecialization, they also work together to form more general theories of culture and human-machine cognition. One of the consequences of digitization—by no means a mandate—is that it affords the ability to seek more general understandings of human creativity.

When the *Internet Archive was founded in 1996, it promised "universal access to all knowledge." We now know that access to digitized information is not universal, nor does digital information encompass all forms of knowledge. Conversions involve losses as well as gains. The more general insights to be gained from digitization necessarily come at the expense of more particularized knowledge (and vice versa). Perhaps even more important is the fact that just because a machine has read or seen or heard something does not mean a human has understood it. Digitization does not by itself produce new knowledge. We also need ways of understanding the growing heaps and stacks of information stored on "drives" or *"clouds" around the world. This is yet another way that conversion underlies the history of information: the art of how we convert information into knowledge. As the engineers would say, this problem remains nontrivial.

Andrew Piper

See also commodification; computers; data; databases; documentary authority; error; files; information, disinformation, misinformation; photocopiers; quantification; storage and search

FURTHER READING

Mohamed Cheriet, Nawwaf Kharma, Cheng-Lin Liu, and Ching Y. Suen, eds., *Character Recognition Systems*, 2007; Julia Flanders and Fotis Jannidis, eds., *The Shape of Data in Digital Humanities: Modeling Texts and Text-Based Resources*, 2018; Andrew Piper, *Enumerations: Data and Literary Study*, 2018; Herbert F. Schantz, *The History of OCR*, 1982; Claude Shannon and Warren Weaver, *The Mathematical Theory of Communication*, 1998; Jonathan Sterne, *MP3: The Meaning of a Format*, 2012; Ted Underwood, *Distant Horizons: Digital Evidence and Literary Change*, 2019; Hans Vaihinger, *The Philosophy of "As If": A System of the Theoretical, Practical, and Religious Fictions of Mankind*, 1911, translated by C. K. Ogden, 1924, repr. 1949.

DIPLOMATS/SPIES

Diplomats are, and have always been, in the information business. Across history, amid a great diversity of tasks, diplomats have engaged in three areas of activity above all: representation, negotiation, and information exchange. It is the last of these that has consistently consumed the largest share of diplomats' time, and produced an enormous volume of written records. From its beginning, the state has demanded information, and it has been the task of the diplomat "to inform" both those who send them and those to whom they are sent. The worth of diplomats has historically been assessed in part according to the accuracy and utility of the information they provide.

Spies, like diplomats, are information professionals, but traditionally there has been a distinction between their respective brands of information gathering. We generally associate "intelligence" with the work of spies, with a distinction drawn between diplomatic activity and the gathering of intelligence. Intelligence is information collected with a particular end in mind, from sources deemed to have especial authority, access, or insight, in the hope that the resulting knowledge might inform or facilitate the implementation of policy; the purpose of intelligence, whether as human intelligence (HUMINT) or signals intelligence (SIGINT), is to equip decision makers with timely truths, by which to monitor threats, form alliances, and make war. It was a role acknowledged as long ago as Sun Tzu in the fifth century BCE when the Chinese general and philosopher wrote in *The Art of War*: "Thus, what enables the wise sovereign and the good general to strike and conquer, and achieve things beyond the reach of ordinary men, is foreknowledge." The collection of intelligence is often furtive in nature, and its yield regularly subjected to appraisal for its verisimilitude and utility.

This difference between diplomacy and intelligence gathering has been implicit in the many warnings to ambassadors not to be seen as acting like spies. An eleventh-century Persian treatise called the *Siyāsatnāmeh*, or *Book of Government*, which drew in part on sources from the earlier Sassanian period, declared that "it should be realized that when kings send ambassadors to one another, their purpose is not merely the message or the letter which they communicate openly, but secretly they have a hundred other points in view." The fifteenth-century Venetian Ermolao Barbaro, in his treatise *De officio legati*, emphasized that it was in the gathering of information that an ambassador most clearly demonstrated his value to his sovereign, but that he must take care not to cross the line of propriety and look like a spy. In his 1681 treatise *L'ambassadeur et ses fonctions* (The ambassador and his functions) Abraham de Wiquefort described diplomacy as the "the trade of an honest spy," and François de Callières, in a 1716 work on the art of diplomacy, described the ambassador as an *honorable espion*, an "honorable spy," because he was expected to uncover the secrets of the court to which he was sent by winning over those who could inform him.

Although secrecy is sometimes seen as a hallmark of intelligence (hence the "secret service"), and one that distinguishes it from diplomacy, secrecy is not a requirement of the work of spies and intelligence services. And much important diplomatic activity takes place away from public view, and sometimes entirely in secret, as seen in the distress among American policy makers over the release of thousands of diplomatic cables by WikiLeaks. In practice, diplomacy and intelligence work are almost always intertwined.

Some of the earliest written records we have of government document diplomatic activity. The so-called Mari tablets, dating from the eighteenth century BCE, record the travels of Bronze Age diplomats across the Near East, from Mesopotamia to the Aegean. One letter describes the delivery of leather sandals in the Minoan style by an official named Bahdi-Lim to the famed Babylonian king Hammurabi. Unfortunately for the Marian ambassador, Hammurabi rejected the footwear, for reasons not indicated, and a short time later would invade and conquer Mari. This is one of dozens of diplomatic missions recorded in the tablets, an indication not only of active diplomacy four thousand years ago, but also of one of its essential features: the informational paper (or, in this case, clay) trail that it generates.

The *Rigveda*, the great collection of Sanskrit hymns composed in the second millennium BCE, indicates that the various Vedic tribes of India engaged both in espionage and in the regular exchange of envoys to negotiate disagreements over land and form alliances with like-minded partners. In their accounts of the two great wars that convulsed ancient Greece, both Herodotus and Thucydides repeatedly describe the dispatch of spies and the exchange of envoys, sent out not only to negotiate but also to report and gather information. Herodotus tells us that Histiaios, the tyrant of Miletus, sent an envoy with a message tattooed on his head, which would be revealed when its recipient shaved the envoy's head. While typical of Herodotus's partiality to fantastic stories, this tale is nonetheless indicative of the regular long-distance exchange of information in ancient Greece.

While for most of its existence the Roman Empire had no formal, centralized foreign policy apparatus, and there is no indication that the Romans kept systematic records of their diplomatic activity, information furnished by diplomats and spies was vital to the Roman imperial project. The Romans operated an imperial secret service attached to its extensive courier network known as the *cursus publicus*, whose aim was to direct sensitive and useful information and intelligence to the imperial metropole. The sixth-century historian Procopius wrote that both the Romans and their rivals in Sassanid Persia spent significant public monies on spies "to go secretly among the enemy in order to examine their affairs accurately, reporting to their rulers on their return." The Byzantine Empire placed especial importance on information gathering, buffeted as it was for centuries by antagonistic neighbors. Gathering information about the politics and policies of bordering states was regarded as critical and one of the foremost concerns of the envoys dispatched by the Byzantine emperors. The imperial chancery, the *drome*, had the *scrinium barbarorum* (Office of the barbarians), dedicated to drafting letters and keeping records related to the empire's diplomatic and intelligence-gathering activity, and led by an official known as the *logothete*, dedicated to the collection and organization of sensitive information.

The calculus of information for diplomats fundamentally changed in the *early modern period. Starting in Italy in the fifteenth century, and then spreading elsewhere in Europe and beyond, states exchanged ambassadors who remained resident at court, establishing households that in time would develop into permanent embassies. Permanent residence meant that information gathering became a daily concern for diplomats. As early as 1458, Duke Francesco Sforza of Milan, who was the first sovereign systematically to send out resident ambassadors to multiple states, told one of his ambassadors that he wished to become "the lord of the news" (*signore di novelle*). The duke also had within his chancery a team of *code makers and breakers.

The advent of resident diplomacy had informational repercussions that went beyond diplomats' daily tasks. With the constant drafting, exchange, receipt, and copying of diplomatic correspondence, institutions emerged to handle the production and storage of documents. Diplomatic chanceries like that of Louis XIV of France handled "worlds of paper" related to statecraft, and diplomats themselves, like the chancery secretaries, oversaw voluminous paper flows. Diplomatic records became tools to guide policy, establish precedent, and, in some cases, assert political legitimacy.

In the modern world, statecraft, like commerce and finance, increasingly depended on the provision of timely information, with both diplomats and spies playing essential roles. The institutional lines between diplomacy and intelligence, however, tended to become more finely drawn. In nineteenth-century Europe we see the precursors to the intelligence agencies that would emerge in the following century. The Austrian foreign minister and chancellor Klemens von Metternich is rightly famous as the chief diplomatic architect of the nineteenth-century "Concert of Europe," but he also developed one of the continent's most effective intelligence services. Staffed by secret police and a team of *cryptographers operating in a so-called *cabinet noir* (black cabinet) it excelled in the acquisition of both HUMINT (human intelligence) and SIGINT (signals intelligence), the latter through code breaking and the interception of letters. No wonder Metternich referred to himself as the "chief minister of police in Europe." In the next generation, Otto von Bismarck, the master German statesman, also oversaw a two-pronged effort of diplomacy and intelligence. Bismarck's "Prince of Spies," Wilhelm Stieber (1818–82), ran a vast network of underground informants across Europe and even donned disguises to engage in hands-on intelligence work himself. His intelligence reports were vital to Prussian successes in its wars against Austria and France. Building on Stieber's work, Bismarck established the first genuine national intelligence office, known as the Central Information Bureau.

The nineteenth century also saw the appearance of the telegraph, after which "reading the cables" became a daily requirement of diplomats. In the 1840s, the British foreign secretary, Lord Palmerston, after he had received his first telegram, lamented, "By God, this is the end of diplomacy." Palmerston was wrong, but there is little doubt that the telegraph transformed the circulation of diplomatic information. Allowing as it did near-instantaneous communication between the metropole and agents in the field, the telegraph compressed time and space. Over time, it led to a reduction in the autonomy of the ambassador, for he could expect an immediate reply to any information he provided and instructions on what to do. The telegraph also encouraged the centralization of diplomatic decision making, increased the importance of signals intelligence, and accelerated the pace of diplomatic activity (especially during crises). The rapid exchange of information could lead to misunderstanding and miscalculation, especially in an age of mass communication, which energized public opinion. Telegraphy was also vulnerable to tapping, which might yield sensitive intelligence, perhaps most famously with the so-called Zimmerman Telegram of January 1917, a secret message from the German Foreign Ministry to Mexico that proposed an alliance against the United States were the Americans to enter the war against Germany. Decoded by British intelligence, the telegram played an important role in the lead-up to American entry into the First World War on the side of the Allies.

In the twentieth century, it became customary for states to establish a dual-track approach to information from abroad, with separate agencies dedicated to diplomacy and intelligence. The latter became commonplace by the middle of the twentieth century and were given further impetus by the armed peace of the Cold War. Examples include the Central Intelligence Agency, formed by the National Security Act of 1947; the Japanese Public Security Intelligence Agency, founded in 1952; and the KGB, which emerged from the consolidation of several existing bodies in 1954. In some cases, the size and scope of these entities eclipsed those of the foreign ministries. Thus in the United States, the "intelligence community" dwarfs the diplomats on the government payroll.

As communication technologies diversified in the past century, so too did the avenues for intelligence gathering. Phone taps and bugging devices penetrated the most intimate of spaces. Thus, at the Allied conferences at Tehran (1943) and Yalta (1945), listening gadgets at the conference venues gave Stalin unvarnished insight into the American outlook and intentions. In the age of cellular telephony, listening in on the phone conversations of officials and civilians alike is a widespread, and controversial, practice. At the same time, satellites and spy planes gathered imagery intelligence (known as IMINT) from great distances above. In a global Cold War involving the deployment of nuclear assets, IMINT precipitated a number of flashpoints, including the shooting down of an American U-2 spy plane over Russia in 1960 and the Cuban Missile Crisis of 1962, which followed the discovery of nuclear launch sites on the island of Cuba via U-2 flyovers. Satellite intelligence largely replaced spy planes from the 1960s forward, with "eyes in the sky" monitoring everything from nuclear treaty compliance to troop movements. In the course of the Vietnam War, American aerial and satellite assets gathered significantly more IMINT than the available manpower could possibly process. IMINT from satellites is more important than ever, especially for insight into closed societies such as North Korea. Some estimates have suggested that together the National Reconnaissance Office and National Geospatial Intelligence Agency represent the largest tranche of the US intelligence budget, the exact numbers for which are classified.

The age of *digital information has wrought transformations in the roles and conduct of both diplomats and spies. The proliferation of social media networks, the availability of *big data, and digital applications that allow for rapid exchange all combine to generate global connections and information flows. Emails and encrypted digital message have displaced telegraphy, although diplomats still speak of "cables" when describing their communication. The availability of digital media has made diplomatic activity simultaneously easier, in that digital communication does not require the same sorts of investments in personnel and bricks and mortar that traditional diplomacy does, and more complex, given the great increase in potential participants and stakeholders in diplomatic activity, such as NGOs, banks and corporations, academic concerns, and private citizens. It is customary today to speak of "networked diplomacy," which links people, ideas, interests, and audiences through digital communicative mechanisms. The application of "soft power" is an essential concern and requires the broadcast of information not only to fellow state officials, but also to civilian populations and social organizations. In the late twentieth century, economic information assumed a particularly important role for diplomats, who were expected to act as advocates for the national commercial and financial interests. States and major corporations alike became increasingly concerned with commercial and industrial espionage, especially in businesses deemed vital to national security, such as defense contracting and telecommunications. Computer *hacks and malware presented especial vulnerabilities, compromising both intellectual property and the personal data of both employees and customers. The Chinese government, in particular, has been credibly accused of orchestrating widespread espionage efforts against foreign concerns, and Silicon Valley is the target of such intensive Russian and Chinese espionage efforts that it has recently been called a "den of spies." In many cases, such espionage proves to be considerably more time- and cost-effective than R&D.

The business of spying, too, has been changed radically by the emergence of digital information. While boots-on-the-ground human intelligence remains extremely important, a spy is just as likely to be sleuthing for intelligence seated at a computer console or watching incoming footage from a drone. Cybersecurity and online information flows are now fundamental foreign policy concerns that occupy an increasing number of intelligence professionals. This reflects the reality that in modern diplomacy and espionage the key step in the information-gathering process, for diplomats and spies alike, is triage, during which they extract the genuinely important information from amid the noise. This was the challenge, per the 2004 report of the 9/11 Commission, at the heart of the failure to foresee and interdict the terrorist attacks on the World Trade Center and Pentagon. American intelligence agencies "knew," but they did not "know that they knew."

The embassy retains the important role it has had ever since the advent of permanent, resident diplomacy, remaining the primary venue for the exchange of information in bilateral contacts. It also retains important information-gathering capacities, employing a broad range of people in doing so. The "intelligence officer" is a vague category of functionary often assigned to embassies, operating under "official cover." It has been estimated that during the Cold War, the Soviets stationed some eight hundred of these intelligence officers in western European embassies alone; they were, in essence, spies. Embassies thus occupy a gray area—a locale for both diplomacy and espionage, and the official diplomatic presence of a state, granted diplomatic immunity, but often tasked with illicit intelligence tasks, acting as hubs for the acquisition of both HUMINT and SIGINT.

The use of digital information has transformed the contours of public diplomacy, creating new avenues by which to transmit information to the public through cultural exchanges, educational initiatives, and national publicity and advocacy campaigns. In the early twenty-first century, diplomats expend as much time and effort composing messages for virtual audiences on television, podcasts, and online interfaces as they do communicating with other diplomatic officials. While statecraft at the highest level between government representatives remains important, the inclusive and collaborative nature of much of this digital activity suggests a new ethos.

Diplomats in the digital age have been called "bureaucrats of transnational knowledge" and, like so many others, find themselves acting as information managers. The *Economist* magazine in 2012, in surveying the turn of governments toward the use of Twitter feeds, described a new army of "tweeting Talleyrands." Nearly all developed nations now practice what is called Twiplomacy. Consular hashtags are now a diplomatic calling card. The US president Donald Trump regards Twitter as his primary means of communication, not only with domestic supporters and antagonists, but also with foreign nations and leaders. For better or for worse, his Twitter feed has become an instrument of statecraft. The US State Department has an Office of eDiplomacy overseeing its *internet presence and maintains an internal wiki called Diplopedia, to which diplomats and other officials add information relative to their expertise. The State Department also employs massive online open courses (MOOCs) as part of its educational outreach abroad.

Spies in the digital age, in addition to collecting information, expend increasing time and resources on stemming digital threats and interdicting and responding to deliberate misinformation originating from geopolitical rivals. They also have to combat digital *leaks and hacks intending to reveal information they wish to keep secret. Their shadowy adversaries might be WikiLeaks (founded 2006) or Russian hackers in an office basement in St. Petersburg. As WikiLeaks' founder Julian Assange once observed: "The Internet is the biggest spying machine the world has ever seen."

In the longer term, we might ask if the flows of information in the digital age change the fundamentals of diplomacy and espionage. Digital diplomacy raises searching questions over where the boundaries of diplomacy lie and who gets to practice it. Does the surfeit of information and the ease with which it is shared portend a diplomacy without diplomats? Much of the information amassed by foreign and intelligence ministries is *open sources intelligence (OSINT), which does not require the expense, personnel, and subterfuge of long-established information-gathering methods. The traditionally clear boundaries between the diplomat and nondiplomat are being subtly, but steadily, eroded. Diplomats historically have been distinguished by their privileged access to certain categories of information, but in an age when information abounds and is largely open source, that distinction is considerably less clear.

Does the information provided by diplomats and spies end up making a critical difference? Demanding from their diplomats and spies an uninterrupted flow of information, policy makers routinely demonstrate an untenable confidence that possession of certain information assures a capacity to determine the course of events. But intelligence failures are as routine as intelligence triumphs. Even good information does not necessarily lead to good policy. In an age of information saturation, this is perhaps true more than ever.

Paul M. Dover

See also archivists; bureaucracy; computers; data; databases; digitization; documentary authority; governance; information, disinformation, misinformation; networks; secretaries; storage and search; telecommunications

FURTHER READING

M. S. Anderson, The Rise of Modern Diplomacy, 1450–1919, 1993; Jeremy Black, A History of Diplomacy, 2010; Stephen Grey, The New Spymasters: Inside the Modern World of Espionage from the Cold War to Global Terror, 2015; M. Herman, "Diplomacy and Intelligence," Diplomacy and Statecraft 9 (1988): 1–22; Rhodri Jeffreys-Jones, In Spies We Trust: The Story of Western Intelligence, 2013; Garrett Mattingly, Renaissance Diplomacy, 1954; Joseph Siracusa, Diplomacy: A Very Short Introduction, 2010; Michael Warner, The Rise and Fall of Intelligence: An International Security History, 2014.

DOCUMENTARY AUTHORITY

What is a document? What information is it understood to convey? What power does it grant? Each of these contingent questions gestures at the historical intersections between information and power. As defined by the field of information science, documents are objects socially construed to bear evidence. Scrutiny of documents originating in different historical contexts reveals the agendas and intentions of their creation. Still, whereas documents are typically presupposed to truthfully represent their subjects, these informational mediums are rarely neutral and can be subject to willful or incidental distortion, misrepresentation, or confusion. The term *documentary authority* therefore refers to the ways that authors—sometimes individuals, but more often institutions and especially states—pursue and obtain power through the creation and dissemination of evidentiary texts.

Historically, many global institutions claimed documentary authority through their production and circulation of texts. Among these, religious institutions, particularly Christian churches, have long made documentary claims, whether through the issuance of edicts by church authorities or by maintaining records pertaining to land and population. In devoting resources to collecting, documenting, and circulating information in order to claim power and even establish forms of governance, these institutions may be called state-like. In many historical and geographical contexts, the ability to produce, update, store, and circulate documents can be regarded as an index of governing capacity. Documents authored or commissioned by individuals to prove identity (such as notarial documents) or property (such as merchant contracts) rely on mutual acceptance but also on the backing of legal, political, or religious authority.

Documents created by or on behalf of a state are important elements of the history of political development. The documents created by governmental authorities include edicts, legal *codes, gazettes, censuses, tax registers, surveys, passports, and maps. Such documents are material instantiations of state power, describing and facilitating claims to authority over populations, institutions, and territories. States are the primary, although not the sole, social institutions that have historically possessed the organizational power and material wealth necessary to collate information pertaining to their jurisdictions and to produce documents representing these subjects. Other semi–state institutions that have claimed documentary authority through their production and circulation of texts include churches, colonial enterprises like the East India Company, and municipal and urban authorities.

In global historical terms, states that developed bureaucratic traditions usually deployed documents to political purposes. In his influential classification of modes of authority, Max Weber defined the bureaucratic "office" as constituting two equally important parts—the staff of officeholders and the documents, rules, and precedents that substantiated the workings of the office. As states develop more complex bureaucratic systems, they generate and circulate information about their laws and regulations to the subject population. Simultaneously, the multitude of offices that make up the state apparatus build archives and document the history of the state and its institutions. Both circulation and archiving are claims to legitimate authority, even as neither activity guarantees the legitimacy of such authority.

Although Weber understood bureaucratic authority to be a phenomenon of modern social organization and capitalistic development, premodern states and institutions also invoked documents to political use. Whether by using state-mandated coinage or weights and measures in commerce, paying taxes according to an officially compiled register or census, or obeying sentences meted out by an official bearing a legal handbook spelling out the laws of the land, subject populations understood the role of documents in marshaling authority. Documentary authority was particularly important to the rise and lasting power of the bureaucracy in early China. In its rise to become the first imperial power in Chinese history, in the ninth century BCE, the Qin state established weights and measures, coinage, and not only laws but specific guidance for officials charged with enforcement. In this context, documents—texts cast in bronze or inscribed on bamboo strips—became hallmarks of state power and efficiency.

The reasons that states either accumulated and safeguarded or circulated and disseminated documents likewise relate to calculations of political power. In *early modern Venice, the urban council attempted to prevent political information from circulating in public, and it hired only illiterate men to guard archives. In Tokugawa Japan, too, the shogun prohibited the open discussion of state news. In both contexts, the governing body guarded its documents to reduce public scrutiny. By contrast, the early modern English throne, eager to showcase direct communication with subjects, widely circulated royal proclamations. The central state does not always control the means of circulation, nor its result. When imperial elites exchanged state documents in Song dynasty China, they articulated shared understandings of the empire that helped perpetuate the imperial formation despite persistent existential threats.

In both Western and non-Western historical contexts, increased documentation accompanied the development of more complex bureaucratic systems. In early modern China, the population grew rapidly through both territorial conquest and agricultural prosperity. State documents supplemented the sparse manpower of the field bureaucracy to maintain imperial authority. Bureaucratic agents used documents like seals, licenses, and imperial judgments to carry out the will of the state. In fact, the assumption of field office was so closely connected to its documentary apparatus that taking up an office was called "receiving a seal." In order to ease the pains of transmission over long distances, imperial officials corresponded using a densely layered language of quotations and set phrases. And when officials traveled to distant posts, they carried seals and texts bearing archival markers that marked these documents as pieces of an expansive bureaucratic infrastructure. Documents granted power to the bearer only so long as he or she had a legitimate relationship to the state. By specifying a purpose or agenda, documents limited the personal power of the individual.

States often closely guarded the technological processes or material elements of political documents. In early modern Europe, the growing availability of print and paper and the growth of *literacy allowed states to collect increasingly detailed information about their populations and to create and circulate ever larger numbers of documents in order to pursue their agendas. At the same time, such plentiful material and human resources could also undermine state power. By forging, altering, or otherwise misusing documents, individuals subtly disrupted the authority of the bureaucratic state. The problem of forgery and the uncertainty involved in authenticating a document, an individual's identity, or the value of a coin are defining elements of early modern societies. In response, states pursued new administrative techniques to protect and strengthen the authority of their documents. These included seals, signatures, and dates, but also the patterned language and bureaucratic jargon that characterized state texts. Each marked state documents as official and safeguarded against forgery and misuse.

One particular *genre of document—government gazettes—helps illustrate the complexities of documentary authority for early modern polities. Early European examples of state-sponsored periodical publishing, such as the late seventeenth-century *London Gazette* and *Gazette de France* (Gazette of France), are usually treated as state media in contest with popular representations of political news, especially the newspaper. However, like its Chinese counterpart, the *Peking Gazette*, the *London Gazette* primarily published not reporting or opinions, but excerpted state documents. In East Asia, especially China, state gazettes documented state business and were meant to be read by officials of the empire and neighboring states. Once published, these documentary periodicals provided an official vantage on state business to any audience, official or not. Gazettes became particularly important for European travelers to China seeking out the documentation produced by the Chinese state, and especially how these documents portrayed the power of the monarch. In subsequent colonial endeavors, European powers established government gazettes as relatively cost-effective instruments of state authority, recounting laws, judicial decisions, and other correspondence relevant to maintaining the empire.

The publication of excerpted documents in government gazettes challenged the state's desire to avoid forgeries but also facilitated the state's wide circulation of texts. Visual and rhetorical elements of state documents allowed them to be received and evaluated outside the contexts of government offices. In Europe, officially sanctioned periodicals carried stamps and other marks of royal license. In China, a well-versed reader could recognize entries in the court gazette as authorized excerpts from official memoranda and imperial edicts. The interchangeable packaging of state texts in multiple documentary formats of the early modern era anticipated the mutability of format in the *digital age: when text can be copied, stripped of formatting, and restyled in infinite combinations, visual markers become less relevant than one's understanding of genre conventions.

Although the use of documentary authority by historical states is particularly well demonstrated in the early modern era, the question of how documents relate to political power is relevant across the *longue durée* of human society. Indeed, the need for authenticating markers has not been obviated by the seeming disappearance of paper documents from modern society. Digital documents are encoded with layers of authenticating information, such as the *metadata that traces the creation and modification of a document or the certificates, e-signatures, and encryption that each attest that a document is what it claims to be. Present-day examples of manipulated biometric data and *leaked emails make amply clear that documents are multivalent tools—and destroyers—of political authority. Long-standing problems of validity, representation, and legitimacy necessitate that historians and other scholars think carefully about the ways that seemingly neutral documents can be deployed and distorted in contexts of past and present.

Emily Mokros

See also archivists; bureaucracy; censorship; error; forgery; governance; inventories; libraries and catalogs; publicity/publication

FURTHER READING

Michael K. Buckland, "What Is a Document?," *Journal of the American Society of Information Science* 48 (1997): 804–9; Peter Crooks and Timothy Parsons, eds., *Empires and Bureaucracy in World History: From Late Antiquity to the Twentieth Century,* 2016; Lisa Gitelman, *Paper Knowledge: Toward a Media History of Documents,* 2014; Ben Kafka, *The Demon of Writing: Powers and Failures of Paperwork,* 2012; Emily Mokros, *Reading the State: The "Peking Gazette" in Late Imperial China and Beyond,* forthcoming, 2021.

ENCRYPTING/DECRYPTING

A TALE OF TWO MACHINES

The printing press in Europe ushered in what may be described as the first age of mass media and has served for centuries as an engine of open information. In the influential account of Elizabeth Eisenstein, the press put the Bible in the hands of the people and allowed scientists to communicate with precision at a distance; it helped to spread the texts of political dissent and gradually gave the gift of *literacy itself to ordinary men and women. It is generally seen in opposition to the modern computer, which has, according to the prophets of the *digital age, threatened to displace and even destroy the press as the word moves from the printed page to the flickering screens of laptops, tablets, and smart phones.

The Enigma machine, by contrast, ushered in a shadowy world of covert communication, and it has come to serve as the very watchword for secrecy. Its hidden series of alphabetical rotors sent the letters on the keyboard through switches of such complexity that the patterns produced would be utterly illegible to anyone without a version of the same machine and a shared key to its temporary settings. The device was developed by the German engineer Arthur Scherbius (1878–1929), who is all but forgotten today—though his invention is more famous than ever, thanks to renewed interest in Alan Turing, who helped to break Enigma and turn the tide of World War II. Turing's work at Bletchley Park led directly to the advent of modern computing; and it might be said that the promise of information security developed under the pressures of war has been fully delivered in the digital age, which has put a powerful encryption machine inside even the simplest of our portable devices.

At first glance, these two machines have very little in common: they not only come from different periods but seem to take us in opposite directions. But the two machines have much more in common than meets the eye, and they remind us that—in the history of information—secrecy and openness have gone hand in hand from the outset. Indeed, the earliest and strongest evidence linking the printing press and the Enigma machine comes from none other than the archetypal *Renaissance man Leon Battista Alberti (1404–72). Toward the end of his remarkable career he wrote the work that not only offered the first exposition of secret writing in Europe but also described an invention that changed the making and breaking of *codes forever. This slim tract, titled simply *On Ciphers*, was not published until 1568; but it was written almost exactly a century earlier, only one year after the first printing press was established in Italy and in direct response to a conversation about Gutenberg's invention with the pope's secretary Leonardo Dati. In the text's opening paragraph, Alberti recalls:

> When I was in the company of Leonardo Dati in the Pope's gardens at the Vatican . . . we highly praised the German inventor who recently, by means of movable type characters, made it possible to reproduce more than 200 volumes from

one original text in 100 days with the help of no more than three workmen. With a single impression he can indeed obtain a whole sheet of paper of the larger size completely printed. And while we were marvelling at some people's ingenuity about several enterprises, Dati expressed great admiration for those men who, by their talent, can unravel and explain the hidden meanings of messages that people send each other employing those unusual contrived characters known as ciphers. . . . And turning to me, Dati said: "You have always investigated the secrets of nature; what do you make of those who might be called solvers of ciphers and explainers of secrets? Did you ever consider trying your hand at these things?"

What led Dati to jump (without apparent pause for thought) from the setting of type to the cracking of codes? Is this a shocking non sequitur or evidence for lost associations between separate fields and technologies? Perhaps encryption seemed to be another form of "artificial writing" (as printing was called at the time), or perhaps Secretary Dati (who traded, after all, in secrets) wondered how information could remain secure in an age of machine-assisted communication?

In any case, after this fateful exchange Alberti did try his hand at the science of ciphers and mastered it with characteristic speed and flair, producing in the course of some twenty pages a lucid general introduction to the subject, beginning with a definition of the key term in his title: "it occurred to me that *cipher* should be defined as a method for writing secretly by means of arbitrarily chosen signs, the meaning of which has been agreed on between the two correspondents, so as to be unintelligible to others." The idea of encryption using such a system was by no means new in Alberti's day: substituting the letters of the alphabet with an agreed-on set of characters had been known since ancient times, and by the late Middle Ages mercantile and diplomatic networks were drawing on simple keys called *nomenclators*, which provided agents with a set of arbitrary characters for each letter of the alphabet and invented symbols for frequently used words, names, and places.

Alberti explained that the weakness of such systems is that they quickly become predictable and are therefore vulnerable to analysis based on the calculation of letter frequencies (using methods that would later be called statistical). As the pioneers of Arabic *cryptography had known for several centuries, this is the fundamental flaw in the operation known as "monoalphabetic substitution," where one letter is always represented by the same arbitrary character. When Alberti moved from the subject of code *breaking* to code *making*, he went from criticizing the existing system to designing a new one that would put the field on a new footing. His great breakthrough was the creation of a reliable method for substituting individual letters in the "plaintext" with characters drawn from multiple alphabets. Alberti opened the door to what is now known as *"polyalphabetic* substitution," and in doing so he laid down the principles that would lead—with few changes—to the inner workings of the Enigma machine.

Alberti wondered how we can bring many alphabets into play in a device that would be easy to make and operate, and quickly hit upon the idea of the handheld tool that is now known as the Alberti disk. It consisted of a fixed disk with twenty letters in cells onto which a second (smaller and movable) disk would be attached, with a separate and random set of characters in matching cells. The plain alphabet can be keyed to more than twenty different cipher alphabets, with the alignment between the two wheels agreed in advance by means of an "index" (or starting point)—that can be changed between messages or even within a single text.

Alberti's invention took the so-called *ars combinatoria* (strongly associated with the medieval *polymath Ramon Llull) into a new age of information security; and it was taken up by a series of authors in the course of the next two centuries, each of whom improved it in some way. The first of these was the German monk Johannes Trithemius, whose treatise *Polygraphiae Libri Sex* (Six books on the multiple modes of writing), published in 1518, has the distinction of being the first printed book on the subject of cryptography. His *Recta Transpositionis Tabula* (Regular table for transposition) printed an entire alphabet on each of its two dozen lines, with each starting one letter after the one above. The writer can move down through the list of alphabets in order, or jump between them according to some predetermined pattern. And in 1585, a French mathematician named Blaise de Vigenère took Trithemius's invention to its logical conclusion in a method celebrated in his day as "the undecipherable cipher": by selecting a running keyword agreed on with the recipient and using the letters of that word to choose from the available alphabets, the writer will jump between different substitution systems with every single letter.

Most later editions and translations of Trithemius's text returned to the circular format favored by Alberti. Some of these involved volvelles, diagrams with moving parts made out of paper or *parchment. And some of the devices were designed as freestanding machines, including a particularly interesting example in the mid-seventeenth century by the English scientist Samuel Morland—who invented a method for opening and resealing letters during a stint as clerk to Oliver Cromwell's spymaster John Thurloe. After the restoration of the English monarchy in 1660, Morland worked hard to regain the king's favor, and in 1666 he printed two texts describing new inventions, dedicating both to the new king, Charles II. The first, a short folio called *A New Method of Cryptography*, is one of the most visually inventive publications before the twentieth century, and it offered a dramatic math lesson to the king, explaining that by bringing into play the permutations of all letters in the alphabet, the possibilities for coded communication reached *cosmic* proportions: "The Permutations of 24 Letters are so numerous, that a Thousand Millions of able Clerks, in a Thousand Millions of Years were not able to transcribe them! And . . . the Books which might be compiled of the variety of 23 Letters only would do more than twice cover the whole Superficies of the Earth and Sea. Nay further . . . the Paper of those Volumes, laid singly Sheet by Sheet, would cover the very Firmament." Morland's book culminated in a description of a ciphering device that (while operated manually, using a stylus to turn a series of case-mounted rotors) takes us very close to the twentieth-century machines of Scherbius and his competitors (see figure 1).

While the disks developed after Alberti seem to anticipate the mechanical computer, Morland's cryptographic tables were extremely well suited to the technology of the press since a page of printed text is itself a rigid rectilinear grid composed of isolated (and arbitrary) pieces of type bearing characters that become meaningful only when locked in place. And on a more basic level, by greatly increasing the size and scope of the audience for published works, the printing press also called for the opposite, making the need to limit and direct one's readership more pressing than ever.

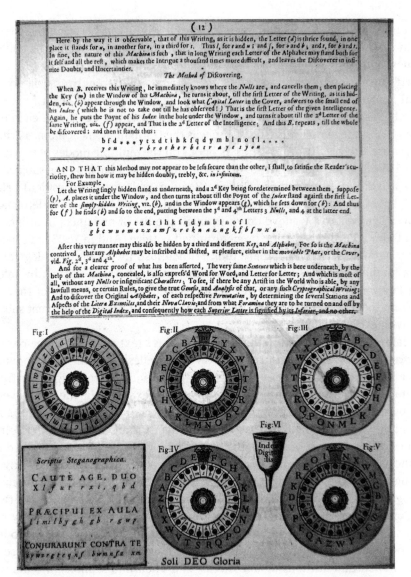

Figure 1. The "Machina Cyclologica Cryptographica" from Samuel Morland's *New Method of Cryptography* (1666). By kind permission of the Folger Shakespeare Library, classmark M2781A, p. 12.

CRYPTOGRAPHY AND STEGANOGRAPHY

Codes and ciphers had been around for centuries, but the first age of print saw an absolute explosion of interest in secret languages of all kinds: the topic of cryptography became closely tied to other aspects of communication, and treatments of ciphers were integrally connected to the art and science of the alphabet itself. Publications on the design of letters almost always included examples of secret characters, whether cipher alphabets or sonnets using visual rebuses to stand in for words (see figure 2). And books on ciphers, for their part, almost always contained long sections on the history of the alphabet—which offered ready-made symbols for simple encryptions.

Figure 2. A rebus-sonnet from Giovanni Battista Palatino's 1566 writing manual *Compendio del Gran Volume de l'Arte del Bene et Leggiadramente Scrivere Tutte le Sorti di Lettere et Caratteri*. By kind permission of the Folger Shakespeare Library, classmark Z43.A3.P3.1566.Cage.

Over the first century or so after the twin inventions of Gutenberg and Alberti, the printed book shared with new readers an astonishing range of novel systems for secret communication. Some moved far beyond the traditional arsenal of letters, numbers, and symbols. For the seventeenth-century English bishop John Wilkins (among others), the notes on a musical staff could be turned into an alphabetical code. Another popular system assigned the letters of the alphabet to different flowers, so a floral wreath could carry a verbal message. One of the most ingenious and enduring methods was the so-called grille, invented in the middle of the sixteenth century by the Italian mathematician Girolamo Cardano. In this system the message itself is not enciphered but plainly written in a series of cutout boxes in a card or stencil shared by sender and recipient. After the secret words are all in place, the card is lifted and the rest of the spaces filled in with innocent words. When the recipient takes the matching template and puts it in the right location, the secret message appears in the windows like magic.

These last few examples take us from cryptography proper to a separate set of techniques that are collectively known as *steganography*. While the etymology of the two words is almost identical (both mean "hidden writing"), the systems are distinct. *Cryptography* refers to systems of secret writing where the message is transformed, either by changing the order of the letters (transposition) or by replacing them with other characters (substitution). *Steganography* is used for systems of secret writing where the message stays unchanged but is hidden. The particular virtue of this latter approach is that the most powerful system of secret writing is one where we cannot see that there is a hidden message at all.

HOW TO MAKE ANYTHING SIGNIFY ANYTHING

The *early modern period produced history's most potent combination of cryptography and steganography. It was invented by yet another Renaissance polymath, Sir Francis Bacon, who not only published the first account of cryptography in English but also invented what is widely considered to be the most powerful cipher devised before the advent of computers. Bacon devised this system of encryption, which he called the "biliteral" (or "bi-literarie") cipher, while still a teenager in the late 1570s, when he spent three years in the entourage of the English ambassador in France. As its name suggests, Bacon's cipher system used only two letters—or, more precisely, represented each letter in the alphabet by some combination of a's and b's. When Bacon realized that it was possible to represent all twenty-six letters in permutations of only two by using groups of five, he generated a standard alphabetic key running from A (=AAAAA) to Z (=BABBB). The crucial point in Bacon's system is that the a's and b's in the ciphered text are not represented by those actual letters; rather, Bacon allowed them to designate the different forms of anything that can be divided into two classes, sorts, or types (which Bacon referred to as the *a-form* and the *b-form*). Indeed, in the biliteral cipher, the cover text need not be "text" at all: the a's and b's can be represented by two types of anything—pluses and minuses, flowers of different kinds or colors, even (literally) apples and oranges. This is why Bacon claimed that it could be used to "signify anything by means of anything," and why it earned the highest praise from no less an authority than William F. Friedman.

Friedman's cryptographic career began in 1915 at Riverbank Laboratories, a privately funded research institute outside Chicago where he served as an assistant to Elizabeth Wells Gallup, then the leading advocate of the theory that Bacon was the true author of Shakespeare's plays—and that evidence could be found by searching for hidden biliteral messages in the First Folio and other texts. Friedman quickly lost faith in this enterprise, but not before reading all the Renaissance had to offer by way of training in the field of cryptography and writing some of the foundational texts that shifted the field to mathematical methods and military applications.

When the US government created its first central agency for signals intelligence in the wake of World War I, it put Friedman in charge, and his subsequent career in Washington, DC, earned him the title of the greatest cryptologist in history. Friedman would lead the team that broke the Japanese equivalent of the Enigma code during World War II; and he proved equally adept at making codes, inventing a rotor-based machine of his own called Sigaba with Frank Rowlett, with whom he would help to create the National Security Agency. After Friedman retired from the NSA in 1955 he returned each year to help train new classes of code breakers. In these classes (published after his death as *Six Lectures on Cryptology*), he started by revisiting his hero Bacon. But by then it was clear where the pioneering biliteral code would lead: "Bacon," he concluded, "was in fact the inventor of the *binary code that forms the basis for modern computers."

CONCLUSION

This short survey shows that codes and ciphers have played an integral (if largely secret and highly specialized) role in the history of information. In recent years, the subject of cryptography has become strongly associated with military history and the history of mathematics; but for some of the most brilliant scholars of the Renaissance period, and for those who revived their work for our own day, the problem of how to encrypt and decrypt messages takes us to the heart of communication itself. Alberti's disk and Bacon's biliteral cipher have now given way to a brave new world in which we use sophisticated cryptography every time we send an email or buy a product online. And not even Friedman could have predicted the emergence of a new economy based on "cryptocurrencies" like Bitcoin: which of our two machines it will most resemble, and whether it will deliver openness or secrecy, remains to be seen.

William H. Sherman

See also cards; computers; diplomats/spies; indexing; letterpress; merchants; privacy; surveilling

FURTHER READING

Leon Battista Alberti, *A Treatise on Ciphers*, translated by Augusto Buonafalce, 1997; Elizabeth L. Eisenstein, *The Printing Revolution in Early Modern Europe*, 1983; Katherine Ellison and Susan Kim, eds., *A Material History of Medieval and Early Modern Ciphers*, 2018; Shawn James Rosenheim, *The Cryptographic Imagination: Secret Writing from Edgar Poe to the Internet*, 1997; Kathryn A. Schwartz, "Charting Arabic Cryptology's Evolution," *Cryptologia* 33 (2009): 297–304; William H. Sherman, "How to Make Anything Signify Anything," *Cabinet* 40 (Winter 2010–11): 32–38; Amador Vega, ed., *The Thinking Machine: Ramon Llull and the Ars Combinatoria*, 2016.

ERROR

Information, as published knowledge, is vulnerable to error at any point in the extended "communications circuit" that connects authors and readers (as Robert Darnton describes it, in the case of print), by virtue of having undergone the error-prone processes of composition, editing, proofreading, printing, binding, selling, and so on. More generally, it is liable to error throughout the even more diverse and open-ended circuits by which it is acquired, analyzed, disseminated in any media, and made use of (to use a four-stage sequence conveniently identified by Peter Burke in the entry "knowledge" in this volume). Some errors along those circuits may be easy to identify as errors, but others raise difficult questions about how to understand past and foreign contexts. The former case includes errors that can be identified through their clear violation of a particular correctness condition in a past context; the latter may involve errors where the very criteria for correctness were disputed in the past or are unclear to us now. To distinguish between errors in the local performance of knowledge and errors in criteria for knowledge requires careful attention and sometimes subtlety, as does identifying them as errors in the first place, since we are at risk of anachronistically imposing onto other contexts our own standards for correctness and our own disputes about criteria for error. Normally we can understand error through the range of practices that have aimed to prevent, correct, or eliminate it; through the diversity of vices and dispositions believed to lead to it; and through its envisaged consequences. Although error criteria often remain implicit in these practices, and can be inferred only with caution, at times they are explicitly identified as such, for example in the literary *genres that exaggerate errors in order to expose them. Satire and comedy, caricature and character types, invective and polemic, and parody constitute rich sources for the explicit representation of error, not of course because they are meant to be plainly believed, but because they offer evidence about what was believable about error and makers of error.

Error may be located in a variety of places in information circuits. It may be discovered, for instance, not in the knowledge itself but in the producer of the knowledge, in some deficiency of character or other personal disqualification. Biography, in some periods, is invoked as a test for the validity of certain kinds of knowledge, the defects of a life implying a failure of that person's knowledge, or at least grounds for suspecting it of error. In courtroom speeches and in political deliberations, for instance, moral and *epistemological error are commonly presented as one. Since the nineteenth century, biography has generally been held irrelevant to the truth of philosophical or scientific statements, but in antiquity the actual course of a philosophical life was a prime arena for testing philosophical knowledge. Errors in other domains of knowledge have also been traced to errors of the knowing subject rather than to the nature of the knowledge itself. The history of the biographies of knowing subjects may illuminate the connections that different ages drew between life errors and knowledge errors and clarify the degree to which legitimate personae of knowers were explicitly established.

When biography is found relevant to error, it is often understood to involve specific epistemological vices. The hardened hearts of sinners blind them to a knowledge of their sin (though some may be cured through repentance and *conversion); the *curiositas* of inquirers leads them in self-trivializing directions where their preference for vulgar knowledge would disqualify them from higher knowledge. Bias is one of the most commonly cited causes of error. Classical historians and orators, for instance, frequently rebut error that they trace to the bias of their rival authors and speakers, whose defects of character, they claim, are manifest in their tendentious and unreliable information; as a result, ancient authors developed a wide range of techniques and rhetoric to distinguish their reliable words from those of their rivals (e.g., by admitting conflicting evidence, insisting on their own independence and impartiality, interrogating sources). However, it is not necessary for a character to be flawed in order to be a source of error in information. For instance, with the emergence in the nineteenth century of mechanical objectivity as a method of truth, any trace of the knowing self in knowledge was regarded as a contaminant; subjectivity itself, the mere presence of a self, was taken to be a ground for error. In addition, error may be understood neither as a specific defect of a character nor as a defect intrinsic to human subjectivity, but rather as the result of the exclusion of some people from the discovery of knowledge: such a democratized knowledge procedure would root error in the inadequate participation of potential knowers in the production of knowledge. It would seek wisdom in crowds or identify coming to consensus as the means to discover valid knowledge.

The converse situation is perhaps more common, when the aspect of character that leads to an error in knowledge is taken to be the result of ignorance, a lack of training, a failure of expertise. Error, in this case, is created because those unqualified for knowledge have participated in producing it. These different ways of locating error within the character of the knower involve the widest range of prophylactics against error, and include diverse examples of spiritual training, disciplined habits of inquiry, repression of self-will, the steady management of a reputation for expertise, the use of torture to elicit truthful accounts from unreliable witnesses (such as slaves or suspects), and the extension or the reduction of the number of qualified knowers.

Alternatively, error may be located not in a flaw within the knowing subject but in knowledge itself. In these cases, the tests that establish the reliability or trustworthiness of knowledge claims are not directed to the character of the person making the claim. Instead, the knowledge has to meet other kinds of criteria: it must be consistent, either internally, or with a body of trustworthy knowledge that is prior to and outside of it; or it must be deducible from principles or axioms (less strongly, justifiable as knowledge by reference to principles); or it must be an appropriate generalization, neither excluding too many cases nor including too many exceptions; or it must be verified by some empirical observation (a prediction or postdiction that may encompass a wide range of possible circumstances); or it must be of the correct age, as both young information and old information may be challenged on the basis, respectively, of insufficient and excessive longevity. Sometimes errors are identified by means of aesthetic criteria: the structure of knowledge may be required to be beautiful, and flaws in information (published knowledge) may be due to aesthetic mistakes, such as a lack of clarity, vividness, narrative skill, or proportion. It is sometimes claimed that knowledge must have potential implications for action, in order to be either genuine knowledge or a higher knowledge.

Knowledge, in such cases, may be subject to additional criteria of wisdom, meaning, or value; to count as knowledge, it must be knowledge of something worth knowing (not, as the title of Lajos Hatvany's early twentieth-century satire puts it, *Die Wissenschaft des Nicht Wissenswerten* [The science of what's not worth knowing]). Ancient denunciations of the idleness or vanity of mere knowledge, separated from the conduct of life or the possibility of redemption, have been regularly renewed. William James (1842–1910), for instance, insisted that a valid difference in truth must correspond to a difference that we can trace elsewhere, one that is concretely imposed on somebody at some time and place. In the twentieth century, Gregory Bateson sought to define information as "any difference that makes a difference." Knowledge, finally, must not be of the sort that is forbidden. Some true things, on penalty of divine sanction, social taboos, or legal liabilities, are to be excluded from the knowledge circuit; that is, they are not permitted to introduce a difference into it: Adam and Eve were forbidden to eat of the tree of the knowledge of good and evil, medical data from Nazi experiments or from unauthorized exhumations have been barred from use, information thought to be pornographic may be banned for that reason, and legal proceedings exclude evidence deemed irrelevant. Other matters may be forbidden on logical or epistemological grounds, as things about which knowledge cannot properly be had.

Error may also be introduced in the reception of information, for instance when it is received by the wrong kind of learner or in the wrong manner. Knowledge correct in itself may nonetheless produce error by being communicated to unfit learners; such communication, it has sometimes been claimed, not only lacks prudence but may even unfit some people, or whole populations, for what was considered to be the proper conduct of their lives, duties, or social roles. (These are cases of epistemological truths yielding moral errors, or what were taken to be moral errors; in the ordinary usage of European languages, "error" encompasses mistakes of both knowledge and action.) The fear that knowledge may be misused or misunderstood, or pose a danger to potential knowers, locates error in people who learn, rather than in the knowledge itself. This fear is often a fear of the risk posed by the unregulated distribution and consumption of information and is typically managed by restricting access to it. Censorship need not be limited to political and legal means; pricing out particular populations may be just as effective in restricting access, as likewise the use of written language to exclude the illiterate, or learned languages or technical jargons to exclude *vernacular speakers. Some groups have been disqualified from both the consumption and the production of knowledge; these disqualifications, however, have divergent histories, and different practices and rationales have been associated with them. For instance, in colonial America, teaching slaves to read (as E. Jennifer Monaghan observed) was legally permitted everywhere, while instruction in writing was sometimes forbidden; after the revolution, a number of Southern states made instruction in reading illegal, thereby barring slaves from the reception as well as the production of written information. (This was often done on the grounds that, as Frederick Douglass's master feared, teaching a slave to read "would forever unfit him to be a slave.")

Forbidding the wide communication of knowledge does not necessarily presuppose defective knowers; it may be a means to establish the value of arcane or secret knowledge. Such an "economy of secrets" (Daniel Jütte's phrase) in the premodern and *early modern periods understands knowledge and publication to be at odds with each other, in contrast to more recent times when they are generally understood as mutually dependent, and with publication as the ground for the self-correction of knowledge. More commonly, however, error is located not in the presence or absence of publication itself but in some defect within potential consumers of knowledge, in the incapacity for truth on the part of some audiences: children, women, enslaved, colonized, and dependent populations, the disabled, the laity or non-coreligionists, for instance. Pedants, bluestockings, opsimaths (who came late to learning), and autodidacts may have accumulated information, but at the cost of becoming spoiled or denatured, and unfit for their assigned roles; as they are not gentlemen, their class or gender (and hence exclusion, in some periods, from formal education) has disqualified them from truly knowing as gentlemen do, that is, from integrating knowledge into their lives without error. Children in particular may be represented as uniquely vulnerable to the ill effects of adult knowledge.

Even capable learners may become flawed as a result of their knowing, if they learn in the wrong way. In the ancient world, Thales fell into a ditch as he was studying the stars: knowledge incapacitated him from everyday life, a theme and an example that, along with Socrates in cloud-cuckoo-land, long persisted in representations of the theorist. The Preacher found that "much study is a weariness of flesh" (Ecclesiastes 12:12), and the Roman procurator of Judea, Festus, complained of St. Paul that too much learning had made him mad (Acts 26:24). Seneca, in the first century CE, in one of the epistles to Lucilius identifies not only immoderate but also hasty or varied reading as the cause of distraction in learners. The eighteenth-century American physician Benjamin Rush believed that booksellers were particularly prone to insanity because their profession led them into the habit of "the frequent and rapid transition of the mind from one subject to another." Enduring stereotypes of melancholy, abstracted, desiccated, emotionally stunted, and asexual or uxorious scholars (Dryasdust, Dr. Syntax, Edward Casaubon, and many others) present the excessive consumption of knowledge as the prime cause of error, while stereotypes of haughty, charismatic, or dangerously predatory scholars tend to place the emphasis on the self-love of the scholar or the forbidden nature of the knowledge.

Wherever it is located, error elicits different kinds of reactions and different estimates of the danger it poses. When a member of an accredited or expert elite makes a mistake, the error may put into question the individual's expert status, which is what allowed the opinion to have authority in the first place; shame or defensive rage may be an appropriate response, allowing for differences in individual temperament and the gravity of the error. In contrast, in more democratic structures of knowledge, the threat of error may not be a fundamental discrediting of a self but rather an ordinary aspect of life: an error may be corrected in the next newspaper issue, installment of a novel, vote by the citizenry, and so on. The gravity of an error, the interpretation of its significance to the larger society, is also likely to be influenced by social contexts. The cultural theory of risk offers a sociological interpretation of varying responses to the significance of error, taking individualistic societies generally as discounting the danger posed by

error, collectivist egalitarian ones as tending to fear catastrophic scenarios, and hierarchical ones as interpreting error as manageable so long as it falls within an expertly
defined margin.

Some of the errors to which information is prone are specific to the medium by which
it is disseminated. Compared to literate cultures, oral ones have a relatively limited ability to fix utterances and so cannot impose analogous kinds of tests for coherence and
consistency on large corpora of written statements. Tests for errors of consistency can
be facilitated by manuscript and print instruments for making comparisons (e.g., cross-
references, *concordances, annotation, tables); these nonsequential reading practices assisted in making errors visible in new ways. In contrast, written works introduce new
problems of error that arise from the difficulties of establishing the trustworthiness or
authority of text. Speakers or reporters of speech in an oral culture are generally known,
so the question of whether to credit them does not raise to the same degree the problems of anonymity, pseudonymity, and forgery associated with written texts, which are
more easily alienated from the circumstances of their production. (The difference is one
of degree, not kind, of course; the oral transmissions of the Jewish Mishna and Islamic
hadith both placed a strong emphasis on citing original sources.) Readers, for their part,
without an oral informant to guide them or a witness they might cross-examine, may
use a text in ways that are remote from its original purpose and thereby introduce error;
moreover, the use of writing itself may atrophy the memory of readers who rely on it
(cf. the much debated passage in Plato, *Phaedrus* 275a).

The introduction and growth of print amplified anxieties about written errors. It was
feared that readers might succumb to diametrically opposed temptations: their attention may be dissipated by the sheer variety of print matter available to them, or they
may be corrupted or radicalized by their absorption in newly available dangerous texts
(such as vernacular translations of the Bible in the sixteenth century, or novels in the
nineteenth). By virtue of its mechanical *reproducibility, print standardized the information disseminated in any print run (of course there was some variation even within
the run, due to stop-press corrections, the removal or addition of material, or other irregularities); on the other hand, there was no guarantee that the disseminated information was itself free from error, as the *publishers may have chosen a defective source
to print, or carelessly converted it into print. Moreover, printed matter now often existed in competition with alternative texts supplied by other printers. Works that were
designed to be definitive sources could be subject to proliferating ripostes and polemics; learned reference works sometimes inspired the production of counterworks of reference; and a whole genre developed to correct common or popular error (*erreurs popu-
laires, pseudodoxia epidemica*).

The problem of trust that ensued with the proliferation of competing texts was handled in a number of ways: works might obtain an imprimatur or the approval of censors, or the support of prestigious patrons or subscribers; they might be brought out by
a printing house, academic society, or other body with a reputation for the quality of
its authors and members, and which perhaps also employed correctors or, from about
the middle of the sixteenth century, professional proofreaders; royal academies secured
the agreement of peer reviewers prior to the publication of articles from the eighteenth
century, as they did with book publication in the seventeenth century, as Mario Biagioli has shown. More informally, works might advertise their authority through schol-

arly apparatuses, dedications, frontispieces, blurbs, or other displays; they might be published, or claim to be published, in certain locations with a reputation for publishing
works trusted by particular readers (Amsterdam, Paris); or they might be published by
coreligionists (the number of theological works published in the early modern period is
far greater than other kinds of learned books because, for the most part, they appeared
in three different confessional versions, as Ian Maclean observed in *Scholarship, Commerce, and Religion*). In the long history of print, the many changes to practice and technology created many new possibilities for errors and correction. Even a narrow subject
such as proofreading shows much historical diversity: in the use of correctors, authors, or
both, to proofread; in the capacity to produce proofs of an entire work at one time, rather
than in installments, which changed the ability to check for internal inconsistencies; in
the method of proofreading, solitary and silent or joint and aloud; and so on. In general, we may see print as both a stabilizing and a disruptive force in the relationships
of information and error, amplifying both. The same is true of *new media, where
analogous problems of the trustworthiness of information and its capacity to deform
provoke anxiety.

The quantity of information that is mechanically or *digitally reproduced creates new
sources of error in the retrieval of information. There is too much to know. Ann Blair
documented the major techniques of information management in the early modern period (note taking, indexing, compiling, and finding devices). One technique, the index
card or equivalents (*scheda, fiche, Zettel*), has been used since antiquity. As important
as the cards themselves were systems for the storage and retrieval of cards. One of the
most elaborate of these was the large "literary closet" (*scrinium literatum*) devised in
the seventeenth century. Scholars would improvise a number of makeshift solutions over
the centuries (as Ian Jackson documented): cards would be stored in bags placed on
shelves or hung from clotheslines, in baskets suspended by hooks, inside biscuit tins on
shelves, in cubbyholes, or in slip boxes (*Zettelkästen*). With the widespread use of index
cards, the kind of person who made use of the information atomized on them (the *fich-
iste*) became an explicit object of scorn (for example, by Joris-Karl Huysmans, Anatole
France, or Charles Péguy, in the decades around 1900).

In the case of digital information, the crucial difference from print is the availability
of keyword search. This permits the navigation of information on a vastly enlarged scale.
The enormous and unwieldy number of possible results in a keyword search is reduced
to manageable size through page rankings, which has the effect of concentrating knowledge in a few places, whose high rank then tends to be perpetuated. Moreover, page
rankings may be customized to particular users, and even when they are not, a particular phrasing of the keyword may dramatically alter the results; as a consequence, users
may be directed to their preferred version of information in cases where there are competing accounts. Digital information with keyword searching is even more efficient
than print at creating distinct epistemological communities, who employ different error
criteria, trust different authorities, and know different *facts.

Error may be a result not only of the scale of the information but also of its system
of organization. Alphabetical order has had many discontents: in a letter of 1530 Erasmus (Ep. 2260) complained that a pirated version of his unpublished epitome of Valla's
Elegantiae spoiled its usefulness by imposing alphabetical order onto it. Joseph de Maim-
ieux sought to replace the "alphabetical chaos" of dictionaries with his new pasigraphic

order (a proposal from the 1790s that stands in a long history of attempts to construct symbols for a universal language corresponding to ideas rather than sounds). Coleridge (1772–1834) believed that the alphabetical order of *encyclopedias had brought about the "dangerous habit of desultory and unconnected reading." Conceptual orderings are generally contested: the spatialized representation and dichotomized brackets of Ramist texts encountered considerable resistance, speculative dictionaries and encyclopedias were rejected by positivists, and the order of *Roget's Thesaurus* was mocked by Nabokov and others. Critics of historicism may object to chronological arrangement. The absence of order is likewise subject to criticism: Coleridge elsewhere worried over the harm incurred by "the general taste for unconnected writing," which he traced to the *Spectator* (no. 46, 1711); a generation before, James Beattie complained about the new fashion for "uncemented composition," blaming it on Montesquieu; and sometimes even madness was feared to be a possible outcome of reading disorganized information.

Since error is usually traced to multiple sources in any period, many of the changes to how error is understood come about through the reevaluation of the threat posed by existing sources of error, rather than by the discovery of new ones. Christianity, for instance, defined itself in opposition to two kinds of error: the literalism of the Jews and the allegorism of the Greeks. The tension between letter and spirit as sources of error runs through its history, but at different moments the errors due to lawless enthusiasm and those due to the dead weight of the past have been judged differently. Another example is the tension between learning from books and learning from nature or experience, a conflict frequently articulated by historical actors themselves, but which varies in time and among different populations. When one criterion of error is dominant, there is an incentive to forge statements that pass as true by that criterion, a situation that— depending on the quantity, significance, or exposure of the forgeries—may lead to a readjustment of criteria or to the establishment of new ones, which may in their turn invite new kinds of forgeries. The accumulation of knowledge among polyhistors in the seventeenth century routinely incurred the accusation of charlatanry in the early eighteenth century (Mencke's *De charlataneria eruditorum* [1715] was the most famous of these satires); the good manners of the *saloniste in the *Republic of Letters were routinely denounced as hypocrisy by the end of the century. Positivist knowledge (or "mechanical objectivity," as Lorraine Daston and Peter Galison describe it) in the nineteenth century sought to correct errors attributable to the vagaries of the observing subject by removing traces of the self altogether; in turn this criterion for separating knowledge from error was followed, in the early decades of the twentieth century, by one overseen by the trained judgment of experts competent to recognize patterns.

The understanding of error may also change when the authority guaranteeing the validity of information is challenged or alters. One influential argument from the last century (still controversial in its scope) ties the emergence of open-ended inquiry and rhetorics of persuasion in sixth- and fifth-century Greece to the hoplite reform by which members of the warrior class were included in some institutions. Christianity is marked by a central tension as to whether the authority of truth is to be located in the body of believers or a hierarchy within the church, or rather the degree and the domains of these respective authorities to define error. The inclusion of religious minorities in scientific pursuits (Dissenters in nineteenth-century England, Jews in twentieth-century America) changed, and reflected a change in, scientific practices. How error changes as a result of challenges to the trustworthiness of traditional authority is unpredictable; it may either challenge or reinforce the tradition in question. The debate over miracles led not only to Hume's skepticism about whether to credit previously authoritative witnesses of unusual events but also to Bayes's mathematical interpretation of their probability, Babbage's defense of miracles in the *Ninth Bridgewater Treatise* (1837), and Whateley's incisive satire on historical criticism (*Historic Doubts Relative to Napoleon Bonaparte*, 1819).

New sources of error are sometimes discovered. One of the most significant was the protracted realization of the role of randomness in observation and its ability to be quantified. It was a major shift for early modern experimenters to record all the results of their experiments, rather than just the result of the best experiment, as it was contrary to their practice as craftsmen to record good and bad results equally (as Jeb Z. Buchwald and Mordechai Feingold have argued). Including tables of all the discrepant data was a practice slow to develop in the history of the publication of scientific reports (Buchwald and Feingold date it "towards the end of the eighteenth, or the beginning of the nineteenth, century"). The realization that randomness exhibited statistical regularities was even slower: the statistical regularity of nature was controversial even in the nineteenth century, when fundamental laws of thermodynamics took a statistical rather than Newtonian form, and the statistics of human behavior are occasionally controversial even today (it is difficult to assign blame for random errors and thereby prevent or correct them). That error might paradoxically become a source of truth was also an early discovery of *philology: rather than identifying a best text, or combining the best readings from several texts, philological criticism took errors (or rather a special category of error, the *Leitfehler*, or significant variants) to constitute true evidence for the history of the text, permitting the reconstruction of earlier versions that were less error prone than surviving witnesses, at least in theory. Psychoanalysis likewise converted errors (such as verbal slips and other parapraxes) into a previously unsuspected source of truth.

New technologies have changed how error is made visible, as we have seen in the case of the technologies of writing and print, but it is difficult to know whether to attribute to them a larger role as agents of change. The display of information so that error is not removed or corrected but made prominent—for instance, the presence, since the sixteenth century, of a critical apparatus to accompany texts, or the use of the scatterplot in the natural sciences since John Herschel in the nineteenth—did not require technical innovation but a new practice, relatively slow to emerge, of systematically including rather than excluding error. It is sometimes argued that the competition between epistemological communities that have been organized in the wake of massive new disseminations of information, and the consciousness of different error criteria active in different communities, may spur innovation to attempt to bridge them via new techniques of truth finding and error management, but such awareness may instead entrench communities further and increase their remoteness from each other.

This discussion has been limited to inadvertent errors, but mention should also be made of carefully deliberated ones: lies, flattery (regularly depicted in antiquity as a major cause of political and ethical misjudgment), willful mistranslations, typographical errors inserted in order to escape censorship, fictitious entries in reference works to establish priority or *copyright, vandalism (a Wikipedia article about a fake Akkadian demon with striking similarities to Jesus Christ lasted a dozen years, as have three other hoaxes identified so far), and errors in the form of parodies and spoofs designed to escape detection.

Kenneth Haynes

See also censorship; excerpting/commonplacing; information, disinformation, misinformation; knowledge; observing; proofreaders; storage and search

FURTHER READING

Mario Biagioli, "From Book Censorship to Academic Peer Review," *Emergences* 12, no. 1 (2002): 11–45; Jed Z. Buchwald, "Discrepant Measurements and Experimental Knowledge in the Early Modern Era," *Archive for History of Exact Sciences* 60, no. 6 (2006): 565–649; Jed Z. Buchwald and Mordechai Feingold, *Newton and the Origin of Civilization*, 2013; Lorraine Daston and Peter Galison, *Objectivity*, 2007; G. R. Evans, *Getting It Wrong: The Medieval Epistemology of Error*, 1998; Michael Friendly and Daniel Denis, "The Early Origins and Development of the Scatterplot," *Journal of the History of the Behavioral Sciences* 41, no. 2 (2005): 103–30; Ian Jackson, "La repubblica delle cartoline tra Otto e Novecento," *Belfagor: Rassegna di varia umanità* 60, no. 3 (2005): 285–302 and 60, no. 5 (2005): 493–514; Daniel Jütte, *The Age of Secrecy: Jews, Christians, and the Economy of Secrets, 1400–1800*, 2011, translated by Jeremiah Riemer, 2015; John Marincola, ed., *On Writing History: From Herodotus to Herodian*, 2017; E. Jennifer Monaghan, "Reading for the Enslaved, Writing for the Free: Reflections on Liberty and Literacy," *Proceedings of the American Antiquarian Society* 108, no. 2 (1998): 309–41.

ETHNOGRAPHY

It is important to draw a distinction between the wealth and range of the late medieval and *early modern ethnographic discourses recording information about (in contemporary idiom) the various peoples of the world and their rites, customs, and laws, and the particular academic environment that generated *ethnography* as an explicit scientific concern. The early modern European discourse on human diversity, understood as an account of physical traits, racial and national inclinations, religious ceremonies, popular customs, rules of civility, laws, and alternative systems of government, is conspicuous after the sixteenth century. By contrast, even within the *Enlightenment, the neologisms *ethnographia* and *ethnologia* had limited currency and appear almost exclusively in German-speaking lands, together with related *vernacular terms such as *Völkerkunde*, from about the 1770s. What had predominated among humanist-trained scholars of the previous centuries was a focus on human history, either within the framework of natural history or, more specifically, as moral and civil history. Geography, cosmography, and travel writing were essentially conceived as aspects of *historia*; travel accounts in particular, which consisted mainly of descriptive relations organized thematically, could be seen as raw materials to be used for further philosophical interpretation. These various humanistic interests culminated in the *science de l'homme* of Enlightenment writers, including the controversial and often speculative works by Montesquieu, Rousseau, and Voltaire. This was precisely the point at which some Protestant academic historians committed to the ideal of a modern system of learning felt the need to coin the neologisms that clearly distinguished between the descriptive and theoretical aspects of a science of peoples. They also adapted the tradition, already well established among humanists and savants, of providing travelers with questionnaires in order to organize their information methodically, thus furthering new scientific expeditions that usually combined ethnography with natural history.

All this, however, seems to suggest a European story line that awards to a particular cultural tradition the key to the emergence of empirical ethnography—a very misleading assumption. Let us therefore begin by looking elsewhere. The South Indian port cities of the Malabar Coast (modern Kerala), such as Kollam, Cochin, Calicut, and Cannanore, were important locations for cross-cultural commercial intersections in the late medieval and early modern periods. They generated a wide range of descriptions not only of their trade but also of their peoples written by foreign observers in a variety of languages, connecting the Far East to the Far West. In fact, between the late thirteenth and early sixteenth centuries we find significant examples of accounts of Malabar from the three major traditions of medieval and early modern geography and travel writing, Islamic, Chinese, and European. These various descriptions can serve as reminder that literary ethnography—the description of peoples and their religion and customs—was far from exclusive to a single tradition. They also exemplify the very different ways in which the *genres that included these ethnographic materials could be cultivated. For example, in 1342 the Moroccan Ibn Baṭṭūṭa participated in a diplomatic mission to China sent by the sultan of Delhi, but after the presents for the Yuan emperor (for which he was partly responsible) were lost at sea in Calicut, and he also lost track of his personal goods, he was forced to change his plans and spent some months in the region and the Maldive Islands. In his travel account, or *rihla*, the Moroccan noted that the custom of the "infidel" (Hindu) kings of Malabar was to transmit their titles to the sons of their sisters while excluding their own children, a peculiar system of succession via maternal line that he had observed only among a tribe of Berbers in the western Sahara, the veiled Massūfa, or Tuaregs. He also described the trade in pepper—an important local product—and noted the presence of merchants from many countries, including the Chinese with their large junks. Muslims, he observed, were highly respected by the Hindus, but the latter would never share food with them. The traveler also emphasized the safety of the roads and the strict justice implemented by the kings of the region, providing a number of anecdotes to illustrate this. However, these curious observations do not appear in a very systematic fashion. Ibn Battūta's narrative follows the vagaries of his personal itinerary, and he often seems more interested in describing Muslim communities, and even identifying by name learned individuals whom he met, than in dwelling on the customs of other peoples. This is coherent with the underlying logic of the *rihla*, the Arabic genre of travel writing, which was an extended religious pilgrimage within the lands of Islam rather than a geographical survey. For Ibn Baṭṭūṭa, who dictated his travels from memory in 1353 after returning to Morocco, mentioning by name a number of prominent men strengthened his religious authority as a *faqīh* (one learned in the law) as well as the authenticity of his account of events.

By contrast, the observations recorded a few decades later by Ma Huan, a Chinese Muslim at the service of the eunuch admiral Zheng He (a close collaborator of the Ming emperor Yongle), follow a different logic. Ma Huan participated as translator of foreign documents (and probably interpreter) in the extraordinary series of imperial trading expeditions undertaken between 1405 and 1433 and was in Malabar in 1414, 1421, and 1432. He is explicit about the fact that he personally collected the notes about peoples, customs, and natural products that made possible the composition of his *Overall Survey of the Ocean's Shores*. He was not the only observer who wrote about the expeditions of Zheng He—for example, Fei Hsin produced *The Overall Survey of the Star Raft* in 1436 on the basis of similar materials—but Ma Huan's account was geographically more precise and thematically more balanced and may be considered the most developed example of Chinese ethnography in relation to those voyages. In Cochin and Calicut he described the people, their dress, and their houses, and he distinguished various social groups ("five kinds of people"), including Muslims and various Hindu castes, all with different marriage customs and funeral rites. It is clear from his description that he was better acquainted with the communities of traders than with the local military and religious elites, and Ma Huan approved of their way of doing business, which accorded with Chinese ideas of proper conduct. By contrast, he failed to distinguish between Hinduism and Buddhism, encompassing the worship of "the elephant and the ox" under the (to a Chinese) more familiar teachings of Buddha. He seemed particularly fascinated by the yogis and their nakedness. Like Ibn Baṭṭūṭa, he did not fail to note that royal succession was through the sisters of the king as being more certain—"the woman's body alone constitutes the legal family."

Our third example, the extensive description of the towns and peoples of Malabar written by the Portuguese crown official Duarte Barbosa circa 1516 as part of his survey of the lands of East, is exceptional for its accuracy and detail and may be considered a first step toward the possibility of a systematic description of a social system. Barbosa was able to accomplish this because he was—not unlike Ma Huan—a professional interpreter and scrivener at the service of the commercial factor in the town of Cannanore; at the same time, unlike his Chinese predecessor, he settled in India and lived in Kerala many years and had acquired a sophisticated knowledge of the local language, Malayalam, rather than just using Arabic or Persian as a lingua franca. Barbosa's pioneering ethnography was therefore extremely competent when it came to describing different religious, ethnic, and social groups, notably the various castes of "gentiles" and the matrilineal succession of the *nayars*. Nonetheless, there were limits to his understanding of Hindu beliefs, no doubt because he was a layman and—unlike many Catholic missionaries seeking to spread the Christian faith in different parts of Asia under the patronage of the Portuguese kings—he lacked the theological training and authority to engage in religious disputations. Where Ma Huan had confused different forms of infidelity, what we today would call Hinduism and Buddhism, Barbosa saw (like many other European observers) something similar to the Christian Trinity in the supreme God of the Brahmans, the Trimurti—Brahma, Vishnu, and Shiva.

The juxtaposition of different accounts of Malabar helps us to appreciate the variable quality of these early ethnographic writings in terms of "empirical information" and points toward two fundamental variables: the conditions of production of each particular account, and the importance of the genre conventions that developed in each cultural tradition. All the accounts we have considered were ideologically charged, but also informative, in different degrees. The most obvious limitations had to do with linguistic competence, but professional interest and intended audiences also played an important part. Each account illustrates a particular balance between the pursuit of practical information about peoples and their customs by means of the ideal of accurate description, and the ideological value of a discourse on exoticism in which engaging one's own identity—whether for internal critique or for collective gratification, including the legitimation of empire—often counts more than understanding cultural diversity. Ma Huan's preface encapsulated perfectly these two dimensions: he collected notes "about the appearance of the peoples in each country and the variations of the local customs" so that readers would have the facts, but he also aspired to show "how the civilizing influence of the Emperor" had spread beyond that of any previous Chinese dynasty. The interpretation of human diversity, overtly or subtly, is thus an inevitable component of any genre whose aim is to record it, and there is no such thing as an objective account. Nonetheless, we can recognize in these descriptions of Malabar a common desire to be informative and accurate within the parameters of each tradition.

What constitutes "information" is therefore problematic—and this is true not only because any descriptive discourse about human diversity is, inevitably, ideologically charged, but also because fictional elements and hearsay are often found alongside personal observations. Even if we exclude fictional works (including some entirely fraudulent efforts) and restrict ourselves to ethnographic works undertaken with the purpose of recording actual historical conditions, the temptation to amplify the travelers' experience often led to some degree of anachronism and falsification. Ibn Baṭṭūṭa, for example, is very unlikely to have reached China (his chronology of a journey to Quan-zhou, Canton, Hangzhou, and Beijing in 1346–47 is impossible to fit in), but he had good reasons to claim that he had gone there, so that he liberally amplified his pilgrimage narrative by relying on the information about the countries of Southeast Asia and ports in south China that he had collected from other Muslims (some of them Chinese) in India. Some of the information he transmitted in this manner—for example, his descrip-tion of paper money—might have been accurate, but the journey never took place, and his report of the country of "Kawalisi" ruled by a formidable warrior princess who spoke to him in Turkish seems entirely made up. By contrast, even the most honest of travel writers could transmit "false" information when reporting what they learned from local informers and interpreters. When Antonio Pigafetta, author of the first account of Ma-gellan's circumnavigation of the world, in 1521 described the penile implants (*sagra* or *palang*) used by the men in the island of Cebu (modern Philippines), he was being in-formative, however shocking his observations—he had examined them personally, and indeed various other contemporary travelers reported this custom in Southeast Asia. When the same Pigafetta reported that there were islands near the Moluccas whose na-tives ate human flesh, another island inhabited by pygmies, and yet another beyond Java—which he himself never reached—where women lived without men, and got preg-nant from the wind, he was entirely accurate too, transmitting faithfully what he had been told by an old pilot from Tidore (other travelers in the Indian Ocean, including Marco Polo, reported similar stories). It is only from the perspective of the critical ac-cumulation of contradictory reports that some of this information was eventually un-derstood to be "false."

In all cases the emergence of an ethnographic discourse and its impact should not be taken for granted: it was, rather, constitutive of the parallel development of distinct cul-tural and intellectual trajectories throughout many centuries. It is remarkable, for ex-ample, that while European accounts of India would multiply in the centuries following the establishment of colonies by the Portuguese and other Europeans, the Chinese genre was interrupted not long after the death of the Yung-Lo emperor in 1424, when the Ming government completely withdrew its support for the kind of imperial trading expedi-tions that Zheng He had led successfully between 1405 and 1433. In that hostile con-text, despite the existence of a few printed editions from the fifteenth to the seventeenth centuries, the impact of any individual texts such as Ma Huan's was very limited (in-deed, at the turn of the sixteenth century even the copies of the charts produced by Zheng He's expeditions were ordered to be burned by ministerial mandate). The Chi-nese genre of ethnographic writings did of course continue in other, primarily conti-nental, contexts, but the maritime branch no longer flourished, and with it also de-clined the cultural capacity to produce fresh information about very distant lands and to subject it to informed criticism. Compilations relying entirely on previous sources remained a possibility, but their quality as sources of up-to-date historical in-formation could be compromised.

A European equivalent would be those works written in the medieval and early mod-ern periods that continued to refer back to classical sources concerning the marvels of India. When Joannes Boemus, the German canon of Ulm Cathedral, published the first edition of his *Omnium gentium mores, leges et ritus* (The customs, laws and ceremonies of all peoples) (Augsburg, 1520), he primarily worked from authoritative books in Latin that could be centuries old, rather than from the reports about Africa or the New World recently written by explorers such as Amerigo Vespucci. It remains an interesting paradox that Boemus's book proved extremely popular and saw many editions and translations precisely during the same decades that many new accounts about the various parts of the world (including the book of Duarte Barbosa) began to reach Europe. Nonetheless, the Spanish translator of Boemus, Francisco Thámara, saw fit to add new materials extracted from historians of the Spanish Indies, such as Gonzalo Fernández de Oviedo, the self-appointed Pliny of the New World. It was a symptom of the changing perspective. Unlike in China, in western Europe throughout the sixteenth century the vast multiplication and frequent publication of new ethnographic writings created the conditions for an entirely new approach to the analysis of information. Increasingly, sources could be historically and geographically contextualized, a process made possible by the emergence of great compilations of "modern" (as opposed to ancient) travel writing. The highest standards of textual selection and historical criticism were set by the Venetian civil servant and humanist Giovanni Battista Ramusio in the three large volumes of his *Navigationi et Viaggi* (Navigations and voyages) published in the 1550s, and a model for many subsequent efforts. It was Ramusio who made books such as Duarte Barbosa's widely available, while also reclaiming the authenticity of Marco Polo, who in this manner became a pioneer of modern geography, rather than a potential fabulist.

While there may be something universal in the human curiosity about the customs and beliefs of different peoples, we may conclude that the extent to which ethnographic genres were driven by a desire for practical information is a historically specific issue. The early modern European trajectory in this respect was conditioned by an exceptional convergence of new developments. The first crucial condition was of course the development of oceanic navigation and new military technologies, such as artillery and firearms, which facilitated the creation of European commercial colonies and even substantial territorial conquests in many parts of the world. Opportunities for observation, and the impetus for collecting practical information, multiplied, and a global network of communication, through travel or in writing, expanded massively and eventually stabilized.

Second, there was a revival of historical and geographical learning led by the humanists, a revival that took place in a Christian society but embraced many secular themes, and empowered a wide range of social agents. Some of this historical learning, in Latin or Greek, was focused on the classical past and remained extremely elitist, but there was also a degree of popularization through translations, compilations, and various educational genres, even plays and romances. One of the consequences was that traders and other commoners, who were often literate, became crucial participants in the development of the new ethnographic genres, not only as observers (who could report orally) but also, increasingly, as writers. Men like Columbus, Vespucci, and Pigafetta, or the New World chroniclers Gonzalo Fernández de Oviedo and Pedro de Cieza de León, are remarkable examples of lay ethnographers who did not participate directly in the revival of classical learning as intellectuals, but could read historical works and echoed some of their themes. Columbus, for example, in order to interpret his geographical discoveries, read and annotated the fifteenth-century cosmography of Pius II, the humanist pope, who in turn had relied on the recently recovered ancient geography of Strabo, as well as the latest account of India by the Venetian merchant Niccolò de' Conti (ca. 1444).

The third important condition was the consolidation of printing and the expansion of the book market. Manuscripts remained of course essential, and many works were never printed or published, but the availability of books multiplied the dissemination of historical information, not least works with ethnographic contents, which attracted wide audiences. Amerigo Vespucci's letters, rehashed by an opportunistic publisher in the Latin pamphlet *Mundus Novus* (A new world) (1503), became so popular that the new continent discovered by Columbus across the ocean was eventually named after him. No doubt Vespucci's description of the naked cannibals of Brazil who lived "according to nature" like Epicureans, without laws, private property, or any sense of shame, contributed to this popularity. Some institutions, notably the Portuguese crown, were keen to keep some sensitive geographical information away from rivals. However, when in 1524 King John III negotiated with Emperor Charles V the division of spheres of colonial influence in the Moluccas (in the Junta of Badajoz), the book of Duarte Barbosa was made available in manuscript by the Portuguese cosmographer Diogo Ribeiro. It was translated into Castilian by the Genoese ambassador Martino Centurione, and the political negotiations eventually culminated in the treaty of Saragossa of 1529, which by means of a sale of rights awarded the islands to the Portuguese crown. A few years later, Ramusio translated this text into Italian (comparing it to another Portuguese manuscript) and published it, making this major account of the lands and peoples of Asia widely available to the European *Republic of Letters.

Finally, the fourth condition was the mobilization of substantial ecclesiastical resources in support of extremely ambitious evangelizing projects, especially by the religious orders of the Catholic Church, who worked in tandem with the monarchies of Portugal and Castile.

Missionaries would become some of the better-trained and systematic ethnographers of the period, including many missions in areas not under direct European imperial control, such as Persia, northern India, Japan, China, Siam, Vietnam, Tibet, Ethiopia, and Angola. Because their motivation was religious zeal and their theological training often thorough, missionaries were particularly keen to learn foreign languages and engage in religious disputations. In some cases they wrote thematically comprehensive *encyclopedias describing all the aspects of the life of native populations under their charge. The case of the Franciscans in New Spain (modern Mexico) is particularly striking, because it reveals the mechanisms through which concern for effective religious conversion led to a deepening ethnographic ambition. For authors like Friar Bernardino de Sahagún, the initial idea of destroying a devilish, false religion by simply burning all the native books of divination, and preaching instead a new and pure Christian religion, had proved to be a dangerous illusion, because the old idolatrous beliefs were subtly inscribed in everyday cultural practices, such as harvesting, eating, and dancing. The inquisitorial methods used to detect heresy and idolatry were therefore mobilized to interrogate native elders, who acted as informants of the missionaries (in a brutal colonial setting, the implicit coercion was of course overpowering). Sahagún and his native aides—educated as Christians in a special school for the sons of the elite—recorded their information in the original language, Nahuatl, and organized it thematically to cover all aspects of the religious, moral, and natural life of the Mexican Indians. The final product, the famous Florentine Codex, with a Spanish translation and many color illustrations, was remarkably rich and comprehensive and has guided the various efforts of modern historians in the twentieth and twenty-first centuries to reconstruct the culture, beliefs, and daily life of the Mexica (the "Aztecs"). However, the *Universal History of the Things of New Spain*, completed in the 1570s, was not meant to offer neutral information, neither in its interpretative biases (as the Franciscans imposed a Christian concept of religious exclusivism that was alien to the Nahuas), nor in its intended uses. Paradoxically, the Spanish authorities were themselves uneasy about the value of the initiative—a work conceived as a tool to identify and persecute idolatry was, for some critics, a dangerous means of perpetuating it. Its circulation was therefore severely restricted. Nonetheless, the ethnographic research conducted by the Franciscans had already been crucial for those historians who successfully wrote about the conquest of Mexico for a wider European public, such as the chaplain of Ferdinand Cortés, Francisco López de Gómara.

Despite a substantial gap between the many ethnographic materials, written and visual, that existed only as relatively rare manuscripts (quite a few lost to us) and those that circulated more widely in multiple copies or in print, often heavily edited and in some cases censored (notably in Catholic countries where the Inquisition was active), it seems fair to generalize that a considerable proportion of the ethnographic information produced in the early modern centuries found its way to the early modern reading public, and that few parts of the globe reached by Europeans remained unknown to the Republic of Letters—especially to those *polymaths and men of letters capable of reading many languages. By the middle of the eighteenth century, the interior of Africa and the Pacific islands remained as mysterious frontiers, but vast libraries could be assembled with books about the Ottoman Empire, India, Brazil, Peru, or China, and the contours of "the great map of mankind," as Edmund Burke referred to it in 1777, were fairly well understood. Combining the global structures of commerce developed by rival colonial powers, the humanist revival of historical genres, the wide participation of lay and religious travelers as observers and writers, the quick consolidation of relatively cheap means of dissemination by means of printing, and the existence of an extensive and indeed growing reading public and book market, it may be concluded that after the sixteenth century the European capacity to both produce and consume informative ethnography was truly remarkable. In reality some of these trends were already apparent in the late Middle Ages—the possibility of missionaries, merchants, or ambassadors describing in detail exotic peoples and their religion and customs was apparent starting in the thirteenth century, with the precarious Franciscan embassies to the Mongols, and the Portuguese exploration of West Africa in the early 1400s. However, the combination of factors that led to the explosion of the genre throughout the sixteenth century was revolutionary in its synergy and impact. It had a transformative effect on European intellectual culture.

In this essay we have defined ethnography (which is of course, strictly speaking, a modern concept) primarily as a widespread descriptive, information-rich literary practice that could appear in a variety of related genres, from a simple descriptive account of the beliefs and cultural practices of different peoples included in a letter, relation, or travelogue, to the more comprehensive works of natural and moral history, geography, and cosmography composed for an educated public. The intellectual culture of the humanists gave these works an additional antiquarian dimension and comparative power, but the essence of the genre centered on the testimony of an eyewitness, typically a rather humble figure who largely relied on everyday language in order to report what he saw or heard. The step, however, from providing information to suggesting interpretations was always very small. For the Dominican Bartolomé de Las Casas, for example, the "defender of the Indians" in the Spanish Indies, the evidence collected by Franciscans about the native inhabitants of New Spain could be used to prove that they were no less rational and civilized than the ancient Greeks and Romans (an important issue when it came to determining their rights). For Inca Garcilaso de la Vega, a mestizo historian of Peru seeking to claim his double heritage, the solar cult of the Inka suggested a mono-theistic belief that prepared the ground for the arrival of Christianity. The Protestant pastor Jean de Léry in Brazil, adopting the moralistic tone of a strict reformer, noted that the naked Tupinambá were less corrupt in their natural state than the Europeans with their clothes. For Thomas Harriot, writing in 1587 at the service of Walter Raleigh in support of the early English colonial project in Virginia, the description of the coastal Algonquians of Roanoke Island (in what is today North Carolina) proved their capacity for Christianity and civilization, but also their weakness against the Europe-ans and their firearms: the English should not be deterred by their presence. All these were polemical arguments that went beyond a neutral exposition of ethnographic information.

The more philosophically inclined writers did not simply engage in arguments that were politically charged, but also reflected on the nature of civilization. For a *Jesuit in Japan, Luís Fróis, the contrast between European and Japanese customs that he sys-tematically listed in 1585 revealed that it was possible for rational peoples to do many things very differently without necessarily endangering the salvation of the soul (pro-vided the universal principles of divine and natural law were respected). Similarly, a reader of Jean de Léry in France in the same period, Michel de Montaigne, considered that the cannibals of Brazil had a lesson to teach to his contemporaries in Europe: eat-ing human flesh for the sake of revenge was indeed a barbarian action, but Europeans were no better in the manner in which they treated each other, and could hardly equate their own behavior with the dictates of right reason. In fact, all judgments about truth and morality were influenced by one's own local customs, and the claim of the civi-lized to universal rationality was a form of vanity. For that reason, Montaigne preferred the observations about distant lands from a simple man who faithfully reported what he saw to the interpretations of someone more educated, and therefore more preten-tious, who ended up distorting the truth in order to prove his own ideas. Ethnographic information and elite erudition were not always the best of friends.

Joan-Pau Rubiés

See also globalization; merchants; money; observing; publicity/publication; scrolls and rolls; surveys and censuses; translating; travel

FURTHER READING

Anthony Grafton, *New Worlds, Ancient Texts: The Power of Tradition and the Shock of Discovery*, 1992; Margaret Hogden, *Early Anthropology in the Sixteenth and Seventeenth Centuries*, 1964; Donald F. Lach, *Asia in the Making of Europe*, 3 vols., 1965–93; P. J. Marshall and Glyn Williams, *The Great Map of Mankind: Perceptions of New Worlds in the Age of Enlightenment*, 1982; Jürgen Osterham-mel, *Unfabling the East: The Enlightenment Encounter with Asia*, 1998, translated by Robert Savage, 2018; Joan-Pau Rubiés, *Travel and Ethnology in the Renaissance: South India through European Eyes, 1250–1625*, 2000; Justin Stagl, *A History of Curiosity: The Theory of Travel, 1550–1800*, 1995; Han F. Vermeulen *Before Boas: The Genesis of Ethnography and Ethnology in the German Enlightenment*, 2015.

EXCERPTING/COMMONPLACING

The history of excerpting is like that of the book. It is only in the context of *new media that the old book appears as a distinct medium, the particular forms and functions of which can be rediscovered. Only since we have begun to work digitally and do everything by *copy and paste* have we become aware of excerpting. Old methods, deployed in the *analog period to gather readings, pieces of information, and dates, have become the object of new historical interests. What was dismissed for a long time as the concern of learned men has recently been rediscovered as a praxis spanning eras and cultures, as historians came under the influence of and gained experience with *digital media and practices. As a result, a premodern perspective, which Zedler's *Universal-Lexicon* defined over 250 years ago, has now been reaffirmed: excerpting is the collecting of "the thoughts of others," which are necessary for "our own meditation." One who relies only on his "own meditation" cannot become "knowledgeable." The sciences are based on "experience"; no person can "have all of the pertinent experience in front of him." One must build on "the experience of others"; therefore, one must excerpt and compile collections of excerpts. The cultural historian Ulrich Johannes Schneider described the impact of such ideas on the production of literature with lapidary precision: "no writing without reading."

CONCEPT AND TRADITION

Historians who attend to the history of excerpting like to cite a passage from the letters of Pliny the Younger (*Epistles* III, 5, 10) on the reading practice of his uncle, the author of what premodern Europe considered the definitive and trendsetting natural history. In summer, seeking recreation after eating, he lay in the sun and had a book read aloud to him, writing down everything that seemed important to him. Above all, the nephew reports, his uncle's reading was always combined with excerpting, in accordance with the maxim: no book is so bad that it cannot be useful in part. *Early modern texts often cited this ancient model. In those days, excerpting was considered an art (*ars*); treatises were written about it. The great response that the *ars excerpendi* (art of excerpting) awoke in the European world of Latin learning can be explained by the humanists' interest in the *canon of ancient texts. Excerpting was closely related at the time to learning and practicing Latin on the basis of ancient authors.

They marked and underlined "passages" (*loci*) in exemplary texts; they glossed them (between the lines or line by line in the margins of the text); they commented and translated; they memorized and transcribed. These methods were by no means invented by humanist scholars. They were practiced, through the application of various kinds of technologies, in all times and in all cultures founded on writing. If we concentrate on the meaning and role that the appropriation and dissection of the ancient (Latin) textual corpus played for the formation of the religious, cultural, and intellectual spheres in Europe, the time span between late antiquity and the eighteenth century can be seen as one long tradition of excerpting. The Bible and ancient texts provided an orienting model and set standards for what could claim legitimacy as religion and as scholarly knowledge. That is why the intensive appropriation of these texts mattered so much, and the first step in that appropriation was excerpting. This was also true of other cultures (such as the Arabic or Chinese) in which similar prestige was accorded to authoritative texts of the past.

With the rise of the humanist movement, excerpting in Europe became an object of school instruction and of intensive reflection on the norms, methods, practices, and media that played a role in the practice. The humanists saw it as their task to reconstruct antiquity, which they regarded as a practical, moral, and philosophical model, from the surviving textual witnesses. In order to distinguish their work from logic-centered medieval Aristotelian *scholasticism, they developed new methods for their engagement with texts, drawing on the ancient rhetorical and dialectical topics. In his enormously successful work *De duplici copia verborum ac rerum* (On the twofold abundance of words and things, first published in 1512), Erasmus of Rotterdam says that one could be called "learned" (*eruditus*) only if he, at least once in his life, mastered "every kind of author" (*omne genus autorum*) through reading. To undertake this task, one must "equip himself beforehand with as many *loci* as possible" (*prius sibi quam plurimos comparabit locos*).

Printing introduced to humanists new opportunities for the interpretation of the ancient tradition. It set generally identical and standardized texts at one's disposal. If the loci in the tradition of the ancient art of memory were places, each one an individually conceived space of memory, now they could be understood more easily and without further ado as identifiable "passages" in certain writings. In antiquity, loci designated, on the one hand, formal instruments for the discovery and order of arguments; on the other hand, they were fixed turns of phrase (*loci communes*) that should be committed to memory. With printing, they increasingly developed into instruments with whose help texts were searched. Likewise, loci served as important categories for the ordering of identified learned materials, which were stored less in memory than in "secondary" memory media. Excerpting as a humanist practice has two essential components: selecting from learned material with the help of loci and compiling it systematically by loci. Erasmus (in *De duplici copia verborum ac rerum*) and other humanists had printed exemplary models of this method with great success, though scholars also laid them out for private use in the form of bound manuscript volumes.

Today, *excerpting* and *commonplacing* are widely used as synonyms. *Excerpting* and its equivalents in other European languages go back to the Latin *excerpere*, which designates selecting in its many connotations (to select, to make or remove excerpts, to delete), while *commonplacing* refers to the *locus communis* or "common place." This term more strongly accentuates the chosen products and their compilation, which can be explained etymologically: in the early modern period the term *loci communes* not only could signify selected topics, exempla, and sayings, but also was transferred to the *commonplace book itself, the storage medium for loci communes.

In principle, one could understand any element obtained from an arbitrary pattern as excerpts—be they passages out of writings, notes of different kinds and origins, or indeed notes that record experiences and observations—and the activity that produced them as excerpting. On the understanding of early modern scholars, excerpting designated the extraction of certain passages from texts in particular, though a good many also included the collecting and recording of what they had heard and their own thoughts as excerpting. For instance, Daniel Georg Morhof, professor of rhetoric at the University of Kiel, wrote in his *Polyhistor* (The polymath) (first published in 1688) that we should collect "what occurs to us when reading an author or in everyday reflection, also what we have observed or has been told to us by others."

THE RULES OF THE ART OF EXCERPTING

Excerpting is selecting. The question of selection became more urgent in the conditions created by printing. Scholars developed methods and instruments to orient themselves in the face of the increasing amount of available information. For example, the Zurich scholar Conrad Gessner compiled a *Bibliotheca universalis* (Universal library) (1545, followed by the *Pandectae*, 1548), which was meant to put its reader in a position to select information according to his needs and interests. Institutions of church and state took measures to assert their control over knowledge and prescribe selection through censorship. Selection is also an important theme in the *De arte excerpendi* *genre. Readers themselves must select from the wealth of texts and information, but one who wants to select autonomously must pass judgment. Thus, attention to the power of judgment (*iudicium*) comes into play. Excerpting is not simply collecting, so the rule goes, and it is often clarified with a remark from the Dutch scholar Justus Lipsius about his own excerpting: "I don't collect, I select" (*non colligo, sed seligo*). One may not make himself dependent on others—thus reads the principle in the *Aurifodina Artium et scientiarum omnium: Excerpendi Sollertia* (The mine of all arts and science: The skill of excerpting), which the Bavarian *Jesuit Jeremias Drexel first had printed in 1638. The ability to judge, according to Drexel, grows with excerpting, for that teaches slow, thoughtful, attentive reading for comparison and judgment. Excerpting is necessary because it compels a conceptual involvement with texts and an independent appropriation of them. There are indeed many useful printed collections of excerpts, collections of loci communes, and *encyclopedias. However, notes selected by oneself were worth a lot more.

Jesuit scholars like Drexel first drew up instructions for excerpting. They saw this as a matter of providing religious and moral protection for readers left to rely on themselves. Jesuit excerpting manuals were designed to create self-sufficient patterns of thought. This notion gained more precise contours in treatises published in the second half of the seventeenth century, which included some published by Protestant scholars. As early as Drexel, the question of the filing of excerpts (loci communes) did not center on their classification; rather, effective organization stood front and center. For Morhof, it is crucial to have excerpts quickly available, for even in the sciences, there was combat, which required a quick reaction time. The order in which one brought his weapons into position was not so important; when it came to a contest, it was vital to have them in place. The effectiveness of using an excerpt collection is a crucial point; quick searchability of excerpts is more important than the topical system. The English philosopher John Locke concentrated entirely on the question of how collections of excerpts could be easily and effectively accessed with the help of an alphabetical index in his *Méthode nouvelle de dresser des Recueils* (New method of forming commonplace books, first published in 1686). Mere copying made way for an independent treatment in summary form. Excerpts should be short (*excerpe breviter*), recommends the *Sciagraphia de studio excerpendi* (Insight into the zeal for excerpting) from 1699. It ought to consume neither too much paper nor too much time; everything is to be captured in a nutshell (*in nuce*). The emphasis on practicability in excerpt maintenance is bound up with the use of notebooks in which excerpts were listed consecutively without organization (*adversaria*). Conversely, the bound manuscript volumes (*codices*), in which excerpts were organized by ready-made patterns of organization, became less important.

Since the eighteenth century, excerpting has been subject to less and less regulation. No more new treatises dedicated to the subject appeared. Moreover, excerpting ceased to form a discrete subject of academic instruction. Instruction in excerpting now became part of basic training in scholarly reading and writing. For instance, in *How to Write a Thesis* (first published in Italian in 1977), Umberto Eco suggested different types of index cards with whose help scholarly readings could be "cut up into notes." Digitization created a new need for instruction, as the video *Excerpting* on YouTube documents, as well as a revived need for academic instruction in excerpting. In 2011 an expert on pedagogy, John Orlando, demanded: "bring commonplacing back to education."

EXCERPTING PRACTICES AND MEDIA

Scholars and scientists have left evidence of different kinds, much of which historical research has only recently begun to discover, that shows how excerpting really proceeded and how collections of excerpts were actually arranged. As early as the sixteenth century, scholars like Conrad Gessner or the Italian natural historian Ulisse Aldrovandi worked with scissors in hand, cutting up their transcriptions (and pages from printed books). Like many other early modern scholars, Aldrovandi had assistance in excerpting from scribes (*amanuenses*) and also from his wife. He created an enormous form of storage, which he called *Pandechion epistemonicon* (A receptacle for all knowledge) for the preservation of his excerpts. It consisted of folio manuscript volumes—eighty-three of them in total by 1589—into which handwritten slips were pasted in alphabetical order. Therein, Aldrovandi explained, one could find the "whole forest of the disciplines" (*selva universale delle scienze*)—everything that poets, theologians, jurists, philosophers, and historians of nature or art had written and anything about which one might want to write; also everything that he had learned from countless documents (*molti documenti*) sent by scholars in many places.

The *Magdeburg Centuries* (1559–74), and the formation of a Protestant church history as a collection of historical arguments organized by loci, fitted out for the struggle against the papacy and Protestant rivals, took shape as a collaborative project for excerpting on an even larger scale. The network of royal patrons and scholars that launched them was international, stretching from Venice to London, from Prague to Paris, from Vienna to Königsberg. Source material was acquired from everywhere in Europe. The team of excerptors evaluated it according to strictly regulated, methodical standards (stated in a *methodus*) and assigned extracts to fixed keywords (loci). The vision of an excerpting project that engaged the whole scholarly world (*respublica literaria* or *Republic of Letters) underlies the *Theatrum humanae vitae* (Theater of human life, first published in 1565) by the Swiss professor of medicine Theodor Zwinger. He understood his work as a model of information storage (*historiarum promptuarium*) in which scholars stored excerpts of every kind and provenance, some of which were drawn from texts, others from recorded experiences, and retrieved them again when necessary. Projects for excerpting could even be organized together across generations to serve the advancement of the sciences. This was the driving vision behind the ideas and projects that motivated the excerpting by the naturalist *virtuosi* (or *polymathic gentlemen) in the circle of the seventeenth-century Royal Society.

Even in the seventeenth century, excerpts were still ordinarily preserved in bound manuscripts, recorded one after another or topically ordered (by loci); both storage media were most commonly accessed through an index. Excerpting guides discouraged the use of unbound, loose collections of slips. Excerpt books are temporary, intermediate forms of storage, as it were; they relieve the memory, which must nevertheless make sure that the assembled excerpts always come back together as a whole. Thus, the collection of excerpts needed ordering structures that could support the work of the memory and, accordingly, excerpt books were firmly bound. In practice, ever fewer people followed these rules. The mid-seventeenth-century Hamburg naturalist Joachim Jungius noted excerpts from texts, quotations, literary references, definitions, and also his own observations and thoughts on individual octavo sheets (*schedae*). They were furnished with keywords (*tituli*) that indicated their respective subjects. Sheets with identical headings were put into a quarto sheet folded in half with the relevant title noted on its outer side. Jungius called the resulting connected slips "bundles" (*manipulus*); when a number of such bundles came together in an envelope, he called them "stacks" (*fasces*). Only these bundles and stacks with their countless individual titles structured the excerpt collection; there was no preorganized (topical) system, no structured book space, and no internal order for the sheets in the bundles and stacks. In the end, the collection comprised 150,000 single sheets.

This merely cumulative collecting of individual excerpt slips without a systematic order and without presupposition followed a scholarly plan. Jungius understood excerpting as the foundation of an empirically established system of knowledge, like that of Francis Bacon, whom he admired. His excerpt collections, like those of the naturalist *virtuosi* of the Royal Society and the earlier excerpting of scholars like Aldrovandi, documented the formation of the modern culture of "pure *facts." Its ideal is the production of short, isolated textual components without cohesion, of "factoids" and "small facts," which can be combined arbitrarily and can be deployed as evidence for various theories and explanatory models.

The flexibility of excerpt storage systems has been a vital aspect of excerpting since the middle of the seventeenth century. The English teacher Thomas Harrison developed an elaborate cabinet system for the storage of individual excerpt slips in the 1640s. However, this laborious method, which in many respects followed the old, topical system, did not catch on. Instead, the simple slip box with movable topical tabs was used more extensively starting in the eighteenth century and proved a flexible, easily expandable method of managing excerpts. The German sociologist Niklas Luhmann described it in 1981 as a "communicative machine" that made it possible for texts to develop automatically, so to speak. Two German scholars, Johann Jakob Moser and Christoph Meiners, had recommended the slip box already in the eighteenth century with similar arguments. Over the course of the nineteenth and twentieth centuries, it evolved into the predominant instrument for the management of excerpts, notes, information, and dates, for it was deployed by scholars of the *humanities and natural scientists, librarians, and journalists as well as authors, artists, private citizens, and office workers. Standardized index cards increasingly served as record supports instead of sheets of paper. The librarian Melvil Dewey's company, Library Bureau, successfully sold standardized index cards and slip boxes to banks, insurance companies, and other businesses. In 1896, Library Bureau entered into a partnership with Herman Hollerith's Tabulating Machine Company, out of which the company IBM developed. Later, index cards became punch cards, which were adapted for mechanical data processing. Still, not everyone in the nineteenth and twentieth centuries used slip boxes for excerpting. The philosopher Friedrich Nietzsche used excerpt notebooks and other filing systems. So did Karl Marx, whose extensive excerpting output is recorded in thirty-one thick volumes of his collected works (*Marx Engels Gesamtausgabe* or *MEGA*). Especially in the case of literati, artists, and humanistic scholars, filing systems for excerpts and notes were and are different "machines of the imagination," which have to conform to the individual needs of their users and to hold not only excerpted snippets of text, experiences, and thoughts but also materials from other media suited to cutting, such as newspapers and photographs.

The art historian Aby Warburg stuck the photographs he collected for his *Bilderatlas* (Atlas of images) to a black cloth with pins, around which he wrapped woolen thread so that the relationships between the visual motifs became visible. He noted, "I have begun to cut out the whole pantheon." The sociologist of film Siegfried Kracauer wrote notes for books, talks, and observations on flimsy loose slips that he always carried with him in shirt, pants, and jacket pockets. He provided citations with quotation marks and page numbers for the excerpts for his book *Jacques Offenbach and the Paris of His Time* (1937), yet such references are missing from the printed text. The loss of references has befallen many other excerpting artists (for example, Nietzsche). The French author Jules Verne (1828–1905) inscribed twenty-five thousand keyword cards over the course of his life. These chiefly recorded the experiences of his travels and enabled him to publish at least two books per year. The Romanian author Tristan Tzara read aloud from snippets cut out of newspapers, arbitrarily pulled out of his pocket, in Zurich's *Cabaret Voltaire*. He became one of the cofounders of Dadaism with his "slip poems" (*Zettelgedichten*). The British painter Francis Bacon (1909–92) arranged his studio as an accessible slip box. This consisted not of subjects but of zones, layers, and lumps on the floor, which were assembled from various materials like torn-out pages, photographs, X-rays, records, his own paintings, and articles of clothing.

Writers and scholars used the art of excerpting to produce printed books, as well as articles in printed periodicals. This method did not change until the rise of digital methods for excepting. But excerpts arranged in slip boxes also provided the material basis for the numerous large-scale handbook, lexicon, and dictionary projects of this period. One example is the *Thesaurus Linguae Latinae* (Treasury of the Latin language), the most comprehensive dictionary of ancient Latin. Excerpting for it began in Goettingen and Munich in 1894, the first printed fascicle appeared in 1900, and the project is still far from complete. It is now a collaborative international undertaking, but it is still based on a slip archive: currently around ten million slips with excerpts, which are constantly supplemented and revised. The archive thus always contains more and more precise information than the printed volumes.

In contrast to the printed book, the advantages of an expandable and revisable informational system broken down into parts were already clear to an information broker of the highest order, Samuel Hartlib, in his multiple excerpting and publication projects. His Baconian activities helped inspire the Royal Society founded in 1662, the year of his death. Should one dissect all books into small components and compile a general index for them all, it would no longer be necessary to read the books of individual authors. In 1910, the Belgian lawyers and bibliographers Paul Otlet and Henri La Fontaine envisaged a "city of knowledge," built up on an extended Dewey's classification system to house all the world's information and thus liberate bibliographic information from its carrier, the book. From 1919 to 1934, they received funding from the Belgian government and created in Brussels the "Palais Mondial" (from 1924: "Mundaneum"). In its final year, 1934, the Mundaneum had collected more than fifteen million index cards. The cultural critic Walter Benjamin—himself a great practitioner of the art of excerpting on slips—explained in *Einbahnstraße* (One-way street, published in 1928) that the book had become an anachronistic medium: "Today, as the current scholarly mode of production teaches, the book is already an obsolete mediator between two different card file systems. Because all of the essentials are found in the slip box of the researcher who has authored it, and the scholar, who carries on his study in it, assimilates it into his own card file system." In the very same year, the German engineer and mathematician Walter Porstmann advocated the "dispersal of printed works and books into filing sheets" in his *Handbook of Filing Techniques*.

With the advent of digitization, paper excerpt collections and wooden chests for information management have disappeared from offices and libraries. Their disposal can be seen as a media destruction of historic proportions. In a 1994 issue of the *New Yorker*, the author Nicholson Baker already composed a somber firsthand report on the obliteration of public library card catalogs, as well as their contents, under the title "Discards." Has the vision—which leads back deep into early modernity—of a collectively organized and universally accessible pool of information come true now that information circulates on the *internet, now that texts and data are digitized and retrieved, and we all cut and paste online? Office administration today is defined by software companies; there is a bewildering plethora of software tools that allow intellectuals, journalists, and scholars to digitally excerpt, take notes, divide them into pieces, and put them in order. Perhaps automated excerpting processes open up unforeseen opportunities for the acquisition, storage, and analysis of information. Yet, for individuals, this may mean the loss of creative self-determination, for they no longer exercise their own power of judgment in excerpting and simply follow automated patterns.

Helmut Zedelmaier
Translated by Ashley Gonik

See also art of memory; cards; censorship; data; digitization; indexing; learning; notebooks; reference books; scribes; secretaries; teaching

FURTHER READING

Ann Blair, *Too Much to Know: Managing Scholarly Information before the Modern Age*, 2010; Alberto Cevolini, ed., *Forgetting Machines: Knowledge Management Evolution in Early Modern Europe*, 2016; Elisabeth Décultot, ed., *Lire, copier, écrire: Les bibliothèques manuscrites et leurs usages au XVIIIᵉ siècle*, 2003; Heike Gfrereis and Ellen Strittmatter, eds., *Zettelkästen: Maschinen der Phantasie*, 2013 (especially the articles by Gfrereis and Strittmatter, Hektor Haarkötter, and Mirjam Wenzel); Markus Krajewski, *Paper Machines: About Cards and Catalogs, 1548–1929*, 2002, translated by Peter Krapp, 2011; Fabian Krämer, *Ein Zentaur in London: Lektüre und Beobachtung in der frühneuzeitlichen Naturforschung*, 2014 (A centaur in London: Observation and reading in the early modern study of nature; English translation expected 2021); Richard Yeo, *Notebooks: English Virtuosi, and Early Modern Science*, 2014; Helmut Zedelmaier, *Werkstätten des Wissens zwischen Renaissance und Aufklärung*, 2015.

FILES

Max Weber famously, and perhaps with a small dose of provocation, noted the importance of files in his examination of bureaucracy: "The management of the modern office is based upon written documents ('the files'), which are preserved in their original or draft form. . . . The body of officials actively engaged in a 'public' office, along with the respective apparatus of material implements and the files, make up a 'bureau.'" Almost a hundred years later, inverting the ratio of fame and provocation associated with Weber, the computer scientist turned media philosopher Jaron Lanier wrote, "our conception of files may be more persistent than our ideas about nature. I can imagine that someday physicists might tell us that it is time to stop believing in photons, because they have discovered a better way to think about light—but the file will likely live on. The file is a set of philosophical ideas made into eternal flesh." Both Weber and Lanier speak to a relationship between files and order. Neither is interested in the content of files, but instead both approach files as a technology that organizes the production of information.

Weber's comments have been invoked to argue that bureaucratic authority is constituted through files. From this perspective, more than simply enabling the collection and circulation of information, files create authority through their format and the network their circulation forms (Vismann's historical critique of German legal culture and Latour's analysis of the Conseil d'Etat provide examples of this).

Files, in the act of gathering paper, define a space of interaction among people and provide a limit on what it is possible to know. They do this because the authority granted to files in the name of institutional objectivity claims recognition from people. Created through regulations and procedures, files appear to not have an author. As Ilana Feldman illustrates in *Governing in Gaza*, procedures create a paper world of self-referentiality. These procedures are enacted through repetition in what a file is and what files do. Along with content, circulation is guided by procedures and regulations. This produces guidelines for adding or removing documents from a file, for the movement of files in and out of departments, and for how members of the public can access a file.

Although files exist in the service of hierarchical structures of authority and control, as files circulate this authority can be manipulated. Matthew Hull argues that the diffusion of responsibility that gives files authority can be used to deflect individual responsibility as much as it disciplines and shapes workers. Officials can use the authority of files to avoid responsibility or influence cases.

Whether manipulated or not, the various sources and opinions in a file become the grounds for making a decision. The fantasy of a file as a complete record becomes a pragmatic working assumption that all an official needs to know is gathered in the file. Depending on the institutional purpose of files, a file can gather papers such as correspondence, drafts, legislation, legal cases, minutes, memos, petitions, plans, and commentary on the file collected as it circulates. These papers are transformed when they become part of a file. The event or issue that initiates a file reconfigures the papers' purpose and focus.

The specific bureaucratic form and function of files constitute a relatively recent iteration in the history of files. As an object that demarcates space for papers and as an entity that can be acted on, "files" have gathered paper in many different ways and been stored in a variety of places. Early files were usually papers bound by string or folded using specific techniques. Individuals and institutions stored these files in bags, chests, cabinets, or drawers, or on shelves or hooks. The name in English comes from techniques to collect paper introduced throughout Europe at the turn of the fifteenth century. Papers strung on wire or string became known as *files*, from the Latin word *filum*, meaning string or thread, via the French *filer,* to spin and thread. Papers were gathered on a string or wire threaded through a hole punched in the edge of the papers and then usually hung from a peg. In some examples, papers were hung upside down and back to front with the oldest items at the rear. This organization allowed a person to easily access a paper by flipping the papers up from the bottom. It also suggests an interest in privacy. A visitor to an office would not have been able to see the content of the papers. Storing papers in this manner protected them from not only prying eyes, but also the gnawing teeth of rodents; these twin concerns have continued through the history of paper files.

In the late nineteenth century, files underwent a vertical revolution (or at least a vertical reorientation). Under the weight of bureaucratic and corporate reliance on paperwork, loose papers were compiled in binders stored vertically like books on shelves, or in manila folders stored on their long edge in drawers in vertical file cabinets. Alphabetical guides and tabs ordered binders and drawers in advance of the actual storage of paper. The increased attention to planning and order heightened the understanding of files as a form of external memory, particularly as the scale of institutional and business activity generated details beyond an individual's capacity to know and remember. With no need for a separate index, in a nod to the importance of the "machine" to the understanding of the modern office, vertical files were marketed as "self-indexing" or providing "automatic filing." This erased or devalued the work of the female clerical worker who from the turn of the twentieth century had begun working in offices in increasingly large numbers.

These binders and manila folders are what come to mind when most people think of files. Less conspicuously they also produce an association between a file and a modern conception of information as a discrete unit. This association led to *files* being deployed as a metaphor to make sense of data in computing. Therefore, Lanier's nightmare began in the 1940s when punch cards provided the material form for data used in computing. At this time, through a deliberate analogy to paper records, a set of cards became known as a *file*. This use of *file* continued as computing moved away from punch cards to tape and then disks.

File became an important abstraction that provided a unit of data computer scientists could use to manage storage. For a computer scientist a file is not the pieces of data, which are scattered across memory or disks, but a way of grouping data so it can be acted on. By the 1960s, computer files were named with identifying information and organized in a (hierarchal) directory system. The utility of *files* took a different turn in the 1970s when it was bundled into the "desktop metaphor" used to develop personal computers, a metaphor subsequently actualized to make this type of computer more comprehensible to first-time users. The launch of Apple Macintosh in 1984 turned the computer screen into a vertical desktop with images of manila folders and file cabinets (and wastepaper baskets). For users, this cemented the idea of the file as a singular entity not the abstraction for the compilation of data bytes by then familiar to computer scientists.

As Lanier's comments suggest, the integrity attributed to files in the world of bureaucracy and government has long been the focus of critique for some computer scientists. For critics, although the self-contained nature of a file, with its assumption that there is no overlap between issues, might work in an office (with the tweaking of cross-referencing), a computer is not paper. The ontological break that they believe should have occurred in the move from paper to the *digital did not happen as the personal computer, in particular, developed in a world of paper simulations. The flexibility the digital had promised was not at the core of computing, its potential limited by the organizational structure of files and directories. But, with networked computing making a single user working on a file from one device less pervasive, the questions of what to store, how to store it, and where to store it have begun to erode the monopoly that the logic of the file has had on digital data.

The difficulty of thinking of a digital world beyond files only serves to underscore how files in a paper or digital environment have served an important function in managing information. This control has come to depend on a conception of information as a discrete unit that can be stored, circulated, exchanged, modified, and destroyed. This is a consequence of a file's primary function as a technology of gathering. Files have gathered information in the name of integrity. In the case of paper files, this integrity often, but not always, comes with the illusion of completeness. Therefore, in the same way that deleting a file frequently offers only the impression of disappearance (its existence or contents are usually recorded elsewhere in a system), the deletion of "files" as the primary mode in which people understand information storage and management remains an ambivalent possibility hindered by the inability to conceive of information as anything other than a discrete unit.

Craig Robertson

See also albums; bureaucracy; cards; cases; computers; databases; documentary authority; inventories; memos; notebooks; registers

FURTHER READING

Ilana Feldman, *Governing Gaza*, 2008; Richard Harper et al., "What Is a File?," *CSCW '13: Proceedings of the 2013 Conference on Computer Supported Cooperative Work*, 2013, 1125–36; Matthew Hull, "The File: Agency, Authority, and Autography in an Islamabad Bureaucracy," *Language and Communication* 23 (2003): 287–314; Bruno Latour, *The Making of Law*, 2002, translated by Marina Brilman and Alain Pottage, 2010; Cornelia Vismann, *Files*, 2000, translated by Geoffrey Winthrop-Young, 2008; Heather Wolfe, "Filing, Seventeenth-Century Style," *Collation*, March 28, 2013 (online); JoAnne Yates, "From Press Book and Pigeonhole to Vertical Filing: Revolution in Storage and Access Systems for Correspondence," *Journal of Business Communication* 19, no. 3 (1982): 5–26.

FORECASTING

Prediction is a basic human activity that has persisted from antiquity to the present day, with myriad terms for methods of producing information about the future, including *augury, foretelling, presaging, prognosticating, prophecy*, and *soothsaying*. With roots in biblical tradition and classical antiquity, prophetic arts of divination hinged on predictive observation of a range of natural and otherworldly phenomena. Augury relied on recognizing omens in the behavior of birds and other animals, for example, as signals of auspicious or foreboding events. Astrology, a widespread practice spanning classical antiquity to medieval and *Renaissance Europe to the present day, involved reading the stars to foretell an individual's fortune, and early astronomers accurately projected the position of celestial bodies and the return of comets (most famously English astronomer Edmund Halley, who issued his predictive calculations of comet orbits in 1705). The historical record is replete with famous oracles, Cassandras, and prophets, from Pythia, the oracle at Delphi in ancient Greece, to the sixteenth-century French physician Nostradamus, whose ambiguous prophecies are still in print today.

The word *forecast* entered the English *lexicon by the fifteenth century, with an early usage being "contrive or plan beforehand; foreordain, predestine." Yet this obsolete definition of *forecasting* as a mode of determining the future would echo through the subsequent centuries' history of attempts—often futile—to understand and thus control future conditions. Forecasting reflects the ideologies, political priorities, and cultural ideals of its historical context, and so the history of forecasting reveals more about a particular time and place in the past than it does about the future itself.

Forecasting, as both cultural keyword and routinized practice, became more commonplace in the nineteenth century as it was intertwined with broader historical processes of commercialization, quantification, and professionalization. Forecasting was both an economic and an epistemic practice: a mechanism for risk management in the uncertain world of commercial and capitalist exchange, as well as a new form of knowledge production. Forecasters often claimed scientific authority for their methods of prediction, but, given the shifting definition of "science" throughout the nineteenth century, we cannot use present-day standards to retrospectively assess forecasts as "scientific" information or not. Forecasters' claims to scientific objectivity and rationality have been an important rhetorical strategy for constructing professional authority, both historically and in the present, yet forecasting is best understood as a combination of predictive calculation and predictive judgment.

If not strictly scientific, forecasting did become newly systematic in the nineteenth century. Government bureaucracies, paperwork, and what Ian Hacking has termed "the avalanche of printed numbers" were key elements of new predictive knowledge infrastructures. Postal, telegraph, and then telephone networks accelerated the circulation of information and so enabled the production of short-term forecasts that coexisted and competed with existing long-range predictions from the traditions of astrology, almanacs, and prophecy. Alongside forecasts as a form of information were imagined cultural and technoscientific futures. Beginning in the mid-nineteenth century, celebrations of industrial progress at world's fairs, proto–science fiction utopian and dystopian novels, and literary forecasts like Edward Bellamy's *Looking Backward* (1888) and H. G. Wells's *Anticipations* (1901) offered more speculative and spectacular visions of a distant future.

The late nineteenth century witnessed the proliferation of routinized forecasts in daily economic life, from weather to harvest to market. As they circulated outside the scientific and government institutions that often produced them, forecasts generated controversies over their accuracy, value, and legitimacy. In the United States, such controversies generated a shift away from a late nineteenth-century belief in predictive certainty toward an early twentieth-century acceptance of uncertainty as a feature rather than a failure of forecasting, an epistemic shift that parallels the nineteenth-century "erosion of determinism" and the "space . . . cleared for chance" identified by Ian Hacking.

The organization of national weather services in the United States and Europe enabled the production of daily weather forecasts, a form of information used for risk management for weather-dependent businesses and activities, from shipping companies to agricultural producers to outdoor excursionists. Although short-lived networks of weather observation stations existed in Europe and North America in the late seventeenth and late eighteenth centuries, they could not aggregate and analyze their data quickly enough to produce forecasts. In the mid- to late nineteenth century, the United States, France, Belgium, Britain, Italy, the German states, Scotland, and Russia established meteorological infrastructures—combining telegraph networks; decentralized networks of observers who conducted standardized synchronous observations of surface conditions including temperature, precipitation, and barometric pressure; and a centralized bureaucracy—that produced and circulated short-term predictions of the next day's weather. Robert Fitzroy (1805–65), the first head of the British Meteorological Department, began using the term *forecast* in 1861 according to this definition: "Prophecies or predictions they are not. The term forecast is strictly applicable to such an opinion as is the result of a scientific combination and calculation." In the United States the daily government forecast, first issued in 1871, was originally called "The Synopsis and Probabilities," but short-term weather forecasting was not probabilistic. The US Army Signal Service's official definition of the daily "probabilities" was "announcements of the changes, considered from the study of the charts . . . as probably to happen within the twenty-four hours then next ensuing." Probability of precipitation forecasts (e.g., 30 percent chance of rain) were not widespread until the 1960s and 1970s and are used to varying extents in countries around the world today as a way to communicate uncertainty about the future to the public.

The advent of short-term government weather forecasts as a public good created direct competition with long-range commercial forecasts long sold by "weather prophets" and almanac *publishers. Although there was no bright line between weather "prophecy" and "forecasting" in the nineteenth century, British and US government officials engaged in "boundary-work" in an attempt to distinguish professional scientific weather forecasting from superstition and fraud. The "war on the weather prophets" was not only a battle over professional authority and respectability but also a political and epistemic conflict over the commercialization of scientific knowledge, the temporalities of short-term versus long-range forecasting, and the nature of foreknowledge itself.

Weather forecasting and crop forecasting are important but often overlooked aspects of the nineteenth-century expansion of state administrative capacity. Beginning in the early nineteenth century, local and then federal agricultural statistics bureaus in Europe and the United States produced volumes of crop estimates that were easily converted into yield forecasts for crops including wheat, barley, corn, oats, tobacco, and cotton. Agricultural statistics bureaus relied on networks of decentralized crop reporters who could be trusted to submit "disinterested" figures on crop acreage and condition. The premise that objective government crop statistics would rationalize agricultural commodity markets—and thwart speculators who profited on commodity futures exchanges by predicting the price of "wind wheat" that they had not grown—did not always come to fruition. Crop forecasts, whether produced by government agricultural statistics bureaus or commercial forecasters, regularly influenced commodity markets, and bear-market forecasters could manipulate cotton prices, for example, with an inflated or fraudulent prediction of the season's yield. Predictive climate and crop statistics were also crucial to imperial expansion, and weather forecasting was the central component of imperial meteorological infrastructures around the globe in the nineteenth century, as *Jesuit observatories, nation-states, and local experts contributed to systems for tracking and predicting cyclones, typhoons, and hurricanes.

Economic forecasting had its origins in late nineteenth-century theories of cycles that, if not widely accepted in academic circles, had enough popular influence to be considered the antecedent of the professional business forecasting industry that emerged in the early twentieth century. In the 1870s and early 1880s, the English economist William Stanley Jevons (1835–82) posited predictive theories of correlation between sunspots and business cycles, declaring, "it becomes almost certain that the two series of phenomena, credit cycles and solar variations, are connected as effect and cause." In the United States, an Ohio farmer, Samuel Benner (1832–1913), became a household name after the 1876 publication of *Benner's Prophecies of Future Ups and Downs in Prices* (subsequently reprinted in over fifteen updated editions), which equipped readers with long-term predictions of the directionality of commodity markets in pig iron, hogs, corn, cotton, and provisions. Benner's price forecasts hinged on his claim that ups and downs in prices recurred in a symmetrical and predictable pattern that could be calculated as precisely as the return of a comet. Benner's method, based on a theory of electromagnetic meteorological cycles set forth in a weather almanac by John Tice, illustrates what Peter Eisenstadt has identified as the "meteorologizing" of the business cycle. The "business barometers" of the early twentieth century were predicated on the metaphorical assumption that both atmospheric and economic pressure could be measured and used to anticipate future conditions.

Although professional economic forecasters like Roger Babson, Irving Fisher, John Moody, and Warren Persons rose to prominence in the United States in the wake of the Panic of 1907, the business forecasting industry overall did not predict the US stock market crash of 1929 (with the exception of Roger Babson). And perhaps this is not surprising, given the performativity of markets and economic models: business forecasts can easily become self-fulfilling prophecies, as gloomy outlooks issued for any economic indicator can influence the behavior of corporations, investors, and consumers so as to cause a downturn. As business and government leaders increasingly studied business cycles and predictive economic indicators during the first half of the twentieth century, so too did advertising professionals on both sides of the Atlantic develop new strategies for using market research and consumer surveys in a predictive capacity (the forerunners of late twentieth-century trend forecasting).

In the context of late nineteenth-century professionalization, forecasters often claimed the imprimatur of science to establish authority and credibility with a consuming public, and the question of whether predicting the future was a legitimate practice bedeviled the worlds of meteorology and fortune-telling alike. The late nineteenth and early twentieth century witnessed the intensified policing and prosecution of fortune-tellers—primarily women—in France, the United States, and Australia, for example. Antidivination laws based in Elizabethan legal tradition and the Napoleonic *Code were applied arbitrarily throughout the nineteenth century and used to enforce nativist and white supremacist moral reform agendas in urban spaces well into the twentieth century. For example, the wealthy white astrologer Evangeline Adams (1868–1932)—known as the "Society Palmist"—was acquitted of "pretending to tell fortunes" in New York City, while the successful Black businesswoman and character reader Adena Minott (1879–?) was targeted by a white supremacist home owners' protective association who sought to drive her Clio School of Mental Sciences out of its original Harlem neighborhood. The resurgence of Spiritualism on both sides of the Atlantic during and after World War I generated new debates over the legal status of occult foreknowledge, and a more liberal jurisprudence emerged to accommodate both the indeterminacy of fortune-telling and the religious freedoms of Spiritualist investigations of "the future life." The American law professor Blewett Lee, who wrote extensively about occult foreknowledge, posited in 1923 a ubiquitous future orientation: "All of us predict the future more or less, from the astronomer with his nautical almanac to the lawyer who foretells the outcome of a lawsuit, or the physician the result of an operation. The weather man makes a calling of predicting, and all who sit down and count the cost of a proposed undertaking are trying to unravel the future." By the end of the World War I era, forecasting had become an *epistemology of the everyday.

World War II marked a key turning point in the history of forecasting. The scope of forecasting became increasingly global from the mid- to late twentieth century, as catastrophic geopolitical and ecological futures were predicted by a range of institutions and individuals across the public and private sectors. The future of the world itself became at once a newly urgent moral category as well as a new terrain to be observed, calculated, and manipulated. The possibilities of nuclear annihilation were anticipated through Cold War geopolitical scenarios, nuclear evacuation drills, and cultural expressions of the atomic age. Dire forecasts—perhaps self-negating—of a nuclear World War III that would obliterate major cities and cripple entire societies never came to fruition. Malthusian warnings of disastrous demographic futures were part of the postwar emergence of global environmental prediction that hinged on a new concept of "*the* environment" as a totalizing ecological and planetary entity as well as on new interdisciplinary modes of expertise required to imagine and protect the environmental future. The apocalyptic famines of Paul Ehrlich's "population bomb" never happened in the 1970s and 1980s, but his 1968 book was representative of a postwar genre of future crises including Rachel Carson's 1962 *Silent Spring* and Alvin and Heidi Toffler's 1970 *Future Shock*.

The new postwar study of the future coalesced in a constellation of self-proclaimed futurists and practitioners of futures studies who combined quantitative and qualitative methods into a new form of social-scientific knowledge applied to problems of planetary, national, and local scope. Beginning in the mid-1960s, new organizations like the World Future Society, the Institute for the Future, and the World Futures Studies Federation held conferences and published academic journals (like *Futures* and the *Futurist*) alongside the work of dozens of less well-known futurist think tanks. Alongside Cold War attempts to strategically anticipate and ultimately control a shared global future, contests over long-term political and social futures emerged in myriad contexts, such as Pan-Africanist socialist development planning in Ghana in the 1950s and 1960s, USAID-funded simulations of the Nigerian agricultural economy in the 1960s and 1970s, and forecasts of a Czechoslovakian postsocialist future and a communist Romanian future in the 1970s and 1980s.

Although the postwar era was not the first instance of predictive calculation, the use of *digital computing technology for simulation and modeling brought the long-term future into sharper focus in a range of contexts, from successful numerical weather prediction in the 1950s to RAND's Delphi method in the 1960s to the production of global climate data that powered the first climate modeling in the 1970s. The twenty-first-century rise of *big data and predictive analytics has created new methods of prediction as well as new digital marketplaces for buying and selling information about the future. Weather futures, options, and derivatives trading began at the turn of the twenty-first century and use government weather data (a public good) to profit from the practice of betting on future weather. Predictive analytics, which employs algorithmic modeling of big data to forecast human behavior, is widely used in the retail, health-care, and social media industries, among others. But as scholars and critics of algorithmic bias have recently noted, predictive analytics' promise of objectivity is unfulfilled, as its application to the US criminal justice system reveals. Big-data techniques of "predictive policing" (which law enforcement uses to target neighborhoods where they expect crimes to happen) and "crime forecasting" (which state prisons use to predict recidivism rates of incarcerated people) perpetuate the centuries-old structural racial discrimination that is the foundation of the prison-industrial complex in the twenty-first-century United States.

Temporalities of forecasting have shifted once again at the turn of the twenty-first century with the advent of *nowcasting* (a term that migrated from meteorology to economics), which compresses the time horizon of short-term forecasting even further to an assessment of the present and immediate future. Meteorological nowcasting predicts the weather within six hours within a square kilometer, and central banks in Europe, North America, and South America use macroeconomic nowcasting for GDP and inflation. Yet even with the increasing speed, precision, and hyperlocal scope of routinized forecasting in the twenty-first century, unforeseen "Black Swan" events like the Great Recession, Brexit, and the 2016 US presidential election defy both probabilistic forecasting and the art of predictive judgment, reminding us that certain futures always remain unpredictable.

Jamie L. Pietruska

See also knowledge; observing; reference books

FURTHER READING

Katharine Anderson, *Predicting the Weather: Victorians and the Science of Meteorology*, 2005; Jenny Andersson, *The Future of the World: Futurology, Futurists, and the Struggle for the Post–Cold War Imagination*, 2018; Jenny Andersson and Eglė Rindzevičiūtė, eds., *The Struggle for the Long-Term in Transnational Science and Politics: Forging the Future*, 2015; I. F. Clarke, *The Pattern of Expectation, 1644–2001*, 1979; Walter A. Friedman, *Fortune Tellers: The Story of America's First Economic Forecasters*, 2014; Ian Hacking, *The Taming of Chance*, 1990; Jamie L. Pietruska, *Looking Forward: Prediction and Uncertainty in Modern America*, 2017.

FORGERY

"Oh, what a tangled web we weave, when first we practice to deceive!" So wrote Sir Walter Scott in his historical romance "Marmion: A Tale of Flodden Field" (1808, VI.17). Tangled, motley, multifarious, labyrinthine—these and any number of similar adjectives, nearly all pejorative, might describe the preternatural handmaiden of the history of information that is *forgery*. An allied term of more recent vintage, *fake news*, connotes untruth and illegitimacy while dismissing, in the same breath, verifiable *facts as imagined political conspiracies. Mendacity trumps reason. Inconvenient verities become tall tales, hard data distortions, and facts mere fantasies, as information is distributed and consumed instantaneously through prefiltered digital and social media. Soon, it seems, any version of the "truth" is possible—past, present, and future—even documentable, from the Flood to the Apocalypse.

But in fact forgery has always been with us, at least since the beginning of written histories and through all recorded time. Indeed, if there is one telltale characteristic (albeit one among many) that often distinguishes forgery from other forms of historical information, it is the obsession of so many forgers to *prove* that they are indeed quite true. The arts of persuasion often constitute a suppressed premise within any thoughtful imposture. Scratch just below the surface, and a far more existential anxiety reveals itself about perceived legitimacy and ostensible documentary origins. Prior to *Enlightenment rationalism and empirical systems of new knowledge, the prevailing standard for judging the probity and authority of any historical claim was rooted in its antiquity. True genius invariably came into the present day through a tradition of thought relayed across centuries and millennia, from an impossibly remote moment in the distant past when giants still presumably walked on the earth and God still spoke directly to mankind. Much as the phrase "it is written," forgery thrived on the implication of self-authorization, whose weight coincided, indubitably, with antique origins.

Another red flag of forgery has been its particular talent for filling in glaring lacunae within the historical record, offering newly concocted, but ostensibly ancient, evidence of things that may have been, at best, only semipreposterous. Jesus never set pen down to paper in the Gospels, but we are given from the third century his sole (surely dictated) correspondence with King Abgar of Edessa (attested in Eusebius's *Historia*, I.13.6–9). Another apocryphal epistle of the sixth century, Jesus's "Letter from Heaven," altered the Sabbath from the Jewish Saturday to the Christian Sunday, while all but assuring its future success, doubling as one of the first "chain letters" in Western history—divinely blessed were those who copied and circulated it, and damned were those who did not. The Gospels are also frustratingly silent about the precise visage of Jesus, and so there appeared by about the eleventh century an apocryphal eyewitness description of the color and disposition of Jesus's hair, skin, and eyes by "Publius Lentulus," a fictitious "Governor of Judea," recorded in a letter to the Senate of Rome. Tens of thousands of paintings of Jesus Christ are indebted, either directly or indirectly, to this short text, which is notably preserved in scores of medieval manuscripts. Similarly, the contemporaneous lives of arguably the two most famous letter writers of ancient Rome, Seneca the Younger (also much admired by medieval thinkers as a proto-Christian moral philosopher) and St. Paul eventually precipitated a lively imagined epistolary exchange between the two. Its most prominent invalidation in print had to wait until the appearance of Desiderius Erasmus's second edition of Seneca's *Opera* in 1529.

The scribal culture of the Middle Ages greatly circumscribed access to comparative textual evidence regarding apocryphal, misattributed, or otherwise forged texts. There were few great libraries to speak of, and those that did exist were far-flung. *Literacy was something of a monopoly carefully protected by the Roman Catholic ecclesiastical elite. Correspondingly, as the prolific medievalist T. F. Tout observed, if homicide was the crime of choice among ambitious knights, then forgery was the preferred transgressive mode for medieval clerics. Prelates could lean heavily on their cultural capital and social prestige as they backdated false charters written on official-looking *parchment membranes signed and sealed, claiming long-established land tenures and grants of privileges that were never so. An effective apparatus of diplomatics enabling the detection of such documentary fakes seemed almost suddenly to appear only with the Benedictine paleographer Jean Mabillon's *De re diplomatica* (On the study of documents, 1681).

Most premodern forgeries of scholarly interest today were less concerned with pecuniary interests than with heralding the triumph of Christianity in the West, and the prestige of the Roman Catholic Church most of all. The most well-known of these was the so-called *Donatio Constantini* (Donation of Constantine), an apocryphal gift bestowed on Pope Sylvester I by the Emperor Constantine granting all the lands of Italy and Europe upon Constantine's departure to his new eponymous capital in the Byzantine East. The omnicapable quattrocento humanist Lorenzo Valla undertook a withering forensic levelling of the *Donatio* on *philological as well as rhetorical grounds, proving impossible linguistic anachronisms and its many risible breaks from the decorum of the ancient imperial Latin language. Many subsequent demolition experts in the history of forgery were profoundly indebted to Valla, though apologists, such as the prefect of the Vatican Library Agostino Steuco, soldiered on over the subsequent century devising more elaborate critical props for the *Donatio* in order to support latter-day papal claims and ambitions. Just as opportunistically, others, including the early religious reformers Martin Luther and the indefatigable Ulrich von Hutten, went on to resuscitate the long-dead horse of the *Donatio* only to sacrifice it once more on the altar of Protestant antipapalism.

The novel technology of print may have facilitated as many forgeries as it did critiques of them. Geoffrey of Monmouth's twelfth-century fabulist *Historia regum Britanniae* (History of the kings of Britain) is a case in point. Based partly on a "very ancient book" he professed to consult in the Welsh language (to which no one else apparently had access), Geoffrey's text, and its considerable medieval influence, inspired robust debates that lasted at least a century between humanist critics like Polydore Virgil and John Selden, and inveterate English antiquaries such as John Leland and John Price who were keener to valorize Geoffrey's romantic accounts of King Arthur's Camelot than to see them go. Other medieval authors experienced similarly mixed receptions in the era of print; the political philosopher John of Salisbury's hugely influential twelfth-century *Policraticus* borrowed considerably from a false work of Plutarch but also preserved entirely legitimate textual witnesses of the otherwise lost ancient Roman *Satyricon* by Petronius. The authenticity of the *Satyricon* was, in turn, ferociously contested throughout the second half of the seventeenth century, following the discovery of the substantial "Trau Fragment" containing over fifty missing chapters. These were dismissed as modern forgeries that betrayed the French or Italian native tongue of their latter-day author before Nicolaas Heinsius revealed in 1676 on philological grounds that they were genuine and that their solecisms were deliberate: Petronius's way of characterizing the semiliterate character Trimalchio.

After more than a century in print, several lingering classical Judeo-Christian impostures were not finally razed to the ground until the later seventeenth century. Prominent among these was pseudo-Aristeas's "Letter of Philocrates" ostensibly relaying the precise circumstances surrounding the biblical translation of the Greek Septuagint from the original Hebrew, and Richard Bentley's masterful annihilation of the impossibly ancient sixth-century BCE Greek "Letters of Phalaris" in 1699. In proving on philological grounds that the Phalaris text dated only from the second century CE, Bentley weakened an essential plank of the argument favoring the most ancient literary authorities over modern authors in what Jonathan Swift famously entitled the "Battle of the Books." So, too, had fallen the ancient Egyptian mystique of Hermes Trismegistus, who was for many centuries thought to have been a contemporary of Moses himself. The optimistically syncretic *Corpus Hermeticum* was shown by the great hammer of forgers, Isaac Casaubon, in 1614 not to have been translated from an impossibly early Egyptian, but once again to have been written in late antique Greek.

Not all forgeries were concerned solely with sorting authentic pagan and early Christian literature from lore. More ambitious impostures methodologically cut huge swatches of human history from whole cloth in the service of their inventors' personal fame, and the promise of patronage from the great and the good. Primus inter pares among these was surely Annius of Viterbo, who came to the attention of Pope Alexander VI, particularly after staging a 1493 excavation in his hometown (also, conveniently, a papal summer retreat) in which he unearthed, inter alia, a false stone "hieroglyph" offering primordial evidence of the presence there of Isis and Osiris. Annius's "mastery" of ancient Etruscan, and his transcription and edition of eleven "lost" treatises by ancient Egyptian, Chaldean, Persian, Jewish, Greek, and Roman authors revealed Viterbo to be the chosen capital of Noah's postdiluvian global empire. Obtaining the mysterious works of "Berosus Chaldaeus" and "Manetho of Egypt" from an Armenian monk in Genoa, and others from the imagined medieval miscellany of "William of Mantua," Annius wrote learned commentaries on them all—or, rather, wrote the works themselves (all in Latin "translation") based on what he had then intended to be their commentaries. His was a tangled web indeed. Dozens of editions of Annius's impostures were printed, with and without his commentaries, into the seventeenth century. Sidestepping the prestigious ancient Greeks as mendacious newcomers, Annius favored the presumably ultra-ancient Etruscans, and Noah himself, to fashion for Viterbo the ultimate historical pedigree after the Flood.

A host of other syncretistic and patriotic mythographers paid Annius the highest compliment of imitation, circumventing altogether any Greco-Roman traditions of authoritative descent to which their native lands were, in the extant classical literature, either barbaric or irrelevant. In their place, they elevated their own more ancient ancestors chosen, as they wished, whether from the sons of Noah, the Trojans, or the Etruscans or Celts, et alia. Annian "reforgeries" appeared across Europe, including texts of the sixteenth-century French authors Jean Lemaire de Belges and Guillaume Postel, and the Noachian and early Saxon contrivances of the Elizabethan Catholic exiles Richard White of Basingstoke and Richard Verstegan. This Annian enterprise persisted despite a long and formidable line of proficient critics, including Pietro Crinito, Beatus Rhenanus, Melchor Cano, and Gaspar Barreiros.

The allied archaeological and textual foundations of Annius's seminal inventions are admirably reflected in ever-expanding *syllogae* (collections) of lapidary inscriptions transcribed and, very often, illustrated in engraved printed "facsimiles." Authentic inscriptional facts were invariably mixed and buried together with creative epigraphic fictions in any number of humongous compendia, notably those of Petrus Apianus and Bartholomaeus Amantius (1534), and Jan Gruter and Joseph Scaliger (1603). Of course, the vast majority of these were nigh impossible "to check" physically against the originals (where there were originals), scattered across the great cities, country palaces, and private collections of Europe.

The precocious Volterran Curzio Inghirami took all this a step further, planting "scariths" (i.e., time capsules fashioned from bitumen, wax, and other preservative materials) containing ancient Etruscan manuscripts (à la Annius) around his aristocratic estate, which were then duly discovered with friends on digs. The result was a magnificently illustrated 1637 folio of still more scribal "facsimiles" of these manuscripts written by the pagan Etruscan priest-prophet Prospero of Fiesole, including his scribal auguries of the coming of Jesus Christ. Attracting immediate and scathing criticisms in print, the irrepressible phenom Inghirami went on to publish a monumental one-thousand-page defense of his own forgery (albeit, printed in a large-type quarto format). Literary forgery had, by the seventeenth century, reached quasi-epic proportions.

The eighteenth century inspired perhaps the widest modern scholarly literature of the whole "House of forgery," as Horace Walpole termed it. Following on the imaginative ancient travel fables of Euhemerus and Ctesias, and the ubiquity of the late medieval Sir John Mandeville, unprecedented long-distance trade and European imperial conquests stimulated latter-day imposters to do much the same, only in far more sensational and elaborate detail. The French refugee to England George Psalmanazar posed for years as an exotic "Formosan" (i.e., Taiwanese), whose account of the Formosan language and alphabet may constitute the earliest "constructed language" (much as latter-day Klingon and Esperanto) in print, beginning with his *History of Formosa* (1704). Bristol's Mary Baker in 1817 perpetuated this unique sort of hoax, impersonating "Princess Caraboo," who had apparently been kidnapped by pirates and was capable only of speaking her native, impenetrable "Far Eastern" language.

These "travel liar" concoctions inspired several of the earliest English novels but also stood in counterpoint to contemporary efforts to bound, if not across oceans, then across centuries of history to "discover" great *vernacular British verse where it had never been. James Macpherson's *Fingal*—more commonly known by the name of its imagined third-century blind bard of Argyllshire, Ossian—was in truth a neo-Gaelic pastiche drawn from a host of latter-day sources. Almost universal admiration was showered on this newly recovered Scots Homer, regardless, perhaps most hyperbolically by Emperor Napoleon and the American Founding Father Thomas Jefferson. Jefferson not only excerpted from the Ossian forgeries in his *commonplace books but, in one letter to Macpherson's brother, proclaimed that "I think this rude bard of the North the greatest Poet that has ever existed." Inspired imitation poured forth from the pens of Coleridge, Byron, Blake, and many others, inspiring the broader question, even after his exposure in the later eighteenth century, "Was Macpherson really a forger?" Or was he, who had remained fairly reticent about his efforts, simply a creative author of imaginative literature?

Less ambiguous were the material English literary forgeries of the teenaged medieval fantasist Thomas Chatterton, who fabricated on old and artificially aged *parchment eccentrically spelled and paleographically crabbed fragments of an invented fifteenth-century English vernacular poet-priest Thomas Rowley. Chatterton's no-holds-barred struggle for literary prestige and patronage was quickly quashed after he failed to lure Horace Walpole into his imaginary web. Chatterton died young in a London garret from a drug overdose only to be lionized by the later Romantic poets as an archetypal artist crying out into the wilderness. The much longer lived forger and poetaster William Henry Ireland was even more impressive for the boldness of his bardolotry. He "discovered" numerous manuscripts in the very hand of William Shakespeare, which usefully filled in glaring gaps in the patchy historical record surrounding Shakespeare's life and literary career. Numerous manuscript copies of Shakespeare's "Confession of Faith," a love letter to Anne Hathaway enclosed with a lock of his hair, signed and annotated books from the playwright's library, and even Shakespeare's "lost" play *Vortigern* count as high points in the surviving corpus of Ireland's superproductive, quasi-literary imagination.

The nineteenth century introduced a "golden age" of forgery undertaken increasingly for pecuniary purposes focused on the scions of a new aristocratic "bibliomania." These largely aristocratic collectors were encouraged to spend unprecedented sums, both by one another in an acquisitive sort of competition, and by the diasporic sale of the great French libraries just after 1789. George de Gibler (aka "Major Byron") specialized in a particular vogue for the almighty literary autograph, leaving behind scores of manuscript "letters" and books bearing the Romantic effusions of Lord Byron. Bolder still was the Frenchman Vrain-Denis Lucas, whose stock of manuscripts for sale included implausible "transcripts" of the epistles of Aristotle and his student Alexander the Great, Julius Caesar and Cleopatra, Mary Magdalene, Judas Iscariot, Joan of Arc, Dante, Montaigne, and the list goes on—some twenty-seven thousand in all, for which Lucas spent two years in prison. "Ancient" Greek manuscripts on aggressively aged parchment were sold by the forger Constantine Simonides to the great collector Sir Thomas Phillipps, including textual fragments of Homer and Hesiod that Phillipps even printed on his private press at Middle Hill in 1855.

As with manuscript, so with print, impossibly rare pamphlets and limited private press productions of works by contemporary *canonical authors attracted collectors. Thomas Wise and Harry Forman did not so much corrupt the literary corpora of Tennyson and the Rossettis as capitalize on their popularity through the antiquarian book trade. The gullibility of such collectors was perhaps nowhere more delightfully satirized than in the hoax of Renier Hubert Ghislain de Chalon, who issued in 1840 a famous provincial auction-sale catalog in the tiny Belgian village of Binche, comprising an imaginary collection of "unique" imprints from the private library of the legendary Comte de Fortsas. Copies of this ultimate bibliomaniacal forgery are, true to its very nature, scarce in the trade even today and irresistible to in-the-know antiquarian collectors.

Recent jaundiced "fake news" epithets in digital media also had their (very real) counterparts in mass print production. David Croly's and George Wakeman's storied 1864 *Miscegenation* pamphlet (which apparently coined the term) pretended a radical Republican program to promote racial intermarriage in order to drive mainstream support from the antislavery party of Abraham Lincoln. Such bare-knuckled racism proved a potent power a half century later with the appearance of the *Protocols of the Elders of Zion* "documenting" a global Jewish conspiracy to usurp control over all human civilization. Adolf Hitler and the American industrialist Henry Ford helped assure a vast readership for this anti-Semitic venom throughout the second quarter of the twentieth century. Political hoaxes proved to be equal opportunity employers in the right hands, as with the Baltimore-born African American Joseph Howard Lee. Lee reinvented himself, in defiance of the Jim Crow South, with his fake autobiography as the African prince Bata Kindai Amgoza ibn LoBagola, which he subtitled "An African Savage's Own Story" (Knopf, 1930). Also claiming to be a "Black Jew" directly descended from the diaspora following the destruction of the Temple in Jerusalem, Lee signed copies and responded to fan mail, in an affected pidgin English encapsulated in his personal motto: "struggle begats strength."

The Regius Professor of History at Oxford Hugh Trevor-Roper was not immune to the attractions of documentary fakes. Though he reversed his former authentication of the so-called Hitler Diaries, he was later taken in by the "Secret Gospel of Mark," which had implied a homosexual affair between the historical Jesus and an acolyte. That sexual politics "gospel hoax" was echoed more recently in the 2012 sensation launched by Harvard's Hollis Professor of Divinity regarding the so-called Gospel of Jesus's Wife—a Coptic *papyrus fragment suggesting Jesus had been married. In this more recent tangle in the great web of forgery, recent scholarship has dismissed this gospel truth as yet another fake.

Earle Havens

See also books; diplomats/spies; documentary authority; error; plagiarizing; professors; readers; travel

FURTHER READING

Arthur Freeman, *Bibliotheca Fictiva: A Collection of Books and Manuscripts Relating to Literary Forgery 400 BC–AD 2000*, 2014; Anthony Grafton, *Forgers and Critics: Creativity and Duplicity in Western Scholarship*, 1990, new ed., 2019; Earle Havens, ed., *Fakes, Lies, and Forgeries: Rare Books and Manuscripts from the Arthur and Janet Freeman "Bibliotheca Fictiva" Collection*, 2014, 2nd ed. rev., 2016; Jack Lynch, *Deception and Detection in Eighteenth-Century Britain*, 2008; Ingrid D. Rowland, *The Scariths of Scornello: A Tale of Renaissance Forgery*, 2004; Walter Stephens and Earle Havens, eds., *Literary Forgery in Early Modern Europe, 1450–1800*, 2018.

GLOBALIZATION

Globalization is a fluid and much-debated term. In general, it indicates the increasing interdependence of economic, cultural, and social relations across the world, and it is at once a cause and consequence, together with technology, of the compression of time and space that has been seen as the defining factor of the "information age." While the roots of globalization reach deep down in history, the real acceleration of global entanglements began with the new economic world order that emerged in the aftermath of the Second World War, and the technological and informational revolutions that followed.

Early on in this period, globalization was perhaps most visible in the rapid diffusion of American (popular) culture across the world. Film, music, television and radio programs, and advertising were the tools of American soft power in the ideological battles of the Cold War, forming the content of the electronic mass media carried through to populations in the Western, Soviet, and nonaligned spheres, and beginning the creation of what Marshall McLuhan called the global village. This phase of cultural globalization is ongoing and increasingly diverse, with many more centers emerging, large and small, to challenge the United States as the primary source of global cultural trends. Another visible form of globalization, trade and finance, also garners considerable public attention and thrives, despite a continuing backlash against it. However, the globalization of technology and information arguably exerts the more profound and lasting influence on society, and it is worth exploring its origins.

Beginning with the diffusion of manufacturing outward from the United States and Europe, the increasing complexity of truly global supply chains, made possible by faster *internet-supported flows of information, connected the various production and consumption nodes in a worldwide network. *Information* itself is a term just as ambiguous, fluid, and contested as *globalization*. It used to be a fairly local concern, generated and used within small geographical boundaries, and its meaning was tied to particular localities. Now, however, it is not only one of the enablers of globalization; it has become itself a global commodity, portable, sellable, and immaterial. Its origins as a material product of social relations, whose value and meaning stem in part from these very relations, is forgotten; it can now be frictionlessly applied anywhere in the world, its qualities unchanged even though detached from their original locale.

In the dominant narrative of globalization in the information age, there are centers, for the most part advanced economies in the West, and there are peripheries, the so-called global South of emerging, developing, and less developed countries. Information has been singled out as the resource that is lacking in the global South, and that, accessed and deployed correctly, can change poor countries' position in the global economy. This is the "idea gap," in the formulation of the Nobel Prize–winning economist Paul Romer, as distinct from an "object gap" (i.e., a lack of factories, machinery, and other material resources) as an explanation of poverty: ideas that generate wealth are not available in poor countries, contributing to their underdevelopment. Ideas are abstract and independent of local circumstances, thus can travel and be effective anywhere, and are transmitted in the form of information, framed as an all-powerful commodity that can unlock access to the global economy; acquiring it, passive observers at the periphery are transformed into nodes in the network. Access is chiefly provided by information and communication technologies (ICTs) such as computers, mobile phones, and the internet, which allow information to be reproduced and to reach every corner of the world at negligible cost. The barriers to access are lowered, and the potential benefits for those who were previously excluded from it—or at least perceived to be excluded—potentially life changing.

This is the familiar narrative of "haves" and "have-nots" that emerged in the early days of the internet as part of the debate on the *digital divide. Some people had access to ICTs and thus could bridge the idea gap by accessing information and leveraging it to improve their lives, but others did not. Closing the gap between the haves and have-nots became then a matter of providing access to information, especially by building infrastructure and programs to bring hardware such as computers into schools and libraries that did not have them. Once again, the debate and policies on the digital divide started within the United States but were soon reproduced globally, particularly in the global South. Lack of access to information, and thus to education, resources, and markets, became one of the key problems to tackle in order to unlock the potential of poorer countries. Blurring the lines between information technologies, information/information society, and knowledge/knowledge economy, international organizations such as the United Nations and the World Bank began in the 1990s to codify "expert knowledge," that is, knowledge that came from Western experts and institutions, into databases and programs that would allow its transfer from the information rich to the information poor (note the interchangeability of "information" and "knowledge," which is a common feature of the plans and documents from this period).

In the 1990s, information- and ICT-related projects in the field of development were scattered and left to the initiative of individual organizations. In the early 2000s, however, the United Nations began to organize projects and actors that were related, however vaguely, to information and information-driven economic development under the umbrella of the World Summit on the Information Society (WSIS). The summit started as two general conferences, held in Geneva in 2003 and in Tunis in 2005, with representatives of governments and civil society, to discuss the role that ICTs and access to information could play in reducing the gap between rich and poor countries, thus providing new areas of economic growth for the global South. These summits resulted in eleven "Action Lines" that emphasized the potential of ICTs to trigger and support economic development, the need to build adequate infrastructure and provide access to all citizens, and the benefits for both individuals and nations that come from "access to information and knowledge" (Action Line Three). Those years also saw the beginning of ambitious programs to bring digital devices to poor places, programs such as the high-profile One Laptop Per Child (OLPC). The brainchild of the exuberant MIT professor Nicholas Negroponte, who once enthusiastically proposed to airdrop OLPC laptops off helicopters to remote villages to give rural children a chance to access education, the quirky and cheap green-and-white machine was designed to be a low-cost computer able to go online but also function off grid. The OLPC prototype was in fact presented at the

WSIS meeting in Tunis, where its most distinctive feature, the crank handle that was supposed to power it, promptly fell off. Despite the perplexity expressed by some of the summit participants as to how appropriate the device was for the reality of the rural global South, given the US-centric assumptions about infrastructure, education, time, and "useful information" inherent in it, the OLPC was hailed as a game changer that could solve thorny educational issues in resource-poor areas. Whether the OLPC was successful or not in changing the course of education in the countries where it was deployed is a debatable (and still heatedly debated) matter. But the philosophy behind it—to give direct access to information to those who do not have it, through ICTs—persists, embodied in a succession of new digital technologies, each imagined to overcome the flaws that led to the failure of its predecessors.

The first wave of post-WSIS ICT deployments was followed by a certain disillusionment, when it became clear that maintaining open-access technology in low-resource and environmentally challenging places was an expensive and labor-intensive endeavor. But this was quickly forgotten once mobile phones became widespread. The same rhetoric deployed in the early 2000s, when computers were the technology that would give access to information to the "have-less," was now repurposed for mobile phones. These had the advantage of being cheaper and more portable than computers, and they spread quickly even in poorer and more rural areas of the global South—although it is useful to keep in mind that about 42 percent of the world, as of 2020, still did not have access to any kind of mobile phone, much less an internet-connected one; and that the ways of using mobile phones among rural, marginal communities in the global South differ substantially from how they are used in urban areas everywhere. Still, the dream of connecting those who are at the margins of the global economy remains, now best captured by the philanthropic efforts of technology corporations racing to bring connectivity and access to information to increasing numbers of previously neglected people, who are not only information have-less, but also potentially lucrative customers.

In the examples above, information is explicitly framed as badly distributed across the world, as difficult to access, and at the same time as the key to development—the source of knowledge about agriculture, education, and health care, but also the source of (better) jobs and increased participation in the value-added parts of the global economy. Information is concentrated in some places and among some groups (the information rich), but lacking or kept inaccessible by gatekeepers in other places and among other people, the information poor. Once the barriers to access are eliminated, then information has the potential to unlock growth, in particular economic growth. Information is also posed as binary: it exists, or it does not; it is the right information, or the wrong; and it is, once again, abstracted from any social interaction.

So far, this has been the story of information as global commodity as told from the perspective of the center, that is, the countries that are considered information rich and ICT rich, and as such the source of information for those without. From the periphery's perspective, this narrative has been embraced by some countries in the global South. In the years following WSIS in Tunis, there has been a surge of national strategies on information, and on digitization and informatization (another vague term that indicates strategies to increase the weight of information technologies and jobs connected with the digital and knowledge economy). The content of these strategies varies from vague gesturing toward creating a more digital economy to very detailed goals such as increasing the percentage of the global flow of information that should pass through a country. Still, perhaps as a side effect of often being written by global consultancies, these strategies remain remarkably similar in embracing the idea of information poverty, and ICTs and information as the essential ticket to escaping the periphery and joining those at the center(s) of the global economy.

Countries that try to forge their own path vis-à-vis globalization and information, and so provide alternatives to Western-driven models, are few. China is one of them, helped of course by its size, but also by the fact that it has struggled with issues related to development, center-periphery relations, and technologies for over a century. In fact, already in the 1880s, during the last imperial dynasty, whose sovereignty had been severely challenged by Western powers, Chinese intellectuals had developed a strategy for reforming the nation that would rely on what they referred to as Chinese "essence" and foreign "means," following the dictum that originated in the mid-nineteenth century: "Chinese knowledge as a basis, Western technology for practical use" (*xi yong zhong ti*). What Chinese intellectuals of that age had focused on was the need to appropriate Western technologies, and eventually develop native ones, but repurpose them in a manner that reflected local values and cultural norms, and focused on national priorities. Policies in the Republican era (1912–49) and especially the postrevolution years (1949–76) continued to emphasize technology and self-reliance in developing technology as important tools for the nation to forge its own path, independent from other countries. From Mao's death in 1976 through the beginning of Deng Xiaoping's economic reforms in the early 1980s, there was a sudden surge of interest in information. Alvin Toffler's book *The Third Wave* was translated into Chinese (and made into a popular television program), and Toffler himself visited the country to present to enthusiastic audiences his ideas on the postindustrial society, where information processing would be a primary economic activity. Although the success of Deng's economic reforms was founded on the exploitation of physical labor—the industrial workers in the factories that the global logistics chain had located in China—the idea of increasing automation in production and thus moving up the value chain to more "informational" and less physical work was already taking form. Information became the theme of many science fiction stories published around that time, while some of the scientific ideas developed in the wake of *The Third Wave*'s popularity went back to earlier cybernetic tropes of the human body as a complex information system, to be integrated with computers and synchronized with information flows. Other ideas, however, found their way into concrete policies that went on to shape the future of the country. While the South and the East of the country were from 1980 on becoming the factory of the world, the government started infrastructure investments and policies aimed at becoming a driver of globalization, not just a peripheral part of it, especially after the political upheaval of Tiananmen began to settle in the early 1990s. Information and informatization were at the center of a series of policies—or rather long-term programmatic documents—that began with the Tenth Five-Year Plan 2001–5. This plan made informatization of the national economy a strategic priority and included the creation of a national informatization index evaluation center, the first such place in the world. In 2006, the Building a New Socialist Countryside framework focused on bringing ICTs to rural areas in order to give farmers more and better access to information, in particular about markets and agricultural technology, and thus decrease the income gap that existed between urban and rural areas. In 2006, the government also launched a National Informatization Development Plan 2006–20, which aimed at setting up "a scientific concept for information resources, that is, to raise the importance of information resources development to equal that of energy and materials, thereby creating the necessary conditions for the development of a knowledge-intensive industry," making it clear that information and access to information is as important for the future of the country as natural resources. Even though many of the technologies and much of the information that is at the core of these plans was still coming from foreign (that is, Western) sources, each subsequent version increased the emphasis on the need for self-reliance. The latest plan, Made in China 2025, thus stresses the necessity to develop indigenous technology, and to create technological standards that are adopted outside China. In the global whirlwind of information, China is thus carving its own path and trying to position itself as a source, rather than a recipient, of information and ICTs, still within the parameters of globalization, but with "Chinese characteristics," such as strong state control over the direction of the economy and a belief in the primacy of politics over economics.

Whether articulated in neoliberal or in Chinese terms, however, both versions of a global information system see information as an abstract, tradable type of knowledge. The reality on the ground, at the periphery of the network, however, is that information remains stubbornly attached to local meanings and interpretations, even when it comes from far away, and it resists detachment from the bodies and social relations that produce it. Market information systems that attempt to bring market price information to global South farmers have more often than not failed; information about prices, it turns out, is not necessarily what is lacking, nor what, as such, farmers prize most. Countries that adopt the sleek information strategies produced by global consultants are also places where information labor, the glue that holds together the global network of capitalist production, is the domain not of the desired highly skilled "value added" worker, but rather of blue-collar workers toiling in cottage factories effectively indistinguishable from piecework manufacturing sites. Information laborers in the Philippines, Thailand, Indonesia, and other global South countries are low-paid workers spending their days creating social media accounts and commenting, liking, or clicking on behalf of their clients, or "farming gold" by playing massive multiplayer online games to acquire virtual currency and then selling it for real money. They might have the ICTs and the connectivity to access the "right" information, but their livelihoods remain strictly dependent on using an essentially manual set of skills, while the world they live in remains dependent on local information, tied to the workplace and the social and economic relations around it. Information—global, abstract, immaterial, and tradable— has not made a significant impact: in rural China farmers might play Farmville online, but they are still farmers. Whether in the future they will also be able to leverage the opportunities always promised by the information society, and yet still not delivered, remains to be seen.

Elisa Oreglia

See also computers; cybernetics/feedback; data; digitization; governance; knowledge; learning; media; networks; quantification; telecommunications; travel

FURTHER READING

Michael K. Buckland, "Information as Thing," *Journal of the American Society for Information Science* 42, no. 5 (1991): 351–60; Manuel Castells, *The Rise of the Network Society*, 2011; Jan Cherlet, "Epistemic and Technological Determinism in Development Aid," *Science, Technology, and Human Values* 39, no. 6 (2014): 773–94; Benjamin A. Elman, *A Cultural History of Modern Science in China*, 2009; Xiao Liu, "Magic Waves, Extrasensory Powers, and Nonstop Instantaneity: Imagining the Digital beyond Digits," *Grey Room*, no. 63 (Spring 2016): 42–69; Paul Romer, "Idea Gaps and Object Gaps in Economic Development," *Journal of Monetary Economics* 32 (1993): 543–73; Janaki Srinivasan, Megan Finn, and Morgan Ames, "Information Determinism: The Consequences of the Faith in Information," *Information Society* 33, no. 1 (2017): 13–22.

GOVERNANCE

Discovered by economists and political scientists in the 1990s, the notion of "governance" has had a surprising career. Despite its rather arbitrary definition, it was used to scrutinize the performance of companies, administrations, and eventually any kind of institutional arrangement. The concept's fuzziness itself seemed useful since it allowed focus on processes and structures alike. Focusing on "governance" makes it possible to highlight the ways in which legislation, culture, discourse, society, or traditions frame and shape institutions. It also tacitly turns away from approaches that center on the personal skills of managers, rulers, or commanders. The concept's popularity is also built on its capacity to assess and weigh everything in the light of ultimately just one single factor, which is success.

Both qualities, its fuzziness and its broad applicability, are a legacy of antiquity. Literally, the Greek term *kybernáo* and the Latin *gubernare* signify "to steer a ship." As a metaphor, it set the pilot's navigation skills against the background of rough waters. But since the safe arrival of the ship never depends on the pilot's skills alone, the metaphor also reminds us to take other factors into account, like the crew's training and order, the ship's construction and condition, and, not least, the available resources: the charts, navigational instruments, and knowledge aboard.

This article aims to trace the roles historically ascribed to information within concepts and practices of governance through a focus on examples from Western and Chinese history. Its two main concepts, information and governance, are fuzzy, and the objects and ideas they refer to have undergone many transformations in the course of history. The path chosen here is to select a set of typical constellations between information on the one hand and tasks of governance on the other. This opens up the opportunity to discuss different theoretical and scholarly approaches along the way.

THE ART OF GOVERNING—INFORMATION WITHIN POLITICAL THEORY

With interesting parallels to the Western classical tradition, the Chinese character of *si*, literally "to direct," "to have charge of," or "to manage," was used for a range of official titles during the period of the Western Zhou, a ruling dynasty in ancient China (ca. 1045–771 BCE). In these times ideals of governance derived, at least in part, from the necessity of justifying a new ruler. The "Mandate of Heaven," for example, was instrumental for the Zhou kings in order to counter the rule of the competing Shang dynasty. It remained a justification for several dynasties of Chinese emperors until the twentieth century and depended almost exclusively on the conception of a dynasty's "generally good character" and its success in governing the land and its people.

In European history information and knowledge are often seen as the true basis of good and effective government. Cicero (106–43 BCE), in *De Re Publica* (On the commonwealth), argued that "as the farmer knows agriculture, and the scribe knows penmanship, and both seek in their respective sciences, not mere amusement only, but practical utility; so our statesmen should be familiar with the science of jurisprudence and legislation, even in their profoundest principles. But he should not embarrass himself in debating, arguing, and lecturing and scribbling. He should rather employ himself in the actual administration of government, as skillful superintendent, and become a farmer of the revenue, so as to make the state as flourishing as possible by a wholesome political economy."

Information was also crucial for government in the thinking of Francis Bacon (1561–1626), the English scholar and politician best known for embracing empiricism as a means to reform natural philosophy. While Bacon never developed a theory of government, he clearly favored quantification on the one hand and administration on the other in his *Essays*: "the greatness of an estate, in bulk or territory, doth fall under measure; and the greatness of finances and revenue doth fall under computation. The population may appear by musters, and the number of cities and towns by charts and maps." Bacon's views on governance and information were subtle and complex. He warned the reader not to take such numbers at face value, and he gave a more nuanced advice in practice. Serving as attorney general and later as Lord Chancellor of England until 1621, he had considerable influence over King James I as well as over his favorite George Villiers, First Duke of Buckingham. In 1616, Bacon wrote a "Letter of Advice" to Villiers instructing the "new-risen star" at court and intimate friend of James I about the ways of government, in which he now took a leading role as "the Favourite of the time." The duke should use his outstanding social position to influence the royal government not in the fashion of secretively whispering to "him in the ear and say[ing] nothing," but methodically in observing the rules of government. First, every procedure of importance should be put in writing. Second, petitions should be sorted, answers prepared, and the secretary instructed to keep the papers in order, for example, in underlining matters of concern. Third, this procedure should be performed by only a few chosen persons, among whom duties of preparing petitions should be divided. The division of labor should guarantee, as Bacon explains in his fourth point, an objective handling of the papers. And fifth, to "return answers to petitions of all natures as an oracle." Such a genealogy of governmental knowledge, reaching from the Roman Republic to modern empiricism, fits well into the history of the modern state. Yet it obscures the fact that knowledge and information were not only scarce in political practice but also of little interest to the art of government from ancient times until the modern era.

Medieval and *early modern scholarly treatises on the art of government were mainly addressed and dedicated to monarchs. They focused on the ruler's personal ability to provide justice and to form decisions guided by values and faith. Authors praised wisdom (*sapientia*) and prudence (*prudentia*), education, some personal experience, and, above all, the ability to surround oneself with the right advisers, in brief: everything that was thought to lead to a reliable and good decision. It might come as a surprise to the modern reader that this did not include acquiring as much knowledge as possible or accumulating empirical information. For example, in the Middle Ages mirrors of princes (a *genre of political advice literature) often remarked only that the knowledgeable prince was supposed to possess elementary genealogical and geographical information.

In a different but not completely dissimilar manner, Chinese thinkers were often far from envisioning that a ruler should acquire much knowledge and information about the state of his realm. Indeed, Sinologists have stressed the importance of a Daoist concept called *wu wei*, literally meaning "without exertion," which was supposed to make the art of statecraft look like "effortless action." The Chinese statesman and philosopher Shen Buhai stated in the fourth century BCE that a good ruler should rely on his ministers and not exert himself in trying to learn everything about his subjects. Rather he should "refrain from taking the initiative, and from making himself conspicuous— and therefore vulnerable—by taking any overt action" (Creel, 66–67).

The Chinese art of governing was thus based on a seemingly uninformed ruler who depended on able ministers and administrators. At the same time the emperor could resort to his mandate from heaven, which made him immune to criticism in managing everyday affairs of his government. According to the Confucian scholar Mencius (ca. 370–ca. 290 BCE) this ideology of governance was founded on a moral basis and entailed commitments to the people in order to secure their livelihood and their support for the government. Thus good governance in the land depended not on short-term administrative successes to sustain the livelihood of the people, but ultimately on the wisdom of the emperor and his ability to maintain the social order as an equilibrium within the limited technologies of rule available.

This lack of interest in a theoretically elaborated concept of governmental knowledge and information is easier to understand in the light of two long-term developments that we overlook when we focus just on a few peaks of thinking marked by Cicero and Bacon, or on the scholarly art of government. The first is a semantic one: alongside sensory metaphors in China and later in Europe, new terms for knowledge did not arise before the late Middle Ages, among them "information" in a modern occidental sense. The second is practical: secular and ecclesiastical administration grew dramatically starting in the late Middle Ages, based in no small measure on the availability of cheaper writing materials with the introduction of paper. Both of these phenomena are highly relevant.

THE SEMANTICS OF GOVERNING—INFORMATION IN THE LANGUAGE OF RULE

The topical use of visual and auditory metaphors in relation to governance dates back at least to the short-lived Qin dynasty (221–206 BCE), which first ruled the whole of China. Han Fei (ca. 280–233 BCE), whose works were popular during the rule of the Qin emperor, wrote "because the ruler sees with the eyes of the entire state, there is none who can see more clearly; because he hears with the ears of the entire state, there is none who can hear more keenly" (Ames, 144).

In 1573, the Venetian ambassador in Madrid reported home that the Spanish king Philip II "has such an intelligence, that there is no thing that he does not know or see." Two generations later the young Louis XIV of France had himself depicted as a face in the sun with the emblematic title *digna deo facies* (a face worthy of God). This emblem meant that he, like God in the world, was visible to everyone. Other emblems and medals extended the solar metaphor to the sphere of knowledge and information. Later in life, Louis reflected in his memoirs on the information overload that resulted from his announcement in 1661 that he would govern alone, signing every document himself. In a collection of texts from the 1660s meant to instruct the dauphin (his heir), the king is styled as the focal point of all knowledge, who wants "to be informed about everything (*informé de tout*)." Now it was considered the king's job "to keep open eyes on the entire world," "to be informed [about an] infinite number of things," and not least to "discover the most remote views of our own courtiers, their darkest interests."

The allegorical self-fashioning of Louis XIV as "sun king" also included a paradoxical stance maintaining that, while needing to be informed about everything, he could also not afford to engage in every detail of the affairs of state. Similarly, "to govern by virtue," according to Confucius (ca. 551–479 BCE), could be compared to the "North Star staying in its place, while the myriad stars wait upon it" (*Analects* 2.1). The polar star, like the sun, signified the immobile constant in the universe that guaranteed the glory or virtue of the ruler. The metaphor implicitly relates to the concept of wu wei: that the less the king or emperor does, the more gets done. He remains the calm center around which his subjects turn while he allows everything to run smoothly without having to interfere with the individual parts of the whole.

In Europe in the sixteenth and seventeenth centuries, kings were regularly referred to as all-knowing and well-informed rulers. The claim to know everything has itself a remarkable history. In papal documents from the end of the twelfth century, we can find a striking formulation that the pope makes decisions *ex certa scientia*—"on the basis of secure knowledge." In fact, the papal administration in Rome had lost track of earlier decisions, and new papal decisions tended to duplicate or contradict earlier ones. Under Pope Alexander III (1159–81), it was thus determined that a letter had validity only if it contained a specific reference to previous letters on the same issue. Without this, the documents issued earlier would remain legally in force. Instead of explicitly mentioning all individual letters, one could also formulate a general statement that the pope was acting ex certa scientia. Claiming omniscience in such a formulaic way deprived all previous documents of their validity. What at first glance looks like an explicit tie to knowledge actually meant the very opposite: it was used especially when the pope himself had *no* complete knowledge of previous determinations and so was in no position to invoke them. It signified a detachment from such knowledge and from all possible normative restrictions in that matter. The decisive element of the formula hence was not "certain knowledge," but rather the absolute and imperative will of the pope. The formula of ex certa scientia quickly entered into the toolbox of rulers who wished to emphasize the sovereignty of their decision making. It soon formed part of the Castilian and French kings' edicts, the latter starting by expressing the king's "certaine science, pleine puissance & authorité Royale (certain knowledge, full power and royal authority)."

Many other formulaic postulates of knowledge served similar purposes. They helped either to derogate existing (local) law or to enhance the effectiveness of orders by anticipating any possible objection that the ruler might lack information or that he was wrongly informed. It was within the same logic that the Latin term *informatio* gained a new meaning in late medieval times. The term's old meaning of "teaching" or "instructing" was now complemented by a newer concept, in which informatio was closely connected to formal procedures. This novel understanding was supported by

the new inquisitorial procedures, which were based on strict interrogation, exact memoranda in writing, and the idea of a formal legal truth. Similar procedures in politics
and administration now fell into a sequence of three steps, whereby "information" was
first collected, then encapsulated in written records, and finally offered as basis for
making a rational and ostensibly objective decision—whether by a judge or a ruler. The
semantics of information was tied in with these practices so closely that the word could
designate all three stages of such an empirical procedure: its start (the interrogation),
the resulting document (the report), and finally the goal of being informed and having
mastery over that information. To a certain degree, the legacy of these procedures is
still perceptible in our modern concept of information, especially if we associate information with rationality and truth.

In China, as in the Ottoman Empire and Mughal India, bureaucratic administration
based on information gathering has a much longer history than in Europe. Since the
first century BCE China had a centralized administration that was staffed by a professional bureaucracy drawn from all strata of society after the introduction of the civil
service examination system. The administration, with the imperial chancellor at the
center, amassed statistics; figures on land and population; maps of the empire; reports
on harvests, banditry, and finances from all the provinces. The sources manifest little
reflection, however, about the specific character of these bureaucratic procedures and,
for that matter, about the semantic history of the Chinese term for information or knowledge. For the earlier periods it remains unclear if these administrative procedures were
an early expression of a certain empirical spirit in Chinese government and if they reflected philosophical notions of truth or rationality in practice. Roy Bin Wong has remarked that for viewing the history of Chinese state formation it is necessary to choose
a middle path between a Eurocentric model and Sinocentric exceptionalism. For him,
Chinese political aspirations were connected to the moral and material order of society. The central administration depended on local means of implementing morally fueled ideals of governance across the different parts of the empire.

DOES INFORMATION EQUAL POWER?
THE PRACTICE OF GOVERNING

Among the earliest rulers in Europe, it was the advisers of the Norman kings of Sicily
who in the twelfth century adapted techniques of administration from the Arabs, such
as the *diwan*, the bureau of the Ishmaelite caliphate. To establish a government, monarchs did not select its members by birth, strength, or wealth but preferred qualified
people who were able to read, write, and control the administrative procedures. The
Norman kings used an administration of this kind not only to collect taxes and exercise
control over land and populace, but also to reinforce, as Jeremy Johns has argued, an
autocratic and despotic monarchy in which the king's power was protected by the Arab
minority in the kingdom (and vice versa).

Starting with Pope Innocent III (1198–1216), the papal administration similarly underwent a process of refinement largely based on the Sicilian model. The apostolic chancellery and penitentiary were tasked with processing grievances and establishing a
professionalized procedure of supplication and response. In the early seventeenth
century, however, a more elaborate administration based on a system of nuncios and

legates was established to govern the different cities and territories of the papal state. Relatives of the pope often filled these posts.

In such regimes, however, officials whose duty it was to inform and advise a superior could extend their scope of participation and influence in a micropolitical environment. They were able to secure their position at court as skilled administrators while avoiding appearing too ambitious or powerful. In the Spanish Empire, for example, information was a means of regulating and controlling government over large distances. The metropolitan administration possessed a considerable amount of information about its most remote territories and subordinates. The more systematically such information had been collected, however—for instance, by using printed questionnaires—the less it was actually used in politics. What was used instead was the stream of correspondence from abroad, often sent by ordinary subjects. Such a practice had several advantages. It allowed the king to respond to actual needs at the periphery, needs that he could otherwise know of only on the basis of a dense and costly institutional network. And it established a low-cost system of mutual control on the ground, based on the subject's readiness to report deviant behavior to the Crown, which, in turn, set and maintained incentives for reporting. Such "triangles of vigilance" were extremely flexible and cost-effective and thus appropriate for colonial expansion. They did not, however, optimize the Crown's knowledge as channels were overloaded with information of private interests and full of contradictions.

The practice of government in China depended similarly on its administrative resources, which were more extensive than in Europe, but nonetheless limited for the purposes of a centralized state. Given its vast size, the Chinese Empire faced many of the same problems of rule as the Spanish Empire. Qing China (1644–1912) is a case in point. According to Wong, the creation of domestic order was a complex task, and the number of local officials was not sufficient for ruling across the whole of the empire. Rulers had to rely on collaboration with the local administration and gentry.

The local governments in the departments and districts of the Qing Empire provide one example of this dependency on local experts. There were—in simplified terms— two important groups of administrators, the magistrates and the clerks. Both had to adhere to the control of their superiors and had to abide by the code of administrative regulations issued by the Board of Civil Office in the central government. While the magistrates were outsiders recruited from among the graduates of the metropolitan or provincial examinations, the clerks were recruited from within the department or district and were of lower social status. This led to a typical conflict for all information-based governance systems: clerks had not only more local knowledge than the magistrates, but also more control over the exchange of documents, since it was the clerks who prepared and received the files. They could also manipulate the information and thus local government affairs. Furthermore, they monopolized information in the documents by declaring them secret, and they regarded private copies of, for example, land tax records as their private property. In Qing China, officials were thus classified according to their distance from the central administration and proximity to the people. Local officials were even addressed as *Fumuguan*, literally "father and mother officials," who had firsthand knowledge of the people's condition and of the administration's successes or failures.

Information thus played two central roles in early modern governments. On the one hand, it enabled the collector, keeper, and conveyor of information to achieve a position of power, and it could also function as a means of justifying an informed and rational rule. In some cases, information might help to make a decision. But on the other hand claiming to be informed also helped to keep the suspicion of arbitrariness at bay. The mere fact that a ruler or government accumulated information thus does not tell us to which of these ends such information was used in practice.

INFORMATION, GOVERNANCE, AND MODERN STATE BUILDING

At the outset of this article, it was argued that both concepts, information and governance, lack a clear definition and are therefore not easy to reconcile. Nonetheless, at first glance, the use of information in governance in order to achieve a more efficient, functional, and rational system of rule seems to fit compellingly into the narrative of the formation of the modern state.

Since Max Weber (1864–1920), historians have looked for structures, discourses, and mentalities that could be responsible for the formation of both the state and the loyal citizen-subject. Weber's articulation of the problem of modern state formation highlighted the role of bureaucracy and a certain rational administrative approach toward governance as the most important requirement. Information in the hand of bureaucrat-ministers and experts thus contributed to the undermining of charismatic and traditional forms of legitimate rule and helped to establish the third type of rule, rational-legal authority. Historians have followed this narrative, exploring the idea that the rational handling of information by administrations helped to form an impersonal state apparatus.

In drawing a comparison in English history between the eleventh-century Domesday Book, the great collection of information under William the Conqueror, and the Orwellian dystopia of total surveillance societies in the twentieth century, Edward Higgs challenged the Weberian interpretation. He grants that new systems of taxation and data collection enabled the modern state to consolidate its central power to an extent unknown to medieval and early modern rulers. Many sociological and historical accounts assume, he argued, that state information gathering is synonymous with the surveillance state and therefore connected with modernity. He points out, however, that historians of the period 1500 to 1800 often misinterpret the extent of information gathering, "mainly because they neglect the essentially decentralized nature of governance." For Higgs, Britain in the twentieth century shows that "although information gathering expanded rapidly in this period, the British state did not always prove itself to be the sort of rational, Weberian state that some sociologists would have us believe."

The multifaceted, practical uses of information prompt a reconsideration of not only the long-term narrative of the history of early modern state formation, but also other variations of informed governance in commercial enterprises and other networks, such as the early modern *Republic of Letters. Studies of early modern trade corporations such as the English and Dutch East India Companies underline the state-like nature of such enterprises largely based on their use of information in governance. Commercialization of information could thus create certain conditions that enabled the rise of colonialism and commercial empires based on epistemic supremacy over other societies.

The cases of local administration in Qing China and also in the early modern Spanish Empire illuminate the functions of information in binding local and imperial levels of government to each other. Chinese officials in the central administration had no access to information of local affairs, not only because they had too few magistrates and clerks to exercise direct control, but because it proved much more efficient to shape power into patterns of coordination, cooperation, and conflict. Nonetheless the limits of this form of long-distance administration surfaced, both in China and in the Spanish Empire, at the close of the early modern period. Grain seizures, tax resistance, and social revolutions were only three major factors responsible for the great transformation in governance experienced in nineteenth-century China and Europe. The Chinese imperial government proved unsuccessful in resisting foreign intervention and domestic challenges to central authority like the Taiping rebellion (1850–64).

Similar problems between the local and central administrative units can be observed in Europe. Governance in cities and church administration was much more efficient in controlling people by laws, statutes, and statistical records than were the large monarchical states in early modern times. Parish records, for example, "good public policy" ("gute Policey"), tax control, and supervision of schools and judicial affairs were managed closely and most of the time equally independent from the royal or imperial authorities as they were in Qing China. The interplay of information and governance thus enabled municipal autonomy, an independent clerical administration, and also the empowerment of the estates and thus helped to form self-governed polities in Europe. In China, however, as in Ottoman Turkey or the independent nation-states of postimperial America, the state struggled to uphold the older administrative functions during the period of transformation and was not able to successfully adapt them to the new political and social order. Instead, these polities turned to the Western model of governance.

Forms of political or economic governance in the modern era certainly used information in manifold and significant ways. Information was now systematically gathered and processed, stored in archives and desk drawers, and transformed into charts and tables, as well as finally called for, retrieved, and consulted at the hour of decision. It was an essential part of the tool kits of power. Such information management, however, did not always underpin good government or rational and efficient rule. The relatively fuzzy and open concept of governance asks us to put information into context. Doing so shows that information could serve very different and even contradictory ends. As we have seen, it could help to make a rational decision or to create the mere appearance of such decision making.

That both of these ways of using information could prove successful is visible in the case of the first circumnavigation the world, by Ferdinand Magellan. Antonio Pigafetta, one of the few survivors of the journey, reported that nobody on board really believed Magellan could find a passage to the Pacific. He then described how Magellan persuaded them to head onward nonetheless. Magellan pretended to have secret information about a small passage and told the sailors that he had seen that passage on a map made by the famous mapmaker Martin Behaim, a map that probably never existed. The illusion of information was sufficient for success in this case.

The historical instances we have chosen show that in many cases, the relations between information and the tasks of governance remained complex and obscure. Neither in China nor in Europe did the concepts of government make any reference to something like information. Only late in the Middle Ages did a semantic transformation set in that gave the term *information* something like its modern functional sense. Practices of government give an even more fragmented picture of how information was linked with rational government. The helmsman used information not only to determine the course of his ship, but also to secure the political order on board; and to achieve that second end a rhetorical claim of exact knowledge could prove more effective than the real thing.

Arndt Brendecke and Benjamin Steiner

See also bureaucracy; coins; documentary authority; memos; petitions; quantification; surveilling; surveys and censuses; teaching

FURTHER READING

Roger T. Ames, *The Art of Rulership: A Study of Ancient Chinese Political Thought*, 1994; Arndt Brendecke, *The Empirical Empire: Spanish Colonial Rule and the Politics of Knowledge*, 2009, translated by Jeremiah Riemer, 2016; T'ung-tsu Ch'ü, *Local Government in China under the Ch'ing* [1962], 1988; Herrlee Glessner Creel, *What Is Taoism? and Other Studies in Chinese Cultural History*, 1970; Edward Higgs, *The Information State in England: The Central Collection of Information on Citizens since 1500*, 2004; Jeremy Johns, *Arabic Administration in Norman Sicily: The Royal Diwan*, 2002; Edward Slingerland, *Effortless Action: Wu-wei as Conceptual Metaphor and Spiritual Ideal in Early China*, 2007; Roy Bin Wong, *China Transformed: Historical Change and the Limits of European Experience*, 1997.

GOVERNMENT DOCUMENTS

Archives have to do with government. Indeed, the word comes from the Greek *arkhḗ* (government) from *arkhō* (to rule). Government or governance by whom, for whom? This essay is restricted to government as the action of directing the affairs of a polity (state, province, city) and the people living there. Such government may be a democracy, a monarchy, an oligarchy, or a tyranny. Each of these is dependent on information. Much of that information is oral, stored by the human memory. This was the case in ancient Greece, but also in western Europe, after Roman culture and Roman script had been superseded by a *vernacular, oral tradition. The Carolingians reestablished documents as tools of government. However, for a long time the written word was regarded merely as a support for a memory trained in processing information orally. A document and its seal were considered to be memory-retaining objects. Only gradually did documents become records, providing evidence of events and transactions. By the eleventh century European emperors and kings were using documents for granting privileges, for sending letters, and occasionally for taxation (Domesday Book, 1086). The twelfth century settled the change "from memory to written record" (the title of Michael Clanchy's classic book).

The history of government documents has been studied for different rulers, at different times, and in various regions across the globe. One of the few general overviews was presented by Cornelia Vismann, while studies of pragmatic *literacy (i.e., literacy and the culture of writing not for literary but pragmatic purposes), social and cultural history, media archaeology, communication studies, political science, and so on are often valuable for the history of government documents. Other studies have dealt with specific *genres of government documents like documents for registering and identifying people, accounting, and propaganda. Studies on the history of government records and archives abound, most of them based on archivists' intimate knowledge of the material in their custody.

Very often government documents are treated as the tools of bureaucracies traditionally associated with the monarchies and empires of the late sixteenth and early seventeenth centuries. However, in this essay I focus on the history of the production and use of documents by and in the city—from the eleventh century to today's "smart city"—which may serve as a companion to the general history of government documents as information devices.

The communal age in western Europe began in the eleventh century with the creation of civic institutions in Milan, Rome, Pavia, and other Italian communities as well as (a bit later) in cities in Flanders. The level of urbanization was remarkable: by the late twelfth century there were some two hundred to three hundred city-states between the Alps and Naples. Management of documents in the Italian cities and (in the thirteenth century) in cities in the Low Countries focused on the city's foundation charters, privileges, treaties, and other charters. These were transcribed into the city's *liber iurium,* allowing the originals to be safely stored, mostly in the local church. Another early documentary genre was the book of statutes. For writing these books and other documents the city relied on religious institutions whose *clerici* acted as clerks to feudal lords and communes.

Beginning in the twelfth century and continuing in the thirteenth, Europe experienced a documentary revolution, caused by various factors. The first was the rapid increase in population and the allied need to regulate social interaction. Recent research considers the urge of city governors to prevent internal and external conflicts and to develop instruments for handling conflict as the main drive for pragmatic literacy. Documents constituted a "legible" citizen—several centuries before the state developed its panoptical gaze. The city deemed accurate registration necessary because citizens had other rights and obligations than noncitizens (residents) and because the status of people played an important role in conflicts with or about people from other cities. Also, for fiscal and military reasons the magistrate had to know who were citizens and who were not. Finally, the fees for granting citizenship had to be accounted for. At first the names of new citizens appear in the accounts of the town, but sooner or later separate citizens' registers were begun (Augsburg 1288, Bremen 1289, Kampen 1302, Cologne 1355, Luzern 1359).

Citizens wanted public accountability for the town's management, and this led to financial control, accounting, and recording. Civic officials surrendered their offices after short terms, but only after having left written memoranda for their successors. Archiving these served the continuity of government and the administration of justice, and this *"archival consciousness" was also influenced by the church's insistence on keeping written records. Another factor for the scriptural revolution was the extension of mercantile activities beyond the city. Trade and banking became an international endeavor in which much previously oral communication was replaced by writing.

Finally, newly established urban chanceries (in the Low Countries they appeared at the end of the thirteenth century) developed new documentary *genres and introduced new technologies (like the use of paper and the vernacular) to meet new information needs.

The revolution took place on two axes. Next to the cartularies (registers with transcripts of received documents), registers of outgoing charters began to be kept by state rulers and cities. Second, instead of the static keeping of charters, civic authorities developed practices of dynamic record keeping in the administration of executive, legislative, and judicial acts: registering new citizens; listing office bearers, soldiers, and guild members; keeping track of the exploitation of town assets; statutes, court proceedings, judgments; and so on. In cities regular accounts in book or roll form began to be kept.

Another cause of the scriptural revolution was the development of a new document genre for recording and retrieving information: the register. The technology of the book form (*codex) was, as we have seen, used to transcribe privileges and statutes. In the thirteenth century Italian cities invented a new usage for the book, in order to register all sorts of communal administration. Various specialized *libri communes* were set up: *liber bannorum* (banishments), *liber accusationum* (accused), *liber dispendii* (expenses), *liber debitorum* (debtors), and so on. In most cities these may originally have formed a component part of a general *liber civitatis*. Cities in northern Europe experienced a comparable differentiation of registers from the end of the thirteenth century, and their use increased thereafter. The Stralsund *liber civitatis* (1270) soon after its start divided the business of private debtors from town income and registered them separately (1278/88). The specialized registers developed often in connection with the differentiation of city government through the establishment of specific offices. All these registers formed one intertextual system in which one event (for example, the admittance of a new burgess) was recorded in several different registers. The accessibility of the registers was enhanced by the use of new technologies such as foliation, tabs (markers fixed to the fore edge of a codex), and alphabetical tables—little tools of knowledge first developed in the High Middle Ages by *Scholastic erudition and gradually introduced into chanceries. Further innovations in record keeping stretching into the *early modern period were the work of ingenious town clerks and the effect of manuals written by record managers like Jacob von Rammingen (1571).

A special category of government documents comprised the registration of acts of voluntary jurisdiction. In southern Europe this was done by *notaries public. In northern cities citizens appeared before the city bench to have their transfers of property and other acts witnessed and recorded (Cologne 1135, Ghent 1169). The difference between north and south, however, should not be overestimated, given the role of notaries as semiofficial scriveners in Italian cities. For example, in Bologna the *libri memoriales* were kept by notaries serving the city. The registers include private business transactions, with over a million entries in the years 1265–1399.

Very often the introduction of a town book coincided with the separation of the original charters from the business records. The charters were to be preserved in special repositories, but the administrative records were kept at hand in the registry, where they were stored in sacks and in cabinets with pigeonholes and drawers, or filed—literally by putting documents on a string (*filum*). The introduction of the book as an archiving technique led to the duality of *Urkunden* (charters) and *Akten* (records). This duality has had a significant effect because premodern and modern scholarship in diplomatics and medieval history focused on the charters while neglecting the other records.

The accounts were normally kept separate from the town register. The oldest city accounts in Italy date from the end of the twelfth century. In the beginning they were read aloud in public, like the city's bylaws. North of the Alps towns started keeping accounts from the second half of the thirteenth century. French and Flemish towns did so at the instruction of the king, but the magistrates in Lübeck (1262), Koblenz (1276), Dordrecht (1283), and Osnabrück (1285) did not need such a directive.

In England eleven towns are distinguished by the systematic keeping of records from before 1272. The earliest surviving civic records are the registers of guilds, later followed by court rolls of various kinds. Registration of deeds of title starts in Wallingford in 1231; the London Husting roll begins in 1252. In Ireland one finds rolls of admissions to the merchants' guild of Dublin from circa 1190 to 1265 and the rolls of admission of free citizens from the early thirteenth century.

Urban records were communal texts often read aloud and performed in public rituals. This social function is neglected by many writers who do not fully acknowledge that the creation, storage, and use of government documents were—and still are—social and cultural practices, embedded in and constituting communities of memory in cities.

The city registers served different purposes, as Prokop, a fifteenth-century city clerk of Prague, wrote in his manual: *ad bonum honestum, ad bonum utilem,* and *ad iustum.* In the first category—for the truly good, one might say serving accountability—were put the *liber memorialis* and the book of accounts. The second category—for expediency, or what we might call for the service of the community—consisted of the registers of real estate, of servants, of citizens, and of leases. Finally, the judicial registers addressed what was righteous. The three categories overlap: the registers in all three categories benefit the city and its citizens.

Every citizen could request a search of the registers or an extract from them, as regulated for example in Florence (1289) and Padua. In Siena (1298) the city government decreed that everyone could use all acts and documents and city registers for his own defense whenever he needed to prove his rights. In Venice and elsewhere, city registers were duplicated or even triplicated. One copy was accessible to the public but secured with a chain. Only later, when city government in Italy came under the control of lords, princes, and kings, did secrecy become the norm.

But secrecy was not absolute. For example, the Dutch East India Company (VOC) instructed its captains, mapmakers, and officials to keep the records secret from competitors, especially the British and the French. However, VOC directors had copies of journals and maps made for private use, and foreign agents acquired valuable information, profiting from the open information society that was the Dutch Republic. In Amsterdam information from all corners of the world was collected, exchanged and compiled, stored and analyzed; new information was created, and finally, information was disseminated from the city. Amsterdam and the other cities participating in the VOC (and in the West India Company) were hubs in an information network covering Southeast Asia, Asia Minor, West and South Africa, and large parts of the Americas and the Caribbean. Nodes in that network were trading posts and settlements developing into colonial cities. Administering these cities differed from governing metropolitan cities mainly because of the space-time distance to the mother country. The knowledge that an instruction or any other document would take several weeks or even months to arrive in the colony influenced the power relations in decision making and accountability. It left much freedom of action, which was curbed by imposing extensive documentation of the governance of the colonial city.

Like any colonial state, the Netherlands was an information-hungry machine. In the 1860s both the Ministry of Colonial Affairs and the General Secretariat in Batavia (now Jakarta) were reorganized, mirroring each other in competencies and processes, including their filing systems. The head of the General Secretariat resembled the chief (colonial) secretary in the British colonies. These colonial secretariats survived decolonization as a model for the state secretariat in the independent states.

Record-keeping practices also survived decolonization. Just as the British had built their regime of surveillance and control over India on the elaborate written procedures of the Mughals, many of the bureaucratic inscriptional practices from the colonial period have remained in the contemporary period, as Matthew Hull convincingly demonstrates in his case study of the governance of Islamabad. Hull's book is titled *Government of Paper,* referring to the enduring reliance by bureaucrats and citizens on the materiality of paper and other graphic artifacts.

Following the rise of unified dynastic states in Europe in the sixteenth and seventeenth centuries, the majority of self-governing cities had to yield most of their powers to the state. Outside Europe, the state left much of the actual urban administration to the nonstate sector. This is apparent, as Ebru Boyar shows (in *The Oxford Handbook of Cities in World History*), in the administration of Ottoman cities (Cairo, Damascus, Aleppo, Baghdad, Thessaloniki, Belgrade, and others), which "centred round a troika of Istanbul-appointed officials: the *bey* (the top provincial official), the *kadi* (judge/administrator), and the *subaşi* (the official in charge of security). Other important officials appointed by the center were the *muhtesib* (the market inspector) and the *mültezim* (tax collector), together with the *mimarbaşi* (the buildings inspector). Below them came the deputies and other administrators, locals appointed by the Istanbul-appointed officials." Apart from these officials, there were also nonofficial elements that played an essential role in the running of the city: corporate bodies such as the *guilds, religious and ethnic bodies, and pious foundations. The *kadi* representing the sultan was the main channel for the information flow from Istanbul to the city and vice versa. Of course, the farther from Istanbul, the more "autonomy" an urban community would enjoy. Extensive record keeping not only bridged the distance from Istanbul but also kept the citizens under surveillance and control. The combination of vertical control by the sultanate and a horizontal network of local communal institutions and "civil society" made the Ottoman Empire into one of the best-administered empires of the premodern and early modern era.

Comparable to the role of nonstate agency in the Ottoman city is the way in Japan aggregated bodies of merchant delegates functioned in urban administration. At the start of the eighteenth century the urbanization rate may have reached over 15 percent (only the Netherlands, and England and Wales had urban densities as great as Japan). In Edo many administrative functions were entrusted to the senior councilors (*rōjū*), who constituted the chief policy-making board in the shogunate. They, in turn, as James McClain writes in *The Oxford Handbook of Cities in World History*, "relied on a variety of samurai functionaries, most notably the city magistrates (*machi bugyō*), . . . to oversee day-to-day activities in commoner neighbourhoods, punish violent criminals, and sit in judgement on important civil lawsuits and petitions." In the neighborhoods, merchants and artisans carried out various administrative functions, supported by an elaborate set of offices. One of these was the neighborhood chief who, among other things, maintained property and census records.

Thus, in the Ottoman cities, in Japan, but also in premodern China, a large part of urban administration was executed by nonstate agents. The documents they created were strictly speaking not government documents, but rather governance documents. The boundaries between the two were blurred. That is also the case today, as an effect of the privatization and outsourcing of public functions, and the growing impact business has on civic life. That public-private osmosis (or intrusion) is intensified by modern information and communication technologies.

These technologies subject the "legible" citizen/customer/client to the panoptical gaze of various governmental agencies and commercial parties. The "datafication" of people happens through the continuous and mostly automated collection, organization, and combination of data concerning people's activities in society. Modern "smart cities" are datafied cities: all activities, situations, incidents, conversations, and interactions are being turned into data. Political scientist Albert Meijer proposes the concept of the "datapolis": a public governance perspective on the smart city "understood as a complex set of interactions between private, public and civil society actors. They all have systems for collecting and processing data and they also exchange and use data from other actors. Governance of the smart city is not only about public structures but about influencing all these interactions in modern cities."

The content, structure, and form of *digital documents exist not in or on a physical medium, but embedded in a digital representation, which serves as a generator for various ways in which the document can be made visible. Digital documents are *potential* documents, coming into existence only by virtue of software that understands how to access and display them. The software sooner or later becomes obsolete, which necessitates "refreshing" the documents through migration or other techniques. Moreover, a digital document may contain links to other documents; it is variable and changeable, fluid and unstable, and links themselves decay rapidly. The document often resides in *the cloud or in a third-party backup service, out of control of its creator(s). Thus, ensuring access to digital documents over time is an enormous challenge. Only by meeting that challenge can society ensure that government documents continue to serve accountability, community, and righteousness—the three goals of record keeping identified by Prokop, the Prague city clerk in the fifteenth century.

This summary of the history of government documents in cities deals with issues that are relevant in research of the history of government documents more generally. Such research has to answer diachronically questions such as, Which government or institution are we dealing with, at what time? Which were the documentary genres? How were documents created, used, and managed? Who were the agents in these processes? Considering the production of documents one may ask, What were the societal factors driving the increase or decrease of the volume of documents and also the differentiation of genres and documentary practices? Documents are produced to be used: By whom, for what purposes? How can information from the documents be retrieved? The intertextuality of documents and their interaction with citizens are also central to their use and storage. In the production and use of documents, public agents use media and technologies that shape the documents but also shape governmental action and citizens' behavior.

Government documents are the instruments for public authorities, both for their internal organization and for the provision of services to society, but also for their disciplinary and surveillance power. In a totalitarian system these documents gain fearful power, the power George Orwell prophesied in his *1984*. Even when these documents provide evidence of oppression in their original contexts, in a "second life" they also serve as evidence required to gain freedom, evidence of wrongdoing, and evidence for reconciliation and restoration of justice.

Eric Ketelaar

See also accounting; archivists; art of memory; bureaucracy; data; files; governance; memos; newsletters; registers; scrolls and rolls; secretaries; surveilling; surveys and censuses

FURTHER READING

Paul Bertrand, *Documenting the Everyday in Medieval Europe: The Social Dimensions of a Writing Revolution 1250–1350*, 2019; Michael T. Clanchy, *From Memory to Written Record: England 1066–1307*, 2nd ed., 1993; Peter Clark, ed., *The Oxford Handbook of Cities in World History*, 2013; Matthew S. Hull, *Government of Paper: The Materiality of Bureaucracy in Urban Pakistan*, 2016; Eric Ketelaar, "Records Out and Archives In: Early Modern Cities as Creators of Records and as Communities of Archives," *Archival Science* 10, no. 3 (2010): 201–10; Albert Meijer, "Datapolis: A Public Governance Perspective on 'Smart Cities,'" *Perspectives on Public Management and Governance* 1, no. 3 (2018): 195–206; Cornelia Vismann, *Akten: Medientechnik und Recht*, 2000; shortened English edition, translated by Geoffrey Winthrop-Young: *Files: Law and Media Technology*, 2008.

HOROSCOPES

The casting of horoscopes, diagrams containing information about the position of celestial bodies at a specific time and place that were consulted and reinterpreted over centuries, has a long history that goes back to antiquity: its origins can be firmly placed in ancient Babylonia, from where astrological practice spread to Egypt, Greece, and the Roman and Abbasid Empires, stretching as far east as India. After being condemned by the Christian emperors as a pagan divinatory practice in the fourth century CE, and having temporarily been eclipsed from sight within the confines of the Roman Empire by the sixth century, astrology and the casting of horoscopes flourished again in medieval and *Renaissance Europe starting in the twelfth century, arguably reaching its peak in popularity in the late fifteenth and sixteenth centuries. Twelfth-century Iberia represents the cradle of this revival, as a significant number of Arabic and Judaic astrological texts were first translated into Latin here and later disseminated across Europe through manuscript and print. By the fourteenth century, astrology was firmly embedded in the university curriculum of many European universities, and the casting of annual astrological predictions and natal horoscopes was one of the routine tasks assigned to Italian university professors teaching the science of the stars.

The Hellenistic origin of casting horoscopes is clearly revealed by the modern-day term, which derives from the Greek *hōroskopos*, from *hōra*, "hour," and *skopos*, "observer." As the composite word suggests, the term refers to the observation of a specific time, more precisely to the mapping of the position of the heavenly bodies in the sky in a particular place at a particular time.

From the Middle Ages onward the mapping of the heavenly bodies was generally represented by a figure made up of three squares, each inscribed within the other (in the sixteenth century a different form of visualization, made up of a circle and some lunettes, became a fashionable albeit less common alternative) (figures 1 and 2). While the central square contained vital information for the casting of horoscopes such as the name and place, day, and time of birth of a client, or the place and time of an event, the twelve equilateral triangles that framed the central square divided the horoscope in "houses," each with a specific meaning and quality. In astrology, the houses represent sections of the ecliptic plane, the circle on the celestial sphere representing the sun's apparent path throughout the year. The constellations of the zodiac (and the corresponding astrological signs) are distributed along a nine-degree band on either side of the ecliptic. The intersection of the ecliptic with the eastern horizon marks the cusp of the first house, called the ascendant (also called the degree of the horoscope), followed by the other houses moving counterclockwise. There was a wide range of methods that could be adopted to calculate house divisions, including the very popular system of the tenth-century Arab astrologer Alcabitus (al-Qabīsī, d. AD 967), and the less popular one of equal houses suggested by the Latin writer and astrologer Julius Firmicus Maternus (fourth century AD), which was later adopted by the Renaissance *polymath Girolamo

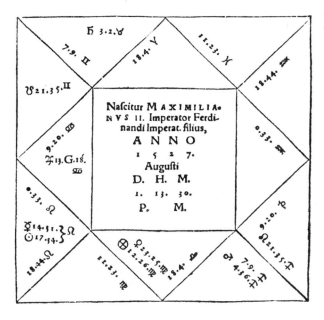

ALIVD THEMA COELI, QVOD NON.
NVLLI TRIBVVNT INVICTISSIMO
IMPERATORI MAXIMILIANO II.

Nafcitur MAXIMILIA-
NVS II. Imperator Ferdi-
nandi Imperat. filius,
ANNO
1 5 2 7.
Augufti
D. H. M.
1. 13. 30.
P. M.

Figure 1. Horoscope of Emperor Maximilian II, August 1, 1527 (square). Johannes Garcaeus, *Astrologiae methodus* (Basileae: Ex Officina Henricpetrina, 1576), n.p. Biblioteca Nacional de Espana.

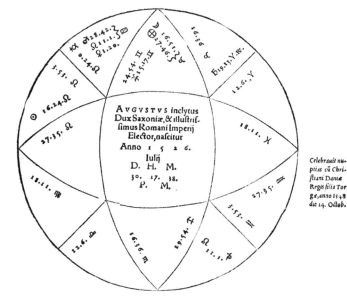

AVGVSTVS inclytus
Dux Saxoniæ, & illuftrif-
fimus Romani Imperij
Elector, nafcitur
Anno 1 5 2 6.
Iulij
D. H. M.
30. 17. 38.
P. M.

*Celebrauit nu-
ptias cũ Chri-
ftiani Daniæ
Regis filia Tor
ge, anno 1548
die 14. Octob.*

Figure 2. Horoscope of Emperor Maximilian II (round). Johannes Garcaeus, *Astrologiae methodus* (Basileae: Ex Officina Henricpetrina, 1576), n.p. Biblioteca Nacional de Espana.

Cardano (1501–76). A lively debate ensued in the Renaissance about the preferred method of house division, as different methods, clearly, led to different interpretations of the chart.

Within the triangles representing the twelve houses, the astrologer mapped the degree and sign of each cusp as well as the precise location of the heavenly bodies by sign and degree. In order to plot planets and stars within the horoscope, astrologers rarely relied on direct observation. Rather, from an early time, astronomers produced tables of houses indicating the zodiacal locations of the house cusps and tables of ephemerides providing the positions of the planets by calendar date and time of day. The use of these tables and basic mathematical computation allowed astrologers to determine the positions of the stars and planets for a particular place and time to be transferred onto a horoscope chart.

The interpretation of this celestial information is based on the basic principle not only that the stars and planets exerted a distinctive influence over the world below, but also that they interacted and influenced one another in specific ways. The interpretation of the astrologer's chart thus centered on a complex web of relationships between the planets and the luminaries (the Sun and the Moon), the signs of the zodiac in which these were placed, and their astrological houses. A further element was that of the angular relationships between the planets, the so-called aspects, which determined their reciprocal influence, which could be positive, neutral, or negative.

This specific set of data, and the complex rules of interpretation that accompanied it, constituted the raw material of the astrologer, whose skill was to translate celestial information into a meaningful narrative that could explain or predict things as varied as the character and physical complexion of a person, major life events such as illnesses or professional successes and setbacks, the length of a person's life, or, alternatively, determine the most favorable moment to undertake an action. The latter practice, called elections, had a distinctly Arabic pedigree and was very popular in the Renaissance, especially among the elites. Elections were often used to choose the most propitious time for the celebration and consummation of a marriage, for initiating warfare, to start a journey, or to place the foundation stone of a building. Thus people, but also cities and buildings, had their own horoscopes, each telling a specific story and each worthy of analysis, interpretation, and reinterpretation (figure 3).

It is no exaggeration to say that horoscopes were gold mines of information related to the event that the astrologer set out to investigate. While individuals' birth charts (also called *genitures*) remained the most popular form of horoscope, there was no limit to what the astrologer could investigate. To this effect, we have ample evidence that buildings and cities possessed horoscopes. Historical reports by the Muslim geographer and historian Aḥmad al-Yaʿqūbī (d. 897 CE) and the polymath astronomer Aḥmad al-Bīrūnī (973–1050 CE) preserve written "horoscopes" for Baghdad and al-Mahdiyya in Tunis, with al-Bīrūnī adding the actual chart of Baghdad, on the basis of which, it was said, astrologers had incorrectly predicted that no caliph would ever die in that city. The death of two caliphs, al-Amīn (d. 813) and al-Mutawakkil (d. 861), in the city later gave ample ammunition to the detractors of astrology, who often cited these cases to cast doubt on the discipline.

Buildings, much like cities, also merited horoscopes, a practice that is documented both for medieval Islam and for Renaissance Italy. It is significant to notice that both the Roman architect Vitruvius and the Renaissance architect and polymath Leon Battista Alberti included astronomical and astrological concepts in their architectural texts. Vitruvius openly instructed the architect to understand the heavens in order to choose the best site in which to situate a building as, he believed, celestial influence would determine the optimal or suboptimal characteristics of the edifice. Similarly, Alberti referred to the radiation of the stars when discussing how to choose a healthy site, plac-

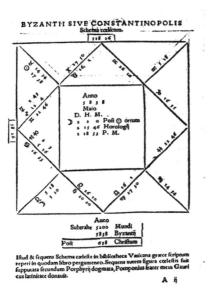

Figure 3. Horoscope of the foundation of Byzantium, May 2, 638. Luca Gauricus, *Tractatus astrologicus* (Venice: Bartholomaeus Caesanus, 1552), fol. 2r. Bibliothèque nationale de France.

ing particular importance on the moment when construction commenced. Following these principles, Pope Julius II founded the new St. Peter's Basilica on a specific day and at a specific time, more precisely on April 18, 1506, at 10:00 a.m., in a clear attempt to coordinate Heavens and Earth and refound the church at the most auspicious time (figure 4). Julius apparently chose a date that had a profound meaning for the original edifice, which was founded by Constantine on the movable feast Sabbato in albis, the first Saturday after Easter. The same feast in 1506 fell on April 18, thus marking the ritual rebirth of the most important church of Christianity. While the date could not be chosen astrologically, the time was selected carefully to make the *cardines* of the chart (the cusps of the four angular houses, which are the most powerful) coincide with those of the birth horoscope of Christ. The planet Mercury, generally associated with Christianity, moreover, was placed in the powerful tenth house, or Midheaven, together with the benevolent Sun and Venus. The foundation horoscope, moreover, correlated with the pope's own birth horoscope, thus creating an ideal set of celestial relationships between Christ, St. Peter's, and Julius's birth chart.

Years later, when the construction of the basilica was floundering, the Neapolitan astrologer Luca Gaurico proposed a rectified chart that placed the time at 9:21 a.m. Mercury was still favorably placed in the tenth house, but Jupiter, the benevolent planet that was originally in the second house, that of wealth, had moved to the third house, that of siblings. This, for Gaurico, represented one factor that could explain why the construction of St. Peter's had stalled.

Together with birth, death was also a common object of investigation. It was not unusual for astrologers to be asked to calculate the duration of life of a client or a client's enemy. Numerous cases can be documented for the Renaissance, the most notorious of which was probably that of another pope, Urban VIII, whose death was predicted astrologically in 1630. The rumor mill generated by this prediction came to an abrupt end when the pope ordered the incarceration of those whom he deemed responsible, and particularly of the unfortunate Orazio Morandi, the abbot of the convent of Santa

Figure 4. Horoscope of the new foundation of
St. Peter's Basilica under Julius II, April 18, 1506.
Luca Gauricus, *Tractatus astrologicus* (Venice: Bartholomaeus Caesanus, 1552), fol. 6r. Bibliothèque
nationale de France.

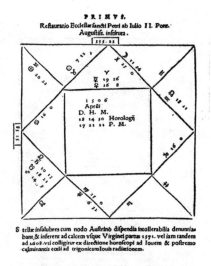

Prassede in Rome, who was deemed responsible for fueling the rumors. The case generated abundant documentation and was punctuated by the unfortunate and rather suspicious death of Morandi only a few months into the trial.

As this brief series of examples illustrates—and many more could be cited—horoscopes
were used as sources of valuable information. As maps of the past, present, and future
open to interpretation and reinterpretations, horoscopes constituted crucial sources of
information that required skillful interpretation, but this process of interpretation was
not necessarily completely reliable, let alone without risk. As the Morandi case demonstrates, making sensitive astrological information publicly available to third parties had
the potential of having practical repercussions for those who manipulated this information for their own ends and handled it inappropriately.

Monica Azzolini

See also diagrams; error; forecasting; learning; maps; observing; teaching

FURTHER READING

Monica Azzolini, *The Duke and the Stars: Astrology and Politics in Renaissance Milan*, 2013; Tamsyn
    Barton, *Ancient Astrology*, 1994; Brendan Dooley, *Morandi's Last Prophecy and the End of Renais-
    sance Politics*, 2002; Anthony Grafton, *Cardano's Cosmos: The Worlds and Works of a Renaissance
    Astrologer*, 1999; Darin Hayton, *The Crown and the Cosmos: Astrology and the Politics of Maximil-
    ian*, 2015; Mary Quinlan-McGrath, *Influences: Art, Optics and Astrology in the Italian Renaissance*,
    2013; Michael Ryan, *A Kingdom of Stargazers: Astrology and Authority in the Late Medieval Crown
    of Aragon*, 2011; George Saliba, "The Role of the Astrologer in Medieval Islamic Society," *Bulletin
    d'études orientales* 44 (1992): 45–67.

INDEXING

In a dedication preceding his *Natural History* (70s CE), Pliny the Elder speculates modestly that the emperor Titus might have more important things to do than to read the vast work from start to finish:

> As it was my duty in the public interest to have consideration for the claims upon your time, I have appended to this letter a table of contents of the several books [*quid singulis contineretur libris*: what is contained in the individual books], and have taken very careful precautions to prevent your having to read them. You by these means will secure for others that they will not need to read right through them either, but only look for the particular point that each of them wants, and will know where to find it.

The listing that follows breaks down the *Natural History* effectively into chapters, giving topics in the order they appear, each epitomized in a phrase, for example, "The world—is it finite? is it one? its shape; its motion; reason for its name." This is not the first table of contents in antiquity; indeed Pliny notes that he took the idea from Valerius Soranus's *Epoptides* (now lost; meaning is debated, perhaps: Initiated Women). Nevertheless, Pliny's description of it expresses nicely both the point of an index—readers' time is finite, and in much of our reading we need only part of a book, not the whole thing—and the basic principles of indexing: abstraction and arrangement. The table represents the work in miniature, with its captions naming the parts of the text that they stand in for. At the same time, because it mirrors the structure of the main work, the table indicates where to go to see any of its entries expanded. An item near the start of table can be traced to a location near the start of the work, and so on.

This brings us up against the difference between what, in modern terminology, we would speak of as a table of contents and an index proper. Both, we might say, are the products of *indexing*—they both work by abstraction and arrangement—but in the former, the arrangement comes ready-made: it is one of similarity with its referent; in the latter, however, the terms are reorganized, most commonly into alphabetical order, so that the ordering, in relation to the source, is arbitrary. By severing the relationship between content and arrangement, remapping the material instead onto a sequence that any literate person will have learned during his or her schooling, alphabetical order offers a universal, text-independent navigation system for verbal information. What may feel intuitive to us has certainly not always seemed so, and we can find instructions for use prefaced in alphabetically arranged works as late as Robert Cawdrey's English dictionary, *A Table Alphabeticall*, of 1604: "Nowe if the word, which thou art desirous to finde, begin with (a) then looke in the beginning of this Table, but if with (v) looke towards the end."

Clay tablets discovered in northern Syria have shown that the sequencing of the letters in the Ugaritic alphabet—which carries through to the Hebrew and Greek, and ultimately Roman alphabets—was established by the middle of the second millennium BCE. In Hebrew, we can see this order structuring some of the acrostic sections of the Hebrew Bible—the book of Lamentations, for example, and several of the psalms. In Greek, abecedaria—that is, simply, rows of the letters of the alphabet in order—have been discovered dating from the eighth century BCE onward. However, the *use* of alphabetical order in Greece—other than as an aid for the acquisition of basic *literacy— seems not to have come until rather later. The rise of the alphabetically ordered list, spreading out from Alexandria during the third century BCE, has led to the suggestion that it was developed in response to the vastness of the newly founded library there, a way of bringing the collection under control. Our first significant instance of indexing, then, comes in the form of not a book index, but a library catalog.

Compiled around the middle of the third century, the *Pinakes* of Callimachus (ca. 303–240 BCE) was a huge bibliography that is said to have taken up 120 rolls itself. Although only short fragments of the original work survives, we can derive a sense of its arrangement from the couple of dozen fragmentary references to it in other works. From these we can deduce that it was organized firstly into *genre—rhetoric, law, epic, tragedy, and so on—and within these classes, authors were arranged alphabetically by name. Under each name, Callimachus listed biographical information relating to that author (e.g., father's name, birthplace, nickname, profession), followed by a list of their works, distinguished into genuine and spurious, along with their first few words and their length in lines. Rolls in the library would have been stored in racks of pigeon-holes, and it has been suggested that these shelves would have been labeled with tablets (Greek *pinakes*) indicating genre and author. If this is the case, Callimachus's title nicely expresses the spatial relationship between an index and its referent: what you see *here* can be found *there*.

Thus, in antiquity, we find both alphabetical order and the table of contents. The tools of indexing are in place, and yet it will be a long time before the arrival of the book index proper. Although certain works, notably glossaries, were organized alphabetically during the first millennium of the Common Era, ordering beyond the initial letter (so that, for example, *ant* comes necessarily after *aardvark*) seems to have been lost in western Europe. When Papias the Lombard boasts, in the mid-eleventh century, that his dictionary, the *Elementarium doctrinae rudimentum* (Basic rudiments of learning), is alphabetical to the third letter, he is able to claim this as an innovation. Papias's precision will be important, a century and a half later, when the arrival of two institutions—the universities and the mendicant orders—will necessitate a new way of reading, more like the one envisaged by Pliny of his time-poor emperor.

As the requirements of preaching and teaching demanded a more efficient type of reading than the meditative monastic mode, the decades around the turn of the thirteenth century saw an extraordinary series of innovations on the page. Mary and Richard Rouse reel off a few of these—"running heads, chapter heads in red, initials in alternating red and blue, different sized initials, marked paragraphs, references, names of cited authors"—but the same moment also sees the division of the books of the Bible into chapters, accomplished by the English cleric Stephen Langton in around 1200. With this chaptering in place as a suitable locator, the stage was set for the first great indexing milestone of the Middle Ages, the Bible *concordance.

The first concordance to the Bible was compiled by the friars of the Dominican priory of St. Jacques in Paris. The work was begun under the direction of Hugh St-Cher, dating it to between 1230 and 1235, and completed no later than 1247. Using Langton's Bible chapters and then applying a further subdivision into sevenths, labeled *a* to *g*, the concordance gives roughly 129,000 locators for around ten thousand keywords. Some leaves of preparatory materials, discovered as binding waste, show how the labor was divided up, with different parts of the alphabet compiled in different hands. These notes were collated, their ordering tightened up, and then retranscribed in full, so that the finished work runs from *A, a, a* (an exclamation usually translated as *Alas*) through to *Zorobabel*.

The St. Jacques Concordance uses a large amount of abbreviation so that the entire work can be crammed into a single volume. Nevertheless, it suffers from a significant drawback (one that still dogs bad indexes today). Entries are presented as single, undifferentiated lists of locators, often running to the hundreds. A reader wishing to track down a particular instance of the word *Deus* (*God*) or *Peccatum* (*Sin*) will find the St. Jacques Concordance almost useless as a time-saver. And so, a few decades later, a second concordance was produced, again at St. Jacques, this time by the Englishman Richard of Stavensby and his accomplices, hence its name, the Concordantiae Anglicanae or English Concordance. The innovation of the second concordance was to include, for each reference, a few words of context: the phrase in which the given term appeared. So, for example, the first entry for *Regnum* (*Kingdom*) appears as "Gen. x.c. fuit autem principium .R. eius Babilon et arach," telling us that it appears just before the mid-point of Genesis 10, in a sentence that runs (to use the King James translation), "And the beginning of his kingdom was Babel, and Erech." Essentially, this is what we would now call a keyword-in-context or KWIC index: a snippet view of the surrounding text.

The drawback here is that each reference, formerly a simple abbreviated locator, has ballooned into a whole line of information. With over a hundred thousand of these, the English Concordance was, of necessity, a large, multivolume work, far from portable, and too cumbersome to be convenient. A third version, then, whose contextual passages were limited to four or five words, was compiled and completed by 1286. Neither too small nor too big, it was the Third Concordance that would become the model for Bible concordances for centuries to come.

In 1230, just as the friars of St. Jacques were beginning the first concordance, across the channel in Oxford, the scientist and theologian Robert Grosseteste was applying the principles of abstracting and arrangement in a rather different way, compiling not an index to a single book, but one that would map the great swathe of his *encyclopedic reading. Unlike the word index of the Dominicans, Grosseteste's was a true subject index, one that identified several hundred topics, such as *fate*, or *tithes*, or *the unity of God*. For each of these, Grosseteste devised a small but distinctive glyph (the symbol for *imagination*, for example, is a six-petaled flower) that he could then jot in the margin whenever he encountered a particular topic. Scanning these margins, Grosseteste was then able to compile a master record of all the appearances of each icon. Now in the Bibliothèque municipale de Lyon, what survives of Grosseteste's Tabula (MS 414 ff. 17–32) shows the entries for the first few dozen of these entries. The arrangement is not alphabetical, but rather topics are grouped into nine major classes: *God, creatures, the holy* *scriptures*, and so on. Under each topic, a list of scriptural and patristic references appears first, with classical and Arabic texts in a separate section to the side.

Thus, by the middle of the thirteenth century we have both alphabetical and topical indexing. Over the next century, the two will come to be commonly applied together, with readers writing indexes into their own books, and using foliation or preexisting divisions of the text as locators. Papal records from the 1320s show payments being made for the compilation of tables—indexing had become a profession—and when print arrives, it is not uncommon for incunables essentially to reissue the work of earlier indexers. The index to Caxton's *Polychronicon* (A chronicle of many ages) of 1482, for example, is drawn from a Latin manuscript of Higden's text and simply translated into English (without being fully realphabetized, so that some entries end up under the wrong letter). The first printed index appears in Fust and Schöffer's edition of Augustine's *De arte praedicandi* (On the art of preaching) (Mainz, no later than 1465), but of greater moment perhaps is another work printed five years later. The *Sermo ad populum predicabilis* (Sermon ready to be preached to the people) (Cologne, 1470) is a short printed sermon in which a printed numeral—a folio number, forerunner to the page number—appears in the right-hand margin of every recto page. As Margaret Smith has shown, printed foliation or pagination was not widely adopted until the early sixteenth century; nevertheless, the innovation was a crucial one for indexing. Different manuscript copies of the same work rarely have the same pagination, so manuscript indexes rely for their locators either on shared textual divisions (book; chapter) that lack granularity, or on foliation that is copy specific. Printed pagination, stable across the whole print run of an edition, meant that *any* text came already provided with a uniform, highly granular system of locators. As long as they were using the same edition, page 16 would be the same for any reader, whether they were in Venice, Paris, or Oxford.

The story of the index in the print era has been one of deepening complexity and growing pervasiveness. From the late sixteenth century, indexes begin their migration from the front to the back of our books, while standardization affects the syntax of keywords such that, by the late nineteenth century, Lewis Carroll can spoof it in his index to *Sylvie and Bruno* (1889), for example, "Scenery, enjoyment of, by little men." Following a period of proliferation (for example, the multiple indexes of Alexander Pope's *Iliad*, with separate tables for "Persons and Things," "Fables," "Characters," "Speeches," "Descriptions," and "Similes") index form contracts into the single consolidated table we generally find today. Alongside these developments, there is also an emerging anxiety that the convenience that Pliny foresaw—that we would not need to read right through our books—is in some way dangerous, undermining deeper modes of reading or learning. We find it in Pope's jibe that "index-learning turns no student pale," as well as in Galileo's dig at "that herd who, . . . in order to acquire a knowledge of natural effects, do not betake themselves to ships or crossbows or cannons, but retire into their studies and glance through an index or a table of contents to see whether Aristotle has said anything about them." The convenience of the index, and its efficiency as a mode of information retrieval, is seen as a threat to other, older modes of reading.

Nevertheless, the march of the index has been irrepressible, and efficient retrieval as important an object for Chinese lexicographers of the twentieth century and for the architects of the *digital revolution as it was for the Dominicans of the late Middle Ages. In China, the index movement spearheaded by Wan Guoding in the 1920s addressed itself to the problem of ordering in a character system that is nonalphabetic. Multiple approaches have subsequently been adopted based on, for example, the simplified description of the shapes found in the corners of a given character (the four corner method). In the *big data age, meanwhile, we find Google summarizing the two basic operations of its flagship search product as "Crawling and Indexing." The latter is explained with the aid of a familiar model: "It's like the index in the back of a book—with an entry for every word seen on every web page we index." The friars of St. Jacques would surely recognize the approach; so too would those veteran detractors, the Galileos and the Alexander Popes. In the era of the digital index, out of sight, but underpinning every search we perform online or on our laptops, this anxiety—that attentive, sustained "deep" reading is under threat—is being felt with a new keenness.

Dennis Duncan

See also books; data; files; learning; libraries and catalogs; lists; readers; storage and search; teaching

FURTHER READING

Rudolf Blum, *Kallimachos: The Alexandrian Library and the Origins of Bibliography*, translated by Hans H. Wellisch, 1991; Lloyd W. Daly, *Contributions to a History of Alphabetization in Antiquity and the Middle Ages*, 1967; Joseph A. Howley, *Aulus Gellius and Roman Reading Culture: Text, Presence, and Imperial Knowledge in the "Noctes Atticae,"* 2018; Mary A. Rouse and Richard H. Rouse, "La Naissance des index," in *Histoire de l'édition française*, edited by Henri-Jean Martin and Roger Chartier, 4 vols. (1983), 1:77–85; Margaret M. Smith, "Printed Foliation: Forerunner to Printed Page-Numbers?," *Gutenberg-Jarhbuch* 63 (1988): 54–70; Hans H. Wellisch, "Incunabula Indexes," *Indexer* 19, no. 1 (1994): 3–12; Francis J. Witty, "The Beginnings of Indexing and Abstracting: Some Notes toward a History of Indexing and Abstracting in Antiquity and the Middle Ages," *Indexer* 8, no. 4 (1973): 193–98.

INFORMATION, DISINFORMATION, MISINFORMATION

To speak of the history of information is to conjure something that is present in all the periods and places that can be said to have histories, whether or not they happen to have had a word for it. But the appearance of the word does suggest that society had "entered into the self-conscious possession of a new concept," as the historian Quentin Skinner puts it. Thus, in what follows, I'll focus on the English word *information*, and particularly on the American setting. The development of its cognates in other nations and other Western languages was roughly parallel, though with some differences.

Over the eighteenth and nineteenth centuries, "information" was elevated to a kind of communication that played a crucial role in public life. At the same time, it was being reconceived as a self-sufficient and autonomous agent, as something "present" in the world. This is the sense of the word that we have in mind when we speak of information as essential to the health of democratic societies—something distinct from the kind of "information" we get from a weather channel, though the two are connected in important ways. It is the former sort of information that we have in mind when we speak of misinformation.

In the eighteenth century, excluding its legal meanings, *information* oscillated between two relevant primary senses. It could refer to an impression on the mind, "the formation or moulding of the mind or character," as the *Oxford English Dictionary* puts it—and particularly, to the moral education instilled by reading (a meaning that was sometimes glossed with Latin *educatio*). As Emerson wrote in "The American Scholar," "great and heroic men have existed, who had almost no other information than by the printed page."

Through association with books and print, information came to denote their content, via a metonymy of "cause for effect"—that is, it was what induced the "information" of mind and character. The eighteenth-century essayist Vicesimus Knox pronounced his era "this age of information," noting that the ease of acquisition of books made oral instruction (and, by extension, the university) less necessary. As such, the diffusion of information assumed a public importance; in *The Idler*, Samuel Johnson wrote: "National conduct ought to be the result of national wisdom, a plan formed by mature consideration and diligent selection out of all the schemes which may be offered and all the information which can be procured."

That view of the role of information was the kernel of the modern understanding that emerged in the nineteenth century. In "The Storyteller," Walter Benjamin described information as a "form of communication" that emerged with "the full control of the middle class, which has the press as one of its most important instruments in fully developed capitalism." This description points to the two conditions that the modern phenomenon of information rests on: the rise of a large middle-class citizenry and the appearance of new forms of representation that served its interests. Benjamin is among those who stress the appearance of the modern mass newspaper—ostensibly apolitical, increasingly "objective" and professionalized, uniform in style and organization, and sold to a vast readership for a low price on a copy-by-copy basis.

But the new notion of information was also connected to the appearance of the modern "reference work," such as the "national" dictionaries and *encyclopedias of Brockhaus, Webster, and Larousse. It battened, too, on the census reports, parliamentary blue books, and other government publications that engendered what the philosopher Ian Hacking has described as "the avalanche of printed numbers," which brought the term *statistics* into general usage. In the commercial sector, the growth of managerial organizations led to the emergence of printed schedules, work rules, and forms.

Still, "information" was most closely associated with the role of the press, a relation made explicit in other languages. The French distinguished between a *presse d'information* (focused on reporting) and a *presse d'opinion* (devoted to commentary); the function of the former, Emile Zola wrote in 1886, was "to bring information to public awareness." In the singular, the French *information* could be used to refer to a bit of news (as it could in English until the nineteenth century); in the plural *les informations* referred to news reports (in recent times truncated to *les infos*). More broadly, in French and Italian the word could denote as well the collection of news or the instruments of its diffusion, as in *une information libre*, "a free press." Jules Verne depicted the intrepid American journalist hero of his 1874 novel *The Mysterious Island* as an *un véritable héros . . . de l'information*, "a true hero of news."

The association of information with the press and other printed documents shaped the way it was perceived, as a self-sufficient substance detached from its source and independent of any individual consciousness. This is one of the important ways in which information differs from knowledge, which always requires a knowing subject—an individual, a collectivity, or at the limit a text, which serves as a proxy for its author. We speak of "human knowledge," for example, but we don't ordinarily speak of "human information"—we don't identify information in terms of its possessors. "Medical knowledge" refers to the body of knowledge possessed by members of the medical community, whereas "medical information" refers simply to information about medical matters, wherever it happens to reside. As the sociologist Alvin Gouldner observed, information doesn't require a specific knower: it is "a product that can be found in a cardfile, a book, a library, a colleague, or some other 'storage bank.'"

The self-sufficiency of information altered its evidential value in a way that Benjamin was getting at when he compared information to intelligence: "The intelligence that came from afar . . . possessed an authority which gave it validity, even when it was not subject to certification. Information, however, lays claim to prompt verifiability. The prime requirement is that it appear 'understandable in itself. . . .' It is indispensable for information to sound plausible." The authority of a piece of intelligence rested on one's trust in the reliability of its source, in the same way the value of a note of hand rested on the credit and reputation of the person who signed it, whereas the authority of information is folded into the form of the communication itself. We walk past a window and hear a voice on the radio announcing the result of a local election; we accept the statement unreservedly, without having to know who the announcer is or what station we're listening to, solely in virtue of the form of communication. The sound of the announcer's voice is sufficient to evoke the whole apparatus of commercial broadcasting.

In the same way, the style and material form of a nineteenth-century newspaper report evoked the apparatus of print journalism; one was supposed to be able to take a report on faith simply because it appeared in the (right) newspaper—it was, as Benjamin put it, "understandable in itself." In whatever form we encounter it—in a newspaper, a book, a broadcast, a road sign, a statistical table—we describe a representation as information only when its form alone seems to index the reliability and authority of the institutions that created it. We should bear in mind that this is a phenomenal experience that neither Adam Smith nor Condorcet could ever have had. They knew only "intelligence" and would not have thought of accepting the truth of a text on the basis of its form alone, in the absence of any knowledge of its source.

While the "moral instruction" sense of *information* had largely disappeared by the mid-nineteenth century, it left its traces in the implication that the "information" provided by printed documents was an essential component of citizenship. By the time of the US Civil War, the political importance of information had become an article of national faith. It was by diffusing information that the press and analogous institutions shaped the political consciousness of the public and enabled public opinion to crystalize and make itself known. In 1884, an article in the *Century* magazine called "The Political Education of the People" noted: "We are indebted to the press for nearly all our information about the condition of public business and the course of events at home and abroad; and it is safe to say that without such a source of information the conduct of popular government, in so large a country as ours, would be very difficult, if not impossible."

A similar conviction animated the American public library movement, which was to provide a model for other nations. In 1852, the trustees of the Boston Public Library proclaimed that "it is of paramount importance that the means of general information should be so diffused that the largest possible number of persons should be induced to read and understand questions . . . which we, as a people, are constantly required to decide." Educators stressed the importance of achieving universal *literacy (a term that first appeared in the United States in the 1880s in the sense "ability to read and write"), while at the same time numerous states instituted literacy qualifications for voting, which in some notorious cases were used to disqualify minority voters.

The more reliant society became on the "informational system" that coordinated the diffusion of information and the formation of public opinion, the more anxious people became about its limits and breakdowns, as reflected in the emergence of a new vocabulary to describe informational abuse and misfire. Some of these words were old ones repurposed. English *misinformation* went back to the seventeenth century to refer to the act of misinforming someone or to a misleading report. But the word was rare until the late nineteenth century, when it came to be used for false or misleading press reports and official communications; its frequency in major American newspaper stories rose more than tenfold between 1870 and 1920.

"Fake news" emerged in the 1890s, when *fake* itself caught on, first in America, as a slang term for something that masquerades as the genuine thing. *Propaganda* was an obscure and recondite word until World War I, when it was attached to the public relations campaigns of the contending governments. Given wide currency by the international press, it rapidly "passed into the vocabulary of peasants and ditch diggers and began to acquire its miasmic aura," as the journalist Will Irwin wrote in 1936.

I will use *misinformation* here as a cover term for this vocabulary, though the word is unique to English. Other languages have coined phrases or adapted colloquial words to similar effect: Italian *cattiva informazione* and *balle*, German *Fehlinformation* and *Quatsch*, French *fausses nouvelles* and *bobard* (a fabrication aimed at deceiving the public). *Disinformation* and its cognates entered Western languages during the Cold War period as a translation of the Russian *dezinformatsiya*, originally used by the KGB to describe false reports concocted to mislead public opinion (the word is sometimes credited to Stalin himself). The English *fake news* was universalized, initially to refer to misleading or deceptive stories circulating on social media, then, following President Donald Trump's precedent, adopted by autocrats to dismiss unfavorable coverage of their regime, a usage that in turn has led media organizations and some governments to cease using it.

The choice of one or another of these words can depend on, among other things, whether the claims referred to are false or simply misleading, whether they are deliberate attempts at deception or widespread misconceptions, or whether they are produced by governments or corporations or individuals. Nonetheless, the words share two defining features, which *misinformation* exemplifies. First, misinformation is obviously a kind of information, in the same way that a misconception is a kind of conception and a misspelling is a spelling. In particular, moreover, it's the sort of information that is diffused by a public medium such as a newspaper, a government report, or a radio broadcast, distinguishing these words from the older vocabulary of mendacity, words like *lie*, *falsehood*, *untruth*, *prevarication*, and the like, which can apply to speech acts between any individuals, in private or public, and touching on any subject. A teenager who falsely tells her parents she was studying at the library can be said to have told them a lie, but not (other than in jest) to have conveyed misinformation or fake news. Of course, we can apply *lie* and *falsehood* for the remarks of specific public figures, as well. But the agent who diffuses misinformation is often unknown and may not even be discoverable (a problem that haunts efforts to contain it on social media).

But the prefix *mis-* also indicates that misinformation is an aberrant form of information, with the implication that in the normal case, information is regarded as correct or reliable. Or, to paraphrase the slogan of the cyberlibertarians who insist that "information wants to be free," we might say that information wants to be true. That is both a descriptive and a normative statement. As a rule, I assume that the statements you label as information are more often true than not, unless you qualify the word with a modifier like "questionable." Unlike *report* or *account*, that is, *information* carries with it a presumption of confidence in the forms and institutions that report it. Indeed, information in this sense of the term is better thought of as an evidential as opposed to an *epistemological notion.

But we also hold, normatively, that information *ought* to be true, or even more urgently, that it *needs* to be true. Yet we're always aware how leaky the system is. The history of *misinformation* and related terms reflects a ceaseless series of crises of faith in the informational order.

In the late nineteenth century, the dangers of misinformation were most often raised in diatribes over the influence of the popular press, for which every nation coined its own disparaging name: the yellow press, the gutter press; the *presse à scandale*, the *Boulevardpresse*, the *riooljournalistiek*, and so on. In an 1896 commentary, for example, the

New York Times drew the attention of "every true and patriotic citizen" to the partisan press that sought to mislead the people with "whole columns of 'fake' news [and] sensational 'stuff,'" whose editorial policies were dictated by commercial interests. Such things, it said, were "shocking to our ideals of democracy." The *Times* urged readers to forswear their reverence for print: "distrust of the press is the cure for the evil." Such complaints often conveyed a certain Olympian condescension. The decorous *Times* trafficked in *facts and was aimed at the "great cultivated, well-to-do class," as one admirer put it—its early motto was "It does not soil the breakfast table"—as opposed to the sensational penny press, bristling with cartoons and color illustrations and flavored with publicity stunts, jingoism, and political scandal for the entertainment of the urban masses.

In one form or another, those themes recur in polemics about misinformation from the nineteenth century to the present day, apportioning blame between the partisan or mercenary promulgators of misinformation and the credulous and easily distracted public whose members are unequipped to evaluate it critically. Often, as in the *Times*'s commentary, it was the establishment press and institutions that were exalted as the sources of reliable information. But the argument could also be turned around.

The flood of Allied and German propaganda in World War I provoked a heated debate over the abuse of propaganda—the systematic effort of governments, or often corporate interests, to manipulate public opinion. The word *propaganda* itself soon fell into disrepute; in most languages, it evoked jingoistic ballyhoo aimed at whipping up public enthusiasm for war and sacrifice. (In some languages, like Spanish and Portuguese, the word simply means advertising.) Governments avoided it—during the war the British propaganda efforts were consigned to the Ministry of Information, and when America entered the war, Woodrow Wilson created the Committee on Public Information, charged with rousing support for the war effort—though its press releases, which often played fast and loose with the truth, led the *Times* to dub it the "Committee on Public Misinformation."

After the war, concern focused on less dramatic techniques for controlling public opinion. Some still spoke of propaganda, but a better name for this would be misinformation, which is indistinguishable in its form from legitimate information. This was the era of the birth of the modern press agent and "scientific" advertising (which had played a role in shaping British and American war propaganda); in 1932, the city editor of the *New York Herald Tribune* estimated that half the news items in the daily press originated with public relations firms. Some maintained that such intervention was necessary. In 1928, Edward Bernays wrote approvingly of the "invisible government" charged with "the conscious and intelligent manipulation of the organized habits and opinions of the masses [that] is an important element in democratic society." Left to their own devices, he said, the masses would be unable to come to a conclusion about anything. Walter Lippmann underscored that point, arguing that the ordinary citizen was more-or-less helpless before the complexities and subtleties of matters of public concern, and largely indifferent to them: as he put it, "The facts far exceed our curiosity." Others found the prospect abhorrent. In *The Public and Its Problems* (1927), John Dewey inveighed against those who were skilled at "enlisting upon their side the inertia, prejudices and emotional partisanship of the masses by use of a technique which impedes free inquiry and expression" so as to create "a state of government by hired promoters of opinion" and which produced "a social situation in which neither truth nor the basic values of civilization get a fair hearing." In 1929, the psychologist Everett Dean Martin warned that "a public ruled by an 'invisible government' becomes like its rulers. . . . Its hero is anyone who, by whatever cheap device, succeeds in capturing its attention. In this manner it is encouraged to worship itself, its own power, and the cheap greatness it can bestow."

Those debates prefigure a long line of commentary and polemic that subjects the dominant discourse of "legitimate information" to critical scrutiny. The advent of the *internet initially promised to give new life to this counterdiscourse: as one influential blogger wrote, "The power of elites to determine what [is] news via a tightly controlled dissemination system [has been] shattered." In the event, however, the spread of the *internet and the rise of social media have triggered a widespread sense of a "misinformation crisis," as signaled in ubiquitous headlines like: "How the Information Age Became the Disinformation Age," "L'ère de la désinformation," "La Disinformazione, vero virus di quest'epoca," and "Eine Zeit der Fehlinformation." These breakdowns in the informational order are usually seen as effects of the internet and social media, but some of the causes antedate them: a decades-long decline in trust in government, the media, and other institutions and the increasing political polarization of the public and the media. Those tendencies are more marked in some countries than others, but they everywhere encourage a degree of public skepticism about any single dominant narrative.

But the internet clearly amplifies those tendencies by eliminating constraints on the production and diffusion of information. The effect is to democratize both misinformation and its remedies. The internet bristles with rumors, canards, hoaxes, misapprehensions, falsehoods, and fallacies as well as with refutations and debunkings of them. But most lack the signs that formerly enabled people to discern legitimate information in the world of material communication, and for a great many people the fact that something appears "on the internet" is good enough, if it's congenial to their worldview. At the limit, the new climate fosters a pathological cynicism: the precept "Don't believe everything you read" has yielded to "Believe whatever you like."

Technology has made it easy to "spoof" legitimate sources (a term that numerous languages have adopted from computer science to refer to forging or emulating a web page, a phone number, or an email address). In the past, no one could produce a plausible-looking newspaper or television news show without considerable resources, much less circulate it to a large or remote public. At best, a marginal group could promote its ideology only by sending a newsletter to the people on its mailing list or passing it around as underground samizdat. Now anybody anywhere in the world can work up a credible-looking home page for a fictitious *Denver Guardian* or Action12news.com, fill it with spurious news stories and sensational headers, and count on the members of a sympathetic network to pass it along to others in their political ecosystem, whether in the hope of influencing an election or merely harvesting clicks for ads. Facebook estimates that 126 million people might have seen the material posted by the Russian troll farm known as the Internet Research Agency between 2015 and 2017, a figure that exceeds the reach of any domestic source of legitimate information.

Debate over how—or whether—the current flood of misinformation can be stanched, throttled, or made less detrimental has led to both supply- and demand-side proposals. Algorithms can help identify misinformation, with the assistance of human reviewers;

its promulgators can then be blocked from posting to a social media site, demoted in search, or disincentivized by preventing them from running ads. On the demand side, citizens need to be able to evaluate what they read more critically. Stanford University researchers have described students' inability to assess online information as "bleak," "shocking," and "a threat to democracy," in an uncanny echo of the words of the *Times* commentary about the yellow press more than a century earlier. Educators have stressed the need for teaching media literacy, reviving the kinds of programs that took off after World War II to counter the effects of propaganda on the public: the French Ministry of Culture has launched an extensive program aimed at enabling students to spot junk information online. But such programs can be caught up in ideological firestorms over the very facts that students are supposed to be learning to discern.

At present, though, it is difficult to see how any of these expedients—technological, institutional, or economic—can restore the informational order that emerged in the mid-nineteenth century. It can be argued that the challenge of a "post-truth" era has actually strengthened the legitimate press and other institutions of the traditional informational order, but their authority is increasingly circumscribed. It may be, as the book *Network Propaganda* suggests, that "as a public we have lost our capacity to agree on shared modes of validation as to what is going on and what is just plain wacky."

Geoffrey Nunberg

See also algorithms; digitization; learning; libraries and catalogs; media; newspapers; public sphere; reference books; social media; teaching

FURTHER READING

Walter Benjamin, *Illuminations*, translated by Harry Zohn, 1968; Yochai Benkler, Robert Faris, and Hal Roberts, *Network Propaganda: Manipulation, Disinformation, and Radicalization in American Politics*, 2018; Richard D. Brown, *The Strength of a People: The Idea of an Informed Citizenry in America, 1650–1870*, 1997; Alvin Gouldner, *The Coming Crisis*, 1970; Alice Marwick and Rebecca Lewis, "Media Manipulation and Disinformation Online," research report, Data and Society, 2017; Michael Schudson, *The Good Citizen: A History of American Civil Life*, 1998; Richard Terdiman, *Discourse/Counter-discourse*, 1985.

INFORMATION POLICY

The phrase "information policy" is not entirely commonplace in contemporary English. It does not possess the same self-evident significance as "foreign policy" or "public policy," which point to a government's respective interactions with international actors and with its domestic inhabitants. By contrast, a certain ambiguity sets in when we speak of information policy. Does it refer to a state's efforts to gather information within its borders? The control of what information is available to its residents? The use of information for diplomatic purposes? International standard setting? The public's protections against governmental and corporate abuses of power, in the form of transparency and privacy laws? At times its constituent parts even seem to pull in opposite directions: *information*, as the word is deployed in the digital age, often seems to be characterized by a tendency to transgress national borders and contravene government planning—in other words, to subvert precisely the kinds of strategic designs for which policy is the instrument.

The eagerness of some in the Silicon Valley to portray information as an ungovernable substance should give us pause. Information has indeed been governed—amassed, censored, manipulated, distributed, surveilled, and so on. The umbrella term for this nexus, *information policy*, may offer a conceptual corrective to some of the antiregulatory distortions of late twentieth- and early twenty-first-century information discourses, provided we clarify what we mean by *information*. First, it might be deployed as a transhistorical and transcultural category of analysis, which when paired with *policy* points to phenomena ranging from the censorship of manuscripts and woodblock prints in Song dynasty China to the efforts of Louis XIV's finance minister Jean-Baptiste Colbert to amass financial, industrial, and other records in the service of governing seventeenth-century France. In this sense, information policy is not a modern innovation. Policies intended to control what can be known within and enumerate what is knowable about a given territory have been bound up, historically, with *longue durée* processes of state formation.

Understood as a self-conscious or historically embedded concept, on the other hand, information policy is distinctly modern. As the linguist Geoffrey Nunberg has noted, in English, for much of the nineteenth century, *information* typically either referred to instruction (a process of becoming informed about substantive matters) or was used with a prepositional phrase specifying its subject (information *about* such and such). The abstraction familiar to us from clichés like "the information age" and *"information overload" is a more recent usage. It bears the imprint of the mid-twentieth-century information theory of American mathematician Claude Shannon, who conceptualized information as a quantifiable entity. The phrase "information policy" also gained—more limited—currency in the twentieth century, a period of intensifying attention to the role of mediated knowledge in social and political life. It offers a discursive indication of the widening range of media and communications technologies and issues causing concern for governments.

Instances of governments collecting information about their territories date to premodern times. One notable example of premodern information policy comes from the late eleventh century, when William the Conqueror ordered a voluminous survey of the people and resources of England—the Domesday Book—in order to gain a more accurate picture of his new kingdom. The collection of information in the *early modern period, inflected by expanding state bureaucracies and the spread of printing and movable-type technologies (among other factors), points to an ambiguity that recurs in information policy making through the present day: Were such initiatives intended to augment the power of the state itself? Or did they also benefit public audiences? In the France of the Sun King, Colbert's vast information apparatus, which deployed innovative organizing and indexing techniques to render searchable tens of thousands of printed books and manuscripts, was erected solely for the use of the state. But at around the same moment in Tokugawa Japan, the results of detailed government cadastral and cartographic surveys were finding their way into printed commercial materials—including *encyclopedias, travel guides, and almanacs—destined for an expanding reading public. Historians have discerned the roots of both the modern security state and the modern public sphere in the information policies of the seventeenth century.

Governments' efforts to manage what could be known within their territories also antedated the early modern period. Burnings of works occurred in places ranging from Qin dynasty China (221–207 BCE), where the emperor sought to suppress his Confucian critics, to medieval and early modern Europe, where Catholic authorities repeatedly staged the public destruction of the Talmud. The diffusion of printing and movable type sharpened the official focus on the perils of uncontrolled information. Hilde De Weerdt has indicated that in Song dynasty China (960–1279 CE), the increasing commercial production of texts coincided with a mushrooming number of legal regulations pertaining to both print and manuscript materials. Similarly, in early modern Europe, state and ecclesiastical authorities fashioned a complex mesh of pre- and postpublication censorship mechanisms, their textual anxieties exacerbated by the ruptures of the *Reformation.

The slipperiness and *leakiness of information—its tendency to subvert the desires of regulatory authorities—are often associated with digital technologies. But historians have discerned these qualities in *analog media at least as far back as the early modern era. Publishing restrictions in Old Regime France, for instance, spawned a flourishing illegal trade with printers based next door in Switzerland, who fed the French public's taste for illicit reading materials. These included publications on the scandalous personal lives of elites (*chroniques scandaleuses*, the Old Regime equivalent of the gossip column) and the related *genre of *libelles*, which were vitriolic denunciations of important political figures up to and including the king himself. According to Robert Darnton, though the libelles did not directly bring about or anticipate revolution, they formed an expression of popular dissatisfaction that helped to strip away the monarchy's moral authority in the years leading up to 1789.

A distinctive feature of information policy in the modern age has been the explicit impetus to democratize the use of information and public access to it. In the premodern era, censuses had typically been taken for purposes of taxation and conscription. In the age of revolutions, they became an essential tool for apportioning electoral representation. A decennial census was written into the US Constitution, as was the federal prerogative to create a national postal system, which encouraged the circulation of news and information among ordinary citizens across the new republic. In reformist Britain, meanwhile, numerous royal commissions and official investigations inquired into the plight of the urban poor, child laborers, and other marginal subjects; and the results of these were published in the belief that the circulation of social knowledge would foster social progress.

The new communications tools of the nineteenth and early twentieth centuries—chiefly telegraphy, radiotelegraphy, and voice radio—raised new concerns for political elites around the globe. How should these tools be regulated at home? How could they be used to best advantage in diplomatic and colonial contexts? Patterns emerged in nineteenth-century telegraphy that would shape the structure of telecommunications into the late twentieth century. First, in many countries land telegraphy became a monopoly of the state, an arrangement that subsequently provided a template for public telephone and broadcasting monopolies. Submarine cables followed a second path: private ownership by well-capitalized corporations. By the fin de siècle British firms dominated undersea telegraphy on a global scale, from cable manufacturing to the ships called in to repair broken lines. Unsurprisingly, British infrastructural supremacy affected the content traveling across the wires. The London-based news agency Reuters held a monopoly on the dissemination of news in the British Empire as well as Asia.

One nineteenth-century response to proliferating telegraph networks was interstate cooperation, a policy innovation with lasting implications. Technical coordination was vitally important to smoothing the traffic of telegrams across national borders, particularly in the patchwork quilt of Europe. Various bilateral and regional agreements anticipated the creation, in 1865, of the International Telegraph Union (ITU), which later expanded its focus to include radiotelegraphy and broadcasting. The ITU, renamed the International Telecommunication Union in 1932, was absorbed by the United Nations in the late 1940s and remains its oldest specialized agency.

But concurrent to the birth of telecommunications internationalism, the supremacy of British and more generally Western interests in long-distance telegraphy was engendering new tensions and rivalries. In British India, officials had celebrated the telegraph's contribution to the crushing of the Rebellion of 1857. But in the ensuing decades the rapid transmission of news and information via cables would help to foster nationalist politics on the subcontinent. In late Qing China, meanwhile, conservatives suspicious of Western technologies clashed with modernizers eager to build domestic telegraph lines. In these and other instances, the international scene presents a dialectical picture of technological innovation, policies designed to exploit new technologies, and unintended social and political consequences.

In the nineteenth century, governmental authorities had often assumed more of a supportive or secondary role than a supervisory one in relation to international communications. As mentioned above, the extensive British cable network was largely in private hands, while—more surprisingly—in Prussia and then unified Germany the autocratic state also mostly left long-distance cable matters to business interests. State involvement with international communications would transform around the turn of the twentieth century, with the intensification of national and colonial rivalries and their

apotheosis in the world wars. Heidi Tworek has shown how turn-of-the-century German anxieties over the British cable network fueled government initiatives in wireless
communications. Kaiser Wilhelm II encouraged the 1903 creation of the manufacturing and research firm Telefunken, which was subsequently subsidized by state investments. By the summer of 1914 the European powers were primed to wage communications warfare. Berlin's fears proved prescient in the sense that Britain wasted no time
in cutting Germany's undersea cables following the outbreak of World War I. The conflict also involved pervasive censorship and—for the first time—significant efforts by
combatants to disseminate propaganda both at home and abroad. Britain channeled pro-
Allied news stories to neutral countries, notably the United States, and British intelligence decrypted the famous Zimmermann Telegram, a proximate cause of the United
States' official entry into the war in April 1917. Soon after, Washington had its own propaganda agency, the Committee on Public Information (CPI), which relentlessly blasted
Americans with patriotic hoopla and painted opposition to the war as un-American.

The creation of powerful agencies explicitly devoted to information management and
dissemination during World War I points to mounting policy consciousness of the ways
in which information might mold public opinion. Nowhere was the epochal shift toward
government involvement in the information field more marked than in the United States,
though it would take another world war and the onset of cold war for American policy
elites to institutionalize peacetime information diplomacy. They did so through the Cold
War continuation of the Voice of America radio service, started during World War II,
and the creation of new executive entities like the US Information Agency (USIA), established 1953. In a country where media were typically privately owned and commercially supported, such initiatives were justified on the grounds that securing "freedom
of information" and the "free flow of information" abroad was key to defeating the
United States' totalitarian enemies: the idea was that properly informed publics, with
access to diverse and plentiful information, would willingly choose liberal democracy
over fascism and communism. Around the same moment Washington also helped frame
article 19 of the 1948 UN Universal Declaration of Human Rights, which announced an
individual right to "seek, receive and impart information and ideas through any media
and regardless of frontiers." The Universal Declaration was a statement of principles,
not a legally binding convention; and the cold war subsequently waged by the United
States often veered far from its ideals. Yet free-flow talk endured as a rhetorical wedge
for opening international markets to American media and technology.

The rise of the twentieth-century propaganda state sparked citizen backlashes with
important consequences for information policy. In the United States, the CPI's contentious legacy and the ongoing repression of dissent after World War I helped inspire a
nascent community of legal activists to form the American Civil Liberties Union (ACLU),
founded in 1920. During and immediately after World War II, the most vociferous critics
of US information policy came from the right, accusing government information programs of crowding out commercial media and encroaching on free enterprise. Both of
these varieties of criticism of state power—civil libertarian and economic libertarian—
fueled policy demands for more accountable and transparent governance, and these too
were formulated in informational terms. The Freedom of Information Act (FOIA) was
signed into law in 1966 and strengthened in 1974, giving citizens the right to access
federal records. Though not the first, the US law was at the leading edge of a wave of

public records laws passed around the world in the late twentieth and early twenty-first centuries that have aimed to draw back the curtains on governance.

A brief appraisal of contemporary information controversies suggests a continuation of the tension between state and public prerogatives, though in new forms. In the same postwar moment when the principle of transparency embedded in contemporary FOIA laws was gaining cultural purchase in the United States, for instance, government secrecy was exploding in terms of the volume of information summarily classified out of the reach of ordinary citizens. And such secrecy has been the handmaiden of digital-age surveillance and propaganda efforts. The tentacles of the twenty-first-century US (cyber)security state reach around the globe, as Edward Snowden's revelations showed, though so do those of Russia and China. Since the mid-twentieth century, we have been accustomed to speaking of information in a naturalized fashion—it "flows," like a river—but in the early twenty-first, episodes of cyberespionage and cybersabotage have served as reminders that it is anything but natural, shaped by institutions of state and international politics. Information was and remains a policy concern.

Diana Lemberg

See also bureaucracy; censorship; diplomats/spies; governance; information, disinformation, misinformation; newspapers; surveilling; surveys and censuses; telecommunications

FURTHER READING

C. A. Bayly, *Empire and Information: Intelligence Gathering and Social Communication in India, 1780–1870*, 1996; Mary Elizabeth Berry, *Japan in Print: Information and Nation in the Early Modern Period*, 2006; Robert Darnton, *The Literary Underground of the Old Regime*, 1982; Hilde De Weerdt, *Information, Territory, and Networks: The Crisis and Maintenance of Empire in Song China*, 2015; Oz Frankel, *States of Inquiry: Social Investigations and Print Culture in Nineteenth Century Britain and the United States*, 2006; Peter Galison, "Removing Knowledge," *Critical Inquiry* 31 (2004): 229–43; Daniel Headrick, *The Invisible Weapon: Telecommunications and International Politics, 1851–1945*, 1991; Michael Schudson, *The Rise of the Right to Know: Politics and the Culture of Transparency, 1945–1975*, 2015.

INSCRIPTIONS

Inscription is the term given to a piece of writing on a durable material, such as metal, terra-cotta, or stone. The people who decipher, classify, and publish inscriptions (with an exception of those on coins, studied by numismatists) are known as epigraphers, and their field as epigraphy. Inscriptions have a central role in the history of information for two related reasons: first, people in nearly all literate societies have written on durable surfaces, often hoping that by so doing they would preserve their texts; and second, those durable surfaces are much more likely to survive today than writing on materials such as *papyrus, cloth, or paper. As a result, historians of ancient societies in particular rely on the work of epigraphers. We would know very little about the histories of ancient Mesopotamia or Egypt, or pre-Muslim India, for example, without the evidence of inscriptions, and even where plenty of other texts survive, as in the cases of ancient Greece and Rome, we can use inscriptions to complement those sources and to provide information about questions that the texts do not address. Although scholars had used the evidence of inscriptions before, it was in the nineteenth century that the field blossomed and epigraphers showed Greek and Roman historians just how much they could learn from objects of this sort. Historians of other premodern societies followed the lead of the classical epigraphers and adopted many of their techniques.

Often, inscriptions are casual creations: graffiti at tourist sites, for example. But because inscribing words in stone or metal gives them the impression of permanence (hence the metaphor "set in stone") and is usually a time-consuming procedure, many inscriptions record deliberate pronouncements. They disseminate information to a broad audience, whether set up by individuals—most commonly, funerary inscriptions preserving the deceased's name, age, and achievements—or state institutions. Inscriptions record the texts of treaties and laws, and honors awarded to individuals. The law code of the Babylonian king Hammurabi (d. 1750 BCE), for example, was carved into a seven-and-a-half-foot-tall piece of basalt underneath an image of the king being invested by Shamash, the god of justice (figure 1); to encourage future students, the fifteenth-century Vietnamese emperor Lê Thánh Tông established the practice of inscribing the names of graduates of royal exams on large steles or *stelai* (stone slabs) in the Temple of Literature, Hanoi. Inscribed stones could serve other communal functions, acting as boundary stones, or providing details of the organization of time. Scholars have suggested that the earliest steles found in the Zapotec site of Monte Albán, in the Oaxaca Valley, include calendrical notation. The Parian Chronicle is a monumental inscription providing a year-by-year countdown of events in Athens and other classical Greek cities from 1581/80 BCE to 264/63 BCE (figure 2). Sometimes inscriptions recorded longer, sanctioned narratives. The Roman emperor Augustus (d. 14 CE) gave orders that his first-person account of his achievements, the *Res gestae*, was to be inscribed on bronze on columns outside his mausoleum. The bronze originals are lost, presumably melted down after the fall of the Roman Empire by scavengers eager for the metal; but because

Figure 1. Stele with the text of Hammurabi's code. The text is dominated by the image of Shamash and the king, above. https://commons.wikimedia.org /wiki/File:Code_of_Hammurabi _11.jpg, licensed under Creative Commons (BY-SA 2.0).

respectful communities in the empire then displayed their own versions of the text on stone, historians can use it today. The Aihole Inscription of King Pulakesin II (634–35 CE), composed by his court poet, the Ravikirti, presented a panegyrical account of the Chalukya dynasty's achievements in central India. In Islamic areas, inscriptions play a crucial role in the decoration of religious buildings. Other inscriptions provide information about the object on which they appear, ranging from artists' signatures to the texts on votive dedications.

Historians today read and exploit the texts of these inscriptions, interpreting them as public communications. They also use the texts in ways their creators might not have expected. The large-scale study of names in Roman inscribed texts, for example, can reveal how people from different linguistic backgrounds moved around the empire. Incidental references to women in inscriptions can illuminate their societal roles in ways that conventional narratives do not. Collectively, the records of individual transactions on clay tablets have allowed historians to reconstruct the workings of Mesopotamian

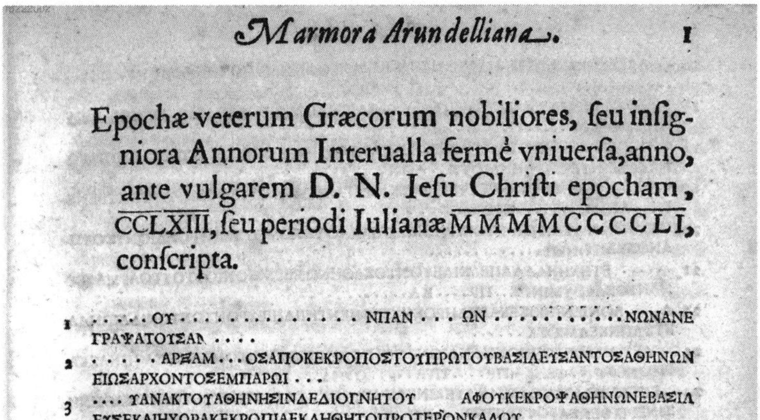

Marmora Arundelliana. I

Epochæ veterum Græcorum nobiliores, seu insig-
niora Annorum Interualla fermè vniuersa, anno,
ante vulgarem D. N. Iesu Christi epocham,
CCLXIII, seu periodi Iulianæ MMMMCCCCLI,
conscripta.

1 . . . . . . OT . . . . NΠAN . . . ΩN . . . . NΩNANE
ΓΡΑΨΑΤΟΙΣΑΝ . . . .
2 . . . . . ΑΡΞΑΜ . . . ΟΣΑΠΟΚΕΚΡΟΠΟΣΤΟΙΠΡΩΤΟΥΒΑΣΙΛΕΥΣΑΝΤΟΣΑΘΗΝΩΝ
ΕΙΩΣΑΡΧΟΝΤΟΣΕΜΠΑΡΩΙ . . .
3 . . . . ΤΑΝΑΚΤΟΥΑΘΗΝΗΣΙΝΔΕΛΙΟΓΝΗΤΟΤ   ΑΦΟΤΚΕΚΡΟΨΑΘΗΝΩΝΕΒΑΣΙΛ
ΕΥΣΕΚΑΙΗΧΩΡΑΚΕΚΡΟΠΙΑΕΚΛΗΘΗΤΟΙΠΡΟΤΕΡΟΝΚΑΛΟΤ
4 ΜΕΝΗΑΚΤΙΚΗΑΠΟΑΚΤΑΙΟΥΤΟΥΑΤΤΟΧΘΟΝΟΣΕΤΗΧΗΗΗΗΔΠΙΙΙΑΦΟΤΔΕΤΚΑΛΙΩΝ
ΠΑΡΑΤΟΝΠΑΡΝΑΣΣΟΝΕΝΑΤΚΩΡΕΙΑΙΕΒΑΣΙΛΕΥΣΕ . . ΣΙΛΕ . .
5 . . ΝΤΟΣΑΘΗΝΩΝΚΕΚΡΟΠΟΣΕΤΗΧΗΗΗΔΑΦΟΤΔΙΚΗΑΘΗΝΗΣΙ . . . ΝΕΤΟΑΡΕΙΚΑ
ΠΟΣΕΙΔΩΝΙΤΙΠΕΡΑΔΙΡΡΟΘΙΟΥΤΟΥΠΟΣΕΙΔΩΝΟΣΚΑΙΟΤΟΠΟΣΕΚΛΗΘΗ
6 ΑΡΕΙΟΣΠΑΓΟΣΕΤΗΧΗΗΙΓ̅ΔΠΙΙΙΒΑΣΙΛΕΥΟΝΤΟΣΑΘΗΝΩΝΚΡ . . . ΟΤΑΦΟΤΚΑΤΑ
ΚΑΤΣΜΟΣΕΠΙΔΕΤΚΑΛΙΩΝΟΣΕΓΕΝΕΤΟΚΑΙΔΕΤΚΑΛΙΩΝΤΟΥΣ
7 ΟΜΒΡΟΤΣΕΦΤΓΕΝΕΓΑΤΚΩΡΕΙΑΣΕΙΣΑΘΗΝΑΣΠΡΟ . . . ΟΝΚΑΙΤΟΤΔΙΟ . . ΤΟ . .
. Δ. . ΜΤΟΤΤΟΙΡ . . ΟΝΙΑ . . . . . . Ο . . ΤΑΣΩΤΗΡΙΑΕΘΤΣΕΝ
8 . . ΤΗΧΗΗΙΓ̅ΔΙΠΒΑΣΙΛΕΤΟΝΤΟΣΑΘΗΝΩΝΚΡ . Ν. .ΟΤΑ . . . . ΚΤΤΩΝΔΕΥΚΑΛΙΩ
ΝΟΣΕΒΑΣΙΛΕΥΣΕΝΕΝΘΕΡΜΟΠΤΛΑΙΣΚΑΙΣΤΝΗΓΕ
9 . . . ΟΤΣΠΕΡΙΤΟΝΟΡΟΝΟΙΚΟΤΝΤΑΣΚΑΙΩ . . ΜΑΣΕΝΑΜΦΙΚΤΤΟΝΑΣΚΑΙΠ . . . .
ΝΟΤ . . ΚΑΙΝΤΝΕΤΙΘΤΟΤΣΙΝΑΜΦΙΚΤΤΩΝΕΣ
10 . . ΤΗΧΗΗΙΓ̅ΠΙΙΒΑΣΙΛΕΤΟΝΤΟΣΑΘΗΝΩΝΑΚΦΙΚΤΤΟΝΟΣΑΦΟΤΕΛΛΗΝΟΔΕΤΚ . . .
. . . . ΩΤΙΔΟΣΕΒΑΣΙΛΕΤΣΕΚΑΙΕΛΛΗΝΕΣ
11 . . ΟΜΑΣΘΗΣΑΝΤΟΠΡΟΤΕΡΟΝΓΡΑΙΚΟΙΚΑΛΟΤΜΕΝΟΙΚΑΙΤΟΝΑΓΩΝΑΠΑΝΑΘ . .Ν̅
ΑΙ . . . . ΩΙΧΗΗΙΓ̅ΠΙΙΒΑΣΙΛΕΤΟΝΤΟΣ
12 ΑΘΗΝΩΝΑΜΦΙΚΤΤΟΝΟΣΑΦΟΤΚΑΔΜΟΣΟΑΓΗΝΟΡΟΣΕΙΣΘΗΒΑΣΑΦΙΚΕΤΟ . . . .
. . . . ΕΚΤΙΣΕΝΤΗΝΚΑΔΜΕΙ
13 ΑΝΕΤΗΧΗΗΙΓ̅ΠΒΑΣΙΛΕΤΟΝΤΟΣΑΘΗΝΩΝΑΜΦΙΚΤΤΟΝΟΣΑΦΟΤ . . . .
ΝΙΚΗΣΕΕΒΑΣΙΛΕΤΣΑΝ
14 ΕΤΗΧΗΗΙΓ̅ΙΒΑΣΙΛΕΤΟΝΤΟΣΑΘΗΝΩΝΑΜΦΙΚΤΤΟΝΟΣΑΦΟΤΝΑΤ . . . . .Η . . .
. . . . . . ΩΝΕΣΑΙΓΤΠΤΟΤ
15 . . ΙΣΤΗΝΕΔΛΑΔΑΕΠΛΕΤΣΕΚΑΙΩΝΟΜΑΣΘΗΓΕΝΤΗΚΟΝΤΟΡΟΣΚΑΙΑΙΔΑΝΑΟΤΘΤ
ΓΑΤΕΡΕΣ . . . . ΩΝΗΚΑΙΒΑ . .

                                        B   . . ΔΔ

Figure 2. Seventeenth-century reproduction of the Parian Chronicle. The page represents the inscribed monument as a text with gaps shown by dots and includes line numbers to the left. John Selden, *Marmora Arundelliana*, 1628, 1 (Bayerische Staatsbibliothek München, 4 Arch. 181, https://reader.digitale-sammlungen.de/en/fs1/object/display/bsb10222002_00025.html).

economies. Famously, multilingual inscriptions have provided linguists with the keys to decipher languages. The *Rosetta Stone includes the same decree in ancient Greek, demotic script, and Egyptian hieroglyphs, which led nineteenth-century scholars to interpret the last of these. At Bisotun, between Babylon and Baghdad, a great relief depicts the Persian king Darius's (d. 486 BCE) defeat of his rivals, and an inscription in Elamite, Babylonian, and Old Persian records the history of his reign, allowing the decipherment of cuneiform (figure 3).

Inscriptions are not simply disembodied texts, although some of the editions that epigraphers have produced, dense with regular capital letters, might give that impression. (As well as reflecting the technological difficulties involved in reproducing inscribed monuments, this approach is also an inheritance of the *philological interests of early

Figure 3. The Bisotun relief. The text records King Darius's conquests in three languages, and the dominant relief makes clear the king's power, showing figures in submission to him. https://commons.wikimedia.org/wiki/File:Behistun_Inscription_in_Persia_ca._520 _BC-_UNESCO_World_Heritage_Site.jpg, licensed under Creative Commons (BY-SA 4.0).

classical epigraphers [figure 2].) As with words in other media, the style of the characters, the use of symbols and decoration alongside letters, and the size and arrangement of inscriptions' texts can affect how we interpret them. The Gothic script used for the Ten Commandments on a 1961 monument at the Texas state capitol, whose display was deemed constitutional by the Supreme Court in 2005, demonstrates the text's venerability. Historians interested in the analysis of individual inscriptions pay attention to the objects on which the texts appear, especially when they are investigating societies with low levels of *literacy. An inability to read the words of an inscription does not necessarily prevent the interpretation of the object. The central message of the Bisotun inscription, for example, Darius's triumph over pretenders to his throne, is clear from the relief, which, unlike the letters, can be seen from a considerable distance away (figure 3); scholars have pointed out that viewers of the stele with Hammurabi's code would have seen the words of the laws surmounted by an divinely inspired lawgiver, making clear the source of authority within the state (figure 1).

Text and object can play off one another. A peculiar dedication by a Roman chief priest (*archigallus*) called Marcus Modius Maxximus is made up of a substantial stone cylinder with a carved cock on top. This is a pun on the man's name and role: the cylinder is a Roman corn measure, a *modius*, and the Latin for cock is *gallus* (figure 4). An inscribed silver casket made in 976 CE for ʾAbū Walīd Hišām, then heir to the caliphate of Spain, features the names of the craftsmen on the underside of the clasp: this is both a sign of humility, and, perhaps, an indication that the two men were under the thumb of the ruler. And the site of the inscribed object matters: in 726 CE the Chinese emperor Xuanzong composed a *moya* inscription (the Chinese term for an inscription on an unquarried rock) that was carved and inlaid with gold pigment at the summit of the

Figure 4. Dedication of Marcus Modius Maxximus. This nineteenth-century reproduction of the small monument allows us to see the cock standing on top of the corn measure. *Monumenti inediti pubblicati dall'istituto di corrispondenza archeologica* 9 (1869): vol. VIIII tav.VIIIa (digitized by the Arachne project [http://arachne.uni-koeln.de/item /buchseite/655585], licensed under Creative Commons [BY-NC-ND 3]).

holy Mount Tai, commemorating his sacrifices and addressing deities and spirits. He thus inserted himself into a holy landscape at the end of an arduous climb; its placement testified to the emperor's piety and power.

Inscriptions are objects, therefore, usually made for particular sites, and should be interpreted as such. They can also make demands on the viewer, requiring him or her to interact with the setting in which they were placed. On Mount Gang in Shangdong Province, China, passages from a Buddhist sutra were inscribed on a series of rocks going up the mountain: reading the text thus requires climbing from one to the next, making a metaphoric parallel with the route to *enlightenment that sutra describes. Other inscriptions invite the visitor to engage with their texts. In Sasanian Iran, a high priest made an addendum to an inscription commissioned by Shapur I (d. 276 CE), saying that whoever read it out loud should feel more confident in his soul. Many Roman funerary monuments beseech travelers to stop, read their inscription, and reflect on the fate of the deceased, addressing passersby in the second person. A tomb in Pompeii features one inscription recording that Publius Vesonius Phileros built it for his patron, himself, and a "friend," Marcus Orfellius Faustus; beneath, he added another, presumably after his Faustus's death. "Learn what to avoid," he wrote, "the man who I had hoped was my friend, I am forsaking: a case was maliciously brought against me. . . . May neither the household gods nor the gods below receive the one who misrepresented our affairs" (Carroll, 52). Some of the makers of medieval and *early modern Christian inscriptions followed the Romans' lead, telling readers to stop and pray for the deceased's soul, although without invectives such as Phileros's. The Latin inscription commemorating the architect Sir Christopher Wren (d. 1723 CE), in St Paul's Cathedral, London, famously advises the reader to do something else. "If you seek his monument," it concludes, "look around" (Lector, si monumentum requiris, circumspice): the visitor has to turn away from the inscription to admire the cathedral that serves as Wren's best memorial.

Wren's son, also called Christopher, composed the epitaph. After the elder Wren's death, the younger devoted much time to securing his father's reputation, commissioning engravings of his buildings and collecting documents related to his career, to which he gave the telling title *Parentalia*. None of this, though, had anything like the impact of his aphoristic inscription. His tribute to his father demonstrated the ongoing power of an inscribed text, displayed in public, to commemorate, engage, and inform.

William Stenhouse

See also archaeological decipherment; coins; money

FURTHER READING

Mary Beard, "Vita inscripta," in *La Biographie antique*, edited by Widu Wolfgang Ehlers, 1997, 83–114; Sheila S. Blair, *Islamic Inscriptions*, 1998; John Bodel, ed., *Epigraphic Evidence: Ancient History from Inscriptions*, 2001; Maureen Carroll, "'Vox tua nempe mea est': Dialogues with the Dead in Roman Funerary Commemoration," *Accordia Research Papers* 11 (2007–8): 37–80; Robert E. Harrist Jr., *The Landscape of Words: Stone Inscriptions from Early and Medieval China*, 2008; Christopher Woods, ed., *Visible Language: Inventions of Writing in the Ancient Middle East and Beyond*, 2015.

INTELLECTUAL PROPERTY

The term *intellectual property* came to be widely used in the last quarter of the twentieth century as an umbrella term to describe a group of rights, including patents, *copyright, designs, and trademarks, each of which has its own legal specificities, its own statutes, jurisprudence, theory, and history. Despite those specificities, these have often been associated (at least since the eighteenth century), and categorization of them as "intellectual property" reflects the fact that each of the rights seeks to confer exclusive control over the exploitation of certain intangible entities—"inventions," "works," "designs," and "trademarks."

The characterization of the subject matter as "intellectual" is misleading, particularly in relation to trademarks, which, as we see below, do not necessarily involve any mental effort or creativity. The description of the rights as "properties" is also not always adequate, in so far as some rights (such as authors' "moral rights") are not assignable and some rights are merely rights to remuneration. Despite these caveats, the term *intellectual property* seems to have become fully established, being used in treaties, in statutes, and as the name of government institutions and nongovernmental organizations, as well as in law reviews, legal textbooks, and common parlance.

The categorization of these specific regimes together as "intellectual property" is not uncontroversial, with many commentators worrying that the umbrella term somehow implies that all creative productions warrant legal protection (a normative position they would not endorse). Certainly, the emergence of the term *intellectual property* has coincided with a proliferation of additional "sui generis" systems, such as the protection of plant breeders' rights, "supplementary protection certificates" (for pharmaceutical products), "data exclusivity," performers' rights, database rights, the artists' resale royalty right, rights in the topographies of semiconductor chips, collective and certification marks, geographical indications, rights in sports events, and even press *publishers' rights.

This entry focuses almost exclusively on the development of these laws in Europe and North America. One reason for doing so is that there is little evidence of similar practices in the ancient world, or in non-Western civilizations. Indeed, the historian Carla Hesse has observed that "a tour of the other great civilizations of the premodern world—Chinese, Islamic, Jewish, and Christian—reveals a striking absence of any notion of human ownership of ideas." Another reason for this narrow focus is that, whatever the position may have been in more ancient and Eastern cultures, they have had little influence on the international norms that are prevalent today.

"Intellectual property law" has rarely been viewed explicitly as a subset of the legal rules concerned with regulating the production, circulation, and consumption of *information*, the primary motivating concerns being articulated in terms of the protection of authorial genius, or at least literary and artistic creativity; the promotion of technological progress through incentivizing invention; and the prevention of free riding and consumer deception. However, on closer inspection, the regulation of information has had an important but distinct place historically in the development of each field. This essay seeks to highlight the ways in which the history of intellectual property is part of the history of the legal regulation of information.

PATENTS

"Patents" are legal rights, acquired by individuals (and corporations) through a process of registration, to control the making and use of "inventions," understood as either products (such as machines or chemicals), processes (ways of making things), or even new ways of using existing substances. The term *patent* refers to the practice of the grant being by "open letter" (letters patent). Today, in most countries, an applicant must describe how to carry the invention into effect and identify the precise subject matter for which protection is sought in short statements called "claims." Applications are usually examined by a relevant granting authority, which will conduct a search so as to ascertain whether the relevant application identifies an invention that is new and inventive (or at least not "obvious"). The maximum term for a patent is typically twenty years, though only around 10 percent are renewed for the full term; some jurisdictions have arrangements to prolong the term.

The earliest grants of exclusive rights over inventions are traced to early Italian city-states, perhaps most notoriously to the 1421 grant to architect Filippo Brunelleschi by the state of Florence of a three-year exclusive right to build and use a new ship for transporting goods. Venice codified its practices for the grant of such privileges in a 1474 statute that has often been described as the first patent law. Significantly, the grant of exclusive privileges was premised on standardized criteria, the invention or introduction of "any new and ingenious device, not previously made," registration at a state office, and a ten-year term of exclusivity. By 1600, Venetian authorities had received over one thousand applications. While these regimes can claim to be precursors of modern patent systems, careful accounts acknowledge that these *early modern privileges were different from modern patents.

Scholars disagree on exactly when, how, and in what ways Venetian privileges came to influence the development of laws elsewhere. One common claim is that Venetian practices spread across Europe as a result of the movement of Italian craftsmen, especially glassworkers, who sought similar protections in their new homelands. The first patent awarded in France in 1551 was to an emigrant from the Venetian jurisdiction, Theseo Mutio of Bologna, for the production of glass "according to the manner of Venice," while England was influenced directly by the movement of Venetian silk workers.

England's Statute of Monopolies, 1624, is frequently treated as a key moment in the history of patent law, regulating, as it did, the Crown's freedom to grant patents to "manners of new manufacture" and limiting the term of any such grants to a period of fourteen years. The time is reputed to represent two terms of apprenticeship, the premise being that a master would teach his apprentices and, following the expiry of the patent, they might use that learning to establish themselves. Thus, already, it seems an assumed benefit of the grant of patents was not just the practice of particular techniques but the idea of training of others, preserving and disseminating the relevant skills or

practices. Of course, this dissemination occurred largely within the regulatory limitations of guild control prevalent in Europe until the eighteenth century.

With the revolutions of the late eighteenth century in France and the United States,
the grant of patents came to be conceptualized as a matter of right rather than grace.
Formal bureaucratic systems were established; the United States operated a system of
examination from 1836. In England, where the system had developed incrementally,
the procedure for the granting of patents was complex, and the level of examination
variable. The numbers of patents granted in England remained relatively small until
the nineteenth century. In response to various pressures, including increasing numbers of applications, the organization was reformed in 1852 with the establishment
of a Patent Office, and the English, Irish, and Scottish regimes consolidated into a
single system.

By this time, with the free trade movement at its height, the benefits of the patent
system came under significant scrutiny, and a movement emerged in favor of the abolition of patents (famously succeeding in the Netherlands, where the 1817 patent law was
repealed, and not replaced until 1910). Paradoxically, what emerged in Britain from this
debate was a reformed system that bore great resemblance to that which we have today.
Building on the experience of the United States and Germany, Great Britain introduced
examination of patents to assess novelty in the first decade of the twentieth century
(and later the requirement of an "inventive step").

Bilateral trade treaties between European states led to foreign inventors being entitled to file for national patents on the same terms as nationals of the relevant state,
generalized in a multilateral treaty signed at the Paris Convention of 1883 on the protection of "industrial property." The effects were not always uncontroversial: many countries found their own manufacturers inhibited by foreign patents and responded by
introducing requirements for local working and provision for compulsory licensing at
rates set by an independent adjudicator. Gradually, international treaties limited the freedom of nation-states to modify their patent laws in this way.

In 1970, a system was established for international application, search, and examination of patent applications through the World Intellectual Property Organization, leading to grants of national patents. The late twentieth century also witnessed the emergence of regional patent arrangements, such as the European Patent Convention (1973),
and greater levels of harmonization of patent law, in particular through an annex to
the World Trade Organization Agreement, known as TRIPS (Trade Related Aspects of
Intellectual Property).

While patents are most commonly understood as incentives for "research and development," a persistent aspect of the history of patent law has been concern with the circulation and survival of information as to how things are made and processes carried
out. Accounts of the early Venetian laws situate the privilege system in a context dominated by guild structures that operated to restrict the circulation of information about
production techniques and draconian laws designed to prevent the emigration of skilled
workers. In that context, in which information about how to make things was embodied in the workers, the movement of information was intimately connected with the
mobility of people. Privileges were regarded as mechanisms to attract foreign skills,
that is, to induce the movement of foreign artisans who carried with them valued technology. Indeed, privileges to foreigners to practice trade are found much earlier (for ex-

ample, the 1331 grant of "Letters of Protection" by Edward III to John Kempe, a Flemish weaver). The 1474 Venetian statute specifically referenced persons who come to Venice "every day from different places . . . who have most clever minds, capable of devising and inventing all kinds of ingenious contrivances."

If these early privileges were frequently mechanisms to induce migration of skilled workers who carried their technologies, from the eighteenth century a similar function was sought to be achieved through textual means. The patent "specification," a document that describes how to implement the invention, first emerged in English patent practice in 1710 and became required from the 1730s. The United States and France adopted similar requirements in their laws of 1790 and 1791. With this move, it became common to characterize patents in contractual terms, according to which a patentee is granted exclusivity *in return* for disclosure of mechanisms and processes that might otherwise have been kept secret. In an era when restrictions existed on migration of workers and machinery, the disclosure requirement—though opposed by some important inventors, such as James Watt—appeared to recognize the public benefits from certain forms of "openness."

In practice, the drafting of such documents soon became the preserve of "patent agents," practitioners versed sufficiently in both science and law and able to steer patent applications past the objections raised by the offices—a process known as "patent prosecution." Patent agents professionalized during the second half of the nineteenth century.

Jurisdictions have varied in the demands placed on disclosure, with some insisting that the "best method" known to the applicant be disclosed, while others only requiring that the disclosure "enable" the performance of the invention. Some legal systems have required, or provided for, nonverbal mechanisms for disclosure, such as through the provision and exhibition of models, and for some time patent regimes were linked to national museums of inventions. In adumbrating standards as to the adequacy of such disclosure, courts appealed to notional figures, such as the "ordinary workman" and latterly the "person skilled in art." As early as 1790, the United States specifically embraced the idea that such specifications should be accessible to "the public," and even in England (where access to such documents was more complicated prior to 1852), specifications came to be copied and circulated through the growing periodical press. The usefulness of the system was significantly increased through processes of indexation not just by inventor or chronology but also by subject—and printed publication. In England, this did not occur until October 1852. Apart from organizing its informational outputs, patent systems have also played an important role in standardizing and cataloging information about such things as chemicals or computer programs, in order to facilitate assessments of the novelty and inventiveness of the material disclosed in a patent application.

The patent system was not merely directly concerned with incentivizing disclosure of valuable information (from inventor to those interested), but itself came to be seen as a repository of information about society. In particular, economic historians have sometimes treated these patent registers as proxies for levels of "innovation," allowing comparisons to be made about different levels of innovation in different countries, and correlations to be made with potential causes. However, others have pointed out that most patented inventions are never exploited, and many exploited inventions are not patented (propensity to patent varying significantly from sector to sector). Indeed, in the case of innovations in the process of manufacturing something, it has often been possible for inventors to practice their inventions in relative secrecy and thereby to secure a longer period of exclusivity than that provided by the patent system (with its obligatory disclosure).

COPYRIGHT

Copyright laws do not tend to conceptualize themselves as protecting information. Rather, copyright laws give exclusive rights over "works" or "works of authorship" understood as "expression," typically on condition that the expression is "original," that is, in some (minimalist) sense "creative." Examples of such works include novels, poems, plays, musical compositions, paintings, sculptures, and cinematographic works. Copyright includes the exclusive right to make reproductions of a work, distribute it to the public, perform it in public, and communicate it to the public, as well as to make adaptations of, and derivative works, from it. In modern copyright laws, copyright arises on creation (or, possibly, recording or fixation), so is conditioned on neither publication nor registration; and protection exists from creation (recording or fixation) throughout the life of its author and for a set period thereafter (most often fifty or seventy years). Associated with copyright are certain specific rights reserved to the author, often called "moral rights," that protect the personal tie between authors and their work: these rights include the right to be named when the work is exploited, and the right to object to modifications of the work that are prejudicial to the author's "honor or reputation."

Extensive work has been conducted on the history of copyright. The two precursors of the modern idea of copyright (a right conferred by statute on authors) are printing privileges and practices of the guilds that controlled printing starting in the fifteenth century. Long before then some ancient authors manifested a sense of moral rights to their compositions, as in the complaints of Martial (first century CE) against those who recited his poetry as their own, or Galen (second century CE), who protested the sale of works on medicine falsely attributed to him.

Printing privileges operated in the same manner as privileges over inventions, as state or royal grants of exclusivity. As with invention privileges, the earliest examples come from Venice, including most notoriously a monopoly over printing itself conferred on the German printer Johannes of Speyer for five years. In the late fifteenth and early sixteenth centuries similar privileges were granted in Würzburg (1479), Spain (1487), Portugal (1502), France (1507), Brussels (1516), and England (1557). Alongside these there were papal privileges (from at least 1509) and the first rabbinic reprinting privilege (1518). Frequently such privileges were closely associated with receiving permission to publish.

In England, the printing trade was subject to control by a London guild, the Stationers' Company, founded in 1557, whose monopoly was reinforced by statutes prohibiting others from operating printing presses. The company allocated rights to print approved texts to particular printers, thereby endowing them with a form of exclusivity. The term *copy-right* was coined in the eighteenth century as a reference to the Stationers' Company's (or perhaps author's) right in the "copy," a manuscript intended for publication (rather than the right to control "copying," as might be assumed).

The control of printing by the Stationers' Company was challenged in the late seventeenth century when the Licensing Acts lapsed. After a period of fifteen years in which printing was unregulated, the Statute of Anne, 1710, restored to publishers the right to control the reprinting of books, though with two important qualifications. First, the right (for works published after 1710) was conferred on authors, publishers being entitled only as their assignees; second, the right was limited to a term of fourteen years, and, should the author be alive at the end of that period, a further period of fourteen years. In effect, the 1710 Act created a *"public domain" for books in which exclusive rights had expired. The Stationers' Company did its best to circumvent this limitation, arguing for a perpetual right at common law, but in *Donaldson v. Beckett* in 1774 the House of Lords rejected such a claim, at least for published works.

During the eighteenth and early nineteenth centuries similar rights were adopted in France, the United States, and the German states, often accompanied by sophisticated debate over the justification for recognizing such rights. Various rationales for copyright were embraced, varying from utilitarian conceptions of incentivizing creativity, to the recognition of the innate rights of authors in the results of their own creativity. Most legal systems developed toward offering protection to music, plays, and artistic works, as well as books, and to conferring protection for at least the life of the author. Those countries that saw themselves as granting protection to authors, as such, recognized special rights (so-called moral rights) of attribution and integrity and gave special protection to artists allowing them to claim a profit on the resale value of artworks (known as the "droit de suite").

In the mid-nineteenth century, some of these countries sought to obtain recognition of the rights of copyright holders in nearby states, and, in 1886, ten states (including France, Germany, and Great Britain, but not the United States) established an international arrangement, the Berne Convention. A 1908 revision took the dramatic step of prohibiting registration (and other formalities) as a condition of protection (other than in the country of origin), and most of the countries that still had registration systems abolished them. The Berne treaty was revised a number of times, but the United States remained outside the arrangement until the late twentieth century, reluctant to forego requirements that, in order to be protected, works be marked with notices and that, in order to be enforced, they had to be registered.

In the twentieth century, copyright became a model on which claims were made to protection of investment in a host of productions: "cinematographic works" were treated as creative and thus within the Berne Convention's ambit, while sound recordings and broadcasts were protected, along with the rights of performers, by so-called neighboring or related rights. As noted, similar rights have more recently been conferred on publishers, the makers of "databases," and even producers of press publications.

Not conceptualized as protecting information, copyright instead holds as a key premise that it protects "works" understood as "expression," typically on condition that the expression is in some (minimalist) sense "creative." Indeed, a key premise of most contemporary copyright regimes is that the law protects expression but not ideas, information, or *facts as such. The Berne Convention itself states that it "shall not apply to news of the day or to miscellaneous facts having the character of mere items of press information," a sentiment that can be traced back to the treaty's original text.

While copyright law may not protect information as such, there can be no doubt that, historically, copyright law has been an important mechanism for regulating the production of "works of information." Indeed, although the requirement of minimal creativity today holds sway as the condition for copyright, for much of its history copyright regimes have offered sanctuary to productions, for example, almanacs, directories, maps, calendars, and compilations of laws. The 1790 US Copyright Act extended to "maps, charts and books," the former subject matter clearly being prized for its informational accuracy. Looking back from the end of the nineteenth century, the British politician Augustine Birrell noted that the case law on "literary larceny" was made up chiefly of "disputes between book-makers and rival proprietors of works of reference, sea charts, Patteson's 'Roads,' the antiquities of Magna Graecia, rival *encyclopedias, *gazetteers, guide books, cookery books, law reports, post office and trade directories, illustrated catalogues of furniture, statistical returns, French and German dictionaries, Poole's farce, 'Who's Who?' [and] Brewer's 'Guide to Science.'" The position was little different in France: of thirty-seven disputes over copyright between 1793 and 1814, twenty-one of them concerned what the scholar Jane Ginsburg classifies as "informational works." Moreover, since 1948 the Berne Convention itself requires protection of encyclopedias, anthologies, and other compilations "which, by reason of the selection and arrangement of their contents, constitute intellectual creations."

Although copyright laws mostly offer control over the form ("expression") of a work rather than its informational content, in one obvious respect they seek to offer control over information, specifically information about "authorship." The Berne Convention (since its Rome Revision in 1928) has required members to protect the moral rights of authors, including "attribution rights" (also known as "paternity" rights), and, as a condition for the availability of certain exceptions (such as quotation), requires that the authorship and source be acknowledged. These rights and obligations, historically almost always justified in terms of the natural rights of the "authors," can equally be seen as critical components in a system of information norms, "authorship" being the dominant system for organizing cultural outputs, through catalogs, bibliographies, and thus "meta data" or—in recent terminology "rights management information" or *metadata.

TRADEMARKS

While the practice of marking goods is ancient, less is known about the history of the legal protection of trademarks than that of copyright and patents. In England, it seems, some protection was available through *guilds or manorial courts, in particular sectors, from the sixteenth century. Moreover, it appears that from a similar time it was possible to bring proceedings for damages for misusing marks so as to deceive consumers though traders were able to obtain orders to prevent such behavior only from the early nineteenth century. By then, advertising through bills, posters, and newspapers had become common, initially for medical cures, but then also for boot polish, sauces, food, and drink.

With courts hearing increasing numbers of complaints as to deceptive use of the names or marks of competitors, attention turned to ways to make the system of protection simpler, quicker, and cheaper. Proceedings before civil law courts were often supplemented by criminal law regimes, allowing for quick if rough justice against "counterfeiters." In France, a system of registration of trademarks was adopted at the beginning of the nineteenth century, and after the middle of the century such systems spread through the Anglo-American world—with the United States establishing a federal register in 1870 and Britain a comparable register in 1875. Such systems, in turn, gave rise to a specialist class of advisers—"trademark agents"—as well as workers employed to watch the register to ensure others did not seek protection for marks that might interfere with one's own operations or plans.

Although the movement of goods across markets had long had an international dimension, as this became stronger so traders sought protection beyond their own shores. As with patents, bilateral arrangements were developed, but their effectiveness also required registration schemes. Protection of trademarks was included within the scope of the Paris Convention of 1883, and early in the twentieth century members of this convention committed themselves to offering protection also against unfair competition and similar deceptive practices.

The protection of trademarks was initially justified by reference to the harm caused to established traders from the unauthorized use of the same or similar marks to deceive purchasers. The core wrong—deception—was largely understood in moral terms. Comparisons were frequently made in the middle of the nineteenth century to fraud, forgery, and the counterfeiting of currency. However, as later scholars would observe, notions such as deception can easily be reconceptualized in terms of information: deception is the behavioral consequence of misrepresentation or misinforming. Indeed, trademarks were themselves frequently recognized to be vehicles for communicating information, particularly information about the origin or quality of the goods to which they were applied. In the final quarter of the twentieth century, trademarks came to be seen as valuable precisely because of their role in supplying the marketplace with information, the dominant account being that trademarks reduce purchaser "search costs." As the economic and legal scholars Landes and Posner argued: "The value of a trademark is the saving in search costs made possible by the information or reputation that the trademark conveys or embodies about the brand (or the firm that produces the brand). . . . If the law does not prevent it, free riding will eventually destroy the information capital embodied in a trademark." Trademark law is seen as conferring protection to trademarks because by doing so they enable traders to improve the quality of information in the relevant market, and thereby make the market more competitive.

Such an account, however, is not without its critics. One important mid-twentieth-century commentary sought to draw a line between informational and persuasive advertising: the protection of trademarks may well be socially beneficial in so far as it incentivizes traders to better inform consumers as to the properties and qualities of the goods; but protection is not needed in so far as trademarks were a vehicle for persuasive advertising to generate artificial desires and needs. Other critics recognized that trademark rights could be vehicles for reducing information available to consumers by privileging the trademark owner's ability to shape its own message.

As with patents, trademark registration systems have distinct informational roles. In principle, they are supposed to offer traders a means of finding out about existing exclusive rights. This is achieved through a combination of representation of the mark and identification of a list of goods and services in relation to which a mark is used (or intended to be used). In the era of digitization, information about the use of signs by other traders is probably more easily accessed through the *internet than via the networks of trademark registers. In contrast with patents, no claims are made that the collecting of information about trademarks in a central register has other benefits, and some commentators have begun to express doubts as to whether the costs associated with these information systems are justified.

Lionel Bently

See also commodification; globalization; indexing; information, disinformation, misinformation; learning; public sphere; publicity/publication; reference books; registers; teaching

FURTHER READING

L. Bently and M. Kretschmer, eds., Primary Sources on Copyright (online); A. Birrell, *Seven Lectures on the Law and History of Copyright in Books*, 1899; S. Bottomley, *The British Patent System during the Industrial Revolution, 1700–1852: From Privilege to Property*, 2014; O. Bracha, *Owning Ideas: The Intellectual Origins of American Intellectual Property Law 1790–1909*, 2018; R. Deazley, *On the Origin of the Right to Copy: Charting the Movement of Copyright Law in Eighteenth Century Britain (1695–1775)*, 2004; Jane Ginsburg, "A Tale of Two Copyrights: Literary Property in Revolutionary France and America," *Tulane Law Review* 65, no. 5 (1990): 991–1032; Carla Hesse, "The Rise of Intellectual Property, 700 B.C.–A.D. 2000: An Idea in the Balance," *Daedalus* 131, no. 2 (2002): 6–45; W. Landes and R. Posner, *The Economic Structure of Intellectual Property Law*, 2003; B. Sherman and L. Bently, *The Making of Modern Intellectual Property: The British Experience*, 1999.

INTELLIGENCE TESTING

In 2018, one of the leading behavioral geneticists, Robert Plomin, proclaimed that the time would soon come when intelligence testing could be abandoned. Plomin had spent much of his career analyzing the genetic bases of intelligence, and so this prediction could have signaled the final demise of an enterprise that had been embroiled in controversy since Alfred Binet and Théodore Simon's invention of the modern intelligence test in 1905. Plomin was not conceding, however, that those criticizing intelligence testing were right and that all such tests were inextricably culture bound. Rather, he foresaw their abandonment in favor of another form of testing and information extraction, genome-wide association studies carried out on DNA snippets, a technique that he imagined might eventually allow parents to use direct-to-consumer DNA tests to know the intelligence level of a child from birth (or even in utero).

Putting aside some of the technical issues with Plomin's claim (by his own admission, for example, genes might account for at most 50 percent of measured intelligence), his turn to DNA as the gold standard for determining an individual's intelligence is an indication of how closely intertwined intelligence measurement and information are and have historically been. A person's DNA code and his or her intelligence level not only are themselves pieces of information about that individual but also, in principle, provide access to important aspects of what the person can and will become, at least in the eyes of those such as Plomin who are convinced of the primary influence of these elements. Genes, for Plomin, constitute a way of escaping the culture-bound nature of intelligence tests by drilling down to the information bedrock that each individual carries within him- or herself, regardless of when or where born. While the conception of DNA as the "code of life"—or pure biological information—is relatively recent, the underlying idea that an individual's external physical and behavioral manifestations are largely products of particular internal states or features has a long history. Genetic testing could thus realize intelligence testing's long-sought goal: to provide reliable knowledge about a fundamental characteristic of an individual's nature, one that explained and helped determine significant aspects of his or her destiny. This article will briefly sketch the history of intelligence testing as an information technology in order to place Plomin's endeavor in historical perspective and to explore what it is about this form of information gathering that has remained simultaneously so alluring and so problematic.

Although intelligence testing in its modern form dates from the early twentieth century, it is rooted in a tradition of attempting to gain knowledge about central and difficult-to-observe aspects of human nature that stretches back in the Western tradition for centuries. Classical Greek medicine, for example, used *humoral theory to postulate the existence of four basic types of temperament: choleric, melancholic, sanguine, and phlegmatic, states that were at once psychological and physiological. Individuals might have their own particular combination of the four humoral elements—hot, wet, cold, dry—but each could be understood as fitting one of these broader types, and thus conclusions about their strengths and weaknesses, as well as the kinds of medical treatments they might need, could be derived from the broad classification. This postulation of some set of internal factors that could provide information about the externally manifested behaviors of an individual, as well as the turn to groups or categories of individuals to give meaning to the internal signs, has remained a hallmark of investigations into attributes such as intelligence up to the present day.

Intelligence itself as a particular characteristic of individual minds (human and nonhuman) became the subject of sustained scientific exploration starting in the early eighteenth century, when Carl Linnaeus and other naturalists began to compare animal types systematically in order to construct *taxonomies of the living world, and used intellectual capability as one of the differentiating features. The Dutch anatomist Peter Camper in the 1760s was among the earliest to attempt to quantify intelligence differences by proposing that a particular physiological feature, the facial angle, would allow a variety of human and animal types to be ranged into an intelligence hierarchy, with ancient Greeks at the top, Africans at the border with nonhuman animals, followed by apes and then down to dogs and other lower mammals. The facial angle was but the first of a number of bodily measures proposed during the late eighteenth and nineteenth centuries that were presumed to provide some information about the mental power of the group being measured and that were most frequently used to justify a racial hierarchy with white Europeans at the top and African peoples at the bottom. Cranial capacity and brain weight quickly came to dominate and were occasionally used to explain the mental prowess of individuals; nonetheless, these quantifications and most others could reveal patterns only when measurements of many different individuals were combined so that statistical regularities could emerge. And by the end of the century, significant variability both within and between the groups of interest (typically ethnoracial) suggested to most practitioners that these physical measures were not providing the information necessary to explain why some groups or individuals seemed (to them) more intellectually capable than others.

The turn to more psychophysical or purely psychological approaches to extracting information about individual intelligence blossomed in the late nineteenth and early twentieth centuries, primarily based on the work of two individuals, Francis Galton in England and Alfred Binet in France. Beginning in the 1860s, Galton conducted a variety of statistical and anthropometric studies on individual differences in mental as well as physical characteristics to show that psychological attributes varied in a population, as did physical ones, according to the bell-shaped normal distribution curve, and thus that mental attributes such as genius were biological in origin and heritable. Where Galton's goal was to explain eminence and why it ran in families, Binet's, at least initially, was to identify children of subnormal intelligence for the purposes of special education. The intelligence scale that he and Simon devised in 1905 and then revised in 1908 and 1911 eventually produced a single number, the mental age (MA), meant to characterize the intellectual level of any child administered the examination and thus to reveal a significant and previously difficult-to-isolate feature of his or her nature. Like the purely physical measures, however, the information provided by these individual psychological assessments was at its core statistical: a comparison of the performance of the individual tested with that of "normal" children of the same age.

The Binet-Simon Intelligence Scale was quickly adopted and modified in Britain, the United States, and eventually wherever so-called scientific psychology flourished. The most significant early refinement of the scale came at the hands of the Stanford psychologist Lewis M. Terman in 1916. His Stanford-Binet intelligence test was standardized on 905 California school children and helped introduce the concept of the intelligence quotient (IQ), a ratio of mental age to chronological age developed by the German psychologist William Stern, as a way to provide a measure of intelligence that was in theory constant over time. Subsequently revised in 1937, 1973, 1986, and most recently 2003, the Stanford-Binet has remained one of the preeminent ways in which an individual's intelligence is assessed. Its main rival has been the tests of child and adult intelligence developed by the American psychologist David Wechsler, the Wechsler Intelligence Scale for Children (WISC) and the Wechsler Adult Intelligence Scale (WAIS).

Both the Stanford-Binet and the Wechsler instruments require one-on-one interactions between the examiner and individual being examined; they have found their main uses in clinical settings. A second branch of intelligence testing developed out of the Binet-Simon during World War I: group-administered examinations, often employing multiple-choice questions. Created by a team of psychologists led by Robert M. Yerkes to aid the US war effort, the principal group test, Army Alpha, was used to screen almost 1.75 million soldiers during the war, providing information relied on by some commanders to balance military units according to intelligence or to select soldiers as candidates for officer training. Although many military leaders were skeptical about the value of the information the tests provided, during the post–World War I period intelligence testing flourished. Public school systems in the United States, Britain, and other nations adopted intelligence testing for the purposes of placing students in educational tracks; industries employed testing for personnel decisions; and after the Princeton psychologist Carl C. Brigham developed the Scholastic Aptitude Test (SAT) in 1926, colleges and universities increasingly incorporated intelligence assessments into admissions decisions. In virtually all these settings, intelligence testing was employed in order to rationalize (and perhaps legitimate) some form of rationing of limited resources based on the presumption that intelligence level provided information that could serve as a stand-in for merit, thereby ensuring that the "best" were chosen. The ethnoracial and class implications of relying on such information, however, were visible from the start. Group-level analyses of the data from the army testing program were interpreted as demonstrating that intelligence ratings reproduced standard class and ethnoracial hierarchies, even though many of the results seemed to correlate closely with level and quality of education. Many psychologists believed the hierarchies confirmed the legitimacy and accuracy of the tests as measures of native intelligence; others, particularly a number of African American scholars, argued that the group-level results provided information about familiarity with English, level of educational attainment, and quality of education far more than about intrinsic mental ability.

Throughout the interwar period, and indeed up to the present day, psychologists, educators, and laypeople debated these questions about whether intelligence testing provides any real information about individuals or groups and, if so, what exactly it reveals. The test results themselves can be analyzed to demonstrate that intelligence is a single mental entity, or composed of a small set of separate abilities, or the product of an almost unlimited number of different factors. The strong correlation of IQ scores with socioeconomic status has been used by some to argue for the meritocratic nature of Western societies, while others have emphasized the culture-bound character of all intelligence measurement instruments and thus their inability to provide a true picture of an individual or group. Although scientific (though not necessarily popular) support for the existence of inborn group-level differences in intelligence has largely receded, Plomin's turn to DNA analysis as the next frontier in intelligence testing is a pointed reminder of how unsettled the question of nature versus nurture remains within scientific and popular circles at the level of individuals and how powerfully real the differences that intelligence tests have revealed (or generated) have become. The tests themselves are, in a double sense, information technologies: not only are they designed to assess some combination of the amount of information an individual possesses plus their ability to process that information, but they also are represented by their advocates as providing a new kind of information about the individual tested, a measure able to reveal a person's basic intellectual potential, and by their critics as revealing the ways in which bias and privilege can be occluded through the invocation of scientific objectivity.

John Carson

See also knowledge; learning; quantification; teaching

FURTHER READING

John Carson, *The Measure of Merit*, 2007; Nicholas Lemann, *The Big Test*, 1999; Erik Linstrum, *Ruling Minds: Psychology in the British Empire*, 2016; Annette Mülberger, "The Need for Contextual Approaches to the History of Mental Testing," *History of Psychology* 17, no. 3 (2014): 177–86; Richard E. Nisbett, Joshua Aronson, Clancy Blair, William Dickens, James Flynn, Diane F. Halpern, and Eric Turkheimer, "Intelligence: New Findings and Theoretical Developments," *American Psychologist* 67, no. 2 (2012): 130–59; Robert Plomin and Sophie von Stumm, "The New Genetics of Intelligence," *Nature Reviews Genetics* 19, no. 3 (2018): 148–59; Adrian Wooldridge, *Measuring the Mind*, 1994; Leila Zenderland, *Measuring Minds*, 1998.

INVENTORIES

An *inventory*, as the Latin etymology of the word indicates, is a list of things that have been found. Today, we often associate the word with the commercial practice of keeping track of stock on hand. This association is the legacy of *early modern business practices: in Luca Pacioli's 1494 treatise on *bookkeeping, the goods inventory constituted a key element of a system known as "early perpetual inventory recording." But the habit of making lists of found things long antedates the commercial function. Ancient temples and sanctuaries kept lists of the objects held within the precinct. Medieval European popes, bishops, and monasteries made inventories of their treasures. By the thirteenth century, royal courts and noble houses had picked up the habit, producing inventories of their wardrobes, household effects, and libraries. The custom persists today in the Oxbridge colleges, whose officers periodically conduct inventories of their colleges' silver plate.

One of the most ubiquitous types of inventories in the Arabic and Christian societies of western Eurasia and northern Africa was the postmortem or probate inventory. Records of the Cairo Genizah reveal instances of people making postmortem inventories in Fatimid Egypt, and the practice is attested in Islamic documents from fourteenth-century Jerusalem. In Europe, numerous ecclesiastical inventories survive from throughout the Middle Ages, and inventories of the laity appear in archival sources from the thirteenth century onward. The number of extant inventories increases exponentially during the early modern period, and the legal *genre leapt the Atlantic and spread to all parts of the globe touched by European settler colonialism.

The surge in inventory making in early modern Europe was paralleled in the Ottoman world. Here, the words for the genre—*muhallefat* and *tereke*—come from Arabic roots that mean "to leave (behind)." In China, similar types of documents, called *fendan* or *yizhu*, were generated by the process of household division, *fenjia*. The people who made these documents, the earliest of which dates to the tenth century, were especially interested in lands, buildings, fishponds, and so on, but they also paid attention to the kinds of movable goods that feature in Ottoman and European sources, such as furniture, livestock, tools, books, and utensils. The documents produced by European, Ottoman, and Chinese legal customs are similar in function. The fact that they draw on different conceptual roots, however, raises the philosophical question of whether it is appropriate to assimilate them into a single genre.

By the eighteenth century, complex changes in law and society were beginning to conspire against the practice of keeping postmortem inventories in European societies. Among other things, the growing volume of household objects, coupled with the declining value of goods relative to the value of financial investments and properties, made full inventories less useful from a financial perspective. Postmortem inventories remained a legal requirement in some regions of the world into the twentieth century, however, and the practice has persisted informally.

The practice of keeping inventories of things or goods is associated with the understanding that goods have value and that they are mobile. This is why goods attract the regulatory instincts of commercial and inheritance law. Yet the genre should not be limited by the horizons of legal or practical necessity. An inventory is a device we use to order and in some cases to commemorate the world of things. When people decide to make inventories of things, they do so in part because the very act of making an inventory is a statement about oneself or one's loved ones. As the anthropology of consumption has demonstrated, identity is intimately associated with the penumbra of things that envelops all of us. An inventory, in short, is more than just a list of things. It is an act that defines the contours of personhood.

The taking of any inventory, for this reason, can have important symbolic dimensions. During the occupation of France in the Second World War, Nazis entered the households of Jewish families and stripped them of artwork, furniture, clothing, and other things. After the war, members of the families whose goods had been plundered were asked to create inventories of the stolen objects. They did so by entering the palaces of their own memories and listing what they found there retrospectively. The inventories that resulted were ostensibly made in the hopes of recovering the families' things or laying the groundwork for reparations. As Leora Auslander has suggested, however, the process also provided an opportunity for grieving people to commune with lost things and to take stock of the world that was.

An inventory, as mentioned above, is a list of things that have been found. Each element of this sentence merits attention. As a list, an inventory partakes in a genealogy as old as writing itself. An essential quality of all lists is that they are paratactic, since the ordering of their elements is not derived from verbs or coordinating conjunctions. As Jack Goody has suggested, when lists came into being they invited a form of cognition different from that which governs normal speech. Parataxis also promotes the tabular layout that we often associate with list making. In addition, some lists include typographical devices such as bullet points, stock words such as "item," and indentations. A list does not have to be tabular, of course. Lists kept in paragraph form are especially likely to include typographical devices that mark the beginnings and ends of object phrases.

A variety of conceptual objects are list worthy: things of many kinds; people (class rosters; censuses; king lists); references (bibliographies; *encyclopedias), and abstract or timeless entities (the periodic table of elements). Regardless of their contents, almost all lists, inventories among them, aspire to completeness. A dictionary, for example, seeks to be a complete list of the words of a language; it would make no sense to have a dictionary that ends with the letter Y. But completeness is a difficult thing to achieve. Unless a given list seeks to record everything there is in the universe, it can aspire to be complete only within a defined domain. For this reason, list making inspires habits of categorization and classification. Contemplating the extant corpus of European postmortem inventories, we can make out an important stage of this history, as the spatial system of classification typical of the late medieval inventory gradually expanded to include systems based on monetary value and object typology.

Although all inventories are lists, not all lists are inventories. No one would say that shopping lists, to-do lists, and wish lists are inventories. More challengingly, a strict definition of the genre would probably exclude catalogs and collection guides kept by librarians and curators. To appreciate the difference, imagine a collection damaged by fire, flood, or theft. Not knowing the extent of the loss, the curator may commission an inventory in order to find out what remains. The resulting inventory could subsequently serve as the basis for a new catalog, of course, but that is a subsequent stage in the life cycle of the document. Some of the earliest catalogs of European library holdings began life in the fifteenth century in just this way, that is to say as components of postmortem royal inventories. With the passage of time, the book list emancipated itself from the inventory, thereby transforming itself into a catalog. The difference is subtle but important: where a catalog describes what purports to be there, an inventory describes what was actually found.

As a list of found things, an inventory results from an inquiry into a single facet of a thing's identity, namely, the facet of belonging. In a paradoxical way, a postmortem inventory provides a list of things at the very moment when the underlying principle of classification—that they belong to someone—has just winked out of existence. As this suggests, inventories often provide lists of things that will soon be on the move. Since the results of any inquiry into inherently mobile things will be valid for only so long, the early modern postmortem inventory, unlike a dictionary or a catalog, was not designed to record the enduring or the universal. Like a radioactive element, an inventory should be thought of as having a half-life that describes the decay of its own informational utility. Much the same is true for the commercial inventory, although the half-life of utility will vary depending on the type of goods in store.

The inherent ephemerality of the genre raises questions about the informational service that inventories performed. Information consists of sets of things that are given or discovered. In the early modern era, postmortem inventories provided crucial information for probate and related processes. They made it possible for the executors to repay the creditors of the estate and distribute goods among the beneficiaries. But it is crucial to understand that inventories were never designed to record durable information about things. After a few weeks or months, an early modern postmortem inventory will, in theory, no longer carry any meaningful information whatsoever, at least where its original function is concerned. Like all archival sources, early modern inventories survive today because people found it possible to repurpose them for different informational ends, including symbolic ones. The lesson is important: we use inventories today for reasons undreamt of by their makers.

Daniel Lord Smail

See also appraising; archivists; art of memory; book sales catalogs; documentary authority; indexing; libraries and catalogs; lists

FURTHER READING

Leora Auslander, "Beyond Words," *American Historical Review* 110 (2005): 1015–45; Mary Carolyn Beaudry, ed., *Documentary Archaeology in the New World*, 1988; Jack Goody, *The Domestication of the Savage Mind*, 1977; Ad van der Woude and Anton Schuurman, eds., *Probate Inventories: A New Source for the Historical Study of Wealth, Material Culture and Agricultural Development; Papers Presented at the Leeuwenborch Conference, Wageningen, 5–7 May 1980*, 1980; David Wakefield, *Fenjia: Household Division and Inheritance in Qing and Republican China*, 1998.

JOURNALS

A journal is a specialized periodical that prints articles researchers have written for an audience of their scholarly peers. As such, they are principal sources of scholarly information. Scholars in fields from physics to law regard publishing in journals as an essential part of a research career. Journals are particularly important in the sciences, where journal articles are the overwhelmingly dominant form of communication between researchers. The research journal has a complicated history, however, and even today the seemingly simple label of "journal" can belie an enormous diversity in content and format, especially across disciplinary boundaries.

THE EARLIEST JOURNALS

The *Philosophical Transactions of the Royal Society* and the *Journal des Sçavans* (Journal of the learned), generally regarded as the first journals, began publication in 1665 in London and Paris, respectively. Other journals such as the German *Acta Eruditorum* (Proceedings of the learned) followed close behind. Articles in seventeenth-century journals were often not accounts of experiments or original research, as we would expect today. The first issue of the *Philosophical Transactions*, for example, contained an account of recent improvements in optical glass making, a notice about Robert Boyle's new book *An Experimental History of Cold*, and a story about the birth of a monstrous calf. The first number of the *Journal des Sçavans*, a publication focused on political and historical commentary, included a first-person account of a trip through Spain, an essay about a collector's personal antiquities, and a poem about gardening.

For much of the seventeenth and eighteenth centuries, most journals either were affiliated with *learned societies, such as the English Royal Society or the French Académie des Sciences, or were the personal projects of passionate editors who wanted to publish interesting knowledge. Learned society periodicals were slow to publish, often issuing just one volume per year or even less. Editor-run journals published more frequently—often quarterly or monthly—and their contents tended to be somewhat more eclectic, reflecting the interests of the person who chose their articles.

THE RISE OF JOURNALS IN THE NINETEENTH CENTURY

The scholarly journal system that researchers use today began to take shape in the natural sciences in the nineteenth century. At the beginning of the nineteenth century, important scientific discoveries could be announced in a range of formats, including monographs, *encyclopedia articles, public lectures, popular magazines, and pamphlets. By the end of the nineteenth century that was no longer true—the journal article had become the standard *genre for announcing new scientific findings.

The rise of the journal was related to several major shifts in the social and intellectual status of science during the nineteenth century. As science became seen as a more respectable intellectual pursuit, researchers no longer felt the need to present their work to a lay audience in popular periodicals or accessible pamphlets. Instead, because more paying posts for scientific research were being created at universities and in governments, researchers' professional advancement increasingly depended on impressing their scientific peers. Publishing in a specialist journal for an audience of fellow researchers therefore became more desirable than publishing in any other format. Concern for scientific priority also drove the shift to publishing shorter journal articles instead of longer monographs, as researchers sought to publish their work as quickly as possible in order to secure their scientific reputations.

The natural sciences were not the only research discipline where journals grew in number and importance during the nineteenth century. Members of newly formed disciplines in the social sciences, such as psychology and sociology, generally founded journals early in their discipline's history. Examples of such journals include the *Psychological Review*, founded in 1894, and *L'Année Sociologique* (The year in sociology), founded in 1896. In history, the *Historische Zeitschrift* (Historical journal) began publication in Berlin in 1859 and quickly became a major site of historical scholarship; it was followed by the *Revue Historique* (Historical review) in France in 1876, the *American Historical Review* in 1884, and the *English Historical Review* in 1886. In the *humanities, however, journal publishing remained (and still remains) only one of several genres of scholarly communication. In history, classics, and literary studies, for instance, books are still considered essential vehicles for new research findings.

PEER REVIEW AND SCHOLARLY CREDIBILITY

The practice of sending submissions to journals out for referee reports—opinions about the paper from the author's fellow experts—also dates from the nineteenth century. That practice began first in learned society journals, where members of societies wanted to ensure that their periodicals reflected well on their organization as a whole. However, the earliest referee reports were often considered confidential documents for a society's internal use and were not usually given to the author.

Most editor-run journals did not adopt refereeing during the nineteenth century. Editors generally felt themselves qualified to evaluate any contribution that came their way. Significantly, during the nineteenth and early twentieth centuries, journals that used refereeing were not seen as more legitimate or scholarly than those that did not. Refereeing was an optional bureaucratic process, not a requirement for scholarly respectability.

During the Cold War, refereeing—or "peer review," as it was increasingly called—slowly became seen as an essential part of scholarly journal publishing. The idea that a journal had to be peer reviewed to be credible seems to have its origins in the United States. As public interest in science rose during the Cold War, American scientists looked for a way to maintain autonomy over scientific funding decisions without surrendering their new public status. They promoted peer review as an indispensable part of the scientific process, arguing that scientific research would be corrupted if it was evaluated by anyone other than a scientific researcher.

Nonscientific disciplines tended to maintain their trust in editors and were more reluctant to adopt systematic peer review. In 1969, only a quarter of rejected papers at
the prestigious *American Historical Review* had been sent out for referee opinions; the
rest were rejected on the editor's authority. A 1979 survey of history journals found that
only 12 percent of them employed external referees to help decide which articles would
be printed. Journals outside the United States were also less likely than American ones
to employ external peer review in the 1970s and 1980s. The British scientific weekly
Nature, for example, adopted systematic external refereeing for all articles it printed
only in 1973. As late as 1989, some readers and editors outside the United States viewed
the American emphasis on peer review with bemusement. In a 1989 editorial, for instance, the British medical journal the *Lancet* complained that "in the United States far
too much is being asked of peer review" and proudly assured readers that at the *Lancet*,
"reviewers are advisers not decision makers." Despite such concerns, however, by the
mid-1990s few academic journals in any field, or any country, remained peer-review
holdouts.

JOURNALS IN THE LATE MODERN PERIOD

The rise of peer review was only one of the important changes that occurred for journals in the second half of the twentieth century. The number of scholarly journals expanded rapidly, as did the size of many prominent journals. For instance, the 1950 volume of the *Annual Review of Psychology* contained 310 pages; the 1970 volume contained
628 pages. Even more dramatically, the 1940 volume of the physics journal *Physical Review* had 2,310 pages, but in 1969—the last year the American Physical Society attempted to publish just one unified *Physical Review* instead of *Physical Review A* through
Physical Review D—the journal published a whopping 24,533 pages.

The rising number of journals and articles led to overwhelmed readers and librarians, and to attempts to quantify the importance of individual journals in order to prioritize reading lists and subscription money. Most famously, in 1972 the bibliographer
Eugene Garfield began publishing lists of *"impact factors," the average number of citations to each article published in a journal. The implication was that journals with
high impact factors were more widely read and more important than journals with low
impact factors.

In the late twentieth century journal publishing in the natural and social sciences
shifted from a multilingual system, in which important scientific findings might be
printed in a number of different languages, to a system in which English is the overwhelmingly dominant language of scientific communication. This period also saw the
rise of *"publish or perish" culture in most scholarly disciplines. Hiring and promotion
for scholars became increasingly dependent on a scholar's publication record—with only
peer-reviewed publications considered valid.

JOURNALS MOVE ONLINE

For most of their history, journals existed entirely in print, but beginning in the early
1990s *publishers began experimenting with electronic journals. Early attempts to distribute journals via CD-ROM were expensive and folded quickly. However, online jour-

nals proved to be a far more cost-effective and accessible format. Today, few scholars read print issues of journals cover to cover. Instead, they access most of their reading online through personal or institutional subscriptions to electronic journal databases. Many journals also permit researchers to purchase access to individual articles for a fee, often $30 or more per article.

Since the advent of online publishing, the cost of journal subscriptions for libraries has consistently outpaced inflation. Many scholars are voicing frustration with the economic side of journal publishing. Because researchers are expected to receive professional rewards for their publications directly from their employers, journals do not pay their authors. Most journals also do not pay their peer reviewers (although a few disciplines, including economics, have started compensating referees more regularly). For-profit publishing giants like Springer Nature and Elsevier have increasingly come under scrutiny for their high subscription costs and their impressive profit margins. Some observers argue that all scholarly journals should be *"open access," with their contents freely available to any interested reader. Open-access journals such as *PLOS One* are starting to gain some traction; however, the long-term impact of the open access movement on the journal format remains to be seen.

Melinda Baldwin

See also books; commodification; libraries and catalogs; newspapers; professors; publicity/publication; readers

FURTHER READING

Melinda Baldwin, *Making "Nature": The History of a Scientific Journal*, 2015; idem, "Scientific Autonomy, Public Accountability, and the Rise of 'Peer Review' in the Cold War United States," *Isis* 109, no. 3 (2018): 538–58; Alex Csiszar, *The Scientific Journal: Authorship and the Politics of Knowledge in the Nineteenth Century*, 2018; Aileen Fyfe, Julie McDougall-Waters, and Noah Moxham, "350 Years of Scientific Periodicals," *Notes and Records: The Royal Society Journal of the History of Science* 69, no. 3 (2015): 227–39; Michael Gordin, *Scientific Babel: The Language of Science from the Fall of Latin to the Rise of English*, 2015; Margaret F. Steig, *The Origin and Development of Scholarly Historical Periodicals*, 2005; Anne Weller, *Editorial Peer Review: Its Strengths and Weaknesses*, 2001.

KHIPUS

Khipus—multicolored threads that record information—represent one of the longest-lasting Native American forms of inscription, having been used in the Andes for over a millennium, from the Wari Empire (600–1100 CE) to the mid-twentieth century. Fashioned from cotton, maguey, camelid, deer, or sheep fibers, khipus have taken a variety of configurations over their thousand-year history. However, the most common khipu structure is that referred to as a "standard Inka style," where multiple pendant cords hang down from a horizontal "main cord" (figure 1). Pendants may be different colors and may contain knots that indicate decimal numbers.

During the Inka Empire (c. 1400–1532 CE), when khipus were the predominant way to record information, experts known as *khipukamayoqs* created two kinds: one for encoding economic and accounting data, and another for recording narratives, history, and poetry.

1. ACCOUNTING KHIPUS

According to Spanish and native Andean chroniclers, accounting khipus recorded demographic data, labor tributes, inventories, and other types of numerical information throughout the Inka Empire. While many mysteries remain about how they encoded information, scholars have deciphered some basic principles.

In 1923 Leland Locke decoded how to read numbers on accounting khipus. Generally there exist three kinds of khipu knots: simple overhand knots, long knots, and figure-eight knots. In a long knot, a cord is wrapped around itself two or more times, making a cylinder with two to nine turns, depending on what number is intended. A figure-eight knot, where the cord forms the shape of the numeral eight, indicates "1." The decimal value of a knot is determined by its place along the pendant, with knots closest to the top cord possessing the highest value. If, for example, there are three groups of knots on a pendant, the knots nearest the top cord have a value in the hundreds, the middle knots have a value in the tens, and bottom knots in the ones (see figure 1). For example, a pendant with a single overhand knot in the hundreds place, three overhand knots in the tens place, and a long knot with eight turns in the ones place would equal 138.

One of the two most frequent color patterns of the pendant cords is "color-banding," where multiple pendants of one color are followed by multiple pendants of another color—for example, four cream, four blue, four brown, and so on. In the other common color pattern, "seriation," a sequence of pendant colors is repeated over and over—for example, cream, blue, brown; cream, blue, brown; and so on. While researching twentieth-century accounting khipus, I deciphered the meaning of these patterns: color banding indicates individual information, whereas seriation signifies aggregate data from numerous color-banded khipus. For example, in a color-banded khipu, each band

Figure 1. "Inka style" numerical khipu with a seriated color pattern. #1931.32.1, Pitt Rivers Museum, Oxford University. Photo by author.

of one color might indicate a particular villager, with each pendant representing a different task fulfilled by that person. In a seriated khipu, however, each sequence might indicate a particular task, with each cord showing the contributions of all the individuals in the village. Seriated khipus represent the combined information of multiple color-banded khipus.

A Peruvian scientist, Mariano Eduardo de Rivero, discovered that special threads or needlework bundles at the beginning of the top cord indicated a khipu's subject matter. Writing in the nineteenth century, he suggested that the meaning of other signs varied according to the particular topic. Rivero's insights about subject markers had been largely forgotten by scholars. However, recent investigations into modern accounting khipus have confirmed that *kaytes*—the special markers on the top cord—indicated the khipu's subject; the structure of the top cord probably did as well. The meaning of secondary symbols, such as color, ply direction, and knot direction, depended upon the type of khipu. The significance of a crimson pendant, for instance, was contingent on whether it was an inventory of food, a record of tribute labor, or a list of ritual offerings, to name a few possibilities. Binary markers, like the difference in ply direction (twisted to the right or the left) signified binary contrasts, such as the distinction between male and female animals. The specific meanings of these binary markers depended on the type of khipu and where the cord was placed. These intricate devices could express complex information with great sophistication and nuance.

2. NARRATIVE KHIPUS

Andean chroniclers claimed that Inka khipus encoded historical narratives, biographies, poetry, and songs in addition to economic and demographic information. They also described the existence of khipu missives sent from one individual to another,

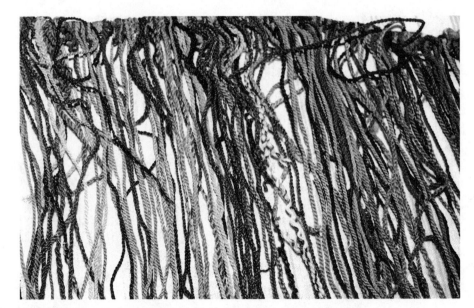

Figure 2. Khipu A pendant cords, Collata, Peru. Photo by author.

which implies that these letters could be "read" by persons other than their creators. How these narrative khipus inscribed such literary forms of information remains a mystery.

However, a clue to how Inka khipus recorded narratives has appeared in San Juan de Collata, a remote highland community in central Peru. In 2015 village elders invited me to study their two khipus, which had been kept secret from outsiders (figure 2). According to traditions formally passed on to young men when they accept their first major ceremonial role in the community, the khipus were missives sent among local leaders. Lineage (*ayllu*) chiefs, they say, created these epistles during a revolt against Spanish rule led by a claimant to the Inka throne, Felipe Tupa Inka Yupanki, in the 1780s. It is believed that one may have announced the beginning of the revolt while the other invited neighboring officials to render homage to Felipe Tupa Inka.

These complex khipus, which lack knots, were fashioned from the fibers of six different animals (vicuña, alpaca, llama, deer, guanaco, and vizcacha); in many cases, the type of fiber can only be identified by touch. Villagers refer to the khipus as "a language of animals." They have characteristics that correspond to logosyllabic writing systems, which use a combination of phonetic (syllabic) and nonphonetic indicators to express the sounds of speech. They possess over ninety-five syllabic characters, each one consisting of a pendant with a unique combination of color, ply direction, and fiber type. I have been able to decipher the final three pendant cords on each khipu, which phonetically spell out the names of two prominent lineages (A-LLU-KA and A-KA-PAR).

Similar missives were made for a previous revolt in the same region, suggesting that these phonetic khipus represent a tradition of some antiquity. However, it is currently unclear whether the cords' phoneticism was a colonial innovation or descended from pre-Columbian khipus. The largest catalog, Harvard's Khipu Database (KDB), contains information on slightly more than a third of all extant khipus (550 out of approximately 1,450). The KDB lacks consistent data on the materials from which the khipus were made, so it is impossible to determine whether it includes others with a degree of diversity in animal fibers that is similar to the Collata khipus. It is also unknown whether khipus with features similar to those of the Collata cords exist among those in museums and universities that have not yet been studied. Efforts are underway to utilize artificial intelligence and computational linguistics to decipher the remainder of the Collata khipus and to identify other potentially phonetic khipus.

NATIVE AMERICAN PHILOLOGY

Khipus represent one of many Native American forms of inscription, a category that encompasses Maya glyphs, Nahua pictographs, Zapotec script, Ojibwa birch bark scrolls, Haudenosaunee wampum, and Lakota day-counts, among others. As Elizabeth Hill Boone has stated, studying texts that are "executed in graphic registers other than alphabetic writing, specifically histories that are painted, knotted, and threaded" promises to reveal new insights into the epistemologies of the Indigenous peoples who have created them. Nonalphabetic methods of conveying information are not "failed" attempts at alphabeticism; rather, they consist of artifacts that are inherently closer to Native American systems of knowledge and thus convey this knowledge more accurately. In the Andes, for example, the sense of touch plays a crucial role in Indigenous epistemology; it is likely that the tactile nature of khipu coding is one of the reasons why Andean people continued to make khipus even when they had access to alphabetic writing. As scholars gain a greater understanding of the inscriptive traditions of the Americas, we can develop a truly global philology, one that embraces the ancient information systems of the Western Hemisphere.

Sabine Hyland

See also accounting; archaeological decipherment; documentary authority; inscriptions; inventories; letters

FURTHER READING:

Elizabeth Hill Boone, "Presidential Lecture: Discourse and Authority in Histories Painted, Knotted, and Threaded," *Ethnohistory* 59, no. 2 (2012): 211–37; Galen Brokaw, *A History of the Khipu*, 2010; Sabine Hyland, "How Khipus Indicated Labour Contributions in an Andean Village: An Explanation of Seriation, Colour Banding, and Ethnocategories," *Journal of Material Culture* 21, no. 4 (2016): 490–509; Hyland, "Writing with Twisted Cords," *Current Anthropology* 58, no. 3 (2017): 412–19; Frank Salomon, *The Cord Keepers: Khipus and Cultural Life in a Peruvian Village*, 2004; Gary Urton and Carrie J. Brezine, "Khipu Accounting in Ancient Peru," *Science* 309, no. 5737 (2005): 1065–67.

KNOWLEDGE

What do we mean by *knowledge*? The term is sometimes used as a synonym for information. In the United States, this book is one of a number of books on the "history of information," implying a pragmatic approach, but in Britain a more common phrase is the "history of knowledge," implying a concern with philosophical debates about the question *How do we know?* In similar fashion to the British, the French write the history of *savoirs*, and the Germans, that of *Wissenschaft* (referring to organized knowledge and not simply to natural science). Scholars who read Chinese, Japanese, Arabic, and other non-Western languages will be able to add to these examples. The studies themselves, though, often distinguish between information, which is relatively "raw," and knowledge, which has been woven or "cooked": in other words, transformed into a relatively finished product. Sometimes a third term is added, raw "data," implying that information is half-cooked while knowledge is fully cooked. In any case, what is believed to be knowledge varies a great deal between places, periods, and social groups. In sixteenth-century Europe, for instance, it was virtually taken for granted that witches existed. As the Hungarian sociologist Karl Mannheim (1893–1947) argued, everyone's knowledge is socially situated, shaped not only by personal experience but also by the surrounding culture.

VARIETIES OF KNOWLEDGE

Different kinds of knowledge are often distinguished—implicit and explicit, for instance, or knowing how and knowing that. The phrase "implicit knowledge," sometimes known as "implicit memory," refers to knowledge that has become habitual and so unconscious, to skills such as driving a car or making a pot, for example. Much practical knowledge or "know-how" takes this form, in contrast to knowledge that is explicit, academic, and often theoretical. Academic knowledge has often been described as "learning"; in German, *Gelehrtheit*, and in Latin, *litterae*, a term that was not confined to what we call "literature." The *early modern phrase *Respublica Litterarum* is best translated not as the *"Republic of Letters" but as the "Commonwealth of Learning."

Historians have long concerned themselves with explicit knowledge. Histories of philosophy go back to the seventeenth century, and histories of science to the nineteenth. What is new is the turn from concentrating on the history of academic knowledge (in German, *Wissenschaftsgeschichte*) to including all kinds of knowledge (*Wissensgeschichte*), thinking of knowledges in the plural rather than knowledge in the singular. Some scholars now concern themselves with the history of what they variously call "orders," "regimes," or "cultures" of knowledge, in short with the relation between different kinds of knowledge in a given place and time, including their hierarchies. In late medieval universities, for instance, theology was regarded (at least officially) as the queen of the sciences, in other words the highest form of knowledge, while the academic disciplines, known as the *liberal arts, were considered to be superior to "mechanical arts" such as weaving, cooking, or trade. Again, from the eighteenth century onward, some individuals and groups distinguished between what they called useful knowledge, which they regarded as superior, and knowledge for its own sake, which they rejected. The debate continues.

This expansion of interest in the varieties of knowledge has brought problems in its train. How, for example, can one write the history of implicit knowledges? Individuals acquire these knowledges by following the example of the already skilled, punctuated by a few words of advice, a process of learning that leaves no traces for historians to study. They have to work at one remove, reading how-to books on good manners, cookery, calligraphy, medicine, diplomacy, building, and so on; examining artifacts, the deposits of past skills, like archaeologists; or observing skills in the present, like anthropologists, and then trying to adjust what has been observed to the technologies and mentalities current in earlier centuries.

KNOWLEDGE IN THE MAKING

The example of skills vividly reveals how knowledges are created, transmitted, and refined. Other kinds of knowledge can also be studied in this way. In what follows I shall concentrate on the processes that have transformed relatively raw data or information into knowledge. These processes, which vary according to the kind of knowledge that is sought, may be summarized, roughly, as gathering, storing, verifying, and analyzing.

Gathering the data that will be turned into knowledge is already a form of processing, since it involves selection as well as accumulation. It has taken many forms, including the literal gathering of plants for study, alongside catching butterflies, obtaining specimens of rock, excavating the remains of former cities, and so on. Collecting is a form of gathering objects, whether natural or the work of human hands, displayed in what were known as private *cabinets of curiosities in the seventeenth century or in public museums from the nineteenth century onward. Metaphorical gathering includes observation (of the stars, for instance, the symptoms of illness, or the behavior of animals and humans). *Fieldwork* is a convenient term to describe old practices that have become formal methods in a number of academic disciplines: archaeology, anthropology, botany, ethology, folklore, geography, geology, sociology. *Gathering* includes the interrogation of witnesses by inquisitors, detectives, colonial administrators, and anthropologists. Experiments may be viewed as a form of interrogation, famously described by Francis Bacon (1561–1626) as "putting Nature to the question," in other words, torturing her in order to reveal her secrets.

The gathering of knowledge has become more and more systematic since the end of the Middle Ages. Offering a questionnaire to travelers or fieldworkers, a practice that became increasingly common from the seventeenth century onward, encouraged a focus on what was relevant for a particular purpose. Scientific expeditions, rare in the sixteenth century, multiplied from the later eighteenth century onward, the age of Captain Cook's voyage to the South Seas (1768–71) and that of Alessandro Malaspina to the Americas, from the Falklands to Alaska (1789–94). In the nineteenth century, expeditions were launched to study the depths of the oceans, and in the late twentieth century, into space. These expeditions, often funded by governments, illustrate both the cooperation and the competition between nations in discovering the secrets of nature and the resources of the earth. They returned with many specimens—animal, vegetable, and mineral—many of them still to be seen in museums. Scientists also became increasingly concerned to measure what they observed. On his expedition to Spanish America (1799–1804) Alexander von Humboldt took over forty varieties of measuring instrument, among them an altimeter to measure altitude, a hygrometer to measure rainfall, a magnetometer to measure the earth's magnetic forces, and even a cyanometer to measure the blueness of the sky.

Selection continues in the later stages of processing knowledge. Indeed, different cultures may be regarded as so many systems of selection, sieves or filters that exclude some information because it is viewed as irrelevant or because it challenges the assumptions or the values of the culture. A second stage in the processing of knowledge is storing it in some retrievable form, from learning by rote or the use of mnemonics such as the *khipus* (clusters of colored and knotted strings) used in Peru before the Spanish conquest to different forms of writing, drawing, or photography. Putting knowledge in writing (textualization) facilitates retrieval, allowing the creation of major storehouses such as archives and libraries: the archive of Simancas, for instance, the Vatican Library in Rome, the Imperial Library in Vienna, and so on. It also facilitates classification. The process of textualization often goes through several stages, from the rough notes that journalists, doctors, detectives, diplomats, or anthropologists jot down on the spot to increasingly elaborate dispatches and reports. The translation into words of what is observed—like other forms of translation—involves a certain loss of knowledge, but this loss has been compensated, at least in part, by making sketches, plans, and maps and later by taking photographs.

Writing, especially after cheap paper became available in the West in early modern times, transformed the practice of government, making possible the early modern paper state in which written orders replaced oral ones. In similar fashion, writing transformed the practice of business. In both business and government, written messages that could travel long distances encouraged the gradual centralization of decision making at the expense of the autonomy of local agents, a process that became still more rapid in the age of the telephone. The proliferation of printed handbooks transformed many practices, from painting to cookery. In architecture, for instance, *Renaissance patrons studied treatises by the ancient Roman Vitruvius or the Renaissance Italian Sebastiano Serlio before giving instructions to their masons and carpenters.

A third stage in the production of knowledge is the evaluation of what has been discovered. Evaluation includes verification. The observations of an astronomer or the experiments of a chemist are repeated by others in order to ensure their reliability. Detectives and attorneys try to turn clues into evidence of guilt or innocence. Historians return to the sources in order to test one another's assertions. For a time, individual anthropologists such as Bronisław Malinowski (1884–1942) in the Trobriand Islands were the only witnesses of what they observed who were also in a position to communicate it to the world of Western scholarship, but later on, other anthropologists entered the same field, while literate Trobrianders read and criticized their publications. At a more general level, philosophers from ancient Greece onward have concerned themselves with *epistemology (in other words, knowledge about knowledge). Some, the skeptics, or as they were known in the seventeenth and eighteenth centuries, the Pyrrhonists, believed reliable knowledge to be impossible, while others, like René Descartes (1596–1650), placed it on what they believed to be secure foundations.

A fourth stage in the making of knowledge is analysis. For example, anthropologists do not think that their task is finished when they have described the society in which they carried out their fieldwork; they also want to move from description (ethnography) to theory, or at least to test general theories by means of description. Quantitative analysis is also important, as in the case of social surveys such as the census, breaking down the data into categories of different sizes and importance that allow comparisons to be made with similar surveys made in other places or at other moments in time. "Statistics" owe their name to the fact that from the eighteenth century onward, Western governments have increasingly relied on figures in order to orient their policies.

A major form of analysis is classification, viewing separate items as parts of a greater whole. A major contrast between orders of knowledge, such as the traditional Chinese system and the Western one, consists in their systems of classification. Some scholars, like the Swiss humanist Conrad Gessner (1516–65), classified books, contributing in the process to the rise of a new discipline, bibliography. Others, more ambitious, tried to classify nature itself, like the Swede Carl Linnaeus (1707–78), best known for his contribution to botany. The German Franz Bopp (1791–1867) divided languages into families, while the Russian Dmitri Mendeleev (1834–1907) classified the elements. Even clouds were classified. So was knowledge itself, most famously by the Frenchman Auguste Comte (1798–1857), following in the footsteps of earlier classifiers such as Bacon but revising their systems. In his turn, Comte inspired the work of the American librarian Melvil Dewey (1851–1931), whose system, the Dewey Decimal Classification, is still used in many libraries, and the Belgian Paul Otlet (1868–1944), an enthusiast for Dewey's work who attempted to extend it to classifying the world, liberating the organization of knowledge from dependence on books.

Practices such as verifying or classifying knowledge are generally associated with particular places, sometimes described as centers of calculation. These sites of knowledge have often been located in major Western cities such as Rome, Amsterdam, and London, centers in which scholars and scientists process information gathered from the periphery and turn it into knowledge. Rome, for instance, was the headquarters to which Catholic missionaries returned to give accounts of their experiences, as well as the center of presses producing religious books in a variety of non-European languages. The German *Jesuit *polymath Athanasius Kircher (1602–80) was able to publish an important book about China (*China Illustrata*, China illuminated, printed in Amsterdam in 1667) without leaving Rome thanks to his conversations with Jesuit colleagues on their return from that mission field. Amsterdam was the headquarters of the Dutch East India and West India Companies, where statistics concerning the price of spices and other commodities for import and export were carefully analyzed.

DISSEMINATING KNOWLEDGE

After knowledge has been fully processed, it is ready to be communicated or disseminated. Some of it may be classified as secret, but that term really means that dissemination is supposed to be confined to a particular group. These groups include not only secret services such as the CIA, MI5, or KGB but also early modern communities of alchemists, members of persecuted religious groups, or the Venetian Senate, to whom returning ambassadors read their reports or *relazioni* about the strengths and weaknesses of the state in which they had resided. In any case, secrets are difficult to keep. *Leaks have often occurred, not only in our own age of WikiLeaks but long before. Some of the Venetian relazioni had already found their way into print in the sixteenth century.

Other knowledges are public, available to everyone, at least in principle, and spreading more and more widely thanks to printing (block printing in China and Japan, printing with movable type in Korea and the West). The handpress associated with Johannes Gutenberg (ca. 1400–1468) was replaced in the nineteenth century by the steam press, which produced a flood of cheap print, available to the increasing number of western Europeans who were able to read (the *literacy rate was much lower in Europe east of the Elbe). The nineteenth century was a time of the popularization of science, thanks to organizations such as the Society for the Diffusion of Useful Knowledge (founded in Britain in 1826) to popular *encyclopedias, public lectures, exhibitions, and periodicals such as the *Scientific American* (1845). Authors and *publishers became increasingly concerned with their intellectual property, protected by *copyright laws that have had to be rewritten in the age of the *internet.

The process of communicating knowledge has often been described as diffusion, in other words as a kind of flow. This metaphor has the disadvantage of implying that the flow was one way, and today it is often replaced by the term *circulation*, referring to movement in more than one direction. All these terms have another disadvantage, that of implying that the knowledge that is received in a new place is the same as the knowledge that was sent. The metaphor *dissemination* has the advantage of suggesting that seeds that are sown grow into something different. As theorists of cultural reception remind us, knowledge is often transformed during the process of communication, whether the medium is oral, written, visual, printed, or *digital. Translation between languages is often necessary; misunderstanding often occurs while both individuals and groups consciously adapt what they learn to their own purposes.

Take the case of missionaries, who travel to foreign parts in order to convert their inhabitants, in other words to persuade them to replace their form of religious knowledge with a new one. A recurrent dilemma faced by Christian missionaries emerged from the need to speak about God in the local language. To employ a local term such as the Chinese "Lord of Heaven" (*Tianzhu*) might encourage listeners to think of Christianity as an extension of their own beliefs rather than an alternative to them. On the other hand, to use a foreign word such as *Deus* (God) might discourage potential converts. Jesuit missionaries, ready to adapt or, as they used to say, to "accommodate" Christianity to the local order of knowledge, were sometimes described by other Catholics as having been converted by the Chinese instead of converting them.

Missionaries traveled in order to teach, but other Westerners traveled to Asia, Africa, or the Americas in order to learn. They have sometimes been viewed as working by themselves and as bringing back raw information, but it has become increasingly apparent that the visitors learned from local experts and that the knowledge that they brought back was embedded in local classification systems. For example, the twelve-volume herbal *Indian Garden of Malabar* (1678–1703), associated with Hendrik van Rheede, the Dutch governor of that region of southwest India, was the result of collaboration between Western physicians and botanists and local healers in the Ayurvedic tradition. Like Kircher's *China Illustrata*, Rheede's *Garden* vividly illustrates a general trend, the increasing globalization of knowledge. So does the work of Linnaeus, who stayed in Sweden, at the University of Uppsala, but received regular reports from his so-called apostles, former students who studied botany in the field in Egypt, China, Japan, South Africa, Surinam, and elsewhere.

OVERLOAD AND SPECIALIZATION

In every successive century since the late Middle Ages, more knowledge has become available, especially in the West. The invention of the telescope and the microscope, like the discovery of the Americas by Europeans and their increasing contacts with Asia and Africa, led to awareness of new worlds of knowledge. In order to contain this knowledge, encyclopedias had to become larger and larger: the seven volumes of the *Encyclopaedia* (1630) compiled by Johann Heinrich Alsted were followed by the seventeen volumes of the famous French *Encyclopédie* (1751–65) (with an additional eleven volumes of plates) and the thirty-two volumes of the fifteenth edition of the *Encyclopaedia Britannica* (2010 version), dwarfed by *Wikipedia* (2001–) and its online rivals.

The awareness of new knowledges also had a downside, the anxiety that there was too much to know. The problem of overload is not a new one, even if it has become more acute in the last generation and a more frequent topic of debate. Some knowledge considered out-of-date has been discarded, as an inspection of successive editions of an encyclopedia will reveal, but this does little to reduce the load, not only *information overload (the raw data arriving too fast to be processed into knowledge), but also what might be called knowledge overload, too much for individuals to digest. Complaints about the proliferation of publications have multiplied from the sixteenth century onward. Recurrent metaphors include the flood of books in which readers feared drowning and the forest in which they felt themselves to be lost.

Various means were devised to cope with the problem. Guides through the forest included printed bibliographies of books on law, theology, history, politics, and so on, some of them labeled as "select" rather than complete. Note taking by readers became more systematic. The traditional *commonplace books, in which excerpts from books read were collected under a few main headings such as "friendship" or "war," were replaced by paper slips ranged in alphabetical order. The slips were followed in their turn by record cards of a standard size, popularized by Melvil Dewey for use in library catalogs but soon taken up by scholars to organize their notes. Books designed to be consulted rather than read (reference books) proliferated. Reading itself became more rapid and less intensive. The skimming of books that was preached and practiced by Samuel Johnson (1709–84) is not so different from the online "scanning" of today.

The most important of the responses to overload was specialization. Until the seventeenth century, it was not unusual for some scholars, known as polyhistors or *polymaths, to study a variety of disciplines and even to make original contributions to several of them, like Gottfried Wilhelm Leibniz (1646–1716), whose interests included history, theology, linguistics, and Sinology as well as the philosophy and the mathematics for which he is best known. All the same, scholars such as the Czech Jan Amos Comenius (1592–1670) were already lamenting the fragmentation of knowledge, and the trend has been accelerating ever since. The line between the *humanities and the natural sciences gradually became a gap, recognized by the coining of the term *scientist* in Britain in the 1830s. Between what became known as the "two cultures" (a term coined in 1959), a third culture, that of the social sciences, became established. At university level, in the second half of the nineteenth century, a general education was gradually replaced by the study of a single discipline. The age of the polymath was followed by the age of the "expert" (a term coined in the 1820s) and the "specialist" (coined in a medical context in French in the 1840s and in English in the 1850s, but soon spreading more widely).

Although the knowledge of most scholars became less general, polymaths did not disappear altogether, as a few remarkable examples may suggest. The Russian Pavel Florensky (1882–1937) studied mathematics, philosophy, and theology before turning to art history, electrical engineering, and chemistry. The Englishman Gregory Bateson (1904–80) moved between anthropology, biology, psychology, and what was known in his day as cybernetics. The French Jesuit Michel de Certeau (1925–86) was trained in philosophy, theology, and history but moved into psychoanalysis, anthropology, and sociology. The American Jared Diamond (b. 1937) was a physiologist before his curiosity led him to ornithology, anthropology, and finally comparative history. Polymaths may have become an endangered species, but they are not yet extinct.

Peter Burke

See also archivists; art of memory; bibliography; cybernetics/feedback; data; excerpting/commonplacing; globalization; indexing; intellectual property; khipus; learning; libraries and catalogs; manuals; observing; quantification; reference books

FURTHER READING

Ann Blair, *Too Much to Know*, 2010; Peter Burke, *A Social History of Knowledge*, 2 vols., 2000–2012; Michel Foucault, *The Order of Things*, 1966; Christian Jacob, *Lieux de Savoir* [Sites of knowledge] (2007–11); Frank Kafker, *Notable Encyclopedias*, 1981–94; Bruno Latour, *Science in Action*, 1987; Karl Mannheim, "The Problem of a Sociology of Knowledge," in Mannheim, *Essays on the Sociology of Knowledge*, edited by Paul Kecskemeti, 1952; Kapil Raj, *Relocating Modern Science*, 2007.

LANDSCAPES AND CITIES

Twenty-first-century information systems occupy virtual rather than physical space. The structures for collecting, organizing, and storing knowledge that shape our everyday lives depend on *digital technology and *internet access. Linked by a multiplicity of wireless computers, these ethereal networks exist in *the cloud. They are part of a global "information landscape" that is ever more complex, intricate, pervasive, and dense. There is growing demand for electronic tools that analyze and present data geographically. Modes of visualizing and mapping knowledge, geographic information systems have applications in engineering, planning, logistics, telecommunications, business, and scholarship, notably in the fields of archaeology and history. They have proliferated alongside technologies that permit accurate geospatial positioning by receiving satellite signals. Such systems are rapidly superseding maps as the principal means by which we navigate movement through the urban and rural environments that surround us. London black cab drivers study for years to acquire the *encyclopedic "knowledge" of the city's streets required for a taxi license. But the mental maps of its topography on which they pride themselves are increasingly rivaled by the machine memory of the satellite-navigation devices on which their Uber competitors rely. These inventions are arguably eroding our capacity to orientate ourselves in relation to space, even as they are enhancing the status of virtual space as a key matrix for the interpretation and management of information. And yet material location has always been at the heart of how we conceive, arrange, communicate, and retrieve information. Long before the transformative developments of the last half century, landscapes and cities served as information systems.

The physical environments in which people live and work determine the conditions in which knowledge is circulated. Prior to the Industrial Revolution, the continent of Europe and its adjacent islands were predominantly rural. Especially in Italy and the Low Countries, urbanization was on the increase, driven by commercial and mercantile growth and by economic migration from the countryside of people in search of employment. Tiny in comparison to the huge agglomerations of population that count for cities today, the largest city in 1500 was Naples, with 150,000 people. By 1600 it had been overtaken by Paris, which boasted half a million; in due course this was eclipsed by London, in which some seven hundred thousand people lived by 1750. But the majority still inhabited villages and small settlements surrounded by the agricultural land that provided their livelihoods and hedged about by wild places—mountains, moors, forests, and bogs—that proved more troublesome to tame.

Altered by human habitation over several millennia, such landscapes were repositories of folklore, archives of information about customary rights and inherited rules, and storehouses of communal memory. They were littered with natural and human-made landmarks that served to demarcate boundaries and functioned, alongside place names, as a compass for travelers. Ritual perambulation of the parish limits also helped to ingrain geographical knowledge in local communities, and the furrows ploughed in fields established a template for sowing crops in future years. The legends that accumulated around trees, stones, springs, rocky outcrops, and other distinctive topographical features provided pointers to distant and more recent history. In Europe, many were linked with the Christian faith, which left an enduring footprint on the face of the landscape in the guise of places of worship, pilgrimage shrines, wayside crosses, and sites hallowed by association with local saints. A canvas filled with hagiographical information, the material world was an important mnemonic tool in contexts in which the majority were illiterate. Popular perceptions of the past in the premodern period were more closely tied to location than date. A sense of place took precedence over precise identification of chronology, hence the many mythical stories that accumulated around prehistoric megaliths, burial mounds, and barrows.

Such traditions were transmitted down the generations by word of mouth, which was also the principal medium by which news circulated in the countryside. Farmers exchanged it at fairs and markets, and it also penetrated rural areas via seasonal workers and itinerant tradesmen and salesmen. From the sixteenth century onward, peddlers carried ballads, pamphlets, almanacs, and other inexpensive books in their packs, providing even humble villagers with access to textual knowledge. But acoustic communication continued to play a vital role: church bells were rung to mark deaths and warn of approaching armies. Beacons and bonfires were other devices for alerting neighboring communities to impending danger, and lighthouses served the same purpose for ships off treacherous stretches of coastline. In seventeenth-century north Yorkshire, Catholics devised an ingenious system of semaphore: white sheets were laid out to dry on sloping fields and hedges to signal to the faithful members of this persecuted minority where Mass would next be celebrated. Without local knowledge, it was easy to get lost. Anti-invasion measures ordered by the Ministry of Information in World War II Britain included the removal of signposts and milestones to confuse the enemy.

As an information system, the landscape is never static but in constant flux. The rise of capitalist agriculture and the advance of enclosure, for instance, profoundly transformed its physical appearance, obliterating features that were fillips to local memory. Drives for "improvement" in the form of reclaiming land from the sea and draining fenland likewise eroded the knowledge encoded in the local environment, as did mining, quarrying, deforestation, and later major engineering schemes to create dams and reservoirs. No less corrosive in its effects was the Protestant *Reformation. Especially in countries that embraced Calvinism, this was accompanied by a war against idols. Iconoclastic destruction of monuments of "superstition" and sites of pagan veneration combined with natural processes of weathering and decay to reduce redundant architectural structures such as monasteries to crumbling ruins. Sacred landscapes became secular ones, migrating from ecclesiastical into lay possession and becoming arenas in which the social elite displayed their status and power. Catholic reformers responded by rehabilitating battered shrines and by creating new holy places, including vast spiritual theme parks such as Mont Valérien in France, where devout visitors prayed in an array of chapels and tableaux that reconstructed Christ's route to Calvary.

The damage done by military conflict and revolution further eroded the landscape as a repository of inherited memory, even as it overlaid it with new connotations. *Early modern wars left ecological scars, though these pale in comparison with the devastation wrought by artillery and bombing in modern times. Battlefields from Bosworth and Naseby to the flat fields of Flanders, where thousands of World War I soldiers lie in official cemeteries close to where they fell, serve as memorials to the dead, admonishing present and future generations to give thanks for their sacrifice and preserve the peace for which they paid so high a price.

European projects of colonization and conquest were likewise often accompanied by the deliberate destruction and alteration of physical environments, the obliteration of which was a symbol of triumph over a rival information order. In Ireland, plantation was a process designed to efface Gaelic culture; in the New World, the curiosity of initial encounters gave way to aggressive campaigns of imperialism and acculturation that entailed the demonization of Indigenous knowledge. Colonial violence could not, however, entirely efface the capacity of subjugated native peoples to remember through the land. In North and South America and Australia, the *vernacular, nontextual memories of displaced Indian and aboriginal tribes have remained resilient. In these ways, the landscape was and is a field in which ideological and territorial politics are visibly played out. More recent examples of this ongoing phenomenon include the destruction of Buddhist shrines in Afghanistan by the Taliban and the huge red-and-white flag emblazoned on the mountain overlooking the divided city of Nicosia in Cyprus, laying claim to Turkish sovereignty over the northern part of the island.

From the fifteenth century, the growth of *literacy and the advent of the mechanical press converged with other processes to inspire attempts to transfer the information system enshrined in the medieval landscape onto paper and into print, lest it be lost in oblivion. Environmental change and human-made disaster served as powerful stimuli to recording and writing. Revived in the course of the *Renaissance, the classical tradition of chorography was itself rooted in a spatial theory of knowledge. It reflected an intellectual outlook in which geography was regarded as the eye of history and its inseparable twin and in which memory was frequently imagined as a theater or palace. Early modern antiquarianism fostered the compilation and publication of many "surveys," "perambulations," and "itineraries." From Petrarch onward, it facilitated archaeological excavation of the ancient past, "re-membering" it by reassembling its fragments and traces. The product of book learning as well as active fieldwork, the texts these impulses generated were structured in ways that underlined the idea that information had a location and that the past was a place that it was possible to inhabit in the imagination. The prospects, drafts, and engravings with which these texts were illustrated were another way of making topographical knowledge visible, and of reproducing the experience of visiting these living repositories of history for the armchair traveler. In the seventeenth century, the Dutch word *landschap* denoted a *genre of painting: a scene viewed from the perspective of a particular spectator. Only later did it come to be used to describe actual places rather than their two-dimensional simulacra. The disappearing legacy of popular "antiquities" collected and written down by aristocratic, gentry, and clerical compilers was similarly filtered through a lens that fundamentally distorted it.

The same observations apply to the growing impulse to map the landscape. Assisted by its sister arts of surveying and mathematical measuring, cartography was another critical mechanism for representing geographical information. Far from neutral and objective depictions of space, maps must be understood as subjective projections of authority. An instrument of reconnaissance and governance, the map is a semiotic system that reflects the aspirations of those who create it and that turns them into pictorial truths. Linked with the commodification of land for monetary gain and with the pretensions of expanding nation-states and empires, mapping at all levels—continent, country, region, and private estate—occluded alternative ways of delineating the landscape. It suppressed the cartographies of subaltern and dispossessed peoples, laid claim to contested frontiers, and reordered the center and periphery in ways that vindicated particular political and administrative objectives. Early modern mapmaking also helped to construct geographical contrasts that reified hierarchies of knowledge: subordinating east to west, and locating it backward in time as well as in space. The "dark corners of the land" and "Indies within our midst" whose ignorance flummoxed sixteenth- and seventeenth-century bishops were compared with heathen places in a manner that instinctively linked civilization and *enlightenment with the art of cultivation. In nineteenth- and early twentieth-century Germany the settlements of "healthy" Saxons were similarly contrasted with the wastelands inhabited by "indolent" Slavs and "parasitic" Jews. Such racial assumptions laid the foundations for Nazi ethnic cleansing.

The idea that the environment determines human behavior also found expression in the cities that early modern Europeans built in Latin America. Models of symmetry based on rectangular grids, their layout was a strategy for discipline and socialization: Spanish *reduccíons* in the Andes were spatial manifestations of the desire to create order out of diabolical chaos. Others had avenues radiating from a central square that provided clear sightlines from every direction. Perhaps the most perfect realization of this ideal was the Venetian military outpost of Palma Nuova established in 1593. Town planning of this kind was itself a device for maximizing the gathering of information by observation.

Most medieval cities, however, had grown up more haphazardly. A tumble of houses in a maze of meandering lanes and streets, they were full of hidden nooks and crannies and encrusted with multiple sedimentary layers of memory and meaning. Warfare and fire sometimes provided opportunities for clearance and rebuilding, as in London following the great conflagration of 1666, while the reconfiguration of Rome in the sixteenth century was a papal project embodying the pretensions of the resurgent Counter-Reformation Church. The steady growth of some cities as a result of economic migration, mercantile prosperity, and later industrialization presented significant challenges to the capacity of their inhabitants to gain a mental map of them in their entirety. Comprehending these sprawling metropolises became increasingly difficult, providing an incentive for portable directories and guidebooks that substituted for firsthand knowledge of their topography and buildings. The pocket companion compiled by William Stow in 1722, for instance, was designed to meet the needs of coachmen and porters in London, Westminster, and Southwark and to prevent deliveries from going astray, their suburbs and liberties having become so expansive that no one was familiar with every inch of them. Robert Kirk, the Scottish visitor who commented in 1690 that the city was "a great vast wilderness" articulated a sentiment that must have been widely shared.

Cities and towns progressively ceased to be face-to-face communities and became conglomerations of strangers living in discrete and disaggregated neighborhoods, but they maintained their status as engines and exchanges of information. Hotspots for literacy and the headquarters of the printing industry, they engendered a range of other institutions associated with the production and dissemination of textual knowledge: bookshops, libraries, archives, schools, academies, and universities. The birthing chambers of serial newspapers, they engendered and sustained a host of professional scribes, notaries, writers, and journalists. They also spawned sites of sociability and spaces in which public opinion about current affairs was regularly aired: from inns, taverns, *coffeehouses, and *salons, to pharmacies and barber shops, squares and piazzas. Inquisitive Londoners in search of gossip and rumor walked up and down the aisles of St. Paul's Cathedral and haunted the Royal Exchange. Oral information circulated freely alongside manuscript tracts, printed broadsides, and petitions, which were pinned or pasted to prominent landmarks to attract attention. The pinning of Martin Luther's ninety-five theses on the church door in Wittenberg may be a retrospective invention, but the posting of government proclamations in public places was a standard technique for releasing information in urban settings. Large cities such as Venice, Cologne, and Hamburg functioned as resonating boxes in which information moved back and forth across different media and across the porous boundaries between the literate and illiterate.

By contrast, the information flows that linked early modern Istanbul with Western capitals via ambassadors, diplomats, scholars, and traders were largely oral and epistolary. Increasingly cosmopolitan in character, cities were entrepôts into and from which knowledge was imported and exported by road and water, paper and whispers. They were crossroads for interchange between cultures. Established as an encampment in 1575, Luanda, capital of modern-day Angola, was a hub of Portuguese imperial power and a major port of embarkation for slaves at which African and Atlantic circulatory networks converged. But cities were sites of apartheid as well as coexistence and diversity. A strategy for preventing ideological contamination and facilitating surveillance, the physical segregation of the religious and racial minorities who resided within them also served to control and channel the passage of information. In Nagasaki in Japan, meticulous documentation of the illicit Christian population between 1665 and 1871 was a mode of inquisition and coercion by the Tokugawa shogunate.

Everywhere urban information systems relied on the senses of both sight and sound. Medieval and early modern cities were auditory environments, filled with street sellers, minstrels, town criers, and open-air pulpits. Bells regulated the division of the day into times of work and play and, together with drums and cannons, signaled the nightly curfew, though new technologies such as personal watches and newspapers gradually superseded these functions and the level of noise from traffic and machines increased. As in the countryside, physical landmarks such as prominent buildings and symbolic shop signs were aids to navigation. Increasingly, though, cities became spaces into which visible words penetrated and by which they were saturated. Though it had a precursor in ancient Rome and Greece, the reemergence of a public "graphosphere" began in Renaissance Italy and spread steadily across the continent, reaching Russia in the eighteenth and nineteenth centuries. Initially, inscriptions on stone slabs, façades, and pillars carried the voice of princes, tsars, rulers, and oligarchs; supplementing if not superseding the theatrical and ceremonial spectacles for which the streets provided a regular stage, they were emanations of political authority. Later, they proliferated for commercial and practical purposes and, in the guise of graffiti, were a tool of protest and resistance. As the state stretched its tentacles into the lives of its citizens, it devised more mathematical methods of gathering information about them. House numbers replaced names as a more efficient mechanism for taking censuses and levying taxation. This also facilitated the development of modern postal systems, which delivered letters to the door of individual residences and businesses, sometimes twice daily.

Finally, it is necessary to focus attention on movement between different locations as a mode of obtaining and conveying information. Circulation must be understood in both a literal and a metaphorical sense. Whether on foot or horseback, by carriage, boat, homing pigeon, car, train, or plane, mobility has always been integral to the creation and spread of information. Pilgrims, merchants, migrants, and missionaries were key mediators and brokers, translating it linguistically and physically into new settings and bringing it into contact with other cultures. A sense of disorientation is a prerequisite for the forging of knowledge. The speed with which ideas and news traveled along paths and roads, canals, rivers, and oceans before the nineteenth century was slow by comparison with that enabled by railways and by mechanized transport and flight. In turn, the inventions of the telegraph, telephone, radio, television, and internet have led to an exponential increase in how quickly news and ideas can be transmitted around the globe. They have enabled us to transcend the tyranny of distance, be in different time zones simultaneously, and explore locations in every continent vicariously. The very terms we use to describe how we interact with the *World Wide Web, from *surfing* to *superhighways*, are resonant of the centrality of space and place to the way in which we conceptualize and acquire information.

Alexandra Walsham

See also art of memory; bells; bureaucracy; commodification; globalization; governance; maps; networks; public sphere; travel

FURTHER READING

Liam Matthew Brockey, ed., *Portuguese Colonial Cities in the Early Modern World*, 2008; Filippo de Vivo, *Information and Communication in Venice: Rethinking Early Modern Politics*, 2007; Simon Franklin and Katherine Bowers, eds., *Information and Empire: Mechanisms of Communication in Russia, 1600–1854*, 2017; David Garrioch, "Sounds of the City: The Soundscape of Early Modern European Towns," *Urban History* 30, no. 1 (2003): 5–25; John-Paul A. Ghobrial, *The Whispers of Cities: Information Flows in Istanbul, London, and Paris in the Age of William Trumbull*, 2013; Walter Mignolo, *The Darker Side of the Renaissance: Literacy, Territoriality, and Colonization*, 1995; William J. Smyth, *Map-Making, Landscapes and Memory: A Geography of Colonial and Early Modern Ireland, c. 1530–1750*, 2006; Alexandra Walsham, *The Reformation of the Landscape: Religion, Identity and Memory in Early Modern Britain and Ireland*, 2011.

LAYOUT AND SCRIPT IN LETTERS

Interpersonal communication was one of the earliest functions of writing across the world, and the letter was a versatile *genre serving that function across a wide range of social contexts. Letters ranged from official to personal in purpose and tone and carried information not only through words but also in the physical form and layout of the text.

In the written culture of East Asia, literary Chinese functioned as a shared learned script for educated elites for about two millennia. Most terms referring to letters in literary Chinese allude to various material supports older than paper that made writing and reading possible: bamboo strips, wooden panels, wooden tablets, silk, brushes, and so on. The usage of these terms suggests that letter writing is as old as the history of writing itself. Just as letters functioned as a synecdoche for writing in lexicographical traditions of some European languages, *shu* (Korean *sŏ*, Japanese *sho*)—the term most commonly used to refer to epistles in literary Chinese—means "to write" as a verb and "the act of writing" or "writing" itself as a noun.

Literati across East Asia had good reason to sharpen their letter-writing skills. The official positions that they would take required them to be effective letter writers. In one way or another, most official documents took epistolary formats, with designated senders and addressees. The drafts of outgoing letters together with received letters thus formed the fundamental decision documents in the premodern polities of East Asia. The operation of the Chinese tributary system, moreover, required scholar-officials to draft flawless diplomatic letters using the appropriate epistolary *protocols, to prevent unnecessary diplomatic tensions.

The emergence of new linguistic environments in Korea and Japan by virtue of the invention of *vernacular scripts further expanded the scope of epistolary networks. The invention of Japanese *kana* script, which originated from eighth-century attempts to express Japanese sounds with Chinese characters, precipitated an exuberant vernacular literary culture during the Heian period (794–1185), which aristocratic women actively joined as both poets and letter writers. Elementary textbooks taking the form of exchanged letters (*ōraimono*) promoted both popular *literacy and correspondence in *early modern Japan. Likewise, the ease of learning the Korean alphabet, invented in the mid-fifteenth century, allowed women and nonelites to express their thoughts and feelings in written forms. As prolific letter writers, Korean elite women could maintain their own social networks separate from their positions in the patriarchal structure within their husbands' families. For the users of vernacular script, letters must have been the most accessible genre, which did not threaten the male elites' dominance in the literary Chinese classical tradition. Most letter writers other than male elites wrote nothing but letters.

When the sheer number of epistles circulated increased exponentially, something exciting began to develop from the seemingly mundane and trivial practice of letter writing.

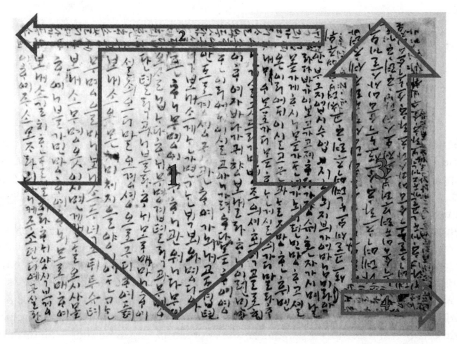

Figure 1. One of the two oldest existing vernacular Korean letters written in spiral form, purportedly in the 1490s. 49.9×34.9 cm. Photo courtesy of Daejeon Municipal Museum. Effects added by the author.

The users of vernacular scripts in both Korea and Japan experimented with the physical layouts of their letters. Some users of the Korean alphabet created nonlinear epistolary forms starting in the late fifteenth century (figure 1). Korean people did not even name this particular layout, probably because of its mundane and ubiquitous usage, which I call "spiral letters." Letter writers had to rotate the texts counterclockwise by ninety degrees several times to complete their messages, which divided a single text into several sections. This spiral movement in writing letters brought about the same bodily motion in reading them. Spiral forms developed in elite women's vernacular Korean letters first, then carried over to male elites' literary Chinese letters. Considering that male elites disdained the easy Korean alphabet as unsuitable for serious Confucian scholarship, women letter writers could have devised this new textual technology to make their letters appear complex visually, whatever their contents. These complex layouts dovetailed with the contemporary scholarly culture that prized painstaking learning.

Some epistles written by aristocratic women in Heian Japan also used nonlinear textual layouts. The writers indented radically to the middle of the page, leaving a generous upper margin. When there was no space left at the lower left edge, they continued to write in the upper margin and then moved on to the blank space on the right side of the page—"sleeve writing" (*sodegaki*). Besides sleeve writing, "scattered writing" (*chirashi gaki*) also developed in kana composition and spacing, in which the columns of text neither start at the same height nor stay straight all the time. Such quaint and unpredictable textual layouts might have expressed the emotional sensitivity of the writer. Thomas LaMarre, however, has claimed that scattered writing presents the Heian variation of the Chinese calligraphic model by relaxing the strict striation of space.

Aesthetic values attached to Japanese scattered writing made this form appear intact in both manuscript and printed form. When Korean spiral letters were printed, however, they were straightened up and rearranged into linear reading order and their contents extensively edited. Just as the vernacular grammatical and syntactic apparatuses were removed from manuscripts when they were printed, these vernacular textual layouts were undone to incorporate the texts into the Sinicized world of books. The process of devernacularization turned informal messages in unusual textual layouts into formal information inscribed on printed pages.

The manipulation of textual space can be observed globally across diverse periods. In some contexts in early modern Europe, for example, letter-writing protocols governed not only verbal forms of address but also the layout on the page. Jonathan Gibson called attention in 1997 to the clues that "significant space" in a manuscript letter offered about the social standing of sender and recipient—information that is typically lost in any printed edition from the time or since. Vernacular letter-writing manuals starting in 1521 in French and in 1568 in English called for the subscriptions (or sign-offs) of letters to social superiors to be placed as low as possible on a page, and higher up on the page as the standing of the sender was equal or superior to that of the recipient. Similarly in the especially elaborate hierarchical system of the French royal court under Louis XIV in the late seventeenth century, letter writers showed deference by leaving space between the address to the recipient ("Dear . . .") and the beginning of the letter itself—the greater the deference, the greater the opening interval left blank. As Giora Sternberg has brought to light, in letters among social equals the text simply began on a new line. By contrast when the king wrote, he started the letter immediately following the address, since he outranked everyone else; but out of gender courtesy he "gave the line" when writing to the queen. When members of the court wrote to social superiors they left a variable amount of blank space depending on their standing relative to the recipient. A duke would leave seven or eight lines, or fingers, when writing to the king; five or six lines when writing to the king's brother; and three lines for princes of the blood. Similarly spelling out abbreviations was a sign of deference. Breaches of this protocol had serious consequences—insults taken and redress sought—as can be traced through disputes preserved in the archives. When distinctions of rank were uncertain, communication could break down altogether. An alternative mode of communication developed that bypassed the strict epistolary conventions: the "billet" or short note was meant for rapid and easy communication, although it worked seamlessly only when there was goodwill on both sides. While Louis XIV was personally involved in the explicit codification of these among other courtly protocols, epistolary conventions concerning layout both predated and postdated his reign.

The usage of blank space to express deference to the addressee also appears in Tibetan Buddhist correspondence. Tibetan epistolary manuals in the early modern period instruct letter writers to leave a vertical space or "hierarchy" space (*gong'og*) after the opening line. Just as in letters in early modern France, this hierarchy space in Tibetan letters was measured by one's finger's breadth (*sor*): eight fingers of hierarchy space when addressing a lama or a king, two fingers of hierarchy space when writing to friends, and so on. These manuals also advised using a large piece of paper, preferably white and fragrant, when writing to superiors. Likewise, calligraphic styles were attuned to the hierarchical distance between sender and addressee. When an inferior wrote to a superior, small handwriting with lines stacked densely together conveyed the soft voice of humility and deference. By contrast, superiors exhibited their elevated status and authoritative voice through large letters with sweeping tails and wider spaces between lines. As in the case of Korean spiral letters, all these spatial manifestations of hierarchical relationships between the senders and addressees in manuscript letters collapsed into continuous lines of script when the letters were published in print editions. The above examples attest that letter writers across many different contexts performed what James Daybell calls "the social politics of manuscript space in the physical layout of letters," which was closely related to letter writers' social status, gender, and intimacy with the addressee as well as the purpose of the given letters, and the circumstances of correspondence.

Another distinctive form of layout in European and American letters of the nineteenth century was crossed writing, in which a second text was written over the first at a right angle. Jane Austen's 1808 letter to her sister, Cassandra, preserved in the Morgan Library and Museum, for instance, contains two paragraphs of writing, one written over the other at a right angle. British and American letter writers produced these "crossed letters" to save postage, which was charged by the number of sheets of paper. This layout, however, remained popular even after the introduction of Penny Black postage in 1840, which charged a flat rate of one penny for letters of up to half an ounce. Crossed letters likely also appealed to some letter writers for reasons other than saving textual space. In *Emma*, for instance, Austen described how Miss Bates admired the exquisiteness of crossed letters that she received from her niece, Jane Fairfax. Writing a perfect crossed letter without ruining the appearance of the page took skill, which made the exchange of letters more enjoyable. The layouts of letters added crucial elements of meaning to their contents, although their connotations varied under different sociocultural circumstances.

Letter-like exchanges today, from email to text and social media messages, have dropped most of these earlier epistolary conventions in favor of a stated preference for informality, speed, and directness, but they have spawned conventions of their own, using symbols and layout in addition to words to convey information beyond the words themselves.

Hwisang Cho

See also bureaucracy; diplomats/spies; governance; letters; networks

FURTHER READING

Hwisang Cho, *The Power of the Brush: Epistolary Practices in Chosŏn Korea*, 2020; James Daybell, "Material Meanings and the Social Signs of Manuscript Letters in Early Modern England," *Literature Compass* 6, no. 3 (2009): 647–67; Jonathan Gibson, "Significant Space in Manuscript Letters," *Seventeenth Century* 12, no. 1 (1997): 1–9; Christina Kilby, "Bowing with Words: Paper, Ink, and Bodies in Tibetan Buddhist Epistles," *Journal of the American Academy of Religion* 87, no. 1 (2019): 260–81; Thomas LaMarre, *Uncovering Heian Japan: An Archaeology of Sensation and Inscription*, 2000; Antje Richter, *Letters and Epistolary Culture in Early Medieval China*, 2013; Giora Sternberg, "Epistolary Ceremonial: Corresponding Status at the Time of Louis XIV," *Past and Present* 204 (2009): 33–88.

LEARNING

Learning is a term used in contemporary educational theory to describe the ability to build up and add to a foundation of concepts, beliefs, and applicable skills. Techniques of argumentation and other means of communication are seen as a relevant part of these skills, but so too are motor skills that help control the use of the body and its parts, including the senses and brain. The faculty of learning applies to animals, humans, and some artificial technologies; but we will focus here on human learning, which has been scrutinized and discussed for the longest time. Information, or messages to which the receiver attends, plays a crucial role in the acquisition and development of knowledge and mental habits, but it can also disturb and disorganize them.

Memory has long been and still is an integral part of the learning process by allowing for both storage and retrieval in the mind and in external media of many kinds—from cave walls and notched stones to electronic devices. Natural memory depends on the physiology of the human brain but also on the training specific to cultural habits of child rearing and education. In many, perhaps most, cultures before the recent reliance on finding aids and electronic devices, a strong memory was considered one of the greatest intellectual and moral virtues. One of the principal goals of education was to develop natural memory; as a result, we have records of feats of memory that seem nearly impossible today. In short, human mnemonic capacities have varied over time, as have the various forms and media of external memory.

Individual learning depends on interactions with the world and with others. This article will examine the recent theory of connected learning and show how kinds of connected learning operated in practice in historical contexts, in particular in the community of sixteenth-century Zurich. It will then consider the possibility of self-learning (or autodidacticism), in particular through the example of the self-taught Cambridge PhD Tara Westover and her memoir *Educated*, published in 2018.

CONNECTED LEARNING THEORY

Modern theories of information tend to overwrite the traditional concept of knowledge with a more flexible concept of information as bits of knowledge, associated with a technology of storage and transmission. As "information" is transferred, the means of its transfer are important—they codefine (and thus manipulate or on a positive note help formulate) any message or observation.

Connected learning theory is a recent ideal of learning that encourages learners to make decisions and respond quickly as new information is continually acquired. Connected learning theory values the ability to create connections amid a diversity of inputs, to distinguish important from unimportant information, and to recognize whether newly gathered information should alter decisions already made. The capacity to acquire new knowledge is therefore more critical than the amount of knowledge that has been acquired; and maintaining and augmenting connections to sources of learning are crucial techniques to facilitate continual learning. The theorists of connected learning aim to integrate *machine learning with human learning. They thus stray from the field of psychology, in which modern theories of learning developed, notably in the wake of seminal work of Jean Piaget (1896–1980) on cognitive development. Instead these theorists strive toward practices of collecting as the basis for connected learning. This theory focuses on learners as collectors of information and on their process of gathering objects and information as just as constitutive of learning as the knowledge that is collected.

Although the theory is new, the practice of connected learning is anything but. Good examples include *encyclopedic practices in many cultures that gathered information from many sources, the various *"republics of letters" formed by personal and remote interactions among scholars from different backgrounds with shared intellectual interests (including European *Renaissance and *Enlightenment), and the participation in a burgeoning public sphere. Other entries in this volume give overviews on those topics. Instead I will use as an example of premodern connected learning communities a mid-sized city, sixteenth-century Zurich, with about five thousand inhabitants, which served as the economic and cultural capital of its region. Connected learning operated through the civic community, but the records that survive about oral and other nontextual learning habits are very sparse. Most of the developments that we can reconstruct today were recorded by learned scholars working with texts. They thus present modern researchers with a scholarly technology rather than, say, a public response to news and information.

CONNECTED LEARNING: A SIXTEENTH-CENTURY CASE

Sixteenth-century Zurich was not a democracy, but neither was it a completely authoritarian society. A culture of diversity was fostered through its status as a free imperial city and its late medieval organization into twelve guilds, with the aristocratic landowners (and other citizens not belonging to another guild) being one of them; other guilds included those for merchants, apothecaries, or shoemakers. Together, the guilds' representatives governed the city. Vertical and horizontal social mobility allowed sons and daughters to follow different career paths from their elders. Litigation courts managed diversity of opinion, in particular when opinion clashed with town laws. These courts heard and pondered each side of the argument and imposed penalties in order to maintain internal peace. As long as the laws of state or church were not at issue, people discussed opinions openly on the street.

One central activity in the community of Zurich was a process of connected learning, one that involved a diversity of contributions. In the early years of the *Reformation in Zurich, one endeavor of the learned church elite was to engage in a public discussion of how to translate the Bible, the most important basis for wisdom and moral instruction. Four designated scholars used the daily mass in the Grossmünster Church to come together to discuss in front of an audience of citizens, men and women of all social ranks, the best way of translating the Holy Book, sentence by sentence. In their collective deliberations, they compared the Bible transmitted in the learned languages (Hebrew and Aramaic, Greek, and Latin) and translated passages into German to make them accessible to the public. In their open dispute, the scholars detailed and compared differences in each version. The Greek and Hebrew specialist Theodor Bibliander (ca. 1506–64) was one of them, and he was especially interested in the comparison of different versions. He understood the philological approach of comparing languages for a true understanding of the Bible, which he believed would lead in the end to world peace.

Alongside such events attended by a wide range of community members, the scholars of Zurich (as in many other cities of *early modern Europe) were concerned to store and transmit the information they accumulated. Drawing on models from antiquity and the inheritance from medieval institutions, sixteenth-century Zurich had a significant cathedral library, a growing city archive, and a number of compiling projects carried out by individuals. These can be considered nonhuman memory appliances, equivalent to our various electronic media today. In the sixteenth century these collections increased significantly for a number of reasons, including the growth of official record keeping and the production of printed books, the circulation and trade in specimens and objects within Europe and beyond, and most fundamentally a genuine enthusiasm for the accumulation of information in many forms. This growth of information posed problems of organization and retrieval and motivated new experiments in the methods of managing books, archives, and information of many kinds.

Thus the catalog of the Grossmünster library, with its unusual *taxonomy that offered lists organized by author, title, and topic, may have inspired the famous Zurich encyclopedist Conrad Gessner to compile a reference book that sorted all known books by the topics they treated (the *Pandectae* [All-receiver] of 1548, sorting the contents of his *Bibliotheca universalis* [Universal library] of 1545). At the same time, Gessner also tapped a pan-European network of correspondents and readers whose contributions of information about animals and plants made possible the large *encyclopedias of natural history that he published. As he thanked contributors in print for sending him specimens or images of text extracts, he encouraged further contributions from existing but also new contacts. Through his letter writing and his explicit thanks to informants in his publications Gessner nurtured and maintained the connections needed to facilitate continual learning.

Sixteenth-century Zurich offers just one example of the kinds of connected learning that occurred in a myriad of places in the early modern world, in Europe and elsewhere. In applying the notion, our learning today indicates that we all are (largely unconsciously) using premodern academic techniques that rely on textual sources rather than experiences, and that store our information in organized external memory. Scholars developed these techniques before the sciences and the *humanities separated, and before the term *research* was used to characterize their work.

AUTODIDACTICISM

Learning was closely associated with teaching in the long tradition of European pedagogy in all European languages: a learning person, according to the philologists Jacob and Wilhelm Grimm's *Wörterbuch* (Dictionary, 1854), was synonymous with a pupil, student, or apprentice, and this person would always have a master as interlocutor. The intellectual circles of late seventeenth- to nineteenth-century Europe, however, integrated a certain type of student, who earlier had a rather marginal role and negative connotation. These came to be called "autodidacts," named after the Greek, those who self-learned or were self-taught. This term was applied both to people who published and taught in university disciplines such as astrophysics or economics, even though they had not received a formal school or university education, and to those who from a humble and illiterate background had taught themselves how to read and write. Compared with the sixteenth century, where many scholars were self-taught but did not broadly discuss the topic, the frequent usage of the term in the later scholarly discussions shows that formal education was now the norm for reaching professional excellence in the disciplines, and for being able to read and write.

An influential source for the idea of the autodidact as not only being self-taught, but also having learned to reason without outside help, was Ibn Ṭufayl's *Philosophus Autodidactus* (The self-taught philosopher), a book originally written in the twelfth century that Edward Pocock translated in 1671 from Arabic into Latin. The book tells of a child who grew up on a desert island without any human contact. By the sole use of his own reason and experience, the young man not only learned the rules necessary for living but also penetrated into the most hidden secrets of the sciences. When he was accidentally discovered, it turned out that by his natural judgment he had far surpassed all ordinary philosophers. The book was influential in the eighteenth century on presentations of castaway narratives, not least the learning theory that Jean-Jacques Rousseau (1712–78) presented in his book *Emile*, where the teacher arranged learning scenarios to stimulate the boy Emile to learn by experience and through his own rationalizations and conclusions. Crucial for the success of this didactic method was the exclusion of Emile from human society, so that his tender mind would not be spoiled or corrupted.

Already at the end of the seventeenth century scholars and pedagogues debated whether the self-learners could read or understand the disciplines they studied without a teacher's guidance. The fear was that they would misunderstand their readings and give bad advice to those whom they served professionally. This fear diminished during the eighteenth century, and innovative pedagogical approaches were encouraged, especially in the sciences and economics, where agricultural progress was based on a creative reading of new and old sources together with an open mind for new experiments and calculations. The Royal Society, which awarded membership to the most innovative scientists of its day, had many autodidacts among its members, including artists who became published science illustrators and mining engineers. Examples include the famous polymath Gottfried Wilhelm Leibniz (1646–1716), self-educated in mathematics, and the astronomer John Hellins (1749–1827). To integrate autodidacts meant to accept (and prefer) a diversity of opinions and to be open to judgments that deviated from the standard *protocol or *canon.

Today, in spite of the rigorous formal training that modern educational systems typically involve, we are self-taught in many of our daily practices. Once we have mastered the basics of reading and writing, methods of thinking, and gained familiarity with the computer and *internet, then we can teach ourselves through our networks, our reading, or how-to videos. In her memoir *Educated* (2018), Tara Westover describes growing up without a formal education or access to the networks of information in modern society. She was deprived of both because her father, a radical Mormon survivalist, prepared his family for the last judgment, which he considered imminent. Largely self-taught, using books and materials supplied by her elder siblings, she made her way into college and finished with a PhD in history at Cambridge University. She finally thought of herself as educated when she had developed an independent voice to formulate opinions and beliefs of her own, which she based on her experiences, readings, research, and rationalizations. To be self-taught helped her to be passionate about her learning but was also an obstacle because she lacked basic historical knowledge (she had never heard of the Holocaust or the civil rights movement) and had little sense of how problems might admit of more than one interpretation.

The *facts and stories that she learned were less important for her than the process of self-finding. When asked how she would conceptualize education, she answered that she would be in favor of open-ended learning materials, so as to offer the full breadth of possibilities.

Once admitted into college, Westover had a few understanding teachers who helped her. But even in her formal-learning phase, she did most of her learning via self-motivated reading of textbooks. Her doctoral thesis was an account of coming to terms with her past. She analyzed her religious background of Mormonism and put her early readings of the Book of Mormon and other religious literature into a historical and philosophical context. By historicizing her religious reading, she was able to make sense of it as useful and important, and she found a voice as a historian thinking and making sense of her past experiences. Westover represents a new form of autodidacticism that is based on connected learning: her learning rests in diversity of opinion; she connects specialized nodes or information sources; she values the capacity to know more as more important than what is currently known; she maintains connections needed to learn; and she ties together different fields and ideas, linking her religious upbringing to her methodic study of history. Connected learning enabled Westover to free herself and obtain an education.

Anja-Silvia Goeing

See also algorithms; appraising; art of memory; diagrams; digitization; excerpting/commonplacing; globalization; knowledge; manuals; media; professors; reference books; storage and search; teaching

FURTHER READING

Avner Ben Zaken, *Reading Hayy Ibn-Yaqzan: A Cross-Cultural History of Autodidacticism*, 2011; Ann Blair, "Printing and Humanism in the Work of Conrad Gessner," *Renaissance Quarterly* 70, no. 1 (2017): 1–43; Connected Learning Alliance, https://clalliance.org/about-connected-learning/; Anja-Silvia Goeing, *Storing, Archiving, Organizing: The Changing Dynamics of Scholarly Information Management in Post-Reformation Zurich*, 2017; Jacob and Wilhelm Grimm, *Deutsches Wörterbuch*, 1854–1961 (online); George Siemens, "Connectivism: A Learning Theory for the Digital Age," *International Journal of Instructional Technology and Distance Learning* 2 (2004): 3–10; Hans Rudolf Velten, "Die Autodidakten: Zum Aufkommen eines wissenschaftlichen Diskurses über Intellektuelle gegen Ende des 17. Jahrhunderts," in *Intellektuelle in der Frühen Neuzeit*, edited by Jutta Held, 2002, 55–82.

LETTERPRESS

Printing has long been considered a crucial agent of the circulation and transmission of information. The principle of letterpress, printing from a raised surface onto paper or cloth, was known by the seventh century in China and was used for metal movable type in China and Korea by the twelfth and thirteenth centuries. Wooden blocks were applied to the decoration of cloth in India by perhaps the fourth century BCE, and in western Europe by the fourteenth century CE.

The separate development of movable type in mid-fifteenth-century Europe depended partly on the adaptation of a series of existing metalworking processes. First, a punch was cut, with the appropriate letter or other mark on the end. From this a matrix, of softer metal, was made. This matrix was inserted into a mold and type metal was poured in so as to create the piece of type. Once a large number of pieces of type (or "sorts") had been made they were planed down so as all to sit at exactly the same height, with their faces upward, when they were printed. Separate punches and so on were required for each size of letter as well as for each design. Punchcutting, like typefounding, was a quite separate skill from printing. In Italy, Francesco da Bologna worked with Aldus Manutius to create roman and the first italic type. His Greek types, based on the work of skilled contemporary scribes, successfully overcame the difficulties posed by highly ligatured handwriting. By the sixteenth century the names of some craftsmen such as the Frenchmen Robert Granjon or Jean Jannon were celebrated: several of Granjon's types were used by Christophe Plantin in Antwerp. By the end of the eighteenth century names such as Caslon in England, or Didot in France, not only were internationally celebrated; they also became synonymous with particular families of designs.

In the fifteenth century printers could usually be distinguished by the types they used, whether of different designs or showing evidence of having been cast at different times. The first English printer, William Caxton, for example, used eight different fonts along with assorted decorative initials, but some of the largest printers used many more: in Nuremberg, Anton Koberger (active by 1471) owned an exceptionally large printing house with two dozen presses and perhaps a hundred workmen. He has been identified with almost thirty different sizes and designs of type by the end of the century. The development of an international trade in matrixes and typefounding meant that by the mid-sixteenth century the same designs were to be seen in many different towns.

Printers needed large supplies of type in order to make books. Type metal was heavy, and expensive. Until the nineteenth century it was customary to set a given number of pages, and after printing them off to distribute the type so that it could be used for another setting.

Type that had been cast was distributed into pairs of cases, the upper case (mostly containing the capitals) and the lower case: hence the modern terms uppercase and lowercase. Using a setting stick, the compositor set a few lines and then transferred them into a wooden or (later) metal tray known as a galley. From this, pages were made up, arranged in such a way that when printed onto large sheets the paper could be folded into sections with the pages in the correct order. The form of type was transferred to the bed of the press, locked in place, inked, and printed. While in the smaller printing houses no doubt skills were transferable, it was normal for the compositor to be quite separate from the two pressmen: he was also often better educated. Each sheet was laid on the press and printed first one side and then the other, the form of type being inked by hand between each impression. Because this could be paused at any time, text could be corrected easily: the result was that an edition might well contain many minor variants. This phenomenon has been most studied for Shakespeare and early English drama, but it is equally applicable to all kinds of text, and this remained so for as long as books were printed by hand. Further alterations could be made by means of replacement leaves or even whole gatherings ("cancels"), by printing corrections on slips of paper and pasting them in, or simply by pen. All are frequent in early printing and mean that no individual copy in the handpress period can be confidently regarded as part of an exactly repeated sequence.

Letterpress printing brought an immediate and immense increase in the numbers of books in circulation, and in the speed with which they could be produced. The wooden, or common, press was developed also in the 1450s and remained in use until the introduction of iron presses in the early nineteenth century. But the latter brought no essential technical change, and the speed of printing remained much the same, with about 1,250 sheets printed per day. Larger editions were possible, but agreements with workmen were designed to ensure a balance between compositors and pressmen. So after a day's work the type was redistributed. Any reprints (strictly called new editions) had thus to be reset, though in fact sheets from two settings could be easily confused, as excess sheets from the earlier printing were redeployed in the reiteration.

Speeds altered dramatically with the invention of the cylinder press, first installed at the *Times* in London in 1814. Output increased dramatically, to over one thousand impressions an hour, and steam was replaced by electricity for newspaper printing in the 1890s. Old methods of stop-press correction were usually no longer feasible. The newspaper press was responsible for many of the innovations during the century. When curved stereotype plates were introduced after 1816, and were linked to machine-made paper fed on a continuous roll, presses were developed that could run very much faster.

It took longer for typesetting to be speeded up. Several ideas were tried, both in casting as one those letters frequently used together (logography) or in combining manual and machine setting, until in the 1880s Ottmar Mergenthaler of Baltimore invented the Linotype machine, which set lines in solid slugs of metal, and in the 1890s another American, Tolbert Lanston, invented the Monotype, which cast each piece of type separately, as it was needed. The latter drew several of its principles from the Jacquard loom, where the machine was instructed by punched card. In the Monotype this card was replaced by a punched paper spool, created by the compositor sitting at a keyboard. The spool was then fed into a separate machine to cast the letters and make up the lines of type. Linotype was much used in newspaper work, and in setting cheap paperbacks. Monotype, with a huge mixture of traditional, modern, and specialist typefaces, dominated book printing. Both were used worldwide, latterly even for the complexities of setting in oriental languages.

The printing of illustrations was transformed with the invention of the halftone process, whereby photographs could be reproduced as a series of raised dots, the size of the dots, and hence the density of ink, dictating shadows, darkness, and light. The principle was suggested by William Fox Talbot in 1852, but it became commercially as well as technically successful thanks to Georg Meisenbach, a German working in England in the 1880s. Color printing, which had hitherto depended on lithography, was transformed with the introduction in 1893 by William Kurtz of three-color separation for half-tones.

Letterpress, where type, line blocks (whether of wood or metal), and half-tone photographs could all be printed simultaneously, lay at the heart of printing worldwide until the last quarter of the twentieth century. Its dependence on a host of specialist skills made it increasingly expensive in equipment and manpower alike. It was overtaken by new technical developments in both setting and machining and could no longer compete in price. Within a very short time it was replaced for all but specialist work mostly by fine printers, as lithography and offset lithography, computer setting, and eventually *digital printing took its place.

David McKitterick

See also books; printed visuals; publicity/publication; stereotype printing; xylography

FURTHER READING

Paul Goldman, "The History of Illustration and Its Technologies," in *The Oxford Companion to the Book*, edited by Michael Suarez, 2010; Richard E. Huss, *The Development of Printers' Mechanical Typesetting Methods*, 1973; David McKitterick, *Print, Manuscript, and the Search for Order, 1450–1830*, 2003; Richard Southall, *Printer's Type in the Twentieth Century: Manufacturing and Design Methods*, 2005; Michael Twyman, *The British Library Guide to Printing: History and Techniques*, 1998.

LETTERS

Letters exploit two features of writing: its capacity to preserve speech across time, and its capacity to make speech portable. They have existed as long as writing itself: it cannot be a coincidence that the only reference to a letter in the Homeric poems is also the only specific mention of writing in the poems (*Iliad* 6.167–70). The letter, however, is not simply speech at a distance. Its defining characteristic is the fact that the author is not present when the letter reaches its destination and goes about its purposes. The absence of the author is embedded in the assumptions of the *genre, and it often preoccupies the letter writer to a degree that is rarer in other modes of writing. For most of the history of the letter, the uncertain period between its composition and its delivery has tended to make letters more self-conscious about the passage of time, and more likely to speculate about the circumstances prevailing when they arrive. This gap between writing and receiving has been largely eliminated by modern technology.

The material on which letters have been recorded has varied according to the resources and ingenuity of their senders. Ovid tells us that the Greek youth Acontius transmitted a message to his beloved Cydippe by inscribing it on an apple (*Heroides* 20.9–10). Ancient letters were more often written on wooden tablets, either directly on the wood or inscribed in a shallow layer of wax, a format that could be folded and sealed with wax or cords to protect the fragile medium and to secure its content against unintended or unwelcome readers. Wax tablets were designed to be easily erased and reused, marking the status of such letters as ephemeral. If the letter was felt to be important, of course, it could be transferred to more expensive semipermanent storage, usually in the form of *papyrus, *parchment, or paper. Letters on papyrus have been preserved in the sands of Egypt for two thousand years, and wooden tablets from the first and second centuries CE have been preserved at Vindolanda on the Roman frontier in the British Isles. Such survivals show something of the tenor of the vast majority of ancient letters, written in the belief that their content had no permanent value.

The manuscript tradition has transmitted a very large number of letters from antiquity and preserved examples of many different types. The most familiar category is represented by Cicero's private correspondence, unpublished during his lifetime, but issued posthumously by his secretary Tiro. Other letters were published, and partly composed, by their authors as public demonstrations of their literary talents: into this category fall, for example, the letters published by the younger Pliny. In Greek, there are categories less familiar to modern readers. We have collections of "imaginary" letters, self-evidently fictitious letters written for literary purposes by writers such as Alciphron, Aelian, Philostratus, and Aristaenetus. We have "pseudonymous" letters, such as those ascribed to Hippocrates, Socrates, and Diogenes the Cynic. The Greek letters attributed to the tyrant Phalaris were shown to be late imposters by Richard Bentley in 1699, in a treatise that was a landmark in the development of modern historical and linguistic scholarship.

In medieval Europe, Latin letter writing came increasingly to be codified from the eleventh century by the so-called *ars dictaminis* (art of letter writing). Influential manuals emphasized the use of formulas and attempted to identify and standardize the parts of letters that were shared by all letters devoted to similar tasks. Letters written according to these conventions showed some tendency to elaborate the introductory and closing formulas of the letter while abbreviating and simplifying the intervening material. The manuals emphasized the task that the letter was intended to achieve, and they looked to ancient rhetorical principles to guide the letter's composition and structure. By standardizing certain types of official communication, the manuals reduced the scope for misunderstanding, but only at the cost of marginalizing the personality of the sender. Because it was often difficult to separate the official capacity of senders from their personal capacity, the tone and structure of personal letters was also influenced by the formal requirements of the conventions. In these circumstances, a mode of communication constructed for bureaucracies and institutions became a model for communication between individuals, and the private letter acquired some of the characteristics of the public pronouncement.

It was this medieval context that made Francesco Petrarch's rediscovery in 1345 of Cicero's private correspondence with Atticus a revolutionary event. The discovery reasserted the role of the letter as a component in a private conversation between friends, and it contributed to Petrarch's increasing self-consciousness about the nature and the audience of his own letters. Among its first fruits, however, were a series of public letters addressed to figures of the ancient world, starting with Cicero himself. This letter to Cicero was the first of a number of public addresses to the illustrious dead, written in the tone of a conversation with a learned friend. Petrarch thus turned the central conceit of the letter form on its head: the absence of the author presupposed by the letter was used instead to focus attention on the absence of the recipient. This unprecedented mode allowed Petrarch to select his particular friends from among the greatest figures of the ancient world, and to present himself as one for whom such conversations were natural and proper.

Letters were one aspect of manuscript culture that flourished and expanded in Europe following the advent of the printing press. Improved communications and the relative cheapness of paper were certainly factors, but the place of letter writing in the classrooms of the period was also of central importance. Letter writing was taught in the schools as a valuable social skill, but it also had practical advantages as a classroom exercise: it could be relatively brief and self-contained, and it combined simple rules and rigorous imitation with opportunities for innovation and imagination. This confluence of the preferences of the educators with the priorities of the educated led to large numbers of new letter-writing manuals in all languages. Some of these were regularly reprinted, including the work of Carolus Virulus (1476), Erasmus (1522), Juan Luis Vives (1534), Georgius Macropedius (1543), and Justus Lipsius (1591). *Vernacular versions soon followed: from England, for example, we have William Fullwood's *Enimie of Idlenesse* (1568) and Angel Day's *English Secretary* (1586). A century later, Henry Care's *Female Secretary* (1671) formally invited women into a genre they had long inhabited and provided model letters that he believed voiced their concerns. By the seventeenth century, the letter was among the most highly theorized genres in existence. Like any well-defined genre, it was easily parodied: the notorious Latin satire *Letters of Obscure Men* (1515–17) has many targets, but along the way it takes aim at the conventions of the letter form.

During the same period, the most common public letter of all, the letter of dedication, underwent some internal reorganization. It had been a prominent and specialized instance of the letter proper since ancient times. Its traditional role was to praise the dedicatee, to make a plausible connection between the dedicatee and the work in hand, and thus to foster a relationship between the dedicator and the dedicatee. As the document that mediated the reader's approach to the work, the dedicatory letter was often assigned a further role: to examine the purposes and methods of the work it prefaced. However, these two roles were quite different and their conjunction sometimes awkward. During the sixteenth century, the dedicatory letter bifurcated into the dedication and the preface *To the Reader*, where both jobs could be done separately and more conveniently. The dedicatory letter, freed from the obligation to perform scholarly tasks, could now move further in the direction of eulogy.

Most private letters were autographs, and the hand of the sender was both a guarantor of the letter's authenticity and a projection of intimacy. The sealing of letters, a practice common to all ages, generated a sense of privacy that encouraged writers to commit sensitive matters to paper. Those who maintained large correspondences would often file them alphabetically by sender and chronologically by date in order to facilitate regular and timely replies. In the process they accidentally created substantial biographical archives and bequeathed them to their literary executors. Because letters were so often authoritative, semiconfessional, precisely dated, and carefully organized, they came to occupy a central position in the art of biography. The letter collections of religious figures, statesmen, and scholars could become vehicles to illustrate exemplary lives. In the seventeenth century, artful editors shaped the biographies of men like Joseph Scaliger and Isaac Casaubon by excluding awkward letters and inconvenient material from their collections. In doing so, they constructed and transmitted an ideal of the scholarly life that remains influential.

As this idea of the scholar took shape in the seventeenth and eighteenth centuries, letters emerged as a mechanism for communicating new research and discoveries. In this role, letters were gradually superseded by the learned journal, but for a time scholars could claim to feel part of an international conversation maintained through correspondence and might identify themselves as members of a "respublica litterarum," a *"republic of letters" or a "republic of the learned." A number of modern projects devoted to understanding the phenomenon are detailed in the entry "networks" in this volume. The term *republic of letters* is often misleading as a tool for examining the history of the letter: it is part of an elaborate recurring metaphor rather than the name of an informal international club.

Handwritten letters are unusual historical documents because we often have precise information about how they were read by their recipients. The audiences of plays leave few impressions of their experiences, and the readers of books rarely do more than write notes in the margins, but the recipients of letters often supply us with detailed accounts of their immediate reactions in their replies. The process that constructed these replies may also be studied: letter readers often annotated the letters they had received in order to prepare their response, and large numbers of drafts survive from all periods that record an intermediate stage in the process between the receipt of the letter and the composition of a reply.

The immediacy of letters, the sense that they represent a timely response to the issues raised by a correspondent, has always been part of their attraction. In the heyday of the printed newspaper, editors regularly published letters from their readers because the immediacy of the genre was consonant with the purposes of the publication as a whole. With news organizations now providing their readers with facilities for online comment, the role of the letter to the editor is very much reduced.

The expansion of electronic messaging has transformed the letter. The traditional letter tended to address a range of subjects, but an email is more likely to be a shorter piece of text addressing fewer issues. Electronic messages are often less carefully composed, and they leave fewer traces of the process of composition. They are more easily stored and retrieved than paper letters, but they are seldom retained for long by their recipients, and the chances of long-term preservation for the overwhelming majority are slim.

Paul Botley

See also bureaucracy; documentary authority; files; forgery; journals; layout and script in letters; learning; networks; privacy; secretaries; teaching

FURTHER READING

James Daybell and Andrew Gordon, eds., *Cultures of Correspondence in Early Modern Britain*, 2016; William Fitzgerald, "The Epistolary Tradition," in *The Oxford History of Classical Reception in English Literature*, vol. 2, *1558–1660*, ed. Patrick Cheney and Philip Hardie, 2015; Judith Rice Henderson, "Defining the Genre of the Letter: Juan Luis Vives' 'De Conscribendis Epistolis,'" *Renaissance and Reformation* 7 (1983): 89–105; Carol Poster and Linda C. Mitchell, eds., *Letter-Writing Manuals and Instruction from Antiquity to the Present*, 2007; Carol Poster and Richard Utz, eds., *The Late Medieval Epistle*, 1996; Stanley K. Stowers, *Letter Writing in Greco-Roman Antiquity*, 1986; Ronald Witt, "Medieval 'Ars Dictaminis' and the Beginnings of Humanism: A New Construction of the Problem," *Renaissance Quarterly* 35 (1982): 1–35.

LIBRARIES AND CATALOGS

A remarkable chapter of the Austrian writer Robert Musil's *The Man without Qualities* (1930) bears the title "General Stumm invades the State Library and learns about the world of books, the librarians guarding it, and intellectual order." Vexed by the lassitude of the government committee on which he served, the besabered Stumm ventured into the Imperial Library in Vienna. The general expected quick results from a state information repository. He instead encountered "book stands and library tables piled high with catalogs and bibliographies, the concentrate of all knowledge, don't you know, and not one sensible book to read, only books about books." With technical precision he reported that the place "positively reeked of brain-phosphorous."

By Musil's time, libraries had emerged as the central information-processing centers of the industrialized West. Modern technological developments—the mechanical cylindrical printing press, integrated rail and postal systems, the telegraph, electric power, telephones, typewriters—coupled with social changes in the professionalization of knowledge created a communications environment in which increased volumes of information moved with unprecedented rapidity. Libraries served as both warehouses and clearing centers for the mass of information contained in books, periodicals, and the myriad publications of industry, commerce, and government.

The modern library aimed not simply to stockpile learning but to connect knowledge sites and manage information flows. Its creators recognized that the production of knowledge was a dynamic, ongoing process. Professional training, "scientific" methods, and "modern" procedures were confidently introduced into the space of the library. Stumm himself had been admitted into the library's catalog room—"the holy of holies"— only after asking "about some sort of railway time-table that would make it possible to get cross-connections between ideas going in every direction." The librarian, a sometime professor of library science, mistook Stumm for one of his own and steered the general toward a "bibliography of bibliographies."

The largest of the new libraries—the British Museum Library (1857), the Bibliothèque nationale in Paris (1868), the Library of Congress (1897), the New York Public Library (1911)—were sprawling book machines that processed thousands of new books and periodicals each year thanks to specialized staff and devices such as card catalogs, conveyor belts, book lifts, and pneumatic tubes delivering call slips.

Libraries were everywhere. The popular lending libraries that dotted the urban landscape furnished day-to-day familiarity with library practices and paraphernalia. Government, business, and industry were served by specialized libraries—sometimes called "information bureaus"—that provided access to technical reports, scientific documentation, and institutional records. Meanwhile a large research library was regarded as the intellectual center of the modern university. Though differing in size and scale, libraries were the ubiquitous, everyday information-processing sites of the predigital age.

LIBRARIES, SPACE, CATALOGS

From the perspective of the history of information, libraries furnish an important example of sites where the recording, ordering, and sharing of large quantities of disparate data was an organized social activity. Library technologies such as catalogs and indexes were sometimes adapted to the organization of knowledge in other social spheres such as government and commerce. And library data management practices contributed to the early *digital landscape in meaningful ways.

Even before industrialization libraries functioned as sites of interconnectivity that managed information flows and provided an interface between people, books, and knowledge. Libraries grew exponentially in size from the *Renaissance to the early twentieth century. Remarkably the core practices for accumulating and structuring bibliographic data—describing, classifying, abstracting, indexing—remained much the same. Libraries combined assemblages of manual procedures with a variety of handwritten and printed media to structure information, order collections, and guide readers to books. Though catalogs changed in form and function over the centuries, they were always intimately connected to library space.

The physical space of the library was an essential element of library "information architecture." Premodern libraries offered a deeply embodied experience of knowledge. Standard library furnishings of the Renaissance featured long, sloped lectern desks with books stored on shallow shelves either above or below the reading surface. Books were often chained in place, and readers were accustomed to moving around a library to read. By the seventeenth century books were more commonly kept on wall shelves and read at tables. Many libraries adopted a plan of jutting alcoves with accompanying desks in order to maximize shelf space. Books were normally arranged by subject: theology, law, philosophy, and so on. It was a rare library that possessed more than a few thousand volumes.

Catalogs were normally topographical inventories that itemized books according to their physical arrangement in the library. There was little preoccupation with elaborate description or complex classification. When the French librarian Gabriel Naudé observed in 1627 that the best order for a library was "that which is the most common," he spoke the library wisdom of the ages. Classification schemes aimed to reflect shared intellectual categories. Memory, visualization, and embodied familiarity with library space played an important role in finding books.

Even as collections grew in size over the course of the seventeenth and eighteenth centuries, the cognitive contours of the library changed little. Library architecture enhanced the embodied encounter with knowledge. The Benedictine scholar Oliverius Legipontius observed in 1747 that "looking at a book collection should be like seeing the entire history of learning in a mirror." Catalogs, in turn, sought to replicate and enhance a library's visual order. A subject catalog reflecting shelf order was often the only working tool available to librarians and readers. As Naudé explained, subject catalogs allowed readers to see "in the twinkling of an eye" all books available in a given area. Library architecture responded with visual and spatial cues. Subject headings or pressmarks were inscribed above bookcases. Copies of catalog pages on individual sheets that were sometimes posted on library furnishings underscore the close relationship of catalogs and the spatial environment.

Figure 1. A bird's-eye view of the interior of Leiden University Library in 1610. Books are visibly arranged in the subject order of the library's printed 1595 catalog. The lettering on top of the cases, which in reality would have been visible to no one, is an engraver's conceit—subject classification was no doubt communicated differently. Engraving by Willem van Swanenberg. Image courtesy Leiden University Libraries (COLLBN Port 315 3 N22).

The apotheosis of this phenomenon lies in the fantastical sculpted baroque libraries whose galleried, often curved library walls seemingly enfold the reader in bibliographic embrace. Books not only were stored openly; they were displayed. "Knowledge lies here" was the tantalizing promise, quite literally within grasp, even when guardrails and librarians intervened. There was no pretense that a library might contain all books. Rather, the library constituted a prism of universal knowledge that refracted but did not reproduce a larger order.

PRINT, DATA, ORGANIZATION

The *early modern print explosion meant that the informational tools used in libraries were called on to manage increasing volumes of data. Basic procedures for making catalogs remained the same for centuries. The first step was to arrange books in subject order. Most classification schemes were thematic and hierarchical. Books were grouped into broad subject areas—theology, law, history, literature, and philosophy were fairly

Figure 2. The English architect Sir Christopher Wren designed an influential interpretation of alcove library architecture for the library of Trinity College, Cambridge (1695). Reading desks are situated in the midst of each alcove, with books an arm's length away. At the end of each bay the Roman lettering used for shelf notation is prominently displayed. Wooden tablet-like leaves beneath open to reveal written lists of the contents of each bay. Photo: James Kirwan. Image courtesy Wren Library.

standard—and subdivided into further subclasses that varied according to the size and nature of the collection. The next step was to draw up a shelf list to serve as a subject catalog. Empty shelf space was left to accommodate new acquisitions, and blank pages were left in catalogs. Alphabetized author tables or keyword indexes might be made afterward. This method was used, for example, to organize the Bibliothèque du Roi in Paris in the seventeenth century (twenty-three subject classes in fourteen volumes, cataloging some sixty thousand volumes; accompanied by a twenty-one-volume alphabetical index) and the library at the University of Göttingen in the eighteenth century (eighty-five subject classes in 147 volumes). While loose slips or cut sheets—the embryonic elements of the modern card catalog—were used as aids to sorting and arranging, a bound catalog in book form remained the habitual media support for storing bibliographic information.

Each bank or case of shelves was assigned an identifier, very commonly a capital Roman letter. In some cases it served secondarily as a subject class *code. Individual shelves were assigned a distinct identifier such as a lowercase letter or Roman numeral, with individual volumes on each shelf assigned a number using Arabic notation. In other instances books were numbered sequentially within each class. In isolated cases super-script notation (a precursor of decimalization) was used to incorporate additions. What is now called the shelf notation or call number might serve at least four different functions: to provide a distinct alphanumeric identity for an individual volume; designate a book's physical location; indicate a subject class; and furnish a universal notation for cross-referencing bibliographic data across different types of catalogs and finding aids.

To modern eyes the system is perplexing. The fixed character of both the physical arrangement of books and the bound catalog appears to condemn librarians to a purgatory of endless shelf rearrangement and recataloging. Yet new accessions were the exception rather than the rule in premodern libraries. Systematic shelf arrangement also offered frank recognition of the fragility of catalog systems and the enormous labor involved. No matter how approximate a physical subject arrangement, rooting around on library shelves could be the first as well as the last resort of any investigation. The alcove architecture adopted by many medium-sized libraries in the seventeenth century, and that endured as a model for more than two hundred years, actively fostered this sort of wandering, tactile encounter with books. It is telling of the entire system that some regarded catalogs as intellectual crutches, a poor substitute for the flexible, multifaceted "place" memory of the librarian.

The tools developed by Hernando Colón, son of the famous navigator Christopher Columbus, provide a snapshot of available premodern library information practices. Colón inherited his father's wealth as well as his name and amassed a large library—some fifteen thousand volumes of printed books by the time of his death in 1539. Just as importantly, he devoted money and energy to its organization. An unusually large number of staff worked in the library and under Colón's direction produced an ambitious array of catalogs, indexes, and other works. The primary information tool was a register of accessions where bibliographic data was recorded as books were purchased and assigned a number. The accession number signaled the physical location of a book and served as an identifier for cross-referencing in other catalogs. The register was supplemented by a suite of author, title, and subject catalogs and indexes. The most remarkable of Colón's working tools is the recently discovered *Libro de los Epítomes*, or "book of summaries." Assistants were employed to read Colón's books and prepare abridgments. These were then reviewed, corrected, and copied into the *Libro*. Though the contours of the system changed slightly as the collection grew in size, its essential elements remained in place. A torturously complex system of numbers and symbols purportedly enabled staff to move from one informational device to another and to locate books on the shelves.

Colón's system was complex and unique. It nonetheless shows how catalogs and indexes could be used to organize a large number of books and share knowledge-building information. Tellingly, many of Colón's catalogs remain unfinished. Labor intensive, they were the work of years rather than months. Most early modern libraries had a sole, usually ill-paid, librarian who often performed other duties. Only larger institutions might have assistants, copyists, and the like.

Conrad Gessner provides a strikingly different example of how bibliographic data could be adapted and organized. While Colón sought to bring order to his library in Seville, Gessner sought to catalog the world of books writ large. When he coined the term *universal library* a few years after Colón's death, it was not because Gessner had access to a fabulously stocked library but because he did not. The town library in his native Zurich possessed a meager one thousand volumes.

Hailed as a landmark of bibliography, Gessner's *Bibliotheca universalis* (1545–48) offered readers a panorama of the world of Renaissance books. Published at the tail end of the first century of print, Gessner's bibliography inventoried the available stock of learning and assembled what we would now consider a virtual library catalog. Of interest are the tools Gessner employed: earlier printed bibliographies; printers' catalogs; handwritten library catalogs; a network of correspondents; the book collections of members of his circle in Zurich and nearby Basle. He also distilled data from title pages, *colophons, and tables of contents. And in the manner of Colón's *Epítomes* he furnished readers with the fruits of his own reading. A reference tool intended for scholars, the *Bibliotheca* itemized some twenty-five thousand Hebrew, Greek, and Latin titles. Gessner intended his "universal library" to furnish a guide to library acquisitions, and he suggested that it could be adapted to serve as a library catalog.

Gessner showed how bibliographic data could be disaggregated from the localized space of the library and assembled to create an independent tool of knowledge. After Gessner a range of publications established norms for the description and classification of books that intersected with the technical practices of libraries. The year 1564 witnessed the publication of the first printed catalog of the semiannual Frankfurt Book Fair. Printed library catalogs furnished another important source of bibliographic information. The earliest of these were the catalogs of the University of Leiden (1595) and the Bodleian Library at Oxford (1605). Book reviews soon became a staple of the new periodical press, while subject bibliographies diffused more specialized bibliographic information. Like Gessner's "universal library" many works embraced the ideal of a virtual library: *Bibliotheca medica, Bibliotheca theologica*, and so on.

The *Bibliotheca universalis* and its successors were the precursors of the "bibliography of bibliographies" that later confounded General Stumm. During the centuries that separated Gessner's Zurich and Stumm's Vienna, this informal network of bibliographic information coalesced into a regulated system that seemingly found its natural home in the bowels of the centralized state library. The transition was gradual, spanning almost four hundred years.

CARDS, STACKS, NOTATION

From the Renaissance to the *Enlightenment the ideal of a well-ordered library changed little. The visual display of a collection was of paramount importance. Books were arranged by subject order and accompanied by classified catalogs, alphabetical indexes, and other finding aids.

In the nineteenth century increased volumes of new acquisitions placed urgent pressures on the processing of bibliographic data and the physical storage of books. It is estimated that industrial print technologies triggered a sixfold increase in the annual production of books and other materials over the course of the century. In Germany, which dominated the field of scientific and technical publications worldwide, the number of journal and magazine titles increased by a factor of eighteen, effectively doubling every twenty-five years.

Shifting knowledge paradigms together with increased production capacity meant that new acquisitions were a daily occurrence rather than a rare and privileged exception. By the early twentieth century periodical publications played an unprecedented role in the dissemination of knowledge. The triumph of disciplinary knowledge meant that researchers no longer strived to master defined traditions—which libraries had sought to map and mirror—but to create new knowledge.

The crux of the problem lies in the relationship between multiple enterprises: processing a rising tide of bibliographic information; incorporating accelerating rates of new acquisitions into established collections; storing and locating unprecedented numbers of materials on library shelves; and somehow communicating endlessly shifting pools of information to library patrons through catalogs and indexes.

Librarians experimented and theorized in response. The most important architectural innovation was the invention of the book stack. Built of iron or steel, compact book stacks stored rather than displayed books. The first book stack was erected in the new British Museum Library that opened in 1856. Readers were seated in a single vast, circular reading room. The library's bound catalogs ringed a central reference desk. Rows of reading desks radiated from the catalogs, while reading room shelves displayed some forty thousand reference works. Invisible to readers was a warren of forty-two kilometers of multitiered iron shelves that surrounded the reading room. The stack system was incorporated into the construction of the new Bibliothèque nationale in Paris (1868) and was rapidly advocated by German and American librarians. From Helsinki to Melbourne, stacks furnished the dominant architectural model for libraries across the Western world.

The arrival of the book stack reflected a wider preoccupation with the differentiation of function in the organization of library work and the distribution of library space. Just as books and readers were separated, so too were work spaces: librarian's offices, acquisitions and cataloging departments, catalog rooms. In tandem with the increased professionalization of librarianship—library schools, cataloging manuals, professional associations, and the like—the reorganization of library space triggered experiments with the storage, manipulation, and display of bibliographic information.

Removing books from public view meant that catalogs now furnished the sole access point to books. This was true not only for readers, but also for librarians—"stack work" was carried out by clerical staff. This opened the door to the end of systematic shelf arrangement by subject. In the British Museum Library books were originally sorted into 650 subject groupings and then shelved by size and order of accession. Accession-order shelving was taken to further extremes elsewhere. Shelving by size and accession order alone was adopted by the new Bibliothèque nationale facility. It was soon introduced into other Parisian libraries, and even enshrined in law. Instructions for university libraries issued by the French Ministry of Education in 1878 mandated that books be arranged by size and order of accession only.

In this system the accession number becomes an integral part of the physical volume, which permanently identifies it. The accessions register was the lynchpin of the enterprise. Much as the book stack warehoused books, the register archived rather than organized information and "mechanically" generated a number that functioned as a stable identifier for an individual volume. The principle became known as the *numerus*

Figure 3. The New York Public Library (1911) was one of the largest new book palaces of
the modern era. This cover illustration from the popular magazine *Scientific American*
shows the seven-tiered fortress of steel book stacks that fed—and physically supported—
the library's monumental reading room. Stacks, book lifts, pneumatic messaging tubes,
and library staff are all in plain view. The central reading room, depicted upper left, is
glimpsed through a rear view of the arched portals of the book delivery desk. Image courtesy New York Public Library.

currens (running number) system. The manipulation and display of bibliographic information was an entirely separate endeavor. This was performed by author and subject catalogs that referenced the accession number.

Though pragmatically compelling, there was resistance to accession-order arrangement. It never really took hold in the English-speaking world. In Germany, where book stacks were enthusiastically adopted, many librarians considered accession-order shelving an act of *epistemological violence. In 1912 Georg Leyh, a leading German academic librarian, launched a concerted attack on what he called "the dogma of systematic arrangement." Leyh argued that the system served no one. Readers had long been denied access to library shelves, while the clerical staff employed to fetch books used systems of shelf notation without referencing classification systems. Most large libraries in western and central Europe gradually abandoned arrangement by subject order. Books were placed in broad subject groupings upon accession, assigned an accession number (the numerus currens), and varyingly cataloged by author, title, and subject.

The arrival of book stacks intersected with the rise of the card catalog. Recording bibliographical data on paper slips was not a new idea, though it was usually reserved for the preliminary stages of cataloging. Preparatory materials for one of Colón's catalogs, for example, record information on cut sheets that were subsequently stitched together for safekeeping. By the end of the nineteenth century the use of cards and slips had become the norm. Individual catalog entries were recorded on stiff cards and inserted in drawers in standardized wooden catalog furniture. Nonetheless in many quarters card catalogs were regarded as an administrative efficiency rather than a terminal solution. Library manuals of the late nineteenth century usually advocate the use of cards, often in duplicate and triplicate, for the accessions catalogs and alphabetized author catalogs maintained by library staff. It was still foreseen, however, that the principal public catalog would be a classed subject catalog in bound book form. If printed, all the better. Critics of public card catalogs complained that cards were easily lost or misfiled. It was argued that information stored in tightly packed drawers was difficult to read and unduly limited the number of readers able to consult the catalog. Some found that isolating bibliographic information on cards impeded the visualization of aggregate data afforded by the display of multiple entries on a single page.

Even in Germany, where the ideal of the bound, classified subject catalog or *Realkatalog* had reigned supreme for over two hundred years, the combined advantages of cards, stacks, and numerus currens notation was gradually recognized. Critics of the bound catalog pointed out that in most libraries a bound subject catalog remained little more than a pipe dream. In 1906 the *philologist Hermann Diels mocked the entire system, referring to the "arcanum" of modern library catalogs and the "bibliographic hieroglyphics" that linked catalogs to one another. By midcentury most large European libraries used a combination of numerus currens shelf notation, closed stacks, and card catalogs.

The Anglo-American library world went in another direction entirely owing to the implementation of "relative" classification systems. The brainchild of Melvil Dewey (1851–1931), the most vocal exponent of the American "library movement," relative classification systems used a standardized number of subject areas that were assigned either a numeric or alphabetic value. Dewey's system used ten categories, which were assigned numbers: 001–099 (general), 100–199 (philosophy), and so on. Charles Cutter (1837–1903), a librarian first at Harvard and subsequently at the Boston Athenaeum, created a rival system of "Expansive Classification" using alphabetical codes. The range of codes could expand or contract depending on the size of the collection being classified. A modified version of Cutter's method became the *Library of Congress (LC) Classification system. Similar systems were adopted in the United Kingdom. In all cases, numeric or alphabetic class codes are followed by forms of numeric or alphabetic notation (sometimes in combination) that allow a book to be assigned a unique alphanumeric identifier and inserted into an appropriate position in its subject class.

Though the relationship between card catalogs and the development of relative classification is unclear, the two were intimately connected. Dewey and Cutter were both card evangelists. It is possible that habituation to the ease of inserting new cards into an alphabetized author catalog without disrupting the catalog's principal ordering sequence prompted experimentation with subject classification along similar lines. In this regard the truly unique aspect of the American innovation was the application of information management techniques to physical shelf arrangement.

The advantage of the various relative classification systems is that the "mechanically" generated notation does not refer to the fixed location of a book. It instead provides an "address" for a book defined by its relative proximity to other books in the same class. New books could be added without resequencing the entire class. When coupled with the card catalog, the new methods allowed for systemic efficiencies. Cards and books alike could be added at any time without disrupting established order.

Cards, stacks, and notation schemes assumed varied configurations. A version of the Dewey Decimal Classification system—the *Universal Decimal Classification (UDC)— was developed in Europe, where it was often employed in conjunction with the numerus currens shelving system. In other words, UDC was used to index rather than order a library's holdings. In the English-speaking world the convenience of classified shelf arrangement was not lost on readers. Public libraries gradually acquiesced in allowing readers access to book stacks, and the practice spilled over into university research libraries. Globally, public libraries and specialized research libraries normally adopted some version of decimalized classification and open stacks. Decimal classification has proven especially adaptive to non-Western cultures where Roman lettering does not enjoy "universal" recognition value. Both Korea and Japan, for example, employ decimalized national cataloging codes.

The new library systems had important social implications. The vast reading rooms of the large public book palaces emphatically housed people rather than books. The promise of access to material resources combined with the cultural power of libraries— reinforced through imposing, monumental architecture—made libraries important sites of social interaction that acted as a magnet for researchers across the social science and *humanities disciplines.

Invisible to readers, the work of cataloging proved relentless. Cataloging departments routinely complained of underfunding and staff shortages. Backlogs were endemic. Though card catalogs, numerus currens shelving, and relative classification solved the problem of incorporating new items, the pace of accessions increased relentlessly. The number of physical cards required was enormous. Some manuals recommend at least four catalogs, all kept on cards. An accessions catalog and alphabetical author catalog were kept behind the scenes for library administration. A second author catalog and a subject catalog were normally made available to the public. To boot, author catalogs were sometimes interfiled with alphabetized title cards. Library of Congress and Universal Decimal Classification systems employed faceted subject indexing—the use of multiple entry terms for a single item. In that case two or three cards were needed for the subject catalog alone. Ambitious libraries required as many as eight or nine cards for each volume that entered the library.

There were efforts to reduce the burden of cataloging. The Royal Library in Berlin and the Library of Congress, for example, developed standardized "codes" for generating catalog entries that were adapted by other libraries. Other strategies included collective cataloging and the distribution of printed cards. When the new Library of Congress building opened in 1897, it had eight hundred thousand books and no catalog. In 1901, under pressure from other American libraries, it was decided to make the library a center for the distribution of bibliographic information. Printed catalog cards—nearly seventy thousand a year—were made available for purchase. The Library of Congress coordinated with other card-printing institutions such as Harvard, the John Crerar Library in Chicago, and the information service of the US Department of Agriculture. The circulation of stable forms of bibliographic data laid the groundwork for the development of union catalogs and interlibrary loan networks. In 1913 the general catalog of the books housed at Columbia University libraries contained over two million cards. A companion union catalog included cards from the Library of Congress, numerous federal bureaus, other major American libraries, and of New York City libraries not at Columbia. The Columbia example is by no means exceptional. It was reported that the University of Chicago Library, which employed a complex system of cross-indexing with departmental libraries, needed as many as twenty-eight individual cards for each item that entered the collection. By 1920 the Library of Congress had nearly three thousand subscribers and distributed over six million cards annually. Many European countries had similar schemes for collective cataloging, card distribution, union catalogs, and interlibrary loans.

The system worked in conjunction with new schools of library science, classification schedules, cataloging codes, indexing services, standardized forms of academic citation, and other material and social mechanisms of knowledge production. The goal was to produce a stable container for the dynamic transmission, storage, and retrieval of bibliographic data that could be generated and accessed by multiple users. The midcentury library system was a decentered and open-ended network. In principle it was capable of reproducing itself at any point. The only requirements were cash and labor, both in chronic deficit.

Familiarity with the management of large volumes of data and experience with alphanumeric notation rendered libraries well placed to experiment with early computational technologies. By some estimations catalog systems were on the verge of collapse in many places by the mid-twentieth century. Largely in response to a mounting cataloging crisis, the Library of Congress developed digital records in the 1960s—MARC, or *M*achine *R*eadable *C*ataloging standards—that could be read by computers and shared with other libraries. Though computerization was initially adapted for internal systems management and in order to accelerate the production of physical data records, the digital interface was soon made public. By the 1980s the first hands-on experience with computers and digitized information for many people, the present author included, occurred at a public library catalog terminal.

The arrival of the *internet and the digitization of content has had an even more profound impact. Catalogs, books, and articles are available remotely, and libraries now manage vast virtual collections. Digitization has triggered extensive and controversial deaccessioning of physical stock. Meanwhile systems maintenance and digital subscription services loom large in cataloging and acquisitions budgets. Though libraries, books, and librarians have become all but invisible, the "digital revolution" has proven expensive. The need for funding and expertise will not diminish. In 2012 nearly half ($3.4 billion) of the total expenditures of academic libraries in the United States went to salaries and wages. Another $2.8 billion (40 percent) was spent on "information resources"—a combination of print and digital purchases and subscriptions. The number of digital publications acquired was nearly double the number of print publications. Nonetheless the cultural power of libraries remains remarkably strong in the public imagination. Facing the combined pressures of deaccession and depopulation, library spaces have been reimagined to perform new and sometimes unexpected social and cultural functions.

Paul Nelles

See also archivists; art of memory; bibliography; books; book sales catalogs; cards; computers; digitization; indexing; knowledge; readers; reference books; storage and search

FURTHER READING

Andrew Abbot, "Library Research Infrastructure for Humanistic and Social Scientific Scholarship in the Twentieth Century," in *Social Knowledge in the Making*, edited by Charles Camic, Neil Gross, and Michèle Lamont, 2011; Alistair Black, Simon Pepper, and Kaye Bagshaw, *Books, Buildings and Social Engineering: Early Public Libraries in Britain from Past to Present*, 2009; John Willis Clark, *The Care of Books: An Essay on the Development of Libraries and their Fittings, from the Earliest Times to the End of the Eighteenth Century*, 1901; Eric Garberson, "Libraries, Memory and the Space of Knowledge," *Journal of the History of Collections* 18, no. 2 (2006): 105–36; David Kaser, *The Evolution of the American Academic Library Building*, 1997; Catherine Minter, "Systematic or Mechanical Arrangement? Revisiting a Debate in German Library Science, 1790–1914," *Libri* 67, no. 3 (2017): 193–203; Felix Reichmann, "The Catalog in European Libraries," *Library Quarterly* 34, no. 1 (1964): 34–56; Wayne A. Wiegand, "The 'Amherst Method': The Origins of the Dewey Decimal Classification Scheme," *Libraries and Culture* 33, no. 2 (1998): 175–94.

LISTS

Many current discussions of lists begin with anthropological accounts that set lists as the ur-genre of all texts. The literary theorist Walter Ong suggests that most cuneiform script that has survived is account keeping and that writing was largely invented for that purpose. According to the anthropologist Jack Goody, lists help demarcate the "great divide" between oral and literate cultures. Goody and Ong have argued that lists allow for novel forms of cognition by decontextualizing words from their discursive contexts. By making objects discontinuous, lists allow them to be levered out of their normal settings and to be rearranged, classified, and analyzed. Even Goody and Ong would not deny the existence of some lists in oral cultures, such as catalogs of warriors in epic poetry, but they emphasize that such lists do not separate the objects on the list from their narrative framing and thus are not truly discontinuous. Classic examples of lists, such as Homer's catalog of ships, would therefore not be lists at all according to this definition.

Decontextualized from nature and narrative, the argument goes, each object on the list can be closely examined and controlled, thus making the history of list making a frequent topic in accounts of state control of information. The pared-down structure of the list stands in for the movement of things through monitored points of access, such as merchants filing through points of entry and exit in an ancient Sumerian walled city, forcing their goods to be paraded before governmental inspection. The historian Arndt Brendecke has compared such Mesopotamian list making to flows of information in the Spanish Empire, and to certain choke points in port towns and bureaucratic offices.

More recent work in anthropology and linguistics has sharply questioned the thesis of the great divide in general, and the link between list making, writing, and a new rationality in particular. Many types of textual lists are not as discontinuous as Goody claimed. Lists can call up tacit knowledge that, to the period reader, filled in the blanks of a seemingly discontinuous list, but which may not be as obvious several centuries later. Many premodern lists, whether oral or written, can be understood to have embedded within them a preorganized, continual hierarchy, whether of society (king lists; genealogies; and military, bureaucratic, and noble ranks), of space (itineraries), of time (chronologies), or of all three combined (entries, parades, and processions).

In fact, it is not at all obvious that these various genres would have been seen as various forms of one entity, the list. Historians have included a vast array of specialized historical terms, many of them now obsolete or nearly so, within studies of lists. In French alone, Gregorio Salinero has noted "almanach, armorial, billet, bulletin, cadastre, catalogue, cens, chronique, chronotaxis, classement, *codex, collection, compilation, dictionnaire, état civil, feuille, *florilège, galerie, index, inventaire, livres, mémoire, minte, obituaire, pragmatiques, propositions, recensement, relation, répertoire encyclopédique, registre, répartitions, rôle, scalae, série, souscriptions, syllabaire, synopsis, table, tableaux, table chronographique, tablettes chronologiques, témoignage, vignette, vies." Many of the terms that Salinero includes under the rubric of the list, however, were specialized for qualitatively different, incommensurable subject matters. They appeared in specific historical circumstances that do not make them interchangeable.

Many treatments of lists, such as Umberto Eco's *The Infinity of Lists*, written to accompany an exhibition at the Louvre Museum in Paris, stress the dizzying cornucopia of visual and textual forms that lists have taken. Such all-encompassing groupings of lists, such as in Eco's essay, or in Salinero's list of terms, expand the genre to such an extent that it becomes difficult to trace or analyze. As a result, the scholarly investigation of lists does not proceed further than reiterating that lists are meant to organize but in fact subvert order—with an obligatory reference to Borges's Chinese *encyclopedia. No tradition of premodern reflexive writing about lists in general exists, and thus it is difficult to assess whether contemporaries would have recognized all the terms Salinero listed as instances of a list.

Approaching the topic from linguistic and conceptual history, however, allows for a sharper view of what has counted as a list. According to this perspective, the list was not to be found everywhere; rather, it was, literally, marginal. The word itself, from the Old English *liste*, meaning a hem or border, is of remarkably recent vintage. The term came to be applied primarily to a written grouping of people, not objects, at the turn of the seventeenth century, such as the "list of laweless resolutes" Fortinbras compiled in *Hamlet*. However, its older meaning as the hem of a garment remained primary. In 1598, John Florio defined a list as "a list or selvage of any cloth, a list where tilting or turneaments are used, a role, a checkrol, or catalogue of names, an inventorie." We might consider his dictionary itself to take the form of a list, but evidently Florio did not. In a later dictionary, Edward Phillips did not include the term in 1671 and 1678; in 1696, he defined it as "A Scrowl of the Names of several persons of the same Quality with whom we have Business, or with whom we have some Relation. A List of the Slain and Wounded in such a Battel. A list of such a ones Creditors. A List of the Prisoners in such a Prison. It is also the Bordering of a Piece of Cloath that limits the Breadth of it." Over the course of the century, the listing of people had come to replace the hem of a garment as the primary meaning of the term. To Phillips, it meant the names of individuals who belonged to a particular social group.

This nominalist approach, in contrast to Liam Young's "ontic" or civilizational perspective, restricts the study of lists. The historical question to answer becomes not what the function of lists in human society has been since the emergence of *literacy. Rather we might in a more targeted fashion explore the obscure origins of this term in *early modernity, its specific use in listing people, and the way it eventually replaced and rendered obsolete so many other terms for collected serial information.

The early modern emergence of the list seems to offer some support for another great divide in which lists have figured in historiography, that is, the shift from manuscript to print with the invention of the printing press in the 1450s. Elizabeth Eisenstein, for example, has emphasized the information-finding aids that appeared in tables, registers, and indexes of printed works. However, here too, some series are more internally organized and hierarchical than they might appear to modern readers. The historian

Richard Oosterhoff, for instance, notes that certain series in printed textbooks that appear to us as lists are "are not *simply* lists, but serve as a conceptual map," complete with an inherent hierarchy.

Given that the early modern list applied primarily to human subjects in various social configurations, rather than the contents of books, I suggest a sociopolitical explanation for the rise of the term, rather than an explanation drawn from the history of the book. The term *list* also emerged alongside market society, the public sphere, and finally, national taxation, all developments calling for listing many previously unenrolled parts of society. Compared to many other literate societies, postclassical Europe reserved its listing of people for a small fraction at its social edges, that is, the highest echelons included in genealogies and lists of officeholders, or the extreme fringe to be found among wanted felons, heretics, and authors to be censored. The bulk of the population was not listed. Perhaps for reasons of its novelty, representations of society in list form initially appeared a chief way to indicate a distasteful, new social chaos in early modern Europe, replacing a traditional, qualitative order based on natural structure and divine fiat with the fungibility of monetary exchange and disordered feasting and brawling associated with the marketplace.

François Rabelais made lists a key feature of the marketplace aesthetic that Mikhail Bakhtin termed "carnivalesque." Rabelais made his farcical lists compete with and upend more traditional social registers; Gargantua and Pantagruel were the progeny of fifty-nine giants, outdoing Jean Bouchet's fifty-seven kings in his *Anciennes et modernes genealogies des roys de France* (Ancient and modern genealogies of the kings of France, 1528). Numerous satires inspired by the market scenes in the *Advertisements* of Trajano Boccalini (1556–1613) likewise criticized consumer society as an ungovernable stampede, overwhelmed with long lists of desirable objects. These were lists that did not have the implicit order of the great chain of being and feudal hierarchy underlying them. They, like the "list of laweless resolutes" in *Hamlet,* are thus qualitatively different from previous genres that tacitly included such orders.

From a means of showcasing disorder, the list became a tool for imposing a new order on this previously unorderable population. State projects for investigating the bulk of the populace have thus been rich in such lists. One edited volume, *Le temps des listes* (The age of lists), emphasizes two such projects: Spain's quest to gain complete information of America and the listing and reordering of society in the French Revolution. To these we might add, from late seventeenth-century England, the political arithmetic of William Petty, who used lists for studying and remaking society, and the demographic studies of John Graunt, who analyzed the "bills of mortality," or annual accounts of births and deaths in London first mandated in 1603. Studies of modern governmentality continue to stress the political technology of the list. Only after the list became a tool for ordering and controlling the disordered populace did lists begin to dominate our notion of ranked and ordered texts, rendering obsolete many older terms.

Vera Keller

See also book sales catalogs; censorship; governance; indexing; inventories; public sphere; registers; scrolls and rolls; surveys and censuses

FURTHER READING

Arndt Brendecke, *The Empirical Empire*, 2009, translated by Jeremiah Riemer, 2016; Umberto Eco, *The Infinity of Lists: An Illustrated Essay*, 2009; John Florio, *A World of Wordes*, 1598; Richard Oosterhoff, *Making Mathematical Culture: University and Print in the Circle of Lefèvre d'Étaples*, 2018; Edward Phillips, *The New World of Words*, 1696; Gregorio Salinero, "L'octogone des listes," in *Le temps des listes: Représenter, savoir et croir à l'époque moderne*, edited by Gregorio Salinero and Miguel Ángel Melón Jiménez, 2018; Kenneth Werbin, *The List Serves: Population Control and Power*, 2017; Liam Young, *List Cultures: Knowledge and Poetics from Mesopotamia to BuzzFeed*, 2017.

LITHOGRAPHY

The late Qing journalist Huang Shiquan spoke of it in terms poetic: "stone plates from the West, rubbed smooth like a mirror . . . millions of pages of books are not hard to do in a day, fine like an ox's hair and sharp as a rhinoceros horn." What Huang had in mind was a multifaceted printing process that was radically changing information orders around the world: lithography. Coined in French at the beginning of the nineteenth century, the word derived from the ancient Greek words for stone, *lithos*, and "to write," *graphein*. "Printing from stone" was also the expression used in Arabic; "stone printing" the literal compound in Chinese and Japanese. Yet an emphasis on stone alone does not fully capture the process. The credited inventor of lithography, an aspiring playwright named Johann Alois Senefelder (1771–1834), first described the technique as "chemical printing" (*chemische Druckerey*), and it is this label that is most apt for tracing lithography across its diverse metamorphoses. For independent of the printing substrate, lithography rested on the principle that oil and water are mutually repellent. From this seemingly everyday observation arose a host of methods whereby the contents of one flat surface could be reproduced on or transferred to another, without the intervention of relief blocks, type, or intaglio plates. Lithography transformed *how* one could print. And in doing so, it also transformed *who* might enter the world of printing, as well as *what*, fundamentally, printing might faithfully reproduce.

Geographical contingencies were essential to lithography's emergence. Too poor to hire the services of job printers, much less acquire movable-type equipment himself, Senefelder began experimenting with alternative methods of printing from his base in Munich at the beginning of the 1790s. His trials eventually brought him in 1796 to experiments with Kelheimer limestone, abundant in the Solnhofen district of his Bavarian surroundings. Senefelder's initial instinct was to employ an acid etching process to produce a relief plate from the stone. Over the course of the next three years, however, his approach changed. This culminated in 1799 with the discovery of a new method for treating limestone, the chemical principles of which would remain central to lithographic printing throughout the nineteenth century.

At its core, Senefelder's new method comprised two innovations. The first was a process that allowed for planographic printing from stone. Content that one desired to print was drawn in reverse on limestone with a greasy substance. Water was next applied to the stone, seeping into its porous surface except where the grease repulsed it. Thereafter, one rolled a special ink onto the stone that would adhere only to the greasy areas on its surface. Paper might then be pressed onto the stone, resulting in a mirror-reflection of the inked image.

The second of Senefelder's innovations, which he dubbed "autography," considerably lowered the skill required to print by obviating the drawing of reverse images onto the stone. For this method, one used a greasy ink to write normally on paper treated with gelatin. This sheet, which came to be known as "transfer paper," would then be pressed onto the stone's surface and wetted, washing away the gelatin but leaving the ink's grease. Transferred thereby onto the stone was a mirror image of the paper's contents, allowing for copies of what had originally been written on the page to be printed.

In time, these processes would come to be adapted for a variety of other materials, such as zinc plates, photographic negatives, and rubber blankets. But even in its early limestone stage, lithography already presented several distinct advantages over existing techniques of printing. Obvious among these was its suitability for heavily graphic *genres, a usage made all the more appealing after the emergence in 1830s France of chromolithography, which allowed for the use of different colored inks. In Persia, lithography enabled a rich printed illustrative tradition to blossom. Apart from images and artistic compositions, this facilitated the printing of maps, technical diagrams and plans, musical scores—a field in which Senefelder himself was involved—and not least calligraphic and non-Latin scripts. Lithography also served increasingly as the backbone for a teeming world of ephemera such as visiting cards, stamps, permits, bonds, circulars, calendars, labels, playbills, posters, and even pornography. In this capacity, lithography proved a central component of global revolutions in commercial and retail technology during the nineteenth century.

More broadly, during its early stage, lithography opened the boundaries of participation in printing, lending itself to the reproduction of a wide range of content without imposing heavy demands on economic and human capital. Compared to letterpress printing, startup costs for lithography were relatively small. Limestone was the most expensive fixed component, but these stones withstood large print runs, and their surfaces could furthermore be ground down for reuse with new content. Beyond this, the range of requisite tools was minimal: a roller, a sponge, a scraping knife; special ink, transfer paper, and printing paper. Dispensed with also was the need for compositors, imposers, press operators, woodcutters, engravers, and other skilled artisans. Cheap, portable, and easy to master in comparison to movable type, lithography allegedly made "Every Man His Own Printer"—so, at least, claimed the title of a popular 1854 manual on the process.

By sharply lowering entry costs to the world of print, lithography changed the dynamics of a radically asymmetrical process of globalization. As indicated by an 1864 Mumbai handbook addressed to the "Indian amateur," lithography promised in theory to foster the emergence of small native-run private presses against the monopolizing backdrop of colonial and Indigenous states. This held especially true in areas where local scripts, whether by their inherent qualities or by their numerousness, posed a challenge to the adoption of movable type. Indeed, Christopher Reed has helpfully suggested that lithography be thought of as a "compromise technology"—one that allowed non-Western actors to negotiate the transition to print capitalism on their own terms, culturally and economically. Placing lithography, rather than movable type, at the center of analysis therefore yields a substantial revision of our narratives of modern printing. Specifically, instead of a deficit model of the world marked by movable type's "haves" and "have-nots," lithography proposes the existence of a coeval and connected print modernity, wherein "the West" and "non-West" were simultaneously newcomers to a mode of textual and graphic reproduction, the meanings of which had yet to be articulated, and the possibilities of which thus remained open for determination by a plurality of cultures around the world.

Yet asymmetries remained that shaped the spread and reception of the new technology. At first, global networks of expertise privileged European actors. In the case of Egypt, for example, it was the Parisian engineer and cartographer Edme-François Jomard who may have encouraged the provincial Ottoman state to import lithography in the 1820s. This man had traveled with Napoleon Bonaparte's army to invade Egypt from 1798 to 1801, and in 1803 he watched Senefelder himself demonstrate how lithography worked in the city of Regensburg. Some years later, he served as an adviser to Egypt's governor, shaping the curriculum for the state's student missions in Paris when it began purchasing presses from Europe. Once these presses were set up in Egypt, the state mainly applied lithography to diagrams, forms, and maps, printing most Arabic typographically perhaps on account of European influence. In the Ottoman imperial capital of Istanbul, lithography was likewise imported in the early 1830s by the French orientalist Henri Cayol, who, backed by the sultan, bought the equipment necessary to establish a government atelier for reproducing technical drawings. He had learned the art from his cousin, who had in turn served as a French consul to the Ottomans in Bârlad. Private ownership of lithographic presses in these cities began in the 1850s, a development that helped to spread the technology to places in the Islamic world that it had not already reached. For example, Tunisians traveled to Cairo, Alexandria, and Constantinople to commission lithographic printings, while the first lithographic press in Morocco arrived via Egypt alongside an Egyptian printer named Shaykh Muḥammad al-Miṣrī, who trained others in its use.

A similar story might be told for late imperial China, this time focused on missionary activity. The lithographic production of Chinese texts commenced at the London Missionary Society's Malacca press in 1829, with stations in Macao and Canton quickly following suit. American Presbyterians likewise established lithographic facilities in Ningbo after the First Opium War. Foreign missionary control remained the pattern until 1877, which witnessed the founding of China's first native-owned and privately operated lithographic printing house—the Dianshizhai Studio in Shanghai. From this point onward, native commercial lithography thrived and formed the basis of the modern Chinese print industry.

As for Japan, the earliest lithographic traces date to the Dutch printing house at Dejima in 1857. The impact of the Dutch, however, was minor compared to investment from the Japanese state and native entrepreneurs after 1860, the year when lithographic presses and stones were provided to the shogun by a Prussian diplomatic expedition. Admittedly, lithography was not the only technology of interest. Unlike China, Japan concomitantly and successfully pushed for the adoption of movable type. Lithography never exercised decisive sway over the establishment of the country's modern printing industry. Nevertheless, by the early 1870s, Japan had established a firm regional reputation in lithographic production through specialists such as Matsuda Atsutomo, Umemura Suizan, and firms such as the Gengendō Studio. In subsequent decades, Japanese lithographers came to be employed as key advisers in Chinese printing houses.

What changes in information orders resulted from lithographers' activities? On the one hand, lithography had the ironic consequence of multiplying the old. In the Ottoman Empire, private printers working in Arabic overwhelmingly used the new technology to reproduce standing titles from both the handwritten and the typographical traditions, largely on commission from the religious scholars who were the main users and

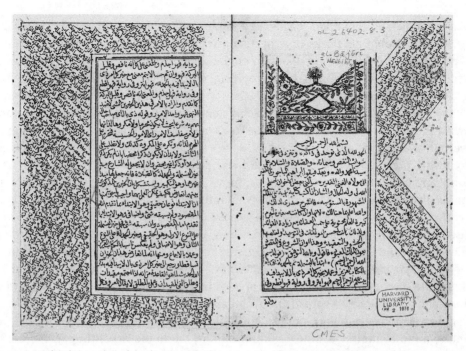

Figure 1. Multiplying the old, along with the new: the first page opening of the supercommentary of the Azhari Shaykh Ibrāhīm al-Bājūrī (d. 1860) on the *Introduction* of the theologian Muḥammad ibn Yūsuf al-Sanūsī (d. 1490). Lithographed in the style of a manuscript by an unnamed press, likely from Cairo, in 1863. I. Bājūrī, *Ḥāshiyat Ibrāhīm al-Bājūrī ʿalā al-Muqaddimah al-Sanūsīyah* (n.p.: n.p., [1863]).

producers of books through the end of the nineteenth century. Presses composed their lithographs in the style of manuscripts, as seen in figure 1, with elaborate ornamental or floral headpieces at the start of texts, and triangular or circular *colophons at their ends. They also took advantage of shorter print runs that lithography made economical as typography had not. But with time, those presses that could afford to purchase movable type gravitated to it because of its prestige. Analogous trends were visible in East Asian contexts, in particular after the rise of photolithography, which allowed the contents of a negative to be transferred onto a lithographic surface. Photolithographic techniques spurred a market for facsimiles of older texts, now priced more affordably and available in larger quantities. The mass reprinting of early Qing examination essays, for instance, was a hallmark of China's lithographic industry, much to the chagrin of late nineteenth-century native reformers, who branded lithography an ally of "traditional" knowledge. Japanese actors, meanwhile, consciously differentiated between genres. Lithography was typically deployed in ways coterminous with xylography, replicating the look and feel of a centuries-long woodblock print culture, while movable type was reserved for works deemed more "modern" or "Western."

Whether or not lithography really favored old or new knowledge, the speed and simplicity of reproduction that it enabled unquestionably reconfigured information orders by undermining nascent regimes of global intellectual property. Lithographic reprints circulated promiscuously. In Egypt, presses reprinted one another's works many times over, and these in turn could be found lithographed anew from presses in Persia and South Asia, still preserving within them the colophons of their printed forebears. Western printers in China lithographed Chinese books for sale on the local market. Japanese printers imported Chinese books and lithographed them for reexport. And as late as 1934, Chinese photolithographs of works such as Hall's *International Law* (1880), Raleigh's *Elementary Politics* (1886), and the *Concise Oxford Dictionary* (1911) were still being sold on the Indian market. Trademarks, commercial designs, and other objects of industrial property also became the frequent target of lithographic copying. Known for the obsessive protection of its mark, Bass Beer waged a protracted campaign from 1875 to 1888 against Japanese wares bearing its label, urging the confiscation of lithographic stones from native presses.

Throughout this long century of global lithography, the medium experienced a series of technological metamorphoses that ultimately altered its relation to conditions of print participation again. These metamorphoses largely stemmed from the discovery of methods of transference other than Senefelder's transfer paper, and printing surfaces other than limestone. Anastatic printing, the first major development in the former arena, rested on the discovery that nitric acid could release the residual grease in dried ink. Any existing texts and images in ink, manuscript or print, might therefore be treated with nitric acid to transfer their contents onto a lithographic printing surface. The acid, however, had the drawback of frequently destroying the original paper, and anastatic printing all but disappeared from use following the development of reliable photolithography by 1859. Photolithography redefined the nature of facsimile printing and took over the bulk of work in European and East Asian lithographic industries. In Istanbul and Egypt, photolithography emerged by at least 1873, without the need for "factories which produce chemical products," bragged the Frenchman Antoine Laroche, through the partnership between him and Pascal Sébah, an Ottoman. They used photolithography to print maps, handwriting, and a newspaper, and they relied on French technical books translated into Turkish to develop from their laboratory a way of using photolithography to reproduce engraved photos.

Meanwhile, by the mid-1830s, a move to using zinc plates rather than limestone as a lithographic surface was already underway. The switch was in part motivated by the realization that only Bavarian limestone possessed a rate of water and grease retention suitable for quality lithographic printing, spurring the search for a more widely and cheaply available substitute. Zinc, moreover, was significantly lighter and easier to transport. Consequently, although limestone usage persisted selectively because it offered a better tonal range, zinc proved more commercially popular during the second half of the nineteenth century, with aluminum as a second candidate. China transitioned largely to zinc after 1882, Japan after 1890, and Egypt as late as the 1900s under the British occupation.

Of even more far-reaching impact were lithographic methods for printing from curved surfaces, rather than flat stones or plates. An early impetus for this arose out of a desire to print designs directly onto tin cans. A process of treating rubber for lithographic printing was invented in 1903. Printing from curved surfaces proved to be advantageous because these surfaces could be wrapped around the cylinders of steam-powered, and later on electric-powered, rotary presses, ultimately enabling the full incorporation of lithography into industrial print production. Partnered with advances in photographic typesetting, this offset method of lithography eventually came to replace relief printing itself, dominating the commercial market after the 1960s. Modern print's long good-bye to movable type, initiated over a century and a half earlier by "chemical printing," had ended at last.

Yet the lithography that triumphed in this final farewell was structurally distinct from the kind that, during the century prior, had powered the emergence of small native-run private presses across the world. Initially, lithography had altered global information orders by bypassing obstacles of movable type and enabling local actors to adopt printing on their own terms. Now part of the sprawling technological assemblage of mass printing, the new lithography instead demanded extensive photographic apparatuses, complex rotary presses, and other forms of financial, mechanical, and human capital that by default excluded the amateur and everyman. There is, therefore, an untold history of information that would situate lithography as a central axis along which to grasp global reconfigurations of participatory power in modern print. Here, we have outlined its basic points in reference to Ottoman Istanbul and Cairo, Qing China, and Meiji Japan, in the hope that its broader tale will find future tellers and tellings.

Hansun Hsiung and Kathryn A. Schwartz

See also cameras; commodification; diagrams; globalization; intellectual property; letterpress; maps; photocopiers; printed visuals; public sphere; stereotype printing; xylography

FURTHER READING

M. Nakane, *Nihon insatsu gijutsu shi*, 1999; C. Reed, *Gutenberg in Shanghai: Chinese Print Capitalism, 1876–1937*, 2004; A. Senefelder, *Vollständiges Lehrbuch der Steindruckerey*, 1818; U. Stark, *An Empire of Books: The Naval Kishore Press and the Diffusion of the Printed Word in Colonial India*, 2007; M. Twyman, *Breaking the Mould: The First Hundred Years of Lithography*, 2001; G. Zellich and A. Senefelder, *Notice historique sur la lithographie et sur les origines de son introduction en Turquie*, 1895.

MANUALS

Manuals offering instruction or information originated in ancient times and proliferated widely in both premodern and modern eras. Their readers have ranged from diverse individuals who have wanted to know how to make or do something to specialists using standard professional guidebooks. Manuals have a history of their own. Their cultural and historical significance goes far beyond the hugely varied specific topics that they treat. Historians have found in them rich sources for understanding practices, technologies, cultural attitudes, beliefs, and ideas.

The word *manual* derives from the Latin *manualis*, pertaining to the hand, and in late Latin, *manuale*, a handbook. Manuals are printed instructions (or often now, the *digital equivalent) on how to operate equipment such as, for example, a camera or a dishwasher. They include "how-to" books—how to repair your Toyota, how to fix the toilet, how to embroider, how to play golf, how to draw animals, how to build a chair. They frequently focus on manual tasks, but they are by no means so limited—how to write a sentence, how to sell your novel, how to speak effectively in public. Although they are often oriented toward the general public, providing instruction on something someone would otherwise not know how to do, some are aimed at specialists. Molecular biologists use *Molecular Cloning: A Laboratory Manual*, which sold ninety-five thousand copies in its first two editions (1982 and 1989). It is now in its fourth edition (2012), with parts published online. The best-selling *Chicago Manual of Style*, the handbook of writers, including historians, and editors, appeared in its seventeenth edition in 2017. The controversy-producing *Diagnostic and Statistical Manual of Mental Disorders*, first published in 1952 and now in its fifth edition, is a mainstay of the profession of psychiatry and related fields.

Manuals for both the general public and specialists are ubiquitous. They accompany products, are available online, and often sell millions of copies. They are also avidly sought as collectables and as needed guides to such things as antique cars. But until relatively recently, scholars did not consider them interesting beyond their very specific concrete topics. Historians at one time viewed manuals from premodern times in the same restricted way—created as instruction for particular needs and without great import beyond this. This view has changed primarily for two reasons.

First, historians of science, of technology, and of culture have become interested in the practices and the processes detailed in these manuals and in their accompanying intellectual frameworks. Experimental re-creation of craft recipes and instructions (such as for making a blue pigment, for example) have shed much new light on craft and technological practices in the premodern world and have illuminated attitudes toward those practices. An ongoing focus of research is the role of the artisan in the development of the new empirical sciences of the seventeenth century (including the adoption of artisanal values such as an appreciation for handwork, for observation and experience, and for experiment). Craft handbooks and technical manuals constitute important sources for this research.

Second, deeper study of premodern manuals has brought an understanding of how richly diverse the *genre is, not only in particular subject matters such as navigation or painting or fortification, but in the authors and readers of such books, who ranged from the humble to the high elite, and even royal, from skilled practitioners to scholars and princes. During the fifteenth and sixteenth centuries, practices, technologies, machines, and instruments gained an allure, a cultural fascination that developed for complicated reasons. These included an increasing appreciation for objects, the growing practice of conspicuous consumption by elites, and the rising status of certain kinds of practically trained individuals such as painters, sculptors, architects, printers, and engravers. In addition, in an era before modern professionalization and specialization, certain practitioners achieved a kind of professional mobility—sculptors could become architects, carpenters could become cartographers, printers and engravers could become architects and designers of gardens. There was also increased interchange on substantive matters in locations such as printshops and arsenals—what have been called trading zones—between workshop-trained artisans and university-trained men.

All this was facilitated by the great proliferation of practical and technical writings. Some were in manuscript; some were printed in pamphlets on cheap paper. Others were printed on high-quality paper and even leather bound. Many were illustrated, some strikingly so. Such manuals did not originate with printing—there are substantial numbers of ancient and medieval examples—but printing did bring about their huge proliferation. Although some were directed toward practitioners, many were not. Topics were wide ranging, from falconry to fencing, from hunting to silk making, from gardening to winemaking. Beyond artisanal subjects (or subjects that involved making something) there were many others, including secretary manuals for government officials, manuals for writing or calligraphy, and mirrors for princes providing advice on how to rule.

One reason for the great popularity of manuals has to do with the information that they contained. University-educated humanists, for example, did not have access to workshop apprenticeships where hands-on practice was acquired. Some of this heretofore tacit knowledge, which they desired for a variety of reasons, was now explained in craft manuals. Similarly, individual householders could learn the rudiments of beer making and remedies for illnesses. Recently employed secretaries and other officeholders could learn how to best execute their new duties. Professional mobility and the rising status of arts such as painting, sculpture, and architecture meant that there was an ongoing need for new information when individuals moved from one profession to another or when they acquired an interest in a practical art for which they had no practical background.

One kind of manual that proliferated in the premodern world were books of recipes, often called "books of secrets." These books contained recipes and formulas of all sorts—for craft processes such as cloth dying, pigment making, food and drink preparation, and medicinal recipes. They originated in late antiquity but were published in the thousands in the sixteenth and seventeenth centuries. Many households owned such books. Men and women used, modified, exchanged, discussed, and experimented with the recipes, making households important centers for empirical knowledge and experimentation.

In addition to the medicinal recipes contained in books of secrets, hundreds of manuals on health and healing were printed and used both by medical practitioners including physicians and by laypeople. These books included manuals for midwives such as Nicholas Culpepper's often reprinted *Directory for Midwives* (1651). Another subset of manuals addressed surgery, including Ambroise Paré's *Dix livres de la chirurgie* (Ten books of surgery, 1564), which contained detailed illustrations as well as discussion of instruments.

Practical manuals of other kinds circulated in response to particular technologies. Accompanying the fourteenth- and fifteenth-century development of gunpowder artillery were numerous handbooks for gunners, including many manuscript examples from German lands. The bastion fortification that was invented and widely constructed in the sixteenth century as a response to that artillery saw the emergence of manuals in both manuscript and print emphasizing the importance of measurement for this new type of fortification, as well as the importance of designing forts adapted to the unique topographies of particular sites. An important example is Francesco de Marchi's *Della architettura militare* (On military architecture, composed 1545–65, published 1599).

In some cases, manuals overlapped with more formal treatises. Architects and patrons collected architectural treatises and commentaries on Vitruvius's *De architectura* (On architecture), the only complete ancient architectural treatise to survive. They also collected illustrated manuals containing architectural instructions and exemplars (such as images of diverse forms of capitals to be placed on columns). The line between manuals, conceived as books of instruction and practical information, and treatises, larger, more systematic writings, is blurred, in part because the latter often contained plenty of practical information. A subgenre that stands at the border between manuals and treatises comprised machine books and "theaters of machines." These books explained how machines were built and how they could be used and illustrated possible variations of their component parts.

Shipping and navigation was a developing area that produced numerous manuals. Muslim nautical manuals (*rahmani*) proliferated from the eleventh century. They provided sailing instructions and information about specific coasts and features, especially in the Indian Ocean but also far beyond. Manuals on navigation appeared much later in European countries, as transoceanic exploration and commerce exploded from the late fifteenth century through the eighteenth, and as European navies expanded to enormous size. European navigation manuals, often used in pedagogy, served the urgent need to train sailors and navigators. They also reflect an ongoing conflict about who should control navigation—skilled practitioners who had extensive oceanic experience or mathematically trained scholars who could chart courses on paper.

In early fifteenth-century European painting, sculpture, and other decorative arts, the new classicizing approaches and new methodologies such as artists' perspective led to the proliferation of manuals and other writings on these topics. Both practitioners and nonpractitioners produced books on the arts, including painting, sculpture, goldsmithing, and ceramics. In the late 1390s, Cennino Cennini, a painter in the school of Giotto, wrote his craftsman's handbook (*Il libro d'arte*, The book of art). In the 1430s,

Leon Battista Alberti, a learned humanist, dedicated his *Della pittura* (On painting) to Filippo Brunelleschi, inventor, goldsmith, and architect of the Florentine Duomo. The painter Piero della Francesca wrote tracts on perspective and on mathematics. In the sixteenth century, the artist from Nuremberg Albrecht Dürer wrote manuals on painting, mathematics, and the proportions of the human figure; the goldsmith Benvenuto Cellini wrote not only his autobiography but tracts on goldsmithing, sculpture, and casting. An author on ceramics, Cipriano Piccolpasso, was a humanist and military officer whose brother was a master of majolica (the elegantly painted ceramics of the Italian *Renaissance). Piccolpasso's treatise on pottery (written around 1557 but not published until the nineteenth century) was filled with practical instructions and illustrations.

Other subgenres developed out of other circumstances. Agriculture and gardening manuals emerged along with new crops, new foods from around the world, new systems of agriculture, new systems of irrigation and hydration, and magnificent villas surrounded by gardens. These include the Arabic *Katub al-Filāh* (Books of husbandry), which proliferated on the Iberian Peninsula (al-Andalus) and in the eastern Mediterranean.

Manuals on mining and ore processing accompanied the central European mine boom that developed after 1450 and then the development of huge silver mines by the Spanish in Potosí in the New World (present-day Bolivia). They were written by learned humanists such as Georg Agricola, whose *De re metallica* (On metals, 1556) contained striking illustrations; by mine overseers such as the Sienese Vannoccio Biringuccio; and by practicing assayers and minters of coins such as Lazarus Ercker. The consumers of such books were not primarily miners, but princes whose territorial income depended on mining, mine investors, and undoubtedly also the many midlevel people who lived and worked in the mining areas of central Europe.

In China, Song Yingxing's *Tiangong kaiwu* (The works of Heaven and the inception of things, 1637) treated practical crafts, including the fabrication of ceramics and of sweeteners, the construction of carts, papermaking, and jewelry making. It was not a book of instructions but one in which universal principles and the cosmological order were connected and understood though practical technologies.

In all, manuals were published in the hundreds and thousands and cannot be simply categorized as instruction books directed at people who wanted guidance in making something. Rather, the complex variety of such books is matched by an equally complex crowd of readers from diverse walks of life, who used and understood them in diverse ways.

Despite this great variety, developments in manual writing can be discerned from premodern times to the modern. Premodern manuals often explicated an entire craft or practice, such as painting, or metallurgy, or agriculture. Modern manuals more frequently instruct on a single piece of machinery, equipment, or tool, such as a car or drill press, or they provide specific *protocols to highly specialized professions such as molecular biology. Premodern tool or equipment use was frequently preceded by informal or formal apprenticeships in a trade that used the object, making a manual superfluous. Modern use is frequently preceded by the delivery of a package to a relatively unskilled person, making a manual essential. (Galileo's military compass and the manual he wrote to be purchased with it were prescient!)

For both premodern and modern manuals however, diagrams and visual images have often been essential. Indeed, technical diagrams and illustrations have undergone a striking development within the pages of manuals from the fourteenth century until the present.

Pamela O. Long

See also accounting; coins; diagrams; files; knowledge; maps; media; observing; printed visuals

FURTHER READING

Rudolph Bell, *How to Do It: Guides to Good Living for Renaissance Italians*, 1999; Ricardo Córdoba, ed., *Craft Treatises and Handbooks*, 2013; Angela N. H. Creager, Mathias Grote, and Elaine Leong, eds., "Learning by the Book: Manuals and Handbooks in the History of Knowledge," special issue of *British Journal for the History of Science* 5 (2020); Elaine Leong, *Recipes and Everyday Knowledge*, 2018; Pamela O. Long, *Openness, Secrecy, Authorship*, 2001; Joad Raymond, ed., *The Oxford History of Popular Print Culture*, vol. 1, *Cheap Print in Britain and Ireland to 1660*, 2011; Dagmar Schäfer, *The Crafting of the 10,000 Things*, 2011; Margaret Schotte, *Sailing School: Navigating Science and Skill, 1550–1800*, 2019; Pamela H. Smith, *The Body of the Artisan*, 2004.

MAPS

The concept of mapping is used so widely as to be almost meaningless in its capaciousness. At the same time, perceptions of the purpose of a map in the spatial sense—a representation of geographical rather than of metaphorical or discursive space—are very limited. Many twenty-first-century persons see today's maps as straightforward, objective tools for way finding, and premodern exemplars that look "different" by dint of their unfamiliar conventions and visual elements as modes of propaganda or of imagination rather than as modes of information. Yet for thousands of years, maps have had a much wider range of uses, across cultures, than merely way finding. In order to understand geographical maps from the point of view of the history of information, it is important to be mindful of the wide spectrum of purposes to which maps were put.

A map—in both the narrower geographical and the broader metaphorical senses—is essentially a diagram that orients things or concepts in relation to one another, or within a physical space, be it a village or the world. A map may be composed of words, lines, illustrations, symbols, or concepts, and a map can take a variety of physical or virtual forms. A map is not an attempt to replicate the real world with the exactitude of a trompe l'oeil painting, but rather a reconstruction of space, one that selects and organizes information in ways that make it visible and usable for particular purposes. Maps necessarily emphasize and enlarge some features and represent them using visual *codes rather than via images devised to look as naturalistic as possible. Readers are expected to know these codes: for example, a printed map may contain numerous instances of the identical schematic stamp to denote houses, but viewers are expected to know that this does not imply that all these houses looked the same, or even that each house stamp necessarily indicated a single house. These variations between the "real world" and the map are more productively understood as practical and strategic decisions that are essential for and inherent to cartography, rather than as distortions of what the eye would see on the ground or from a fixed point above it.

What distinguishes the geographical map, in the context of the history of information, is that it selects and positions information on a diagram that represents physical space. Maps also organize space into named, digestible chunks—into the "Orient" and the "West," into continents (where do they start and end, and which islands are included?), and even into the boundaries between named oceans, seas, and rivers (figure 1). These organizing spatial structures or metageographies, as Martin Lewis and Kären Wigen termed them, do not exist in nature but rather are cartographic constructions that essentialize regions and devise boundaries so as to make topographical information legible and powerful within the viewer's geopolitical framework.

Geographical maps across cultures and periods take a great diversity of forms in many media, from manual engravings on (relatively) hard objects composed of metal, stone, wood, glass, or clay; to representations drawn or painted on pliable material such as *papyrus, bark, animal skin, or paper; to maps co-constituted alongside their medium,

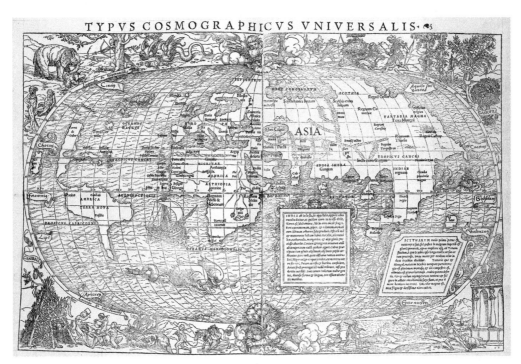

Figure 1. Sebastian Münster, "Typus cosmographicus universalis" in *Nouus orbis regionum ac insularum ueteribus incognitarum*, edited by Johann Huttich (Basel, 1532). Beinecke Rare Book and Manuscript Library, Yale University, call no. 1986+106.

as in the case of textile maps. Maps may be two-dimensional sheets, multidimensional, or virtual, taking the form of globes, time-lapse video maps, and *digital maps. Their contents may be applied manually in ink, paint, or other substances (in the case of manuscript maps), or transferred by a mechanical printing process onto multiple exemplars. Textual geographies, such as those that ripple through conquest literature and weighty geographical tomes penned in sixteenth-century Spain, conjure up maps, from words, in the mind's eye of the reader. Mural maps on walls, such as the late fourth-century BCE Mayan example in La Sufricaya, a royal residence in Petén, Guatemala, lay out a culture's—or patron's—view of the world or the cosmos and their place in it. Maps from such disparate contexts as La Sufricaya and late medieval Europe represented, on maps, not just topography but also people, cities, structures, events, and cosmology, while also making political claims.

One type of map did not gradually become extinct in order to give way to another, better mode. Rather, a number of cartographic modes tended to coexist in a given time and place. In thirteenth-century Europe, for example, one might encounter *mappaemundi* (world maps), regional itinerary maps, portolan charts (on which most information pertained to coastal regions), and local maps produced for legal or administrative purposes. Medieval maps were primarily artifacts of contemplation, not of navigation (figure 2).

On a map that encompasses both land and water, topographical forms (representations of physical or natural features) shown are likely to include the boundary between land and sea, or the courses of rivers. Words may delineate place names, historical events,

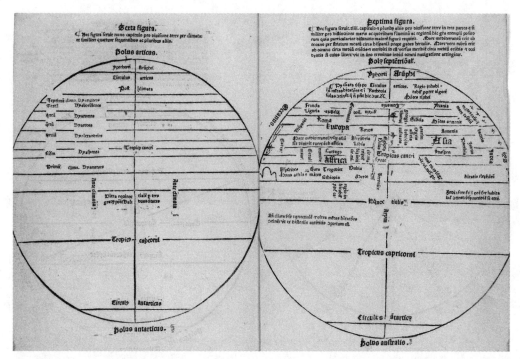

Figure 2. Zonal medieval map: *Sexta figura. Hec figura servit nono capitulo pro divisione terre per climata. Septima figura. Hec figura servit xiiii. capitulo & pluribus aliis pro divisione terre in tres partes* . . . In Pierre d'Ailly, [Ymago Mundi], ([Louvain?], [1483?]). Courtesy of the John Carter Brown Library at Brown University, call no. A483 A293i/1-SIZE.

or explanations of symbols and illustrations, but they can also serve rhetorical purposes—assuring the viewer of the map's newness or efficacy, or proclaiming ownership, for example. While a map is often devised around a geographical grid, this does not require the information on it be positioned with a particular level of precision. Nor does the cartographic representation of space presume any particular scale, magnification, technique, or style. What devising a map does require, more urgently perhaps than does devising a book, is selection: what does one put in a finite space? The contents of maps reveal choices about what labor and expenses to shoulder—clues about their makers, patrons, and *publishers, and about the multifarious purposes to which maps were put. Conversely, attending to makers, audiences, and purposes helps to explain the what, how, and why of information on maps.

Not everything on a map is about space per se. Maps encode information about things beyond topography (physical elements of the terrain), such as peoples, plants, animals, and human-made structures (figure 3). In the case of premodern maps, historians of cartography have traditionally assumed either that nontopographical elements were decorative ways of filling spaces for which no information was available, or that they functioned solely as propaganda. More recently, historians of science, literary scholars, and art historians have challenged these assumptions and worked to analyze and historicize visual aspects of maps. Consequently, there has been a move away from dismissing these elements using such terms as *decoration, myth,* and *legend,* and toward

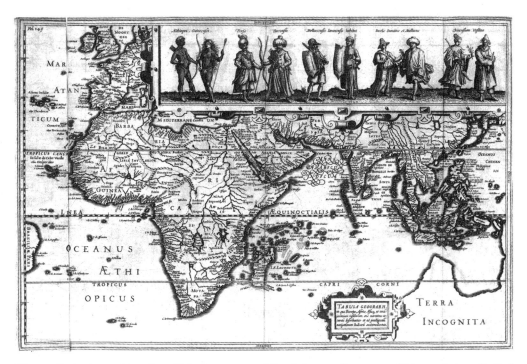

Figure 3. Jodocus Hondius, *Tabula geograph[ica], in qua Europae, Africae, Asiaeq[ue] et circu[m]jacentium insularum orae maritimae accurate describuntur et ad intelligentia[m] navigationum Indicaru[m] accommodantur* (Amsterdam, 1611). Courtesy of the John Carter Brown Library, at Brown University, call no. F611 P811r/1-SIZE.

analyzing these images in relation to a wide range of textual and visual sources in order to uncover the cultural work they performed. In this way, scholars are shedding light on how map illustrations also performed the work of making knowledge, and thus how they form part of the broader history of information.

Both the types of information maps contained and the visual codes via which this information was expressed varied with the uses of maps. Maps for legal and administrative purposes were made not just by professional artists and mapmakers, but also by local civic officials and townspeople. In the final quarter of the sixteenth century, the Spanish crown commissioned two surveys of its domains: the *Relaciones Geográficas* (Geographical Accounts) of Spain's overseas empire, and the *Relaciones Topográficas* (Topographical Accounts) of peninsular Spain. The crown dispatched lengthy questionnaires across its domains, requesting information about populations, history, and the built environment. A number of the replies that returned included local maps, often devised by the region's inhabitants. In seventeenth-century Muscovy, local inhabitants made hundreds of detailed manuscript sketch maps of small areas, in the service of property disputes. These contexts often emphasized natural features such as trees, rivers, and changes in elevation that served as boundary markers.

Perhaps the most panoramic form of map is the world map. These maps conjure up an imaginative viewpoint far above the earth, a bird's-eye view that sees the entirety of a globe in one sweep of the gaze. Flat, physical exemplars—rolled, in sheets, or bound into codices—allow one to look both deeply and broadly at maps as bearers of information.

In the early Middle Ages, zonal maps, drawing on the writings of such Greco-Latin authors as Ptolemy, Pliny, and Aristotle, as well as on the works of medieval scholars like Albertus Magnus and Pierre d'Ailly, laid out the earth's geography in the form of zones of habitation (figure 2). Advocates of zonal theory divided the spherical earth into five zones: uninhabitable zones at the two poles, an impassable torrid zone at the equator, and two habitable, temperate zones that separated the torrid zone from the polar zones. These maps occasionally subdivided the northern temperate zone into seven climates (*climata*) in order to show how, as one approached the two extremes of latitude, it became increasingly difficult to sustain civil human societies or even properly formed bodies.

Such maps transmitted, in graphic form, aspects of the geoclimatological framework known as *humoral theory. Classical humoralism, based on a fifth-century BCE corpus associated with the physician Hippocrates, was undergirded by a theory of bodily humors. Four humors—blood, phlegm, black bile, and yellow bile—were affected by external factors such as local climate, astrological constellations, and geographical latitude, and they linked the minds and bodies of individuals to their environment. Thus, from at least the Middle Ages, world maps in Europe were visual diagrams via which the mutability of the human body was articulated. These maps illustrated the geographer Ptolemy's assertion that life at the same parallels would have similar characteristics. By extension, they made implicit arguments about how nature and culture varied across space.

In the late twelfth century, a new mode of world mapping depicted human—and particularly biblical—history within a geographical framework. Often denoted as the mappaemundi tradition, this mode showed the inhabited world as a circle circumscribing a T-shaped area formed by the River Nile, the Black Sea, or River Don, and the Mediterranean Sea. These waterways dissected known lands into the three portions said to have been populated by Noah's three sons. Mappaemundi placed Jerusalem at the (spiritual) center of the world and were oriented to place the East—the location of the Earthly Paradise—at the top. With Jerusalem—a region perfectly placed within the northern temperate zone—at the center, the further one traveled toward the outer, northern and southern edges of the map, the more extreme the climate became. Mappaemundi often placed representations of monstrous peoples at these edges, and particularly at the southern edge of the world. Medieval mapmakers drew here from works of classical natural history such as Pliny the Elder's *Natural History* (ca. 77–79 CE). Pliny extrapolated that regions most distant from the Mediterranean were inhabited by a variety of species of monstrous peoples deformed in body or in behavior (and therefore in mind) by the unsavory latitude or climate of their local environment. This theory could be squared with biblical tradition: for example, the descendants of Cain (who killed his brother Abel) and of Ham (who jeered at his father, Noah) were thought to have been cursed by God. By the fifteenth century, there emerged a tradition that Noah had given Africa to Ham, and that Ham's descendants began to turn black as a lasting sign of Ham's sin. Mappaemundi thus functioned as analytical spaces in which information about geography and humankind could be fused with biblical *exegesis. They appeared in geographical treatises and religious books; a hand-sized example known as the Psalter Map

appears in a late thirteenth-century book of psalms in the British Library. At the other
end of the scale, enormous exemplars hung on cathedral walls or in palaces; the Here-
ford Map, circa 1300, continues to hang in the eponymous English cathedral.

During the fifteenth century, the *Geography* of the second-century CE Greco-Egyptian
geographer Ptolemy began to circulate in Latin translation. Contained within it was a
system for representing the world on a plane, using lists of latitudinal and longitudinal
coordinates for places. Ptolemaic maps made it a simple matter to see which regions lay
at the same latitude and which, by extension, could be expected to have a similar climate. Such expectations would perplex sixteenth-century European travelers to the
northeastern seaboard of what would later be called North America; settlers struggled
to tend Old World crops that had not been bred for the swampy summers and frigid
winters of the region they optimistically called New England, whose temperatures were
more extreme than those in European regions that lay at the same latitudes.

During the late fifteenth and sixteenth centuries, mapmakers in Europe faced the
prospect of evaluating new information about geography and the natural world, which
had been amassed via oceanic voyages, with ideas about distant regions that had long
circulated in writings from classical antiquity, religious scripture, and medieval travel
and natural historical works. The long sixteenth century witnessed an efflorescence of
world maps. A number of sheet maps and atlases survive from Spain, Portugal, and Normandy in manuscript form; Venice and Rome were early centers of printed maps and
atlases, as were the German-speaking lands, soon followed by the Low Countries in the
second half of the sixteenth century. Maps that depicted the world's peoples would essentialize the appearance and characteristics of peoples of the Americas. By devising
distinct motifs for each region—the city of Tenochtitlán for Mexico, eaters of human
flesh for Brazil, giants for Patagonia, and so on—these maps made visual and explicit
the humoral connection between climate, geography, and human bodies (figure 4).

The era of European oceanic exploration, colonization, and empire was also one of
maps that attempted to hem in and claim lands that had barely been visited by the states
that purported to have surveyed them. Through maps, monarchs and administrators
made arguments about territory and identity. Yet not only were distances such as longitude at sea difficult to measure, but establishing fixed points in desert, jungle, or forest was far from straightforward. The nineteenth-century British surveyor and explorer
Robert Herman Schomburgk's survey of what became known as British Guiana—a traverse survey, or a survey made by transcribing a route through difficult terrain, and
the sight lines taken from it—involved constructing fixed points (landmarks at known
coordinates) in the terrain, even though few if any would be able to replicate the journey and authenticate them. On the other side of the globe, European mapping in the late
eighteenth and nineteenth centuries invented the "Indian subcontinent" as a region.
The nineteenth-century imperial cartographic ideal of the trigonometrical survey—a
new mapping technique that bound a series of control points to each other without
reference to astronomical features, deemed to be systemic, coherent, and exact—was
observed in cartographic rhetoric more than it could be enacted on the ground. In the
Americas, Indigenous peoples' geographical knowledge was embedded in European
cartography, gathered in dialogue or via coercion, with the aid of guides, or via Indigenous maps. Place names were often adopted, but in many cases were later excised, to
be replaced with European ones. In imperial settings, cartography was a technique

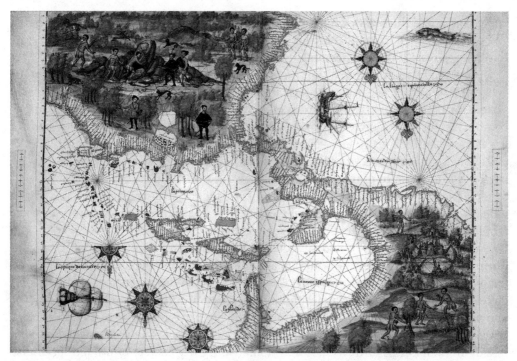

Figure 4. *Vallard Atlas*, 1547, map 10, Central America. The Huntington Library, San Marino, California, call no. HM 29.

practiced in negotiation with local elites, guides, and informants, even if these activities go unmentioned on the maps.

In the early twenty-first century, the ideal of cartographic objectivity persists, despite the tensions created by digital mapping, which offers almost infinite ways of performing cartography as bespoke tailoring—or as manipulative skewing—of information for particular purposes and audiences. What the seeming redundancy of having a sense of direction or locational memory will do to mental and externalized maps in the future remains to be seen.

Surekha Davies

See also albums; books; diagrams; ethnography; globalization; governance; inventories; knowledge; landscapes and cities; notebooks; observing; travel

FURTHER READING

D. Graham Burnett, *Masters of All They Surveyed*, 2000; Surekha Davies, *Renaissance Ethnography and the Invention of the Human*, 2016; Matthew H. Edney, *Mapping an Empire*, 1997; Evelyn Edson, *The World Map, 1300–1492*, 2007; Valerie Kivelson, *Cartographies of Tsardom*, 2006; Martin W. Lewis and Kären E. Wigen, *The Myth of Continents*, 1997; Barbara E. Mundy, *The Making of New Spain and the Relaciones Geográficas*, 1996; Ricardo Padrón, *The Spacious Word*, 2006.

MEDIA

In the early twenty-first century there is perhaps no more burdened a concept than media. In part, this reflects the technological upheavals that have rendered mediated communication a more or less constant presence in everyday life. It also reflects the enormous influence afforded those messages, and the devices behind them, in contemporary discourse. Above all, though, it reflects the extent to which, beginning in the mid-nineteenth century and continuing to the present, the term *media* was invested with layer upon layer of meaning. The result is a dual definition in which *media* refers to the formal, or technical, conduits that enable communication *and* to the organizations and industries through which certain communicative activities—in particular, the production and circulation of news and entertainment—are orchestrated in their most technologically advanced states.

Sometimes, these uses of the term are relatively discrete. Formally, the artist may work in the medium of acrylic, but neither the artist nor the paint manufacturers who supply the artist are what we have in mind when we talk, institutionally, about *the* media. More often though, and certainly outside the realm of specialists, media's dual formal and institutional meanings overlap. In a kind of nesting-doll fashion, the film, the studio, the movie business, the symbol-construing economic sector to which Hollywood belongs, and the broad swath of public culture that that corner of the economy accounts for are all media. The same rippling pattern holds true for the news story, the sitcom, the TV commercial, the video game, and the status update. In this regard, each generation of *"new media," among other things, has generally meant more things count as media. This expansion has come at the expense of terms that once parsed messages and their makers into neater categories. Phrases like "the press," "show business," and even "the web" might remain useful, but to use them in everyday speech is to risk dating oneself.

Alongside this narrowing of terminology, *media*'s growing definitional scope has muddled the line demarcating it from concepts that, though related, remain fairly autonomous. Information may be the most complicated of these. In the one sense, mediated information can refer to the enormously diverse variety of messages that deal with factual content, or at least appear to. The news, in its myriad forms, would be the foremost example, but nonfictional media could include everything from a documentary to an emoji. Beyond this subset, information has also come to refer in a much broader sense to the encoded version of *all* mediated messages. A pop song may not have been produced with much intent of informing the listener, but when transformed into the ones and zeros of an MP3, it becomes information. Finally, information, in the media context, also includes the data that communication institutions create about their activities, products, and audiences. Much of this information comes in forms, such as patents and earnings statements, that are generic to the bureaucratized workings of corporate capitalism. A substantial portion, however, is fairly distinctive to institutional media, which has been something of a breeding ground for new modes of public inquiry. Public opinion polling, audience studies, market research, and database profiling were all developed or greatly advanced within the framework of nineteenth- and twentieth-century mass media.

FROM ENVIRONMENT TO INDUSTRY

From antiquity to the *early modern era, *media* and its root terms referred to the physically situated environment or the middle ground connecting one entity to another. For Newton and his students, this in-between was a carrier of everything from light to gravity. Remnants of this earlier, elemental usage still color our speech today—sometimes I listen to music over the air and sometimes I stream it—but by the nineteenth-century a medium increasingly meant the instruments and institutions that linked humans, and their thoughts, across time and space. In concert with these changes, *information* was redefined as well. Where it once referred to the *process* of becoming informed, *information* came to mean *what* one was informed about. Generally, this brought to mind paper-based documentation. *Information*, in this new sense, had a catchall quality, describing references to reality in the aggregate—the figures on a ledger sheet, the goods listed on a bill of lading, the stories published in a newspaper, the writing on a census form. Media were constituent elements of this larger body. They were paper instruments, such as the printed forms and ledgers crafted for use in information compilation efforts, as well as formats and *genres that printers, merchants, scholars, clerics, administrators, and others who worked with paper had developed over the course of centuries.

But also, the term was increasingly applied to electrically, mechanically, and chemically engineered channels, in particular telegraphy and photography, through which information was conveyed and retained in mysterious new ways. Entering public consciousness in the same era as the Spiritualist movement of the mid-nineteenth century, the technical medium and the clairvoyant medium, or celestial telegraph as the clairvoyant was sometimes called, commonly enacted what seemed to be a magical interconnect across time and space. As the boundaries between the supernatural and scientific became less porous in the late-nineteenth century, it was increasingly the technical qualities, and the aura of industrial progress they carried, that made a medium a medium.

Nowhere were these trends more evident than in the publishing offices of the mass-circulation daily newspapers. Printed periodicals had been part of the Western social landscape since the sixteenth century, yet it was only in the nineteenth century that the size, scope, and reach of these publications exploded as never before. Between 1850 and 1900, daily newspaper circulation increased by roughly twentyfold. At the same time, city papers grew longer, doubling from four pages to eight, then again to sixteen. Mammoth Sunday editions sprawled across more than one hundred pages. Not surprisingly, many readers struggled to keep pace. A half century before Claude Shannon crafted his elegant equations of information and entropy, a writer for *Harper's Weekly* could describe the newspaper press as "infinity on parade."

Given the ephemerality of daily papers and the volume of news they put into circulation, information had a spectral quality—it was both out there and not. Mindful of this, a growing number of libraries and private archives dedicated space and labor in the late nineteenth century to preserving periodicals for later reference. The press clipping bureaus that sprouted up in the same era had a more timely solution: industrialize the reading process. Collecting hundreds of periodicals from across their home regions, hiring dozens of women to scan them for keywords, and sharing their clips with partners elsewhere, the clipping bureaus treated the media landscape writ large as one contiguous field of information to be mined each day for usable scraps of data: reviews for the artist, evidence for the scholar, leads for the salesman. Yet newspapers supplied more than just *facts, accounts, and reports. They furnished informational guidance, such as how to conduct oneself on a date or in a department store, that helped readers navigate the environs of modern life.

For their part, *publishers relished their image as purveyors of modernity, turning their buildings into the great technological hubs of their times. But if the newspaper was the archetypal informational medium of fin de siècle modernity, the synonymy of print media and information was already hard to reconcile. After all, much of what appeared in the paper arrived at the publisher's office as blips of electricity transmitted by wire services like the Associated Press, Reuters, and Wolff. Although ordinary readers' direct contact with the telegraph was minimal, especially in the United States, they knew full well that the wires draped above city streets and disappearing into the horizon coursed with information. As early as the Civil War, crowds began gathering outside to catch word of the latest telegraph dispatches. In the decades ahead, many publishers encouraged such crowds, developing public display technologies that incorporated chalkboards, magic lanterns, and other visual media.

Such scenes, which created a spectacle out of the convergent and industrialized nature of new communication technologies, rendered it perfectly clear that there was a subset of an emerging corporate order that dealt in the business of mass-produced messages. Though there was still no singular term to describe them in aggregate, the contours of *a media*, or interconnected set of technologies and institutions that seemed to be reshaping social experience, were abundantly clear in the traits Progressive intellectuals ascribed to modern communication. "Expressiveness, or the range of ideas and feeling it is competent to carry," the sociologist Charles Horton Cooley enumerated in 1909. "Permanence of record, the overcoming of time. Swiftness, or the overcoming of space. Diffusion, or access to all classes." Cooley, like many others before and since, was attentive to media's spatiotemporal contortions. But he also noticed something else: its ubiquity. Everyday life was not only being rescaled by media; it was becoming saturated with it as well.

Of Cooley's four characteristics, two in particular—documentation and diffusion— would prove particularly useful toward understanding how media, as a cohort of interrelated forms and technologies, took shape in relation to similar constructs like information and communication. In the case of the former, media could be understood as storage devices. They were things that preserved information across time. Traditionally, this implied some combination of script, type, ink, and page. After the mid-nineteenth century, these base ingredients were no longer necessary. With the advent and advancement of photography, information could be captured on polished plates or panes of glass through processes that were more photochemical than linguistic in nature.

Indeed, the photograph, widely interpreted as a visual fact, placed imagery on par with language. "To see is to know," boasted the leading stereograph-card manufacturer Underwood and Underwood.

Sound recording, introduced in the 1870s, added a new wrinkle by essentially disassociating inscription from the human senses. The eye could decipher a photographic negative or a film reel's celluloid frame, but the grooves etched into a shellac canister were neither audible nor readable without the required playback device. Mediated information, at least in its most technologically current forms, would only become more illegible over the course of the twentieth century as sounds, images, and text migrated onto the airwaves, magnetic tapes, and microchips. If in the nineteenth century media was a constituent element of information, information was now a constituent element of media—the ones and zeros that provided a kind of universal building block for mediated sight and sound in general.

Diffusion would prove equally important to twentieth-century conceptions of media. What counted in this case, however, was the publicness of a message, not its documentation. Thus a long-distance phone call and a network radio bulletin were categorically different forms of communication, even though both traversed the same wires. The former was interpersonal communication. The latter was a broadcast medium. This equation of media and diffusion was made explicit in the term *mass communication*, which came into vogue after the 1920s to describe messages that were centrally produced and widely disseminated. Forms and genres that shared these cardinal traits, whether they be the photo-essays of a *Life* or *Picture Post* or the variety programs aired by an NBC or BBC, were media. Although this one-to-many characterization would prove frustrating to new media scholars in the early twenty-first century, it was exceedingly useful to midcentury theorists eager to understand how large corporations and states shaped, bent, and distorted the information landscape.

After World War II, cybernetics and information theory gave the media concept a distinctly kinetic quality. Paper-based information had been anything but static—often circulating in unpredictable ways. But information moved differently for these theorists. Instead of perambulating, it ricocheted, looped, and unfurled, moving continuously rather than intermittently. Furthermore, the mathematical origins of both fields gave information a quantifiable character. And, of course, what could be counted could be valued, argued the prophets of an emerging information economy. Pushing for as capacious a definition of *copyright as possible, media conglomerates found a receptive audience among Western policy makers who saw their nations' knowledge sectors as the cure to a dwindling industrial base. The result was a series of legislative measures, such as the US Copyright Act of 1976, that collapsed the legal distinctions between media, information, and intellectual property. Stretched to encompass everything from gene sequences to Gene Simmons, information was much like the "manufactures" of the nineteenth century: a teleological framework for grouping together the many activities of those "knowledge" businesses—software firms, biotech labs, media conglomerates, and others—that seemed to be pushing modernity forward. As unrelated as these industries may have appeared to the layperson then, they no longer appear so discrete in a smart phone age when simply watching "television" might well require some act of biometric authentication and an update to one's operating system.

AUDIENCES AS INFORMATION

The passage from analog to *digital has meant that media more readily produce information about their own use. In today's media environment, that data exhaust can be every bit as valuable as the content itself, if not more so. In collecting this audience information, *internet platforms have followed the lead of the publishers and broadcasters before them, who began positioning themselves as experts on audiences, markets, and publics in the early twentieth century. Collectively, these surveillance initiatives have made media into not only vessels of information, but tools for generating knowledge about the thoughts, tastes, and behaviors of those who use them.

In part this owes to the logistics of long-distance communication. Messages need somewhere to go. That destination could be somewhere as placeless as the ether. Usually, though, media operations have needed something more specific: a name and place of residence, a particular terminal, or an IP address. This basic locational data provided something of a peg on which other pieces of information could be hung; gradually, a more detailed picture of the individual behind that address could take shape. Mass publishers were quick to recognize that these profiles had value independent of their own fulfillment operations. As early as the 1870s, mail-order magazine firms developed a thriving trade in the names and addresses of subscribers. Standard practice was to sell bundles of letters, sometimes numbering in the tens of thousands, to one another. The purchaser would then add names and addresses harvested from those letters to its mailing lists and use these in future marketing campaigns. Like any other commodity, these names were graded for desirability and worth, taking such factors as freshness, génder, and class into account. In the meantime, a similar trade took shape among the mailing-list brokers that sprang from the directory-publishing field. Fed by clipping bureaus, automobile registries, and hundreds of other sources, the list houses were, in turn, an important source of names and supplementary data that mass publishers incorporated into their subscription drives. The onomasticians, or name specialists, behind these projects were the forerunners of today's number crunchers, whose facility with massive data sets is nearly as sought after on Madison Avenue as it is in Silicon Valley. Aided by the internet's basic two-way architecture, a host of tracking technologies, and a contemporary culture of public divulgence, firms like Alphabet (Google) and Facebook have built information dossiers on their users rivaled only by the consumer credit-rating bureaus.

Efforts to profile audiences as individuals were paralleled by efforts to describe them in aggregate. Throughout the first half of the twentieth century, US media organizations built research arms and participated in cross-disciplinary projects that brought the social sciences to bear on the reading, listening, and viewing public. After spending much of its first decade crafting mammoth studies of various industries, the market research division at the Curtis Publishing Company turned its gaze toward the audience in the 1920s. To learn more about readers of the *Saturday Evening Post* and *Ladies' Home Journal*, Curtis researchers carried out surveys, interviews, and even censuses of their household trash in hopes of yielding a composite picture of middle-class buying habits. Curtis's activities were widely emulated in the decades ahead, laying the groundwork for the psychographic profiles and lifestyle typologies into which consumers were slotted in the late twentieth century.

As mass publishers were honing the tools, techniques, and genres of market research, social scientists were developing the first large-scale academic studies of media audiences. Payne Fund researchers in the sociology and psychology departments at Ohio State University, the University of Chicago, and the University of Iowa used everything from electrodes to interviews to analyze children's emotional response to motion pictures. Endowed by a mass-culture-wary philanthropist, the studies offered a prototype for foundation-funded media research.

Nowhere was this cross-fertilization of industry and academic research more apparent than the US broadcast industry of the 1930s and 1940s. Funded by a Rockefeller Foundation grant, the Office of Radio Research (ORR) was established in 1937 by the social-psychologists Hadley Cantril, Paul Lazarsfeld, and Frank Stanton at Princeton University. There, and later at Columbia, the ORR took a big-tent approach to audience research, employing surveys, in-depth interviews, polygraph readings, and textual analysis. For Lazarsfeld, the ORR offered a means of advancing his work on class stratification and his methodological experiments with statistical analysis. For Stanton, who headed up the research department at CBS and later served as the network's president, ORR research added nuance to the methodologically woeful audience ratings furnished by the telephone surveyors of the era. Those ratings would soon get their own methodological upgrade at the hands of A. C. Nielsen, which teamed with the Census Bureau in the 1940s to create a statistically representative sample of US households. Ratings and shares facilitated the truck and barter in audiences by providing broadcasters and advertisers a standard of exchange: a numerical score representing the volume of households tuned into a program. Along with similar measures, including the best-seller lists, record charts, and box-office tallies, ratings also functioned as feedback mechanisms, informing the common sense at networks, publishing houses, labels, and studios as to what "works" with audiences.

Almost unique among industry standards, media metrics have taken on a public life, providing a ready, if imperfect, snapshot of popular tastes and sentiments. Today's digital platforms even incorporate them into their user interface, showing the number of times a video has been viewed or a song streamed. Against such baselines, individuals have been able to evaluate their own preferences and sense of self-distinction. Here, media metrics have much in common with public opinion polling, which shared the same deep links to the broader world of institutional inquiry. Before establishing his American Institute of Public Opinion, for instance, George Gallup had earned a doctorate in psychology, honed a namesake method of studying reading habits, and headed up an advertising agency research department. In the same years Gallup's polls became a mainstay of news reporting, he and his contemporary Elmo Roper built up lucrative consultancies in market research. As evidenced by such activities, there was never a clean line separating the commercial, academic, editorial, and political strands of audience research within and around media.

Richard K. Popp

See also cameras; cybernetics/feedback; data; databases; files; newspapers; platforms; printed visuals; public sphere; social media; surveilling; telecommunications

FURTHER READING

Ann Blair and Peter Stallybrass, "Mediating Information, 1450–1800," in *This Is Enlightenment*, edited by Clifford Siskin and William Warner, 2010; Daniel J. Czitrom, *Media and the American Mind: From Morse to McLuhan*, 1982; Susan J. Douglas, *Listening In: Radio and the American Imagination*, 2004; Julia Guarneri, *Newsprint Metropolis: City Papers and the Making of Modern Americans*, 2017; John Nerone, *The Media and Public Life: A History*, 2015; John Durham Peters, *The Marvelous Clouds: Toward a Philosophy of Elemental Media*, 2015; Richard K. Popp, "Information, Industrialization, and the Business of Press Clippings, 1880–1925," *Journal of American History* 101, no. 2 (2014): 427–53; Douglas B. Ward, *A New Brand of Business: Charles Coolidge Parlin, Curtis Publishing Company and the Origins of Market Research*, 2010.

MEMOS

The humble memo was a ubiquitous feature of American business life throughout the twentieth century, though it has faded in salience, if not necessarily in use, in the twenty-first as electronic media replace paper. Variations of this *genre existed before its American heyday, however, and have continued past it. According to the *Oxford English Dictionary* (*OED*), the *memorandum* genre has been referred to in the English-speaking world since at least the fifteenth century, with its shortened name, the *memo*, appearing by at least the eighteenth century. The term can refer to several genre variants, with different socially agreed-on purposes and recognizable form features, however, and the preponderant variant has changed over time, at times reflecting organizational developments and at times technological ones. Its earliest purpose was as a note that served as an aid to the writer's memory, whereas its primary use in the twentieth century was as correspondence to another person within the same organization, generally with a secondary documentary purpose. It has legal, diplomatic, and commercial senses, as well, with one of those acquiring renewed salience in the Trump era.

One early and basic use of the term *memorandum* was to refer to a note a person made about something he or she wanted to remember in the future—for example, a shopping list, observations, or an account of an event. Although some memorandums were written for a single occasion (such as a note about a single important event), others were more regular. On the title page of the fictional *Moll Flanders* (by Daniel Defoe, 1722), for example, the subtitle claims this account of her life was "Written from her own Memorandums," apparently referring to an ongoing series she (putatively) wrote during her lifetime. A daily entry in a diary was often referred to as a memorandum, too, and both individuals (e.g., Clarissa in Samuel Richardson's 1748 epistolary novel by that name) and commercial entities (e.g., Hudson's Bay Company) referred to *memorandum-books* in which regular notes of events were recorded. Such memorandums included a date and possibly time of day as a standard form feature. The term *memorandum* has been used to refer to this version of the genre much less frequently in the twentieth and twenty-first centuries than in earlier centuries.

Since at least the sixteenth century, another variant was the legal memorandum, a type of legal document that recorded an agreement or transaction for future reference. In this case, the genre was more formal and intended not just to help the person writing it to remember its contents later, but also to attest to the agreement for other audiences, including courts. Such use required specificity in dates and details of the agreement, as well as more formal, precise language. Although this legal memorandum variant existed almost as early as the personal memorandum for use only by the writer, it has survived more visibly and is still used for some legal matters, particularly when combined with other terms, as in *memorandum of understanding* or *memorandum of agreement*.

The world of diplomacy adopted a related version of the memorandum genre. According to the *OED*, in this sense the memorandum might summarize a question or issue, or recommend a course of action (e.g., the 1876 Berlin Memorandum between Germany, Austria-Hungary, and Russia). Its purpose was less formal than that of a treaty. Like the legal memorandum, the diplomatic memorandum was not written solely for the benefit of the writer, but for others, as well.

Around the turn of the twentieth century, the genre most familiar to most of us emerged in the realm of American business. The business memo, as it was most often termed, did not exist in the mid-nineteenth century. At that time, most firms were very small and could be managed by word of mouth, supplemented by correspondence over distance. Letter correspondence in American firms communicated information, opinions, and instructions between partners when one was traveling, or between an owner and sales agent at a distance. The form of the business letter genre included conventional openings (e.g., "Your esteemed favor of the 16th ult. duly to hand") as well as elaborate sign-offs (e.g., "Most humbly and devotedly yours") and tended to be long and wordy. Letters of this form were also used between firms.

By the last two decades of the nineteenth century and the first two of the twentieth, many American business organizations had grown and acquired more hierarchical layers. A new philosophy of management, systematic management, was developed and expounded in articles appearing in engineering and management publications. Proponents (sometimes called systematizers) advocated (1) depending not on individual initiative or memory but on systems mandated and documented by management, to be communicated in writing to those at lower levels; and (2) monitoring performance by recording data regularly at the lower levels and passing it up to higher levels for comparison and evaluation. This movement created new demand for written correspondence and documentation *within* firms. At the same time, technologies of written communication, many of which had been available for some time, were adopted to make creating such written documents more efficient. Typewriters, carbon paper, and stencil copying, along with new methods of storage such as vertical filing cabinets, facilitated the creation, distribution, storage, and retrieval of internal correspondence.

The philosophy soon extended to making the correspondence itself more efficient, by stripping away the opening and closing flourishes of traditional letters and developing a new format for internal memorandums or memos, as they were called. This format included the now familiar *to*, *from*, *date*, and *subject* lines, intended in part to aid clerks filing this internal correspondence for later reference. Systematizers within firms as well as textbook treatments outside them advocated brevity and conciseness that contrasted with the old norms for letters. The increasing numbers of managers within firms also used memos to communicate and document lateral, as well as vertical, interactions and relations. Indeed, a cynical view of memos, captured by the description of their primary function as "CYA" (cover your ass), was that their authors wrote them to *document* a particular view of an event or interaction for later defensive use rather than to *communicate* with the recipient in the first instance. For better or for worse, memos became a ubiquitous feature of twentieth-century organizational life.

By the end of the century, however, the advent of electronic mail, followed by other electronic media in the opening decades of the twenty-first century, challenged the dominance of the memo, in name if not in function. Although the format of electronic mail adopted the now traditional heading of the memo, many in business saw emails as a genre themselves, and one that drove out the memo. Reflecting a more historicized view, we can say that the memo genre migrated into the email medium, but not every email message exemplifies the memo genre. Businesspeople can use email (and now increasingly other messaging applications) for quick, coordinating messages that they would once have conveyed in person or by telephone, as well as for more extended messages with the same purpose and even form as paper memos, but now sent electronically. The increased linguistic informality introduced in many personal emails has bled over into what used to be a more concise, business-like style in memos. In addition, many other genres of external communication (e.g., the sales letter, the fund raising letter) now take the form of email, as well. So all email messages are certainly not memos, but memos are still one genre seen among the many email messages in our inboxes.

The legal memorandum has also undergone changes from the twentieth into the twenty-first century. During much of the twentieth century, long and relatively formal typed legal memorandums analyzed the issues in a case for clients. Law students were taught to write such legal memorandums, just as business students were taught to write business memos. By the early twenty-first century, however, such documents have given way to email communication with clients, along with occasional informal (and electronic rather than paper-based) memos.

Another use of the memo genre in law and government that has received considerable recent attention reflects both the memo as a record of an event to augment the writer's memory and the memo as documenting an event for others. James B. Comey, at that time director of the FBI, wrote a series of memos, the first of which was addressed to three colleagues at the FBI and the others (as released) not including addressees, to document his conversations with President Donald J. Trump about the Russian dossier and other issues. Comey wrote these memos immediately after each of his meetings with Trump in January 2017 and intended them as contemporaneous documentation, to be used defensively if needed. As such, they were much discussed in the news after Trump fired Comey a few months later. This use of the memo to document a person's view of what happened, like the business use of the memo, is unlikely to go away, whether the document is paper or electronic, suggesting that the memo still has an important future.

JoAnne Yates

See also diplomats/spies; governance; letters; merchants; observing; office practices; photocopiers

FURTHER READING

Kristen Konrad Robbins-Tiscione, "From Snail Mail to E-Mail: The Traditional Legal Memorandum in the Twenty-First Century," *Journal of Legal Education* 58, no. 1 (2008): 32–60; JoAnne Yates, *Control through Communication: The Rise of System in American Management*, 1989; JoAnne Yates and Wanda J. Orlikowski, "Genres of Organizational Communication: A Structurational Approach to Studying Communication and Media," *Academy of Management Review* 17 (1992): 299–326.

MERCHANTS

Information about market conditions, about prices and quality of goods, about the reliability of partners, and about what is in demand and what is not has always been essential for the trade in goods. Consequently, merchants, perhaps more than those in any other occupation, have been dependent on information in order to conduct their business. However, as the forms of commodity exchange evolved, the forms and functions of trade-related information changed too.

In its earliest forms, the trade in goods was carried on in person. Merchants traveled with their goods on the back of horses or camels or on board vessels. Exchange of goods took place at agreed marketplaces or along the road. Trade did often take the form of bartering, in which the value of the goods exchanged was volatile. Accumulated trade knowledge was embodied in the merchants' experience, and much of the transfer of this knowledge was informal. It was exchanged in the daily practice, by talking, or with the help of customary arrangements such as apprenticeships. Information was stored in the minds of men, with all the problems this entails. The bulk of trade was carried on in a customary way based on know-how. The organization of long-distance trade by the Silk Road can illustrate such a kind of commodity exchange.

By the late Middle Ages, another form of trade developed. Instead of traveling with their commodities from place to place, merchants settled in commercial centers. They sent their agents (commission agents) with goods abroad, and correspondence or messengers provided means to keep in contact. In due time, the predominant form of long-distance trade in Europe took the form of merchant networks. The commission agents were lesser partners or employees of the merchant firm; they were very often relatives—sons, brothers, or sons-in-law. The incorporation of family relationship increased the level of trust in the merchant networks; it was also a way to pool a firm's capital.

A crucial means of the introduction of this form of trade (merchant network) was an exchange of letters. Letters transferred a vast amount of information: on the general conditions of trade; on prices and quality of goods; on demand and supply situations; on the marketplace and safety of transport; on insurances, politics, trade duties, and laws. Letters also of course included specific information of relevance to the firm's agents: how to treat clients, which partner or clients were reliable and creditworthy, and who were not. Letters, too, gave orders to the agents about what to do, what to buy and sell, and at what prices. The exchange of letters between the firm's main office and its commission agents was reciprocal. Agents suggested to the main office what to do or could argue with the principal about the business strategy.

Already in the fourteenth century, the scope of merchant letter writing and exchange could be very extensive. From the end of the fourteenth century, we have the archives of the Italian merchant firm of Francesco Datini from Prato. Datini started his career as a merchant in arms, luxury goods, and arts in French Avignon, where the papal court was centered at the time. In 1383 Datini moved to Prato in northern Italy, and until

1410 he managed his trade from his hometown. His firm traded in a vast number of articles. Datini's surviving archives contain about 150,000 letters; most of them are concerned with business. The Datini merchant firm had eight agencies, so-called *fondaci*, in Avignon, Prato, Pisa, Florence, Genoa, Barcelona, Valenza, and Majorca, which together corresponded with 267 marketplaces in Europe, North Africa, and the Middle East. The letters were mainly written in the Tuscan version of Italian, but many other languages were used too (Latin, Catalan, Castilian, Arabic, and Hebrew). The example indicates the extent to which vast amounts of business information were collected and used already by about 1400.

The correspondence of the Datini firm illustrates the transformation of the merchant's role, from a traveler to an office keeper. Trade required the employment of personnel dedicated to letter writing, individuals who ended up spending many of their working hours in one of the firm's eight offices, which together produced more than five thousand letters a year on average.

Written documents, such as letters, contracts, and accounting books, entailed a formalization of trade. Later on, the material could be used to enforce agreements with contractors. Letters could even be used in court proceedings to prove one party's claim on another. This is one of the reasons why copybooks of letters were kept so carefully. The correspondence and accounts were stored in the merchants' offices because they provided useful information. New "paper technologies," ways to organize information on paper, and types of papers in archives evolved. This represented a step forward, away from the customary transactions of previous stages of trade. Yet it is important to stress that the new merchant practices based on paper technologies (correspondence, copybooks, written contracts, account books, etc.) belonged to big and midsize firms, firms engaged in long-distance trade. Most of the small-scale trade and bartering among common people was still based on the customary practice of the "bazaar economy," without or with very little written documentation.

When studying the role of information for merchants, we have to distinguish between historical changes in the form of, for example, the new paper technologies discussed above, *and* in the form of institutional changes. While an interdependence existed, these were two different processes. The role of institutional change in studying information is highlighted in institutional economics (Douglass C. North, Oliver E. Williamson, Ronald Coase, and others). Institutionalists point to the so-called transaction costs as a key cost factor in trade. The job of a merchant is to manage transaction costs so as to make a profit. Institutionalists divide the transaction cost into a number of key cost components. "Search and information costs" include costs for accessing useful information about goods. "Contract costs" entail costs directly related to the transaction, for example, the legal costs of contract signing. There are also "enforcement costs," in other words, the costs of making sure that parties stick to the contract. Transport costs are also costs handled by merchant firms, and they might be added to the transaction costs. From an institutional perspective, the history of trade expansion after 1500 is a history of a decline in transaction costs, which also encompasses a very significant decline in information costs.

Perhaps the most revolutionary innovation before the introduction of modern information technology was the introduction of movable print, just about fifty years after Francesco Datini's death. Printing influenced merchants' access to information in a number of ways. The most obvious was in the introduction of printed commercial news. Such news appeared already in the mid-sixteenth century in Antwerp in the Low Countries, in the form of the first printed lists of prices of goods—so-called price currents. Such prints were produced commercially and sold in cities, in a similar manner to modern newspapers. The price currents were attached to letters and distributed through merchant correspondence networks. In due time the scope and quality of information included in such business prints developed, and distribution expanded.

By making price information available broadly the merchant business changed in a fundamental way. It introduced benchmark prices to which all traders related. A price was no longer an outcome of a momentary negotiation; instead there was a price baseline that traders referred to. This made trade more predictable and merchants' accounts safer. Such predictability attracted merchants to the same marketplaces. Publicly available information was thus good for business, something the rise of Antwerp, Amsterdam, and London as central marketplaces in the *early modern period attested to. In the seventeenth century, business prints arrived in Britain, France, and other European countries, and by the late eighteenth century in the United States. The information provided via business prints was not free, but it is very likely to have significantly reduced information costs for merchants. And the information provided was reliable; otherwise, the business prints would have disappeared. Moreover, the amount of information was much greater than what a commission agent could possibly offer in letters.

The key innovation in the distribution of correspondence and prints was the introduction of post services. These started in the Holy Roman Empire in the early sixteenth century, when the noble house of Thurn and Taxis secured the license to carry mail in the Holy Roman Empire and Spain. Other European countries followed suit and developed similarly regulated postal systems. Early modern postal services delivered both private (business) and government intelligence in a combined service.

Reliability was high and postage rates low in comparison with the costs associated with employing messengers, but delivery was slow. In this respect there was little difference between how information was communicated in the sixteenth century and how it was in the early nineteenth century. Only with the invention of the telegraph in the 1830s did the speed of information distribution increase significantly; the change was immense. Yet, from a business point of view, in its first decades the telegraph was very expensive; and thus it was used only when a high cost of information transmission was deemed tolerable.

The expansion of correspondence networks together with the introduction of reliable postal services are two explanations for the successful development of merchant network trade in Europe in the seventeenth and eighteenth centuries. But this way of organizing trade had its problems. The scope of trade was limited by the access to relevant, up-to-date information and timely conveyance of instructions from the firm's headquarters to commission agents. In transcontinental trade this posed a particularly large problem; the distances between European merchant centers, such as Lisbon, Cadiz, London, and Amsterdam, and markets in Asia, Africa, or South America were too great. It took months, sometimes years, to send a message with relevant information to European headquarters and to receive instructions on what to do. Transcontinental trade also required specific local knowledge of markets.

Chartered companies (for example, the English East India Company and the Dutch East India Company) were one solution to the problem of information asymmetry. This form of trade organization provided the company employees at a distance with more freedom to act independently. Company agents in Asia or Africa had access to local information, and they knew local markets. But the same information advantage also made the company agents disposed to make money on their own, and to ignore the instructions from their companies. The company directors (principals) attempted to limit such behavior by stricter regulations of the agents' employment and by introducing control mechanisms. None of these measures worked perfectly because of the distance and the headquarters' dependency on their local agents. Information asymmetry between headquarters (principals) and local agents persisted. The problem is characterized as the principal-agent problem and is common in any complex economic organization, not only the chartered company. The chartered company as a business form was only a partial solution to the problem of information asymmetry in long-distance trade. But in the seventeenth and eighteenth centuries, it was a working solution for the conditions of transcontinental trade.

In the nineteenth and twentieth centuries, the access to business information was primarily characterized by technical innovation, and by a broadening of information markets. Business information became "better, faster, cheaper." Better meant that information was more reliable, was more accessible, and had a wider scope. Naturally, the introduction of information technology in the late twentieth century vastly increased the amount of stored and searchable information.

While the amount of business information has grown steadily since 1500, the speed of information transmission did not change much until the breakthrough of the telegraph in the mid-nineteenth century. But ever since then the speed of information transition has continued to rise, owing first to the telegraph, then the telephone, and most recently to *internet and mobile phone technology. Today information on global commodity and capital markets is accessible in real time; that can be compared with the six to eight months it took to deliver price information from Canton in China to northern Europe at the end of the eighteenth century.

Steamboats, railways, automobiles, and travel by air revolutionized the transfer of business information too. Information costs also declined as a result of the increasing size of information markets and increasing competition among information suppliers. But once again, the biggest historical change was the introduction of information technology, which immensely reduced costs of information storage, distribution, and searches.

The fact that much of the information on the internet is cheap, or even free, does not mean that everybody has the same access to all of it. In one sense, access to information has not changed over time. Business competition has been characterized not by equal access to information but by information asymmetries. It was exclusive "insider" information, or information asymmetry, that provided a merchant firm with a competitive advantage. The information advantage has been one of the key factors of business profitability. Consequently, trading firms did their utmost to keep specific business information private. From a public point of view, such a strategy might often be perceived as immoral or even illegal, and bad for the economy in general. Today, the abuse of insider information on the stock market entails very serious legal consequences.

How should one assess the age-old contradiction between, on the one hand, the information revolution—making business information better, faster, and cheaper—and, on the other hand, the continued competitive advantage of information asymmetries? The use, and abuse, of information asymmetries is advantageous only to individual firms while information asymmetries in general harm markets and hinder economic development. Institutional and technical innovations in information processing, storing, and transmission (merchant correspondence, print, postal services, telegraph, information technology, etc.) improved the functioning of market economies, and consequently they indisputably promoted economic growth to everybody's benefit.

Leos Müller

See also accounting; commodification; globalization; letters; networks; newspapers; postal customers; telecommunications; travel

FURTHER READING

John Seely Brown and Paul Duguid, *The Social Life of Information*, 2000; Ann M. Carlos and Stephen Nicholas, "Agency Problems in Early Chartered Companies: The Case of the Hudson's Bay Company," *Journal of Economic History* 4 (1990): 853–75; Michael Hobart and Zachary Schiffman, *Information Ages: Literacy, Numeracy, and the Computer Revolution*, 2000; Seija-Riitta Laakso, *Across the Oceans: Development of Overseas Business Information Transmission 1815–1875*, 2007; John J. McCusker, "The Demise of Distance: The Business Press and the Origins of the Information Revolution in the Early Modern Atlantic World," *American Historical Review* 110, no. 2 (2005): 295–321; John J. McCusker and Cora Gravensteijn, *The Beginnings of Commercial and Financial Journalism: The Commodity Price Currents, Exchange Rate Currents, and Money Currents of Early Modern Europe*, 1991; Leos Müller and Jari Ojala, eds., *Information Flows: New Approaches in the Historical Study of Business Information*, 2007; Simone M. Müller, *Wiring the World: The Social and Cultural Creation of Global Telegraph Networks*, 2016.

MONEY

Money is a vital carrier of economic and political information: coins or banknotes typically not only convey the currency metrology of the polity where they were issued but also bear the image of eminent personalities associated with the history of the polity in question. Whether it be kings, prime ministers, scientists, authors, or emblematic flora and fauna—money imagery can tell us much about the mind-set of the place where it was issued, and about the evolution of monetary sovereignty therein.

By no means linear, the evolution of money can nevertheless be roughly abstracted into six main stages: nonmetallic or commodity based; metallic protocurrency (hacksilver); coinage; bills (paper); fiat (bills without metal backing); and virtual (electronic). Money has taken both material and *digital forms to convey information about the value of goods. Intertwined with these discrete stages one invariably finds tension between private-order and state-issued (chartalist) currency, where the former derives from the need to facilitate trade and the latter is primarily aimed at enriching the rulers' coffers (seigniorage). To this day, one cannot determine with certainty which of these two exigencies catalyzed the emergence of money to a greater extent.

In ancient Sumer, barley volume units had famously been used to project monetary value onto other commodities. However, of the three oldest premodern centers of urban civilization—pharaonic Egypt, the Indus valley, and Mesopotamia—it is believed that only in the latter had silver ingots (hacksilver) and weights been systemized into semi-uniform currency. This is despite the fact that metallurgy as such was developed for other purposes in all three. Notably, metallurgy was developed autochthonously in pre-Columbian South America, but metal seldom acquired monetary-exchange qualities there.

Arguably inspired by Mesopotamian hacksilver, the earliest form of coinage was made of an alloy of gold and silver (electrum) and was struck by the Greek city-state of Lydia in present-day Anatolia around 650 BCE. Striking a coin involved hammering a plain coin-sized disk between two dies so that the coin was imprinted on front and back with the inverse of the patterns that had been cut into the dies. Greek-style coinage, which was round in shape and incorporated not just script and numerals but also a rich vein of animal and anthropomorphic imagery, then diffused across Europe, North Africa, and the Levant. Following Alexander the Great's conquests (336–323 BCE), Persian and later Indian currency also broadly evolved from metallic protocurrency into round struck coinage, and Greek impact may have played a critical role in that transition.

Chinese civilization appears to have broadly transitioned from cowrie and metallic protocurrency (e.g., "knife money" or *daoqian*) into round coinage predominantly cast from bronze around the fourth century. Yet foreign impact is much harder to establish in this setting, as contemporaneous Greek-style coinage has not been excavated in China proper as yet. The case for "separateness" is perhaps plausible on technological grounds too. While bronze metallurgy itself was not developed endogenously in pre-imperial China, the fact remains that Chinese coinage was *cast* rather than *struck*, that is, it was formed by pouring the molten metal into a mold to produce the patterns on the coin. Not only was the production technique quite different from the European preference for striking coins; Chinese coins were also virtually devoid of anthropomorphic imagery until the late nineteenth century.

That gold and silver were hardly ever made into coinage in premodern China suggests a key difference in the evolution of coinage in the rest of Eurasia, which may have had to do with the relative endowment of low-lying metal deposits. Mining-technology factors are moot, as are explanations more "institutional" in nature: after all, low-value cast bronze coinage, as well as the strict regulation of copper mining, held a particularly strong appeal in traditional Chinese statecraft.

In *early modern Europe, the use of precious-metal currencies, on the back first of African gold and later of Mexican silver, afforded the state greater seigniorage potential. This occurred in conjunction with improved minting technology—first horse powered, and from 1788 steam powered. By contrast, Chinese statecraft arguably entertained a much stronger prejudice against the very notion of the state profiting from currency. Otherwise put, better minting technology was sought by early modern European polities to differentiate sanctioned currencies from forged or foreign ones. In the Chinese setting, however, incentives to improve the quality of coinage were less compelling because bronze coinage possessed a priori lower seigniorage potential.

Early coinage in the Islamic world was predicated on Sassanid prototypes in much the same way that early medieval European coinage still harkened back to Roman designs. While gold and silver as well as bronze were employed across the Islamic world with local variations, anthropomorphism was largely stamped out in the eighth century. In that sense, both Islamic and Chinese coinage could be described as expressively frugal. Within the Islamic world, Mughal coinage was of particularly high quality thanks to advanced craftsmanship, yet steam-powered mechanization of minting caught on only in the early twentieth century.

This was all part of a much wider *global* progression through which the notion of money had initially been all but synonymous with coined metal, then augmented with paper bills (ca. eleventh century CE in China, seventeenth century in the West, nineteenth century in the Ottoman Empire), and has more recently become associated with much more abstract constructs such as public debt, the nation-state, or transnational monetary unions. Ordinarily, paper bills had been backed against metal reserves (i.e., bullion or specie) in private or state coffers. But, especially at times of war, bills could be issued without reserves. For example, the assignats issued during the French Revolution to ward off bankruptcy were initially backed by the church lands seized by the revolutionary government; but as more and more assignats were issued between 1790 and 1796, they depreciated precipitously.

Following the establishment of the Bank of England in 1694 as a lender of last resort, early modern Western currencies started to gradually shed their conceptual metallic anchorage. But, *epistemologically, the linkages between metal and money had been fraying earlier as evidenced, for example, in Nicholas Oresme's (1320–82) exhortations against the scourge of medieval debasements, and his calls for an unadulterated currency belonging with the public; Jean Bodin (1530–96) similarly envisioned money creation as the prerogative of the sovereign at a time when privately owned mints were not uncommon.

Between the 1870s and the 1930s, following the discovery of new gold deposits in California, Australia, and South Africa, the gold standard was adopted by the world's advanced economies, whereby paper bills became mostly of public-order, fiduciary nature. Namely, they were partially backed against gold reserves in state coffers and could be fully redeemed in principle.

Following the deflationary upheavals of the Great Depression, and the ravages of World War II in Europe, the gold standard articulated into a gold-exchange international mechanism. Known as the Bretton Woods system, after the town in New Hampshire in which delegates from the Allied nations gathered in July 1944 to formulate rules for international monetary standards, that mechanism was administered by the United States with the price of gold fixed at US$35 per ounce. Subsequently, the US dollar became the most widely used foreign currency around the world.

However, the fixed price of gold became increasingly difficult for the United States to maintain because it rendered the US dollar rigid vis-à-vis the government budget balance or the bullion reserves. On the other hand, other countries devalued or revalued their currencies, including major economic powers such as the United Kingdom (in 1967), Germany, and France (both in 1969). As a result, President Richard Nixon severed the tie between the US dollar and gold in 1971, thus abolishing the Bretton Woods system and ushering the fiat stage in its currency, where the state rather than metal would become the ultimate guarantor of all forms of money.

Although previous phases in which currency inconvertible to metal had been recorded in different parts of the world—Marco Polo's or Ibn Battuta's impressions of China under Mongol rule might perhaps spring to mind right away—never before had full-blown fiat money been so universally and sustainably accepted, and never before had the inconvertibility of currency into specie seemed so unquestionable as in our age. In the face of Irving Fisher's dire predictions in the late 1910s, even celebrated free-marketeers such as Milton Friedman and Anna Schwartz would come to conclude by 1986 that government monopolies over currency in the developed world were to remain in effect. It is this consensus among economists that has all but relegated "free banking" to historical trivia. Namely, the late nineteenth-century notion that private banks are more responsible than state institutions when printing money as a form of debt no longer carries much weight.

What was to be enduringly unique after the collapse of the Bretton Woods accords is, however, of great magnitude: For the last four decades we have grown accustomed to think of and value money virtually inextricably from the nation-state as its ultimate arbiter, whereas through much of the previous twenty-six-hundred-odd-year period, money ultimately implied base or precious metal mostly in the form of round metal coinage or in the form of metallic reserves backing notes. The premodern insignia of rulership on coinage had represented, in that context, a guarantee of *metallic* quality much more than of value par excellence.

Today, however, if one were to look beyond the most basic quantity-of-money index in any OECD country—the M1—one would quickly realize the increasingly abstract nature of money. That is to say, in highly urbanized modern societies, the great bulk of current wealth is embodied in electronically digitized interbank flows, partially backed by central-bank guarantees. Only a fraction of the "money" thereof actually circulates in tangible form as banknotes, let alone as subsidiary coinage.

Against this backdrop, the most recent stage in the evolution of currency can be traced to the spread of the *World Wide Web in the late 1990s. This led to the creation of private-order computer-generated currencies such as the Bitcoin (est. 2008) that are highly speculative in nature and completely unbacked by central banks. It is estimated that around two million people around the world currently own Bitcoins, but virtual currencies have also been accused of being computer-chip-disguised Ponzi schemes. Whether they signal a historical rebound of "free banking" or perhaps a further sustainable abstraction of money as a whole remains to be seen.

Niv Horesh

See also bureaucracy; coins; commodification; computers; digitization; governance

FURTHER READING

Glyn Davies, *A History of Money*, 1994; Catherine Eagleton, Joe Cribb, Elizabeth Errington, and Jonathan Williams, *Money: A History*, 2007; Niall Ferguson, *The Ascent of Money*, 2016; Dennis O. Flynn, Arturo Giráldez, and Richard Von Glahn, *Global Connections and Monetary History, 1470–1800*, 2003; William N. Goetzmann, *Money Changes Everything*, 2017; Eric Helleiner, *The Evolution of National Money*, 2003; Niv Horesh, *Chinese Money in Global Context*, 2014.

NETWORKS

What do we mean by a "network"? Is it a metaphor, concept, cultural construction, heuristic device, model, structural entity, or relationship between people and things defined socially or mathematically? Is the network a revolutionary technology of social organization, or merely a means to enhance what we already do? Or is it all the above? The elasticity and mutability of the term (and of networks themselves) have made them both an attractive tool and a compelling object of interest to many academic disciplines, not only the hard sciences, but psychology, social anthropology, sociology, economics, and, more recently, history. In practice, networks tend to be viewed in several overlapping ways: as a metaphor—just as the image of a web or net was used in the eighteenth and nineteenth centuries to characterize the integuments of human society; descriptively—as a particular account of sets of social relations; analytically—as a means of explaining their strengths and weaknesses; and prescriptively, as a superior means of social organization. As we shall see, it has been a common feature of discussions about networks that they have elided the network as phenomenon and the network as analytic tool, and have been far more concerned with the supposed virtues of networks in both senses than with the problems they pose.

Networks and networking are everywhere. The terms have increased exponentially in everyday speech, in N-diagrams of usage in Google Books, in newspapers and magazines (nearly a fourfold increase in their appearance in the pages of the *New York Times*), and in academic publications. A major social theorist, Manuel Castells, argues that we have entered a new epoch, that of "network society." Figures 1 and 2 plot the increased use of the terms "networking" and "social+network" by decade in the Web of Science, the combined citation indexes of the major academic disciplines. The trend, especially in the new millennium, is stark. If in Adam Smith's commercial society of *The Wealth of Nations* (1776) he viewed everyone as potentially a trader or merchant engaged in "truck, barter and exchange," in contemporary information society we are all in some way seen or see ourselves as networkers.

The rise of the network, and particularly of social networks—first identified as such by Elizabeth Bott in the 1950s, as opposed to those systems of trains, ships, telegraphs and cables, radios, and televisions that were described as the key networks of the nineteenth and twentieth centuries—has, of course, been enormously facilitated by *digital information technology. The central thesis of Castells's work is that information and communications technologies have enabled networks, that have had a long history, to overcome their limitations (chiefly of scale), and thereby to become the dominant form of economic, political, and social organization.

Digital networks began as a series of systems designed to facilitate communication and data sharing within the scientific community but quickly spread into the public sphere. The building of the ARPANET in 1968–69 by the Advanced Research Projects Agency in the United States, the invention of email programs, and, some years later,

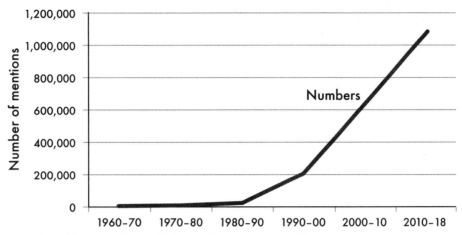

Figure 1. Use of "networking." Web of Science, 1960-2018.

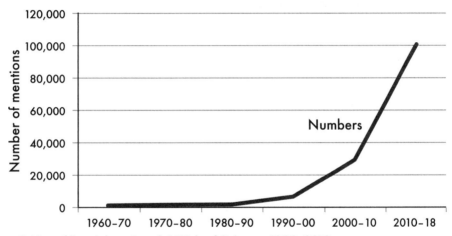

Figure 2. Use of "social+network." Web of Science, 1960-2018.

the development by Tim Berners-Lee and Robert Cailliau at CERN, the European Laboratory for Particle Physics in Geneva, of a system of *hyperlinks and hypertext that underpinned the *World Wide Web, created the platform on which a commercialized *internet was built in the 1990s. The dissemination of personal computers and smart phones, along with a raft of technologies, means that today individuals are constantly and inexorably reminded of their networked being, just as the very technologies that enmesh us also provide us with the capacity to access, analyze, and build networks for ourselves.

It became a largely unquestioned assumption, especially among organization theorists, that networks were good: both a good way to understand the workings of the world, and an effective means of acting within it. This view predated the internet—it became current in the late 1970s and 1980s when experts argued that the best way to deal with the economic ills of stagnant growth and inflation, and with the shifting nature of the economy, away from commodities to information, from mass production to niche markets, was to replace the traditional and inflexible hierarchies of business organizations with informal networked enterprises. These were seen as "flat" (relatively egalitarian), flexible, adaptable to changing tastes and circumstance, and (a favorite term) nimble. Such attributes were a wish list, not an accurate historical account of how all networks functioned. Nevertheless networks were crucially seen as more receptive to information, able to spread it faster and react to it more quickly, to be both nimble and creative—an insight taken up alike by political activists and the new social movements, and by critics of such cumbersome entities as the nation-state. Even before the internet, speed and mutability were of the essence.

At the same time the insights of graph theory and topology (and their popularization by authors like Malcolm Gladwell and in such games as Six Degrees of Kevin Bacon) reinforced the notion that the world was a small place in which everyone is connected, and whose structures—virtual, biological, economic, and social—were self-organized networks that followed certain mathematical rules. Social network sites became the preferred portals through which to connect to this world. Network euphoria, a new species of technophilia fueled by the tech industries, focused, understandably, on the enormous potential unleashed by the availability of information exchange on an unprecedented scale and at astonishing speed. Who would not prefer, it was assumed, to be "information rich" rather than "information poor." This was, of course, the latest iteration of the myth—found earlier in the promotion of the telegraph and the telephone—that technology is inherently emancipatory, that it would create a more democratic world, expand freedom, dispel ignorance, and enhance human understanding. (The assumption here is that social conflict derives from isolation and insufficient communication, but that technology can annihilate space and time.) This vision also manifested a disturbing tendency to elide the distinction between information and knowledge or wisdom. The fact that the content, context, history, and purpose of networks were every bit as important as their configuration and scale tended to be overlooked. These concerns re-emerged in public discourse only as it became apparent that virtual networks suffered from the same ills as their material precursors: the need to maintain their integrity, avoid disintegration, secure trust, avoid malevolent and covert manipulation, and identify misinformation and mendacity.

Absorption in networks and fascination with their contemporary capabilities have transformed the sense of how things worked in the past, revealing networks and relationships that had hitherto been obscured. Different or various sorts of entity—cliques, circles, coteries, cells, cartels, friends, patrons and clients, and correspondents—have all come to be seen as having common features *as* networks. So the recent sense of their importance has spawned scholarly networks to study historical networks, among them the Harvard University Visualizing Social Networks project; Oxford University's Cultures of Knowledge: Networking the Republic of Letters 1550–1750; Stanford University's Mapping the Republic of Letters; Six Degrees of Francis Bacon at the Carnegie Mellon University; and the Dutch universities' and academy's consortium the Circulation of Knowledge and Learned Practices in the 17th-Century Dutch Republic. Some of these networks are substantial. The network News Networks in *Early Modern Europe has involved more than thirty scholars from nine different countries. Such historical initiatives are recent. The journal *Social Networks* was founded in 1979, but the *Journal of Historical Network Research* only in 2018.

What are the problems that networks can and have addressed? First, networks can help solve problems of information over distances; they can be used to address problems of scale. Thus when the nineteenth-century Parisian naturalist Georges Cuvier needed fossil skeletons for his work on comparative anatomy he used a (preexisting) network of geologists to which he belonged and that included English, Scots, Irish, German, Scandinavian, Swiss, and Italian savants to find him specimens from all over Europe. Second, they can provide collective assurance and insurance. They can offer a sense of belonging or identity, secured by mutually supportive actions, and shared narratives and values (as, for example, in the US civil rights movement of the 1960s). This has often entailed collective obligations to mutual protection, as in the case of political and social movements like the revolutionary European Carbonari or the American women's suffrage movement of the nineteenth century, and among religious sects and minorities, whether sixteenth-century Protestants or twentieth-century Jews. Third, whatever their purpose—the pursuit and dissemination of learning, the creation or enjoyment of art, the consolidation of kinship or friendship networks, the hunt for profit, the provision of credit, or the acquisition of different sorts of power—networks can reduce uncertainty and risk by pooling sources of information and establishing conventions of acceptable conduct. The information embedded in the dense and interconnected neighborhood, familial, political, and economic networks of merchants and traders in fourteenth-century Florence made lending money less risky and borrowing more readily open to scrutiny. Fourth, in reducing risk and uncertainty, networks can enhance trust—in other members of the network, in the network itself, and in the reliability of information. So, in a way, a network historically has often been a form of information management.

All these benefits and access to them are described in the technical literature as "social capital," a resource that network members do not *own* but can use to their advantage. A network is not just a connection; it entails exchange over time: reciprocal, preferential, and mutually supportive action and conversation; in short, friendship (admittedly a slippery concept), a connection that is informal rather than official. Social capital can be accumulated, but it can also be depleted, or even lost. Networks offer not just the promise of inclusion, but also the possibility of exclusion—hence the contemporary fear of not being connected, often seen as something akin to social death. The fear is not new. As the fourteenth-century Tuscan author and merchant Paolo da Certaldo wrote, "a man without a friend is like a body without a soul," and "a man who loses his friends is worse than dead." Access to social capital is not distributed evenly. It is easier for the privileged to acquire it, and when they do so, they gain further advantages over others.

Not least because they are not institutions (though they may depend on them), networks are also very much in the business of conserving and sustaining themselves. Communication among members of a network has often included extended discussions about how best to keep the network intact, how to maintain contact and to ensure the circulation of information and goods among its members—by internet, email, encryption, post/mail, private courier, friends and business associates, the diplomatic bag—and how to avoid obstacles to its transmission, such as censors, police, spies and customs officials, marauding warriors (cyber or real), or clumsy and incompetent carriers.

Equally important to networks is the question of how best to conserve, secure, and stabilize information, both when it is moving and when it needs storing. This might seem a much less significant obstacle in a virtual world than in one made up of networks of paper, print, and things. Transferring a series of electronic files from Shanghai to Rio de Janeiro by computer is clearly easier and swifter (though not necessarily safer) than shipping a container full of paper. But the networks of the virtual world, like almost all social networks, have a large and vulnerable material component; using an ineffable term like *"the cloud" brilliantly conceals the phone lines, fiber optics, satellites, thousands of miles of cables, and vast data warehouses (in 2015 data centers used 3 percent of the world's electricity and produced 2 percent of global emissions, almost the same carbon footprint as the airline industry) that underpin virtual communication. All this requires maintenance. And virtual information is, as yet, more difficult to conserve over time than its traditional precursors.

But network maintenance and conservation have never been merely a matter of technical support. Above all they have involved interpersonal activity to sustain social bonds—acts of friendship and trust, gift giving and kindness, the sharing of knowledge and technique—that help sustain the network. One of the most important ways to extend this, as evident in the twenty-first as in the fourteenth century (though its style, form, and content have changed), has been the letter of introduction and recommendation.

What does the network do for the student of networks rather than for the networkers themselves? It makes visible and tangible what is often concealed. It is a cliché of network analysis that those inside a network, though they can see those who are closest to them, are often unable to envisage the network as a whole, or see its full extent and ramifications. But this emphasis on formal structure conceals the degree to which the network is often a powerful imaginary for networkers, made up of circulated stories, shared values, and activities, in which content matters to them more than form. Networkers can be perfectly well informed about what is necessary to make networks more or less effective without knowing their boundaries. These become important only when a network begins to fragment or fail.

There have been two main approaches to network analysis (though they rarely acknowledge one another): social network theory (SNT), sometimes and more accurately called social network analysis (SNA), and actor network theory (ANT). The former is chiefly concerned with the relationship between social behavior, network structure, and its outcomes; the latter with explaining how, through the use of instruments, tools, and particular work practices, certain scientific facts and insights come to be made, disseminated, and accepted. The two approaches have sometimes been rigorously applied in writing the history of information, but more usually their insights have been used selectively as helpful analytic tools.

Social network analysis seeks to map the ties, the constraining and enabling dimensions and distribution of patterned relationships, and to express them with varying degrees of mathematical precision. A key concept for this analysis is "homophily"—"birds of a feather flock together"—based on the observation that the same kinds of people are drawn to one another and often inhabit the same space: courtiers in a sixteenth-century ducal court, humanists in a university, philosophes in an eighteenth-century Paris *salon, business entrepreneurs in a nineteenth-century international exhibition, scriptwriters in a Hollywood coffee shop, and "friends" on a social media site. The combination of homophily and proximity (which media like the written letter and the internet free from geographical constraints) leads them to influence one another, so they become more and more alike. Such groups, made up of nodes (people or groups), and connected by ties (or edges), make up networks that configure in different ways, and which are often most easily understood through graphic visualization. There are three main types of such networks: ego networks attached to an individual person or node, like the remarkable correspondence networks of European savants such as the jurist Hugo Grotius (7,725 letters), the religious reformer Ignatius Loyola (six thousand letters), the humanist Desiderius Erasmus (three thousand letters), and the Enlightened historian, critic, and philosophe Voltaire (nineteen thousand letters to and from fourteen hundred correspondents); bounded networks within organizations, such as the employees at CERN that Berners-Lee helped connect; and open networks such as the *Republic of Letters whose boundaries are flexible and indeterminate.

For the social network analyst looking at the operations of a network as a whole, its distribution and density are vital—the number and type of connections between nodes, the extent to which they work reciprocally or involve more than one type of connection (say employment, kinship, religion), the distance between those that are furthest apart, the ease with which nodes can link through others—all these affect a network's capacities and function. A densely connected network aids social cohesion and shared ideas, but within it there may be points (so-called structural holes) where two different parts are joined through one individual person, an essential go-between if the network is to survive. Another position of equal importance is occupied by those with weak ties to the network. They are sometimes bridges between tightly knit network segments or connect one network to another and are therefore more likely to bring new information, knowledge, and insight into the network. For example, the network of geologists that Cuvier relied on for his anatomical fossils included a cluster of mutually acquainted Italian savants scattered through the Italian peninsula, but the key figures in sparking new initiatives and new connections within the Italian network were two figures who connected the Italians to the rest of Europe: a Swiss watchmaker and amateur savant in Geneva, Stefano Moricand, and a young Irish geologist, Joseph Barclay Pentland, working for Cuvier, who shuttled between Paris, England, and Italy.

Even when historical source constraints have prevented full-blown SNT analysis, the method has confirmed the importance of go-betweens and intermediaries bridging boundaries, figures on the margins (in several different senses) who are anything but marginal: interpreters and translators, diplomats and spies, international bankers, and anyone on the cusp of different cultures, like the Cantonese compradors (agents) in nineteenth-century Hong Kong, whose combination of language skills in English and Cantonese, and local expertise in employment, insurance, shipping, and banking, made them indispensable to the British and American trading houses in China. The importance of such figures is one of the few areas shared by SNT and actor network theory.

The more intermediate skills a go-between was able to use, the greater his or her ability to connect different networks. Johann Georg Wille (1715–1808), a German engraver who lived and worked in Paris, linked three overlapping networks: an international community of engravers and artists from all over Europe, more than seventy of whom were his pupils; a wealthy community of art collectors and their dealers, notably German, Russian, and Danish aristocrats, in which Wille was a prominent *marchand-amateur* (gentleman dealer); and a body of critics and writers, including his friends Denis Diderot, the philosopher Johann Gottfried Herder, and the art critic Johann Joachim Winckelmann. His place at the junction of these networks enabled him to become one of the most important cultural brokers between the French and German *Enlightenments. Wille's movement among networks was not geographical—after 1739 he never left Paris—but the result of juggling a congeries of identities, a stratagem often associated with the role of intermediary, whose opportunities for reinvention were great. He enjoyed, of course, working in a medium that was both reproductive and visual—not constrained by language. He was at once German and French, an artisan teacher of manual skills, the conveyor of tacit knowledge, and a connoisseur whose taste was expressed in his collections and his criticism (written in both French and German). He promoted French engraving outside France, and Flemish art and German criticism within it. An art dealer and factotum to the European aristocracy, he still retained his independence as a critic. His importance as a sedentary intermediary not just within but between networks was sustained by the constant movement of his pupils, fellow collectors, literary friends, objects, and texts, whose circulation spread and nurtured his reputation. Although he refused frequent invitations to travel, he was indefatigable in encouraging the movement of everyone and thing except himself.

Johann Georg Wille, as the steady but protean center of a constantly moving network of people—pupils, critics, and collectors—and objects—books, journals, paintings, reproductive engravings—makes a suitable object not just for social network analysis but for actor network theory. This theory is best known for two controversial claims: first, that *facts and knowledge are not found but made (constructivism), and that their status therefore depends less on their truth than on the ways in which they secure acceptability within a community or network; and, second, that in networks inanimate and non-human objects—natural or artificial—enjoy the same status as persons as "actants" making facts. Rather than adjudicating these claims, it is more constructive to consider how these sorts of assertion contribute to an understanding of networks more generally. (This seems apt given that many proponents of ANT have argued that it is not a theory, but rather a changing "repertoire," and that this is precisely its strength.) If SNA points to the importance of network *structure* in understanding how networks work, then ANT argues for examining their *processes*—whether of creation or discovery—in order to comprehend their role in knowledge production, dissemination, and legitimation, what is described as "the work of ordering." The view is dynamic and sees travel and circulation—like the movement of Wille's friends, pupils, and artifacts—as vital to the spread of information and the creation of knowledge, while also grappling with the vexed question of the stability of knowledge that circulates. Hence the interest in "immutable mobiles," texts, images, and objects whose combination in "centers of calculation" makes possible the creation of scientific knowledge, fabricated from materials from a variety of peripheries. (The view has rightly been criticized as somewhat "imperial" in its perspective.)

Given the rapid advance of *artificial intelligence, and that "bots" now send us birthday greetings, and tell us what we need (after a recent accident I was advised of the need for burial insurance), it is not hard in the world of AI to see nonhumans as actants. But networks have invariably depended on a complex relationship between technologies, material culture, and human agency. The technical and material environment, broadly conceived, can at the very least be seen as a necessary condition or as an affordance of certain sorts of network: writing, paper, and posts for correspondence networks; printing and graphic media for a public sphere; precious metals, coin, and paper money, or certain sorts of commodity for mercantile and business networks. More specifically, materials like Wille's designs and engravings, which circulated with his former pupils through Europe, helped constitute networks of knowledge and taste, shaping, for instance, the designs to be found on Meissen porcelain. Examining these interrelations (while avoiding technological determinism) is essential in understanding the historically specific nature of networks—their operations, powers, and constraints.

Clearly networks are a powerful mechanism of social action and for the dissemination of information, and an illuminating way to analyze them. The proponents of networks (those who take a prescriptive view) lavish on them an abundance of positive qualities: efficiency, flatness, speed, adaptiveness, and the revelation that knowledge often depends less on individual genius than on flexible cooperation or vigorous rivalry. Questions of cause and effect, of how networks come into being rather than what they do when they exist, tend to take a back seat; too often networks just "are." And network thinking has rightly been criticized as too insular, formal, and abstract, paying insufficient attention to issues of difference or reducing them to a question of access to or exclusion from the network. Networks may appear (or be represented as) flat, but as only the most superficial glance at Wille's networks demonstrates, actors are not equal; they are teachers and pupils, aristocrats and commoners, savants and artisans, all mindful of their standing. Networks are not a class-free zone, nor are they just made up of individuals. And it is not clear why or where networks begin or end. Yet the boundaries we draw—who is in, who is out—significantly affect how we understand such processes as knowledge creation. Writing a history of botanical knowledge, do we include the findings of Indigenous collectors and informants, or confine our network to better-known (to us) European collectors? The shape and extent of the network affects the story that we tell. Or, perhaps more accurately, the story we tell affects the network we build. In short networks and network analysis are powerful tools but need to be exercised with caution, a prudence best exercised by treating them less as ideals and more by attending to their specific histories.

John Brewer

See also computers; digitization; globalization; knowledge; letters; money; newspapers; public sphere; social media; travel

FURTHER READING

Manuel Castells, *The Information Age: Economy, Society and Culture*, 3 vols., 1996–2002; Bonnie Erickson, "Social Networks and History: A Review Essay," *Historical Methods* 30, no. 3 (1997): 149–57; Niall Ferguson, *The Square and the Tower: Networks and Power, from the Freemasons to Facebook*, 2018; Charles Kadushin, *Understanding Social Networks: Theories, Concepts, and Findings*, 2012; Hannah Knox, Mike Savage, and Penny Harvey, "Social Networks and the Study of Relations: Networks as Method, Metaphor and Form," *Economy and Society* 35, no. 1 (2006): 113–40; Mike Michael, *Actor-Network Theory: Trials, Trails and Translations*, 2017; W. Powell, "Neither Hierarchy nor Market: Network Forms of Organization," *Research in Organizational Behavior* 12 (1990): 295–336; Simon Schaffer, Lissa Roberts, Kapil Raj, and James Delbourgo, *The Brokered World: Go-Betweens and Global Intelligence 1770–1820*, 2009.

NEWSLETTERS

The newsletter is a *genre that communicates a particular kind of information within a particular kind of relationship. The information involves events, which are understood to be relevant and factual. This need not imply, however, that the news is current or recent, or even reliable or trustworthy, as much that passed in *early modern news exchange was neither of these things. Anything that was mutually recognized as news in a communication, whether by word of mouth, by letter, or in print, anything that was accepted in answer to the question *What news?* was news. A newsletter communicates news in writing, in manuscript or print, from one or more correspondents to one or more recipients, sent by post or messenger. The conventions of the form, which originate in purely practical circumstances, were soon appropriated for imaginary purposes, so the writers and recipients as well as the post or messenger could be fictional. These elements were turned into imaginative devices to create the illusion of personal communication, much as the letter form transforms the human voice into writing, to imply a virtual presence.

A letter involves speaking across distance in order to communicate to a real or implied reader what he or she wants or needs to know—so there is a way in which almost all letters involve news. However, a *newsletter* is something more than the area where these two terms overlap. Angel Day wrote in 1586 that the letter was "the messenger and familiar speeche of the absent." The messenger brings news, which complements "familiar speech," by which Day means personal, informal, sociable (and relating to the family). However, the early modern newsletter was a narrower and more precise form than this suggests. The newsletter was a material vehicle in which news was conveyed, and a set of conventions for presenting news. The medium is not reducible to the news it contains, and news isn't reducible to the medium that conveyed it.

There were forms of newsletters in medieval Europe. We find them—intermittent and informal—in the communications in England among the Paston family, 1422–1509, sent by couriers and friends between Norfolk and London. Before Marin Sanudo's famous diary, covering 1496–1533, there was that of another Venetian, Antonio Morisino, from the first half of the fifteenth century, who recorded various pieces of news extracted from newsletters usually reporting on a single event. And in the archive of Biagio Dolfin, Venetian consul in Alexandria 1418–20, there survive both single-topic newsletters and digests containing multiple paragraphs of impersonal news. These forms of communication passed among and between merchants and state officials. "It is impossible to trade without news," wrote one merchant in 1401; so understood was this that mercantile companies formally established shared carrier services, named *scarsella* after the bags used to transport letters. Anticipating the postal service, scarsella systems are at least as old as the early fourteenth century, when they developed in Tuscany. Thus when the formal, semipublic *avvisi* system developed, as discussed below, this was the outcome of a rich group of existing practices, not the start of entirely new ones.

The newsletter as a form or medium of communication evolved and spread rapidly across Europe from 1450 to 1600, then remained consistent until about 1800. Personal letters containing news changed a great deal during this same period, but the newsletter as a genre remained recognizable and flourished in a stable form because it served an essential social function in Europe—and indeed can be said to have shaped the geography of Europe. The newsletter was one of several *complementary* vehicles, that is, newsletters were read alongside other documents, or received with spoken reports, in order to obtain the news an individual reader wanted. And the openness to complementary communications is one of the things that defines early modern news media. There was no notion that one might communicate "all the news that's fit to print," because readers always received news from multiple sources, and frequently compared them.

There were two kinds of newsletters, both in manuscript and in print, whether personal or commercial: those that described a single event, and those that described several events, or reported news from several places, in distinct paragraphs. In *Too Much to Know*, Ann Blair describes how information in this period circulated and was recycled in "morsels," and the morsel of news was not the event but the paragraph. This is because of the uses of news in European politics, and to understand why these uses necessitated both the paragraph and the newsletter we must turn to two fields that developed regular newsletters to facilitate the conduct of their business: diplomacy and international trade.

With the introduction of resident ambassadors in late fifteenth-century Europe, states developed a semiformal means of communication. Ambassadors would send to their home city weekly reports of locally accumulated news; these reports would then be gathered up and sent back to all ambassadors, in paragraphs headed by source date and location (which was not always the place that the news concerned). Ambassadors then knew where the intelligence—which was an invaluable currency in the conduct of their office—originated and how old it was. Thus began the convention of paragraphs of news with the *metadata preserved. (Earlier merchants' paragraphs of news, though sometimes similar, were less diligent on this point.) The diplomatic system was a *leaky one, and both the news it gathered and the practices associated with it seeped into broader society. The paragraphs were recycled by other professional news writers, and when news, originating with an ambassador or another scribe, was passed on, this metadata was preserved and added to. A typical paragraph of news might begin: "Amsterdam, 23 May. By letters from Venice dated the last week we hear news of a battle in Ragusa, where the Turk. . . ." The newsletter form that originated in ambassadorial communications was known as the *avviso*—a term with equivalents in most western European languages— and the avviso became the standard form for all newsletters reporting multiple events.

Merchants had relied on the exchange of information over distance, communicated by (irregular) messenger, from the fourteenth century or earlier. Mercantile news combined morsels of news, relating to war and politics, with specifically financial and commercial news. The latter was regularized into a variety of forms that accompanied newsletters, including bills of entries or customhouse bills (daily lists of commodities that were imported or exported at any given port), price currents (lists of commodities and their prices on the local market), and exchange rate currents (weekly lists of exchange rates). This kind of data was increasingly kept distinct from the more general news exchanged within and between merchants' communities. *Lloyd's List*—a printed weekly journal listing the ships arriving in and departing from British and overseas ports— was founded by the coffee merchant Edward Lloyd in the 1690s and still survives; while certainly innovative, it was also precisely typical of specialization of news forms that were intended to supplement newsletters. The famous collection of newsletters belonging to the Fuggers, dated 1568–1605, which were once thought to be the product of the family's own news-gathering networks, is in fact made up of merely standard avvisi, commercially available across Europe. This shows the scholarly predisposition to mistake the routine for the exceptional; but it also shows that the rise of the avvisi provided an important and transformative service for merchants, allowing them to replace an expensive source for *some* of their news with a cheaper, general product.

Paragraphs of news were shared in marketplaces, church porches, barbershops, and, later, *coffeehouses. In cities with merchants, early modern *scriptoria, and printing houses, paragraphs were copied by hand, translated, recombined, added to, and printed. The entrepôts were the nodes in a network of news communication that traversed Europe. When a major news event provided reports that were longer than the typical diplomatic dispatch of paragraph—such as the battles of Chioggia, Lepanto, or Chaldiran—a single-subject news report would be written; this would be communicated as a "separate," an independent document that could accompany a personal letter or an avviso or both, or be sold separately, or turned into a printed pamphlet. The separate was frequently in letter form, containing an eyewitness account, or an account gathered from several sources but digested within an authorial or editorial voice; alternatively, it might assume the form of an impersonal document, though the news content was similar or identical in both cases.

The content of these newsletters, in both forms, included politics, ceremonial reports from courts, military dispatches, and news of trade, disasters, and to a lesser extent crimes and news of wonders and sensation. In early seventeenth-century Oxford Robert Burton would describe the news as a burdensome superfluity:

> I hear new news every day, and those ordinary rumours of war, plagues, fires, inundations, thefts, murders, massacres, meteors, comets, spectrums, prodigies, apparitions, of towns taken, cities besieged in France, Germany, Turkey, Persia, Poland, &c., daily musters and preparations, and such like, which these tempestuous times afford, battles fought, so many men slain, monomachies, shipwrecks, piracies, and sea-fights; peace, leagues, stratagems, and fresh alarms. A vast confusion of vows, wishes, actions, edicts, petitions, lawsuits, pleas, laws, proclamations, complaints, grievances, are daily brought to our ears. New books every day, pamphlets, currantoes, stories, whole catalogues of volumes of all sorts, new paradoxes, opinions, schisms, heresies, controversies in philosophy, religion, &c.

The *hyperbole* and *copia* express the wonder, but the summary is representative.

The development of this culture of news depended on improving transport infrastructure, and especially on the creation of postal services in the early sixteenth century, which replaced earlier, more expensive carriers. States and rulers discovered the benefits of outsourcing the use of staging posts as a means of sending messages. These postal services were opened to the public as a means of defraying costs and improving efficiency. By the early seventeenth century much of Europe was covered by long-distance postal services (which could be complemented at the local level by private messengers and carriers). Some involved international transport, but even where this was not available it was possible to send letters by more than one postal service. The geography of early modern news is closely related to the geography of the early modern post. This is also true of temporality: the weekly periodicity of postal services shaped the practices of gathering news and determined the speeds at which it jumped across Europe. It is because of this communications network that we can find the same paragraph of news in a manuscript newsletter in Italian in Venice one month, and in a printed newsletter in Spanish in Madrid two months later.

The newsletter forms were developed within manuscript communication in the fifteenth and early sixteenth centuries, beginning in Italy and then moving north and west. From the early sixteenth century both avvisi and separate newsletters were occasionally printed, initially when a significant event happened. The early printed forms of news were entirely derived from the manuscript culture and were an opportunistic response by printers and *publishers to the resources—of text, paper, and printing equipment—that were at hand. When printed news periodicals appeared in the early seventeenth century—in Germany, the Netherlands, England, France, and, later, Spain and Italy and other European states—they were printed versions of avvisi. The reliability or credibility—and we shouldn't underestimate the careful skepticism of early modern newsreaders—depended on the system that communicated the news, not on the personal authority of the reporter. This printed form developed over decades, and different regions of Europe gradually acculturated the form, adapting it to local printing practices, and adding local news, but the form remained embedded in the printed newspaper through to the end of the handpress period.

There is an important degree of continuity here. Paragraphs have a continuous life as they move among cities, genres, languages, and modes of reproduction, even while they are transformed and recombined in different ways. The forms move too, and the newsletter continues to exist in manuscript and printed forms even as it changes. The newsletter was an international form in essence, and it constituted a community of shared news among writers and readers who did not directly communicate among themselves, but instead participated in a network. It was this that gave Europe a political identity in the early modern period.

The newsletter—as something other than a personal communication—disappeared into commercial media in the age of nationalism, of revolutions, and of capital. If we look for it in the industrial and postindustrial world we can find analogs, though that vital continuity with the earlier newsletter does not exist. We can, however, find corporate newsletters, in which an artificial body, such as a university, brings together a community of customers and employees, albeit these units do not necessarily participate voluntarily. An analog can be found on the *internet in the form of news digest websites, or services such as Nuzzle, which identify news stories that are shared by people with whom you are virtually connected. It is the algorithm that has replaced the newsletter in the twenty-first century.

Joad Raymond

See also journals; letters; networks; newspapers; postal customers; public sphere; readers

FURTHER READING

Ann M. Blair, *Too Much to Know: Managing Scholarly Information before the Modern Age*, 2010; "Die Fuggerzeitungen: Ein Frühneuzeitliches Informationsmedium und seine Erschließung," (online); Mario Infelise, "From Merchants' Letters to Handwritten Political *Avvisi*: Notes on the Origins of Public Information," in *Cultural Exchange in Early Modern Europe*, vol. 3, *Correspondence and Cultural Exchange in Europe 1400–1700*, edited by Francisco Bethencourt and Florike Egmond, 2007, 33–52; idem, *Prima dei Giornali: Alle Origini della Pubblica Informazione, secoli XVI e XVII*, 2002; Juraj Kittler, "Caught between Business, War, and Politics: Late Medieval Roots of the Early Modern European News Networks," *Mediterranean Historical Review* 33, no. 2 (2018): 199–222; Joad Raymond and Noah Moxham, eds., *News Networks in Early Modern Europe*, 2016; Will Slauter, "Le paragraphe mobile: Circulation et transformation des informations dans le monde atlantique du 18e siècle" and "The Paragraph as Information Technology: How News Traveled in the Eighteenth-Century Atlantic World," *Annales HSS* 67, no. 2 (2012): 253–78, 363–89.

NEWSPAPERS

In 1605 Johann Carolus of Strasbourg applied to the local magistrates for permission to print his weekly news service. This is now universally accepted as the first newspaper. Europe already had a lively market for printed news, and an established *genre of manuscript news services (known as *avvisi*). Carolus himself ran one such news agency, so his new print version was in effect mechanizing an existing service. The Strasbourg *Relation* is the first newssheet taken to meet the criteria that distinguish a newspaper from other forms of printed information: regularity, frequency, general availability (in contrast to the limited readership of the manuscript avvisi), and a miscellany of news reports.

The new innovation spread very quickly, particularly in the German Empire (Strasbourg was at this point a German city). The year 1631 saw the foundation of the Paris *Gazette*, a state-sponsored venture that would, with regional reprints, hold an effective monopoly of printed news in France for 150 years. The newspapers also found a ready audience in the Dutch Republic. By 1618, Amsterdam had two competing weekly newssheets, each of which would be in continuous publication for over fifty years (elsewhere, newspapers often failed to find a sustainable commercial model and quickly failed). The Dutch were also the first to introduce paid advertising, first for newly published books, then for other goods and services. This showed the way toward commercial viability: elsewhere in Europe newspapers often depended on government subsidy to continue publishing. In England, confusions of royal policy inhibited the growth of the press, but with the foundation of the London *Gazette* in 1665, the English press embarked on a trajectory that would, with the growth of London and precocious party politics, soon place it at the center of the newspaper world.

The seventeenth century also saw the development of an embryonic code of journalistic ethics. The difficulties of news supply obliged newspapermen to pay special attention to the accuracy and reliability of news reports. Newspapers were careful to record when a report was uncorroborated or uncertain. The first papers relied on a miscellany of reports from around the European news hubs. Those who gathered the news, often also the suppliers of the more exclusive manuscript news services, remained largely invisible: none of the reports in the newspapers, headed only with a terse dateline ("from Rome, 3 January") were signed. The editor played no organizational role beyond choosing which news to place in the newspaper, typically a miscellany of ten to fifteen short paragraphs totaling around two thousand words. The reports were presented with no commentary or explanation. Newspapers had no opinion: the concept of the editorial lay far in the future.

This high-minded austerity began to break down in the eighteenth century, first in England under the pressure of party politics, then with the American and French Revolutions. In London, the audience for news was large enough to sustain competing Whig and Tory papers. To defend his policies, Prime Minister Robert Walpole assembled a stable of newspapers whose editorial loyalty was ensured by government subsidy.

Despite the high-profile campaigns by John Wilkes for liberty of speech, most London newspapers remained paid instruments of either government or opposition to the end of the century. In the American colonies, the high-minded principle of political neutrality, eloquently encapsulated by Benjamin Franklin, was sustained until the Stamp Act Crisis of 1765. The attempt to impose on the colonial papers the same regime of taxation applied in London united the colonial press in indignant opposition. Although the Stamp Act was quickly withdrawn, the newspapers remained politically engaged. In France, the revolutionary years produced a torrent of new publications, many essentially publicity vehicles for revolutionary leaders such as Robespierre, Marat, and Brissot. Yet some principles survived the revolutionary assault: although newspapers engaged in vigorous mutual denunciation, they did not compete on price.

One of Napoleon's first acts on taking power was to rein in the press. The reactionary regimes established in continental Europe after the Congress of Vienna (1815) generally followed suit. In the United States, in contrast, the newspapers were rewarded for their patriotic fervor by a constitutional guarantee of press freedom. As important, and uniquely, the federal post office was obliged to transport newspapers at low cost: this was a conscious attempt to create an informed political nation. Between 1776 and 1800, the number of newspapers in the United States increased from twenty-five to 230. By 1850, this had grown to twenty-five hundred, including 373 dailies.

In many respects, the nineteenth century was the golden age of the newspaper. Innovations in design and business practice, technological breakthroughs, and a huge advance in male and female *literacy created a true mass market. Newspapers led political debate and became by far the most important suppliers of news. On the production side, the most crucial innovation was the incremental introduction from the 1820s of the steam press. This allowed a huge multiplication of the number of copies that could be printed in a day, crucial in the major metropolitan markets, London, Paris, and New York. But the costs of the new technology were prohibitively high, and traditional handpresses continued to be used in the smaller markets (here, the substitution of an iron frame for the wooden handpress had already doubled production capacity).

The advent of the railways improved distribution and offered some improvement in the speed of news gathering. Here the crucial, transforming innovation was the invention of the telegraph (1837). In contrast to the telephone at the end of the century, the telegraph spread quickly. Access to news improved immeasurably, particularly for newspapers outside the metropolitan hubs. In the 1860s and 1870s, the introduction of wood-pulp paper reduced production costs.

Newspapermen were not slow to realize the opportunities of the new reading public. In 1830s New York, two innovative editors, Benjamin Day (the *Sun*) and James Gordon Bennett (*New York Herald*), published papers that mixed trenchant political commentary with reports of lurid crimes and local scandal: certainly there was no return to the age of innocence, and little pretense of objectivity. Most newspapers took a strongly political stance, and many editors, among them Horace Greeley and Whitelaw Reid, harbored political ambitions. In continental Europe political turbulence, especially the revolutions of 1848, were propelled by a mass of newly published newspapers. When the revolutions were extinguished, so was the radical press.

Outside the United States, press controls, either by taxation or by prepublication censorship, were dismantled only in the period 1860–80. Even after this, most newspapers were solid supporters of the prevailing political and social orthodoxies. This was even more the case as newspapers expanded over the globe with the imperial powers. India had its first paper, the *Bengal Gazette*, in 1780; in Australia the *Sydney Gazette* was established in 1803. Newspapers reached New Zealand with the first major immigrant settlement in 1839; Hong Kong had its government *Gazette* in 1841. Another enduring legacy of the nineteenth century was the establishment of the press agencies: Reuters in 1851, the Associated Press in 1848, and the Press Association in 1868. They continue to play a vital role today in providing newspapers around the world with a supply of copy.

In the twentieth century, the birth of radio, then television, challenged the newspaper monopoly of fresh news. Newspapers adapted, with more pages and new features, reflecting the new appetite among customers with increased leisure time and spending power for sports news and soft lifestyle stories. Improvements in photography opened further new avenues for reporting and more attractive designs. Journalism finally became a recognized profession, with the first training courses, and attempts by men like Walter Lippmann to adumbrate new theories of ethical journalism. These ethical principles were sorely tested by the great world conflicts of 1914–18 and 1939–45. In Soviet Russia, Germany, and Italy the press became the supine vehicle of government propaganda; in the fighting democracies, the search for victory imposed irresistible pressures toward conformity. In occupied countries such as the Netherlands, a vibrant underground press helped salvage battered self-respect, as it would again in communist Eastern Europe between 1945 and 1989.

None of these existential challenges damaged demand for newspapers. Despite the competition of broadcasting, circulation remained strong, though a consolidation of local markets gradually reduced the number of titles. The *digital challenge, at the end of the twentieth century, was of a different order. The inexorable progress of the *internet giants gave new consumers unmediated access to multiple sources of free news, and, most crucially, ravaged newspapers' advertising income. The number of journalists employed fell precipitately as newspapers frantically cut costs. Some were able to compete by entering the digital market as purveyors of online news, trading on their established authority and professionalism. This was all the more welcome as the cacophony of news stories placed the core values of truth telling and objective reporting under ever greater strain. For the first time in over four centuries, the place of newspapers in the ecology of news and political debate seems seriously under threat.

Andrew Pettegree

See also censorship; newsletters; political reporting

FURTHER READING

Siv Gøril Brandtzæg, Paul Goring, and Christine Watson, *Travelling Chronicles: News and Newspapers from the Early Modern Period to the Eighteenth Century*, 2018; Filippo de Vivo, *Information and Communication in Venice: Rethinking Early Modern Politics*, 2007; Julia Guarneri, *Newsprint Metropolis: City Papers and the Making of Modern Americans*, 2017; Richard John and Jonathan Silberstein-Loeb, *Making News: The Political Economy of Journalism from the Glorious Revolution to the Internet*, 2015; Andrew Pettegree, *The Invention of the News*, 2014; Arthur der Weduwen and Andrew Pettegree, *The Dutch Republic and the Birth of Modern Advertising*, 2020.

NOTEBOOKS

Notebooks have been used both to capture fleeting and inchoate information at the start of intellectual projects and to make extracts from already sanctioned bodies of knowledge. The former role may explain the special power notebooks have exercised over our imaginations: they promise something not contained in books and other records, perhaps something lost or suppressed, or an insight into the creative process. Hence biographers and historians of art, music, and science have scrutinized the diaries and working papers of individuals such as Leonardo da Vinci, Ludwig van Beethoven, and Charles Darwin. The second function is equally important: notes taken from published material have been recombined with notes from various sources—testimony, observation, experiment, reflection—to generate new knowledge.

Note taking has a longer history than the notebook. From the eighth or seventh century BCE, Babylonian scribes made nightly observations of the sky in monthly reports now called "astronomical diaries." The earliest surviving example dates from 652 BCE. Evidence of what might also be regarded as note taking is found on Egyptian *ostraka*—fragments of pottery (usually limestone). One of these dated to circa 1250 BCE, held in the British Museum, is a register of workmen's attendances over a 280-day period. In the heart of Roman London, wooden writing tablets (ca. 140 mm wide × 110 mm high) dated to the first century of the Common Era were found in the excavations of a temple to Mithras (built about 240 CE). A recess was carved into the faces of these tablets and filled with a thin layer of blackened beeswax; a needle-pointed stylus was used to scratch a short message (often about provisions and financial transactions) on the waxed surface. Pliny the Elder (23–79 CE), the author of *Natural History* (in thirty-seven books), collected extracts from his reading in *commentarii* (notebooks). Pliny the Younger reported that his uncle bequeathed to him "160 notebooks of selected passages." It is likely that these extracts were copied on to *papyrus rolls rather than bound in *codex form; the latter was a practice not regularly preferred for another two centuries.

It was not until the mid-1500s that the notebook took the form of a small bound "paperbook" comprising pages of blank paper. According to the *Oxford English Dictionary* (*OED*), this word was first used in about 1548, slightly before "notebook" (or "note-booke") in 1568. Since then there have been two main kinds of notebook—the *commonplace book and the journal (or diary). In principle, commonplace books stored information under categories and topics, whereas journals of various kinds were predicated on *daily* entries. The words *journal* (*OED*, ca. 1540s), *day-book* (1571), and *diary* (1581) betray this focus, as do *diario* and *Tagebuch*.

Explicit discussion about the format of commonplace notebooks was evident from the time of the European *Renaissance. Thanks to the legacy of the Roman rhetoricians Cicero and Quintilian, humanist authors such as Erasmus of Rotterdam promoted the habit of making notes under *tituli* (titles) or headings, adapting the Latin notion of *loci communes* (common places). By the late 1500s, this practice was established in grammar schools, universities, and private scholarship as a way of storing *copia* (abundant material) for the purposes of conversation, oratory, and literary composition. The terms *book of Common Places* and *commonplace book* (1578) referred to a notebook in which excerpts from classical Latin authors such as Ovid, Virgil, Horace, Cicero, and Seneca the Younger (and also contemporaries such as Michel de Montaigne and Francis Bacon) were kept under topical headings, such as friendship, honor, and constancy. In his *De ratione studii* (1512), Erasmus urged that students "have at the ready some commonplace book of systems and topics, so that wherever something noteworthy occurs he may write it down in the appropriate column." This method of keeping like with like was believed to assist memory in two ways: first, to stimulate recollection (a process of searching, distinct from immediate recall) of both the information summarized and other related details and ideas, which themselves provoke trains of thought; and second, to serve as external records of information that dispense with the need for memorization via regular rehearsal of content. The benefit, therefore, of a carefully kept notebook was that it could function as a *secondary memory (memoria secundaria)*, or what Jonathan Swift in his "Letter of Advice to a Young Poet" (1721) called a "supplemental memory." Many manuals from the early seventeenth century on extolled the virtues of various methods of taking notes—some recommended immediate storage of excerpts under headings, others a register in the order in which one read; the transfer of these latter notes to a commonplace book was compared with the procedure of merchants who entered daily transactions in a "waste book" before recording them systematically in a journal and ledger. Practices were as varied as the men and women who compiled the notebooks.

Conversely, the terms *journal, diary,* and *day-book* referred to notebooks that registered day-by-day (diurnal) events, natural phenomena, and ideas. Moreover, whereas commonplace books were mainly for private use, journals served both personal and institutional functions. *Jesuits and Puritans inculcated the habit of keeping spiritual diaries in which individuals entered both sins and prayers. In a sermon of 1631 John Donne underlined one rationale: "God . . . sees their sins . . . and in his Ephemerides, his journals, he writes them downe." Outside strictly religious practice, almanacs (usually small duodecimo booklets) were often stitched into diaries, some providing blank pages for annotation, as in *A Blancke and Perpetuall Almanack* (1566), which promised to act "as a memorial . . . for any . . . that will make & keepe notes of any actes, deedes, or things that passeth from time to time." The *OED* gives 1581 as the earliest instance of "diary" as a notebook for recording "matters affecting the writer personally," a use that matches a line in Ben Jonson's *Volpone* (1605–6): "This is my diary, wherein I note my actions of the day." On almost every day in the diary he kept between 1672 and 1680, the experimental philosopher Robert Hooke noted his diet, health, and medical complaints—for example, "slept well but had windy pains in stomach and belly next morn . . . voided much urine" (January 28, 1673). In 1712 Joseph Addison declared that daily note taking was crucial to personal development, recommending to readers of the *Spectator* (no. 317, March 4, 1712) "the keeping a Journal of their Lives for one Week."

In institutional contexts, journals were incontestably the notebook of choice in the cases of parliamentary records, merchants' account books, ships' logbooks, travel reports (such as the Venetian *relazioni* [relations]), and weather registers. Bacon signaled this in 1605 when he said that "in enterprises memorable, as expeditions of Warre, Navigations, and the like, [it was usual] to keepe *Dyaries* of that which passeth continually." Published travel advice from the late 1500s, issued under the rubric of *ars apodemica* (the art of travel), provided explicit directions on what to note. The usual presentation of this advice under topics—for example, climate, ports, trade, fortifications, the structure of the society—indicates the abiding influence of the commonplace method even though, by the early 1600s, the *journal* became the more usual notebook for travelers. Some of the great scientific voyagers of the nineteenth century—Nicolas Baudin, Alexander von Humboldt, and Charles Darwin—chose journals as their notebooks of first response.

From the *early modern period, note taking played an important role in the collection of empirical information. Individuals engaged in scientific inquiry gathered material from books, testimony, observation, experiment, and their own thoughts. By the mid-1600s, notebooks included lists of things-to-do, *desiderata* (things desired), and "queries" or "inquiries." Increasingly, the information thus generated was entered in journal or diary form, even if later transferred to a commonplace book under a topic. Especially in the observational sciences, this method suited the need to record information (also "informations," in seventeenth-century usage) quickly as discrete "particulars," with an emphasis on storage and retrieval, rather than to impose a systematic or topical organization prematurely. With further analysis postponed, the imperative of rapid collection favored rough notes, often including time and place of events, observations, or experiments. To be effective, however, "*Diaries* of *wind* and *weather*" (as Robert Plot called them in 1677) demanded detail and discipline. The English physician and philosopher John Locke began to keep such a diary, or "Register," from June 24, 1666. He reserved a large number of pages in the back of a folio-sized commonplace book and ruled up columns for date and hour, for readings from a thermometer, a barometer, and (by July 30) a hygrometer, for observations of wind direction and velocity, and for general remarks, such as "rain," "fair," "cloudy." Locke displayed rare commitment, sometimes adding entries up to three or more times a day. Aware of the demands entailed by constant observation, the astronomer and architect Christopher Wren envisaged a self-recording device that would replace human note taking by making "a *Thermometer* to be its own *Register*." It was recognized, however, that personal notes could not contribute to a collaborative project unless they followed agreed conventions. Especially during the eighteenth century, scientific and medical societies in Europe attempted to standardize the manner in which empirical information was collected by issuing questionnaires and by giving instructions for ruling up notebooks. This stress on *protocol eventually governed all procedures in scientific laboratories, as the chemist Michael Faraday prescribed in 1827:

> A blank writing paper book should be upon the table, with pen and ink, to enter immediately the notes of experiments. . . . The Laboratory notebook, intended to receive the account of the results of experiments, should always be at hand, as should also pen and ink. . . . The practice of delaying to note until the end of a train of experiments or to the conclusion of the day, is a bad one, as it becomes difficult to accurately remember the succession of events.

The commonplace and journal formats do not exhaust the range of note taking evident from the 1600s. There were "loose" notes on slips and sheets of paper stitched together, as in the *zibaldoni* of Italian merchants from circa 1400. In his *Bibliotheca universalis* (Universal library) (1545–48), the Swiss humanist Conrad Gessner recommended a version of this technique as a way of indexing books and composing new ones. The Italian naturalist Ulisse Aldrovandi kept twelve thousand *cose diverse* (various things, including specimens, ideas, and observations) on slips stored in sacks. There were also numbered lists of queries or experiments, some in sets of one hundred items ("centuries"), as seen in the writings of Bacon and Robert Boyle. Loose notes did not necessarily break with all previous conventions: they could preserve chronological arrangement or carry topical headings; with numbering or coding, they could be linked to bound notebooks. Moreover, despite being loose, they retained the ability to trigger recollection, as Bacon recognized when he said in 1620 that "a host of circumstantial details or tags help the memory, as writing in discontinuous sections." Another advantage was that such notes could be physically moved and re-sorted, allowing reclassification of data and new combinations of ideas. This potential, however, depended on adequate storage and retrieval. In his *De arte excerpendi* (On the art of excerpting) (1689), a review of note-taking advice, Vincent Placcius promoted the invention of the Oxford graduate and rector Thomas Harrison, as outlined in a manuscript of 1640. Harrison's "Arca studiorum" (Ark of studies) was a cabinet that stored loose slips of paper on hooks fixed to thin brass plates bearing labels arranged in alphabetical order. In the examples Harrison gave, the headings on the labels were conventional ones (such as Love, God, Faith, Virtue) but he also mentioned assigning numerals to single slips, thereby implying that these alone, not topics or categories, could be effective markers. Some of Gottfried Wilhelm Leibniz's loose notes still bear the holes created by pinning them into a cabinet similar to the one designed by Harrison.

Paper slips, and then index cards, encouraged the notion of a note as a record of a discrete piece of information. In the mid-1600s, the German mathematician and philosopher Joachim Jungius used loose notes without a cabinet but stressed that each slip should contain only one *fact or idea, a principle forcefully stated in 1926 by the English historian Beatrice Webb. The use of slips and cards to register and store units of information was central to the work of the Belgian lawyer and bibliographer Paul Otlet. With Henry La Fontaine, he created the "Répertoire Bibliographique Universel" (Universal bibliographical directory), aiming to document information for worldwide access. Otlet sought not just to capture the publishing details of every book, but "to detach what the book amalgamates, to reduce all that is complex to its elements and to devote a page to each." At its foundation in 1895 the "Répertoire" contained some four hundred thousand entries on single pieces of paper and index cards; by 1914 there were eleven million. Searches of these entries relied on an elaborate version of Melvil Dewey's *universal decimal classification. In 1945, the American engineer Vannevar Bush put the emphasis on personal selection rather than universal repositories of information. His *"memex" (a contraction of either "memory extended" or "memory index") was a photoelectric machine designed to link documents (on microfilm) chosen by the owner, thereby superseding both index cards and library classification. Its "essential feature," according to Bush, was "the process of tying two items together"; multiple documents could be "joined together to form a trail" (before *"hypertext") that preserved the mental associations made by the user. Bush emphasized the capacity to revisit these trails, but the consequent repetition—of what William James called "habit-worn paths of association"—lacked the suppleness of loose notes in combination with notebooks.

From the 1970s, when new information technologies promised to displace the paper notebook, the word itself (or its variants) remained irresistible—as witnessed in the Tandy Corporation laptop computer the "Notebook" of 1983, the Xerox "NoteTaker" of 1978, and the Samsung "Galaxy Note 8" of 2017. These, and subsequent electronic devices, were marketed as personal machines that facilitated note taking, in part by offering greater speed of entry and retrieval. However, these benefits were questioned in an experimental study of 2014 that compared groups of individuals who took longhand notes at lectures with those who used a keyboard. The former group made shorter, less verbatim, and more considered notes and subsequently showed better recall of concepts—thereby possibly confirming early modern advice that such notes prompt recollection and thought. It may be that it is not the speed, but the interactive potential of *digital note taking that delivers the most significant advance: individuals can share notes in real time, thus fostering collaboration. We may not yet appreciate how the tasks of selecting, entering, storing, classifying, recollecting, reviewing, and retrieving information—supported over centuries by notebooks—have been affected by reliance on digital devices.

Richard Yeo

See also accounting; albums; art of memory; cards; computers; excerpting/commonplacing; files; indexing; journals; lists; memos; merchants; observing; secretaries; sermons; storage and search

FURTHER READING

Ann M. Blair, *Too Much to Know: Managing Scholarly Information before the Modern Age*, 2010; Vannevar Bush, "As We May Think," *Atlantic Monthly*, July 1945, 101–8; Noel Malcolm, "Thomas Harrison and His 'Ark of Studies': An Episode in the History of the Organization of Knowledge," *Seventeenth Century* 19 (2004): 196–232; Ann Moss, *Printed Commonplace-Books and the Structuring of Renaissance Thought*, 1996; Pam A. and Daniel M. Oppenheimer, "The Pen Is Mightier Than the Keyboard: Advantages of Longhand over Laptop Note Taking," *Psychological Science* 25 (2014): 1159–68; Paul Otlet, *International Organisation and Dissemination of Knowledge: Selected Essays of Paul Otlet*, edited by W. Boyd Rayward, 1990; Adam Smyth, *Autobiography in Early Modern England*, 2010; Roger S. O. Tomlin, *Roman London's First Voices: Writing Tablets from the Bloomberg Excavations, 2010–14*, 2016; Richard Yeo, *Notebooks, English Virtuosi, and Early Modern Science*, 2014.

OBSERVING

Human beings everywhere and always have observed: the clouds that portend fair or foul weather; the heft and texture of the animal fur that will spin into the finest wool; the faint markings that distinguish a succulent from a poisonous berry; the path of the sun through the ecliptic that heralds the seasons; the slightly raised eyebrow that betrays a courtier's intrigue; the effects of an herb on stomach pains; the discrepancies between words or hands that signal a variant text. Long before and long after scribal techniques such as writing, institutions such as libraries, and methods such as statistical correlation were invented, observers discerned subtle correlations between present signs and future events in both the natural and the human worlds. Because observed phenomena were often highly variable and sometimes unfolded on superhuman timescales, such correlations were the work of generations, codified, remembered, and transmitted in the form of proverbs: "Red in the morning / Sailors take warning." Observational proverbs both antedate and postdate written versions, whether in the exhortations to sow and reap in conjunction with the movements of heavenly bodies in the Hesiodic *Works and Days* (ca. 700 BCE) or in the recommendations of the latest editions of the *Farmers' Almanac*. Before the invention of reading and writing, sagacious observers were reading the world.

Observational knowledge is first and foremost correlational and predictive, rather than causal and explanatory. The Roman philosopher and statesman Marcus Tullius Cicero (106–43 BCE) described the correlations based on observation as "natural divination," which he deemed more reliable than divination based on dreams, auguries, sacrifices, and prodigies. But this distinction between reliable and spurious correlations among observations has always been blurred, whether in the case of medical observations of the symptoms of a patient that point to a diagnosis or financial observations of the stock market that indicate boom or bust. Observation and divination seem to have been intertwined since ancient times, and the correlations that survive from that period exhibit the same difficulty in sorting out reliable from unreliable conjecture that bedevils modern analyses of *big data. In ancient Mesopotamia scribes correlated bad harvests with the likelihood of war and other misfortunes; in ancient Rome and in many other cultures portents as diverse as the flights of birds and the entrails of sacrificial animals were read as heralding future events. Some of the most ambitious, systematic, and long-lived observational projects ever mounted, such as the six-hundred-year continuous tradition of the astrometeorological diaries kept by Babylonian scribes from the sixth century BCE to 60 CE, mingle the most stable (astronomical) and unstable (meteorological) phenomena. The art of observation consisted not only in the careful, persistent monitoring of things and events but also in the choice of those phenomena likely to yield strong, durable regularities.

Observation has always been an art, dependent on sagacity, attention, and the trained senses, and no one has ever doubted that it is a useful, indeed essential art. But its status as a scientific practice has been more controversial, rising and falling as the definition of science itself changed. In the Latin Middle Ages, *scientia* was understood by university-trained Aristotelian scholars as certain knowledge of universal causes, in the best instance knowledge that could be shown to be necessary through demonstration. According to this scheme, scientific knowledge was explanatory but rarely predictive. Although the Aristotelian corpus of books about nature is rich in observations of all kinds, from the color of various animals' eyes to the variety of smells and tastes, Aristotle himself considered such particulars to be history (*historia*, which embraces natural history as well the study of the past), a branch of knowledge preliminary and inferior to philosophy and even poetry, which deal in universals. Because Aristotle's empirical remarks aim at philosophical universals, they are almost always generic in character, about species rather than specifics. The other great treasure trove of empirical particulars bequeathed by Greco-Roman antiquity to later learned traditions in the Middle East, Mediterranean, and later in northern Europe, Pliny's *Natural History* (70s CE), did contain occasional items about individual cases (for example, a dog so loyal that it fished up its master's corpse from a river) but for the most part also described genera rather than specifics. Only in the ancient medical literature, notably in the Hippocratic corpus, were individual cases recounted in detail, a tradition that was to be enormously consequential for scientific observation when Hippocratic medicine enjoyed a revival in sixteenth-century Europe.

It is notable that these empirical remarks in ancient Greek and Latin and medieval authors are seldom called "observations": Aristotle used the Greek word *teresis* rarely, and then mostly in connection with animal behavior; the Latin word *observatio*, in keeping with its associations with the natural divination practiced by farmers, shepherds, sailors, and other outdoor laborers, was also not generally considered a learned activity, much less a philosophical category. The two most important exceptions were astronomy and medicine. In astronomy, observations of heavenly bodies stretching in some cases back to Babylonian as well as to Greco-Roman sources were at least partially transmitted through the works of the Alexandrian astronomer, astrologer, and geographer Claudius Ptolemy (ca. 100–ca. 170 CE) into learned traditions in, among others, Arabic, Persian, and Latin. However, the difficulty and expense of making new observations, much less of improving the sighting instruments (e.g., the sextant and quadrant) needed to improve their accuracy, meant that sequences of continuous observations were rare until the sixteenth century in Europe. Only a wealthy nobleman like the Dane Tycho Brahe (1546–1601), whose passion for astronomy was unusual enough within his aristocratic circles to have to be hidden from his family and tutors, could afford to devise new instruments like his great mural quadrant and to maintain a permanent staff of assistants (briefly including Johannes Kepler [1571–1630]) to conduct the long-term series of observations that eventually made Kepler's remarkable innovations in the *Astronomia nova* (New astronomy) (1609) possible. Galileo's (1564–1642) spectacular telescopic observations, reported in his *Sidereus nuncius* (Starry messenger) (1610), took the learned world by storm and also glamorized the once humble word *observation* in both academic and courtly milieus.

In medicine, the sect of the Empirics and the Skeptical philosophical school of Sextus Empiricus (ca. 160–ca. 210 CE) used *observation* as a term of art, and the word gained currency in learned circles in the mid-sixteenth century when Sextus's works were partially recovered and translated into Latin. It is also notable that the Latin words *experimentum* and *observatio* were rarely found together in medieval texts, and neither referred primarily to learned practices: an experimentum was a test of the sort that an artisan might make in the workshop of a new recipe for dyeing cloth or tempering steel; an observatio took note of something or event, usually outdoors tilling fields, navigating by the stars, or watching flocks. Although university-trained scholars certainly observed their own world constantly, they did not theorize the word and practice as a path to scientia: observational knowledge was too contingent, variable, local, noncausal, and uncertain to qualify.

In the sixteenth and seventeenth centuries, this situation changed radically as voyages of exploration, commerce, and colonization to the Far East and Far West, technological inventions such as the printing press, religious *reformation and counter-reformation, and theoretical upheavals in astronomy, medicine, geography, and *philology deluged Europeans with novelties of all kinds: new flora and fauna, new peoples and languages, new drugs, new religions, new inventions, new stars, new continents, new cosmologies—as well as the rediscovery of old texts from antiquity read in new ways. Amid this ferment, the meaning of "science" began to shift, if only because knowledge once considered unshakably certain—for example, the geography of Ptolemy and Strabo or the cosmology of Aristotle—was revealed to be false on the basis of the observational discoveries of Columbus, Galileo, and others. The stock of observation as a learned practice rose accordingly.

Systematic observation structured by instructions, questionnaires, tables, and *genres emerged in several contexts in the sixteenth century. Northern European humanists wrote treatises on the art of travel, the *ars apodemica*, for their students about to embark on grand tours of Italy and other parts of southern Europe, full of minute instructions on what to observe and how to act: converse with everyone, but don't divulge your religion, and take no books except your journal of observations; note the chief commodities of each region and their prices, the manners of its people, the court beauties and other favorites of the prince, the climate, the value of local coinage, and "infinite other particularities." Such instructions aimed to improve the culture and character of the young gentleman and keep him too busy to frequent taverns and whorehouses in the sinful south. More economic and political in character were the questionnaires prepared at the order of Philip II of Spain in the 1570s to collect information about his possessions in the New World, with an eye toward governing colonies and exploiting resources. A century later, the Royal Society of London issued similar questionnaires to travelers in order to standardize natural history reporting.

Starting in medicine and astronomy in sixteenth-century Europe, and spreading to jurisprudence, natural history, philology, travelogues, and eventually natural philosophy by the mid-seventeenth century, the word *observations* started to feature prominently in the titles of both Latin and *vernacular books. Although the new genre was as diverse as its subject matter, its exempla exhibited certain common features: the observations were often collections, gleaned either from the author's own experience or from other publications; they were organized as short, often numbered, entries, with little or no attempt at systematization; even in collections, firsthand observations (by *autopsia*) were granted privileged status; novelty was emphasized; and conjecture concerning the import of the observations was notably absent or even explicitly withheld.

A seamless lineage connects these books of observations, increasingly designated as such in their titles, with the articles that appeared in the earliest scientific journals of the latter half of the seventeenth century. For example, the aptly named *Miscellanea curiosa* (Miscellaneous curiosities), sporadically published by the Academia Naturae Curiosorum (Academy of those curious about nature, later the Leopoldina, established in Schweinfurt in 1652, Germany's oldest academy of sciences), was composed entirely of mostly medical *observationes*, numbered and titled as such, sent in by doctors from all over the Holy Roman Empire and beyond. "Observations" also featured prominently in the *Philosophical Transactions* published by Henry Oldenburg, secretary of the early Royal Society of London (established 1660) and the *Histoire et mémoires* (History and memoirs) of the Paris Académie Royale des Sciences (established 1666).

Along with the words *experiment* and *history, observation* emerged as a key practice in the self-styled new science of the late seventeenth century, and one increasingly theorized in relationship to the other two terms. Although Francis Bacon's (1561–1626) call for a reformed natural philosophy based on a vastly expanded natural history influenced many of the proponents of the "new experimental philosophy" in the latter half of the seventeenth century in the Royal Society of London and elsewhere, his own use of the words *historia, experimentum*, and *observatio* had been quite fluid. By the late seventeenth century, however, these had become terms of art, designating refined forms of empiricism that were learned (as opposed to popular), distinct from each other, and grounded in *epistemological reflection. Whereas *historia* increasingly referred to compendious collections of information, both first- and secondhand, on a given topic (e.g., the winds), on the model of the natural histories sketched in Bacon's own uncompleted *Sylva Sylvarum* (Forest of forests) (1627), *experimentum* and *observatio* referred to more particular inquiries. *Experiment* referred to an "artificial" (the word was Bacon's) intervention in nature in order to produce a certain effect and thereby tease out its causes; *observation* referred to the close monitoring of nature undisturbed. Although the two words had rarely been conjoined in earlier centuries and still more rarely associated with *scientia*, by 1700 they were an inseparable and complementary pair, both emblematic of a new kind of science that produced probable rather than certain knowledge, aspired to prediction as well as explanation, and was pursued collectively through systematic inquiry into particulars.

The rise of observation as a scientific practice was propelled by a battery of techniques, some as old as note taking and intense attentiveness, others as new as making tables (well known in astronomy and other mathematical sciences since antiquity but new to disciplines like chemistry and natural history) and image making. Already in the sixteenth century, botanists, most of them physicians familiar with the new genre of medical observations, had lavishly illustrated their publications with the then-new image technology of woodcuts. By the late seventeenth century, the word *observation* could refer to an act of attentive perception, the verbal description of such an act, or an image (usually an engraving) accompanying the description. Works of observation, especially in anatomy, geography, and natural history, but also in booming new fields in physics such as the investigation of electricity and magnetism, were lavishly illustrated, and eighteenth-century savants such as Linnaeus vied for the services of the best artists. Observation also still carried resonances to a much older sense of the word as the faithful execution of certain obligations, especially carrying out religious rites. During the *Enlightenment, when the prestige of scientific observation was at its zenith, observation was more than a scientific practice; for virtuoso observers like the Swiss anatomist and naturalist Albrecht von Haller (1708–77) or the Dutch natural philosopher Pieter van Musschenbroek (1696–1761), it was an arduous way of life, demanding great dedication and often the sacrifice of money, social life, and health. Writing to von Haller in 1757, the Genevan naturalist Charles Bonnet (1720–93) vaunted observation as "the universal spirit of the arts and sciences"; observational prowess was the yardstick by which savants took each other's measure; it was even possible to become a "genius of observation."

Although observation never ceased to be an essential and steadily evolving practice in the arts and sciences, sharpened into a precision instrument for collating evidence, detecting patterns, and mounting arguments in the hands of great naturalists such as Georges Cuvier (1769–1832), Alexander von Humboldt (1769–1859), and Charles Darwin (1809–82), its star waned in nineteenth- and twentieth-century science—or at least philosophy of science. Prominent nineteenth-century men of science distinguished observation sharply from experiment, describing the one as passive and requiring minimal skill and the other as active and demanding the utmost ingenuity. In his *Introduction à l'étude de médecine expérimentale* (Introduction to the study of experimental medicine, 1865), the French physiologist Claude Bernard emphasized that "the mind of the experimenter must be active, that is to say he must interrogate nature and pose questions in every sense, following the various hypotheses that suggest themselves to him," whereas the observer embodied "the passive senses that obeyed the intellect in order to realize an experiment designed with a preconceived idea in view." The British astronomer John Herschel, in his *Preliminary Discourse on the Study of Natural Philosophy* (1830), demoted observation to an amateur activity, to be discharged by an army of volunteers who would diligently "observe regularly and methodically some particular class of *facts" and fill out standardized forms consisting of "distinct and pertinent questions, admitting of short and definite answers." Twentieth-century philosophers of science took the devaluation of observation in science a step further by positing a "neutral observation language" that barely differed from mere looking—a form of empiricism too rudimentary to be suspected of being "theory laden." In the late nineteenth and early twentieth centuries, new tools of mathematical statistical inference were developed that eventually led to the partial mechanization of the discernment of reliable correlations—for example, through significance tests, which had been the backbone of the long tradition of observation for millennia.

One sign of the waning scientific prestige of observation has been the massive enlistment of amateurs, most recently under the banner of "Citizen Science" and via websites like Zooniverse, in observation-intensive disciplines such as entomology and astronomy. Enormous trawls of data from satellites, CCTV cameras, and space-based telescopes have created an urgent need for volunteers to register new insect species, monitor video footage, and classify galaxies, and professional scientists are increasingly dependent on such assistance. To date, pattern recognition algorithms cannot rival the acuity and sagacity of the trained human eye of a conscientious observer: once again, sensory, epistemic, and moral qualities blend to make a virtuoso observer.

Whatever its fortunes as a scientific practice, the cult of observation flourishes among travelers, ethnographers, physicians, connoisseurs, detectives, and of course spies.

Whether the task at hand is detecting a new disease such as AIDS or SARS on the basis of a scatter of symptoms in individual patients or the forensic examination of clues at the scene of a crime or judging whether a putative Vermeer painting is a forgery, the lynx-eyed observer detects what others overlook. As Sherlock Holmes famously reproached Watson: "You see, but you do not observe."

Lorraine Daston

See also algorithms; cases; data; horoscopes; journals; knowledge; learning; libraries and catalogs; notebooks; printed visuals; teaching; travel

FURTHER READING

Susan Dackerman, ed., *Prints and the Pursuit of Knowledge in Early Modern Europe*, 2011; Lorraine Daston and Elizabeth Lunbeck, eds., *Histories of Scientific Observation*, 2011; Anthony Grafton and Nancy Siraisi, eds., *Natural Particulars: Nature and the Disciplines in Renaissance Europe*, 2000; Christoph Hoffmann, *Unter Beobachtung: Naturforschung in der Zeit der Sinnesapparate*, 2006; Gianna Pomata, "A Word of the Empirics: The Ancient Concept of Observation and Its Recovery in Early Modern Medicine," *Annals of Science* 68, no. 1 (2011): 1–25; Gianna Pomata and Nancy Siraisi, eds., *Historia: Empiricism and Erudition in Early Modern Europe*, 2005; Hans Poser, "Observatio, Beobachtung," in *Historisches Wörterbuch der Philosophie*, edited by Joachim Ritter and Karlfried Gründer, 1984, 6: cols. 1072–81; Arno Seifert, *Cognitio historica: Die Geschichte als Namengeberin der frühneuzeitlichen Empirie*, 1976; Justin Stagl, *A History of Curiosity: The Theory of Travel 1550–1800*, 1995.

OFFICE PRACTICES

Information storage, access, and security have always been central to office practices. Throughout the twentieth century, secretaries, executive and administrative assistants, file clerks, and other types of office workers (including specialists and executives) used a variety of tools and systems for information management in a business or other professional organizational setting. This entry offers an overview of key office tasks, and the technologies that facilitated them, in the twentieth and twenty-first centuries.

STUDYING OFFICE PRACTICES

The role of the secretary provides a focal point illuminating the modern office as a collaborative workplace across a variety of office environments. Starting in the late nineteenth century, secondary schools and specialized training programs offered coursework to prepare students—especially young women—for careers as office workers. Alongside courses in literature, mathematics, and foreign languages, students could elect to study *bookkeeping, stenography, and typing. Commercial diplomas were offered to students who could complete their secondary education. While most young people who completed commercial diplomas were women, these programs were also designed to prepare men for office-based careers.

In 1911, John Robert Gregg, inventor of the eponymous Gregg *shorthand system, and Rupert P. SoRelle published the first textbook for secretarial studies, which appeared in two editions. In 1934 they expanded it into *Applied Secretarial Practice*, a textbook used in both secondary schools and secretarial colleges. It was published in seven editions through 1974, twenty-six years after Gregg's death in 1948. Gregg's textbooks document evolving office technologies and practices throughout the twentieth century, and evolving social and cultural perspectives on office and secretarial work. Gregg also published books teaching typing and shorthand, which document the conventions for the preparation of a variety of document types—from letters, to legal documents, to literary manuscripts—on a typewriter, and exercises for practice. His books were translated into French, Spanish, and German.

Training for office work instructed students in tasks such as answering the phone, composing letters, scheduling, taking dictation, transcribing and editing dictated texts, conducting research and writing reports, preparing and editing material for publication, and arranging transportation of goods and services. Secondary schools were typically unable to train students in the most advanced of these tasks, which were taught in specialized secretarial training courses. Aspiring office workers could obtain more sophisticated training in secretarial colleges, which flourished in the twentieth century. In secretarial colleges students could learn a wider variety of skills (for example, different filing systems), practice them, and build expertise.

The many training manuals for secretaries are valuable sources for tracking the shifts in the conceptions of office work over time. Pre–World War II editions of the Gregg textbook used "he" as a gender-neutral pronoun to refer to both employers and their secretaries. Chapters addressing professional dress also offered advice to both men and women job seekers who might be transitioning into a white-collar workforce. By contrast, the 1968 edition of the *Applied Secretarial Practices* gendered all aspiring and practicing secretaries as female. Guidelines for professional dress and grooming were offered to women only and advised secretaries to work diligently so that their personal successes and good ideas would be credited to their bosses, who were gendered as male. Illustrations of people at work in these books are also revealing. The 1968 textbook, for example, pictured ethnically diverse women working as secretaries alongside ethnically diverse executives, while earlier manuals are illustrated exclusively with pictures of white people.

American high schools appear to have stopped offering commercial diplomas at around the time that Gregg's manual ceased publication. Secretarial colleges have also moved from brick-and-mortar organizations to online training programs in the *digital age. In the United Kingdom, Pitman Training (established in 1837 by Sir Isaac Pitman, inventor of the Pitman shorthand method) offers programs to certify administrative assistants, secretaries, bookkeepers, and IT workers, as well as one-off courses in office software, management, web design, IT support, and other business-related skills. Perhaps because computers and office productivity software are now so widely used, twenty-first-century guidebooks for administrative and executive assistants focus more on professional relationships, time management, and productivity than on specific skills and business machines.

OFFICE PRACTICES IN ACTION

In the machine age, office workers used a variety of tools to record, reproduce, circulate, retrieve, and store information; such tools were designed to expedite work and minimize errors. In every office, all employees gathered and shared information about their activities in a variety of formats, and to groups or audiences of various sizes. School textbooks, secretarial desk references, and locally produced handbooks were regularly updated to keep up with current office technologies. Common typewriters and duplicators such as the mimeograph, ditto, and Multilith machines, and, later, photocopying machines and scanners appeared with brief descriptions of models available, their functions, and applications to a variety of printing tasks. Bookkeeping machines and calculators, used by bookkeepers and accounting staff in offices to document organizational finances, were similarly described in detail. Offices also made great use of technologies that recorded and transmitted sound. Telephones, sound-recording devices like the Dictaphone, intercoms, and audio-conferencing technologies were key tools for aural information sharing. In 2006, Skype offered video-conferencing services over the *internet for the first time.

In 1968, *Applied Secretarial Practice* offered information on punch-card systems and electronic computer systems. By the late 1980s, offices everywhere used fax machines to quickly share information on paper, and some office workers were expected to understand how to select, operate, and maintain (but not repair) them. The Prentice-Hall

Secretary's Handbook of 1983 provided detailed advice on the use of computer software for different tasks, spreadsheets for financial records, for example, and databases for business records. By the 1990s, manuals included information on the use of local area networks, dial-up internet, and email.

Just as many universities employ a staff of trained technology specialists (better known as IT professionals) to maintain their battery of computers, printers, and similar equipment, large businesses, such as Hollywood motion picture studios before the 1948 antitrust ruling, often employed their own technicians to repair broken office machines before the internet age. Most businesses, however, have always worked with external vendors who specialize in business machine repair. Often, though not always, business machines like printer-copier-scanners are rentals that come with a maintenance and repair contract; this has been the case since the Xerox machine first appeared in offices in the mid-1960s.

Offices have been sites of tremendous technological change in record-keeping practices and technologies. Today individuals and organizations use *cloud-based file storage services such as Google Drive, Dropbox, and Amazon Web Services to store documents on a remote server accessible via an internet connection. Overall computers have dramatically reduced the physical footprint of information within the office itself, but the environmental footprint of digital data is vastly larger. Records that once filled an entire room of filing cabinets with paper can now fit on a server the size of a large microwave onsite, or remotely in massive data centers sometimes called *"server farms," which host the digital files of multiple users. This transition has had a tremendous environmental impact because of the energy required to power and cool thousands of computers within a single building. In the United States alone, server farms use more than ninety billion kilowatt hours per year, the equivalent of thirty-four giant coal-powered plants. Server farms are staffed by technicians and janitors who keep these machines operating safely day and night, year-round.

During the twentieth century, numerous filing systems were designed to meet different organizational needs. Most organizations organized files by name, place, or number. The Social Security Administration used the phonetic Russel-Soundex system to maintain a file of sixty million names, some of which might sound alike but have vastly different spellings. Most other systems relied on visual aids. The consistent use of filing guides (markers made from cardstock with a rectangular tab protruding from the top), and file folders with tabs in varying positions provided visual cues to help record seekers to quickly zero in on a desired folder's location within a drawer. The Variadex system, for example, specified the tab positions of filing guides and folders and used a color *code to highlight the start of new letters of the alphabet. An orange guide tab in the first position on the far left indicated the start of a new letter (for example, R). Subdivisions within that letter (for example, Ra-Red) would be marked following sequencing of colors in the rainbow. Yellow (Ra-Rip), green (Rit-Rob), blue (Rod-Rum), and violet (Run-Ry) tabs would be sequentially repeated until the next letter began with an orange tab (S).

In the twenty-first century most offices store information in a variety of digital formats in databases on individual computers and servers that connect them within a closed network. Many businesses are now "paperless." By reformatting physical files into electronic documents using scanners, and creating databases or local filing systems to index and store company records, businesses exclusively maintain electronic records, though office workers routinely use desktop printers and produce an enormous quantity of print in the office. Digital reformatting is not the first instance of this practice, however. In the late twentieth century, some offices reformatted paper records into microfilm for higher-density information storage.

Clerks' expertise in the local filing system facilitated information gathering and retrieval. Before filing, secretaries and clerks were responsible for indexing, sorting, and cross-referencing documents to ensure that they were filed correctly and findable later. Documents were first annotated with standardized marks to show that they were ready for filing. Secretaries and file clerks read all documents to be filed and used their expertise in local practices to identify the name or place under which a document should be filed or cross-referenced. Filing clerks were also called on for information retrieval and used "out" cards to mark the location of withdrawn files, recording the pull date and name of the requester and crossing them off when the file was returned.

The correct use of these systems was key not only for information retrieval, but also for security. Many documents retained by businesses or organizations contained sensitive information about clients, products, and the organization itself, and had to be guarded to ensure privacy. Shredders are now ubiquitous machines in offices and homes; they destroy paper-based documents containing sensitive information such as social security or credit card numbers. In the late twentieth century and today, offices write cybersecurity policies to protect information stored on networked computers and install software designed to protect their information from loss and theft. Nevertheless, in recent years many organizations have been subject to *hacks and data breaches that have seriously compromised their own reputations along with the privacy and financial security of their clients.

Unlike paper records, moreover, digital files, easily duplicated and passively stored, can be difficult to permanently destroy. In the 2016 US presidential election, FBI officials discovered US State Department emails on the personal computer of Anthony Weiner, the husband of Huma Abedin, deputy chief of staff for presidential candidate Hillary Clinton. Simply by using her husband's computer to check her email, Abedin passively saved correspondence thought to be lost in March 2015, when a technician employed by Clinton's personal computer services provider erased them from Clinton's personal server.

In addition to business files, mid-twentieth-century corporate offices often maintained small libraries or book collections. Office workers, from secretaries to specialists, relied on these informational storehouses for general research purposes to produce reports for internal or public circulation. Reports could be very brief or quite lengthy, requiring input from a variety of staff members and sometimes even external consultants. If a report first circulated in draft form, it would then be transformed into a neat, presentable printed version, reproduced in the appropriate number of copies, and distributed or used as a visual aid to an oral presentation.

Secretaries and administrative assistants were usually responsible for gathering resources, editing drafts, and producing the final physical document. Other professional staff were responsible for in-depth research, analysis, and composition, though this was not always the case. Business reports use charts, tables, graphs, and other graphics to represent quantitative information in business reports. Computers make it easy to produce colorful, detailed charts and tables, but before their ubiquity, typewriters and tools for hand drawings were commonly used. Secretarial handbooks offer detailed instructions for creating these images for professional presentation using typewriters, stencils, and transfer lettering and graphics (e.g., Letraset). Methods for presenting images within offices migrated to overhead projection and then to digital tools. Today elaborate digital images are prepared to present data and plans to internal and external audiences— each of them called a "slide" in a case of skeuomorphism—notably through the spread of software programs such as Microsoft's PowerPoint, which has been included in its "Office" bundle of software since 1988.

Offices have seen tremendous changes in the way in which collaborations take place. Computerized tools have transformed the office from a defined central location and information repository to a networked entity facilitating work between collaborators even when separated by great distances. Yet offices have been and remain collaborative workplaces that rely on information storage, access, and security to function. Though they now use different tools, office workers remain engaged with tasks that would be eminently recognizable to their predecessors.

Erin McGuirl

See also accounting; data; databases; digitization; files; indexing; inventories; manuals; photocopiers; secretaries; storage and search

FURTHER READING

Lillian Doris, *Complete Secretary's Handbook*, 1983; John Roberts Gregg et al., *Applied Secretarial Practice*, 1934–74; John Roberts Gregg and Rupert SoRelle, *Secretarial Studies*, 1911, 1928; Jonathan McIlroy, *The New Executive Assistant: Exceptional Executive Office Management*, 2018; Julian E. Orr, *Talking about Machines: An Ethnography of a Modern Job*, 1996; Anthony Vlamis, *Webster's New World Office Professional's Desk Reference*, 1999.

PETITIONS

In June 1648, a crowd of supplicants approached Tsar Aleksei Mikhailovich as he returned to Moscow from a pilgrimage. Rather than accept their petitions, his retinue waved them off and rode into the Kremlin. Still hopeful, the crowd approached the tsaritsa, who followed her husband into the city. This time, the guards drove them off by force. The refusal of the traditional right to petition the tsar proved costly: the city erupted in insurrection. When the ash settled, half of Moscow had burned, and thousands of people had died. Spurning petitions was not the sole cause of the uprising, but it provided the spark.

Disappointed petitioners might seem an unlikely set of rebels. A petition, after all, is an exercise in groveling. It is a document or speech that asks, begs, or humbly requests. According to the *Oxford English Dictionary*, it can be "a supplication or prayer; an entreaty; esp. a solemn and humble prayer to the Deity, or to a sovereign or superior." In Muscovy, petitions were called *chelobitnye*, literally, forehead-beating documents, and indeed the supplicants ritually bowed their foreheads to the ground before the tsar. Moreover, the potential benefits of petitioning would seem too low to be worth a rebellion. Even if the tsar had personally received their supplications, there was no guarantee that their requests would have been granted. Yet Muscovite subjects energetically availed themselves of what they saw as their ancient and inalienable right to hand petitions to the tsar, and, moreover, they expected the ruler would attend to their woes.

Petitions historically have served as a primary means of conveying information from below, funneling news upward and allowing rulers to measure the pulse of their people. The expectation that those in power would attend to the information contained in petitions was not unique to Russia or to the seventeenth century. Shakespeare had Julius Caesar hurry into the Capitol, leaving petitioners futilely proffering their "humble suits." His murder follows immediately after. Charles I's refusal of petitions added an irritant to already tense relations in seventeenth-century England, contributing at some level to his ultimate demise. Back in Russia in 1905, another group of humble petitioners marched, crosses and icons aloft, to present a petition to Nicholas II, only to be gunned down by the Cossack guard. Revolution ensued.

Most scholarly work on petitions considers the significance of petitions as informational instruments intended to provoke political action. In older work, petitioning is often represented as a lesser, "immature" form of political engagement, one invoked by those without other forms of redress. Yet a fascinating body of recent scholarship has upended this impression, showing that petitions can provide a powerful basis for rights claims. Studies demonstrate not only the ubiquity of petitioning practices but also the obligation, both ideological and practical, of those in authority to respond. Norms of reciprocity in such situations are not just polite fictions but are observed as both important cultural touchstones and hardnosed pragmatic strategies of state building and survival. As we have seen, historically monarchs ignore them at their own peril.

Despite their usual vocabulary of humility, petitions can make strong bids for recognition on the grounds of firm, nonnegotiable rights. It is not at random that the right to petition is included in the English Bill of Rights of 1689, the First Amendment of the US Constitution, and the Charter of Fundamental Rights of the European Union. Petitions and the law might seem to work at odds with each other: the first entreats with pathos and hopes for merciful response; the latter rests on objective rules, positive rights, and expectations of impersonal justice. Yet the two spheres are far closer together than might first appear. Petitions frequently salt their "humble" appeals with strong legal claims and clear demands. Historically, even where the language of petitions was relentlessly abject, petitioners did not stint in pointing out when they had the law on their side. In many cultures, petitioners did indeed have legal standing. In Qing China (1644–1912), for instance, local magistrates were legally obliged to attend to the petitions they received, and the power of the law, rather than capricious whim, dictated their rulings. This relatively recent finding upends earlier presumptions about the arbitrary authority of Qing local officials and corrects the idea that magistrates could simply ignore their constituents' petitions or could refuse to accept them at will.

Reanimated by the possibilities of mass organization via the *internet, petitions circulate widely today, popping up in our email and Facebook feeds. These online petitions inform and animate targeted publics and also convey a sense of the scale of mobilization. As has been true historically, political leaders are free to consider or ignore these collective expressions, but the very fact of their circulation guarantees that a broad population will be made aware of the issues and will have taken a stand. As with any petition campaigns, these contemporary iterations may register legal claims or ignite moral indignation, or both, and in either case, aim simultaneously to inspire popular support and to press high officials for positive resolution.

Recent studies have gone a long way toward recuperating petitions as a form of fully fledged political engagement. This is important work but in some ways has constrained the horizon of investigation. When we limit our definition of what constitutes true political engagement narrowly to fit modern, Western, rights-based frameworks, we risk overlooking other, equally vibrant forms of political life. In many undemocratic societies, petitions testify to alternative forms of membership in a polity, membership based on personal appeal and on reciprocal acknowledgment. Rulers in nonegalitarian societies commonly have to recognize an obligation to protect and affirm the status of each petitioner or group and to protect the entitlements incumbent on that status, negligible and manifestly unequal though it might be.

Petitions not only operate on a political level but also play an active role in the creation and circulation of information. Through their petitions, subjects air their grievances to those above, while reports of their reception communicate important information to their communities back home. This exchange of information can work smoothly, consolidating the status quo, or it can threaten that precarious balance. Disillusioned petitioners disseminate their resentments and can fuel the work of activists who challenge the system. As Francis Cody writes of Dalit petitions in South India, "The textual structure of petitions themselves constitutes a zone where competing models of social power are also rendered evident."

Petitions can produce information that goes far beyond the pragmatic two-way flow between center and periphery or ruler and ruled. Petitioners can craft their narratives to satisfy the demands and expectations of the people who will decide their cases, or in very different ways, to suit purposes quite distinct from the ostensible goals of their suits. Natalie Zemon Davis famously developed these ideas in her *Fiction in the Archives* (1990). The fictions she explored were those elaborated in petitions seeking royal clemency in *early modern France. Along the same lines, in his trenchant examination of petitions for clemency for death row inmates in the United States, Austin Sarat sets out several distinct narrative strategies. He asks why the inmates and their lawyers bother with these petitions when their success rate is close to zero. He identifies in the petitioners a desire to dictate the terms of their own life stories and to memorialize their own being, even in the face of imminent execution. Caroline Wigginton brings the skills of literary analysis to bear on nineteenth-century Native American petitions and uncovers a similarly potent motivation, distinct from the documents' apparent aims. "Through these petitions," she writes, "Natives assert their active presence. . . . They assert their intellectual right to tell their own stories. They assert their ability to construct their own versions of history." Petitions, then, can create or reinforce ideas of self and of community.

If we consider what motivates people to go through the often costly and difficult process of submitting petitions, we can better understand what information mattered to the petitioners themselves, what information they chose to communicate, to what audience, and to what purpose. These self-abnegating documents communicate powerfully, pushing us beyond the issues of law and rights that generally preoccupy scholars. They demand that we attend to the ideas of inclusion and reciprocity that they advance and that we listen to the ways their authors, whether the petitioners themselves or hired scribes, narrate their own histories.

Products of radically unequal power, petitions can crack open the field of political participation and claims making, allowing the disempowered some limited degree of enfranchisement and self-assertion. Viewed in this way, petitions offer a crucial insight into contributions of information not only, as is widely recognized, to democratization, but also to the stability and success of nondemocratic regimes, whether in the past or the present.

Valerie Kivelson

See also bureaucracy; governance; public sphere; publicity/publication; scribes

FURTHER READING

Valerie Kivelson, "'Muscovite Citizenship': Rights without Freedom," *Journal of Modern History* 74, no. 3 (2002): 465–89; Linxia Liang, "Rejection or Acceptance: Finding Reasons for the Late Qing Magistrate's Comments on Land and Debt Petitions," *Bulletin of the School of Oriental and African Studies* 68, no. 2 (2005): 276–94; Austin Sarat, "Memorializing Miscarriages of Justice: Clemency Petitions in the Killing State," *Law and Society Review* 42, no. 1 (2008): 183–224; Caroline Wigginton, "Extending Root and Branch: Community Regeneration in the Petitions of Samson Occom," *Studies in American Indian Literatures*, ser. 2, 20, no. 4 (2008): 24–55; David Zaret, "Petitions and the 'Invention' of Public Opinion in the English Revolution," *American Journal of Sociology* 101, no. 6 (1996): 1497–555.

PHOTOCOPIERS

In marked contrast with the attention paid to writing, printing, and telecommunications, the impact of copying has remained largely undocumented and unexamined by historians. The ability to make facsimile copies mechanically has had an enormous impact on commerce, education, bureaucracy, and scholarship as a convenience, for preservation, and by enabling further products.

Tracing paper and tracing parchment were known already in the Middle Ages and were used to aid the making of engraved facsimiles; images were also transferred by pouncing, which involved poking holes to outline an image and spreading colored dust through them onto a sheet below. From the early seventeenth century the *pantograph*, a pen mechanically linked to a pointer tracing an existing diagram, would create a copy or, if linked to a writer's pen, a copy of what was being written. The first widespread copying technique developed in the eighteenth century was the *copying letter press* (entirely different from letterpress printing) in which a thin moist paper was pressed on top of a freshly written letter such that enough of the ink on the original would seep through to the front of the moistened paper to create a copy. Thomas Jefferson was a well-known user.

Copying options were transformed once techniques for enduring photographic images were developed in the 1830s. Joseph Nicéphore Niepce made lithographic plates from photographic images, and John Benjamin Dancer promptly made daguerreotype microphotographs of texts. But before 1900 photocopying was little more than a novelty, occasionally used for the urgent copying of military battle plans, responding to interlibrary loan requests, and, famously, by René Dagron for sending microphotographed news over enemy lines by homing pigeons during the siege of Paris in 1870.

Widespread use of photocopying began with the *photostat* process developed by the French orientalist René Graffin to aid his editing of Syriac manuscripts. Photostat, which was both a generic name and a trade name, used a large camera to photograph documents directly onto sensitized paper without using a negative as an intermediate step. One simply fixed the exposed paper to obtain a negative print of any desired size showing white text on a black ground. Left-to-right reversal was corrected by using a forty-five-degree prism attached to the lens. If desired, a photostat of a photostat would reverse the reversal to produce a black text on a white ground. Graffin's camera won a prize at the International Exposition on Paris in 1900, and the process was prominently endorsed by a US federal efficiency commission in 1912. At that time the US government was sending staff to transcribe foreign archives by hand or by typewriter. Photostat's overwhelming superiority in speed, simplicity, efficiency, accuracy, and versatility, especially for copying images, was obvious. Photostat cameras became commercially available in 1910, were widely adopted, and remained the copying technique of choice until at least the 1930s. Copying speeds of up to six hundred pages an hour were claimed for advanced equipment. Photostatic prints had additional advantages over the use of photographic film: For a while photostats were accepted as legal evidence, whereas prints made using a negative, being indirect copies, were not. More importantly, the storage of images on photographic film, then nitrate based and inflammable, was effectively prohibited by insurance companies.

Widespread use of *microfilm* had to await improvements in photographic technology and the commercial availability of acetate safety film. Major applications during the late 1920s and 1930s included banks' filming of presented checks to reduce fraud, the reduction of space needed for storing business records, and libraries' use of microfilm to copy newspapers and other documents. Microfilm was more compact, more easily transported, and easier to reproduce than photostats.

High-profile microfilming initiatives by individual historians include Fernand Braudel, who aroused attention in 1927 by using an old movie camera to microfilm up to three thousand pages a day in the General Archive of the Simancas, which he later reviewed at leisure using a projector. Vernon D. Tate's extensive filing of Mexican port archives for his doctoral research led to a lifetime leadership role in micrographic developments. The Library of Congress undertook a number of high-profile microfilming projects starting in the 1930s.

Other microforms, notably *microfiche* (small sheets of film, typically 105×148 mm or 75×125 mm, reproducing some one hundred pages) and *microprint* (like microfiche but printed on opaque white cards) were used after 1945, primarily as publication media. In practice the benefits of microfilming are conveniently achieved at reductions of 1:10 or 1:20, but smaller is technically possible. In 1925 Emanuel Goldberg demonstrated extreme reduction *microdots* with a resolution equal to fifty Bibles per square inch, an achievement that J. Edgar Hoover prominently and inexplicably attributed to a mythical "Prof. Zapp." Such tiny images are hard to find, which led Goldberg to develop an electronic search engine for use on photocopied documents on rolls of 35mm film, a technology popularized by Vannevar Bush's imaginary desktop *memex information system.

Much simpler than photostat or microforms, life-sized *contact prints* were made without a camera by placing sensitive paper on or under the original. In the simplest case, light shone on to the original would pass through the paper except where ink marks absorbed the light creating a silhouette recorded on the light-sensitive sheet placed behind the original. Cyanotype engineering "blue prints" used this method. When paper had ink marks on both sides or was opaque, a reflex method was used. The sensitive sheet would be placed in front of the original and record light reflected by the paper except where absorbed by ink. A similar method (thermofax) used heat-sensitive paper to record where ink had been heated by absorbed light.

In 1937 Chester F. Carlson developed an *electrostatic copying* process. Light temporarily increases the conductivity of selenium, so projecting patterns of light creates patterns of increased conductivity on a selenium surface. Negatively charged particles of ink (toner) cling to the surface in proportion to the increased conductivity. The toner pattern is then transferred to and fused into a sheet of paper, replicating the pattern of light originally projected. When offered this technology, Kodak declined, preferring to concentrate on its technical leadership in photochemical processes. The Haloid Photographic Company, a maker of photostat paper seeking to escape Kodak's overwhelming market presence, made a strategic decision to invest in a product different from Kodak's and adopted Carlson's "electrophotographic" technique. Because this process avoided the use of wet chemicals, it was renamed xerography ("dry writing"), and after many difficulties Haloid, renamed Xerox, brought it to market. It became the technology of choice for copiers and computer printers.

Duplication refers to a variety of late nineteenth- and twentieth-century techniques for making multiple nonfacsimile copies of texts or line drawings, typically in runs of twenty to one hundred copies. Best known are the spirit duplicators ("ditto"), in which typing transfers waxy ink onto a sheet used for printing; stencil duplicators ("mimeo"), in which typed incisions in an ink-proof paper allow ink to flow through on a rotary press; and hectographs, in which waxy ink is laid on a flat gelatin printing surface. These and similar processes create a new master and are more properly considered small-run printing.

Photocopying techniques can achieve much more than the making of copies because the image made can also serve as input for other *derivative procedures*, especially the production of photolithographic plates for printing and the special case of "halftone" plates familiar in newspaper illustrations, in which tiny black dots (pixels) of increasing density produce the effect of a continuous graduation from white through increasingly dark grays to solid black—and similarly in color printings.

Strictly speaking, copying is not simply making a copy but a rendering or a version of the original, and any such process might introduce errors or distortions. The significance of this is that versions or renderings can be used for specialized purposes of image enhancement such as changing the size or increasing contrast. Use of wavelengths outside the visual spectrum can be used to make erased text visible, to read through censor's redactions or inkblots, to detect forgeries, to read charred records, and in many other forms of forensic analysis. The classic example is the development by Raphael Kögel (aka Gustav Kögel) of improved techniques for reading medieval texts that had been erased on recycled parchment (palimpsests). Kögel found that ultraviolet light generated fluorescent light except where the writing had been and so was able to convert the resulting effect into a legible text. Lodewyk Bendikson used infrared light to reveal the text written underneath a huge blot where Benjamin Franklin had spilled his ink pot on a page of his manuscript autobiography. Similarly, when the ink used by a censor when redacting a printed work was chemically different from printer's ink used in the printed original, Bendikson made a copy using a wavelength that penetrated the former but not the latter and so was able to read the redacted original.

The history and impact of photocopying techniques have been unduly neglected. Photographic techniques, notably photostat, microfilm, photolithography, and, now, electrostatic processes, have pervaded our daily lives and have transformed what can be done with both graphic and textual records.

Michael K. Buckland

See also archivists; cameras; digitization; documentary authority; error; forgery; lithography

FURTHER READING

Michael K. Buckland, *Emanuel Goldberg and His Knowledge Machine*, 2008; idem, "Lodewyk Bendikson and Photographic Techniques in Documentation, 1910–1943," in *International Perspectives on the History of Information Science and Technology*, edited by Toni Carbo and Trudi Bellardo Hahn, 2012; Percy Freer, *Bibliography and Modern Book Production*, 1954; Herbert William Greenwood, *Document Photography: Individual Copying and Mass Recording*, 1943; William R. Hawken, *Full-Size Photocopying*, 1960; David McKitterick, *Old Books, New Technologies: The Representation, Conservation and Transformation of Books since 1700*, 2013.

PLAGIARIZING

It is often said that "imitation is the sincerest form of flattery." But to the ancient Romans, a *plagiarius* was a kidnapper, a slaver who carried off the children or servants (including slaves) of another for his own selfish purposes. It is impossible for a banker to trust a thief, and practically unthinkable for a scholar to trust a plagiarist. Plagiarism is generally deemed a crime, sometimes a tangled, even sophisticated one, but a crime nonetheless. It can be neatly summarized, as by the literary historian Christopher Ricks: "The morality of the matter, which asks of us that we be against deceit and dishonesty, is clear, and is clearly defined."

A deeper look into the history of information can hardly bring into dispute this essential ethical point, though greater context may also admit greater complexity and allow for greater subjectivity. Poets need muses; mathematicians, numbers; astronomers, stars. All scholars, furthermore, need books and libraries—spaces, both material and intellectual, fitted and singled out as essential repositories that capture and preserve the proof of literary and philosophical res gestae, whether great or modest. Like scholars, plagiarists have also always needed libraries to ply their trade, though preferably of the less well-cataloged variety.

Not all forms of theft are purely repugnant or derivative. There have always been blundering thieves, but also very talented ones. The *canons of classical literature, and their *Renaissance revival during the fifteenth century, admit to this, particularly through the sophisticated notion of a skillful, even ingenious *imitatio* (imitation, and in Greek, *mimesis*), though forms of genius in one age can inspire mockery in the next. As popular *vernacular literary forms and *literacy expanded dramatically by the eighteenth century, Alexander Pope relegated a small army of everyday literary imitators to membership within a mock-heroic "Dunciad." The sentiment was echoed by his fellow Scriblerian Jonathan Swift's famous mantra: "When a true genius appears in the world, you may know him by this sign: that the dunces are all in confederacy against him."

Plagiarism is indeed stealing another's ideas and words, and claiming them as your own. That much is clear. But at what point does one person's recombobulation of another's thoughts become something else, even across a spectrum—from a dunce-worthy parroting, to an inspired tertium quid that becomes a new great idea and singular contribution shaped from an admixture of the thoughts of others? The poetical *locus classicus* for plagiarism from the ancient Roman Martial (*Epigrams*, I.52) offers some insight: "I commend you my little books—that is, however, if I can call them mine when your poet friend recites them. If they complain of harsh enslavement, come forward to claim their freedom. . . . If you shout this three or four times, you will make the kidnapper ashamed of himself." Martial's "little books" were only as powerful as they were numerous, made so by placing them into the hands of those who could commission further scribal copies honoring their original author. Fidentius, the "poet friend" of Martial's addressee Quintianus, apparently recited Martial's epigrams as his own, thus enslaving the poet's verses. The credit of Martial's literary genius subsisted within a predominantly oral premodern literary culture.

Anxiety about literary fame continued to loom large throughout the manuscript age, and for good reason. The ancient Roman elegies of Propertius hung by the thread of one, perhaps two, known medieval scribal copies. Petronius's *Satyricon* seemed lost altogether, save the apparently solitary medieval witness in John of Salisbury's *Policraticus*. Early monastic *scriptoria inspired bustling urban scribal industries beyond the cloister, and as Renaissance "bookhunters" rediscovered and commissioned multiple scribal copies of theretofore "lost" ancient texts in out-of-the-way libraries, literary survivals—and subsequent opportunistic imitators and plagiarists—could flourish.

The mechanical and intellectual corruption of texts through manuscript copying occurred within a near monopoly over literacy and scribal activity by the medieval Roman Catholic Church. Orthodox and traditional knowledge could predominate over "new" forms of knowledge, and some medieval textual forms took on corporative and anonymous generic qualities. The literary accumulation of Christian *auctoritas* (authority) in *florilegia and preaching manuals could be interpreted as plagiaristic, where original sources were inconsistently referenced, though many collections such as Thomas of Ireland's popular *Manipulus florum* (Handful of flowers) were often fairly meticulous in crediting sources. Vincent de Beauvais's *encyclopedic *Speculum maius* (Greater mirror) cites hundreds of sources, but with some imperfections of quotation since all his references came from unique, and potentially flawed, manuscripts.

Renaissance critiques of these pressures on literary invention (often unfairly characterized as atavistic) found much medieval literature to be inimical to the individualizing virtues of personal *inventio* (invention) and *ingenium* (talent) more readily associated with the fifteenth-century revival of classical learning in the West. A dynamic and increasingly efficient public sphere, such as we associate with the mature era of *early modern print, was less in evidence in the medieval West and, thus, contemporary authorial accusations or documented commissions of plagiarism are not so easy to discover or to reconstruct. Plagiarism was simply easier to find, if also more complicated fully to comprehend, with the advent of rapid-fire printing with movable type from the mid-fifteenth century onward. The concomitant diversification of reading audiences (albeit still quite elite and erudite) across a wider geographical range coincided with the emergence of a new authorial demographic, and corresponding readership, of humanists dedicated to the textual revival, and critique, of sources from any historical period. Polyglot *philologists adept in languages ancient and modern, and learned editors and commentators, turned these critical analytical methods to pagan and Christian texts. The "arch-humanist" Desiderius Erasmus (1466–1536) attained his tremendous reputation (and lucrative career in scholarly publishing), in part, through his reliance on sophisticated stationers capable of carrying his exacting standards on to the printed page. Erasmus praised as Herculean the skills of Aldus Manutius and leaned on his Basel printer Froben as the primary *publisher of his great Christian humanist works.

Even still, Erasmus himself stood at the heart of one of the major disputes over plagiarism of the early modern period regarding rival claims to the invention the runaway best-selling academic *genre of "adages"—pithy ancient quotations with accompanying philological essays. Technically, the Italian humanist Polydore Vergil came first with his *Proverbiorum libellus* (Booklet of proverbs, 1498) containing fairly concise entries on three hundred ancient wisdom sayings. Erasmus's *Collectanea adagiorum* (Collections of adages, 1500) followed shortly thereafter with a similar format, by then eight hundred entries strong (140 overlapping with Polydore's selection). Erasmus's *Adagiorum chiliades* (Thousands of adages, 1508), printed by the great Aldus, quadrupled his earlier piece in size, though Polydore did not raise the red flag of plagiarism in print until 1521 (citing a 1519 letter to an English diplomat). Polydore's salvo was anticipated two years prior in a letter from Erasmus to Guillaume Budé, claiming he had never heard of Polydore until long after his 1500 *Collectanea*. Erroneously, Erasmus claimed precedence for his 1500 first edition, perhaps confusing Polydore's 1498 *Proverbiorum libellus* with a later Venetian edition of the same. Such disputes would become legion in the era of print and often remain unresolved. Not without irony, in his famous 1508 Aldine *Adagiorum chiliades* Erasmus relocated the proverb *amicorum communia omnia* ("friends hold all things in common") to the first position (I.1.i). Regardless of who may have taken the very first draught, all lovers of ancient wisdom, it seems, will have drunk from the same spring.

Accusations of plagiarism often take to extremes commonplaces of readerly and authorial practice within the interplay of the imagination, memory, and the love of language. Though he venerated classical literature, Michel de Montaigne deployed a less proprietary approach to humanistic literary activity than many of his contemporaries. He, too, held his favorite authors "in common," simply carving their wise proverbs into the ceiling rafters of his famous tower library (including several also in Erasmus's *Adages*) without explicit attributions. So, too, in many of Montaigne's *Essais* (composed ca. 1570–92; first ed., 1580) are there similarly excised and decontextualized nuggets of the ancients, often quoted explicitly, but also paraphrased, perhaps unwittingly "stolen," or simply reworded in some textual variation. Echoing Erasmus on *amicitia*, Montaigne reminds his reader that "truth and reason are common to everyone, and no more belong to the man who first spoke them than to the man who says them later" (*Essais* I.26). Following the classical apiarian metaphor of the scholar as a honeybee who gathers nectar from various flowers to make honey and wax (running straight through Seneca, Macrobius, Erasmus, and, indeed, Montaigne himself), his resulting "attempts" (*essais*) at formulating original thoughts were, often, just that, efforts to bend the arts of humanist reading to original self-explorations and syntheses. Montaigne's first language was Latin, not French; he was steeped profoundly in ancient literature, so much so that it may have been impossible for him to credit all to all, even if he had intended to.

Quiet, scholarly retreat to a well-stocked personal library was not the first option of every reader or writer who wished to scale the ever-competitive and often slippery ladder to literary fame. Few who wished to be remembered like a Montaigne may have shared Montaigne's ecumenism about the imperfect nature of authorship and originality. In the English vernacular, early etymological confusion conflated "plagiarism" in Sir Thomas Elyot's *Dictionary* (1538) with the Latin *plaga*, a wound caused by a whip, presumably a classical punishment for kidnapping. That punitive association was readily extended to the office of the schoolmaster and his scourge by generations of Latin grammar students, and frequently deployed in the titles of literary satires for whipping and punishing as derivative any lesser claimant to literary achievement. Charges of plagiarism would emerge as a commonplace within these satires and invectives throughout the early modern period, inspiring a procedure of literary outing and punishment that relied on an adept mixture of wide reading, apparent native cleverness, and a certain delight in public shaming made possible on a massive scale through print.

Still, even by 1646 Sir Thomas Browne envisaged no "epidemic" of printed plagiarism in his *Pseudodoxia epidemica or Enquiries into very many received tenets and commonly presumed truths*, since plagiarism, itself, was as old as the hills and well preceded the creation of a public sphere driven by movable type: "Thus may we perceive the ancients were but men, even like ourselves. The practice of transcription in our days was no monster in theirs: plagiary had not its nativity with printing, but began in times when thefts were difficult, and the paucity of books scarcely wanted that invention." Mendacity, ancient and modern, could be found in "a certaine list of vices committed in all ages, and declaimed against by all authors, which will last as long as human nature, or digested into common places may serve for any theme, and never be out of date until Doomsday" (I.6.21–22). Neither Montaigne nor Browne was an apologist of plagiarism, though their broad-minded sentiments on originality were perhaps tempered by firsthand experience of their own brutally partisan historical moments amid the French Wars of Religion and the English Civil Wars.

Charges of plagiarism in print were forever problematized by the absence of formal legal intellectual property rights that favored authors over publishers. In England, primary power over mainstream print (and its implicit censorship) devolved to the private monopoly of the London Stationers' Company, at least until the Licensing Act of 1662 was allowed finally to lapse in 1695 and succeeded by the Copyright Act of 1710. The latter effectively transferred *copyright from publishers to authors and shifted press control into the regulatory hands of government and the law courts. Gradually, public conceptions of an "authorial text" could be seen as integral to the creative powers and personal well-being of original authors. This sentiment could even elide with a kind of protonationalism, as when the dramatic critic Gerard Langbaine, in his *Momus triumphans: or, The plagiaries of the English stage* (1688), decried as the very "worst of plagiaries, [those] who steal from the writing of those of our own nation. Because he that borrows from the worst foreign authors, may possibly import, even amongst a great deal of trash, somewhat of value: whereas the former makes us pay extortion for that which was our own before."

These events coincided with a broader, and often retrospective, impulse to identify within postclassical vernacular literary and philosophical traditions a well-defined, native canon of authorial genius. In England, Sidney, Shakespeare, and Milton were arrayed alongside Bacon, Locke, and Newton, in a continuous expression of "national" *virtù*. To these bright flames of literary distinction were drawn many plagiarist moths, from the obscure to the infamous. Much as Martial's Fidentius, the teenaged Robert Baron cut whole swathes from the verses of Waller, Lovelace, Suckling, and Milton, claiming them as his own in his *Cyprian academy* (1647) and *Pocula castalia* (Cups of Castalian waters, 1650). The cantankerous Scottish neo-Latinist and literary critic William Lauder unleashed a far more sweeping plagiaristic controversy, however. What began simply as his promotion of the verse psalm translation of the Scots poet Arthur Johnston grew to a stupendous cause célèbre that embroiled several of the leading figures of the Augustan age. Where Alexander Pope had lavished great praise on Milton's poetry, that came at the great expense of Johnston in his *Dunciad* (4.111–12), setting

Lauder off into a seven years' war to establish the epic poet Milton as, in fact, the *pla-giarorum princeps* (prince of plagiarists) of English letters.

The vehicle of Lauder's venom was the respectable *Gentleman's Magazine*, a ubiqui-tous periodical digest of news, literature, and criticism. There Lauder accused Milton of lifting much of the structure, and thousands of lines of verse, of *Paradise Lost* from several neo-Latin texts of the first half of the seventeenth century, including epic poems by Hugo Grotius and the Jesuit Jakob Masen. Resting as it did on books obscure to the point of being nearly unobtainable (and, thus, impossible to interrogate further) in mid-eighteenth-century England, Lauder's twisted obsession to rip to shreds Milton's authorship of "things unattempted yet in prose or rhyme" could not resist detection for long, however. It soon emerged that the ostensible filching was in fact a sequence of citations stolen by Lauder from William Hog's *Paraphrasis poetica* (Poetical paraphrase, 1690), a latter-day translation of Milton into Latin. Several confessions of guilt for the imposture by Lauder, including one dictated by Dr. Samuel Johnson himself (albeit largely retracted by Lauder in a postscript) could not blunt John Douglas's *Milton Vin-dicated* (1751), an utter demolition of Lauder's literary critical sand castle.

Plagiarism motivated by commercial profit, rather than literary fame, was hardly alien in the eighteenth century, particularly in the realm of erudite literary compila-tions. Even the greatest of them all, the massively ambitious **Encyclopedia* of Diderot and d'Alembert, borrowed significantly (not always with explicit citation) from Ephraim Chambers's earlier *Cyclopaedia* (1728). This may not have pained Chambers though, who explained of "dictionary-writers" (Chambers's term for authors of encyclopedia entries), in his own entry on "Plagiarism," that their "occupation is not pillaging, but collecting contributions."

At the dawn of industrial mass print publication, critical estimations of plagiarism could remain mixed and muddled amid expansive notions of human subjectivity and authorship. Lamenting the exponential production of cheap print, the great Parisian bibliographer Charles Nodier published his *Questions de littérature légale: Du plagiat* (Questions of legal literature: On plagiarism, Paris, 1828), condemning plagiarism, but with the caveat that "it would be unjust to qualify as plagiarism what is truly only an extension or a useful amendment" to what another has written. There was room for a kind of "plagiat autorisé" (authorized plagiarism) since "there are ideas that can gain from a new expression; established notions that a more felicitous development may clarify." Here, Nodier notably juxtaposed plagiarism with discussions of au-thors' contractual rights, pirated editions, spurious printed rarities designed solely for gullible *bibliomanes*, which combined to form a widening, not-so-creative corner of the marketplace of ideas.

Ironically, Nodier himself dabbled in what he might have condemned. His *Histoire des sociétés secrètes de l'armée* (History of the secret societies of the army, 1815) pre-sents a fabulous spy-versus-spy "history" of a military coup against the Napoleonic re-gime. The far more pernicious conspiratorial *Protocols of the Elders of Zion* (1903) told of a global Jewish cabal bent on worldwide economic and cultural domination. This double-plagiarism drew on the anti-Semitic, mid-nineteenth-century writings of Mau-rice Joly, his *Dialogue aux enfers* (Dialogue in hell, 1864), and Eugène Sue's novel *Les Mystères du peuple* (Mysteries of the people, 1849–56), unleashing a "warrant for geno-cide" popularized, variously, by Adolf Hitler and Henry Ford.

In the twenty-first century, plagiarism seems to receive greatest attention in the cut-throat competitive world of higher education. Policy standards against plagiarism are often attached to procedures for adjudication and sanctions, though these are hardly standardized across institutions. They rely implicitly on the discretion and interpretation of teachers in the classroom who often face increasing teaching loads and class sizes, and the seemingly limitless increase of online content. The double-edged sword of complex search functions and instant data retrieval on the *internet may have ushered in a "golden age" of plagiarism. Countervailing "Plagiarism Detection System" (PDS) software deploys a complex array of methodologies from the fields of computer science and computational linguistics that include "fingerprinting" "bag of words" vector space retrieval, citational pattern analyses, and stylometric analyses for authorship attribution. The cost propositions of real investment of human resources and operational vigilance in the detection and prosecution of plagiarism are nevertheless real and often prohibitive. And, thus, plagiarism remains, as perhaps it has always been—an intellectual, practical, and subjective snarl rooted in a desire for justice, expressed to promote creativity, but undermined by the inexorable increase of information in all its forms.

Earle Havens

See also books; computers; documentary authority; excerpting/commonplacing; forgery; intellectual property; money; readers; teaching

FURTHER READING

Trevor Cook, "The Scourge of Plagiary: Perversions of Imitation in the English Renaissance," *University of Toronto Quarterly* 83 (2014): 39–63; Kathy Eden, "Literary Property and the Question of Style: A Prehistory," in *Borrowed Feathers: Plagiarism and the Limits of Imitation in Early Modern Europe*, edited by Hall Bjøornstad, 2008; Kathy Eden, *Friends Hold All Things in Common: Tradition, Intellectual Property and the Adages of Erasmus*, 2001; Paulina Kewes, *Authorship and Appropriation: Writing for the Stage in England, 1660–1710*, 1998; Robert Macfarlane, *Original Copy: Plagiarism and Originality in Nineteenth-Century Literature*, 2007; Scott McGill, *Plagiarism in Latin Literature*, 2012; Richard Terry, *The Plagiarism Allegation in English Literature from Butler to Sterne*, 2010.

PLATFORMS

To some, the web promised to provide an unmediated and unfettered information landscape. Traditional media systems funnel information through a bottleneck of professional production and editorial selection. This funnel can be gripped by concentrated economic power, government control, or both. The *Word Wide Web appeared to be the opposite: the opportunities for contribution wide open and freewheeling, the tools of production simple and distributed, the editorial oversight nearly nonexistent and easily skirted. Participation would displace consumption, anyone could contribute as they pleased, and decentralized communities would flourish. A public sphere, a celestial jukebox, and a "marketplace of ideas" that would naturally generate knowledge and variety and truth—all seemed on the horizon.

The web was not without intermediaries, but at first they all appeared to be infrastructural, telecommunicative: network nodes and domain name registrars that ushered the *bits around, web hosts and *internet service providers that charged for access but remained agnostic as to what users did with it. But new intermediaries soon emerged, designed to host, facilitate, and profit from this unfettered bounty of information: search engines, blogging tools, content archives, and social media sites. These intermediaries did address some of the drawbacks of the open web. Some simplified the tools and expertise needed to produce information online; some alleviated the burdens of finding information in a rapidly expanding web. A few even figured out how to be financially solvent, in an ecosystem where users blanched at paying for services directly, and rejected attempts to own content as a land grab. These intermediaries professed fealty to the spirit of *digital culture: access for all, evaluation on meritocratic grounds, governance through rough consensus, and a decentralized structure more like a "bazaar" than the "cathedral" that was traditional media.

Since then, over more than a decade, the kinds of encounters with information and people that were once scattered across the web have been largely gathered up onto a handful of "platforms" run by a handful of companies. These platforms have worked hard not just to facilitate, but to ingest the flows of information the web itself used to handle. To be free of intermediaries, we accepted new intermediaries.

A term like *platform* does not drop from the sky. It is drawn from the available cultural vocabulary, by particular stakeholders with particular aims, and carefully massaged so as to resonate with particular audiences. Like other structural metaphors (think *network*, *broadcast*, or *channel*), the term is amorphous and malleable, but not empty. Through the boom and bust waves of *internet investment (of both capital and enthusiasm), platforms promised users an open playing field for the free flow of information, promised advertisers a wide space in which to link their products to popular content, and promised policy makers that they would be a fair and impartial conduit for all that information—requiring no further regulation. Social media companies have embraced the term, and it has even expanded to refer to services that broker the exchange not just of information or sociality but of material goods, transportation, housing, and labor.

Terms like these matter as much for what they hide, however, as for what they reveal.

First, *platform* downplays the fact that these services are not flat or unfettered. Their core offer is to organize, structure, and channel information, according to arrangements designed both by the platform (newsfeed algorithms, featured-partner arrangements, front-page placement, categories) and by the user, though structured or measured by the platform (friend or follower networks, playlists, trending or popularity metrics). Platforms architect every aspect of the information exchange: the technical standards of the content, what counts as a commodity, what is measured as value, and the depth and duration of the relationship—all of which can change at the whim of the designers. The idea of a platform captures none of this, implying that all activity is equally and meritocratically available, visible, public, and potentially viral. In other words, platforms are intimately involved in the exchange they claim to merely facilitate.

Second, platforms are driven by their economic imperatives, not the demands of users. In the West, these platforms are, of course, nearly all for-profit operations. Advertising still powerfully drives the design and policy decisions of many platforms. But most have discovered that they can better target this advertising by gathering and mining the lucrative data that users leave behind—the content they post, the search queries they enter, the traces of their activity through the site and beyond, the preferences they indicate along the way, and the "social graph" they build through their interactions with others. This makes platforms interested in not only supporting their users' participation but sustaining their "engagement," luring them back, expanding the community, all so as to elicit more data, and more kinds of data, and sell it all to advertisers and content partners.

Third, their relationship with the state is not one of independence or antagonism, as some like to proclaim—a common rhetorical tactic for US information providers. The classified National Security Agency documents *leaked by Edward Snowden in 2013 revealed that many major platforms had reluctantly granted data access to the NSA. More informal confluences of interest and approach between platforms and the state have since become apparent: soft pressure to safeguard the democratic process; allied efforts to restrict terrorist recruiting, hate speech, and propaganda; and the growing entanglement of politicians and platforms through online advertising. In China, Russia, and other parts of the world, where government oversight of communication systems trumps the protections of free expression, there is far less illusion about the way social media platforms work intimately with governments to surveil and constrain users in particular ways.

Fourth, platforms are not entirely open or entirely impartial. They do, indeed they must, moderate the content and activity of users. Anyone can make a website to which any user can post anything he or she pleases, with no rules or guidelines. But such a website would, in all likelihood, quickly become a cesspool of hate and pornography and subsequently be abandoned. To produce and sustain an appealing platform requires moderation of some form: Platforms are defined not by what they permit but by what they disallow. For the larger platforms, this requires a complex and largely opaque logistical arrangement of detection, review, and enforcement. Moderation is not unique to social media. Analogous interventions made by traditional information producers similarly weave together questions of propriety, legality, and the wants of the audience: industry "standards and practices" norms, bleeped profanity in broadcasting, movie and television ratings systems for children, black bars across images and brown paper around magazines, and edited, Photoshopped, and forged political and news photographs. And like these older forms, platform moderation must also be obscured and disavowed, to maintain the illusion of an open platform and to avoid greater legal and cultural responsibility.

Finally, platforms obscure much of the labor that goes into producing and maintaining these services. As with the great and powerful Oz, the audience is not supposed to see the director or the set decorators or the stagehands, only the actors in the spotlight and the technical apparatus that supports them. So it is with platforms: faith in the algorithms that manage the circulation of information at this scale allow these platforms to present as systems that can run themselves. But social media platforms are in fact the product of an immense amount of human work, whether it be designing those algorithms, cleaning that data, or policing away prohibited content.

Given all these characteristics, platforms are a fundamentally distinct information configuration—materially, institutionally, financially, and socially. Scholars, activists, and policy makers have had to develop a new critical vocabulary, to unwind the claims platforms make about themselves and pinpoint the ways they shape public discourse and social life. It is useful to think of platforms as *media*, as *markets*, and as *infrastructures*—or as all three, often at the same time. These understandings help highlight the nature of platforms' hidden investments and explain their preferred solutions to intractable social problems.

Platforms may structure the distribution of information differently than broadcasting and publishing, but they offer the same basic deal as traditional media: we'll handle distribution for you—terms and conditions apply. Like media, platforms benefit from making themselves appear as essential spaces of community and engagement. Their influence, and their vulnerability, revolve around occupying this middle position. And like media, they shape the flow of public information in important but subtle (and deniable) ways. This makes platforms the kind of institution that, historically, we have held responsible to a degree for the information they circulate, like broadcasters, newspapers, scientific publications, or radio.

But if traditional media are funnels, platforms are brokers. Economists have noted that social media platforms are "multi-sided markets," in which a broker (i.e., the platform) profits by bringing together sellers and buyers, producers and audiences, or those in charge of tasks and those with the necessary skills to accomplish them. So just as Uber profits by pairing independent drivers with interested passengers, coordinating their interaction, and taking a fee off the exchange, Twitter does much the same: pairing independent speakers with interested listeners, coordinating their interaction, and taking a fee off the exchange—in the form of valuable user data. It is a position that can be, in a few instances, extremely lucrative: the largest platforms are more than brokers in a market; they are in some ways markets in and of themselves.

And if platforms mediate and broker the exchange of information, they also stand beneath and beyond these information flows, providing a social infrastructure on which communities can be built, and a technical infrastructure on which additional tools can be designed. Some build identity architectures (profiles, login mechanisms) that extend out to other sites, computationally linking themselves to the rest of the web. These are strategic attempts to counter the economic risks of being a mere intermediary, by turning themselves into an ecosystem that keeps users using their services and makes their data collection more comprehensive and therefore more valuable. Protected from the market and regulatory forces that might impose obligations on them, platforms are not just too big to fail, but too deep to dismantle.

Tarleton Gillespie

See also algorithms; censorship; commodification; computers; cybernetics/feedback; data; databases; networks; public sphere; social media; surveilling

FURTHER READING

Annabelle Gawer, ed., *Platforms, Markets and Innovation*, 2011; Robert W. Gehl, "The Archive and the Processor: The Internal Logic of Web 2.0," *New Media and Society* 13, no. 8 (2011): 1228–44; Tarleton Gillespie, *Custodians of the Internet: Platforms, Content Moderation, and the Hidden Decisions That Shape Social Media*, 2018; Jean-Christophe Plantin, Carl Lagoze, Paul N. Edwards, and Christian Sandvig, "Infrastructure Studies Meet Platform Studies in the Age of Google and Facebook," *New Media and Society* 20, no. 1 (2016): 293–310; Eric S. Raymond, "The Cathedral and the Bazaar," *First Monday* 3, no. 2 (1998); Sarah T. Roberts, *Behind the Screen: Content Moderation in the Shadows of Social Media*, 2019; José van Dijck, *The Culture of Connectivity: A Critical History of Social Media*, 2013.

POLITICAL REPORTING

Political reporting is the art of gathering and disseminating information about the state and its rulers while maintaining at least some degree of independence from them. When states seek out this kind of information for themselves, often in secret, it is better described as intelligence; when statesmen and politicians publicize information to advance their own interests, often selectively or misleadingly, it is propaganda. Political reporting therefore challenges the state's control of information. Its history bears the weight of arguments about the rise of civil society and the public sphere, the making of democratic political cultures, and the proliferation of such antidemocratic dangers as polarization, sensationalism, and apathy.

Oral cultures of political reporting both predated the rise of written news and persisted long afterward. Gossip originating in courts, councils, and parliaments routinely found its way into script and print. In *early modern London, the *coffeehouse served as the primary waystation for this traffic, where clerks and courtiers sold the latest information and news writers transcribed rumors for the benefit of their subscribers. In Paris, some *Enlightenment-era *salons doubled as news bureaus, where guests filed items as they entered and the results were compiled into nationally circulated newsletters (*nouvelles à la main*). The ubiquity of the phrase "we hear" in English publications, mirrored by *on dit* in French, attests to the porosity of the boundary between conversation and reportage. In the reception of political news, too, spoken and written communication was symbiotic. Well into the nineteenth century, people commonly pooled resources to buy newspapers, which were then read aloud in clubs, pubs, and other public spaces—a practice that enabled a measure of political participation even for those with no formal political power and little formal education.

In a similar way, scribal modes of political reporting long preceded and coexisted with print. Even when printing technology was readily available, material that might attract the notice of censors was often disseminated in manuscript. In seventeenth-century London, manuscript copies of royal addresses and parliamentary speeches reached tens of thousands of readers at least; so did handwritten pamphlets purporting to pierce the veil of official secrecy with intercepted letters or purloined documents (not all of them genuine). In eighteenth-century France, likewise, the nouvelles à la main evolved from intelligence reports for aristocratic patrons into subscription-based news services without passing through the printing press along the way. Manuscript and oral communication fed off each other as well as print: the most trenchant contemporary commentary on the reign of Louis XV came in poems that were scrawled on bits of paper and sung on street corners.

Examples like these help to explain why the eighteenth century has often been seen as a formative moment for political discourse beyond the reach of the state. And yet, the circulation, reliability, and independence of political information in that period remained limited by later standards. Politics usually played a marginal part in the textual culture that reached the vast majority of people: the broadsheets and ballads filled with colorful tales of crime, the supernatural, and the occult. In publications aimed at the commercial and professional classes, meanwhile, the heavy hand of the state kept a lid on potentially subversive reporting. Across the European continent, censorship, licensing, and privilege systems rendered independent reporting on domestic politics a tenuous prospect at best. The only legally permissible way to publish a newspaper story about government in prerevolutionary France, for instance, was to reprint items from the official *Gazette de France* (Gazette of France). It is true that a lively extraterritorial press, whose Francophone output was printed in the Low Countries and then flowed across the border, circumvented this restriction to a great extent. But many European newspapers avoided potential complications by simply transcribing official documents without commentary, leaving practical-minded merchants and lawyers to calculate the consequences for themselves. Printers' dependence on government advertising and other contracts offered another incentive for political quiescence.

Britain was unique in the European context as the home of a robust in-country press that regularly and critically covered domestic politics before the end of the eighteenth century. After the 1695 lapse of the Licensing Act, which provided for prepublication censorship and the registration of printing presses through the Stationers' Company, a lively new crop of newspapers sprang up to rival the official *London Gazette*, not just in the capital but in provincial cities as well. While the threat of postpublication censorship by prosecution persisted for more than a century—along with the use of fiscal policy to hamper radical titles—the shift away from the systematic prior regulation of political print proved decisive. "Of publick transactions," Samuel Johnson could write in 1773, "the whole world is now informed by newspapers." (It was, of course, a less triumphant story in Britain's colonies overseas, where the seizure of presses, the prohibition of subversive publications, and the imprisonment of dissenters constrained press freedom for as long as the British ruled.)

The growth of the public sphere in eighteenth-century Britain was closely linked to the rise of partisan media. As Whigs and Tories vied for power, deep-pocketed patrons on both sides subsidized newspapers and paid off journalists. Savvy governments learned the lesson that "managing" press coverage—not only with bribery, but also through the dissemination of favorable stories, the cultivation of sympathetic writers, and the dangled promise of access, prestige, and advancement—had certain advantages over the brute force of censorship. As the press became more political, the information it provided did not necessarily become more reliable; gossip, innuendo, and character assassination loomed large. Alexander Pope, in his 1743 satire *The Dunciad*, identified "three chief qualifications" for political writers (whom he revealingly termed "Party-writers"): "to stick at nothing, to delight in flinging dirt, and to slander in the dark by guess."

The métier of the journalist—to summarize and clarify events, constructing narratives out of disorderly experience—itself encouraged the definition of ideological battle lines, the labeling of factions, and the identification of heroes and villains. In debates over the ratification of the US Constitution in the 1780s, as in in the French revolutionary tumult of the 1790s, the number and circulation of newspapers exploded. The overwhelming majority of them staked out identities as Federalist or anti-Federalist, revolutionary or counterrevolutionary, even when they also bemoaned factionalism and paid lip service to national unity. British radicals like John Wilkes and William Cobbett made their name as writers and editors, touted their publications as the lifeblood of popular sovereignty, and transformed their battles against sedition charges into causes célèbres. Partisanship was not only a subject of political journalism, in other words, but also a creation of it.

A corollary to this development, in the nineteenth century, was the idealization of political rhetoric. Britain again offers a paradigmatic case. As parliamentary liberalism fostered romantic visions of enlightened men debating their views in a reasoned way, conveying those debates to ordinary people emerged as a major function of the liberal press. While circulation grew with the gradual elimination of levies on cheap print (the so-called taxes on knowledge) between 1836 and 1855, newspapers devoted a significant portion of their columns to reprinting the text of political speeches, reflecting a paternalistic ambition to elevate and improve the values of an expanding electorate. One indication of this civic-mindedness is that the parliamentary reporters who scribbled *shorthand notes in the gallery above the House of Commons were regarded as the elite of the journalistic tribe; most were university educated, and many, like Charles Dickens, went on to prestigious careers in other fields. When platform addresses outside Parliament became common in the 1870s and 1880s, newspapers printed them verbatim as well. With the advent of the telegraph, readers across the country could pore over the text of a speech within a few hours of its delivery.

For all the attention lavished on their rhetoric, Victorian political leaders never communicated with the electorate in a totally unmediated way. It was political identity, not the quality of stenography, that distinguished newspapers from one another; everything from editorial commentary to the choice and placement of stories reflected a clear ideological slant, a partisan affiliation, or both. Even so, the pronouncements of political leaders received overwhelmingly respectful treatment. The "penny press," which supplanted the more radical "pauper press" after 1855, was both a crucial base of support for the Gladstonian Liberal Party and a champion of small-*l* liberal values. The didactic sensibility of these newspapers, urging humble readers to prove themselves worthy of the franchise, injected a lofty sense of purpose into political journalism—though, notably, without any hint of the later belief that journalists themselves were mere observers rather than participants in politics.

Only in the final decades of the nineteenth century did newspapers across Europe and the United States begin to deemphasize their identity as political actors. That is when liberal-style political journalism was eclipsed by novel forms of commercial journalism. The economics of the newspaper business changed as brash newcomers—the *Daily Telegraph* and the *Daily Mail* in Britain, *Le Petit Journal* (The little daily) and *Le Petit Parisien* (The little Parisian) in France, the *New York World* in the United States— chased the widest possible circulation, trading steady subscription fees from modest but dedicated readerships for the advertising-driven revenue of the mass market. These papers soft-pedaled ideological and partisan loyalties to avoid alienating potential readers, pinning their hopes on the appeal of compelling stories instead. (In Britain, moreover, the 1883 passage of the Corrupt Practices Act prevented parties from buying off editors as they had routinely done in the past.) "News" accordingly displaced opinion on many front pages, elevating journalistic values of detachment, impartiality, and neutrality to newfound prominence. At the same time, "news" itself had less and less to do with politics, as *publishers found better luck boosting sales with human-interest stories, celebrity profiles, and the old standbys of crime and catastrophe. The rise of colorful *faits divers* (miscellaneous, often sensational human interest stories) came at the expense of the comparatively dry rhetoric recorded in parliamentary debate columns, which steadily shrank. The advent of objectivity, in other words, had less to do with the ethical reformation of political journalism than with the intensification of a struggle for the public's attention. Although few newspapers renounced their political voice altogether, politics no longer furnished their raison d'être, and commercialism imposed constraints on their ability to intervene in politics.

Discontent with political reporting in the present often stems from a desire to recapture the civic purpose of nineteenth-century liberal journalism without replicating the conditions that made it possible: deference to the authority of political leaders; unabashed partisanship; rootedness in the associational life of parties and clubs; and insulation from the pressures of a mass market. Every one of these conditions became far more elusive in the twentieth century. A newly adversarial style of reporting—especially pronounced after the 1960s—treated politicians with skepticism and attached little significance to their rhetoric, devaluing the ideas behind the speeches along the way. Ever more restrictive notions of objectivity, meanwhile, discouraged reporters from expressing ideas of their own. As party organizations withered, journalists had to appeal to atomistic news consumers rather than tapping into existing loyalties, favoring decontextualized novelty over intellectual coherence. The increasingly capital-intensive character of the news business, in print and even more dramatically in broadcasting, only strengthened incentives to cover politics as entertainment. So did the digitization of media, which unbundled stories from newspapers and made each one a commodity to be valued in clicks, "shares," and "likes." In much of the world, political reporting freed itself from the grip of the state, only to end up under the dominion of the market instead.

Erik Linstrum

See also bureaucracy; commodification; digitization; governance; newsletters; newspapers; public sphere; publicity/publication; readers

FURTHER READING

Hannah Barker and Simon Burrows, eds., *Press, Politics, and the Public Sphere in Europe and North America, 1760–1820,* 2007; Jean K. Chalaby, *The Invention of Journalism,* 1998; Noah Millstone, *Manuscript Circulation and the Invention of Politics in Early Stuart England,* 2016; Jeremy D. Popkin, *News and Politics in the Age of Revolution: Jean Luzac's "Gazette de Leyde,"* 1989; James Vernon, *Politics and the People: A Study in English Political Culture, c. 1815–1867,* 1993; Stephen Ward, *The Invention of Journalism Ethics: The Path to Objectivity and Beyond,* 2015.

POSTAL CUSTOMERS

Although mail services now pose as democratic systems for exchanging information, the original users of the mail were royalty. Whereas literate persons of all ranks might compose letters, and masses of ordinary men and women could transmit them, to be an authorized user of a postal network was a rare privilege. In antiquity, postal networks were mouthpieces of empire, instruments of rule, technologies for extending political power from palaces and courts to distant locales. Herodotus's celebrated couriers, who worked the gloom-of-night shift and delivered mail in bad weather, bore the authority of the Persian king, because by definition any message conveyed in their hands hailed from the absent, invisible ruler. Those same Persian deliverymen, mounted on fast steeds, also appear in the Hebrew Bible. In the book of Esther, political power lies in a postal system featuring an army of letter carriers and a single postal patron. Only King Ahasuerus gets to use the mail.

In subsequent periods in the history of the West, mail systems accommodated more users, but those systems remained restricted. Monastic orders, universities, the papal curia, or consortia of merchants established regular circuits of mail exchange in medieval and *early modern Europe. Such mail circuits were closed to outsiders. Meanwhile, in other parts of the world, larger, organized systems of postal relay transmitted the word of the Mongol rulers in the late thirteenth century in such places as China and Iran. None of these mail systems created cultures of popular use, nor did the legendary postal service of the Taxis family of northern Italy, commissioned by the Habsburgs in the late fifteenth century to establish a long-distance network across Europe. The Taxis post, whose routes dominated mail exchange over much of the continent for three centuries, oversaw and underwrote an expansion of private user and uses; this expansion made possible the increased exchange of letters and books among scholars who increasingly perceived themselves as forming an interconnected *Republic of Letters. Nonetheless states claimed monopolies over the right to post letters over fixed routes, though they might grant special privileges to companies to provide this postal service, which entailed guaranteeing regular, reliable delivery and, crucially, regulating access.

In the course of the nineteenth century, a very different model of postal service took hold through much of the Western world. Mail service had already expanded (along paths blazed by global capitalism) in volume, extent, and frequency throughout the early modern period. But a series of innovations at the national level, inaugurated and epitomized by the British postal reforms of Rowland Hill from 1837 to 1839, ushered in a new era of mail exchange. In advocating cheap, uniform, prepaid postage, Hill envisioned unprecedented volumes of correspondence, which he promised would provide a higher return on the fixed costs of letter delivery. Hill was not simply altering the business model of the British Post Office, however. He was also promoting mail exchange as a mass activity rather than the special domain of merchants. Cheap, uniform, pre-paid postage soon became structuring norms in the canton-level postal systems of Zurich, Geneva, and Basel, then of national ones in Brazil, the United States, Belgium, France, Spain, Denmark, Holland, and Luxemburg. Over the span of two decades, a new mass mail system came into being. By the 1870s, it had gone practically global, subsuming new or modernized postal networks in other parts of the world (Russia, Egypt, Japan, Turkey, Persia) within a World Postal Union, thereby creating single continuous postal space on Rowland Hill's model of cheap postage and broad participation.

Beyond its massive popularity as an interactive medium, two crucial features distinguish this communications system. The first is universal access—the institutionalized expectation (sometimes codified in law) that, in principle, everyone is entitled to send and receive mail, subject only to the requirements of payment. The second, subtler development in the nineteenth-century mail system was the establishment of vast zones in which letters, printed forms, and objects could circulate with minimal friction. Rather than imagining the mail as a set of routes and trajectories of varying distance and difficulty, postal bureaucracies in Europe and the Americas increasingly redefined the mail as a homogeneous space of continuous circulation, which users simply and cheaply paid to enter.

Within this renovated landscape of information circulation, a new representative figure emerged—not the letter carrier of classical pedigree, but the modern postal user, defined and recognized both as a customer who could pay to send or receive letters and objects and, even more abstractly, as an ever-present potential addressee.

What it meant to be an implied potential user of a modern mail system varied by place and time. In the United States in the mid-nineteenth century, when postal service shifted dramatically from broadcasting news to facilitating mass interactivity, the creation of a single rate of postage across a vast nation precisely at the moment of its transcontinental expansion turned a highly mobile and predominantly literate population into a world of postal users. Consumers of all classes were expected to have access to paper, pen, stamps, and postal facilities. And any individual—a relative living across the country, a credulous rural customer, a celebrity in the news, a stranger on a train—could in principle be reached through the mail system. All one needed to address fellow postal users was their personal (though rarely unique) name and the name of the town or city where they might be expected to inquire for mail at a post office.

In that respect, American mail users were users of particular spaces, and access to mail was mediated by the people and forces that monitored or regulated access to those spaces. In large cities, the anonymous, promiscuous, and bustling character of the purpose-built post office stigmatized the appearance of women at letterboxes and counters, and it led in many places to gender-segregated entrances and windows. In smaller towns, by contrast, where post offices were often located in general stores, taverns, or postmasters' homes, personal relations might place additional constraints on users' attempts to send or receive mail, especially in the cases of children, wives, or enslaved persons seeking to access the mail without the authorization of parents, husbands, or masters. Modern mail systems may have erased distance as a determinant of cost, but they did not thereby facilitate placeless or frictionless telecommunications. Nor were American mail users geographically indeterminate, although the system presumed and allowed considerable mobility, since the postal address designated as a domain a broadly accessible post office rather than a fixed residence.

Frequent users often found this feature of US mail service inconvenient, especially urban merchants, who paid additional fees to private delivery services to avoid trips to the post office. Users of other modern postal networks also protested what the English novelist Anthony Trollope (himself a longtime postal clerk and official) branded a "deficiency" in the American mails. "The United States Post-office does not assume to itself the duty of taking letters to the houses of those for whom they are intended," he noted in 1862 with a mix of bemusement and outrage, as if describing the customs of a primitive civilization, "but holds itself as having completed the work for which the original postage has been paid, when it has brought them to the window of the Post-office of the town to which they are addressed." Among other costs of this system, millions (literally) of pieces of uncollected mail washed up annually in the Dead Letter Office in Washington, DC, the great postal cemetery that fascinated Herman Melville's narrator in "Bartleby, the Scrivener" (1853).

The alternative model, which British and French postal patrons took for granted by 1860, subsumed home delivery into the act of mail transmission and (as Trollope implied) included its cost in the price of postage. This model may have been more feasible in European countries, where mail use was overwhelmingly urban and disproportionately local. But in the United States, where the postal system had been designed from its inception as a medium for connecting a dispersed rural population, and where mail use remained, even after the postage reforms of 1845 and 1851, notably long distance (though still disproportionately urban), free home delivery lay beyond the means or goals of mail service. Nonetheless, in 1863, just one year after Trollope published his critique, Congress introduced delivery in close to fifty large American cities. Other cities would soon be added, and by the mid-1880s mail delivery was standard throughout urban America. By century's end, free delivery would extend to rural users as well, thus completing the slow but steady transformation of the US post into what Trollope would recognize as a thoroughly modern mail system: a network in which private homes and businesses, rather than personal names and public post offices, served as the primary exchange sites and constitutive addresses of most users and uses.

By linking postal participation with residence, modern mail systems (unlike telegraphy at the time or email in more recent years but quite like telephones for much of the twentieth century) entered the home and provided standard domestic amenities, facilitated and represented by mailboxes on front lawns and letter slots built into front doors. The incorporation of residential space into mail networks in the form of an *address*, a communicative act that has become a metonym for a geographical location, has carried important legal and political consequences in many modern mail systems—for commercial transactions and debts, voting, jury service, and relations between governments and citizens/subjects more generally. Postal *codes continue to designate neighborhoods in major Western cities (notably Paris, London, and Berlin), and in the United States knowing one's place in a mail system (in the form of a billing zip code) is necessary for online commerce or for purchasing gasoline with a credit card. Even with the ascendancy of rival communications media, which have allegedly consigned the mail system to obsolescence or even irrelevance, it is still as postal users that most modern subjects and their homes remain accessible, legible, and exposed to contact and scrutiny. To be a modern mail user is thus to enjoy dizzying mobility and circulation and, at the same time, to be profoundly fixed.

David M. Henkin

See also letters; merchants; newsletters; privacy; public sphere; readers; social media; telecommunications

FURTHER READING

Monica Cure, *Picturing the Postcard: A New Media Crisis at the Turn of the Century*, 2018; Konstantin Dierks, *In My Power: Letter Writing and Communications in Early America*, 2009; Catherine J. Golden, *Posting It: The Victorian Revolution in Letter-Writing*, 2009; David M. Henkin, *The Postal Age: The Emergence of Mass Communications in Nineteenth-Century America*, 2006; Richard R. John, *Spreading the News: The American Postal System from Franklin to Morse*, 1995; Bernhard Siegert, *Relays: Literature as an Epoch of the Postal System*, 1993, translated by Kevin Repp, 1999; Paul Starr, *The Creation of the Media: Political Origins of Modern Communications*, 2004; David Vincent, *Literacy and Popular Culture: England, 1750–1914*, 1989.

PRINTED VISUALS

More than a generation before Johannes Gutenberg (ca. 1400–1468) supervised the printing of the first books using movable type in the 1450s in Mainz, multiple copies of visual images were printed on paper and distributed in substantial numbers in Europe. Although it is often argued that the invention of movable type initiated a revolution in the transmission of information throughout Europe, the role of printed images in the dissemination of information is only beginning to be understood. Historians disagree about such matters as whether prints were a necessary precondition for the emergence of the Protestant *Reformation or just one factor that facilitated it and whether prints engendered the international *Renaissance style, a hybrid ensemble of physical characteristics that juxtaposed elements from classical, Gothic, Italian, and Flemish works and presented particular inflections in various sites. William Ivins Jr. (1881–1961), one of the earliest and most passionate advocates of the importance of prints in intellectual endeavors, argues in *Prints and Visual Communication* that "exactly repeatable pictorial statements" were a prerequisite to certain scientific advances. In response, Ernst Gombrich (1909–2001) contends that Ivins exaggerates the roles of printed pictorial statements at the expense of verbal communication. In *The Art of Philosophy*, I underline the importance of both text and image in the organization and exchange of information. Printed text and image—often in tandem with one another—played crucial roles in some of early modern Europe's most influential movements, whether ideological ones like the Reformation or artistic ones like the international Renaissance style. They were also integral to the spread of information beyond the European continent and to the interrelations between Europe and other parts of the world.

The term *printed visual* denotes images, texts, designs, or combinations of these that are impressed onto a support, such as a piece of paper or fabric. This notion encapsulates a broad range of methods employed to create numerous copies of a scheme. Printed visuals not only have played an important role in the organization of information and the transmission and generation of knowledge, but their technologies have also functioned as enduring metaphors for cognition and memory. At the same time, printed visuals were often viewed with suspicion and understood as entities that could increase confusion and multiply errors and misunderstanding.

To create a woodcut, a design is drawn onto a block, and the areas that are meant to be white in the print are removed from the block with a knife or a chisel. Rather than being drawn onto the block directly, the design can also be transferred to the block in a variety of ways, such as carboning, incising, or pouncing. The cut woodblock is coated with ink, and in the process of printing, its design is inverted. Because both woodcuts and movable type are printed in relief, they could be placed together within a single form, making it possible for printers to impress images and texts concurrently and also to integrate images inside of texts. As Lucille Chia has emphasized, in Chinese imprints from the Song dynasty (1127–1279) onward the physical relationship between text and *tu*—an untranslatable term that could refer to a map, picture, diagram, portrait, chart, or table—is arguably still tighter, insofar as the tu were often inscribed on the same block as the text.

Whereas woodcuts and movable type are relief-printing technologies, engravings are a technique of intaglio printmaking—that is, a technique whereby an image is incised into a surface and the sunken image is made to contain the ink. In the creation of engravings, a burin is employed to inscribe metal (typically copper) plates. By contrast, in producing etchings—another intaglio printmaking technique—artists used corrosive acids to incise plates. In either case, pressure is then employed to push the paper into the inked lines below the plate's surface. By the end of the fifteenth century, the roller press was used to ease this printing process. A disadvantage of intaglio prints as compared to woodcuts for the production of books was that they could not be printed concurrently with movable type.

Textual and pictorial seals, technologies that produce printed visuals, existed already in the Western Han period (206 BCE–9 CE) in China. By the Eastern Han era (25–220 CE) woodcut blocks were used to print textiles; and they were employed on paper toward the late seventh century CE. Woodblock printing prevailed as the most widespread type of relief printing in China until the nineteenth century. Most of the oldest surviving Chinese prints are Buddhist. From the Song (960–1279) and Yuan (1279–1368) periods, prints survive in classical Confucian works and publications on governments. Printed portraits can also be found in biographical works. In addition, prints of plants, animals, maps, city plans, architecture, and bronze vessels appear in works on such topics as medicine, agronomy, and local history. In the late sixteenth and early seventeenth centuries, Chinese book illustration and printmaking flourished; in this era, woodcuts came to be integrated into works of fiction and drama, handbooks, and manuals for artists.

Woodblock printing arrived in Japan during the eighth century via China or Korea. Intaglio printing came into use there only during the twentieth century. Until the late sixteenth century, the clergy and the aristocracy patronized Japanese printmaking, barring the period from the late eighth to the eleventh century when the practice of printmaking briefly stopped. Movable type entered Japan in the last decade of the sixteenth century from Europe, through Catholic missionaries, and from Korea, where the technology had existed for some time. Although movable type was initially used in Japan, by the mid-seventeenth century, it was abandoned as printmakers opted to cut all the elements of a page onto a single block. Secular woodblock printing thrived in the Edo period (1600–1868) with its shifting sociopolitical conditions. The *genre of ukiyo-e or "pictures of the floating world," for instance, presented the enjoyments of food, theater, brothels, and other entertainment sites in Japanese towns. According to Elizabeth Mary Berry, a sense of national community arose among readers in Japan between 1590 and 1700 thanks to the proliferation of printed genres that produced a wide-ranging "library of public information" pertaining to public and private life. Other historians, by contrast, have not tied this shift to printed visuals and have argued instead that this sense of national cultural identity emerged only in the late nineteenth century.

The earliest likely handling of woodblocks in Europe occurred in the thirteenth century, when they were adopted to impress patterns on fabrics. The first paper prints in Europe were probably produced in the second half of the fourteenth century. Wood-cuts came to be made in sizable quantities in central Europe and southern Germany at the latest by 1425. Engravings probably started to be fabricated in Germany in the following decade, and etchings were likely invented around the turn of the sixteenth century in Germany.

Initially, woodcuts produced in Europe visualized devotional subjects, such as Christ, the Virgin and Child, and saints. Engravings likewise showed devotional themes, but in addition engravers manufactured secular representations, including ornamental designs, grotesque alphabets, and satires. In the years between 1470 and the mid-sixteenth century, an understanding of prints as independent artworks developed. Two important prints that functioned as artworks in their own right were Martin Schongauer's (1448–91) *Large Procession to Cavalry* and Andrea Mantegna's (1431–1506) *Entombment*. The technical achievements of both these artists were developed in subsequent years by Albrecht Dürer (1471–1528) and Marcantonio Raimondi (1480–1534).

European missionaries and colonial forces brought techniques of mechanically printed texts and images into South Asia, although Chinese block printing was already employed in Tibetan regions prior to European interventions. In Goa, for instance, printing was introduced in 1556 and became an important tool in the dissemination of Christianity. In addition, the influx of European prints into South Asia from at least 1556 onward made it possible for artists to examine and to absorb visual information concerning European artistic practices. In 1580, *Jesuit priests, for example, gave a copy of the Royal Polyglot Bible printed by Christoph Plantin in Antwerp between 1568 and 1573 to Emperor Akbar (r. 1556–1605); the book's eight volumes contained multiple engravings that imperial artists examined closely.

As printed visual representations were produced in ever growing numbers throughout early modern Europe and other parts of the globe, critics and historians, eager to understand their benefits and drawbacks, began to theorize and analyze them. In a chapter entitled "De l'utilité des Estampes, & de leur usage" (On the usefulness and use of prints) in the treatise *L'idée du peintre parfait* (The idea of the perfect painter, 1699), the French art critic Roger de Piles (1635–1709) comments on the multiple functions of prints. Among their benefits he lists their capacities to instruct, to persuade, and to strengthen the memory. Other theorists, from Peter Ramus (1515–72) to Thomas Hobbes (1588–1679) to the Abbé Michel de Marolles (1600–1681), champion these and other advantages in the ways that prints categorize and convey information. Indeed, printed visuals accumulated and conveyed myriad units of data and ideas to European viewers, from quotations of ancient texts to the forms and colors of plants to definitions of concepts to physiognomies.

Siegmund Jacob Apin (1693–1732), rector of the Aegidienschule (in Braunschweig, Germany), composed an especially helpful synoptic overview of diverse kinds of pedagogical and mnemonic printed visuals produced in sixteenth- and seventeenth-century Europe. This work, entitled *Dissertatio de variis discendi methodis memoriae causa inventis earumque usu et abusu* (Dissertation on various methods of learning, invented for the sake of memory, and on their use and abuse), was published first in 1725 and in a revised and augmented edition in 1731. In his first chapter, Apin presents accounts of more than one hundred engravings, woodcuts, and illustrated books that he organizes into twenty different subjects that range from philosophy, to history, to geography, to astronomy. Apin's treatise displays the enthusiasm that early modern scholars and educators shared for the ability of prints to order and disseminate information. But he is also conscious of the shortcomings of visualization. In this vein, the second chapter of *Dissertatio* outlines some of the dangers inherent in the prints discussed in chapter 1. Apin argues, for instance, that mnemonic images cause confusion and augment the labor of students when they do not resemble the things that they are meant to denote. In addition, he contends that when teaching abstract notions, visual representations can never capture conceptual theories fully. He is concerned that such prints will cause students to confuse particulars for universals.

Apin singles out one engraving for its misleading imagery: *Clara totius physiologiae synopsis* (Clear synopsis of physics in its entirety, 1615), designed by Martin Meurisse (1584–1644), a Franciscan professor of philosophy at the Grand Couvent des Cordeliers in Paris, in collaboration with the engraver Léonard Gaultier (1560/61–35) (figure 1); the broadside was published by Jean Messager (1572–1649), and an anonymous engraver of lettering inscribed its texts. Apin was likely upset by such details as *Synopsis*'s representation of prime matter, through the partially formed woman at the bottom of the broadside, who acts out the process of substantial change: whereas her head, neck, and hands are formed, the rest of her is not yet. The detail uses lines to show prime matter, even though it should not have any form at all; consequently, Meurisse and Gaultier fail to capture this philosophical concept accurately and risk misleading or confusing observers.

In conveying and organizing information through printed representations, scholars and artists often relied on two especially crucial mechanisms that aided visual thinking. First, they used the space of the page to exhibit and to map out theoretical relationships. *Artificiosa totius logices descriptio* (Artificial description of logic in its entirety, 1614) of Meurisse, Gaultier, Messager, and an anonymous engraver of lettering exemplifies how early modern authors ordered concepts across the space of the page to visualize connections (figure 2). This broadside, which shows and comments on Aristotelian scholastic logic, allows viewers to understand at a glance how the discipline of logic can be divided into its parts and how the parts pertain to each other and the whole. The lowest area shows Meurisse, his students, and various personifications of logical concepts approaching a walled garden. The inside of this garden represents the realm of proper logic. The text and images within the garden space summarize the activity of the first operation of the mind, through which the conception of an object or term is brought to the mind. Above is another garden that explicates the activity of the second operation of the mind, through which terms are combined and divided to form propositions. The uppermost area pertains to propositions that are organized into syllogisms or arguments, through the activity of the third operation of the mind. The print's particular sections cannot be understood completely when seen in isolation; rather, they obtain their meanings from their place within the broadside's spatial order.

Second, designers of early modern printed representations often thought through the mechanism of visual commentary, whereby their text and imagery not only illustrated concepts that already existed, but also presented enriching interpretations of preexisting ideas. Consider, for instance, the two flute players to the right of the garden hedge in *Descriptio* (see figure 2). This visual representation and its inscription produce an analogy between the deceptive arguments of Sophists and musical performance that draws on the ancient suspicion of flutes, which deform the face and obstruct the mouth,

Figure 1. Meurisse and Gaultier, *Clara totius physiologiae synopsis* (Clear synopsis of physics in its entirety), 1615. Engraving printed on paper, 25.5×18.5 in. (64.8×47 cm). Bibliothèque nationale de France, Cabinet des Estampes, Paris [AA4].

Figure 2. Meurisse and Gaultier, *Artificiosa totius logices descriptio* (Artificial description of logic in its entirety), 1614. Engraving printed on paper, 22.4×14.4 in. (57×36.5 cm). Bibliothèque royale de Belgique, Cabinet des Estampes, Brussels [S. IV 86231].

the organ required for rational discussions. The observer's understanding of sophistry is enhanced and augmented through this comparison between Sophists and performers who are both focused on how things appear rather than on how they are.

If Meurisse and Gaultier's interpretations of abstract philosophical principles make use of visual thinking through spatial constructs and visual commentaries, printed representations belonging to a genre known as the *imago contrafacta* (counterfeit image) deploy a rhetoric of visual persuasion instead. As Peter Parshall has shown, this image type developed in the sixteenth century in northern Europe and aimed at convincing observers of the credibility of visual information by capturing the truth of particulars. Counterfeit images tended to be works of portraiture, topographies, representations of particular events, and images of natural and supernatural occurrences; they were understood to have been derived either from direct observation or from an image taken from direct observation. Insofar as they claimed to be based on immediate acts of witnessing, counterfeit images were designed to persuade observers that they conveyed trustworthy information.

Another type of printed visual involved the representation of nature by printing drawings made from life. An early such example is a work by the German theologian and botanist Otto Brunfels (1488–1534), *Vivae eicones herbarum* (Images of herbs made from life, 1530–36), featuring woodcuts designed and cut by Hans Weiditz (1495–1537). Its German translation of 1532 bore the title *Contrafrayt Kreütterbuch* (Counterfeit herbal). The noun *contrafactum* and the verb *contrafacere* do not appear in classical language. The term *counterfeit* is derived from the medieval Latin verb *contrafacere*, which could mean "to imitate" either as an accurate likeness or in the more negative sense of a forgery or an intended deception, akin to the meaning of the word *counterfeit* today. Both neutral and negative connotations of the term existed in the fifteenth and sixteenth centuries. The peculiar visual rhetoric of Brunfels's counterfeit images includes the wormholes, bent stems, and shriveled leaves of the representations of such plants as the *lappa major* (burdock plant) (figure 3). These blemishes were meant to convince observers that they were viewing a representation based on firsthand experience of this particular plant.

Whereas the creators of counterfeit prints aimed to convey persuasive information concerning particular objects of study, other artists and scholars produced printed visuals that juxtaposed text and image to generate visual arguments that attempted to capture information on their objects of study completely and in general terms. As Sachiko Kusukawa has explained, this category of printed visual representation, characterized as an *icon absoluta* (absolute image), offered an ideal account of an entity based on numerous firsthand experiences. Both Leonhart Fuchs's (1501–66) *De historia stirpium* (On the history of plants, 1542) and Andreas Vesalius's (1514–64) *De humani corporis fabrica* (On the fabric of the human body, 1543) feature woodcuts that are not representations of individual specimens with eccentricities, such as those found in Brunfels's *Vivae eicones herbarum*; rather, they depict objects of study in an ideal and general form. Vesalius and Fuchs aimed to elevate the knowledge generated by medical botany and anatomy to the realm of *scientia*, or theoretical knowledge, from that of *historia*, a descriptive kind of knowledge; it is for this reason that they include "absolute" images in their works, that is, images that capture plants and bodies in ideal and general terms, seeking to embody something essential about their objects of study.

Figure 3. Brunfels, "Burdock plant," in *Vivae eicones herbarum* (Images of herbs made from life), 1532. Woodcut printed on paper. 7.5×12.38 in. The Huntington Library, San Marino, California.

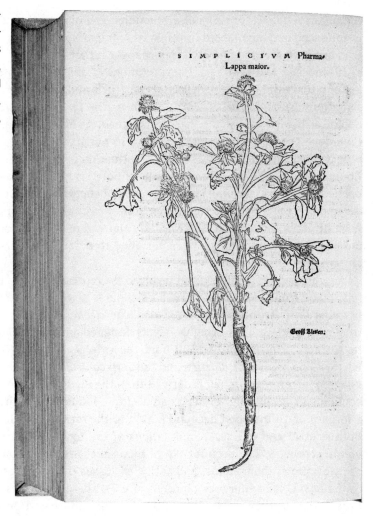

Not only did printed visuals enable observers to instruct, remember, think, persuade, and make arguments, but their technologies also acted as important metaphors to explain the processes of cognition. The association between thinking and printing technologies goes back to antiquity: in his treatise *On Memory* (450a31–450b25), for instance, Aristotle likens mental images to wax impressions. By the early modern era, the Aristotelian printing metaphor was often updated with more recent technologies, as scholars, such as the French Jesuit Louis Richeome (1544–1625), described thoughts as being "engraved" onto the memory.

The metaphorical association between technologies of printed visuals and cognition continues into the present, as evinced by such phrases as "photographic memory" or "flashback," which derive from photographic technologies. During the nineteenth century, novel reproductive techniques came to replace or supplement standard graphic technologies such as engraving, mezzotint, and etching. Photography (invented and developed in the mid-nineteenth century) and lithography (invented in 1798–99), as well as technologies that enabled illustrated books and the illustrated press to reach large numbers of people at a low cost, contributed to a massive increase in the dissemination of printed visuals. During this period of enormous transformation, photography soon developed into a popular metaphor for cognition and memory. For example, early in the 1880s, Adolf Kussmaul (1822–1902), a German physician and clinician, likened sensations to "the invisible images, which the sun makes on a prepared silver surface." Moreover, as Kate Flint has shown, the metaphors of the flash and the flashback were developed as well to capture the kinds of memory that offer an often unexpected and undeliberate incursion of a past time into the present moment.

Beyond building on preexisting metaphors of cognition and memory, the advent of novel technologies that enabled the mass reproduction of visuals for the first time in history further contributed to the often-vexed relationship between visuals and knowledge. On the one hand, posters, photographs, illustrated news, and other printed visuals made it possible for massive numbers of individuals to gain access to unprecedented amounts of information. On the other hand, the dramatic shift in the scale of possible communication brought worries about the dangers of widespread manipulation. Joseph Stalin (1878–1953), for instance, carefully doctored photographs to advance his political interests and delete representations of his adversaries. Much like the technology of movable type, and much like the *digital information technology today, the printing of visuals was simultaneously progressive and regressive. The printing of visuals ably facilitated the transmission of information, but it encouraged the spread of disinformation as well.

Susanna Berger

See also art of memory; books; cameras; cards; coins; diagrams; error; knowledge; lithography; maps; media; money; newspapers; observing; photocopiers; teaching

FURTHER READING

Elizabeth Mary Berry, *Japan in Print*, 2006; Kate Flint, *Flash!*, 2018; E. H. Gombrich, "Review of William M. Ivins, Jr., 'Prints and Visual Communication,'" *British Journal for the Philosophy of Science* 6 (1954–55): 168–69; William Ivins Jr., *Prints and Visual Communication*, 1953; Sachiko Kusukawa, *Picturing the Book of Nature*, 2012; David Landau and Peter Parshall, *The Renaissance Print*, 1996; Chia Lucille, "Text and Tu in Context: Reading the Illustrated Page in Chinese Block-printed Books," *Bulletin de L'Ecole française d'Extrême-Orient* 89 (2002): 241–76; Peter Parshall, "*Imago* contrafacta: Image and Facts in the Northern Renaissance," *Art History* 16, no. 4 (1993): 554–79.

PRIVACY

In the "information age," privacy is a public problem. Economic and political fortunes depend on how we understand it, and on how our legal and political systems define and defend it. Debates rage over the various outrages against it that are perpetrated by some of the world's most famous companies, and fears are rife about criminal intrusions into the financial and administrative systems on which everyday commerce depends. But the greater cause of anxiety may be less the infractions than the systems themselves. "Surveillance capitalism," as it has become known, is the systematic collection, investigation, and circulation for profit of information that is gleaned algorithmically from our everyday actions on- and offline. To be a citizen in our era is to live in a world in which privacy is a paramount concern, yet cannot possibly exist in the way that it did for our grandparents. To accept that is to acknowledge a responsibility to tackle one of the most pressing issues of the contemporary world.

But we are not necessarily as well informed as we may suppose about what that issue really is. The first problem with privacy is its notoriously elusive character. Legal efforts to arrive at a conceptual definition have not been wholly successful, because the nature of privacy is not primarily conceptual at all, but historical. Privacy was first projected as an important area of legal, political, technological, and moral concern in America during the Gilded Age. To worry about how our grandparents' sense of privacy has been lost, then, only gets us so far, because most of us know less than we should about what that sense of privacy really was—and about how much it differed from what *their* grandparents had experienced. As we struggle to address privacy's challenges in our own time, we would do well to rest our decisions on a defensible account of how it has evolved.

We may not be sure quite what privacy is, but we do feel that we can tell when it is violated, invaded, stolen, lost, or threatened. The conceptual definitions that have circulated have tended to be occasional, advanced for instrumental purposes, to fight specific battles. However, we can discern trends in how definitions have altered in tone over the centuries. Two stand out. First, beginning in the 1880s and 1890s jurists and writers came to speak conventionally of a *right* of free citizens to remain out of the sight of powerful surveillance. When Samuel Warren and Louis Brandeis coined the phrase "the right to be let alone" in 1890, they were thinking primarily of journalism posting everyday lives of East Coast elites onto the pages of the daily press. But the state might also be the instigator of surveillance: in 1886 the Supreme Court also issued its first interpretation of the Fourth Amendment (prohibiting arbitrary search) since the original passage of the Bill of Rights a century earlier. The conjunction of these two concerns was captured in Warren and Brandeis's remarkably successful slogan. Second, in the years after World War II a conviction developed that privacy was fundamentally *informational*. It had always been so, in a sense. Medieval townsfolk, embedded in a complex world of gossip and rumor, worried about what their neighbors were saying about them. But "information age" discourse came to focus explicitly on this informational character as definitive. That is, privacy was something that inhered, not in a place that could be invaded or an object that could be seized—the home, the intimate letter—but in disembodied traces, collected, perhaps at a distance, via some mediating technology. Privacy was now imperiled by a phone tap, by a computer database, or by an infrared camera aimed at one's house from across the street.

Anxiety that privacy is endangered has been sempiternal. But it should also be acknowledged that the gatherers and users of information—police, researchers, statisticians, corporations, and states—have just as frequently expressed concern at the opposite trend. That is, they have feared that technological and cultural changes might enable people to escape the reach of their vision altogether and, as the FBI has put it, "go dark." Before there were professional police forces at all, for example, British officials voiced their fear that criminals might become invulnerable if customs officers lost the ability to enter homes that was granted by general warrants and "writs of assistance"; the fiscal health of the imperial state itself would be put at risk. Investigators in the early and mid-twentieth century insisted on the need to listen in to telephone conversations between illicit bookies or smugglers of prohibited alcohol, to cite two of the best-known American cases. Those fears about going dark only intensified after 9/11, as was exemplified by the controversy over Apple's refusal to decrypt the cell phone of the San Bernardino terrorist in 2015–16. *Plus ça change*, one may be forgiven for thinking: the Apple case was in fact brought under a revolutionary-era law called the All Writs Act, introduced partly to replace the old powers lost with independence. The Harvard scholar Ian Samuel has dubbed the government's demands "the new writs of assistance."

It would certainly be a mistake to claim that privacy did not exist before the modern era. People in earlier periods acknowledged the importance of a place out of general view, to which one could retreat to regroup, reflect, read, pray, and carry out the body's various functions. Moreover, they also acknowledged degrees and kinds of publicity, privacy, confidentiality, and secrecy. In *early modern diaries one can find fairly consistent distinctions between prayer carried out "secretly," "privately," or "publicly." These distinctions changed over time, however.

Medieval and early modern town dwellers often lived in close proximity to each other within their small, walled enclaves. Villagers too lived in Jane Austen's "neighbourhood of voluntary spies" (by 1803 this was magnified because, as Austen continued, "roads and newspapers lay everything open"). To be alone often required going not into the home but outside, into the field, which in a society like colonial New England became what David Flaherty called "the safety valve" for personal autonomy. Law courts commonly heard cases about neighbors whose windows overlooked a home, or who tossed rubbish into a litigant's yard. Such cases, however, were typically between groups, not individuals: a household was a stratified community within stratified communities, nested like Russian dolls, containing people of different ages, genders, and ranks. In feuds about privacy it was community against community. An individual had no absolute right to privacy as such, and even the household's claim had to be weighed against other desiderata. A medieval London householder might want not to be overseen, then, but at the same time had to coexist with neighbors. It was a matter of balance, not principle.

It is often said that a modern principle of privacy first began to emerge in the sixteenth and seventeenth centuries. Certainly, the built environment of Europe's towns and cities does contain clues to important shifts. Wealthier citizens could aspire to a library, set aside in a discrete room. Separate jury rooms made their appearance in Shakespeare's age. So, in Catholic Europe, did confessionals. More telling is probably the evidence of increasing resistance to intrusions by state officials into domestic spaces. It became a matter of civic and then national pride that royal officers could not legitimately enter a home. The notion that the house was one's "castle" seems to have become proverbial in the late sixteenth century, receiving legal sanction in Coke's *Institutes* in the early seventeenth; it was cemented into political mythology by Blackstone and Pitt in the eighteenth. The family that lived there was a little commonwealth, and its "private and familiar discourse" (as one preacher put it in 1766) was fundamental for the state's very existence.

Before about 1850, then, *privacy* and its cognates qualified substantial things: places, things, or people. One could be a private gentleman; such a man lived in a private house and wrote private letters. The facts that many others lived in the house and that the letters would routinely be steamed open by officials in the post office were secondary (in part, this may be because the term *private* still carried the old connotation of ownership rather than impenetrability). Starting in the late sixteenth and seventeenth centuries, privacy might be attributed to *interests* too. Political culture came to recognize a "public interest," contrasted to the "private interests" of particular political actors. A complex process articulated "reason of state" and the propertied subject. Privacy came to be commonly invoked either because private interests were allegedly being favored over the public one or because officers were entering a space they had no legal right to enter. The resulting outrage might certainly be couched in far-reaching terms. Think, for example, of James Otis's 1761 denunciation of writs of assistance (instructing an official to carry out a search or seizure, for example) as "the worst instrument of arbitrary power, the most destructive of English liberty and the fundamental principles of law, that ever was found in an English law-book." (John Adams remembered this speech as the one that lit the fire of revolution.) But there is no sign that privacy per se was broadly identified as a theme worthy of major, sustained political attention.

That changed in the late nineteenth century. We owe to that era the idea of and jurisprudence concerning a right to privacy. The trigger was the emergence of new institutions and technologies devoted to communication and preservation. The telegraph, telephone, and phonograph promised to record and transmit sounds and messages with an ease, speed, and fidelity never before possible. Steam printing, linotype, and the emergence of the mass press promised to bring those messages to the attention of a far greater public, offering salacious details of the lives of Boston brahmins and other elites. And advertisers helped themselves to images of elite people to sell wares. Henry James called the whole congeries "newspaperization." The same media that created modern celebrity also threatened to expose society's cultural leaders as fallible human beings. Moreover, a substantial number of people seemed actively to *want* to collaborate in the exposure of their lives, in both the United States and Europe. Deborah Cohen has revealed the enterprising ways in which Britain's *Mirror* went about securing what it called "confessions."

In reaction, the United States and Britain saw a rise in complaints, both about individual revelations and about the state of morals in general. The canonical statement to emerge from this era was the 1890 *Harvard Law Review* article by Warren and Brandeis entitled "The Right to Privacy." It was prompted by Warren's distaste for journalism as applied to himself, but the influence it exerted proved profound and lasting. After 1890, a series of legal cases and political gambits addressed privacy in this sense. The first wave concerned "kodak fiends"—people who used the box camera to take and circulate photographs of others without permission. The initial articulation of the principle had been notably paternalistic, but women were prominent among those complaining that their likenesses were being used for advertising copy. Through these cases, Warren and Brandeis's notion of a "right to be let alone" gradually took greater hold as the practices of *publicity* were changing, and not only in the media. Police, administrative, and social-scientific methods were taking advantage of the possibilities of photography, bibliography, new printing technologies, and sociometrics to bring into practice techniques aimed at knowing more about the citizenry. Public health researchers claimed a prerogative to know about household practices; police created "rogues' galleries"; boards of education investigated the health of pupils citywide. The expansion of state information gathering during and after World War I—a central pillar of the modern state itself—built on these initiatives. Coming in the wake of the nineteenth-century news media, this array of increasingly centralized informational practices made "privacy" seem an urgent political issue, essential to the definition of a free society. By 1902 a Chicago newspaper could declare that the very idea of a private citizen was obsolescent, because the old role of the gentleman with a "public" life was now being forced on everyone. In the twentieth century that lament would become ubiquitous.

Through the twentieth century, legal and political arguments about privacy waxed with developments in these two domains: the capitalist world of telecommunications and the administrative/scientific world of social science surveys, information accumulation, and analysis. This process is traced in Sarah Igo's *The Known Citizen*. It did not trace out a smoothly rising graph of intrusion and anxiety. There were peaks of concern, such as the 1890s. Another came in the 1930s, when the expansion of the state during the New Deal led critics—including notable intellectuals on both right and left, but mainly on the right—to warn against the erosion of individual autonomy. Was the advent of the social security number in 1935 the end of the road for Warren and Brandeis's "right"? If so, it joined a number of other such endpoints, roughly one per generation from 1890 to the present. Each had its signature fear: journalism in the 1890s, the overweening state in the 1930s, computers and databases in the 1960s and 1970s, and ubiquitous data mining since 2010.

By the late 1960s, ambitions for data collection and analysis had reached a height sufficient to provoke seriously urgent critiques on an informational plane. One of the most important of these was University of Michigan jurist Arthur R. Miller's *The Assault on Privacy* (1971). Miller's book, which became a best seller, emerged from his experiences as an adviser for the federal government on so-called *data banks. To read it in the twenty-first century is a slightly uncanny experience because Miller identified several anxieties that have since become pressing; but he did so not as prophecies but as reminders of things past. His point was that fears of data integrity, inaccuracy, and inescapability were *already* justified, and had been so for some decades. Computers—and networked computers in particular, which were only just starting to become visible—certainly made these phenomena more evident, but Miller pointed out that they merely magnified a "threat to informational privacy" that long predated the cybernetic age, arising with the expansion of government in the first half of the century. Miller went on to warn that a balance between individual rights (privacy) and "the need for societal efficiency" would come to rest, not on the state, nor on the law, but on "the conduct of the computer professions." The fate of privacy lay in the hands of working coders themselves, and the corporations that employed them. What would decide society's fate was not formal, designed, explicit policy, but the everyday practical ethos of the experts who made information work. It was a matter of social ethics quite recognizable to the generation of the sociologist Robert Merton, who was trained in the 1930s. But Miller, not nearly as sanguine as Merton, concluded that asking coders to honor privacy would be like expecting car manufacturers to embrace emission-control devices out of the goodness of their hearts.

Information privacy thus emerged as a major issue of public debate in the period from the 1950s to the 1970s, partly because of the rise of computers, to be sure, but also because that rise occurred in the wake of at least two generations' worth of anxiety at the tendency of midcentury states, sciences, and corporations to obliterate the distinction between private and public selves. These years also saw the rise of a disciplined approach to the *history* of privacy. The first official parliamentary report on privacy in the UK, issued in 1972, claimed that there had never been a historical treatment of the subject at all. The same year, Flaherty's influential *Privacy in Colonial New England* opened with a pointed reference to how "technological advances in the making of surveillance devices" threatened personal information. Flaherty invoked a series of projects launched by the political scientist (and author of *Privacy and Freedom*, 1967) Alan Westin at Columbia University, directed at understanding privacy's history across the classical, medieval, and early modern worlds.

The most authoritative historical treatment of privacy came out of a quite different tradition, however—that of the French Annales school. Emerging from a fruitful meeting between the medievalist Philippe Ariès and the sociologist Norbert Elias in Berlin in 1983, the five-volume *History of Private Life* ranged from ancient Rome to contemporary France. The concerns about modernity, technology, and social science that so motivated Anglo-American work had relatively little place here. At its core was a neo-Kantian conceit that in the seventeenth and eighteenth centuries "private life" and "public life" underwent transformations so fundamental that it could even be said that such things had not really existed before—and that modernity itself emerged through that shift. It looked like the Anglo-American emphasis on sciences of the state and the Francophone emphasis on the Kantian *Enlightenment were quite incommensurable. Today's plight shows that this is a misapprehension.

Prescient as Miller seems today, the practices of data gathering and analysis used routinely by twenty-first-century states, corporations, and even individuals go far beyond anything envisaged in the late 1960s. Citizens in both the developed and the developing worlds live accompanied constantly by *digital devices that are connected wirelessly to the *internet, and hence to an unknowable array of institutions that seek to collect, preserve, circulate, "mine," and monetize our behaviors. In 2018 the *New York Times* found that smart phones might send location data fourteen hundred times per day to a repository. However anonymized, it would not be hard for a curious investigator with access to such a database to reach conclusions about an adult who, say, left a certain residential area at 7 a.m. every weekday and spent the hours between 8 a.m.

and 4 p.m. in a public school building a few miles away. The *Times*' journalists could certainly do it.

This is the world of surveillance capitalism. It makes the delineation of private and public perhaps *the* issue of contemporary political thought. According to that *Times* report, location-based commerce is soon to be an industry worth tens of billions of dollars. Scandals about Facebook's insouciant approach to the data it garners in unimaginable quantities have helped to make clear that records, once collected, are not going to remain "private." Facebook has provided access very widely to other companies despite the expressed preferences of users. Even the recipient organizations seem to have been unaware of how much access they were given. And this was no exception. The company's "instant personalization" practice involved altering the privacy settings of four hundred million people so that their information could be shared. This earlier exposé had led to Facebook's being obliged to create a "comprehensive privacy program" under two senior "privacy officers," with a biannual "privacy audit" to be carried out by an independent company. Somehow this triplicate oversight of privacy failed to spot continuing practices that were even worse. In mid-2019 the company was fined a record $5 billion—which sounds like a lot, but seems to have been regarded as a tacit acceptance for those practices. Facebook's stock price went up on the news.

Like the newsmen of the late nineteenth century, the data mongers capitalize on an active willingness of citizens to go along. For example, several companies urge us to embrace their use of cameras to photograph shoppers entering a supermarket, using facial recognition software to sort potential shoplifters from reliable customers—who, it suggests, might be approached by staff bearing cappuccinos and special offers. The bargain between convenience and confidentiality may seem Faustian, but the vast majority of people are content to make it.

American society has responded in the way it often does to social problems, by creating a civil society marketplace—an arena in which overlapping or rival organizations see themselves as engaged in a competition for attention in the community. An industry of digital privacy advocacy now exists, comprising such bodies as EPIC (the Electronic Privacy Information Center) and the more general-purpose EFF (the Electronic Freedom Foundation). But Miller's argument from the 1960s remains valid: laws and policies are nothing without practical intervention. The idea that the problem can be solved by tweaking "privacy settings" has already been proved insufficient.

Perhaps the fundamental issue is the one that has dogged privacy campaigners since the 1890s: that many of us *want* our privacy compromised. There are real benefits to having it so, whether they be a degree of fame in the late nineteenth century, the provision of social security and public goods in the mid-twentieth century, an ability to get to a conference on time in the early twenty-first century, or—effectively—the ability to have a "social" life at all nowadays. And an ideology of radical openness has attracted a large popular following too, aided by associations with cognate movements in software and content. It may well be that a fully open culture would be the nightmare portrayed in Dave Eggers's transposition of *Nineteen Eighty-Four* to the Googleplex. But there are plenty who would opt for it. Radical openness and total withdrawal—a retreat to that old notion of one's home as one's castle—are equally unrealistic options. Paradoxically, only the most privileged could hope to succeed at either. For the rest of us, withdrawal would be a dead end, either simply failing (because it is hard not to be connected in *some* way) or, if it succeeded, leading to isolation and, quite possibly, madness.

This being so, three less crude strategies merit note. The first is to defy the data gatherers by using *encryption*. If the information we preserved or transmitted digitally were encoded in some way that could resist decoding, we could preserve a realm of privacy. The technique of so-called public-key *cryptography offers this possibility (quantum computers may qualify this, but they are some years away from public adoption). Originating in academic and defense-related research in the 1980s, public-key cryptography has since been widely circulated, and it has been embedded in various everyday technologies. (The *https* moniker used by websites indicates that data transfer is protected in this way.) Public-key cryptography was championed by a range of visionary thinkers connected by early digital networks. As a result, today one does not have to be an expert coder to encrypt one's email, and it is fairly simple to use an encrypted system for SMS messaging or web browsing. But practical difficulties remain, and they continue to deter many.

The other two strategies are far less ambitious. Each involves appropriating the capabilities of digital information media and putting them to use against the practices of the data gatherers. The first of these is to address the ubiquity of surveillance through what has been called *sousveillance*. Here, individuals use small instruments—usually cameras—to record events involving the agencies that typically record them. The best-known example is the use of small wearable cameras to record interactions between citizens and police officers. This clearly does nothing directly to preserve the privacy of the wearer—rather the reverse, if anything—but it does even the odds by compromising the privacy of the institutional party to the interaction.

The final strategy is *obfuscation*, outlined in the book of that name by Finn Brunton and Helen Nissenbaum. This strategy does not block access to one's information, nor record the recorders, but rather generates so much information, most of it spurious, that it becomes more trouble than it is worth for data harvesters to sort the wheat from the chaff. This can be done online, for example, by using software that mimics a click on every advertisement on a web page and thus obscures whatever the user may actually choose to do. But it too has its costs; in particular, it can interfere with things that we want to work, like spam filters.

Privacy seems always to be defined in terms of a binary between antonyms, but the other term in the binary changes. Is *public* the opposite of *private*? Not always. Sometimes the opposite seems to be something like *tracked*. The variation arises because such binaries do not capture adequately the nature of privacy in everyday life. There we encounter tensions between different kinds, degrees, and extents of privacy and openness. For a particular *fact to become public—to become, in effect, a recognized "fact" at all—generally requires a *transition* between a more closely held domain and one that is less so. Although, for example, Julian Assange's WikiLeaks came to prominence as a location for unaccountable whistle-blowing and championed an ideology of informational openness, it relied on its own strict rule of privacy in order to sustain that radical openness. Contrariwise, the suppressing—the rendering private—of information by censors has generally relied, and probably must always rely, on local and limited *openness*, for example between policing and judicial institutions that must collaborate. Privacy depends on situated publicity; publicity depends on situated privacy.

In other words, our regular language about privacy misdirects us. We would do well to recognize that what matter are traversals across boundaries, rather than boundaries themselves. The classic sociology of Erving Goffman offers examples, showing how we rely on such transits for the "presentation of self." In the sciences, one could point similarly to a good deal of historical and sociological work indicating that facts emerge from processes of circulating between relatively private and relatively public spaces. Michael Faraday is a particularly good example, because we still have the building (the Royal Institution in London) in which he rehearsed and then staged his experimental performances before audiences. Visitors can retrace the literal steps from his basement lab to his public theater, by which his trials gave rise to science. Steven Shapin makes a similar account about experiment in general. Sociologists and historians of laboratory science argue a similar case about contemporary sciences. And one does not have to think too hard to come up with examples in other disciplinary enterprises, like history itself. Kant argued in his famous answer to the question "What is Enlightenment?" that the process depended on the "public use of one's reason," which could happen only in a private space, but must be manifested in the sphere of published print. Many—perhaps all—epistemic practices could be described in similar terms. The circulation between private and public is *epistemologically essential. Ariès meets Elias. *That* is what we need to protect.

Adrian Johns

See also censorship; commodification; computers; databases; digitization; encrypting/ decrypting; networks; public sphere; publicity/publication; surveilling; telecommunications

FURTHER READING

P. Ariès and G. Duby, eds., *A History of Private Life*, 1985–87, translated by A. Goldhammer, 5 vols., 1987–91; Finn Brunton and Helen Nissenbaum, *Obfuscation: A User's Guide for Privacy and Protest*, 2015; Deborah Cohen, *Family Secrets: Living with Shame from the Victorians to the Present Day*, 2013; D. H. Flaherty, *Privacy in Colonial New England*, 1972; Erving Goffman, *The Presentation of Self in Everyday Life*, 1959; Sarah E. Igo, *The Known Citizen: A History of Privacy in Modern America*, 2018; Michael McKeon, *The Secret History of Domesticity: Public, Private, and the Division of Knowledge*, 2005; J. Turow, *The Aisles Have Eyes: How Retailers Track Your Shopping, Strip Your Privacy, and Define Your Power*, 2017; David Vincent, *Privacy: A Short History*, 2016.

PROFESSORS

The Latin term *professor* was used as early as the first century CE to describe a paid teacher and to indicate a trained proficiency in the subject "professed." Both elements are evident in the current Anglophone use of the word denoting a member of a university faculty. It is from the evidence posed by "professors" of this sort, and their predecessors in the European universities of the medieval and *early modern period, that this entry is written.

Other parameters are certainly possible. A full accounting of the word *professor* and its cognates in the nineteenth century alone would have to include also secondary-school teachers of a certain rank, to say nothing of an (antiquated) designation for a particular academic degree; an exhaustive treatment of the word's scope in antiquity, meanwhile, would need to deal with its religious associations. If, on the other hand, we loose ourselves from the term and simply look instead for some constellation of the functions and characteristics that, at various times and places, have attended the professorial title—publicly funded lecturing, for example, or institutionally anchored pedagogical activity on the part of leading scholars—the field grows even wider. We might find the professorial chair in the imperial salaries extended to certain high-level teachers in antiquity, such as the great rhetorician Quintilian in Rome, those installed in Athens in the second century CE by Marcus Aurelius, or those officially appointed in Constantinople as early as the fourth century. We would have to do with learned individuals like Ioannes Xiphilinus and Michael Psellos (1018–78?), active in schools sponsored by the Byzantine emperor. And we would be profitably engaged with figures in sites such as the academies of premodern China and the madrasas of eleventh-century Baghdad. One of the tasks for the history of information and its practices will be to elaborate how some of the themes presented here look different when the frame is changed. But for now, an outline.

THE "TRADITIONAL" AND THE "MODERN"

Standard narratives about the history of the university begin in the twelfth and thirteenth centuries in Italy and France and spot a principal pivot point for the professor in late eighteenth- and early nineteenth-century Germany, at which time and place a research emphasis is said to have gained currency. Some combination of factors—competition between the German states, a social pressure to define disciplinary standards, increasing invigilation by bureaucratized ministries, a particular scholarly ideology—conspired to make original, written production for a specialized audience henceforth a crucial component of the professorial identity. According to this view, the professors (or *magistri* [masters] or *doctores* [doctors]) in the medieval and early modern university were predominately teachers. They lectured to students on set texts, reading them aloud, explicating them, offering a sort of running commentary on any questions they raised. They participated in and presided over the verbal jousting exercises known as disputations. All the while they are supposed to have remained more focused on polishing and passing on established truths than on generating fresh ones. Their positions, often owed in no small part to family connections within the university, carried legal privileges and a measure of dignity and could be switched, over time, for others in subjects in which they had little experience. When they wrote, an activity to which they were not compelled, they inclined to treatises, textbooks, and commentaries based on their lectures and disputations, or else (this in the early modern period) to translations and other works meant for a general rather than a specialized readership—productions that would generate broader fame and, indirectly, more students and income for themselves and the universities of which they were a part. The "traditional" professor becomes, in this telling, a manager of information for the purpose of systematization and transmission.

The modern professor, on the other hand, is said to be a researcher, a handler of information for the purpose of creating new information. At a certain point it was no longer sufficient to teach: a faculty position came to require the writing and publication of specialized, often highly esoteric investigations that yielded original results. Such efforts, largely inaccessible to the general reader, were assessed by expert colleagues, whose reactions guided the decisions of the government bureaucrats controlling professorial appointments with filed and foldered efficiency, putting an end to old systems of local favoritism and corporate fellow feeling. Professors still gave lectures, but the disputation had all but disappeared, and the university landscape had new features—seminars and laboratories where the methods of research were exemplified and taught in hands-on ways, spurring students to their own original research. The modern professor was still a charismatic figure, one vested with a certain sort of authority, but now that authority inhered comparatively less in traditional symbols, dress and processions and titles, and comparatively more in a certain type of written academic production that could be peer reviewed, tallied in dossiers and tables, and translated into salary by ministerial decision makers.

There is much that this account captures, both about how professors and universities have viewed their own histories, and about the very real differences in attitude and orientation between the publish-or-perish, specialized faculties of today and those of several centuries ago. But there is also much that it risks flattening, and many other ways to tell the story. In particular, scholars have shown that a detailed attention to the "everyday" practices and concerns of professor and student inside and outside the classroom tends to blur the line between traditional teacher and modern researcher, or at least to suggest new patterns of resonance and dissonance between them. The following will adopt a structure in line with this "everyday" approach, portraying the modern professor not as the *after* to a putative *before*, but instead as a cross section of a continually evolving set of considerations, waged in the *longue durée*, about the communication, generation, conduction, and use of information within and beyond the university.

COMMUNICATION: THE LECTURE

The modes of professorial communication are many: disputations, seminars, exercises, monographs, conferences, popular writing, informal exchange in "office hours." A particularly durable mode of information transfer has been the lecture: the professor's "reading" of a subject, author, or work before an auditor or group of auditors. The lecture's history is one of back-and-forth motion along many, often interrelated axes: between reader and auditor, content and form, oral and written, presence and absence. The difficulty of finding the right equilibrium is amply attested: lecturers could be too difficult, too quick, too uninviting, or too long-winded (one early modern Tübingen scholar spent twenty-five years working through the book of Isaiah). The auditors, meanwhile, had their own ways of influencing the proceedings: in fourteenth-century Paris, "clamor, hissing, noise, [and the] throwing of stones" were conceivable ways of protesting a lecturer's delivery. Later accounts have students intervening by placing slips on the professor's lectern with doubts or questions; by stamping their feet or scraping them across the floor to indicate approbation, confusion, or disapproval; or by absence—when an eighteenth-century Jena professor insisted on using Aristotle's *Rhetoric* as a manual for preaching, and when he lingered for three hours on a single word, the students simply stopped coming.

The matter of the lecture's orality further illustrates its perpetually negotiated character. Many modern lectures play out as the oralization of an existing text or script, a phenomenon with analogies already in the medieval university, where, for instance, the set text for a course might be read out—"dictated" or "pronounced" or "given to the pen"—so that students, if they wished, could generate a copy for themselves, and where it was not unknown for a scholar (or deputized student) essentially to read off another's course. But the idea that the lecture itself should not simply be a vocalized form of the written word also has a venerable tradition. Merely reading aloud could earn the early modern Italian professor a monetary penalty and the derogatory title "paper doctor": there were regulations against dictation in Paris and in German universities as well. Hybrid written-oral forms were common: medieval professors in the higher faculties might expect students to have a book before them; some early modern professors lectured according to printed textbooks (sometimes their own), commenting orally on the printed contents. The Göttingen professor Johann Matthias Gesner (1691–1761) printed a book that offered only an outline of his lecture because he believed students fared better if something remained to be found out "from the mouth of [the teacher] alone, by paying attention, or to be learned through their own inquiry." Students, that is, still needed to be present for the oral part of the lecture if they really wanted to get ahead.

Their activity once there was oriented around the capture of the information that the professor presented, often in the form of notes. This was an operation that could involve everything from particular equipment (the medieval student's wax tablets or *parchment scraps, for instance, and the pouches or "wallets" that may have held them), to styles of writing adapted for rapidity, to the furniture of the lecture hall (which might include slanted desks for propping a book and writing). There was no shortage of attempts to regulate the exchange from the professorial side. A 1355 statute of the Paris faculty of arts references a test of two ways of delivering lectures, one too quick for the note taker's hand to follow, one deliberate enough to allow transcription. The decision, later superseded, was for the former method, so that lecturers were enjoined to speak "as if no one were writing in front of them." But one suspects that regardless of statute, it proved difficult to elude the recording hand, as was certainly the case at other times and places. The Jena theologian Johann Andreas Danz (1654–1727), for example, reportedly used to complain that students made a record of everything, even when he cleared his throat: some auditors, apparently unfazed, duly recorded the complaint.

Serious students would spend time refining the results of these note-taking efforts, working up an elaborated version after the lecture itself. A thirteenth-century collection of Aristotelian works belonging to Henry of Renham at Oxford shows what is possibly the result of such a multistage process: while listening to the lecture Renham apparently made notes with a stylus (more easily handled in a classroom than pen and ink), later enhancing them into penned glosses. Such *second-order notes were partly the product of the student's own reflections and could take far longer than the lecture itself. In 1853, Ernst Haeckel reported spending at least three to four hours on every one hour of the lecture of his teacher Rudolf Virchow, "chew[ing] and digest[ing]" what he had transcribed. Students' role in the lecture, therefore, did not begin and end in the lecture hall. Instead, they transformed spoken words into written documents—in German, so-called *Hefte* (notebooks)—that could be bound, circulated, even sold. The lectures of a notable professor, "traditional" or modern, might well end up in circulated or published versions based in part or in toto on these student copies. Thus the (more or less) oral event that emerged at the nexus of professorial practice, ministerial regulation, and student desiderata was often transformed into other information-delivery tools, including manuscript notebooks and printed books or commentaries.

The question of what is lost or gained in these media transformations of the lecture is a sort of Rorschach test for pedagogical convictions still on display today in debates about how to handle the filming and *internet broadcasting of course components. If the lecture is modeled as a pure information transfusion from professor to auditor, its migration onto more widely diffusible platforms is enticing. But the tendency to see something more there—a need for spontaneity, orality, participation—is centuries old. Indeed, for many the information transmitted into the *Heft* was of decidedly secondary importance to the general "catalytic effect" of witnessing a great teacher. An example: an eighteenth-century report of the lectures of the *philologist Christian Gottlob Heyne (1729–1812) saw the chief takeaway, regardless of the material treated, as the "art of finding the point that matters." Here was something, after all, for future bureaucrats and businessmen, and it was something to be taught not declaratively but rather in modeling the process, for example, of investigating the meaning of an unassuming Greek particle. What exactly, in the end, δέ meant in one passage or the other was not really the issue. The key thing was to learn "to feel around for the spring" that could undo a difficult problem. Watching Heyne at work was apparently good for that.

GENERATION: PROFESSORIAL EQUIPMENT

"We look for the researcher and find the collector," went an unflattering faculty assessment of a candidate for a Munich professorship in 1904. The message was clear: a professor was expected to generate new information, not gather what was already available. One can and should historicize the "newness" at issue, as well as its policing and emphasis, but we should also appreciate that the pantheon of professorial virtue has for centuries included the ability to deliver artful and productively distinct scholarly results. In the eighteenth century, it was inconceivable to a young Alexander von Humboldt that Heyne could be equaled by a scholar he deemed a "tasteless compiler."

In the seventeenth, it was cause for mordant pity to Joseph Scaliger (1540–1609) that a Zurich professor had managed, in a book on numismatics, to say nothing that was not already said: "Oh the poor man!"

Information generation did not happen ex nihilo; it demanded equipment. The prolific German sociologist Niklas Luhmann (1927–98), for decades a professor in Bielefeld, said as much of his own production. He relied on a legendary card index full of notes—some ninety thousand slips, components of a filing system that he credited with the role of a *"secondary memory" and accorded a key place in his academic productivity: "Without the cards, just by contemplating, I would not come up with these [new] ideas." For scholars in many disciplines, libraries have served a similar productive purpose. The faculty at Göttingen was lampooned at the end of the eighteenth century for supposedly believing professors came there because it was an honor: in reality the draw was the pay and the library, where one could often "from nine books make a tenth—a business at which [one] see[s] the Göttinger get so fat." Scholars, in short, were inclined to come to places that afforded them productive apparatus, a fact that helped determine the shape of the university landscape. One of the conditions of the deal to bring the scientist Hermann von Helmholtz as professor to Berlin in 1871 was a ministerial promise to build him a new physics institute. His contemporary, the Munich philology professor Eduard Wölfflin, worked in the 1890s to ensure that a collaboratively assembled collection of millions of slips documenting the use of Latin words would be housed in Munich, writing to the ministry of the "honor and advantage" conferred thereby: "there will deposited here such a material for Latin-language studies that numerous scholars will be forced to seek out the university in Munich."

The machinery of information production had living and breathing components. Professors could rely on correspondence or reports from other scholars to supply their work. The Latinist Wölfflin, for instance, drew for years on an extensive correspondence network to outfit him with information about words' occurrences for his lexicographical studies. The American psychologist G. Stanley Hall attended the seminar of the noted professor Wilhelm Wundt at Leipzig in the 1870s and recalled how the students became in effect prosthetic readers: Wundt's method was to take "incessant and voluminous notes" when seminar participants reported on the literature "so that in a sense [the students] read for him." At still closer quarters, professors have long relied on helpers, sometimes from their own households—including their wives and children—or among the students who might have their lodgings there. But the need for personnel assistance has become particularly visible in vast modern university laboratories that have demanded legions of professors, engineers, technicians, and graduate students to collect, curate, and interpret new information. In the 1960s, experiments on the seventy-two-inch hydrogen bubble chamber supervised by the Berkeley professor Luis Alvarez could involve one hundred people. While Luhmann's card index was formidable, he had built it himself, could operate it from his desk, and could serve as sole author of the results; for mid-twentieth-century professors specializing in areas like high-energy physics, issues of construction, use, and authorship were considerably more complicated and would become still more so as subsequent decades brought collaboration to paradigm-shattering levels.

The importance of equipment cannot be underestimated, not least for some of its "side effects." Early modern professorial aides, as Martin Mulsow has indicated, sometimes circulated things that their supervisors would not have, providing an alternate information byway. Another problem was overabundance. Wölfflin's correspondence network generated so much information that by the 1890s he was revising his enthusiasm for comprehensive lexical collection: the seven boxes of material documenting citations for the humdrum preposition *a, ab* presented an apparatus so formidable that nobody wanted to work with it. The twentieth-century bubble chamber also became cause for second thoughts: as Peter Galison has shown, Berkeley's Alvarez became disenchanted with the "factory world" required to work with the detector: the necessary routine had become "just a little dull." Instruments—human, paper, or otherwise—could circumvent, overwhelm, or stifle the researchers meant to manage them. In the laboratory and in the study, the message is the same: not always did the tools of information creation do the bidding of those meant to wield them; sometimes they forced the professorial hand.

CONDUCTIVITY: PROFESSORIAL PARA-INFORMATION

"Accumulation and distribution of information are integral components of practical life in the academic field," wrote Heidrun Friese, in an anthropological account of an academic workshop in the 1990s. The "information" in question included details communicated in the social interludes built into the academic gathering. Such details, which constitute part of what Friese calls the *"paratext" of the conference, were of many sorts: name-dropping, allusion, personal confidences, and "gossip," all constantly deployed, registered, stored, and exploited in plays, long and short, for influence. This too is part of the messy business of professorial information management, an entrée to the phenomenon of para-information—the collection and circulation of information *about* professors. Information does not arise and move of its own accord: one can think of para-information as helping to establish the conductivity and reach of the lines that it travels. It is part of the equation by which some scholars cultivate position and influence as professors and others do not, making their prospects for communicating and creating disciplinary information *stricto sensu* better or worse.

Professorial para-information has its own long history. As the Göttingen theology professor Johann Lorenz Mosheim (1693–1755) told a visitor, one judged scholars far better with the benefit of personal knowledge: "when one has inquired about their circumstances, situation, conditions and has had the opportunity now and then to speak with them and to surprise them in a state of *undress*, so to speak." Here, too, professors could rely on assistants to help gather material: students on the move between universities delivered dispatches humming with news of scholars in all states of undress. Göttingen's Gesner "hates pretty much all good men, and all hate him in turn" went the helpful report of a transplanted Basel student who had met the man in his own home—he was writing to his former teacher (also a professor, and Gesner's competitor in the field of Latin lexicography). The concern to control talk like this, to ensure that the right sort of reports made the rounds, is evident in the case of still another Göttingen professor, the mathematician Abraham Kästner (1719–1800), who knew that "all the world wanted to hear clever ideas from him" and felt "embarrassed" before visitors when he was not in the mood to muster them.

Para-information has been of particular interest to professorial employers seeking individuals regarded as stars. When the Duke of Braunschweig-Wolfenbüttel saw fit, in

1650, to compensate Hermann Conring with a second professorial chair at the University of Helmstedt, a key motivation was Conring's favor with Queen Christina of Sweden. His lot, that is, was bettered most directly not by what he had per se done as a professor but by the information about where that stood him and how others responded to him. To keep track of such information, ministries developed tools such as the professorial dossier: files for individual professors and professorial candidates complete with testimonies and assessments from colleagues. Once professors were installed, it was often necessary to determine how they performed and whether they behaved. In Bologna in the fifteenth and early sixteenth centuries, an official—the *punctator*—was responsible for checking classes to make sure lecturers were present and had enough auditors. Other early modern measures included everything from paying "spies" to sit in on lectures, to requiring the submission of *Professorenzettel* (professorial slips) in which professors accounted for the term's work, to visitations—in which ministerial emissaries were sent to a university to report on the doings there.

It is the power of para-information that helps account for one apparently deep-seated professorial phenomenon: that of the public celebrity commanded by figures from the swaggering Peter Abelard of the eleventh and twelfth centuries to the bald-pated Michel Foucault of the twentieth. One may wonder whether those reportedly inclined to call out *Ecco Montsene!* ("Behold, Mommsen!") behind the internationally renowned German historian Theodor Mommsen (1817–1903) in the streets of Rome had ever read the man's celebrated Roman history, let alone his more technical publications. But they knew and admired him nevertheless. The same goes for the Italian thieves who supposedly stopped short of robbing Mommsen when he told them his name: a big reputation could be a boon for a professor's wallet, in more ways than one.

The inverse of this extraordinary amplitude outside the university has been, of course, the sort of para-information that keeps some from entering such an institution or ascending its professorial chairs altogether. One thinks of statutes like the one dating from the fifteenth century at the University of Leipzig, which specified that those examined for the master's degree must be "born legitimately and otherwise morally commendable." But there is no need to look so far into the past. The modern histories of the obstacles faced by Jewish scholars, by women, and by other minorities in ascending the academic ladder are a reminder of a simple truth: professors' ability to create and transmit information (or not) in the subjects they profess, and indeed to be professors at all, has been and continues to be regulated and dimensioned by an extensive ecosystem of para-information, one that is sometimes flatly oppressive.

USE: INFORMATION IN THE WORLD

Finally, we must turn to what is done with professorially generated information, which has never been merely confined to the classroom. Medieval and early modern regents recognized that they could benefit from the opinions and advice of university teachers. The ample seventeenth-century portfolio of the Helmstedt professor Conring included services to the archbishop of Mainz, the French crown, Sweden, the cities of Lindau and Cologne, and others besides: his legal and diplomatic skills allowed him to do work with palpable territorial and political implications—work that could earn him a tidy sum. The arrangement parallels roles filled by professors acting as paid consultants for governments and private companies today. The spectrum of such relationships is wide: in their crasser forms they have led some universities to regulate the ways in which professors may seek to apply their status and expertise outside the academy. But of course the "right" and the "wrong" use of information, the proper mode of its production and trafficking, is not always perfectly clear. This was true centuries ago when the ask-me-anything disputations known as quodlibets saw medieval professors weighing whether they committed mortal sins by treating interesting questions instead of those concerning salvation, and whether one could refuse inquiries potentially offensive to the rich and powerful. It is just as true in our own times, not least of all when the stakes are highest. The obvious example: several of the physicists whose extraordinary mobilization helped deliver crucial military technology in the 1940s, including the atomic bomb, were or would be professors. The information produced by these civilian scientists was used to help win the war and brought with it a high profile reflected not only in ballooning federal support and access to government, but also in a new disciplinary posture back on campus. "The college professor, you think, is a dreamer," read part of a contemporary poem passed about—as Galison relates—in the physics department at the University of Wisconsin, "but see the shellacking he gave Hiroshima." The use of certain kinds of professorial information could be breathtakingly consequential—and unsettling indeed.

Unsettling enough to make high-profile physicists query seriously what price they had paid for their new prominence on and off campus. J. Robert Oppenheimer (1904–67), whose wartime work as the director of the Los Alamos Laboratory abutted professorships at Berkeley and Caltech, represented the postwar concerns of certain of his scientific colleagues in describing further weapons work as "against the dictates of their hearts and spirits." There was a feeling, a nervous Oppenheimer said to President Harry Truman, of "blood on my hands." A feeling, too, he wrote elsewhere, that the war with its dislocation and emphasis on technical application had meant a temporary disaster for "the prosecution of pure science," and "a more total cessation of true professional activity in the field of physics" in America than in any other country. The influx of money from government and industry for university research carried its own risks: a Stanford physicist, William Hansen, worried prior to war's end about preserving "our soul" while accepting financial "help . . . from the outside." The concerns are a classic indication of some of the tensions around information from "inside" the university: the clash of idealistic and often imprecise commitments to a "pure" sort of scientific activity undertaken by a clean and "professional" scientific soul, with the needs—sometimes dirty—of the societies that support such activity. They point up inevitable gray areas in the consideration of just what kind of information professors are meant to make, how it should be supported, and how it should move.

Christian Flow

See also books; cards; diplomats/spies; indexing; knowledge; learning; libraries and catalogs; notebooks; secretaries; teaching

FURTHER READING

C. Burnett, "Give Him the White Cow: Notes and Note-Taking in the Universities in the Twelfth and Thirteenth Centuries," *History of Universities* 14 (1995–96, pub. 1998): 1–30; William Clark, *Academic Charisma and the Origins of the Research University*, 2006; Holger Dainat, "Mitschrift, Nachschrift, Referat, Korreferat: Über studentisches Schreiben im 19. Jahrhundert," *Internationales Archiv für Sozialgeschichte der deutschen Literatur* 40, no. 2 (2015): 306–28; Heidrun Friese, "Thresholds in the Ambit of Discourse: On the Establishment of Authority at Academic Conferences," in *Little Tools of Knowledge: Historical Essays on Academic and Bureaucratic Practices*, edited by Peter Becker and William Clark, 2001; Peter Galison, "Laboratory War: Radar Philosophy and the Los Alamos Man," and "Bubble Chambers: Factories of Physics," in *Image and Logic: A Material Culture of Microphysics*, 1997; Anthony Grafton, "Polyhistor into Philolog: Notes on the Transformation of German Classical Scholarship, 1780–1850," *History of Universities* 3 (1983): 159–92; Kristine Haugen, "Academic Charisma and the Old Regime," *History of Universities* 22, no. 1 (2007): 199–228; R. Steven Turner, "The Growth of Professorial Research in Prussia, 1818 to 1848—Causes and Context," *Historical Studies in the Physical Sciences* 3 (1971): 137–82.

PROGRAMMING

"Good programming," the eminent Dutch computer scientist Edsger Dijkstra snidely noted sometime in the 1970s, "is probably beyond the intellectual abilities of today's 'average programmer.'" Despite having computerized airline reservations, financial accounting, early warning systems, and countless other business and government functions, working programmers were deemed hopeless, for they had "been lured into a profession beyond their intellectual abilities." Such elitism was not universal. A few years earlier, in 1971, the inaugural issue of the People's Computer Company newsletter demanded a more demotic computing, with an image of a diverse protest of men, women, and children of many races on the march holding signs insisting "BASIC" is the people's language" and "Use computers *for* people, not against them."

Computer programming often exemplifies a vision of creation in which a thinking being implements a mentalistic plan. The history of electronic computing in its early years largely comprises the failures of just such a vision of labor and creative work. Computer programming involves iterative work with machines, work that fits easily neither as labor nor as ideation, even when that work involves deployment of sophisticated logical and mathematical forms. Both the image of programming as fundamentally pure thought stuff and the quotidian reality of its implication are historically, sociologically, and legally crucial. Programming steadfastly cannot be reduced either to math or to labor practices; as an object of study, it proves challenging for intellectual and labor historians in equal measure.

HUBRIS

Pioneers in the 1940s briefly believed that programming the new electronic *digital computers would be as simple as communicating logical and mathematical operations to coders to implement. "It had not occurred to me that there was going to be any difficulty about getting programs working," the English computer pioneer Maurice Wilkes quipped. "And it was with somewhat of a shock that I realized that for the rest of my life I was going to spend a good deal of my time finding mistakes that I had made in my programs." By the 1950s, the craft-like qualities of most industrial programming led to the understanding of the activity, in the words of the IBM researcher John Backus, as "a black art, a private arcane matter." Programming is a skilled intellectual craft, and it is, for any project of reasonable complexity, a social effort, demanding constant intercommunication—an effort resistant to hierarchy and standardization. In a major polemic entitled the *Mythical Man-Month*, Frederick Brooks argued, "Men and months are interchangeable commodities only when a task can be partitioned among many workers with no communication among them. . . . This is true of reaping wheat or picking cotton; it is not even approximately true of systems programming." Unlike many other industries, programming does not scale by throwing more people at a programming task; expansion willy-nilly is likely to promote, not foreclose, failure.

In the 1960s, computer scientists drew on logic and algebra to refashion programming, culminating, as Mark Priestley describes, in "a move away from a step-by-step approach to computation to one based on higher-level operators which were described in terms of their overall effect." This shift altered fundamentally both the control structures of programs and the ways that large databases were envisioned and manipulated. While moving programming further from coding in machine language, this mathematical infusion did not result in programming being less a craft.

From the 1950s onward, a passel of programming philosophies has waxed and waned, and a panoply of management philosophies have been celebrated, tried, and found wanting. Typically, new solutions arose from a diagnosis of a crisis in programming, an intellectual, a social, or a business crisis—often a tangle of all three. Diverse social groups of programmers and managers have diagnosed the failures of programming in radically different ways. For academic computer scientists, such as Dijkstra, programming was inadequately mathematical and scientific; for commercial computing, programming was inadequately managed and organized. From structured programming to software engineering, no solution has proven adequate, whether for academic, scientific, or industrial needs; plenty involve a simple rebranding of earlier business philosophies; some reek of academic condescension and imperialism; some involve dramatic reworkings of thinking and business practices; most remain aspirational; each proposes, in varied measures, combinations of social and technological solutions to the collective creation of functioning software systems.

Drawing on "lean" manufacturing approaches, prominent efforts in the last twenty-five years have promoted iterative and incremental approaches rather than top-down bureaucratic and mathematical design philosophies and work processes. In 2001, to take a still influential example, seventeen software practitioners came together to *canonize a "Manifesto for Agile Software Development" centering on iteration in business and coding cycles alike, drawing on a variety of practices stretching back to the 1950s. "Through this work," they argued, "we have come to value":

Individuals and interactions over processes and tools
Working software over comprehensive documentation
Customer collaboration over contract negotiation
Responding to change over following a plan

These values in turn undergirded twelve principles intertwining the individual motivation and skills of programmers, their social organization, and their relationships to customers. "Working software is the primary measure of progress." Rather than organization from above, the "best architectures, requirements, and designs emerge from self-organizing teams." Each claim resonated against earlier bureaucratic and industrial orders of software design and spoke to developers in the flatter corporate structures of the early twenty-first century.

Initially far from corporate life, advocates of "free" software—free as in freedom, not free as in beer—sought technical architectures for collaborative programming that promoted adaptability and creativity rather than planning, and that substituted collective self-organization for top-down control. "Whereas controlled design and hierarchical planning represent the domain of governance—control through goal setting and orientation of a collective of a project—adaptability privileges politics," the anthropologist Chris Kelty notes, "properly speaking, the ability to critique existing design and to propose alternatives without restriction."

For all the attention to practices for creating new software, a vast edifice of legacy *code, often in old-fashioned languages such as COBOL, has long demanded and continues to demand maintenance. No code is every truly finished. "Because maintenance does not involve design," Nathan Ensmenger notes, "it was (and is) generally considered routine and low-status activity," even as it commands something estimated to be 60–80 percent of budgets for programming. Open source programming and agile programming, in never-ending development, often elides any distinction between discrete design and maintenance stages.

PROGRAMMING PEOPLE

Before computers were machines, computers were people performing calculations, and many of those people were women. During World War II, such women operated early mechanical calculating machines in computing ballistic trajectories, for example, and then became the first electronic computer operators in the *cryptographic effort at Bletchley Park in the UK and the scientific calculations of ENIAC in the USA. The division of labor predictably followed a gendered partition of origination and implementation. The percentage of women programmers has waxed and waned since, and in recent years the low numbers of women in the field in the United States has been an object of concern. Despite, or perhaps because of, their utopian pretensions, programming cultures outside corporations and academia have proven even worse for women. The open source and free software communities have had very few women indeed: in the early 2000s, around 1.5 percent of programmers as opposed to 28 percent in commercial software development. The causes remain up for debate; unquestionably, the collaborative culture of open source draws heavily on norms of masculine sociability, including the most toxic, from flame wars to the denunciation of newbies. And yet, the gendered quality of programming is hardly universal: in India, women made up 42 percent of computer science and engineering students in 2011, and, as Roli Varma and Deepak Kapur have argued, programmers are not broadly understood to share naturally the interests and forms of sociability central to American geek culture.

BETWEEN MATERIALITY AND IMMATERIALITY

Punching cards, plug boards, and repetitive stress injury from too much typing: programming calculating machines and computers has always been a physical human practice. Software might be thought stuff, pure ideation, math in a machine, but the process of making it is anything but, and it always runs on computers drawing energy, prone to fail, and possessing distinct material affordances. Facets of this materiality, Matthew Fuller in the *Software Lexicon* argues, include "the particular characteristics of a language or other form of interface, . . . how its compositional terms inflect and produce certain kinds of effects such as glitches, cross-platform compatibility, or ease of sharing and distribution; how, through both artifact and intent, events can occur at the level of models of user subjectivity or forms of computational power, that exceed those of pre-existing social formatting or demand new figures of knowledge." Historians, media scholars, and anthropologists stressing such material embedding of all programming argue in surprising parallel to corporate lawyers and lobbyists who have sought for decades to demonstrate that software is far more than mathematics, in order to gain patent and other intellectual property protections. Even if they may misconstrue or misunderstand programming, arguments concerning the tangibility and intangibility of software undergird alternative visions of the generation of knowledge and technology production, including those that challenge the intellectual property regimes in place since the nineteenth century.

THE "PROGRAMMER AS NAVIGATOR"

In 1973, the business information visionary Charles Bachman proclaimed that data storage was undergoing a "Copernican Revolution" that "is changing the programmer from a stationary viewer of objects passing before him in core into a mobile navigator who is able to probe and traverse a database at will." Rather than envisioning data as something examined serially, the advent of new random-access storage technologies like disk drives meant that digital computers could escape the traditions of serial information storage and retrieval inherited from early technologies of punch cards. Older technologies of retrieval, such as the index, featured elsewhere in this volume (see "indexing" and "storage and search"), could find analogs in digital technologies, if only programmers could shift their worldview. From this perspective, the task was to organize and store data for diverse programs and programmers to use.

A generation of development brought the database technologies, based primarily on the relational model, to the robustness and security that enabled global business throughout the end of the twentieth century. By the 1990s, many observers were announcing a crisis: programmers had figured out how securely to store data but they hadn't done nearly enough to provide tools for investigating that data.

COMPLEXITY, INSECURITY, AND TECHNICAL DEBT

By the late 1960s, consultants associated with the US National Security Agency (NSA) and the US Air Force began worrying about security issues associated with software systems, particularly as networks began to interconnect those systems. A 1970s report noted, "operating systems are very large, complex structures, and thus it is impossible to exhaustively test for every conceivable set of conditions that might arise." Complete design is impossible: "inadvertent loopholes exist" that "have not been foreseen by the designers." An attacker, this study predicted, "could mount a deliberate search for such loopholes with the expectation of exploiting them to acquire information." Computer systems quickly had proved far beyond any human capability to audit and to understand—even though the NSA tried, and tried, and tried. As with questions of maintenance, the complexity of existing software systems proved to be a gilded cage, a structure that human beings built that is outside of their control and understanding. Any software project of sufficient scope becomes for programmers, to borrow from Marx, "an alien force existing outside them, of the origin and goal of which they are ignorant, which they thus cannot control, which on the contrary passes through a peculiar series of phases and stages independent of the will and the action of man, nay even being the prime governor of these." Our current condition of computer insecurity speaks to a complexity far outside our ken. "Program formulation is thus rather more like the creation of a bureaucracy," Joseph Weizenbaum wrote, "than like the construction of a machine" that can be comprehended as a whole.

Capital, if not *Kapital*, provided a metaphor now commonly used for understanding complexity of development and implementation of software systems. As the American developer of agile software Ward Cunningham wrote, "Shipping first time code is like going into debt. A little debt speeds development so long as it is paid back promptly with a rewrite." Dealing with debt is expensive—in future developer time. "The danger occurs when the debt is not repaid. Every minute spent on not-quite-right code counts as interest on that debt. Entire engineering organizations can be brought to a stand-still under the debt load of an unconsolidated implementation, object-oriented or otherwise."

FROM AUTOMATIC PROGRAMMING TO MACHINE LEARNING

"More and more, computers will program themselves," Herbert Simon predicted in 1961, "and direction will be given to computers through the mediation of compiling systems that will be completely neutral so far as the content of the decision rules is concerned." From the 1960s onward, ever more powerful tools enabled human beings to program at higher levels of abstraction from the physical hardware of machines, but the vision that computers might program themselves has proven elusive, both as an industrial practice and as project of scientific hopes. These dreams powerfully promoted, early on, the *conversion of mathematical language into higher-level languages without having to machine code oneself. Complaining of the "dull labor of writing and checking programs," Admiral Grace Hopper, pioneer of compilers, envisioned that the "programmer may return to being a mathematician." She was too sanguine. Generations of programming tools permit ever higher level work, but programmers have never returned to being mathematicians.

In his epochal 1950 paper on machine intelligence, Alan Turing noted that human beings will have programmed a computer to start acting intelligently just at the moment it ceases to act mechanically: "most of the programs which we can put into the machine will result in its doing something that we cannot make sense of at all, or which we regard as completely random behavior. Intelligent behavior presumably consists in a departure from the completely disciplined behavior involved in computation, but a rather slight one, which does not give rise to random behavior, or to pointless repetitive loops."

Producing computer systems capable of programing themselves in ways that appear to emulate or reproduce human intelligence has long been a desideratum of *artificial intelligence and has remained elusive—productively so. Those seeking to create computers capable of reasoning or emulating human reasoning have found themselves confronted with the difficulty of translating human knowledge and skills of all kinds into fully articulated descriptions capable of being programmed in the form of explicit rules. In the 1970s, the problem was diagnosed as the "knowledge-acquisition bottleneck," which underscored the same ineffability of skill as did the sociology of scientific knowledge of Harry Collins. In the early 1980s, the machine learning pioneer Donald Michie explained, "The inductive learning of concepts, rules, strategies, etc. from *examples* is what confers on the human problem-solver his power and versatility, and not (as had earlier been supposed) his powers of calculation." Today inductive algorithms trained on large data sets predict the judgments of human reasoners with no pretense of reproducing the thought processes and somatic judgments of human beings. Machine learning researchers have been most successful in creating programs capable of mimicking the outcomes of expert judgment precisely as they abandoned the effort to make computers proceed through hard-coded logical procedures and ceased to be priests of the high church of symbolic logic. Replicating decision making with the help of statistics, not the subordination of reasoning to logic and mathematics, fuels the ethical and political dangers of the explosion of machine learning all around us.

Using the example of the development of linear perspective in the art of the European *Renaissance, Dijkstra described how the "virtuoso coder" of the 1960s "feels like the medieval painter that could create a masterpiece whenever his experience enabled him to render proportions well, who suddenly found himself overtaken by all sorts of youngsters, pupils of Albrecht Dürer and the like, who had been taught the mathematical constructions that were guaranteed to surpass his most successful, but intuitive, renderings." The coming of mathematics to painting and sculpture provided a good analogy for the development of programming, but not for the reasons Dijkstra gave. Explaining the quality of Renaissance perspective in practice, the art historian James Elkins explains, "Laws, examples, and rules of thumb commingled, and there was a welter of more-or-less independent methods rather than a single mathematical set of axioms and a logically antecedent set of applications." So too with programming in the last half century. However much mathematically inspired techniques reshaped programming, they never could substitute for the welter of practices and knowledge undergirding our software-mediated world, any more than the tool kit of linear perspective dictated the content of paintings.

Matthew L. Jones

See also cards; computers; data; databases; indexing; intellectual property; networks; storage and search

FURTHER READING

Janet Abbate, *Recoding Gender: Women's Changing Participation in Computing*, 2012; Barry Boehm, "A View of 20th and 21st Century Software Engineering," in *Proceedings of International Conference on Software Engineering 2006*, 2006, 12–29; Wendy Hui Kyong Chun, *Programmed Visions: Software and Memory*, 2011; Geraldo Con Diáz, *Software Rights: How Patent Law Transformed Software Development in America*, 2019; Nathan Ensmenger, *The Computer Boys Take Over: Computers, Programmers, and the Politics of Technical Expertise*, 2010; Christopher M. Kelty, *Two Bits: The Cultural Significance of Free Software*, 2008; Mark Priestley, *A Science of Operations: Machines, Logic and the Invention of Programming*, 2010; Joy Lisi Rankin, *A People's History of Computing in the United States*, 2018.

PROOFREADERS

Proofreader originated as jargon from the world of printing. It designates the person reading through a trial version (a proof, galley, or galley proof) printed in one copy so that typographical and other errors can be corrected before the final print run. The related act of correcting before publishing, however, was performed on texts long before the advent of movable type in the mid-fifteenth century, and it has been adapting to the *digital era. In this light, proofreading can be defined more generally as the thorough search for linguistic inaccuracies in a written text regardless of its features (date, length, purpose, *genre, materiality, production technology, etc.), commonly after its completion and before its circulation or storage; this can be repeated as many times as one wishes, or is able, or is asked. By adopting this broader definition, we can appreciate the deep historical and sociological roots of the phenomenon and retrace its global spread, persistence, and variety. As a process of spotting errors, proofreading is intertwined with reading, marking, correcting, editing, and publishing. Its history recurrently overlaps with the development of textual tradition and the book trade. For centuries, a person dealing with proofreading—and a great many other editorial tasks—was called *corrector*, a Latin term that was also applied to scholars who emended texts by means of *philological conjectures and comparison between manuscripts (collation). *Diorthotes* (διορθωτής) was the Greek equivalent.

Notwithstanding their production of long-form texts, Greeks and Romans did not have anything resembling a modern publishing system. Although Cicero's friend Titus Pomponius Atticus (110–31 BCE) occasionally provided the famous orator with feedback, Atticus was neither a *publisher nor a corrector. There were, of course, copyist-booksellers, retailers, and authors willing to "publish" their works through public readings. How about *correctores*? Evidence is thin and mostly refers to the Roman Empire. The restricted group of proficient readers, including Cicero and Seneca, lamented the poor quality of the available copies. Strabo noted that booksellers in Rome and Alexandria made use of cheap scribes and neglected to check their work with reference to good-quality originals. This comparative form of proofreading was probably more frequently practiced in scholarly centers with a notable noncommercial textual activity, beginning with the most celebrated of all, the *Musaeum* of Alexandria. It was there that the emperor Domitian sent a team of scribes to take and correct copies for the library he wished to build in Rome. Very few copyist-booksellers were renowned for the quality of their items; those who were ostensibly achieved accurate copies through effective revision. For instance, the Greek books written in Rome by Atticus's employees were so free of errors that they were marketed to native speakers of Greek in Athens. As for originals, ancient authors preferred to revise their works themselves after dictation, as attested by Horace, Martial, and Pliny the Younger. The Epicurean philosopher Philodemus may have even organized the dissemination of his own writings, with a team of scribes drawing from corrected exemplars in Herculaneum. Early Christian texts, too, were normally corrected by authors. In Caesarea, Origen employed over seven scribes for his biblical comparative enterprise and yet read through final drafts in person. The cases of Pamphilus and Eusebius illustrate how the first copyists of biblical and *exegetical works were prone to checking and collating with particular care, while the twilight of the Roman imperial culture increasingly led readers to take responsibility for improving their books.

At the present state of research, the flourishing of monastic *scriptoria across medieval Europe does not appear to have given impetus to proofreading. In the absence of clear prescription on the matter, scribes had probably no concern with systematic countercheck of finished copies; the most attentive of them corrected themselves while reporting what was dictated or copying in silence. Monks specifically devoted to proofreading were not part of the picture. The closest to playing that role were elders who occasionally went through a newly or recently written manuscript, as in Montecassino under Abbot Desiderius. So far, the only solid evidence of consistent internal revision concerns the scriptorium of St. Martin's at Tours, in which numerous codices repeatedly bore the Tironian symbol for "looked after," as in checked after the copy was finished. As a rule, marginal and interlinear corrections in medieval manuscripts are to be taken as by-products of contemporary and later users, the act of *emendatio* (emendation) pertaining to the reading and teaching practices inherited from late antiquity. Identifying the work of irregular in-house correctors is hard, unless they cared to inscribe their names at the end of the *codex or where they stopped revising. The few recognizable cases of such annotations are scattered over time and space, though they grew in number between the thirteenth and sixteenth centuries and involved not only clerics but also laypeople. Kindred inscriptions have been noted on several Arabic manuscripts, in line with Ibn Khaldūn's statement that deft copyist-booksellers attended to any aspect related to their books; yet in the Arabic world, freshly copied texts would also be read aloud to a reputed scholar and thus be "proofheard." In the reunified China of the sixth and seventh centuries, three or four proofreaders (whether students, officials, clerics, or copyists) often scrutinized a single copy of Confucian classics, sutras, and imperial documentation and then wrote down their name just after that of the scribes with whom they had teamed. The same happened in the main Japanese centers during the Nara period (710–94). Going back to Europe, we can reasonably infer that official documentation produced in medieval chancelleries was somehow proofread to avoid ambiguous proclamations, perhaps by the high ranks entrusted with authentication. To be sure, the remarkable growth and diversification of the lay and religious book market from the early thirteenth century onward called for novel textual accuracy. Scholastic authors started to write their elaborate works in person, and a larger number of commercial manuscripts underwent tight control. Most notably, the textbooks issued for university students in Bologna, Paris, Oxford, and Naples had to be collated with the originals entrusted by faculties to the *stationarii*, the stationers licensed by the universities to sell or rent books

In their pursuit of the purest Latin, humanists established an innovative practice: submitting works to learned friends for language and content check; indeed, both formal and substantive errors came to be perceived as a diminishment of the scholarly self already in the early years of the *Republic of Letters. Printing with movable type ushered in a new era in which proofreading became a necessary mechanical step and eventually a specialized job. Owing to the high cost of paper, printers sought to avoid wasting it and thus sought to correct the typesetting before printing hundreds of copies that might have to be redone if a serious error were found. The first printed specimen of a newly composed sheet—a proof—was read through, marked, and passed over to the compositor to insert emendations. A few such proof sheets survive in archives and crop up in broken bindings where they were inserted as filler, the earliest such examples dating to the late 1450s, just a few years after Gutenberg's invention. Stop-press corrections were also made during printing, generating variants of the same leaf/page within the same edition. After printing, manual adjustments were still possible by writing, scribbling, stamping, pasting in paper slips, or even replacing the incorrect leaf (cancelland) with another specially printed (cancel). Some late fifteenth-century humanists feared printing would trigger the proliferation of mistakes: Niccolò Perotti went so far as to invoke centralized proofreading by the papacy (to no avail). Others, like Giovanni Antonio Campano, directly engaged with the new medium and tried their best to carry out flawless classical texts. From 1494, humanist printers, first among them Aldus Manutius, followed by his descendants, as well as the Estienne, Froben, Plantin-Moretus, and Elzevir families, were particularly keen to advertise the correctness of their editions. By mid-sixteenth century, correctores had been handling proofreading and preparing final lists of mistakes (errata) for all major presses. In addition, they often standardized spelling (especially that of the rising *vernaculars), arranged and divided texts, and ghostwrote dedications and printers' addresses to readers, as well as drafted titles, indexes, tables of contents, and blurbs. In other words, they shaped the *paratext, exerting considerable influence on how books conveyed meaning. They rarely got credit for their intervention, which stirred up animosity among authors and printers/publishers every time it was deemed too invasive. Several of them were respected scholars, translators, and authors in their own right.

From Shakespeare's folios to the Encyclopédie, the mirage of fixable texts and perfectly emended books haunted the European publishing industry of the ancien régime, with typographical manuals describing unrealistically smooth systems of three rounds of proofs. By contrast, proofreaders' social status decreased so drastically that they ended up assimilated into the common, anonymous manpower working directly in the printshop. The seismic transformation of the book market and printing technology over the nineteenth and early twentieth centuries brought no significant change to proofreading techniques, though the rise of mass newspapers can be considered as the turning point for the differentiation of the editing tasks performed by correctores since the *Renaissance: proofreaders, filling drafts and galleys with their increasingly consistent and distinctive marks, were relegated to the bottom of the chain and deprived of any critical voice with regard to contents and style. Above them, now stood copyeditors, subeditors, and editors. Modern proofreaders partook in union fights, not always in peaceful conjunction with printers, and established professional societies. In the meantime, their literary personae started appearing in witty memoirs and columns (J. W. Lea's *Notes from a Proofreader's Diary* and Frederic Brown's *Proofreader's Page*), provocative defenses of linguistic uprightness (Orwell's *Politics and the English Language*), and metafictions (Saramago's *History of the Siege of Lisbon* and George Steiner's *Proofs*).

The digital era marks another watershed. It shows that proofreading is not inextricably linked to printing, but to written texts: enterprises such as the volunteer community

Distributed Proofreaders flanking Project Gutenberg with two pairs of eyes for each digitized page are there to prove it. One major challenge entails the hastiness of web publishing and posting in the information age. The fact that online texts can be changed after publication seems to encourage even authoritative news websites to postpone indefinitely the tasks of revision and emendation that were once tightly scheduled ahead of the moment of publication. The risk of splitting the timing of making a text accurate across multiple moments before and after publication is that errors will remain unnoticed and ultimately become accepted or even acceptable. At length, this cultural trend might endanger proofreading. Nowadays, common writing programs and apps provide autocorrection, which may easily trick users and give rise to amusing or dramatic misunderstandings; and although more sensitive tools are in the air for spell-check and stylistic improvement, machine *codes and algorithms have not been able to replace trained, experienced proofreaders, as yet.

Paolo Sachet

See also books; error; information, disinformation, misinformation; letterpress; newspapers; readers; scribes

FURTHER READING

Brian S. Brooks and James L. Pinson, *The Art of Editing in the Age of Convergence,* 11th ed., 2017; Guglielmo Cavallo and Roger Chartier, eds., *A History of Reading in the West,* 2003; Anthony Grafton, *The Culture of Correction in Renaissance Europe,* 2011; Anthony Grafton and Megan Williams, *Christianity and the Transformation of the Book: Origen, Eusebius, and the Library of Caesarea,* 2006; Lotte Hellinga, *Texts in Transit: Manuscript to Proof and Print in the Fifteenth Century,* 2014; David McKitterick, *Print, Manuscript and the Search for Order,* 2003; Adam Smyth, *Material Texts in Early Modern England,* 2018; Rex Winsbury, *The Roman Book: Books, Publishing and Performance in Classical Rome,* 2009.

PUBLIC SPHERE

When data are shared with and explained to others, they are publicized and hence they gain a social significance that transforms *facts into knowledge. For this reason, the history of the public sphere is a crucial aspect of the history of information. Understanding the role of publics and publicity in the socialization of information helps illuminate the ways in which forms of knowledge have been created. While the role of publicity in knowledge formation plays a key role in most social histories of knowledge, the major studies of publicity or public formation have not been explicitly conceived of as interventions in the sociology of knowledge. They developed out of an interest in media history and particularly studies of the invention of news and the proliferation of print (and later electronic) media in the modern era. Work of this kind has developed into a substantial body of scholarly studies detailing the emergence of a "public sphere" that was a product and perhaps even a defining feature of the modern age.

The concept of a public sphere developed in the postwar era primarily as a result of the publication of Jürgen Habermas's famous thesis *Strukturwandel der Öffentlichkeit* (1962), a work better known in English translation as *The Structural Transformation of the Public Sphere* (1989). Habermas posited that the modern age saw a "structural transformation" of the ways in which publics and publicity were both imagined and practiced. Habermas's original German text did not use the phrase "public sphere," choosing instead to use the less spatially oriented term *Öffentlichkeit*, which could be better (albeit rather awkwardly) translated into English as "public-ness" or the state of things being made public. Habermas noted that in German "the noun *Öffentlichkeit* was formed from the older adjective *öffentlich* during the eighteenth century, in analogy to '*publicité*' and 'publicity.' . . . If the public sphere [*Öffentlichkeit*] did not require a name of its own before this period, we may assume that this sphere first emerged and took on its function only at that time, at least in Germany." A differentiation between what is public and what is private, however, was a much more enduring distinction. Thus Habermas briefly detailed a history of the ancient and medieval public spheres before moving quickly to his main subject of interest, the emergence of a bourgeois public sphere in the modern era.

Bourgeois public-ness (*Öffentlichkeit*) was distinctive because it was discursive. In contrast to premodern concepts of publicity, which Habermas called the representative public sphere (*representative Öffentlichkeit*) because it simply involved the repetitive presentation of things by the powerful before their passive audiences, the bourgeois public sphere was shaped by the sharing of information among different people who could decide among themselves what this information meant and ultimately what should be done with that knowledge in mind. The bourgeois public sphere both enabled and legitimized the socialization of knowledge. It created public opinion as social fact, as an object of study, and ultimately, as an object of political manipulation.

For Habermas, the emergence of the bourgeois public sphere coincided with, and indeed to a large degree was constitutive of, the philosophical project of *Enlightenment. Not only was the bourgeois public sphere formed collectively and discursively, but it developed out of a sense that private individuals could and should discuss matters of common concern in a rational and disinterested manner, and that in doing so, better policies and, ultimately, better polities would result. In its ideal form at least, the bourgeois public sphere would also be a rational public sphere. It emerged through "rational-critical debate" and ultimately became "the organizational principle of the liberal constitutional state."

Although rationality was at the heart of the bourgeois public sphere, Habermas also argued that it was enabled through the growing sympathy that members of the Enlightenment public felt for others. Fiction emerged at this time as a cognitive category that was distinct from deliberate falsehoods, fakes, or shams: it became a psychologically complex means of exploring subjective interiority in narrative form. A new kind of prose fiction called "the novel" emerged as the epitome of this new sense of realistic fictionality. Sentimental novels such as Samuel Richardson's *Pamela* (1740), Jean-Jacques Rousseau's *La Nouvelle Héloïse* (The new Heloise, 1761), and Johann Wolfgang von Goethe's *Werthers Leiden* (The sufferings of Werther, 1774) were symptomatic of this emergent sphere of public sympathy, while at the same time helping to develop a new and more interactive relationship between authors, works, and publics. A crucial part of Habermas's argument is that the public sphere emerged first in the literary realm (*literarische Öffentlichkeit*), beginning "as an expansion and at the same time completion of the intimate sphere [*Intimsphäre*] of the conjugal family."

If the origins of the bourgeois public sphere were in the private sphere of family life, the public sphere quickly assumed an intermediary space between the private realm (*Privatbereich*) and the sphere of public authority (*Sphäre der öffentlichen Gewalt*), or in other words, the domain of state power. The bourgeois public sphere had a political dimension, particularly insofar as it could influence public opinion on matters of political concern, but it was distinct from the state. This aspect of his argument has provoked some of the most vociferous criticism from historians of the eighteenth century, many of whom have argued that it was in fact the state (itself a newly burgeoning sociopolitical entity at the time) that enabled the growth of the public sphere. States regulated publishing, sociability, and even family life in the private sphere at both the national and the local levels. The Habermasian narrative of the emergence of the bourgeois public sphere is at heart a liberal one—the state, at least in its "absolutist" old regime form, is seen as in some way antithetical to the civil society exemplified by the public sphere. The bourgeois public sphere ultimately became the forum for a new form of political consciousness that was opposed to absolutist monarchy and in which the universal sovereignty of "general and abstract laws" supported by public opinion came to be understood as "the only legitimate source of this law." In its fully developed nineteenth-century form, the bourgeois public sphere became the source of legitimacy for the liberal democratic state.

An important aspect of Habermas's thesis is that there was both a normative and a practical aspect to the making of the modern public sphere. The public sphere was both imagined and realized through the new social practices of public making that emerged in the seventeenth and eighteenth centuries, roughly during the century and a half between the English Revolution and the French Revolution. Although always existing more as an ideal than as a realized practice, it is crucial to the Habermasian argument that the normative ideals of the public sphere were at least attempted to be put into practice in real places by real people. Hence the importance for his thesis of the emergence of new forms of sociability and new forms of communication in the *early modern era. The paradigmatic spaces in which bourgeois publicity was practiced included the English *coffeehouse, the French *salon, and German dining clubs (*Tischgesellschaften*). Social spaces such as these offered new opportunities for individuals to come together to exercise their reason through discussion and debate. They were particularly important because they provided a place free from interference from the state or other forms of political control or repression in which matters of public interest could be debated. They also encouraged the discussion of new ideas that circulated in print, particularly in newspapers and pamphlets. In this way, the sociable institutions of civil society allowed for people to practice public opinion making through the sharing of information, attitudes, and opinions with one another over a cup of coffee at an urban coffeehouse or at a convivial dinner at an aristocratic salon. Coffeehouses and salons came to be seen as little commonwealths, or as refuges from the constraints on free-thinking normally imposed by the state on civil society. They offered a model for how a liberal state, founded on the rock of public opinion rather than royal majesty, could function.

Despite the importance of this practical dimension to the emergence of the public sphere, the virtual (or imaginary) public sphere was possibly even more important for its ultimate fruition. This is because the idea, and the ideals, of a public opinion based on rational-critical debate was free from the messy realities of a civil society that could never live up to the utopian ideals of a reason-based political order. In the minds of Enlightenment thinkers, the virtual public sphere could truly flourish. Publicity was above all a state of mind; it was a means by which collectivities could be imagined. This "virtual" aspect of the Habermasian public sphere concept would be developed further in different ways by later theorists of modern identity formation. For Benedict Anderson (1983), it would form the basis for his understanding of modern nationalism as the product of the always strained and artificial process of imagining new communities. For Charles Taylor (2004), publics are a key "social imaginary" that comprise modern identities and particularly the modern sense of selves that come together as individuals with a common set of beliefs or interests. Modern people imagine themselves to be part of a panoply of different kinds of communities that are variously understood as nations, publics, faiths, or other interest groups.

Habermas's public sphere concept, and his historical argument about the structural transformation of the bourgeois public sphere that occurred in the seventeenth and eighteenth centuries, has been immensely influential, but part of the explanation for its extraordinary success both as theory and as history lies within the ambiguities of the original work. Precisely because Habermas's arguments were chronologically imprecise, many scholars have quarreled with the details of his historical narrative, in some cases going to the extreme of using the phrase but denuding it of any relationship to the broader historical vision of a transition from representative to bourgeois publicity, or its claim that the ideals of publicity began in the nonpolitical intimate sphere of private life and sympathetic imaginations. This approach has the benefit of allowing for a much more nuanced understanding of premodern media culture, particularly since it encourages the study of a much more diverse media ecology than the highly print-centered perspective offered by the Habermasian model. Gossip, theatrical performances, and manuscript circulation, for example, were all important aspects of information circulation both before and after the seventeenth and eighteenth centuries. Post-Habermasian studies of the public sphere emphasize this intermediality and particularly the numerous ways in which these forms of publicity interacted with the rise and efflorescence of print and the press in the modern era.

Related to this attention to intermediality and interactions is a greater recognition of the multiplicity, variability, and temporal limitations of any given public sphere. Rather than speaking in terms of a unitary public with its own clearly recognizable opinion, it is much more common today to think of many publics, each of which competes for members, recognition, and influence. From these post-Habermasian perspectives, the public sphere is not the product of a grand structural transformation in social and economic relations as Habermas's original Marxist thesis posited; it is rather a multivocal, constantly evolving marketplace of attention in which new publics are continually formed and re-formed. It is now common to speak of publics, rather than *the* public.

With this more pluralistic public sphere model in mind, post-Habermasian perspectives have devoted greater attention to the reasons why publics were formed in the first place. What brought people together to see themselves as participating in something that they understood to be a public? The answer is: things. Drawing on Martin Heidegger's theory of the thing, scholars such as Bruno Latour and others have stressed that a key property of "things" is that they bring people together—they are objects of attention that can create publics. This line of thinking reminds us of the original meaning of the Roman *res publica* as "the public thing" as discussed by Heidegger: republics do not begin as states fully formed; they emerge out of "that which, known to everyone, concerns everybody and is therefore deliberated in public."

The material aspect of things also plays a role in post-Habermasian public sphere theory. Although things need not necessarily be material objects, they may be, and as such they offer a physical instantiation of what would otherwise be only a virtual reality. Obviously, the material forms of knowledge collection, such as books, newspapers, databases, and so forth, are key things that help bring publics together when these works are read, used, or discussed. But things are as multifarious as publics, and they need not be material objects. As Heidegger noted, "the Romans called a matter for discourse *res*." Public-forming things could be discursive as well as material.

The idea of a public sphere is here to stay, even if the concept is now used in ways that Habermas could not have imagined in the context of postwar Germany, where it was first conceived. What was once an attempt to salvage the Kantian Enlightenment project of explaining how rational-critical debate could guide the way toward better public policy in a liberal democratic society has in the twenty-first century become something different—the public sphere concept offers a valuable guide toward thinking about how ideas and information have been disseminated, debated, and ultimately turned into new forms of common knowledge. What was once thought to be a unitary phenomenon produced by an inexorable historical dialectic is now more commonly understood to be something that can be found in many different times and places, each with its own local complexities and variability. Post-Habermasian understandings of the public sphere are more pluralistic and less rooted in a narrative of European historical development, and they are more inclined to see the relationship between publics and states as mutually constitutive rather than separate entities or even antagonists.

The history of information should attend to the histories of public formation. Without a public to receive it and discuss it, the meaning and significance of information remains limited to those select few individuals who have it. While the history of secret information—*arcana imperii* (secrets of government) classified information, and the like—is an important counterpoint to the history of information in the public sphere, even secrets gain resonance through their oppositional relationship to publicity. The act of concealing information in itself recognizes that it is too sensitive to be revealed to a wider public.

It is not an exaggeration to say that publics turn information into knowledge; if so, then the role of public spheres needs to play a key role in the history of knowledge formation. Equally so, histories of public spheres are enhanced by the history of information. While few historians of the public sphere today believe that rational-critical debate was at the center of the activities that brought publics together, even during the supposed rational high-water moment of the Enlightenment era, publics are fundamentally communicative entities. Therefore, if we are going to understand what publics were up to in the past (as well as in the present), we must know what kinds of information they were interested in communicating, and we should attend to the various ways in which that information was communicated. The answers may not confirm Habermas's view of what a public sphere should look like, but they will lead to better histories.

Brian Cowan

See also information, disinformation, misinformation; journals; knowledge; media; networks; newsletters; newspapers; privacy; publicity/publication

FURTHER READING

Benedict Anderson, *Imagined Communities: Reflections on the Origin and Spread of Nationalism*, 1983; T.C.W. Blanning, *The Culture of Power and the Power of Culture: Old Regime Europe 1660–1789*, 2002; Jürgen Habermas, *The Structural Transformation of the Public Sphere: An Inquiry into a Category of Bourgeois Society*, 1962, translated by Thomas Burger and Frederick Lawrence, 1989; Martin Heidegger, "The Thing" (1951), in *Poetry, Language, Thought*, translated by Albert Hofstadter, 1971; Bruno Latour and Peter Weibel, eds., *Making Things Public: Atmospheres of Democracy*, 2005; Charles Taylor, *Modern Social Imaginaries*, 2004; Michael Warner, *Publics and Counterpublics*, 2002; Bronwen Wilson and Paul Yachnin, eds., *Making Publics in Early Modern Europe: People, Things, Forms of Knowledge*, 2010.

PUBLICITY/PUBLICATION

Publication should be distinguished from "communication." The latter designates the bidirectional sharing of information at relatively high rates of exchange, commonly across multiple channels simultaneously; it may have the primary function of creating common meanings (as, for example, in a conversation between friends, in which verbal, visual, and physical information is shared and adjusted synchronously, and the result of which may be primarily affective); publication, by contrast, takes the form of an expositing or setting forth of information at much slower rates, with reduced capacities for feedback, and often using a single medium or channel. One cannot communicate by standing on a hill and speaking to an empty plain, although one certainly can publish by placing an inscribed stone in such a place; in the latter case we may presume an intention to have one's text "copied," as it were, in the minds or the practices of its readers when or as they arrive at the stone, which thus functions as a kind of exemplar for psychic or practical reproductions (a law is "practically reproduced" when a named transgression is punished or a prescribed penalty is imposed). Publishing should also be distinguished from "archiving." "Archiving" designates taking steps to preserve a text for posterity without the necessary implication of any collective readership or popular address, while publication implies an expectation, or perhaps it is no more than a hope, that one's text will reach a public (I understand *public* as a collective noun implying a plurality of people; whether this public is real or imagined is a question I take up below).

Overwhelmingly, textual publication in the West has been oral (we would have to tell a quite different story if we were to speak of the publication of images or music): through legal or political rhetoric in courts and city forums, through the proclamation of decrees or the pronouncement of the sacred word, through sermon and homily, the voice was the primary means of making public and of marking a public. We need not ascribe to any form of technological determinism to recognize that the voice's capacity to broadcast information made it a powerful tool for social cohesiveness even before the age of radio and electric amplification. Indeed, it has only been in the last two centuries that the pulpit was rivaled by the press as a channel for the dissemination of information and the performance of community. (This rivalry could well be programmatic: one of the primary scripts of the *new media after the age of auditory recording and dissemination has been the claim that this form of publicity reaches more people—reaches, indeed, "the mass" of people. On some of the contradictions inherent in this claim, see below.)

Non-oral publication was long a matter of state. The Law Code of Hammurabi (ca. 1700 BCE), which was displayed on a monumental stele (as well as being copied within the scribal culture for centuries), invoked a public: like Wallace Stevens's jar in Tennessee, it gathered a community around it, both by its material form—an imposing basalt stele—and by its content, combining a first-person panegyric of Hammurabi and a set of regulations governing social behavior ("laws"). Similarly, the Greek city-state of Gortyn had its law code inscribed on the walls of a civic building in the mid-fifth century BCE. Here, as in the case of Hammurabi, the gesture of monumental inscription seems impossible to dissociate from a desire to make the rules regulating a community open to all, to invoke and consolidate a public through the display of text.

Texts we habitually (though not always accurately) call "literature" were also occasionally published in the sense outlined above. The Greek songwriter Pindar's early fifth-century panegyric of the Rhodian boxer Diagoras was inscribed in bronze and publicly displayed in Diagoras's hometown. The outside wall of the Athenian treasury at Delphi was inscribed with two hymns to Apollo, complete with musical notation—an extremely rare act that is hard not to understand as advertising the high levels of technical attainment of Athenian musicians. Even philosophy could be published in such a way: in the second century CE, a wealthy citizen of the mountain town of Oenoanda by the name of Diogenes built a public portico and had essays on Epicurean ethics and physics inscribed on the back wall. This Diogenes made his motivations clear in the inscription. Individual contact—ideal, it would seem, for philosophical therapy—being impossible owing to the massive number of those suffering from their ignorance, Diogenes opts for the (by his time) millennia-old practice of creating a public space covered in text, effectively broadcasting his message to an invoked public in a kind of philosophical public health initiative. At the same time, however, as he resorts to public address, he also replaces specific, individual (we might say "real") interlocutors with a fictive public, enacted within the text of the inscription and perhaps—but only perhaps—associated with actual readers who might have visited the portico.

On soft media such as *papyrus or *vellum, "literary" publication was rare and unpredictable in the ancient world. Often it was accidental, its consequences uncontrollable. Usually textualization coincided more closely with what I above referred to as communication, or else with archiving: authors merely shared texts with friends, or (if they were teachers) had their lectures inscribed for one or a few students; these lectures could then circulate among interested readers, or be stored in libraries, effectively disappearing for centuries (as with Aristotle) or millennia (as with Philodemus). Cicero, who did intend broader circulation outside his immediate social circle, used his friend Atticus as his main channel of distribution. Atticus was useful not as a "bookseller" but as a wealthy Roman with an unusually robust network among the political classes. The sharing of a book with Atticus could lead, if Atticus was willing, to its being circulated to major policy makers or their proxies. Such social publication remained the paradigm well into the later medieval period; even in monastic contexts new works were often distributed first to close circles of friends and then outward along international networks.

Ancient and medieval publishing did not mean necessarily that a text was fixed; it often meant just the opposite of this, as texts circulated beyond the authors' control and were altered as seemed best to their copyists and readers. Perhaps transforming a few local remarks in Cicero's letters into a conventional gesture, writers such as Boccaccio invited dedicatees and members of their reading circles not only to disseminate but also to correct their texts, in effect authorizing both dissemination and fluctuation within textual traditions. Universities seem to have sought to contest this trend: in a context where teachers wanted students to have uniform copies of the texts they explicated (and also of the explications themselves), mechanisms were developed to ensure a certain amount of textual stability, such as the so-called *pecia* system in Paris (whereby stationers had texts copied from authoritative exemplars, in sections) or the careful regulation of dictation or *pronunciatio* in the north and east.

The revolutionary effect of printing has often been exaggerated: it seems equally reasonable to observe that movable type was a response to a growing desire for books in the European context (see Blair, chap. 4, and Slauter, chap. 7, in this volume). What may matter most about printing is the fact that it interposed between a manuscript and its publication an assemblage of technical, social, and legal routines, including the establishment of warrant to publish, editing, typesetting, printing, and proof checking, with which the producer of a manuscript text had little business before the publishing process began. With print, publishing came to coincide with the labor-intensive technological transformation of a text. In fact, publication had often involved some kind of transmediation in which verbal expression was transferred from one modality to another, and with transmediation there was also commonly a kind of remediation, in which the new media form metaphorically recalled an older one. In the ancient world, transmediation most often took the form of inscribing spoken words, and remediation involved the presentation of written text as though it were spoken. The frequency with which ancient texts invoke the fiction of oral speech, whether as samples of rhetoric or as dialogue or diatribe, still challenges classical scholars, some of whom continue to fail to recognize the complex intermediality at work there. But ancient transmediation was not associated exclusively with publication: in many cases, primarily where literary texts and soft media were concerned, the association was primarily with archiving. With print, transmediation and publication seemed to coalesce to such a degree that in recent memory "to publish" simply meant "to have printed in book form," with little distinction made between whether the book is addressed to a public (as with commercial publication) or an archive (as with academic "publication").

Publishing not only transmediates; it also condenses, reducing expression into a packet of information aimed at others. But a book, once bought, need never be read, and an audience, though listening, might not hear. Thus the compression of literary activity into a commodifiable format can resemble an act of abandonment. Because publication evokes an audience (unlike archiving) but does not come with a natural way for that audience to speak back (like communication), a published text may be difficult to distinguish from a text that has just been left behind, given up, as it were, for adoption. This is a risk recognized as early as the fourth century BCE, when Plato described written texts as orphans; it became a central part of the authorial self-representation of the Neronian poet Martial, who spoke of his poems as eager to leave him and enter the crowd; and it was still at work in the much-repeated (and rewritten) cliché attributed to Paul Valéry in the early twentieth century that a poem is never finished but only abandoned. This cliché can be meant in any number of senses, including that a writer is never satisfied with her or his work (a sense most movingly developed by Ernst Cassirer in "The Tragedy of Culture"); what it means in the context of the act of publication is that a published work cannot be erased or taken back, and its *fortuna* cannot be limited or controlled.

One consequence is that it is difficult for *publishers to retain credit, both financial and cultural, for their work. Martial was already intensely aware that once it began to circulate a poem could be passed off as the work of others, and he wrote poems attacking plagiarists who stole his work; in the modern period, booksellers needed to be aware of the possibility that texts they had edited or acquired would be reprinted by others, and they developed various means to prevent this from happening—eventually leading to the evolution of legally defined *copyright. But even with robust legal protections for copyright, bootlegging and unauthorized and unremunerated circulation poses an existential threat to publishing, a fact experienced with great immediacy by the music industry, which was brought to its knees by the rise of person-to-person sharing of *digital content in the 1990s and 2000s.

A second consequence of the similarity between publication and abandonment is the fact that while a publisher pretends to present texts to a public, there is no inherent way to know that a connection has been made with anyone real. Various compensations for the resounding silence that follows a book being publicly exposed have developed. First, a kind of self-reflexive narration of a public became part of the "public sphere": even ancient authors paused to remark on the wide circulation of their texts within the circulating texts themselves, as though to reassure themselves and their readers that a public truly existed somewhere, somehow. Similarly, from the eighteenth century the ephemeral press took pains to report (or create) feedback from "actual readers," as Michael Warner has compellingly shown, in effect creating a public that is narrated within the pages of the texts supposedly circulating to that public (on periodical printing, see Slauter, chap. 7 in this volume).

Publication's orientation toward publics conceals a remarkable and significant paradox: outside state publication (like the ancient law codes discussed above), publics have tended to be constituted by strangers who have in common little more than an intense form of privacy and interiority. If, as I have suggested, the earliest forms of publication in durable media were political or statist in origin and function, "literary" publication is rooted in personal processes of reflection and creation that for a long time were considered primarily ethical, part of the work of self-fashioning. Outside of dramatic forms, most ancient literary forms (including rhetoric) were closely associated with what Pierre Hadot called "techniques of the self" and Brian Stock has analyzed under the heading of "contemplative practices": writing and reading were components of philosophical practice whose aim was the attainment of a relatively unperturbed, autonomous self, free of the most extreme passions. Such forms of exemplary self-fashioning were still central in the work of Petrarch and Montaigne in the *Renaissance and are often assumed in the age of mass publishing, where reading—even of entertainments such as novels—is taken as an inward, private act. If the act of publishing creates a public, that public, in as much as it is a "reading public," is constituted by a turning away from any kind of open commonality (even if the turn to privacy is itself a shared act). This oxymoronic fact has a cultural and political importance that is difficult to underestimate, for it is thanks to the inwardness and autarchy of its members that "the reading public" acquired moral and political clout in the nineteenth century and after. Arguably an important, if unacknowledged, element in the culture of listening documented by Jonathan Sterne was the interiority associated with reading books: radio listening was a private act intimately involved with the experience of subjectivity. This occurred only at the far end, as it were, of large-scale textual culture and could be called an auditory modulation of print publishing.

With an increasingly hegemonic electronic network of communication, publication is again rare and unpredictable. What happens online, even when it is initiated by institutions with historical roots in the publishing industry, cannot easily be called "publication" in the same sense as when the word was used for print or stone. The real-time nature of electronic communication, with what amounts to instantaneous feedback and "living texts," makes it much more like communication than publication. Privacy, notoriously, is vanishing in digital media: in principle, every ocular saccade can be tracked. Not only privacy, but the very nature of subjectivity is transformed in this new context. Digital platforms rely heavily on models drawn from neuroscience (particularly, but by no means exclusively, having to do with addiction), and the result has been a twisted version of McLuhan's prediction that electronic communications would become "extensions of the human nervous system"; electronic communication does extend the human nervous system outside of human bodies, but in the process it has come to dominate and redefine it, porting subjectivity into a new form that old subjectivities can barely recognize. At the very least it is possible to say that this new technical and social environment is not one to which one can "publish." It is, rather (as our softwares tell us), one in which we may "share," thereby participating in the real-time creation of a new cultural and subjective world. When we release texts to the web we participate in an unmanageably complex interactive network of communication—one whose consequences are fundamentally different from those of publication.

Noticeable as well is the disappearance of any meaningful form of transmediation. Though it is true that an early and important moment in the rise of the electronic regime was a massive process of "scanning," in which a significant proportion of mainstream print materials were digitized and made available online, most new digital texts have an extremely brief existence in nonelectronic form—in many cases amounting to little more than the passage from brain to keyboard or microphone. (We cannot quantify the number of recent texts that began with pen or typewriter; but that very fact indicates a major difference between the contemporary regime and that of modern publication: writing and typing are secret activities, inherently part of the paradoxical world of publication.) In a significant twist, "publications" that could well be entirely digital, from initial composition right through purchase and use, are still presented online in a format that largely recalls the visuals of print and are often mediated by levels of production that mimic those of the publishing house. Transmediation itself has become the object of a kind of nostalgic remediation, a seemingly desired but entirely metaphoric moment in a new set of procedures for textual sharing that retain the gestures, but not the content, of publication.

Sean Gurd

See also archivists; books; commodification; computers; cybernetics/feedback; digitization; inscriptions; letterpress; libraries and catalogs; media; newspapers; plagiarizing; public sphere; readers; scrolls and rolls; social media

FURTHER READING

J. David Bolter, *Remediation: Understanding New Media*, 1999; Sean Alexander Gurd, *Work in Progress: Literary Revision as Social Performance in Ancient Rome*, 2012; Pierre Hadot, *Philosophy as a Way of Life: Spiritual Exercises from Socrates to Foucault*, 1995; Daniel Hobbins, *Authorship and Publicity before Print*, 2009; Marshall McLuhan, *Understanding Media: The Extensions of Man*, 1964; Jonathan Sterne, *The Audible Past: Cultural Origins of Sound Reproduction*, 2003; Brian Stock, *After Augustine: The Meditative Reader and the Text*, 2001; Michael Warner, *Publics and Counterpublics*, 2002.

QUANTIFICATION

Over the last century, one key definition of information has come to depend on the idea that anything and everything can be represented by a *binary number sent humming through wires or optical fibers. Quantification has been built into the foundations of information technology. But digitization in the "information age" is but one episode in a much longer history of filling the world with numbers while making sense of the world through numbers.

The earliest examples of quantification date back to near the dawn of agriculture and well before the advent of written history—indeed some scholars argue that quantification acted as a stepping stone toward writing. In the beginning, categories were narrow, and each came with its own means of counting. Looking at the ancient Near East between 7500 and 3500 BCE, Denise Schmandt-Besserat explains that every class of goods had to be represented by a particular token. A person counted grain with grain tokens and garments with garment tokens. With the rise of cities came clay tablets bearing marks for counting and keeping track of debts. On those tablets, the symbols for quantities of grain—themselves already standardized—broke free of their specificity and became instead abstracted numerals fit to be used in counting within any or all classifications. Techniques for quantification laid claim to people and their labor as well. The discussion of Inka *khipus* in this volume explains how twisted and knotted cords were employed to track thousands of hours of work owed as tribute to the empire.

In the modern era quantification became inescapable and often industrial in character. For example, one of the largest life insurance companies in the world in the early twentieth century developed a technique for assessing the risk of individual lives and called it the "numerical method." The numerical method's "human treadmill" began working each day when the company's mailroom received a flood of standardized forms filled in by applicants, agents, or examining physicians—each already abounding in numbers from earlier quantifying processes and sorted by gender, race, and class. Those forms eventually made their way to white women in white blouses and white men in vests, jackets, and ties sitting in row upon row of desks in the office tower in a New York City skyscraper. Those workers disassembled each application into its key questions and determined how to classify each answer to each question, assigning a point value (often derived from consulting a table of printed numbers) to the resulting classifications. Then the worker added and subtracted these preliminary ratings according to a fixed algorithm to determine the extent to which each applicant departed from a standard set for healthy, white men. The resulting number stood in for the insurance applicant and in most cases justified, on its own, the company's decision to accept, reject, or impose a penalty on the applicant. What is striking in this description is not only the vast scale of the quantifying operation, but also how many numbers had to be made and how many others consulted in the process. A person—or a commodity, or a physical phenomenon—became a number, but only after becoming a number many times before.

The processes that filled the modern world with numbers depended on widespread observation mediated by specialized instruments and new techniques for managing and presenting numerical data. When the naturalist Alexander von Humboldt traveled to South America in 1799 determined to reveal the laws linking life to its surroundings, he carried with him an observatory's worth of thermometers, barometers, chronometers, and sextants borne on the backs of mules guided by Indigenous workers. To make sense of all his measurements, Humboldt drew maps on which he could plot his figures and trace "isolines" connecting them. The subsequent invention of graph paper in the early nineteenth century facilitated further reliance on observational data and the use of graphical techniques to make sense of proliferating observations. Astronomers and actuaries alike, in the name of science or business, defined natural laws with curves drawn by hand through plotted numbers.

In the early nineteenth century, Victorian bureaucracies responsible for reforms meant to hold off revolution precipitated an "avalanche of printed numbers" in Europe, according to Ian Hacking. With more numbers came the possibility to look for and discover patterns or regularities, many of which became new objects of study in themselves. Hacking's key example was sickness, a state of being that came to be seen as explicable by statistical laws in the context of the avalanche and, once in the grasp of standardizing bureaucrats attending international statistical congresses, produced a host of new and newly defined kinds of illness. Over the second half of the twentieth century, for instance, high blood pressure evolved from an indicator of high risk for later heart disease to something like the status of a disease in itself requiring sustained medical treatment.

Corporate offices set off their own avalanches of printed numbers in the mid-nineteenth century. Railroads and telephone companies built vast networks for coordinating the flows of both goods and information. They—and the mass marketers who grew along with them—sent agents to far-flung peripheries, built branches, and advertised widely. Quantification offered a means for disciplining dispersed employees. Home offices that did not trust their field divisions to keep the corporation's best interests at heart forced them to fill in complicated blank forms, many of which accepted only numbers. Relying more on figures from account books or objective instrumental measures also meant relying less on the judgment of ill-trained or deceiving agents. States responded to corporate expansion with their own systems for measuring the honesty and probity of big business and, with the advent of cost-benefit analysis and elaborate twentieth-century budgeting systems, of government itself. Of course, those who provided the figures could still doctor them, or game them, to win some advantage. And quantification caused new distortions when it encouraged governance based on numbers that, even if faithfully rendered, privileged whatever was most readily quantified rather than what experts, bureaucrats, or ordinary people judged to be most significant. It was in the context of a heavily regulated corporate network—the Bell telephone system—that Ralph Hartley and Claude Shannon made "information" itself into a reliably quantifiable entity, as Paul Duguid explains in this book (see chap. 12).

The twentieth century nurtured bigger, nimbler networks of observers and instruments supported first by empires, then new international governance bodies (like the League of Nations and the United Nations), and later by Cold War alliances. Such networks invented new globe-spanning numbers that helped make debates about international politics look more like engineering problems. With the calorie serving as a standard unit, for instance, national and global indexes of hunger could be created and used to justify humanitarian interventions or the distribution of food aid (which also subsidized agriculture in rich countries). To take another example, world population figures eventually fed major efforts by nation-states teamed with philanthropic foundations to curtail or control fertility. But determining such a figure after World War II required first reconciling national censuses of varying quality, coverage, and organization. Similar challenges confronted efforts to represent global climate or assign and then track annual average global temperatures. To meet those challenges, researchers across fields integrated computer-powered data models into their quantifying treadmills. In the early twenty-first century, much quantification results from people and things who, via the *internet, act as unceasing observers of themselves and their surroundings. Some of the numbers they produce remain private, some combine to form risk profiles in various national security databases, and many are stored by a new breed of corporations for whom such data acts like capital.

Over the last few hundred years, quantification has been closely associated with objectivity. Such associations have proven particularly useful to bureaucrats and scientists alike who sacrificed a modicum of professional judgment in favor of allowing numerical criteria—from credit scores to risk ratings to p-values—the power to make more defensible, because less subjective, decisions for them. Focusing on the way quantification constrains subjectivity, however, distracts from one of the most important explanations for quantification and its effects. A complex range of emotions drive people to make numbers. Nathaniel Bowditch, for example, embraced the task of calculating numerical tables that American sailors used to find their longitude at sea in the early nineteenth century. He ferreted out errors in others' tables and made his own extraordinarily precise. While others considered such work drudgery, Bowditch approached his long hours as an aesthetic or spiritual pursuit, according to Tamara Plakins Thornton.

Numerical tables could also communicate emotions and aesthetics to readers, like those described by Jacqueline Wernimont, who found a glimpse of the sublime and hints of human mastery even in John Graunt's tallies of those who died from plague in seventeenth-century Britain. Or, as Caitlin Zaloom discovered, commodity traders in Chicago and London at the end of the twentieth century lived in a world awash with market numbers, but most learned to interpret them less as individual *facts than as a mass whose motions must be watched and judged, all as part of getting a feel for or telling a story about the "market." On a larger scale, numbers like those produced by pollsters and marketers often shaped how ordinary people, like those discussed by Sarah Igo, understood themselves, their communities, or their nation. Numbers are not inherently objective, and to assert that they are only further hinders us from fully understanding how quantification works.

Numbers often seem entirely natural and quantification an elementary process, but only because so many tools, techniques, institutions, and infrastructures have developed over millennia—and especially over the last few hundred years—to churn out numbers and make the world intelligible through them.

Dan Bouk

See also accounting; bureaucracy; commodification; data; error; governance; khipus; observing; surveilling; surveys and censuses

FURTHER READING

Ian Hacking, "Biopower and the Avalanche of Printed Numbers," *Humanities in Society* 5, nos. 3–4 (1982): 279–95; Sarah E. Igo, *The Averaged American*, 2007; Emily R. Merchant, "Prediction and Control," PhD dissertation, University of Michigan, 2015; Theodore M. Porter, *Trust in Numbers*, 1995; Denise Schmandt-Besserat, "Tokens and Writing," *Scripta* 1 (2009): 145–54; Tamara Plakins Thornton, *Nathaniel Bowditch and the Power of Numbers*, 2016; Jacqueline Wernimont, *Numbered Lives*, 2018; Caitlin Zaloom, *Out of the Pits: Traders and Technology from Chicago to London*, 2006.

READERS

In his 1967 essay "The Death of the Author" (*La mort de l'auteur*) the French literary critic Roland Barthes attacked those who believed that the task of criticism was to extract and identify the authorial intent that lurked behind a text. To put it in the terms of this book, Barthes rejected the notion that information about authors—about their biographies, habits, ideologies, the other books they read, liked, or disliked—should equal information about their *texts*. Instead he proposed a new unit of interpretation. He called for replacing the author with his or her analog or antithesis: the reader. It was only at the point of reading, not composition—of consumption, not production—that a text acquired meaning: "A text consists of multiple writings, issuing from several cultures and entering into dialogue with each other, into parody, into contestation; but there is one place where this multiplicity is collected, united, and this place is not the author . . . but the reader." Barthes issued a call to arms, and many in the last half century responded with enthusiasm: "We know that to restore to writing its future," he declared, "we must reverse its myth: the birth of the reader must be ransomed by the death of the Author."

In many respects, Barthes's prediction of the "birth of the reader" was prophetic. Two years later, Michel Foucault famously critiqued what he labeled the "author function." In the ensuing decades, developments across academic disciplines granted readers new centrality and visibility. From theories of reader-response in literary studies, to the rise of reception studies in classics, to the emergence of book history and the study of *marginalia and other forms of readerly engagement with the physical copies of their texts, readers now enjoy a prominence that seems unprecedented. And the rise of *digital media—and with it the so-called information revolution—has drawn new attention to how readers consume, and sometimes re-create, the texts they read across *genres, layouts, and formats.

To adopt Barthes's terminology, how had the author achieved so vaunted a position that his death was necessary for the reader's birth? In other words, why were the two figures opposed to one another? Barthes, like Foucault and others, identified authorship with some usual suspects. The author was that quintessential "modern figure," whose birth was traceable to certain textbook *early modern developments: "English empiricism, French rationalism and the personal faith of the *Reformation." In other words, he judged the author the product of a species of individualism derived from the likes of Luther, Locke, and Descartes.

But this schema raises some questions: what was the status of readers and their relationship to the producers of what they read (whether or not they considered these producers *authors*) during the millennia of written culture that *preceded* these developments? For instance, how did readers in classical antiquity and the Middle Ages understand what they were doing when they read? And how did readers and authors interact in the subsequent period—now called early modernity—that Barthes identified as fun-

damental to the triumph of the latter? As argued here, the history of reading during
these periods might complicate the dichotomies we sometimes imagine between the production and consumption of texts. Where does readership end and authorship begin,
and vice versa? For instance, how should we classify early modern annotated books that
contain more marginalia (by anyone from a well-known scholar to an anonymous student in a lecture hall) than printed words? Or medieval manuscripts in which the sheer
quantity of commentary and gloss on a given folio overwhelms the few lines of underlying text commented on? Or what might we say of hermeneutic strategies, such as those
that Christian readers applied to pagan writings, which interpreted texts as elaborate
allegories for phenomena of which their authors were ignorant? For instance, what did
it mean to read Virgil's Fourth Eclogue as a prophetic account of Christ? Just *who* exactly counted as an author in these cases?

All this raises another, still more basic question, which strikes at the very heart of
this volume: what was reading *for*? Barthes's scheme imagined reading as a discursive
phenomenon: one presumably read for things like narrative, argument, and interpretation. But readers—whether premodern, modern, or postmodern—have also always engaged in another form of reading, which, even if it feels less glamorous, is nonetheless
no less important. And this was a kind of reading that is actually broader, insofar as it
is not limited to the reading of things we would unambiguously label coherent texts or
stable authors. In other words, this was reading for information, in the hopes of extracting from written material anything from technical knowledge to quotidian *facts. Its
history is equally visible among ancient encyclopedists like Pliny the Elder or modern
tools for content aggregation on the web. And the purpose of this kind of reading (of a
reading without authorship, we might say, or a reading that renders authorship irrelevant) has also been debated from antiquity to the present.

Space does not permit an exhaustive survey. Instead, in what follows I examine several discussions and definitions of readers and reading advanced by critics and theorists writing in Latin, from Roman antiquity to the early modern period. This reflects
not just the specialization of the present (hopefully not dead!) author, but also the profound importance of these prescriptive statements in shaping basic expectations about
what reading was and what it could accomplish—even for modern readers operating in
a world where Latin had lost its status as a lingua franca. Traces of it are found even in
twentieth-century critics like Barthes himself, who contrasted the author (derived from
the Latin *auctor* and hence etymologically linked to *auctoritas* or "authority") with someone he termed the *scriptor* (i.e., Latin for "writer") and defined as nothing more, or less,
than his or her text: "the modern writer (scriptor) is born simultaneously with his text;
he is in no way supplied with a being which precedes or transcends his writing, he is in
no way the subject of which his book is the predicate."

Much research on reading in classical antiquity has focused on the basic *how* of the
operation, and what it might tell us about the relationship between orality and textual-
ity in worlds very different from our own. In particular, scholars have long debated
whether ancient readers read as we often do—that is, silently—and what the relative
presence or absence of such silent cogitation might tell us about how the ancients viewed
their texts. By now, the claim that the ancients read aloud exclusively has largely been
debunked, even if it remains impossible to quantify just how, or how often, they read
silently. Yet as the classicist William Johnson has argued in an important study of Roman

reading communities, disproportionate focus on this question of silent reading or its absence has obscured other avenues of inquiry into what the ancients thought they were doing when they read. To put it in our terms, how did readers in classical antiquity conceive of the relationship between reading and information gathering?

Perhaps one of the most explicit descriptions of the relationship between the two was offered by the Roman rhetorician Quintilian (ca. 35–100 CE) in his *Institutio oratoria* (Oratorical institutes). At the beginning of his *Institutes*, a kind of how-to manual for rhetorical education, Quintilian explained what being a reader entailed: he argued that proper reading was a prerequisite for discerning meaning or what he styled *enarratio*— literally "exposition" or "setting forth" (1.4.2–3). As he put it, "correct reading precedes exposition" (*enarrationem praecedit emendata lectio*). Such *lectio* embraced many things, from the proper sounding of vowels to the proper attribution of authorship. Elsewhere, in a section (1.8.1–2) specifically devoted to lectio, he did discuss the fundamentally oral nature of such reading, noting that—when it came to poetry, for instance—reading must be "manly and grave with a certain charm." Yet he prefaced these admonitions with a reminder to his would-be pupils that such efforts would be for naught if they failed to grasp reading's interpretive function: "In order to be able to do all these things [i.e., carry out readings with the proper deportment or intonation], one must understand them" (*ut omnia ista facere possit, intelligat*). In other sources, we also find variations on lectio, deployed not to characterize an oral, performative mode of reading, but rather to describe the activity of information *gathering*—this was lectio done in its literal sense of "choosing" or "selection." For example, Pliny the Elder famously advertised at the beginning (praef.17) of his *Historia naturalis* (*Natural History*) that he had assembled that massive work "from the perusal of approximately 2,000 volumes" (*lectione voluminum circiter duorum milium*), and hence had assembled nothing less than twenty thousand distinct facts. Lectio could also possess a multiplicative property.

Yet the locus classicus for discussions of reading in the ancient world actually comes from a slightly later moment: a world that we might no longer consider classical, even if it was still profoundly influenced by the practices of a Quintilian or Pliny. In his *Confessiones* (Confessions), Augustine (354–430 CE), theologian and bishop of Hippo, described the events that precipitated his conversion to Christianity. In a garden in Milan, he famously recounted that an angelic voice instructed him, "Pick up, and read" (*Tolle, lege*), and so he picked up a copy of Paul's epistles (8.12.29). There is perhaps no more famous injunction in the history of reading. Yet he did so in a fashion that had profound importance to the history of what we would term information. Here Augustine read the Bible in a manner akin to how Romans often read Virgil: he practiced a biblical variation on the so-called *sortes Vergilianae* (Virgilian lots), in which one would open to a passage of Virgil at random and then interpret the significance of such a passage to one's own fortunes and life. Augustine had heard that Saint Anthony had employed this same practice on the Bible, and hence he followed his lead and opened to a chapter of Paul's letter to the Romans.

Scholars have often focused on the fact that Augustine described this reading as silent ("and I read in silence the first chapter on which my eyes were cast") (*et legi in silentio capitulum quo primum coniecti sunt oculi mei*), much as he had famously described Ambrose of Milan reading silently several chapters earlier (6.3). However, it is also worth noting the kind of information selection that Augustine, having picked up and read, here performed. The *sortes* might seem a fitting example of Barthian reading. Or perhaps it resonates with still more recent practices. Not unlike the time-pressed student who performs a keyword search on a text in Google Books or another digital repository, but fails to read the surrounding paragraphs once locating the desired citation, the sortes were not only a form of reading by chance, but also a form of decontextualized reading—blithely unconcerned with squaring any hermeneutic circles. Their reader did not need to fit the particular passage into the text as a whole, in order to divine its author's intent. Rather, it sufficed to interpret the decontextualized significance of a given passage or line *for the reader*—that is, the passage was to be contextualized not via the remainder of the author's text, but rather via the progress and circumstances of the reader's life, just as Augustine did in the garden. In a fashion that would have made Barthes proud, meaning was created by the reader, not the author.

Augustine's reading practice reveals something else important to the history of information. The *Confessions* feature readerly encounters not only with the Bible and other Christian sources, but also with pagans like Virgil. When it came to the latter, Augustine drew an important distinction, which anticipated medieval practices. Describing his elementary instruction (1.13), he distinguished between the *contents* of that which he read and the *skill* of reading itself he gained from them. Whereas he was scornful of the former, he was grateful for the latter. Instruction in letters "gave me the capacity and then the ability that I still possess, of reading anything written I come across" (*ut et legam, si quid scriptum invenio*). Divorced from its contents, reading at this basic level functioned as a technology for information gathering: it did not matter from what sort of text, however harmful it might be, one had initially learned the skill.

These sentiments persisted throughout the Middle Ages and became a powerful component of Christian reading practice in the medieval West. In his massive seventh-century *encyclopedia, the *Etymologiae* (Etymologies), the Spanish scholar and bishop Isidore of Seville (ca. 560–636) described reading as intimately related to letters and literature. And he perpetuated that Augustinian optimism about the durability of reading, contrasting it with the ephemerality of memory, voice, and sound (1.3.2). In his formulation, "the use of letters was invented for the sake of remembering things (*usus litterarum repertus propter memoriam rerum*), which are bound by letters lest they slip away into oblivion. With so great a variety of information (*tanta . . . rerum varietate*), not everything could be learned by hearing, nor retained in the memory." (It is worth noting that the recent Cambridge translation, which I have followed here, renders *res* or "things" as "information," making them reminiscent of Pliny's "facts" and aptly conveying the connotations of the term for Isidore.) But what exactly were those things to be remembered? Were they the contents of texts themselves, or rather other things that readers could select—and extract—from them? Granted, this was not always an either/or question in practice, and different medieval readers found different things worthwhile in ancient pagan works. In her study of medieval reading, Suzanne Reynolds has examined commentaries—especially commentaries on the Roman poet Horace—in which pagan literature was instrumentalized in this fashion. One of these commentators even declared that he would read ancient pagan texts *propter aliud* or "on account of something else." That *aliud* or "something else" took many forms, yet extracting it was made easier by the development of a specific technology of information gathering: the so-called *accessus ad auctores* or "introductions to authors." An *accessus* featured answers to key questions about a text, ranging from the number of books it contained and the genre to which it belonged to the intent of its author and its usefulness to the reader. Hence, while defining authorial intention or *intentio* was an important component of medieval *exegesis (and a technique with important antique precedents, as shown for example in the commentator Servius's contention that Virgil's intentio when composing the *Aeneid* was to imitate Homer's *Iliad* and lavish praise on Augustus), the *usus* or use the reader assigned a text enjoyed equal prominence.

The early modern period certainly witnessed some dramatic changes in the history of reading. We saw that Barthes and others highlighted their ostensibly epochal significance. These were related above all to the invention and dissemination of print by movable type. Yet much of the scholarship in the history of books and reading in more recent decades has pushed back against formerly broad claims of this nature. Instead, we now have a better sense of how features of print continued to formalize a relationship between text and reader that had been set in the Middle Ages and antiquity. For instance, features of the medieval accessus survived in the so-called *Ad lectorem* or epistle to the reader that constituted the prefaces of many early modern books. And the tools that printers refined to guide readers through books—indexes, contents lists, even quotation marks and paragraphing—all derived from the manuscript culture of the Middle Ages.

How do we know how early moderns read and extracted information from their books? Many physical, material traces of early modern reading still survive today, especially in the form of books annotated with marginalia. Their quantity might surprise modern readers, especially since not all of us still use annotations as our default means of extracting information from texts. For instance, as William Sherman has noted in his study *Used Books*, of the approximately seventy-five hundred titles in the STC (Short-Title Catalogue) collection at the Huntington Library, printed between 1475 and 1640, more than one-fifth contain annotations of one form or another. Marginalia are records of reading that blur the lines between author and reader, reflected in the difficulties that some modern librarians face over whether to classify heavily annotated books as printed works or manuscripts. Whatever their status, many marginalia are not only records of reading, but often also explicitly *about* reading. A few examples—worthy imitators of that Augustinian injunction "tolle, lege"—will here suffice.

Some of early modernity's most famous—and prodigious—of annotators liked to make notes concerning their own reading. The classical scholar Isaac Casaubon adorned his books with phrases like *lectu dignissimus* or "most worthy of reading." He then explained—not unlike the medieval accessus—the given text's worth or utility. In a note jotted on the title page of his copy of the late antique poet Claudian (now in the British Library), Casaubon inscribed his verdict: "this poet is most useful (*utilissimus*) for the history of his time, and for ancient fables, and is most worthy of reading (*lectu dignissimus*)." In other words, if you wanted information on either classical mythology or the history of the tumultuous years around 400 (two very different purposes indeed), Casaubon suggested that you consult Claudian's poetry. Similarly, in one of his many notebooks (now in the Bodleian Library, Oxford) he summarized the work of the early medieval historian Gildas and declared "on account of both the gravity of the argument and the erudition of the man, this is most worthy of reading." Hence Casaubon memorialized the particular utility he had extracted from his many *lectiones*. Another prodigious early modern reader, the Elizabethan John Dee (who assembled one of sixteenth-century England's largest libraries) similarly memorialized his own readings via marginal notes. For example, when he reached the end of Josias Simler's revised edition of the massive *Bibliotheca universalis* or *Universal Library* of Conrad Gessner (copy now in the Bodleian Library, Oxford), he recorded not only when he had read it, but also *how* he had done so—in other words, with what degree of intensity he devoted to it: "I began to read this book in passing (*obiter*), and to excerpt certain things from it, on the 24th day of June, and I finished on the 29th day." One early modern way of reading a book—perhaps Augustinian, perhaps Barthian, or both—was to record one's own reading of it.

The history of reading reveals that readers do not just make meaning from texts, but that they also extract information from them, and then use this information to make meaning in realms far beyond the text itself. Reading for information is a long-standing practice, but it has gained intensity at moments of intellectual and cultural transition—that is, moments such as the end of the ancient world or the emergence of Christianity that have exacerbated the gulf between authors past and readers present. Today we face a different, though just as consequential, kind of transition: reading for information has become more and more salient as more and more information—preserved via the "use of letters" that Isidore of Seville praised—is no longer presented in narrative form. The history of reading offers us a useful tool for understanding how such information will be interpreted and disseminated. As Quintilian put it, lectio must always precede enarratio, yet interpretation may look very different in a world in which physical books and texts are no longer defaults or givens. Still, the basics of lectio enjoy many continuities across periods. And so its history may offer salutary guidance as information producers, compilers, and consumers navigate an uncertain future.

                                                                   Frederic Clark

See also art of memory; books; documentary authority; excerpting/commonplacing; files; knowledge; learning; storage and search

FURTHER READING

Guglielmo Cavallo and Roger Chartier, eds., *A History of Reading in the West*, 1995, translated by Lydia G. Cochrane, 1999; Robert Darnton, "First Steps towards a History of Reading," in *The Kiss of Lamourette: Reflections in Cultural History*, 1990; Anthony Grafton and Lisa Jardine, "'Studied for Action': How Gabriel Harvey Read His Livy," *Past and Present* 129 (1990): 30–78; Martin Irvine, *The Making of Textual Culture: "Grammatica" and Literary Theory 350–1100*, 1994; William A. Johnson, *Readers and Reading Culture in the High Roman Empire: A Study of Elite Communities*, 2010; Suzanne Reynolds, *Medieval Reading: Grammar, Rhetoric and the Classical Text*, 1996; William H. Sherman, *Used Books: Marking Readers in Renaissance England*, 2008.

READING AGAINST THE GRAIN

In describing how they make sense of information about the past, historians often deploy a woodworking metaphor: they claim to "read against the grain." It is a curious comparison, because woodworkers prefer to cut with the grain, whenever they can, and use special tools when they have to cut against it. Following the grain is rarely simple or self-evident; woodgrain can be straight, irregular, diagonal, spiral, wavy, or interlocked, and of these, any can boast comparatively open or closed pores. Woodworkers must intuit something of their material's character, then, before making the first strike with the blade. Irregularities in the fibers only make the task more challenging. Burls, knots, dimples, bird's eyes, and other types of figuring in the grain, usually caused by fungus or stress suffered by the tree, make the work unpredictable, sometimes even dangerous. Yet the wood bearing such complexities is highly prized by skilled artisans, who transform these unassuming lumps of timber into handsome collector's pieces. Guided by the grain, the crafters aim to showcase the wood's naturally occurring qualities, revealing a beauty innate rather than conjuring their own new creation.

This is not what historians do. Rather than allow ourselves to be led by the "grain" of our archival materials, or to see it as "natural" and "innate," we are taught to resist it—to see it, in Arlette Farge's words, as "an adversary to fight." Historical documents, at least those that survive long enough for us to encounter them, have ideas of their own. They want to lead us along particular lines of inquiry, to spin us around in their whorls and knots, to make us see their features as naturally occurring, to have us take them at their word. Moreover, the archival traces with which we work are hardly raw specimens hacked from virgin forest (a metaphor long critiqued by historians of women and gender). They are, instead, highly mediated: first, by way of decay, neglect, disorganization, or purposeful destruction, and second, through the appraisal process, by which professional archivists cull at least 95 percent of the documents that come in over their transoms. Archives, unlike trees, do not spring forth from the soil. They are made by humans. Those humans, incidentally, have employed rather varied practices of "reading" at different sites and times, as we shall see.

What traps await us if we succumb to the temptation to follow the archival grain? We know that its lines map but a deeply partial and incomplete route into the past. The records that survive the historical events they document are disproportionately those created by powerful individuals and groups: states, empires, militaries, police forces, courts, churches, banks, presidents, and the like. They privilege the gaze of the wealthy, the male, the official, the landed, the white. And the creation of such records was usually instrumental, not incidental, to the exercise of power: imperial administrators generated paperwork to govern colonial subjects, police kept records to monitor dissent, courts produced files that upheld and reproduced legal regimes. The same goes for the institutions preserving those records: national archives were born with the modern nation-state, their symbolic and informational power used to legitimate the exercise of governance. We seek to understand how historical actors and institutions thought, but without unintentionally replicating or reifying the categories of knowledge on which they relied.

When historians say that they "read against the grain," therefore, what they mean is that they interrogate documents in a critical spirit, questioning the original objectives of institutional documentation in order to excavate and reconstruct the histories of individuals and groups marginalized from political power. This is not to say that reading "along" the grain is without its value; quite the opposite. But working around the limitations of the official record was and is the basic work of social history, which has privileged recovering the voices and experiences of women, people of color, oppositional political movements, and other subaltern actors from archival traces that tend to be fragmentary at best. Because of these foundational generations of scholarly work, we know that the surviving documents of any period are notable less for their inclusions than their exclusions, less for what they say overtly and more for what they silence or distort. As such, historians have developed techniques for reading against the documentary grain, which is to say, using records in ways that resist their original purposes. By now this method is considered to be, quite simply, good history. Of late, historians have also deployed *digital tools to *hack archives, using mapping and data-mining programs not only to generate new visualizations of old data, but also, in their best iterations, to enable different and complementary forms of analysis.

The pioneers of these critical approaches were historians of empire and historians of women and gender. How, they asked, could women's pasts be discerned in records created primarily by, for, and about men? How did the representations of colonized people spun by imperial bureaucrats compare to those colonized people's lived experiences? How had ideas about what counted as the proper objects and methods of historical study been shaped by the very historical processes that informed patriarchy, class struggle, and empire—and how could they be subverted? And, importantly, how might bodies of records generated for the purpose of social control actually reveal the fragilities, inconsistencies, and vulnerabilities quivering below the surface of those seemingly all-powerful systems of domination?

That scholars should treat individual documents with these questions in mind is now a commonplace of historical practice. But what about the archives housing those documents? These are not, after all, simply buildings that store documents, much as the documents therein are not just the randomly accumulated flotsam and jetsam of the past. Rather, archives are historically constituted entities, active sites for the construction of meaning, collections heavily shaped by archivists, provocative metaphors for the social practices of remembering and forgetting, and politically charged symbols of statecraft and sovereignty. Moreover, the specific contours or character of particular archives— their histories, their compositions, their access norms, their locations, their guiding missions—impact the kinds of stories that scholars can write using the records they contain. This realization has spurred some historians, archivists, and anthropologists to urge a shift in approach: to treat archival research less as an extractive enterprise, as Ann Laura Stoler writes, and more as an ethnographic one. This involves complementing the long-established view of the "archive-as-source," which largely focuses on archival content, with analyses of the "archive-as-subject," which involves an attention to archival form and organization.

I have elsewhere referred to this type of engagement as *archival thinking*, a phrase borrowed from a Guatemalan archivist. The archivist, who was training human rights activists in the norms of archival processing as part of an effort to safeguard a massive new cache of secret police files from the country's long civil war, was speaking of the challenges of transforming the way her activist charges thought about record keeping. Initially, the "students" had little patience for the lessons on archival structure and organization; they simply wanted to access smoking-gun documents to facilitate war crimes prosecutions, and they were frustrated by the archivist's insistence that it was less important to identify individual records than to understand and preserve the larger flow and system of information gathering of which any single page or file was a part. The archivist noted, however, that once her students had learned to see past the words on the pages to perceive how and why the records had been created, maintained, and organized in the way they had, they had begun, she said, to "think archivally": to see the documents not only for their content, but for their form, for their organizational structure, for their politics, for their metaphoric power both as a synecdoche for a broader state terror apparatus and as a symbol for the possibilities of postwar healing, and for the role they played in the larger social orders of both past and present. They came to envision the archives not as a static repository of evidence, but as an active site for the construction and reconstruction of social meaning, with powerful cultural and political implications. This realization led them to conceptualize and use the archives differently.

Archival thinking, then, is an approach to archives based on the proposition that historians should ask questions about how our archives, as collections and institutions with their own histories and realities, shape the pasts we study and the stories we tell. A useful starting point for archival thinking, if an obvious one, is the argument that archives are never neutral. As a result, we must always be thinking of the constructedness, the noncompleteness, the absences, and the suspicious presences of the archives we consult. Just like the records themselves, the archives are always mediated, whether by historical circumstance (burst water main, insect infestation, war, defunding) or by the purposeful interventions of record producers, keepers, subjects, and objects (archival appraisal, purges of incriminating records, *leaks, and, again, war and defunding). These acts of mediation, whether accidental or purposeful, shape not only what ends up being preserved, but, over time, what ends up being considered preservable or worthy of preservation. What we encounter in most archives consists of the accretion of thousands or millions of individual decisions about the historical value, incriminatory potential, or veracity of particular bodies of documentation and pieces of information as captured in individual records or record categories, decided by particular individuals or institutions at specific points in time. The history of these archival decisions is thus the history of power itself—how it is deployed, understood, enacted, ossified, and contested over the years in the documentary record.

Historians are not immune to the contemporary echoes of those historical power dynamics, which, in structuring the archives, also help structure our own ideas about worthy subjects of inquiry, hegemonic narratives, and presence and absence. There are certain stories that a particular archives will "want" us to tell by virtue of what was included and what was not, as well as by how it was included; it is not uncommon to hear historians remark that they selected a particular topic because of the rich available source base. This is why scholars should examine not just what a document says but why it exists at all, and the history of how it was used. It requires considering the stakes at play in the moment of a record's creation, but also in any subsequent "activations" of that record—for example, the opening of a surveillance file by a police force for purposes of social control, but also a justice activist's encounter with that same file, for starkly different ends, several decades later. Adopting a forensic, investigative approach to the analysis of the available archival record—to its systems of categorization and which histories these inflate or diminish, its gaps and silences both purposeful and accidental, its underlying organizational logics and how these may have changed over time, and the nature of our interaction with it—brings us closer to our historical subjects.

By now, we have traveled a fair distance from the metaphor of "reading against the grain." After all, wood is hard and solid, while, as we have seen, archives are contingent and malleable. Wood has a preexisting grain pattern that can be cut and polished differently but not fundamentally altered, while archives and the documents they contain can be variously reorganized, bought, sold, destroyed, or censored in ways that shape the stories that can emerge from them. Perhaps it is time to retire the turn of phrase?

While we ponder the matter, it is worth pointing out that how historians "read" also has its own history of significant change over time, as other essays in this volume attest. Additionally, while I have focused here on written or printed documents for the sake of economy, oral and visual sources of course involve distinct practices of interpretation that are incompletely captured by the notion of "reading." And this is to say nothing of the digital revolution in information technology, which has dramatically altered the preservation, storage, and management of historical records, while simultaneously shifting the role of archives both in society and in the practice of professional history. How does the historian engaged in large-scale mining of, say, the *metadata of classified, *born-digital US State Department records read them against the grain? Must a massive born-digital corpus be "read" differently than, say, eighteenth-century French judicial archives, or Guatemalan police files, or *early modern diocesan cause papers, or personal correspondence, or colonial records from the Dutch Indies? What are the pitfalls and advantages unique to the forms of reading required by the technology-fueled profusion of records in the postwar period—to say nothing of the new practices these technologies have enabled, including text searching, the consultation of digitized sources formerly accessible only in person, and *optical character recognition (OCR)? Professional historians still debate these matters of method as they relate to documentary and archival form, and they will continue to do so as *new media and new storage possibilities further expand the possible horizons of historical investigation.

In its foregrounding of the historian's agency and perspective, the concept of reading against the grain recalls a question posed by Marc Bloch: Is history a science or an art? It is neither, even if at different points in time it has been cast as primarily one or the other. Instead, it is an act of knowledge making, one thoroughly suffused with relations of power. What it means to read, and what is understood by the grain, depends on the specific historical moment in which historians perform their labors. And it is driven by the knowledge makers themselves, by their motivations and subjectivity, their archival thinking. What is the kind of knowledge they wish to make? Whose are the voices they want to listen for and to amplify? What do they hope to find, and why? To which wrongs do they aspire to bring some form of historical redress? Like woodworkers, historians are constrained by the grain of their material. But unlike woodworkers, historians aim less to showcase beauty than to reveal complexity. The past is no more "natural" or "innate" than is the historian's approach to interpreting it. Historians subvert power by exerting a force of their own.

Kirsten Weld

See also appraising; archivists; art of memory; bureaucracy; data; documentary authority; knowledge

FURTHER READING

Walter Benjamin, *Illuminations*, 1955, translated by Harry Sohn, edited by Hannah Arendt, 1969; Marc Bloch, *The Historian's Craft*, 1949, translated by Peter Putnam, 1953; Terry Cook, "The Archive(s) Is a Foreign Country: Historians, Archivists, and the Changing Archival Landscape," *Canadian Historical Review* 90, no. 3 (2009): 497–534; Mary Douglas, *How Institutions Think*, 2012; Arlette Farge, *The Allure of the Archives*, 1989, translated by Thomas Scott-Railton, 2015; Lara Putnam, "The Transnational and the Text-Searchable: Digitized Sources and the Shadows They Cast," *American Historical Review* 121, no. 2 (2016): 377–402; Ann Laura Stoler, *Along the Archival Grain*, 2009; Michel-Rolph Trouillot, *Silencing the Past*, 2015; Kirsten Weld, *Paper Cadavers*, 2014.

RECORDING

We live in a world saturated with recorded information—both audio and video—but too seldom do we reflect on the meaning of these objects in our lives. To understand and evaluate the power that recordings hold over us today, we need to examine the curious history of recording technology and its development. In doing so, it will become clear that recordings constitute not simply a mirror that reflects our lives, but a magnifying lens through which we can examine ourselves, our actions, and our choices.

When Thomas Edison's phonograph was first presented to the public in 1878, the magic of recording was obvious. The device was proclaimed a miraculous invention, even more astounding than the still-new telephone (1876). The phonograph was strictly a mechanical device, a cylinder covered with metal foil rotated by a simple wind-up motor. Subjects spoke into a small horn that channeled the sound energy of their voice down to a flexible diaphragm, a thin disk, at the horn's apex. The vibrating diaphragm drove an attached needle up and down and, as the foil-covered cylinder spiraled beneath this needle, the foil was impressed with a record of the voice. To play this recording back, the process was simply reversed. The moving needle set the diaphragm into motion, and its vibrations re-created in air the same sound waves that had originally been spoken. The horn now served to amplify the faint sounds generated by the diaphragm, so that a group of people clustered around the device could all hear the words originally voiced.

The simplicity of the setup begged the question: Why hadn't anyone invented this before? None of its technology was particularly new, nor even unusual. What was new was the idea that one could store up sounds and then call them forth again, at a different time and place. The essentially ephemeral nature of sound had presented conceptual obstacles to the phonograph's discovery, and Edison's real accomplishment was one of imagination, not mechanism.

So why hadn't others imagined this technology before? Perhaps necessity is indeed the mother of invention: no one had articulated a compelling need for what the phonograph did. Many had ventured close. A long tradition of scientific experimentation had been devoted to rendering visible acoustic phenomena. Some simply wanted a visual means to study sound itself. Others sought a new kind of written language; a direct rendering of spoken words onto a medium, which could then be read like words on a page. Such sound writing would also capture the purely acoustic aspects of expression, such as tone and emphasis, which words set in type fail to transit (for example, the sonic difference between *record* the verb and *record* the noun). In the mid-nineteenth century, Léon Scott, a bibliographer and typographer working in France, had constructed a device mechanically similar to Edison's later machine. Scott's *phonautograph* let the "sounds write themselves" by transforming aerial vibrations into inscriptions on a soot-covered plate of glass. It never occurred to Scott to try to turn those scribbles back into sound. A fellow Frenchman, the poet Charles Cros, did imagine that possibility, and he wrote up his thoughts in a dated, sealed letter. But he never acted on those ideas, and all Cros could do after Edison's phonograph was presented to the world was to open the letter and show everyone that he had thought of it first.

Alexander Graham Bell was also familiar with work on sound writing, for his father had written a treatise on "visible speech." But the younger Bell was devoted to solving a different problem, that of moving voices across vast distances. He approached this challenge by converting the acoustic energy of the voice into an electrical signal for transmission over a wire, and then reconverting that signal back into sound at the other end of the line. When Bell first learned of Edison's phonograph, he expressed to a colleague astonishment that he had failed to discover this simple device.

So what led Thomas Edison to a device that had eluded so many? As a professional inventor, Edison—and his team of technicians—always had numerous projects under way, and Edison was able to see new possibilities that fell between specific problems and solutions. The phonograph grew out of their work on increasing the information-carrying capacity of a telegraph line. By recording *Morse code messages as indentations on a strip of paper, an operator could increase the speed of the transmission by rapidly passing the paper under a telegraph key. Edison discovered that the recorded dots and dashes of *code made an audible noise as they passed under the transmitting key. Following his curiosity, he attached a telephone diaphragm to the embossing key and made an indented record of his voice. When this paper was passed back under the mechanism, he heard a faint sound that resembled human speech. Edison's laboratory notes confidently assert that, having now proven the principle of voice recording and reproduction, his ultimate perfection of the device was a given. Unlike Cros, Edison would follow up on this claim, and by the end of 1877 a functional model was ready to present to the public.

The public was amazed at this talking machine that recited poetry, sang songs, and played musical instruments, even spoke French. But after the novelty wore off, no one was really sure what to do with it. Predictions were made: talking books and clocks, court transcriptions, language instruction, musical interludes, spoken correspondence, voice archives. Nonetheless, the miraculous machine was simply set aside, and for the next ten years few even noticed that it was gone.

In 1888, the phonograph reemerged in a new and improved version that utilized rigid wax cylinders in place of the fragile foil, the result of a competition between Bell's laboratory in Washington, DC, and Edison's people in New Jersey. Both parties now declared that the phonograph was a piece of office equipment. It was to be used as a dictating machine that would mediate between bosses and typists to generate business correspondence. But the office phonograph didn't really offer significant improvements over human stenographers. In 1890 a frustrated salesman in San Francisco took one of his unmarketable machines and added a coin slot mechanism to operate it. He loaded in a recording of some entertaining musical novelty and left the device in a public location. A nickel at a time, the listening public decided what they wanted from sound recordings, and what they wanted was easy and inexpensive entertainment. By the turn of the century a new industry had been born.

The recording industry sold the machines as well as the recordings that those machines transformed into musical sounds. Music stores now offered phonographs and records alongside musical instruments and sheet music, and some musicians began to worry that the former might supplant the latter. Composers earned royalties on sheet music sales, but not on sales of sound recordings of their compositions. Congress rewrote *copyright laws to accommodate the economic implications of the new technology, but while the new laws protected the property rights of composers, they failed to acknowledge any rights of the performing artists. Music, as intellectual property, was defined exclusively as notes on a page, not sounds on a record. A record could thus be only a copy of a creative work, never an original creation itself.

The bandmaster John Philip Sousa questioned whether "mechanical music" was music at all. If a recording sounded exactly the same every time, Sousa argued, was it capable of transmitting the emotional soul of music? But for some artists, the disembodiment of their voice onto a record was a musical opportunity, not a loss. Some of the best-selling recordings of the early twentieth century featured African American performers whose records traveled places their bodies could not, expanding the cultural reach of Black music. Nevertheless, the phonograph did not open up a new "color-blind" appreciation of musical sounds; instead it became more important than ever for consumers to know the "color" of the voices they heard when listening to records, and through sonic segregation—ultimately via the category of "race records"—the industry sorted those absent bodies as vigilantly as ever.

Unlike Sousa, most listeners accepted their records as real music, and their desire for recordings—by Black and white artists alike—prompted a change in format from cylinder to disc. Mass production of flat discs via stamping presses was far more industrially efficient than the molding process required to manufacture hollow cylinders, and discs were preferred by consumers, who began to build collections of records, to own musical sounds in ways never before imagined. Edison first offered disc records in 1913, asserting they were not "recordings" but "re-creations" of the sounds of live musicians. He demonstrated this claim through Tone Test recitals, where Edison recording artists performed alongside their records and challenged audiences to hear any difference between the two.

Fidelity, or faithfulness to the original, had long been a fundamental metric of the quality of a sound recording. The criterion assumed—like the new copyright laws—that a record was never something original in itself. But one need only consider the very different history of optical recording, or moving pictures, to discover an alternative approach in which the notion of fidelity held much less sway.

Visual artists, of course, had long sought different ways to evoke the passage of time and a sense of movement in their static subjects. But the first "moving images" in our modern sense of the concept are best located where scientists and showmen alike began to exploit the optical phenomenon of the persistence of vision, whereby a person observing a rapidly changing sequence of images will knit the static pictures together in their mind and experience the sequence as a single moving image. The Zoetrope, a nineteenth-century parlor toy, disseminated the phenomenon far and wide, but such representations fell within the realm of tricks and illusions. When photographic images of bodies in motion, however, were printed sequentially onto long strips of plastic film and viewed through more complex mechanisms with gears and shutters, moving images came to be perceived as registrations of reality. These optical recordings were first viewed individually through peep-show boxes that stood alongside early "nickel-in-the-slot" phonographs at the turn of the century. Indeed, Edison's own work on moving pictures was prompted by his desire "to do for the eye what the phonograph does for the ear." But even as optical recording joined sound recording in the new realm of mechanical entertainment, the criterion of fidelity found much less purchase within this new visual culture.

Moving pictures quickly moved beyond the mimetic. While newsreel companies offered realistic records of each week's news, most filmmakers took advantage of the plasticity of their medium to create something totally new. Time sped up and slowed down or moved backward in a cinematic presentation, and vast distances could be traversed in the blink of an eye.

The phonographic disc was less amenable to such manipulations, but by the mid-1920s, electroacoustic technologies began to play a role in the recording and reproduction of sound. The new sound signals were much more malleable, particularly when registered as an optical sound track—long strips of light and dark patterns printed onto cinematic film—for the new sound movies. Technicians in the film industry became adept at cutting and mixing different sound recordings to create the unique, original kinds of sounds needed to accompany highly manipulated images.

Technological developments within the music industry—such as experiments in stereo sound—by contrast were dedicated to achieving ever greater fidelity to the original. With stereo recording and reproduction, the spatial distribution of musicians could be re-created in the space between the two loudspeakers that broadcast the sound of the record, adding spatial realism to the sonic record. After the Second World War, the quest for fidelity was superseded by the new goal of "high fidelity," an unprecedented degree of sonic realism enabled by a wide range of wartime developments in acoustics and electronics.

Affluent and middle-class men, many of them veterans of the war, took refuge in the new hobby of assembling "hi-fi" systems to engineer the best possible illusions of reality out of their records. But as the culture of high fidelity reached its apex, the fallacy at its foundation was revealed: any "original" that is recorded is necessarily changed by the very act of recording. This had been true since the earliest days of tinfoil and wax. Pieces were shortened to fit onto a cylinder or disc; selections were rescored for instruments that recorded better than others; performers learned to control their voices and instruments in new ways suited to the horn, and then to the microphone, to create more compelling recordings. Many years after she performed her last Tone Test, Edison recording artist Anna Case recalled that she would shape her voice, as she sang live in these recitals, to imitate the sound quality of her records.

Some in the sound recording industry now began to celebrate hi-fi recordings as "better than real." Spatial effects and movements and layerings never encountered in real life began to be heard on records, and innovations in studio recording technology were dedicated to enabling the manipulation of sound. New music was not really recorded, but rather created in this environment, composed on tape rather than paper. Rock bands in the 1970s were faced with the challenge of performing live the studio-crafted sounds of their records. Their fans wanted nothing less: the recorded sound was now the "original" that they sought to hear. Musicians had to learn to reverse engineer their recordings into performances or abandon the stage altogether, as the Beatles famously did in 1969.

Another group of artists working in the 1970s with far fewer resources developed a very different way to create new kinds of original music out of recorded sounds. They turned the record player into a musical instrument. The earliest hip hop DJs built on a West Indian musical culture that featured highly manipulated studio recordings that accompanied live performers who sang and chanted along with the recorded beats. Within US immigrant communities, this practice was transformed by performers like Kool Herc and Grandmaster Flash to feature the live manipulation of phonographic playback in order to transform the recorded sounds into something totally new. They created musical mixes as sonically complex as any Hollywood sound edit, and they did it all live in front of dancing crowds. As before, many complained that this was not real music; at best it was technological fiddling, at worst outright theft of the work of the artists whose records the DJs spun. But if this new sonic practice were a form of theft, that charge assumed that the recordings on a DJ's turntables were original creative properties, and in fact the law had just come to acknowledge this view.

In the 1970s, Congress once again rewrote its copyright laws, this time to acknowledge that the actual sound of a recording was not simply a copy of something else, but could itself be an original creation and thus deserving of legal protection. This new view was prompted, not by hip hop aesthetics, but by the establishment of magnetic tape as a dominant medium for the production, storage, and dissemination of audio and video recording.

Even as magnetic tape enabled new sonic possibilities in recording studios, where video was concerned the medium was mainly devoted to the long-subsidiary task of representing reality. Cinematic newsreel technology was expensive and cumbersome, and it took time to edit and disseminate each film program. For those in the news business, magnetic tape now offered a cheaper and faster way to introduce moving images into their broadcasts. The earliest televised news focused mainly on the men who delivered the stories on camera, but by the 1970s TV news featured video recordings of what was happening each day around the world. This brought a new sense of immediacy and graphic objectivity to the medium, encapsulated in news anchor Walter Cronkite's famous sign-off, "And that's the way it was."

Magnetic tape also became a popular consumer format for both audio and video recordings. Manufacturers now disseminated recorded sounds and images to audiences via compact audio cassettes and VHS ("video home system") cartridges. But these new consumer media presented new problems for the recording industry. They were easily and inexpensively copied by individuals or by bigger and more organized industrial pirates. Bootlegged recordings had always existed, but the threat they posed had been minimal because the number was so small. Few had the resources to turn an off-the-shelf disc record into a mold for a pressing plant, and with motion picture film the task was even more expensive and technologically complicated. Once sounds and images were captured as magnetic patterns on plastic tape, however, it became far easier to make copies. And it didn't take a lot of money for unscrupulous entrepreneurs to tool up such activity on a scale that could affect a manufacturer's profitability. Congress had made this kind of rerecording illegal in 1971 by declaring a recording a form of intellectual property, an original creation. Pirates still roamed the global seas of commerce beyond US jurisdiction, however, and the new law was hard to enforce domestically at the consumer level. But magnetic tape recordings—like all *analog formats—had physical limitations that still kept the problem in check.

Analog recording depends on direct physical processes to turn one form of sonic or optical energy into another. The undulating groove on a phonograph record is a physical analog of the vibrating air molecules of the sound wave that has been captured. Continuously variable patterns of microscopic magnetic particles suspended within a tacky fluid painted onto the surface of a plastic tape, while perhaps less materially compelling, are also physical analogs of sound waves in air. Each time one analogous representation is transformed into another, something is lost along the way. The physical forces involved exert a kind of informational friction that wears away a bit of the content. String together too many such transformations and, as in the party game of "telephone," the original message is lost.

Even as Congress was rewriting the law to recognize intellectual property inherent in analog recordings, researchers had begun to explore fundamentally new ways of recording in order to transcend the physical limits of those analog processes and enable endless transformation and manipulation, duplication and dissemination with no loss of content along the way. This new kind of recording—digital recording—turned sounds, not into another physical analog, but instead into a stream of data, of information that described the sound but did not physically embody it. This description was shaped by algorithms, mathematical rules written by man, not nature. The data was numeric and deployed in a *binary system that required just two numbers—zero and one—to express any quantity. A digital system was thus required only to distinguish between these two values (albeit very often and very rapidly), in contrast to the infinite variations of values at play within analog systems. For this reason, within the digital realm, copies of copies ad infinitum can be made without limit or loss.

Within production studios, digital technology brought ever more powerful creative tools whose manipulations of sound and image were virtually seamless. New consumer formats—CDs and DVDs—promised more permanent storage with no degradation over time or through use. And for many consumers the quality of these new digital recordings was better than ever. Audiophiles, however, took issue with the fact that the algorithms at the core of digital recording—particularly the sampling rate—put an absolute limit on the accuracy of any reproduction. There was now a ceiling; it was high, but its presence was a new and insurmountable obstacle to the endless pursuit of perfection.

By the 1980s and 1990s, for most consumers this desire for fidelity was no longer compelling. Particularly as audio and video were folded into the more general digital culture and content of home computers, the quest for quality was overwhelmed by a new appetite for quantity. When home computers were first linked together by the cables of the *internet, people used these connections to gather up and store as many recordings as possible, defying the law as they did so. Some utilized *compression algorithms that further compromised fidelity but enabled them to download data as quickly as possible and to fit as much content as possible onto a hard drive. By the turn of the new century, digital devices like the iPod put that hard drive into people's pockets, allowing them to take all that data with them wherever they went. Immediate access to as much content as possible became a new means by which to measure recording technology.

Digital wireless networks were developed to move data without the encumbrance of cables, and cell phones took over the roles that home computers and iPods had originally occupied within recording culture. Now, the data need not be stored on one's own personal devices, since one could always access it via the wireless network. This massive, invisible collection of data has been characterized as a *"cloud," a benign vaporous entity that seems to dissolve all previous physical media of recording as if some all-powerful wizard had waved a magic wand. But this cloud is itself an illusion: that collection of data is captured and nurtured on the hard drives of a vast number of machines, consuming space and electrical energy with an appetite as voracious as our own hunger for content.

To generate ever more recorded content, digital recording devices have proliferated too, listening to and looking at our lives at home, in our workplaces, and on our city streets. The cell phone camera in virtually everyone's hands today is a recording device far more powerful than any Edison could imagine. Each of us is a combination of a Hollywood movie mogul, a record executive, and a television news producer, and the products of our recording efforts can effortlessly be manipulated, shared, or both. Everything, it seems, can now be captured and retrieved, and some people may be at risk of spending more time engaging with these recordings than they do with the real world that still surrounds them.

Digital recording technology fundamentally disrupted the commercial economy of sound and video recordings, and we are only beginning to sort out how to value and protect property that eludes control through its very ubiquity. But perhaps more importantly, our moral economy has also been transformed, and in ways we may not yet fully recognize. How can we protect the identity and value of truth from within a web spun of such easily malleable representations? How can we locate a physical foothold, a reassurance of reality, as the sea of digital data rises ever higher around us?

Perhaps a modest start is to remind ourselves that this web is not real, but rather a trick of the eye and ear that has been spun out before us for over a century. It is a technological artifice, made of artificial representations of the sights and sounds of our lives. The challenge before us is to remember this history so that we can distinguish for ourselves what is real and true, and thereby act accordingly.

Emily Thompson

See also algorithms; commodification; computers; data; digitization; governance; intellectual property; networks; newspapers; plagiarizing; telecommunications

FURTHER READING

Raymond Fielding, *The American Newsreel: A Complete History, 1911–1967*, 2nd ed., 2006; Lisa Gitelman, *Always Already New: Media, History, and the Data of Culture*, 2006; Mark Katz, *Capturing Sound: How Technology Has Changed Music*, rev. ed., 2010; Charles Musser, *The Emergence of Cinema: The American Screen to 1907*, 1990 (as well as subsequent volumes in the series History of the American Cinema); David Suisman, "Co-workers in the Kingdom of Culture: Black Swan Records and the Political Economy of African American Music," *Journal of American History* 90 (2004): 1295–324.

REFERENCE BOOKS

"Information fatigue" has been called a distinctively modern phenomenon, but reference works—a culture's most visible attempts to manage *information overload—are found written in cuneiform on clay tablets and in Egyptian hieroglyphs on *papyri. The putatively modern phenomenon is nearly as old as writing itself.

Reference as we know it, however, can be no older than writing; it is necessarily a written form. Oral cultures may have to reckon with their own forms of information overload, but their solutions differ from those of literate cultures. Those without access to writing can manage only as much information as fits in memory but writing makes it possible to store the overflow in books. Beyond reference works' origins in writing, though, it is notoriously difficult to make generalizations about them, and there is no widely accepted definition of the form. They are so diverse in their contents, organization, and readership that it is probably wrong to refer to them collectively as a *genre. Any area of endeavor in which the amount of important information is too much for one memory—whether as elevated as the vocabulary of patristic Greek or as demotic as the market prices of baseball cards—will eventually be treated by at least one reference work. Reference books define words (whether of the entire vocabulary of a language or some specialized subset of it), identify library holdings, name stars and galaxies, locate half-remembered quotations, predict the phases of the moon, warn about the counterindications of medicines, compile the results of mathematical functions, and provide elaborately indexed tables of folkloric motifs and postage stamps and Jewish surnames and French watermarks.

No one has ever enumerated all the varieties of reference works—dictionaries (monolingual and polyglot, general and subject specific), *encyclopedias (general and specialized), bibliographies, atlases (terrestrial and celestial), classifications of maladies (physical and mental), almanacs, *concordances, chronologies, legal compendia, compendia of sports statistics, biological *taxonomies, trigonometrical tables, artists' *catalogues raisonnés*, collectors price guides, and so on—let alone provided a comprehensive bibliography of the individual titles. Such a list would surely run into the millions and would include works in most of the world's written languages, living and dead. There is, moreover, no agreement on the outer periphery of the category: are cookbooks, real estate listings, railway timetables, and newspaper horoscopes properly reference books? It would be difficult to make a principled case for excluding them, though in practice we reserve the term for works of a certain magnitude and gravitas.

Every reference genre has its own history or, more accurately, histories, since similar forms are often developed independently in distant cultures. Dictionaries tend to follow a pattern in most places where they appear: the earliest ones are either bilingual, subject specific, or devoted entirely to "hard words"; only later do general monolingual dictionaries that strive to cover the entire vocabulary appear, and historical scholarly *lexicons are a product of nineteenth-century scholarship. Legal *codes typically mark the high-water marks of empires; imperial conquest and exploration spur the production of new bilingual dictionaries and *gazetteers. Perhaps the most complex history is that of the encyclopedia, a term that was first applied to a reference genre in the seventeenth century, though countless ancient works—Greek, Latin, Sanskrit, Chinese, Arabic—can be called "encyclopedic," leaving open the question of what precisely constitutes the genre. Some, like Pliny's *Naturalis historia* (ca. 77–79 CE), inhabit the boundary between encyclopedia and science textbook; others, like the Chinese *leishu*, combine encyclopedic scope with the form of copious anthologies sometimes running to hundreds of millions of words.

The boundaries between the various reference genres are often unclear, and different languages demarcate the field in different ways. Speakers of English use Greek *lexicon*, for instance, as a synonym for *dictionary*, often with the connotation of a dictionary of the classical languages; in German, *Lexikon* is often used where Anglophones would use *encyclopedia*. Peter Mark Roget repurposed *thesaurus*—also used for dictionaries, medical texts, and textual corpora—to serve for what had been called a *synonymy*. Speakers in English sometimes limit *dictionary* to alphabetically organized works covering the vocabulary of one or more languages, but in many compounds—*biographical dictionary, historical dictionary*—it overlaps with *encyclopedia*, and *dictionaries of proverbs* and *dictionaries of quotations* are other kinds of compendia altogether.

Not content, however, but organization is paramount: a reference book is a work structured to facilitate rapid consultation. This means its parts—"entries"—are discrete, comprehensible individually, and organized to make finding them as efficient as possible. Because reference books are meant to be consulted in parts, the works as a whole often seem unreadable. Most books have *readers*, but reference books have *users*. Their creators, too, are often thought of not as *writers* but as *compilers*. While the names of a few lexicographers and encyclopedists are familiar and a few of their works express something of the character of their creators, the twenty-first-century norm is that reference books are prepared by teams of scholars—dozens, hundreds, even thousands—working in near anonymity.

It is the responsibility of those teams not only to write the entries but to put them in a useful order. Some information has an obvious ordering principle—tables of logarithms and chronologies, for example—but for information not intrinsically ordered, some structure must be imposed to make rapid access possible. History is full of examples of struggles to find "natural" modes of organizing complexity. Ancient encyclopedias and glossaries are often organized topically in an effort to keep like with like. In 1852 Roget followed a number of ancient models, including Philo of Byblos's Greek synonymy (early second century CE?) and the Sanskrit *Amarakosha* (Immortal Dictionary) (ca. fourth century CE?), when he worked to classify nearly the entire English vocabulary: the top-level classes of his taxonomy are "abstract relations," "space," "matter," "intellect," "volition," and "affections," with dozens of subheads covering more than a thousand categories. Such systems, though, however perspicuous they seem to their creators, have proven difficult for users, and so many compilers give in to an arbitrary order—since the fourteenth century, typically the one provided by the alphabet. Though it offers ease of use, alphabetical order has the disadvantage of scattering related terms throughout the work (*cat, feline, tiger*) while grouping unrelated terms through accidents of orthography (*casuistry, cat, catachresis*), and so the quest for rational organizations persists.

We usually speak of "reference books," but reference has been embodied in virtually every kind of information technology, and reference books are more liable than most written forms to be shaped, enabled, and sometimes threatened by developments in the technologies of the word. The earliest surviving *glossary, the bilingual *Urra=hubullu* from the second millennium BCE, translates between Sumerian and Akkadian in a series of clay tablets; the oldest surviving Chinese dictionary, the *Erya*, was probably written on bamboo strips sometime around the third century BCE. Many thousands of reference works date from Greco-Roman antiquity, including geographical surveys (Claudius Ptolemy's *Geography*, composed ca. 150 CE), legal codes (Tribonian's *Corpus iuris civilis* [Corpus of civil law] dates from the early sixth century CE), and proto-encyclopedias (Isidore of Spain's *Etymologiae* [Etymologies] appeared in 636 CE). While the earliest of these may have first circulated on papyrus scrolls, none such survive. Instead the *codex form of a *parchment manuscript, bound at the spine, spread across the ancient world starting in the second century, along with Christianity, and encouraged the kind of random access that was difficult with scrolls. Vast works like the Domesday Book, more than sixteen hundred pages, compiled in 1086, and biblical concordances, a genre that dates to the early thirteenth century, became practical with the advent of easily turned pages. Paper appeared first in China and spread to the Islamic world, where it was the medium of choice for Avicenna's medical compilation the *Qanun* (Canon) (1025) and Muḥammad ibn Mūsā al-Khwārizmī's adaptation and expansion of Ptolemy, the *Kitab surat al-Ard* (Book on the appearance of the earth, early ninth century). The arrival of paper in Europe (the eleventh century in Italy and the fourteenth century north of the Alps) was a crucial prerequisite to the success of printing in the fifteenth century. Printing created new norms, including pagination and indexes that could serve every copy in an edition. In the nineteenth century the steam press and cheap wood-pulp paper helped to place dictionaries and encyclopedias in every middle-class household. Stereotype and electrotype changed the economics of reprints and revised editions.

We are only beginning to understand some of the consequences of the electronic revolution. Printed reference works are economically inefficient: almost by definition, they are useful to their readers only in parts. The user of a twenty-volume encyclopedia might, over the course of a lifetime, consult only a few hundred of the work's ten thousand pages. For centuries, therefore, there has been an imperative to keep reference works as concise as possible to minimize materials costs. The *digital dispensation has changed those calculations, though, and freed from print, we have no need to "save space." The materials cost of a ten-thousand-entry encyclopedia is now effectively the same as for a one-hundred-thousand-entry encyclopedia.

The change in the economics of the materials, however, has had a spillover effect on the economics of compilation. Reference works are often huge projects that stretch out over decades. The *New English Dictionary*, intended to be completed in four volumes and ten years, grew over the course of seventy-five years into the thirteen-volume *Oxford English Dictionary*, at which point it was time to begin a new edition—and as soon as that one was finished, the project began again, occupying hundreds of professionals over the course of a century and a half. Even without substantial materials costs, therefore, someone has to pay for the intellectual labor that goes into reference publishing. But the distribution of old reference works online and the creation of new ones, without any cost to the user, has depressed the value of that labor and inspired a mantra for demoralized twenty-first-century "content providers": "You can't compete with free." We are now participating in a culture-wide experiment to determine whether reliable reference works can be assembled by unpaid and uncredentialed volunteers without central oversight. The number of specialized reference works continues to grow, their costs generally borne by institutional libraries, but more general works—dictionaries, encyclopedias, atlases—struggle to produce enough revenue to sustain their creation.

Still, constant creation is a necessity, for new reference works will always be needed to replace the old ones. Reference books are uncommonly subject to obsolescence, and only a very few older examples are as useful now as when they were created. Reference works are valuable for the information collected in them, but *facts themselves, our understanding of facts, and our interest in various kinds of facts are all constantly changing, making old reference works ever less useful. The most many reference works can hope for is to go through multiple editions before becoming obsolete. Novelty sells reference books: dictionaries tout their thousands of new words since the last edition, and encyclopedias boast of up-to-the-minute currency.

Obsolete works, however, have their own attractions for historians of information, for they give remarkable insights into the mentalities of their creators. If we want to know facts about the world there is no reason to turn to Isidore of Seville or the *Encyclopédie* of the French *Enlightenment. If, however, we want insight into how the church fathers or *les lumières* saw the world, few sources are more valuable than the reference books they created, both for what they consciously chose to tell us and for what they unintentionally reveal about the way they saw the world. Their selection tells us what information they considered most vital, and their method of organization gives us insight into how their creators mentally organized their worlds. Though we may read them for very different reasons than those of their original users, even the most obsolete reference books demand attention.

Jack Lynch

See also bibliography; excerpting/commonplacing; indexing; letterpress; maps; scrolls and rolls

FURTHER READING

Ann Blair, *Too Much to Know: Managing Scholarly Information before the Modern Age*, 2010; John Considine, *Dictionaries in Early Modern Europe: Lexicography and the Making of Heritage*, 2008; Bill Katz, ed., *Cuneiform to Computer: A History of Reference Sources*, 1998; Sidney I. Landau, *Dictionaries: The Art and Craft of Lexicography*, 1984; Tom McArthur, *Worlds of Reference: Lexicography, Learning and Language from the Clay Tablet to the Computer*, 1986; Foster Stockwell, *A History of Information Storage and Retrieval*, 2001; Richard R. Yeo, *Encyclopaedic Visions*, 2001.

REGISTERS

The term *register*, as either noun or verb, refers to a fundamental operation that is part of creating and organizing recorded information. The word's origins lie in the post-Roman tradition in Europe, first appearing in late Latin and spreading to most European languages by the High Middle Ages. The term *register* was defined in DuCange's dictionary of medieval Latin as "a book in which whatsoever commentaries are recorded" or "a book containing notes on other books." Calling something a register thus identifies it as a written product with several key features: first, a register generally collects distinct entries, rather than consisting in a single work; second, the resulting collection takes a coherent form, often with abundant *metadata; and third, the register serves for future reference as a source of information (rather than being, say, a spiritual resource or a work of art). Because similar written products have been important for record-keeping regimes around the globe, the term *register* is often applied to various practices outside of western Europe. European registers, however, especially those in book form, sometimes also took on social roles that went beyond their administrative function, such as ceremonial and representational contexts. Before labeling Chinese, Ottoman, or other records "registers," therefore, it is important to consider the full range of contexts involved, which may differ from European registers.

In Europe, the term *register* was long associated with the medial form of the *codex, although registers may take many forms ranging from book to card file to database. The broad resonance of the term is illustrated in *Piers Plowman*'s evocation of a "Registre of hevene" around 1378, which implied that God and the saints were maintaining an organized record of individuals' sins and merits. Today, the principle that a register is a collection of entries has been generalized, so that we can speak of registering to vote or simply "to register" in the sense of taking note of something for future reference; in German, *Register* can refer to the index of a book. As this breadth of usage makes clear, the term can be applied to diverse records, media, and actions and is therefore best approached by considering its functional, formal, and social dimensions. The term's wide range also means that its referents through history and around the globe share family resemblances rather than fitting under a single definition. Ultimately, the presence of registers in any historical context—either functionally or through contemporary use of the term—provides prima facie evidence that systematic record keeping for informational purposes is being attempted.

Functionally, registers are characterized by the assembly of multiple entries, which may or may not be related, into a single body. Many premodern empires already produced material matching this criterion, often for tracking land ownership, military service, or other documents. For example, the Ottoman Empire's records of land ownership such as the *tahrir defterleri* or the *defter i-hakâni* are routinely referred to as registers in English. Similarly, the Chinese Qing dynasty's finding aids for Grand Council records, whose Chinese name signified "Record of items as they come to hand," are called the

"Document Register" by Western scholars. In Europe, a common early form of register gathered records about issued charters or letters from a single authority or office over time as serially inscribed entries (either in full text or in summary) in a book. Generally, multiple offices in premodern bureaucracies produced separate registers; in Europe, in consequence, principalities and cities could produce hundreds of diverse registers over the centuries.

A key early form of registration in Europe involved notaries, whose registers authenticated the records of private and public agreements. When two parties created a contract and submitted it to a *notary, the latter summarized the agreement's content along with specific formal attributes into a register that provided a public record for the future. When a dispute arose later, the notary's register could confirm the authenticity of the parties' own copies of the agreement or could serve as evidence in itself about what had been agreed. Protocol books that recorded the decisions of an urban or princely council, which emerged across Europe by the thirteenth century, were another common form of register, although often called by other names—in German cities at first simply called the "city book" (*Stadtbuch*). Treasuries and fiscal offices also began creating daily registers of transactions in the late Middle Ages, often called journals or diaries. The verdicts of a court could be recorded in a register for future reference, such as the registers of the Geneva consistory court after the *Reformation. All these types of register shared the feature that they grew organically over time as records about certain kinds of acts accumulated on the pages of a book.

The term *register* is not confined to such serial forms. Very common were registers that served as inventories or finding aids to some other body of material, like the Qing Document Register. The city chancellor in Lucerne, Switzerland, produced a "Register of Charters in the Chancellery" (*Register der Brieffen in der Cantzley*) in 1514, which both summarized charters and provided a means to find the originals. Whether officials undertook investigations in the world or gathered together existing records, the result was a register. From the massive registers produced by the church Inquisition against the Cathars of Languedoc after 1240 CE to modern registries of voters and motor vehicles, the compilation and organization of information is crucial in defining a media product as a register.

As these examples suggest, the formal characteristics of a register typically involve accretion, referentiality, and the abstraction or simplification of referents. In addition, many registers are characterized by relatively abundant metadata to aid in their use. Accretion refers to the fact that the production of a register typically begins with an open media substrate, such as a prebound but empty book, an empty card file, or an unpopulated database, which is then filled sequentially with records over a short time or over centuries. Depending on the creator and purpose, the entries that accrete can be similar or wildly heterogeneous, though over time, registers have tended to become more homogeneous in their contents. Referentiality follows from the fact that entries in a register typically refer to something outside the register. Creators expected that they or others would refer to a register in the future in order to gain information about something else of interest, whether persons, actions, objects, or other documents.

The expectation of future reference shapes two additional formal characteristics found in most registers. First, a register generally (but not necessarily) simplifies whatever its entries refer to. A typical European register of outgoing charters (emissions register), for example, left out most of the language found in the individual charters it recorded, such as the formal titles of the issuer and recipient. By the High Middle Ages, many emissions registers took on a highly compressed form that included only the date, parties, and any nonstandard elements in the charters involved. Second, deploying various kinds of metadata about the entries in a register is a common and effective way of increasing a register's power. In the registers of the Cathar Inquisition, the inquisitors added dates, cross-references, marginal notes, and indexing to allow them to track individual suspects across space and time. The multivolume inventories that Wilhelm Putsch prepared for Austrian Habsburg chancelleries in Innsbruck and Vienna before 1550—known as the *Putschregister*—included both metadata on each volume's pages and a separate alphabetical index to the whole. *Digital media allow register metadata to overlap completely with contents through global or keyword search algorithms, though additional coding to enhance search, such as tagging, can also be employed.

Since creating metadata in manuscripts is highly labor intensive, its presence provides evidence that such registers were valued for future reference. The primacy of referential functions also meant that many registers are relatively unprepossessing in material form, inscribed on flawed *parchment or cheap paper, and using hasty handwriting or underpaid data-entry clerks. Nevertheless, late medieval Europe in particular also saw the production of registers, such as the Lisbon *Leitura Nova* after 1512 or an illuminated parchment finding tool in Würzburg, the *Hohe Registratur*, completed in the 1550s, that also fulfilled representational and ceremonial functions. Both were carefully inscribed on fine parchment at great expense, using highly decorative writing and graced by *illuminations and rubrication. Referential and performative functions were not mutually exclusive in the European tradition.

While European registers were inescapably connected to the book and its associated organizational tools until the nineteenth century, ongoing expansion of formal record keeping transformed the scope and form of registers produced in later periods in two important ways. First, capacious *systems* for gathering and managing administrative records emerged in Europe in the seventeenth and eighteenth centuries, which came to be known as registries. Even when they still relied on book technologies for their organization, such systems comprised far more than a single book or series and included many kinds of record. The term *registry* also denoted specialized institutional arrangements and the emergence of specialists in record keeping. Second, new or intensified techniques such as card files, binders, and filing cabinets enabled the further expansion and generalization of the term *register*. A nineteenth-century register of eligible military recruits or of authorized businesses in a city might not take book form and might not be operated by a state. More and more, the term *register* simply denotes a structured assemblage of multiple informational records and their metadata, as well as the persons responsible for operating such a register as an institution. Regardless of the scope and media technologies involved, therefore, the use of the term *register* or the appearance of the functional characteristics that define a register provides evidence that systematic record keeping was taking place.

Randolph C. Head

See also accounting; cards; data; databases; excerpting/commonplacing; governance; indexing; lists; quantification; scrolls and rolls

FURTHER READING

Richard Britnell, ed., *Pragmatic Literacy, East and West, 1200–1300,* 1997; Markus Friedrich, *The Birth of the Archive: A History of Knowledge,* 2013, translated by John Noël Dillon, 2018, esp. chap. 2, "Documents: Filling Archives," 2013; Randolph C. Head, *Making Archives in Early Modern Europe: Proof, Information and Political Record-Keeping, 1400–1700,* esp. pt. 1, "The Work of Records (1200–)," 2019; Geoffrey Yeo, *Records, Information and Data: Exploring the Role of Record-Keeping in an Information Culture,* 2018.

SALES CATALOGS

Purveyors of books and all other sorts of consumer goods continue to offer their stock to prospective buyers and to facilitate sales by issuing catalogs in both print and digital media. While the virtual catalog is the preferred point of sale and purchase for many businesses and shoppers today, in many respects what is still a text- and information-driven marketplace for print and other consumer goods has relied on a combination of strategies born in the handpress period, expanded in the era of industrial printing machinery, and networked in the era of high-speed digital connectivity. This short entry will explore a few milestones in the emergence of a digital book market, and connect the dots between printed advertisements, periodical publications, sales catalogs, and digital marketplaces like Amazon.

As with any commodity, advertisements have been used to encourage book sales and to share information about forthcoming information since the beginning of printing; handbills advertising Caxton's "Pies of Salisbury" (1477) still survive. Books are also on offer in the first advertisements in the earliest European newspapers in the seventeenth century and are still advertised in many serial publications today. Such advertisements most often come from two distinct business groups: booksellers and *publishers. While it was difficult to distinguish between the two in the *early modern period and even through the nineteenth century, the divisions were fairly clear throughout the late nineteenth and twentieth centuries, with lines blurring again with, for example, Amazon's Kindle direct publishing service. In general, booksellers purchase and sell new or used books, while publishers seek out and produce textual products in print and digital formats. Distributors may act as wholesalers or warehousers of one or many publishers' titles and control rights to distribution for print-on-demand or e-books.

In the nineteenth century, literary magazines and popular periodical publications noted the appearance of new books in bookish columns and also sold ad space to publishers. Throughout the twentieth century in particular, ad space marketed new books to a massive reading public in national and regional newspapers and magazines. Such advertisements for books have declined alongside print ads for products and services more generally. Yet in the twentieth and twenty-first centuries, academic and commercial presses advertise in printed periodicals devoted to book reviews like the *New York Review of Books* and *Times Literary Supplement*, and on *internet blogs like Literary Hub. Such advertisements remain an important resource for the study of information in the modern period.

Academic and commercial presses, as well as book distributors like Distributed Art Publishers, continue to issue print catalogs that librarians and booksellers use to stock their shelves. Around the turn of the twenty-first century, publishers decreased printed catalogs' availability owing to production and distribution costs and encouraged buyers to browse and shop their online catalogs. In both formats, book descriptions typically consist of the now-ubiquitous "blurb," that is, a pithy endorsement of the work by a well-known authority on the subject or a successful peer of the author. As with early sales catalogs, works are typically arranged by subject, and, viewed as a whole, catalogs document changes in approaches to the categorization of knowledge, and the emergence of new disciplinary and general-interest categories.

In the twentieth century, antiquarian bookshops emerged as distinct businesses within the broader book trade. Trade organizations such as the International League of Antiquarian Booksellers (ILAB, founded 1948) and Antiquarian Booksellers Association of America (ABAA, founded 1949) organize book fairs, help antiquarian booksellers build credibility and clientele, and, in the digital age, provide online bookselling platforms. While at one time focused almost exclusively on manuscripts and rare books printed during the handpress period, or the *canonical literary writers of the nineteenth and twentieth centuries, today's booksellers offer goods that are perhaps best understood as textual material culture. Diaries and photo albums compiled by ordinary people, as well as ephemera like flyers and zines, are commonplace, sometimes high-priced items in their catalogs. Many booksellers also sell stuff, for example, vinyl record albums and a souvenir belt buckle from Bob Dylan's Rolling Thunder Review tour. Most booksellers specialize in a narrow range of subjects, while larger operations like Quaritch and Maggs Brothers staff dedicated subject departments with experts in those areas.

Antiquarian booksellers describe the objects they sell in terms of their physical makeup and informational content. Descriptions of handpress printed books and many nineteenth-century books typically include collational formulas; pagination statements; detailed notes on condition, which use standardized terms; and historical notes about binding and provenance. Descriptions of informational content might provide, for example, a comparison between the edition offered and the first or subsequent editions, or situate the content within a broader intellectual landscape. Modern booksellers' catalogs contain a wealth of copy-specific information about the material culture of information, and the marketplace for it. While the vast majority of this information is confined in historical printed catalogs within library collections like the Grolier Club's, booksellers now offer digital catalogs on their websites and use platforms like AbeBooks to sell their stock.

Both in print and online, the modern catalogs not only for books, but also for all sorts of other goods, operate as a means of publicity and advertisement and as a point of sale. Printed instructions helped buyers make purchases by mail or telephone, and many catalogs included printed order forms that calculated shipping costs and facilitated advance payment. This became commonplace in the United States and Europe following the development of postal services and railways, enabling retailers of all sorts to offer goods to customers on a national scale.

Also commonplace was offering books alongside a massive array of other types of goods. Companies like Sears-Roebuck sold everything from wood-burning stoves to shoes and even houses. Sears offered books in a designated "Book Department" and remarkably made efforts to ensure that African Americans and other minorities had the information they needed to mail their orders and circumnavigate local barriers to doing so. During a time when schools and public libraries in the United States were segregated, the Sears catalog allowed all Americans to purchase books for home study and self-improvement in a wide range of topics. Early on, Sears also encouraged buyers to cooperatively purchase books in a "club order." Such orders encouraged individuals and booksellers to collaboratively purchase larger quantities that would cheaply ship by freight. Perhaps to encourage these orders, the Book Department aimed to offer something for everyone. At the same time, the range of authors and, to some extent, topics, nonetheless centered on the experience and tastes of white men and women.

The 1902 catalog, for example, offered English- and European-language dictionaries, *encyclopedias, and other reference books; fiction, poetry, medical handbooks; palmistry and hypnotism books; cookbooks; and practical guides to agriculture, building, and blacksmithing. By the 1940s, catalogs also included books for children; many were educational. Catalog entries appear with small illustrations and a brief content description; prices ranged from 20¢ (equivalent to $6.02 in 2019) to $9.98 ($300 in 2019) for a fifty-volume set. Like book-only catalogs, mail-order catalogs of Sears and other companies operated as both textual points of sale and publicity tools, building awareness of a range of commercially available products and their retailers. They also contextualized books as desirable commodities within a quickly growing world of tools and technologies. Stereoscopes, electric lights, typewriters, phonographs, radios, washing machines, and power tools were part of an ever-expanding universe of goods in the Sears catalog.

Following the Second World War, civil and cultural unrest gave rise to new demands for information and goods in the United States. Broadly speaking, those who were involved or identified with the civil rights, Black power, American Indian, Chicano, antiwar, new left, gay liberation, back to the land, women's, and hippie movements actively distributed print ephemera—for example, pamphlets and flyers—and even started their own publications to counter established information outlets. Alternative periodicals like the *Berkley Barb*, the *Ladder*, *Modern Utopian*, and the *Black Panther* offered outsider views on current political and cultural affairs and created spaces for dispersed countercultural communities to gather in print. Classified ads and narrative reports, for example, allowed readers from new communes to attract residents. This was so effective that communes like Drop City in Trinidad, Colorado, were overrun with visitors and shut down or relocated. Alt-weeklies' cultural calendars were the source for information about art, music, literary, and activist events, and important points of exchange for diverse countercultural groups, many of which were working for political, social, and cultural change.

The *Whole Earth Catalog* emerged from this landscape in 1968 and uniquely envisioned technological tools as driving forces for change. While this viewpoint was not unique to the *Whole Earth* group, its Sears-like catalog of books, goods, and high- and low-tech tools was innovative in creating a textual focal point for reference and community exchange that went on to influence a generation of early denizens of the internet. Largely influenced by experiences with LSD, as well as writing by architect Buckminster Fuller and cybernetics theorist Norbert Wiener, the *Whole Earth Catalog* has understood the book itself, and the tools it describes, as stimuli within a responsive, networked system of human consciousness and environment that is constantly exchanging, processing, and reacting to information. Despite the well-known marginalization of minority groups, however, it imagined this network of human consciousness and environment as totally unified, rather than stratified and hierarchical. Espousing a do-it-yourself ethos that encouraged people to eschew traditional modes of employment (especially within corporations) and find freedom in designing their own lives according to a higher natural order, it imagined a primarily white, heteronormative readership that was financially and socially positioned to thrive even as outsiders to mainstream American culture. The catalog intentionally ignored the social and political struggles that women, LGBTQ, and minority communities were engaged in.

This catalog was published from 1968 through the mid-1980s in several incarnations—the *Whole Earth Catalog* and its *Supplement*, the *Whole Earth Epilog*, the *Whole Earth Software Catalog*, *CoEvolution Quarterly*; the best known and National Book Award–winning *Last Whole Earth Catalog* is generally considered representative of the *Whole Earth* enterprise. Published in 1971, the *Last Whole Earth Catalog* contained over four hundred pages of products with reviews written by editor Stewart Brand, *Whole Earth* readers, and experts within Brand's techno-hippie social sphere. When it started in 1968, the catalog simply directed readers to the point of sale for each item it listed; by 1969 the Whole Earth Truck Store in Menlo Park, California, was selling most of the goods listed in the catalogs, which contained order forms. The *Supplement*, published between 1968 and 1971, mimicked alternative serial publications by printing readers' book and product reviews and news items alongside essays by, for example, environmentalist Wendell Berry, the avant-garde architecture collective Ant Farm, and geodesic dome builders Steve Baer and Lloyd Kahn.

In the history of the internet, the *Whole Earth Catalog* is well known for popularizing the concept of the computer as a networkable, personal information storage, access, and communication tool. Like the catalog, the networked personal computer could offer user-supplied information about anything to anyone, from anywhere. Unlike printed texts, however, networked computers would connect a world of people sharing texts describing their own experiences, opinions, and information in real time. In 1985, Stewart Brand and Larry Brilliant founded the Whole Earth 'Lectronic Link (WELL), a dial-up bulletin board system (BBS), the first available to Americans. The WELL offered virtual community to its users who valued tech-oriented conversation and as such created a tool for information exchange. Rather than requiring browsing through categorized information, networked personal computers allow people to search for exactly what they're looking for, or to consult their peers for references and expect quick answers. For the first time, dispersed communities whose members were not well known to each other could connect without using the postal system, so-called snail mail.

Nine years later, Jeff Bezos founded Amazon as an online marketplace for books. The website quickly expanded to offer the same range of goods that Sears and Whole Earth did, and it has radically changed the way that consumers all over the world purchase goods, especially books. Unlike smaller distributors or publishers, whose stock is limited, Amazon is a clearinghouse for books from everyone and everywhere. It even offers everyone the opportunity to publish their own book in print-on-demand or e-book formats, incentivizing this service by offering authors a substantial share of royalties.

Today, Amazon's *digital platform typifies the modern shopping experience. Websites across the internet gather information about and then share the user-guided browser's preferences with retailers like Amazon by using cookies. These packets of data, sent by an internet server to a browser, are returned by the browser each time it subsequently accesses the same server and can thus identify the user or track the user's access to the server. Algorithms then populate users' browser screens with items like those they are purchasing, have purchased, or have viewed. Search engines like Google do the same thing, and customized search results cater to known tastes and beliefs rather than challenge or surprise them. Cookies help internet retailers to populate ad space on websites across the internet with products and services of interest to the person behind the web browser. These digital ads function much like printed flyers. Digital ads sometimes appear in logical contexts and also show up in in seemingly random places. For example, a digital ad for the sunglasses viewed in one browser you considered purchasing, and an author you've written an email about in that same browser, might both pop up in the sidebar when that browser navigates to a literary blog. But hasn't this always been the case? The checkout counter in a book shop might offer printed flyers for a tax preparation class beside a notice about an upcoming author reading. Internet browsers act as lenses through which an individual or community may view a customized digital information landscape. To this point, an annotation on the John Rylands Library copy of the "Pies of Salisbury" advertisement implores the reader, "Supplico stet cedula" ("Pray, do not pull down the advertisement"). Perhaps it was pinned up in a strange place. One is more likely to encounter diverse products and perspectives in a browser on a publicly accessible computer than on one's own laptop.

As it has partially subsumed its print predecessors, the digital marketplace has retained and expanded many of the print catalog's and the periodical's most noteworthy features. Sellers of books and other stuff have always been eager to share information about their wares and encourage sales by sharing information, and all text-based media have played a starring role in their efforts to do so. The internet has transformed catalogs from a categorized, static, browsable, and periodically updated printed object to a digital tool that connects users via their browsers to a wealth of information and opportunities to shop in a high-speed environment. Cookies and algorithms facilitate that with greater personalization and frequency than ever before, but a good rare book dealer often recognizes something a well-established client wants before the client does and knows just how to sell it to just that person; cookies and algorithms remind readers of the socks they meant to order while reading a book review online. The old-fashioned sales catalog is the same thing, just slower. As the online catalog has partially subsumed its print predecessors, however, the digital marketplace has retained and expanded many of the catalog's and the periodical's most noteworthy features.

Erin McGuirl

See also algorithms; book sales catalogs; commodification; computers; data; digitization; inventories; manuals; newspapers; postal customers; reference books; storage and search; surveilling

FURTHER READING

Uriel Heyd, *Reading Newspapers: Press and Public in Eighteenth-Century Britain and America*, 2012; Louis Hyman, "How Sears Helped Oppose Jim Crow," *New York Times*, October 20, 2018; John McMillian, *Smoking Typewriters: The Sixties Underground Press and the Rise of Alternative Media in America*, 2011; Fred Turner, *From Counterculture to Cyberculture: Stewart Brand, the Whole Earth Network, and the Rise of Digital Utopianism*, 2006; James L. W. West III, "The Expansion of the National Book Trade System," in *A History of the Book in America*, vol. 4, *Print in Motion: The Expansion of Publishing and Reading in the United States, 1880–1940*, edited by Carl F. Kaestle and Janice A. Radway, 2009; Michael Winship, "The Rise of a National Book Trade System in the United States," in *A History of the Book in America*, vol. 4, *Print in Motion: The Expansion of Publishing and Reading in the United States, 1880–1940*, edited by Carl F. Kaestle and Janice A. Radway, 2009.

SCRIBES

In the many historical contexts when writing was a rare and difficult skill, scribes were the specialists entrusted with producing written documents. They played crucial roles both in creating the first written record of an oral text or transaction, and in making copies of an existing text for transmission across time and space. Scribes developed special skills for the physical act of writing (including the preparation of the surface, the posture and tools for writing) but also for the composition of texts. They mastered and honed the protocols for legal documents, conventions of polite address, and spelling and punctuation, among other topics. In some contexts, they were also responsible for reckoning and keeping accounts and for managing documents. Scribes are viewed as brokers and transmitters of information, but in writing and copying texts they also shaped and transformed them, both intentionally and unintentionally.

Writing is one of the longest-lived tools of information management, defined as the representation of spoken language with signs and symbols. Most writing systems can be classified as logographic (as in Chinese characters), syllabic (as in the Linear B script of Mycenean Greek), or alphabetic. When writing was a recent invention (e.g., starting in Mesopotamia or Egypt ca. 3500 BCE, China ca. 1200 BCE, or Mesoamerica ca. 300 BCE), scribes were highly respected and powerful figures. The scribe's skills in making cuneiform marks on clay tablets or inscribing stone or bamboo strips or *papyrus required extensive training, often passed on from father to son. Political and religious leaders relied on scribes to produce authoritative documents and records. Sumerian scribes active circa 2100 BCE were also responsible for the oldest surviving work of literature, the *Epic of Gilgamesh*, inscribed on clay tablets discovered and deciphered in the nineteenth century. Statues and bas-reliefs of Egyptian, Sumerian, and Assyrian scribes—seated or standing and ready to write—attest to their elite status although we rarely know their names. Their activities also ranged from divinatory and religious practices to codifying languages in dictionary-like lists.

Alongside this direct evidence of ancient scribes in durable media like stone and clay, we have indirect evidence of the activities of generations of scribes throughout the ancient world from the transmission of texts that they copied over and over again on fragile media such as papyrus, palm leaves, or plant-based paper. Most ancient texts we know—including Greco-Roman literature and philosophy, the Hebrew Bible, the Indian Vedas, and the Chinese classics—have come down to us only because scribes had made new copies of these texts by the time the old ones wore out. The papyrus roll, for example, which was the principal medium for long-term storage in ancient Greece and Rome, rarely lasted two hundred years in ordinary circumstances, judging from Pliny the Elder's surprise at seeing such an old roll in the first century CE (*Natural History*, XIII.26.83). Texts had to be copied onto new rolls every few generations in order to remain available. As a result many ancient texts have been completely lost, and even the knowledge of their existence has been lost. In the European tradition the ancient texts that have come down to us were those copied onto much more durable *parchment, by early Christian scribes in the fourth to sixth centuries, and importantly again in the new minuscule scripts introduced during the Carolingian *Renaissance of the ninth and tenth centuries. Those Carolingian copies were most often the ones that the humanists recovered and put into circulation again some five hundred years later.

We know very little about the work of the scribes responsible for the first and many subsequent copies of ancient texts that preceded the earliest copies that can be examined today. Nonetheless we know that in Greco-Roman antiquity educated slaves served as readers and scribes and also as teachers of *literacy to both free and enslaved children. Reading and writing texts were often two-person activities, as depicted on Attic vases, with slaves available to read aloud from and take dictation on scrolls held open on the lap. Whereas in Greco-Roman antiquity the scribe was generally distinct from the user of the text, early Christians often copied or corrected themselves the texts they wished to own and use, perhaps in some cases (e.g., when they otherwise would have had the means to hire a scribe) owing to their special concern for accuracy in copying a sacred text. Early Christian scholarship also produced some long and unusually elaborate scribal projects, such as the hexapla of Origen (184–253), in which six different versions of the Old Testament (one in Hebrew, one in Hebrew transliterated into Greek, and four in Greek) were laid out in parallel columns, or the chronicles of Eusebius (ca. 260–340), in the second part of which the histories of different ancient peoples were laid out in a table format. Each of these projects was carried out by a group of highly skilled scribes working collaboratively in the best possible conditions, in Caesarea with access to the rich resources of the library there and with generous funding from a wealthy lay patron named Ambrose (in the case of Origen) and the emperor Constantine himself (in the case of Eusebius, who served as presbyter in Caesarea).

The survival of tens of thousands of manuscripts from medieval Europe makes it possible to study more closely the impacts of scribal copying. Medieval scripts varied considerably by time and place. Thanks to scholarly analysis of scripts underway since the seventeenth century and the dates recorded in some manuscripts, the handwriting and scribal habits displayed in a manuscript serve as crucial evidence for locating the place and date of its production. While many identifications offer estimates of a half century and a region, in some cases scholars can identify the production of specific monastic *scriptoria (e.g., Wearmouth-Jarrow in England in the seventh and eight centuries or Mont Saint Michel in Normandy in the late tenth to twelfth centuries). Monastic scribes worked mostly in anonymity for the greater glory of God and their order. Women also worked as scribes and illuminators in convents, including Guda, a German nun who named and depicted herself in a manuscript in 1180. Scribing was physically difficult and slow; in a closing statement or *colophon scribes occasionally recorded relief at finishing a manuscript or complained of a sore hand. A considerable survival bias has favored the transmission of beautifully produced and illuminated manuscripts over more ordinary ones, which were likely produced in much larger numbers than are now extant. *Illuminations were often produced by scribes with specialized skills. The nobles commissioning manuscripts would pay dearly for the work of sought-after scribes and illuminators and could negotiate specific requests for the cost and production values, including particular colors or themes in illuminations. By the later Middle Ages manuscripts were also produced commercially in major centers. The spread of literacy created new readers and buyers of manuscripts who valued speed, functionality, and lower cost over beauty and prestige. Scribes working for them favored new *cursive scripts, which were about twice as fast to write as the earlier *"book hands" and also packed more text onto a page, leading to lower production costs. Paper became available across Europe starting from Italy in the thirteenth century and spreading northward, cutting the cost of materials by a factor of four by 1500. Paper was first used for archival documents and letters, then spread into *genres of all kinds.

In copying scribes often introduced changes. Some were no doubt unintentional errors—among them words or lines skipped or repeated or reversed. But there is also good evidence that scribes in medieval Europe often felt it was appropriate for them to improve the text while copying it. When faced with a passage they did not understand, they might add an explanation in the text or in the margin, which might be integrated into the text by a later scribe; they could also transform the text to make it more easily understood, for example, by changing a word or two. These practices documented in the stemmata of medieval manuscripts led to the formulation of two philological principles still valued today: *"brevior lectio potior"—that the shorter version is the better one (coming earlier in the chain of transmission since scribes usually added to rather than shortening a text); and *"difficilior lectio potior"—that the more difficult version is the better one (because scribes tended to make a difficult passage more intelligible and simpler to understand). *Philologists, starting in the Renaissance, have been motivated by the awareness of these changes to correct the "errors of the scribes," which in the case of ancient and biblical texts had accumulated over centuries of copying. Overzealous correction provided opportunities for further interventions by later scholars, and for continued discussion of optimal critical methodologies.

Nevertheless, in some contexts scribal copying was remarkably free of changes. Daniel Wakelin documents examples of scribes working in English literary texts who replicated originals with great care not only to the text but also to punctuation and layout, which were generally expected to be variable. The *sofrim* or scribes of the Torah scrolls used in Jewish worship were famously attentive to strictly accurate copying following numerous rules to ensure that each copy reproduced the authorized text and its layout with precision.

The introduction of printing in mid-fifteenth-century Europe was rapidly perceived as a challenge to existing scribal practices. Although autography had been on the rise since the thirteenth century as a means of composing a text, scribes were still responsible for making multiple copies of a text for sale or gift. With printing the task of making multiple copies could be mechanized thanks to the financial investment of the printer and the labor of all those working in the printer's shop. Surprisingly, just as the computer revolution has mainly increased our use of paper, the printing press also encouraged the use of handwriting by the elites who used it not for mere copying, but to signal an especially personal or private form of contact. Scribes scrambling to monetize their skills given the competition from printing used the new medium to disseminate manuals about the virtues and methods of handwriting. Contemporary humanist pedagogues also lent their weight to the notion that handwriting was a skill appropriate for the elite to master. Once the merely mechanical function of handwriting could be filled by printing, the art of handwriting gained a new prestige. Fewer scribes were needed, but the profession perdured.

Figure 1. Jean de Beauchesne,
calligraphic specimen, 1575.
Harvard University, Houghton Library Ms Typ 232.

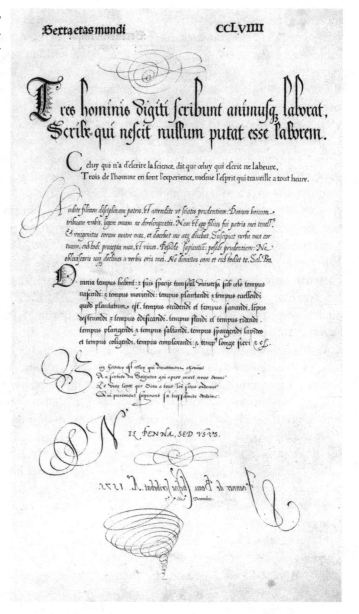

Scribes taught handwriting, and some devised systems of *shorthand, which were
marketed in England starting in 1588 and spread to the continent only after 1800.
Through the seventeenth century scribes were also employed to produce multiple manuscript copies of texts that could not be printed, because they were dangerous (owing
to political or religious content) or were designed to be secret (alchemy, or private newsletters) or were needed in only a few copies (such as musical parts). Through the eighteenth century the Vatican scriptorium produced illuminated parchment manuscripts
of liturgical texts commissioned by cardinals on their appointment, perpetuating the
skills developed for the production of medieval manuscripts. Strong writing skills were
also valued in amanuenses and secretaries hired by individuals, and in the legions of

clerks working in offices at every level of the state or other bureaucracies through the nineteenth century. A good scribe could write in different scripts, as Jean de Beauchesne, a French Huguenot in London, advertised in a one-page sampler of seven elaborate scripts, including mirror writing (see figure 1). A scribe's ability to imitate the hand-writing of his employer, whether an individual or an official, was another valued skill, which generated apparently autograph manuscripts without the personal effort that they represented; but occasionally the skill could be turned to dishonest ends, as a few court cases attest. Indeed, forgeries emerged wherever written documents carried authority, for example as early as the ninth century in England when documents started to be valued over oral witness in legal proceedings. But the ability to forge a document successfully depended on a mastery of the shifting conventions of scripts and layout. That expertise was present long before it was formalized in seventeenth-century reference works of paleography and diplomatics, which surveyed past forms of handwriting and document production.

In the twenty-first century the merits of handwriting are under discussion as school systems decide how much to emphasize a skill long valued for the discipline of hand and mental attention that it instilled. The term *scribe* surfaces mainly in the names of software and hardware tools for recording and writing. But any transition of a text into writing or a new copy, whether aided by a person or a device, has the potential to introduce modifications (as can be experienced in scans resulting from *optical character recognition rather than photographic reproduction, for example), so verification and an understanding of the sources of error remain essential measures of quality control, continuing a tradition in which scribes have been engaged since the beginning of writing.

Ann Blair

See also archivists; documentary authority; error; proofreaders; scrolls and rolls; secretaries; teaching

FURTHER READING

Peter Beal, *In Praise of Scribes: Manuscripts and Their Makers in 17th-Century England*, 1998; Christopher de Hamel, *Scribes and Illuminators*, 1992; Malcolm Parkes, *Their Hands before Our Eyes—a Closer Look at Scribes: The Lyell Lectures Delivered in the University of Oxford 1999*, 2008; L. D. Reynolds and N. G. Wilson, *Scribes and Scholars: A Guide to the Transmission of Greek and Latin Literature*, 4th ed., 2014; Colette Sirat, *Writing as Handwork: A History of Handwriting in Mediterranean and Western Culture*, 2006; Daniel Wakelin, *Scribal Correction and Literary Craft: English Manuscripts 1375–1510*, 2014.

SCROLLS AND ROLLS

The terms *scrolling* and *information* appear together everywhere nowadays. Ever since the PC revolution of the 1980s, we have scrolled up and down our files to find what we need. Some experts believe that scrolling will eventually replace the traditional form of reading. No one doubts that scrolling to find a *fact or term on a computer is faster and more efficient than finding a traditional *codex book and opening it. In the thirteenth century, attitudes to scrolls and codices were very different. The theologian and canon lawyer Guillaume Durand explained that in Christian art, the Hebrew patriarchs and prophets were depicted holding scrolls, to show that their knowledge was imperfect. "But because the apostles were perfectly taught by Christ, therefore they can use books, to signify this perfect knowledge." Durand saw the superiority of the reading experience provided by codices as clear. Yet the scroll had been in use for almost four thousand years when Durand wrote. For much of that time it had been the standard form of written record, and it remained vital long after Durand's death for preserving and accessing information of many kinds.

Scrolls—rolls of material used for writing—are as old as the formal writing systems of the ancient Near East. In Egypt, sheets of writing material were made from two layers of fibers from the *papyrus reed, laid across one another at right angles and pressed together. A series of sheets, attached end to end, became a scroll. The oldest surviving ones have been dated to around 2500 BCE. They were used for both documents and texts: scribes wielded brushes to write hieroglyphic texts and add images of gods and humans, animals and artifacts. In Asia, the oldest Hindu and Buddhist religious texts were written on so-called sutra scrolls, lengths of cloth or, later, paper that were folded like accordions. By the fourth century BCE, scrolls were being widely used in South Asia: short, illustrated ones hung in temples, and longer ones, designed for extended narratives, were unrolled to be read. By the beginning of the Common Era, scrolls were being made in China, and from there they spread to Japan and Korea.

Mycenean Greeks, like their Babylonian contemporaries, wrote on clay tablets. But by the eighth century BCE, Greeks adapted the Phoenician alphabet, adding vowels, and rapidly employed it to record the texts of their earliest epic poems, the *Iliad* and the *Odyssey*. Blank papyrus scrolls from Egypt, bought ready-made, became their standard writing material. Each scroll consisted of a set of sheets, glued end to end. Greeks normally wrote, with reed pens, on one side of the papyrus—the one on which the strands of papyrus reed were horizontal, and on which sheets overlapped one another from left to right, making it easier to write. In the last centuries BCE, forms of treated animal skin began to be used, alongside papyrus, for writing: most of the Dead Sea Scrolls, for example, are on *parchment. Whatever the medium, Greeks wrote in columns, usually five to ten centimeters wide, so that when holding a scroll open one could see two of them at a time—more or less what would be the typical content of a modern page laid out in two columns. One scroll could be as long as thirty feet: large enough to hold two to three books of one of the epics, or one book by the historians Herodotus or Thucydides. Complete texts of such long works always filled a number of scrolls. Fairly soon it became standard practice to keep such related scrolls in a single container of leather or wood, to prevent loss or confusion. Greek vases depict readers who sat, unrolling the text with their right hand and rolling it up again with their left hand: one of the Latin terms for a book, *volumen*, derives from the verb *volvo*, to turn or roll. It seems a cumbersome method, and wealthier Greeks, and later Romans, relied on slaves to read aloud to them. Yet it worked. Virgil—whose epic the *Aeneid* is a mosaic of artful allusions to the works of Homer and other Greek poets—obtained his knowledge of the poetic tradition entirely from scrolls (whose contents he seems to have committed to his capacious memory, perhaps by repeated recitation).

The Derveni papyrus, the earliest surviving Greek manuscript, preserves part of an Orphic poem with allegorical commentary. It was written around 340 BCE. By then written texts had become widespread, though not inexpensive. Socrates estimated that a manuscript of the philosopher Anaxagoras would cost one drachma—a day's wage for a laborer—in the Agora, and the comic poet Aristophanes joked about how easy it was to buy the texts of the tragedians in written form. In the decades after 300 BCE, when the Ptolemies, the rulers of Hellenistic Egypt, built up a vast library in their new city of Alexandria, they collected their texts as scrolls—490,000 of them, by one account, in the main collection. In the next century, their rivals, the Attalids of Pergamum, did the same. So, from the first century BCE onward, did the Romans. The Jews used scrolls to record and standardize both their holy books, which took shape in the last centuries BCE, in Hebrew and in Greek translation, and an increasing range of other religious texts, including Aramaic translations of the biblical texts. Their libraries, in the Temple and elsewhere, also consisted of scrolls.

The use of scrolls was not confined to a small *canon of texts. In Egypt, archives of legal documents also consisted of papyrus scrolls. Letter writers across the Hellenistic and Roman worlds committed thoughts and information to short papyri, which were rolled up, tied with a single strand pulled out of the paper, and sealed with wax. As scrolls of all sorts accumulated, scholars began to collect information from them. First, they had to be sorted. Tags identified scrolls, and in Alexandria bibliographies were compiled to list the works of known authors and to separate forged ones from the genuine (the library's demand for new books had created a lively trade in fake classics). In Aristotle's school, in Alexandria and elsewhere, scholars interested in subjects from politics to health compiled new books, moving information from one scroll to another. Scrolls were not easy to use as sources, since finding and marking a particular passage was difficult. But the demand for information overcame all the difficulties. A Roman savant, Pliny the Elder (d. 79 CE) took the notes for his massive *encyclopedic work, the *Natural History*, by assigning a slave to read sources aloud while he took notes. He produced more than 160 volumes of extracts, written tightly and, unusually, on both sides of the papyrus scrolls, which served as the basis of his compendium. Collections of letters—for example, those of Cicero—were also assembled, as the contents of the original small scrolls (one for each letter) were transferred to and organized in longer ones. Letters too had a distinctive value as sources of information: the Roman historian Cornelius Nepos noted that Cicero's correspondence with Atticus formed the best single history of Rome in the late Republican period.

From the first century CE, a second form of book—the codex, originally made up of wooden boards coated with wax—began to appear. While a small bound set of wax tablets was useful for temporary notes, a bound set of pages made of papyrus or from parchment could be substituted for the scroll as a permanent storage medium. Romans used codices for traveling copies of literary works. More important, though surviving fragments show that some early manuscripts of the New Testament were scrolls, the majority of them were codices. In the third and fourth centuries, the percentage of codices rose. The codex, as Peter Stallybrass has argued, favored "discontinuous reading": searching the scriptures for a single text and marking it. In the late fourth century, when Augustine, struggling to convert in a north Italian garden, heard a child sing "Take and read" and opened a text of the letters of Paul, he used a codex—as we know because he tells us that he stuck his finger in it to keep his place.

Codices—hard to destroy and easy to consult—had real advantages. When Romans and Greeks made fine manuscripts of the classics in Augustine's time and later, they used the codex form, which soon came to dominate the libraries of the Roman world and continued to do so in the Middle Ages. Guillaume Durand recognized that fact implicitly when he insisted on the superiority of the codex. But the same advantages were recognized in Egypt, where the codex replaced the scroll for use in Coptic texts by the sixth century, and in East Asia, where the codex (developed independently) came to dominate Chinese and Japanese book production.

As in many other cases, however, a medium that looked obsolete to some continued to develop new functions. In both China and Japan, scholars greatly valued aesthetically pleasing scripts. They cultivated this art extensively, producing calligraphic scrolls that combined writing with images. In Japan, these provided the material basis for experiments with fiction, such as the *Tale of Genji*, which was first created as an illustrated handscroll, parts of which still survive, in the first half of the twelfth century. In China, immense, vividly detailed series of pictorial scrolls depicted the travels of emperors as late as the eighteenth century. Jews never stopped using scrolls of the Torah in their synagogues. The oldest surviving ones, which deviate in small respects from those produced according to modern rules, are eight hundred and more years old.

In the Latin West, scrolls served, first and foremost, to preserve information of clear social importance. For records that had to be kept over long periods, the scroll was more convenient than the codex: new pieces could simply be laid over or glued onto old ones. From the twelfth century onward, accordingly, English administrators kept legal and financial documents in roll form. Collections of practical information—recipes and cures, for example—were also produced by adding one bit of material to another and often took scroll form. So did mortuary scrolls: death notices for prominent monks, which were carried from one monastery to another, each adding its own prayers on to those of others. Small scrolls bore the scriptural verses worn during prayer by Jews in their phylacteries—as well as a wide range of blessings and curses that could be preserved or cast on others as their purpose demanded.

Scrolls were also well adapted to recording and presenting particular forms of information that mattered to medieval and *early modern readers. Histories of the world, for example, were linear texts that began at Creation, moved through generations and dynasties and finished either with the Apocalypse or with the story of a modern town or institution. Scrolls, as Peter of Poitiers noticed in the twelfth century, could record this story in a visually dramatic and easily intelligible form that helped young students master it. They could do the same for genealogy, the basis of precedence and hierarchy in the social order. Royal and noble families prized and paid for magnificent scrolls that recorded their marital connections with other branches of the good and the great. On a smaller scale, scrolls were used for the scripts for ritual processions and theatrical performances, especially since they were relatively light.

In the late medieval and early modern West, as in East Asia, scrolls permitted experimentation. Painters and sculptors used banderoles, or winding scrolls, to identify the characters in their religious images or to put appropriate words in their mouths. Alchemists filled scrolls with vibrant, colorful images that allegorically depicted the properties of matter and the processes of its creation and transformation. Perhaps they chose the form of the scroll to dramatize the explanations that they would offer to their patrons, unrolling as they spoke. Twenty-two of these scrolls, on paper and parchment, were ascribed to a fifteenth-century Englishman, George Ripley, by the collector and alchemist Elias Ashmole, who owned five of them. Humanists tried to imagine what ancient scrolls had looked like: a fifteenth-century manuscript of Virgil now in Princeton University Library takes the form of a scroll—though the text is written not, as it would have been in ancient Rome, column by column across the roll, but in one long vertical stream, like the entries on a medieval documentary roll. *Renaissance scholars also mistook the "golden roll," a medieval Torah scroll, then as now held in Bologna, for the original scroll written by the scribe Ezra. But scrolls could also point forward. During the English Revolution of the mid-seventeenth century, religious radicals like Abiezer Coppe revived the term, if not the form, of the scroll when they launched their most apocalyptic pamphlets, the *Fiery Flying Rolls*.

Even in more recent times, scrolls have continued to find practical uses—in registers of attorneys and other professionals, in seismographs, and in the dot-matrix printers that were attached to the first desktop computers. They also serve ceremonial purposes: as diplomas, for example, and in synagogues. In the new *digital world, finally, the scroll—or at least scrolling—has had its revenge on the codex, making possible efficient and rapid, if discontinuous, forms of reading that codex users like Augustine could never have imagined.

Anthony Grafton

See also computers; documentary authority; files; forgery; letters; scribes; storage and search

FURTHER READING

Roger Bagnall, *Early Christian Books in Egypt*, 2009; Thomas Forrest Kelly, *The Role of the Scroll: An Illustrated Introduction to Scrolls in the Middle Ages*, 2019; Frederic Kenyon, *Books and Readers in Ancient Greece and Rome*, 2nd ed., 1951; Brent Nongbri, *God's Library: The Archaeology of the Earliest Christian Manuscripts*, 2018; Jennifer Rampling, "A Secret Language: The Ripley Scrolls," in *Art and Alchemy: The Mystery of Transformation*, edited by Sven Dupré, Dedo von Kerssenbrock-Kosigk, and Beat Wismer, 2014, 38–49; Victor Schmidt, "Some Notes on Scrolls in the Middle Ages," *Quaerendo* 41 (2011): 373–83; Peter Stallybrass, "Books and Scrolls: Navigating the Bible," in *Books and Readers in Early Modern England: Material Studies*, edited by Jennifer Andersen and Elizabeth Sauer, 2002, 42–77; E. G. Turner, *Greek Papyri: An Introduction*, 1980.

SECRETARIES

The work of making and managing written information, including letters, drafts, notes, documents, and administrative records, is time consuming and may require special skills such as good handwriting and spelling, and mastery of organizational systems. As a result, those responsible for this work, whether in official positions or as private individuals, have often relied on helpers to carry it out. The terms by which these helpers were called have varied by context and emphasized different qualities. In ancient Greece and Rome educated slaves often performed these functions; Tiro worked for Cicero both as a slave and after his manumission in 53 BCE, taking dictation, checking references, and crucially safeguarding and editing Cicero's speeches and notes after his death. The Latin term *amanuensis* was commonly used to designate those who served "a manu" (by their hand, i.e., by writing); another term, *exceptor*, designated one who could "catch" (*excipere*) spoken words. The Roman official "a libellis" dealt with petitions and the like. The term *secretarius* and its *vernacular equivalents originated in the medieval Europe and emphasized the helper's role as a confidant entrusted with secrets.

Under Elizabeth I the office of "secretary of state" was created; the trend of calling various high-ranking officers "secretaries" (and variants like undersecretaries, as the hierarchy became more complex) spread across many kinds of governments down to the present. These officers typically relied on a staff comprising further secretaries (with or without the title) to carry out their duties. Outside officialdom well-to-do and middling households relied on one or more servants among whom the division of labor was often fluid; secretarial work such as writing, reading, reckoning, or filing were performed alongside other duties in the household. Family members, including sons, daughters, and wives, could also help in these tasks. By extension from these characteristic tasks the term *secretary* has also designated manuals for writing business letters (starting in the late sixteenth century), a type of handwriting (eighteenth), and a writing desk (nineteenth).

In the nineteenth century offices tended to be small: the male business partners relied on and worked in close proximity to their male clerks. By contrast, in modern parlance, "secretary" conjures up the vast number of mostly female employees, hired at lower wages than male clerks had been, to work in offices of all kinds starting in the late nineteenth century. They worked with *shorthand (present in England since 1588 in many different systems, but standardized only much later, e.g., with Pitman's system of 1837), the typewriter (first marketed by Remington in 1878), and various duplicative and communicative technologies (Dictaphone trademarked in 1907, mimeograph, telex, among many others). The secretarial ranks were segmented by task (in patterns often correlated to social class, with stenographers at the bottom of the hierarchy). Work in large "pools" of typists all but eliminated a personal relationship with an individual employer or the content of the work. The work of the secretary was depersonalized and mechanized in the quest for efficiency and lower costs.

In the twenty-first century *secretary* has waned in favor of other terms like *office assistant*; in 2000, for example, National Secretaries' Day, established in the United States in 1952, was renamed Administrative Professionals' Day. The people they work for are now called "principals." The spread of personal computers used directly by said principals in addition to their assistants has generally reduced the numbers of office helpers, as software can handle many of the tasks that once required human labor. Nonetheless high-ranking leaders still often rely on executive administrative assistants. Meanwhile, IT (information technology) help services have grown apace instead; and the bulk of keyboarding has often been outsourced to offshore locations, including to workers who cannot understand what they are typing on the grounds that they may be more reliable, but certainly also because their wages are lower.

Throughout the many social and technological changes over the centuries secretaries consistently played a crucial role in carrying out paperwork and managing it. Equally consistent has been the conception of their work as mechanical, ideally carried out so well that no one would notice their role as intermediaries between the person they served and the work attributed to him or her. It is thus often difficult to determine exactly all the work that secretaries performed, and with what amount of independence or direction from their employer. Our best evidence for their work often lies in the surviving manuscripts that they wrote or that discussed them (such as letters seeking to hire a secretary or letters of recommendation). Even in the modern period, when a secretarially produced business letter typically included the initials of the secretary under the principal's signature, we cannot tell whether the secretary typed the letter based on a draft written or dictated by his or her employer or instead composed the letter based on more or less detailed instructions. Sinclair Lewis offers a memorable depiction of this work in *Babbitt* (1922) when Miss McGoun expertly transforms the lead character's dictation of a few ungrammatical clauses into a coherent business letter. Uncertainty about the independence of secretarial work is all the greater for earlier periods when even fewer records survive: we can often identify the handwriting of a secretary by its neatness compared to that of the principal, but we cannot tell how the text was composed.

These close yet hierarchical relationships included many oral interactions invisible to the written record, but occasionally the exchange of ideas in both directions is visible in surviving drafts. In his study of early seventeenth-century English letter writing, James Daybell documents, for example, secretaries both receiving feedback on letters they had drafted and in turn offering comments on letters drafted by their employers. In the early periods secretaries across many different contexts were expected to be intellectually versatile and well informed as needed to help their employers. The huge scope of their potential purview is evident in the thirty-volume *encyclopedia written by a clerk in fourteenth-century Cairo; as Elias Muhanna has shown, al-Nuwayrī's *Ultimate Ambition* grew out of his experience as a secretary and encapsulated the knowledge that others in this line of work might need, addressing a massive range of topics, from history and politics to natural science and medicine, in 2.5 million words.

Until the late nineteenth century secretaries were predominantly men, although wellborn women also relied on maidservants for similar services (Shakespeare's *Twelfth Night*, for example, hinges on the ability of the servant Maria to imitate the handwriting of her mistress Olivia). The rise of *Renaissance Italian diplomacy generated many new secretarial positions in which skill at writing in humanist prose was especially valued. A position as secretary could constitute a career or an entry into a life of writing or administration. Thomas Wolsey (1471–1530), whom his enemies identified as the son of a butcher, rose to become Lord Chancellor of England by dint of his administrative skills. Edmund Spenser (1552–99), author of the *Fairie Queene* and other major works of poetry, served as secretary to multiple aristocrats. Secretaries were also responsible for organizing written records and managing access to them. They created individual or shared systems for marking letters received and outgoing, for example, and for sorting them by date, or recipient, or topic, according to their purposes and preferences. Secretaries served as de facto gatekeepers to these papers as well as to their employers themselves. In case of the principal's death secretaries played a crucial role in the disposition and possible publication of the remaining papers; they might even clash with the wishes of the family, on the strength of their mastery of the content and organization of the papers.

One of the longest-running roles of secretaries has been to record speech in writing, whether by taking dictation or by making a written record of oral delivery, for example in sermons, lectures, or court proceedings. In ancient and medieval Europe dictation was the norm for compositions of all kinds, including letters, documents, and treatises. The complaints of the ancient orator Quintilian or the church father Jerome about dictation—that it encouraged the author to compose too fast and thus required revision—confirm that assessment. Nevertheless, autography (or writing in one's hand) was also practiced throughout these periods, and valued for giving the writer more privacy and more leisure and control in composing, and the recipient a more personal connection to the author. The thirteenth-century Dominican theologian Thomas Aquinas had famously illegible handwriting, which was another reason to dictate. Aquinas could rely on the help of fellow clerics, like his companion Reginald, who reported that Aquinas could dictate to three or four people at once. The latter skill had already been attributed to Julius Caesar by Pliny and Plutarch although they were writing decades after Caesar's death—the skill likely signaled a "great man" instead of an actual practice. In a rare depiction of this activity one of Erasmus's former secretaries depicted himself as a young man of twenty-six taking dictation from the great humanist at the age of seventy; the image printed almost twenty years after the relationship it depicts (and after Erasmus's death) may well involve a certain idealization of the interaction (see figure 1).

In the Renaissance a humanist education included emphasis on good handwriting, as advocated by Petrarch and Erasmus among many others, and we have more evidence of autography. But composition by dictation remained a good option—for John Milton in his blindness, or Winston Churchill in his great haste to compose his lengthy histories before and after World War II. Business letters were commonly dictated to clerks or secretaries, who used stenography to take down regular speech. In the twentieth century the Dictaphone made it possible to separate the dictating from the transcribing in time and place. In the twenty-first century speech recognition software has replaced a person taking dictation in many circumstances, although court reporters and medical assistants continue to perform this work in person. Transcriptions by machine may be accompanied with disclaimers about garbled results, and with good reason. Similarly, *early modern authors warned of the errors of amanuenses, whether past, present, or

Figure 1. "Gilbert Cousin of Nozeroy [France], amanuensis of D. Erasmus, age 26 in the year 1530. Desiderius Erasmus of Rotterdam, age 70 in the year 1530," Gilbert Cousin, *Effigies Des: Erasmi Roterodami* (Basel: Oporinus, 1553). Reproduced with permission from Universitätsbibliothek Basel, AN VI 4a, pp. 7–8.

future. The making and managing of texts has long been a collaborative enterprise; the work of secretaries, often ignored as merely mechanical, is an integral part of the history of the creation and diffusion of information.

Ann Blair

See also archivists; documentary authority; error; letters; office practices; scribes; sermons

FURTHER READING

Douglas Biow, *Doctors, Ambassadors, Secretaries: Humanism and Professions in Renaissance Italy*, 2002; James Daybell, *The Material Letter in Early Modern England: Manuscript Letters and the Culture and Practices of Letter-Writing, 1512–1635*, 2012; Paul M. Dover, *Secretaries and Statecraft in the Early Modern World*, 2016; Arnold Hunt, "The Early Modern Secretary and the Early Modern Archive," in *Archives and Information in the Early Modern World*, edited by Kate Peters, Alexandra Walsham, and Liesbeth Corens, 2018; Markus Krajewski, *The Server: A Media History from the Present to the Baroque*, 2018; Elias Muhanna, *The World in a Book: Al-Nuwayri and the Islamic Encyclopedic Tradition*, 2010, translated by Ilinca Iurascu, 2018; Leah Price and Pamela Thurschwell, eds., *Literary Secretaries/Secretarial Culture*, 2005; Sharon Hartman Strom, *Beyond the Typewriter: Gender, Class and the Origins of Modern American Office Work, 1900–30*, 1992.

SERMONS

Sermons have long been and remain a central and regular (typically weekly) feature of religious observance in Christianity, Judaism, and Islam, as well as other religions. They are an oral *genre, delivered by a person vested with religious authority, to an audience of congregants gathered for worship; the oral event can also be transmitted in writing or, in modern times, through audio and video recording. Sermons have been powerful vectors for the diffusion of information—on religious but also other topics, including politics and general knowledge—given the authority attributed to those delivering them and the high turnout of listeners, notably in contexts where attendance was socially or legally expected or required. Sermons were often the principal means of reaching audiences who had limited *literacy or access to writing. The impact of oral delivery was immediate and cost-free to the listener and ideally could be transformative emotionally as well as intellectually. The lived experience was more complicated: church visitations recorded complaints about inattentive parishioners, and in Puritan contexts "tithingmen" walked among the congregation armed with staffs to which feathers, foxtails, or thorns were attached to prod listeners to attention.

In addition to their role in persuading and in diffusing information, sermons prompted the development of new information technologies designed to ease the burden experienced by preachers who needed to compose and deliver them at a relentless pace. While today many congregations expect a twenty-minute sermon once a week, in medieval and *early modern Europe sermons lasted one hour or more and were more frequent. Theology students at the university of Paris in the thirteenth century attended an estimated one hundred sermons per year while the rituals in some monasteries featured two sermons per day. Much less was expected of laypeople of course, but the numbers of medieval sermons produced remain staggering, especially considering that only a small fraction of the sermons delivered have been transmitted in written form. About one hundred thousand medieval sermons are extant today (only 5 percent of which date from before 1200); from the thirteenth century on we commonly have four hundred sermons from a given preacher, with a record of twelve hundred sermons extant by Odo of Chateauroux (1190–1273), who was a prolific preacher of crusades. Preaching was even more central to many Protestant denominations and, given their shift from Latin to the *vernacular, these sermons reached a broader audience. There was so much preaching in Puritan circles in early modern England that one enthusiastic artisan, Nehemiah Wallington, attended nineteen sermons in one exceptional week and filled fifty volumes totaling twenty thousand pages with notes from the sermons he attended between 1618 and 1654. All that preaching fueled the development of aids to preparing sermons in medieval Europe, including lists of examples and keywords from the Bible, methods for outlining and memorizing a sermon, and collections of model sermons. And all that listening to sermons prompted practices of note taking, from the *reportationes* (transcripts) that survive from medieval sermons, to new techniques such as *shorthand and note taking in teams in the early modern period.

Sermo meant "discourse" or "conversation" in classical Latin. Early Christians were the first to use the term as the designation of and title for a particular genre. Sermons were attributed to Jesus by his followers, most famously the passages in Matthew 5–7 called the "Sermon on the Mount" at least by the time that the church father Augustine (354–430 CE) wrote a commentary on it. In the fourth and fifth centuries, bishops dominated preaching in urban basilicas. Augustine himself was a famous preacher as bishop of Hippo in North Africa. He preached extemporaneously, taking as his point of departure a biblical passage read in the service that day, and combining *exegesis, comparison with other passages cited from memory, a doctrinal message, and some heartfelt exhortation. Augustine's sermons were in high demand at the time and circulated in written form based on the notes taken by listeners, probably in many cases a secretary designated for the task. Augustine's sermons were transmitted throughout the following centuries, although sometimes with modifications made to the style and to the object of his critique, as the heretics of the early Christian period (Manicheans or Donatists) faded in importance.

The sermons of Augustine and other church fathers long remained important models, but new patterns also appeared along the way, including: Carolingian sermons based on a catena or a string of extracts from multiple authoritative sources; monastic sermons focused on the monk's spiritual progress; university sermons featuring theological arguments and elaborate argumentative structures; and, starting in the thirteenth century, the energetic preaching of Dominican and Franciscan friars who addressed a broader lay audience and warned against heresies. The written versions of sermons are mostly in Latin before the fifteenth century (along with some macaronic or mixed-language notes) but it is possible that the note taker engaged in translation when recording vernacular elements of a sermon. Preaching manuals, which multiplied starting in the thirteenth century, recommended adjusting the level of discourse to one's audience, and a shift to the vernacular when preaching to a broad lay audience would have been advisable on those grounds. Certainly religious and civic authorities were well aware of the power of the sermon and arrested preachers who spread messages of which they disapproved, such as John Wycliffe (d. 1384), who preached in English about reading the Bible in the vernacular, or Girolamo Savonarola (1452–98), who inspired Florentines with his call to purify the church in preparation for the end times.

Preaching was one of the main purposes for which medieval reference works were first developed. The oldest of these were *florilegia, collections of authoritative sayings (e.g., from the Bible, church fathers, and some ancient authorities), organized by topics alphabetically arranged for easy retrieval. The headings varied but usually emphasized the vices and virtues, which were commonly discussed in sermons. In the twelfth century *distinctiones* listed important words in the Bible alphabetically, along with their allegorical meanings and the scriptural passages in which they appeared for easy insertion into one's preaching. Sermon manuals featured advice on organizing sermons including the use of visual aids. They explained how to divide a topic into logical parts using branching diagrams (figure 1) and how to conjure up an image in the mind's eye that would help both preacher and listener retain the different parts of the sermon, each

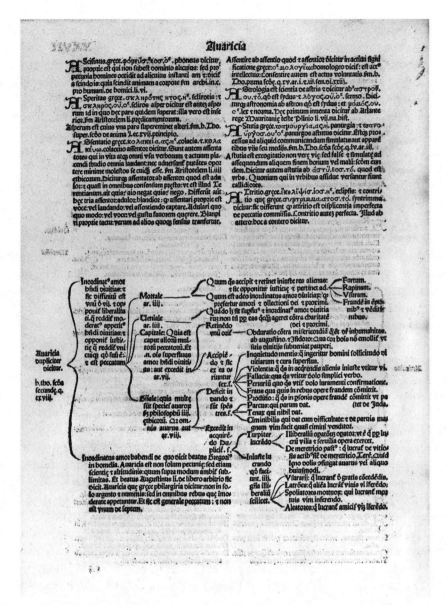

Figure 1. A diagram outlining the parts of a discussion of avarice, one of the seven vices, in an alphabetized florilegium designed to provide material for preachers among other readers. Domenico Nani Mirabelli, *Polyanthea* (Venice: Petrus Liechtenstein, 1507), fol. xxvii verso. Image courtesy of Bayerische Staatsbibliothek Munich 2.P.Lat.1065, digitized on MDZ.

corresponding to a part of the image. More prosaically, collections of sermons, whether arranged around one author, or around a theme, liturgical event, or scriptural pericope/excerpt, offered models and also ready-made material that could be lifted in case of need—hence the title of one such collection, by the German Franciscan Johannes von Werden (d. 1437): *Dormi secure*, "Sleep soundly." These tools spread from manuscript into print and from preaching to other branches of textual creation, forming models for the expansion of alphabetical indexing, branching and other diagrams, and ordered compilations of many kinds.

As central as preaching was to medieval Christianity, it was even more so to the Protestant reformers who preached in the vernacular to spread their ideas for religious reform. Through the many often violent disagreements between Catholics and Protestants and among the numerous Protestant factions that resulted from the religious schism, sermons remained a crucial tool of persuasion. Printed sermons were a hugely successful genre in many Protestant contexts, ranging from large learned collections to cheap single-sermon imprints. For the Middle Ages as well as the age of print we know very little about the relation between the oral delivery of a sermon and the written forms that have come down to us. But that relationship was occasionally explicitly mentioned, when a few early modern English imprints boasted that the sermons had been recorded in shorthand, with the implicit claim that this ensured a verbatim rendering of the text. Shorthand had existed in antiquity, but the sixteenth century knew only the term and concept of those "Tironian notes" named after Cicero's manumitted slave Tiro. Despite the lack of ancient models to imitate, the concept was inspiring: one Timothy Bright was the first of about forty authors of shorthand systems active in England (and only in England) between 1588 and 1700.

How many sermon goers actually used shorthand to take notes is hard to gauge, given that such notes would have readily been discarded once transcribed. But the regular references to sermons taken down in shorthand attest to the association of sermons with this new method of note taking. Less evident, because it was barely discussed in print, was the practice of group note taking developed in Halle circa 1700 in order to record the hundreds of sermons delivered by Hermann August Francke in the pietist orphanage and school he founded there. Eight to twelve note takers worked as a team, with each recording about a dozen words at a time on a slip of paper, thus creating a distributed record of the full text, which could be reconstructed from the slips to fill dozens of volumes of manuscript sermons. This technique was also used by university students to take down lectures, including courses offered by Kant and Hegel, which were later printed.

Preaching remained a site of important innovations in later centuries, including the first explicit embrace of women as preachers by Quakers and then Methodists in the eighteenth century (there were earlier instances of female preaching but generally without official support), the multiday events of the great revivals that began in the eighteenth and early nineteenth centuries, early uses of radio and then television in the twentieth century, and most recently the nondenominational megachurches that gather in sports arenas to listen to a preacher who is most visible from the projections on big screens. The *internet now offers a vast array of materials for composing sermons and of sermons delivered in countless denominations ready to be watched or listened to.

Sermons are not specific to Christianity. Jewish preaching has a long history, but our earliest manuscripts date from the thirteenth century. Since Jews were prohibited from writing on the sabbath, listeners did not take notes as Christians did. The medieval sermons we have were mainly written by the preachers themselves, sometimes in preparation for the oral delivery but most often after the event for future circulation and transmission. As a result, scholars estimate that most of the oral elements were removed, with citations and more complex arguments inserted, and that the text was translated from the vernacular used for delivery to the Hebrew of the written version. Islamic sermons originated with Muḥammad himself. Traditionally the Khutbah was limited to the Friday prayers in a designated "cathedral mosque" in an urban center; this facilitated control of the preacher by civic and religious authorities. In recent times these restrictions are less enforced. Preachers are active in many mosques, and even if denied that institutional support they can diffuse sermons through print, audio, and video media. The language of preaching has also shifted increasingly away from classical Arabic toward the colloquial forms more accessible to a broad audience.

Sermons vary in their contents, rhetorical forms, and specific purposes across different time-place and religious contexts. What sermons have in common is their deployment of oral and performative strategies (including movement, gesture, and tone) designed to move the listener emotionally as well as convey information intellectually. Sermons typically seek to inspire change in personal behavior, for example, by defining and condemning vice and exhorting to virtue. Because they identify vice and virtue across daily life, sermons have long been vehicles for political and social messages: by exhorting listeners to vote in a certain way, or to shun or embrace various categories of people or behaviors. Sermons are often associated with the authorities in power, but preachers have also exhorted rejection of the status quo including violent rebellion. Sermons seek to inspire action and can succeed in doing so by tapping the authority that listeners typically invest in the person delivering the sermon and their eagerness to be swayed by the preacher. Across many media landscapes the spoken rhetoric delivered by a preacher is a powerful means of conveying information and inciting to action.

Ann Blair

See also art of memory; diagrams; knowledge; learning; notebooks; reference books

FURTHER READING

Ann Blair, "Note-Taking as an Art of Transmission," *Critical Inquiry*, 2004; Lina Bolzoni, *The Web of Images: Vernacular Preaching from Its Origins to Saint Bernardino da Siena*, 2004; Patrick Gaffney, *The Prophet's Pulpit: Islamic Preaching in Contemporary Egypt*, 1994; Arnold Hunt, *The Art of Hearing: English Preachers and Their Audiences, 1590–1640*, 2010; Beverly Mayne Kienzle, ed., *The Sermon*, 2000; Meredith Neuman, *Jeremiah's Scribes: Creating Sermon Literature in Puritan New England*, 2013; Kimberly Rivers, *Preaching the Memory of Virtue and Vice: Memory, Images, and Preaching in the Late Middle Ages*, 2010.

SOCIAL MEDIA

In one sense, all media are social, and all media forms have always been social. As a species, we learned to sing and recite stories and poems in a circle, around a fire, as a way of forging social bonds through cultural exchange. Movie theaters have been sites of courtship for more than a century. Films don't end as credits roll. People continue to discuss them around offices and barbershops. Mail, telegrams, telephone calls, and emails all connect individuals to each other, each media form more conveniently than the last.

So when we refer to Facebook, Twitter, Instagram, or even Tinder as "social media," what do we mean? How are these services distinct from other, older forms of connectivity and information assimilation? What's so "social" about social media?

The operative definition of a social media service within the field of social media studies was established in 2008 by two researchers in the emerging field of *internet studies, danah boyd and Nicole Ellison. They defined social media services as bounded systems that allow people to enroll and construct a profile of themselves, let them choose other profiles with which they would interact, and allow them to view material posted by their chosen list of profiles. Ellison and boyd generated this broadly applicable definition when most social media services were websites, before most of the activity moved to freestanding applications that run on mobile platforms like smart phones or tablets. But, just as importantly, they chose not to include one of the most important aspects of the most dominant social media services around the world: algorithmic amplification.

Ellison and boyd emphasized the choices that users make to construct their profiles and to interact with select other members of a service. But as the second decade of the twenty-first century rolled in it became clear that the most important relationship in social media services such as Facebook, Instagram, Twitter, or even the employment service LinkedIn is that of user to algorithm.

Users often unwittingly feed their information to a database. The database thus contains deep and broad records of user preferences, desires, queries, and patterns of interaction with other users' profiles and with sources of information and commercial service. Through phones social media platforms track users' movements, locations, and even communication via text message outside of the platform itself. All these data help the algorithms not only predict but also shape what a user might want to read, view, or buy. Social media services design their algorithms to feed users more of what they have habitually expressed interest in, keeping users fully engaged and offering them constant affirmation through a count of "likes" and comments from fellow users. Algorithms select posts that generate significant engagement—clicks, shares, likes, and comments—to spread them faster and further than other posts, landing in front of more users. This selective amplification structures the experience of using Facebook, Instagram, or Twitter. It keeps people using the service. It focuses interest and limits exposure to expressions and opinions beyond what a user has desired. And it positions advertisements effectively and efficiently before likely consumers. Overall, the relationship among users, the data, the algorithms, and advertisements is synergistic and revolutionary. The rise and global scale of Facebook and other social media services is unlike any previous media form.

SOCIAL MEDIA DOMINATE

These platforms have risen in the first two decades of the twenty-first century to dominate the global media ecosystem. By 2020 Facebook had more than 2.5 billion users—nearly one-third of the population of the Earth. WhatsApp and Instagram, both owned by Facebook, enjoyed more than 1.5 billion users each. And WeChat, the largest social media platform in China, had the loyalty of more than 1.3 billion people. Facebook hosted content in more than 110 languages by 2020.

Through these services people share accounts of their lives and desires, clips of videos they had made or watched, links to articles they had written or read, and expressions of emotion ranging from joy to rage. That meant that social media platforms contain and carry the content of previously dominant media forms: text; recorded music; video. But more than that, social media platforms record and relate the feelings and opinions that people express about that content.

While films live on around the water cooler, content on Facebook arrives via Facebook and conversation around and about that content remains on Facebook. The water cooler is now in the theater, and the audience need never leave. Facebook and Twitter first arrived as websites, designed to be used on personal computers attached to keyboards that sat on desks. This model worked well in the early years of these services (2004 through 2010 for Facebook; 2006 through 2010 for Twitter) as they grew in North America and western Europe, where computers and broadband data connectivity were ubiquitous and affordable.

By 2010 most social media services had turned their attention to becoming chiefly mobile platforms, used mainly through telephone handsets like the iPhone, which was introduced by Apple in 2007, or those using the Android operating system introduced by Google in 2008. By 2011 the majority of Facebook usage was through the mobile application rather than the traditional websites. That growth has continued as Facebook expanded around the world and made its service available in more languages. By 2018 more than 75 percent of Facebook usage was mobile. This shift meant that Facebook users no longer considered Facebook a "place" to "go" at particular times of the day, whenever one happened to be sitting in front of a computer. Facebook by 2018 went everywhere that users went. The time that Facebook would not be available to users would be infrequent, and its presence would be constant and ubiquitous.

THE RELATIONSHIP

The relationship between those who engage with social media platforms and the platforms themselves is complex and unlike that between any previous media industries. Film viewers are a paying audience for the experience of watching a film. Commercial television viewers are the product that stations and networks sell to advertisers. Telephone and telegram companies relied on paying customers to provide the connections and content that made paying for the service worthwhile in the first place. For social media companies, all these relationships complement each other. Users work for social media platforms, as they post all the text, images, and video that constitute the content of the medium. Users also are a commodity to social media companies, as they provide the target for advertisements. And social media users choose the fellow users with whom they wish to communicate. But there is one aspect of the relationship that is new to social media and absent media forms that predate 2000: social media companies engage in total surveillance of users.

This surveillance, the ability to record every user's location, movements, internet activity, and preference—as well as the patterns of interactions between and among users—allows these companies to map social relationships and predict which products, services, ideas, and expressions a user might desire. This allows for two revolutionary aspects of the commercial activity of social media platforms. They can ensure that advertisements only reach those who have expressed interest in a type of product, service, or political candidate. Surveillance enables a revenue-generating process that not only made Facebook one of the most highly valued corporations in the history of the world by 2020 but subtracts that revenue from some older advertising-driven media industries such as newspapers, magazines, television, and radio broadcast companies. The second aspect is just as important. Data accumulation lets these companies predict which types of content are likely to generate responses from particular users, thus encouraging them to come back to the service frequently.

Therefore the "social" in "social media" refers not merely to the fact that people assemble their groups of friends and followers and contribute almost all the content that makes the services worthwhile. It more properly describes the ways in which computer algorithms deploy vast collections of user-created data to forge the experience of interacting with the mediating service, rather than with other people directly. Every interaction within a social media service is governed by algorithms. These services choose what users will see, read, and with whom they will most frequently interact. Data run through algorithms dictate the terms of those experiences. It turns out that what makes social media distinct from previous media forms is the opposite of what we usually think of as "social." It's not about relationships among people. It's about relationships between people and machines. Social media are more antisocial than social.

THE SOCIAL MEDIA MOMENT

The phenomenon of social media arose in the first decade of the twenty-first century only because of a confluence of technological, economic, and ideological forces, each of which amplified the other. The *World Wide Web was conceived in 1990 as a collection of documents, linked within text, and indexable by tracking relations among terms. By the late 1990s many who contributed to the development of the web considered ways to make it "social," by emphasizing connections among people rather than among documents. Much of this work was inspired by the work of social scientists like Stanley Milgram, who explored the "small world" phenomenon and posited that everyone is separated from everyone else by six degrees, and Mark Granovetter, who mapped relationships and described how networks of people work together. The idea of making the web social was to enhance collaborative creativity. Much of the infrastructure of the internet and many of the most impressive software projects of the 1990s had been built along *"open source" principles. Open source meant that the computer *code was open to revision by any member of a coding community. It would not be controlled by any single company or person, but firms could build on open source software to engage in commercial activities. This idea, that dozens or hundreds of authors could do better, cleaner, more efficient, more elegant work than any single creator could, grew to be a canonical belief in Silicon Valley and beyond. If networks of people could find each other and collaborate, amazing things would emerge.

Many of the early developers of what would become the major social media platforms emerged from a "hacker culture" that celebrated such open source styles of development. They applied such principles easily from software to society. People, it seemed, were objects to be tagged, classified, arranged, and managed.

An influential strain of psychological and social science also influenced the idea that electronic networks could bond and manage people, not just pages. Sociologists and psychologists worked to extend some fascinating early work on the makeup of social cohesion, including the famous "six degrees" experiments in the 1960s by Milgram and others. This work inspired popular thought about what the internet could do if people could communicate and collaborate over long distances at no marginal cost.

Not coincidentally, the earliest web platform that explicitly asked members to create a profile and choose their connections was called sixdegrees.com. It debuted in 1997, but it developed no way to generate revenue, and its technical infrastructure failed as its popularity grew. The same issues condemned the next few platforms that arose in the last years of the twentieth century: LiveJournal; AsianAvenue; BlackPlanet; and MiGente. By 2002 there was enough broad interest in social media interactions that a service called Friendster managed to generate significant attention and enrollment, only to collapse by 2008 just as MySpace and Facebook rose to dominate the industry. The Friendster collapse was the result of weak infrastructure that could not handle its rising popularity along with a lack of any source of dependable revenue. Frustration with fake profiles and frequent service interruptions drove users in North America to MySpace and Facebook, but Friendster continued to thrive for several more years in the Philippines, Singapore, Malaysia, and Indonesia. Meanwhile, a Google project called Orkut grew to dominate the social media market of both Brazil and India, only to be displaced in both countries by Facebook by 2013.

When MySpace launched in 2003 it was just another one of dozens of social media platforms, many of which attracted venture capital investments, but few of which created sustainable revenue. MySpace differentiated itself from others by allowing users to customize the design of profiles. This appealed both to musical acts and to young people who followed those acts. Youth interest drove enrollment in MySpace into the millions and ultimately attracted Rupert Murdoch's News Corporation, which purchased the service in 2005 for $580 million. MySpace, which focused heavily on young users and thus limited the extent of its "network" in contrast to its rivals was worthless and out of operations by 2011. It had been replaced by an insurgent that had learned from the mistakes of Friendster and MySpace: Facebook.

POLITICS

Facebook started in a Harvard University dormitory in 2004 and served mainly US university students for the first two years of its existence. Its founder, Mark Zuckerberg, resisted growing too quickly before upgrading servers and connectivity so that the service would rarely crash even at peak usage times. By 2007 the general public could use Facebook in English. By 2010 Facebook was available in more than twenty languages. And by 2011 Facebook had spread to much of the world.

In the first few months of 2011 Western coverage of popular uprisings in Egypt, Tunisia, Morocco, Syria, Libya, and Bahrain inspired an assumption, largely unsupported by data, that Facebook and Twitter had sparked them. Journalists in Europe and the United States assumed, because they learned of these demonstrations through Twitter, and because a small group of Egyptian expatriates gathered on a Facebook group, that these services were essential to what were a series of complex political events. Most analysis of these movements at the time ignored long-developing tensions, labor unrest, civic organization, the role of the Al Jazeera news network, and the role of soccer fan clubs in rallying public opposition to an array of authoritarian governments across many Arabic-speaking countries. The focus was on the new: social media. Once governments fell in Egypt and Tunisia (despite surviving in most of the countries in which uprisings sprouted) the myth was sealed. The misnamed "Arab Spring" was a social media phenomenon. The assumptions spread that Facebook and Twitter energized movements that favored democracy and free expression. They were the tyrant's foes.

Social media research revealed a very different phenomenon. As early as 2010, researchers saw how authoritarian governments used Facebook and Twitter to monitor and surveil dissent. Facebook groups were easy to infiltrate. Many dissidents and activists urged confederates to avoid Facebook and Twitter if they feared arrest or surveillance. By 2014 authoritarian leaders across central and Southeast Asia discovered that the algorithms that drove Facebook favored content that sparked strong emotions. Nationalism, xenophobia, racism, and other forms of bigotry traveled fast and furiously across the platform, making Facebook the best possible propaganda tool. In 2014 Narendra Modi used Facebook to drive his Hindu nationalist electoral victory in India. Soon others took note. By 2016 Facebook's targeted advertising system and algorithmic amplification contributed centrally to the election of Rodrigo Duterte in the Philippines and Donald Trump in the United States. Facebook also played a central role in the surprise victory of the "Leave" campaign in the referendum on the future of the United Kingdom's membership in the European Union. Also by 2016, Russia had mastered the art of using Facebook to inject divisive propaganda into democratic electorates, first in Ukraine and Estonia and later in the United States. The Russian Facebook-driven campaign to undermine civic trust continued from 2017 well into 2019 across Europe, with significant success in Poland, Spain, and Italy. Meanwhile, Facebook-driven campaigns helped promote nationalist leaders' rise to power in Brazil and Indonesia. In 2019 Modi won reelection in India using Facebook and WhatsApp just as effectively as he had in 2014.

THE OPERATING SYSTEM OF OUR LIVES

As social media platforms, chiefly Facebook and WeChat, grew to dominate the attention of more than half of the population of the world by 2020, they structured many social, cultural, political, and economic relationships. People began to purchase goods and services through these services. And by 2019 Facebook began developing its own encrypted currency in an effort to control, monitor, and monetize even more human activity. These services became more than just media through which we shared photos of children and pets. They became the operating systems of our lives. Not coincidentally, awareness of and resistance to this concentrated power grew as well. Governments around the world considered measures to weaken or dismantle Facebook and its affiliate services, Instagram and WhatsApp. As Facebook fought off such proposals, its leaders invoked the specter of its only remaining competitor, WeChat, and its close relationship with the government of China. The prospects for democracy remained unclear by 2020 for many reasons. The remarkable power of Facebook and WeChat are among those reasons.

Siva Vaidhyanathan

See also algorithms; censorship; cybernetics/feedback; data; databases; files; information, disinformation, misinformation; media; money; networks; platforms; programming; public sphere; surveilling

FURTHER READING

danah boyd, *It's Complicated: The Social Lives of Networked Teens*, 2015; Taina Bucher, *If . . . Then: Algorithmic Power and Politics*, 2018; Tarleton Gillespie, *Custodians of the Internet: Platforms, Content Moderation, and the Hidden Decisions That Shape Social Media*, 2018; Zizi Papacharissi, *Affective Publics: Sentiment, Technology and Politics*, 2015; Siva Vaidhyanathan, *Antisocial Media: How Facebook Disconnects Us and Undermines Democracy*, 2018; José van Dijck, *The Platform Society: Public Values in a Connective World*, 2018.

STEREOTYPE PRINTING

Exact duplication of typeset words through stereotyping promoted accurate reproduction of information and enabled this information to be transported across continents and stored for future printings. Stereotype plates are a printers' technique for reproducing typeset words by taking a mold of the raised letters of a letterpress form. The advantage of making a mold is that it preserves the compositors' labor for subsequent printings and editions. Stereotype plates, known as stereos, became an important vehicle in the distribution of syndicated news for regional newspapers and the export of books for printing in other countries.

Early eighteenth-century experiments in stereotyping used a plaster mold over oiled type. The pages were laid out to avoid hollows when the plaster was poured on; the oil prevented the plaster from sticking to the type. Once removed, the plaster was baked hard and then placed on an iron plate and put into a casting box. Typefounders called the technique "cliché" from the sound the molten metal made when it came in contact with the matrix. As the process was refined, the plates were cast curved instead of flat to fit round a cylinder for faster printing, and later still, the plates were nickel faced for increased durability.

The invention of the technique has been ascribed variously to William Ged of Edinburgh 1725 and to Firmin Didot of Paris, who first used the term *stereotyping* and printed an edition of Callet's *Tables of Logarithms* in 1795 from stereos. It is known, however, that Karl Hildebrand von Canstein was printing Bibles from stereos in 1712, and it is likely that some method of taking a mold of a typeset page was in use earlier. Ged met considerable resistance from his compositors and typefounders, who thought they would be out of work when he published his edition of the Roman historian Sallust in 1739. While some books were published using stereotype plates, there was little economic benefit in investing in the additional equipment, enlarging the foundry, and skilling the typefounders for the short editions printed at handpresses unless it was to ensure the necessary accuracy. Stereoplates of the Bible were first cast in America in 1814, and T. C. Hansard illustrated the method in his *Typographia* (Typography) in 1825.

A cheaper mold made of a material called flong made the process more efficient. Flong is made of alternating layers of thin and absorbent paper pasted together and felted over the top of the type. It was then hardened by heating while still on the type. The result was a less crisp, but flexible, negative mold of the type. This was a considerable advantage for larger rotary and cylinder steam-powered printing machines of the nineteenth century, as curved plates could be cast and affixed to the drums. Holes were left in for illustration blocks and the late news. Stereos could be corrected by punching out the letters and welding in smaller plates or slugs from the typecasting machines. For Bibles and backlist titles a "master" stereo could be made from which others could be cast to ensure that the books were always in print.

Printing machines were able to trade on the economic advantages of stereotype plates as their print runs were longer, and they enabled the presses to run faster. From the 1830s stereos were frequently used for magazine and newspaper printing, which required print runs above a hundred thousand. Looking back in 1854, the printer Charles Knight credited the stereotype with the transformative growth in the availability of useful knowledge and dissemination of cheap literature. From the 1840s stereotyping became common: by then the cost of stereos was less than half of the cost of composition, and if printers chose to simply make the molds, then the outlay was just a fifth. Flat column stereos with syndicated news, reviews, or serialized stories were bought by and distributed to provincial printers, and they came into general use in the 1860s. Stereotyping offered brands a way of making and duplicating illustrated advertisements to send to newspaper offices across the nation, and newspapers willingly accepted the variety of pictorial illustration, eye-catching typography, and revenue that came with it. In 1863 William Bullock constructed a cylinder press to print from stereos for the *Philadelphia Inquirer*, and in 1876 the weekly edition of the *Toronto Globe* was printed from plates.

Trade between book publishers and printers was affected by stereotyping. Rather than risk sending printed sheets on long sea voyages, British publishers such as Chatto and Windus and George Bell and Sons made two sets of plates from their popular books, one to be exported to America. Others went for the lighter but more vulnerable option and sent flong molds overseas. Printers warehoused the stereos for their clients, seeking repeat business, and charged only a nominal fee. This meant that stereos were kept for decades, melted down only when the printer required the metal or the space. For the publishers, owning stereos meant that whole series of books could be bought and sold, as stereoplates of classics that were out of *copyright were transferred between owners while remaining in the warehouse. Bohn's Libraries in Britain were sold from publisher to publisher following their owner's retirement; similarly, in America, the printer Houghton Mifflin received plates in lieu of payment after the financial crisis of 1857. Transferred books and series were refreshed by a new title page, prelims (front matter), and binding, and sometimes by a new introduction or foreword. In 1828 it was estimated that William Clowes, the British book printer, had on his premises between seven hundred and eight hundred tons of stereoplates worth around £200,000. By 1843 this quantity had increased to around twenty-five hundred books, valued at around £500,000.

By the mid-nineteenth century a common alternative to stereos were electros, or electrotype plates, in which a wax impression of the type was coated with graphite to make the electrode on which the copper was laid. The technique preserved finer detail and was originally used for making copper facsimiles of cuts. Publishers on both sides of the Atlantic operated a mixed economy, sometimes combining new setting with stereos or putting stereos of the text with electros of the cuts. Reuse of texts, whether printed from duplicate plates or reset from the printed edition, was common practice and in the nineteenth century shaped American literary culture. Such practices extended where publishers had branches in Africa and India for example. They were also in use in Australian newspapers for pictorial advertisements, and sales of the stereos of whole books or individual advertisements were held. In China and Korea, however, older, traditional methods remained in use.

*Digital detection of duplicate news stories, short fiction, and poetry in newspapers and periodicals demonstrates the variety of interest, from Washington's farewell address and the inaugural address of President James Buchanan to a recipe for making starch with gum Arabic, to poetry by Edward Bulwer Lytton. Sheets printed from the set type and from stereos were combined, as in the case of Thackery's *Vanity Fair* (1847–48) and *Mrs. Beeton's Book of Household Management* (1859–61). Griswold's *Works of the Late Edgar Allan Poe* in 1850 used stereos of twelve stories from Wiley and Putnam's *Tales* (1845). The cost saved, however, became less significant as markets increased. In 1834, 46 percent of Harper and Brothers volumes were stereotyped, but by 1855 the publisher had adopted the more hard-wearing electros. In Canada, the Montreal Type Foundry was making both stereos and electros in 1863. In Britain, Oxford University Press used electroplates for its Clarendon Press series in the 1860s, and in the 1870s Macmillan was making electros of its new work.

In the twentieth century lithography and offset presses replaced the technologies of letterpress and stereotypes, though these continued to be used commercially until the 1970s.

Alexis Weedon

See also books; commodification; layout and script in letters; lithography; newspapers; platforms; printed visuals

FURTHER READING

Richard Altick, "From Aldine to Everyman: Cheap Reprint Series of the English Classics 1830–1906," *Studies in Bibliography* 11 (1958): 3–24; Philip Gaskell, *A New Introduction to Bibliography*, 2007; Thomas C. Hansard, *Typographia: An Historical Sketch of the Origin and Progress of the Art of Printing*, 1825; Harris B. Hatch and A. A. Stewart, *Electrotyping and Stereotyping*, 1918; Meredith L. McGill, *American Literature and the Culture of Reprinting, 1834–1853*, 2007; Jeffrey A. Savoye, "Reconstructing Poe's 'The Gold-Bug': An Examination of the Composition and First Printing(s)," *Edgar Allan Poe Review* 8 (2007): 34–48; Peter L. Shillingsburg, "The Printing, Proof-Reading, and Publishing of Thackeray's *Vanity Fair*: The First Edition," *Studies in Bibliography* 34 (1981): 119–45; Alexis Weedon, *Victorian Publishing: The Economics of Book Production for a Mass Market, 1836–1916*, 2003; Michael Winship, *American Literary Publishing in the Mid-nineteenth Century: The Business of Ticknor and Fields*, 1995.

STORAGE AND SEARCH

All information history can be seen as the augmentation of direct communication (speech and gesture) with a relentless increase in indirect communication, either store-and-forward communication (letters, publications, email) or store-and-search communication (archives, libraries, personal notes, and now *"big data"). The pervasiveness of this development has been accompanied by such wide differences in terminology that the essential identity of the underlying structure has been obscured.

Direct communication in the form of speech and gestures is transient, even if the effect may be lasting, but recordings and documents endure for a greater or shorter period, and much of information history is concerned with the consequences. One consequence is that what endures will tend to have a more lasting influence than what is transient, provided that it is preserved and discoverable. The steady growth of information objects afforded by writing, printing, telecommunications, photography, and recording equipment using *digital and other technologies has created and progressively exacerbated two challenges: how to store them and then how to find the items most suited for some purpose. The robustness and durability of records vary greatly by medium and circumstances. Repeated loss through disasters, such as the loss of the library of ancient Alexandria, and deterioration have gradually led to best practices for preservation and conservation. The long preeminence of the printed book in *codex format meant that techniques for storage and search (notably bibliography and cataloging) have been narrowly focused on that medium. Work remains to be done generalizing these important techniques to newer media.

ORDERED AND UNORDERED STORAGE

As the number of items stored increases, the task of finding any particular one, or any that have desired characteristics, becomes progressively more difficult. In the simplest case of items stored at random a *serial search* will be more reliable and more efficient than searching randomly, but the average effort per search rises steeply as the collection size increases unless there is an ordered arrangement enabling one to go directly to a desired item at whatever location it occupies (*random access*). But a single ordering can support search only by the criterion used for that ordering and fails to support other preferences. For example, large libraries can economize on space needs by sorting books by size then shelving books of each size in the order received (*numerus currens*), but this is not helpful for readers seeking books on a topic.

Providing multiple copies for multiple sequences for multiple purposes is unaffordable, but the same effect can be achieved by adding virtual copies in any ordering desired (*index, inverted file*). Libraries, for example, typically shelve books in a classified subject arrangement and then provide additional virtual arrangements using as surrogate copies catalog records pointing to the book on the shelf. Traditionally, virtual arrangements by author, by title, and by verbal subject headings have been provided either as separate author, title, and subject catalogs or interfiled into a dictionary catalog for readers in addition to a shelf list for library staff. Similarly, bibliographies usually provide a single primary sequence augmented by multiple orderings provided via indexes. In a digital environment, the ease of generating multiple indexes and of displaying parts or all of the stored items means that the primary ordering, typically a sequentially assigned identifier for administrative purposes, is irrelevant for the searcher. The relationship between the descriptive indexing (*metadata) assigned to each document and the document itself is, in effect, inverted to constitute a crucial form of infrastructure whereby the systems of metadata are navigated to find the documents associated with each descriptive term.

Computer-based data sets are used the same way. A search command locates specified values in a serial search, with or without *inverted files* (indexes) for efficiency. Relational database management systems provide for multiple alternative virtual arrangements.

DYNAMIC COLLECTIONS

Useful collections are typically dynamic as new items are added and in some cases old ones removed. Unless items are merely added in the order received, new items disrupt the ordering. Librarians leave some space on the shelves for expansion but cannot predict reliably where expansion will be needed. Until the nineteenth century libraries used *fixed location*, whereby books were arranged by topic but assigned to a specific shelf location. The call number would specify the section of shelving, the shelf, and the position on the shelf. It did not require many additional books to disrupt this system. The decimal classification of Melvil Dewey solved this problem in two ways. First, books were shelved by classification number and so were ordered relative to each other (*relative location*) and not to any particular shelf. Moving a collection to different shelves does not affect the classification-based call numbers, nor therefore the shelving order. Second, since the classification system used a decimal notation, it is indefinitely hospitable to the insertion of new topics at any point at any time.

Scholars have long developed dynamic storage systems for their notes based on slips of paper or cards to allow flexibility for expansion and rearrangement for use or as a convenient way to prepare copy for printed bibliographies or other reference works.

CLASSIFICATION AND INDEXING

Arrangement by author, by title, and by date are relatively straightforward compared with arrangement by topic. Classified arrangements were long preferred to verbal subject headings, and there was little use of alphabetizing beyond the initial letter until after printing developed in Europe. By the end of the eighteenth century reliance on scholar librarians and their knowledge of the literature, especially as represented in the local collection, was failing in the face of expanding knowledge, the relentless growth in publication and collections, and the increasing numbers of readers wanting to search and to discover by themselves. The technical development of librarianship by Martin Schrettinger, who coined the term *library science* for it in 1808, and others, was a deliberate response to this crisis.

Classification systems have three requirements: the ordering of concepts into a linear sequence; a form of notation; and, if verbal headings are not used, an index from natural language terms to that notation (e.g., Dewey's "relativ" index; today a search term recommender).

Well-curated databases and other collections ordinarily have a carefully prepared and assigned set of categories. Nevertheless, effective and efficient searching depends on experience and familiarity with the categorization system used. The development of the *internet increases access to a wider range of resources, but this inevitably introduces additional systems with unfamiliar categorization. Providing a mapping to terms in alien vocabularies from familiar terminology is very expensive, does not scale well, and is inherently obsolescent. Statistical methods used in search-term recommender services can provide a cost-effective and easily updated alternative.

By the 1950s, very powerful and precise classifications ("indexing languages") had been developed using *facet analysis* (e.g., using separate components for what, where, when, and who) and syntax (for distinguishing between, say, "man bites dog" and "dog bites man"), as well as ingenious mechanisms using edge-notched cards and optical coincidence ("peek-a-boo") systems. But these powerful systems were hard to use and could not compete with the ease and economy of using punch cards and then digital computers to simply search text for any character string, with, later, some support for spell-checking, synonyms (*vocabulary control*), and specifying combinations of concepts at the time of search (*postcoordination*), which avoided the need to create these at the time of indexing (*precoordination*) and is more flexible.

TERMINOLOGY

No single arrangement by subject can suit equally well all needs or the differing perspectives of specialists in diverse fields. Not only does each specialized community have its own particular use of words, but subjects and the relationships among them are always evolving. Similarly, subject terminology inherently faces obsolescence as both subjects and language itself change. The subject indexer, like Janus, must base terminology on established discourse (the past) in order to provide for future needs. Any assigned index term recedes, fixed into the past, while knowledge, language, and searchers evolve in new and unforeseeable ways.

SCALE

The vast scale of contemporary digital resources (e.g., the web, Google Books, Amazon's offerings, *"the cloud") and increasing ability to search for fragments within resources as a result of the move from printed to digital media make consistent human categorization impractical, so we have to fall back to basic search for character strings, augmented with elementary spell-checking prompts, mechanical surrogates for relevance (e.g., counting of citations or links), and, now, relentless inference from data collected from the searchers' behavior.

Michael K. Buckland

See also algorithms; bibliography; books; cards; data; databases; diagrams; digitization; files; indexing; registers

FURTHER READING

Michael K. Buckland, *Information and Society*, 2017; Ronald E. Day, *Indexing It All: The Subject in the Age of Documentation, Information, and Data*, 2014; Daniel N. Joudrey and Arlene G. Taylor, *The Organization of Information*, 4th ed., 2017; Markus Krajewski, *Paper Machines: About Cards and Catalogs, 1548–1929*, 2002, translated by Peter Krapp, 2011; Henry Petroski, *The Book on the Bookshelf*, 1999.

SURVEILLING

Surveillance derives from the French *sur* (over) and *veiller* (to watch). The latter, which comes from the Latin *vigilāre*, is the root of English words such as *vigil* and *vigilance*. The term *surveillance* gained currency during the French Revolution, notably in the name of a provisional committee charged with public security. Though it is now used in scientific contexts—the surveillance of infectious disease and ecological change, for example—it is more conventionally associated with efforts to "watch over" other humans. Broadly speaking, surveillance encompasses efforts to describe, classify, store, and recall information about people, their past behaviors and future intentions, and other phenomena bearing on social relations. The history of surveillance is the history of human efforts to organize techniques of prediction and to exercise social control.

Surveillance is often discussed in connection with technological developments, but surveillance practices are always rooted in embodied experience. The body, therefore, is the principal site of surveillance. Whenever we interact with strangers or those familiar to us, we look for clues in our counterpart's physical appearance and speech. We infer meaning from body language and attire, from which we make assumptions about identity, status, and trustworthiness. Likewise, we manage our own speech and appearance to conform to social expectations. During these interpersonal performances, we signal our understanding (or misunderstanding) of socially approved roles and behaviors and are judged accordingly.

These judgments are often based on ingrained cultural ideas and power dynamics. We are on guard against those who fit our mental portrait of a criminal; we are deferential toward those who appear respectable; we accept those who seem to belong. At a basic level, then, surveillance is concerned with identification and classification. In this way, surveillance activities seek answers to two questions: *Who is this person?* and *What kind of person is this?* The answers to these questions determine one's treatment in a given social context, whether chatting with a colleague or interacting with an algorithm. The answers can also have profound implications depending on who is doing the asking—the powerful or the marginal—and particularly when applied to questions of citizenship, criminality, social legitimacy, and economic value.

HISTORICAL CONTEXTS

Though modern surveillance is often attributed to post–World War II computerization and later *digital technologies, this perspective is misleading. In fact, surveillance has become increasingly instrumental and pervasive since the 1700s. The origins of this change are complex and vary across place and time. However, four interrelated historical developments stand out. The first is the rise of the nation-state. As governments in western Europe consolidated during the eighteenth and nineteenth centuries, record keeping became crucial for coordinating administrative power and controlling subject populations. As a result, state bureaucracies documented more of everyday life, from tax collection and military service to matters of law, criminality, public health, education, city planning, territorial security, and colonial rule. A second development is the rise of capitalism. At nearly the same time, new forms of industrial production, business management, and accounting fostered a growing reliance on commercial record keeping to track material, labor, and profits. Personal relationships, in many cases, were replaced by impersonal market information, which could be calculated in terms of price and risk.

A third development involves urbanization. As more people moved to industrializing cities during the nineteenth century, populations became denser and more anonymous. Unlike small rural communities, where individuals were known and easily recognized, large cities involved more frequent—and potentially hazardous—encounters with strangers. A fourth development involves technology. During the nineteenth century, a variety of new information transmission and storage devices were introduced. These include novel filing systems, which gave old forms of documentation new uses; the telegraph and telephone, which permitted instant communication at a distance; and image- and sound-recording technologies that captured new types of evidence.

These four developments—the rise of nation-states, capitalism, urbanization, and new information technologies—are key features of modernity. Together, they also provide the context and conditions of modern surveillance. More than anything, modern surveillance has grown out of efforts to exert control over increasingly large, diffuse, and mobile populations. Drawing on a concept provided by the political scientist James C. Scott, these efforts can be usefully summarized as attempts to make society "legible"— that is, to make individuals and groups visible and knowable to governments, businesses, and other social actors. This process can be seen in the development of identification and classification systems.

IDENTIFICATION: WHO IS THIS PERSON?

During the nineteenth century, individual identities were documented with growing regularity and consequence. Though governments had long identified citizens through tax rolls and censuses, these practices were episodic and generally limited to specific groups—free men, for example. The passport, perhaps more than any other document, signaled the state's effort to identify its subjects and to regulate movement across its borders. These documents evolved from letters of safe passage to standardized forms with rubrics for legal names, nationalities, physical appearances, signatures, and, eventually, photographs.

States also took increasing interest in overseeing administrative systems for registering births, marriages, and deaths—information formerly dispersed among various religious and local authorities—as well as systems for registering criminals, political dissidents, and recipients of social and medical welfare. Personal identification was further imposed by standardizing the use of first and last names, through fingerprinting (after 1850), and by reordering urban space to make the location of specific addresses (and people) more efficient.

While nation-states sought to identify those within their borders and in colonized territories, the business community also took greater interest in identifying employees,

other businesspeople, and consumers. The expansion of free-market wage labor, for example, required more information about the productivity of specific individuals, and
the growing complexity of work processes and management encouraged the development of formal systems for defining individual responsibilities. At the same time, the
growth of impersonal credit relationships, particularly in the United States, encouraged
the creation of systems for identifying prospective borrowers, and insurance companies probed more deeply into the identities and behaviors of their policyholders. By the
end of the nineteenth century, the identities of consumers also became a focus of business information gathering. Mass retailers, mail-order companies, and magazine *publishers, in particular, sought to boost profits by targeting their sales and marketing campaigns at specific individuals.

All these efforts to identify individuals were intensified through the use of new information technologies. Writing and record keeping, beginning with ancient list making, have been powerful tools of surveillance throughout the history of civilization. For
reasons already noted, however, these activities proliferated during the eighteenth and
nineteenth centuries, drawing more social interactions into systems of administrative
documentation. One of the most significant technical developments involved information storage. Information, after all, is valuable only if it can be found. New office technologies like vertical filing cabinets expanded surveillance capabilities by making records about people more accessible and, by extension, more useful, inciting still more
information collection. The filing revolution was felt in contexts as diverse as criminal
identification and retail customer accounts.

Surveillance also expanded through new electric communication technologies, beginning with the telegraph in the 1830s and the telephone in the 1870s. The possibility
of instant communication extended the power of state authority, including military operations and the governance of distant colonial populations, and accelerated the transfer of commercial information about trading partners and management activities. These
wired technologies were easily tapped, opening the door to new forms of illicit eaves-
dropping and criminal investigation. Electric signaling was also employed in alarm systems and police call boxes, and, more generally, electrification affected embodied surveillance through its application in lighting, which deterred crime by illuminating dark
spaces.

While electric communication "annihilated" the constraints of time and space, photography and phonography inscribed identity in new kinds of records. Photographic images, beginning with the daguerreotype in the 1830s, offered new possibilities for reproducing human likenesses. Photography became a popular medium not only for
memorializing family and famous figures, but also for documenting the bodies of criminals and suspect populations, sometimes in the guise of medical or ethnographic research. By the late nineteenth century portable cameras, including so-called detective
cameras, made candid, surreptitious photography a reality. In the 1870s, phonographic
devices captured sound for the first time in human history. Voices and conversations
were no longer ephemeral; they, too, could be recorded and reproduced as evidence,
with or without the subject's knowledge.

While observing the growth of identification systems over several centuries, one persistent obstacle is worth noting. This is the difficulty of connecting bodies to texts.
Even as official documents became important for identifying individuals, these same

documents were hardly foolproof. Identification systems—from medieval seals and badges to today's identity cards—are always at war with fraud. The handwritten signature illustrates the problem. Though easily forged, these self-attesting scribbles still function as proof of the signer's physical communion with the text, whether the text is paper or the face of a touchpad. During the nineteenth century, fingerprints, bodily measurements, and photographs were adopted to more reliably attach individuals to their disembodied records. The subsequent development of unique numbering systems, DNA testing, passcodes, and biometric readers all reflect efforts to pin down shapeshifting bodies and to link each to a verifiable identity.

CLASSIFICATION: WHAT KIND OF PERSON IS THIS?

Identification is primarily concerned with authenticity—Is this person who she claims to be?—but classification is more broadly concerned with categories. Classification, of course, is implicit in identification. Individuals may be *identified* through physical characteristics—gender and height, for example—which are themselves *categories* for making sense of human variety. While some categories seem to be untouched by human interpretation—some people are objectively taller than others—others are the product of social invention. Gender, for instance, is no longer a self-evident binary classification. Where once it was possible to exist only as male or female, the concept of gender now includes additional categories of personhood.

In the context of surveillance, classification is inseparable from power. By sorting people, things, and ideas into sense-making categories, classification systems shape social reality itself. Classification delimits what we see, what is ignored, and what is valued. Those who define the terms of classification therefore wield extraordinary power over others. This is especially consequential when applied to questions of group membership and deviance. During the eighteenth and nineteenth centuries, classification systems, like those for identification, took on new significance as governments, commercial interests, and the scientific community sought more detailed knowledge about citizens, markets, public health, and human behavior. This knowledge, it was hoped, would render populations more legible, more predictable, and more easily controlled.

To better "know" their subjects, modern states sorted their populations into new and more elaborate categories. In the United States, for example, an ever-expanding list of census questions reflected government efforts to classify the nation's population. The first census in 1790 consisted of just four questions; in 1890, it swelled to thirty. Importantly, the categories themselves reveal the power of classification. This is well illustrated with regard to race. In the 1790 census it was possible to be classified as only white or Black. In 1890, it was possible to be "white, black, mulatto, quadroon, octoroon, Chinese, Japanese, or Indian." Not only was race treated as an essential category—something real and immutable—but the category itself changed over time, splintering into subcategories. In this way, classification creates the conditions of possibility—and impossibility. Those without categories are, by definition, nonexistent. Prior to 1870, there were no Native Americans ("Indians") in the United States. The category simply did not exist on census forms.

During the nineteenth century, the enthusiasm for classification also extended to the scientific study of crime, illness, psychology, and social problems. Inspired by

*Enlightenment ideals of rationality, intellectuals and reformers looked for clues to criminal types—"jug ears," according to an influential Italian criminologist, were a distinguishing trait—and cataloged a growing inventory of maladies and dysfunctions, from sexual perversion to suicide. Classification, from this perspective, advanced the cause of scientific progress and intersected with the project of governance. The development of statistical analysis further encouraged classification, as states, social scientists, and businesses (especially insurance firms) sorted people and phenomena into countable categories. Statistics gave those armed with numbers not only the ability to observe previously unnoticed relationships—correlations between crime rates and education, for instance—but also the power to predict future events.

The rise of statistics-driven classification would be one of the most consequential developments in the history of modern surveillance. This is the case for several reasons. First, because statistics rely on numbers, statistical analysis is often assumed to be purely objective. Questions about the validity of the categories themselves—race, intelligence, or personality, for example—are easily overlooked and naturalized. Here, again, classification can be seen as an expression of power. Intelligence tests, for instance, are useful only insofar that they help those with authority—the state, psychological experts, educators—"see" and measure the invisible mental abilities of those in their charge. Indeed, statistical knowledge may be promoted in the name of democracy and fairness while at the same time cloaking the values and interests of those in control.

Additionally, because statistical analysis required accumulations of data, statistical knowledge demanded the collection of more information. The hunger for data, in turn, encouraged more surveillance and more extensive classification. Though early statistical analysis was incredibly time and labor intensive—all counting, transcriptions, and calculations were done by hand—new information-processing technologies changed this. Tabulating machines, notably late nineteenth-century punch card systems, automated data-handling functions and presaged the development of electronic computing. Statistical analysis would provide the foundation for later algorithmic decision-making programs, from risk-scoring systems to the delivery of social media content.

SEEING AND BEING SEEN

The intensification of administrative record keeping and new communication technologies between 1700 and 1900 meant that more of an individual's life was documented. The individual, in other words, was becoming increasingly "legible." This was a gradual and uneven process, to be sure. Some lives and populations, such as public figures, middle-class shoppers, laborers, and criminals, were more aggressively documented than others. Many others remained largely invisible. While surveillance is often viewed negatively, particularly in terms of privacy violations, it is important to acknowledge the positive dimension of being known. Citizenship and legal rights, for instance, depend on one's recognition as a legitimate member of society. The fight for social change often hinges on a marginalized group's right to be seen and accepted.

Whether in the service of social control or demands for equality, surveillance would become a defining feature of modern society. By the end of the nineteenth century, the size of an individual's information footprint was quickly growing. Compared to a person in 1800 or 1700, individuals in 1900 generated far more recorded evidence about themselves in government records; commercial transactions; school, employment, and medical files; official credentials; civic memberships; photographs; and other documentary traces. This trend accelerated throughout the twentieth century. The *internet and digital communication would vastly increase the variety and volume of such evidence production—from text messages and videos to *metadata and biometrics—but these developments represent a continuation, rather than a break, in the longer history of modern surveillance.

Josh Lauer

See also appraising; bureaucracy; cameras; cards; documentary authority; files; governance; indexing; lists; privacy; quantification; surveys and censuses

FURTHER READING

Jane Caplan and John Torpey, eds., *Documenting Individual Identity*, 2001; Michel Foucault, *Discipline and Punish: The Birth of the Prison*, 1975, translated by Alan Sheridan, 1977; Edward Higgs, *The Information State in England*, 2003; David Lyon, *Surveillance Studies*, 2007; Torin Monahan and David Murakami Wood, eds., *Surveillance Studies: A Reader*, 2018; James C. Scott, *Seeing Like a State*, 1998.

SURVEYS AND CENSUSES

To survey the history of surveying practices is to explore the multifarious quest—across time and space—to grasp a sense of the whole through the aggregation of its parts. To *survey* is to gain a general or comprehensive view of the landscape, whether physical or social. In late Middle English, the verb meant to "examine and ascertain the condition of." The noun form connoted oversight or supervision. Indeed, the word *survey* still carries three distinct meanings, the first being to measure or count. The two other definitions point in opposite directions. On the one hand, surveying means to *oversee*, or examine closely. On the other, it refers to *seeing over* in order to gain a broad perspective.

The thing being examined or ascertained is itself less significant. The subject of a survey, especially in early usage, was often a plot of land, a coastline, or a set of topographical features. Land surveying, among the oldest of the mathematical arts, dates to ancient times. Exploration and mapping, transportation, and communications all depended on surveyors' tools for assessing the distances, angles, and features of specific terrain. A survey might settle a dispute between contending owners of a field, for example, or the proper boundaries of a village, painstakingly marked out with a chain and a compass. On a broader—indeed, global—scale, surveying was a crucial technology of empire, enabling colonizers to map and engineer, and thereby attempt to master, unfamiliar, far-off places.

Increasingly, surveys were pressed into the service of gathering information about the human inhabitants of those places as well. A surveyor might simply want to tally the people in a given territory. In the West the population registers we know as censuses are as old as the biblical account of Mary and Joseph's journey to Bethlehem, the purpose of which—before miraculous events interceded—was to be included in such an enumeration. As surveying techniques were developed and refined over time, however, the object was just as often people's characteristics, behaviors, or attitudes. Sometimes these were gleaned by observation, but more often by asking human subjects directly via interviews or questionnaires.

Social statistics are close companions of the survey, emerging originally as a "science of state." Systematic attempts to catalog the entirety of a realm can be found stretching back at least as far as William the Conqueror's Domesday Book of 1086, which cataloged both property and people. In that case a "Great Survey" was conducted by men who fanned out across England and Wales in order to discover "how many hundreds of hides were in the shire, what land the king himself had, and what stock upon the land; or, what dues he ought to have by the year from the shire." The Florentine *Catasto* of 1427, an extensive tax survey of the citizens of that city, amassed household-level data on debts, property, business interests, and family background.

Military service or taxation motivated these early efforts. But the survey's uses proliferated alongside the functions of governance. The seventeenth and eighteenth centuries saw the systematic collection of birth and death rates, or "vital records," in order to track epidemics and devise insurance tables. The age of revolution introduced another purpose for such tabulations: ensuring accurate political representation. In the United States, the federal census established in the 1780s was coincident with the nation itself, the empirical undergirding of the principle of representative government. Sir John Sinclair's ambitious *Statistical Account of Scotland*, published between 1791 and 1799 and inspired by German state surveys, aimed rather to measure his nation's quantum of happiness.

The social survey, prominent by the later nineteenth century, was the nonstate counterpart of official population counts. Western nations in the nineteenth century saw a wave of surveying by private citizens and philanthropists, triggering what Ian Hacking calls an "avalanche of numbers" in the service of industrial and social reform. These investigations sought a comprehensive view of modern conditions through local studies and firsthand data collection. They were undertaken by budding statistical societies and individual reformers certain that systematic social knowledge was the key to solving problems ranging from urban poverty, crime, and disease to cultural assimilation and unsafe factory work.

Charles Booth's monumental self-funded survey *Life and Labour of the People in London*, its findings released in seventeen volumes between 1889 and 1903, was one of the most comprehensive. Predating Booth's survey was Frederic Le Play's six-volume *Les Ouvriers Européens* (The workers of Europe, 1855), which relied on interviews as well as observation to offer a representative portrait of French society. German mass polls in the 1870s as well as detailed neighborhood studies by American surveyors—Jane Addams's block-by-block study of Chicago's immigrant communities in her settlement house work at Hull House and W.E.B. Du Bois's *The Philadelphia Negro* (1899), for instance— speak to the range of nineteenth-century information-collecting efforts transpiring under the sign of the social survey.

In the twentieth century, this species of social investigation, along with its ameliorist and amateur bent, would be supplanted by *scientific* or *sample* surveys and academically accredited institutions of survey research. Whereas earlier social surveys typically had been conducted by those outside the academy, the modern survey was the province of professional social scientists in the newly distinct fields of sociology, demography, psychology, economics, and political science. And where prior efforts had necessarily been fairly localized, the modern survey often aimed to speak to national trends or aggregate behavior.

Twentieth-century survey researchers would narrow the definition of what counted as a scientifically legitimate survey even as they sought to expand those instruments' authority in public life. Touted as statistically representative, rigorously quantitative, and resolutely empiricist rather than reformist, sample surveys became in Jean Converse's words "an instrument of special power for viewing mass populations in industrial societies, especially in their character as social facts, political publics, and economic markets."

Newly precise methods for measuring variability and assessing the reliability of responses enabled the rise of modern survey research. In particular, the application of probability theory in the form of scientific sampling and data-weighting techniques allowed for more powerful extrapolations from parts to wholes. Keen interest in attitude measurement in the early 1920s by sociologists and psychologists as well as government agencies and commercial interests led to an intense focus on questionnaire and interview design. Whole new technical fields sprouted around constructing attitude scales and assessing respondents' candor.

The advance of professionally trained social scientists into authoritative positions in the academy and government shuttled these techniques into the realm of policy. Scientific surveys responded to political and bureaucratic demands for what James Beniger termed "technologies of mass feedback" that might elucidate phenomena such as soldiers' morale and consumer behavior. Seemingly neutral, nonpolitical instruments for decision making, statistics and surveys became useful tools for all manner of agencies, both private and public.

Ethnographic and narrative surveys of social life would persist. One key instance was the Mass Observation project in Britain, created in 1937 as an "anthropology of ourselves" on topics ranging from wartime clothes rationing to pub socializing. But quantitative sample surveys would overtake the field in the mid-twentieth century.

Major academic and government survey centers flourished, especially in the United States, where figures like Paul Lazarsfeld and Rensis Likert built major survey outfits before and after World War II. The Survey Research Center and Institute of Social Research at the University of Michigan were exemplary, spurring innovation in survey techniques and housing longitudinal data such as the National Election Study and the Survey of Consumer Attitudes. Likewise, the National Opinion Research Center at the University of Chicago has since 1972 through the General Social Survey monitored both the demographic characteristics and the political and social attitudes of US residents.

Universities, foundations, and states all invested heavily in survey technologies in the latter half of the twentieth century. Indeed, survey-based social science touched almost every area of inquiry and a remarkable array of social questions, from race relations to mental health, consumer confidence to sexual behavior. It transformed commercial fields like marketing, advertising, and journalism as well. Opinion polling, and electoral polls in particular, became a major sector of the survey enterprise in the United States, playing an increasingly important—some would argue outsized—role in political campaigning and strategy. Although initially resisted by other governments, polling would become an essential political technology in most industrial nations.

Employed to assay everything from coastlines to candidates, the survey has been both a flexible and a durable tool. There are discernable turns in its long history from antiquity to the present: surveys shifted in focus from physical terrain to human beings, passed from the hands of rulers to survey research centers, and made growing claims to scientific rigor. But the surveyor's promise to offer a better, more comprehensive view of whatever she or he beholds has remained constant.

Sarah E. Igo

See also data; databases; governance; maps; observing; quantification

FURTHER READING

James Beniger, *The Control Revolution: Technological and Economic Origins of the Information Society*, 1986; Martin Bulmer, Kevin Bales, and Kathryn Kish Sklar, eds., *The Social Survey in Historical Perspective, 1880–1940*, 1991; Jean M. Converse, *Survey Research in the United States: Roots and Emergence, 1880–1940*, 1987; Sarah E. Igo, *The Averaged American: Surveys, Citizens, and the Making of a Mass Public*, 2007; Theodore M. Porter, *The Rise of Statistical Thinking, 1820–1900*, 1988; Andrea Rusnock, *Vital Accounts: Quantifying Health and Population in Eighteenth-Century England and France*, 2002; Paul Schor, *Counting Americans: How the U.S. Census Classified the Nation*, 2017; James C. Scott, *Seeing Like a State: How Certain Schemes to Improve the Human Condition Have Failed*, 1998.

TEACHING

The guiding of learners is an activity as old as human society and a crucial means of conveying not only information but also the methods for finding and managing it from one generation to the next. Teaching is connected to information in a basic and general sense, as teachers are intermediaries between selected information and those who need to use it, though teaching may also involve the imaginative faculties. We distinguish between formal and nonformal education to describe instruction and learning. In this usage, formal and nonformal education are connected to educational institutions and teachers, along with a third type, so-called informal learning, in which everyone and everything can be perceived as a teacher. This entry is about teaching in the formal and nonformal senses only. (To read more about informal learning, see the entry on learning in this volume.)

As defined by UNESCO (2012), both formal and nonformal education are "institutionalized and intentional." Both "respond to requirements and standards that are set by national or sub-national educational authorities." Formal education is usually "initial [comes first] and presents programs recognized by the relevant national educational authorities." The defining characteristic of nonformal education is that it is an addition, alternative, or complement to formal education "within the process of the lifelong learning of individuals." It "caters to people of all ages, but does not necessarily apply a continuous pathway-structure; it may be short in duration and/or low intensity, and it is typically provided in the form of short courses, workshops or seminars." Nonformal education mostly leads to "qualifications that are not recognized as formal qualifications by the relevant national educational authorities or to no qualifications at all." Formal education, for example, includes K–12 and higher education, whereas nonformal education encompasses learning opportunities in many media, including online courses.

Teaching in formal and nonformal education provides information to students that educational authorities deem worthy of exercising and memorizing. It includes guided mastery of predefined ways of rationalizing and arguing, and also the transmission of traditions and technical know-how from one generation to the next. Students might use these pools of information to build up new ideas and experiments, and thus form part of technical innovation, but there is also the possibility that they might primarily learn to live like their ancestors. The Chinese imperial examination system is an example of a national regulated system of tests that shaped what people strove to learn (mainly the mastery of the Confucian classics). This examination system selected candidates for the state administration, starting around 681 CE in the mid-Tang dynasty. It was abandoned in 1905 as archaic, ending Confucianism as an official state ideology. The exams had constituted the value system of all Chinese local elites, because most of them had learned for and committed to the values presented in the exams.

Another way to look at teaching from generation to generation is to explore reciprocity, by examining parenting. In her book *Growing Each Other Up: When Our Children Become Our Teachers* (2016), Sara Lawrence-Lightfoot highlights the shifting dynamics of authority in the postmillennial years, which brought new ways of learning interaction between children and their parents. One example is the balance of emotional closeness and distance that parents learn while interacting with their children; another lies in the challenges of dealing with different identities, such as when a mother is taught patiently by her autistic son about his abilities, feelings, and desires, or a father is mentored by his lesbian daughter.

In its ideal form, teaching in both formal and nonformal education is based on one or more methods, which make it easier for students to understand very difficult and closed contents. The long-standing discipline of didactics studies these methods and their contexts and applications. Methods include cutting content to its roots, starting with memorizing simple statements and vocabulary, often in visual and categorically or associatively organized forms; solving single-track problems; and ending with more complex contexts and arguments. In many formal and nonformal contexts, these steps are marked by exams, grades, and promotions to the next level. The *Jesuits, or Society of Jesus, a Catholic order originating in Spain, were early advocates of a regulated school system of grades and promotions in the Western world. Between 1551 and the official abrogation of the order in 1773, the Jesuits built a network of schools in Europe, the Americas, Japan, and China. The Ratio Studiorum, with its system of grading and testing, had been the authoritative guide to Jesuit education worldwide since 1599.

While teaching programs ending with grades and exams are applied in most formal educational contexts, they are not necessarily part of nonformal education. Martial arts training is one context that brought nonprofessional sports coaching (which is by definition an add-on and informal training for almost all age groups) to a level with formal education by introducing national regulations. Exams determine the belt color that a student wears as part of the sports uniform: the color represents the level of mastery the student has reached. When students reach the grade of the black belt, they are qualified to teach less skilled pupils.

Other sports have equally differentiated systems of achievement. German horseback riding training provides exams and promotion from level 10 (which informs and tests the most general way of keeping and treating of horses) to level 1 (which tests the internationally most difficult performance level of riders in dressage or jumping). The tests of skills and knowledge, practical and theoretical, and the preparatory textbooks are nationally standardized and lead to certificates. The upper levels serve as an entrance phase for those who want to become professionals: they will do additional training and tests. The upper levels are connected directly to the international standards of the disciplines of dressage and jumping and are aligned with the skills needed to compete internationally. Some of the nonformal education fields such as martial arts training and the German horseback riding teaching system are highly regulated and come very close to formal education.

Nonformal education often happened where the unwritten traditions of society had been stable over centuries, relying more on tacit knowledge than in nontraditional societies. In *early modern Habsburg Austria, youth took residence at a court of a related aristocratic family, where they learned manners, dress, and sports so as to perpetuate distinctions between themselves and the lower classes. Communities that experienced the disruption or suppression of values by governments also used forms of education outside the official classroom, such as in communities in exile, or among disadvantaged genders. Communities in diaspora, like the Jews and Muslims after their expulsion from Spain in 1492, offer prime examples of ancestral traditions maintained in the home, sometimes with a diminishing understanding of their origins. The transmission of information was perforce clandestine and oral instead of written out or published. With this lack of written record, the information cannot be easily recovered or reconstructed by outsiders, because it is not visibly stored or archived. Finally, poor or remote parts of society do not always have access to schools and therefore have developed and used alternative forms of teaching and learning.

TEACHING WITHIN INSTITUTIONS IN EARLY MODERN TIMES

In the context of late medieval Christian Europe, the learned were also the professional elite of a town, serving the government and aristocracy (as the powerful owners of landed property). Belonging to this service elite opened up a career path facilitated by the standing of the learner's family, and by the access to schools and higher learning in society. The body of educational institutions was manifold, built up either by the church, with branches in cathedral schools and monastery schools, elementary education, and universities; or by the town, with apprenticeship systems of town *guilds, and secular merchant schools. After the *Reformation, the amount of town-managed higher education increased. Following elementary school, higher education targeted boys from fourteen years onward. Girls usually did not participate in higher education or trade school, but households did train them privately, provided interest and money were available.

European ideals of education developed from the ancient Roman notion of the "seven *liberal arts" comprising the trivium of disciplines of the word (grammar, logic, rhetoric), and the quadrivium, the four disciplines of the number (arithmetic, geometry, astronomy, music). At universities (which developed across Europe after the first foundations of Paris, Bologna, and Oxford in the late twelfth century), students spent three years in the Faculty of Arts studying advanced curricula of the seven liberal arts and philosophy (principally the four branches of logic, ethics, physics, and metaphysics). They could then enter one of the three higher faculties devoted to law, medicine, or theology (often called the queen of the disciplines). This system weathered changes in the material being taught—from *scholastic emphases of the medieval period to humanist ones starting in the sixteenth century and the new sciences introduced in the late seventeenth century. In the nineteenth and twentieth centuries, European universities centered on research, shaping the modern *research university. The most influential university models in the nineteenth century were the Humboldtian (German) style, which focused on philosophy as a core subject and leave the students free and alone to start thinking methodically and creatively, and the French model, centering on the sciences of the Polytechnic with strict discipline and examination.

In medieval and early modern Islamic societies, the centers of learning were Quran schools for the young, and madrasas for the higher education, both geared toward boys. Girls usually did not participate in formal education, but many of them were trained with private teachers at home. Madrasas were buildings supported by the ruling classes, not communities like the European universities; their origins go back to the ninth century, they flourished in the eleventh to fourteenth centuries, and their science had great impact on European thought in all disciplines, from philosophy, mathematics, and astronomy to law and theology to medicine.

Damascus in 1517 had about 130 madrasas and about ten thousand inhabitants. By contrast Basel had only one university; and Zurich, with about five thousand inhabitants, had no institute of higher education. The schools of Damascus were generally smaller than universities in Europe, and they included fewer teachers, teaching not only one, but more subjects than in Europe. For example, one teacher would teach law, physics, and theology at the same level. The Islamic school masters competed against each other, so that there were different schools of Islamic *exegesis typically in one place, each giving out its own certificates or *ijazas*, which authorized its students to become teachers in turn.

When the Ottoman Empire disintegrated, the madrasas reacted with a stricter religious schooling. Studies in religion, literature, and Arabic language dominated the curriculum, and teaching consisted mainly of reiterating past knowledge as the authority. In this environment, reforms of Islamic education happened on a national basis. Egypt, for example, embraced Western models of scientific education in the late twentieth century and placed religious education in schools on a secondary footing, with, in 2003, three hours a week spent on religious studies of thirty hours per week in total.

TEACHING THAT IS HARD TO TRACK

Education outside the institutions, such as with tutors or through parents, is harder to track, and we often know about it through personal archives, or by reading court trial records against the grain. Documents about content and the daily how-to of education are scarce, especially where the transmission of knowledge or information was orally or physically administered. We know about healers, for example, mostly because of their conflicts with the law, when they were accused of heresy and brought in front of the law court, because we have the trial documents. Only from the details of these law court documents can we infer how the next generation of healers might have been trained, by word of mouth.

In medieval and early modern times, the experience of diaspora and exile provided a challenge to those concerned in setting and adjusting goals for achievement and teaching. Religious exiles link together the experiences of Muslims, Jews, and Christians of many confessions. Exile communities developed three main strategies: tactics of inclusion to fit into the new environments, often connected with learning a new language; programs to restore their religious and social identities, connected with teaching traditional lore, or in extreme cases teaching the students to become martyrs; and finally, methods of coping with the new realities, for example, dealing with poverty. Teaching plans and institutions followed each of the three directions. Jan Amos Komenský (or Comenius, as he Latinized his name) (1592–1670) had educational ideas that were born out of religious exile. He revolutionized the way to think about education, by formulating a comprehensive philosophy to contextualize and rationalize his goal to teach everything to everybody. He called it *Pansophia*, all-knowledge. As a side product in 1658 he published a textbook for children—*Orbis Sensualium Pictus* (World of the senses in pictures)—that contained diagrammatic pictures on every page explaining daily life and work to young children. By naming the objects and situations drawn out in the pictures, he built up their vocabulary simultaneously (and playfully) in many languages.

A SIGN OF MODERNITY: COMPULSORY EDUCATION

Traditional societies, such as many Indigenous cultures in the nineteenth and twentieth centuries, continued to rely on unwritten or tacit approaches to teach most or all of their children in an unregulated way. But at the same time modern industrialized societies introduced compulsory attendance at schools for pupils up to a certain grade or age, related to the extent of local or territorial government control. With origins in different regions of Europe, more comprehensive laws for both genders came into place after the Reformation; so in 1592 a compulsory school law was introduced for both sexes by the German duchy Palatinate-Zweibrücken. Scotland followed in 1616 with the School Establishing Act, which demanded that schools in every parish of Scotland be established to educate everyone. The parishioners were to pay for them and the church bishops to supervise classes and curriculum (thus leaving decisions about the size and levels of the school to the parish); and in 1647, Massachusetts passed the first compulsory schooling law in America, geared toward a comprehensive system of schools, not individual attendance of pupils. Prussia is usually cited as instituting the first modern compulsory education system, in the years 1763–65, when Frederick the Great signed the decree known as the "Generallandschulreglement." Girls and boys were to go to school from age five to age thirteen or fourteen. By 2018, a large number of the world's nations had adopted the system of compulsory education. Entry age was usually about six years, and exit age varied from eleven (Haiti) to eighteen years in Turkey, Israel, Poland, and Mexico and other industrialized countries. In the United States, the ages varied in 2018 between states, with an entry age of five to seven and an exit age of sixteen to eighteen years. Such requirements have sometimes been met with resistance. The home schooling movement in the United States is one sign of opposition to the mandatory requirements of government.

TEACHING METHODS

Teaching methods based on memorization including visualization of objects and processes, and interactive performance (by participation and by audit), are as old as teaching itself. Some methods focus on drill and on the teacher's role as the focal figure for a group of students, sometimes (as in the Oxford and Cambridge tutorial method) even using a teacher-student ratio of 1:3 to 1:1. Some methods need a peer group, especially methods concerned with emotional intelligence and morals; others, such as many experimental methods, use feedback directly from the outcome of the students' quest: Did the water turn pink when they mixed in the solution? If yes, follow up with the next chemical exercise; if no, go back to the start. In the computer age, algorithms are able to take over parts of the teacher's role to assign and grade or give feedback to exercises that individual students or groups of students take within specific computer programs, and to customize the schedule so it fits the analyzed needs of the student. The *internet educational organization Khan Academy, named after its founder, Salman Khan, uses one of these algorithms for courses in mathematics and a wide range of fields. Students who sign up repeat easy exercises in the subject they want to learn until they can solve them without thinking, and the program decides according to the results what exercise the student should do next. Without reading theory, the student thus learns immediately like a child in trial-and-error manner, one step at a time.

GOALS AND VALUES

Goals and values guided the standards for education. Earlier goals of compulsory education were teaching essential skills for the industrialized society; giving youth social skills and moral values; and bringing "outsiders" into a mold, such as immigrant children, to fit into their new environment. With new considerations of diversity in the age of internet society, providing a melting pot to shape and reeducate all citizens toward similar morals and values seemed unnecessarily restrictive. But to allow students to reject restrictive state regulations, and therefore weaken compulsory education, has the downside that the governmental support for poor families to send their children to school would diminish if regulations were cut.

With new goals of globalization and diversity in mind, as suggested by the information age, the floor would be open to discuss teaching methods and offer gains of knowledge and skills from a standpoint outside the national school system. The new communication skills of computer coding and internet *literacy are valid globally, as is internet etiquette as a basic moral *code, and they call for standardized programs worldwide. The challenge remains to connect international learning programs with nationally or regionally controlled funds and access policy.

Anja-Silvia Goeing

See also algorithms; art of memory; diagrams; digitization; excerpting/commonplacing; globalization; learning; manuals; media; professors; reference books; storage and search

FURTHER READING

Benjamin Elman, *A Cultural History of Modern Science in China*, 2006; Timothy G. Fehler et al., eds., *Religious Diaspora in Early Modern Europe: Strategies of Exile*, 2014; Eric Hilgendorf, "Islamic Education: History and Tendency," *Peabody Journal of Education* 78, no. 2 (2003): 63–75; "International Standard Classification of Education," UNESCO Institute for Statistics, 2012; Sara Lawrence-Lightfoot, *Growing Each Other Up: When Our Children Become Our Teachers*, 2016; Karin J. MacHardy, "Cultural Capital, Family Strategy and Noble Identity in Early Modern Habsburg Austria 1579–1620," *Past and Present* 163 (1999): 36–75; Ebrahim Moosa, *What Is a Madrasa?*, 2015; Timothy Reagan, *Non-Western Educational Traditions: Local Approaches to Thought and Practice*, 4th ed., 2018.

TELECOMMUNICATIONS

For centuries, people and governments have tried to quickly transmit short messages in one direction, using smoke signals, fire towers, tom-toms, flags, and other means. Not until the late eighteenth century were the first effective systems devised that could communicate any message in either direction further than the human voice could carry and faster than a letter could be transported. We call these systems telecommunication, and their modern descendants underwrite our contemporary information infrastructure.

PRE-ELECTRIC TELECOMMUNICATION SYSTEMS

The first effective bidirectional open-ended telecommunication systems were created—and not by coincidence—during the wars of the French Revolution and Napoleon. Two new systems, one on land and the other at sea, arose out of the demands of war and, just as importantly, from the belief that reason and ingenuity could conquer time and distance.

The creator of the first land-based telegraph system was the Frenchman Claude Chappe. It consisted of stations positioned on towers or church steeples a few kilometers apart, each one visible to two others. Each station had a set of boards that could be moved by ropes and pulleys into ninety-eight different positions, each position corresponding to a word or phrase in a *code book. After many attempts, Chappe persuaded the French National Convention to fund his system. Beginning with a line from Paris to Lille built in 1794, the network was extended to all the major cities of France and, under Napoleon, to neighboring countries as well. By the 1840s, the French network consisted of 530 stations covering five thousand kilometers. Spain, England, and Sweden also built lines, most of them between a royal palace and the capital city, but abandoned them when peace came in 1815.

New lines were erected in the 1830s and 1840s. Those built in continental European countries were reserved for administrative and military use. In Britain and the United States, private individuals erected lines to signal the approach of ships or to transmit commercial and financial information. Nowhere were these early telegraph networks open to the public, though the New York and Boston lines did provide users with access to the information they conveyed in return for the payment of an annual fee.

The other pre-electrical telecommunication system was naval flag signaling. For centuries, warships had communicated by hoisting flags and other objects, but such communications involved unidirectional prearranged messages, and were often confusing. During the 1780s and 1790s, several British officers came up with sets of flags and signal books for use during naval maneuvers. Rear Admiral Sir Home Popham's *Telegraphic Signals or Marine Vocabulary*, first issued in 1800, made it possible for ships to communicate with one another and allowed the admiral of a fleet to direct the movements of his ships even during the course of a battle. After several editions, it became the official code of the Royal Navy in 1813. It was followed in 1817 by Captain Frederick Marryat's *Signals for the Use of Vessels Employed in the Merchant Service*. These systems remained in use until the early twentieth century, when they were gradually replaced by radiotelegraphy.

ELECTRIC LANDLINE TELEGRAPHY

Even as the French were building their optical telegraph network, several inventors tried to use electricity to send messages at a distance. The demand for rapid communication, the science and technology of electricity, and the ingenuity of inventors coalesced in 1837–38 with the introduction of two practical and commercially profitable electric telegraph systems.

One of these was created by Charles Wheatstone and William Fothergill Cooke in England in 1837. It consisted of a battery and a set of wires, a board with needles pointing to letters or numbers, and, at the receiving end, another board with needles that moved in response to the positions of the needles on the sending board. This system was rapid and effective and did not require highly trained operators. It proved especially useful for railroad operation and was widely adopted in Great Britain and the British Empire.

In the United States at the same time, Samuel Morse and Alfred Vail presented a system that required only one needle (with the Earth forming the return), a battery and a key (or switch) at the sending end, and an electromagnet and sounding device at the receiving end. The basis of this system was the *Morse code, with electric pulses (dots and dashes) corresponding to letters and numbers. The system was less expensive than Wheatstone and Cooke's, a consideration in the United States where distances were much greater than in Britain, but it required trained operators who could turn written characters into dots and dashes and who could hear the incoming signals and write down the corresponding characters. The Morse system spread quickly. By 1852, telegraph lines covered twenty-three thousand miles throughout the eastern United States. It was also adopted in Europe and around the world. Because it worked at night and in bad weather, the electric telegraph was able to transmit ten times more words per day than the optical telegraph, which it soon replaced. Since it could carry far more messages than governments needed, it was opened to the public and was widely used by merchants, financiers, newspapers, and ordinary people.

Though very fast in comparison to the optical telegraph, the early electrical telegraphs offered many opportunities for improvement. One was to reduce the dependence on operators prone to making mistakes. David Hughes and Emile Baudot introduced keyboards that simplified transmission and devices that printed incoming telegrams. Thomas Edison's quadruplex system allowed four messages to be sent through the same wire simultaneously. Teleprinters, introduced in the 1880s, eliminated the need for operators trained in the Morse code. Telex machines, introduced in the 1930s and sold to businesses, allowed typists to send telegrams to other telex machines without resorting to the telegraph office. Inventors also built various devices to transmit images through telegraph lines. Such facsimile (or "fax") machines remained very complicated until the 1960s, when American and Japanese companies introduced simple and inexpensive machines as household consumer items.

SUBMARINE CABLE TELEGRAPHY

After 1838, landlines spread quickly. In North America, Western Union's lines reached the Mississippi and Ohio Rivers in 1860 and the Pacific coast a year later. By 1900 it operated one million miles of landlines. In other countries, landlines were operated by governments.

Inventors sought to fill the gaps between land masses with telegraph wires laid on the seafloor. To do so, they insulated copper cables from the surrounding water with gutta-percha and protected them by wrapping them with iron wires. The first successful submarine cable, laid across the English Channel in 1851, encouraged entrepreneurs to lay cables across the Mediterranean, down the Red Sea, and, in 1858, across the Atlantic Ocean. All these early cables failed, and it was only in 1866 that a successful cable crossed the North Atlantic and in 1870 that cables connected England and India.

After 1870, cables were laid to Australia, China, and Japan, to South America and the Caribbean, around Africa, and finally across the Pacific Ocean. By 1908, 473,108 kilometers of submarine cables linked every continent and most islands in a global network. Of these, 82 percent were owned by private companies, over half by Eastern and Associated, a British conglomerate.

The global telegraph network played an important part in the great expansion of world trade in the decades before World War I. Until the 1920s, to defray the enormous cost of manufacturing and laying cables, the cable companies set their rates so high that only governments, news agencies, and businesses could afford to send intercontinental messages. The British dominance of the world's cables also rankled rival nations, first France and Germany, and later the United States, leading them to lay their own cables and, in the early twentieth century, to invest in radiotelegraphy. Nonetheless, copper submarine cables remained in use until the 1960s, for they were more secure than radio, especially in wartime, when radio signals could be intercepted, but cables could not.

TELEPHONY TO THE 1960S

No sooner did the electric telegraph become practical than inventors sought ways of transmitting sound through wires. The first person to obtain a patent for an instrument that transformed a human voice into electricity and back again, albeit only over short distances, was Alexander Graham Bell, in 1876. Improvements followed rapidly. Thomas Edison's carbon microphone, invented in 1878, permitted sound to be carried over much longer distances. That year also saw the introduction of the telephone exchange with a switchboard that allowed an operator to connect any two subscribers. Telephony spread rapidly in the United States as operating companies were licensed by the Bell Telephone Company, which had been founded to commercialize the patents held by Alexander Graham Bell. As more telephones were installed, the number of possible connections rose exponentially, greatly increasing the demand for switchboard operators. To expand the market, Bell managers in the 1890s experimented with innovative calling plans (including "measured service" and pay-as-you-go telephones), sophisticated operator-assisted switchboards, and elaborate advertising campaigns. As a result of these innovations, telephones proliferated. By 1904 the United States had over three million telephone subscribers.

Telephony had social and cultural consequences. Unlike telegraphs, telephones were designed to be used in homes as well as offices. In most families that could afford a telephone, women stayed home when their husbands went to work. Though businessmen and telephone company executives complained that housewives clogged the lines with useless chatter, in fact it was office boys crowding the lines to gamble, gossip, or discuss the latest baseball scores who posed the biggest problems in the early days at the most highly congested big-city exchanges. However, the telephone did also allow housebound women to reach out to one another and form networks of friends more easily than before. Later, as phones proliferated, teenagers also took advantage of the new technology to stay in touch.

After two of Bell's most important patents expired in 1893–94, numerous companies with no connection to Bell sprang up to provide service in local areas, and, in some instances, entire regions. Some of these companies relied on rotary dial phones and the Strowger automatic telephone exchange—inventions that had yet to be introduced by Bell. Bell would eventually acquire many of these local companies, though thousands would remain in existence for decades. Bell's long-distance subsidiary, the American Telephone and Telegraph Company (later AT&T) put up lines that reached from New York to Chicago in 1892 and to San Francisco in 1915. By the First World War, the Bell-AT&T combine would become the dominant telephone network provider in the United States. European nations, burdened by government-owned telegraph networks, lagged far behind.

Though long-distance telephone became a reality early on thanks to repeaters along the major trunk lines, crossing oceans was a greater challenge. After World War II, cable companies developed repeaters that could be installed along a submerged cable and that permitted the transmission of voice as well as dots and dashes. Several copper-core telephone-and-telegraph cables were laid across the Atlantic between 1955–56 and 1978 and across the Pacific in 1964 and after. They were soon made obsolete, however.

RADIO TELEGRAPHY AND TELEPHONY

Unlike telegraphy, which was born in a time of war and was later improved by scientific discoveries in electricity, radio arose from scientific researches in electromagnetism and was later developed to serve both commerce and warfare.

Guglielmo Marconi is rightly praised as the inventor of radio, but he based his invention on several major discoveries, especially the electromagnetic theory of light by James Clerk Maxwell and the demonstration thereof by Heinrich Hertz. What Marconi did was use electromagnetic waves to transmit information in code. His invention closed the gap in telegraphic communication, namely with ships at sea. After moving to England in 1896 and patenting his invention, he quickly attracted the attention of the British Admiralty, of major shipping lines, and of the maritime insurer Lloyd's of London.

Marconi's success soon bred competitors and stimulated further technological advances. Inventors knew that radio waves could bend around obstacles, yet reaching around the curvature of the earth, for instance, across the Atlantic Ocean, would require very long radio waves produced by extremely powerful transmitters and emitted by enormous antennas. By 1907 Marconi had achieved that goal and was able to compete with the cable companies for transatlantic traffic.

Meanwhile, others sought to overcome a flaw in the Marconi system—namely, the radio waves produced by sparks that sounded like the static emitted by lightning. Several inventions—the alternator, the electric arc, and the vacuum tube—produced continuous, that is, pure, waves. In 1906, using an alternator, Reginald Fessenden was able to transmit the human voice. The first transatlantic telephone conversation became possible nine years later, albeit at enormous expense.

As companies competed to build ever more powerful long-distance stations transmitting kilometric waves (that is, up to 300 kHz), they left shorter wavelengths to amateurs to play with. After World War I, using the newly invented vacuum tubes, amateurs found they could communicate around the world, though too erratically and unreliably for commercial use.

While experimenting with waves as short as ten meters (up to 30 MHz), Marconi and others discovered three important features: with parabolic antennas, such waves could be concentrated in a "beam" rather than being scattered in all directions; although they traveled in a straight line, they were reflected off the ionosphere, hence could bounce around the world at certain times of day; and, most importantly, their equipment cost one-twentieth as much to build and operate as long-wave stations. From the mid-1920s on, shortwave wireless began to replace the enormous and costly long-wave systems and even telegraph cables. From then on, shortwave radio became ubiquitous around the world, even in airplanes.

THE POSTWAR TELECOMMUNICATIONS REVOLUTION

Since World War II, telecommunications have been transformed as radically as they had been by the introduction of electricity in the nineteenth century. Several innovations combined to make telecommunication rapid, global, and inexpensive. In this section we will consider three innovations: microwaves, satellites, and fiber optics.

Microwaves, that is, very short waves (between one meter or 300 MHz and one millimeter or 300 GHz), were first produced in the 1930s. These waves travel in straight lines, even through clouds and fog, but are reflected by most solid objects. Hence they were first applied to radar installations used to detect enemy airplanes during World War II. Starting in the 1950s, strings of towers were erected between cities, for microwaves could transmit telephone calls and television programs much more cheaply than cables could. Later, they were used to communicate with satellites.

The idea of launching artificial satellites dates back to the nineteenth century. Only in the 1950s were rockets available that could put a human-made object into orbit, the first being the Soviet Sputnik in 1957. The first direct communication satellites were launched in 1962–63; by 2000, there were over two thousand of them. We can distinguish three distinct types. Low Earth Orbit (or LEO) satellites, orbiting between 160 and 2,000 kilometers above the Earth, are inexpensive to put into orbit but move fast relative to the surface of the Earth and therefore need to be numerous and communicate with costly tracking stations. Medium Earth Orbit (MEO) satellites, between 2,000 and 35,786 kilometers above the Earth, move more slowly relative to the surface but cover a larger area. And Geostationary Earth Orbit (GEO) satellites remain directly 35,786 kilometers above a fixed point on the planet. For a time GEOs were used for transoceanic telephone calls but suffered from annoying delays while signals traveled up to a satellite and down again. Since the 1990s they have been used mostly to beam television programs.

The third innovation is fiber-optic cables. Not only does light travel faster than an electric current, but it can also carry much more information. The challenge was to confine a light beam in a strand of glass that could carry it around corners and over long distances without scattering or fading. The first cables encasing a strand of super-pure glass were developed in the 1970s. By the late 1980s, the technology of fibers and repeaters had advanced sufficiently for companies to lay cables between distant cities and across oceans. The first transatlantic fiber-optic cable, TAT-8, laid in 1988, was capable of carrying forty thousand simultaneous telephone conversations. The world's cable network reached 250,000 kilometers of cables by 2002 and has been growing ever since. Today, the cost of communicating between any two places on Earth is almost insignificant; what costs is switching and administrative expenses.

Making these innovations possible, indeed tying them together, is the *digital revolution, which allows any medium to be digitized and processed by computers. The *internet, with which computers everywhere communicate with one another, can therefore carry all types of information: voice, data, images, and video. With satellites and fiber-optic cables, the internet now reaches almost every place on Earth that governments allow.

MOBILE TELEPHONY

All the technologies described in the previous section belong to infrastructures of which most customers are unaware. In the 1980s came a new consumer device, the most revolutionary since the invention of the telephone: the mobile or cellular phone.

Inventors and companies had long been interested in detaching the telephone from its wire. Portable two-way radios ("walkie-talkies") became available after World War II, but they were heavy and expensive and had a limited range, and the radio networks that served them could handle only a few calls at once; they were used mainly by the military and by police and public works departments. These restrictions were lifted in 1979 when the Nippon Telephone and Telegraph Company introduced a cellular network in which a radiotelephone automatically switched from one transmitter to another as the user moved around. As improvements made handheld devices cheaper, faster, and more versatile, mobile telephony quickly spread around the world. Mobile networks were so much easier and cheaper to build than landlines that they penetrated even into the poorest countries. By 2014, there were eighty-five mobile telephones per one hundred inhabitants in the developed countries, and thirty per one hundred in the poorer countries of the world.

Meanwhile, mobile telephones morphed into smart phones. These handheld devices combined mobile telephones, text messenger devices, GPS devices, clocks, cameras, video games, internet-accessible computers, and dozens of other features. The first full-featured smart phone, the Apple iPhone introduced in 2007, was soon followed by many others. Smart phones became one of the most popular inventions in history, with 1.2 billion sold in 2014 alone. They allowed people not only to communicate, but to find their way, play games, check up on their "friends," send texts and emails, shop online, and stay entertained around the clock, even while walking down the street, eating lunch, or driving a car. They are the indispensable tool of modern life.

CONCLUSION

The innovations introduced since World War II have made telecommunication faster, cheaper, and more ubiquitous, especially over long distances. The promise of the telegraph in the nineteenth century, that it would overcome time and distance, has now been achieved, or soon will be, for most of the world's people. But telecommunication has gone far beyond transmitting messages from point to point. As costs plummet, it is bringing information of all kinds, in almost infinite quantities, within reach of almost everyone, subject only to political restrictions. How the relations between politics and information will play out is an issue for future generations to resolve.

Daniel R. Headrick

See also commodification; digitization; encrypting/decrypting; globalization; networks

FURTHER READING

Claude S. Fischer, *America Calling: A Social History of the Telephone to 1940*, 1992; Daniel R. Headrick, *When Information Came of Age: Technologies of Knowledge in the Age of Reason and Revolution, 1700–1850*, 2000; Peter J. Hugill, *Global Communications since 1844: Geopolitics and Technology*, 1999; Richard R. John, *Network Nation: Inventing American Telecommunications*, 2010; Robert MacDougall, *The People's Network: The Political Economy of the Telephone in the Gilded Age*, 2013; Simone M. Müller, *Wiring the World: The Social and Cultural Creation of Global Telegraph Networks*, 2016; Heidi J. S. Tworek, *News from Germany: The Competition to Control World Communications, 1900–1945*, 2019; Dwayne R. Winseck and Robert M. Pike, *Communication and Empire: Media, Markets, and Globalization, 1860–1930*, 2007.

TRANSLATING

Long before Google Translate enabled anyone with an *internet connection to take words from one language and—with little more than a click—translate them into another, translation as a practice was one of the fundamental building blocks for making information intelligible and useful for diverse communities the world over. From religious texts meant to be read aloud in community worship to histories designed to make foreign communities comprehensible (or inimical) in an age of increased commerce between nations, translations before the modern age were achieved with tremendous effort and scrupulous attention to their ultimate effects. Within Europe and the Euro-American world, these translations have come to represent one of the most complete archives of the spread of information about events of significance in the *early modern period.

Translation, however, was never a neutral practice; indeed, it was regularly carried out with ideological overtones as well as pragmatic aspirations. The gradual, often violent, process by which a European presence grew in the Americas made coming to terms with the cultures and knowledge found in the New World particularly essential. The readers of these first accounts—and those who were subjected to their discourse—required much more than mere translation to understand the impact of a powerful clash between worlds and cultures. But textual translations often worked to justify ideological exertions of power and to soften the blow, at least in theory. Rather than focusing on translations in all places and under all circumstances, this entry will focus on a series of interventions made in the context of the early Americas—an important sphere for transimperial translations—with an eye toward showing not only how Europeans translated phenomena they encountered there but also how the American experience—including that of Indigenous and Creole populations—transformed European understanding into new idioms.

A first distinction about translations in an age of early modern information exchange is the form in which the "original" information was held and how in turn—and into what—it was eventually transformed. Turning back to the original Latin meaning of *translation* (*trans-lat,* "to carry across"), it is important to recognize that carrying information across a boundary, from one medium to another, could occur in a variety of contexts and across a multiplicity of boundary types, each of which had the potential to transform the ultimate message or information received. Whether in the form of oral communication (whereby the translator or go-between would be the boundary affecting the communication) or in the form of physical or textual formats, messages might often be fluid and dynamic as they passed across linguistic, geographic, and ideological borders. This was as much the case when what was being discussed related to ideas about the natural world—where the purported veracity of the observations being made by on-the-spot naturalists and local populations was subjected to scrutiny by narrators (in different languages) and translators alike—as it was in the context of religious persuasion and proselytization, especially common for the temporal and geographical context that this article will examine: the early modern Americas.

A second distinction, related to the first, is understanding the materiality of translation. What material tools and skills were utilized to undergird the textual translation process, and how did these materials impact the ultimate form such processes took? How did scribes with their pens play a role alongside printers and interpreters? How in turn can we think of material objects that change their meanings as they circulated between worlds? In the context of early modern natural history, objects that traveled from one site to another often did so as containers of information that would adapt to the different circumstances in which they found themselves. Amulets and beads that had one purpose in Africa found themselves being used for radically different purposes once they arrived in the Caribbean, in Brazil, and in the Andes. Being attuned to these different contexts—and the fluidity that existed between textual and material formats—can open up the broad meanings of translation as a tool for information exchange.

A third and final distinction in understanding translation in an age of information exchange relates to the ideology of translation, and how a particular subject may affect the circumstances of its own transmission. Do all topics translate—and travel—as effectively as others? What makes a good translation and how do particular actors in the translation process negotiate complicated topics in the process? Translation in the context of colonial expansion or violence, for instance, quickly loses the lofty idealism that Walter Benjamin and others may have ascribed to its practice. In a colonial setting, translation sooner becomes the handmaiden of a zealous observer in search of the required conquest rather than a poetic aspiration through which an original text is preserved and even uplifted. Much translation in the early modern shadow of European colonial administration is prosaic and perfunctory, meant to describe what are doubtless already caricatures of objectified populations, bloated by the crude language that proclaimed the superiority of European perspectives over those of native views. Given the absence of many contemporaneous (printed) accounts, one side of the cultural equation was often left silent in the information wars that ensued (the *requerimiento*, discussed below, is an excellent example of this process).

To provide focus to this short article, we will examine in particular the long history of translation for an event that was recognized at the time as one of the most significant in human history: the arrival of Europeans in the Americas and the complex series of processes that transpired in its wake. In the sixteenth century Lopéz de Gómara referred to the discovery of the New World as "the greatest event which has happened since the creation of the world," while in the eighteenth Abbé Raynal considered the arrival of Europeans in the Indies to be one of the most significant events "for the human species in general and for the peoples of Europe in particular." Even Abraham Lincoln was inspired to put the discovery of America before the advent of print in world-historical significance. But prior to turning to one of the most iconic texts of the New World expansion by Europeans, we begin with the role of African interpreters in early Portuguese Atlantic exploration, which would eventually lead to the multigenerational phenomenon that got going well before Columbus's arrival in the New World known as the Atlantic slave trade.

Simply put, the process by which African men and women were sold into captivity and later brought across the Atlantic to work in New World plantations would have been unthinkable without the process of translation: African interpreters were used by the Portuguese—and later by others—to facilitate the operations of an economy that relied on captive Black bodies sold into servitude. As early as the mid-fifteenth century, Alvise Cadamosto made reference to African interpreters along the West African coast who had been brought to Portugal by early expeditions, and who then participated as shipboard translators for further voyages. These opportunities continued to increase along the coast as European empires made inroads in the slave trade and required more intermediaries to assist them at the outset of the slave trading cycle. Interpreters were also of great significance on slaving ships that plied the middle passage: according to a 2003 *Anthropological Linguistics* article by Joan M. Fayer, they were useful in "calming the newly purchased slaves, giving information and commands from the captain and crew, and preventing and suppressing insurrections."

For the "Enterprise of the Indies," one document symbolizes communication across global borders more notoriously than any other: the letter Christopher Columbus wrote in 1493 describing his discoveries of a set of "Indian Islands" newly encountered beyond the Ganges ("De Insulis Indie supra Gangem nuper inventis"). This letter serves as a paradigmatic example—in many ways, *the* paradigmatic early modern example—of how the arrival of Europeans to what were new worlds for them, and the near-contemporaneous spread of printing press technology in Europe, led to an explosion of editions and translations that recast European knowledge about the shape of the globe and its inhabitants, in the Western Hemisphere and beyond.

Columbus's initial letter in the Spanish language to Luis de Santangel, published in Barcelona on February 15, 1493, and preserved in a single copy at the New York Public Library, was produced in order to describe the extraordinary islands Columbus had come across in the Indies to one of his principal funders (in addition to King Ferdinand and Queen Isabella themselves, for whom Santangel worked). This initial letter—and the translation fervor it set off in its wake—represents one of the most significant translations of an experience the world had seen until that point: the attempt to describe a geographical phenomenon, and resident populations, that another part of the world had not acknowledged to exist. The letter is also significant in that Columbus struggled with how to express to his distant audiences the extraordinary differences he found in the islands he had discovered: "[The island of] La Española is marvelous [*una maravilla*]: the hills and mountains and the valleys and the fields and such beautiful and abundant lands to plant and harvest, to raise cattle of all kinds, for the construction of towns and sites." The hyperbolic language he used was in and of itself a strategy of translation: by emphasizing the marvelous landscapes and their potential for transforming a New World terrain into "lands to plant" and "sites to construct," Columbus was reaching into his own linguistic arsenal to make faraway readers understand what he had seen in person.

Soon after the appearance of Columbus's letter to Santangel, the first translation (Rome, 1493, in Latin) went through a series of contemporaneous Latin printings—first in Paris (1493), later in Basel (1494), and eventually in other editions as well. The Paris edition of 1493 also included woodblock images, another way in which early modern printed matter sought to make New World landscapes familiar to Old World readers. Indeed, the idiom that woodblock printers used relied quite often on the use and reuse of stock images, which took on new meanings as the texts that they accompanied changed around them. The iconic images of the *Nuremberg Chronicle*, also published in

1493, brought large-footed giants and curious demonic persons into the conceptual vocabulary of the early modern reader. In the wake of the Latin texts, the Columbus letter
was translated to other languages, and the Indies as a global concept was born. It became clear that the West Indies was a new geographical reality that would give rise to
new projects of colonization and cultural expansion, just as Raynal would claim three
centuries later. Following these initial Latin printings, the letter began making its way
into European *vernaculars. In 1497, for instance, the German text "Eyn schön hübsch
Lesen von etlichen Insslen die do in kurtzen Zyten funden synd durch de[n] Künig von
Hispania" (A very nice account of some islands that were recently found by the king of
Spain) was printed in Strasbourg, containing not only an edited version of Columbus's
original Latin text but a woodcut on the title page that shows a Christ-like Columbus
with his apostles in European garb.

While European presses began to churn out multiple translations of these initial—
and largely iconic—texts, European invaders, missionaries, and colonizers sought to employ translation as a weapon to enforce submission and conversion. And the silence of
translation in these processes—or, indeed, its absence—could be just as potent as its
presence. During the reading of the *Requerimiento*, a document that required native
populations in the Caribbean either to submit to the tenets of Christianity and salvation or to resist and be punished in this world and the next, there was little attempt to
translate into vernacular languages. The arriving Spaniards, who sought to claim both
terrestrial and spiritual sovereignty over these subject peoples, made no effort to provide a clear translation for those populations whose land and title were being stolen
from them. While the complexity of these situations of cross-cultural persuasion has
been underscored by recent scholarship, the requerimiento as a phenomenon still depended fundamentally on a translation that was utterly unintelligible to the audience
in question.

These attempts at forced adherence through translation—translation without comprehension by the local communities—gave way to a more serious attempt to translate
European conceptions into American vernacular forms. The evangelization campaigns
of newly arrived friars in Mexico and elsewhere brought sophisticated dictionary, vocabulary, and *catechism projects into being, including the first dictionary printed in
the Americas: the 1555 Nahuatl-Spanish dictionary by the Franciscan Alonso de Mo-
lina. Such masterworks of transcription and compilation not only enabled religious
agents to search for analogous terms in the vernacular languages of central Mexico;
they also became *lexicons of native knowledge systems at the time of the Spanish conquest and as such serve today as tools for understanding how Indigenous cultural and
intellectual concepts came to be co-opted and transformed through European idioms.

While efforts at religious proselytization generated translation projects in order to
write catechisms and other doctrinal texts in native tongues, another project begun a
few decades after the publication of Columbus's letter and the earliest use of the requerimiento led to a translation project in reverse. Rather than describing the triumphant tales of the European conquistadors to unwitting Indigenous audiences, or using
Indigenous languages to enable proselytization through dictionaries and vocabularies,
the Friar Bernardino de Sahagún worked to translate the customs and beliefs of the native Mexicans—known as Mexica—from their native language of Nahuatl into Spanish
for other purposes. The Florentine Codex—so-named for its having been preserved since

the 1790s in the Biblioteca Medicea-Laurenziana in Florence—was the fruit of a process of European and Indigenous collaboration at the Royal College of Santa Cruz in Tlatelolco (Mexico City). In a series of twelve books ranging from the origin of the Mexica gods to astronomical observations, Sahagún coordinated an ambitious effort alongside other Franciscan friars and their native counterparts to encapsulate what he called *General History of the Things of New Spain* (completed ca. 1577). Conscious of the fact that "this history . . . was written at a time when those who took part in the [Spanish] Conquest were alive," Sahagún set out to capture the terms and terminology that were known and used by "those who were conquered," emphasizing the lack of awareness that the invading Spaniards had of those whose cultures and societies they had sought to destroy. "I desired to write [the history] in the Mexican language . . . in order that the terms and proper modes of expression for speaking on this subject in the Mexican language can be derived therefrom." Part of this translation was performed through graphic images—a gesture toward the distinctive nontextual languages by which the Mexica had for generations expressed their cultural norms. Chapter 11, on animals, used a visual discourse to express features of the Mexica cultural universe, especially the way in which animals—and the central figure, Huitzilopochtli, which often appeared in the form of a hummingbird—interrelated with human activities in the larger *encyclopedic context that the *codex represented.

Translation and compilation often went hand in hand, especially as translation and transcription projects sought to bring together not only descriptions but also artifacts that had been collected across myriad contexts in the Americas. From the colossal natural historical project of Francisco de Hernandez in New Spain to Georg Marggraf and Willem Piso's *Historia Naturalis Brasiliae* (Natural history of Brazil, printed in Leiden in 1648), greater efforts were made to bring together natural knowledge of the Americas across geographic boundaries, and translation projects sought to unify natural knowledge under one tome. Marggraf and Piso's *Historia* accumulated materials in a far more complex way than even Hernandez's text allowed for, especially as the articulation of natural historical objects came to draw not only on descriptions that were made from other texts—translated into Latin and represented succinctly by both naturalists—but also on the Indigenous populations of northeastern Brazil in their central role as participants in the *palimpsest that was created through their work. Thus, translation came to function as one component of a larger project that was weaving together cultural and scientific practices of local populations with firsthand observations by passing travelers and philosophical prose from European academies, who were increasingly seeing themselves as arbiters of value in a transatlantic conversation about the role of imperial powers in managing interactions on an increasingly global scale.

As the fervor to compile and consolidate overtook more and more authors in the wake of the eighteenth-century *Encyclopédie*, and descriptions of the Indies became more and more geared toward a general audience, the range of activities described in multivolume accounts of European colonization and conquest of the Americas—from the political to the philosophical—increased as well. The culminating account was undoubtedly Guillaume Thomas François Raynal's *Histoire philosophique et politique, des établissemens & du commerce des Européens dans les deux Indes* published initially in Amsterdam in 1770 (in six volumes). Although there were many authors who contributed to the multivolume endeavor (including Denis Diderot), Abbé Raynal could not have achieved what he did without translating many sections of his account from other texts that described parts of the world that had been subjected to European empires over time. Nearly thirty years after the initial publication, in 1798, a ten-volume London edition of Raynal's *Deux Indes* was published under the title *A Philosophical and Political History of the Settlements and Trade of the Europeans in the East and West Indies*, with a clear indication on the title page that this edition was "revised and augmented" from the original. In the "Advertisement of the Translator," William Thomas emphasized that "the translation is . . . almost totally a new work," owing to the new (currency) calculations as well as a series of new maps, including seven maps of the world, Europe, Africa (with European settlements), "one of the European settlements in the East Indies," and similar quantities for South America, Mexico and the West Indies. A final new map contained documents on the United States of North America, with adjoining dominions of Britain, France, and Spain "according to the treaty of 1783." As is evident, the creation of a new translation (into English) and the inclusion of new peripheral materials—including maps and other prefatory remarks—were understood as functioning on the same level. That is, they were both providers of information in digestible form, aiding the eventual readers to see and understand the landscape of what had gone before. The similarities between these tomes and those that had been published nearly three decades earlier were enough to bind the two editions together but were not sufficient to preclude Thomas from proclaiming their distinction.

Only a few years later, the process of translating New World nature—and the world's nature for the New World—would come to an elegant close for the Luso-Brazilian world with the founding of the Arco do Cego Printing House, a two-year intensive publication effort designed to provide Portuguese agents across the broader Portuguese world—including Africa, Asia, and Brazil—with the pragmatic tools they needed to bring order and prosperity to certain colonial projects that had yet to fill the coffers of the monarchy. During the three years of its brief existence, from 1799 to 1801, the Arco do Cego produced a wide range of texts, published under the auspices of the Portuguese minister of overseas and naval affairs, Dom Rodrigo de Sousa Coutinho. Texts were produced on the acclimatization of new species, maritime commerce, and works of a nautical nature, all of which served to legitimate the publication project as part of the minister's dossier. But the texts published by the Arco do Cego also included treatises on pasigraphy (which were systems of writing meant to be intelligible to speakers of any language, like mathematics) and translated treatises on the blanching of fabrics. What the diversity of texts produced at the Arco do Cego shows is the multiplicity of uses to which translation was put at the end of the eighteenth century, and the high hopes that imperial agents and monarchs alike had for how it could transform economies and political dynamics from the metropole to the farthest shore of the empire.

More broadly, it is clear that translations were a fundamental part of Europe's long engagement with the New World across several centuries, and that different objects and different communities became integrated into the historical record in distinctive ways based not only on the translator employed but on the nature of the political, cultural, or intellectual context being translated. What is distinctive about the broader American context discussed in this short essay is that the economic and political stakes were always at the fore when Europeans sought to make sense—often in the vernacular—of phenomena that they witnessed either firsthand or through their agents. The sheer diversity of translated documents and translated experiences make it difficult to draw any overarching conclusion. But what remains is a spectacular corpus of books and other materials that were made intelligible to broad communities through their translators, even if the empires they represented did not always see their image shining brightly in the lucid light of different idioms.

In many ways, translated idioms are part and parcel of the interconnected virtual world we live in today. With the flip of a switch, websites appear in different languages to facilitate comprehension across a wide range of readerships, often to great—and by and large positive—effect. But the disclaimers that accompany this translated information as new words and phrases flash on our screens—including messages such as "Google Translate cannot translate all types of documents, and may not provide an exact translation," or even "Anyone relying on information obtained from Google Translate does so at his or her own risk"—remind us that the early modern adage of translation as betrayal has not gone away entirely; it has merely shifted forms, transmuted into a graphic medium where pop-up windows and predictive text are the new normal. Studying the early modern origins of our contemporary translational dilemmas may help us to understand the challenges we face today as we communicate in so many mediums that were foreign to our forebears. But it also helps us to appreciate the simple but essential challenge in our cosmopolitan age of finding words in other languages that express our most common thoughts—and doing so preferably with élan and not ennui.

Neil Safier

See also ethnography; knowledge; letters; maps; observing; printed visuals; publicity/ publication; scribes; travel; xylography

FURTHER READING

Jaime Marroquín Arredondo and Ralph Bauer, eds., *Translating Nature: Cross-Cultural Histories of Early Modern Science*, 2019; Harold J. Cook and Sven Dupré, *Translating Knowledge in the Early Modern Low Countries*, 2012; "Focus Section: Historians of Science Translating the History of Science," *Isis* 109 (December 2018): 4; "Focus Section: Translating Science over Time," *Isis* 109 (June 2018): 2; Niall Hodson Fransen and Karl A. E. Enenkel, eds., *Translating Early Modern Science*, 2017; Patrick Manning and Abigail Owen, eds., *Knowledge in Translation: Global Patterns of Scientific Exchange, 1000–1800 CE*, 2018; Karen Newman and Jane Tylus, eds., *Early Modern Cultures of Translation*, 2015; E. Nathalie Rothman, *Brokering Empire: Trans-imperial Subjects between Venice and Istanbul*, 2011.

TRAVEL

Travel is commonly defined as the movement of people from one place to another. Migrations, warring expeditions, tourism, to give but a few examples, are all forms of travel. Historians pose a variety of questions about these movements, regarding issues such as motivations and aims, center versus periphery, the scale of distances covered, or the means of travel. Throughout most of human history major movements of individuals, groups, and whole peoples often went unrecorded, or minimally so, beginning with our species' foundational story, the "Out of Africa" theory of human dissemination. When, however, we consider the more specific nexus of travel and information, as this essay will do, a new set of definitions, both narrower and broader, is required. Narrower, in the sense that it would be more useful for our purposes to consider not just any human movement, but particular forms of travel that are meaningfully linked to information, such as travels that are recorded, by either the traveler or others, travels intended to gather specific information, or travels that provide the basis for other studies. Historians have for long mined travel accounts in order to reconstruct the geographical history of various regions and past cultures, languages, and economies. We require broader definitions, too, because travel and information are related to a wide range of historical phenomena that do not necessarily require physical human movement: vicarious and spiritual travel, and travel as an organizing conceptual form, for example. Moreover, information itself travels and is shaped by the spatiotemporal conditions of movement. The technologies of the late nineteenth century, which freed information from human movement, will not be addressed here.

FACT COLLECTION AND POWER

The first theme for discussion will be travel in the context of politics, power, and information gathering. A few paradigmatic ancient examples can help us sketch the main factors at play. The first example provides a biblical model for an official *fact-finding mission and its troublesome reception. Following God's command, Moses, leading the Israelites in the desert, sent twelve prominent men "to spy out the land of Canaan." Their task was to "see the land" and, following a questionnaire, bring back detailed information about its natural and human conditions. The spies searched Canaan and returned after forty days, bringing with them a sample of fruits. They reported back to Moses and the people and could confirm God's word about the fertility of the land. They were divided, however, in their recommendations for action against the strong peoples they had met. The majority view, based on an exaggerated, "evil report," doubted the Israelites' ability to overcome the "men of great stature" of Canaan.

The second ancient example continues the theme of the interpretation of travelers' information. In the second century CE, the Alexandrian scholar Claudius Ptolemy wrote a guide to geography and mapmaking, known as the *Geography*. In his theoretical introductory chapters, Ptolemy evaluated travel accounts as a source for accurate data. The mathematical geographer, he wrote, had to reduce distances reported by travelers on land and sea because they never followed straight lines. Moreover, Ptolemy claimed, astronomical data always surpassed travelers' estimations. Short distances on a common, often traveled route should be trusted. Another basic rule Ptolemy set down was that "it is necessary to follow in general the latest reports that we possess, while being on guard for what is and is not plausible in both the exposition of current research and the criticism of earlier researches." In other words, Ptolemy demonstrates the role of travel as a source of information for the production of theoretical knowledge at a centralized institution.

While these two ancient models are far from exhaustive, they enable an overview of the many meaningful resonances between travel and information. Although I will concentrate on travel in or after the late medieval period, informational travel and doubts over travel data also occurred in earlier periods.

Governments and imperial centers were deeply dependent on information gathered in remote provinces and regions under their rule, or that they aspired to conquer. For example, the Spanish crown in the age of westward expansion and colonization was acutely aware of the need to collect and protect information about new lands, commodities, and routes. In 1503, Spain established the Casa de la Contratación, which was tasked with regulating navigation and trade with the New World. Officials in the Casa interviewed returning pilots and sailors and established the secretive *padrón real*, the official route chart. Besides the collection and redistribution of empirical data, the Casa was, uniquely, a stage for encounters between practitioners and theoreticians, or seamen and cosmographers. The Casa was thus in charge not only of the handling and processing of navigational data, but also of regulating sailing methods and scientific knowledge. Later in the sixteenth century, the cosmographer of the Council of the Indies, López de Velasco, sent the Spanish officials in the colonies the *Relaciones Geográficas* (Geographical Accounts) (1578–84), a detailed administrative questionnaire, in order to systematically accumulate data regarding topography, vegetation, demography, political organization, and much more. Some of the maps that he received had noticeable Amerindian influence, drawn perhaps by locals.

Early Ming China, too, had expansionist ambitions and sponsored major maritime expeditions commanded by the eunuch admiral Zheng He (1371–1433). The Chinese fleets sailed toward South Asia and East Africa, subduing pirates and creating a network of tributary rulers. Some members of these expeditions recorded their progress and provided ethnographic descriptions as well as geographical directions for future sailings. Later Chinese travelers left records of their journeys in areas such as Java and Taiwan, covering climate, flora, and fauna, and with ethnographical notes.

The republic of Venice is famous for its institutionalized system of political reportage. In addition to daily and weekly correspondence, Venetian governors (*rettori*) and ambassadors were required, upon the end of their tenure, to provide the central government with detailed reports (*relazioni*) about the regions and cities they had served in. These relazioni, which regularly contained also geographical and ethnographical materials, often circulated in manuscript and print and were in high demand by a curious reading public. In the nineteenth century, Venetian ambassadorial relazioni were collected and edited in print and became a favorite source for political historians. Leopold von Ranke, for example, purchased manuscript relazioni collections in Venice and treasured them (wrongly) as unbiased sources.

*Early modern Catholic missions were quick to follow and even go beyond European political expansion. Such ventures depended on an elaborate system of correspondence between center and periphery. The *Society of Jesus, in particular, developed a mandatory and highly regularized information network, which channeled reports and correspondence from across the globe up the organizational hierarchy, and then redistributed them. Letters, reports, instructions, edifying news, and objects traveled up and down the global Jesuit administrative and educational network and became a hallmark of Jesuit identity. Jesuits were not ordinary travelers, because they stayed for extended periods in remote regions, and tried, moreover, to familiarize themselves with local customs and languages (e.g., Alexandre de Rhodes in seventeenth-century Vietnam). Many had learned interests, which they viewed as serving, first, their Christian mission, but also the broader *Republic of Letters in Europe. For example, in the early eighteenth century the superior of the Jesuit Cairo mission, Claude Sicard, mapped biblical and contemporary Egypt.

In his scientific utopia *The New Atlantis* (published posthumously in 1626), Francis Bacon described a model society based on a highly regulated economy of knowledge. One of its secrets and keys to success was a system of industrial espionage, whereby twelve "merchants of light" sailed into other countries in disguise and brought back valuable information. Indeed, scientific societies, which emerged across Europe throughout the seventeenth century, were deeply involved with travel and correspondence with travelers. In 1666, a short essay titled "General Heads for a Natural History of a Countrey, Great or Small" was published under Robert Boyle's name in the young Royal Society's *Philosophical Transactions*. The Royal Society continued to publish such lists of inquiries and queries, which then inspired a range of more popular publications in England and Europe. These questionnaires, following Baconian ideals of data collection under "heads," listed the necessary items for establishing a proper natural history of a place: longitude and latitude, waters, topography and size, population, local traditions and skills, and so on. For Boyle, Henry Oldenburg, and other fellows of the Royal Society, travelers had to be properly instructed about useful observation, which would then generate true empirical (natural historical) and theoretical (natural philosophical) knowledge. These questionnaires demonstrate the tension already disclosed in Ptolemy's attitude to travel reports, as a source that was at once indispensable and suspect.

In the eighteenth century, the Royal Society and other learned organizations (together with the state and the military) became more directly involved in the planning and sponsorship of specific scientific missions. Such was the French expedition to (current-day) Ecuador, which was sent in 1735 to determine the roundness of the Earth, sponsored by the Académie des sciences and Louis XV. In 1768 the first of three expeditions under James Cook's command, sponsored by the Royal Society and the navy, left England in order to observe the transit of Venus in the Pacific. On board were an astronomer and a botanist. The increased involvement of the government in such focused missions was matched by a growing press coverage of such initiatives. The Danish Arabia mission (1761–67), sponsored by Frederik V, aimed to explore biblical landscapes in their natural and historical settings. The only survivor of the scientific crew, the German Carsten Niebuhr, was able to publish his travels and findings after his return. The Danish expedition was eclipsed in scale and scope by Napoleon's military-scientific conquest of Egypt (1798–1801), which included around 150 scholars. The mission was justified by the idea that modern France, in the name of reason and science, had a right to their birthplace, ancient Egypt. The failed military expedition resulted in the multivolume *Description de l'Égypte* (Account of Egypt) (1809–29), covering areas such as astronomy, zoology, anthropology, commerce, and cartography, to mention only a few. Its publication proved a complex and lengthy process, which required the establishment of an official commission. The nineteenth and early twentieth centuries saw a significant proliferation of scientific expeditions, spurred by a mixture of blatant colonial, economic, and religious motivations. For example, the various searches for the sources of the Nile (by figures like Stanley) or the study of central Asia (Aurel Stein) were part of a larger effort to create imperial spheres of influence and control.

TRAVEL, THE TRAVELER, AND TRAVEL ACCOUNTS

The relations between physical travel and travel writing present another area where travel and information are at play. As we have seen, data gathering, organization, and interpretation have been integral to physical travel as an institutional and political practice since antiquity. Representing travel, however, in textual and visual forms, is not a straightforward process. Cultural conventions, media, and the nature of the audience determine the ways in which travel is digested into information. The study of travel and its representations has flourished in the past three decades, as increasing numbers of (mainly) historians and literary scholars have begun to acknowledge their value for understanding not only regions visited, but also the intellectual makeup of the traveler. In this section I look more closely at the figure of the traveler and his or her retelling of the voyage within a broader cultural-intellectual context.

Again, we may turn to an ancient model, Herodotus's mid-fifth-century BCE *Histories*—a Greek narrative of the Persian wars, which is also based (most probably) on extensive travels in Egypt and Mesopotamia. In his account, Herodotus covers geography, natural history, ethnography, and folklore, while identifying his sources of information, such as his own eyewitness accounts and discussions with locals. Sections in the *Histories*, especially the description of Egypt, provide a model for the first-person travel account. Its reception offers an important example, too, of the deep suspicion toward travelers' tales. Herodotus was famously criticized already in antiquity as a peddler of fables and lies. Lucian of Samosata, writing in the second century AD, was relying both on the established state of travel writing as a *genre and on its questionable authenticity when he wrote the satirical *True History*, which described his journey to the moon. Between the ideal-typical Herodotus (the first-person, eyewitness travel account) and Lucian (satirizing such an account) we find many other possibilities and combinations of travel and its digestion into informational form, for example, real travelers who entrusted others with the task of compiling their accounts, often based on older texts (Bernhard von Breidenbach's pilgrimage, 1486); or stay-at-home authors who compiled earlier accounts couched as the supposedly authentic reports of real travelers (Mandeville's *Travels* of the late fourteenth century). Even "Herodotean" travelers, who dutifully took notes while on the move, would eventually be expected to convert them into a narrative or learned treatise form, with the help of an extensive shelf of books tapped as sources.

Travel collections complicate the picture even further, as the figure of the editor takes center stage in the presentation of travel knowledge, often at the expense of the traveler. These massive compilations developed in response to the increased volume of geographical information from the early sixteenth century. Montalboddo's *Paesi novamente retrovati* (The newly found lands, 1507) and Peter Martyr's *De orbe novo* (On the new world) (1530) marked the beginning of the trend, which continued to thrive well into the modern period. Travel collections were linked both to the interests of a growing reading public and to commercial and political agendas of expansion, as Ramusio's *Delle Navigationi et Viaggi* (On the navigations and voyages) (1550–59) and Richard Hakluyt's *Principal Navigations* (1589) demonstrate. Cosmography, comprising descriptions of the world, was a contemporary learned genre that also relied heavily on travel accounts. Cosmography was much indebted to the geographical conceptual schemes offered by Ptolemy and Strabo, on the one hand, and to late medieval world histories, on the other. Sebastian Münster, editor of the most famous cosmography of the sixteenth century (1544), also relied on an extensive network of collaborators who sent him descriptions of individual regions.

Travel collections and cosmographies included political reflections as well, as they invited thoughtful comparisons between systems of rule and custom. It is perhaps not surprising that Thomas More's *Utopia* (1516) is framed as a travel account of "nowhere" told by a fictional traveler to a fictional "Thomas More." Toward the end of the century, the political theorist (and ex-Jesuit) Giovanni Botero's *Relazioni universali* (Universal relations) (1591–96) provided a historical account of the world, geographically organized as a series of reports. Political thinkers continued to excavate examples from travel accounts and collections in order to substantiate their theories ("the state of nature," and "Oriental despotism," for example). Historians, too, embraced travel as a central form of knowledge about human affairs. Some scholars were also keenly interested in the history of travel itself and studied and published ancient travel texts (Roman itineraries, the Peutinger Table, or Benjamin of Tudela's travels). The proliferation of travel narratives also inspired the development of early fiction literature. Swift's *Gulliver's Travels* (1726) and Voltaire's *Candide* (1759) were philosophical satirical works that employed the theme of travel and the conventions of the genre to describe the evolution of a character facing the world's vagaries. The literary scholar Percy Adams famously argued that the emergence of the novel at large is deeply indebted to travel, in terms of narration, progression, and characters. Some scholars argue that all literature is, in fact, travel literature.

Reflection on others' voyages is found also in the tradition of vicarious or armchair travel, which is another pivotal component of the information-travel nexus. Twenty-first-century travelers (en masse) rely on instant availability of information about their destinations, accessed on location. In earlier periods, staying at home and traveling in one's mind's eye was more common. The tradition of pilgrimage set an early model for mental or spiritual travel. Already in late antiquity, church fathers recommended imagining Jerusalem rather than traveling there. Other regimens of devotion, such as Ignatius Loyola's *Spiritual Exercises* (1548), also relied on setting oneself in particular locations and scenes. A few decades later, the Lutheran pastor Heinrich Bünting encouraged readers of his highly informative biblical geography (*Itinerarium Sacrae Scripturae*; A travel book of sacred scripture, 1581) to follow as pilgrims the wanderings of biblical figures, from Adam to the Apostles. Such imaginings, however, were dependent on actual pilgrims, who brought home information about the sacred sites: relics, replicas, measurements, views, and narrative accounts of the journey, often told in person to eager listeners. During their fund-raising journeys, for example, Jewish emissaries (*shadarim*) from the Holy Land to Mediterranean and European communities carried illustrated booklets and scrolls about the sacred sites.

Since around 1500, the increasing availability of maps, atlases, cosmographies, and travel accounts and collections has allowed stationary readers access to information about locations they could not physically reach. To give a notable visual example, the *Civitates orbis terrarum* (Cities of the world, published in six volumes, starting in 1572, by Georg Braun and Frans Hogenberg) allowed educated European readers to study and enjoy town views from four continents, each adorned with images of local figures in costume and supplemented by short historical texts. Heavily illustrated books in this genre often also explicitly invited the readers to travel themselves, whether for education, for entertainment, or to settle elsewhere. Thus, Henry Blount in *Voyage into the Levant* (1636) declared that he had extended his itinerary outside Europe in order to experience real cultural and political alterity. In the nineteenth and early twentieth centuries, the medium of photography brought new possibilities to vicarious travel. In particular, series of stereographs of (often staged) foreign scenes, depicting ancient biblical lands or the western American frontier, were very popular.

Beginning in the sixteenth century, travel developed into a legitimate form of elite education, and, in parallel, there emerged a genre of travel advice and method, the *ars apodemica*. Practical advice (exchange rates, *lexicons, political updates, and road security) for merchants and other moving agents was common much earlier. The educational traveler required more guidance by way of moral direction and the refinement of observational skills. In his well-known essay "Of Travel" (1625) Francis Bacon wondered why men were filling their diaries during sea voyages "where there is nothing to be seen but sky and sea," whereas on the more exciting land journeys they neglect this important task. In other words, Bacon, like others writing in the genre, called for systematic and meaningful note taking as part of educational travel. He also recommended maintaining correspondence with worthy foreign acquaintances. By preparing to travel and then leaving for an extended period, under the close eye of a tutor, the young gentleman could experience cultural, linguistic, and religious difference and practice observation of ancient sites, local customs, and political institutions, as the literature advised. Thus, methodized travel could help aspiring young members of the elite to sharpen their political sensibilities before entering careers in law, foreign trade, or the court.

Traveling to an institution of learning or to join the household of a renowned scholar is also a long-standing practice that meaningfully ties travel to information. In such cases, the experience of travel was secondary to the challenge of learning in a different intellectual environment. Early rabbinic sources tell us about pupils who left their homes to study with authoritative figures. Such was R. Eliezer ben Hurcanus (first century CE), who, despite his father's protestations, went to Jerusalem to train with R. Yohanan ben Zakai (*Avot of Rabbi Natan*). Roman elites' "study abroad" in Athens was a well-established phenomenon, which Aulus Gellius recorded in *Noctes Atticae* (Attic nights) (second century CE). The medieval university, most famously in Paris, institutionalized the diverse geographical background of its student body by dividing it into nations. In his *al-Muqaddimah* (The Prolegomenon), the fourteenth-century Arab thinker and historian Ibn Khaldūn highly recommended travel to multiple teachers as the best way to gain deep knowledge, for two reasons: first, personal contact with different learned men allows the student to observe and imitate good scholarly practices; second, coping with divergent technical terminologies helps develop comparative sensibilities, which, in turn, facilitate reaching the science behind them. Such ideas seem to have guided a few Jewish physicians of the same century, such as Abraham Abigdor and Leon Joseph, who traveled to the university of Montpellier to study medicine from the mouths of Christian doctors.

Travel to study with learned authorities and visit institutions of learning became very common in the early modern period. As several recent studies point out, learned travel, or the *peregrinatio academica*, became a central practice of members of the *Republic of Letters. On the one hand, this scholarly web was held together by the movement of letters, printed books, manuscripts, and various objects between sedentary figures. This type of connectivity heavily relied on merchant and postal network infrastructures. On the other hand, many scholars, especially during their formative years, physically moved between central hubs of learning, often carrying introduction letters and the above items as curiosities or gifts. Some would perform tasks on behalf of other scholars: the well-traveled Jacques Bongars, a Huguenot diplomat, served as courier and manuscript checker to the Dutch scholar Joseph Scaliger. This mobility, too, helped strengthen the rather nebulous Republic of Letters. Some academic pilgrims would enroll in foreign universities for short periods of study. To give one of many possible examples, the seventeenth-century Zurich orientalist Johann Heinrich Hottinger (1620–67) traveled to stay with Jacobus Golius (1596–1667) in Leiden and matriculated at that university. In the fruitful fourteen-month stay, Hottinger transcribed a good number of Oriental manuscripts, which would furnish his studies for many years. These manuscripts were collected during Golius's own extensive travels in the Levant. Moving in the opposite direction and a few centuries later was the *polymath and collector Abraham Shalom Yahuda (1877–1951), born in Jerusalem to an Iraqi family, who traveled to study and then teach in Europe. Modern "study abroad" and exchange programs continue to develop this tradition.

Early modern academic travel, and the range of scholarly practices it entailed, was as much an intellectual as a social enterprise and rite. Scholars on the move often obtained and shared their information by spending time with local virtuosi—visiting libraries, appreciating ancient sites, performing scientific experiments, and attending academic gatherings. *Cabinets of curiosity were particularly attractive focal points, allowing the collector and visitor to converse and exchange while observing the global cornucopia of natural and human-made objects. En route to the court of Christina of Sweden in 1652, for example, the French pastor Samuel Bochart visited the famous Copenhagen collection of Ole Worm in the company of the younger Pierre-Daniel Huet, who recounted the story in his memoir. These collections were in themselves the product of far-reaching travel networks, facilitated by merchants, diplomats, and other mobile agents. In the eighteenth century, public museums, with extensive natural historical and ethnographical displays, replaced and popularized the smaller learned collections. A century later, in an imperial age, officially sponsored international grand exhibitions (for example, London, 1851; Paris, 1900) brought together many colonial displays, including replicas of villages populated by living subjects. In the 1904 St. Louis Exhibition, a real-size model of Jerusalem was a major attraction. Like the earlier cabinets, these huge fairs became travel destinations in themselves, spawning a documentation and souvenir industry (including stereographs) that replicated the replicas.

CONCLUSION

This short survey, following the travel-information nexus in political and intellectual contexts up to the twentieth century, attempts to demonstrate the multiple, intertwined, and at times contradictory ways in which the two categories interacted. Travel was, and still is, a major source of information for various purposes, private and public. Effective production and control of travel information requires the institutionalization of reportage and interpretation methods. Travel management thus helped develop the broader idea that knowledge was infinite, and it prompted the creation of open systems of information storage and retrieval, which in turn enabled research that led to unpredictable results. Such ideals were often frustrated by the chaotic nature of premodern travel and by conflicting notions of what constituted valuable information. These ingrained ambiguities were only heightened when the volume of travel information increased after 1500. Moreover, travel not only produced but also consumed information. Travelers, whether lay or learned, were dependent on previously established bodies of knowledge. As a cultural-intellectual practice, in a less fact-oriented setting, travel proved to be a fruitful arena for personal education. It supplied a topic for reflection and provided a useful organizing blueprint for systematizing thought. In other words, it was both an object of scholarship and a scholarly method.

Zur Shalev

See also cameras; commodification; diplomats/spies; ethnography; governance; learning; maps; merchants; notebooks; observing; political reporting; postal customers

FURTHER READING

Percy G. Adams, *Travel Literature and the Evolution of the Novel*, 1983; Mary B. Campbell, *The Witness and the Other World: Exotic European Travel Writing, 400–1600*, 1991; Nandini Das and Tim Youngs, eds., *The Cambridge History of Travel Writing*, 2019; Jaś Elsner and Joan-Pau Rubiés, eds., *Voyages and Visions: Towards a Cultural History of Travel*, 1999; Justin Stagl, *A History of Curiosity: The Theory of Travel, 1550–1800*, 1995; Richard Yeo, *Notebooks, English Virtuosi, and Early Modern Science*, 2014.

XYLOGRAPHY

Xylography, or woodblock printing, is a process of transferring graphic content from incised wood to a flat surface. The printing block, with a raised mirror image of the content, is coated with ink, then the target medium, usually a sheet of paper, is pressed onto the block and peeled off. Xylography was the principal mode of printing in East Asia until the twentieth century, for books as well as stationery, posters, and ephemera. It enabled the production of nearly identical documents in huge quantities and facilitated the development of print cultures based on wide access to written material by diverse readers and intensive engagement by specialists with large volumes of information.

In *early modern China, Korea, Japan, Vietnam, Tibet, and Mongolia, woodblock printing on paper was the most common technique for book production, especially of books intended for a large readership, and for documents such as calendars, playing cards, and bureaucratic forms. It supplanted, but never replaced, hand copying; it coexisted with reprographic technologies such as rubbings of stone inscriptions and with movable type. By comparison with the latter it is well suited to the Sinographic ("Chinese character") scripts of East Asia, with thousands of distinct graphs, and those like Mongolian, Manchu, and cursive Japanese in which each word is written in a single ligatured whole.

Some Arabic block prints of the ninth to fourteenth centuries and European block books of the eleventh to fifteenth centuries represent a similar technology, but neither dominated textual production in those regions. In early modern Europe, woodblocks were also the principal means of reproducing images that were mingled with typography, by contrast with copper engravings, which required a separate kind of press. The point at which xylography became dominant in East Asia is difficult to ascertain; for China, McDermott estimates that in elite book collections imprints outnumbered manuscripts from the turn of the sixteenth century.

The technological sources of xylographic printing lie in two well-established technologies: seals used to authenticate documents and blocks used to stamp textiles. With the advent of paper as writing medium around the first century CE, seals—previously used to create a relief impression in soft clay—were adapted to apply ink directly to this more affordable writing surface. And especially in religious contexts, such as the production of charms or talismans, seals grew from brief names and titles to longer passages of multiple sentences or complex series of glyphs.

Even when stamped directly on a document, a seal impression (*sealing*) tends to perform different informative work than the printed text in, for example, a book. The material fact of the sealing provides information about the document as object: it was issued by the party controlling the seal; if the seal is intact, the document has not been opened. The sealing's function is the same whether it is attached to a document or to something without informational content, such as a bottle whose wax sealing proves that the wine is unadulterated. It may be infinitely duplicated, but detached from a host object, a sealing ceases to inform. The same is true, mutatis mutandis, for the other main form of mass-duplicated text in the ancient world, numismatic inscriptions. These were copied in the millions but produced value less by what they said than by where they said it. Likewise, the power of a magic talisman is embedded in its physicality and does not travel with the simple repetition of its verbiage.

Printing may thus be distinguished from mere impression by the decreased *semiotic involvement of the substrate. The paper and ink with which a book is produced, by printing or handwriting, are a material necessity, but users need not refer to them to make sense of a book's words. In these terms, xylography is the world's oldest and longest-used technology for the mechanized dissemination of information.

Most of the earliest (seventh- to tenth-century) printed books and references to printing in China involve the reproduction of sacred, especially Buddhist, texts. In Buddhism the dissemination of scriptures and icons was a meritorious act whose karma could redound to the party commissioning them. Woodblocks thus enabled patrons to perform good deeds on an industrial scale. In some cases the intent was more talismanic than communicative, as in the "Million Pagoda Dharani" commissioned by Japanese empress Shōtoku between 764 and 770. Each printed text was sealed inside a bronze stupa; their creation was a ritual rather than a communicative act. Other projects were, however, clearly intended to spread Buddhist doctrine, most notably editions of the complete Sinitic Buddhist canon produced by various ecclesiastical and state institutions. For example, the Haeinsa, a temple in Korea, preserves a set of over eighty thousand woodblocks carved between 1237 and 1248 that still yield readable prints of the Korean Buddhist canon.

By contrast with religious evangelism, scholarly practice often favored copying texts by hand. This remained so in China even after the state-sanctioned printing of core *canonical works. In the Song period (960–1279) printing offices issued standard versions of key texts, notably ones from the curriculum of the civil service examinations, but printed books were just one part of the textual ecosystem, and a majority of texts remained in manuscript form. Printed books often served as models for handwritten copies, but many bibliophiles preferred texts proofread by a careful copyist to mechanically made books that thoughtlessly perpetuated mistakes.

At the same time, a commercial printing industry developed that produced cheaper editions of texts issued by the state (sometimes in nominal violation of the law) and a range of other books for a wide readership. These included study aids for examination students, classical and historical texts of all sorts, literary collections, *vernacular fiction, drama, and books on useful arts such as agriculture and medicine. Some regions became notorious for books printed on inferior paper from crudely executed woodblocks, a clear sign of a competitive market. Such productions boomed in the latter half of the Ming period (1368–1644) and until the end of the Qing (1644–1911), when mechanical printing techniques imported from the West began to supplant xylography.

Woodblock printing spread from China to its neighbors, including both regions in which Chinese was widespread as a language of scholarship, religion, and government (Korea, Japan, and Vietnam) and other areas such as Mongolia and Tibet. Unlike movable type, xylography requires no additional equipment to produce diverse graphic styles and sizes, or even multiple scripts. In Japan, where woodblock printing boomed in the Edo period (1600–1868), it was used to manufacture books in a variety of linguistic modes: Classical Chinese works nearly identical to their continental models; these same texts with interlinear, *marginal, or running Japanese-language commentary in the *kana* syllabary or a mix of kana and Sinographs; texts in various mixed forms with both Sinographs and kana; and Japanese texts in pure, *cursive kana. Any of these could incorporate illustrations in configurations ranging from figures set on their own page to a melding of image and text resembling modern comics.

Compared to most other printing methods, xylography presents a low economic and technical barrier to entry. Unlike letterpress, it does not require large capital investments for type or even a press. Blocks can be incised by craftspeople of varying skill and with little or no understanding of the content. In early modern China, for example, different artisans might cut the vertical, horizontal, and diagonal strokes. Once carved, typically on both faces, a block could produce thousands of copies. The yield depended on the hardness of the wood, quality of the carving, and frequency of use. Blocks could also be modified to fix damage, correct errors, or censor content.

Xylography is thus a robust technology for making graphic information rapidly and widely available in identical form. Transferring information from other media to woodblock prints inevitably entailed transformations. For example, multicolor printing was expensive and technically demanding, so the vast majority of xylography in East Asia was monochrome, mainly using soot-based black inks similar to those for handwriting and drawing. Multicolor printing using different pigments was a complex undertaking reserved for decorative works, stationery, and a small minority of books, notably texts with annotations and punctuation from multiple commentators distinguished by color. Variegated shading, too, was usually lost in the move from brushstroke to print, which tends to be either black or white, so xylography promoted a view of the document as a monochrome entity. The uniformity of block sizes also favored the standardization of the page as a frame for text and images and aided a shift from the scroll to the spine-bound volume in East Asia. Tibetan books, by contrast, were typically stacks of wide, short sheets on the model of Indic palm-leaf books; this form needed little modification for printing.

Different technologies tend to emphasize certain graphic features for replication. If typography isolates by doing something akin to digitization—engaging with text as a sequence of glyphs drawn from a finite set—xylography is indifferent, like photography, to the semantics of language and imagery; its domain is the whole page. Nonetheless, at other scales xylography shaped graphic design, promoting both visual styles that were easy to execute in wood (straight lines rather than curves, for one) and forms that conveyed information efficiently, such as "typefaces" that were graphically spare and confounded calligraphic aesthetics but made small, dense text more readable. It took writing out of the hands of the scribe and put it into the hands of millions.

Bruce Rusk

See also books; layout and script in letters; letterpress; proofreaders; scrolls and rolls

FURTHER READING

Cynthia J. Brokaw and Peter F. Kornicki, eds., *The History of the Book in East Asia*, 2013; Susan Cherniack, "Book Culture and Textual Transmission in Sung China," *Harvard Journal of Asiatic Studies* 54, no. 1 (1994): 5–125; Peter F. Kornicki, *The Book in Japan*, 1998; Joseph Peter McDermott, *A Social History of the Chinese Book*, 2006; Kurtis R. Schaeffer, *The Culture of the Book in Tibet*, 2009; Tsuen-hsuin Tsien, *Science and Civilisation in China*, vol. 5, *Chemistry and Chemical Technology*, part 1, *Paper and Printing*, 1985.

GLOSSARY

analog. *See* digital/analog.

archival thinking/consciousness. An approach to historical research that assumes that historians should ask questions about how archives, as collections or institutions with their own histories and realities, determine the understanding of the pasts for which they not only provide evidence but also shape the stories told.

artificial intelligence (AI). A branch of science and research that focuses on producing computer systems that are assumed to respond with human-like thinking when addressing human tasks.

big data. A set of data that owing to its enormity requires special computing power and analytical attention to be manipulated or understood. A key goal of big data collection and analysis is to unearth underlying patterns or trends that are invisible to other research approaches.

binary. The foundational system of 0s and 1s that is used to make information readable for computers.

bits. A term coined by the mathematician John Tukey for binary digits, the fundamental units of digital encoding. Made of 1s and 0s, they originally reflected whether a switch was on or off or a signal was "long" or "short." Computers are designed to work with groups of bits. The conventional grouping is made of eight bits and known as a "byte."

book hand. A formal script used in copying books or documents, usually by trained scribes.

bookkeeping. The practice of maintaining accounting records of debits and credits that allow for future access and use.

born digital. A qualifier used to describe texts that were first produced for a digital platform, as opposed to those that might be translated into a digital form from their original analog state.

brevior lectio potior. A foundational tenet of textual editing, from the Latin meaning that "the shorter version is the better one" because it comes earlier in the chain of transmission. It captures the assumption that scribes usually added to rather than shortened a text.

cabinet of curiosities. An early modern collection of items considered interesting or valuable, including natural specimens and items created by human crafts. Whether formed by monarchs or private collectors, cabinets of curiosities offered materials and models for the development of museums.

canon. A body of religious works, literature, or artistic productions (e.g., sculptures, films, paintings) that is considered culturally authoritative or of exceptional quality.

catechism. A religious text, typically in question-and-answer form, containing important doctrinal positions and often used in an educational setting.

cloud, the. A metaphor commonly used to invoke a ubiquitously accessible system in which large volumes of data are stored in centralized data banks, linked by the internet, rather than on individual computers. The ethereal term *cloud*, it is often pointed out, obscures the physical reality of thousands of miles of cables, and vast, energy-consuming data warehouses, all of which require frequent physical maintenance.

code. A set of rules for inscribing information, usually to promote more efficient transmission or resist unwanted recipients. Code could refer to the translation of information for communication (e.g., "Morse code") or to a secret cipher, such as ones that governments have long used to encrypt information. It can also refer to the underlying symbolic representation of information in a computer system or program, that is, machine code.

codex. A book constructed of a number of quires of paper, or similar writing surface, bound together at the spine. The term derives from the Latin *caudex* for "trunk of a tree" or "block of wood."

coffeehouse. An establishment, formed in the early modern Ottoman world and then in Europe, where people (at first only men) gathered to drink coffee, read, and talk about news. As a location for the interchange of political views, the coffeehouse has been used as an emblem for the early "public sphere."

colophon. A short statement placed at the end of a manuscript or printed work, announcing some details about the text, such as title, author, producer (e.g., scribe or printer).

commonplace book. An early modern notebook in which users stored textual excerpts under topical headings to facilitate retention or retrieval. The excerpts were often copied from books (e.g., by famous authors) but could also include personal observations.

commonplaces (*loci communes*). Fixed turns of phrase to be committed to memory. In the early modern period, the term designated selected topics, exempla, and sayings. The commonplace book was the storage medium for loci communes.

compression. The practice of producing a digital representation of information, often by eliminating redundancy, to achieve more efficient storage or transmission. The process is said to be either "lossless" or "lossy" depending on whether the result sacrifices some of the quality of the original.

concordance. A reference tool, first developed in the thirteenth century for the Bible, that collects in alphabetical order all the occurrences of the words in the text so they can be found easily without reading the whole work. A variety of concordances, many of them digital, also exist for examining word usage in classical Latin and Greek texts and in works in many other tra-

ditions, such as the Talmud, the Quran, and the corpus of Vedic Sanskrit texts.

conversion. The means of representing a communication in a new medium, such as translating written letters into electric signals for transmission over telegraph lines.

copia. Meaning "abundance" in Latin. The term refers to the storehouse of phrases and elements of knowledge that Renaissance intellectuals encouraged students to gather from classical authors and store in their notebooks and memories.

copyright. A legal construct that gives exclusive rights, usually for a limited time, over authored "works" understood as an "expression," typically on condition that the expression is "original," that is, in some (minimalist) sense "creative."

copy text. The version of a work that was selected as the basis of a published work, most often because it was presumed to be closest to the author's intentions.

cryptography. A means of encoding content so as to preserve privacy. Cryptographic practices, though widely used for modern databases, date to antiquity and have taken many different forms.

cursive. A manner of writing that conjoins adjacent letters within a word. By eliminating the spacing between individual letters, cursive saves a writer space on the page, as well as time spent writing.

data banks. Repositories of valued digital content, usually with highly restricted access. Given the value of the data, they are often subject to attack by people seeking illicit access. Consequently, the strength of security and upkeep for these databases faces continuous and constantly changing challenges.

dead media. Media forms that have been superseded and so present significant barriers to access (e.g., the contents of a floppy disk cannot be easily accessed by a modern-day laptop).

difficilior lectio potior. A maxim of editing from the Latin that "the more difficult version is the better one" because scribes tended to make a difficult passage simpler to understand.

digital/analog. Terms to describe the operating character of mechanisms. *Digital* describes mechanisms that offer particular, preset states—such as a light switch that can be on or off, or a keyboard that can be set to all capitals or all lowercase. *Analog,* by contrast, indicates devices with continuous settings—such as a light dimmer or a thermostat that can be turned up or down across an undivided spectrum. Most modern computational devices are underpinned by a binary digital system, where the fundamental settings are either 0 or 1, which nonetheless allows them to produce apparently continuous settings. The terms are also used, by extension, for a broad division of history into two eras. The phrase "digital age" is used to describe the era of widespread digital computing, often assumed to coincide with the growth of the public internet. All that comes before is then treated as if it shared traits of a contrastingly "analog" era.

early modern period. The period of history from roughly 1400 to 1800, thus named on the notion that various features of "modernity" originated then, including new intellectual movements, religious schism, the formation of nation-states, voyages of exploration and colonization, and early global capitalism. Though this periodization originated as a way of describing European history, its use has expanded to cover a more global context.

encyclopedia. A term that nineteenth-century European scholars applied to works of large scope with various ordering principles from around the world, including examples from East Asia and the Middle East. Although the term was formed from the Greek for "all-around education," it was associated from its first use in the Renaissance with the "circle of learning" and works that covered a large range of topics, often with a systematic arrangement to match the order of the disciplines as each author conceived it. The *Encyclopédie* of Diderot and d'Alembert (1751–75) gave the term a new set of associations with a large and usually alphabetically ordered reference book.

encyclopedic order. An arrangement of knowledge into a hierarchical scheme by discipline or another system of classification, typically contrasted with alphabetical order.

enlightenment. A term used to describe a period of increased or especially noteworthy intellectual and philosophical activity. "The Enlightenment" often refers specifically to eighteenth-century France, while "the early Enlightenment" refers mostly to late seventeenth-century thinkers like Isaac Newton, John Locke, and Pierre Bayle.

epistemology. A branch of philosophy that examines the foundations and properties of knowledge, and a central concern of philosophers since ancient Greece. Among other questions, epistemology examines how humans know when something is true or false.

exegesis. The practice of critically examining, interpreting, and explicating a text. Practitioners of exegesis, called exegetes, in ancient as well as contemporary times have most often focused on sacred scriptures or canonical literary texts.

fact. From the Latin verb *facere* meaning "to make" or "to do." A fact is that which was done, occurred, or exists.

fair use. A common-law principle that under certain circumstances (e.g., educational use) allows copyrighted text to be used without the explicit approval of the copyright holder.

florilegia. From the Latin for a "collection of flowers," florilegia were collections of authoritative sayings organized by topics and alphabetically arranged for easy retrieval.

free speech/freedom of speech. A legal principle that protects, within certain limits, an individual's ability to express ideas and opinions. Within the US legal system, this protection is enshrined in the First Amendment to the Constitution.

gazetteer. A textual compilation concerning the geography, peoples, history, and other features of a particular locality, culled from texts, in situ observations, or conversations.

genre. A category to describe a kind of text or artwork with certain shared characteristics of form or content. Mysteries and romances are examples of genres for novels. Outside of literature, the term can also refer more broadly to a specific form or style of text.

glossary. A reference element, often at the end of a book, that features brief definitions of selected terms.

guild. An association of skilled workers that regulated the practice of their trade. This kind of organization was the norm in medieval and early modern Europe. In England, for example, the printing trade was controlled by a London guild, the Stationers' Company, which was granted a monopoly by statute allowing it to prevent nonmembers from operating printing presses and to force members to conform to certain norms.

hacking. In the pejorative meaning of the word, the unauthorized engagement with a digital system or data repository, often with the goal of gathering or destroying privileged or personal information. "Hack" also has a positive meaning as an unauthorized or unexpected solution to a difficult problem.

House of Wisdom. A palace library founded in eighth-century Baghdad and staffed mainly by officials of Iranian descent, responsible for collecting books about Persian heritage and ancient Arabian lore. Recent scholarship has rejected the view that it served as a research academy and translation hub; instead it probably designated a library modeled on those of the Sasanian Empire and reflects the influence of the bureaucratic traditions of Iran on the new Islamic empire.

humanities. A set of disciplines that was thought to foster ethical qualities in leaders, and which derived from the Renaissance pedagogical program known as the *studia humanitatis* (humane studies). These disciplines included classical and modern languages, history, philosophy, and literature.

humoral theory. The theory used in classical Greek medicine to postulate the existence of four basic types of temperament that described psychological and physiological states: choleric, melancholic, sanguine, and phlegmatic. Individuals could each have a unique combination of the four humoral elements—hot, wet, cold, dry—but could be fit into one of these broader types, which indicated their strengths and weaknesses, and the medical treatments they might need.

hypertext. Interlinked digital text that allows a reader to navigate to preselected and interrelated information. Hyperlinks are markers within digital documents that allow users to connect to other documents. Connections are usually achieved by clicking on the link. The related document then appears on the screen. Hypertext is text that relies on such links and the interrelated documents to fulfill the purpose for which the document was designed. The word was coined by Theodor (Ted) Nelson, an early internet pioneer.

illumination. The ornamentation using colored and gold pigments of a manuscript or printed work.

impact factor. A measure of supposed academic worth built around the number of citations that each article receives in a particular journal. The measure assumes that journals with higher impact factors are more widely read and thus the articles they contain more important than journals with low impact factors.

indulgence. Remission of temporal punishment for sin, often recorded in a certificate issued by the Catholic Church and attesting to an act of charity, a pilgrimage, or the use of a rosary or other set objects. Indulgences were printed in great numbers (including by Johannes Gutenberg) as single sheets, which have a very poor survival rate.

information overload. The sense or feeling that there is simply too much information for one to grasp and recall given the resources available. Complaints about overload are not unique to the so-called "digital age" but can be found in various premodern contexts.

internet. An interconnected network of computers and related devices to transmit and process digital communications. The modern internet is the outcome of a vast number of connections among multiple different networks, though current use of the term evokes an all-embracing, single network.

leak. The unauthorized disclosing of information classified as private or secret.

learned societies. Associations of the learned around a shared interest, such as poetic performance, or the study of language, or of science. Three principal examples still active today, the English Royal Society, the French Académie des Sciences, and the German Academia Leopoldina, were formed in the late seventeenth century and disseminated findings of their members in the form of a periodical.

lexicon. A reference book devoted to explaining terms in a foreign (mainly classical) language or terminology specific to a particular field of knowledge.

libel. A legal term used to designate false or defamatory statements that are recorded in writing or other fixed form. Libel differs from slander, which encompasses verbal, gestural, or unrecorded defamation.

liberal arts. An ancient Roman notion of education comprising the trivium of disciplines of the word (grammar, logic, rhetoric), and the quadrivium, the four disciplines of the number (arithmetic, geometry, astronomy, music). Today it designates a conception of education that spans multiple disciplines and is not oriented toward specific professional skills.

Library of Congress subject headings. A controlled vocabulary of subject headings assigned to every publication entering the purview of the US Library of Congress. These headings first appeared in the late nineteenth century and are still in active use today in many libraries.

literacy. The ability to read and write. Historians distinguish many types of literacy. "Pragmatic literacy" was sufficient for managing basic legal and business affairs. "Mercantile literacy" involves reckoning and reading in the vernacular. In Europe, before the modern period, to be "literatus" meant to possess the ability to read Latin, which was expected of all clergy and students.

longue durée. Literally "long duration," a term introduced into historical practice by the French historian Fernand Braudel and now widely used. It refers to a historical method that emphasizes developments that take place over the very long term, such as changes in climate, which both shape human society and are shaped by it. Cultural phenomena may also act on long time scales.

machine learning. A statistical and computer-based method that uses inductive algorithms trained on large data sets to extract patterns and adapt machine behavior in response to these patterns. In particular, when used in the fields of artificial intelligence or natural language processing, it enables machines to infer the judgments of human reasoners with no pretense of reproducing the thought processes and somatic judgments of human beings. More generally machine learning algorithms are designed to "improve automatically through experience" (Tom Mitchell, 1997).

marginalia. Annotations left by readers in the margins of a written or printed text. Marginalia can be studied as records of one person's reading but also of methods of reading typical of a given context.

memex. A contraction of either "memory extended" or "memory index," referring to a photoelectric machine envisioned by the engineer Vannevar Bush to link documents (on microfilm) chosen by the owner, thereby superseding both index cards and library classification. As such, it was a precursor of hypertext systems and the World Wide Web.

memory palace. An ancient technique for memorizing whereby a user associates knowledge to be remembered with distinctive locations (loci) visualized in the mind. To this day, this technique is famous for helping facilitate impressive feats of memory.

metadata. From the Greek *meta-* for "behind." These data "about data" record details about the items being cataloged. Book metadata, for example, usually include the place and year of publication, the format, and authorship. Metadata help structure the data in a collection according to items' relationships with one another.

Morse code. A telecommunication system developed in the nineteenth century by Samuel Morse and Alfred Vail that used combinations of electric pulses (dots and dashes) to encode letters and numbers.

new media. A term applied to digital media, with the implication, not always correct, that they either displace or replace older forms.

notary. A person invested with the authority to create, authenticate, and store documents with legal significance.

open access. A form of publication committed to making documents, including scholarly research in peer-reviewed journals, open to any interested user to read, copy, or circulate, without the need for permission, payment, or proof of institutional affiliation.

open source. Both a principle and a practice according to which a piece of computer code is open to adoption and adaptation. Open source codes, programs, or scripts are not controlled by any company or person. Instead, all are free to use the code for their own purposes, on the understanding that what is produced is also made available on similar terms.

optical character recognition (OCR). The process by which a machine "reads" a document, converting, for instance, the analog lettering on a page into digital bits and bytes that can then be, for instance, digitally searched or reorganized.

palimpsest. A manuscript in which an initial layer of writing has been either partially or completely erased, often through scraping, and a more recent text inscribed over it.

papyrus. The dominant writing material used in ancient Egypt, Greece, and Rome, made from the pith of a plant native to the Nile delta. Texts written on papyrus rolls often required recopying owing to the fragility of the medium. Nonetheless, thousands of papyrus fragments have survived (particu-

larly in dry desert conditions) and are studied by papyrologists.

paratext. Textual material, usually but not always at the front and back of a book, that refers to the main text, such as the frontispiece, table of contents, dedication, prefaces by author or printer, commendatory odes, illustrations, alphabetical indexes, and errata lists.

parchment. A writing surface made from animal skin, including calf skin (vellum) but also the skin of sheep, goat, or pig. Even after the availability of paper, parchment was used for transcribing particular types of documents (e.g., classical texts, charters, bulls) deemed especially important. *See also* vellum.

philology. From the Greek for "love of words," a discipline devoted to studying the histories, contexts, and developments of ancient or classical languages and literatures.

polymath. A scholar who studies a variety of disciplines and makes original contributions to several of them, such as Gottfried Wilhelm Leibniz (1646–1716), whose interests included history, theology, linguistics, and sinology as well as the philosophy and mathematics for which he is best known.

protocol. A standardized set of rules allowing different machines within a network to communicate with each other. Rather than needing to accommodate the diverse workings of all the machines in a network, each machine has only to respond to the agreed-on protocols to transmit and receive communications.

public domain. The cornerstone of copyright law designating those materials to which no legal restrictions on use or reproduction apply. The public domain denotes what is left over after all other rights have been defined and distributed.

publishers. The person(s) or company that manages publication or the public dissemination of a text (in print, digital, or another format). Though not a universal phenomenon, certain rights have historically been reserved to publishers, including, to varying degrees, copyright and the control over reprinting a work.

publish or perish. A colloquial academic expression that communicates the expectation that scholars must publish their work in articles and books in order to advance their academic careers.

Reformation. A movement of religious reform, begun by Martin Luther in 1517, that resulted in a schism of the Western Christian church into Roman Catholic and many Protestant branches.

Renaissance. From the French for rebirth. The term describes a revival of learned and artistic culture. In the European context, the Renaissance refers to the period circa 1300–1600, during which humanists, with their focus on classical antiquity, recovered and studied not only texts but also architecture (e.g., the dome) and art (sculptures large and small), coins and inscriptions, and other cultural remains. The term also occurs in the "Carolingian Renaissance" (around 800 CE), noted for the foundation of new schools offering instruction in Latin; and the "twelfth-century Renaissance," which featured the transmission of Aristotelian philosophical works to the Latin West from the Arabic translations circulating in Spain. The term has also been applied to other cultural contexts.

reproducibility. The extent to which material can be copied and then disseminated. Reproducibility presupposes that information is independent of its source and does not change as it travels.

Republic of Letters. An international and self-described network of early modern scholars, philosophers, and thinkers who communicated with one another via letters and personal contact.

research university. A model for a university developed in late eighteenth- and early nineteenth-century Germany and widely adopted around the world since then that places a high emphasis on research. Today, the professor at such a university not only teaches but is expected to generate new knowledge and train others to do so.

Rosetta Stone. A stone inscription dating to the second century CE that includes the same decree of Ptolemy V Epiphanes in ancient Greek, demotic Greek, and Egyptian hieroglyphs. Its discovery in 1799 allowed the decipherment of previously unintelligible hieroglyphics.

salon. A private gathering of literati, often hosted by women in seventeenth- and eighteenth-century France. Some historians consider salons crucial spaces for the discussion of ideas under fewer constraints than were common in public settings; others see them more as forms of sociability dominated by the aristocrats who assembled them.

scholasticism. A method of analysis practiced in medieval universities in Europe, focused on disputation and logical commentary of authoritative texts, including Christian theology and Aristotelian philosophy.

scriptorium/scriptoria. Site(s) in which scribes copied texts, whether in medieval monasteries or in the commercial enterprises that sought to create multiple copies of manuscripts for sale in urban centers, in late medieval and early modern Europe among other contexts.

secondary memory. An object, such as a notebook or hard drive, that stores data and thus serves as a supplement or extension of the user's memory.

second-order notes. A reworking or reorganization of an existing body of notes. Second-order notes are usually neater and sometimes longer than the first-order notes and might include the note taker's personal reflections on the material. The notes that survive from oral events like sermons or lectures are often second-order notes as opposed to the first-order notes written in haste while listening.

semiotics. The study of signs, which proved important for understanding and developing nineteenth-century communication technologies. It features in multiple disciplines, from philosophy to computer science and marketing.

server farm. A massive collection of computing devices, often located in a remote location, that stores and processes digital information for individual organizations or many users.

shorthand. A method of recording speech in abbreviated form through different symbols and notes.

skeuomorphism. The presentation of content or an interface that aesthetically resembles an older medium. The majority of online books and electronic resources, for example, resemble the page-based and paratextual forms of codices, with traditional formatting parameters.

Society of Jesus/Jesuits. A Catholic order founded in the sixteenth century famous for its secondary schools and for the system of regular reports generated by its missionaries in Europe, the Americas, and Asia.

structured data. Data organized and stored as information in certain specified classes. In contrast, **unstructured data**, like materials on the web, are heterogeneous, conforming to no predetermined subject categories.

taxonomy. A means of structuring the world or its representation hierarchically. In biology, for example, the taxonomy of Carl Linnaeus (1707–78) sorted the organic world into a nested hierarchy of categories (families, genera, species, etc.) that to some degree have a real, if abstract, existence.

Universal Decimal Classification (UDC). A bibliographical system developed in the late nineteenth century to categorize content internationally using numeric categories to classify library holdings by content and location.

vellum. A writing surface manufactured from calfskin. Vellum was the medium of choice for manuscripts in medieval Europe. A text could also be printed on vellum, but this was done only occasionally during the early decades of printing to create a copy of special value. Vellum was also used in book bindings, as it was more flexible, more durable, and less expensive than alternatives like boards covered in leather.

vernacular. A language used in daily life as one's primary means of communication. The vernacular is often contrasted with so-called dead or world languages (e.g., Latin), or older variants of a mother tongue usually reserved for particular ceremonial or religious occasions (e.g., Classical Arabic vs. Modern Standard Arabic).

World Wide Web. The networks developed within the internet that use shared protocols to standardize document formats and provide unique addresses for documents or other dynamically generated content, allowing users to reach those resources from any computer on the network.

INDEX

Pages in bold denote an entry devoted to the term. An asterisk signals that the term appears in the glossary.

Muybridge, Eadweard, 185
MySpace, 780
Mythical Man-Month (Brooks), 703

Nabateans, 5
Nagasaki, 48, 204
Napoleon, 148, 372–73, 461, 823
Nappi, Carla, 38–60
Nathan, Isaac, 263–64
National Association for the Advancement of
Colored People (NAACP), 200
National Election Study, 798
National Geographic, 195
National Geospatial Intelligence Agency, 410
National Opinion Research Center, 798
National Physical Laboratory (NPL), 248–49
National Reconnaissance Office, 410
National Science Foundation (NSF), 247, 251
National Secretaries Day, 769
National Security Act, 410
National Security Agency (NSA), 422, 666, 706–7
National Technical Information Service, 266
Natural History (Pliny), 10, 14, 78, 491, 730, 747, 765
Naudé, Gabriel, 341, 568
Naven (Bateson), 382
Nazis, 200, 202, 213, 219–20, 225–27, 232–35, 243,
426, 528, 548
NBC, 204–5, 209, 604
N-diagrams, 620
Necker, Jacques, 292
Negroponte, Nicholas, 465
Nelles, Paul, 567–78
Nelson, Theodor Holm (Ted), 252, 261–62, 273
Neoplatonism, 26, 35–36, 288, 320
Neopythagoreans, 26, 35–36
Nepos, Cornelius, 765
Nestorius, 7
networks: **620–27**; accounting and, 88, 91; actor
network theory (ANT) and, 624–26; advertising
and, 199–200, 204; ARPANET, 251, 273, 620;
books and, 86–87; capitalism and, 91; Catholics
and, 88, 92–94, 98; censorship and, 193, 200,
204, 623; China and, 92–94, 194, 198–200,
206–7, 245, 625; Christians and, 92, 98, 100–2;
coins and, 99–100; commercialization and,
144–47, 621; computers and, 621, 624, 757–58;
correspondence, 141; credit, 167–69; digital,
620–22; diplomats/spies and, 407–12; Egypt
and, 89, 100, 674; Enlightenment and, 626;
Europe and, 98–102; expanding, 144–47;
globalization and, 86–89, 103, 191; imperialism
and, 89, 91, 99, 194, 626; Islamic world and,
87–88, 92, 95–102; Japan and, 193–94, 196,
198, 203–4; Jesuits and, 86, 92–94, 801; Jews
and, 88, 202, 623; journals and, 190–96, 200–9,

622, 626; letters and, 95–97; libraries and, 101–2;
literacy and, 193, 199, 204; making of connectedness and, 86–103; maps and, 622, 624; merchants and, 86–103, 140, 145, 192, 196, 290,
476, 482, 541, 613–14, 620, 623; money and,
102, 190, 192, 201, 203, 627; news and, 86, 91,
93–94, 98–99, 190–209, 622; newsletters and,
101, 199; newspapers and, 190–209, 620;
Ottomans and, 86–88, 91, 95, 98–102; periodicals
and, 144–47; Persia and, 96, 99–101; photography and, 195–96, 201–2, 208; Portugal and, 86,
89, 92–96, 194; printing and, 96, 193, 198, 207,
627; radio and, 199, 204, 206, 620; role of,
620–27; scholarly, 57; secretaries and, 98–99;
sixteenth-century, 86–103; social media and,
777–82; social network theory (SNT) and, 624–26;
Spain and, 87, 93, 97–98, 194, 200; spice and,
3–10, 89, 96; submarine cables and, 177–78,
213–14, 505, 808; Syria and, 89, 99–101;
telegraphs and, 191–95, 198–200, 204, 209,
620–22; telephones and, 622, 725; trading
companies and, 89–91, 100, 140, 145, 290, 476,
482, 541, 614; translating and, 86, 90, 95, 98,
101–2, 195, 204, 209, 625, 627; travel and, 86;
World Wide Web, 244, 252, 254, 259, 261–62,
328, 338, 550, 619, 621, 779
Neumann, John von, 246–47, 380, 385
New Deal, 689
New English Dictionary, 748
New Method of Cryptography, A (Morland), 419
news, 15; algorithms and, 298–99; Asia and, 41, 52,
58–59; authority and, 414–15, 610, 712; bells
and, 325; censorship and, 367; commercialization and, 129–32, 135–49; duplication of, 785;
Europe and, 61, 66, 68, 71; fake, 225, 258, 458,
463, 498–500; global, 190–209, 780–81; Great
Firewall and, 367; hot media and, 191; intellectual property and, 519; Islamic world and, 21;
journalism and, 669 (*see also* journalism);
learning and, 556; letters and, 566; media and,
601–2, 606; merchants and, 613; networks and,
86, 91, 93–94, 98–99, 190–209, 622; petitions
and, 652; photography and, 351 (*see also*
photography); plagiarizing and, 663; platforms
and, 667; postal service and, 12, 129–32, 135–39,
148, 150, 505, 628–30, 674; power of elites
and, 501; printed visuals and, 685; privacy
and, 689, 691; propaganda and, 506 (*see also*
propaganda); public opinion and, 212–13,
216–36, 384; public sphere and, 713; search and,
279, 282; sensationalism and, 201, 669; state, 414;
syndicated, 783–84; technology and, 176–78;
telegraphs and, 176; television and, 204–5; travel
and, 822; word of mouth and, 546, 550
News Corporation, 780